CRITICAL SURVEY
OF
DRAMA

CRITICAL SURVEY

OF

DRAMA

Second Revised Edition

Volume 8
Essays

Resources

Indexes

Editor, Second Revised Edition
Carl Rollyson

Baruch College, City University of New York

Editor, First Editions, English and Foreign Language Series
Frank N. Magill

SALEM PRESS, INC.
Pasadena, California   Hackensack, New Jersey

Library of Congress Cataloging-in-Publication Data

Critical survey of drama / edited by Carl Rollyson.-- 2nd rev. ed.
    p. cm.
Previous edition edited by Frank Northen Magill in 1994.
"Combines, updates, and expands two earlier Salem Press reference sets: Critical survey of drama, revised edition, English language series, published in 1994, and Critical survey of drama, foreign language series, published in 1986"--Pref.
Includes bibliographical references and index.
ISBN 1-58765-102-5 (set : alk. paper) -- ISBN 1-58765-110-6 (vol. 8 : alk. paper) --
1. Drama--Dictionaries. 2. Drama--History and criticism--Dictionaries. 3. Drama--Bio-bibliography. 4. English drama--Dictionaries. 5. American drama--Dictionaries. 6. Commonwealth drama (English)--Dictionaries. 7. English drama--Bio-bibliography. 8. American drama--Bio-bibliography. 9. Commonwealth drama (English)--Bio-bibliography. I. Rollyson, Carl E. (Carl Edmund) II. Magill, Frank Northen, 1907-1997.
PN1625 .C68 2003
809.2′003—dc21   2003002190

Fourth Printing

PRINTED IN THE UNITED STATES OF AMERICA

CONTENTS

VOLUME 8

COMPLETE LIST OF CONTENTS

VOLUME 1

VOLUME 2

VOLUME 3

VOLUME 5

VOLUME 6

VOLUME 7

AMERICAN DRAMA

VOLUME 8

CRITICAL SURVEY

OF

DRAMA

EUROPEAN DRAMA

PRECLASSICAL DRAMA

Although theater is a comparatively late phenomenon in the history of human culture, its origins are obscure. Drama in the Western world goes back to Greek origins scarcely more than twenty-five hundred years ago—well within the period of recorded history—but information about the origin of Greek drama is scant and not always reliable, coming as it does from sources such as Aristotle, who wrote long after the fact. Other cultural traditions, however, though never fully documented from the beginnings to the appearance of a fully developed theater, have provided a series of models that suggest not only what may lie behind Greek drama but also what social and psychological impulses underlie all drama. Subdramatic rituals and performances in various parts of the world have illuminated several aspects of drama and theater.

The study of the origins of drama is therefore only in part a historical undertaking. Because of its appeal to the emotions and other functions of the mind that are not strictly rational, even fully evolved theater may be comparable in some ways to the rituals of prescientific peoples. Students of the theater hope, therefore, to learn something of the first principles of drama by investigating the theatrical performances of undeveloped cultures. Such cultures, often designated "archaic" to indicate their preliterate condition, invariably observe rituals of a theatrical character.

One of the great universals in such predramatic rituals is dance, described by Sheldon Cheney as "the great mother of the arts" and documented in artifacts such as cave paintings as early as 15,000 B.C.E. Although the motions of dance may be as purely formal and abstract as the sounds of music, most dance traditions have a demonstrably mimetic element. War dances that are mock contests, love-pantomimes related to fertility rites, and the animal dances of hunting societies testify to the mimetic use of dance. The horned, phallic dancer on the wall of the Trois Frères cave in southern France is our earliest example of such imitation. There is no way of telling at what point these dances were accompanied by the rhythmic chants of poetry or by the sound of musical instruments; the combination of dance, music, and song in rituals may be as old as human culture itself.

As it is no more than a step from imitation to illusion, the mimetic intention of a subdramatic song and dance may have the effect on a spectator of belief—for example, that the animal spirit represented in a buffalo-dance is real and not merely an imitation. A small child might easily be so deluded, but it is in the nature of religious ecstasy for an adult spectator, and even the performer himself, to make the additional step from self-conscious fantasy to a belief in the reality that is imitated. Modern theater succeeds even when a rational audience accepts the fiction that the action imitated on the stage is the real thing. By the same token, a religious congregation believes in the transubstantiation of bread and wine into the body and blood of its deity, just as the community witnessing a buffalo-dance accepts the reality the dancers before it are imitating. As an aid to such quasi-dramatic illusion, costume is a common adjunct to archaic performances. The dancer on the wall of the Trois Frères cave is dressed in an animal skin, complete with a mask and the antlers of the animal he represents. The mask is notably widespread in dance customs throughout the world. Representing the features of an animal, an ancestral spirit, or a god, masks symbolize the transformation and the illusion that are common denominators of ecstatic ritual and actual theater. A vestige of the theater-mask tradition remains in the playbook convention of listing the cast of characters as the *dramatis personae*, or "masks of the drama."

An important difference between the mimetic performance of a preliterate dancer and the representations of true drama is the level at which the mimesis is accepted. Where the audience of a play believes in the symbolic correspondence between the actor and his role, archaic audiences—and often the performers themselves—take the correspondence further. As Johan Huizinga points out in *Homo Ludens*, when a certain form of religion accepts a sacred identity between two things of a different order, say a human being and an animal, the relationship is not adequately expressed by calling it a "symbolical correspondence" as *we* conceive this. The identity, the essential oneness of the two goes far deeper than the correspondence between a substance and its symbolic image. It is a mystic unity. The one *becomes* the other. In his magic dance the savage *is* the kangaroo.

The magical content of much predramatic activity has led some investigators to the study of shamanism as the earliest type of theatrical performance. The shaman, whose name originates in the title of the Siberian spiritual healer, is a kind of medicine man who deals with the spirits; he does his work in a trance state, using rituals chiefly for healing the sick. Shamanism is believed to have originated in central Asia and Siberia in paleolithic times and to have spread through Eurasia and over the Alaskan land bridge into the Americas. It is also found in Africa, Australia, and New Guinea, and is so widespread that it probably arose spontaneously in many cultures. Its techniques include singing or chanting, dancing, costuming, storytelling, and many forms of illusionistic tricks. It has been called the oldest technique of theatrical performance because of its similar repertory of skills. E. T. Kirby's *Ur-Drama: The Origins of Theatre* explains the links between shamanism and theater in India, China, Greece, and Europe. Kirby distinguishes the shaman or controller of spirits from the medium, who is possessed by spirits who speak or act through him and determine his actions. His thesis is that "it is shamanism as it is most rigorously defined which has almost invariably been the antecedent of established theatre forms." Kirby calls attention to the importance of an audience in shamanic rituals— they contribute to more than a séance between the shaman and his patient. Such rituals differ from theatrical rites of passage or other ceremonies in that shamanism depends on "the immediate and direct manifestation to the audience of supernatural presence, rather than its symbolization." Dialogue is a particularly significant feature of shamanic ritual: The shaman converses with the spirits he has summoned or arranges conversations between his spirits and partic-

ipants in the ritual. An important corollary of shamanistic theatricality is that it imitates not the existing reality but the "reality" of another world. If Kirby's thesis is correct, theater in its origins was not concerned with ordinary reality, but with some transcendent and stylized spirit world, and with the abstract rather than the realistic: "Shamanistic illusionism, with its ventriloquism and escape acts, seeks to break the surface of reality, as it were, to cause the appearance of a super-reality that is 'more real' than the ordinary." Ur-theater was surrealistic before theater was realistic.

Most theories of the origin of drama assume that in its earliest stages a dramatic performance fulfilled a social function more important than mere entertainment. The classical Greeks believed that their own tragic drama should serve as an inspiration to noble behavior, and Aristotle, writing at the end of the classical period, proposed a theory of group therapy: that tragedy effected a catharsis of pity and fear in audiences prone to an excess of those emotions. Modern anthropologists have tended to see both serious and comic theatricality in functionalist terms, as a mechanism for promoting group solidarity. Important religious beliefs are acted out at yearly seasonal festivals, clowns act out the expulsion of the community's enemies, and by such dramatizations of commonly held views the spiritual life and emotional coherence of a group are periodically renewed.

Victor Turner has challenged this belief as a "flat" view of ritual. Rather than promoting "a gross group solidarity," he argues, some theatrical forms work as a mechanism for resolving social conflict. Turner associates such performances with a "social drama," which he describes as recurring "on all levels of social organization from state to family." Taking its beginnings in ritual and juridical procedures, a form of representation evolved that was "agonistic, rife with problem and conflict." Various kinds of theater, including puppetry and shadow theater, dance drama, and professional storytelling, became a means to "probe a community's weaknesses, call its leaders to account, desacralize its most cherished values and beliefs, portray its characteristic conflicts and suggest remedies for them, and generally take stock of its current situation in the known world." Turner conjectures that the various genres of cultural performance are potentially active in the phase of social drama concerned with redressive processes, when ritualized forms of authority such as litigation, feud, sacrifice, and prayer are invoked to contain a conflict and render it orderly. Social drama is by this definition a generic crisis in any community consisting of breach, crisis, redress, and restoration of peace through reconciliation or a mutual acceptance of schism. It is the cultural response to this social process, particularly in its third phase of redress, which generates the various genres of performance, including tragedy and comedy. Turner's hypothesis is not arguable on the basis of observed evidence, though it fits the agonistic character of Greek tragedy and comedy as well as the socially conscious drama of the twentieth century. It is more appropriate to a dynamic society than to traditional, authoritarian, or stable communities. In any case, the end product of performance in Turner's social drama is not so different from what other functionalists have found: the maintenance of an orderly and harmonious society.

Drama historians no longer believe that drama derived from a universal ritual in which, according to J. G. Frazer's *The Golden Bough*, the New Year king or vegetation sprite deposed his predecessor. This theory has been shown to be synthetic, based on evidence that is not complete for a single culture, and though some handbooks still repeat Frazerian formulas, the theory as a whole can no longer be accepted. The same is true of William Ridgeway's hypothesis in *Dramas and Dramatic Dances of Non-European Races* that theater originated in the worship of the dead. Theodor H. Gaster's *Thespis: Ritual, Myth, and Drama in the Ancient Near East* argues that all drama in the Near East descended from seasonal rituals, but, like previous monolithic theories, this is little credited by modern scholars. Under the influence of Bronisław Malinowski and later anthropologists, students of preliterate drama have rejected the assumption that all cultures go through the same stages of development. It is also acknowledged that true drama, as opposed to theatrical ritual, is a more secular creation, likely to have been decisively molded by storytelling

and the artistic performance of narrative poetry. Observers of African performing arts have promoted a view of drama as only supplementary to ritual, presenting secularized and popularized versions of beliefs that underlie ritual, thus giving ritual more meaning but in no way supplanting it. Psychologists, partly in response to Aristotle's characterization of man as a mimetic creature, call attention to the human penchant for fantasy that reshapes reality into more satisfying forms. A greater appreciation of the complexity of human culture and creativity has thus reduced the appeal even of the newer monolithic theories. Nevertheless, many of the beliefs commonly held by later scholars still reflect the position of Frazer and his followers that the source of theater is ritual, and some of the most challenging modern theories proceed from a renewed search for universal patterns in the development of drama.

Preliterate society offers a wealth of opportunities to observe rituals with dramatic or theatrical elements: song with a narrative element, dance that imitates via mime, music that dramatizes the action of dancers, costumes and masks that aid the impersonations of performers, and magical tricks to support the illusion of an action represented to an audience. Even playing areas, ranging from round dancing-floors ringed by spectators to the contrived theatrical enclosure of a shaman's tent, suggest the settings of true theater. The scenario of a sacred or shamanic ritual is close to the action that Aristotle identified as the "heart and soul" of tragedy, the earliest true dramatic form known. There are performers, and there is something like an audience—although ritual does not make the same distinction that theater makes between audience and performers. In spite of many similarities, historians of the theater are reluctant to call these archaic performances true drama; for this, they look for autonomous, exclusively dramatic performances in which theatrical art is free from the requirements of ritual.

THE ANCIENT NEAR EAST AND EGYPT

Because of their proximity to Greece and their role as the home of the first great civilizations, the Near East and the eastern Mediterranean basin have been closely scrutinized for performances that may have influenced the Hellenic inventors of drama. Greece was in fact the meeting place of three powerful traditions, though it is not always easy to distinguish them in detail. The latest to be identified may be the oldest, and it is not to be confused with the so-called cradle of civilization, a conception of the ancient Near East that has been to some extent discredited. Before the Indo-European Greeks migrated into the southern Balkans in the beginning of the second millennium B.C.E., the inhabitants of what are now Greece, Crete, the Aegean islands, and western Anatolia shared a culture with the southeastern Europeans that can be identified through a family of artifact types, including religious figurines and other paraphernalia of ritual. Marija Gimbutas identified this as the Civilization of Old Europe in *The Gods and Goddesses of Old Europe*. The roots of this cultural complex reach back into paleolithic times, but between about 7000 and 3500 B.C.E., "the inhabitants of this region developed a much more complex social organization than their western and northern neighbors, forming settlements that often amounted to small townships, inevitably involving craft specialization and the creation of religious institutions." Many artifacts from this early period bear significant resemblances to those of the classical period that are connected with classical drama. Though not unique to this part of the world, the presence of masked figures and animal masks in a region whose earliest dramatic actors wore masks and (in comedy) animal costumes is probably no coincidence. As Gimbutas observes, "masks and masked figures, life-size or in miniature, of ancient Greece, Minoan Crete and Old Europe, imply liturgy and drama whose emphasis is theatrical. It is quite conceivable that all three belong to the same tradition."

The second tradition to establish itself in Greece was that of the Greeks themselves, who brought with them the Indo-European language and myths that would provide the raw material of the earliest true drama. These people were to distinguish themselves from their neighbors in historical times by their passion for language, poetry, and debate; their extreme individualism; a love of the arts; and their secular temper. The aggressive and entrepreneurial character of the Greeks eventually brought them into contact with the more highly developed civilizations of Egypt and Mesopotamia, which provided the third great component in the context from which theater was to take shape. Their possible contributions to the origins of Greek theater have been perhaps overemphasized in the past because of a diffusionist ideology of Western civilization. All civilized arts did not necessarily flow from the East, and it is impossible to establish any positive links between the pageantry of Egypt and the Near East, on one hand, and the theater of Greece, on the other. Still, it is certain that Greek culture was stimulated in various ways by contacts with Egypt and the East in two formative periods: first, in the Minoan-Mycenaean age (c. 1600-1100 B.C.E.), and later, from the Orientalizing period in Greek art (c. 750-650 B.C.E.) through the time in the sixth century when the dramatic festivals were instituted in Athens.

Both Egypt and Mesopotamia have traditions of predramatic activity at least as early as the third millennium B.C.E., centuries before the Greeks themselves arrived in the southern Balkans. These traditions fall into two categories, with some overlap: literary dialogues of the sort that later produced the Song of Songs and the Book of Job, and sacred liturgies and pageants that followed a semidramatic scenario. In Mesopotamia, the Sumerian pageant of the "sacred marriage" solemnized each year the divine royalty's mystical union with the gods in what is fancifully described as a "mystery play" and a "great religious drama" with pantomime, incantation, and music. Although this ritual was discontinued by Hammurabi at about the beginning of the seventeenth century B.C.E., observances of this type became common throughout the Near East; a vestige of it survived even in classical Athens, where the wife of the King Archon was ritually "married" to Dionysus and had the duty of spending the night with him in his temple. A Sumerian festival of the New Year continued into Babylonian times; there was a celebration in Babylon in the time of King Nebuchadrezzar I (twelfth century B.C.E.), which included showy processions, a recitation of the myth of creation, and pantomimic performances. All of this is far from what today's audience would recognize as drama, but a small number of texts from Sumeria deserve mention because of their dramatic quality. In one such text, titled "Hammurabi's Conversation with a Woman," the great legal reformer is represented as captivated by the charms of a woman with whom he converses. This may have been a kind of court play, though nothing is known of any performance. There is also a Sumerian epic in dialogue form, "Enmerkar and the Lord of Aratta," which may have been a secular drama. Seven "divine disputations" have also been discovered that have a theatrical character. These represent humanized Sumerian gods in debate with one another, each praising his own merits and belittling those of the other. Dialogue literature became widespread in the Near East and, like other literary forms, is likely to have been known to Greeks who came into contact with the commercial centers of the Levant.

The roots of drama go back even further in Egypt than in Mesopotamia. A group of documents known as the Pyramid Texts were claimed in 1882 by the Egyptologist Gaston Maspero to have a dramatic character. The earliest of these sepulchral hieroglyphs were written on the interior walls of royal pyramids, and later in the tombs of nobles. Portions of some can be dated on the basis of internal evidence as having been composed as early as about 4000 B.C.E., though the actual inscriptions were made in the early third millennium. They are concerned with the resurrection of the dead and contain what appear to be stage directions and a script for a dramatic liturgy in which various divinities speak, frequently identifying themselves by name ("I am Horus"). It is speculated that the lines were recited by priests who wore animal masks representing the theriomorphic gods involved, although nothing is known of the actual rituals. These lines were evidently endowed by tax revenues set aside for the purpose, and there are accounts of misappropriations of such endowments for similar rites on behalf of more recently deceased nobles.

The Memphite drama is also of great antiquity, dating to about 3100 B.C.E. It was first rediscovered in the eighth century B.C.E. by an Ethiopian pharaoh in a worm-eaten leather or papyrus copy. Although this pharaoh had little notion of its age, he had it copied on a stone, which was eventually used by modern Egyptian peasants as a nether millstone and was later rescued after much of it had been worn away. This text, probably written as a coronation festival play, celebrates the gifts of the god Ptah, who was believed to have influenced the early development of religion and culture and to have aided the development of Egypt.

A later coronation festival play celebrated the elevation of a Middle Kingdom pharaoh to the throne in about 2000 B.C.E. A similar political ritual text has survived, a *Heb Sed* celebrating the coronation jubilee of King Osorkon II in the twenty-second year of his reign. *Heb Seds* symbolized the renewal of a king's power through an imaginary death and resurrection after a long period of his reign. They are believed typically to have taken a dramatic form.

Another type of dramatic ritual is medicinal drama, of which a single example is recorded on the Metternich stele. This shamanic drama tells how the goddess Isis's child Horus is stung by a scorpion and cured by a combination of magic and artificial respiration. This divine paradigm would have been used to promote the healing of a real patient.

The Abydos passion plays were perhaps the largest and showiest of the Egyptian liturgical dramas. This great pageant celebrated the death and resurrection of Osiris and the coronation of the god Horus. Abydos became the principal seat of the cult of Osiris, but similar liturgies were acted out at Busiris, Heliopolis, Letopolis, and Sais. No single document gives a complete account of the Osiris legend, but evidence that the legend was dramatically reenacted in considerable detail comes from a stele set up by a court official named Ikhernofret in the twelfth-dynasty reign of Senwosret III (1887-1849 B.C.E.). In this stele, Ikhernofret records his accomplishments as organizer and participant in the Osiris mysteries, beginning with the words "I organized the departure of Wapwawet as he goes to the rescue of his father," evidently in an early stage of the complex pageant. It has been conjectured that the full enactment of the Osiris story took place over an extended period in the religious year. The legend had considerable potential for dramatic elaboration because Osiris was the most humanized of the Egyptian gods, having evolved from a fertility god into a Christlike or Promethean figure, a special friend to humankind who suffers betrayal and death. The tears and laments of his mourners bring about his resurrection, and he becomes the ruler of the dead. This passion play of Osiris was a regular feature of Egyptian popular religion from about 2500 B.C.E. and was performed at Abydos until about the middle of the sixth century B.C.E. Herodotus knew of two other passion plays in Egypt a century later, and similar pageants were celebrated well into the Christian era.

The ingredients of drama were at hand in Egyptian ritual and letters, but the special cultural conditions that gave rise to theater in Greece were not present in Egypt. A stagnant culture, authoritarianism, and a preoccupation with religious ritual have variously been blamed for the failure of drama to germinate. As for the influence of Egyptian or Near Eastern dialogues and liturgies, there is no evidence that the Greeks were imitating anything outside their own culture when they did invent theater. The institutions suggestive of drama were only part of a milieu that the Greeks, particularly at the time of the birth of tragedy, were inclined to dismiss as barbaric.

THE ORIGINS OF GREEK TRAGEDY AND COMEDY

The cardinal fact for the study of Greek dramatic origins is Aristotle's remark in the *De poetica* (c. 334-323 B.C.E.; *Poetics*, 1705) that tragedy developed "from the leaders of the dithyramb," a song and dance in honor of Dionysus. There were other Greek cults whose rituals included mimed scenes from the life of the gods, such as the mysteries of Demeter and Persephone at Eleusis and the Delphic combat of Apollo with the Python. These rituals or liturgies were comparable to similar presentations in Egypt, but only the Dionysiac cult developed the capacity for myths from which the dramas of tragedy sprang. The worship of Dionysus was a late arrival in Greece, possibly coming from the northern regions such as Epirus, Macedonia, and Thrace. Definite cult forms did not take shape in Attica, where tragedy devel-

oped, until the sixth century B.C.E. By that time, it was able to incubate in the hothouse conditions of a civilization already distinguished by a highly developed epic tradition and a mature lyric poetry. With literary siblings of this quality, the dithyramb had not only a rich base on which to develop but also a high standard of taste to meet. Accordingly, the dithyramb developed a larger repertory of events from the life of Dionysus than the archaic hymns composed in honor of the other gods. Moreover, for reasons that are not clear, the dithyramb became a more open-ended form than the older hymns. The Athenian tyrant Cleisthenes assigned to it a chorus originally sung for the hero Adrastus, and in the fifth century Bacchylides made the Athenian hero Theseus the subject of his Seventeenth Dithyramb. As far back as the early seventh century B.C.E., the great lyric poet Archilochus was already a regular leader and participant in dithyrambic performances: "I know how to lead the fair song of Lord Dionysus, the dithyramb, when my wits are fused with wine." The poet's emphasis on intoxication is significant, because the worship of Dionysus, unlike the other major Greek cults, was ecstatic. Wine stimulated the religious rapture of the god's worshipers, who surrendered their personal identities: The men imagined themselves to be Satyrs or goat-men, the women maenads ("ravers") or bacchantes (from the cult name Bacchos). This element of transformation grew out of the ecstatic character of Dionysiac religion and led to the role-playing of regular drama.

It is a great irony that a form of art demanding as much discipline and calculation as drama should have developed from the wild abandon of ecstatic dancers, but it was the freedom from the rigid formulas of ritual that gave Dionysiac worship its initial promise as a medium of artistic development. The mythic stories that were to be its raw material came from epic and heroic poetry, which was highly developed even as early as the mid-eighth century B.C.E., when writing was first introduced to Greece. Homer's *Iliad* (c. 750 B.C.E.; English translation, 1611) and *Odyssey* (c. 725 B.C.E.; English translation, 1614), composed in the formulaic style of oral poetry in the latter half of that century, set a literary standard for all time: His language and themes recurred in every literary genre throughout the rest of antiquity. The dramatizing style of Homeric narrative, particularly in the *Iliad* (more than half of which is direct dialogue), is echoed in tragedy, which in turn employed the long messenger-speech as a medium of narrative. In the generations after Homer, rhapsodists traveled around the Greek world giving dramatic recitations of scenes from Homer, further cultivating a Greek taste for theatrical performances.

Lyric poetry was another major influence on the original form of Greek drama. "Lyric" is a generic term for both personal monody (such as the poems of Sappho and Alcaeus) and choral song. As the name implies, both forms were recited to the accompaniment of the lyre, and both were identified with the word *ōidē* (whence "ode"), or song. The word survives in the second part of trag*oidia*. All poets were songwriters—even Homer called on his muse to sing, and the education of every well-born boy included instruction in the lyre. Homer's fiercest and angriest warrior, Achilles, is also represented as an accomplished musician and singer of heroic song. The songs of lyric were less narrative than the verses of epic and more obviously meditative in the sense that they explored the meaning and the ramifications of a situation or an emotion, sometimes finding mythic paradigms for immediate experience and always looking for language precisely suited to what they sought to express. The style and rhythms of lyric poetry provided the main idiom of early tragedy, whose primary content was choral lyric. Choral song and dance were a part of the cultural life of every Greek, both male and female. Any public event of importance was marked by choral performances, either by adults or by groups of girls or boys. Sophocles himself sang and danced as a boy in a choral celebration of the Athenian victory at the Battle of Salamis, and it is reported that he took to writing because his voice was too weak for performance. Although choral dance is illustrated on many Greek vases, the details of choral dance are as little understood today as are those of early Greek music, but it is clear that most performances called for a dozen or more dancers, often holding one another's hands as in some folk dances of modern Greece and its neighbors. The words *strophe* and *antistrophe* ("turn" and "counterturn"), used to denote stanzas of the choral interlude in mature Greek tragedy, suggest that the original movement of the dance was circular. The circular form of the orchestra ("dancing-place") in many Greek theaters also suggests a kind of circle dance.

The Greek proclivity for the performing arts promised a ready audience for a deritualized Dionysiac performance. The work of adaptation has been attributed to a series of more or less shadowy individuals, the first of whom is Arion, a celebrated performer on the cithara who lived at Corinth around the end of the seventh century B.C.E. Sources point to Arion as the first poet to have written out dithyrambs, to have named the form, and to have produced them in Corinth. He may also have made alterations in the form of the dithyramb that brought it a step closer to tragedy; one source indicates that his songs came to be called "tragic drama" and his singers *tragoidoi*, but the evidence is problematic. Lasos of Hermione, an Argive, is believed to have introduced dithyrambic contests in Athens during the time of the tyrant Hipparchus. If this is true, Lasos can be credited with bringing the dithyramb to the city best suited to its development, as Athens was already the largest of the city-states and the Pisistratids had an active performing arts program. Under them, the City Dionysia became the great Athenian festival of musical and poetic contests, among which the dithyramb had a naturally preeminent place. The festival retained its importance in 510-509 B.C.E. after the expulsion of the tyrants. Simonides became the most successful of many composers of dithyrambs for the Athenian contests, claiming in one of his own epigrams to have won fifty-six dithyrambic victories. These performances at Athens were danced and sung by choruses of fifty men or boys; women of the citizen class were excluded from public life in Athens, and this kind of performance remained the sole prerogative of males throughout the fifth century, with men playing all female roles. The poet whose dithyramb won the first prize was awarded a bull. For the most part, however, the dithyramb remains something of a mystery. No complete specimen survives except for some possible later versions by Bacchylides, and the sources of information are late and unreliable.

Thespis is the name (probably a nom de plume meaning "inspired") associated with the invention of tragedy proper, because the writer and impresario who adopted this name wrote in a role for a *hypokritēs*, or "answerer," who played opposite the *exarchos*, or leader of the chorus. The dialogue between the chorus leader and his answerer now appeared as a series of "interpolations," or episodes. This new dialogue-drama was introduced to Athens (or at least won its first victory there) under the tyrant Pisistratus in 534 B.C.E., possibly after a period of time in which Thespis and his troupe wandered around Attica with a wagon that served as a kind of float or stage for his performances. There is some evidence that Thespis performed in Athens as early as 560 B.C.E., before the organization of dramatic competitions. Thespis is said to have tried various methods of disguising the faces of his actors, first with white lead and other dyes, then with masks of white linen.

Thespis's successor, Choerilus, made additional experiments with masks, and another early tragedian, Phrynichus, introduced masks representing female characters that were shaded lighter than the masks of male characters. This concern with masks shows that from the earliest stages of tragedy the role of actors was primarily recitative, and that the use of facial expression to convey character or emotion was alien to the form. The first known attempt to represent anything other than mythic action occurred in 492 B.C.E., when Phrynichus wrote about Persian reprisals against the Ionian revolt in *The Capture of Miletus*. The performance so distressed the Athenian audience that the playwright was fined. After the Persian defeat in 480-479 B.C.E., both Phrynichus's *Phoenissae* (476 B.C.E.) and Aeschylus's *Persai* (472 B.C.E.; *The Persians*, 1777), which represent the defeat through Persian eyes, were performed. These plays are early exceptions to the rule that only mythic subjects are suitable for the tragic stage. An early form of tragedy is evident in Aeschylus's *Hiketides* (c. 463 B.C.E.; *The Suppliants*, 1777), long believed to be his earliest surviving play until a papyrus discovered in 1952 showed that it was produced after 470 B.C.E., proba-

bly about 463. The dominant role of the chorus, not only as a commentator but also as the chief character, and the relatively minor role of other characters in dialogue with one another indicate the strongly choral nature of the form that Aeschylus inherited. It was he, according to Aristotle, who added the second actor. This change, which made possible the evolution from chorus-drama to actor-drama, was to have far-reaching consequences for Greek theater and by itself justifies the characterization of Aeschylus as the "father of Greek tragedy," but other innovations—in scene-painting, costuming, and special effects—suggest a flair for theatrical showmanship that compelled imitation and left an indelible stamp on Greek stage conventions. Subsequent developments, such as Sophocles' introduction of the third actor, were little more than refinements of Aeschylus's idea of the theater, and though his greatest successors had their own poetic vision, the Greek tragic theater remained Aeschylean in conception to the end.

Tragedy was the highest development of the original song and dance in honor of Dionysus. The dithyramb, from which it evolved, maintained a life of its own long after Thespis made tragedy a separate dramatic form, and a third kind of performance, the satyr play, survived as an adjunct to tragedy. The satyr play may in fact have been the earliest form of drama; as its name implies, the actors retained their dithyrambic character as satyrs, the phallic goat-men who follow Dionysus, who drink large amounts of wine, and who take indecent sexual liberties with maenads. The basic content of satyr drama consisted of unseemly outrages that the mischievous satyrs, the demons of misrule, visited on the venerable characters of Greek mythology. These performances had less to do with satire (a word derived from an unrelated Latin root) than with mythological farce. They seem originally to have been unscripted scenarios, though two examples of a later, more premeditated form survive in Sophocles' *Ichneutae* (fifth century B.C.E.; the hunting dogs or trackers) and Euripides' *Kyklōps* (c. 421 B.C.E.; *Cyclops*, 1782). Like the cartoon show, which was for years appended to American motion pictures, the satyr play was part of a tetralogy that a tragedian would offer at the annual dramatic competition, consisting of a trilogy of tragic dramas and a single satyr play. Euripides' *Alkēstis* (438 B.C.E.; *Alcestis*, 1781) was submitted instead of a satyr play in 438 B.C.E.; its plot and themes are suitably countertragic.

Satyr drama proved to be an artistic dead end, eclipsed by the serious drama to which it was attached. Its themes and point of view were more successfully exploited in comedy, which was also a part of the dramatic festivals in honor of Dionysus. Its name, *kōmoidia*, or *kōmos*-song, is derived from the name of another Dionysiac celebration, the "revel." A scene in Aristophanes' *Acharnēs* (425 B.C.E.; *The Acharnians*, 1812) illustrates how the early *kōmos* may have looked when it was a simple rural procession in which the main personage sings a licentious song to Dionysus's phallic companion, Phales. Aristotle adds that the *kōmos* included derisive songs making fun of prominent or unpopular persons. The comasts disguised themselves in masks and animal costumes to protect themselves against reprisals. This story accounts for the theriomorphic choruses of Aristophanes' *Sphēkes* (422 B.C.E.; *The Wasps*, 1812), *Ornithes* (414 B.C.E.; *The Birds*, 1824), and *Batrachoi* (405 B.C.E.; *The Frogs*, 1780) and for the conspicuous presence of political satire in Old Comedy, which is known only in the late fifth century works of Aristophanes. The animal choruses have parallels in theatrical rituals all over the world, however, and their original purpose may not have been disguise. Somewhat less is known of the development of comedy than of tragedy, perhaps because, as Aristotle said, it was taken less seriously by the first historians of theater, but like tragedy (which uses a Doric dialect in the lyric portions and Attic in the dialogue), comedy appears to be a composite form. One element of comedy was the *kōmos* of Dionysus's revelers; another was improvised Dorian farce, combined by Epicharmus of Syracuse (c. 530-440 B.C.E.) with a comic *agōn*, or debate-scene. Another distinctive feature of Old Comedy is the parabasis, a kind of entr'acte structurally related to the *agōn* in which the chorus lay aside their dramatic role and make a speech to win the favor of the audience. As this feature tends to become less prominent and finally disappears entirely in Aristophanes' later comedies, it may be surmised that it was an early component of Old Comedy. The prominence in the parabasis of political commentary suggests that it may have been a means of bringing political discontents into the open under the protection of a kind of carnival privilege. Another early feature is the comic Old Man, an established citizen and paterfamilias who hatches a fantastic scheme to rid himself and his fellow citizens of some common affliction in the body politic. Here, too, the pattern tends to break down as Aristophanes' later comedies become less formulaic. A type-scene that occurs in the later portions of many of Aristophanes' comedies shows the beating and expulsion of supposed undesirables. Performances of this type are common worldwide in rituals of mockery and are related to customs involving scapegoats in which a criminal representing all the wrongs of the community is led around, beaten, and killed. A ritual of this kind is reported to have existed in early Athens, and the symbolic chastening of informer, creditors, and other supposed delinquents in Old Comedy may well be a substitute for the earlier ritual executions. The padded costumes and red-tipped *phalloi* worn by the actors of Old Comedy are also common features of humorous performances in various parts of the world. In the Attic theater these are believed to be survivals from Dorian farce, but like other features they may go back to much earlier fertility rites.

It is rash to form any but the most tentative theories about the origin of Old Comedy because the evidence available is so late and incomplete. The examples of the form that survive from the last quarter of the fifth century, composed by a brilliant poet for a sophisticated audience, are highly eclectic and much influenced by mature tragedy, which is tirelessly parodied. Aristophanic comedy combines refined lyricism, literary parody, political satire, and licentious humor with a sublety that defies archaelogical analysis.

All Greek dramatic performances were technically and originally religious acts, performed throughout the fifth century at festivals of Dionysus, the de facto patron of theater. The first comedies were performed at the lesser or Rural Dionysia in December or early January. In Athens itself, comedy was first improvised at the Lenaea, a festival in January or February named after the *Lenai*, or maenads. Tragic performances were added to this festival about 442 B.C.E. The principal dramatic festival was the great or City Dionysia, celebrated in late March or early April. This festival was observed throughout Attica, and its direction was the responsibility of the *archon eponymos*, the highest state official, who selected the plays that were performed. Dithyrambs, comedies, and tragedies were presented, tragedies in the morning and comedies in the evening.

An ancient proverb has it that Greek tragedy as it is known today has "nothing to do with Dionysus." Except for Euripides' *Bakchai* (405 B.C.E.; *The Bacchae*, 1781), the last play of the last great tragedian, and Aristophanes' *The Frogs*, Dionysus or his worship is not the subject of extant Greek plays. Gilbert Murray proposed in 1912 that the basic scenario of tragedy followed the outline of a ritual in which the year-daemon suffered and was killed in the form of a sacrificial animal, then resurrected. This attempt to apply Frazer's anthropology has as few adherents today as the belief that Euripides' *The Bacchae*, representing the persecution and triumph of Dionysus, reproduces the original pattern of early tragic ritual. The most plausible aspect of such hypotheses is that the suffering of many tragic characters that is displayed after the fact in a spectacular way, such as the bloody corpses in Aeschylus's *Oresteia* (458 B.C.E.; English translation, 1777) or the mutilated eyes of Oedipus preserves the traditional *sparagmos*, or dismemberment, of live animals by frenzied worshipers of Dionysus. Most students of the Greek stage are ready to agree, however, that the extant plays are essentially independent of their ritual origins and can be understood properly only if they are read as literary and dramatic artifacts.

BIBLIOGRAPHY
Bergmann, Bettina, and Christine Kondoleon, eds. *The Art of Ancient Spectacle.* New Haven, Conn.: Yale University Press, 2000. In nineteen essays, explores events as combat in the arena, festivals, theatrical productions, processions, and banquets in terms of their forms and the visual arts created for them.

Bieber, Margarete. *The History of the Greek and Roman Theater.* Princeton, N.J.: Princeton University Press, 1961. Explores the ancient roots of Greek and Roman drama.

Cheney, Sheldon. *The Theatre: Three Thousand Years of Drama, Acting, and Stagecraft.* New York: McKay, 1972. Provides history and interpretation of the development of performance and stage acting. Bibliography.

Kirby, E. T. *Ur-Drama: The Origins of Theatre.* New York: New York University Press, 1975. Discusses ancient origins of theater.

Lexova, Irena. *Ancient Egyptian Dances.* Translated by Diane Bergman. New York: Dover, 2000. Using numerous illustrations, investigates the origins, nature, and role of dance in Egyptian culture, including gymnastic, imitative, dramatic, and lyrical performances. Bibliography.

Pickard-Cambridge, Arthur W. *Dithyramb, Tragedy, and Comedy.* 2d ed. Oxford, England: Clarendon Press, 1962. Provides history and criticism of Greek tragedy and comedy.

Schechner, Richard, and Mady Schuman. *Ritual, Play, and Performance.* New York: Seabury Press, 1976. Explores a host of topics related to the very early origins of theater, including shamanism and meditation, social dramas and ritual metaphors, and magic.

Wilson, Edwin, and Alvin Goldfarb. *Living Theater: A History.* 3d ed. New York: McGraw-Hill, 1999. Traces the development of theater in a contextual manner, examining the social, political, and economic conditions of each era. A small chapter on early theater, followed by more substantial chapters on Greek and Roman theater.

Daniel H. Garrison

CLASSICAL GREEK AND ROMAN DRAMA

Little is known about the origins of Greek tragedy. Anthropologists point to fertility rites, masked ceremonies, and other primitive rituals as containing the seeds of drama, but these phenomena, common to many early societies, in themselves do not adequately explain the unique evolution in Attica of a highly developed tragic form. In the absence of other credible information, historians must rely on the testimony of Aristotle, who discusses the origins of drama in the fourth chapter of his *De poetica* (c. 334-323 B.C.E.; *Poetics*, 1705). Aristotle maintains that tragedy originated with the leaders of the dithyramb, a choral song sung in the worship of Dionysus. He also adds a second element to these origins, the satyricon: This was an early forerunner of the satyr play, a form that might have dropped into oblivion were it not later restored by Pratinas. Support for Aristotle's theory of a dual origin is found in the figure of Arion, a Corinthian who raised the dithyramb to an artistic form of choral lyric. Arion's dithyrambs were performed allegedly by satyrs, and this seems to show a clear point at which dithyramb and satyricon converged.

The dithyramb in the hands of Arion probably had a narrative content (as it does in the later, extant works of Bacchylides), and this, too, makes it a likely precursor of tragedy. Further support for Aristotle is found in the Dionysiac character of both the dithyramb and the satyricon, because tragedy, from its inception, was always performed at Athens in connection with the great festivals honoring Dionysus. The content of tragedy, however, almost never deals with the mythic stories of Dionysus, but evidence from Herodotos links the choral song of hero-cults with the worship of Dionysus in one specific case, and this might help explain why heroic mythology provides the substance for songs and, later, plays performed in the worship of Dionysus. Epigenes of Sicyon, an obscure figure who predates Thespis, is said to have been the first tragedian; scholars believe that he may have been connected with this early stage at which heroic mythology became linked with the service of Dionysus.

Tragedy, then, began with choral singing, but at some point it became true drama with the introduction of dialogue. An ancient account based on Aristotle reconstructs that momentous step in the following manner: Because the choral song eventually came to include complex mythological material, demanding much knowledge on the part of the listener, it was convenient to add a prologue to lead the audience into the song; in like manner, a speaker could be brought on between songs to explain transitions, and eventually, the narrator and the chorus leader began to speak with each other. Tradition names Thespis, in the last half of the sixth century B.C.E., as the inventor of the tragic actor; it is more likely that he was an important innovator who deeply affected a process that was essentially evolutionary in nature. He was the first to present a tragedy at the Greater Dionysia (established c. 535 B.C.E.) and thus is connected with Pisistratus's institutionalization of tragedy in Athens as part of official religious life, and it is suggested that he was also associated with the introduction of masks for the actors. Because the tragic presentations at the festivals took the form of competitions, inscriptions recorded the winners and their play titles (*didascalia*), and much of this evidence has survived, providing the names of other early tragedians. Among these is Choerilus, a figure of the late sixth and early fifth centuries B.C.E. He competed with Pratinas and Aeschylus, and one of his tragedies, titled *Alope*, dealt with a local Attic legend. Phrynichus was another tragedian of the same era, and many of his titles show the same mythic subject matter later used by Aeschylus and Euripides. Phrynichus also tried his hand at dramas of historical content: *The Capture of Miletus* (pr. 492 B.C.E.) evoked among the audience such painful recollection of a recent military disaster that Phrynichus was fined and the play banned. A final playwright of the pre-Aeschylean era is Pratinas, who wrote tragedies, although he was best known for his reform and restoration of the satyr play.

THE ORIGINS OF COMEDY

Even less is known about the origins of comedy: Aristotle confesses in his _Poetics_ that by his own day, the early stages of comedy were already obscure and unknown. He does, however, offer two important clues. He traces comedy back to the phallic songs, fertility rites that persisted in his own time, much as he found the origins of tragedy in the dithyramb. He also supports the etymology of the word "comedy" deriving from the Greek _kōmos_, the song of a train of revelers. This notion is supported by the relatively late dates of institutionalization of comedy at Athenian festivals—442 B.C.E. for the Lenaea and 486 for the Greater Dionysia—which suggest that comedy was for a long time informal and improvisational in nature.

Something is known of the phallic processions that Aristotle views as the starting point of comedy. One passage in Aristophanes' _Acharnēs_ (425 B.C.E.; _The Acharnians_, 1812) includes such a celebration. Semos of Delos describes two kinds of phallic processions: the _phallophoroi_, garlanded youths who followed one young man wearing the phallus, with his face blackened, and _ithyphalloi_, performers wearing masks that represented drunkenness. Both types of processions were accompanied by singers, and the _phallophoroi_ involved audience abuse; because Attic comedy employs choral singing, the phallus, and invective aimed at the viewers, it seems likely that Aristotle was, at least in part, correct.

In modern times, classical scholars, with the aid of the resources of archaeology, have compiled a list of other rituals, celebrations, and miscellaneous phenomena that may also have contributed to the development of comedy in its earlier stages. Animal masquerade, an Attic form of the sixth century B.C.E. documented by a series of vases, looks forward to the theriomorphic element common in the choruses of comedies of the fifth century. Further, a number of Greek festivals involved the hurling of obscene abuse at the participants, and one custom had groups of jesters travel the countryside in wagons, abusing bystanders. These rituals, rooted in the very ancient idea that obscenity held some apotropaic magic, show their influence in both the obscene and the invective

elements of the later, developed comic genre. All the phenomena discussed above are associated with singing, dancing, and speaking by groups, rather than individuals. This reflects the view held by most scholars that comedy, like tragedy, began with the chorus: An analysis of existing comedies makes clear the original importance of the chorus and their participation in prominent structural parts of the plays, especially the parabasis.

Scholars have also examined many predramatic forms in quest of the origin of the actors and the episodic component of Greek comedy. One important influence, often overlooked, must surely be the parallel, but slightly advanced, development of tragedy, which is also characterized by an alternating arrangement of choral parts and actors' episodes. Other early forms that scholars suggest as possible influences on the episodic scenes in comedy include the Spartan _deikeliktai_ described by Sosibius, the mimic dances described by Xenophon, and the antics of the padded actors seen on a Corinthian vase in the Louvre; all three involve simple dramatic representations of brief, humorous stories. Another possible ancestor of the episodic component of comedy is the Megarian farce, which was apparently very slapstick and obscene in character; similarities to Old Comic humor, as well as explicit comments about Megarian farce by Old Comic playwrights, confirm some sort of connection. In addition, an offshoot of the Doric comic tradition (of which Megarian farce is a part) was the phlyax play of southern Italy. The costume of the phlyax actors included both the body padding and the phallus found on Greek Old Comic actors; this, in addition to certain parallels between specific phlyax vases and scenes from existing Greek comedies, as well as the presence of Attic dialogue on one vase, seems to argue for a connection between the Doric tradition and the Attic comic drama. Alfred Körte, a German scholar of the nineteenth century, was so convinced by this evidence that he hypothesized a dual origin for Greek comedy, with the choral element deriving from animal masquerade and other Attic forms and the episodic scenes descending from Doric farce. Such a clear-cut fusion of Attic and Doric elements is unlikely, and other scholars have disputed Körte, some maintaining that all the prerequisites of comedy existed on Attic soil. In fact, it is most probable that a number of predramatic forms, including Aristotle's phallic processions, as well as animal masquerade and various festive improvisations, eventually evolved into Old Comedy. Non-Attic influences, such as Doric farce, surely cannot be ruled out, especially in view of the continuous contact among the city-states of Greece (as well as their Greek colonies in southern Italy) in the sixth century.

The Attic comedy of the archaic period was a vigorous combination of various influences, but it lacked unity, especially in comparison with the surviving comedies of the last quarter of the fifth century. Tragedy probably was very influential in helping comedy to become more coherent. Aristotle suggested that Epicharmus, a Sicilian of the late sixth and early fifth centuries B.C.E., was associated with the development at Attica of unified comedies. The surviving fragments of Epicharmus are not sufficient to allow evaluation of Aristotle's claim, but they do show a predominance of ribald mythological travesty, especially involving Heracles, traces of which can be found in scenes from the plays of Aristophanes. Other characteristics demonstrated by the fragments include philosophical discussions and elements of Doric farce. These plays do not seem to have had choruses, except possibly in rare cases. While it is probable that Epicharmus had some influence on Attic comedy, it is impossible to determine to what degree. The mimic element of this playwright was continued on Sicilian soil by his fellow Syracusan, Sophron, the fifth century writer of mimes favored by Plato. The true culmination of ancient Greek comedy, however, is to be found in the Attic political comedy of the late fifth century, dominated by the figure of Aristophanes.

TRAGEDY IN THE FIFTH CENTURY B.C.E.

Greek tragedies were presented as a part of the official religious festivals honoring Dionysus, the Greater Dionysia and the Lenaea (from 432 B.C.E.); thus, tragedy must always be viewed as having a religious and an Athenian state context. The tragic presentations were competitions that climaxed the festivals, though they were by no means the only events of these festivals. At the Greater Dionysia, three poets competed, each presenting three tragedies and a satyr play. Because the Lenaea was mainly devoted to comedy, only two tragedians participated, with two tragedies each. An archon of the Athenian city-state chose the competitors from among those poets who "applied for a chorus." The archon appointed for each of the chosen poets a choregus, a wealthy citizen who provided the money for the trainer of the chorus; the training, sustenance, and costuming of the chorus members; and the flute player. These were the greatest expenses involved in a tragic production, and the office of choregus imposed a heavy financial obligation as well as conferring a great honor. The remaining expenses, especially for the actors, were paid by the state. The poets sought the favor of the audience, but the contest was decided by judges, chosen by lot from among those nominated by each tribe. It is not known what monetary reward was given, but the victors received olive crowns and, undoubtedly, great honor among their fellow Athenians. First-place and second-place awards were given.

The plays were presented at the Theater of Dionysus, on the south slope of the Acropolis. In the fifth century, the theater was very rudimentary: It was made of wood rather than stone and consisted of the orchestra, a round area for the choral dancing, and the theatron, where the audience sat. At the rear of the orchestra was a simple building called the *skene*; the actors made their entrances and exits through doors in the front of the *skene*, and on occasion, characters even appeared on the roof. Corridors along the sides of the orchestra, called parodoi, provided entryways for the chorus. There were no curtains, no lights, and no darkness to help focus the attention of the audience. The plays began at dawn and were played in the open air. Scenery was rudimentary. The audience was reportedly rowdy and festive, and food was served in the theater. These difficult conditions placed a great weight on the words of the playwright, the skill of the actors, and the performance of the chorus.

The actors were always men, even when the characters were female. In the early part of the century, the playwright acted in his own dramas; Thespis, and probably Aeschylus too, produced their plays in this manner. At this stage in the development of tragedy, there was only one actor, though Aeschylus soon added a second actor, and Sophocles, a third. Additions ceased after this, because it was decided that three actors should be the canonical number. The number of characters, however, was not limited to three, because actors usually played more than one role in a single play, using the mask in making transformations; the "three-actor rule" did, however, mean that no more than three characters could be onstage at the same moment. With Aeschylus's addition of the second actor, the playwrights ceased to participate in the plays, and professional actors, chosen by the poets, came into use. Around the middle of the century, when actors' competitions were added to the festivals, the state assumed responsibility for the actors: The protagonists (actors playing the most important roles) were selected by officials and then allocated to specific playwrights by lot.

The most important asset for a tragic actor was a good voice for the speaking parts (iambic trimeter) and the recitative. Gesture derived special importance from the fact that masks were always worn, precluding the use of facial expression. The masks, to which wigs were attached, were lightweight and boldly painted; tradition attributes to Aeschylus the innovation of coloring the masks. The costumes featured chitons with fitted sleeves and ornamental designs, clothing very unlike that of the ordinary Athenian. Sometimes the actors wore no shoes, but often high boots were worn, though not of the high-soled variety, as some scholars allege.

The chorus, an important component of tragedy, was in Aeschylus's day composed of twelve members; Sophocles later increased the number to fifteen. The chorus members were costumed in accordance with their role in the play (in satyr plays this involved the phallus and a horsetail), and they were accompanied by an unmasked flute player. The chorus sang and also danced, and their parts were written in anapests (for marching) as well as in more complicated lyric meters, accompanied by the flute.

The structural parts of a tragedy show alternation between choral portions and actors' dialogue. The play began with a prologue, whose purpose was usually to introduce the plot and supply background information. This was followed by the parodos, or entrance-song, of the chorus. Thereafter, episodes alternated with choral odes (*stasima*), with the ode generally containing comment on the substance of the preceding episode. Near the end of the play a *kommos*, or song of mourning, was often sung by actor and chorus in combination. The play closed with an exodos.

AESCHYLUS

Greek tragedy derived from choral performances to which actors were subsequently added; in fact, the history of tragedy in the fifth century B.C.E. is characterized by the gradual but steady decline of the chorus and the consequent elevation of the actors. In the plays of Aeschylus, the chorus is the dominant element, but by the time of Euripides, the choral odes were reduced to lyric interludes between the episodes. It was once thought that Aeschylus's *Hiketides* (c. 463 B.C.E.; *The Suppliants*, 1777), in which the chorus portrays a group main character, was his earliest play; this seemed to support the notion of a declining chorus by showing a very early play in which the chorus was clearly dominant. Because subsequent papyrus discoveries have moved the date of *The Suppliants* to 463 B.C.E., however, it has been established that Aeschylus's earliest surviving play is *Persai* (*The Persians*, 1777) of 472 B.C.E., written when Aeschylus was in his early fifties; there is no extant work from his early period.

The peak years of Greek tragedy coincided with the great period of Athenian supremacy under the leadership of Pericles, a period bounded at both ends by wars: The Persian Wars, in which the Greeks, led by Athens, defeated the Persian invaders, effectively ended in 480 B.C.E. and 479 B.C.E. with the great victories at Salamis and Plataea; the Peloponnesian Wars, in which Athens came to blows with its fellow city-state Sparta, started in 431 B.C.E. The conclusion of the Persian Wars ushered in an era of peace and prosperity in Athens that provided the money, the leisure time, and the faith in the abilities of humankind needed to produce great art and literature. The beginning of the Peloponnesian Wars, and the plague of 430 B.C.E., greatly diminished those resources, and the great years of the Pentacontaetia ("the period of fifty years") were over. Aeschylus's earliest surviving play, *The Persians*, therefore stands at the commencement of the golden era of Greek tragedy. Moreover, it celebrates the Battle of Salamis, the event that marked the opening of that era.

The Persians, the only surviving example of a historical, rather than mythological, tragedy, tells the story of the Battle of Salamis from the Persian point of view. Xerxes, the Persian king, is the central character, and there are appearances also by the ghost of Darius, by his mother, Atossa, and by a messenger. Lengthy catalogs of foreign-sounding names and Eastern costumes lend the play a Persian flavor, but the central ideas retain their Greek quality. The play is somewhat static, with its alternation between choral odes and two-character dialogues, but it is also stately and grand in its language and characters.

The Persians was not part of a connected trilogy; the titles of Aeschylus's other two tragedies for this occasion suggest completely unrelated topics. The trilogy structure, for which Aeschylus later became famous, was probably still in the conceptual stage. *The Persians* does, however, exhibit two other characteristics that later became hallmarks of his work: the devices of suspense and extended climax, and the worldview in which *ate*, a kind of doom or ruin, deludes a man and speeds him to his destruction, aided by his own *hybris*, or hubris—overweening pride. This philosophy permeates tragedy even after Aeschylus, and it is also found in the works of the great historian of the Persian Wars, Herodotus.

In 467 B.C.E., Aeschylus presented a tetralogy, detailing the story of Laius and the house of Oedipus, of which only the third play, *Hepta epi Thēbas* (*Seven Against Thebes*, 1777), has survived. This does not make it possible to evaluate the structure of the tetralogy, but passages from *Seven Against Thebes* show that Aeschylus emphasized the notion of the family curse, to be worked out over several generations, much as he did later in the *Oresteia* (458 B.C.E.; English translation, 1777) trilogy. *Seven Against Thebes* is characterized by a slow pace in the early

portions, and then a more rapid movement toward a dramatic climax, a structure also found in *The Persians*. On the thematic level, the play shows the main character, Eteocles, laboring under an awareness of his destruction, but still compelled to act. Thebes, led by Eteocles, prepares to defend against the Argive-based attack led by Polyneices, the brother of Eteocles (both are sons of the cursed Oedipus). In the assignment of battle stations, Polyneices and Eteocles are set against each other, and this ultimately leads to a double fratricide. Eteocles senses his imminent destruction, with its unholy aspect, but he surrenders to the necessity of action, and sped by the curse of Oedipus, he rushes on to his doom.

The Suppliants, a play whose dating has already been discussed, is also the sole survivor of a trilogy; because it was the first of three plays, little can be deduced about the development of ideas in the trilogy as a whole. The play is quite static, dominated by the chorus of Danaids who flee an unwanted marriage with their relatives, the sons of Aegyptus. The evidence permits one to conclude that ultimately the trilogy ends with the submission of the Danaids to the will of the gods and with reasonable reconciliation of opposing forces, themes that point toward the *Oresteia*. A similar conclusion is hypothesized for the trilogy of which *Promētheus desmōtēs* (date unknown; *Prometheus Bound*, 1777) is the only surviving play. *Prometheus Bound* shows the Titan chained to a rock, victim of the outrageous tyranny of Zeus. Very little is known of the remainder of the trilogy (not even the precise titles and order of the plays), but scholars believe that ultimately the Titan was released and that the two opposing forces, Prometheus and the Olympians, reached a reconciliation.

The *Oresteia* of 458 B.C.E. is considered to be Aeschylus's masterpiece. With *Agamemnōn* (*Agamemnon*), *Choēphoroi* (*Libation Bearers*), and *Eumenides*, the trilogy structure reaches perfection. The first two plays, each climaxed by a murder, show human actions leading to a confounding web of blood guilt and retribution, and the third shows divine grace, embodied by Athena and Apollo, working out a reconciliation. The *Oresteia* exhibits advances over the static quality of earlier plays. There, the third actor is used effectively for the first time among surviving tragedies. The prologue, once a mere vehicle for communicating information, is now used to set the mood for each play. Even the set shows progress, because the *skene* building is here used for the first time to represent the front of a palace, with a large central door.

Agamemnon tells of Agamemnon's return from Troy to Argos, and of his murder by Clytemnestra and her lover, Aegisthus. Once again, as in *The Persians*, the early scenes are spacious, later quickening to a climax. The plot shows a human being compelled to act and surrendering his will completely to that destructive compulsion: Agamemnon's decision to sacrifice Iphigeneia recalls Eteocles in *Seven Against Thebes*. Agamemnon's involvement in an inextricable chain of guilt and retribution recapitulates the motif of a god who speeds humanity to destruction, as seen in *The Persians*.

Two other aspects of this play merit discussion here. The first is the remarkable use of imagery: yokes, nets, lions, and snakes are used to characterize actions and individuals, creating a rich network of images that enhances the poetry and underlines the connections between seemingly separate events. The second is Aeschylus's craftsmanship in bringing in past events that have a bearing on the incidents here dramatized. The choral odes are used to tell of the sacrifice of Iphigeneia and of Helen and the origins of the war. Most interesting is the mad raving of Cassandra, Agamemnon's prophetic concubine: She moves back in time to tell of Atreus and Thyestes, then uses her clairvoyance to describe the murder of Agamemnon as it happens; this eliminates the need for a messenger's speech, the usual device for depicting murder on a stage where violence was, by tradition and convention, never portrayed directly.

The second play in the trilogy, *Libation Bearers*, tells the story of Orestes' return to Argos and his killing of Aegisthus and Clytemnestra. Once again, the opening scenes are slow and expansive: They build first to the *anagnorisis*, or recognition, of Orestes by his sister Electra, and ultimately to the two murders. In the climactic scene of the play, Clytemnestra and Orestes meet in a confrontation full of tension and emotion. Orestes' hesitation in the face of his mother's plea is ended by Pylades, breaking for the first time the silence of the third actor. Orestes' ethical problem in this play is very great: He is under divine compulsion to avenge his father's death (the Delphic oracle has so ordered him), but his own will recoils from the deed of matricide. In Homer, the will of the gods and the actions of men are always shown as potentially conflicting, but they never do; instead, they form a cosmic unity. In tragedy, however, human will and divine decree do collide, and this collision is the very essence of tragedy; only a solution from the gods can undo a tragic web of events.

This leads to the final play in the trilogy, *Eumenides*. *Libation Bearers* ends with Orestes being pursued and driven mad by the Erinyes, the Furies that traditionally persecuted perpetrators of kindred murder. Seeking refuge at the Delphic oracle, Orestes is told to go to Athens. Aeschylus, up to this point conservative in his use of the mythology, now departs boldly from the tradition to endow the story with a uniquely Athenian concept of Justice (Diké). A trial is held, in Athens, at the Areopagus, with Apollo as advocate for Orestes. In conflict are the very primitive Greek religion, which held that the mother was all-important, and the newer, father-dominated religion, here represented by Apollo. After the presentation of cases, the jurors cast their votes; Athena votes for acquittal, and the resulting tie is declared an acquittal by the rules of the Areopagus. The Erinyes are still angry and unappeased, but Athena's gentle persuasion soothes even them: They will now be called the Eumenides, "the kindly ones," and they will be held in special honor by the Athenians. Thus, the opposing forces achieve reconciliation, and the curse of the house of Agamemnon is, at long last, lifted.

The *Oresteia* demonstrates a tragic worldview that is, finally, optimistic: The world is full of conflicting forces that give rise to tragic situations, but reconciliation is possible, through the wisdom of the gods. Aeschylus articulates this philosophy through dramas that are elevated in thought as well as language. The language is ornate and filled with rich imagery. The chorus is dominant and vital. Aeschylus's craftsmanship shows an awareness of drama and spectacle. The poet provides the grand form to match and complement his important content, and in so doing achieves greatness.

SOPHOCLES

Sophocles, the second of the great Attic tragedians, lived a long life that nearly spanned the fifth century. He quickly attracted and held a favorable audience, and he was also a vigorous participant in the life of the Athenian polis (city-state), holding several public offices. Thus, Sophocles, more than any other playwright, embodies the character of Athens in its proudest moments.

Sophocles introduced his own innovations in the genre of tragedy: He increased the chorus from twelve to fifteen members, and he added the third actor (in which Aeschlyus, though older, followed him). Sophocles also abandoned the trilogy framework perfected by Aeschlyus, producing instead single plays of taut structure. His language is less ornate than that of earlier tragedy, and the chorus begins to recede slightly, focusing more of the attention on the individual characters.

Only seven plays survive by which to judge the skill and accomplishment of Sophocles, the same number extant for Aeschylus. *Aias* (c. 440 B.C.E.; *Ajax*, 1729), considered the earliest of the surviving plays, tells the story of the title character's anger and despair at not receiving the arms of Achilles, of his suicide and the subsequent debate over the treatment of his body. The suicide of Ajax takes place halfway through the play, so that the drama falls into two parts: The first part deals with Ajax's deluded attempt to avenge himself on Agamemnon and Menelaus; his anguish at discovering that, in his madness, he has captured and tortured not his enemies but their cattle; and finally his death. The second half deals with attempts by Ajax's wife, Tecmessa, and his half brother, Teucer, to secure proper burial, and their success, aided by the advocacy of the man who defeated Ajax in the contest for the arms, Odysseus. The play has often been criticized as having a "diptych" structure, two distinct parts only loosely welded together. In fact, however, the play coheres properly. Ajax, in

the form of a corpse, continues to dominate the tragedy, even in the second half, and his destiny is not completely resolved with his death, because a Greek would regard the issue of disposal of the body as an important part of the individual's fate. It is, however, proper to note that *Ajax*, like other early plays of Sophocles, lacks the tight unity of his later tragedies, especially *Oidipous Tyrannos* (c. 429 B.C.E..; *Oedipus Tyrannus*, 1715; also known as *Oedipus the King*).

On a thematic level, Ajax shows the overweening pride, the hubris, of Aeschylean tragedy, and he surely suffers as a result. There is more here, however, than the Aeschylean hubris and *ate* motif: Odysseus's refusal in the prologue to gloat over Ajax's catastrophic situation points the way to a more complex philosophy. Odysseus take the plight of Ajax as a reminder of his own difficult lot as a mortal, and Athena compliments his self-restraint. Even in a society that believed in harming one's enemy, Odysseus shows great compassion and humanity. Sophocles demonstrates his debt to Aeschylus in this play, but he also shows the ability to move beyond these roots.

One interesting point of craftsmanship in this play, later to become a Sophoclean trademark, is the moment of premature joy and relief, when it appears that disaster might be averted, only to be followed by complete catastrophe. The moment comes in this play when Ajax, realizing that he has been deluded, comes out of his tent and makes a speech: He has learned, through suffering, the laws of the universe, and he now intends to purify himself, bury his sword, and make peace with Agamemnon and Menelaus. The speech itself has led to much scholarly debate (Can Ajax be lying? Is he merely speaking figuratively, knowing his words will be taken literally?), but the chorus responds with an ode of joy, to be followed quickly by Calchas's ominous words and the suicide of the hero. The same device, an ironic manipulation of the audience's emotions that also serves to emphasize the Sophoclean theme of the fallibility of human reasoning, would be used later in *Oedipus Tyrannus*.

Like *Ajax*, *Antigonē* (441 B.C.E.; *Antigone*, 1729) has been criticized for a lack of unity: Some see separate tragedies here, that of Antigone and that of Creon, which do not cohere completely. The story begins in the immediate aftermath of the expedition of the seven against Thebes, the battle in which Polyneices, the invader, killed and was killed by his brother Eteocles, defender of Thebes. Creon, now king of Thebes, has declared that Polyneices shall remain unburied. In the prologue, the sisters of the slain brothers, Ismene and Antigone, discuss these events, and it becomes clear that while Ismene feels powerless in the face of Creon's power, Antigone is determined to act. This scene, similar to one in *Ēlektra* (418-410 B.C.E.; *Electra*, 1649), is crucial because it eliminates a possible ally and helps to place the tragic figure, Antigone, in isolation.

Antigone's defiance is largely symbolic, but it makes clear her disregard for Creon's edict: She sprinkles dust over the corpse of Polyneices, thus performing a ritual burial. When the messenger reports this to Creon, the chorus marvels at the human ingenuity that has made this act possible, in spite of Creon's guards: The famous choral "Ode to Man" speaks of humankind's greatness and strangeness, of people's abilities to tame their environment and their boldness in confronting nature. These words reflect the humanism of the mid-fifth century B.C.E.: "Man is the measure of all things," Protagoras said. This was the era of Athenian imperialism, of the rise of sophism, and humanity's potential seemed limitless. Sophocles' anxiety over these developments is clear in the final lines of the ode, which remind the audience that humankind is ultimately subject to the law of the gods.

Antigone, here the representative of the immutable divine law and thus not cowed by human pretensions of power, persists even in a face-to-face confrontation with the king; as a result, she is sentenced to be buried alive. Haemon, the son of Creon and betrothed of Antigone, attempts to dissuade his father, but he meets with failure and departs in anger. The prophet Tiresias gives stern warning against the pollution of the unburied corpse, but he, too, is rebuffed. An eleventh-hour change of heart comes too late: Antigone hangs herself in the underground chamber; Haemon kills himself on the body of his beloved; and Eurydice, hearing of her son's death, curses Creon and dies also. Creon alone survives, a broken man.

Some critics have argued that the play derived its tragedy from a clash between two forces of equal moral validity: the state and the family. In fact, Creon does not represent the legitimate interests of the state, because he breaks divine law in depriving the dead of burial. Sophocles reminds his audience and his city that every ruler, however strong, remains subject to a higher law. Creon, in his hubris, breaks that law, creating a web of tragedy that destroys everything he loves.

Trachinai (435-429 B.C.E.; *The Women of Trachis*, 1729) tells story of Deianira, the wife of Heracles, who lives in Trachis with their son Hyllus while the hero is off on his adventures. Word comes to Trachis that Heracles will soon arrive, but Deianira learns that he is bringing with him his new love, the nymph Iole. She remembers the dying words of the centaur Nessus, who had promised that his blood could be used as a love-philter, should Heracles' affections every stray. She sends her husband a robe smeared with Nessus's blood, but it has far from the desired effect. Heracles begins to die in agony, and Deianira, hearing this, kills herself. The hero finally arrives onstage, where he bids that Hyllus marry Iole, and then dies.

Sophocles has clearly moved beyond the world of Aeschylean hubris and "learning through suffering." Deianira is guilty of nothing more than trying to secure her husband's love, yet every action brings her closer to doom. What can be the meaning of this? The gods' ways may seem obscure and even reproachable to people, but Sophocles never wavers in his religious faith. The play closes: "In all this there was nothing that was without Zeus." This deep religious acceptance, as well as the concept of people's active role in bringing about their own downfall, looks forward to Sophocles' greatest tragedy, *Oedipus Tyrannus*.

The exact date of *Oedipus Tyrannus* is not certain, but scholars place it somewhere between 429 B.C.E. and 425 B.C.E. As such, it stands at the very climax of the classical era, at the last moment of undisputed Athenian supremacy. The art of Sophocles also reaches a climax with this work, whose classic unity remains unparalleled in Western literature. Gone are the diptych structures of *Ajax*, *Antigone*, and *The*

Women of Trachis: The play coheres perfectly around the character of Oedipus, who stands before the audience in nearly every moment of every episode. Oedipus, seeking a murderer, is himself the very murderer he seeks. This taut, ironic mystery story is enhanced by equally ironic imagery. Sight and blindness lose their traditional meanings in a world in which the blind can see while the sighted are blind. Walking and foot imagery focuses attention on Oedipus's ancient ankle injury, which holds the key to his identity. The Delphic motto, "Know thyself," becomes a leitmotif as Oedipus, the great riddle-solver, searches for the man who is really himself. The imagery, structure, and expert plotting of the play result in such a strong, compact composition that *Oedipus Tyrannus* became even in ancient times a standard by which other plays were judged. Indeed, in the fourth century, Aristotle, in his *Poetics*, organized his methodology for criticizing tragedy around this play, his paradigm for excellence.

Most of the important events that contribute to the tragic situation have already taken place before the point in time when *Oedipus Tyrannus* begins. Laius and Jocasta, fearing a prophecy that Laius's own offspring will one day kill him, exposed their infant son, Oedipus ("swell-foot"), piercing his ankles with a thong. The servant charged with disposing of the child, overcome with pity, disobeyed his orders and handed Oedipus to a Corinthian shepherd. The shepherd gave the infant to his childless king and queen, Polybus and Merope, who reared him as their own. As a young man, Oedipus left Corinth, troubled by a drunken remark impugning his legitimacy. Seeking help from the Delphic oracle, he was told that he was destined to kill his father and marry his mother; in order to spare his beloved Polybus and Merope, he resolved never to return to Corinth. On leaving Delphi, he encountered Laius and his entourage. A scuffle ensued, in which Oedipus killed Laius and all in his bodyguard with the exception of one man. Soon after, he arrived at Thebes, where he rescued the city by solving the riddle of the sphinx. As a reward, he was made king and became the husband of the widowed Jocasta; they have lived together happily, bearing four children.

The play opens with a group of Thebans gathered at the palace of Oedipus, seeking relief from the plague that has gripped the city. Oedipus emerges to say that he sympathizes with them and has anticipated the suggestion that he seek aid from the oracle; in fact, he is now awaiting the return of Creon from Delphi. This speech immediately establishes Oedipus as a leader of compassion, energy, and intelligence. Creon soon returns with the message that the plague is caused by moral pollution: Laius's murder remains unsolved. Oedipus at once sets out to discover the identity of the murderer, calling down a curse on the guilty man. He sends for the blind seer, Tiresias, whose hesitation to speak frustrates Oedipus, and angry words are exchanged. Tiresias's anger leads him to blurt out an accusation: Oedipus himself is the murderer, and he lives in incest. The outburst surprises Oedipus; his intelligent mind darts in an erroneous direction, and he leaps to the assumption that Creon has conspired with Tiresias to unseat his government. A rancorous confrontation between Oedipus and Creon follows, but it is interrupted by Jocasta. On hearing about the revelations of Tiresias, the queen attempts to comfort her husband by deriding prophecy and prophets: After all, did not a prophecy predict that Laius would die at the hands of his son, when instead he was killed by robbers at a triple crossroad? Her attempt to comfort Oedipus plants a seed of doubt in his mind; he recalls the incident at the crossroad, but he clings to the hope that Laius was killed by more than one man and sends for the servant who survived the encounter.

At this point, a messenger arrives from Corinth, announcing the death of Polybus. Oedipus, sad yet relieved, refuses to return to Corinth, still fearing incest with Merope. The messenger now attempts to comfort Oedipus by telling him that Polybus and Merope were not his real parents: The messenger himself, once a shepherd, received the infant Oedipus from a servant of Laius. Here Jocasta leaves the scene in ominous silence, and Oedipus assumes that she is troubled by some "womanly" fear that her husband may prove to be of low birth. The chorus sings a jaunty song of wonder at Oedipus's birth: Perhaps he is the child of god. (The happy ode ironically prefiguring doom is reminiscent of a similar pattern in *Ajax*.) The servant of Laius now enters. He resists speaking, because he is in a unique position to know everything: Not only did he witness the death of Laius, but he is also the very servant once charged with the exposure of the infant Oedipus. The king interrogates the servant, and even when the truth is nearly apparent, he presses on until all is known. Oedipus cries out his misery and leaves the stage. A messenger soon reports the denouement: Oedipus rushed into the palace, saw that Jocasta had hanged herself, and struck his eyes repeatedly with her garment-brooches. The blinded Oedipus now returns, bids his daughters farewell, and prepares to go into exile.

A summary of the plot reveals several points of Sophoclean craftsmanship. The play is structured so that every effort to provide comfort merely brings the web closer around the participants, and Oedipus's own intelligence and vigor plunge him into the abyss; this structure provides a fine vehicle for Sophocles' superb use of irony. On the negative side, critics have often pointed out that in order to achieve such a compact composition, Sophocles was forced to make two of his characters perform double functions: The servant of Laius who was charged with the exposure of Oedipus is also the survivor of the incident at the crossroad, and the Corinthian shepherd who received the infant is the same man later sent to bear the message of Polybus's death. All of this is very contrived, yet it does not interfere with the believability of the play.

On a deeper level, what does the play mean? Surely, the concepts of Aeschylean hubris and *ate* do not apply here. Oedipus is guilty of nothing more than being himself, and yet, this terrible fate befalls him. As always, Sophocles finds his answer in the great, impenetrable ways of the gods. After Jocasta's speech deriding prophecy, the chorus sings an ode questioning the truth of the gods and their oracles: If these things are not valid, the chorus asks, what is the point in performing in a tragic chorus? Ultimately, the play proves the veracity of all the oracular predictions. Human reasoning is fallible, as seen in Oedipus's repeatedly erroneous conclusions, but

Zeus's wisdom is perfect, and his justice is valid. The deep religious faith of Sophocles persists.

Electra is usually grouped with Sophocles' late works. Like Aeschylus's *Libation Bearers*, *Electra* tells the story of Orestes' return to Argos and the vengeful killings of Clytemnestra and Aegisthus, but there are many differences between the two plays. *Electra* focuses on the title character rather than on her brother—her suffering in the household of Clytemnestra and Aegisthus, her anguish when she believes her brother is dead, her bitterness toward her mother, and her joy when the lovers have been killed. Moreover, the moral view has changed: Whereas Aeschylus saw the act of killing Clytemnestra as a classic dilemma, fraught with problems whether Orestes acted or refrained from acting, Sophocles' Clytemnestra is wholly evil, and the matricide is simple and laudable. Another Sophoclean innovation is the addition of the character of Chrysothemis, a sister who is mentioned in very early descriptions of the family of Agamemnon but who does not appear in Aeschylus or in Euripides' *Ēlektra* (413 B.C.E.; *Electra*, 1782). Like Ismene in *Antigone*, she is a foil whose cowardly withdrawal adds to the isolation of the heroine while also emphasizing her bravery.

Electra bears certain similarities to the other plays of Sophocles' old age. The characters interact with one another in a more meaningful way than in earlier plays, replacing the static speech making of previous dramas. Ultimately, they are still subject to the gods, but the divine element has receded to the background of the action. The deep emotions of Electra dominate, and there is less mention of oracles and prophecies. Another important change that characterizes the plays of Sophocles' old age is the disappearance of the tragic situation in which human action and divine ordinance come into conflict, to be replaced by insights into the way a profound human soul responds to momentous changes in its circumstances and situation.

This is true also of *Philoktētēs* (*Philoctetes*, 1729), for which there is a firm date of 409 B.C.E. The story, based on the Cyclic Epics and also the subject of earlier lost tragedies by Aeschylus and Euripides, goes as follows: On the way to Troy, the Greek expedition abandoned the warrior Philoctetes on the deserted island of Lemnos because a snakebite had given him a malodorous wound that did not heal. A prophecy having declared that Troy could not be taken without Philoctetes and the bow of Heracles, then in Philoctetes' possession, Odysseus and Neoptolemus, the son of Achilles, are sent to bring Philoctetes to Troy. In the Sophoclean play, Odysseus is devious and unappealing, and he forces the noble and straightforward Neoptolemus to aid him in luring Philoctetes to the ship under the pretense of bringing him back to Greece. Neoptolemus feels unexpected sympathy for the stricken man and is moved both by Philoctetes' joy at meeting another human being and by his anguish from the painful wound. When Philoctetes entrusts him with the sacred bow, he cannot betray this sick man and hand it to Odysseus. He finds, further, that he cannot continue as an accomplice to deception, for to do so would be to deny his own innate character, or *physis*. Agreeing instead to take Philoctetes home to Greece, in the face of Odysseus's angry objection, Neoptolemus shows the true nobility of his nature; a timely epiphany of Heracles redirects events back to their traditional course, sending all three heroes back to Troy. Thus, Sophocles upholds the conservative, aristocratic view that heredity (*physis*) is a more important determinant of character than environment (*nomos*); the sophistic movement of the late fifth century B.C.E. argued that the opposite was true, and the debate continues even today.

Oidipous epi Kolōnōi (*Oedipus at Colonus*, 1729), the final tragedy of Sophocles' long career, was produced posthumously in 401 B.C.E. The play is a gentle, melancholy approach to death, reflecting the poet's advanced age and his inevitable confrontation of his own mortality. Oedipus, a blind old beggar attended by his loving daughters, at last arrives in the grove outside Athens where his peaceful death has been prophesied. He is greeted by the Attic king, Theseus, symbol of Athenian humanity. Because Oedipus has been endowed with special powers, he is sought by both sides in the developing conflict between Eteocles and Polyneices. Creon and Polyneices both attempt to secure the old man's talismanic aid, but he angrily rebuffs these villains. He meets a heroic and mystical death, accompanied only by good Theseus.

Though the play lacks the structural compactness of Sophocles' finest works, the figure of Oedipus provides unity. Moreover, *Oedipus at Colonus* contains some of Sophocles' finest lyric poetry, in particular the famous "Ode to Athens," the poet's eloquent farewell to his city. No truly tragic situation, such as that of *Oedipus Tyrannus*, is to be found here; rather, the poet presents a sequel to the earlier play, in which a great soul who has suffered as no other finds special favor in the eyes of the gods. In death, he finds both strength and peace, the hope of all men of deep religious faith.

Sophocles, then, moves from an early era of Aeschylean influence to find an identity of his own in the restrained language, spare imagery, and coherent structures of his best plays. The dominant theme of his tragedies is a relentless faith in the ultimate justice and wisdom of the gods. Even Oedipus, that most miserable creature among mortals, finds ultimate solace in the special favor that comes through acknowledging the wisdom of Zeus.

EURIPIDES

One tradition holds that Aeschylus fought at Salamis, that Sophocles performed in the youth-chorus that celebrated the victory of Salamis, and that Euripides was born on the very day of that celebration. Although the tradition is probably not accurate with regard to Euripides' birth (dated about 485 B.C.E.), it does underline the generational gaps that separated the three great tragedians: Euripides is very far removed from the immediate memory of the Persian Wars. The conservatism and deep religious faith of Aeschylus and Sophocles yield to the intellectual restlessness of Euripides, and the rise of sophism makes itself felt even in the tragic theater. The plays are full of passion but also of rationalism. Characters are closer to the ordinary human level. The catastrophes and joys of mortals are no longer viewed as part of an important divine plan for the cosmos: Euripides has deep uncertainties about the gods and their universe. The poet's doubts encompass not only religious issues but also the life of the Athenian polis.

Unlike Sophocles, Euripides was withdrawn and somewhat alienated from the state. He produced plays for more than ten years before winning first prize, and he achieved four victories in his career as a playwright. His plays were controversial and disturbing, and he never achieved the popularity of his predecessors. He died in Macedonia, far from Athens.

Euripides has a surviving corpus of eighteen plays. The Euripidean corpus is large, relative to the extant corpus of Aeschylus or Sophocles, and it is possible to examine Euripides' greatest plays alongside those of lesser caliber.

Euripides' earliest surviving play is *Alkēstis* (*Alcestis*, 1781) of 438 B.C.E. *Alcestis* poses a problem of genre, because the *hypothesis* (a summary in the manuscript) shows that it was the fourth play in a tetralogy; it therefore took the position normally occupied by a satyr play. Further, the play has a happy ending and contains burlesque elements, especially in connection with Heracles, often a buffoon in comedy. It is, then, a very special type of tragedy, but the serious issues it raises leave no doubt that it is a tragedy. The play deals with Admetus, a man whose generous hospitality to the gods has earned for him a reprieve from death, provided that he can find another person willing to die in his place. His wife, Alcestis, has agreed to this supreme sacrifice, and she bids farewell to her family and home. In the meantime, the hero Heracles arrives, and Admetus, unwilling to be inhospitable, welcomes him to the household without explaining the current problems. Pheres, the father of Admetus, comes to the palace with funeral gifts, and he and Admetus argue: The rancorous discussion takes the form of an agon, a formal debate in which two characters follow a format of alternating long speeches, short speeches, and, finally, *stichomythia*, or alternating lines. Euripides was a master of this device, and it recurs often in his plays. Following the agon and the exit of the funeral procession, Heracles learns the truth and sets out to wrestle death for the prize of Alcestis. He succeeds, and a veiled Alcestis is returned to her husband.

The play shows a marked contrast with the works of Aeschylus and Sophocles. The gods have receded far to the background, and humankind is now the fo-

cal point. The main character of the play poses insuperable difficulties for the modern reader. Admetus not only is willing to permit his wife to die in his place, but he also grieves and expects sympathy because of his impending loss. This makes him a very unsympathetic character, and one wonders why Alcestis is willing to die for such a man. The problem finds no ready solution, but it is important to remember that Euripides inherited the character of Admetus from mythology and from earlier tragedy.

Euripides won only third prize with *Mēdeia* (*Medea*, 1781) of 431 B.C.E., but it is considered to be one of his masterpieces. Following the adventure of the golden fleece and the death of Jason's uncle, Pelias, Jason and Medea have come to live in Corinth with their children. Jason has just become engaged to marry the daughter of Creon, the king. Medea is predictably furious at this turn of events, and her anger increases at the news that she is to be exiled. In a scene with Creon, however, she manages to have her departure postponed for a crucial twenty-four hours. A bitter confrontation with Jason follows, and Euripides once again shows his mastery of the agon. Aegeus, the king of Athens, enters in the next episode: Critics point to the contrived nature of this appearance and to its lack of relevance to the play, but it advances the plot in that it provides Medea with a much-needed place of refuge. Medea continues her plan by summoning Jason, pretending to a change of heart, and offering to send the children with gifts for the bride. Through all this, the chorus supports and abets the efforts of Medea. A messenger soon announces the deaths of Creon and his daughter, caused by the gifts of Medea, a poisoned robe and diadem. Medea now strikes her greatest blow, killing her children. Jason returns to find Medea on the roof, with the bodies of the children, intent on escaping to Athens in the magic chariot of her grandfather, Helius. Her final speech deals with the establishment of a cult for her children at Corinth, and later plays confirm Euripides' fondness for cult-etiologies.

The tragedy derives from the conflict between Medea's great passion and her rational, deliberate consideration: The victory of passion makes the situation truly tragic. Once again, the plans of mortals are the focal point, and no divine design is at work behind the scenes. The character of Medea alone contains the conflicting elements that cause catastrophe. Ultimately, Medea is repugnant as she stands gloating over the bodies of the children, and this creates a problem similar to that involving the character of Admetus in *Alcestis*. Even so, it is a tribute to Euripides' skill that the audience remains in sympathy with Medea for a long time—until she becomes at once more than human and less than human.

Like *Medea*, *Hippolytos* (*Hippolytus*, 1781), of 428 B.C.E., tells the story of an erotically obsessed woman. The play begins with a prologue by Aphrodite: She has been spurned by the chaste Hippolytus, who cleaves only to the virgin Artemis, and accordingly, she has planned a revenge that will begin with Phaedra, Hippolytus's stepmother, falling in love with him. Hippolytus and his companions enter, and the audience witnesses his worship of Artemis and his deliberate and dangerous neglect of Aphrodite. Phaedra's nurse informs the audience that her mistress is wasting away with a mysterious disease. In a scene of exquisite craftsmanship, the nurse manipulates an unwilling Phaedra into confessing her passion, and then speaks soothingly of "magic charms" that will solve her problem. Phaedra soon overhears the end of a conversation between the nurse and her stepson: Hippolytus angrily rejects a sexual proposition delivered by the nurse on behalf of Phaedra. The heroine now kills herself in despair, leaving for Theseus a note containing a false accusation of rape against Hippolytus. Theseus returns from abroad, reads the note, and denounces his son, calling on Poseidon to destroy him. Hippolytus, bound by an unwilling oath to the nurse, cannot defend himself, and a sea monster causes his chariot to crash, killing him; this disaster is narrated in an ornate, highly wrought messenger's speech. At the close of the play, the dying Hippolytus is brought into the presence of his father, and Artemis, appearing *ex machina*, reveals the truth to Theseus and announces the foundation of a cult to honor Hippolytus. Hippolytus forgives his father and dies.

As in *Medea*, the tragedy derives from the central character's failure to maintain rationality in the face of great passion, but the struggle of Phaedra—unlike that of Medea—is ennobling. Euripides had been soundly defeated several years earlier in his presentation of another play about Hippolytus in which Phaedra boldly approached Hippolytus herself, without the mediation of the nurse. In the later play, Phaedra's hesitation and her willingness to die rather than succumb to passion elevate her character. In addition, the other characters in the play demonstrate different types of excess that also contribute to the tragic outcome: Hippolytus's fanatical chastity and his hubristic rejection of Aphrodite speed his doom, aided by the quick temper of Theseus. The role of the two goddesses is problematic, for it appears that they use Phaedra as a pawn in a careless and petty contest between themselves. One solution is to view the goddesses as representatives of opposing forces in human nature, sexuality and chastity, rather than as literal depictions of actual deities.

Two other aspects of *Hippolytus* merit brief comment. The first is the loveliness of the choral lyrics, in particular the imagery of the inviolate meadow that is used to portray human chastity near the beginning of the play. Another is the misogynistic speech given by the angry Hippolytus on hearing the proposition of the nurse. Speeches such as this, and Euripides' powerful depictions of female characters like Medea and Phaedra, led to accusations of misogyny against the poet himself, even in ancient times. It should be remembered that the speech of Hippolytus, while written by Euripides, does not necessarily reflect the poet's personal views; moreover, the character of Phaedra is noble, human, and complex, not patently irredeemable.

Heklabē (*Hecuba*, 1782), of 425 B.C.E., is also dominated by a woman of great passion. In the aftermath of defeat, Troy's great matriarch must suffer two additional griefs: Her daughter, Polyxena, goes heroically to death as she is sacrificed to the shade of Achilles, and the body of Hecuba's son, Polydorus, is discovered in Thrace, where he has been betrayed and killed through the greed of the Thracian king, Polymestor. Hecuba has her revenge, blinding the king and killing his children. The play is often criticized for its failure to integrate its two parts, each of which contains a formal agon, or debate. An important development here is the taking over of some of the lyric by the characters, further diminishing the role of the chorus. Also worthy of note is Hecuba's speech on the nature of human nobility: Euripides raises the old question of *nomos* versus *physis*, no longer adhering to Sophocles' belief in the power of heredity, but leaving the issue open.

Andromachē (*Andromache*, 1782), of 426 B.C.E., which describes the fates of Andromache, Neoptolemus, Hermione, and Orestes in the years after the Trojan War, is more correctly criticized for disunity. Andromache has been living as captive with Neoptolemus, to whom she has born a son. Hermione, Neoptolemus's childless legal wife, attempts with the aid of her father, Menelaus, to ruin Andromache while Neoptolemus is absent at Delphi. The attempt fails, primarily as a result of help from the aging Peleus, Neoptolemus's grandfather. In the second half of the play, Orestes comes and claims Hermione to be his wife, and it is revealed that Orestes' ambush has killed Neoptolemus. Thetis appears at the close of the play to complete the plot. Most interesting here is the virulent anti-Spartan feeling that emerges in the portrait of Menelaus, a reflection of Athenian chauvinism in the early years of the Peloponnesian Wars.

Another play of the same period is *Hērakleidai* (c. 430 B.C.E.; *The Children of Heracles*, 1781), which shows Alcmena and the children of Heracles still pursued by Heracles' great enemy, Eurystheus, even after the death of the hero. The Heraclidae, as the children are known, find refuge at Athens with the gracious and humane king, Demophon. This, too, is an expression of Athenian patriotism from the early years of the Peloponnesian Wars. The play contains the narrative of a battle, in which the Heraclidae, led by Hyllus and the aging Iolaus, and augmented by Athenian aid, are victorious. Macaria, a daughter of Heracles, sacrifices herself in compliance with divine conditions, and, during the battle, the old Iolaus is miraculously rejuvenated. Eurystheus is captured and brought before Alcmena, but Athenian pleas for humanity fail, and in a Hecuba-like moment of rage, she demands his execution. He dies with a promise of proper Athenian burial.

Hiketides (c. 423 B.C.E.; *The Suppliants*, 1781), a third play of the same period, also emphasizes Athenian justice and humanity, here embodied in the person of the Athenian king, Theseus. In the aftermath of the failed expedition of the seven against Thebes, the Argive king, Adrastus, wishes to have military support; the mothers of the dead Argive heroes wish to ensure the proper burial of their sons. Theseus will not aid Adrastus, but he will not surrender him to the Thebans either, and he also agrees to provide the suppliants with the funeral rites they seek. In doing these things, Theseus has the opportunity to defend his humane actions, and further, the very nature of democracy, in an agon with the Theban herald. In many ways, his enlightened leadership recalls that of Pericles, the Athenian statesman who succumbed to the plague at the very beginning of the Peloponnesian Wars. A battle narrative tells how Theseus forced the surrender of the Argive bodies for burial. Adrastus gives an eloquent funeral oration, stressing the importance of education in contributing to the greatness of the individual: Here Euripides, following the tenets of the enlightenment, chooses *nomos* over *physis*, a point of view that separates him from Aeschylus and Sophocles. As the funeral continues, Evadne throws herself on the pyre of her husband, Capaneus, adding a note of passion to contrast with the oratorical rationalism elsewhere in the play. The tragedy closes with an appearance by Athena, *ex machina*, who solemnizes a sworn treaty between Athens and Argos. Although Euripides is not a propagandist, *Andromache*, *The Children of Heracles*, and *The Suppliants* all reveal an attitude of high praise for Athenian values and ideals, reflecting the patriotic feelings of that city-state as it embarked on a lengthy conflict with its rival state, Sparta.

Hērakles (*Heracles*, 1781), a play presented some time around 420 B.C.E., shows the great hero of mythology in two very different aspects: In the first half, he returns triumphant from his adventures to rescue his wife, Megara, and their children from the tyrant Lycus; in the latter half, Hera sends Lyssa, the personification of madness, to drive Heracles into a fury, during which he murders his wife and children. His situation on returning to a state of lucidity is analogous to that of Ajax in the play by Sophocles, but whereas the Sophoclean Ajax, bound by heroic notions of honor, had only the recourse of suicide, the more enlightened world of Euripides shows that Heracles can continue to live in spite of his grief, and at the conclusion of the play, he is led off by Theseus to Athens. *Heracles* also invites comparison with Sophocles in that it shows a once-great hero faced with total misery and distress, but here there is no deep religious faith in the ultimate wisdom of the gods, only a profound questioning of the vicissitudes of human existence.

In the same period, Euripides presented at one performance three plays dealing with the Trojan War, of which only the third, *Trōiades* (415 B.C.E.; *The Trojan Women*, 1782), has survived; fragments of the other two show that the three plays were only loosely connected and did not constitute an Aeschylean trilogy. The play is similar to *Hecuba* but is less unified, detailing an assortment of the traditional events connected with the fall of Troy: Polyxena's death, the allotment of Trojan women to Greek warriors, and the death of Andromache's son, Astyanax. In the middle of the play, Hecuba and Helen engage in a highly rhetorical agon. The audience also hears of the misery yet to befall the victorious Greeks, partly through the prophecies of Cassandra and partially through the prologue speeches of Poseidon and Athena. In 415 B.C.E., on the eve of the disastrous Sicilian expedition, Euripides wished to demonstrate to his audience the full horror of war, for victor and vanquished alike. Most interesting here is a prayer by Hecuba, in which she articulates Euripides' searching doubt about the nature of the divine.

In 413 B.C.E., Euripides presented his *Ēlektra* (*Electra*, 1782), which contains a probable reference to the Sicilian expedition. It is not known whether the Sophoclean *Electra* was earlier or later than this play, but along with Aeschylus's *Libation Bearers*, the two *Electras* provide an excellent opportunity to compare the three great tragedians as they treat the same myth. Euripides is innovative, adding a poor farmer of noble birth as a "husband" for Electra (the marriage is not consummated); here he shows his expertise with "low" characters and a less aristocratic viewpoint,

which endows even a poor man with nobility. In his moral outlook, Euripides harks back to Aeschylus: The act of matricide is abhorrent, whatever the deed it may avenge. Though Electra's bitterness is clear during her great agon with Clytemnestra, she and Orestes both are consumed with horror in the aftermath. The Dioscuri appear *ex machina* to ensure the traditional ending (Electra will marry Pylades; Orestes must go to the Areopagus), but in place of Aeschylus's grand plan in which the gods find a way to justice, there is only Euripides' questioning of the wisdom of Apollo, the god who motivated Orestes to commit matricide. Thus, *Electra*, like *Heracles* and *The Trojan Women*, shows Euripides to be an iconoclast, a restless and searching man who lacks the great religious faith of his predecessors.

In *Helenē* (*Helen*, 1782), of 412 B.C.E., Euripides expands on the unusual history of the Trojan War found in Stesichorus's *Palinode* (early sixth century B.C.E.): Helen never went to Troy, but a phantom was sent in her place, while she spent those years in Egypt. As the play opens, Helen's stay in Egypt has reached a crisis. Her original protector, Proteus, is now dead, and his son Theoclymenus has courted Helen so aggressively that she now seeks refuge at Proteus's tomb. An incorrect message reporting Menelaus's death frightens her further, but the hero himself soon appears, shipwrecked on return to Greece, and a dramatic recognition occurs. With the aid of Theonoe, the king's sister, the reunited couple contrive an escape by deception, and the Dioscuri appear *ex machina* to prevent Theoclymenus from venting his anger on Theonoe. The recognition (*anagnorisis*) and intrigue (*mechanema*) motifs look forward to the New Comedy of Menander. The controlling force in these events is not the gods or destiny, but a new component in the universe, chance (*tyche*).

Iphigeneia ē en Taurois (c. 414 B.C.E.; *Iphigenia in Tauris*, 1782), a play of the same period, also employs motifs of recognition, deception, and escape. Iphigenia, the daughter of Agamemnon, was surreptitiously rescued at Aulis, and she now serves as priestess to Artemis in the far-off land of the Taurians, where she is charged with the consecration of strangers for sacrifice. Orestes, driven by the Furies even after his trial, comes to this place on the orders of Apollo in order to obtain the cult statue of Artemis. Accompanied by Pylades, he is about to become a sacrificial victim when brother and sister recognize each other. Employing intrigue and deception, they escape the pursuit of Thoas with the statue in their possession. Appearing *ex machina*, Athena establishes the cult of Artemis.

Another of Euripides' "*tyche* plays" is *Iōn* (c. 411 B.C.E.; *Ion*, 1781), also of the same period, a drama of highly complex plot and recognition. Creusa, the daughter of Erechtheus, bore a son to Apollo, and the child was later taken by Hermes to serve as a priest at Delphi. Creusa was married to Xuthus, king of Athens, and their childlessness drove them to seek help at Delphi. The oracle induces Xuthus to accept Ion into his house as a son, but in its subtlety it miscalculates, for Creusa, thinking Ion to be Xuthus's illegitimate son, flies into a rage and attempts to poison him. About to be executed, Creusa flees to the altar, where the priestess of Apollo brings forward the chest in which Ion was exposed as an infant; the tokens show that Ion is the son of Creusa, and Athena clears up the remaining details. The use of recognition tokens, once again, looks forward to New Comedy, and again, the predominant force in the universe, which interferes even with the plans of the gods, is chance.

Phoinissai (c. 410 B.C.E.; *The Phoenician Women*, 1781) and *Orestēs* (408 B.C.E.; *Orestes*, 1782) are Euripides' latest surviving plays written before his departure from Athens to Macedon. Both exhibit an almost frantic attempt to pack as much material as possible into the plot framework. *The Phoenician Women* is yet another play built on the myth of the attack of the seven against Thebes: Included are an eleventh-hour attempt by Polyneices to avoid conflict; the necessary sacrifice of Menoeceus, the son of Creon; messengers' speeches describing first the attack of the seven and later the double fratricide of Polyneices and Eteocles, which causes the suicide of Jocasta; the exile of Oedipus from Thebes; and Creon's edict prohibiting the burial of Polyneices. A problem is posed by Antigone's simultaneous plans to bury her brother and to join Oedipus in exile, but

the conjecture that these lines are spurious is no longer widely accepted.

In *Orestes*, Orestes and Electra cower in the wake of the matricide. Orestes suffers madness, and the people of Argos are angry with the brother and sister. Menelaus, a possible champion, enters, but Tyndareus, father of Clytemnestra, persuades him to abandon Electra and Orestes; Menelaus accedes mainly out of personal cowardice, and his baseness of character serves to increase the audience's sympathy for Electra and Orestes, who now are joined by the noble Pylades. In desperation, they attempt to kill Helen, but this fails, and they decide to seize Hermione, the daughter of Helen and Menelaus, as hostage. From the roof of the palace, they force Menelaus's capitulation, but only the intervention by Apollo, as *deus ex machina*, can clear up this mess: Orestes will obtain justice at the Areopagus and marry Hermione. The play is complex and, in places, illogical, hinting at a slight decline during the poet's last years in Athens.

Iphigenia ē en Aulidi (*Iphigenia in Aulis*, 1782) and *Bakchai* (*The Bacchae*, 1781) were both written in the last years of Euripides' life, in Macedon; they were produced in 405 B.C.E. at Athens, posthumously, by a son also known as Euripides. These plays are far superior to *Orestes* and *The Phoenician Women*. *Iphigenia in Aulis*, a play of many reversals, describes events at Aulis, where the Greek fleet is becalmed by Artemis, who has demanded the sacrifice of Agamemnon's daughter in order to provide favorable winds for the journey to Troy. On the pretext that Iphigenia is to be married to Achilles, Agamemnon has sent for his wife and daughter. A change of heart causes him to send a second message canceling the first, but this is intercepted by Menelaus, for whose adulterous wife the war will be fought. The brothers argue, but when Clytemnestra's arrival is announced and Menelaus sees his brother's despair, he argues against the sacrifice, and Agamemnon returns to his original position, believing that Iphigenia's death is inevitable. A chance meeting between Clytemnestra and Achilles proves embarrassing, because Achilles knows nothing of the prophecy that he is to become her son-in-law. Mother and daughter soon learn the real reason that they have been summoned, and

Clytemnestra lashes out at Agamemnon while Iphigenia begs for her life, declaring that it is better to live in shame than to die in glory. Achilles, meanwhile, is prepared to defend Iphigenia, because he cannot allow the misuse of his name and honor. The expedition to Troy is soon revealed as having a deeper significance than the mere retrieval of an adulterous wife—it is a battle against Asian despotism. Iphigenia now changes her position: She will die willingly, and she will not allow Achilles to incur the wrath of the Greek fleet in her defense. She goes off proudly to her death. The ending of the play is plagued with manuscript problems, but it is probable that Euripides followed the version in which Artemis miraculously rescues Iphigenia, substituting an animal in her place. The most interesting thing about the play is that, for the first time, there is true character development; there is no step-by-step evolution, but Iphigenia is shown in two separate stages of a psychological process; on a stage where consistency of character was highly valued, this was indeed an exceptional innovation.

The great era of Greek tragedy, and with it the career of Euripides, concludes where it began—with the worship of Dionysus: Euripides' final play, *The Bacchae*, draws from the mythology of that great god. Like most of the legendary stories of Dionysus, this one concerns itself with the initial resistance that greeted the introduction of Dionysus to the Greek world. Pentheus, king of Thebes, doubts the divinity of the new god, as do his mother Agave and her sisters; these women are the sisters of Semele, the mother of Dionysus. Appearing in the prologue, Dionysus explains that he will vindicate himself, coming to Thebes in human disguise. Pentheus is contemptuous of Tiresias and of his grandfather, Cadmus, both of whom readily follow the god. His annoyance gives way to shock and anger when he learns by messenger that his mother and aunts have taken to the woods, where they rage as frenzied followers of the very god they spurned, but he also reveals a deep curiosity, and even lust, to observe the women. He goes to the forest and hides in a tree, but, led by Agave, the women discover him and tear him to pieces. Agave returns triumphantly with the head of Pentheus on her thyrsus,

and with slowly dawning horror, she returns to a state of lucidity and comes to understand what she has done. The ending of the play is incomplete, but it is known that Dionysus appeared once again, sending Agave into exile and promising future rewards to Cadmus. One interesting point here is that the chorus, which generally lost ground in the Euripidean era, becomes once again integral to the tragedy, and the play includes much choral lyric. *The Bacchae* shows Euripides once again dealing with the tension between the rational and the emotional; perhaps there is also an indication here that the old iconoclast flirted with mysticism at the end of his long life.

The surviving plays of Euripides, then, exhibit certain distinct characteristics that separate them from the works of Aeschylus and Sophocles. The individual parts of his plays stand out rather sharply, though this does not mean that the plays lack unity. These parts include the prologue, which tends in Euripides' plays to be of the informative type, spoken by one character; the agon, a formally structured debate; the elaborate and rhetorical messengers' speeches; and the endings, which often involve a *deus ex machina* who appears on the roof of the *skene* building (transported there by the "machine," a stage crane), or a cult etiology. Although the chorus is no longer the dominant component of tragedy, generally the songs show some relevance to the episodes, with a few exceptions; the focus is on the episodes and the actors. Finally, the most remarkable quality of Euripidean drama is the brooding presence of his searching and restless intellect, which finds expression in plays of great form and craftsmanship.

OTHER FIFTH CENTURY B.C.E. TRAGEDY WRITERS

Modern knowledge of other writers of tragedy in the fifth century B.C.E. is limited to short fragments, comic lampoons, comments by Aristotle, and inscriptional evidence. The Hellenistic canon of tragic playwrights included, in addition to the three great masters, Ion of Chios and Achaeus of Eretria. Of the latter, almost nothing is known, but Ion was a writer of Aeschylus's era who experimented with other types of poetry as well as tragedy. Agathon, a tragedian of the late fifth century, is known primarily through the parody of Aristophanes, who made the poet a main character in one of his comedies. Agathon was greatly influenced by the later dithyramb and also by Gorgias and other rhetoricians of the enlightenment. Aristotle praises him but criticizes his plays as having overly complex plots. An interesting phenomenon is Agathon's *Antheus*, which Aristotle maintains had no mythic content; the story was entirely invented by Agathon.

THE SATYR PLAY

The satyricon, an early precursor of tragedy, also led to the evolution of a separate form called the satyr play, which was reformed and restored by Pratinas in the late sixth century B.C.E. By the fifth century B.C.E., the three tragic playwrights competing at the Greater Dionysia each regularly presented a satyr play after their tragedies; satyr plays were not performed at the Lenaea.

The most distinctive feature of the satyr play is the chorus of satyrs, lusty woodland creatures who were half man and half goat or horse. The plays are somewhat shorter than tragedies, and their lighthearted, burlesque tone must have provided a welcome emotional relief in the wake of three tragedies. Fragments of Aeschylus's *Promētheus Pyrphoros* (472 B.C.E.; *Prometheus the Fire Bearer*) show that in this play Prometheus brings fire to man while the satyrs praise his new invention. *Proteus*, of which little is known, was presented at the end of Aeschylus's great *Oresteia* trilogy in 458 B.C.E., and the Theban trilogy of 467 B.C.E. closed with *The Sphinx*. More substantial remains of *The Drawers of Nets*, part of a Perseus tetralogy, allow a glimpse at the genre: One fragment shows Dictys and another fisherman struggling to pull in an unusually heavy catch, the chest containing Danaë and her infant son Perseus. Another fragment, from later in the play, has Silenus attempting to woo Danaë, while Dictys is temporarily absent, by pointing out his own good qualities and amusing her child. The chorus of satyrs cheer him on, interpreting Danaë's hesitation as a sign of hidden passion. These fragments show the charm and humor of the satyr play, and they also demonstrate Aeschylus's tendency to extend the theme of the tragedies into the satyr

play, so that all four form a unified tetralogy. *The Spectators at the Festival* has the satyrs planning to escape the service of Dionysus in order to participate in the Isthmian Games. Aeschylus was considered a great master of the satyr play.

From Sophocles, there are extensive remains of a satyr play called *Ichneutae* (c. 460 B.C.E.; English translation, 1919), in which the chorus of satyrs join Apollo in the search of his cattle, which have been stolen by the precocious infant Hermes. Attracted to a cave by the sounds of a new musical instrument, the lyre, the satyrs speak with Cyllene, the nymph guarding Hermes. The ending of the play is lost, but it probably contained a reconciliation of the two gods, and a reward and freedom for the satyrs; their servitude and desire for freedom were apparently regular features of the genre. Euripides occasionally used a tragedy with a happy ending in lieu of a satyr play (for example, *Alcestis*), but his work with this genre is also documented in one play of fairly substantial remains. *Cyclops* refashions Odysseus's adventure with Polyphemus so that a chorus of satyrs serve as slaves to Polyphemus. Although the play is certainly a burlesque, it lacks the lightness and charm of the Aeschylean and Sophoclean fragments. The Cyclops behaves as he does out of an ideological adherence to crude, natural law rather than out of whim. Here, too, the highly individual intellect of Euripides separates him from his predecessors. Ion of Chios wrote a satyr play called *Omphale*, which showed the gluttonous Heracles of farce during his enslavement to the Lydian queen.

These fragments of satyr plays are supported by a large corpus of vase paintings depicting the antics of satyrs, but there is still much that is not known about the genre. In the Hellenistic period, the satyr play was revived by Lycophron of Chalcis; a few lines of his *Menedemus*, which lampooned the philosopher of that name, remain. Sositheus also wrote satyr plays in this period, and sources indicate that his works were an attempt to return to the original satyr play.

POLITICAL COMEDY

Like tragedy, comedy was presented at the festivals of Dionysus, and it, too, must be viewed as having a religious and an Athenian state context. Comic playwrights competed both at the Greater Dionysia and at the Lenaea, with five poets each presenting one play; the Lenaea was thus dominated by comedy. Most of the arrangements for choosing the competitors and covering the costs, as well as the theatrical circumstances, were the same for comedy as for tragedy. Because it is playful in its use of dramatic illusion, comedy offers overt evidence of two of the devices of the Athenian stage: the *mechane*, or crane, used to deliver actors to the roof of the *skene* building and also, on occasion, to simulate flight, and the *ekkyklema*, a movable platform that could be used to present an entire tableau at once by wheeling it into view.

The situation of the actors was much the same in both comedy and tragedy, except that the "three-actor rule" was less rigidly enforced. Again, all parts were played by male actors, but the costuming was quite different. The clothing was that of the ordinary Athenian, but body padding in front and in back and a leather phallus for male characters added to the burlesque atmosphere. The chorus, sometimes depicted as people and sometimes as theriomorphs, numbered twenty-four rather than twelve or fifteen, as in tragedy.

The extant comedies of Aristophanes show an extremely formalized structure. They begin with a prologue followed by a parodos, as in tragedy, followed by the usual alternation of choral songs and actors' episodes. Most of the plays contain an agon, or debate. The most important and distinctive structural feature of comedy is the parabasis, in which the chorus addresses the audience on behalf of the playwright, often commenting on contemporary political issues. Both the parabasis and the agon are characterized by an interlocking internal structure called the epirrhematic syzygy. Through the history of Old Comedy, the chorus gradually declines in importance, and the parabasis eventually disappears. The closing scenes of comedy often contain a symbolic marriage, with a strong erotic element.

The history of Greek Comedy has been divided, since the Alexandrian period, into three phases: Old, Middle, and New Comedy; the term "Old Comedy" refers to the political comedy of the fifth and early fourth centuries B.C.E. Old Comedy is characterized

by the structure discussed above, by its political (that is, relating to affairs of the polis) subject matter, and by a unique brand of humor that combines obscenity and scatology with personal invective and tragic parody and criticism. The plots are simple and fantastic. Old Comedy is a unique product of a particular time and place, and it gives testimony to the vitality and freedom of speech that characterized Athens in its proudest moments.

CRATINUS

The ancient canon of comic playwrights included Cratinus, Eupolis, and Aristophanes. In addition, the names of three of the very earliest Old Comic playwrights, Magnes, Chionides, and Ecphantides, are known. Magnes' titles show the use of theriomorphic choruses, and the fragments of Ecphantides reveal a claim to comedy superior to that of old Megarian farce, but Cratinus is the first playwright who emerges with any real clarity. Cratinus, who flourished between 450 B.C.E. and 423 B.C.E., was especially fond of lampooning Pericles, the great Athenian leader. In *The Nemesis*, he presented Pericles as Zeus, intent on carrying out disastrous schemes; in *Dionysalexandros* (pr. c. 430 B.C.E.), a burlesque of the judgment of Paris, he attacked Pericles as well as his mistress, Aspasia, and Pericles' oddly shaped head was a subject of humor in *The Chirones*. His obscene attacks were not, however, limited to one target: He also inveighed against foreign cults, in *The Thracian Women*, and against the sophists in *The Panoptae*. The fragments show a combination of personal attack, mythological burlesque, and a strong fantasy element. Aristophanes attacked Cratinus in the parabasis of *Hippēs* (424 B.C.E.; *The Knights*, 1812) for becoming old and drunk and unskilled at the comic art, but Cratinus rejoined with spirit in the following year with *The Pytine* (pr. 423 B.C.E.), in which he depicted himself as married to Comedy, who is jealous of his new mistress, Drunkenness. The judges awarded him first prize for this brilliant self-parody.

EUPOLIS

Between Cratinus and Eupolis, a group of names and fragments allow only a glimpse at Old Comedy in its developing stages. Crates was a relatively tame comic writer who abstained from personal invective but made a contribution to unity and clarity of plot in Old Comedy. Teleclides restored the attacks on political figures to the genre, and also criticized poetry in his plays. Hermippus carried his criticism of Pericles' mistress Aspasia from the comic stage into the law court. Plato Comicus, a contemporary of Eupolis and Aristophanes, criticized individual politicians and treated more general political issues as well; fragments of *Phaon* also show a more whimsical, fantastic side. Pherecrates criticized the movement of the New Music and also wrote several plays named for *hetaerae*, or prostitutes, which seem to point to the concerns of Middle and New Comedy. Phrynichus (not to be confused with the author of *The Capture of Miletus*) presented a play similar to Aristophanes' *Batrachoi* (405 B.C.E.; *The Frogs*, 1780), in which the merits of Sophocles and Euripides were compared.

Eupolis was a patriotic Athenian, interested in political affairs and not prone to fantasy. In *The Taxiarchs*, he attacked Pericles, under the guise of Dionysus, for cowardice, and the demagogue Cleon was the target of *The Golden Age*. The attack on Hyperbolus in *The Lad* caused a rift between Eupolis and Aristophanes, who accused him of plagiarizing from *The Knights*. Eupolis's anger at the sophists is characterized by attacks on individuals and groups rather than on the intellectual movement as a whole, as far as can be determined from the fragments. Eupolis's last play, *The Demes*, was written in the wake of the Sicilian disaster, and it contemplates the future of Athens in melancholy tones; the Athenian past, on the other hand, is glorified, as its former leaders (Solon, Miltiades, Aristides, and Pericles) are shown in the underworld, and the plot revolves around the summoning of these men to return to Athens and solve the great problems that plagued the city in 412 B.C.E.

ARISTOPHANES

Although the other writers of Old Comedy survive only in fragments, eleven plays by Aristophanes are extant. The last of these are really Middle Comedies, so the corpus of Aristophanes encapsulates the devel-

opment of Old Comedy from its climax until its virtual conclusion. *The Acharnians*, Aristophanes' earliest surviving play, was the first of his several antiwar comedies. The play was presented in 425 B.C.E., by which time it had become clear that the Peloponnesian Wars would not end in an easy Athenian victory. The Periclean policy of bringing the farmers of surrounding areas to live within the walls of Athens had created crowded living conditions in the city and contributed to the spread of the plague. Aristophanes, who was always alert to the special hardships that war brought to the poor and the powerless, chose as his main character for this play Dicaeopolis, a peasant. When it becomes clear, in the prologue, that the Athenian Assembly will do nothing to bring about peace, Dicaeopolis declares his own personal truce, and so, fantastically, lives a happy life filled with the bounties of peace, while the war continues for everyone else. The chorus of Acharnian charcoal burners opposes Dicaeopolis, and this results in an agon over the issues and continuation of the war. To help his cause, the beleaguered protagonist obtains from the tragedian Euripides the costume of a beggar; this scene provides an opportunity for parody and criticism of Euripides' lost play *Telephus* (438 B.C.E.), in which the hero appeared in the guise of a beggar. In the parabasis, where the chorus speaks directly to the audience on behalf of the playwright, Aristophanes lays claim to his own greatness, and chides the Athenian audience for their susceptibility to flattery; included is a poignant rebuke on the ill-treatment of the old.

It was traditional for the post-parabasis episodes to illustrate the major reversal of the play—in this case, Dicaeopolis's private declaration of peace. Accordingly, Dicaeopolis sets up a marketplace through which he can resume free trade and enjoy commodities unavailable in wartime. He is visited by a Megarian, whose attempts to sell his own daughters confronts the audience with the painful consequences of the harsh blockade of Megara, initiated in 431 B.C.E. Dicaeopolis is kind to the Megarian but less patient with the Sycophant who follows, a representative of the despicable class of men charged with the exposure of contraband goods. A Theban visitor provides the market with many kinds of delectable goodies, among them a Copaic eel, unavailable in Athens during the war. General Lamachus soon appears, a figure who represents the empty glory of war. He provides a stark contrast to Dicaeopolis as he prepares to go off to battle while the hero makes ready to attend a feast. In the denouement, Lamachus returns to the scene injured and in pain, while Dicaeopolis arrives home from the feast fed and tipsy, in the company of two naked flute-girls. The final scene of the play includes the customary emphasis on the erotic.

The Acharnians illustrates the complete structure of Old Comedy—prologue, parodos, agon, parabasis, and episodes. It also demonstrates the full range of Old Comic humor: sexual and scatological, slapstick, literary, and personal. The humor is carefully used to enhance the serious ideas of the playwright, allowing him to advise and chastise the polis with impunity. An element of very beautiful choral lyric also contributes to the whole. The plot is simple, and the episodes cohere only loosely, but the comedy is perfectly bound together by the eloquent message that war is evil, a bringer of unhappiness and deprivation, while peace provides life's greatest joys. In this there is no ideological rigidity, but a clear-eyed emphasis on the sensual pleasures of food and sex and feasting: War is finally wrong because it deprives humanity of the most basic joys of life.

The Knights is a political allegory. It opens with two slaves who complain that a new slave, called Paphlagon, has mesmerized their master, Demus, and now holds undue influence over the household. Paphlagon is a transparent persona for Cleon, the Athenian demagogue, and Demus, as his name indicates, represents the Athenian people. As the play progresses, a sausage-seller enters, competes with Paphlagon in many debates, and ultimately supplants his rival. Near the end of the play, Demus reveals that he is aware of the manipulations of the slaves, and shortly thereafter, he is miraculously rejuvenated as a man of the Marathon era of Athenian greatness. The sausage-seller, too, has changed, becoming a wise and sincere adviser. The play, which mercilessly attacks Cleon and his policies, thus closes with an optimistic hope for the future, provided that the polis jet-

tison Cleon and act more sensibly than it has in the past.

Aristophanes met sound defeat with *Nephelai* (423 B.C.E.; *The Clouds*, 1708); the surviving play is a rewrite that was never performed. The extent of the revision is not known; it can be said with assurance only that the parabasis, which alludes to the failure of the original, must belong exclusively to the revision. *The Clouds*, which attacks Socrates and the new philosophical movements in Athens in this period, begins with the resilient Strepsiades, a poor man plagued by debts accrued through the horsey activities of his son, Pheidippides. Strepsiades proposes to escape his creditors by learning the sophistic ability to "make the worse argument appear to be the better." Pheidippides initially refuses, so Strepsiades goes off to the Thinkery, a school where Socrates and his pale disciples study and meditate. The inmates of the Thinkery are depicted as sly ascetics involved in the study of trivial points of natural science, and Socrates appears in a basket, engaged in astronomical investigation. The philosophers deny the traditional gods, introducing new divinities, among which are the Chorus of Clouds. Through all this, Strepsiades proves to be a hopeless student, literal-minded and totally incapable of grasping abstractions. It is decided that Pheidippides, after all, should be the student, and for his benefit a great agon is staged, in which Unjust Reasoning, the representative of Socrates and sophism, defeats Just Reasoning, a conservative and old-fashioned educator. Pheidippides quickly becomes so adept at the new philosophy that he mistreats his father, all the while offering glib rationalizations for his behavior. In the Aeschylean tradition, the Clouds explain to Strepsiades that they have contributed to his delusion so that he might learn through suffering. He responds by going off to burn down the Thinkery, thus providing a very unorthodox ending to the comedy.

The major question raised by the play is in the portrait of Socrates. Aristophanes obviously wished to ridicule the philosopher in a manner that would be humorous, but there is much in the characterization that is inaccurate, and even dangerous: Plato has Socrates say in *Apologia Sōkratous* (399-390 B.C.E.;

Apology, 1675) that Aristophones' caricature contributed to the general misunderstanding of his purpose and character that eventually led to his accusation and trial. The scholarly controversy on these points is complicated, but it can be said that the comic playwright has attributed to Socrates many characteristics that he really possessed; the confusion of Socrates with sophism is incorrect, but Aristophanes wrote comedy, and some license must be allowed in the interests of adding humor to the presentation. It should be noted also that Plato showed Aristophanes and Socrates together in *Symposion* (388-368 B.C.E.; *Symposium*, 1701).

In *Sphēkes* (422 B.C.E.; *The Wasps*, 1812), Aristophanes reiterates the motif of the opposition of father and son, but here his target is the law-court system of Athens: Cleon had recently raised the wage paid to those serving jury duty, and, in the play at least, this has created a class of loafers who lived on jury wages. Philocleon ("loves Cleon"), the father, is such a man, as are his cronies, the Chorus of Wasps, so named and costumed because they love to convict; Bdelycleon ("hates Cleon"), the son, opposes his father's vocation and has shut him up in the house, under guard, to keep him from the law courts. The early scenes in the play are taken up with various comic attempts by Philocleon to escape, and by the arrival of the Wasps, who wish to rescue their friend. An agon parodies the new jury system: In order to satisfy and amuse his father, Bdelycleon sets up a mock trial, in which one dog prosecutes another for stealing cheese, with kitchen implements serving as witnesses; names and other clues indicate that this is a parody of an action brought to court by Cleon in 425 B.C.E. After the parabasis, Bdelycleon attempts to elevate his father socially, teaching him new ways to dress and speak. The educational experiment backfires, and the audience discovers that Philocleon has misbehaved outrageously at a dinner party; he returns for a chaotic final scene of song and dance.

In 421 B.C.E., the deaths of Cleon and his Spartan counterpart, Brasidas, led to an uneasy peace, soon to be broken; *Eirēnē* (421 B.C.E.; *Peace*, 1837) reflects the doomed hopes of Aristophanes that the war had really ended. Trygaeus, an Attic farmer, desires peace,

and he has conceived a scheme that matches that of Dicaeopolis in *The Acharnians* for its fantastical and ingenious nature: He will ride to heaven on a dung beetle and make a personal appeal to Zeus. The scenes of preparation and flight are filled with scatological humor, and the hero soon alights in Heaven, only to find that the gods have moved in order to distance themselves from the wars of the Greeks; Hermes alone receives Trygaeus. Peace has been imprisoned in a pit, and Trygaeus now enlists the aid of Hermes, as well as of the chorus, in freeing her. After a protracted struggle, accompanied by song, the group succeeds in retrieving the statue of Peace, along with her handmaidens, Opora and Theoria, who are played by actors. The parabasis grants an opportunity for Aristophanes to boast of his own skills, although it lacks several components of the syzygy, thus pointing the way to the eventual decline of the parabasis form. In the episodes that follow, Trygaeus bestows Theoria on the Athenian Council (the Boulé); an oracle-interpreter is unceremoniously thrown out; arms sellers fail while those who deal in more peaceful commodities succeed; and, finally, the play closes with the usual erotic union—in this case, joining Trygaeus and Opora. The play raises some important questions concerning Athenian stagecraft: Most scholars believe that the flight of the dung beetle was effected by means of the stage crane and that the "heavenly" scenes took place on the roof of the *skene* building, but the buried statue of Peace and its retrieval pose problems that are much debated.

This first series of surviving Aristophonic comedies is followed by a gap; the next extant play, *Ornithes* (414 B.C.E.; *The Birds*, 1824), was presented soon after the initiation of the Sicilian expedition, which was to end in catastrophe for Athens. Though the play does not allude to this momentous political event, it is characterized by a mood of adventure, expectancy, and hope that perhaps reflects the feelings of the polis at that precarious moment. Two Athenians, Pisthetaerus and Euelpides, have fled their native city out of disgust with the litigiousness and *polypragmosyne* ("bustling busyness") that characterized fifth century B.C.E. Athens. They meet a hoopoe, and after considering and rejecting a number of suggestions, they decide to found a bird city in midair. The Chorus of Birds enters, creating a spectacle with their individual costumes, and they engage in an agon with the interlopers. Pisthetaerus convinces them to join in his venture, and it is decided that he and Euelpides will take a magic herb and turn into birds. The parabasis intervenes, presenting a history of the world in bird terms and praising the freedom from legal and social restraints inherent in bird life. The play is unusually lengthy, and many episodes follow the parabasis. Pisthetaerus and Euelpides return to the scene, now attired in laughably incomplete bird costumes, and found their new city, Cloudcuckooland. The usual scoundrels flock to the founding rituals and are quickly dispatched, walls are constructed, and a plan emerges to exploit the location of the new city by blocking earthly sacrificial vapors from reaching the gods. Iris is captured and sent back to Zeus to inform him of the new turn of events. Various individuals enter seeking wings, symbols of release and freedom, and these are dealt with in different ways. Prometheus arrives to tell of Zeus's consternation, and an embassy of gods—a stuffy Poseidon, a gluttonous Heracles, and a pidgin-speaking Triballian—comes to negotiate terms. Zeus agrees to give up Basileia, a personification of sovereignty, and the play closes with the expected union of Pisthetaerus and Basileia. *The Birds* is a play of exceptionally lovely choral lyric and close unity in spite of its length and variety.

Aristophanes presented two plays in 411 B.C.E., *Thesmophoriazousai* (411 B.C.E.; *Thesmophoriazusae*, 1837) and the more famous *Lysistratē* (411 B.C.E.; *Lysistrata*, 1837). *Thesmophoriazusae* returns to the parody of Euripides that served as a subordinate theme in *The Acharnians*. As the women of Greece prepare to attend their exclusive annual festival, Euripides becomes anxious that they will plan some retaliation for his ill-treatment of them in tragedies. He decides to infiltrate the rites, choosing the tragedian Agathon, a notorious effeminate, to serve as his spy. Agathon is rolled out on the *ekkyklema*, in the midst of composing, but he refuses the request of his colleague. Instead, Euripides' relative, Mnesilochus, will embark on the dangerous mission. Accordingly, he is

shaved and singed and clothed in feminine garb, with the aid of Agathon's extensive wardrobe, in a scene of ribald humor. Mnesilochus attends the festival, and speeches against Euripides are followed by the impostor's defense of the playwright, in which he confides that Euripides, at least, did not reveal some of the worst aspects of women and their intrigues. The women become suspicious, and they unmask the unwanted visitor; an attempt to hold hostage a wineskin fails, and Mnesilochus is placed in the custody of a foolish Scythian. In the episodes that follow the parabasis, Euripides attempts to rescue his kinsman by repeating famous rescue scenes from his plays: He plays Menelaus to Mnesilochus's Helen, and Perseus to his Andromeda. At last, a pretty flute-girl distracts the Scythian, Mnesilochus escapes, and Euripides and the women are reconciled. Throughout, the play combines ribaldry and transvestism with sophisticated tragic parody and criticism.

Lysistrata is the last of Aristophanes' surviving antiwar plays, following *The Acharnians* and *Peace*. Its tone is at once more urgent and more conciliatory than those of the previous plays, because the war had by then been going on for more than fifteen years and the Sicilian expedition had ended in disaster. Lysistrata, an Athenian woman of strong will, intelligence, and initiative, leaves her home at dawn to meet with women of Athens and other Greek cities, including Sparta. Her dedication to peace is well received, but the women hesitate when they hear her plan: a sex strike. Her persistence, together with that of her Spartan friend Lampito, wins the day, and the women solemnize their agreement, groaning at the prospect of their own deprivation; an auxiliary plan will have the older women occupy the Acropolis, where the treasury is kept, in order to cut off the financial resources that make the war possible. The parados reveals an unusual feature, two opposing choruses of old men and old women, who enter quarreling. The theme of conflict extends into a debate between Lysistrata and the Proboulos, a government official, and then the choruses return, their arguments taking the normal place of the parabasis. The episodes that follow show the attempts of several women to escape to their husbands, and in one hilariously ribald episode a young matron, Myrrhine, teases her husband, Cinesias, and leaves him unsatisfied. The Spartan ambassadors arrive in sorry plight, and Lysistrata brings about a reconciliation, aided by the allegorical figure of Forgiveness. The play ends with a happy feast that consummates the new harmony, and even the opposing choruses unite in joy and mutual need.

The play is well written and compact, with all of its various elements contributing effectively to the whole. The focus on the feminine point of view again emphasizes the ramifications of war for the powerless and the disenfranchised: Men make policy, but women must sacrifice their husbands and sons and the joys of married life, and this is serious. The ribald element, far from undercutting the serious intent of the playwright, actually enhances it: The sexual eagerness of the deprived Greeks, both male and female, is a metaphor for the urgency of the need for peace. The opposed choruses contribute to the atmosphere of conflict at the beginning of the play, and their tender rapprochement prefigures the ultimate reconciliation of Spartans and Athenians. Aristophanes dares to speak well of the Spartans in this play, a courageous move indeed, and for this reason the play is said to be Panhellenic in its vision, but it is more than that: It shows through clear eyes the need that men and women have for one another, a need that is physical but also natural and dignified. Once again, Aristophanes advocates peace in the interests of retrieving the true joys of life.

In *The Frogs*, the comic fun is tempered by an atmosphere of melancholy: Athens was on the brink of surrender, and Euripides was already dead; Sophocles died while the play was being written. In a reversal of the normal arrangement, the more humorous episodes precede the parabasis, and the agon comes later. Dionysus, the god of drama, longs for the art of Euripides and, accompanied by his slave, Xanthias, has undertaken to journey to the underworld and bring back the tragedian. Because Heracles had succeeded in a similar mission, the capture of Cerberus, Dionysus appropriates a lionskin and club, traditional attributes of the mythological strongman. A brief visit to Heracles underlines the hilarious contrast between the Heraclean and the Dionysiac. Dionysus

continues his journey by crossing the Styx in the bark of Charon, while a chorus of frogs, perhaps unseen, sing a croaking swamp-song. On arriving in the underworld, the cowardly Dionysus soon encounters the main chorus of the play, a group of Eleusinian initiates, who sing a lovely hymn. Several episodes follow in which the Heracles disguise is met with varying reactions, inducing Dionysus to exchange clothing several times with Xanthias; in all this, Dionysus shows great cowardice. The servant of King Pluto, Aeacus, soon appears, intent on discovering which of the two is really a god by flogging, but when the issue remains in doubt, he sends the two into the palace. A partial parabasis follows, in which Aristophanes urges forgiveness for political offenders, and, knowing that the end is near, a spirit of dignity and fairness for Athens. The plot now changes, as the audience learns of a dispute between Aeschylus and Euripides for the underworld's "chair of tragedy." Dionysus, emerging in more dignified state from his earlier buffoonery, will serve as judge in a great agon between the two tragedians; Sophocles' very recent death has kept him from playing a major role in the plan of the play, and his absence from the agon is gently excused. The remainder of the comedy is taken up by the contest, which treats first the general principles of tragic poetry and then the technical points of composing the individual parts of tragedy. Dionysus has great difficulty in arriving at a decision, even when the scales show Aeschylus to be far "weightier" than his rival. The play closes with the ultimate victory of Aeschylus, who is escorted back to the upper air to improve the public morals of Athens. Though Aeschylus wins the contest, Dionysus's hesitation betokens a great affection for Euripides on the part of the comic playwright. Aristophanes parodied Euripides relentlessly, making of the tragedian a comic character on at least three occasions, but through his criticism there shines a deep awareness of the greatness of his target.

Old Comedy was inextricably bound to a particular time and place: With the surrender of Athens and the destruction of the Long Walls in 404 B.C.E., that time had passed away. Aristophanic comedy then became Middle Comedy, with the loss of the parabasis, the vast diminishing of the chorus, a loss of obscenity and political topicality, and the rise of stock slave characters. Of the two surviving plays from this period, *Ekklesiazousai* (*Ecclesiazusae*, 1837) is tentatively dated at 392 B.C.E. Praxagora, an Athenian matron, conspires with other women to infiltrate the Assembly and push through legislation that will put the women in charge, as in *Lysistrata*, and that will also set up a state of pure communism. Disguised as men, the women succeed in their purpose, and Praxagora later defends her policies to her husband Blepyrus in an agon. The new arrangements are borne out in a series of episodes that show, among other things, a handsome young man forced to make love to a series of hags before he can mate with his beloved, because love, too, has been communized. The play ends with a communal feast. *Ecclesiazusae* raises again the question of the relationship between Plato and Aristophanes, because communism and, to some degree, recognition of the abilities of women are both treated in *Politeia* (388-368 B.C.E.; *Republic*, 1701). Rather than posit a direct relationship between poet and philosopher, it seems best to assume that these ideas were being discussed in Athens at this time; in any case, it is not very wise to view Aristophanes as a serious theoretician of political systems.

The last surviving play of Aristophanes is *Ploutos* (388 B.C.E.; *Plutus*, 1651), in which Plutus, the god of wealth, is miraculously cured of his blindness. His new moral vision elevates the good to positions of wealth while the bad suffer the opposite fate. In lieu of choral odes, this play has only manuscript notations indicating the insertion of a song and dance to separate the episodes, and there is no parabasis. The play includes almost no obscenity or personal invective, and the main thrust of the plot is social allegory rather than political statement. The slave Carion is an officious manipulator in the mode of New Comedy. *Plutus* clearly shows Aristophanes' movement away from the structures and the spirit of Old Comedy.

FOURTH CENTURY B.C.E.

Evidence shows that tragedy came to be performed widely in the Greek world in the fourth cen-

tury B.C.E., especially in the Greek colonies of the west. Both in Athens and elsewhere, revivals of fifth century B.C.E. tragedy were performed, and this custom was institutionalized at the Greater Dionysia beginning in 386 B.C.E. Of plays written in this period, only fragments and titles remain, with the possible exception of *Rhesus*, which many scholars believe to be a fourth century B.C.E. tragedy, although it has been passed on in the corpus of Euripides. This play retells the Homeric spy tale of the Doloneia, and the killing of the Trojan ally Rhesus by Odysseus and Diomedes. The titles associated with the playwrights Meletus, Carcinus, Astydamas, and Antiphon show a tendency to rework the same mythological material perfected by the fifth century B.C.E. masters, with an emphasis on the blatant and theatrical. There was a trend also to borrow from the later plays of Euripides a stress on chance, intrigues, and recognitions; larger religious issues were ignored. Tragedy in this period was also characterized by a vastly diminished chorus with the music quite independent from the play, and great importance was vested in the actors and stagecraft, a sign of the decline of the art.

The only Middle Comedies that survive complete are the last extant plays of Aristophanes, discussed above, which are characterized by the omission of the parabasis, the independence of the choral element from the episodes, and the diminishing of political focus and personal attack. The most important and prolific writers of Middle Comedy were Antiphanes, Alexis, and Anaxandrides. The playwrights were no longer exclusively Athenian, and performances were given in many cities, although Athens remained a center of dramatic art. Although the plays do not focus on affairs of the polis, they include references to contemporary events and public policy. Personal invective, too, receded but did not vanish, and Middle Comedy includes attacks on public figures, philosophers, and others. Mythological travesties, especially involving Euripidean parody, were very popular, though this trend tapered off in the middle of the fourth century B.C.E. Middle Comedy also borrowed from Euripides, especially in his fondness for intrigue and recognition plots. The fragments show the seeds of the stock-character system that was to become so important in New Comedy. Finally, Middle Comedy dropped the obscene language of the Old Comic period and, with it, the phallic costumes.

THE HELLENISTIC AGE

The death of Alexander the Great in 323 B.C.E. is traditionally considered to mark the beginning of the Hellenistic era. From this time on, there was a rapid growth of new political and cultural centers outside Athens. The old polis structures had changed, and politics were now very remote from the personal control of the average citizen; this led to a turning inward and a new focus on the individual. There was also a sharpening of social contrasts, placing a new importance on social class. Finally, the unlocking of the East allowed the Greeks to become aware of a larger world, and there was a new source and flow of cultural exchange.

Menander, the only poet of New Comedy who survives in nearly complete plays, epitomizes the spirit of the new age; indeed, the contrast between Old and New Comedy says much about the effects of these profound political changes on the average Athenian. Menander lived in turbulent times, but his plays contain few direct references to political upheavals, focusing instead on the hopes and concerns of the individual. Modern scholarship at one time depended on short fragments, combined with Roman adaptations of Menander's plays, for knowledge of the poet; in the twentieth century, however, Egyptian papyrus finds broadened the picture with several very large fragments, and in 1959, a nearly complete papyrus of *Dyskolos* (317 B.C.E.; *The Bad-Tempered Man*, 1921; also known as *The Grouch*) was discovered.

The Bad-Tempered Man, which is divided into five acts, begins with an informative prologue by the god Pan, whose rural Greek shrine provides the setting for the drama: An old grouch named Cnemon lives in a poorhouse near the shrine with his young daughter, while his wife and stepson, Gorgias, have moved to the city. Pan has arranged for a wealthy young man called Sostratus to fall in love with the daughter. The surly Cnemon is difficult to approach, but Sostratus finds a way to meet the girl. Gorgias's

slave tells his master what has happened, and Gorgias suspects Sostratus of trying to take advantage of their family because of their poverty. On direct meeting, however, Gorgias learns to trust the young man's intentions, and Sostratus, though a wealthy fop, goes off to work in the fields in an attempt to convince Cnemon of his worthiness. Meanwhile, the family of Sostratus arrives to plan a sacrifice, preceded by an officious cook, a stock figure of New Comedy. In the third act, Cnemon rebuffs repeated attempts by the sacrificers to borrow utensils for their banquet, and the audience learns that Cnemon has fallen into a well. In the fourth act, matters reach a climax: Cnemon is rescued by Gorgias and, having learned a valuable lesson about his need for other people, agrees to allow Gorgias to find a husband for his daughter; Sostratus, sunburned from his fieldwork, is chosen. Act 5 adds a second betrothal, that of Sostratus's sister to Gorgias. Cnemon at first refuses to attend the festivities (his conversion has not been total), but the cook and the slave harass him and force him to participate. This ending is unusual for Menander, but it contains some elements from the more traditional banquet scene, inherited from Old Comedy.

The plot of *The Bad-Tempered Man* is simple, and the events are probable, if not totally realistic; they are everyday happenings, and they follow one another logically. The setting is contemporary Greece, not necessarily Athens, and the problems of the play are private and domestic. Love provides the occasion for the plot. Social class plays an important role, although in the end the love of the young couple is shown to overcome social barriers, and Gorgias, a poor man, displays great nobility of character. The lesson in the end is that understanding, tolerance, and generosity are the keys to happiness in human relationships. All of this is very far from the Old Comedies of Aristophanes.

Significant fragments from other plays by Menander also survive. *Epitrepontes* (after 304 B.C.E.; *The Arbitration*, 1909) is a complex rape and recognition story, in which a young man, Charisius, returns from a voyage undertaken before the consummation of his marriage to discover that his wife, Pamphila, has given birth and exposed the child out of shame; deeply distressed, he moves to the home of a friend and hires a prostitute whom he never touches. Meanwhile, the child is discovered, and among its birth tokens is a ring that Pamphila grabbed from the hand of the unknown man who raped her during a festival. With the aid of the good-hearted prostitute, Pamphila soon recognizes that the assailant and father of her child, is, in fact, her husband. All ends happily, and Menander's humanity stresses the basic love of the husband and wife. In Menander's *Perikeiromenē* (314-310 B.C.E.; *The Girl Who Was Shorn*, 1909), Glycera, a young woman who lives with a braggart soldier, Polemon, is seen kissing a young man whom she knows to be her twin brother, from whom she was separated at birth. Polemon, misinterpreting this affection, cuts Glycera's hair to stigmatize her, though he comes to regret his hastiness. At the end of the play, a citizen named Pataecus is discovered to be the father of the twins, and Glycera, now considered to be a citizen also, is reconciled and properly married to Polemon. *Samia* (321-316 B.C.E.; *The Girl from Samos*, 1909) deals with an exchange of infants and a series of misunderstandings that end with the reconciliation of all concerned.

The small corpus of Menander allows some conclusions about his plays. He was fond of preparing the audience for his complex plots by means of an informative prologue that usually followed several initial scenes, although the prologue of *The Bad-Tempered Man* actually opens the play. The audience is addressed directly in Menander not in the style of the Old Comic parabasis but rather in monologues and asides. The plays were customarily divided into five acts, with the climax coming in the fourth act. Menander's plays are middle class in milieu, with an emphasis on money, especially as it influences choice of spouse. Events are controlled by chance, as in the later plays of Euripides. Menander's realistic humanism and his depiction of Greek life and thought caused Aristophanes of Byzantium to ask: "Oh Menander, Oh life, which of you imitates the other?" Even more telling evidence of Menander's great spirit is his own credo: "I am a man: nothing human do I deem alien from me."

Other important writers of New Comedy are known mainly through Roman adaptations of their works. Philemon (c. 368-c. 267 B.C.E.), born in Syracuse and later made an Athenian citizen, employed the same type of plots as those of Menander, with the addition of some mythological burlesque. His plays are characterized by a moralizing tone, neat construction, surprise, caricature, and wit, and he often competed successfully against Menander. Diphilus (c. 360-c. 300 B.C.E.) was born at Sinope on the Black Sea, and his early plays deal with mythological burlesque, but most of the titles indicate middle-class comedy, and he was especially fond of recognition plots. His works are characterized by vivid imagery, concentrated action, and a love of spectacle. Apollodorus of Carystus, who began producing around 285 B.C.E., later became a favorite model for the Roman Terence. He favored plots of misconception and false assumption, and his plays stress family relations to the detraction of comic effect.

Greek New Comedy was performed in stone theaters, with two-story scene buildings, and convention determined that one direction led to the harbor and the other to the *agora*. The costumes lacked the phallus and padding of Old Comedy, and the masks were more realistic, with a characteristic wide mouth. The masks and wigs aided the implementation of an important stock-character system, which included young men, stupid and clever slaves, old men, parasites, matrons, prostitutes, pimps, cooks, and soldiers; the stock system in no way prevented the development of character, which was very important in New Comedy. The plots were complex, involving lost children, rape and intrigue, love, slaves, and recognitions, but the events were probable and causally logical, as opposed to Aristophanic flights of fantasy. The milieu was Greek middle class, but with an awareness of the outside world and frequent reference to travel and voyages. There was no chorus, although groups of revelers occasionally performed a choral function. Political references were rare, reflecting the loss of political control by the people. New Comedy lacks the political import, the vigorous freedom of speech, the choral lyric, and the pointed invective of Old Comedy, but its interesting plots and developed characters, its transcendence of time and place, make it the distinguished ancestor of European comedy.

Tragedy in the Hellenistic age was centered not at Athens, but at Alexandria, under the patronage of Philadelphus. The Pleiad, a selection of the best tragedians of the period, included Alexander Aetolus, Lycophron of Chalcis, Homer of Byzantium, Philicus of Corcyra, and Sositheus. Only nine fragments have survived, and the titles show some use of fifth century B.C.E. themes as well as the addition of a few new ones. Lycophron survives in *Alexandra* (third century B.C.E.; *The Alexandra*, 1806), a tragic fictional messenger's speech, in which Cassandra prophesies the fall of Troy and later events. Other remains of the period include fragments of *Exagoge* (second century B.C.E.; *The Exagoge*, 1983) by Ezechial, a tragic depiction of events from Jewish history, and fragments of a Gyges drama that follows Herodotus.

The formal genre of New Comedy did not completely satisfy the needs of the audiences in the Hellenistic cities, and a thirst for variety, as well as a desire for coarse fun and more realistic scenes from everyday life, led to a wide variety of mimetic forms. The many surviving terms for other dramatic forms are bewildering, because these entertainments included speech and song, prose and poetry, monologue and scenic performance. *The Maiden's Complaint*, a surviving solo song, tells of a woman who laments outside her lover's door after a quarrel. The best-known practitioner of the solo speech was Sotades of Maronea, whose invectives aimed at Philadelphus eventually caused his death. Considerable remains of the iambic mimes of Herodas, called *mimiambi*, survive; these are "slices of life," short scenes on a wide variety of subjects, probably recited rather than dramatically enacted. Evidence also shows that mimes of continuous plot, without masks, were performed in this period, and that female actresses appeared onstage.

UNDER THE ROMAN EMPIRE

Under the empire, tragedy rapidly declined, and those Greek tragedies that were written were intended for recitation rather than dramatic presentation. The mime was the most important dramatic form of the period, and much of it was improvisational. Philistion of Nicaea was a famous composer of mime from the time of Augustus. A papyrus survives that details a mime similar in plot to *Iphigenia in Tauris* of Euripides: A young Greek woman has fallen into the hands of barbarians near the Indian Ocean, and she is rescued by her brother. There is much making fun of the barbarians and their speech. Another mime depicts a scene between a woman who has attempted to poison her husband and a slave. Pantomime also flourished in this period, with a masked dancer acting out a story through his movements, to the accompaniment of an orchestra. Bathyllus of Alexandria won fame as a pantomimist in the early empire, especially for his comic dances.

EARLY ROMAN DRAMATIC FORMS

Roman drama in its developed form is closely modeled on Greek drama; this is not surprising, because the Greeks had colonized Sicily and southern Italy, known collectively as Magna Graecia, from the sixth century B.C.E. Moreover, drama achieved such perfection at the hands of the Greeks that Hellenic influence on Roman drama was inevitable, even when Roman political power had eclipsed that of Greece. Even so, Italy had indigenous entertainment forms that are interesting cultural documents in their own right, and that also contributed, albeit in a small way, to formal Roman drama.

Fescennine verse was a merry, impromptu entertainment that grew out of wedding and harvest celebrations. An important element of this form was alternating song, sung by rival groups; the rivalry was good-natured but contained an abusive aspect that was probably apotropaic in origin. Fescennine verse was sometimes sung in meter, originally Saturnian, but later trochaic, and the flute provided accompaniment. Performers wore rudimentary masks, but Fescennine verse remained improvisational in nature and was never elevated to a literary form, though it was occasionally used in the celebration of military triumphs. Most scholars believe that the name "Fescennine" derived from that of an Etruscan town, and the etymology that connects it with *fascinum*, a term for procreative magic, has been soundly repudiated.

The Satura, which is documented by Livy, was a country stage entertainment. Its name derives from the *Satura Lanx*, a mixed platter of food for offering to Ceres and Bacchus: The Satura was a medley of song, dance, and dialogue. Though it lacked a connected plot, it was not mere improvisation, with dramatic elements more developed than in Fescennine verse. It is likely that Satura would have evolved into Roman Comedy, had the influx of Hellenism not intervened with the import of New Comic models. For a time, the Satura was used as an afterpiece in the performances of formal Roman Comedies, but eventually the evolution of the Satura carried it in two different directions: It led, on one hand, to the development of literary satire, and on the other, to Italian mime, which eventually made a contribution to Roman Comedy.

The *fabula Atellana* (Atellan farce) is perhaps the most dramatic of the indigenous Italian forms. Originating in rural Campania, it flourished in the third century B.C.E. There was dialogue and music, and the masked performers acted out short plots based on country life. Cheating and trickery were important components of the plot, and riddles occurred often in the dialogue. The most distinctive feature of *fabula Atellana* was a set of fixed characters: Maccus, a fool; Pappus, a silly old man; Dossenus, a clever swindler; and Bucco, a glutton. The fixed characters retain their basic personalities, as in a Punch-and-Judy show, but their occupations, marital situations, and circumstances vary according to the plot. Nothing survives of the third century B.C.E. farce, but in the first century B.C.E., Novius and Pomponius elevated the *fabula Atellana* to a literary form, and these fragments are helpful in reconstructing the earlier farce.

The Italian popular mime, whose actors were called *phlyakes* ("gossips"), descended from the old Doric farce that influenced Attic Old Comedy, and Epicharmus, a writer of this type of mime, is believed to have had some influence also on Old Comedy; phlyax, then, is not a wholly Italian form, but from its earliest beginnings was connected with activities on the Greek mainland and the Peloponnese. These mimes, skits without choruses, began in Sicily and Tarentum, later moving northward to Paestum and Campania and, finally, to Rome. Under the influence of Doric farce, they included travesties of mythology and also of daily life. The mythological travesties eventually evolved into tragic parodies, primarily under the influence of the frequent stagings of Athenian tragedies in the region, especially the plays of Euripides. Epicharmus first gave these mimes literary form, and fragments of his works survive, as do remains from Rhinthon of Tarentum (early third century B.C.E.), who specialized in tragic parodies known as *hilarotragodia*. The best evidence for the *phlyakes* comes from a great corpus of cartoonlike phlyax vases of the late fifth and fourth centuries, which vigorously depict the antics of the performers. Mythological figures such as Odysseus and Heracles are burlesqued, and one humorous vase depicts the arrest of Antigone—followed by the revelation that she is really a man. Travesties of daily life are represented, too, with bustling slaves, thieves, drunks, old men, and domineering wives. The vases show a padded, phallic costume similar to that of Greek Old Comedy, worn with tights and comical masks, and also a portable wooden stage. The peak years of the vases (350-330 B.C.E.) precede the fragments of Rhinthon. Therefore, while the old Greek farce was reaching literary perfection at Athens, it continued in a lower mode in Sicily and Southern Italy, remaining essentially at the level of farce.

These are the most important dramatic and predramatic forms of early Italy, but other phenomena merit brief mention here. Livy tells of Etruscan dances, accompanied by the flute, to which Roman youths later added dialogue and gestures. Gladiatorial contests, introduced from Etruria, can be said to contain basic mimetic elements. Finally, there are miscellaneous forms of casual mime, such as juggling, acrobatics, and animal imitation. The mimes and entertainments described above surely contained the seeds of drama that would have evolved into an indigenous Roman drama, had not the Greek drama, in its developed form, invaded Rome in the third century B.C.E. Even after the impact of Hellenization was fully felt and the development of these forms was short-circuited, many of them continued a vigorous existence, in the shadow of the drama imported from Greece.

THE PIONEERS OF ROMAN DRAMA

The invasion of Hellenism into Roman life and letters was an event of enormous impact. During the period from 241 B.C.E. (the end of the First Punic War) to 70 B.C.E. (the consulship of Pompey), Rome rose to world power, completing the conquest of the Italian peninsula and extending its dominion in every direction. The result was an influx of wealth and ideas from all over the Mediterranean world. The Roman Flamininus declared Greece to be free in 196 B.C.E., but Greece and Rome continued their close contact, with Greek art, literature, and ideas flowing continually to Rome. Though the absorption of Greek culture by Rome was a profound process, it was also a slow one, because temperamental differences led to a certain initial resistance on the part of the Romans, the more conservative of whom tended to regard Greek culture as decadent, effete, and unmanly. Even so, the Hellenization of Roman culture continued in spite of this early distrust, and few cultural areas reflect this process more clearly than does Roman drama. Moreover, the new Hellenism made itself felt on dramatic forms quite early; in fact, the most significant historical event in the Hellenization of Roman drama occurred before the First Punic War, in 272 B.C.E.: In that year, the fall of Tarentum, a seemingly insignificant element in the conquest of Italy by the Romans, brought to Rome one Livius Andronicus, and with him, a knowledge of Greek tragedy and New Comedy that in time led to the domination of Roman drama by Greek models and the consequent suppression of all but a few of the native Italian dramatic forms.

Though Livius Andronicus arrived in Rome as a slave, following the fall of Tarentum, he was eventually manumitted, and in 240 B.C.E., when it was decided to expand the customary *Ludi Romani* (Roman Games) in honor of the victory in the First Punic War, Livius presented one tragedy and one comedy, both Latin adaptations of Greek originals, a fifth century B.C.E. tragedy and a New Comedy. The event established among the Romans a taste for such adaptations; in addition, a precedent was set for the use of New Comedy, rather than Old, as a model, with the resulting Latin comedies to be known by the term *fabula palliata* (literally, "a play in Greek dress"), because the Greek *pallium*, a cloak not worn by Romans, was retained onstage. At this point, a single playwright would often write both tragedy and comedy, though increasing specialization followed soon afterward. The remains of Livius are few, but it is known that the plays were adaptations and not mere translations. Of the tragedies, eight titles survive; they show a preference for Sophocles, and also for the Trojan cycle. There are also fragments of comedies with titles such as *The Actor*, *The Gladiator*, and *The Virgin*, many of which were translated in *Remains of Old Latin* (1936).

Gnaeus Naevius began producing plays in 235 B.C.E., showing more independence and originality than his predecessor. Seven titles of tragedies based on fifth century B.C.E. originals survive, and these show an emphasis on the Trojan cycle. Naevius's native spirit asserts itself in plays called *fabulae praetextae*, tragedies based on historical Roman events; in fact, he invented the genre. Naevius's many comedies included *fabulae palliatae*, some of which mixed several Greek sources in one play (a phenomenon later known as *contaminatio*), as well as *fabulae togatae*, "plays in Roman dress," which were original dramas performed in native Roman costume. Among his works, of which only fragments survive, all dating from the period c. 250-205 B.C.E., were *Ariolus* (*The Soothsayer*), *Carbonaria* (*The Collier Maid*), *Colax* (*The Flatterer*), *Dementes* (*The Madmen*), and *Quadrigemini* (*The Quadruplets*). The comedies are populated by parasites, braggart warriors, slaves, masters, and lovers, and a vigorous, coarse spirit abounds. Naevius recalls Aristophanes in his free use of political invective, but Rome in the third century was quite unlike the Athens of Aristophanes, and a comic gibe at the Metelli led to Naevius's incarceration, though intervention by the tribunes later brought about his release.

The fragments of Quintus Ennius include two comic titles, a *fabula praetexta* called *Sabinae* (*The Sabine Women*), and some twenty tragedies. Of the latter, a number show Euripidean themes. Ennius's tragedies demonstrate great originality in spite of their reliance on models, and their weight and passion caused them to be revived in the Augustan period. Also known for his *Saturae* (translated in *Miscellanies*, 1935) and the epic *Annales* (*Annals*, 1935), Ennius advanced the use of meter and language, and his tragedies mark an important stage in the development of Roman drama. Following Ennius, the writing of drama became specialized, and the composition of tragedy and comedy became separate skills.

ROMAN COMEDY

Formal Roman comedies in the era of Plautus and Terence were, like their Greek precursors, always presented at state religious festivals. The most important of these were the *Ludi Romani*, in September, and the *Ludi Plebei*, in November, though the spring *Ludi Megalenses* and summer *Ludi Apollinares* also included dramatic presentations in the second century B.C.E. One play was presented each day, and it began at noon. Originally, the playwrights produced their own plays, but a system quickly evolved under which a producer/troupe manager purchased the play and then contracted with the appropriate aediles for its presentation. The actors, all of whom were men, were organized into a *grex*, or troupe, usually under the leadership of a freedman; the actors were often slaves, and even when this was no longer true, the profession of acting was generally held in low esteem among Romans; out of season, the troupe continued to earn a living as informal entertainers. There was some doubling up on roles by the actors but not as much as in Greek drama. The costume of the actors, which gave the *fabula palliata* its name, consisted of a tunic with a Greek *pallium*, or cloak, worn over it: slaves wore no cloak, women wore a white or yellow chiton, soldiers wore military clothing, and country folk were distinguished by rough cloaks. Sandals or other informal footwear was worn, and wigs helped determine the age and sex of the character. There is some controversy on the matter of whether masks were worn in this period.

The Roman theater began with a temporary wooden structure that faced a hillside on which the audience sat. In the middle of the second century B.C.E., a stone theater under construction was demolished by Senatorial decree; thereafter, temporary tiers of wooden seats were constructed for specific festivals, to be taken down and reconstructed when needed. These practices underline the Roman ambivalence toward theater, because they were based on the notion that a permanent theater might encourage loitering and have a detrimental effect on Roman social fabric. It was not until 55 B.C.E., under Pompey, that the first stone theater was erected at Rome. In Plautus's day, the crowd sat on the slope, and a long, narrow wooden stage provided the place for the production. There was always an altar onstage, and at the rear was a simple building to house the dressing rooms. The front of this building, which was the backdrop for the play, had two or three doors, representing two houses and an alley between them. By convention, the actor's right-hand side entrance represented the way to the harbor, and the left-hand entrance, the way to the forum; the stage itself stood for a city street. There was no curtain. These arrangements were enhanced by certain conventions: Events supposedly taking place within the houses could be made vivid by an actor emerging from a doorway and shouting back into the house, entrance cues to off-stage actors were extended by comments about the creaking doorpost, and asides and eavesdropping were also used.

Music was more prominent in Roman Comedy than in its New Comic models; plays were accompanied throughout by the double-flute, except for the most prosaic dialogue, and all the actors could sing. This represented a marked change from the Greek New Comedies, which used musical intervals only to divide the five acts. The spectators at Roman Comedies of this period were a rowdy group drawn from every level of society; servants were used to keep order, but the crowd was noisy and easily distracted.

Titus Maccius Plautus, whose name indicates an early connection with theater, possibly as an actor of Atellan farce, was one of the two great masters of Roman Comedy. Of this prolific playwright, there are twenty surviving plays and substantial fragments of a twenty-first; all are *fabulae palliatae*, based on Greek

New Comedies. The best of Plautus's plays include *Amphitruo* (*Amphitryon*, 1694), the only mythological travesty in existence, the story of the title character's impregnation by Jupiter (the result was Hercules) and her husband's subsequent suspicion of her fidelity; *Aulularia* (*The Pot of Gold*), a character study of a miser, Euclio, whose stolen treasure of gold is restored to him in time to become his daughter's dowry; *Bacchides* (*The Two Bacchides*), a hilarious double-deception play involving two young men, two fathers, and two prostitutes called Bacchis, with the identity of names leading to a misunderstanding, and the usual need of the sons to deceive their fathers; *Captivi* (*The Captives*), a more serious drama, in which confusion of slave and master plays an important role in a deception that has a noble motive, rare in Roman Comedy; *Menaechmi* (*The Twin Menaechmi*), in which the arrival of a long-lost twin brother leads to a merry round of confusion, ending in a happy recognition; *Mostellaria* (*The Haunted House*), a play dominated by the bustling slave Tranio, who attempts to keep his master out of the house where his son is reveling by claiming that it is haunted; *Miles Gloriosus* (*The Braggart Warrior*, 1767), in which the soldier of the title, who has purchased another man's sweetheart, is foiled by the lovers, who continue to meet, aided by various forms of deception; *Pseudolus*, in which the title character, a clever slave, helps his young master to outwit an evil pimp, Ballio; *Rudens* (*The Rope*), a play with a romantic seaside setting, in which an evil pimp is outwitted and a young girl is restored to her father and her rightful citizenstatus; and *Trinummus* (*The Three-penny Day*, 1767), a quiet, family play in which a young man sells his father's house, unaware that it contains a buried treasure. Of lesser quality are *Asinaria* (*The Comedy of Asses*, 1774), *Casina* (English translation, 1774), *Cistellaria* (*The Casket*, 1774), *Curculio* (English translation, 1774), *Epidicus* (English translation, 1694), *Mercator* (*The Merchant*, 1767), *Persa* (*The Girl from Persia*, 1774), *Poenulus* (*The Carthaginian*, 1774), *Stichus* (200 B.C.E.; English translation, 1774), and *Truculentus* (English translation, 1774).

Much of Plautine scholarship centers on the relationship of the playwright to his sources; in no case are both a Plautus play and its model extant. *The Merchant*, *The Haunted House*, and *The Three-penny Day* are based on plays of Philemon, and *Casina* and possibly also *The Rope* and *The Braggart Warrior* come from Diphilus. *Stichus*, *The Two Bacchides*, and *The Carthaginian* derive from Menander, while *The Comedy of Asses* is modeled after Demophilus. It is clear that Plautus was no servile translator and that he endowed the New Comic plots with his unique *vis comica*, or comic vigor. The Greek elements of the plays include the plots, the meters, the settings, the costumes, the clever slaves, the tragic echoes, and the general attitude toward life. On the other hand, there is much that is Roman and specifically Plautine: the use of language, the modification of the plots, the dialogue repartee, the severe treatment of slaves, the coarseness, the injunctions for the attention of the audience, and the specific references to Roman customs, institutions, and historical events.

The characters of Plautus's comedies conform largely to the New Comic stock system, though there is less serious development and exploration of character than in Menander. The characters include the young man (*adulescens*), of either the exemplary or spendthrift type; the old man (*senex*), sometimes strict and sometimes liberal; the prostitute (*meretrix*), either greedy or sincere and affectionate; the pimp (*leno*), invariably evil; the kidnapped young girl (*virgo*), whose true identity is always discovered; the matron (*matrona*), usually a suspicious shrew; the slave (*servus*), either loyal or scheming; the braggart soldier (*miles gloriosus*); and the self-serving parasite (*parasitus*). The plots, usually occasioned by love, involve deception, trickery, mistaken identity, and false assumptions, with money an important motive. The humor, which often grows out of the plot, includes broad farce, extravagant caricature, wordplay, sarcasm, witty retort, satire, parody, and occasional obscenity. In all this, there are serious points as well: The sanctity of family life is upheld; there is great sympathy for certain characters; and, in general, self-sacrifice, loyalty, and love are rewarded, while greed and the worst vices are defeated.

The plays were written in meters adapted and transformed from the Greek. The basic meter of the plain dialogue and soliloquy (the *diverbium* portion) was the iambic senarius, with iambic and trochaic septenarii and octonarii used to show greater degrees of excitement. The *cantica*, or songs, were written in different meters, to be accompanied by the flute; divisions into five acts are a modern addition to the text. The language of the plays was based on that of daily life, with homely sayings and lower-class slang. In general, the plays have tremendous comic vigor and a natural sense of joy, enhanced by sure theatrical instincts, which overcome occasional problems of carelessness and loosely cohering plots.

TERENCE

Publius Terentius Afer, known as Terence, a manumitted slave born at Carthage in North Africa, was a member of the Scipionic Circle, a literary coterie organized around Scipio Africanus the Younger, for which Greek refinement and education were the standard. Terence's comedies, as a result, are less boisterous, more refined, and closer to the Greek New Comedy models than were those of Plautus. All six of the plays were produced by Ambivius Turpio. Of these, the earliest is *Andria* (c. 166 B.C.E.; English translation, 1598), in which a father, Simo, wishes his son Pamphilus to marry the daughter of Chremes, but Pamphilus loves an Andrian girl named Glycerium. The relationship between father and son is severely tested, but fate interposes a solution when Glycerium turns out to be, in fact, a daughter of Chremes; Pamphilus can both marry the woman he loves and honor his promise to his father. Very important here are the machinations of the slave, Davus. *Hecyra* (*The Mother-in-Law*, 1598), first presented in 165 B.C.E., failed when the audience became distracted by a rope-dancing performance, and was revived, unsuccessfully, in 160 B.C.E. In this fairly serious treatment of married life, a bride has returned to her parents' home during the absence of her husband, and a quarrel between her and her mother-in-law is suspected, though the real problem lies in the past of the bride and groom. The play has very little in it that is humorous. *Heautontimorumenos* (*The Self-tormentor*, 1598) of 163 B.C.E. has a double-strand plot (*duplex argumentum*), with two fathers, two sons, and two young women. After a good bit of trickery, deception, and mistaken identity, the sons are married, one to his lover and the other to a woman more conventional than his original choice. The play presents various thoughts on how to rear and discipline one's sons, a topic to which Terence was to return in *Adelphoe* (160 B.C.E.; *The Brothers*, 1598).

Terence's most successful play, *Eunuchus* (161 B.C.E.; *The Eunuch*, 1598), is more boisterous and closer to Plautus than any of his other comedies. In this *duplex argumentum* plot, Phaedria loves Thais, a courtesan. Phaedria's brother disguises himself as a eunuch in order to enter Thais's establishment and ravish a new young girl there. The young girl is revealed to be freeborn, and the couple marry, while an arrangement is made for Phaedria and a soldier to share the favors of Thais. While the latter portion of the denouement is less than satisfying, the fine character of Thais is compelling. *Phormio* (English translation, 1598), of 161 B.C.E., is a well-constructed *duplex argumentum* in which the two strands are well-integrated, primarily through the character of the parasite Phormio. With his help, two young cousins obtain their young women, one through a phony court action and the other by a deception to gain the needed money. *The Brothers* of 160 B.C.E. tells of two brothers, Micio and Demea, and the antics of their sons, Aeschinus (Demea's natural son, adopted by Micio) and Ctesipho (Demea's son). Micio, the liberal father, is far more appealing than Demea and holds the sympathies of the audience through most of the play, especially as the audience learns that Demea's Ctesipho is no real model, though strictly reared. Demea later appears to relent and change to Micio's more genial style, but surprisingly, he draws out his new liberality *ad absurdum*, exposing the problems inherent in Micio's approach to education. Many scholars consider this to be Terence's finest play.

It has already been noted that the plays of Terence are close to their Greek models both in treatment and in spirit: Caesar referred to him as "Menander halved." The plays, all of which are set in Athens, derive from the following sources: *Andria* from a combination of two Menander plays; *The Mother-in-Law* from a play by Apollodorus; *The Self-Tormentor* from a Menander comedy of the same name; *The Eunuch* from two Menander plays; *Phormio* from Apollodorus; and *The Brothers* from a Menander play and parts of a comedy of Diphilus. The practice of using more than one Greek model for a single play, called *contaminatio*, was apparently controversial in Terence's day, though there was solid precedence for doing so.

The prologues of Terence's comedies are unique because, instead of pleasantries and plot introductions, they take up literary matters, responding especially to criticisms of the poet's work; in this, they recall parabasis passages from Aristophanes. Terence is especially concerned with the criticisms of his rival, Luscius Lanuvinus. To the accusation of *contaminatio*, he responds that he is guilty as charged, preferring to copy the "negligence" of Plautus, Naevius, and Ennius rather than the "diligence" of others. To the charge of using a Greek passage already translated by a previous Roman playwright, he replies that the passages involved centered on stock characters, such as the parasite and the soldier, which are common in comedy. The accusation of receiving help from his friends receives an aloof statement of pride in his literary relationships, though it is likely that the Scipionic members offered only advice, rather than substantial aid, in the writing of Terence's plays. To Luscius's attacks on his style, Terence responds by moving to the offense, inveighing against his rival's literal translating. Also included in the prologues is information on the failure of the first presentation of *The Mother-in-Law*.

The characters of Terence's plays are more subtle, humane, and refined than those of Plautus. There is more serious interest in relationships, especially that between fathers and sons. The stock characters are no longer caricatures: Slaves are treated fairly, soldiers boast more plausibly, parasites are more realistic, and prostitutes are more refined. The humor, consequently, is quiet, more socially satiric and less boisterous; the style is clear, correct, and refined, but Plautus's theatrical instinct is lacking. The use of meter is more regular in Terence than in Plautus. Though Terence's plays were, in general, too subtly artistic to hold the interest of his contemporary Roman audience, subsequent ages have found much to admire in his work.

OTHER WRITERS

Caecilius, Statius falls chronologically between Plautus and Terence, and indeed, his surviving titles and fragments show a transition to the more Hellenized comedy of Terence. He employed the standard stock characters, and later Latin writers speak of his strength in composing plots and his weakness in the use of the Latin language. Gellius's side-by-side comparison of passages and aspects of Caecilius's *Necklace* and the Menandrian model emphasizes the superiority of the latter. Other writers of *palliatae* in this period, of which little is known, include Quintus Trabea, Marcus Atilius (who wrote *The Woman-Hater*), Aquillius, Licinius Imbrex, and Terence's nemesis, Luscius Lanuvinus. Terence was followed by Juventius, Valerius, and Sextus Turpilius, whose fragments show a strong Menandrian element. There were few attempts at the *palliata* after this time, though the plays of Plautus and Terence were occasionally revived. The *fabula palliata* had become so Hellenized that it was beyond the reach and tastes of the people of Rome.

OTHER DRAMATIC FORMS

Fabulae togatae (native Roman comedies), which became popular after Terence, were much more Italian in character, as their name ("plays in Roman dress") makes clear. Only fragments of this genre survive, but a few characteristics emerge: an interest in country folk as the butt of humor, a diminished emphasis on the cleverness of slaves, and a new prominence for women. The important authors include Titinius; Titus Quinctius Atta, reputedly highly skilled in depicting female characters; and, most important, Lucius Afranius (born c. 150 B.C.E.). Afranius was fond of Menander and brought back the Greek element to Roman Comedy once again, though in a very subtle way. The titles and fragments of *togatae* suggest a bourgeois Italian drama: Husbands and wives bicker, families go on holiday, and there are marriages, divorces, elections, and other reflections of Roman social and political institutions.

The late Republic saw other dramatic forms as well. The *fabula tabernaria*, close to the *togata*, was the comedy of the tradesmen and their ways. Also in this period, the old *fabula Atellana* (see above) was raised to a composed and rehearsed literary form, with verse replacing prose, by Pomponius and Novius; the titles and fragments show the old characters (Maccus, Pappus, Dossenus, and Bucco) involved in a wide variety of situations, including rural farce, mythological burlesque, and middle-class comedy, and an element of vigorous obscenity persists. After the literary *Atellana* had run the course of a generation, it yielded to the mime, a form of Greek origin that came to Rome by way of the southern cities of Magna Graecia. At this time, the mime was popularized in a degenerate form, with real women taking the female parts. Typically, the plots involved the deception of a doltish cuckold by a woman and her paramour. A more reputable type of mime emerged in the age of Julius Caesar. The element of gesticulation became progressively more important in mime, and ultimately the form degenerated into the wordless pantomime, thus ending the history of Roman comedy.

ROMAN TRAGEDY AFTER ENNIUS

The works of Marcus Pacuvius are represented by the survival of fragments and thirteen titles; of these, one belongs to a *fabula praetexta* (Roman historical tragedy), *Paulus* (after 168 B.C.E.), and twelve to tragedies based on works of Sophocles and Euripides. The fragments, and the comments of later Roman writers, indicate that Pacuvius was prone to elaborate phrasing and ornamental flourishes. His popularity was the result of his powerful characterizations and the universality of the reflections in his stage soliloquies. Cicero was especially impressed by his dramatic power.

Lucius Accius, a younger contemporary of Pacuvius, survives in a large number of titles and fragments. The titles of two *praetextae*, *Decius* and *Brutus*, survive, and the tragedies modeled on the Greek include *Atreus*, *Andromeda*, *Medea*, and *Philoctetes*. Several of these titles were translated in *Remains of Old Latin*. Accius was known in ancient times for his loftiness of style and the grandeur of his dramas. The plays contained excellent speeches, used as models for students of rhetoric. The remains of Accius allow certain conclusions about Roman tragedy in this period: The chorus, which was located on the stage rather than in an orchestra, came and went freely, intervening at suitable moments to participate in the dialogue or to provide a group of people when one was needed for any purpose. The usual meter of dialogue was the iambic trimeter, as in Greek tragedy, with anapests and cretics dominating the *cantica*, or songs. Tragedy persisted on the Roman stage in spite of the popular preference for lighter entertainments, primarily because of the interest and support of the Roman aristocracy, who found its ideas agreeable, especially the fear of tyrants; when the early empire brought about the decline of the old Roman families, and also of freedom of speech, tragedy faded from the stage into a strictly literary form. During its existence as a dramatic genre, Roman tragedy stayed close to fifth century B.C.E. Greek models, especially Euripides, and the *fabula praetexta* was a comparatively rare phenomenon.

Accius influenced the tragedies of the orator Gaius Titius, in the period of Cicero's boyhood; other writers of tragedy include Atillius, Gaius Julius Caesar Strabo, Cassius, and Santra. In Cicero's time, the tragedies of Pacuvius and Accius were revived during the peak years of the actor Aesopus. Roman figures famous in other spheres tried their hands at writing tragedy, including Asinius Pollio; Varius Rufus, who wrote a *Thyestes*; and Ovid, who wrote a *Medea*, but few traces remain of these efforts. From this point, Roman tragedy was an exclusively literary form, not written for stage presentation.

MIME IN THE PERIOD OF CAESAR AND CICERO

A brief history of the mime, from its origins in Magna Graecia to its decline into pantomime, has already been given. During the period of Caesar and Cicero, mime was very popular on the Roman stage, partly because of the scantily clad female performers, whose costuming caused the form to be known also as *fabula riciniata*. An important mime writer of Caesar's day, Decimus Laberius, was by social class a knight, or equestrian. His political outspokenness provoked Caesar to force him to appear onstage in one of his own mimes, in a competition with the newcomer Publilius Syrus; Caesar awarded the prize to Laberius's rival but restored him to his equestrian status. There are forty-four known titles of Laberius's mimes, some showing interests similar to those of Atellan farce, some common also to the *fabula togata*, and others resembling *palliatae*. A second mime writer of the same period was Publilius, Laberius's rival in the competition commanded by Caesar. Proverbial lines from his plays, mostly iambic senarii, were gathered into a corpus of *sententiae* in the first century C.E.

THE EARLY SILVER AGE

During the Silver Age of Latin literature, which lasted from the death of Augustus in 14 C.E. to the death of Hadrian in 138 C.E., many important changes took place in the Western world: The Roman Empire spread and became firmly established; trade and provincial administration led to many cultural contacts between Rome and its provinces; and the emperors became so powerful that their individual capacities to influence the literature and the arts were very great, in some cases leading to positive developments (most were well educated and interested in literature), and in some cases stifling the growth of learning and creativity through their absolutism and the free exercise of their whims. From the early Silver Age, there are only scraps of information concerning the history of the drama. Germanicus (15 B.C.E.-19 C.E.), the nephew and adopted son of Tiberius, wrote Greek comedies, of which no fragments survive. Formal drama had declined, opening the way for the coarse and popular mime: The mime in this period, though not intellectually or morally uplifting, was often praised for its "slice of life" authenticity. Under the reign of Caligula, Catullus was an important mime writer, and there survive two titles, *Phasma* (first century C.E.; the ghost) and *Laureolus* (first century C.E.), the latter a play about a bandit that was made notorious when a real-life criminal played the title role and reportedly was actually crucified onstage. The *fabula Atellana* also enjoyed a resurgence of

popularity at this time, with an occasional line or phrase covertly directed against an emperor. Tragedy was carried on through the *fabulae salticae* and also through dramatic recitations. The *fabula saltica* was a form in which a dancer pantomimed a story, while a chorus supplied the story line. The *salticae* were often based on unsavory stories from mythology, such as the tales of Pasiphaë and Leda, but prominent poets, such as Lucan and Statius, were among the authors. Little is known about the dramatic recitations of tragedy, beyond the fact that Nero favored them as a personal amusement.

The writing of drama was no doubt stifled by the arbitrary actions of the emperors: One Mamercus Scaurus came into severe disfavor for a line in his *Atreus* (first century C.E.) that alluded to a ruler's folly, and Caligula had a writer of Atellan farce burned in the amphitheater for an insult. Pomponius Secundus, a writer of tragedy, survived surveillance by the emperor Tiberius but was later attacked by a mob in the theater, for unknown reasons; he survives in a single title, *Aeneas*, probably that of a *fabula praetexta*.

SENECAN TRAGEDY

Seneca, a great writer, philosopher, satirist, and poet of the Neronian period, also wrote tragedies, of which nine survive. The plays of Seneca were written for recitation, between 45 and 55 C.E., and not for presentation on the stage; the long, elaborate speeches and scenes clearly unsuited for the stage make this obvious. Seneca's favorite model was Euripides, a somewhat kindred spirit, but Aeschylus and Sophocles also provided source material on occasion. Seneca's adaptations go well beyond mere translation to include major plot modifications as well as complete changes in spirit and emphasis. The plays are clever, rhetorical, and outwardly philosophical, but they never approach the profound genius and moving examination of the deepest problems in the human universe found in Greek tragedy of the fifth century B.C.E.

Hercules furens (wr. c. 40-55 C.E.; *Mad Hercules*, 1581) was based on Euripides' *Heracles*, with a few modifications: The tyrant Lycus has proposed marriage to Hercules' wife, Megara, in his absence (rather than threatening the lives of his sons); a lengthy description of the adventures of Theseus and Hercules has been added; and the killing of Hercules' wife and children is imagined in dramatic portrayal rather than in messenger's narration. *Troades* (wr. c. 40-55 C.E.; *The Trojan Women*, 1581), based on Euripides' *The Trojan Women* and *Hecuba*, drew also on two lost Sophoclean plays on the aftermath of Troy. Some scholars suggest that Seneca was, in addition, influenced here by Accius, the early Roman playwright, but there is no clear evidence of this. *Phoenissae* (wr. c. 40-55 C.E.; *The Phoenician Women*, 1581), based on Sophocles' *Oedipus at Colonus* and Aeschylus's *Seven Against Thebes*, is preserved in somewhat fragmentary condition, but it is clear that Jocasta has not committed suicide in the immediate aftermath of Oedipus's blinding, as she lives to attempt vainly to reconcile Polyneices and Eteocles. In *Medea* (wr. c. 40-55 C.E.; English translation, 1581), modeled on Euripides' play of the same title, the visit of Aegeus has been eliminated; a long passage on the magical powers of Medea has been added; and Medea's children are not sent into exile, but Jason expresses his desire to keep them with him, and thus reveals his fatal vulnerability to his wife. *Phaedra* (wr. c. 40-55 C.E.; English translation, 1581) looks back to Euripides' *Hippolytus*, though not to the extant play, but to the unsuccessful earlier drama in which Phaedra confronted Hippolytus directly; in Seneca's version, she also denounces him to Theseus in person and lives to clear Hippolytus in the end. The grotesque closing scene, in which the dead Hippolytus is reconstructed (with the exception of one piece of unknown anatomical identity), demonstrates the sometimes comical results of Senecan literality.

Seneca's *Oedipus* (wr. c. 40-55 C.E.; English translation, 1581) compares poorly with the Sophoclean masterpiece. Much space is devoted to the gruesome description of sacrifices and necromancy, in an attempt to replace the classic Sophoclean suspense with the establishment of a gloomy atmosphere. Jocasta and Oedipus face each other after the revelation of their kindred relationship, and Jocasta kills herself openly, again circumventing the Greek convention of the messenger's speech. Seneca's *Aga-memnon* (wr. c. 40-55 C.E.; English translation, 1581) also pales beside its famous predecessor. The watchman's prologue is replaced by an appearance of the Ghost of Thyestes, in another attempt to set a spooky tone. Clytemnestra wavers in her resolve to kill Agamemnon, but Aegisthus convinces her to proceed. The purple carpet scene is replaced by a lengthy storm description, and the play climaxes with Electra's daring rescue of her younger brother. Because several of these modifications are found also in Accius and Livius Andronicus, scholars have argued that they influenced Seneca, but the evidence is scarce, and a common post-Aeschylean Greek source cannot be ruled out. In his *Thyestes* (wr. c. 40-55 C.E.; English translation, 1581), Seneca took up a legend popular among Roman writers, the cruel revenge of Atreus, who forced the unwitting title character to feast on his own dead sons. The Greek plays dealing with this material have not survived for comparison. Finally, *Hercules Oetaeus* (wr. c. 40-55 C.E.; *Hercules on Oeta*, 1581), a lengthy play that shows signs of reworking, either by Seneca himself or by another, derives from Sophocles' *The Women of Trachis*. Here, Deianira loses her nobility to become a jealous shrew, Alcmena has been added as a character, and the deification has been incorporated into the play. It has been suggested that Ovid influenced Seneca in his treatment of this plot.

There are many weaknesses in Seneca's tragedies: the artificial treatment of human nature, the pedantic use of a dramatically exhausted mythology, the monotony of character, the bombastic rhetoric, and the lack of straightforward dramatic depiction. Even so, Seneca's plays contain some excellent speeches and interesting ideas, and the use of meter, both iambic trimeter and choral verse, shows polish and care. Most important is Seneca's profound influence on postclassical Western drama, for Seneca provided the important link between Greek tragedy and the theater of the modern era.

NERONIAN PERIOD DRAMA

Octavia, the only extant *fabula praetexta* (historical tragedy), survives with the corpus of Seneca, but the appearance of Seneca himself as a character, and the very accurate and detailed prophecy of Nero's death, argue convincingly that the play must be dated after the death of the emperor. Both the presence of ghosts and nurses and the meters imitate Seneca, but the repetition and the paucity of epigrams are uncharacteristic. The true author of the play remains unknown, and the date of composition is uncertain, though the years immediately following Nero's death are most likely.

The play, set in Nero's palace in 62 C.E., focuses on Octavia, the popular but ill-fated young woman who had already lost her father, the emperor Claudius, and her brother Britannicus, and had also been taken from her betrothed and forced to marry Nero, all through the machinations of Nero's mother, Agrippina. Octavia now faces Nero's plan to marry Poppaea and his consequent condemnation of Octavia to death, spurred by the spontaneous popular demonstration of support for the doomed empress; the death of Seneca is also a major event in the drama. The play ends with the lament of Octavia as she is led off to exile and death. *Octavia* is marred by endless repetition and grotesquely pedantic use of mythology.

In general, serious drama continued to be replaced by lesser forms in the Neronian period. In addition to the mimes, pantomimes, and *fabulae salticae* (discussed above), there was Nero's personal ascent to the stage, described by Suetonius: The emperor appeared as Orestes, Oedipus, and the mad Hercules, probably reciting long passages rather than participating in full-length tragedies; in his farewell performance, he appeared as *Oedipus in Exile*, reciting in Greek iambics. Curiatius Maternus, an orator-turned-poet who appears in Tacitus's *Dialogus de oratoribus* (c. 98-102; *A Dialogue Concerning Oratory*, 1754), wrote tragedies from the Greek in the Senecan mode, including a *Medea* and a *Thyestes*; two titles of *fabulae praetextae* also survive, *Domitius* and *Cato*. Juvenal and Martial mention the names of several other writers of tragedy, but about these little is known.

STATIUS AND MINOR FLAVIAN DRAMATISTS

Publius Papinius Statius, primarily known as an epic poet, composed a libretto (now lost) for the actor Paris, titled *Agave*, which told the tragic story of Pentheus; the words of Statius were sung by a chorus, while Paris danced and pantomimed the tale. Much of the dramatic poetry of this period is lost, but there were a Scaeva (or Scaevius) Memor and a Canius Rufus, both of whom wrote tragedy, and there are traces of lost *palliatae* and *togatae*. Formal drama had essentially vanished from the Roman stage.

BIBLIOGRAPHY

Beacham, Richard C. *The Roman Theatre and Its Audience*. Cambridge, Mass.: Harvard University Press, 1996. Traces the history of classical Roman theater, analyzing such aspects as staging, scenery, costuming, performance style, and the audiences' reaction to and influence on the nature and occasion of the performance. Particular attention given to Plautus and Terence.

Easterling, P. E. E., and B. M. W. Knox. *Greek Drama: The Cambridge History of Classical Literature*. Reprint. Cambridge, England: Cambridge University Press, 1991. Advances in recent scholarship are incorporated into this reprinted version of a classic text that offers a comprehensive survey of Greek literature from Homer to the third century C.E.. Includes appendix of authors and works, a list of works cited, and an index.

Forman, Robert J. *Classical Greek and Roman Drama: An Annotated Bibliography*. Pasadena, Calif.: Salem Press, 1989. Introductory resource that includes individually authored bibliographies, an overview of Greek and Roman drama, and chapters covering playwrights such as Aeschylus, Aristophanes, Euripides, Menander, Plautus, Seneca, Sophocles, and Terence. Within each chapter there are three sections, one covering translations and commentaries, the other two covering recommended criticism and general criticism.

Grene, David, and Richmond Lattimore, eds. *The Complete Greek Tragedies*. Chicago: University of Chicago Press, 1992. Provides new translations of *Oedipus at Colonus*, *Antigone*, *Oedipus the King*, and *Prometheus Bound*, among several others. Includes introductions to the playwright, to Sophocles' Theban trilogy, and brief critical commentaries preceding the other plays.

Hunter, R. L. *The New Comedy of Greece and Rome.* Cambridge, England: Cambridge University Press, 1985. Places the social comedy of Menander, Plautus, and Terence in its ancient context and considers its universal literary qualities.

Kelly, Henry Ansgar. *Ideas and Forms of Tragedy from Aristotle to the Middle Ages.* Cambridge, England: Cambridge University Press, 1993. Traces the shifting meanings given to tragedy throughout the ages, starting with Aristotle's notions, via Roman ideas and practices, to the Middle Ages. Chapters include "Greek and Roman Poetics," "Aristotle on the Tragic in General," and "Modes and Subjects of Roman Tragedy."

Ley, Graham. *A Short Introduction to the Ancient Greek Theater.* Chicago: University of Chicago Press, 1993. In analyzing the surviving plays of the tragic writers Aeschylus, Sophocles, and Euripides and of the comedian Aristophanes, Ley explores the actor's technique, the power and range of the chorus, the use of theatrical space, and parody in the plays.

Sutton, Dana Ferrin. *Ancient Comedy: The War of the Generations.* New York: Twayne, 1993. An overview chapter explores the origins of ancient comedy in Dionysiac festivals and the development of the comedic form. Subsequent chapters combine lively descriptions of the era's rowdy plays with analyses of the historical context and the ubiquitous theme of intergenerational conflict.

Wiseman, T. P. *Roman Drama and Roman History.* Exeter, England: University of Exeter Press, 1998. Explores early Roman dramatic tradition and its role in creating and recycling the Roman past.

Laura M. Stone

MEDIEVAL DRAMA ON THE CONTINENT

Often set aside as naïve and unoriginal, medieval theater on the European continent kept alive the natural human desire to act, to mimic, and to experience vicariously what could not be known in a given life. For its inspiration, it used two great sources of ideas: the Christian Scriptures and contemporary life. It explored these sources to the fullest and took all sorts of people as its performers: clergy, religious laymen and laywomen, and professional companies of actors. Drama in the Middle Ages was popular, of the people and for the people. Never for such a long period in human history did popular entertainment survive. Rejected as naïve and undeveloped, it left its seeds in the great dramatists to follow, who combined the scholarship and subtlety taught by the classical models with the simplicity, wit, and directness of the medieval theater.

DECLINE OF CLASSICAL DRAMA

Medieval drama, like Greek drama, was born at the foot of the altar and was intimately associated with religious feasts. Despite their common origin, however, classical and medieval drama appear not to be linked, according to all current evidence. The last known writer of tragedy was Pomponius Secundus, who lived during the reign of Claudius I. The great Greek tragedies, although seemingly forgotten, were preserved in a few Western monasteries, notably in Ireland, but there is no evidence to support any performances in the Middle Ages. Their apparent disappearance seems attributable more to the loss of the study of Greek than to any prejudice against their content.

The continued existence of Roman comedy is more evident. Numerous manuscripts of Terence were copied in medieval scriptoria. Some ancient Roman theaters did escape the pillaging of the barbarians, among them Arles, Autun, Narbonne, Orange, and Paris, but their original purpose seems to have disappeared. Early manuscripts speak of actors and acting; however, even before the fall of Rome, entertainment seems to have taken the form of farces, known as the *fabulae Atellanae* (Atellan farces), and mimes. The *fabula Atellana*, not unlike the *commedia dell'arte* (improvised comedy), revolved around four fixed characters and was rather limited. Comic masks in the art of the period have been cited in modern scholarship. The subject matter of the mime seems to have been broader, although there is no mention of farce, mime, or any kind of drama in the West after the sixth century, and there are no records of any dramatic activity between the sixth and ninth centuries. Isidore of Seville (seventh century) mentions *histriones* and *mimi*, but from his use of the past tense, one cannot assume the existence of drama at that time.

In the East, one would expect to find Greek classical drama, but although there are records of four theaters in Constantinople, there is no evidence of any plays. Critics have attempted to cite the play *Christos paschon* (variously ascribed from the fourth to the twelfth centuries) as a mosaic of classical and Christian drama and a link between the two, although there is no evidence of its performance, and it probably belongs to the later period rather than to the earlier. Both in the East and in the West, the profession of actor (*histrio*) changed to *pantomimus* and was little respected. Church authorities were hostile to plays and forbade actors to become Christians. Secular authorities were more lenient, merely limiting performances to certain times. Some critics, among them E. K. Chambers, believe that the *mimus* merged with Germanic entertainers to produce the *jongleur*. Critic Grace Frank supports the existence of such players but does not see them as continuing the dramatic tradition throughout the Dark Ages.

Manuscripts of Terence and Plautus are the most frequent classics preserved in medieval monasteries. Many copies of Terence's work were found in French monasteries such as Corbie, Fleury, Reims, and Limoges. Only about eight manuscripts of Plautus existed before the fifteenth century. It is evident that scholars used these dramatic texts only for study and not for performance. From the fourth century onward, the terms "comedy" and "tragedy" seem to have lost their classical distinction, and many misconceptions developed regarding the manner of classical dramatic performance. There are medieval works known as "elegiac comedies," edited by Gustave Cohen, which are Latin elegiac poems, some written in dialogue. Most are found in the area around Orléans, which is where the manuscripts of Terence were preserved and which was known to have been a cultural center with a cathedral school. The two most popular elegiac comedies are attributed to Vitalis of Blois in the twelfth century. They are called the *Geta* and the *Aulularia* and show affinities with the plays of Plautus. It is uncertain how and if they were performed.

HROSWITHA OF GANDERSHEIM

Unique among the classical writers of the Middle Ages is Hroswitha of Gandersheim, who was born in 935 and who died around 972. An educated nun in the Benedictine monastery of Gandersheim, founded in 850 in Saxony, she was familiar with Christian Scripture, the fathers of the Church, hagiographers, Plautus, Terence, Vergil, Ovid, and Horace. As a direct result of the Carolingian Renaissance, the abbeys of Saxony were centers of culture. The abbess in Hroswitha's time was Gerberg, the niece of Emperor Otto I and a great classical scholar. Hroswitha was directly influenced by her, and in this cultivated atmosphere, she deliberately took Terence as her model to produce six plays in simple but correct Latin prose.

Hroswitha's plays follow well-known legends of the lives of the saints. Three plays, *Gallicanus* (English translation, 1923), *Dulcitius* (English translation, 1923), and *Sapientia* (English translation, 1923), deal with the martyrs of the early Christian period. In *Gallicanus*, the title character is one of Constantine's generals, in love with a Christian, Constance, who has vowed to remain a virgin. Through her example, he is eventually converted to Christianity. *Sapientia*, the best-constructed of the martyrdom plays, has been called by C. Magnin "a ray of Sophocles shining through a Christian mind." Hroswitha shows the dignity of the early martyrs mingled with not a little impudence and portrays the heroic adherence of women to chastity.

Callimachus, though not the best of Hroswitha's plays, is a kind of Romeo and Juliet story and shows a moment of passion rare in the medieval theater. *Abraham* (English translation, 1923) and *Paphnutius* (English translation, 1923) are Hroswitha's finest plays. They are based on the lives of the fathers in the desert and show the war between the flesh and the spirit. Both deal with the fallen woman who is converted through a concerned relative or friend and who becomes a saint. *Paphnutius* shows the height of Hroswitha's dramatic art. It is the story of the conversion of Thaïs and shows excellent characterization, a well-knit plot, and expressive dialogue. The opening scene presents the exposition with classical conciseness and clarity. There are touching scenes in Paphnutius's concern for Thaïs, and passion is treated with warm restraint. The play was performed in England in 1914 and has seen other performances since that time.

Hroswitha's plays are outstanding for their dramatic quality in a period that has no other examples of such achievements. Although there is no indication that the plays were ever performed in her abbey or elsewhere, it is impossible to deny her ability, creative powers, and originality. Her introductions seem to indicate that the plays were merely recited, yet they reveal her own independence of character. Equally surprising are the exuberance of poetic expression and passionate overtones in the plays, which, unfortunately, were without a sequel.

Although research in medieval drama still has important lacunae, it seems evident that the classical theater survived only as a literary form, through manuscripts in certain monasteries. It was known but not performed, nor did it inspire independent writers, with the exception of Hroswitha. Drama existing until the tenth century was apparently comic entertainment, recitation, or poetry with dialogue. It was the inspiration of liturgical services, the faith of the people, and stronger political and religious unity that would bring about the rebirth of drama.

LATIN CHURCH DRAMA

In the eighth and ninth centuries, Charlemagne brought order and stability to Western Europe.

Anointed emperor of the Romans in 800 C.E., he revived the ancient concept of unity and peace. He encouraged monasteries, built churches, and founded schools. He invited the best scholars, notably Alcuin of York, who headed the Palatine School of Aixla-Chapelle (Aachen, in German). Charlemagne attempted to establish an educated clergy and a substantial body of cultivated laymen. During his reign, the service books of the Church were corrected, the Latin text of the Bible was re-edited, and classical works of antiquity were studied and imitated.

As a direct result of this liturgical and educational reform, there is a notable development in church services, which Karl Young in his authoritative work on medieval church drama sees as a first step in the re-creation of the theater. It begins with the liturgical embellishment known as the trope, defined by Young as a "verbal amplification of a passage in the authorized liturgy, in the form of an introduction, an interpolation, or a conclusion, or in the form of any combination of these." Although the origin of tropes is obscure, they seem to have been attached to parts of the Mass rather than to the Divine Office. The most important writer of tropes is Tutilo, from the Abbey of Saint Gall. His tropes are usually written in prose, and he has an *Agnus Dei* also in poetry. Most of his tropes are related to seasons of joy, rather than to the Passion.

In the ninth and tenth centuries, liturgical embellishments were added to the Allelujah verse before the Gospel, called *sequentiae*, and later *sequentia cum prosa*. In France, they were called *prose*; in Germany, *sequentia*, from which comes the English term "sequence." The earliest extant sequences are attributed to Notker Balbulus, from the monastery of Saint Gall. He seems to have put words to complex melodies of the Allelujahs to make them easier to remember. He was evidently inspired by a book brought from the Abbey of Jumièges to Saint Gall in 851. There is evidence of such compositions before this date, probably at Limoges, Luxeuil, Moissac, or Saint-Benoît-sur-Loire. In the eleventh century, sequences took on a poetic form and dialogue. The best example is the Easter sequence *Victimae paschali*, still retained in the liturgy.

Of these various liturgical developments, the earliest with dramatic possibilities is the famous tenth century text, *Quem quaeritis*, found in a manuscript in the monastery of Saint Gall. It is as follows:

INTERROGATIO: Quem quaeritis in sepulchro, Christicolae?

RESPONSIO: Jesum Nazarenum crucifixum, o caelicolae. Non est hic, surrexit, sicut predixerat. Ite nuntiate quia surrexit de sepulchro. Resurrexi

(QUESTION: Whom do you seek in the sepulchre, O friends of Christ?

RESPONSE: Jesus of Nazareth, who was crucified, O dwellers of Heaven. He is not here; he is risen, as he foretold. Go and announce that he has risen from the sepulcher. I have risen.)

Very likely it was sung by different sides of the choir. Its origin is obscure; although the Saint Gall text is the simplest, it is not the oldest. This honor belongs to the Abbey of Saint Martial at Limoges, and it was written during the period from 923 to 934.

The *Quem quaeritis* trope was first attached to the Introit, or entrance, of the Mass. Other, similar manuscripts are from Vercelli, in the twelfth century, an eleventh or twelfth century manuscript from Ravenna, and a tenth or eleventh century, more definitive, text from the Benedictine monastery in the Abruzzi. Unfortunately, there is no information describing the circumstances in which these were sung, but it was probably before some representation of the sepulcher. Such details can be deduced from an eleventh century manuscript found at Monte Cassino and twelfth century directions from Benevento.

There were few dramatic developments in the *Quem quaeritis* trope until it became detached from the Introit and incorporated into the Divine Office. It first appears as an independent liturgical ceremony, following Tierce, as seen in eleventh century versions in Heidenheim, Monza, and Saint Gall. Gradually, the *Quem quaeritis*, greatly amplified, was placed at the end of Matins, the liturgical hour that traditionally marks the passage of night to day. The last responsory refers to the visit of the three Marys to the sepulcher. Appropriately, this became the nucleus for the first genuine liturgical drama, known as the

Visitatio sepulchri. In the very early versions, clerics carry thuribles in addition to, or in place of, the biblical spices. The altar, symbolizing the sepulcher, was thus incensed. Young sees this as a first step toward creativity and free composition.

EASTER PLAYS

The Easter play, *Visitatio sepulchri,* was the most popular of all medieval liturgical dramas. Young cites more than four hundred extant versions and believes that many lie still unexamined, particularly in southern and southeastern Europe. The *Visitatio,* like the later Nativity plays, knows no national frontiers, for the Church was unified in the Middle Ages, and Latin was spoken and understood universally by the educated people. The versions show remarkable similarity, with formalized speeches and standard characters, with diversity only in the stage directions. Young distinguishes three stages in the *Visitatio:* In the first, there is a dialogue conducted by the Marys; in the second, the Apostles Peter and John are added; and in the third, the person of Christ appears.

Early versions of the first type are found at Tours in the eleventh or twelfth centuries; Utrecht, in the twelfth century; Minder and Arras, in the eleventh century; and Saint Gall, in the twelfth century. Fourteenth century manuscripts (unidentified German, Fécamp, and Toul) indicate a sepulcher large enough to accommodate two angels and specify costumes for the three Marys. Many churches retained the simpler version throughout the Middle Ages. The earliest plays go back to the second half of the tenth century and are found even in sixteenth century manuscripts and printed books. Several more elaborate texts show the incorporation of the sequence *Victimae paschali* into the *Visitatio.* In some cases, the congregation seems to represent the disciples to whom the news was announced.

The second stage of the *Visitatio* enlarges the setting to include Peter and John. Manuscripts of this type begin in the twelfth century and seem to have originated in Zurich, southern Germany, and Augsburg, although French and Italian manuscripts have been found from later periods. Congregational singing takes place at the end, and this part seems to be

amplified, with a generous role accorded to the people, as in a sixteenth century text from Aquilea.

At the end of the twelfth century, the figure of Christ appears at the center of the play. This phase seems to be of French origin. The simplest type, as in the Rouen manuscripts, centers on the dialogue between Christ and Mary Magdalen. Perhaps the most highly developed form comes from the famous playbook at the monastery of Saint-Benoît-sur-Loire, at Fleury. It contains all the phases of the Resurrection plays and shows a remarkable fusion of scriptural texts with poetic meters. A manuscript at Nuremberg concludes with a song in the vernacular, "Christ ist erstanden" (Christ is risen), sung by the congregation.

The *Visitatio* plays at this stage also introduce a nonbiblical figure, the *unguentarius,* or spice merchant. In its simplest form, it appears in a thirteenth century manuscript from Prague. Further additions include the soldiers sent by Pilate to guard the sepulcher. This incorporation of laypersons, not found in all versions, seems to have originated no earlier than the thirteenth century, in France, with texts also found later in Germany, and adds color and the beginning of comedy to an otherwise solemn presentation.

As the Easter play developed, it came to include events preceding and following the actual Resurrection narrative. There was a considerable increase in length and characters, and the intrusion of the vernacular. Critics differ as to which plays are actually liturgical dramas. Frank lists only two: a Norman play preserved in a thirteenth century manuscript from Tours (the Tours *Ludus pascalis*) and the other from the convent of Origny-Sainte-Benoîte. Young adds those from Klosterneuburg and Benediktbeuern. The *Ludus* from Origny-Sainte-Benoîte uses female characters for the Marys and a liberal amount of the vernacular, and thus creates more realism and human feeling. The Norman play begins with the setting of the soldiers' watch and includes several merchants. It continues into the Doubt of Thomas eight days after the Resurrection. The Klosterneuburg play includes a vivid presentation of many unusual scenes, especially the famous "Harrowing of Hell," and a genuine role for the soldiers. The Benediktbeuern play is found in the same early thirteenth century manuscript as the joyous and licentious songs known as *Carmina burana*. Although similar to the Klosterneuburg play, it is superior in dramatic elaboration and characters.

Gradually, the Easter play came to include other events from the period surrounding the Resurrection. Among the most famous topics are the Journey to Emmaus (*Peregrinus*), found in manuscripts in Saintes, Sicily, Benediktbeuern, and the Fleury playbook; the Ascension, especially popular in Germany; and the Pentecost, much less fully dramatized. Although one might expect the Passion to be included, there are no Passion plays before the thirteenth century, and representations within the Church were exceedingly rare, yet this theme was to result in one of the most popular of the vernacular plays in the fourteenth and fifteenth centuries. A phase of the Passion does occur in liturgical drama in the form of the *Planctus*, or lament, especially of the Blessed Virgin, known as the *Planctus Mariae*. Young traces the popularity of this theme to the cult of the Blessed Virgin that extended over Christianity from the twelfth century onward.

Although the Easter play shows great development from the simple *Quem quaeritis* trope to the more complex *Ludus paschalis*, it remained relatively faithful to scriptural sources. The solemnity of the subject precluded highly imaginative scenes, other than the introduction of the spice merchant, the soldiers, and the apocryphal descent of Christ into Hell. There was little effort in elaborate staging, other than the sepulcher, with some imagination given to the less popular Ascension scene. It remained for the more human Christmas story to call forth greater dramatic possibilities.

NATIVITY PLAYS

Plays relating to the birth of Christ, which were to have a much broader development than the Resurrection cycle, began in imitation of the *Quem quaeritis* trope. An eleventh century manuscript from Limoges gives a model text and may be among the earliest. The very use of *Quem quaeritis* shows imagination because it has no scriptural model as does the Easter trope. In fact, there is no dialogue in any of the

Christmas Gospels. Very early, personages were invented as interlocutors with the shepherds: *obstetrices*, or midwives. They appear in the second century apocryphal *Protevangelium Jacobi* and were very popular in the East. They appear in Christian iconography from the sixth century onward. They are in earliest versions of the *Quem quaeritis* Nativity trope, as Ivrea, Bobbio, Mantua, and Novalesa, with very little variety.

Like the Easter *Quem quaeritis* trope, the Christmas trope did not achieve real dramatic force until it was transferred to the Office at Matins and became known as the *Officium pastorum* (the Office of the Shepherds). Manuscripts indicate the presence of a *praesepe*, or manager, in the middle of the choir, with canons vested as *obstetrices* and *pastores*. Early texts are found at Padua and Clermont-Ferrand, with the most impressive from Rouen in the fourteenth century, also found in a thirteenth century Gradual. On the whole, however, dramatic representations of Christmas are relatively meager, although the manager became extremely popular.

More impressive was the representation for January 6, or the Feast of the Magi. Plays centering on this theme became known as the *Officium stellae*, or Office of the Star. An early text from Limoges places the Magi in the Offertory Procession. At Bayeux and Besançon, there were dramatic readings of the Epiphany gospel. Other texts place the *Officium stellae* outside the Mass, as in a fourteenth century manuscript from Rouen, which uses the midwives as interlocutors. Additions are also found in the person of Herod, later to become a comic figure. He first appears as a solemn figure in a manuscript from Nevers.

Shepherds begin to appear in the *Officium stellae* in the twelfth century. The most highly developed version comes from Fleury, which has a dignified tone, as befits a church play. A manuscript from Freising in the eleventh century depicts a raging Herod, which was to become typical and which would come to dominate the Christmas liturgies. In a manuscript from Padua, Herod even hurls his spear at the choir. The simplest and oldest manuscripts with Herod appear only in France, where they probably originated, in the twelfth century. Most of the texts in all stages of the *Officium stellae* are French and originated in the eleventh century.

The next theme to follow the *Officium stellae* is the Slaughter of the Innocents, celebrated on December 28. There are fragmentary versions at Freising and Compiègne, with a complete play at Laon, attached to an *Officium stellae*, ending with a Rachel moaning her children. The same theme is found in an eleventh or twelfth century manuscript from Saint Martial de Limoges, the briefest and simplest treatment. The Rachel theme was a very popular series and became known as the *Ordo Rachelis*. The best example is from the Fleury playbook, showing amplification of roles and originality in dramatic staging within the church.

The final addition to the *Officium stellae* appears in the *Ordo prophetarum*, or Procession of the Prophets, which presents prophecies concerning the coming of Christ. Young places their origin in sermons, particularly Saint Augustine's *Contra Judaeos*, used in the readings for the Christmas season. It appeared as a dialogue in Salerno, and it developed verse and music at Limoges. The Laon manuscript (thirteenth century) gives the most dramatic role to Balaam's ass, which became the most popular character. Young does not see this as a comic intervention, but rather as the medieval sympathy for patient and sober beasts. Balaam's ass became the inspiration for the *Festum asinorum*, probably performed for January 1. Frank associates this play with the liturgical revelry of the lower clergy known as the Feast of Fools, associated with the development of comedy. The introduction of buffoonery into some plays of the *Ordo prophetarum* brought variety and animation to otherwise stylized plays.

The most interesting of all Christmas plays is obviously a cycle, including an *Officium pastorum*, an *Officium stellae*, an *Ordo prophetarum*, and an *Ordo Rachelis* from the monastery of Benediktbeuern, found also among the *Carmina burana*. It begins with the prophets, after which an original character called the Archisynagogus becomes aggressively obstreperous and ridicules the prophecies. He returns to counsel King Herod and debates wildly with him. Herod's death is portrayed with horrible realism in a panto-

mime in which he is gnawed by worms. In the actual nativity scene, a *diabolus*, or devil, attempts to corrupt the shepherds as they listen to the angels' message. The play ends with the flight of the Holy Family into Egypt. It is a work unmatched for realism and pageantry, so much so that critics have debated its actual performance, although Young believes that it did exist in dramatic form.

OTHER DRAMATIC THEMES

Christmas and Easter themes represent the greatest number of liturgical plays. Other New Testament themes included the Raising of Lazarus, the Conversion of Saint Paul, and plays about the Blessed Virgin. Highly developed plays about Lazarus are found in the Benediktbeuern Passion Play and in the Fleury playbook. The plays about the Blessed Virgin, destined to attain great popularity in the vernacular miracle plays, followed scriptural or apocryphal texts in the liturgical drama. The four most important feasts celebrated the Presentation, on November 21, the Annunciation, on March 25, the Purification, on February 2, and the Assumption, on August 15. Of these, the drama at Avignon in 1385 for the Presentation is the most ambitious, with twenty-one characters, among them symbols, foreshadowing the later morality plays, and a complete set of rubrics for the stage. The plays for the Assumption are rather limited in scope, and some seem to have been of an indecorous type.

Other than the *Ordo prophetarum*, Old Testament themes were limited in subject. The most important themes were Isaac and Rebecca, Joseph and his brethren, and Daniel. Liturgical plays of nonscriptural origin were based on legends or miracles of the saints. They did not attain great popularity in the church dramas, but they were to reach enormous proportions in the vernacular plays of the late Middle Ages. The only saint to be widely treated in church plays is Saint Nicholas, about whom there are four known legends in dramatic form.

Church drama represents a gradual development from the ninth to the thirteenth centuries, and seems fully developed by the fourteenth. It was a drama essentially in Latin, though some texts in the vernacular appear as early as the twelfth century. For the most part, it followed scriptural texts, with some additions from apocrypha and popular characters, such as the spice merchant in the Easter plays or the midwives in the Christmas plays. The actors were principally clerics; hence, costumes were liturgical vestments. Roles for women were not unknown, especially in monasteries of nuns. Although most of the plays are serious and solemn in nature, a certain amount of buffoonery was tolerated. Church dramas were international, with the same type of play appearing in widely separated geographic areas. Some themes are indigenous to a country, such as the *Officium stellae* to France, but on the whole they extended throughout all of Western Europe and are even known in the East. By the fourteenth century, however, they came to be supplanted by the vernacular drama, for reasons listed below.

THE RELIGIOUS THEATER IN THE VERNACULAR

The change to a theater outside the church and under secular auspices was gradual. The vernacular began to appear side by side with Latin in several church plays, sometimes for a translation, sometimes for amplification. Some early examples are the Benediktbeuern Christmas and Easter plays, the Easter play at Klosterneuburg, and the *Suscitatio Lazari* (*The Raising of Lazarus*, 1975) and *Iconia Sancti Nicolai* (*The Image of Saint Nicholas*, 1976) of Hilarius. The Trier *Osterspiel* (fourteenth century) contains verse paraphrases and translations. In the twelfth century Anglo-Norman fragment of *Adam*, the prophecies are given first in Latin, then in Norman-French.

As early as the twelfth century, clerics objected to abuses in church plays. Gerhoh of Reichesburg objected to the dramatization of sacred events in which women, soldiers, and devils were portrayed by clerics. Another denunciation came from the abbess of Hohenburg, Herrad of Lansberg, in the late twelfth century. She objected that plays had become occasions for buffoonery and general disorder. Clerical disapproval was not the main reason for the transition to the vernacular play performed outside the church. Church hierarchy was on the whole favorable to liturgical drama. The change to the secular theater, according to Young and other critics, came about rather from a natural evolution and from the desire of both playwright and audience for an increase in scope, greater staging facilities, and the use of the vernacular. Plays would be unintelligible to many of the faithful because by that time very few understood Latin. There was also a need for secular surroundings in order to develop comedy, although some buffoonery is found in the liturgical drama. Once emancipated from the Church, comedy developed rapidly, especially in Germany, which already had more comic elements in its church plays than did other countries.

Transitional plays were of great scope and magnitude, often composing cycles, not unlike the Nativity church plays. They were often performed outdoors; hence, spring was the most favorable time. The Feast of Corpus Christi, promulgated by Pope Urban IV in 1264, was brought into prominence in the fourteenth century, and a great many plays, especially in England and Spain, revolved around this celebration. The secular plays, once instituted, took on a national character, quite different from the international similarity of the liturgical plays. The greatest progress in the drama on the Continent was made in France, Germany, and Spain; hence, it is appropriate to examine the development of theater in each of these countries separately.

FRANCE

The tradition of the liturgical theater was very strong in France. The famous Fleury playbook, now preserved in the Bibliothèque d'Orléans and presumably dating from the end of the twelfth or the beginning of the thirteenth century, contains ten of the most finished of all medieval church plays. The book includes a *Visitatio sepulchri*, an *Ordo stellae*, an *Ordo Rachelis*, a Peregrinus, a Raising of Lazarus, a Conversion of Saint Paul, and four versions of the Saint Nicholas story. All the compositions show strong dramatic content and can very easily have been the inspiration for future secular drama. The first known author of liturgical drama, Hilarius, a wandering scholar and possibly student of Peter

Abelard, wrote around the region of Angers. His three extant plays, a Raising of Lazarus, an *Iconia Sancti Nicolai*, and a Daniel, contain some refrains written in the vernacular.

The earliest surviving text that contains a considerable amount of French comes from the Abbey of Saint Martial de Limoges and dates from the first third or first half of the twelfth century. It is in a dialect on the borderline between French and Provençal. Known as the *Sponsus*, it dramatizes the parable of the Wise and Foolish Virgins, awaiting the Bridegroom, who represents Christ. Although based on the Gospels, it nevertheless exploits dramatic possibilities by repetitions, verses in French, and the introduction of additional characters in the merchants. The occasion for its representation is not clear, yet it is preceded and followed by other plays: an Easter trope and an *Ordo prophetarum*, usually associated with Christmas. It is a very representative play, written with skill and artistry.

The first surviving French play wholly in the vernacular is the *Mystère d'Adam*, or *Le Jeu d'Adam*, dating from 1146 to 1174. It is considered part of the semiliturgical theater because it was not performed within the church but rather in front of it, with the figure of God entering and leaving through the main door of the church. It is written in an Anglo-Norman dialect by an anonymous author. *Le Jeu d'Adam* contains three unequal parts: The first, and the longest, represents the Fall of Adam and Eve; the second, the murder of Abel; and the third, incomplete, is a Procession of Prophets. It thus shows affinities with the cyclical plays and suggests an orientation toward the Redemption theme, with the prophets and the figure of Abel representing Christ. *Le Jeu d'Adam* is one of the most original and delightful of all medieval plays, particularly the first section, which shows the human side of Adam and Eve. Adam is a loyal vassal of his Lord, and Eve represents feminine fragility. The most successful scene is the temptation of Eve by the wily serpent, who flatters her feminine nature and entices her curiosity by promising to reveal a secret. On the whole, it has excellent characterization, realism, and lively dialogue, with skillful manipulation of verse.

Other transitional plays from the twelfth and thirteenth centuries are *Les Trois Maries* and *Courtois d'Arras*. *Les Trois Maries* has only forty lines remaining in a fragment and appears to be a translation of some liturgical *Quem quaeritis* and *Victimae paschali*. *Courtois d'Arras* is the story of the Prodigal Son and transposes the parable to the thirteenth century, in a Picard dialect, with many comic accessories and lusty scenes that border on farce. Some theories ascribe the play to Jean Bodel.

By the thirteenth century, the vernacular theater was well established in France. At this time the miracle play became its most important expression. According to J. M. Manly, Young, and others, a miracle play is the dramatization of a legend, setting forth the life, or the martyrdom, or miracles of a saint. Although Young maintains that the germ of miracle plays is already present in the Christmas and Easter plays, Manly believes that they arose spontaneously in the twelfth century. In any event, it is natural that by this time there was more secular intrusion into monasteries, and relationship with the laity was growing. With liturgical models to follow and secular impetus to impel writers, miracle plays became very popular in France, especially in the fourteenth century. The two most popular were the Saint Nicholas and the Blessed Virgin plays.

Saint Nicholas was the patron of students, children, merchants, travelers, and young girls in search of a husband. He was the most favored miracle worker of the Middle Ages, and his cult was popular in the East and the West. The earliest, and the best, surviving French miracle play is by Bodel, called *Le Jeu de Saint-Nicolas* (pr. c. 1200; *Play of Saint Nicholas of Jean Bodel*, 1932). Bodel was from Arras, a great commercial and literary center where he died in 1209 or 1210, after having served in the municipal government. He was a talented writer by profession. Frank places the date of the play between 1199 and 1201.

The play reveals its author's imagination and creativity. Bodel transforms a meager legend of an infidel whose treasure is stolen. After witnessing an apparition of Saint Nicholas, the infidel decides to embrace Christianity. Bodel makes the king a raging tyrant, who "out-Herods Herod." The king has a wily Seneschal and a cruel jailer, Durant. A valiant Christian warrior, anonymously called Le Preud'homme, alone survives a battle of the Christians and Muslims. The king has recklessly exposed his treasure to test Saint Nicholas, so praised by his Christian captive, le Preud'homme. Three thieves, Cliquet, Pincedé, and Rasoir, authentic specimens of Artois lowlife, steal the treasure, but Saint Nicholas forces them to return it fourfold. The king and his courtiers are in this way converted, and Le Preud'homme is saved.

The edifying side of the play is minimal in contrast to the local color, shrewd character portrayal, and witty dialogue. Although the play belongs to the religious theater, it is in fact the ancestor of the comic theater, especially in the persons of the three thieves. There are no stage directions, but it is very likely that the play took place in a series of spots onstage called "mansions," where the scene is indicated by a very simple symbolic device, such as a tree for a forest. Medieval stained-glass windows give evidence of this arrangement. Thus, many scenes could be played at once by a device known as simultaneous staging.

Play of Saint Nicholas of Jean Bodel is an outstanding yet singular example of the power of the medieval theater. Unfortunately, it had no direct influence on succeeding plays. The next important French author, Rutebeuf, was a professional writer, obviously of lower station than Bodel. He wrote lyrical, satiric, and polemical verse; *fabliaux*; lives of saints; and a monologue, *Dit de l'herberie*. He is most famous for the miracle play of the Virgin titled *Théophilus*. Although the Virgin figured prominently in the Nativity plays, this is the first play, in 1260, in which she appears in what was to become her popular role of intercessor for erring mortals.

Théophilus (pr. c. 1260; *Le Miracle de Théophile*, 1971), based on a primitive sixth century Faust-type legend, was extremely popular in the Middle Ages and is frequently represented in medieval iconography, most notably on the façade of the cathedral of Notre Dame in Paris. Théophile, an important ecclesiastic, loses his wealth and invokes the Devil, who in turn promises Théophile wealth and fortune if he renounces God and promises to do evil. Théophile

takes the solemn oath required by the Devil and is restored to his former status. Yet he repents, implores the Virgin, and is saved. This short play of only 663 lines is remarkable less for its plot than for its poetic imagery, especially the "plainte de Théophile" (lament of Théophile), which many critics have considered a description of Rutebeuf's own suffering. The Devil and Salatin are creative portrayals, recalling Satan from *Le Jeu d'Adam* and the king from *Play of Saint Nicholas of Jean Bodel*. Although the play was probably performed in simultaneous stage setting, the disproportionately long role of Théophile may point to a dramatic monologue.

The miracles of Notre Dame are the most popular miracle plays in fourteenth century France. About forty have been found in a fifteenth century manuscript called *Cangé*, yet they obviously date from the fourteenth century. All the miracles of Notre Dame reveal a remarkable similarity in theme. The Virgin always saves a sinner at the last minute, yet each one has its own story of the sin. They were performed by a guild, or *puy*, dedicated to the Virgin, probably for her feasts. The similarity of style has led critics to posit a single author, although recent scholarship suggests fifteen or twenty. Twenty-three plays are accompanied by lyric poems, called *serventoys*. Their exact relationship to the play is unknown but suggests a contest among the sponsors of the plays. Similarity in language and freedom from dialectical traces indicate the region around Paris, and one is ascribed to Amiens. The plays all have musical interludes, and many have sermons that were pronounced very solemnly by lay officials.

The plays are diverse in their themes, inspired by such varied sources as Gregory of Tours, Gautier de Coincy, *chansons de geste*, and folktales. Although the moral is always stated, the development of the sinner provides enormous scope for medieval entertainment. The plays tell of unfaithful nuns, gossiping women, murderers, and robbers, all of whom are ultimately saved by the Virgin. Freed from the limitations of the liturgical drama, these plays make use of surprise and suspense as their dramatic elements. They are the faithful representation of the society of their times, the naïve piety of the people, and their customs and values, and they show tremendous possibilities for character development.

As the fourteenth century was characterized by the great miracle plays of Notre Dame, no doubt the result of widespread Marian devotion and the birth of the courtly love tradition a century or two earlier, the fifteenth century was marked by Passion plays. This theme, rather unpopular in the liturgical theater, attained increasing importance in the vernacular, developing performances of several days. The causes of sudden interest in the Passion are closely linked with the prevailing death theme in fifteenth century art and literature, the *danse macabre* or Dance of Death, and the splendid tombs of the Dijon dukes. This was the period of the Hundred Years' War, the Black Death, and much civil unrest; hence, plays on the Passion were seen as a kind of exorcism. When the Passion plays became cycles, beginning with the Creation and ending with the Last Judgment, they were played by groups of professional actors, or *confréries*, and served as competitions among various guilds.

At the end of the twelfth and the beginning of the thirteenth centuries, the *Passion des jongleurs*, a narrative sung by wandering minstrels, was circulated in France and England. It formed the basis of later Passion plays. The first cyclic Passion play, which shows considerable French influence, is the *Paaschspel de Maestricht*, a Dutch play dating from 1350. The first French Passion play is the *Passion du Palatinus*, dating from the fourteenth century, and it is related to three other fragments known collectively as the *Passion d'Autun*. All these texts point to an earlier, but lost, text. The *Passion du Palatinus* has many lines taken from the *Passion des jongleurs* and is a lively play, with realistic and often witty dialogue, as in Judas's argument that he has received only twenty-eight instead of thirty pieces of silver. Despite these touches of humor, the anonymous writer maintains solemnity and adheres to the traditional portrayal of Christ and other major characters.

Le Jour du jugement, from the late fourteenth or early fifteenth century, resembles the *Passion du Palatinus* but lacks its verve and originality. It is the story of the Antichrist, a theme less popular in France than in Germany. The *Passion de Semur*, found in a Burgundian manuscript of 1488, though the play itself is earlier, is the first model for the great spectacles of the fifteenth century. It contains 9,582 lines and required two days to present, spanning the period from the creation of the world to the Ascension of Christ. It expands Judas's role, contains many *diableries*, or devilish pranks, and invents allegorical figures, such as Orgueil (Pride), Ecclesia (the Church), and Synagogua (the Synagogue).

In contrast to the lively and relatively short *Passion de Semur*, the *Passion d'Arras* by Eustache Mercadé is longer and more ponderous. It is twenty-five thousand lines long and took four days to perform. It covered only the history of Jesus. It is framed within the so-called *Procès de Paradis*, where allegorical figures plead for mercy for the fallen human race. A *Prescheur*, as in many other medieval plays, reads the prologues and epilogues. Although Mercadé's version is very heavy, he portrays feminine characters with unusual skill, especially Mary Magdalen and the Virgin Mary.

The classic medieval Passion is *Le Mystère de la passion* by Arnoul Greban. This Passion play was performed three times in Paris before 1473, by the famous Confrérie de la Passion. Performances also took place in Le Mans, Amiens, Mons, Troyes, and other cities. The bimillennial celebration in Paris in 1951 included Greban's *Passion*. It had more than thirty thousand lines and took four days to perform. Like the *Passion de Semur*, it began with the Creation. Although Greban improved greatly on Mercadé's version, he is indebted to Mercadé for the *Procès de Paradis*. Greban's work is lyrical, scholarly, and swift moving. It is especially noted for its tenderness in scenes relating to the Virgin Mary, whose delicate humanity marks the plays. Greban's play has become the model for all Passion plays, although Jean Michel's work was popular around Paris.

The earliest surviving text of Jean Michel's *Passion* is 1486, when it was played "sumptuously and triumphantly" at Angers. His play is based on Greban's and includes several wearisome amplifications. Less scholarly than Greban, Michel incorporates apocryphal and legendary material indiscriminately, although this adds new life to the theme.

Many other plays of the time included variations of the Passion theme. One of the most noteworthy is the *Actes des Apôtres* (c. 1452-1478), which is said to have taken forty days to perform in Bourges in 1536. It had five hundred roles and created great suspense and excitement among the spectators. References are made in the fifteenth and sixteenth centuries to other plays, notably *Le Vieux Testament*, but no text contains a complete version.

In the fifteenth and sixteenth centuries, guilds, towns, and societies frequently performed plays in honor of their patron saints. Saints' plays from the early or mid-fourteenth century are among the manuscripts in the Bibliothèque Sainte-Geneviève collection and include a Sainte-Geneviève play, a Martyrdom of Saint Denis, and a unique *Vie de Saint-Fiacre*, evidently intended for performance at Meaux. These plays influenced later works. Fifteenth and sixteenth century versions vary in length, from very short—probably intended for small communities—to much longer cyclical plays. Some were written by skillful professionals such as Jean Molinet's *Mystère de Saint-Quentin*, dating from before 1465, and Andrieu de la Vigne's *L'Aveugle et le boiteux*, a morality reworked into the story of Saint Martin. Most saints were apostles or early martyrs. There were important plays about Saint Louis, especially a *Vie*, or *Mystère, de Saint-Louis*, written before 1472 and played by more than 280 actors in Paris. It ends with miracles of the saint, as does Gringoire's sixteenth century play, and is noteworthy for the devil known as Penthagruel, related to François Rabelais's immortal Pantagruel.

The religious theater remained popular in France until well into the sixteenth century, and some plays are even known in the seventeenth century. In 1548, Parliament forbade the performance of *mystères sacrés*, but the famous Confrérie de la Passion continued to perform them under the name of *tragédies* or *tragi-comédies*. Moralities, on the whole less popular in France than in England, were often combined with *mystères* or took the form of *sotties* in the comic theater and continued until well into the seventeenth century. *La Goutte*, by Laffemas in 1605, is described as a *tragédie nouvelle*, but it is really a morality. The religious theater did not end at any definite moment; it simply became transformed into the tragedy of the seventeenth century. Its spirit of realism and spontaneity, the sublime and the grotesque, the tender and the diabolical, returned later in the nineteenth century Romantic theater.

GERMANY

As the earliest Latin manuscript came from the German monastery of Saint Gall, notably the *Quem quaeritis* trope, so some very early manuscripts in the vernacular are in the German tongue. The most famous and the earliest is the Benediktbeuern Passion Play, from about 1200, in which the biblical text is handled more freely and there are songs both in Latin and in German. Germany has a number of transitional plays and shows a different development in subject matter from other countries. The German plays tend to make unusual combinations and groupings. Plays from Trier (fourteenth or early fifteenth century) and Wolfenbüttel (fifteenth century) are examples of simple transitions. The second gives a considerable role to the ointment seller, characteristic of German plays. It also adds scenes of Pilate and a Harrowing of Hell to the Easter Play.

The most significant of the early plays, considered by W. von Creiznach to be the first complete play in the vernacular, is from Kloster Muri in Switzerland, from the early thirteenth century. It used rhymed couplets à la the court epic written in a polished style. Only fragments remain, which indicate a lively scene with the ointment seller, a boastful Pilate with a comic servant, and a Harrowing of Hell. There are elaborate Easter plays, notably from Innsbruck, Berlin, and Vienna. In the Berlin play, only a fragment relating to the ointment seller is preserved. The well-known Innsbruck play, dated 1391, has an *Expositor ludi* and a Pilate who appears as a boastful tyrant. There are examples of buffoonery in the setting of the watch. The Harrowing of Hell is also full of merriment and includes glimpses of contemporary society together with the ubiquitous ointment seller. Although the scene of the three Marys is treated with reverence, it is evident that comedy in Germany made its way very early into the religious theater.

There is an early fourteenth century Vienna Passion play that follows the same form as the English plays, with the usual German comic orientation. The manuscript is incomplete, but it obviously contains the elements of the Fall, the Atonement, and the Resurrection. The fall of Lucifer, while not biblical, is usually found in medieval Passion plays and is especially lively in Germany, where it provides for the presentation of diabolical pranks. In the Vienna play, the role of Satan includes two other devils, and the fall of Adam and Eve also includes a number of villains and cheats intended for Hell. Although all scenes are not extant, it is possible to reconstruct the play from a Czech manuscript obviously borrowed from the Vienna play.

The model for later German Passion plays is the Saint Gall Passion from an undated but fairly early manuscript. It follows biblical sources closely and is essentially reverent in tone, although it is not without its comic elements, particularly in the role of Satan, who seems to have changed sides. It presents scenes of Christ's life from the wedding at Cana through the Resurrection in rather simple yet lively form. It includes events not usually found in other plays, such as the washing of the feet, the suicide of Judas, and a *Planctus*. It also includes much Latin, which suggests a translation.

Also from Saint Gall comes a fourteenth century Christmas play that is rather extensive. It contains a well-developed *Ordo prophetarum* in which each prophet introduces himself as he speaks, and then continues from the Betrothal to the Flight into Egypt. German Christmas and Easter plays seem to have united very early, and Creiznach dates such a play from the middle of the thirteenth century. It comes from Kloster Himmelgarten near Nordhausen and contains fragments of an *Ordo stellae*, Flight into Egypt, the Calling of Peter and Andrew, and the Wedding at Cana.

One of the most complete Passion plays dates from the mid-fourteenth century and includes a set of stage directions, called *Ordo sive registrum*. It is known as the Frankfurt Diregierrolle. The play is intended to take place over at least two days, and goes from a *Prophetae* and an elaborate prologue spoken by Saint Augustine to an afterpiece concerning the dispute between Ecclesia and Synagogua. This play, together with one from Alsfeld (1501), a more scriptural one from Frankfurt, and one from Heidelberg, has led Creiznach and other critics to conclude that there is an established type of Passion play in western and southern Germany. It has no Old Testament plays, usually no plays of the Nativity, and no Last Judgment. Tyrol plays seem limited to the Passion and Resurrection.

Although records are scant regarding Corpus Christi plays on the Continent, other than sixteenth century Spain, there is a late fifteenth century play from Eger in Czechoslovakia that is the fullest of all the German-language plays. It contains elaborate Old Testament plays and has unusual themes, such as Lamech and the death of Cain. It qualifies as a Corpus Christi play, though it is not so called. Corpus Christi plays presented chronologically the story of the entire liturgical year on successive days, by the local guilds. A play from Künzelan (1479) called "ein Frohnleichnamspiel," or Corpus Christi play, is believed to have been connected with the procession and was played at stations along the way. An earlier manuscript, from Innsbruck in 1391, indicates a Corpus Christi play, which Creiznach considers the first of all.

The popularity of the Marian theme in Germany is centered on the Assumption. One of the most significant plays comes from Innsbruck. Because it is found in the manuscript with plays on the siege of Jerusalem and the Acts of the Apostles, it is assumed that these were popular themes and that the Assumption was the starting point. Plays on the Antichrist and the Last Judgment were also frequent, particularly in the fifteenth century, as is seen in a play from Lucerne, Switzerland (1549). Christmas plays show much farce and comedy. Saints' plays were also popular.

Miracle plays are represented by three plays from the fourteenth or fifteenth century: *Theophilus*, *Das Spiel von den zehn Jungfrauen* (the play of the ten virgins), and *Frau Jutta* (Pope Joan). *Theophilus*, a Low German fifteenth century play, has the same theme as Rutebeuf's *Le Miracle de Théophile* and retells the Faust legend of a priest who sells his soul to the Devil to become a bishop. In comparison with Rutebeuf's play, it is poorly constructed and undramatic, yet it is important in its use of the Faust legend. *Das Spiel von den zehn Jungfrauen* was played at Erfurt in 1322. It is a play of Christ's inflexible justice, because contrary to the usual theme of the miracle, he refuses to pardon the foolish virgins even at the request of his mother. The play is said to have so moved the Landgrave of Thuringia that he suffered a fatal stroke. *Frau Jutta* is a Thuringian play written about 1480 by the priest Dietrich Schernberg. Tempted by the Devil to wear men's clothes and study in Paris, Frau Jutta is finally elected pope. She dies in childbirth but is saved by the Blessed Virgin and is carried from Hell by the Archangel Michael. Following the German comic tradition, there is a mirthful scene in which all the devils in Hell dance, accompanied by Lucifer's grandmother.

In contrast to its effect on French and English drama, the Reformation did not bring about the end of the German-language religious theater. In Switzerland, biblical dramas were produced, and in the early sixteenth century, Pamphilus Gengenbach (1480-1524) adopted the *Fastnachtsspiel* to moral and religious purposes. Nikolaus Manuel (1484-1530), a native of Bern, produced religious satires on the worldly ambition of popes in contrast to the simple life of Christ. The highest point in the development of the *Osterspiele* (Easter plays) was not reached until 1583, in Lucerne. In Catholic Germany, religious plays continued. The Oberammergau Passion Play, which began only in the seventeenth century, continues to the present day. The Renaissance did finally sharply curtail religious drama, however, substituting Plautus and Terence, and humanistic themes supplanted religious plays.

SPAIN

Although liturgical Latin dramatic texts are considerably lacking in Spain, Spanish literature has the honor of possessing the oldest vernacular text of a church play. The *Auto de los Reyes Magos*, consisting of 146 lines, comes from a manuscript in the Chapter Library of Toledo. It is generally ascribed to the middle of the twelfth century and was probably played

for the feast of the Epiphany, January 6. Because it shows some resemblance to the liturgical texts of Limoges, Rouen, and Orléans in the twelfth century, it may have been introduced by the Benedictines of Cluny. It has independent aspects, however. For example, three monologues, consisting of fifty-one lines, are attributed to the Magi, who express doubts about the star and try to determine the nature of the king by speculating on which gift he will accept. Herod is portrayed as the usual raging tyrant. The rest of the play no doubt contained the Adoration of the Magi, but it has been lost. It is written in rich metrical structure, with Castilian and Moorish influence.

The law of Las Siete Partidas of King Alfonso el Sabio (1256-1263) prohibits certain abuses in plays and allows members of the clergy to participate in Nativity, Epiphany, and Easter plays. The words of the law give some indication as to the nature of the plays, the dialogue, and the rather primitive manner of dramatization. The reference to prohibition of gain indicates the use of the vernacular. Not until the fifteenth century are there any further manuscripts in Spanish. A few records indicate the presence of plays, such as one from 1360 that says that it was customary for the canons of the Cathedral of Gerona to perform an Easter play titled *Las tres Marias*. Christmas plays are mentioned in Valencia in 1432.

In the fifteenth century, religious plays were also performed in the castles of noblemen. A reference is made to a Magi play in 1462, which was probably performed annually. The earliest extant representation of an *Officium pastorum* in the vernacular is Gómez Manrique's *Representación del nacimiento de Nuestro Señor*, composed between 1467 and 1481 for a community of nuns at Calabanzanos. It follows the traditional shepherd plays, with little dramatic advancement over the *Auto de los Reyes Magos*. It shows originality in the presentation of the gifts: Saint Gabriel, Saint Michael, and Saint Raphael present to the Child the instruments of his Passion. The nuns took part in the play, and they end by singing a charming lullaby to the Christ Child. Another and better Christmas play, dating from about 1480, is Fray Iñigo de Mendoza's *Vita Christi por coplas*, of which only a few scenes remain. Its dialogue is superior, and the fright of the shepherds is animated and mildly comic. The play ends with a narration by one of the shepherds of what he saw in the stable. Christmas plays seemed to be accompanied by costumes and other scenic effects, as shown by an expense account of 1487 preserved in the Cathedral of Saragossa.

Miracle plays, similar to those played in France, are also known in Spain. In 1380, a representation of the martyrdom of Saint Stephen was given at the Cathedral of Gerona. In the fifteenth century, such plays were popular in the kingdom of Aragon. A play known as *Mascarón*, dating from the fourteenth century, is found in the Biblioteca de Barcelona. It includes dialogues between God, the Blessed Virgin, and Mascarón, procurator of Hell. It is similar to the sixteenth century *Auto de accusación contra el género humano*. Both are related to the stories of the man whose soul was sought by the Devil.

Corpus Christi processions were no doubt present in Spain very early, for Catalan and Valencian documents of the first half of the fourteenth century refer to them. Scenes such as the *Sacrificio de Isaac* and *Sueño et venta de Jacob* are mentioned in the records of the Cathedral of Gerona in 1360. Records of the Corpus Christi procession at Valencia date back to 1355; in Palma de Mallorca, to 1371. In the Castilian-speaking part of Spain, the earliest mention of Corpus Christi plays dates from the latter half of the fifteenth century in Seville (1454). The procession of Barcelona in 1391 included scriptural scenes of the Old Testament. Sculptured images were present in 1424. Dramatic interludes known as *entremeses* were very popular, although at first they consisted only of songs and tableaux. The use of the mystery play came much later. The first *farsa sacramental*, or Eucharistic play, was written by Hernán López de Yanguas and has an angel explaining the Eucharist to four shepherds.

The Corpus Christi plays of Diego Sánchez de Badajoz in the sixteenth century show considerable evolution and variety in topics. Old Testament themes, Isaac, Abraham, Moses, and King David all have Eucharistic allusions and use religious symbolism with great skill. The *Farsa de Santa Susaña* was per-formed on a car that represented a garden and tells the story of Susanna from the Book of Daniel. A gardener speaks against idleness and in favor of his own trade. The play contains vivid characters and rare dramatic intensity. Two farces use allegorical motifs, *La farsa de la Iglesia*, with the famous *débat* between the Church and the Synagogue, and *Danza de los siete pecados*, representing the Seven Deadly Sins. All the plays show some relation to the Eucharist, a point not developed in England. Three plays, *La farsa del molinero*, *La farsa del colmenero*, and *La farsa del herrero*, mention the guilds involved. The well-developed plays of Sánchez de Badajoz were performed at Badajoz and at Seville, in 1560.

The only other extant Corpus Christi cycle is Sebastián de Horozco's *Representación de la parábola de San Mateo*, performed at Toledo in 1548. In the Parable of the Vineyard, he inserts characters from everyday life, including two former soldiers released from Algerian prisons who come to work in the vineyard. His story of the healing of a blind man is similar to *Lazarillo de Tormes*, in which a blind man knows that his guide has pocketed food, because he smells it. The guide, in revenge, allows the blind beggar to stumble into a wall. The blind beggar is cured by Christ in a reverent scene. These plays were continually performed until the end of the sixteenth century, and they characterized Spanish prosperity.

Juan del Encina, who wrote in Salamanca, is considered the first Spanish dramatist. His first two plays were presented on Christmas Eve, 1492, in a hall or chapel of the duke of Alba. The first play already shows classical influence and is called an *égloga*, yet shows local color in the portrayal of the shepherds who speak a rude country dialogue and become the model for later comic figures of shepherds. The Christmas play that follows is reverent in tone. In 1493 or 1494, he presented the *Representación a la muy bendita pasión y muerte de nuestro precioso Redentor* and a *Representación a la santisima resurrección de Christo*, which resemble the liturgical plays. In both, Encina does not present Christ, but uses secondary characters to describe the scenes. In his *Égloga de las grandes lluvias* (pr. c. 1494-1513), performed on Christmas Eve sometime around 1500, the realistic element almost overshadows the Nativity theme. After 1512, his plays show great classical influence.

Lucas Fernández, a contemporary of Encina, though much less popular, wrote three pastoral compositions, a Passion play, and two Nativity plays, probably performed between 1500 and 1511. The Nativity plays resemble Encina's *Égloga de las grandes lluvias*, for they portray the shepherds as comic figures. They show more dramatic possibilities than Encina's. The same comic element appears in the plays of the Portuguese dramatist Gil Vicente, who wrote an *Auto pastoril castelhano* (pr. 1502) in Castilian, about incredulous shepherds, and an *Auto dos reis magos* (pr. 1503; *The Three Wise Men*, 1960). His *Auto da sibila Cassandra* (pr. 1513; *The Play of the Sibyl Cassandra*, 1921) mingles classical, biblical, and realistic characters in a Nativity play that is the first example in Spain of the use of religious symbolism in drama.

The outstanding figure in Spanish religious drama in the first half of the sixteenth century is Sánchez de Badajoz, who wrote twenty-eight plays, published posthumously by his nephew. Twelve were performed on Christmas, ten on Corpus Christi, two on saints' days, and four on other occasions. They are all called *farsas* and are difficult to classify. They do indeed display comic elements generally found in medieval farces, yet they have a serious theological side and also contain allegory in the manner of the moralities, such as the *Farsa moral* and the *Farsa militar*. Sánchez de Badajoz also composed Old Testament plays, namely *Farsa de Tamar* and *Farsa de Salomón*. In the Christmas plays, the shepherds have important roles: dramatic, in that they function as vehicles of comedy, and theological, in that their ignorance serves as a pretext for religious instruction.

Although numerous Passion plays did exist in Spain, such as Encina's, the last serial play for Lent by Vasco Díaz Tanco, and Fernández's *Auto de la pasión* (pr. 1514), this theme seems to have contributed less to the Spanish religious theater than did the Nativity, where the comic role attributed to the shepherds grew rapidly. The few plays dealing with Old and New Testament themes seem to be associated with Corpus Christi plays. The Assumption was a popular feast in many cities, but the only complete play honoring it is one by Hernán López de Yanguas, *Farsa del mundo y moral* (pr. c. 1524), which is inserted into an allegorical framework.

Morality plays, the last to arrive in the religious theater, are present in some of Sánchez de Badajoz's farces. They appear both in the Christmas cycle and in the Corpus Christi plays, notably the Dance of the Seven Sins and the *Farsa de la muerte*, in which an old man battles death and seeks release from his sufferings. The most important Spanish morality play in the sixteenth century was written by Gil Vicente and is a trilogy of the three boats, composed from 1516 to 1519. The first two, *Auto de barca do inferno* (pr. 1516; *The Ship of Hell*, 1929) and *Auto de barca do purgatorio* (pr. 1518; *The Ship of Purgatory*, 1929), were written in Portuguese. The last, *Auto da barca da gloria* (pr. 1519; *The Ship of Heaven*, 1929), was composed in Castilian. Each of the three plays tells of various persons who are claimed by Death and set off for Hell on a boat. Death grimly lays bare their faults. In the first and most dramatic play, the exposition of sin is set forth with grim realism. The theme of death remained popular in Spain even in the latter half of the sixteenth century. A dramatic composition was published in 1551 by the Segovian Juan de Pedraza, titled *Farsa llamada danza de la muerte*. In it, a pope, a king, and a lady of questionable virtue are all confronted by Death. The prologue is recited by a jovial shepherd who thus continues the tradition of the Nativity play.

Religious plays remained extremely popular in Spain even up to the second half of the sixteenth century. The most important extant work is a codex of ninety-six plays preserved in the National Library in Madrid, edited by Leo Rouanet. All but one of the plays are religious in theme, and all but one are anonymous. The *Auto de Cain y Abel* bears the name of Maestro Jaime Ferrey. Rouanet also ascribes three to Lope de Rueda. A number may be identified with performances at Madrid (1578) and Seville and may be related to Corpus Christi. They follow traditional patterns, beginning with a *loa* or *argumento*, and end with a *villancico*. They are sometimes divided by an *entremés*. In almost all there is a comic figure called *pastor*, *bobo*, *villano*, or *simple*, whose ignorance provokes theological explanations and whose silly chatter provides comic relief.

Corpus Christi plays remained popular in Spain in the latter half of the sixteenth century. Allegory and symbolism entered into the texts and into numerous *autos sacramentales*, with thirty-three in the Madrid codex. Christmas, Passion, and Easter plays were less popular at the time. Religious plays were even performed across the seas, in the Spanish colonies, both in native tongues and in Castilian. Because Spain was not affected by the Reformation, there was no great movement to end religious plays nor to modify their very Catholic nature. As in other countries, the Renaissance, with its classical inspiration, transformed religious dramas into a secular institution. It was also the passing of an age: Scientific discoveries, travel across the Atlantic, and the wide use of printing were to transform the medieval spirit into the modern, one which did not tolerate the naïve faith and simple comedy of the religious stage.

THE COMIC AND SECULAR THEATER

Although medieval comedy is vastly inferior to the religious theater both in the number of plays and in their quality, it cannot be thus inferred that society in the Middle Ages lacked humor. On the contrary, the medieval mind did not categorize the secular and the sacred and therefore, comic elements exist side by side with serious representations in the plays. Important examples are the spice-merchant in the German Easter plays, the shepherd in the Spanish Nativity plays, and the character of Herod in the Magi plays. From early times local townspeople with their dialects and foibles appear along with biblical characters, and add liveliness and wit to otherwise solemn events.

It is generally admitted that medieval comedy sprang from religious plays, rather than continuing from classical sources through the mimes of the Dark Ages. Comic elements influenced its development, as did the practice of providing interludes, *farces* or *entremeses*, between plays and serious scenes. Although there are comic plays in the twelfth and thir-

teenth centuries, comedy as a separate genre did not emerge until the late fourteenth or fifteenth century, and in the sixteenth century. Though classical models were already in evidence, comic authors continued to write in the spirit of the medieval farces. Most European farces and comedies have basically the same themes, and there is extensive borrowing from one country to the next. Subjects usually include ruses and trickery of all kinds, marital infidelity, and clerical greed, and they draw on such techniques as repetition, gestures, impersonation, and improvisation. The popular farces are often vulgar to the point of obscenity, whereas more literary examples show a more cultivated form of wit.

Although some critics place Bodel's *Play of Saint Nicholas of Jean Bodel* and the anonymous *Courtois d'Arras* (pr. c. 1218) in the comic genre, they are basically religious plays. Bodel draws his humor from scenes of common people drinking, gambling, and quarreling, such as he must have observed in his native Picardy. *Courtois d'Arras*, also a religious play dealing with the Prodigal Son, emphasizes the repentance theme less than the son's loss of his money to experienced *filles de joie* in a local tavern. Indeed, the theme lends itself to such development. Both plays end with the usual *Te Deum laudamus*, the mark of a church play. Because the plays are so similar, critics have suggested common authorship and have cited them as transitions between serious and comic drama.

The first real farce in France, *Le Garçon et l'aveugle*, is a short thirteenth century play that has only 265 lines. It also has only the two characters mentioned in the title, a boy and a blind beggar. The beggar tries to trick the boy, who offers to guide him, and he is in turn robbed by the boy; the humor consists in the eternal theme of the trickster tricked. This story has many parallels in medieval literature, among them the sixteenth century Spanish story *La Vida de Lazarillo de Tormes y de sus fortunas y adversidades* (1553; *Lazarillo de Tormes*, 1576), with a similar version in Sebastián de Horozco's Corpus Christi play, *Representación de la parábola de San Mateo*.

Adam de la Halle, or d'Arras, is the author of two well-known comedies of the late thirteenth century: *Le Jeu de la feuillée* (pr. c. 1275; *The Greenwood*

Play, 1971) and *Le Jeu de Robin et Marion* (pr. c. 1283; *The Play of Robin and Marion*, 1928). Like Bodel, Adam de la Halle came from a cultivated circle in the prosperous town of Arras. *The Greenwood Play* is a loosely connected series of themes involving local townspeople, who very likely played the roles. The action takes place at Pentecost, when the women of the town were accustomed to going to see the fairies in the woods under a canopy of green leaves known as a *feuillée*. Although the action is quite complex, the play has sparkling wit, facile verse, and poetic style.

The Play of Robin and Marion, much simpler, is really a "pastourelle dramatique." It is the tale of Marion, a shepherdess, repelling the amorous adventures of a knight in favor of her rustic lover, Robin. It has been called the first French comic opera, the model of the *pastourelle*, and it influenced the short plays and interludes of Molière. It is characterized by lightness and gaiety and shows both the influence of courtly literature and the realism of everyday life, especially in the persons of the braggart—the cowardly yet crudely affectionate Robin—and the shrewd peasant Marion.

The sophistication and witty comedy of Adam de la Halle is very different from that of the fifteenth century. In the meantime, the Hundred Years' War, attributed to economic rivalries, caused changes in the French class structure, especially in the north and northwest of the country. Professional groups of actors called *puys* appeared that were responsible for the presentation of the *miracles*. A series of festivals also developed that were to influence the comic theater. The "Fête des fous," or Feast of Fools, between Christmas and Epiphany, was the revival of the Roman Saturnalia. Students and minor clerics mocked religious services within the church and elected a pope or bishop who said a burlesque Mass. Begun in the north at the end of the thirteenth century, the Feast of Fools spread elsewhere with great popularity until the Council of Bâle (1435) and the Council of Soissons (1456) forbade it, though it did not meet its demise until the sixteenth or seventeenth century. Many other feasts were instituted: "la Fête de l'âne," or feast of the ass, carnival, May Day (associated

with fertility), and student celebrations called *lendits*. Nonprofessional theater troupes were formed, later called "Enfants-sans-souci" (children without cares) and the "Basociens." These celebrations were popular in various forms all over Europe.

Spontaneous plays called *sotties* or *farces* developed from such feasts. The distinction between the two is not always clear, although *sotties* are so called because of the presence of a *sot*, or fool. *Sotties* are closely related to allegory and to the morality plays. The morality in France is better expressed in comedy than in the serious theater, in pieces such as *Les Enfants de maintenant*, a satire on contemporary children and their parents, and *La Condamnation de bancquet*, against the evils of gluttony. In the *sottie*, characters wear the characteristic cap and bells, asses' ears, staff with bells, and many-colored costumes. Most *sottie* humor is slapstick comedy: quick banter amid cries and blows, dissolute laughter. The *vray sot* was agile, young, and intelligent. Later *sotties* had better developed plots, but the earlier ones are characterized by improvisation, little action, and lively dialogue based on puns, obscenities, and misunderstandings.

Closely related to the *sottie* is the farce, which flourished in the fifteenth and early sixteenth centuries. Unlike the *sottie*, which relied on allegory, the farce used real people. It needed few characters and made fun of local folk and events. Farces are really comic stories about the universal frailties of human nature. They are closely allied to the *fabliaux* and include beatings, disguises, reversed roles, confession to the wrong persons, puns, and often obscenities. Between 1460 and 1560, there are about 150 French farces, most of them anonymous, all in verse, most with octosyllabic rhyming couplets. The majority are quite short, requiring ten to forty minutes of playing time. Because marital infidelity is the most common theme, they abound in scatological and sexual references, sometimes quite clever in their imagery, as pointed out by scholar Barbara Bowen. Gustave Cohen has edited forty farces that date from that period, and because many of the plays have references to the University of Paris, he assumes that students had a major role in their development. He also believes that farces developed from popular songs and a kind of medieval vaudeville, and used masks, though this genre was less popular in France than in Italy. French farces include political, religious, and social satire in the *esprit gaulois* (Gallic spirit), kept alive in Rabelais, Molière, and Voltaire.

The best known of all medieval farces, and far superior in every way, is the *Farce de Maître Pathelin*, which affected the development of comedy both in England and on the Continent. Its witty character delineation and theme of the duped charm audiences of every age. Maître Pathelin is a penniless yet self-confident lawyer with no clients. He vaunts his own talents to his practical wife and promises her a new dress. With equal bravado, he visits a local cloth-merchant and by a series of flatteries gets six aunes of the merchant's best wool. Pathelin promises money and a good dinner. When the merchant arrives, Pathelin's wife joins in the ruse and assures him that her husband has been sick for eleven weeks. Guillaume the merchant succeeds in entering the house and finds a delirious Pathelin who rambles in foreign languages and mistakes the merchant for the doctor. Puzzled, Guillaume retires. In the meantime, Thibaudet l'Agnelet, Guillaume's shepherd, has been rightly accused by his master of slaughtering and eating more than twenty of his sheep. Pathelin becomes Thibaudet's lawyer and instructs his client to say nothing but "baa" at the trial. When Pathelin realizes who his client's master is, he tries to conceal his face, while Guillaume so confuses the story, mixing "six aunes of cloth" with "slaughtered sheep," that the bewildered judge dismisses the case. The final irony comes when Pathelin demands payment of Thibaudet, who responds only with "baa."

The *Farce de Maître Pathelin* is usually dated before 1470, of unknown authorship, although inconclusive evidence has suggested François Villon and Guillaume Alecis. The play was popular in its own day, and expressions such as "revenons à nos moutons" ("let us return to our muttons") and *pathelinage* became part of the French language. Its accurate character portrayal, the use of vocabulary appropriate to the characters (for example, the shepherd's ungrammatical French and Pathelin's intellec-

tual style), the rapid movement, logical development, and surprise make the play a classic of all time.

Nuremberg in Germany is the center for farcical comedy, especially during the last week before Lent, called *Fasching* or *Fastnacht*, the occasion for much merrymaking. In the fourteenth century, *Fastnachtspiele* or Shrovetide plays arose from this celebration, and many fifteenth century examples are preserved. The earliest known is the fifty-eight-line *Neidhartspiel* from Saint Paul in the Lavanthal (Carinthia), which dates from about 1350. The hero is the minnesinger Neidhart von Reuenthal. The play is courtly in tone and contains only two characters, Neidhart and the Duchess of Austria, in addition to the Proclamator, who introduces the action. Neidhart finds the first violet of spring and covers it with his hat while he goes to bring the duchess. During his absence, a peasant steals it, although this action apparently has no stage directions. When Neidhart returns with the duchess to find no flower, she impatiently rebukes him, and he threatens vengeance on the thief. This theme was reworked in later *Fastnachtspiele*, losing its delicacy and courtly tone, with many ungainly lines. Hans Sachs, the best writer of *Fastnachtspiele*, also used the Neidhart theme.

Most plays of this type were primitive, with few if any properties, and were performed by groups of players who went from one inn to the next, raising increasing hilarity. A *Präcursor*, or herald (Ehrenhold in Sachs's plays), introduced the play and briefly outlined the plot. The players then introduced themselves and began a series of comic exchanges and, usually, crude jokes. The range of subjects was wide: from courtly epics and romances to political satire, as seen in a fifteenth century play referring to Charles IV, *Des Entkrist Vasnacht* (the Shrovetide play of Antichrist), which also had a religious theme. Plays also had satire on women and the clergy.

Most *Fastnacht* plays originated in the area of Nuremberg. Hans Schnepperer, a meistersinger who preferred the name Rosenplüt, tried to improve the crude plays of this time and added a social note and references to court epics. Four plays are attributed to him, and six to Hans Folz, a meistersinger of a generation later. A large number of Shrovetide plays were found in the archives of Sterzing in the South Tyrol, in a sixteenth century manuscript copied by the painter Vigil Raber, although they seem to belong to the Nuremberg cycle. Their topics include the quack doctor, love, Kriemhild's rose garden, and the like. A list of plays, believed to be more serious in tone, comes from the Lübeck archives, although the plays themselves have not survived.

The greatest writer of *Fastnachtspiele* is the sixteenth century Hans Sachs. Sachs was a cobbler in Nuremberg who studied Latin and Greek and used classical models in some of his dramas. As a meistersinger he explored German and foreign folklore. He excelled in the *Schwänk*, a short and witty anecdote with a moral, and used it in his *Fastnachtspiele*. Despite the simplicity of his dialogue, Sachs showed the ability to draw characters such as knights and priests, peasants and rogues, jealous husbands, and greedy merchants and deceitful wives. The best of Sachs's plays include *Der fahrend Schüler im Paradies* (pr. 1550; *The Traveling Scholar*, 1910), *Frau Wahrheit will neimanden beherbergen* (pb. 1550), and *Des Krämers Korb* (pb. 1554). Hans Sachs also wrote religious drama, in the manner of mystery plays, as a part of his Reformation apologetics, but he is best known for his portrayal of sixteenth century Nuremberg.

Like other continental cultures, Spain also had its Feast of Fools. A sequel to the famous law of the Siete Partidas forbade the so-called *juegos de escarnias*, or medieval games, held in churches and elsewhere, in which participants wore clerical garb and mimicked the clergy and the sacred rites. The Feast of Fools was held around the New Year. Fifteenth century documents speak of the mock ceremony of the Obispillo, or Boy Bishop, at Gerona and Lérida, and sixteenth century manuscripts tell of the same thing at Seville. Such ceremonies were accompanied by farcing parts of the Mass, and with compositions of tropes in Latin and later in the vernacular called *farsia*, *farsura*, or *farsa*, indicating a comic scene. Church councils condemned this use of farce, but to no avail.

Mime seems to have continued for some time in Spain, despite vigorous protests by the Church. Frequent mentions in documents of *joculator*, *remedadores*, *bufones*, *juglares*, and *locos* attests their presence. These people performed at weddings and festivals, and their repertoire is evident from sixteenth century plays. Closely related to these entertainers were the *mascarás* (masquerades) and *representaciones* (pageants, with or without dialogue) that were held to celebrate important events, such as the entry of Alphonso XI into Seville in 1327 and the coronation of Ferdinand the Just in 1414, in which allegory was associated with the pageant. One of the best allegorical dramatic dialogues in the fifteenth century is Rodrigo Cota de Maguaque's *Diálogo entre el Amor y un viejo*, in which Love offers his goods to a disillusioned old man who at length accepts and is in turn ridiculed by the god. The piece was evidently not written for performance, but it seems to have influenced Encina.

Encina, the author of religious plays, is also important in the field of secular drama. His *El triunfo del amor*, published in 1507 but written in 1497, reworks Rodrigo Cota's theme into a delightful burlesque courtly play in which the boasting Cupid explains his trade to a simple shepherd. Encina performed two carnival eclogues at the palace of the duke of Alba on Shrove Tuesday in 1494. The second presents four shepherds who test the capacity of their stomachs in anticipation of the forty days of fasting. The eclogues humorously tell of the defeat of Carnival by Lent. Encina also wrote eclogues in the style of the courtly *pastourelle* that recall *Le Jeu de Robin et Marion* by Adam de la Halle. Lucas Fernández and other sixteenth century authors continued the pastoral theme. The Spanish pastoral was not original, however, nor did it represent real life or have enough humor to sustain it. Hence it failed to satisfy audiences, who gravitated toward Italian comedy.

In the second half of the sixteenth century, comedy is a regular feature of religious plays and gives them an air of similarity. In almost all these plays there is a clown figure whose ignorance provides occasion for instruction and whose wit offers comic relief. In the secular drama, there were many comedies in the late sixteenth century, yet they can be classified neither as medieval, in the tradition of farces, nor as classical, according to Greek and Roman models. Many resemble the pastorals, with complicated and exaggerated love plots. Yet Spain, despite its broad cultural contacts in the sixteenth century, was slow to accept Italian models, and it was not until Lope de Vega Carpio in the seventeenth century that Spanish drama found its characteristic style.

Although Italy was the model for the Renaissance throughout Western Europe, it had a very important influence on medieval comedy as well and provided a viable expression for the characters from the farces. This was through the *commedia dell'arte*. In the sixteenth century, members of this group formed troupes and traveled widely in Italy, Germany, Spain, and France. Originally, the *commedia dell'arte* had been performed by charlatans, mountebanks, and acrobats in the public squares, but by 1550, it had reached a rather high form of development. Each troupe had stock actors who performed stereotyped roles: the lovers, the braggart captain, the doctor, and the *zanni*, or acrobatic clowns. Each member had his own costume, and the male characters bore masks. The characters had the same names in every comedy, such as Columbine, Doctor Gratiano, Captain Fracasse, Harlequin, and Polichinelle.

By the sixteenth century, actors worked with scenarios written out in great detail, but they would improvise lines as the occasion demanded. Printed speeches of various roles became popular, as in Francesco Andreini's *Le Bravure del Capitano Spavento da Vall'Inferna*, published in 1615. An actor's repertoire included tragedy, pastoral comedy, ballet, and farce. The earliest preserved scenario from 1568 shows a great deal of literary drama. One of the most important contributions of the actors of the *commedia dell'arte* was to keep alive the short farce, which depends on a comic situation rather than on plot, and was well suited to their wanderings. The Italian *commedia dell'arte* was especially influential in Spain and France, and it, along with the farce, had great importance for the comedies of Molière.

At this juncture, the medieval theater faded almost imperceptibly into the humanistic and secular dramas of the sixteenth and seventeenth centuries. In northern Europe, France, and some parts of Germany, the Reformation hastened its demise. In Spain and Italy, the Renaissance moved it into another sphere.

BIBLIOGRAPHY

Beckworth, Sarah. *Signifying God: Social Relation and Symbolic Act in the York Corpus Christi Plays*. Chicago: University of Chicago Press, 2001. Provides a multidisciplinary approach to understanding the Corpus Christi plays, engaging theater history, religious studies, and literary history to provide a contextual backdrop for the plays.

Boucquey, Thierry. *Six Medieval French Farces*. Lewiston, N.Y.: Edwin Mellen, 1999. Translated versions of six farces, with a good general introduction to the collection that provides a history of the genre. Each play also has its own introduction that gives commentary and notes.

Chambers, Edmund K. *The Mediaeval Stage*. 1903. Reprint. New York: Dover Publications, 1996. Published as a two-volume set in 1903, this work still proves to be comprehensive in its treatment of minstrels and mimes, miracle and morality plays, puppet shows, dramatic pageants, liturgical plays, and much more.

Collingwood, Sharon L. *Market Pledge and Gender Bargain: Commercial Relations in French Farce, 1450-1550, Volume 3*. New York: Peter Lang, 1997. Analyzes the thematic importance of economic exchange within the bourgeois literary genre of mercantile and conjugal farces.

Davidson, Clifford, et al., eds. *The Drama of the Middle Ages: Comparative and Critical Essays*. New York: AMS Press, 1982. Provides a general overview and interpretive criticism of medieval drama.

Kipling, Gordon. *Enter the King: Theatre, Liturgy, and Ritual in the Medieval Civic Triumph*. New York: Oxford University Press, 1997. Traces the importance of rites and ceremonies in medieval civilization and their translation into theatrical performances.

Muir, Lynette M. *The Biblical Drama of Medieval Europe*. Cambridge, England: Cambridge University Press, 1995. Provides a detailed overview of major aspects of biblical theater including the theatrical community of audience and players, the major plays and cycles, and the legacy of medieval drama in the modern world.

Ogden, Dunbar H. *Staging of Drama in the Medieval Church*. Newark: University of Delaware Press, 2001. Examines the staging space and physical movement of performers by using ground plans of notable cathedrals throughout Europe. Explores how the unique physical space of each cathedral impacted the liturgical dramas' performance.

Tydeman, William, Louise M. Haywood, Michael J. Anderson, et al., eds. *Medieval European Stage, 500-1500*. Cambridge, England: Cambridge University Press, 2001. The editors bring together a comprehensive selection of documents and analyses to elucidate the survival of classical tradition and development of the liturgical drama, the growth of popular religious drama in the vernacular, and the pastimes and customs of the people.

Warning, Rainer. *The Ambivalences of Medieval Religious Drama*. Translated by Steven Rendall. Palo Alto, Calif.: Stanford University Press, 2000. Examines Easter, Adam, and Passion plays from Spain, France, Germany, and England. The theoretical approach contends that religious theatrical events served as collective rituals of compensation, with the actor portraying Christ taking on the role of the scapegoat.

Young, Karl. *The Drama of the Medieval Church*. 1933 (2 volumes). Reprint. Oxford, England: Clarendon Press, 1967. Provides a collection of extant examples of church drama employed by the medieval church in Western Europe as a part of public worship. Text interspersed with commentary.

Irma M. Kashuba

RENAISSANCE DRAMA

The Renaissance means many things about an amorphous period in political, economic, scientific, and above all cultural history, involving a number of Western countries at various stages in their development. The scholarly attempts to block it off with dates, however roughly allocated, confuse more than they clarify because the phenomenon made itself felt at different times in different places. The single fact of which one can be sure is that it all began in Italy, sometime in the fourteenth century, and then later—more than a century later—spread to other parts of Europe and eventually penetrated deep into the seventeenth century, where it commingled and fused with the Baroque.

Rinascimento, or rebirth—an idea popularized by Jacob Burckhardt's *Die Kulture der Renaissance in Italien* (1860; *Civilization of the Renaissance in Italy*, 1878)—has to do with a spirit of self-rediscovery whereby human beings, putting aside the medieval scholastic cloak, engaged in energetic exercise of mind and limb, viewing themselves as creatures of this world, as they had in antiquity (hence the pagan presence in the lap of Christian belief—an admixture that Dante had promoted in no uncertain terms as early as the very beginning of the fourteenth century). It was self or inner discovery that made possible outer discovery, that of a Christopher Columbus on the seas or a Galileo in the heavens. Rinascimento was a confident state of mind that made human beings the measure and the center, with their own reason for being, and that urged individuals to sign their names to their creations.

Although science acquired fresh vitality in this atmosphere, it was the arts that fostered the *vita nuova*, or at least that symbolizes it for modern civilization. The rise of the middle class and the Maecenaean prosperity of the ruling families of the city-state—Sforza, Visconti, Malatesta, Este, Medici, Montefeltro, Della Rovere, Baglioni, Gonzaga, and others, as well as popes such as Pius II, Alexander VI, Leo X, and Julius II, or cardinals such as Bibbiena (Bartolomeo Dovizi), Giulio de' Medici, Girolamo Riario,

Ottone Colonna, and Ippolito d'Este, who nourished their appetites with art as they endeavored, even in their villainies, to convert life into a form of beauty and pleasure—made the ebullience possible. More than ever before, the arts developed qua arts with a "reborn" inspirational freedom: nature and the open air, the ornate *palazzo* and the gilded cabinet, the magic of inlaid wood and tinted glass, the comeliness of the human body, the lasting splendor of marble, the radiance of color, the freed dynamics of secular sound, the splendid intricacies of polyphonic textures—all aesthetic delights for the eyes and ears—the magnificent artifice of drama and theater, complete with the appurtenant playhouses, stages, machineries, costumes, and sets. The world was a stage, and life a drama—meaning also an art. This is what made the French citizens under King Charles VIII marvel at and loot the Italian peninsula in 1494 when they crossed the Alps, and the Germans and Spaniards of Emperor Charles V plunder it during the 1527 sack of Rome; this is what the English imported zealously even after King Henry VIII broke from the Papacy, for to its credit the Reformation made no attempt to obstruct the pagan revival.

The self-rediscovery stemmed in large part from an aesthetic view of the self, and humanism, absorbing and refashioning the intellectual visions of ancient Greece and Rome or simply reproducing and imitating their accomplishments, kindled a new desire for learning for its own sake. Raphael's Vatican fresco *La scuola d'Atene* (*School of Athens*) reproduced in spirit what the earlier Platonic Academy of Marsilio Ficino in Florence had cultivated in research and philosophy, the reconciliation of antiquity with Christianity. In the glorious Trecento, Petrarch starred as the first humanist, the supposed author of several comedies, and the poet very much in love with life and fame. The Middle Ages, far from being gloomy—intellectually or otherwise—as often depicted, had distinguished itself with directed learning, dominated by concerns of religion, morality, and the Hereafter. The windows of the cloister tended to close to other vital manifestations of living. Now, after Giotto di Bondone had left behind the impersonal Byzantine manner and injected personality and blood, as it were, into his paintings, Leonardo da Vinci (and also Piero della Francesca, Lorenzo Ghiberti, Donatello, Leon Battista Alberti, Bramante, and Filippo Brunelleschi in their respective arts) opened those windows to the geometries of perspective, thereby embracing a limitless worldly range, while madrigals and *frottole* opened music to novel, secular dimensions of tone and expressiveness. To adapt words from Alfred North Whitehead, the new climate "altered the metaphysical presuppositions and the imaginative contents of our minds; so that now the old stimuli provoke[d] a new response," to which one should add: The opportunity for new stimuli lay almost unrestrictedly everywhere. It was natural for drama and theater, then, to make full use of the humanized idioms and fecund inspirations galvanizing the Western world.

STAGE AND THEATER

Though Italy (like France until its Age Classique) cannot boast of the copious and genial drama that characterized Elizabethan England and the Spanish Golden Age, Italian influence shaped dramatic production all over Europe, not only by virtue of its humanistic spirit derived from the classical tradition but also by virtue of how it developed the actor's craft (the actors for medieval religious dramas were guild members—students, academics, scribes, and the like—but not the professionals they became later: *attori di mestiere*, *comici d'arte*, trained in mime, voice, acrobatics, choreography, and other essentials), the stage on which he performed (very often medieval sets were nothing more than wooden scaffolding in various shapes for multiple staging possibilities), and the buildings inside which he exercised his art (much medieval drama was mounted outdoors, in public courtyards or squares, performances not moving indoors until the sixteenth century).

These influences were not, however, always absorbed speedily. By the sixteenth century, for example, Europe beyond Italy still lacked a playhouse as it is known today. Apart from costuming, pictorial

scenography, when performance was not at court, remained primarily an Italian craft, which eventually included sophisticated mechanisms for scene changes and the revolutionary discovery of perspective that allowed the set painting of countless fantasies and optical illusions. In time, tragedy, comedy, and pastoral each had its own established setting: *scena tragica*, *scena comica*, and *scena satirica*. Vitruvius's ten-volume *De Architectura* (c. 27 B.C.E.), discovered in 1484, helped to shape the stage in imitation of antiquity (the Roman *scaenae frons* of access doors in a row) and to arrange the auditorium and the orchestra. Sebastiano Serlio's *Sette libri dell'architettura* (1537-1551) stressed perspective (book 2) and large, fixed edifices as best suited to the peripeteia of great personages in tragedy. Andrea Palladio's Teatro Olimpico in Vicenza, the "most beautiful theater in the world" (completed in 1584 by Vincenzo Scamozzi, who then built another, more intimate theater for Duke Vespasiano Gonzaga at Sabbioneta), with its semielliptical auditorium and the raised perspectives of its long, narrow stage, main lateral roads, and central archway, all in wood and stucco, fulfilled a dream of reproducing a Roman theater that welcomed anything tragic, from the classical *Oidipous Tyrannos* (c. 429 B.C.E.; *Oedipus Tyrannus*, 1715) to the modern *La Sofonisba* (wr. 1515). Commissioned by one of many humanist academies, the Accademia Olimpica di Vicenza, the Palladio-Scamozzi structure housed more than two thousand spectators, and its fine perspectives greatly impressed all travelers, among them Josef Furtenbach, who in 1619 brought its architectural ideas back to Germany with him. The modern playhouse was born in 1618 with Parma's Teatro Farnese—an elongated auditorium that had a sculpted proscenium arch. Indeed, some of the most renowned artists contributed over the years to the scenic splendors of Italian stages: Brunelleschi, Baldassare Peruzzi, Raphael, Leonardo, Bramante, and the Sangallo brothers (Francesco and Antonio Giamberti). Thus drama was transferred from the great halls of the *palazzi* of princes, such as that in Florence's Palazzo Pitti, or even more impressively the court stage built by Bernardo Buontalenti in 1585 for the Medici in the Uffizzi, or from outdoors, such as the Piazza del Campidoglio's ad hoc theater, covered by an awning for Tommaso Inghirami's production of Terence's *Poenulus* in 1513, to the veritable *teatri* abetted by the academies and sponsored by noble patrons.

The move encouraged free inventiveness along all lines, not the least of which were theatrical machinery and decorative effects. The typical Italian stage was characterized by simplicity and classical severity, but the Roman *scaenae frons*, adopted and adapted by the humanist theater, was superseded by more sophisticated elaborations. Buontalenti's contributions to scene transformation (leading later to sliding flat wings), building on the revolving wooden prisms of his predecessors—Giacomo Barozzi Vignola, Sangallo, Daniele Barbaro, and Giulio Danti—were to be magnified by the Baroque theater. Similar innovations took place with decorative effects. In 1518, in Rome, for Leo X, Peruzzi converted the backdrop, or wall, into an "acting area" of perspective by providing a decorated proscenium. The idea grew out of Girolamo Genga's stage set at Urbino for Bibbiena's *La Calandria* (pr. 1513; *The Follies of Calandro*, 1964) five years earlier. Perspective provided the most challenging potential for effect. Into it the Quattrocento poured much of its mathematical and artistic imagination. Vitruvius's book 5 deals with theater; its various editions (1486, 1521, 1556) underlay subsequent treatises on the subject, such as Vignola's *Le due regole della prospettiva pratica* (1583) and its suggestions for distant stage entrances, wooden prisms turning on pivots, and other technical equipment.

By the seventeenth century, scenographers had a full catalog of technological possibilities, and the best were much in demand. Alfonso Parigi could set a stage afire for Prospero Bonarelli Della Rovere's *Il Solimano* (pr. 1619), Gaspare Vigarani and his sons brought heavenly apparitions down from above clouds in mythological scenes that amazed Parisian audiences, Francini managed rapid and stupefying set changes in the Louvre in 1617, and in Venice's Teatro Vendramin, in an anonymous *Dario*, in 1671, thirteen changes were effected by those who had learned Francini's lessons. Giacomo Torelli di Fano, called

"the great wizard," could handle forty scene changes; Ludovico Ottavio Burnacini's very drawings for sets in Vienna are marvels of sumptuousness (now available in the Nationalbibliothek); and the Bibbiena family established a veritable dynasty that covered four generations (two Giovanni Marias, a Ferdinando, Francesco, Alessandro, Antonio, Giovanni Carlo, and two Giuseppes) that combed Europe: Vienna, Prague, Mannheim, Belgrade, St. Petersburg, Lisbon, Paris, Amsterdam, and London. Much of their work benefited opera when melodrama set in and when other architects carried on the work of their colleagues: Andrea Pozzo, Filippo Iuvara, Giovanni Bernini, and Giambattista Piranesi.

Greater elaborateness signaled a commensurate attention to costuming, especially for tragedy, in which costumes were expected to be rich and sumptuous (as compared with common but neat costumes for comedy and humble but graceful ones for pastoral). Special occasions required special paraphernalia, such as Leonardo's fancy costumes to clothe divinities and his fantastic animal masks for Bernardo Bellincioni's setting of Lodovico Sforza's allegorical masque of 1490. The new interest in science together with the obsession for artifice in the good sense—in other words, the conversion of life into art—inspired technological apparatuses designed to facilitate sensational effects. Traps and hoisting machines that would have gratified Euripides' use of the *deus ex machina* were devised, contraptions to be much welcomed by William Shakespeare and Pedro Calderón de la Barca. As might be expected, again Leonardo, in his capacity as inventor and military engineer for the court of Milan, contributed his genius to such enterprises, in one instance a movable planetary system and, for a circling paradise, the world's first revolving stage. He did the same in France in 1518, at the Château Cloux by Amboise, as a guest of King Francis I. As similar ideas carried over to the stages in playhouses, Italian *ingegneri* became more and more ingenious and were hired for many European productions. Lope de Vega Carpio saw machinery as an interference, believing that "carpenters" detract from the spirit of drama. Yet there was no stopping technology. The cardinal rule was always observed, in all the arts: no awkward overlappings. It was not long before these masters of optical illusion, the directors of production pursuing the same "scientific" inclinations, hit on the notion of practiced positioning and choreographed movement by the actor—in other words, blocking—another contribution to the ever expanding craft of performance.

Not to be outdone, comedy borrowed many of the ideas, such as expanding—as in the production of *La Calandria* in 1513—to a rich, urban background of domes and towers to supplement the traditional *scaenae frons* square bordered by a few houses. This was true mainly for learned comedy, for the popular plays of the *commedia dell'arte* were performed originally on open, undecorated platforms capable of only crude scenic changes. With time, however, they, too, changed. With the pastoral, the setting shifted to a somewhat ornate naturalism: trees and rocks, hills and flowers, bowers and brooks. Whatever the dramatic category, any performance was well lighted: A bright stage sparkled in a dimmed hall, varied appropriately according to the moment in the action. Indeed, lighting by candle, oil, and reflectors received careful attention.

In France, popular theater, as in the case of the *parades*, remained outdoors in squares and fairs on improvised stages for some time, serving as a crowd grabber for hucksters selling their potions and remedies. Actors such as Tabarin (Jean Salomon, possibly an Italian) and Gille le Niais were successful plebeian performers with no particular training. Only toward the end of the sixteenth century did some professional groups form—troupes that moved indoors, as in the *jeux de paume* buildings, taking account of Italian innovations. In time, some groups acquired high visibility, such as the Théâtre du Marais and Molière's Illustre Théâtre. Performances took place inside palaces and halls, but no theater structure as such favored their enterprises. Paris had only one theater—the Hôtel de Bourgogne in the early seventeenth century—when London had six. The public was mixed and segregated by class or means (some dignitaries sat onstage—a custom that hampered French productions well into the eighteenth century), and the premises were often dirty; yet activity there

was, primarily in the gallery, not always edifying but activity nevertheless: drinking, arguing, dice rolling, and other "social" pastimes.

The Hôtel de Bourgogne was in the hands of the Confrérie de la Passion, a corporation of theater managers the origin of which went back to 1402, when the organization of amateurs performed religious drama (as the name suggests), biblical plays that events of the religious wars forbade in 1548, when the Confrérie de la Passion began renting the premises to various troupes and visiting companies. There Spanish and English actors were welcomed; there the renowned Italian comedians, the Comici Gelosi, introduced the French to dramatic improvisation. In the following century, the Hôtel de Bourgogne, under Valleran Le Conte, housed a permanent group for popular comedy, Les Comédiens de Roy (Italian *comici*), including the public's favorite stereotypes: the fat clown Gros Guillaume, the amusing and clownish old man Gaultier-Gargouille, and the wily servant Turlupin. The stage, at first a simple platform, imported Italian refinements to supplement the medieval carryovers (such as separate mansions): scene painting and other types of stage setting, backcloth, perspective side-wings, variations of foreshortened space that allowed locations separated by distance to appear simultaneously, and other devices noted by seventeenth century scene directors Laurent Mahelot and Michel Laurent in their *Mémoire*. The first performances of Jean de Rotrou's *Les Occasions perdues* in 1633 demonstrated some of these novelties. Yet in France, drama became more important later in the seventeenth century because genuine dramatic interest centered on the court, where a more restricted and more select class of spectators assembled, headed by the king, who often prescribed and proscribed. After the heyday of Pierre Corneille, drama belonged to Molière and Jean Racine, whose genius did not need the supplement of stage elaborations. Nevertheless, the expert scenographers imported from Italy, such as Torelli di Fano, were certainly no liability.

A similar evolution, again heavily Italianate, may be traced in Spain during the sixteenth and seventeenth centuries, except that there a broader segment of the public concerned itself closely with theater, and the courtly emphasis was not as pronounced as in France. This meant that standards of performance as well as behavior, to the woe of intellectuals, left something to be desired, despite Miguel de Cervantes's efforts to remove drama from the plebs and give it a more sophisticated, classical setting. Actors tended to be adventurers (for example, the "Carro de la muerte" in *El ingenioso hidalgo don Quixote de la Mancha*, 1605; *The History of the Valorous and Wittie Knight-Errant, Don Quixote of the Mancha*, 1612-1620; better known as *Don Quixote de la Mancha*), often of questionable ethics, who pilfered what they could if gate receipts got low. Roving companies performed on platforms, erected for the occasion with rickety supports, in courtyards called *corrales* (such as the Corral de la Pacheca, mounted by Italian *comici* in 1574) or out on the squares.

Two coarse wooden theaters existed in Madrid shortly thereafter, the Corral de la Cruz and the Corral del Príncipe. The windows overlooking the courtyard were the "box seats" for the privileged, while on the ground stood a less distinguished audience, some gentlemen sitting on a few tiers of far benches above which was constructed a wooden gallery, the *cazuela* (stewpan), for less affluent women. In another arrangement, the persons of means or standing sat forward, the commoners behind, armed with anything that they could throw at the stage: hence Cervantes's call to imitate the Italians (meaning the humanists) and their balanced Greco-Roman art, which in turn would invite a sense of decorum. Some improvement, though, did occur when his rival Lope de Vega dominated the theatrical scene, and after him, Calderón. Unhampered by concerns with classical tenets, and given its fundamentally popular orientation (Fernando de Rojas's *Comedia de Calisto y Melibea*, 1499, rev. ed. 1502 as *Tragicomedia de Calisto y Melibea*; commonly known as *La Celestina*; *Celestina*, 1631, with its open forms and shifting settings related to medieval multiple staging, remained a strong influence), Spanish drama at its apogee developed along freer, less academic lines, incorporating many popular themes, and with them came increased audience attentiveness to the plays.

Across the Channel, when the Tudors (1485-1603) opened England to the splendors of the Rinascimento, along with Italian books and scholars came Italian actors; Drusiano Martinelli, for example, gained great popularity at the court of Queen Elizabeth I. Under her father, Henry VIII, the theater was looked down on (part of his decree of 1531 labels actors "vagabonds") because of the unsavory character of many of its practitioners, but in the new atmosphere, actors managed to take advantage of the prevailing interest in drama and seek the protection of court lords, indeed also of sovereigns. Not even the Puritan clergy could prevail. Previously outlawed, strolling players became respectable, enjoying legal protection together with other benefits. King Richard III, Henry VIII (his decree notwithstanding), and Elizabeth I through Lord Leicester (Robert Dudley, who was more interested in players than was the queen) kept companies, some of which might actually go on tour.

Like Molière and Lope de Rueda, Shakespeare too acted, until 1603. Many other companies, like guilds, became "recognized," and a 1572 law, making the recognition exclusive by "privilege," encouraged James Burbage four years later to establish the first public theater at Shoreditch: The Theatre, built circularly of timber. A white flag flown aloft indicated comedy; a black one, tragedy. Also round and unroofed was The Curtain (London, 1577), and this was followed a decade later by Philip Henslowe's The Rose, then The Fortune (Finsbury, 1600), and The Hope (1613), the last unroofed London playhouse. More theaters, to attest Elizabethan passion for drama, were Francis Langley's The Swan (1595), the Globe Theatre (1599), and The Red Bull (1605). After 1620, all playhouses were roofed. With companies flourishing in them, the theaters increased in number from eight to twenty between 1600 and 1616, when Shakespeare died. Theatrical activities took place everywhere, from private homes and public squares to universities. Italian scenography was put to use, imported directly from Italy or later from France, though originally the stages were occasional, placed in courtyards as in Spain, or even in circus structures, following other types of entertainment. As usual, the upper class sat separately from the others, either in lower balconies (the gallery remained for the commoners) or, when French habits encroached, directly onstage. All in all, though the actors had to shout their lines (Hamlet inveighs against the performer who would "split the ears of the groundling [and] out-herod Herod"), English enthusiasm for the theater made the event not as obstreperous as it tended to be in France or Spain. Still, Hamlet could wish for a calm, cultured audience over a low public. From the pit, the "groundlings" would shout their approbation or lack of it, regardless of whether the majority of spectators thought differently. No doubt the actors raised their voices to compete, and the open roof did not help matters acoustically. Accordingly, gestures became broader and more expressive—a positive result of the conditions, along with greater clarity of diction. Another positive development was the "spoken decor," the stylistic feature whereby the scenery was explained in the play's text. In the aggregate, then, the shortcomings were few in comparison with other conditions that, one notes in retrospect, favored the flowering of one of the most significant dramas of the Renaissance, one that elicited creative responses from enthusiastic audiences.

It was probably this enthusiasm that inspired the concoction of multiple mechanisms, particularly for performances at court. A Master of the Revels for Elizabeth's private theater, such as Edmund Tilney, who during his tenure, from 1579 to 1610, could censor all public stages (the practice did not cease until 1968), could mount forests and deserts, mountains and monsters, and fires and lightning. One need only think of the culmination of all this in the way Ben Jonson's masques were staged by that frequent traveler to Italy, Inigo Jones. Yet the bulk of the performances took place in public structures, and here too the enthusiasm inspired a very innovative stage, which may be credited with having stimulated the three-dimensionality of Shakespearean characters as contrasted with the bland two-dimensionality of so many Italian Renaissance characters. Although historical consciousness was not such then as to prescribe chronological accuracy for costumes, the Elizabethan stage indulged itself lavishly in opulent garments, and this condition affected others. The En-glish adopted the medieval concept of a multiple stage and combined it with that of the thrust stage, whereby the proscenium protrudes into the audience, like an acting podium (and where "rounded" characters and costuming assume special importance), omitting the curtain that the Italians had devised. This stage's versatility enhanced the creative imagination along all lines, and, among other things, like Spanish open-form staging, fostered a break with the unities of time and place. The whole occurrence was a veritable spectacle, complete with musical interludes, or even improvisations by a clown or buffoon (to Shakespeare's displeasure), but the overall experience was wholesome and substantial and brought forth actors of true thespian stature similar to France's stellar Montdory (Guillaume Desgilberts), such as Edward Alleyn for Christopher Marlowe and Richard Burbage for Shakespeare.

Toward the seventeenth century's end, companies of English actors—*Englische Komödianten*—made their way to Germany, introducing not only their Elizabethan repertoire but also the notion of the participating spectator, the clown or fool who became the German Narr and who was to enliven the popular stage considerably under an array of different names: Hans Supp, Pickelhäring, the Arlecchino-like Hanswurst, and others. In Munich and Vienna, Italian companies, as well as French companies, appeared during the next century, the latter finally exercising the greater influence (if one does not count the *comici*). With each group, Germany profited by the staging and technical advances that each country had to offer, though the continuous foreign impact—let alone that of the Reformation, which tended to inhibit subject matter—did not inspire the shaping of an indigenous classical theater, authors Martin Opitz, Andreas Gryphius, and director Johannes Velten notwithstanding.

Not to be omitted, for its contrast, is the simple, single-set stage of planks and barrels used for religious drama in many countries, particularly in Germany, where the Lutheran revolt stimulated the use of plays for spiritual purposes. Theater was accomplished with the barest of sets, simple name shingles above doors to identify the characters' houses, and a handful of modest props: a clergyman's chair, a throne, a few bars for a prison, a primitive altar, a crude door—all present simultaneously in the multiple-setting tradition. Examples of striking stage effects continued to come primarily from Italy, such as Brunelleschi's rotating spheres of the microcosm for the *sacra rappresentazione* at the Feast of the Annunciation in Florence in 1438. With the introduction of Italian humanist practices, greater elaborateness eventually became evident north of the Alps. Still, it was not unusual to see college quadrangles used for a religious occasion in the northern countries, where the existing trees and bushes could be incorporated to form part of a would-be wing or backdrop. The emphasis remained more on doing than on seeing.

The German *Meistersinger*, whose acting background dated back to the fourteenth century, worked indoors as well as outdoors, without particular regard for fancy staging. Sometimes attractive staging came about naturally. Hans Sachs, the famous cobbler poet who is often called the founder of the German theater, once employed Nuremberg's Martakirche as a setting; his *Die Enthauptung Johannes* of 1550 was performed there on a podium either under the Gothic choir vault or in the nave, the church itself sufficing as scenery. On another occasion, Sachs, who, on the other hand, did not eschew technology, imitated a performance of Plautus's *Menaechmi* (*The Twin Menaechmi*, 1595) given at the Court of Ferrara in 1486 by having a ship rolled in onstage. In the seventeenth century, in Holland, the *Rederijker* stage (the Rederijker Kamers was the Chamber of Rhetoric) developed considerably under humanist influences and English strolling players, elaborating a rear acting area onstage, with columns, arcades, and drawable curtains. This stage was to accommodate the decorations of processions illustrating a religious, didactic text. It climaxed in Amsterdam's famous Schouwburg. Yet, barring a few exceptions, religious drama as a whole remained technically and aesthetically sparse in comparison with what the Master of the Revels could draw on and with what the *ingegneri* could assemble.

RELIGIOUS DRAMA

Religious drama, which moved into the Renaissance from the Middle Ages, lasted up to the threshold of the seventeenth century and beyond this date in some countries. Mystery plays, miracle plays, and morality plays formed a common denominator for most European cultures because all the works were conceived with a similar fondness for didactic, abstract allegory. Germany especially, which remained relatively impervious to the aesthetic events of the Rinascimento, cultivated religious drama assiduously. In one of his *Tischreden*, Martin Luther made it very clear that he regarded the theater as potentially beneficial and educational. In all lands, a dramatic production sponsored by a lord or a prince often was tied to political purposes; it stands to reason that in a country politicized by the Reformation the weapon of drama was not overlooked. The Bible was explored and exploited for stories destined to provide instruction through entertainment. On the grounds of pure catechism, however, not many differences distinguished these performances along national lines; the Italian *sacre rappresentazioni* were akin to the French *mystères*, which were related to the German *Passionsspiele* and the English miracle plays (as well as the Cornish "guary" plays). Scores of dramatic works formed a cycle taking days to perform, such as the York or Coventry cycles, or the *Passion* of Jehan Michel, the *Mystère du Vieil Testament*, the one at Valenciennes in 1547, the 1536 Bourges *Actes des Apôtres*, or the texts that still in modern times shape the highly wrought productions at Oberammergau.

The French Confrérie de la Passion in Paris was royally commissioned in the early 1400's to interpret and present mystery plays (until the Religious Wars, and also the increased coarseness of the plays, put an end to such devotional exercises). Queen Marguerite de Navarre's humanist, allegorical, and intensely pious plays met with little success in a country riddled with intolerant religious strife, where power was divided politically about equally on both sides. Yet where, in other countries, including Germany, this was not the case and more unanimous or neutral attitudes toward Reformation and Counter-Reformation prevailed, religious drama developed more extensively. It is not surprising, therefore, that professionalism seemed a secondary concern and that, as it turned out in the sixteenth century, those in charge of middle-class education had a strong hand in developing religious (instructional) drama, namely, the Jesuits. Under the guidance of a coach, called a *choragus*, the fathers originally had their students perform tragedies in Latin in the school-drama context: only male parts at first, then adding males playing female roles, but no love scenes. The religious mission, however, appeared more important; more and more didactic works were performed.

Jesuit drama, as it came to be known, appeared everywhere, from Naples to Lyons and from Oxford to Vienna to Kraków. The Society of Jesus came to regard the theater as a tool to attract attention and as a weapon to safeguard people's minds. The school dramas of the Netherlands provided excellent models. First, they emphasized word and message; second, they taught by loud declamation. In addition, a useful festive tradition existed. The sixteenth century annual festival, Landjuweel, promoted allegorical processions and *Vertooninge*, or living scenes, which culminated in morality performances based on chosen topics, such as "What gives a dying man most consolation?" or "What can best awaken humankind to the liberal arts?" The religious magnet was strong; Joost van den Vondel, the dominant Dutch author of this period, steeped in humanism and politics, nevertheless preferred to deal with biblical themes: He began with *Het Pascha* (Passover) in 1610 and triumphed with *Lucifer* (English translation, 1917) in 1654.

This is not to say, however, that all dramas in this context were strictly of religious inspiration, or, if religiously based, that a somber, existential cast, secularly inspired, did not approximate them more to tragedy or pastoral than to religious drama narrowly understood. Either north or south in the Alps, in Latin or the vernacular, the inspirations frequently overlapped. Giovan Battista Andreini's tragic *Adamo* (pr. 1613; *Adam*, 1844), a *sacra rappresentazione* of the first half of the seventeenth century, and Jakob Bidermann's tragedy of free thought and divine faith, *Cenodoxus* of 1602 (English translation, 1963), are cases in point. The works of Calderón show the same overlapping. In this category, too, may be placed the works of the earlier Jacob Grester, the English Jesuit

Joseph Simeons, his follower Nikolaus Avancini, and the Sicilian Ortensio Scamacca, whose influence spread widely over the eighteenth century Jesuit stage. Gryphius derived much from this type of Jesuit drama, if his *Catharina von Georgien: Oder, Bewehrete Beständigkeit* (wr. 1647) is any example.

One must not assume that religious drama took the vow of poverty and was always staged sparsely and modestly. In time, as noted above, its success invited more glamorous settings in the Italian style, especially in the days of the flowering of the Baroque. The Jesuits were associated with this flowering in Italy and elsewhere, and the Baroque in turn cultivated a pomp and ornateness that infused all artistic endeavors, even religious drama, with splendor, just as it paved the way for the development of that supratheatrical genre called opera. In Italy, the *sacro teatro* became a cultural institution along with being a religious one, from Father Basilio Lamagna's *Baldasar* of 1610 to the experiments of Giovanni Maria Cecchi, such as *Il figliuol prodigo* (pr. 1570), or the works of fathers Saverio Bettinelli and Giovanni Granelli one century later. The other countries followed suit, though not necessarily with the same showmanship.

Most didactic plays, however, obediently followed religious directives, often with a combative, partisan fervor: Agricola's *Tragedia Johannis Huss* (pr. 1537), Thomas Naogeorgus's *Pammachius* (pr. 1538), the Swiss Jakob Ruoff's antipapist *Weingartenspiel* (pr. 1539), Sixt Birck's *Susanna* (pr. 1532), Johannes Sturm's play on Lazarus (1535), Alsacian *Meistersinger* Jörg Wickram's *Tobias* (pr. 1550), Johann Rasser's *Spiel von der Kinderzucht* (pr. 1573), and many more. The repertory was rich and enhanced with mounting professionalism. In fact, human gestures, expressions, and parts of the body used for acting and recitation were all analyzed for this purpose by Jodocus Willich in his *Libellus de prononciatione rhetorica* (1555). Finally, Sachs must always be remembered as a genuinely religious playwright whose very sincerity made him a companion and admirer of Luther while not engaging through his varied writings in typically anti-Catholic satire. In England, an equally rich Protestant fare came into being, with John Bale, for example, whose *King Johan* (wr. c.

1531) shows the pope as a usurper of power, or with Robert Greene, who wrote satiric mystery plays. The Catholics, too, marshaled their talents, usually in the form of farce or satire: John Heywood's *The Play of the Foure P.P.: A Newe and a Very Mery Enterlude of a Palmer, a Pardoner, a Potycary, a Pedler* (pb. 1541-1547) and his *The Pardoner and the Friar*, published by John Rastell in 1533 (though Heywood's humor often makes him sound anti-Catholic), and Scotsman David Lindsay's morality *Ane Satyre of the Thrie Estaitis* (pr. 1540), which became a favorite of James V.

The religious spirit in drama reached Prague (see, for example, *Susanna* of 1543 by Matthias Collin, a disciple of Philipp Melanchthon), Hungary (Leonhard Stöckel's *Historia de Susanna* is usually mentioned), Denmark (Peder Jensen Hegelund's *Susanna*), and, during the next century, Sweden, where Johannes Messenius mounted dialogued presentations of historico-religious events. Even in Dubrovnik, in Croatia, inspired by Italian examples, a native drama flourished in the sixteenth and seventeenth centuries, underscoring such names as Marin Držić and Ivan Gundulić.

Not uncharacteristically, the Iberian peninsula presented a different picture. Among his many duties as organizer of his country's court festivities, the Portuguese Gil Vicente wrote an *Auto de la fama* (pr. 1515) and a devotional trilogy, a Dantean morality sequence that did much to influence religious drama in neighboring Spain: *Auto da barca do inferno* (pr. 1516; *The Ship of Hell*, 1929), *Auto da barca do purgatório* (pr. 1518; *The Ship of Purgatory*, 1929), and *Auto da barca da gloria* (pr. 1519; *The Ship of Heaven*, 1929). He was followed by *auto* authors António Ribeiro Chiado and António Prestés. Lope de Vega's religious plays, such as *La hermosa Ester* (pb. 1621), were well received. The typical Spanish religious play, counterpart of but not identical to the *sacra rappresentazione*, was the *auto sacramental*, an allegorical play based on a religious theme, often performed after intermissions in religious processions. Those of Juan del Encina became well known. Tirso de Molina wrote a psychological one, *El condenado por desconfiado* (pb. 1634; *The Saint and the Sinner*,

1952; also known as *Damned for Despair*, 1986). Calderón's *El gran teatro del mundo* (pr. 1643; *The Devotion to the Cross*, 1832) portrayed all the stations of humanity (rich man, king, beggar, laborer, and so on) as allotted by the Author, or God, each properly outfitted, discoursing with abstractions such as Beauty, Discretion, or The Law of Grace on a stage symbolically decked with a cradle and a coffin. Calderón stands out as a most prolific writer of *autos* (he wrote seventy or more); his grave spirit lent itself well to the highly regarded form. His *autos*, which received regular performances on Corpus Christi Day, include *La cena del rey Baltasar*, *La devoción de la misa*, *Lo que va del hombre a Dios*, and *La vida es sueño* (the *auto*, not Calderón's famous philosophical drama). These plays are not to be confused with his other (nearly five hundred) dramas, though the religious subject matter frequently links them conceptually if not formally: *La devoción de la cruz* (pr. 1643; *The Devotion to the Cross*, 1832), *El purgatorio de San Patricio* (wr. c. 1634; *The Purgatory of Saint Patrick*, 1873), and *El mágico prodigioso* (pr. 1637; *The Wonder-Working Magician*, 1959), with its opposition of the pagan and the Christian.

Many of these dramas enjoyed visual or scenographic ostentation—which Calderón liked—as well as musical background. In Spanish hands, then, religious drama took more advantage than the rest of Europe of the luxurious practices of Italian staging. It produced variations, such as the shorter forms (the *jácaras*, short pieces about some famous deed); the praising *loas*, generally prologues, used by Lope de Vega; and other free forms.

Closely related to the religious productions were the processions, or parades, theatrical forms in their own right. The Italians promoted them with all the pomp, excitement, and glitter that they could muster, thereby modifying both psychologically and philosophically the medieval processional theater. It was modified aesthetically as well, for during the Middle Ages the procession rolled past the spectators only once, allowing them but segmental glimpses, while the Italians devised seating so as to allow for the delight of a total, simultaneous viewing. In courtyards and squares, the spectators enjoyed these fifteenth century *trionfi*, or panegyrics, from all angles: the floats and masks, boats and dances, mythological gods and allegorical figures, planets and dolphins, angels and saints. In Florence, the music of the *canti carnascialeschi* of the late 1400's, written by the finest composers, such as Antonio Squarcialupi, Heinrich Isaak, and Alexander Agricola, to lyrics by the finest poets, including Angelo Ambrogini (Poliziano) and Lorenzo de' Medici, accompanied the festivities that took place by day (in places such as Piazza Santa Croce or the Palazzo Pitti) and by night (by torchlight in the streets).

This practice inspired less lavish but significant counterparts elsewhere in Europe. In France, apart from the less pretentious *parades*, they became known as *entrées solennelles* under King Henry III late in the sixteenth century, the dancing and pantomimes emerging eventually in an organization labeled Le Ballet Comique de la Royne. The beautiful gardens of the nobility provided excellent, if restricted, sites for such *entrées*. Thus was founded a tradition of dance-dramas on which Molière and his collaborating Florentine court musician, Gianbattista Lulli (commonly known as Lully), were to base a *comédie-ballet* such as *Le Bourgeois Gentilhomme* (pr. 1670; *The Would-Be Gentleman*, 1675).

In England, these processions or revels became interludes, variations of the *trionfo*, such as John Heywood's *The Play of the Weather* (pb. 1533). Allegorical festivals were also known in Spain and Portugal, where an *auto sacramental* could form part of the total event. Sometimes, too, they assumed a historical character—João Sardinha Mimoso's *Tragicomedia del descubrimiento y conquista del Oriente* (pr. 1581), based on Vasco da Gama and staged by Lisbon's Jesuit Colégio de Santo Antônio, being a noted example. Not different in spirit were the days-long Dutch *Vertooninge*, which ended in competitions of religious dramas, or the German-organized performance enterprises featuring floats—what in one instance Albrecht Dürer on his canvas titled *Triumphwagen*. The humanist Konrad Celtes, much honored along with the Sodalitas Literaria Danubiana academy by Emperor Maximilian I for his Linz production of *Ludus Dianae* (wr. 1501), had absorbed the

best that Rome and Ferrara had to offer and, in 1501, had mounted the first example of the genre outside Italy. This custom continued in Prague and Vienna with the sumptuous *Ludi Caesarei* during the height of the Baroque period. Quite clearly, the religious dimension sometimes seemed lost, given the sense of pagan revelry that accompanied the more excited and magnificent productions, but in point of fact it always underlay the events somehow, historically as well as spiritually, if one takes into account the didactic nature of many of the floats and songs.

Except for the Spanish *autos*, one tends to overlook Renaissance religious drama because it develops as a continuum from its medieval source, as the continuing traditions of the German *Meistersinger* and the Dutch *Rederijkers* suggest. One expects to see more of a break with the past, or at least an eye-catching transformation, such as the elaborations of the *trionfi* and other processions provide. Yet this expectation is a mistake. School drama and Jesuit drama, even if often in Latin, and plain religious drama of a polemical, Reformational, or Counter-Reformational nature, by their very enthusiastic energy or combativeness, contributed to the spirit of rebirth and must be reckoned with as influential forces shaping new theatrical destinies alongside those shaped by the learned humanist and the popular theaters.

HUMANIST DRAMA AND DERIVATIVES

When the Italian humanists set their sights on Greco-Roman antiquity, their admiration became such as to suggest to them that, because perfection precludes improvement, the task of the modern playwright was to emulate and imitate in order to achieve the best work that could be achieved. In Aristotle, they came on the authority who provided the moral justification of tragedy, just as in Vitruvius they found the mentor who made tragedy possible onstage. The problem turned out to be the subservience of the theorists to their interpretation of the Greek philosopher's statements, forgetting that while the Stagirite deduced his observations from a corpus of acclaimed works by the great tragedians, they were interpolating meanings and fashioning rules from those few observations to apply to what was going to be written. Moreover, when they did look into the ancient playwrights directly, they placed more emphasis on the moody Euripides and the sermonizing Seneca than on the austere Aeschylus and the profound Sophocles. Their desire to formulate laws while copying the ancient models may have coincided intellectually with the humanist orientation of the Renaissance, but psychologically it pulled in an opposite direction: The spirit of rebirth, inhibited by such rules, found itself denied the freedom it coveted—a freedom that even the medieval theater had enjoyed. As it happened, perhaps surprisingly and perhaps not, by pouring their creative energies into theaters and staging and their conceptual energies into theory, the Italians wrote next to nothing of note in the category of tragedy, but their theoretical discussions, naïvely argumentative and logical as they often sound, had a significant effect throughout Europe that was not really dislodged until the Romantic revolt in the nineteenth century. John Milton, Ben Jonson, Pierre Corneille, John Dryden, Voltaire, Gotthold Ephraim Lessing, Johann Wolfgang von Goethe—hardly a playwright was spared their influence, though the latter two writers headed in a reformed direction.

As Joseph E. Spingarn, who made a thorough study of Renaissance literary theory, observed, the basis of the Rinascimento theory of tragedy stemmed from Aristotle's definition as found in his *De poetica* (c. 334-323 B.C.E.; *Poetics*, 1705): Not a narration like an epic, tragedy imitates an action that is serious (therefore, not like comedy), unified, and of a certain length; its language is lofty and includes musical elements such as song, in which the medium is not verse alone; and through pity and fear it induces a purgation of the emotions, a catharsis. Then the chain of speculations started. Without touching on Aristotelian observations, Bernardino Daniello, in *La poetica* (1536), distinguished between dramatic modes— tragedy and comedy, excluding ignoble incidents from being shown in the former. Tragedies express the terrible and doleful tales, historically based, of afflicted princes, usually beginning normally and ending with inevitable misfortune; comedies express familiar though invented occurrences in modest, domestic situations pertaining to meaner people, usu-

ally beginning with problems and ending happily (for this reason, Dante, finishing his famous poem with the *Paradiso*, was supposed to have called the whole work "La commedia," a concept related to upward movement). The sublime language of the one contrasted with the colloquial language of the other, just as the bloodshed marring the first contrasted with the love and seduction propelling the second. Basically, the distinction had obtained in the Middle Ages as well, and it continued unaltered through the poetic theories of Jean Vauquelin de la Fresnaye (*Art poétique*, 1605) and the Pléïade in France, and into the speculative works of William Webbe (*Discourse of English Poetrie*, 1586) and George Puttenham (*The Arte of English Poetrie*, 1589) in England.

To this distinction, Giambattista Giraldi Cinthio (*Discorso intorno al comporre delle commedie e delle tragedie*, 1543) added the dignity of the subject matter, its elevated rank that must distinguish tragedy from comedy—a favorite notion, entwined with that of decorum, that marked the whole classical period for two and a half centuries to come. The idea established itself solidly in France, from the works of Étienne Jodelle in the sixteenth century through those of Corneille and Racine during the seventeenth to those of Prosper de Crébillon and Voltaire in the eighteenth, and it appealed especially in England because of its moralizing potential. The rank of the protagonists must also be high. Francesco Robortello (*In librum Aristoteles de arte poetica explicationes*, 1548) referred to the hero's fall as needing to elicit the spectator's compassion, and another commentator, Vincenzo Maggi (*In Aristotelis librum de poetica explicationes*, 1550), applied the notion of rank specifically to the most highly situated men, such as kings, for the same reason. The more elevated the hero's station, the more tragic his decline and, as the English liked, the greater the likelihood of the drama's teaching through admiration and commiseration before the mutability of fortune. Sir Philip Sidney insisted on dignified personages, together with gravity and loftiness of elocution, as did Jonson, Webbe, and Puttenham; Milton, in his prefix to *Samson Agonistes* (1671), adhered to the ancient and Italian tenets and eschewed vulgar people and events in the name of decorum.

Julius Caesar Scaliger (*Poetices libri septem*, 1561) exerted a tenacious influence toward the end of the sixteenth century and later in France, where he lived and wrote and introduced the French to the Aristotelian canon. He stressed the illustrious, historical dimension of tragedy (as opposed to the common invention of comedy), while Antonio Minturno (*De poeta*, 1559, and *Poetica toscana*, 1563), in his paraphrase of Aristotle, stressed linguistic severity of tone to avoid the softening effect of amorous idiom. Actually, in the seventeenth century—without forgetting Minturno—two Dutch scholars promoted Scaliger's ideas in France: Daniel Heinsius (*De tragoediae constitutione*, 1611), a pupil of Scaliger's son Joseph Justus Scaliger, and Gerhard-Joseph Vossius (*De rhetoricae natura ac constitutione*, 1622; *On Plot in Tragedy*, 1971), thereby anchoring in the Italian Renaissance French poetic theory and the structural laws regarding the tragedy of the Age Classique. Much was said about the role played by Cartesian rationalism in all this; the Abbé François d'Aubignac (*La Pratique du théâtre*, 1657; *The Whole Art of the Stage*, 1684), for one, insisted that the rules had nothing to do with authority but rather were based on reason, a contention that Nicolas Boileau-Despréaux echoed in his *Art poétique* (1674), just as Corneille, for another, appealed to logic in his *Discours* (1660), aimed at removing the tyranny of the arbitrariness of unnatural requirements.

Perhaps the most significant influence, not only in France, resulted from Lodovico Castelvetro's publication of his *Poetica d'Aristotele vulgarizzata e sposta* in 1570 (as well as other critical writings), remarkable for its subtle observations. It forms, in a way, a compendium of Renaissance dramatic theory. For alongside the usual topics, he discussed a host of related matters: among others, the fact that tragedy is written to be acted on a stage (a concept that shaped thinking about the three unities), in possibly a huge theater, demanding that attention be paid to acoustics; that verse allows not only aesthetically for delight but also functionally for projection, lest the actor have to resort to the indignity of shouting; that because plays are for recreation, all technical or erudite discussions must be avoided (later, the English,

especially Jonson, spoke of "simplicity") and action must center on humanity's elemental interests; and that because the stage is usually not an extensive platform, violent deeds may not occur conveniently on it, or with decorum, and should therefore not be represented.

Taking a hint from Sperone Speroni and Minturno, Castelvetro gave Aristotle's catharsis an aesthetic interpretation, relying on the theory that emotions are purified through art, through the effect of seeing the terror and sad events heaped on a great man—which leads the spectators to grieve less over their own misfortunes. When people see what happens to others and realize their common nature, it eases their emotions of pity and fear. Vittore Vettori (*Commentarii in primum librum Aristotelis de arte poetarum*, 1560) as well as Robortelli subscribed to this interpretation. Most Italian critics, however, embraced the ethical interpretation, attributing the function or value of tragedy to the moral lesson or example derived from catharsis. This notion follows the opinion of Giraldi Cinthio and of Giangiorgio Trissino in his *La poetica* (1529-1562) that tragedy and comedy both aim to inspire virtue. The former looked to the eradication of vice through catharsis by making the viewer afraid to imitate it, while the latter preferred to avoid the problematics of catharsis by noting that tragedy must admire the good, leaving to comedy the task of chastising the bad.

This ethical interpretation became a literary axiom for the rest of Europe; it is discernible in Lessing and Corneille, Dryden and Racine, and Milton and Voltaire. Unfortunately, at times the ambition to purify by fear engendered the most acute (offstage) atrocities: incest, child murder, patricide, and suicide dominate Giraldi Cinthio's *Orbecche* (pr. 1541). A true descendant of Seneca and Euripides and forerunner of Crébillon, Giraldi Cinthio cultivated what he admitted was full of "horror." Nevertheless, Giraldi Cinthio's treatise laid the foundation for the proper French Age Classique and for Lessing's dramaturgy (to the extent that the latter did not militate against the established form), while his tales provided seminal material for many writers after him, including Shakespeare (*Othello, the Moor of Venice*, pr. 1604).

Maggi and Benedetto Varchi (*Lezzioni, lette nell'Accademia Fiorentina*, 1590) shifted the stress, maintaining that pity and fear themselves were not purged by catharsis but that passions analogous to them were. Tragedy, in other words, afforded a liberation—again an ethical purpose. In an often quoted letter of 1565, Speroni endorsed the cathartic notion of liberation from the bondage of pity and fear, even though Aristotle had merely called for their control. The moral aim of tragedy, however, did not preclude the theorists from underscoring the factor of pleasure. For Scaliger and Minturno, drama must move and delight as well as teach, though an ethical purpose lies at the core of art, and a tragedy's basic function is to reveal how evil invites punishment and goodness reward. Such an end may be facilitated by the use of instructive precepts—*sententiae*—in true Senecan fashion. The spectator learns by example and admonishment. At this point, Italian literary critics, and those beyond the Alps who followed in their footsteps, were conscious of countermanding the sacred authority of Aristotle, for theorists such as Minturno and Milton knew quite well that by catharsis the Greek philosopher implied an emotional instead of a moral effect.

Yet no instruction is possible unless the tragic hero invites sympathy. He must appear neither eminently good nor entirely bad, and his fall must stem from a tragic flaw in his character or a fatal behavioral mistake. Sometimes prosperity or misfortune guides a human destiny, so that the hero might change for the better or the worse—this was the conjecture of Daniello, though Giraldi Cinthio stayed closer to Aristotle when he claimed that the happy or unhappy ending must still inspire pity and fear for the drama to qualify as tragedy. The argument over the necessity of an unhappy ending occupied the larger part of the theorists' discussions. Scaliger insisted on this, and so did another rhetorician, Francesco Capriano (*Della vera poetica*, 1555), who linked misfortune to imprudence. To this Minturno added a further refinement; in his view, calculated imprudence, such as the actions of perfect persons, Christian saints, for example, fits the weighty and admiring character of tragedy and fully deserves treatment in this mode—

an argument not forgotten by Corneille when he wrote *Polyeucte* (pr. 1642; English translation, 1655).

In all instances, however, the protagonists remained as illustrious as the action remained grave, and any deviation from this norm resulted in a jarring, unacceptable impropriety. The Renaissance had much to say about decorum, as had Aristotle and Horace. Propriety requires that characters be realistic and consistent with their own type. An old man, for example, while he may be in love in comedy, may not be so in the serious context of tragedy; low characters may not play roles of importance in tragedy; bloody actions may not be carried out in full view of the spectator lest the latter see the monarch, say, befouling himself. As the practice gained footing, the playwrights' freedom diminished, for an old man or a soldier or a princess or a Roman could possess only certain characteristics, and in the process social distinctions were taken for granted; that is, only those of the highest rank could figure prominently in the action. For Girolamo Muzio (*Arte poetica*, 1551), Daniello, and Marco Gerolamo Vida (*De arte poetica*, 1527; *Vida's Art of Poetry*, 1725), a pleb could never pass as a king. Formulas took over despotically, even in matters of an actor's movement, dress, and talk; Minturno and Scaliger developed the theories in such detail that the notion of personality was smothered, so that what has come to be known as character development had no opportunity to evolve, even during the later neoclassical period, when playwrights were allowed to shed some of the strictures. Jonson's concept of "humours" (defined by Lionardo Salviati in the second half of the sixteenth century as peculiar characteristics) derives from the older formulas.

THE DRAMATIC UNITIES

By far the most extensive debate centered on the question of the dramatic unities. Aristotle intimated a unity of action, referred once to a time limit, and never wrote a word about unity of place. Yet the Italians wrote tomes on the subject. Action is the only unity that can claim ancient authority; time and place were fashioned out of it by inference. One sole plot (no subplots), one sole location (hence no scene changes), and one sole day (either twelve or twenty-four hours) circumscribed and fettered the tragedians, who yet saw no reason to disparage the injunctions. In fact, they balanced off the elaborateness of scenography by catering to the taste for classical simplicity (something that endeared them to the Age Classique in particular). Thus realism juxtaposed fantasy. Trissino's *La Sofonisba* was upheld as a model tragedy.

It stands to reason that for the sake of coherence a single action and not a plurality of plot lines makes sense. If Corneille, Calderón, Marlowe, or Shakespeare introduced secondary plots now and then, regardless of whether they harbored any respect for the unities, they did so with cautious reserve and never allowed the ancillary action to attain any independence. Unity of action simply means good composition.

The same may not be said uniformly about the unity of time, an artificial regulation. The Italians, however, did not see things that way. Giraldi Cinthio first enunciated it, limiting action basically to one day or very little more. Judging from the normal practice of the Greek playwrights, he stood on honored ground, but when the argument's spirit was replaced by chronometrics, its value dissipated. Aristotle's observation of "a single revolution of the sun" became, for Robortelli, twelve hours (because people sleep at night) for both tragedy and comedy. Bernardo Segni (*Rettoria et poetica d'Aristotile*, 1549) argued for a more scientific twenty-four hours (for terrible things do happen at night), a circumscription later endorsed strictly by Milton and more casually by Jonson (who favored allowing the action to grow). So it went, with thirteen Italian rhetoricians eventually joining the controversy. It was Trissino who finally approached the issue more reasonably, suggesting that time must be viewed as an artistic principle aimed at avoiding dramatic formlessness (a weakness of medieval plays).

Up to this time, the critics did not refer to the unity of place. It became recognized as a necessary derivative of action and time when duration of plot was made to coincide with time of representation onstage, all of which led to the consideration that, with time restricted, a character could not go far away from the site of the action without straining temporal credibility. This became Maggi's concern. So with the coming of Scaliger (who made no direct allusion to time), another principle took shape, one that prevailed everywhere in classical Europe: the *verisimile*, the *vraisemblable*, or verisimilitude. The temporal and spacial constraints resulted supposedly in the kind of plausibility that Minturno and Vettori sought and that Milton was to observe, together with the laws of decorum. Such semblable reality of stage representation convinced Castelvetro, the first to fix the unity of place, of the preponderant need for a circumscribed space; he gave it precedence over the other two, and it is to him that European drama owes the final formulation of the three unities as inviolable laws of drama.

Castelvetro put the unities together in 1570; in 1572 they were voiced by Jean de La Taille (in his preface to *Saül le furieux*) in France, and in 1595 by Sidney in his *Defence of Poesie* in England. In introducing his play, de la Taille discussed the propriety of mixing good and evil, passion and sentiment in the light of drama's imitation—a favorite Renaissance principle, especially for the Pléïade—of life, and when he came to the three rules, he attempted to solve the problem of space by reverting to the medieval practice of multiple (simultaneous) sets. For some time to come, however, the theoretical spirit in France reflected thinking south of the Alps. The refined level of Italian criticism influenced the critic Guez de Balzac, but it was Jean Chapelain (*Lettres sur la règle des vingt-quartre heures*, 1630) who carried the torch for the unities and imposed them on French tragedy. Furthermore, he instilled in his countrymen a respect for Castelvetro (as opposed to Annibal Caro in the controversy over versification) and Speroni, as well as for the purveyor of Italian theory, Heinsius. Chapelain promoted Racine, and he was much admired by Corneille. In France, the dramatic unities were there to stay. Clearly, unlike Corneille, the genius of Racine knew how to take advantage of them: simplicity of action, no improbabilities or digressions, and a focus not on his predecessors' sense of heroic admiration but on love as a determining element of plot, all of which easily reduced the action to a short time frame and a single location. This is not to say that the French, like the English and Spanish, avoided the debates that kept Italy astir. Alexandre Hardy may have moved his audiences with his freely conceived adventurous dramas, but Jodelle (*Cléopâtre captive*, pr. 1552), Jean Mairet (*Sophonisbe*, pr. 1634), and most others did not circumvent the precepts upheld by the rhetoricians who wrote with such finality, such as d'Aubignac and Boileau, that spokesman for the French classical program.

Apart from Sidney, who held to the notion of the unities rigidly—he criticized Thomas Sackville and Thomas Norton's *Gorboduc* (pr. 1561) for not observing time and place—the English at first treated the rules somewhat cavalierly. Elizabethan dramatists such as Thomas Kyd, Francis Beaumont, John Fletcher, and Marlowe wrote independently of rules, establishing their own romantic drama, and certainly Shakespeare was above them, though, as it happened, his last comedy, *The Tempest* (pr. 1611), followed them strictly. Although Spanish romantic production had its theorists, that of the Elizabethans did not. With the infusion of French practices, however, the unities became law until well into the eighteenth century. Sidney, then, originated English dramatic criticism; after him, neoclassical tragedy followed Aristotelian lines, in conjunction with the oratorical and gory Senecan orientation that had inspired the playwrights from the earliest days of the Renaissance.

Sidney reacted against the formless outrages and the mixture of modes, let alone the buffooneries of clowns, in the name of gravity, lofty style, and heroic dignity—in other words, decorum. Tragedy might modify history, but not the rules of poetry. He said all this long before the Aristotelian and Horatian Boileau. Milton paid homage to Sidney's point of view, which stressed the common end of both tragedy and comedy: namely, to teach and delight. Jonson did, too, though he behaved more laxly with respect to some of the marginal conditions, such as division into acts and scenes, number of actors, and chorus. Yet in 1603 he constructed his Roman tragedy *Sejanus His Fall* (pr. 1603) strictly according to the rules, and it failed, faring no better than Jodelle's

Cléopâtre captive or Mairet's *Sophonisbe*. Shakespeare was right in taking no part in arguments about theoretical rules, and when Polonius announces the players to Hamlet, he calls them

> the best actors in the world, either for tragedy, comedy, history, pastoral, pastoral-comical, historical-pastoral, tragical-historical, tragical-comical-historical-pastoral, scene individable, or poem unlimited: Seneca cannot be too heavy, nor Plautus too light. For the law of writ and the liberty, these are the only men.

Imitation of the ancients and of the Italians conformed with "the law of writ." Yet not all rhetoricians and playwrights were content to imitate; some preferred "the liberty." The need to compromise when the rules gave rise to untenable situations modulated with some writers to a desire for freedom of inspiration, something with which the Elizabethans, culminating in Shakespeare, were quite familiar. Giambattista Giraldi Cinthio (*Discorso intorno al comporre dei romanzi*, 1549) and his pupil Giovanni Battista Pigna (*I romanzi*, 1554) had argued for an author's intellectual independence of the sacred authorities in treating certain subjects, the *romanzi*, or romances, such as Matteo Boiardo's *Orlando innamorato* (1483-1495; English translation, 1823) or Ludovico Ariosto's *Orlando furioso* (1516, 1521, 1532; English translation, 1591), whose mixture of love with the heroic diverged from the fundamental requirements of long narrative poems and so made them distinguishable from epics. Being unknown to the Greeks and Romans, the *romanzi* constituted a new genre, therefore not subject to the rules. (It is doubtful if historical and pastoral drama would have reached the heights that they did without the absence of many constraints.) This was the romantic "liberty" some playwrights sought. This independence gave the Renaissance proper (before the French Age Classique) its finest drama—in England and in Spain.

Apart from the Elizabethans and Shakespeare, who did not have rhetoricians championing and defending their aesthetics, the most noteworthy dramatic freedoms were taken in Spain, where literary theory was debated. Cervantes, in his theoretical writing, pleaded for a literary, noble theater, "a mirror of human life, a reflection of the customs and image of truth . . . , verisimilitude . . . , the observance of the dramatic rules." In practice, however, Cervantes paid less attention to his learned formalism and thought of theater as an aesthetic and cultural datum; his respect for the dramatic unities was relative, as the character Comedy in his *El rufián dichoso* (pb. 1615) asserts: Seneca, Terence, and Plautus are admirable, but "time changes things, perfects the arts," and they should be imitated only in part. The unities of time and place inhibit the modern dramatic vision. Despite such insights, his best drama, *El cerco de Numancia* (wr. 1585; *The Siege of Numantia*, 1870), for example, can hardly be considered a landmark.

Yet the spirit of romantic innovation and "irregular" drama took shape nevertheless. Juan de la Cueva's *Ejemplar poético* (wr. 1606, pb. 1774), by a man Italianate in matters of poetics but nationalistic in matters of drama, may be read essentially as an apology for Lope de Vega's dramatic practices, in its attempt to encourage his countrymen, because of Spain's special position in Europe, to innovate on classical foundations. The title of Lope de Vega's poetic work *El arte nuevo de hacer comedias en este tiempo* (1609; *The New Art of Writing Plays*, 1914) suggests unmistakably the romantic desire to branch out in new directions (albeit admiring the Aristotelian canon and the Italianized rules). Theater must please. The norms he proposed, however, were not entirely new: freedom of choice in subject matter, mixture of tragic and comic, unity of action, abandonment of the unities of time and place, separation of the work into three acts, division of the argument in two so that the second leads to a resolution without the spectator's awareness, never an empty stage, consistency between characters and their language, avoidance of unverisimilar events, and questions of honor. One hears echoes of Scaliger, Castelvetro, Minturno, Speroni, and Trissino. Furthermore, because the people demand the plays, the people, not the literati, must be satisfied; Lope de Vega put them right into his plays, and in a work such as *Fuenteovejuna* (pb. 1619; *The Sheep Well*, 1936) they constitute indeed the protagonist. Maggi had spoken in favor of the masses mingling with princes. In short, Lope de Vega

Carpio's "new art" lay not in his do's and dont's but in the relative absence of them. In this respect, he served as Spain's Shakespeare.

The "new art" aroused traditionalists, and a series of polemical battles took place involving in the opposition people such as Fernando Nuñez Pincianus, Cascales, Cristóbal de Mesa, Suárez de Figueroa, and even Miguel de Cervantes. Torres Rámila published a libel in 1617 titled *Spongia*, which divided the litigants into Lopists and anti-Lopists, the former attacking the publication with their own *Expostulatio Spongiae*, in which context Alfonso Sánchez made his mark in 1618 by declaring that "the principal precept of art is to imitate nature because the works of poets express the nature, customs, and genius of the century in which they wrote. . . . If Spanish comedy were to abide by the rules of the ancients, it would proceed against nature and against the fundamentals of poetry." For him, Lope de Vega surpassed all the ancient poets.

It was to this liberty—call it a romantic or naturalistic concept—to which the French looked during the seventeenth century before Molière and Racine. To d'Aubignac's displeasure, Hardy insisted on the legitimacy of public taste with the same fervor as François Ogier emphasized the independence of manner of the *romanzi*, or romances. In England, too, the rules came under attack, despite Dryden's strong defense of them; yet Sir Robert Howard (in his preface to *The Duke of Lerma*, 1668; *The Great Favourite: Or, the Duke of Lerma*, pr. 1668) and George Farquhar (*Love and Business*, pb. 1702) scoffed at the rules, particularly those of time and place, and at all pontificators of poetic principles. France and England (after the Elizabethans), however, went classical, after all was said and done; Spain went, or stayed, romantic; and Italy, with its firmly established classical tradition but also with its developed pastoral drama, which tended toward the romantic, kept the debate alive both in theory and in practice.

THE RULES AND COMEDY

Some of the debate on tragedy overlapped with that on comedy or spilled into it. Because of its humbler nature, comedy did not concern itself theoretically with questions such as decorum and sometimes language (which could be colloquial). Yet most other tenets for tragedy applied to comedy as well and were taken equally seriously. The lesser mode attracted the greater audiences. Court society in general, including the Roman Curia, preferred the amusement of comedy to the terror of tragedy and did not care about the polemics of academies, literary circles, and erudite theoreticians. Whether in Florence or in London, the public liked the lucky chance that suddenly appeases distress and gathers joy, as Webbe would have it, and the easier identification with private persons closer to themselves, as Puttenham would. Jonson, for one, paid more theoretical attention to comic than to tragic arguments. Lope de Vega was a master at exploiting what Sidney saw as the common errors of life, and Molière remained unequaled in ridiculing erratic domesticities and wayward social trends.

The central requirement—a requirement that endured into the century of Carlo Goldoni and Ludwig Holberg—was delight, with or without laughter. This notion dated back to Trissino. Yet while the Latins (Italians, French, and Spanish) would accept that which simply delighted and produced laughter, though this might be provoked by sinful events, the English needed to inject the factor of delightful teaching into their conception of comedy. Niccolò Machiavelli's *La mandragola* (pr. c. 1519; *The Mandrake*, 1911) would never do. Jonson would "sport with human follies, not with crimes," and Sidney would use the ridiculous to improve moral life.

On the whole, however, rhetoricians had less to say directly about comedy than about tragedy. Most was by implication, and perhaps this turned out for the better, for after a very slavish beginning in close imitation of the ancients and New Comedy (Menander, Philemon, Plautus, and Terence), in which stereotyping triumphed and verisimilitude suffered, comedy from Ariosto to Machiavelli, from the *commedia dell'arte* to Molière, and from Lope de Vega to Jonson (Shakespeare always apart) energized itself through its own inner dynamics or resources, through its own natural irrepressibility, and as a result the Renaissance produced on the whole a better fare of comedy than of tragedy, because comedy was freer to explore new manners and new materials.

TRAGEDY

Learned humanist theater, called in Italy *teatro erudito*, developed in a threefold way: ancient Latin and Greek plays produced in the original, afterward in translation; dramas written in Latin; and tragedies written in the vernacular, adhering to the rules and in servile imitation of the classical masters, more often than not Seneca and Euripides. It was the dream of the early humanists in Italy, during the fifteenth century, to bring Latin and Greek texts back to the stage. The practice developed on a broad scale. Melanchthon, during the sixteenth century, revived ancient dramas in his academy—Euripides' *Heklabē* (425 B.C.E.; *Hecuba*, 1782) and Seneca's *Thyestes* (English translation, 1581), for example—and in France also, where Seneca's works appeared in 1485, translations were used, such as those by Desiderius Erasmus of Euripides in 1506, before being translated in turn into French (Italian plays, too, were translated, since throughout the Renaissance Italian was considered by the Pléïade a classical language). In England, George Buchanan translated Euripides for the stage, and in Italy, some Greek works were performed in the original.

As far back as the Trecento, Albertino Mussato, a contemporary of Dante, wrote a famous (at that time) tragedy, *Ecerinis* (1315; English translation, 1975), a Senecan story of a recent Paduan tyrant (Ezzelino III da Romano), and by the next century Enea Silvio Piccolomini (later Pius II) was still composing plays in Latin. As professors, masters, and rectors with a school stage available, German humanists in particular did much to promote dramaturgy in Latin: Celtes, Johann Reuchlin, Jakob Locher, Jodocus Badius, Jakob Wimpheling, Philipp Frischlin, his pupil Heinrich Julius von Braunschwig, and others. In the northern countries, humanists lived in an ambience in which the vernaculars took over more slowly in learned circles. Most of them enjoyed repeated visits to Italian centers such as Rome and Ferrara, from which they garnered many useful impressions. The Accademia Romana, with the noted Pomponio Lato (Pomponius Laetus) and disciples of his, the so-called Pomponians, such as Inghirami, were especially influential. In the manner of Celtes, Locher wrote, at the very end of the 1400's, *Tragedia de Thurcis et Suldano*, and during the next century both Jesuit and Protestant drama, while representing a new—religious and polemical—form of dramatic art (Bidermann's *Cenodoxus* and *Cosmarchia*, 1617, among others), expanded the Latin practice. England, too, had its share of Latin drama—the universities of Oxford and Cambridge serving properly as sites—and while the Elizabethan writers monopolized the country's attention, it was not impossible to run across something such as Simeons's *Zeno sive ambitio infelix* and *Leo Armenius sive impietas punita* on the religious side, or Thomas Legge's three-part tragedy *Richardus Tertius* (pr. 1573, 1579, 1582) on the recent historical. Nothing of note, however, has come down to contemporary audiences from these ubiquitous Latin compositions of the Renaissance.

More was attempted with original drama in the vernacular, though here too an inordinate reliance on ancient models, despite significant departures (by Antonio Cammelli, Giraldi Cinthio, Speroni, Cecchi, and Poliziano, to mention but a few), curbed the creative verve that lent excitement to the romantic aesthetic. Indeed, many Italian attempts did exhibit free impulses. The first tragedy in Italian, in fact, was Cammelli's *Filostrato e Panfila* (1499), a Boccaccian echo of love and horror like a Senecan mystery play, if such a hybrid may be conceived. Giraldi Cinthio's *Orbecche* forty-two years later, or Speroni's *Canace* the following year, outdoing their predecessor in gruesomeness, together with Lodovico Dolce's portrayal of jealousy in *Marianna* (pr. 1565) and Luigi Groto's excited crowds in *La Dalida* (pb. 1572), still belonged to those clumsy efforts at tragedy that Shakespeare improved on and perfected with *Titus Andronicus* (pr. 1594) and *Othello, the Moor of Venice*.

Other romancelike efforts, however, fell as flat as their "regular" tragic counterparts: Giraldi Cinthio's adventuresome *Arrenopia* (pr. 1563), with its happy ending, or his sentimental *Altile* (pb. c. 1545) or his *Cli antivalomeni* (pr. 1548), with its impersonations and incognitos, reminiscent—it has been observed—of *Cymbeline* (pr. c. 1609-1610), or Torquato Tasso's chivalric *Il re Torrismondo* (pb. 1587) and Gabriele Zinano's flighty and affected *L'Almerigo* (pr. 1590). However artificially sensational or simply bland, these works at least invite one's attention as curiosities more than the regular, imitative, rule-bound tragedies, such as Giovanni Rucellai's Sophoclean *Rosmunda* (wr. 1515, pr. 1525) and Euripidean *Oreste* (wr. 1515-1520, pr. 1723); Trissino's Euripidean *La Sofonisba*, with its stamp of Senecan moralism; or Giraldi Cinthio's other Senecan works, *Didone* (public reading c. 1541) and *Cleopatra* (wr. c. 1543), not to mention Pietro Aretino's prolix *La Orazia* (pb. 1546). This is not to suggest that the tragedies were without influence. Trissino's *La Sofonisba* was highly regarded in Europe as a perfect model; typical were the French renderings by Mellin de Saint-Gelais and Claude Mérinet. This type of play of antique complexion spread throughout sixteenth and seventeenth century Europe; one may single out at random Pieter Corneliszoon Hooft's *Achilles en Polyxena* (1614) in Holland and Jan Kochanowski's *Odprawa greckich* (pr. 1578; *The Dismissal of the Grecian Envoys*, 1918) in Poland.

Perhaps the only deserving work of this period's *teatro erudito* belonged neither to tragedy nor to comedy, though it was superficially related to the *sacra rappresentazione:* Poliziano's *Orfeo* (pr. c. 1480; English translation, 1879). In this secularized mystery play, the Christian allusions are paganized: An annunciation is made not by the traditional angel but by Mercury, Gabriel is replaced by Jupiter, Avernus appears, a tumultuous Bacchic chorus climaxes the action, and so on. Given its composition as an idealized sequence of scenic, lyric elegies, it is not inopportune to think of it aesthetically as a precursor of opera, its rhythmically narrated love "numbers," popular in flavor yet humanist in inspiration, qualifying as arias. The relatively early date of the work should have augured well for humanist drama, but unfortunately it remained *sui generis*. The mixed genre (pagan classicism and sacred drama)—*Drammi mescidati*—did find many imitators immediately, such as Tebaldeo (Antonio Tebaldi) and Niccolò da Correggio, whose *Orphei tragoedia* and *Cefalo* (pr. 1487) respectively were probably more read than seen.

In fact, the *teatro erudito* as a whole elicited sufficient boredom for producers to start interpolating shows inside the show, between acts—originally called *intromesse*, that is, insertions, which became *intermedii* or *intermezzi*—something the spectators truly enjoyed and came or stayed to see. These were brief, burlesque, choreographed compositions, usually ending with music and ballet. In evolved form, they passed autonomously into France and England (the court revels, or interludes, such as John Heywood's *The Play of the Weather* along with court masques related to the *trionfi*), and the French word *entremets* suggests their entertainment use during meals. The most noteworthy *intermezzi* were Cervantes's *entremeses* (the Spanish cultivated the genre assiduously): satires of conjugal separations, mayors, human cruelty, courtesans, lowlife, deceived husbands, love rivalries—from *El juez de los divorcios* (pr. 1615; *The Divorce Court Judge*, 1919) to *La guarda cuidadora* (pr. 1615; *The Hawk-eyed Sentinel*, 1948), both published in 1615. If the author of *Don Quixote de la Mancha* enjoys a theatrical reputation apart from his theoretical stands, it is because of his eight or ten rapid sketches, the *entremeses*.

In France, anticipating Cardinal Richelieu, the sixteenth century Pléïade group led by Pierre de Ronsard dictated the refashioning of the stage to bring about a *tragédie à l'antique*, following the Italian example. Joachim Du Bellay, Antonie de Baïf, and Jean Bastier de La Péruse looked for distinguishing nobility of language and respect for the ancients and their transalpine imitators. Their delight knew no end in 1552 at the appearance of Jodelle's *Cléopâtre captive*, on a Plutarchan subject, treated in Alexandrine verses by a young author (he was twenty) displaying total deference to the classical laws. Wordy, monotonous, and without dramatic effect, the play nevertheless impressed the Parisian aristocracy and influenced its entire century. Those who followed him had little more to offer the French learned stage—La Péruse (*La Medée*, pb. 1555), Jacques Grévin (*Le Mort de César*, pr. 1561), Gabriel Bounin (*La Soltane*, pb. 1561), André de Rivaudeau, Florent Chrestien, and others. Antonie de Montchrestien and his Huguenot *L'Écossaise* (pb. 1601; Mary, Queen of Scots) and classical *Sophonisbe* (pb. 1596) in the early seventeenth century attracted much attention, perhaps because of his different, elegiac tone reminiscent of Poliziano, and so did Robert Garnier (*Porcie*, pb. 1568; *Hippolyte*, pb. 1573; *Bradamante*, pb. 1582; *Sédécie: Ou, Les Juives*, pb. 1583), whose eloquence and lively dialogue raises his works a notch above the others.

Another author who flirted with freedoms was the prolific Alexandre Hardy of the early seventeenth century, France's first professional playwright, whose enormous output included examples of tragedy, tragicomedy, and pastoral. In the first category, he drew his material from Plutarch, Xenophon, and Flavius Juseppus: *Didon se sacrifiant* (1603), *La Mort d'Achille* (wr. 1605, pb. 1625), *Coriolan* (wr. c. 1605, pb. 1625), and more, some of which remind one of Elizabethan drama, which he did not know but which did not hesitate to use multiple staging or frequent scene changes or to put aside the unities of time and place. His verve did not make up for his lack of dramatic power, but at least his romantic irregularities removed him from the sterilities of Jodelle and Garnier. Yet the drama of romance led to no florescence, and Cardinal Richelieu appointed a commission of five poets, one the well-known Rotrou (whom Voltaire praised as the founder of the French theater), to establish a disciplined, classical drama. Cervantes would have applauded. Rotrou himself catered to the prevailing taste for linear simplicity, as his Sophoclean-Senecan *Antigone* (pr. 1637) or his celebrated *Bélisaire* (pr. 1643) proved sufficiently for him to have been referred to as the unwitting herald of Racine.

Many followed the new guidelines, albeit with numerous solo declamations that held back the action: Mairet with his *Sophonisbe*, the first French tragedy based on the rules, and with his *Marc-Antoine: Ou, La Mort de Cléopâtre* (pr. 1635); Tristan L'Hermite with his *La Mariane* (pr. 1636; English translation, 1856); Georges de Scudéry, who wrote in various modes, though his *La Mort de César* (pr. 1635) and *Didon* (pr. 1636) are better known among the tragedies; Cyrano de Bergerac with his "libertine" *La Mort d'Agrippine* (pb. 1653); the precious Philippe

Quinault, popular among gallant audiences, with his *Stratonice* (pb. 1660), among other tragedies; Théophile de Viau with his tragic *Pyrame et Thisbé* (pr. 1617); and Corneille, whose *Médée* (pr. 1635) preceded by two years the notorious *Le Cid*, which respects the rules but whose bold, romantic undertones, happy ending, and multiplicity of incidents strained verisimilitude and gave rise to heated debates that eventually involved the Académie Française and Chapelain. His liberties aside, Corneille then became the first great name to become associated with the return to a less fanciful and more rigid dramatic construction (*Horace*, pr. 1640; *Cinna: Ou, La Clémence d'Auguste*, pr. 1640; *Polyeucte*, pr. 1642; *Sophonisbe*, pr. 1663), and from him the step to the master of Port Royal was brief. Richelieu's judgment proved correct for France: "instead of an irregular Shakespeare, France was to have a most regular Racine." In many ways, *Andromaque* (pr. 1667, pb. 1668), *Britannicus* (pr. 1669, pb. 1670), *Bérénice* (pr. 1670), *Iphigénie* (pr. 1674), the brilliant *Phèdre* (pr. 1677), and other tragedies may be considered a fulfillment of the finest dreams of the Italian rhetoricians of the Cinquecento. Indeed, in the long run Racine represents for the whole of Europe the only classical dramatist of luminary stature.

The Italian and French attempts at departure from the fixed norms were fully realized in England (and Spain). Although the French wrote in Alexandrines, the English preferred blank verse. Beginning with Sackville and Norton's didactic *Gorboduc* and on through pre-middle-class realistic dramas such as Thomas Middleton and Thomas Dekker's *The Honest Whore, Part I* (pr. 1604) or Thomas Heywood's *A Woman Killed with Kindness* (pr. 1603) or bloody Elizabethan pieces such as Kyd's *The Spanish Tragedy* (pr. 1585-1589), to the gory bombast of Jacobean and Caroline tragedies in the seventeenth century, disregard for classical tenets produced, if not always a decorous and cogent theater, at least a lively and pulsating series of works that the crowds, on all levels, enjoyed passionately. Regular tragedy, such as Buchanan's attempts to revive the drama of antiquity, *Jephthes, sive votum* (pr. 1554) and *Baptistes* (pr. 1539), or Legge's Latin *Richardus Tertius*, seemed too tame or esoteric; the humanist impulse had little to communicate.

Some of the playwrights who imitated classical models left their works anonymous, perhaps because of their being shaped by preexisting subject matter: *Arden of Feversham* (pb. 1592), for example, or *A Yorkshire Tragedy* (pb. 1608), or *Two Lamentable Tragedies* (pb. 1601). During the Jacobean frenzy, it might have been foreseeable that to return to the classical rules would have invited instant failure, as happened with Jonson's *Sejanus His Fall* (pr. 1603) and his *Catiline His Conspiracy* (pr. 1611). Attempts at revival in the eighteenth century were equally doomed: Joseph Addison's *Cato* in 1713 or Samuel Johnson's *Irene* in 1749 fared no better than Agustín de Montiano y Luyando's *Virginia* (pb. 1750), Nicolás Fernández de Moratín's *La Hormesinda* in 1770, Johann Christoph Gottsched's *Der sterbende Cato* in 1732, Voltaire's *Zaïre* (pr. 1732; English translation, 1736), or Crébillon's *Rhadamiste et Zénobie* (pr. 1711); only Pietro Metastasio's work stands out in retrospect—see his *La clemenza di Tito* of 1734—but his lyric genius was to find its way into opera.

What the public wanted was something with sweeping fantasy and bloody action in the manner of Seneca; often the name of Machiavelli, however improperly, was invoked, if not the character himself, as in the case of the introducer of Marlowe's *The Jew of Malta* (pr. c. 1589). Before one of his plays, Thomas Nashe admonishes his audience to ready its ears and tears, for he has never presented something so tragic: hence Elizabethan drama, full of tragic terror, vengeance, dreams and the supernatural, ghosts, and the ineluctability of destiny. Giraldi Cinthio's "Machiavellian" character Acaristo in *Euphimia* (pr. 1554) would have coincided with English popular taste and in a sense turned up in Marlowe's sanguinary Tamburlaine and in so many historical dramas during the reigns of King James I and King Charles I. These dramas were more "Senecan"—and freer. For Seneca also influenced versification, declamation, and the art of repartee, to which were added the coexistence of tragic and comic elements and the mixture of noble and common language, depending on the characters.

English Renaissance theater wisely gave up the academic, humanistic fixations on the unities in favor of multiple scenes, extended time spans, and parallel plots. Older, medieval traditions were revived, and the judge of success was the people—the crowd for which Lope de Vega wrote and that glorified Shakespeare. Romantic practice created strong aesthetic similarities between Spanish and English theater; indeed, on grounds of techniques, Lope de Vega and the Bard of Stratford have often been the subject of comparisons, though the latter unifies idea and execution while the former falls short in execution.

Even the anonymous playwrights who aped classical conventions were never so servile in their imitation as on the Continent. Libertine themselves, the tavern writers had adopted an unrestricted aesthetic. The garrulous Marlowe was one of them: His *Tamburlaine the Great* (pr. 1587), *Doctor Faustus* (pr. c. 1588), *The Jew of Malta*, and *Edward II* (pr. c. 1592) capitalize on horror and grotesqueness, fantasy and sensation, but at the same time they give flexibility to blank verse and striking plasticity to the protagonists, who emerge with compelling vividness. Robert Greene, a writer of romances, was another (*Orlando furioso*, pr. c. 1588; *Friar Bacon and Friar Bungay*, pr. 1589; and *James IV*, pr. c. 1591), and still another was Kyd. Uneven as their works are, their worth can be measured by how they paved the way for William Shakespeare, for the author of *Hamlet, Prince of Denmark* (pr. 1600-1601), *King Lear* (pr. c. 1605-1606), and *Macbeth* (pr. 1606) did not burst onto the Elizabethan scene out of nowhere. He was, rather, the culmination of a literary and cultural process that owed much to the time's moralistic-philosophico-medieval background and to such figures as Marlowe, Greene, Kyd, Garnier, Giraldi Cinthio, Speroni, and Seneca. Still, his brilliance and mastery left all of them far behind. As in classical drama, his characters are great princes, caught in the throes of fortune's instability and in a struggle with their own weaknesses, vices, and flaws, in a world dominated by undeterminable forces and by the eternal conflict between good and evil. Yet he is an author who defies categorization simply because he is Shakespeare.

The romantic urge was cultivated during Shakespeare's time and was continued after him by many playwrights who combined the tragic mode with historical orientations, so that in a sense they produced a form of historical drama—only in a sense, however, because their focus was on effect rather than on history. Strident ironies, frenzied action, grisly passions, and dismaying outbursts characterize the works of Jacobean and Caroline dramatists. George Chapman's *Bussy d'Ambois* (pr. 1604, pb. 1607), Philip Massinger's *The Roman Actor* (pr. 1626, pb. 1629), Thomas Middleton and William Rowley's *The Changeling* (pr. 1622), Beaumont and Fletcher's *The Maid's Tragedy* (pr. c. 1611), *The Duchess of Malfi* (pr. 1614) by John Webster, *The Revenger's Tragedy* (pr. c. 1606) by Cyril Tourneur, *'Tis Pity She's a Whore* (pr. c. 1629) by John Ford, *The Traitor* (pr. 1631) by James Shirley, and *The Cruell Brother* (pr. 1627) by Sir William Davenant are but a few examples of a colorful chain of productions that, with greater or lesser merit, catered to splenetic rhetoric and degenerate sensationalism.

Despite their reverence for the Italians in matters of theory, drama, or poetics in general, the Spanish did not make a serious effort at classical tragedy. "Rules," exclaimed Lope de Vega, "are an excellent thing, but when I write I lock them in a drawer with three turns of the key." At least in theory, Cervantes disagreed and deemed it correct that Lope de Vega should be regarded in Italy and France as an ignorant barbarian. Yet all Cervantes could put together was the unimpressive *El cerco de Numancia*, acclaimed by Friedrich Schlegel for its supposed "Aeschylean grandeur" and by Shelley for the way it arouses pity and wonder, though not for its poetry.

On the Iberian peninsula, Renaissance drama, while not qualifying as tragedy, strikes a tragic note variously in all those plays that, as in England, border on or draw their intitial inspiration from historical and biographical circumstances. Portugal's *A Castro* (pr. 1553-1556; *Ignez de Castro*, 1825) by António Ferreira stands out, and in Spain, one must always turn to Lope de Vega. Some of his darker works are "tragedies," such as *El castigo sin venganza* (pb. 1635; *Justice Without Revenge*, 1936)—again, as in

Massinger and Middleton, with melodramatic sensationalism and somber versification. Love rules at the center of most of his plays, while with Calderón, it is honor that draws attention and dominates the "tragic" atmosphere. This atmosphere lacks the universal, human currents of Lope de Vega but makes up for them in philosophical depth and with a sense of literary theory, in more craftsmanlike form. If *El alcalde de Zalamea* (pb. c. 1640) demonstrates some of the instinctive vigor that made Lope de Vega appeal to his general audiences, Calderón's masterpiece, *La vida es sueño* (pr. 1635; *Life Is a Dream*, 1830), reveals the agile, metaphysical conceptualization that played to a more limited, thinking, and aristocratic audience. In between, with semihumanist awareness, one may place the biblical *Los cabellos de Absalón* (wr. c. 1634, pb. 1684; *The Crown of Absalom*, 1993) and *Las armas de la hermosura* (wr. 1652), the latter on the theme of Coriolanus. Yet on the whole, and again with an author as diversified as Calderón, who deals with equal ease in religion, philosophy, gallantry, cloak and dagger, passion, and honor, one must speak less in terms of categories or modes than in terms of individuals. For Lope de Vega and Calderón rise above classifications; ultimately they wrote independent Reniassance drama, the kind that grew out of the period's romantic spirit. Spanish theatrical production was fantastic and turbulent, quite removed from Greco-Latin disciplined simplicity and equilibrium. There is melodrama and prolixity, pomp and oratory, the results of a romantic spirit often carried a bit too far. Yet in its finest moments—as in England, few, despite the enormous range of dramatic productivity—it made a superb contribution to Renaissance drama through its richness, energy, and unrestrained individuality, as well as through its sense of proud independence.

INDIVIDUALITY IN SPANISH RENAISSANCE DRAMA

Most of the time, the individuality of Spanish writers is such as to remove some plays from under any kind of heading. A good example is Tirso de Molina's *El burlador de Sevilla* (wr. c. 1625; *The Trickster of Seville*, 1923), whose licentious trickster, a dispassionate and impenitent seeker of erotic adventures, finally meets with retribution and is plunged into Hell; the story of Don Juan Tenorio is elevated from a simple morality to a heroic tragedy by those (Molière, Lorenzo da Ponte, Wolfgang Amadeus Mozart, Christian Dietrich Grabbe, George Gordon, Lord Byron, Alexander Pushkin, Francisco de Rojas Zorrilla) who converted it from a comedy ending in moral justice to a metaphysical drama with tragic implications. Lope de Vega wrote many pieces that fit this unclassifiable grouping, such as Molina's *La villana de Vallecas* (pr. 1620) with its pathetic tale of a ravished maiden who sets out to discover her seducer and does, *La bella mal maridada* (pb. 1609) with its untypical intermingling of love and money, *El villano en su rincón* (pb. 1617; *The King and the Farmer*, 1940) with its philosophical switch of authority between peasant and king, and *La Dorotea* (pb. 1632; English translation, 1985) with its autobiographical and psychological manner. The list could be expanded.

The point with Lope de Vega is always his inventiveness that refuses labels: religious, historical, tragicomic, adventurous, love comedy, honor drama, character comedy, symbolic drama—*The Sheep Well*, *El perro del hortelano* (pb. 1618; *The Gardener's Dog*, 1903), *Los trabajos de Jacob* (pb. 1635)—he is all these things individually and at once, rapid, facile, nimble, and occasionally penetrating, and always retaining an engaging kind of medieval ingenuousness. If he is to be labeled, it must be in the category of "independent." Juan Ruiz de Alarcón y Mendoza's noted *La verdad sospechosa* (pb. 1630) would belong to this group, too, with its unconventional twisting of truth and reality, or his *Ganar amigos* (pr. 1621), an edifying story of friendship. Calderón also contributed to this list of works: There is the notion of purity in *El mágico prodigioso*, the rabid sense of justice in *El alcalde de Zalamea* (pr. 1643; *The Mayor of Zalamea*, 1853; not to be confused with Lope de Vega's play), the peculiar honor and social code in *El médico de su honra* (pb. 1637; *The Surgeon of His Honor*, 1853), and more.

Neither tragic nor comic, not tragedies or comedies or historical dramas, these individualistic plays exist on their own by virtue of the free creativity of their authors; they benefit from no established norms of a genre and enjoy an easy independence in that they invite no comparisons. Mainly Renaissance Spain produced them. Though with a substantial overlay of sensational flair, their underlying spirit may be detected in England, too, in the early pages of the chivalric *Clyomon and Clamydes* (anonymous, c. 1570) as well as in the later pages of Massinger, such as *The Virgin Martyr* (pr. c. 1620) or *The Unnatural Combat* (pr. c. 1621), of Middleton in *The Witch* (pr. c. 1610) or in *Women Beware Women* (pr. c. 1621-1627), in Ford's *The Broken Heart* (pr. c. 1627-1631), in Webster's *The White Devil* (pr. c. 1610), and others of that theatrically dark generation of Jacobeans and Carolines. Dekker's *Westward Ho!* (pr. 1604) and *The Roaring Girl* (pr. c. 1610) and Thomas Heywood's *The English Traveler* (pr. c. 1627) were more subdued, and by the same token less colorful and vibrant than were the plays of the Spaniards.

HISTORICAL DRAMA

Renaissance consciousness of the here and now focused attention on history—recent history—as a worthy topic for drama. The overlap with tragedy is obvious, and often a distinction between the two is unwise and unproductive. Shakespeare aside, a noncontemporary subject such as Julius Caesar, Cinna, Mithradates, Saul, or even Bajazet generally was treated with the full decorum of classical rules, while the chronologically more modern material dealing with a King John or a Charles V received the benefit of the independent, romantic style. So it came to be that "historical drama [was] offered in the great manner of tragedy." The humanists accordingly set their sights on ancient subjects. A strict humanist such as Pomponio Leto could not register enthusiasm for Carlo Verardi's *Historia Baetica* (1492), an account of Granada's recent liberation from the Moors, even if it was written in Latin. The normal fare of Italian "historicized" *teatro erudito* included Giraldi Cinthio's *Cleopatra* (pr. 1555) or *Arrenopia*, Rucellai's *Oreste* (pr. 1514), Aretino's *La Orazia*, and the like—a far cry from what Shakespeare and Lope de Vega meant by history. The rules inhibited the varied emotions and complex designs of historical

events. In the seventeenth century, the Dutch managed to impose Aristotelian rules on more modern, national subjects, if one takes into account Hooft's *Geeraerd van Velsen* (1613) or van den Vondel's patriotic *Gijsbrecht van Aemstel* (1637), which formally opened Amsterdam's Schouwburg theater.

John Bale, in England, dug into national history for his *King Johan*, and with the appearance of Raphael Holinshed's *Chronicles of England, Scotland, and Ireland* (1577) a whole generation and more of playwrights indulged in the luxury of readied material, as inviting, diversified, and exciting as could be furnished anywhere. The English, Shakespeare included, need not have searched elsewhere for their historical dramas. There was Marlowe's Edward II and Shakespeare's Richards II and III, John, Henrys IV, V, VI, and, with Fletcher, Henry VIII. If history deals with power, then tragedy deals with destiny: The two elements combined in Shakespeare to give the Renaissance its most passionate historical tragedies, complete with rises and falls, ambitions, murders, and retributions.

On the Continent, the French and Italians did little with this nonhumanist genre. Every now and then a Frenchman courteously turned to English history— Gautier de Costes de la Calprenède's *Jeanne, Royne d'Angleterre* (1638)—just as the English had made their gesture toward France—Chapman's *Chabot, Admiral of France* (1635)—but the productions, however in vogue (especially in France), left little mark. Spain, on the other hand, had more to offer, more naturally attuned as it was to the romantic cape and sword possibilities lying at the heart of most historical developments and waiting to be discovered. Bartolomé de Torres Naharro fathered the cloak-and-dagger intrigue, and Lope de Vega even used it in his comedies, which then established themselves as a representative genre. In his quest for historical realism, Lope de Vega once went so far as to adopt antiquated speech, in *Las famosas asturianas* (pb. 1623). It would seem that anywhere he found history he found a play, not hesitating to alter facts liberally, whether they concerned the burning of Rome (*Roma abrasada*, pb. 1625), Verona's Montagues and Capulets (*Castelvines y Monteses*, pb. 1647), or the tribulations of Boris Godunov (*El gran duque de Moscovia y Emperador perseguido*, pb. 1617). Those who followed Lope de Vega's historical vein, too, had considerable influence, such as Diego Jiménez de Enciso: *La mayor hazaña de Carlos V*, concerning the need for Charles to honor the Lord and encouraging by its example contemporary even more than recent history; *El Príncipe Don Carlos*, in which the author sides with Philip II, and which is an adumbration of Thomas Otway's, Friedrich Schiller's, and Vittorio Alfieri's subjects; *Los Médicis de Florencia*, the Lorenzaccio story that would reappear in Alexandre Dumas, *père*, Alfred de Musset, Sem Benelli, and Guillén de Castro y Bellvís's *Las mocedades des Cid* (1618; the story later adopted by Corneille). The vogue of history onstage, particularly as stoked by the vivid productions of Renaissance England and Spain, has not disappeared, for to this day the genre remains very popular.

THE PASTORAL

Along with tragedy and comedy, the pastoral, informally improvised or formally composed, occupied Italian palace courtyards, aristocratic halls, and theater stages, then those of other countries, from the 1500's through the seventeenth century. Before historical and independent dramas of the romantic variety came into fashion, shepherds and shepherdesses, fauns, satyrs, and nymphs captured the attention of a public tired of the insipid diet of learned tragedies and comedies. Painters such as Sandro Botticelli and Lorenzo Lotto delighted in this kind of pagan vision. Onstage, expressions of unrequited love poured out to confidants; tirades of pride and sorrow, of pain and rejection; and long confessional soliloquies tested an actor's diction and, as in an operatic aria, his sense of musical balance. In fact, musical accompaniment became a natural attribute of these productions. Totally classical in background but romantic in sentiment, the pastoral fable seemed to build idyllically on echoes of Greco-Roman eclogues, the Dante of the *La vita nuova* (c. 1292), and the Petrarch of the *Canzoniere* (1470) and to correspond to the cultured public's desire for evasion, an artificial escape into a naturalistic world of pure feeling, the opposite of the

one presented to them by all other forms of drama. It portrayed an Elysium of tears and rapture.

The pastoral perfected the art of dramatic speech in the context of sentimental charm and delicacy as, for their own didactic purposes, school and Jesuit theater were also doing, though less self-consciously. In Serlio's *Sette libri dell'architettura*, one reads of the needed setting for such *scene satiriche*: trees, grottoes, rivulets, arbors, rocks, laurel bushes, an occasional spring, and flowers. Nature, in all its beauty and coolness, reigned. Sometimes the genre's purity was contaminated by foreign elements tending to drag it toward tragedy through too weighty an emphasis on despair, or even toward comedy through amusing episodes, including a droll use of dialects, as in the work of one of the Cinquecento's most famous actors, Andrea Colmo: *Giocose, moderne e facetissime egloche pastorali* (date unknown). There was, too, the earthy influence in Ferrara of Angelo Beolco, who introduced Paduan peasant dialogue in *La pastorale* (1517-1518) and *La Moschetta* (1528), though the latter is really a regular comedy. By and large, however, the pastoral held to center and represents a respected contribution to Renaissance drama. If it veered anywhere, it veered toward melodrama. (As antecedents, the *intermezzi* were often musical, and sometimes tragedy was given musical injections, to adhere more closely to the manner of the ancients — as in the case of the music composed by Claudio Merulo in Venice in 1574.)

Clearly, Poliziano's *Orfeo*, written for the festivities surrounding the double betrothal of Clara Gonzaga with Gilbert Montpensier and Prince Francesco with Isabella d'Este in Mantua, hovers in the background of the pastoral mode. The bucolic mood of Matteo Boiardo's eclogues and Ariosto's stanzas also had much to do conceptually with the pastoral's development. To Agostino Beccari is attributed the first true pastoral, *Il sacrifizio* (1554), and among the many works that followed, one must note *L'amoroso sdegno* (1597) by Francesco Bracciolini. The masterpiece of the genre was the poetic realization by Torquato Tasso, *Aminta* (pr. 1573; English translation, 1591), for the rest of Europe the model pastoral play, written for the Este family and acted by nobles together with Gelosi professionals. Beautifully fashioned and effusive descriptions reveal character (events are not shown but related), happy expectation shifts to catastrophe and then reverts to a good ending for Aminta and the nymph Silvia, and a chorus intervenes to moralize on the action.

Tasso's successor in Ferrara was Battista Guarini, with whom the Italian pastoral is said to end, for he left simplicity aside and created a complex plot, laced with jealousies and intrigues before Mirtillo wins the beautiful Amarilli. Broadly and disproportionately constructed, verbose but moving, with three plots, a score of characters, and four choruses, *Il pastor fido* (1590; *The Faithful Shepherd*, 1602) thrilled all Europe with its romantic flair the way *Aminta* had elicited admiration with its classical (though somewhat long-winded) containment.

With such examples to lend it both dignity and popularity, the pastoral fable established itself internationally. Most compositions, however, did not match up to those of Tasso or Guarini. The Marquis de Racan, in France, composed a romantic *Les Bergeries* (1619). In Spain, Encina, who liked mythological constructions and rural settings, had his *Égloga triunfo del amor* produced in 1497 at the wedding celebration of Juan de Castilla and Margarete of Austria, and his agitated *Égloga de Plácida y Vitoriano* at Cardinal Arborea's palace in Rome in 1513. Lope de Vega contributed several works, such as *La selva sin amor* (pb. 1629). Vicente gave Portugal a pastoralized *auto* in which the goddess wears the costume of a shepherdess: *Auto da la fama* (pr. 1510), just as Lope de Rueda used shepherds' wear when portraying rustic life. In the seventeenth century, in Germany, one might point to Nuremberg's Georg Philipp Harsdörffer's praise of urban artisans by the Peguitz River, *Pegnesisches Schäfergedicht* (1644), and in neighboring Netherlands to Hooft's Guarini-inspired *Granida* (pb. 1615). Even if they served occasional interests, the genre of lovelorn shepherds spread.

In England, the land that cultivated startling historical dramas, the need for artificial escape was also felt. George Peele was a master of allegorical pastoral: In one, *The Arraignment of Paris* (pr. c. 1584),

the golden pome winds up in the hands of Queen Elizabeth, "our fayre Eliza." It was up to Shakespeare, however—and not surprisingly—to convert the genre into a realization of its best potential as it had existed germinally in Poliziano. Though it contains ironic, antipastoral utterances (by Rosalind) and the idyllic forest is, in the Duke's words, a "painted pomp," *As You Like It* (pr. c. 1599-1600) acquires meaning through the pastoral prism; the leafy greenwood may be rejected ultimately, but not sufficiently not to remain a dream, the kind that permeates that ultrapastoral, *A Midsummer Night's Dream* (pr. c. 1595-1596), with its hypnotic, melodic patterns.

The intent of pastoral was not plot, but the poetic beauty of declamation, the enchanting musicality that fascinated even the public at large. This was *recitar cantando*, as Emilio del Cavaliere put it in his preface to his lyric work *Rappresentazione di Anima et di Corpo* (pr. 1600). The overt or covert "melody" inherent in its aesthetic led a group of Florentines (the Camerata Fiorentina) under Giovanni Bardi, count of Vernio—Vincenzo Galilei, Giulio Caccini, Jacopo Peri, Ottavio Rinuccini—to think in terms of melodrama, or opera. Peri's *Dafne* (pr. 1598, libretto by Rinuccini) became the first opera, followed by his *Euridice* (pr. 1600) and by Caccini's *Il Rapimento di Cefalo* (pr. 1600). The same mythological element evident in pastoral drama dominated, and it was not long before this lyric progeny produced its greatest exponent, Claudio Monteverdi, the genius of musical drama. With this new development, too, one must credit the Renaissance.

TRAGICOMEDY

The term "tragicomedy" is used for lack of a better one, since in point of fact tragicomedy is basically what has been associated with Spanish "independent" drama. The latter ranges in all directions, as the material dictates; tragicomedy refers more limitedly to the mixture of both tragic and comic elements in a play, simultaneously or successively, to the ambivalent mood created by such a mixture, by unhappy scenes punctuated by humorous relief or vice versa. It ranges from something like Raffaello Borghini's amalgamation of valences of the Romeo and

Juliet story in *La donna costante* (1582) to John Lyly's genteel softening of tragic and comic scenes in *Campaspe* (pr. 1584), described by the author as "a tragical Comedie." Eventually, it gets subsumed, thanks to the Shakespearean impetus, in Victor Hugo's dramatic decree of a mélange of "the sublime and the grotesque," in the preface to *Cromwell* (pb. 1827; English translation, 1896). Although tragedy, comedy, and pastoral, especially the latter, all exhibited this combination of ingredients at times, Renaissance humanists devoted much more attention to the purer modes. Others tended to discard the genre, if one goes by the printer of Beaumont and Fletcher's *The Woman Hater* (pr. c. 1606), which he "dare not call Comedy or Tragedy; 'tis perfectly neither; a Play it is."

In their free aesthetic, the Spaniards fell naturally into the tragicomic pattern. Though, like Goethe's *Faust: Eine Tragödie* (pr. 1829; *The Tragedy of Faust*, 1823), not a performable play, Fernando de Rojas's *Comedia de Calisto y Melibea* (1499, rev. ed. 1502 as *Tragicomedia de Calisto y Melibea*; commonly known as *La Celestina*; *Celestina*, 1631) probably set the tone, given its enormous influence. In its lineage appears Lope de Vega, whose tendency toward writing "true-to-life" comedy of manners and whose sense of proletarian concerns favored "hybrid" exposés, making the most of special characters such as the *gracioso*, or clown. More than that, he used plot in surprising ways, to convert a tragic atmosphere into something more bearable, even provoking smiles—an inconsistency that might have raised Castelvetro's or Trissino's eyebrows but which lies at the core of tragicomedy. A case in point is *Lo cierto por lo dudoso* (wr. 1612-1624; *A Certainty for a Doubt*, 1936), as disaster-bound as Shakespeare's *Measure for Measure* (pr. 1604).

Less congenial to the classical trend in France, tragicomedy still made a number of approximate appearances in that country: Before Molière's *Dom Garcie de Navarre: Ou, Le Prince jaloux* (pr. 1661; *Don Garcia of Navarre: Or, The Jealous Prince*, 1714), there was Corneille's *Don Sanche d'Aragon* (pr. 1649; *The Conflict*, 1798), though he thought it better to call it a *comédie héroïque*, and *Nicomède*

(pr. 1651; English translation, 1671); Garnier's Ariosto-based Bradamante, which attempts to give classical form romantic treatment; a number of works by Rotrou and Isaac de Benserade, who strike a balance; and many plays by Hardy, whose enterprising dare places him strictly in the romantic camp. The latter was irregular enough to have become Shakespeare, it is said, had he possessed the genius. While mixing the sublime and grotesque generally in all of his works, Shakespeare had his hand in genuine tragicomedies also, plays that overlap conspicuously with the "independent" Spanish production: *Cymbeline*, which reverses the atmosphere of *King Lear*, and *The Winter's Tale* (pr. c. 1610-1611), which does the same for *Othello, the Moor of Venice*, are, one might say, works penned by a tragedian who aims at a happy ending, while *The Tempest* leaves one with a sense of comedy written by a solemn philosopher.

COMEDY

In his prologue to *La Lena* (pr. 1528; *Lena*, 1975), Ariosto derides those who would attempt to be original on grounds previously trod by Athens and Rome, for "the ancients knew much more [about comedy, in this case] and every other science." Inhibited by such a mentality in a way that popular comedy—culminating in the *commedia dell'arte*—was not, Italian *commedia erudita* stuck to the rules like tragedy, and like tragedy the New Attic Comedy (for Plautus and Terence adopted the themes of Greek New Comedy) produced much of influence though for its bulk little of lasting value. It focused on love and had many *dialoghi d'amore* to dip into for material, but it left unrequited love for the pastoral, while it itself concentrated on obstacled love, like that of the honest youths who cannot get together because an older person also claims to be in love. Comedy laughed not at the suffering lovelorn but at the gross conflict of generations. The scheme set into motion by Menander and ably varied by Plautus and Terence was always good for a laugh, and the Italians handled it deftly enough, despite the rules, to give their humanist comedy more vitality than their *tragedia erudita*; in fact, at least three-quarters of European Renaissance comedy turned out to be adaptations of

Italian Cinquecento pieces. After Shakespeare, the greatest authors of the seventeenth century who gave the West a "new comedy"—Molière, Jonson, Lope de Vega—were disciples of the Cinquecento, directly or indirectly.

Comedy began early in Italy; in the Trecento, Petrarch supposedly wrote two, now lost. The Quattrocento witnessed mainly productions of classical plays, in the original (Aristophanes' *Ploutos*, 388 B.C.E .; *Plutus*, 1651) was done in Greek) or in translation, frequently in Ferrara for the Este family on special occasions (such as the wedding of Alfonso d'Este and Lucrezia Borgia): Plautus's *Menaechmi* in 1486, Terence's *Andria* (166 B.C.E.; English translation, 1598) in 1491, *Eunuchus* (161 B.C.E.; *The Eunuch*, 1598) in 1499; then in the next century, Terence's *Adelphoe* (160 B.C.E.; *The Brothers*, 1598) in Mantua in 1501 for the Gonzagas and Plautus's *Amphitruo* (*Amphitryon*, 1694) and *Casina* (English translation, 1774).

Then came the master of fantasy, Ludovico Ariosto, who paradoxically chose to be limited by the classical rules and, unlike Machiavelli and Molière, had difficulty with the constraints. Nevertheless, he gave us the first modern comedy, *La cassaria* (pr. 1508; *The Coffer*, 1975), in a vernacular. Tito Livio Frulovisi had written a series of Plautine-romantic plays in 1432-1434, again in Ferrara, and a young Alberti wrote a regular humanist comedy in Latin in 1426, *Philodoxeos*. In the next century and farther north, Ariosto followed with several livelier, more mature plays—*I suppositi* (pr. 1509; *The Pretenders*, 1566; used by Shakespeare for *The Taming of the Shrew*, pr. c. 1593-1594), *Il negromante* (wr. 1520; *The Necromancer*, 1975; adumbrating Jonson), and *La Lena* (fixing for the Renaissance the Old Man character and the theme of domestic corruption). Crisply written satires of modern life, they do not strangle in their Latinate fetters, though the whole course of Italian comedy might have changed if Ariosto had broken them. Still, although they lacked vigor, they launched a new fashion. Cardinal Bibbiena joined it early, with his Plautine story of twins, *La Calandria*, used in 1548 for Henry II and Catherine de' Medici, again a vivid document of sixteenth

century life. Yet the masterwork of Italian Renaissance comedy remains Machiavelli's Boccaccian *The Mandrake*—so different from his tamely Plautine *La Clizia* (1525; *Clizia*, 1961)—whose ingenious boldness and wit proved that the rules need not become obstacles. It did more. Its humorous turpitude and deceit created a distinct polarity between comic and sacred drama and gave comedy, beneath its hilarity, a palpable substratum of tragedy. After Machiavelli, audiences have a right to chill at the humor of *Measure for Measure*, *Volpone: Or, The Fox* (pr. 1605), and *Tartuffe: Ou, L'Imposteur* (pr. 1664; *Tartuffe*, 1732).

If the Old Comedy of Aristophanes was provocatively critical, without a softening of the edges as Jonson and Molière could provide, then Aretino's plays, by virtue of their sheer acrimony, fall into the Aristophanic pattern with the bitter attack on the Curia in *La cortigiana* (pb. 1534; *The Courtesan*, 1926); the unsavory practical joking of *Il marescalco* (pb. 1533; *The Marescalco*, 1986), with its valuable enumeration of the types that people the world of comedy—the Pander, the Parasite, the bombastic Officer, the Miser, and so on); the satiric forerunner of *Tartuffe, Lo ipocrito* (pb. 1540), which introduced a new character, the hypocrite; and the obsession-crazed *Il filosofo* (pb. 1546). A free spirit, Aretino was less subject to the intellectual preciosities of humanism and thereby opened the comic tradition to romantic creativeness. Old and young, males and females, nobles and plebeians, clergy and citizens, learned and dumb—all humankind is diseased for this "Scourge of Princes," as the author referred to himself. The Spanish Bartolomé de Torres Naharro thought along similar lines when he penned his hard, satiric critique of cardinals' machinations in their official hall, or *tinelo*, with *Comedia tinellaria* (pr. 1516; *The Buttery*, 1964). "What makes you laugh here," he commented, "you may punish at home."

All Renaissance comedy is a satire of contemporary life or of humankind's eternal foibles. Ariosto saw the humor, Machiavelli suggested the tragedy, and Aretino proclaimed the bitterness with hilarious inventiveness. The other authors, in Italy and in other lands, from Tirso de Molina to Corneille and from Pierre de Larivey to Lope de Rueda, used these qualities in combination, to which Jonson added the need to view life morally. Enea Silvio Piccolomini's *Chrysis* (1444), like Alessandro Piccolomini's *L'amore costante* (pr. 1536), or Giordano Bruno's attack on alchemy and real attempt to break away from the rules, *Il candelaio* (pb. 1582), appears flaccid by comparison with the Machiavellian masterpiece. In the same category are Giambattista Della Porta's many works: the disguise play, *La Cintia* (pb. 1592), the fake astrologer play, *L'astrologo* (wr. 1570; *The Astrologer*, 1615), and the romantic plays, *I due fratelli rivali* (pb. 1601; *The Two Rival Brothers*, 1980), *La furiosa* (pb. 1600), and *Il moro* (pb. 1607). Many of these plays were refashioned across the Alps: for example, Rotrou's *Célie: Ou, Le Vice-roi de Naples* (pr. 1644) and Tristan L'Hermite's *Le Parasite* (pr. 1653).

These plays were lively here and there, provocative here and there, at times satiric or spoofing, even angry, always colorful (by situation, character, or language), and never truly brilliant, though Della Porta's works come close. The fare is abundant, often repetitious (the miser type, for example, recurs even in Yugoslavia, when in the middle of the sixteenth century Yugoslav theater mirrored the morals of the day, in Marin Držić's character comedy *Dundo Maroje* in 1551), though the individual works are saved by a striking portrait, a new twist, a hilarious scene, or an exploding social comment. Girolamo Razzi's pre-Romantic *La Gostanza*, as an example (pr. 1564, Pierre de Larivey's *La Constance*, pb. 1611) brought forth an unusual and courageous expression of one's feelings resulting in generosity and sacrifice—an unexpected departure from the norm.

The prolific production list of comedies in Italy can include Luigi Alamanni's *Flora* (1548), Giambattista Gelli's Boccaccian *L'errore* (1550), Agostino Ricchi's *I tre tiranni* (1530), and Agnolo Firenzuola's *I Lucidi* (1549), conceived from the ancients yet built around ordinary people; the latter two deal with the all too frequent elderly lovers. Perhaps, as in the last example, the more interesting devices employed dealt with language or the infection of popular elements: the use of folk speech and everyday proverbs (Salviati,

Il granchio, pr. 1566), of folk material (Francesco d'Ambra, *I Bernardi*, 1547), and of rustic motifs (Gigio Artemio Giancarli, *La capraria*, 1545, though of classical inspiration, and *La zingara*, 1545, with Venetian, Bergamese, and modern Greek). The most successful of these playwrights, as a result of a classical and romantic admixture and a more liberated aesthetic, which allowed the author to deal realistically with rustic love, was Beolco, known as Il Ruzzante. He mingled the Rome of Plautus with the countryside of Padua, farce with comedy on an earthy level: *Anconitana* (pr. 1522), *Fiorina* (wr. 1529, pb. 1551), and others. With the aid of dialects (Paduan for Il Ruzzante), the path to popular comedy, as opposed to *commedia erudita*, was now paved.

With love at its core and humor as its goal, comedy engaged in raciness as a matter of course. Giovanni Boccaccio's salaciousness in *The Decameron: O, Prencipe Galetto* (1349-1351; *The Decameron*, 1620) rolled easily over onto the stage, where sex, in subtle or bawdy attire, ensured success. The success was generally cheap, unless a Machiavelli dignified it with philosophical stature, but it gave even bad comedy enormous vitality. Renaissance comedy would never die of enfeeblement. The sensual touch made Cecchi's *L'assiuolo* (pr. 1549) popular, like his *Gli incantesimi* (pr. 1550). The European stage was infected by it (it had the Plautine sanction, after all), down to its more unsuspecting wings—in the Netherlands, for example, where the morality tradition was still strong and where one could yet encounter a racily comic play such as Gerbrand Adriaensen Bredero's *De Spaansche Branander* in 1617. In his own spiceless way, Tirso de Molina's Don Juan, more a punished *burlador* than a fulfilled seducer, and more a seeker after material possession than after erotic challenge, still continues the lineage, though he does so by revealing the other side of the coin, without the same degree of titillating amusement. The same might be argued for *Celestina*.

In Portugal, learned comedy brought forth António Ferreira's *Bristo* (pr. 1552-1553; *The Comedy of Bristo: Or, The Pimp*, 1990) and *Cioso* (pr. 1554-1555; English translation, 1825) in the 1500's, as well as the Italianate *Os estrangeiros* (pr. 1526)

and *Os Vilhalpanos* (pr. 1538) by Francisco Sá de Miranda and Luís de Camões's Plautine *Os Enfatriöes* (pr. 1540) on the Amphitryon theme. An even greater assortment of works appeared in Spain, which showed a true genius for combining lyric, romantic, and tragicomic elements in "free" plays. Seminally, Rojas, who within two decades was translated into Italian, French, English, and German, led the way. Then followed a galaxy of talent. "The Great Lope de Rueda," as Cervantes called him, and whom Lope de Vega regarded as the founder of Spanish comedy, meaning of these "free" plays, ranged widely through the countryside with his band of vagabond actors to bring comedies and *pasos* (brief, bizarre, and lively intrigues, like *intermezzi*, enlivened in Rueda's case by his participation as author-actor) to the people; his own works derived largely from Italian sources—Boccaccio, Ranieri and Cecchi, and Giancarli—but not untypically the Spaniards often bettered their sources. Rueda's artistic origin was Italian, and Muzio (Girolamo Nuzio), the famous actor, had employed him in his company; but once he broke away from established scaffolding, his *pasos* in particular sparkled with picaresque delineations.

Another learned author, Bartolomé de Torres Naharro, lived in Rome under the protection of Cardinal Bernardino de Carvajal and Leo X and extolled the Latin classics, but he exercised his talent in the popular field, in lively character sketches, like Rueda, from daily reality, with a strong Erasmian flavor: for example, *Commedia soldadesca* (wr. 1510) for the military, though he also branched out into allegory with *Comedia Trophea* (pr. 1514), chivalry with *Comedia Seraphina* (wr. c. 1508, pb. 1517), love and honor (with the first appearance of the Spanish *pun d'honor*) in *Comedia Himenea* (pr. 1516; *Hymen*, 1903), and gentility with *Comedia Jacinta* (pr. c. 1509).

Lope de Vega Carpio again occupies a central position. Love hides and blossoms all around, and in the process social codes, normally prominent in his "independent" dramas and the tragedies of others, are twisted into merriment, with women often adventuring against respected convention. In Lope's wake one finds his friend and disciple, Juan Pérez de Montal-

bán, among others, as well as Castro, whose *La Fuerza de la costumbre* (pr. c. 1610) underlies John Fletcher's *Love's Cure* (pr. 1647). It is interesting to note how Lope de Vega could handle the theme of honor with due seriousness in his various dramatic modes, not omitting the comic, whereas Calderón's weightier temperament could not weave comedy around it as smoothly. Given a greater propensity, as in the *commedia dell'arte*, toward the creation of types (gallant, *dama*, old man, *gracioso*, servant, confidant), his concept of honor, so central to his plays, has led others to note ironically how easily the Calderónian ethic invites killing for the slightest reason as soon as it is violated.

The real author of the character play and its creator, however, was Juan Ruiz de Alarcón, whose *La verdad sospechosa* (pb. 1630; *The Truth Suspected*, 1927) nurtured Corneille's *Le Menteur* (pr. 1643; *The Liar*, 1671) in his own century and Goldoni's *Il bugiardo* (pr. 1750; *The Liar*, 1963) in the next. A good female study is that of Inés in Ruiz de Alarcón's *El examen de maridos* (pb. 1633). Such character creation, bordering on caricature but full of psychological humanity, was to become a hallmark of Molière and Jonson. The prolific production of these seventeenth century playwrights defies belief. Lope de Vega's creations range into the upper hundreds (470 extant); there are only about twenty by Ruiz de Alarcón. In this kaleidoscopic repertory, Cervantes's *El rufián dichoso* seems docile, though his acclaimed but lost *Comedia de la confusa* might fare better.

France assimilated the best of outside influences, although only with Molière did comedy attain—gloriously—its potential. It carried on translations actively (Jean Meschinot with Plautus's *Amphitryon* in 1500, Terence's *Andria* in 1537, de la Taille with Ariosto's *Il negromante* in 1573, and more). Yet France did more with original works: Grévin's *La Trésorière* (pr. 1559) and *Les Esbahis* (pr. 1561; *Taken by Surprise*, 1985), de la Taille's *Les Corrivaux* (1562), Baïf's *Le Brave* (pr. 1567), and during the golden seventeenth century, Quinault's noteworthy *La Comédie sans comédie* (1655), Racine's satire on lawyers *Les Plaideurs* (pr. 1668; *The Litigants*, 1715), and Corneille's *Mélite* (pr. 1630), *La*

Place royale: Ou, L'Amoureux extravagant (pr. 1634), his good character study *Le Menteur*, and his strangely genial Spanish-Shakespearean *L'Illusion comique* (pr. 1636), with its play-within-a-play, tragic parody, defense of theater, and general mood of romantic divertimento.

Italy and Spain, however, underlay much of the comedic production. Italian by origin, Larivey derived his inspiration from any number of transalpine sources, sometimes resorting to outright translations without even varying the title though claiming authorship: *La Veuve* (pb. 1579; *The Widow*, 1992, like Corneille's) from Giovanni Battista Cini *La vedova* (pr. 1569), *Les Jaloux* (1579) from Vincenzo Gabiani's *I gelosi* (pb. 1560), *Le Fidel* (pb. 1579) from Luigi Pasqualigo's *Il fedele* (pb. 1575), and other works relating later to Jean-François Regnard and Molière. Corneille's *Le Menteur*, as has been demonstrated, is Alarconian, and Spanish themes and treatments stand behind Paul Scarron's *Jodelet* (pr. 1645), Thomas Corneille's *Les Engagements du hazard* (pr. 1657) and *Le Feint Astrologue* (pr. 1650), and so on.

This comic vein was in keeping with the classical theory of purity of genres, and it came to grips with the vagaries of human conduct and social life. Yet it did not quite know how to thrive under the structural and situational uncertainties provoked by the dramatic rules; too many loose ends kept it from crystallizing. The task needed the hand of a master, and it was accomplished once and for all by Molière. Many of his sources lie elsewhere, too: *commedia dell'arte* for *La Jalousie du barbouillé* (1819) and *Le Médecin volant* (1819), or *Les Fourberies de Scapin* (pr. 1671; *The Cheats of Scapin*, 1701); Niccolò Barbieri for *L'Étourdi: Ou, Les Contre-temps* (pr. 1653; *The Blunderer*, 1678), Secchi for *Le Dépit amoureux* (pr. 1656; *The Love-Tiff*, 1930), Lope de Vega for the Terentian *L'École des maris* (pr. 1661; *The School for Husbands*, 1732), Tirso de Molina for *Don Juan: Ou, Le Festin de Pierre* (pr. 1665; *Don Juan*, 1755), Lorenzino de' Medici (the Plautine *L'Avare*, pr. 1668; *The Miser*, 1672).

Yet Molière's comic brilliance lies within himself, and because of this, if one does not take into account Shakespeare's special, "free" compositions, he represents the culmination of Renaissance comedy. In collaboration with Lulli, he gave prominence to the *comédie-ballet* that delighted the court of Louis XIV: *Les Fâcheux* (pr. 1661), *Le Mariage forcé* (pr. 1664), *La Princesse d'Elide* (pr. 1664), *L'Amour médcin* (pr. 1665; *Love's the Best Doctor*, 1755), *Monsieur de Pourceaugnac* (pr. 1669), and *Le Bourgeois Gentilhomme*.

Shakespeare widened the scope of comedy with fantasy; Molière did it through the *comédies-ballet* in the direction of dance, and he also did it in the opposite direction of tragic comedy (as opposed to tragicomedy), comedy whose pronounced gravity begets a feeling of private calamity, as one experiences it when one considers the solitude of *Le Misanthrope* (pr. 1666; *The Misanthrope*, 1709), the atheism of *Don Juan*, the cynical hypocrisy of *Tartuffe*, and the desperate scene of Harpagon's monologue regarding his stolen money-box in *L'Avare*. The tragic tone in Molière, like the essence of his comedy, always has to do with encroachments on common sense, humankind's unnatural injunctions or constrictions against moderation, all the deformations that pit young against old, pupil against master, love against money, social right against social pretension, woman's humanity against man's law. Implying profound comments on humankind, both Machiavelli during the period's ebullient years and Molière during its steadier "golden mean" years brought to Renaissance comedy something true to and yet greater than life by being eminently theatrical.

Combining classical themes with realistic material, as Molière did, was not unusual in England. The combination weaves through the fabric of historical and "independent" drama. This was evident in that forerunner of Shakespeare's tetralogy, *The Famous Victories of Henry V* (pb. 1598), in which the comic actor Richard Tarlton starred. The moral concern always inherent in the English notion of realism gave Jonson, reflecting less the ethical overtones of *Tartuffe* than the severe moral standards of Ruiz de Alarcón, his feisty strength, if not his comicality. If he achieves theatrical power with grotesque figures or caricatures, it is because there is a lusty deliberateness, like Aretino's, in his approach to his subject, producing, however—if one takes *Volpone*—less a criticism than a minisermon. To give it a physiological explanation—an idea quite alien to the Spanish mind—he introduced the concept of "humours," whose excess, according to him, produced eccentricities and personality changes. Hence the medieval verve of this author, despite his classical plan and common utilization of Terentian and Plautine techniques. *Volpone* is a satire near tragedy; the satiric *The Alchemist*'s racy jargon (pr. 1610) invites pity in the spurious context of the plague; *Epicoene: Or, The Silent Woman* (pr. 1609)—for John Dryden, Thomas Shadwell, and Samuel Pepys the perfect English comedy—softens the tragedy of the Greek prototype (who commits suicide) with compromise, but the deceit, whatever the farcical rendering, lingers heavy; and *Bartholomew Fair* (pr. 1614), through its Dutch-like vignettes of petty greeds, surrounds the viewer with an iniquitous reality that gives the viewer, let alone the defrauded Cokes and Waspe, pause.

Yet while Jonson nevertheless remained closer to the humanist spirit of Renaissance comedy, the true spirit of English comedy manifested itself in the category of romance. Less through laughter than delight in the Terentian tradition (perhaps because his plays were performed by boy-players), Lyly anticipated the comedy of romance in the Athenian *Campaspe*. The sheer number of playwrights in this category, many of them followers of Jonson, testifies to its popularity: Into the romantic material, John Day introduced Jonsonian elements in *The Blind Beggar of Bethnal Green* (pr. 1600-1601); Thomas Heywood and Middleton also brought in Jonsonian middle-class realistic ingredients in *The Fair Maid of the West: Or, A Girl Worth Gold* (pr. c. 1610 - c. 1630) and *A Trick to Catch the Old One* (pr. 1605-1606); Massinger made the elements darker with his pronounced social awareness in *A New Way to Pay Old Debts* (pr. c. 1621) or *The City Madam* (pr. c. 1632); Richard Brome pointed to a special social code of manners in *A Mad Couple Well Matched* (pr. 1639); Shirley intensified class-consciousness in *Hyde Park* (pr. 1632) or *The Lady of Pleasure* (pr. 1635)—all bourgeois plays combed with romance. With a sense of the Molièrian comedy of manners, they suggest that William Congreve's *The Way of the World* (pr. 1700) is not far off.

As usual, Shakespeare dominates the romantic column. His comedies transcend the aesthetic concerns of humanist comedy and the social orientations of the Spanish, not to mention the moral preoccupations of some of his compatriots. Locating most of his comedies in Italy rather than on native grounds, as by and large the other Renaissance writers of comedy did, gave his plays an exotic sense of distance that enhanced the subjects' universal significance and at the same time made possible flights of pure fantasy and dream. The early plays have some of the impertinent contempt of human follies of Italian authors—for example, *Love's Labour's Lost* (pr. 1594-1595)—or of their taste for Plautus—*The Comedy of Errors* (pr. c. 1592-1594)—while the chivalric-romantic motif emerged in *The Two Gentlemen of Verona* (pr. c. 1594-1595). Yet, as in Spain, sentimental romanticism gradually acquired more realistic hues, and with the realism came those touches of serious consequence that keep reminding an audience of the existence of evil in this world—those uneasy notes that sound in the Renaissance from Machiavelli to Molière, Aretino to Lope de Vega, from *Celestina* to *The Alchemist*, and *Doctor Faustus* to *Don Juan*. *The Merchant of Venice* (pr. c. 1596-1597) and *Measure for Measure* convey this in subtle ways.

On another level, *Much Ado About Nothing* (pr. c. 1598-1599) and *Twelfth Night* (pr. c. 1600-1602) show by their sophistication that the realistic and the romantic may blend perfectly well. Finally, fantasy takes over in *A Midsummer Night's Dream* and, at least ostensibly, in the sylvan idyll *As You Like It*. As ever, Shakespeare provides a summing up of the Renaissance mode, a transcendent summing up because of his unique individuality, which brands whatever it treats with the stamp of newness. In the words of one critic, "The spirit of Shakespeare's comedy of romance is something entirely new. . . . There is a kind of transcendentalism here, where the objective and the subjective meet; where the author is at one with his characters and yet, godlike, above them; where intellectual laughter becomes emotional; where clowns become wise and wise men fools."

POPULAR DRAMA

The lines between all categories of Renaissance drama are bound to be blurred, since the overlapping of the religious with the tragic, tragic with historical, historical with independent, independent with tragicomic, tragicomic with pastoral, and so on, was natural and inherent in the movements of a genre evolving in all directions, backward and forward in time, from imitation to invention, seeking its own space and identity. It made itself open to novelty, in the face of respected humanistic tenets; the exchange between Prologue and Argument concerning traditional rhetoric versus new ideas in Il Lasca's comedy *La Strega* (wr. c. 1545, pb. 1582) is revealing. In any event, by absorbing adventuresome and sentimental elements, *commedia erudita* flowed into *commedia popolaresca*, just as the latter drifted into farce. Even with dialects, the rustic plays need not be thought of as belonging to the popular or vulgar category strictly speaking, because they were still conceived within a classical framework and were intended for select spectators. By leaning on the romantic and the realistic, however, they drew wider audiences. One needs only to note Lope de Rueda's *pasos*. Comedy's passage into the world of common entertainment was inevitable when its basic ingredient, character portrayal, started aiming at popular types, those that had enlivened medieval farce. Typical was Dellia Porta's change from classical imitation to popular representation: He went from ancient types such as the Pedant, the Servant, and the Parasite to contemporary types such as the Captain, the German, the Neapolitan, and the Rustic. This is what encouraged the inclusion of dialects, not to mention the thrill of playing to packed houses that delighted in making human identifications.

Comedy became "popular" when performed not in royal courts and the halls or courtyards of cardinals and the nobility but out in the theaters, in the squares, or on the improvised planks of countryside stages. It became popular when it created space for attending merchants and peasants, and when the subject matter shed the classical integument and humanist garb and responded to realistic social stimulations, especially those charged with romance and adventure—and ridicule. For this reason, much humanist comedy acquired vulgar hues—the moment intellectual preciosities were abandoned and nature and truth were adhered to in a spirit of mirth. Indeed, with dialects and colloquialisms loosed on the rustic stage, the *commedia popolaresca* joined the extravagantly comic tradition of the farce, in which verisimilitude yields to improbability and circumspection to license.

To be sure, the ancients had their rustic farces and pantomimes—*fabulae Atellanae*—but the first farces in the modern sense that obtained in the Renaissance were French. They were free, without artificial bonds and with much action, often coarse and indecent, like a counterreaction to the decorum and the relative immobility of the *dramma erudito*, drawing from the older *moralités* and *sotties*. The fifteenth century *Farce de Maistre Pathelin* (1469) spread into Europe, into Italy and Germany, and as late as the eighteenth century into England. In the sixteenth century, under King Louis XII, the fraternity of the Bazoche, the *bazochiens*, boasted authors such as Pierre Gringoire and Nicolas de la Chesnaye. The company presented a pointed series of satires against the court, the pope, even the king, almost as if Aretino had turned to farce. The seventeenth century saw the comedies of farceur Raymond Poisson, the Hôtel de Bourgogne farces, and the ludicrous antics of the clown Gaultier-Gargouille with the Comédiens du Roy. Given the kinship with the *moralités*, these plays have been called profane dramas. Nomenclature aside, they corresponded to widespread popular interest and lasted a long time. The flavor of the farce continued in Molière, who ultimately refined it into genuine character comedy.

Germany's Hans Sachs, in the 1400's, contributed considerably to this extreme mode, drawing from the *Fastnachtspiele: Der fahrende Schüler im Paradies* (pr. 1550; *The Traveling Scholar*, 1910) or *Das haiss Eisen* (pr. 1551; *The Hot Iron*, 1910), for example. In Holland, two centuries later, Amsterdam's Bredero, of the "Eglantines" theatrical group, wrote a number of realistic spoofs rich in type portrayal. England had as active a tradition as France, into which fits the early *Lusty Juventus* interlude (these interludes were short, secular, farcical pieces with no ethical moral).

John Heywood's *Johan Johan* (pb. 1533) also fits the tradition, in which one must also mention Shakespeare, whose *The Taming of the Shrew* moves out from Italian farce material, and Jonson, who clearly revels in farcical moments. In Spain there are a wealth of examples, from Rodrigo Cota de Maguaque's *Diálogo entre el amor y un viejo* (1400's) to Lope de Rueda's *pasos* and their stress on caricature.

Farce may never have produced great literature, but it provided spirited theater. Perhaps the most important feature that developed from it in Italy was the phenomenon of improvised comedy, that exercise in spontaneity and invention fostered by the actors themselves, which made Italian touring companies so well known. At this point, comedy was but a step away from the unique *commedia dell'arte*.

COMMEDIA DELL'ARTE

When the playwrights produced only dull fare, and the impositions of eruditeness became inane, the actors took over: no poetry, perhaps, but spectacle. They produced improvised, histrionic, buffoon comedy, often with masks, carrying on like the *jongleurs* who had continued the Roman mimes. They used the *zanni*—servants or clowns, each from his own region, each with his own name, habit, and set of characteristics. Unlike their predecessors, these were professional actors, *attori di mestiere*, who traveled widely in Europe, performing (especially in France) a good part of the local repertory: tragedies, pastorals, and comedies. Yet their specialty was the subject comedy, plays with only the scenario (a plot summary called *canovaccio*) written down, leaving the development of dialogue and mime to the actors' improvisations. This was not the usually botched farce; theirs was a uniquely Italian development: Some things were memorized, destined for use in varying dramatic situations or certain types of events—soliloquies, sayings, oaths, brief responses, poems, Latinized rigamaroles, tirades, conceits, and the like—but although they were suitable for particular occasions and adaptable to various plays, these verbal "formulas" were made to sound different in each context and from the mouth of a master *comico dell'arte* became indistinguishable from the unprepared "text." Timing

was crucial, along with the ability to take advantage of the unexpected, such as a delay, a crying child, a missing prop, a malfunctioning reflector, or a sudden weather condition. The memorized and the improvised were integrated. The Capitano had his collection of rodomontades but would not have lasted long if he had relied mainly on them; the same held for the advices typical of Pantalone, or the servant needing to lie his way out, or the lovers expressing their mutual or repelled affections. As Arlecchino, Domencio Biancolelli was famous for his extemporized variations on characteristic situations. To be sure, many patterns—*lazzi*—had been previously worked out, but not always, and the bag of tricks bulged.

Mime was not impeded by wearing a mask, since the whole body communicated emotion and meaning; but lovers, among others, being generally handsome, were unmasked, and when the speeches became impassioned, a director such as Andrea Perrucci would have his *comici* remove them. With the mime came music; action invited dance and song. Actresses Isabella Andreini and Orsola Cecchini were fine singers, and the most famous Scapino, Francesco Gabrielli, recited his own scenario, *Gli strumenti di Scapino*, in which he played everything from the violin and theorbo to the flute and trombone. Acrobatics heightened the comicality: contortions, pirouettes, somersaults, executed by both sexes. One Arlecchino, Tommaso Visentini, did back flips holding a full glass of wine. As would be expected, with such gymnastic prowess, when mechanical devices were introduced in the 1600's the physical range of farcical performance increased. Magical appearances and disappearances, flying tables, arrivals from the sky, falling trees, walking statues, and metamorphosing animals—all gave the *commedia dell'arte* an untold number of rip-roaring opportunities.

All this inventive extemporization is not to suggest that the *commedia dell'arte*'s mode was purely folk based. The plots still bore much relation to the classical fare, as the more than hundreds of extant scenarios prove. The staging, basically simple from the mid-1600's, when the form began, was the same as for classical comedy; then, in parallel fashion, with the improvement of pictorial arts and perspective during the Baroque (seventeenth and eighteenth centuries), the whole became more elaborate. Moreover, the characters (old men, pedants, boasters, etc.) were carryovers from the *commedia erudita*, except that, unrestrained by prescriptions such as the unity of action, the love triangle looked uneventful before the love pentagon or hexagon. Unbelievable complications, ingeniously locked and unlocked, put an audience in a state of sidesplitting suspension. In a sense, *commedia dell'arte* was vulgarized—in both senses of the word—classical comedy, complete with bombast and beatings, lewdness and incognitos, equivocations and absurdities, sex and somersaults. Obscenities and prurient humor abounded, even after women were introduced on the stage—a welcome innovation at a time when Shakespeare's Ophelia and Juliet were still played by boys. That the ladies who acted out the lascivious parts were often virtuous women in private is an anomaly that neither neutralized the condemnation of Reformation and Counter-Reformation ecclesiasts nor saved the acting profession from being tainted with a bad reputation.

The reason for the *commedia dell'arte*'s uncommon success across a whole continent for more than 250 years among both the common people and the most significant playwrights (let alone the painters—Pieter Pourbus, Jacques Gillot, Théobald Michau, Giuseppe Zocchi, Naiveu, Giovan Michele Graneri, Jean-Antoine Watteau) lay not in its hackneyed plots or respectable roots or unchanging characters or wanton salaciousness; it lay in its actor-designed and not author-designed inventiveness, in its unpredictable spontaneity, and in its colorful masks (by which is meant the characters of this Italian comedy of masks). It echoed Castelvetro's observation that comedy is written to be acted—except that now there was no writing, only acting. Hence *commedia dell'arte* belongs to the history of theater rather than that of drama. The mask became its trademark. The Venetian Pantalone (de' Bisognosi) appears as a rich, miserly, grumpy old merchant, unfriendly toward youth, sometimes ridiculously enamored and accordingly derided (a parody of age). With pointed nose, pointed beard, and pointed shoes, his presence in academic gown hardly occasioned joy. He fathered other old charac-

ters: Bernardone, Pancrazio, the Barone, Pasquale. Gremio in *The Taming of the Shrew* is labeled a "pantalowne." The Bolognese Dr. Balanzon(i)—old Dr. Graziano—a nonsensical, pedantic mask, strutted around as a lawyer, rarely a physician, giving himself donnish airs (a parody of erudition). Along with the old man and the pedant came the warrior: the grotesque Capitano from Naples (with many surnames: Spaccamonte, Coccodrillo, Bombardone, Spezzaferro, Bellavita, Zerbino, Scaricabombardone, and the best known: Matamoros, Rodomonte, Fracassa, and Spaventa da Vallinferna), a vainglorious braggart (a parody of the Spanish occupation trooper). The Neapolitan Scaramuccia was like a second Capitano.

The buffoonish *zanni* (in classical drama, the servants, otherwise clowns), the first of whom was Brighella, the wily valet who came from upper Bergamo, captured most of the attention; from lower Bergamo came the foolish Arlecchino, gluttonous and sensual, idiotic and lazy, the mocked recipient of frequent clubbings. White attire characterized the lackey, but in Arlecchino's case, by dint of constant patching the outfit became the now familiar, multicolored costume. As the *commedia dell'arte* developed, the roles of Brighella and Arlecchino were reversed, even fused, and in the latter case, as a derider and one derided, he came to stand for the almost picaresque, comic antihero of the people. The Neapolitan version of the plebeian *zanni*, one who retained his white attire, was the equally famous Pulcinella, whose ideal of *dolce far niente* and a good dish of pasta dragged him into all kinds of odd circumstances, sometimes involving theft and drunkenness. His nose was curved, his brow wrinkled, displaying a wart. A self-styled philosopher with a cynical view of the world—"he spoke the truth jokingly"—he stood as a parody of his native city.

From this trio emerged a crowd of *zanni*, enumerated in a poem in twelve eight-syllable verses:

> Arlecchino, Truffaldino,
> sia Pasquino, Tabarrino,
> Tortellino, Naccherino,
> Gradellino, Mezzettino,
> Polpettino, Nespolino,
> Bertolino, Fagiolino,

Trappolino, Zaccagnino,
Trivellino, Traccagnino,
Passerino, Bagattino,
Bagiolino, Temellino,
Fagottino, Pedrolino,
Fritellino, Tabacchino.

Even so, some of the more notorious are omitted: Coviello (Giacometto, who had with a drooping nose, large glasses, flapping pants, and beret with long feathers), Scapino from Milan (Molière's Scapin and Covielle), Burattino, Cola, Flautino, Francatrippa, Farfanicchio, Buffetto, Stoppino, Meneghino, Finocchio, Pedrolino, the renowned and bespectacled Neapolitan Tartaglia, and the Tuscan maids Franceschina, Smeraldina, Pasquetta, Turchetta, Ricciolina, Diamantina, Arlecchina, Corallina, and the best-known, Colombina. Then came the Tuscan-speaking, handsome and beautiful lovers: Cinzio, Fabrizio, Ottavio, Flavio, Lelio, Florindo, Angelica, Ardelia, Aurelia, Flaminia, Lucilla, Lavinia, the virtuous Isabella, and the celebrated Rosaura. Finally there were included the generic roles to complete the social coverage: the Turkish or Armenian Merchant, the Notary, Doctor, Shepherd and Shepherdess, Sailor, Messenger, Executioner, and Peasant, then the slaves, barbers, guards, magicians, soldiers, police, and swindlers. Part of the universal fascination stemmed from the fact that culturally and psychologically these characters represented their provinces. In addition to the masks already mentioned, one might add Beltramo (Milan), Zacometo (Venice), Il Bascagliese (Naples), Marco-Pepe and Cassandra (Rome), Stantorello (Florence), Narcisino (Bologna), Giaudaja (Turin), and Nappa (Calabria). The list is long, but even the most prominent companies (the Gelosi, who became the Comédiens du Roy for Charles IX, the Uniti, Accesi, Desiosi, Confidenti, and Fedeli) only numbered about a dozen members. Though the actors specialized in their stock roles, versatility was also part of the game.

To say that the *commedia dell'arte* enjoyed great success in Europe is to understate the truth: Its success was prodigious. Honored in France in 1571, *zanni* Alberto Ganassi passed into Spain with equal laurels; Giulio Pasquati as Pantalone, Simone da Bo-

logna as Arlecchino, Francesco Andreini as Capitan Spavento, and his wife, Isabella, were invited by Henry III and his Isabella, then by Henry IV; others were acknowledged by the King of Navarre, Drusiano Martinelli as Arlecchino by Queen Elizabeth I, and with his multitalented brother Tristano by the Spanish royalty, the latter also by Henry IV and Lousi XIII. Andreini's son Giovan Battista performed in Paris; the great Scaramuccia, Tiberio Fiorilli, was Molière's teacher; the Italians took over the Petit-Bourbon Theater and afterward many more in the capital, eventually by expanding the musical portions of their shows becoming the Opéra-Comique; in 1661 the Paris of Louis XIV welcomed Domenico Biancolelli—Dominique—as its idol; Austria, Bohemia, Poland, and Russia hailed the comedians. In time, various countries modified a particular mask to be more congenial with local, ethnic realities. Thus Arlecchino became Hanswurst in Germany, Pedrolino and Colombina the pathetic Pierrot and dainty Colombine in France, Pedrolino also turned into Petrushka in Russia, and in England Pulcinella changed his name to Punch. Everywhere a pantomime clown made crowds laugh, he was a former Italian *zanni*. François de Malherbe in France may have objected to them, and French actors may not have been too happy with the invasion, but in this the former had no followers and the latter no counterthrust. Playwrights adopted them: Regnard, Charles-Rivière Dufresny. The influence of the *comici* was simply overpowering; their work, after all, underlay much of Lope de Rueda, Shakespeare, and Molière, and it is not surprising that Goldoni grew out of their tradition.

The *comici*, whose profession quite often became generational in individual families, easily established themselves everywhere because their art stemmed from a discipline demanding talent, training, and experience, and because as they organized their spectacles aesthetically they organized their business administratively. Indeed, Benedetto Croce wrote that they gave Europe the very organization of the modern theater. Yet more than that, because of their firm grasp on the essence of comicality, they gave Renaissance drama one of its most vital expressions and an enduring form of theater.

BIBLIOGRAPHY

Andrews, Richard. *Scripts and Scenarios: The Performed Comic Text in Renaissance Italy.* Cambridge, England: Cambridge University Press, 1993. Traces the rise of the unique theatrical form, *comedia dell'arte*, in Italy, examining its influence on European drama, its antecedents, and its audience reception.

Brereton, Geoffrey. *French Tragic Drama in the Sixteenth and Seventeenth Centuries.* London: Methuen, 1973. Provides history and criticism of the role of tragedy in French Renaissance drama.

Cerasano, Susan P., and Marion Wynne-Davies. *Renaissance Drama by Women: Texts and Documents.* London: Routledge, 1996. Seeks to uncover the historical invisibility of women dramatists of the era. Contains texts by women as well as a highly useful collection of documents about the role of English women in theater.

Di Maria, Salvatore. *Italian Tragedy in the Renaissance: Cultural Realities and Theatrical Innovations.* Lewisburg, Pa.: Bucknell University Press, 2002. Analyzes the revival of Greek and Roman tragedy on the Italian Renaissance stage, examining the way in which playwrights modified dramatic elements to make the productions relevant to their audiences.

Gurr, Arthur. *The Shakespearean Stage, 1574-1642.* 3d ed. Cambridge, England: Cambridge University Press, 1994. A comprehensive examination of the staging of Shakespearean drama, including acting companies and styles, playhouses, audiences, and more.

Jondorf, Gillian. *French Renaissance Tragedy: The Dramatic Word.* Cambridge, England: Cambridge University Press, 1990. Examines the originality and literary influence of sixteenth century French playwrights, arguing that by breaking with the medieval tradition of religious and morality plays, these playwrights were meritorious in their own right.

Orgel, Stephen. *The Illusion of Power: Political Theater in the English Renaissance.* Berkeley: University of California Press, 1991. Examines the way in which Elizabethan politics shaped theatrical performance as well as the way politics were aestheticized by the dramatic stage.

Webb, Nick, Roberta Wood, and Peter Elmer, eds. *The Renaissance in Europe: An Anthology.* New Haven, Conn.: Yale University Press, 2000. Provides a contextual backdrop to the Renaissance by exploring the era from the perspectives of political thought, history, philosophy, religion, music, art, drama, and literature.

White, Martin. *Renaissance Drama in Action: An Introduction to Aspects of Theater Practice and Performance.* London: Routledge, 1998. Explores the characteristics of the Renaissance stage and theatrical performance, in turn discussing their relevance and application to contemporary productions.

Jean-Pierre Barricelli

CENTRAL AND SOUTHEASTERN EUROPEAN DRAMA

Historically, the nations of Central and Southeastern Europe have more experience of foreign occupation than of independence. Whether benign or brutal, whether oppressive or relatively liberal, such dominance has retarded the progress of the region's indigenous societies, while simultaneously making the celebration of past glories and future hopes a central theme of artistic expression. In Central and Southeastern Europe, culture and nationalism have been inextricably intertwined, and as a result the history of drama in these countries is intimately connected to the general pattern of their social development.

There are, nonetheless, significant differences among the national theatrical traditions. Poland, Czechoslovakia, and Hungary have been consistently open to Western European cultural influences, whereas Romania, Bulgaria, and the states briefly united as Yugoslavia have been more involved with the Russian and Turkish empires. Poland and Czechoslovakia have produced playwrights whose work appeals to world audiences, while their Bulgarian counterparts are neglected even at home; the countries achieving independence following Yugoslavia's disintegration in the 1990's continue to display distinct theatrical cultures, with Croatia's dominance even more pronounced at the beginning of the twenty-first century than it has been in the past. Whatever their differences and similarities, however, it is clear that the nations of Central and Southeastern Europe have much to offer the world's stage and are poised to make further contributions in the future.

POLAND

Poland has a particularly rich theater tradition. During the Middle Ages, mystery and morality plays were produced under religious auspices; the only surviving example of the genre, Mikołaj of Wilkowiecka's *Historia o chwalebnym Zmartwychwstaniu Pańskim* (pr. c. 1580; the history of the lord's glorious resurrection), is still performed today. Jan Kochanowski's *Odprawa posłów grekich* (pr. 1578; *The Dismissal of the Grecian Envoys*, 1994) was the first secular drama written in Polish, and inaugurated a tradition of court patronage of the theater that lasted until the country lost its independence in 1795.

The National Theater, the first public dramatic company in Poland, was founded in 1765, and was initially directed by foreign managers who concentrated on adaptations or imitations of plays by Molière, Voltaire, and Carlo Goldoni. During the years 1783 to 1814, however, the administration of the Polish actor, writer, and director Wojciech Bogusławski systematically encouraged native plays and playwrights, established the first school for the training of actors, and developed a network of provincial theaters. This policy began to pay literary dividends with such accomplished works as Alojzy Feliński's *Barbara Radziwiłłówna* (pr. 1817; Barbara Radziwiłł), a tragedy based on the life of a sixteenth century Polish queen that has been compared with Jean Racine's *Bérénice* (pr. 1670; English translation, 1676).

In Poland, as elsewhere, the first third of the nineteenth century saw the Romantic movement capture the imaginations of many young writers, of whom Adam Mickiewicz would go on to achieve international as well as domestic success. Mickiewicz is best known as a poet, but his *Dziady* (pb. parts 2,4, 1823; pb. part 3, 1832; *Forefathers' Eve*, 1968) is a four-part dramatic epic that combines folkloric elements with impassioned patriotic pleas. Never performed in Mickiewicz's lifetime, it was nonetheless a widely read and very influential work that helped to set a nationalistic agenda for Polish drama.

Like Mickiewicz, Juliusz Słowacki, and Zygmunt Krasiński were forced to seek refuge in France after the failure of the 1830-1831 revolts against Poland's foreign rulers. Each of these dramatists made important contributions to the theater: Słowacki's *Kordian* (pb. 1834) is a stirring examination of political conspiracy, and *Fantazy* (wr. 1841; English translation, 1977) goes against the period's grain with its anti-Romantic comedy. Krasiński's *Nie-Boska komedia* (pb. 1835; *The Undivine Comedy*, 1846) is a politically engaged attempt to bring about the transformation of his homeland into a truly just society.

The failure of another uprising against foreign rule in 1863 was reflected in the acerbic comedies of Jósef Narzymski, who, in *Pozytywni* (pr. 1872; the positivists), mocks young intellectuals who think they have the key to social reform, and Jósef Bliziński, whose *Rozbitki* (pr. 1877; wreckage) mercilessly satirizes a nouveau riche who tries to buy his way into the aristocracy. By the turn of the century, the impetus toward realism made plays such as Gabriela Zapolska's *Moralność Pani Dulskiej* (pr. 1907; *The Morality of Mrs. Dulska*, 1923) a controversial story of the protagonist's use of sex for social advancement, popular with those who supported societal change.

Poland's return to independence after World War I sparked a new explosion of national cultural pride, and in the theater, remarkable advances were made in actors' training and stagecraft. Experimental theater made its appearance in the work of Stanisław Ignacy Witkiewicz, whose assimilation of contemporary European avant-garde theories and practices would prove extremely influential for post-World War II writers. Many of his plays, including *Kurka wodna* (pr. 1922; *The Water Hen*, 1968) and *Wariat i zakonnica: Czyli, Nie ma złego, co by na jeszcze gorsze nie wyszło* (pb. 1925, pr. 1926; *The Madman and the Nun: Or, There Is Nothing Bad Which Could Not Turn into Something Worse*, 1966), feature characters whose return from the dead haunts the absurd efforts made by the living; a late masterpiece, *Szewcy* (pr. 1934; *The Shoemakers*, 1968) portrays a post-revolutionary world in which it is clear that further momentous changes lie ahead.

Following World War II, strict government censorship permitted only conventional Social Realistic dramas that glorified patriotic workers and attacked subversive foreign influences. The death of Joseph Stalin in 1953 and the widespread antigovernment demonstrations of 1956, however, produced a unique cultural compromise: As long as they did not directly question state policies, creative artists were largely left alone—although the periodic return of more hardline regimes, as in 1968 and 1981, would retard this process—to pursue their individual visions. What followed was an explosion of literary activity in general, and of drama in particular, that resulted in the formation of a world-class theatrical culture.

In the 1960's, the Polish Laboratory Theatre and its director, Jerzy Grotowski, earned international respect for their fresh approach to dramatic performance. In *Towards a Poor Theatre* (1968), Grotowski argued that technical refinements in stagecraft and the resulting emphasis on visual spectacle had broken the desired connection between actor and audience and that the actor's creativity needed to be liberated by thoughtful exercises in basic movement. Theater professionals came from far and wide to study Grotowski's productions and also became acquainted with the work of the two most prominent playwrights in contemporary Poland, Tadeusz Różewicz and Sławomir Mrożek, whose plays receive frequent international productions.

Różewicz is a practitioner of what he calls "open dramaturgy," in which all theatrical conventions are discarded as a means of ensuring a fresh collaboration among writers, actors and directors. *Kartoteka* (pr. 1960; *The Card Index*, 1969), a satirical depiction of Polish postwar intellectual life, and *Białe małż eństwo* (pr. 1975; *White Marriage*, 1977), a complex treatment of adolescent sexuality, are two widely admired examples of his unusual and yet very accessible approach to playwriting.

Mrożek, who continued to write for the Polish stage after leaving the country in 1968, takes a more playful approach to dramatic construction by borrowing materials from melodrama, circus acts, sketch comedy, and experimental theater. This has produced a string of remarkable entertainments that also have substantial intellectual content, including: *Policja* (pr. 1958; *The Police*, 1959), in which a political prisoner terrifies his guards by threatening to reform and make them obsolete; *Tango* (pr. 1965; English translation, 1966), a masterful reenactment of the history of the twentieth century in Europe through the medium of a feuding family; *Milosc na Krymie: Komedia tragiczna w trech aktach* (pr. 1993; love in the Crimea), in which the 1917 fall of the Russian Empire is treated with a combination of screwball comedy and more reflective social satire.

Poland's alternative theaters have provided many of the highlights of the country's late twentieth century drama. The Theatre of the Eighth Day, the Travel Bureau, and the Association of the Otwock Commune are three of the most active companies; the latter's collective production *Trzeba zabić pierwszego Boga* (pr. 1998; the first god must be killed) uses mythological components to construct new rituals for contemporary drama and has sparked a number of similar efforts.

HUNGARY

Dramatic works based on religious ceremonies begin to appear in Hungary in the eleventh century, and by the fifteenth century passion plays were enacted throughout the country. In the 1500's, strife between Catholic and Protestant factions began a tradition of polemical religious theater that found Protestant ministers such as Mihály Sztárai depicting Catholic clerics as ignorant and bigoted in *Az igaz papságnak tüköre* (pb. 1559; a mirror of true priesthood), a play more significant for beginning a national theater tradition than for any intrinsic merit. Catholics, who previously had conducted their anti-Protestant propaganda in Latin, now found it necessary to produce Hungarian-language responses to such attacks; many of these "school plays," as the works on both sides came to be known, include comment on contemporary political or social issues in addition to their dominant concern with defending true religion.

Secular theater until the late eighteenth century featured adaptations of foreign works. Then György Bessenyei's series of nationalistic historical dramas, of which *Hunyadi László tragédiája* (pb. 1772; the tragedy of Hunyadi László) is the first, as well as his cleverly constructed polemic for Enlightenment ideas, *A filozófus* (pb. 1777; the philosopher), sparked an explosion of new plays by Hungarian writers. Károly Kisfaludy earned both popular and critical success with romantic dramas such as *A kérők* (pr. 1819; the suitors) and *Iréne* (pr. 1821), and József Katona wrote what is generally considered Hungary's first great tragedy, *Bánk bán* (pr. 1815; viceroy Bank). Mihály Vörösmarty, an accomplished poet as well as playwright, wrote several complex, moody

dramas that often made excellent use of fantasy elements, as in the case of the fairy-tale philosophers who cavort their way through *Csongor és Tünde* (pb. 1831). Another aspect of his art was revealed in *Vérnász* (pr. 1833; blood wedding), in which sharp psychological conflict is grounded in realistic social settings.

Hungary's tumultuous nineteenth century history, during which the movement for national independence was first brutally repressed in 1849 and then admitted to a form of power-sharing with Austria in 1867, resulted in some correspondingly volatile theater. Some playwrights struggled to rise above partisan politics in works such as Imre Madách's *Az ember tragédiája* (pb. 1861; *The Tragedy of Man*, 1933), a grandiose epic of humanity's history from creation to extinction that is still popular with domestic audiences. Others sought to find the essence of Hungarian identity in idealized portraits of peasant life, although plays such as Ferenc Csepreghy's *A falu rossza* (pr. 1874; bad guy of the village) and Ede Tóth's *A sárga csikó* (pr. 1877; the yellow colt) often seem to be making fun of their subjects' crudities rather than exalting their natural goodness. Gergely Csíky opted for the realistic depiction of middle-class manners and mores. His *Proletárok* (pr. 1880; parasites) and *Cifra nyomorúság* (pr. 1881; fancy misery) are polished examples of the genre that critics have dubbed the well-made play.

At the beginning of the twentieth century a boom in theater construction throughout Hungary stimulated new levels of dramatic activity, as genres as disparate as cabaret, light comedy, classical tragedy, and naturalistic tales of proletarian squalor competed for the public's attention. This creative ferment produced one author who went on to achieve remarkable international success: Ferenc Molnár's entertaining, well-constructed, and intriguingly complex plays are exemplified by *Liliom* (pr. 1909; English translation, 1922), whose title character is a happy-go-lucky circus tout given one last chance to redeem himself after a lifetime of hedonistic excess. Molnár was also capable of more substantial creations such as *Szinház* (wr. 1921; *Theater*, 1937), a set of three short plays that go behind the scenes of what happens onstage, and both his slighter and more serious works continue to be revived both internationally and in his native country.

World War II and the subsequent imposition of communist rule profoundly affected Hungarian theater, with the careers of Gyula Hay and László Németh illustrating the effect of these traumatic changes. Hay's *Isten, császár, paraszł* (pr. 1932; god, emperor, peasant) focuses on the fifteenth century Czech reformer Jan Hus in warning against the evils of authoritarianism. After the communist takeover, however, Hay churned out pro-Stalinist plays before rebelling, serving a prison sentence for anticommunist activity, and then writing the clever Aristophanic comedy *A ló* (pr. 1964; *The Horse*, 1965). Németh walked a more politic line in fashioning plays that blended meditations on the social responsibility of intellectuals with mild criticism of totalitarian institutions; *A két Bólyai* (pr. 1961; the two Bólyáis), which depicts a conflict between authoritarian father and restless son, is an effective example of his ability to weave wider significance out of commonplace domestic situations.

The century's concluding decades were stronger in comedy than in other theatrical forms. Vámos Miklos's tongue-in-cheek portrayals of contemporary fads, *Egszakadás-földindulás* (pr. 1986; the sky is falling down) and *Két egyfelvonásos* (pr. 1989; *Doubletakes*, 1990), and György Spiro's zany farce about capitalist excesses, *Opera mydlana* (pr. 1996; *Soap Opera*, 1999), were among the many works that seemed to reflect a more entertainment-oriented turn in Hungarian drama.

CZECHOSLOVAKIA

Czechoslovakia existed as an independent country only from 1918 to 1993, when the Czech and Slovak Republics went their separate ways. Historically Czech and Slovak cultures have undergone very different patterns of development. Although some Slovakian drama was produced in the nineteenth century, it was only after Czechoslovakia became an independent nation in 1918 that notable playwrights begin to appear. Ivan Stodola, whose comedy of nouveau-riche greed *Kariéra Jozky Pucíka* (pr. 1931) is still per-

formed, and Július Barć-Ivan, whose sentimental but moving *Matka* (pr. 1943; mother) has also stood the test of time, are representative figures.

After World War II, Slovakian theater produced several young talents of note, although none achieved the international reputation of their Czech contemporaries: Peter Karvaš, a skilled comic writer whose *Velká parochóa* (pr. 1964; a great wig) is his most admired work, and Igor Rusnák, whose *Lisky, dobrú noc* (pr. 1964; foxes, good night) sympathizes with the difficulties of Slovakian youth, are important. Since 1990 the Stoka Theater in Bratislava has mounted several acclaimed collective productions; *Eo ipso* (pr. 1994; by itself), which contrasts elitist and popular approaches to the arts, has been toured abroad as exemplifying Slovakia's achievements in the drama.

Czech-language drama began with religious plays, and the integration of the national language into the Latin used in Catholic ritual occurred far earlier than in other Eastern European countries. By the fourteenth century, secular as well as religious works were being performed in a hybrid Latin-Czech idiom, with Czech gradually dominating as lay participation increased. Although none survive in their entirety, there are some manuscript remains that suggest these plays took remarkable liberties in satirizing abuses by the clergy.

After a period of stagnation during which the puritanical Hussite movement suppressed most theatrical activity, Czech drama revived in the sixteenth century. Comedies of contemporary life were popular: Pavel Kyrmezer's *Komedie ceská o bohatci a Lazarovi* (pb. 1566; the Czech comedy about a money-bag and Lazarus) was set amid Prague's slums, and Jiri Tesak Moslovsky's *Komedie z knihy zakona boziho, jenz slove Ruth* (pb.1604; the comedy from the book of God's testament, which is called Ruth) placed a traditional Bible story in a contemporary peasant context.

The incorporation of the Czech state into the Holy Roman Empire in 1620 was followed by more than a century of cultural decline. Although some theatrical activity did continue during this period, it was largely situated in smaller communities where folkloric and religious elements had a comeback vis-à-vis the previously dominant secular tradition. Czech theater revived at the close of the eighteenth century with a spate of plays that dramatized the country's history, and these were followed by much more sophisticated exercises in social comedy. Václav Klicpera's satires of rural bumpkins, *Veselohra ma mostì* (pr. 1828; comedy on a bridge) and *Každy neco pro vlast* (pr. 1829; everyone's duty for the country), went over well with urban audiences; so too did Romantic tragedies such as Josef Tyl's *Èestmir* (pr. 1834), even though his protagonist opts for social conformity rather than Byronic rebellion.

From 1850 to the late 1880's, Czech theater was dominated by historical plays written in the Romantic tradition: Emanuel Bozděch's celebration of Napoleon, *Svĕta pán v županu* (pr. 1876; master of the world in a dressing gown), and Jaroslav Vrchlický's more sophisticated comedy of manners set at the court of Charles IV, *Noc na Karlštejne* (pr. 1884; night at the Karlštejne), are representative. The founding of the national theater in 1883 encouraged dramas less dependent on commercial success, and realistic treatments of peasant life such as Gabriela Preissová's *Její pastorkyna* (pr. 1891; Jenufa) began to appear. Psychological dramas of anguished introspection influenced by Henrik Ibsen and August Strindberg, such as Jaroslav Hilbert's *Vina* (pr. 1896; the guilt) and Jaroslav Kvapil's *Oblaka* (pr. 1903; the clouds), signaled a new responsiveness to contemporary European theater.

Czechoslovakia's achievement of independence in 1918 sparked a renaissance in all the arts, theater included. The brothers Karel and Josef Čapek, writing in collaboration, produced the most enduring work. *R.U.R.: Rossum's Universal Robots* (pb. 1920; English translation, 1923) depicts a dystopia in which enslaved robots revolt against their masters and has become a classic of world theater. *Ze života hmyzu* (pr. 1922; *The Insect Play*, 1923), in which the world of "creepers and crawlers" is equated with that of humanity, is another important drama. František Langer also gained international attention with his comedy *Velbloud uchem jehly* (pr. 1923; *The Camel Through the Needle's Eye*, 1932), an amusing tale of love

among the lower-middle classes, as well as *Periferie* (pr. 1925; *The Outskirts*, 1934), a bleak tragedy about a killer's need to be punished.

German occupation from 1938 to 1945 and postwar communist rule discouraged theatrical activity, but by the late 1950's playwrights such as Josef Topol and Václav Havel were creating important work. Topol's *Jejich den* (pr. 1959; their day) portrayed alienated youth unable to adopt the socialist dream, and Havel's *Zahradní slavnost* (pr. 1963; *The Garden Party*, 1969) and *Vyroizumìni* (pr. 1965; *The Memorandum*, 1967) highlight the debasement of language by authoritarian bureaucrats in a manner reminiscent of George Orwell's novel *Nineteen Eighty-Four* (1949).

A new wave of political repression in 1969 forced many writers either to flee the country or to go underground, and in the ensuing two decades, most creative theatrical activity took place abroad or in clandestine domestic venues. In 1979, Havel was arrested and sent to prison for four years, and Pavel Kohout, the author of cleverly subversive plays such as *August August, August* (pr. 1967; August August, the clown), was forced to emigrate to Austria.

The return to democratic government in 1989 encouraged many stagings of works by Havel and Kohout. Havel's election as president of the Czech Republic in 1993 and 1998 indicated just how far the wheel of political fortune had turned. Female playwrights such as Daniela Fischerová, whose *Náhlé neštĕtí* (pr. 1993; sudden misfortune) and *Fantomima* (pr. 1996; fantomine) use fairy-tale settings to create mythically charged drama, now became prominent, as did the kind of collective production popular in neighboring countries: Theatre Image, a Prague company, dazzled audiences with *Cabinet kuriosit a zázraků profesora Pražáka* (pr. 1997; professor Prazak's curious cabinet of curiosities and miracles), whose protagonist constructs bizarre onstage machines that represent spiritual as well as mechanical miracles.

ROMANIA

Dominated by first Roman, then Byzantine, and finally Turkish cultural influences, it was not until the nineteenth century that any significant indigenous drama appeared in Romania. Before that time, companies of foreign actors were frequent visitors and some Romanian schools put on plays, but generally only European classics were performed. The French Revolution awakened nationalistic aspirations, however, and by 1840 a national theater had been established and dramas in Romanian began to appear.

Three playwrights stand out in the nineteenth century. Vasile Alecsandri was prominent as both a director and a dramatist, writing a sharp comedy about resistance to Western influences in *Iorgu de la Sadagura* (pr. 1844; Iorgu of Sadagura), as well as patriotic historical plays such as *Despot Vodă* (pr. 1879; Voda the despot) and *Ovidiu* (pr. 1885: Ovid). *Dominita Rosada* (pr. 1868; Dominita Rosada) by Bogdan Hasdeu, is the first historical tragedy of note and is still performed today; Ion Luca Caragiale, generally considered Romania's foremost dramatist, combined comedy and incisive satire of middle-class pretensions in *O noapte furtunoasă: Sau, Numarul 9*, (pr. 1879; *A Stormy Night: Or, Number 9*, 1956), *Conul Leonida față cu reactiunea* (pr. 1880; *Mr. Leonida and the Reactionaries*, 1956), and *O scrisoare pierdută* (pr. 1884; *The Lost Letter*, 1956).

The twentieth century saw a number of new influences surface on what has been a consistently lively theater scene. More realistic stories of peasant life appeared in plays such as Ion Slavici's *Moara cu Noroc* (pr. 1908; mill of good fortune); subjectivist theories about the essential ambiguity of experience underlay Ion Minulescu's *Machinul sentimental* (pr. 1926; sentimental puppet) and *Amantul anonim* (pr. 1928; anonymous sweetheart); ironic treatments of standard romantic situations; satirical comedy achieved a sharper edge in George Ciprian's *Omul eu mirtoago* (pr. 1927; the man with the nag), whose grotesque humor was also a hit with the period's German audiences.

World War II and subsequent communist rule temporarily interrupted this development, but by the 1960's political censorship had relaxed and interesting plays once again began to appear: Aurel Baranga's *Opinia publica* (pb. 1967; public opinion), an amusing satire on polling procedures, and Alexander

Mirodan's *Primarul lunii si tubita sa* (pr. 1969; the moon's mayor and his sweetheart), a quirky tale of a lunar socialist society, demonstrated what could be achieved by clever writers. The post-1989 transition to democratic government further freed playwrights from political strictures and was celebrated by the establishment of a national play contest whose winner is guaranteed publication as well as an annual festival in Targa Mures devoted entirely to new Romanian drama.

BULGARIA

Under direct Turkish rule until 1878 and not fully independent until thirty years later, it took Bulgaria some time to develop an indigenous literary culture. Dobri Voinikov wrote and directed several historical melodramas in the 1860's and 1870's, of which *Krivorazbranata tsivilizatsiia*, pr. 1871 (civilization wrongly understood), was an influential defense of Bulgarian nationalism. Another important play from this period is Vasil Drumev's *Ivanko ubietššu: na Asenia I*, pb. 1872 (Ivanko the assassin of Asen I), written in a slangy contemporary idiom that appealed to a wide audience.

The founding of a national theater in Sofia in 1907 created many opportunities for new playwrights. Ivan Vazov's historical dramas received the most performances, although the realistic treatments of social problems in Anton Strashimirov's *Svekurva* (pr. 1907; the mother-in-law) and *Kushta* (pr. 1909; the house) are now regarded as more literarily accomplished. The interwar era saw the emergence of Stefan Kostov, whose comedies blend entertainment with social relevance; *Zlatnata mäna* (pr. 1926; the gold mine) and *Golemanov* (pr. 1927; Golemanov) are still staged today.

The post-1945 communist takeover of Bulgaria produced little more than a number of dull propagandistic plays, almost all of which were forgotten following the return to a more democratic government in 1991. The country's puppet theater is its most vital dramatic form. A high level of government subsidy supports several professional programs as well as companies such as Credo Theatre, which has been warmly received on international tours.

SOUTHERN SLAV NATIONS

The disintegration of Yugoslavia in the 1990's returned the region to a condition that mirrors its historical past, with Serbia, Croatia, Slovenia, and Macedonia actively pursuing the development of their separate cultures.

As in Bulgaria, Serbia's long period of Turkish rule meant that theatrical activity was minimal until the nineteenth century. In 1834 Joakim Vujić established the first Serbian theater at Kragujevac, and in 1869, a national theater was established in Belgrade. Notable playwrights of the era include: Jovan Sterija Popoviæ, whose comedies *Tvrdica: Ili, Kir Janja*, (pr. 1837; the niggard, or Kir Janja) and *Rodoljćupci* (pb. 1849; the patriots) are still staged today; Djura Jakšić, a poet whose verse dramas on historical subjects fueled nationalist sentiment; Laza Kostić, who in plays such as *Maksim Crnojević* (pr. 1863; Maxim Crnojevich) and *Pera Segedinac* (pr. 1875; Pera Segedinac) incorporated sophisticated character development and current political allusions into his work.

The late nineteenth century was marked by the plays of Branislav Nušić, still Serbia's most respected dramatist, including *Narodni posianik* (pr. 1883; the representative of the people), an attack on corrupt officials; *Put oko Sveta* (pr. 1910; a trip around the world), which mocks Serbians who blindly adopt foreign lifestyles; *Pokojnik* (pr. 1937; the deceased), a lament for those denounced for personal reasons by their political enemies). From the beginning of the century to World War II, historical drama, comedies, and musicals based on folklore proliferated on the country's stages, although few individual playwrights of note appeared.

Serbia's bitter experience under German occupation was reflected in many postwar plays lauding heroic guerrilla fighters. In the 1960's Western avant-garde drama became influential, with Velimir Lukić's *Dugiživot kralja Osvalda* (pr. 1963; king Oswald's long life), which uses the language of Aesopian fable to satirize contemporary society, and Aleksandr Popović's *Razvojni put Bore Šnajdera* (pr. 1967: the development of Bora the tailor), a demonstration of how debased popular speech contributes to moral decline, both important works by notable playwrights. More recently, Dušan Kovačević's raucous comedies of human greed leading to inexorable misfortune, of which *Urnebesna tragedija* (pr. 1991; *A Roaring Tragedy*, 1997) and *Doktor Šuster* (pr. 2000; doctor Suster) have been particularly successful, indicate the vitality of Serbian theater.

Macedonia also experienced a long Turkish occupation that effectively repressed most cultural expression until the 1850's, when the nationalist dramas of Jordan Hadži Konstantinov-Džinov articulated the growing support for independence. The more literarily sophisticated plays of Vojdan Černodrimski, notably the stark peasant drama *Makedonska krvava svadha* (pr. 1901; a Macedonian bloody wedding), followed, but until the end of World War II, little else of consequence was produced.

After 1945 Macedonian was officially recognized as one of the founding languages of Yugoslavia, and many new writers tried their hand at the theater. Vasilj Iljoski's satire on soccer mania, *Dva sprema eden* (pr. 1952; two goals to one) and *Čest* (pr. 1953; honor), a slice-of-life love story, were important contributions, as was Tome Arsovski's *Čekor do esenta* (pr. 1969; a step toward the autumn), in which the characters who populated his earlier plays reappear and try once again to solve their problems. Generous state support for the arts in Macedonia is reflected in the country's annual competition for the best new play, which in 2002 showcased sixteen works.

Croatia and Slovenia experienced somewhat less oppressive occupations by foreign powers than did Serbia and Macedonia, and thus both have longer and richer theatrical histories. In Croatia, religious dramas appeared in the fifteenth century, and in the 1500's the city of Dubrovnik had an active theatrical culture; Marin Držić's comedy *Dundo Maroje* (pr. 1550; *Uncle Maroje*, 1967) still receives contemporary stagings. Plays written in the dialect of Croatia's Zagreb region were a prominent feature of eighteenth century dramatic activity and helped to pave the way for the Illyrian movement that began in 1835. This plan for the federation of the Southern Slavs was warmly greeted in Croatia; Dimitrije Demeter's *Teuta* (pr. 1844; Teuta), a mythical account of an Illyrian queen's murder of Roman envoys, exemplified the nationalist agitation that resulted.

The establishment of the Croatian National Theater at Zagreb in 1861 further stimulated Croatian drama. Many historical dramas of minimal literary interest were staged, and it was not until the beginning of the next century that interest in integrating past and present produced significant new playwrights such as Ivo Vojnović, Josip Kosor, and Miroslav Krleža. Vojnović treated historical subjects in a way that emphasized continuities with contemporary events, and his *Dubrovačka trilogija* (pr. 1900; *A Trilogy of Dubrovnik*, 1921) is considered his masterpiece in this style. Kosor's *Nepobjediva ladja* (pr. 1921; the invincible ship) and *Pomirenje* (pr. 1926; reconciliation) dealt with the difficult moral choices posed by modern society. The prolific Krieža created three dramatic cycles that began with the revolutionary fervor of the six-part *Legenda* (pr. 1914; legends), continued with the pessimistic realism of the trilogy *Golgota* (pr. 1922; *Golgotha*), and concluded in the acute socio-psychological analysis of another trilogy, *Gospoda Glembajevi* (pr. 1928-1932; the Glembays).

After World War II, Croatian dramatists were prominent in the Yugoslav theater. *Vašar Snova* (pr. 1958; Vasar Snova) and *Ranjena Ptica* (pr. 1965; *Ranjena Ptica*), Marjan Matković's plays of human alienation and existential despair, spoke to contemporary anxieties, as did Ranko Marinković's *Gloria* (pr. 1955; English translation, 1977), in which a helpless simpleton is manipulated by self-serving bureaucrats. The nationalist agitation leading up to national independence in 1990 was reflected in many plays on political themes; Miro Gavran's *Noč bogova* (pr. 1986; night of the gods), which imagines Molière, Louis XIV, and a court jester wrangling over plays and politics, is both highly relevant and extremely accomplished.

Slovenian drama also has its roots in performances of religious works that gradually incorporate the national language; the anonymous *Igra o paradižu* (the play about paradise), is referred to in seventeenth century records. In the eighteenth century, Antun Tomaž Linhart adapted popular French and German plays into Slovene, but it was only in the following century that indigenous dramas appeared. Although works such as Josip Jurèiè's *Tugomer* (pr. 1876; Tugomer), a romantic tragedy recounting the betrayal of his country's hopes by a misguided leader, did reflect the typical historical obsessions of the era's Southern-Slav drama, Slovenian theater soon shifted its focus to modernist social and psychological concerns. Jože Vošnjak's *Doktor Dragan* (pr. 1890; doctor Dragan), recounted a physician's ethical dilemma in a piece heavily influenced by Ibsen's *En folkefiende* (pr. 1883; *An Enemy of the People*, 1890); Ivan Cankar achieved international as well as domestic renown for the tragicomedies *Za narodov blagor* (pb.1901; for the well-being of the people), an attack on those who manipulate patriotism for political gain, and *Pohujšanje v dolini Šentflorjanski* (pr. 1908; the scandal in Saint Florian's valley), which satirizes the foibles of contemporary intellectuals.

Slovenian drama, perhaps the least developed of the Southern-Slav theatrical traditions, produced little of note after Cankar. Lojz Remec penned a sympathetic portrait of the rural poor in *Magda* (pr. 1924; Magda). Primož Kozak produced an existential treatment of guerrilla warfare in *Afera* (pr. 1962; *An Affair*, 1977). Andrej Hieng pioneered the writing of radio and television plays with *Burleska o Grku* (pr. 1969; burlesque about the Greek). In the 1990's, the Mladinsko Theatre created some notable collective productions, including *Svinènik piše s screm* (pr. 1997; the pencil writes with its heart), an imaginative exploration of the nature of children's creativity.

BIBLIOGRAPHY

Barac, Antun. *A History of Yugoslavian Literature.* Translated by Pavel Miljuskovic. Belgrade: Committee for Foreign Cultural Relations, 1955. The only general history available in English, and still useful although somewhat dated. Includes material on Croatian, Macedonian, Serbian, and Slovenian drama.

Braun, Kazimierz. *History of Polish Theater, 1939-1989: Spheres of Captivity and Freedom.* New York: Greenwood Press, 1996. An insightful account of Polish drama during the German and Soviet occupations, with many engaging anecdotes enlivening a sound scholarly treatment.

Burian, Jarka M. *Modern Czech Theatre: Reflective Conscience of a Nation.* Iowa City: University of Iowa Press, 2000. One of the most comprehensive examinations of Czech drama available in English, it covers the period from the late eighteenth century to the 1990's, and pays substantial attention to concurrent developments in Western European theater.

Calinescu, George. *History of Romanian Literature.* Translated by Leon Levitch. Milan, Italy: Nagard-Unesco, 1988. Although his penchant for expressing idiosyncratic personal opinions can irritate, Calinescu's massive tome, which includes extensive coverage of Romanian theater, is nonetheless factually authoritative as well as elegantly written.

Cizevskji, Dmitrij. *Comparative History of Slavic Literature.* Translated by Richard Noel Porter and Martin P. Rice. Nashville, Tenn.: Vanderbilt University Press, 2000. A brief, cogent introduction to the wider cultural contexts, especially Russia's, that connect all of the region's literatures.

Czerwinski, Edward J. *Contemporary Polish Theater and Drama, 1956-1984.* The seminal influence of Jerzy Grotowski's work is thoroughly explored in a lucid study that describes the effects of censorship on the period's writers. The book also includes many detailed descriptions of plays, plots, and characters.

Goetz-Stankiewicz, Marketa. *The Silenced Theatre: Czech Playwrights Without a Stage.* Toronto, Ont.: University of Toronto Press, 1979. An affecting portrait of authors under siege by government censors that is especially good on the genesis of Václav Havel's plays.

Lengyel, Gyorgy, ed. *The Hungarian Theatre Today.* Budapest: Hungarian Centre of the International Theatre Institute, 1983. Provides valuable information on the cultural background and performance history of Hungarian drama.

Moser, Charles A. *A History of Bulgarian Literature, 865-1944.* The Hague: Mouton, 1972. A crisp overview of major writers and trends, with useful material on the country's playwrights.

Paul Stuewe

FRENCH DRAMA SINCE THE 1600'S

As the eighteenth century began, the influence of the great dramatic poets—Pierre Corneille, Jean Racine, and Molière—was dominant. Their plays continued as the standard fare in the repertory of the Comédie-Française, created by the fusion of Molière's actors and the Hôtel de Bourgogne players in 1680. Yet whereas the seventeenth century had had a predilection for tragedy, the eighteenth century tended to favor comedy, and, with the exception of Voltaire, there are no tragic playwrights of note as tragedy evolved into drama, melodrama, historical, and thesis plays. At the turn of the century, the most prolific tragic dramatist, Prosper Jolyot de Crébillon, while imitating his predecessors in his choice of subjects taken from Greek history and mythology, favored plots with violent deeds and fast-paced action in which passion leads to mayhem. Eschewing the reasoned analysis of passion that lay at the base of Racinian tragedy, Crébillon's works harked back to the early days of the seventeenth century and baroque exaggeration in the style of Alexandre Hardy. Crébillon justified himself in a celebrated dictum in which he posited that since Corneille had taken Heaven and Racine, Earth, there was nothing left for him but Hell. In *Idoménée* (pr. 1705), a father kills his son; in *Atrée et Thyeste* (pr. 1707), a father drinks his son's blood; and in *Électre* (pr. 1708), a son kills his mother. Crébillon's contribution to the development of drama consisted in having prepared French taste for the violent passions that formed the basis of Romantic theater in the nineteenth century.

The comic playwrights at the beginning of the eighteenth century were all disciples of Molière. Chief among these were Jean-François Regnard and Florent Carton Dancourt. Regnard's *Le Joueur* (pr. 1696) and particularly *Le Légataire universel* (pr. 1708; *The Universal Legatee*, 1796) are full of ludicrous situations, riddled with disguises and impersonations. His plays continue the tradition of Molière's stock character, the clever valet, who outwits his betters, saving the day, and money, for his employer. Like Regnard, Dancourt wrote comedies of manners, satirizing the society of the day. The principal butts of his jokes were pretentious ladies in society, the nouveaux riches in *Le Chevalier à la mode* (pr. 1687; English translation, 1927) and, like Regnard, money in *Les Agioteurs* (pr. 1710), a satire on financial speculation. The best comedies of manners were the work of Alain-René Lesage. A keen observer of human foibles, Lesage distinguished himself by favoring character development over plot. He was fascinated by his contemporaries' preoccupation with money, a theme that became central in his best-known play, *Turcaret: Comédie en cinq actes* (pr. 1709; English translation, 1923).

ITALIAN THEATER AND MARIVAUX

Although the Comédie-Française enjoyed a virtual monopoly on theater production throughout the eighteenth century, there was competition provided by two other theater groups: the Italians and the Opéra Comique. The latter theater had been formed in 1713, when the musicians and players of the Théâtre de la Foire won the right to perform their musicals, thus creating a new kind of entertainment, attracting such playwrights as Lesage and later Charles-Simon Favart and Michel-Jean Sedaine, and offering an important market for dramatic writers. The Italians had shared the stage with Molière but had been expelled from France for indecency in 1697. The charge was the result of a play called *La Fausse prude* (pr. 1697), which was thought to ridicule Louis XIV's wife, Mme de Maintenon. The Italians were allowed to return to France in 1716 and eventually took over the theater of the Hôtel de Bourgogne. The musicians and authors of the Théâtre de la Foire and the Italians merged in 1762, to form one company, taking the name Opéra Comique officially in 1780. Three years later, the company moved into the Salle Favart, which—rebuilt twice after fires destroyed it in 1837 and 1887—continues to exist as a major theater for musical productions in Paris.

The return of the Italian theater and the emergence of a new playwright, Marivaux, were a happy coincidence for the French stage. The author of one tragedy and thirty-four comedies, written for both the Comédie-Française and the Italians, Marivaux had the gift of insight into the delicate sentiments of love and self-esteem, which he analyzed in a series of brilliant comedies. His first success, *Arlequin poli par l'amour* (pr. 1720; *Robin, Bachelor of Love*, 1968), set the tone of the plays to follow, in which the psychology of love is expressed in a language unique to Marivaux, an ingenious, subtle, and highly affected style that was given a name of its own: *marivaudage*. Before Marivaux, love was considered a subject fit only for tragedy or low comedy, but Marivaux made love the central element of high comedy. Unlike the great passions described by tragic playwrights, he concentrated on the phenomenon of first love. In plays such as *La Double Inconstance* (pr. 1723; *Double Infidelity*, 1968), *Les Fausses Confidences* (pr. 1737; *The False Confessions*, 1961), and his acknowledged masterpiece, *Le Jeu de l'amour et du hasard* (pr. 1730; *The Game of Love and Chance*, 1907), Marivaux explored the relationship between a young man and a young woman who carefully observe each other and analyze each phrase they speak. The central image is the mask that everyone wears and behind which the lovers hope to peek in order to know the real sentiments of the other without revealing their own.

Marivaux's plays are set in an elegant social atmosphere that is often equated with the delicate interior design and the elegant lines of the French Rococo style. Nevertheless, behind the rarefied manners of the characters, there is a note of cruelty precipitated by pride and manifested in the sometimes underhanded ways in which the heroes achieve their goals. Marivaux's themes also include the relationship of master and servant, who often switch roles or appear in disguise, unveiling the underlying concerns of money and social class that are prevalent in most of the plays of the period.

"TEARFUL" AND SOCIAL COMEDY

A contemporary of Marivaux, Pierre-Claude Nivelle de La Chaussée, like others of his generation, fell under the influence of English sentimental novels, of which Samuel Richardson's *Pamela: Or, Virtue Rewarded* (1740-1741; 2 volumes) was the most widely read. La Chaussée's plays, among which there is an adaptation of *Pamela* (pr. 1743), present a series of virtuous heroines overwhelmed by misfortunes of every sort. The genre is called tearful comedy (*comédie larmoyante*) because it emphasized the pathetic and romantic at the expense of the comic. La Chaussée's theater is anti-intellectual, vaunting middle-class morality even though the characters represent all social classes. The playwright proposed a study of morals, social questions, and the contemporary political scene, thus predating the bourgeois drama of Denis Diderot and playwrights of the nineteenth century: Alexandre Dumas, *fils*, Émile Augier, and François de Curel.

The literary output of Pierre-Augustin Caron de Beaumarchais is modest. Two bourgeois dramas on the theme of money, an opera, and a sentimental drama titled *La Mère coupable* (pr. 1792; *The Guilty Mother*, 1993), written during the revolutionary period, could all have relegated the playwright to oblivion if it were not for his two comic masterworks of worldwide reputation: *Le Barbier de Séville: Ou, La Précaution inutile* (pr. 1775; *The Barber of Seville: Or, The Useless Precaution*, 1776) and its sequel, *La Folle Journée: Ou, Le Mariage de Figaro* (pr. 1784; *The Marriage of Figaro*, 1784). In Beaumarchais's comedy, all the elements in the Molière tradition are present—character, manners, satire, farce—but they make up something new: social comedy. *The Barber of Seville* is a robust romp that introduces the celebrated and archetypical factotum, Figaro, who, in the tradition of the clever servant, helps that young lover outsmart the heroine's guardian. To this end, the charming young Count of Almaviva, disguised as a music student, overcomes numerous obstacles and wins the heart and hand of Rosine. *The Barber of Seville* is as lighthearted and frivolous as *The Marriage of Figaro* is bitter and satiric. The principal characters of the former play appear in the latter, but time has passed, and Almaviva now manifests aristocratic feelings of superiority and privilege, believing that the lower classes exist only to serve. In a play of obvious political dimensions, Figaro refuses to bend to his master's will, and in his victory over his aristocratic adversary, foreshadows the revolution, which was only five years away.

DRAMA BEFORE THE REVOLUTION

From the perspective of historical hindsight, it might surprise the modern reader to know that the great *philosophe* Voltaire—novelist, short-story writer, historian, literary critic, poet, celebrated for his social, political, and philosophical work popularized in such witty prose satires as the famous *Candide: Ou, L'Optimisme* (1759; *Candide: Or, All for the Best*, 1759)—thought of himself, above all, as a man of the theater. Beginning with *Œdipe* (pr. 1718; *Oedipus*, 1761), Voltaire created numerous tragedies in the classical mold. Although emulating the tragic playwrights such as Racine, Voltaire was also influenced by William Shakespeare, whose plays he discovered during a trip to England. Indeed, Voltaire was responsible for introducing and popularizing the English playwright in France. Although refusing to be as violent as his English model, Voltaire nevertheless filled his plays with movement, action, and exaggerated passions tending toward the melodramatic.

As in other genres, Voltaire used his theater as a podium to express his ideas, turning his plays into thesis dramas. In this regard, he reflected the taste of his age, borrowing from La Chaussée and foreshadowing the nineteenth century's use of the stage for preaching social reform. He was attracted by the geographically exotic with plays such as *Alzire* (pr. 1736; English translation, 1763; set in Peru), *Mahomet* (pr. 1742; *Mahomet the Prophet*, 1744; set in Mecca), and even *L'Orphelin de la Chine* (pr. 1755; *The Orphan of China*, 1756; set in China), or the historical *La Mort de César* (pr. 1733), giving an important place to spectacle in his productions. Generally acknowledged as his best play, *Zaïre* (pr. 1732; English translation, 1736) demonstrates how far removed Voltaire was from the classical litotes of Racine and Corneille.

Voltaire played a major role in ridding the French theater of the practice of seating people on the stage. He encouraged good diction among actors and demanded more realistic costumes and sets. In his attempts at faithful re-creation of foreign and exotic sites, he prefigured the Romantic concern for local color. Although faithful to the classical unities of time, place, and action, he violated the rule of propriety in his scenes of violence and refused to use the classical twelve-syllable Alexandrine exclusively.

It was the lot of Denis Diderot to introduce a new kind of play, called *drame*, to the French stage. Because Diderot believed that theater was useful for social reform, he wanted to create a picture of characters and conditions that reflected French society of his day. His plays, written in a natural prose style, had simple plots and no characters extraneous to the central action. His plays, although neither tragedies nor comedies, conformed to the three unities. *Drame* was a deliberate invention meant to appeal to the bourgeois and lower classes by portraying character types they could recognize in dramatic situations that were proper to their social class. Diderot's criticism of classical theater was that it held no interest for the eighteenth century theatergoer, and he railed against the use of verse even in the comedies of Molière. He was more interested in situation than in character, preferred moralizing and philosophical plots, and preached the use of pantomime and fixed tableaux to evoke pathos. His didacticism in *Le Père de famille* (pr. 1761; *The Father of the Family*, 1770; also as *The Family Picture*, 1871) and *Le Fils naturel: Ou, Les Épreuves de la vertu* (pr. 1757; *Dorval: Or, The Test of Virtue*, 1767) foreshadowed the thesis play of the following century.

Le Philosophe sans le savoir (pr. 1765; English translation, 1927), the only serious play by Sedaine, whose principal efforts lay in vaudevilles and comic operas, is widely considered the best example of Diderot's ideas on drama. The play has everything that Diderot wanted: realism, high passion, energetic speeches, and well-delineated characters. In the play, Sedaine defended the bourgeoisie against the disdain of the aristocracy, because the playwright was convinced of the important role played by the middle class in maintaining the country's prosperity. Like Diderot, he prefigured the realistic drama of Eugène Scribe, Augier, and Dumas, *fils*.

Louis-Sébastien Mercier wrote moralizing dramas in the manner of Diderot and agitated for a revolt against classical tragedy and the three unities. His play *La Brouette du vinaigrier* (pr. 1784) is typical: Following the financial ruin of a once rich merchant, the fiancé of the merchant's daughter disappears. A young clerk, Dominique, is in love with the lady. To solidify his son's position, Dominique's father, a vinegar salesman, brings a wheelbarrow full of his life's savings to the merchant's house, and the two young people get married. The play is a plea for the nobility of work and economy and a condemnation of social-class divisions. Like *The Marriage of Figaro*, produced in the same year, Mercier's play contained many of the elements in the great drama of revolution that began with the fall of the Bastille in July, 1789.

FROM REVOLUTION TO ROMANTICISM

At the outbreak of the French Revolution, there were two principal theater companies in Paris, the Comédie-Française and the Opéra Comique, although there were other theaters on the exterior boulevards in which vaudevilles and melodramas were performed. The Comédie-Française had eliminated seats on the stage in 1759, but it was not until 1782 that seats were installed in the orchestra. The Comédie-Française, which occupied the present-day Théâtre de l'Odéon in 1782, moved into its new quarters adjacent to the Palais-Royal in 1790, where it continues to reside.

The revolution also brought the end of censorship on January 13, 1791, leading to an emancipation of actors and the formation of fifty new theaters in Paris. Indeed, the period beginning with the revolution and continuing throughout the nineteenth century was to be the era of great actors. There was the celebrated Talma, who joined the Comédie-Française in 1787. Specializing in tragic roles, his first great part was in Marie-Joseph Chénier's *Charles IX* (pr. 1789). A favorite of Napoleon Bonaparte, Talma helped introduce reforms on the French stage, urging natural acting and period costumes and scenery. Himself inspired by the paintings of Jacques-Louis David, he appeared in classical roles in bare arms and legs, shocking his audiences. The beautiful Mlle George (Marguerite-

Joséphine Weimer) played tragedy at the Comédie-Français but also created principal female roles in the Romantic dramas of Victor Hugo, Alfred de Vigny, and Alexandre Dumas, *père*. Mlle Mars (Anne-Françoise-Hippoyte Boutet) attained renown during the Consulate and Empire periods in the comedies of Molière and Marivaux. Starting as a clown at the Théâtre de Funambules before turning to melodrama, Frédéric Lemaître achieved his greatest success during the Romantic period, when he played such leading roles as Hugo's *Ruy Blas* (pr. 1838; English translation, 1890). Dubbed the Talma of the Boulevards, Lemaître's life was partly chronicled in Marcel Carné's famous film *Les Enfants du paradis* (1945; *Children of Paradise*, 1946). The greatest actress of the first half of the century was Rachel (Élisabeth Félix), who, after an initial success as Camille in Corneille's *Horace* (pr. 1640; English translation, 1656), continued to play tragic heroines and is credited with having revived interest in the genre. Overshadowing all others in the second half of the century, Sarah Bernhardt, who acted frequently at the Comédie-Française between 1862 and 1880, later founded her own Théâtre Sarah Bernhardt. She performed every sort of role—Phèdre, Marguerite in Dumas, *fils*'s *La Dame aux camélias* (pr. 1852; *Camille*, 1856)—even men's roles such as Hamlet. Her most memorable interpretation was as Napoleon's son in Edmond Rostand's *L'Aiglon* (pr. 1900; *The Eaglet*, 1898).

The taste of the theater public during the French Revolution ran to plays with political and patriotic themes and to melodrama. The best exponent of the first genre was Chénier, whose attacks on fanaticism in *Charles IX* followed the fall of the Bastille by only four months. In *Fénelon: Ou, Les Religieuses de Cambra* (pr. 1793; *Fenelon: Or, The Nuns of Cambray*, 1795), Chénier preached clemency and humanity, and his play *Timoléon* (pr. 1792) protested against the excesses of the revolution. The master of melodrama during this period was Guilbert de Pixérécourt, whose *pièces à sensation* appealed to the emotions of fear, terror, and pity by means of threatened heroines, fires, and ghosts in such plays as *Victor: Ou, L'Enfant de la forêt* (pr. 1798) and *Cælina: Ou, L'Enfant du mystère* (pr. 1800; *The Tale of Mystery*, 1802).

Napoleon formalized the hierarchy of Parisian theaters. Only first-class theaters (the Comédie-Française and the Opéra Comique) in the city could produce serious drama, and the second-class theaters on the exterior boulevards were allowed to feature vaudevilles and melodramas. Melodrama stressed strong emotion, theatricality, simple dramatic characters, and spectacular staging, appealing to popular taste and influencing the Romantic theater.

ROMANTIC THEATER

In the short-lived history of French Romantic drama, the honor of having been the first Romantic play belonged to Dumas, *père*'s *Henri III et sa cour* (pr. 1829; *Catherine of Cleves*, 1831; also known as *Henry III and His Court*, 1904), although the theoretical basis was truly contained in the preface to Victor Hugo's *Cromwell* (pr. 1827; English translation, 1896), which had appeared two years earlier. Hugo's dramatic theory called for a mixture of genres to create a combination of sublime and grotesque, because, he stated, everything in nature should be in art. Like Népomucène Lemercier before him, Hugo wanted to do away with the unities of time and place; unity of action, he thought, was dramatically valid. In addition, he raised the Romantics' cry for local color on the grounds that theater needed a living set, situated historically and geographically and emphasizing what is characteristic rather than what is beautiful.

Finally, Hugo preached the liberty of art without models or rules. After the failure of *Cromwell*, Hugo's *Hernani* (pr. 1830; English translation, 1830) was a resounding success, although it caused great controversy when performed at the Comédie-Française, because it violated classical rules. In 1838, Hugo produced perhaps his best play, *Ruy Blas*, a drama of politics and love set, like *Hernani*, in sixteenth century Spain. Hugo is generally praised for his lyricism and painstaking evocation of historical settings. The richness of *Ruy Blas*'s poetry was admirably delivered by the great actor Frédéric Lemaître. The failure of *Les Burgraves* (pr. 1843; *The Burgraves*, 1896) generally marks the end of the public's taste for Romantic theater, a taste that had turned back momentarily to the classics and then had been reinterpreted by the actress Rachel.

Besides Hugo, the pantheon of Romantic playwrights includes Alfred de Vigny, Alfred de Musset, and Alexandre Dumas, *père*. Vigny, better known as a poet, wrote three translations of Shakespeare: *Le More de Venise* (pr. 1829), *Roméo et Juliette* (wr. 1828), and *Shylock: Ou, Le Marchand de Venise* (wr. 1828; pr. 1905), two dramas and one comedy. In the preface to *Le More de Venise*, Vigny put forth his ideas on the theater, positing that plays should present a large canvas of life rather than the specific nature of tragedy. The roles should be created for real characters, not for theatrical personalities, and peaceful scenes should be alternated with comic and tragic ones, all in a natural style. Vigny's best-known play is *Chatterton* (pr. 1835; English translation, 1847), the story of the conflict between middle-class materialism and the downtrodden poetic spirit. It is a thesis play that shows the injustice of society and its culpability in the suicide of the poet, society's outcast and supreme Romantic hero.

Musset was a more prolific playwright than Vigny, producing twenty plays, fifteen of them in prose. His comedies and "proverbs" are among his most successful works, notably *Fantasio* (pb. 1834; English translation, 1853) and *On ne badine pas avec l'amour* (pb. 1834; *No Trifling with Love*, 1890). Perhaps the best Romantic drama of all is his *Lorenzaccio* (pb. 1834; English translation, 1905), set in sixteenth century Florence and based on the assassination of Duke Alexander by his cousin. The play is a detailed picture of the period told in thirty-nine tableaux, but it is also a political drama in which Musset expresses his sympathy for republican government. In this play, Musset, like other Romantics, was inspired by Shakespeare's multiple plots and numerous dramatic characters.

Alexandre Dumas, *père* was a writer of historical dramas, with the notable exception of *Antony* (pr. 1831; English translation, 1904), considered a modern drama of passion, whose locale was Restoration Paris. The hero of this piece is a typically Romantic social pariah, a foundling who loves and pursues a young lady of good family. Although she falls in love with him, the complications of the plot oblige the hero to kill her in order to save her honor when it appears that she will be compromised. Another play, *La Tour de Nesle* (pr. 1832; *The Tower of Nesle*, 1906), was the most popular melodrama of the century, running for eight hundred performances. Despite early enthusiasm for Romantic plays, public taste was turning to prose drama that concerned itself with contemporary society and its problems.

THE TRIUMPH OF REALISM

Eugène Scribe, a prolific writer of nearly four hundred plays for the Théâtre Madame and the Comédie-Française, attempted nearly every dramatic form except the five-act drama in verse. Deemphasizing character development and analysis, Scribe built a reputation based on clever plot construction known as the well-made play, and his stated goal was success as measured by box-office receipts. One of his most popular historical plays, *La Verre d'eau: Ou, Les effets et les causes* (pr. 1840; *The Glass of Water*, 1850), is based on the idea that small events can cause great ones. A misunderstanding between two women concerning a glass of water spilled on Queen Anne's dress leads to the dismissal of the duke of Malborough and to the Treaty of Utrecht that was signed with Louis XIV. Scribe believed that plots should have a large amount of action wrapped in surprises. A historical play, *The Glass of Water* is an exception in Scribe's opus, which values questions of contemporary society. Scribe influenced both Dumas, *fils*, and Augier and, as a result, much of late-nineteenth century French drama. In mid-century, he was, without question, the most popular playwright on the international scene with imitators in every European country.

Émile Augier, a disciple of Scribe, was as adept as his model in creating the well-made play. Although he began writing in verse, he turned to comedies of manners in prose and, in 1854, produced his best-known play, *Le Gendre de M. Poirier* (with Jules Sardeau, based on Sardeau's novel *Sacs et parchemins*; *Monsieur Poirier's Son-in-Law*, 1915), which is a bourgeois drama heavily laced with morality. He tells his audience that marriages should be arranged and

well matched for success, that the family must be defended, that money must be made in an honest fashion, and that a sense of duty and patriotism must be preserved. In this vein, *Le Mariage d'Olympe* (pr. 1855; *The Marriage of Olympe*, 1915) is set in contrast to Dumas, *fils*'s *Camille*. Although Dumas romanticizes the courtesan, Augier depicts a deceitful and sly creature, wholly depraved. Augier also wrote social comedies attacking the press, *Les Effrontés* (pr. 1861; *Faces of Brass*, 1888) and *Le Fils de Giboyer* (pr. 1862; *Giboyer's Son*, 1911), and thesis plays such as *Les Fourchambault* (pr. 1878; *The House of Fourchambault*, 1915), on the fate of illegitimate children.

Like Augier, François Ponsard was a believer in commonsense theater, writing comedies and dramas on the favorite nineteenth century subject: money. He is also the author of a classical tragedy *Lucrèce* (pr. 1843), written for and performed by the actress Rachel.

Alexandre Dumas, *fils*, son of the author of *Antony*, made his literary mark with a novel, *La Dame aux camélias* (1848; *Camille*, 1857), which became a play in 1852. He created a world-famous character and archetypal heroine, Marguerite Gautier, a courtesan rehabilitated by her love for Armand Duval. As in the case of Augier, Dumas followed Scribe's prescription for the well-made play, but he used the theater as an instrument for moralizing and preaching social reform. In thesis plays such as *La Question d'argent* (pr. 1857; *The Money-Question*, 1915), he depicts a family that refuses to share in the profits from unscrupulous financial schemes. Like Augier, he tackled the question of illegitimacy in *Le Fils naturel* (pr. 1858; *The Natural Son*, 1879). Late in his career, his characters took on symbolic, abstract qualities as in *La Princesse Georges* (pr. 1871; *Princess George*, 1881).

Scribe's influence on plot construction extended to comedy and historical plays, of which the works of Victorien Sardou are good examples. Admitted to the Académie Française in 1877, Sardou chose modern Italy and Italian unification as the setting for *La Tosca* (pr. 1887; English translation, 1925), which became the basis for Giacomo Puccini's opera. The plot of his best-known play, *Madame Sans-Gêne* (pr. 1893; *Madame Devil-May-Care*, 1901), is characteristic. It is the story of a laundry girl married to a future *maréchal* in Napoleon Bonaparte's army. When the emperor suggests that her husband divorce her, she stands up to Napoleon, even producing an unpaid laundry bill from years before. His play *Fédora* (pr. 1882; *Fedora*, 1883), set in Russia, starred Sarah Bernhardt. The early realists had an important influence on the drama of Henry Becque and the theater of ideas as represented by Curel and Paul Hervieu.

THE RISE OF NATURALISM

Realist theater—characterized by the well-devised dramatic plot, with its emphasis on psychological truth and human pathos—tended to be sentimental and moralistic and to preach social reform. Like other genres of the period, realist theater evolved toward naturalism, which aimed at overturning theatrical convention. Authors of naturalist theater, while demanding natural acting and realistic sets, tended to produce one-dimensional characters and gave little attention to psychological analysis. As a genre, it professed to be unsentimental and, consequently, anti-bourgeois, showing real life, even at its seamiest, in all its cruelty and degradation. The Goncourt brothers, Edmond and Jules, both better known as novelists, presented *Henriette Maréchal* (pr. 1865), a disturbing story of a young man, aged seventeen, who is loved by a young woman but who is also the lover of the young woman's mother, aged forty. In 1873, Émile Zola's novel *Thérèse Raquin* (1873; English translation, 1947) was brought to the stage, as were the works of other realist and naturalist novelists such as Léon Daudet and Guy de Maupassant.

One of the important figures in the theater of the late nineteenth century is André Antoine, who founded the Théâtre Libre in 1887. Influenced by the naturalists, he aimed at doing away with all theatrical convention, demanding absolute truth in set design and staging. He criticized bourgeois values in cynical slice-of-life dramas that were an essential part of the naturalist concept of theater. His most important contribution, however, was his success at bringing the attention of the French public both to new French authors (Eugène Brieux, Georges Courteline, Curel) and to foreign playwrights (Henrik Ibsen, Leo Tolstoy, and Gerhart Hauptmann). During the life of the Théâtre Libre, between 1887 and 1896, Antoine produced 124 plays.

The best of the naturalist playwrights was Henry Becque, who in two plays, *Les Corbeaux* (pr. 1882; *The Vultures*, 1913) and *La Parisienne* (pr. 1885; *The Woman of Paris*, 1913), had an important impact on the theater. The first is the story of the ruin of a bourgeois family because of the death of the husband and father; in the second, a silly bourgeois woman is caught between her bitter husband and her jealous lover. Becque, like Antoine, did not believe in theatrical convention. The stage should show daily life, a bare-bones art with simple, dense dialogue. In spite of the failure of *The Vultures*, which had only eighteen performances, Becque set a vogue. Henceforth, set design was more precise and acting style more natural. Above all, audiences came to accept the fact that any subject, no matter how low and demeaning, was suitable for drama. Moreover, Becque's hard observations of life were presented without the moralizing that characterized the work of Dumas, *fils*, and Augier. The naturalist playwright did not aim at amusing his audience, and this kind of theater was given its own name: tough (*rosse*). The term "tough" marks an evolution toward the work of Becque's successors: Curel, Hervieu, and Brieux.

CUREL, HERVIEU, AND BRIEUX

An anecdote tells that Curel sent three plays under three different names to Antoine at the Théâtre Libre in the hope of getting them produced. Antoine agreed to stage two of the three. Thus *L'Envers d'une sainte* (*A False Saint*, 1916), a psychological study of sanctity, opened in 1892. In this play, a woman, rather than commit murder, confines herself to a convent, returning only after the death of the man whose wife she contrived to kill. *L'Invitée*, produced in 1893, addresses the problem of broken families when a long-divorced mother returns to her daughters, who do not know her. She is invited to come back by the girl's father, who wants to secure good marriages for them.

Curel is the foremost playwright among the group who evolved from naturalist drama toward a theater of ideas, sometimes designated as symbolic. In *La Nouvelle Idole* (pr. 1899), which poses problems raised by modern science, Donnat, the doctor, represents science, his wife, love, and the patient Antoinette, religion. Like the naturalist playwrights, Curel's style is spare and austere. Like them, too, he avoids sustaining a thesis and moralizing. Preoccupied with abnormal human relations, he seeks out strange occurrences in life, molds the incidents into simple stories, and analyzes the characters' motivations. *Les Fossiles* (pr. 1892; *The Fossils*, 1915) is the story of the useless nobility in modern France.

The plays of Hervieu, like Curel's, are symbolic, but Hervieu used a high moral tone, heightened by exaggerated rhetoric. As a social moralist, he explored the problems of the bourgeois family and saw, in the natural law, that each generation sacrifices itself for the next. In *La Course du flambeau* (pr. 1901; *The Trail of the Torch*, 1915), often considered his best work, he depicted the tragedy of material love in which the characters are analyzed not for what they are but for what they represent.

Brieux, a member of the Académie Française, was the playwright of the period with the most obvious ties to the tradition of Dumas, *fils*, and Augier. His moral stance can be said to reach the level of propaganda, transforming social drama into thesis play. In *La Robe rouge* (pr. 1900; *The Red Robe*, 1916), he addresses the problem of the administration of justice, and in *Les Remplaçantes* (pr. 1901), the duty of a mother in desperate circumstances to kidnap her own children. Brieux's vision is broader than Dumas's, and his choice of subject more daring than those of either Dumas or Augier. This may have resulted from the influence of Antoine's Théâtre Libre, which produced two of his plays. Unlike other playwrights of his time who dealt with the subject of the family, Brieux considered the phenomenon biological: The family must be preserved to perpetuate the race.

COUNTERCURRENTS AND COMIC RELIEF

The naturalist theater of ideas did not have a monopoly on theatrical productions in the late nine-teenth century. In striking contrast, there was the self-styled theater of love (Théâtre d'Amour) of Georges de Porto-Riche and the psychological drama of Félix-Henry Bataille, which examined the conflicts encountered by love. Porto-Riche's theater of love was a series of eight plays that chronicled the perpetual gallantry of men and the deep sensitivity of women. *La Chance de Françoise* (pr. 1888; *Françoise's Luck*, 1915) declared that even though the heroine was lucky to keep her husband despite his desire to be unfaithful, love still would not bring happiness. *Amoureuse* (pr. 1891; *A Loving Wife*, 1921) showed how too much love from a woman can suffocate a man. Porto-Riche was an admirer of Maupassant and, like the great short-story writer, tried to peer into the souls of his characters and reveal their egocentric love. Bataille is sometimes likened to Luigi Pirandello because he dealt with the fundamental duality of what people believe to be real and what is actually the case in matters of love.

Another countercurrent to the realist-naturalist movement was Symbolist drama, which sought to bring to life poetic ideas and allegories in the belief that the theater, with all of its possibilities, was a perfect means for treating the mysteries of the poetic. The first testing ground for Symbolist drama was the Théâtre de l'Art, founded by Paul Fort, who produced plays between 1890 and 1892. The work was carried on by Aurélien-François Lugné-Poë at his Théâtre de l'Oeuvre, a theater that presented a broad range of plays including Ibsen's *Peer Gynt* (pr. 1876; English translation, 1892) and *En folkefiende* (pr. 1883; *An Enemy of the People*, 1890). The great craftsman of Symbolist theater in the French language is the Belgian Maurice Maeterlinck, whose characters act out their tragedies in mysterious castles and haunted woods. Rejecting the positivistic outlook of naturalist drama, the Symbolists embraced the unclear, vague, and unreal atmosphere of dreams.

The third significant countercurrent was comedy and farce in which the genius of comic writers used the same themes as the realists and naturalists (money and infidelity) and turned them into subjects of humor. Like his realist contemporaries, Eugène Labiche was adept at the well-made play, creating frantic chases (*Un Chapeau de paille d'Italie*, pr. 1851; *The Italian Straw Hat*, 1873) and conflicts of rival suitors (*Le Voyage de M. Perrichon*, pr. 1860; *The Journey of Mr. Perrichon*, 1924), in collaboration with Marc-Antoine-Amédée Michel and Édouard Martin, respectively. The author of more than one hundred farces, Labiche achieved the status of a comedic paragon when the philosopher Henri Bergson used his plays to illustrate a theory of comedy in a celebrated treatise on laughter, *Le Rire: Essai sur la signification du comique* (1900; *Laughter: An Essay on the Meaning of the Comic*, 1911). Scenically updated to a turn-of-the-century decor, *The Italian Straw Hat* was made into a silent film classic by René Clair in 1927. In the same tradition as Labiche was Georges Feydeau, who brought burlesque comedy to its highest point. Feydeau's plays are better theater than they are literature and continued to be popular long after his death. They are quick-paced comedies whose central subject is often adultery, including the inevitable chase, misunderstandings, and mistaken identities.

SATIRE, ROMANTIC REVIVAL, AND COMEDY

Alfred Jarry produced satiric farces with exaggerated grotesque characters such as the unforgettable Ubu in *Ubu roi* (pr. 1896; English translation, 1951), performed at Lugné-Poë's Théâtre de l'Oeuvre. In the series of Ubu plays (*Ubu enchaîné*, pr. 1937; *Ubu Enchained*, 1953; and *Ubu cocu*, wr. 1888; *Ubu Cuckolded*, 1953) Jarry's satire is vicious. Through the Ubu experience, which began as a schoolboy farce, Jarry developed a theory that, in general, all dramatic action should revolve around a single character. His sets were reduced to a minimum, simple accessories to the action, and his actors wore masks. Jarry's work had an important influence on Antonin Artaud, who founded the Théâtre Alfred Jarry in 1927.

At the end of the nineteenth century, a single figure, Edmond Rostand, revived Romantic theater, re-creating moments reminiscent of Hugo, Musset, and Marivaux. His best-known plays are *Les Romanesques* (pr. 1894; *The Romantics*, 1899), *Cyrano de Bergerac* (pr. 1897; English translation, 1898), and *L'Aiglon* (pr. 1900; *The Eaglet*, 1898), which starred Sarah Bernhardt. The idealized hero of *Cyrano de Bergerac* is a pure romantic, noble of heart, pushing love to the point of sacrifice, with language full of images and nuances, his heart and words at odds with his unhappy physiognomy. Rostand's theater represents a reaction to naturalism; it is antithetical to the ideas of Antoine, which were the theatrical gospel of the day.

Like Molière before him, Georges Courteline gave his heroes burlesque names and turned them into marionettes. Seemingly no subject escaped his satire. In *Un Client sérieux* (pr. 1897), he satirizes the system of justice and in *Messieurs les ronds-de-cuir* (pr. 1893; *The Bureaucrats: Messieurs les Ronds de Cuir*, 1928), government employees, showing their mindless routine, the uselessness and absurdity of government regulations. Other favored targets, the police and bourgeois life, are pretexts for demonstrating the simpleminded application of rules or the plight of henpecked husbands (*La Paix chez soi*, pr. 1903; *Peace at Home*, 1913).

The tradition of farce continued well into the twentieth century and is best represented by Sacha Guitry, who wrote light comedies on the theme of the romantic triangle: husband, wife, and lover. Author of more than one hundred comedies, his was the most popular name in the Paris theater from World War I into the 1930's with plays such as *Faisons un rêve* (pr. 1916), *Je t'aime* (pr. 1920), and *Quadrille* (pr. 1937). Not limited to comedy, he wrote plays inspired by the lives of famous men: *Mozart* (pr. 1926) and *Pasteur* (pr. 1919; English translation, 1921). Like many theater people of his day, he was eventually drawn to the cinema and turned many of his theatrical triumphs into films.

At the same time, Jules Romains found a standard comic character in *Knock: Ou, Le Triomphe de la médecine* (pr. 1923; *Dr. Knock*, 1925). Romains's career as a dramatist had begun in 1911 when *L'Armée dans la ville*, considered an attempt at modern tragedy, was produced by Antoine. Romains's connection with the philosophy of unanimism transformed him into a celebrated novelist, but it was the comic vein that brought him success in the theater. *Dr. Knock*, a comedy reminiscent of Molière's *Le Malade imaginaire* (pr. 1673; *The Imaginary Invalid*, 1732), in which the title role was played by Louis Jouvet, was followed by other successes in the same genre: *M. Le Trouhadec saisi par la débauche* (pr. 1923), *Le Dictateur* (pr. 1926), and *Donogoo* (pr. 1930).

BEFORE WORLD WAR II

French drama in the twentieth century is in large measure the story of theater directors who, like their predecessors Antoine and Lugné-Poë, set trends and discovered new authors. Jacques Copeau founded the Théâtre du Vieux Colombier, which he administered from 1913 until 1924. Symbolic of Copeau's desire for change, his theater was on the Left Bank in Paris, as opposed to the other theaters of the time. Training other important directors such as Charles Dullin and Louis Jouvet, he sought eclecticism in the repertory: the classics, foreign authors, and unknown and unpublished playwrights. His principles were basic: sincerity, force, depth, and an ensemble company with no stars. Where Antoine believed in precisely realistic sets, Copeau emphasized simplicity and, to this end, had the Vieux Colombier redesigned. He did away with the proscenium arch and the footlights and had the stage extended into the audience to create a space shared by viewer and actor, in order to encourage a sense of participation.

In 1927, his two pupils Dullin and Jouvet joined two other directors, Georges Pitoëff and Gaston Baty, to form the Cartel. Pitoëff, a Russian émigré, founded a company in 1925, specializing in foreign plays in translation. It was he who put on the first French production of Pirandello's *Sei personaggi in cerca d'autore* (pr. 1921; *Six Characters in Search of an Author*, 1922). Dullin created a new company at the Théâtre de l'Atelier as well as a school of dramatic art. Future directors Jean-Louis Barrault and Jean Vilar learned their trade in Dullin's theater. Jouvet left the Vieux Colombier to direct the Théâtre des Champs-Élysées, offering brilliant productions of Romains's *Dr. Knock* and Jean Giraudoux's *Siegfried* (pr. 1928; English translation, 1930) and *Amphytrion 38* (pr. 1929; English translation, 1938). The Jouvet-Giraudoux tandem continued at the Athénée Theater, where Jouvet also reinterpreted many Molière comedies in which he took roles such as

Arnophe in *L'École des femmes* (pr. 1662; *The School for Wives*, 1732). Jouvet also revealed the talents of Jean Genet in his 1947 production of *Les Bonnes* (pr. 1947; *The Maids*, 1954).

Unlike the Cartel's other directors, Baty was quite far from the ideas of Copeau, his notions harking back to the Romantics. In his Théâtre Montparnasse, he gave great importance to sets, costumes, props, lighting, and music. As the objective of the Cartel was mutual support, both moral and financial, in an effort to resist commercial pressure, Baty was not excluded. These four directors sought to make the theater what they called a "place of dreams and imagination," giving primacy to the text, as well as the art and interpretation of the actor. With the exception of Baty, the others embraced Copeau's ideals and extolled the virtue of simple scenery.

THEATER OF CRUELTY AND CLAUDEL

Through his theories published in *Le Théâtre et son double* (1938; *The Theatre and Its Double*, 1958), Antonin Artaud brought to the stage his notion of a total theater that appealed to the whole organism through the senses. His concept of the Theater of Cruelty underlined the arduous task of spectator and actor, the former coming to the performance to participate in the dramatic ritual. Artaud wanted to place the audience in the middle of the theater, with the action taking place all around, and, to this end, he proposed movable sets. Jean-Louis Barrault was influenced both by Artaud and by Dullin, and one sees this most clearly in Barrault's collaboration with Paul Claudel. Like Artaud, Claudel fell under the spell of certain forms of Asian theater, in which the text is minimal or nonexistent and in which the success of the effect depends on a nonintellectual appeal. Claudel's dramas of immense proportion provided Barrault's imagination the latitude to create with music, staging, film, and lighting. With his wife, Madeleine Renaud, he founded a company in 1947 at the Théâtre Marigny, and after 1956, he assumed directorship of the Théâtre de l'Odéon.

A career diplomat whose posts in the Far East (Shanghai, Tokyo, Beijing) had an immense influence on his work, Claudel was the creator of a mystical, religious, and personal theater of universal dimensions. Throughout his career, Claudel was haunted by the problems of love and redemption of sin. In *Partage de midi* (pb. 1906; *Break of Noon*, 1960), Claudel describes the tragic qualities of love and in *L'Annonce faite à Marie* (pr. 1912; *The Tidings Brought to Mary*, 1916), human charity and the pardon of sin through death. In this play, set in the Middle Ages, a young woman meets a man whom she once loved but who has contracted leprosy. She consents to kiss him out of compassion, and when she falls victim to the disease, she is cast out by her family. In death, she becomes the instrument of a miracle as she resuscitates her sister's dead child.

Together with Henry de Montherlant, Claudel ranks as one of the great language craftsmen of the modern French stage, his scripts containing magnificent prose poetry. The collaboration with Jean-Louis Barrault was best revealed in the production of *Le Soulier de satin* (wr. 1919-1924, pr. 1943; *The Satin Slipper: Or, The Worst Is Not the Surest*, 1931) during the Occupation. The play takes up Claudel's recurrent themes: humanity's attachment to the material and the carnal, its defiance of the love of God, and a person's happiness in the ultimate surrender to God's will.

The tendency toward the mystical is present in the work of Montherlant, a novelist who turned to drama with such plays as *La Reine morte* (pr. 1942; *Queen After Death*, 1951). Like his other plays, *Le Maître de Santiago* (pr. 1948; *The Master of Santiago*, 1951), *Port-Royal* (pr. 1954; English translation, 1962), and *Le Cardinal d'Espagne* (pr. 1960; *The Cardinal of Spain*, 1969), *Queen After Death* has important religious elements and a historical plot constructed around the twin themes of punishment and sacrifice. Although Montherlant was often criticized for writing undramatic plays, he is recognized for his sober and understated style. In the same vein, another novelist, Georges Bernanos, entered the realm of mystical theater with his *Dialogues des Carmélites* (pb. 1949; *The Fearless Heart*, 1952).

COCTEAU AND GIRAUDOUX

Jean Cocteau was either a virtuoso genius or a dilettante, depending on one's point of view. Though often accused of frivolity, Cocteau succeeded in everything he touched: novels, poetry, film, and theater. His dramatic work contains elements drawn from Surrealism and from classical Greek theater: *Orphée* (pr. 1926; *Orpheus*, 1933), *Antigone* (pr. 1922; English translation, 1961), and *La Machine infernale* (pr. 1934; *The Infernal Machine*, 1936), an adaptation of the Oedipus legend. Cocteau's surrealism lies in the magical powers he bestows on objects: mirrors, horses, talking statues, and hermetic symbols repeated in both his plays and films. Like the Surrealists, too, he insists on the magical element of coincidence in which people are victims of the elements rather than masters of their own destinies.

Set in Cocteau's time, *La Voix humaine* (pb. 1930; *The Human Voice*, 1951), a one-act play, recounts the telephone conversation between a woman and her lover, who has left her. *Les Parents terribles* (pr. 1938; *Intimate Relations*, 1952) and *La Machine à écrire* (pr. 1941; *The Typewriter*, 1948) describe the viciousness of family life. Even in these plays, however, the realistic only masks the mystical and mysterious.

In a series of fourteen plays from *Siegfried* to the posthumously produced *Pour Lucrèce* (1953; *Duel of Angels*, 1958), Jean Giraudoux, through a world of myth, legend, and imagination, aimed at unfastening the French theater audience from its rationalist ties. Desiring to create an experience that spoke to the spirit and the senses, Giraudoux's plays set up a system of appositions based on the fundamental difference between the material and the spiritual: France versus Germany in *Siegfried*, life versus death in *Intermezzo* (pr. 1933; *The Enchanted*, 1955), the rational versus the imaginative in *La Folle de Chaillot* (pr. 1945; *The Madwoman of Chaillot*, 1947), the real versus the fantastic in *Ondine* (pr. 1939; English translation, 1954), truth versus justice in *Électre* (pr. 1937; *Electra*, 1952). At the center of everything is man and woman in the form of the couple.

Giraudoux leads one to wonder if Jupiter can seduce Alcmène in *Amphytrion 38*, offering to make her a goddess if she will leave her husband, or whether the Trojan War could have been avoided or justified if Helen had only loved Paris in *La Guerre de Troie n'aura pas lieu* (pr. 1935; *Tiger at the Gates*, 1955). Giraudoux's theater is intellectual, a theater of words that have supernatural powers. Even at the end of *Sodome et Gomorrhe* (pr. 1943; *Sodom and Gomorrah*, 1961), voices can still be heard in the ruins of the cities even though everyone has perished.

POSTWAR FORMS AND TRENDS

The importance of theater directors continued after World War II. Jean-Louis Barrault, following his celebrated production of Claudel's *The Satin Slipper* during the Occupation, went on to found his own company and eventually to assume the directorship of a state-subsidized theater. Another director to make his mark was Jean Vilar, who in 1951 took over as head of the Théâtre National Populaire, which had languished since its creation in 1920. When Vilar came to the large (3,500-seat) theater in the Palais de Chaillot, he did what Copeau had done at the Vieux Colombier: He removed the proscenium arch, footlights, and front curtain and had a large apron added to the stage. The effect was to eliminate any separation between actor and audience. Although Vilar wanted minimal sets with actors playing against a black back curtain, his productions exploded with color provided by lavish costumes that were meant also to suggest the characters' personalities.

Vilar's taste always tended toward popular spectacle. Early in his career, when he believed that permanent theater could not survive in the provinces, he fought for the establishment of regular theatrical festivals, founding the Festival d'Avignon in 1947. He also believed that a large public should be exposed to the work of great authors, French and foreign, and he regularly staged works by playwrights such as Corneille, Shakespeare, Bertolt Brecht, and Heinrich von Kleist. One of his most notable successes was Corneille's *Le Cid* (pr. 1637; *The Cid*, 1637), the reputation of which was largely based on the performance of the incomparable Gérard Philipe, one of the most celebrated stage actors of the mid-twentieth century.

Philipe, whose career began in Nice in 1942, won celebrity for his interpretation of the title role in Albert Camus's *Caligula* (pr. 1945; English translation, 1948) in 1945. Although his career was divided between stage and screen, Philipe's greatest triumphs were in the theater. In 1951, he joined Vilar at the Théâtre National Populaire, where, in addition to the part of Rodrigue in *The Cid*, he gave memorable performances in Musset's *Lorenzaccio, Les Caprices de Marianne* (pr. 1833; *The Follies of Marianne*, 1905), and *No Trifling with Love*, the last produced in the year of his death. At the Théâtre National Populaire, Vilar's avowed aim was to provide entertainment and education for those who could not afford tickets in other theaters.

FISCAL CRISIS AND DECENTRALIZATION

The 1960's saw the Théâtre National Populaire pass through a number of financial difficulties. Early in the 1970's, Roger Planchon was hired as its new director, and the production center was moved to Villeurbanne, in the Paris suburbs. At the same time, the theater at the Palais de Chaillot came under the directorship of Jack Lang, former director of the Festival International de Nancy. Yet Lang's expensive remodeling of the theater building resulted in his termination from the position in 1974. In 1981, he became minister of culture at the beginning of the first Mitterrand presidency. He succeeded in doubling the budget for French cultural expenses in 1982 and acted as a flamboyant advocate of the French arts. Controversial as minister, he left in 1986 only to return for a second term, from 1988 to 1993, when the defeat of his Socialist Party removed him from power. Lang's name became synonymous with lavish spending on culture, including France's public theaters, which freed them from many economic constraints.

The move by the Théâtre National Populaire to Villeurbanne, a drab working-class town outside Paris, reflected a government policy of decentralization, a conscious attempt to move theater away from its natural marketplace, where prices and distance made access to theater prohibitive for many. The first production at the new Théâtre National Populaire in 1972 was of Christopher Marlowe's *The Massacre at Paris* (pr. 1593), directed by Patrice Chéreau. Chéreau's subsequent work at the Théâtre National

Populaire, a mixture of classical and modern plays, particularly by foreign authors, won for him an international reputation so that, by the 1980's, he was making important contributions in film, drama, and opera. In 1982, he became director of the Théâtre de Nanterre-Amandiers, where he formed a close professional relationship with playwright Bernard-Marie Koltès.

With one exception, Chéreau directed all of Koltès's plays, many of which were influenced by the playwright's travels to French-speaking Africa. *Combat de nègre et de chiens* (pr. 1983; *Struggle of the Dogs and the Black*, 1982) is set at the site of an African development project, which has come to a halt after the death of a black laborer. While one of the white engineers seeks his missing dog, the brother of the dead man demands to see the corpse. Koltès's last play, *Le Retour au désert* (1988; *Return to the Desert*, 1997) again focuses on the conflict between two different antagonists, this time a brother and his sister. The crisis erupts when the sister returns to the family home in the early 1960's after being displaced from what had been French Algeria.

Chéreau's collaboration with Koltès also signified a return both of directorial interest in contemporary plays and of the critical success of decentralization, which saw important premieres outside of Paris. After Koltès's death from acquired immunodeficiency syndrome (AIDS), Chéreau left the theater at Nanterre to work independently, directing many European classics on international stages. His first English-language film, *Intimacy* (2000), won the Golden Bear for Best Film award at the 2001 Berlin Film Festival, symbolizing Chéreau's dual success as stage director and filmmaker, which is not an unusual career in contemporary French drama.

ANOUILH

Postwar French drama, despite important trends in philosophical theater, anti-theater (sometimes called Theater of the Absurd), and political and experimental drama also held to the old habits and pleasures of bourgeois theater best represented by Jean Anouilh, whose career spanned three decades from the 1930's to the 1960's. Undeniably the French playwright with the widest international appeal since World War II, Anouilh saw his work translated into many languages, and English versions have played with great success in the United States.

Anouilh's *Le Bal des voleurs* (wr. 1932; *Thieves' Carnival*, 1952) was performed in New York in 1954, and *Le Voyageur sans bagage* (pr. 1937; *Traveller Without Luggage*, 1959) became a film called *Identity Unknown* in 1945. *Léocadia* (pr. 1940; *Time Remembered*, 1955) was interpreted by Helen Hayes and Richard Burton on Broadway and *La Valse des toréadors* (pr. 1952; *Waltz of the Toreadors*, 1953) won the New York Drama Critics Circle Award as the Best Foreign Play of the 1956-1957 season. *L'Alouette* (pr. 1953; *The Lark*, 1955) appeared on the stages of Paris and New York in the same year, the American version starring Julie Harris. *Becket: Ou, L'Honneur de Dieu* (pr. 1959; *Becket: Or, The Honor of God*, 1962) had a successful run with Anthony Quinn and Sir Lawrence Olivier playing the lead roles, and it later became a film starring Peter O'Toole and Richard Burton.

Anouilh grouped his plays into four catagories: *pièces roses*, *pièces noires*, *pièces brillantes*, and *pièces grinçantes* (pink, black, sparkling, and grating plays). Although all of his plays contain liberal doses of humor, pessimism, gaiety, and irony, Anouilh's overview is somber. Throughout his work, he describes the striving of the young, particularly, for emotional absolutes in a world of pedestrian sentiments. The young revolt against ugliness and immoral behavior in the society around them. *Antigone* (pr. 1944; English translation, 1946), exemplary of these elements, reinterprets the Greek legend in modern dress. Here Antigone defies the head of state, her uncle Créon, and buries her brother Polynice. Now a criminal, Antigone finds herself before her judge, Créon, who offers her ways of avoiding the death sentence usually imposed in such cases. Standing up to the state's authority, she demands that Créon do his duty as she had done hers, motivated by the pure love she felt for her brother. Resigned, Créon sentences her to death. Demanding happiness and refusing compromise, Anouilh's characters display the grandeur of unselfish love.

EXISTENTIALISM

Jean-Paul Sartre came from the novel to the theater in a series of brilliant plays from 1943 to 1959. He saw in drama an effective means of communicating his ideas, giving human form to his philosophy. At the base of Sartre's notions are the act (which makes thought concrete), good faith (which makes the act conform to the thought from which it emanates), and responsibility (which demands that the author of an act acknowledge responsibility for it). He is the major French exponent of existential philosophy.

Inspired by his experience in a German concentration camp, Sartre wrote *Les Mouches* (pr. 1943; *The Flies*, 1946), a retelling of the Electra myth with ironic twists. His theater is based on the concept of situational ethics, where choices involved in any decision are determined by the particular conditions under which an individual must make a choice. Choosing to act is essential for Sartre, since existence is the emergence from a passive state. Existentialist heroes are condemned to be free because, conscious of the reasons for their acts, they do not hide behind mass thought. In *The Flies*, a political allegory, the hero, Oreste, returns home to find that his father has been murdered by his mother and that his city is infested by a plague of flies. Oreste finally understands that to save the city he must sacrifice himself by murdering his mother and transferring the plague from the city to himself.

Sartre's *Huis clos* (pr. 1944; *No Exit*, 1946), a one-act play set in Hell, teaches the futility of good intentions if they are not realized by action, and the evil of bad faith or hypocrisy by which most people live, according to the playwright. In *Le Diable et le bon dieu* (pr. 1951; *The Devil and the Good Lord*, 1953), the protagonist, Goetz, demonstrates the absurdity of life by committing good and evil arbitrarily. Although espousing a particular philosophical and political point of view, Sartre's theater, like that of Camus, is a continuation of traditional thesis drama, in which the dramatic situations are concrete reflections of metaphysics.

Albert Camus turned to the theater for the same reasons as Sartre, to express his ideas visually. His drama is limited to four plays: *Caligula*, *Le Malentendu* (pr. 1944; *The Misunderstanding*, 1948), *L'État de siège* (pr. 1948; *State of Siege*, 1958), and *Les Justes* (pr. 1949; *The Just Assassins*, 1958), and perhaps, as a result, Camus's theater is often underestimated. *Caligula*, which opened with Gérard Philipe in the title role, illustrates Camus's concept of the absurd: the quest for logic in an illogical world. The madness of the Roman emperor derives from the central problem that humans die, and they are not happy. Forced to face this truth, Caligula revolts against complacency and imposes a whimsical and arbitrary code of justice, leading to destruction and nihilism. Caligula recognizes his failure at the end and posits that his liberty was not the right kind. What was needed was a more balanced approach to revolt and an insistence on the value of human solidarity.

With the exception of *Caligula*, Camus's plays emphasize philosophy over drama. *The Misunderstanding* tells the story of an exile's return to an inn run by his mother and sister who, unknown to him, make a practice of robbing and killing their guests. When he is unable to communicate with them, they murder him. Camus's concern for creating a meaningful dialogue among men is a distant reflection of Eugène Ionesco's concern with the futility of language.

THEATER OF THE ABSURD

In twelve plays performed between 1950 and 1966, Romanian-born Ionesco created a "shock" theater, not unlike Samuel Beckett's, meant to disorient the traditional theatergoer. The central theme of most of Ionesco's early works is the fundamentally insufficient weight of language and its inability to communicate meaning. Ionesco claims, for example, that he was inspired to create the play *La Cantatrice chauve* (pr. 1950; *The Bald Soprano*, 1956) by his attempts to learn English through the audiolingual method. During this experience, he became aware of the linguistic dominance of the cliché and the nonsensical pattern talk that make up the bulk of everyday conversation. The illogical responses to stimuli in *The Bald Soprano* and the mysterious message of the deaf and mute orator at the end of *Les Chaises* (pr. 1952; *The*

Chairs, 1957) point to the fruitless dependence on language as a means of communication.

Ionesco developed a character type, naïve and surprised by everything, who appeared in his plays, beginning with *Rhinocéros* (pr. 1959; *Rhinoceros*, 1959), in which Berenger watches, amazed and helpless, as the inhabitants of the city are transformed into horned beasts, symbols of the dehumanization that goes hand in hand with fascism. Like Beckett and Arthur Adamov, Ionesco created characters who find themselves living in bad dreams. Berenger appears again in *Le Piéton de l'air* (pr. 1962; *A Stroll in the Air*, 1964) and *Le Roi se meurt* (pr. 1962; *Exit the King*, 1963), in which a king of Shakespearean proportions is accompanied in ritual ceremony by his two wives and his doctor-executioner. In *La Soif et la faim* (pr. 1964; *Hunger and Thirst*, 1968), the Berenger character, here called Jean, is forever in search of impossible happiness. Trapped in a hellish world in which executioners keep two clowns caged, each forced by imposed starvation to retract statements previously made, Jean must serve the community without any hope of ever seeing his family again.

In Ionesco's universe, modern people are prisoners in an absurd, illogical nightmare that they cannot control. The nameless hero of *Le Nouveau Locataire* (pr. 1955; *The New Tenant*, 1956) is powerless to prevent the movers from filling his new apartment with furniture it cannot hold, as humanity is the victim of material things. Ionesco's work is sometimes called anti-theater or Theater of the Absurd, a term also applied to a group of playwrights who refused to deal with convention of any sort: linguistic, dramatic, logical. The major proponents of this new theater were Adamov, Beckett, and Genet.

In 1950 Jean Vilar was the first director to mount a production of Russian-born Adamov (*L'Invasion*), a drama about language in which two men, devoted to a lifelong love affair with electronic games, end up as old men unable to communicate except in the language of the machines. In *Paolo Paoli* (pr. 1957; *Paolo Paoli: The Year of the Butterfly*, 1959), Adamov presents two men who begin their careers trading feathers and butterflies. Eventually, the laws

of commerce take command and lead to commodity trading in everything, including wives and mistresses. Influenced by Brecht, Adamov's hallucinatory universe derives from the Surrealists. With other contemporary playwrights such as Beckett and Ionesco, he shares a concern for the function of language and the nature of action. As early as 1953, Adamov was writing plays with political content, although he did not take a political point of view. *Tous contre tous* (pr. 1953) paints a sordid picture of the dishonesty of political discourse that glosses over intolerance and racial exploitation and justifies self-interest.

From a life begun as an orphan, through crime, prostitution, the underworld, and prisons, Jean Genet came to drama by way of prose fiction. Genet, the outcast, rejected traditional Western dramatic convention in favor of the Eastern tradition of Japan, China, and Bali, an enthusiasm he shared with both Claudel and Artaud. In four plays—*The Maids*, *Le Balcon* (pr. 1960; *The Balcony*, 1957), *Les Nègres* (pr. 1959; *The Blacks*, 1960), and *Les Paravents* (pr. 1961; *The Screens*, 1962)—Genet illustrates evil by using two basic themes: illusion and the sacred.

For Genet, the theater is a world of the false and the ritualistic. In *The Maids*, two sisters, employed as maids, construct a model of role-play in which one or the other assumes the character of their female employer and the other the employer's assassin. The two plot the murder, but when they fail, one has to serve the other the poisoned tea destined for their mistress. The poisoner then assumes the role of the celebrated murderess Madame Solange. *The Screens* is Genet's largest-scale play, with twenty-five tableaux and one hundred roles divided among twenty actors. If *The Maids* is the revolt of the maids against their mistress, *The Screens* is the revolt of the Arabs against the French colonial army. In a debate among the social order, groups of characters, at first unknown to one another, are brought face to face, the poor Arabs confronting wealthy white colonialists. Genet's drama explores dramatic form and illusion, rejecting the idea that the theater is an amusement. With both sincerity and sacrilege, Genet posits that there is no greater nor more effective theatricality than in the Catholic Church and the sacrifice of the Mass. The juxtaposition of positive and negative, of creation and destruction, is the central element in Genet's theater.

Nobel laureate Beckett, like Ionesco and Adamov, refused to deal with what his work means. The Irish-born playwright painted a fresco of the loneliness and the interdependence of human beings. In *En attendant Godot* (pr. 1953; *Waiting for Godot*, 1954), Estragon and Vladimir meet each day to await the mysterious Godot, who never comes. Their clownish ritual defines their relationship. Their encounters with the master-slave duo Pozzo and Lucky underscore the variety of dominant and subservient roles that people play. Godot is a fiction that forces them to wait but that also fills up their time. *Waiting for Godot* is also one of the most famous plays of the twentieth century. It has been produced in many local languages and has inspired playwrights all over the world, including Gao Xingjian, winner of the 2000 Nobel Prize for literature. Gao's *Chezan* (pr. 1983; *Bus Stop*, 1996) has been hailed as a Chinese version of Beckett's play, with characters waiting for ten years for a bus that never arrives. Leaving China in the late 1990's, as Beckett left Ireland decades before him, Gao moved to Paris, became a French citizen, and writes in French as well as in Chinese.

Beckett was exemplary of the absurdist and existentialist mentality at the same time. *Fin de partie* (pr. 1957; *Endgame*, 1958) presents a similar array of unfathomable characters: Hamm, paralyzed and blind; his servant, Clov; and Hamm's deplorably aging kin Nagg and Nell, in garbage cans. Beckett said that nothing brings solace to the human condition, not philosophy, not religion. Beckett's theater juxtaposed action and words in plays in which nothing happens and in which words have insufficient power to clarify misunderstandings. Significantly, Beckett's characters are all linguistically alert, quick to pun, and given to poetic evocation and flights of rhetoric which reaffirm life while masking physical decay.

Jacques Audiberti is another exemplar of shock theater. His first play *Quoat-Quoat* (pr. 1946), produced at the Gaité-Montparnasse Theater derives from a Surrealist tradition, revealing evil forces behind the surface of ordinary life. In *Le Mal court* (pr. 1947) a princess traveling to marry the king of a foreign land is deceived by a young man who is disguised as the king. Having fallen in love with him, she discovers that he is a police agent from her fiancé's country. Alert to universal corruption around her, she determines to create evil in her country by every means possible, including murder.

In 1962, the Comédie-Française created a scandal by mounting *La Fourmi dans le corps*, provoking a heated reaction from audiences accustomed to classical repertory. Like the princess of *Le Mal court*, the seventeenth century heroine retires to a nunnery to escape the eroticism of the world, only to discover a society of pagan hedonism within the convent, where she must eventually resign herself to the fact and accept her new condition. Audiberti's intense verbal richness and his re-creation of the baroque have led some critics to compare him to François Rabelais and Shakespeare.

Fernando Arrabal was inspired by Living Theater and other American theater experiments in the 1960's. His first play, a one-act titled *Pique-nique en campagne* (*Picnic on the Battlefield*, 1960), though produced in 1959 did not become widely known until late in the 1960's and became the basis for a German opera in 1997. Works such as *Le Cimetière des voitures* (pr. 1966; *The Car Cemetary*, 1960), *Les Deux Bourreaux* (pr. 1960; *The Two Executioners*, 1960), and *La Communion solonnelle* (pr. 1958; *Solemn Communion*, 1967) are permeated with sexual and religious symbolism. He is part of an important modern movement toward new expression in the theater. His work owes much also to the Surrealist tradition, and like many other avant-garde playwrights, Arrabal cloaks his drama in a decided hermeticism and fantasy, decipherable fully only to him. In many respects, his theater, which he dubs "panic theater," resembles that of Genet. By 2002, he had written nearly seventy plays, published in nineteen volumes in France. His play *Carta de amour* (pr. 1999; love letter) was well received and displayed the versatile talents of a dramatist at the height of his creative career.

Armand Gatti is the pen name of Monaco-born radical playwright Saveur Dante Gatti. Gatti believes that theater can influence society and should be participatory and subscribes to an extreme left-wing ideology. A number of his plays are influenced by his own experience, like that of Sartre, in a German concentration camp during World War II. As in *L'Enfant-rat* (pb. 1960), *La Deuxième Existence du camp de Tatenberg* (pr. 1962; *The Second Life of Tatenberg Camp*, 2000), and *La Cigogne* (pr. 1968), he is less interested in the event than in the long-term effect on the survivors. *La Cigogne* portrays characters searching the ruins of the atomic devastation in Nagasaki and finding objects that allow them to re-create parts of the lives of the owners.

Gatti's theater is extremely politically oriented, describing repressive regimes in *Les Treize Soleils de la rue Sainte-Blaise* (pr. 1968) and recounting the life of an anarchist leader during the Spanish Civil War in *La Colonne Durruti* (1974). Much of Gatti's early production was mounted by the Théâtre National Populaire and directed by Roger Planchon at Villeurbanne, a working-class community. The values proposed by Gatti's works are statements of political commitment and are considerably left of center, meant to speak to the inhabitants whom the theater in Villeurbanne serves. *La Vie imaginaire de l'éboueur Auguste G.* (pr. 1962; *The Imaginary Life of the Street Cleaner Augustus G.*, 1968) is a biographical tale of Gatti's father, a factory worker clubbed to death by the police during a strike. Gatti's vision of the world is in conflict with the portraits of bourgeois life that are the meat of Parisian theater fare. He has been a foremost promoter of the idea of popular, revolutionary theater and his plays are intended for the working-class audiences outside of Paris where he prefers to produce them. He has also been drawn to locations of international conflict and staged his play *Le Labyrinthe* (1982; the labyrinth) in Northern Ireland during a time of sectarian violence.

DIRECTOR'S THEATER AND LITERARY PLAYS

In the 1970's, the French theater scene was very lively. There was a continuing effort toward decentralization and a promotion of theatrical companies in regional centers. Theater festivals such as the one in Avignon, founded by Vilar, contributed to broadening the audience base. French television began to mount special productions of the classics, even telecasting a British series of Shakespeare plays. Television also started to transmit live performances of boulevard comedies directly from the theaters in which they were being performed. Yet if there was one characteristic above all others that described the state of French theater in the 1970's, it was the dearth of new "literary" playwrights and the increasingly dominant position of directors who reinterpreted the classics and standard repertory, marking them with their personal stamp.

One reason for this phenomenon was the way in which government subsidies for theater provided nearly unlimited economic and artistic power to the directors of the theaters. Decentralization supported this trend with the creation of well-funded Centres Dramatiques Nationaux (national drama centers), or CDN, which multiplied available positions for ambitious and creative directors. By 2002, France had nearly three dozen CDNs, each with its own theater troupe and funded to 64 percent by the state and local governments. There are also nine Centres Dramatiques Régionaux (regional drama centers), which are meant to focus on plays with a local theme, and sixty-one *scènes nationales* (national stages), which include stages equipped for multimedia productions and are fully state funded.

By the 1980's, there emerged a new trend: the reappearance of the contemporary literary play. This was in part fueled by the enduring popularity of café theater in Paris, which has provided an artistic outlet for aspiring playwrights since the mid-1960's. At places like the Café d'Edgar, La Vielle Grille, or the Café de la Gare, all in Paris, up to three short plays are shown in the course of the night, while patrons also enjoy food and drink. Occasionally, star actors like Gérard Depardieu have performed in the plays of personal friends. Looking for new, popular material for their theatrical productions, over which they have maintained their economic and artistic power, many theater directors have shifted their interests to include the production of newly written plays. For example, the collaboration between director Chéreau and playwright Koltès at the Théâtre de Nanterre-Amandiers during the 1980's became a widely emulated model. By 2002, a significant invigoration of French drama had occurred, with new plays written and produced in record numbers.

THÉÂTRE DU SOLEIL

The government's policy of decentralization forced the development of new theater companies, among which one of the most successful in the 1970's and 1980's was Ariane Mnouchkine's Théâtre du Soleil (literally, "theater of the sun"). Mnouchkine exemplifies, like Chéreau, the power of the director in contemporary French drama. Ironically, Mnouchkine prides herself on a nonauthoritarian, collectivist approach, and even participated in menial chores at the Théâtre du Soleil, collecting tickets and sweeping the stage. However, this cannot distract from the fact that the artistic identity of her theater is of her own making, and her talent continued to shape the company's successful productions of the 1990's and early twenty-first century.

The breakthrough for the company came with *1789* (pr. 1970), created under Mnouchkine's artistic guidance in a collaborative approach involving herself, theater staff and artistic talent, and the key actors and actresses. Set in the year of the French Revolution, the play experimented with multiple stages and succeeded in intimately involving the audience, who often remained seated at the end of the performance to discuss the well-researched, individualistically reinterpreted events from history. The play was followed by two more historical dramas, again produced as collective enterprises: *1793* (pr. 1972) and *L'Âge d'or* (pr. 1975; the golden age).

With its elaborate productions, which ran up huge costs, the company was rescued from financial ruin with Jack Lang's doubling of the budget for culture and theater in 1981. Reinvigorated, Mnouchkine won critical fame for her series of Shakespeare plays that were staged with an infusion of classical Japanese and Chinese dramatic traditions in the 1980's, exemplifying again the power of the director's theater. From 1990 to 1993, Mnouchkine produced a cycle of plays, *Les Atrides* (the Atrides), based on classical Greek material.

In tandem with the sudden reemergence of original, text-based contemporary plays, Mnouchkine be-

gan to collaborate with the feminist theoretician and playwright Hélène Cixous. In 1985, signaling a nationwide trend back to the production of new literary plays, the Théâtre du Soleil saw Mnouchkine's production of Cixous's epic play *L'Histoire terrible mais inachevee de Norodom Sihanouk, roi du Cambodge* (*The Terrible but Unfinished Story of Norodom Sihanouk, King of Cambodia*, 1994). Chronicling the plight of Norodom Sihanouk, the former king of Cambodia who collaborated with the murderous Khmer Rouge after being deposed by General Lon Nol in 1970 and later broke with them to become king again in 1993, the play focuses on the suffering experienced by the Cambodian people as a consequence of France's colonial escapades. Cixous's collaboration with the Théâtre du Soleil continued, leading to a critically successful production of *La Ville parjure ou le reveil des Erynyes* (pr. 1994; *The Terrible City*, 1994), focusing on government corruption.

By 2002, indicative of its international reputation, Mnouchkine's theater company produced *The Flood Drummers* (pr. 2002) at the Sydney Theatre Festival in Australia. Exemplifying Mnouchkine's lasting interest in Asian theater, the play is based on a fifteenth century Chinese tale. For the Sydney production, the main performers were dressed like Japanese Bunraku puppets and were carried by other performers clad entirely in black. The play also reaffirmed Mnouchkine's dedication to her socialist beliefs and collaborative ideals, which have been a significant trademark of all productions of her "theater of the sun."

EARLY TWENTY-FIRST CENTURY

At the beginning of the twenty-first century, French drama flourished again, invigorated by new plays of high caliber. A new generation of playwrights had come into its own. For example, Michel Deutsch and Jean-Paul Wenzel, who had formed the Théâtre du Quotidien (theater of the everyday) company in 1975 as a countermovement to the then all-powerful director's theater, remained dedicated to the promotion of new plays. Deutsch gained fame with his fragmentary, nonlinear play *Convoi* (pr. 1980; convoy), which explored characters trapped in the conventions of everyday speech. His play *Skinner* (pr.

2002) is set as night entombs a typical French town. While sirens wail off stage, the characters are abandoned in a postexistentialist world in which humanity is confronted with a sense of universal futility. Wenzel's play *Faire Bleu* (pr. 2000), returns to the scene of his first play, *Loin d'Hagondange* (pr. 1975; *Far from Hagondange*, 1994). The steel workers of an industrial town are revisited a quarter of a century later, as a working-class couple faces the issues of retirement after decades of physical labor.

Among playwrights who began work after the tide had turned in favor of original plays is Philippe Minyana, a prolific writer of plays for the stage, television, and cinema and of opera texts. Beginning with *Premier trimestre* (pr. 1979; first trimester), he is known for short plays for the stage. His *Inventaires* (pr. 1988; inventories) was his first drama, widely produced in Europe, Canada, and South America. Minyana's *Habitations* (pr. 2000; houses) and *Pièces* (pr. 2001; rooms), were produced to great critical acclaim at Paris's Théâtre Ouvert (open theater), as were many of the more than thirty plays he had written by the beginning of the twenty-first century.

PRIVATE THEATER AND MULTICULTURAL FRANCE

Eric-Emmanuel Schmitt is one of the few contemporary playwrights who has written for the commercial, private theaters of Paris. Surviving without direct government subsidies, unlike the public theaters that, in the early twenty-first century, still enjoy generous state funding, the private theaters must rely on box-office receipts and depend on popular plays. The only state support comes through the *Fonds du Soutien* (support fund), which helps, for example, with the production of the first three plays of a new author. Yet the productions of private theaters still draw roughly half of France's annual theater audience.

Schmitt's incredibly successful *Variations énigmatiques* (pr. 1996; *Enigma Variations*, 1999) originally starred Alain Delon and has been produced all over the globe. It is a play about two men, a winner of the Nobel Prize in Literature and a journalist, who probe the theme of love as they pursue a mysterious woman. His *Hôtel des deux mondes* (pr. 1999; *Two World's Hotel*, 2001) features an enigmatic doctor looking after the hotel's guests and examines the question of finding meaning in the postmodern world. The play received seven nominations for France's prestigious Molière Award for 2000 and was a runaway hit at the 2001 Festival d'Avignon, a festival that has become an institution of French drama.

Among the next generation of playwrights who established themselves in the early twenty-first century is Marie Ndiaye, who also reflects the increasing multicultural and multiracial aspect of French society and theater. The daughter of a French woman and a man from Senegal, Ndiaye started as a novelist and turned to drama with *Hilda* (pr. 2002) and *Providence* (pr. 2001), two plays named after their female protagonists. As her early plays received critical acclaim, Ndiaye lived in the region of Aquitaine, signifying the success of decentralization, which means that a playwright is no longer required to live in Paris to be known and successful.

Providence is a dark play of a mysterious blond-haired woman returning to a typical French provincial village to search for her long-lost daughter. Mixing elements of mythology and the magical, the villagers are suspicious of Providence, who also sports cloven feet like a she-devil. At the play's end, a local waitress is revealed to possibly be Providence's daughter, but a final answer is never given as the young woman readies to leave the village. *Hilda* and *Providence* focus on the role of the outsider and reflect both racial tensions and the creative vitality of contemporary drama in modern-day France.

BIBLIOGRAPHY

Bradby, David. *Modern French Drama, 1940-1990.* 2d ed. Cambridge, England: Cambridge University Press, 1991. Excellent, comprehensive study and detailed discussion of major themes, major playwrights, and their work. Bibliography, historical table of play productions, index.

Daniels, Barry V., ed. *Revolution in the Theatre: French Romantic Theories of Drama.* Westport, Conn.: Greenwood, 1983. Collection of perceptive essays probing the shape of drama in French Romantic theater. Index.

Gaensbauer, Deborah B. *The French Theater of the Absurd*. Boston, Mass.: Twayne, 1991. Useful survey of major playwrights and their work, with emphasis on authors such as Artaud, Beckett, Adamov, and Arrabal. Bibliography, index.

Harrison, Helen L. *Pistols/Paroles: Money and Language in Seventeenth Century French Comedy*. Charlottesville, Va.: Rookwood Press, 1996. Useful look at some of the primary themes of French comedy of the period. Argues the treatment of money and language in comic drama is related to the social classes of French society and their divergent interests. Bibliography and index.

Knapp, Bettina L., and Frances M. Kavenik. *French Theater Since 1968*. New York: Twayne, 1995. Examines how the years following the 1968 student protests have redefined French theater and discusses the contributions of figures such as Mnouchkine, Gatti, Chéreau, and Antoine Vitez.

Lamar, Celita. *Our Voices, Ourselves: Women Writing for the French Theatre*. New York: Peter Lang, 1991. Excellent study of the plays by French women dramatists, especially between 1975 to 1985. Critically examines issues, artistic influence, and cultural standing of women playwrights. Bibliography and index.

Lyons, John D. *Kingdom of Disorder: The Theory of Tragedy in Classical France*. West Lafayette, Ind.: Purdue University Press, 1999. Scholarly work of French tragic drama from 1600 to 1699. Perceptive and with significant discussion of how individual plays correspond to theoretical demands. Bibliography and index.

Pao, Angela C. *The Orient of the Boulevards: Exoticism, Empire, and Nineteenth Century French Theater*. Philadelphia: University of Pennsylvania Press, 1998. Provocative study of the impact of France's empire in the East on the tastes of its theatergoing audience at home. Argues that the view of the East was deeply shaped by French political and cultural dreams and desires. Bibliography and index.

Poe, George. *The Rococo and Eighteenth Century French Literature: A Study Through Marivaux's Theater*. New York: Peter Lang, 1987. Comprehensive analysis of the work of Marivaux and the dramatic issues of his age. Bibliography and index.

Powell, Brenda J. *The Metaphysical Quality of the Tragic: A Study of Sophocles, Giraudoux, and Sartre*. New York: Peter Lang, 1990. A look at the Greek sources of the plays by the two French dramatists. Scholarly but also accessible and full of relevant insight. Bibliography and index.

Ravel, Jeffrey S. *The Contested Parterre: Public Theater and French Political Culture, 1680-1791*. Ithaca, N.Y.: Cornell University Press, 1999. Brilliant study of the role of drama in pre-revolutionary France. Focus is on the role of theater and its audience in the political conflicts of the time. Bibliography and index.

Wellington, Marie. *The Art of Voltaire's Theater*. New York: Peter Lang, 1987. Useful work on the dramatic output of the French philosopher of the Enlightenment. Relates Voltaire's plays to the intellectual atmosphere leading up to the French Revolution. Bibliography and index.

Henry A. Garrity,
updated by R. C. Lutz

German Drama Since the 1600's

For German drama, the eighteenth century marks the beginning of a new era that culminates in the unprecedented achievements of Weimar classicism. The credit for having moved literature onto this course must be given to Johann Christoph Gottsched, who is the dominant figure of the early Enlightenment, a time when supreme faith was placed on the exercise of reason.

Though trained as a theologian, Gottsched's real interest was in literature and aesthetics. His productivity began early. At age twenty-four, he arrived at Leipzig, then an important intellectual and cultural center. He soon involved himself in the literary and academic life of the city and became a dominant force. When he published his highly influential Versuch einer critischen Dichtkunst vor die Deutschen (1730; attempt at a critical poesy for the Germans), it became the recognized authority for the writing of poetry and drama. The work, a practical guide for the aspiring author, prescribes principles of composition and discusses elements of style. Its basic premise is that literature is the product of the mind acting in accordance with preestablished laws of composition. Gottsched's primary aim was to introduce into German drama something of that beauty of form that he admired in the plays of the French tragedians Pierre Corneille and Jean Racine. To put his theories into practice, he formed an alliance with the acting company of Karoline Neuber. Together they set out to reform German theater. This was not a simple task. The most difficult obstacle lay in bridging the gap between drama and theater, for at this time the two stood apart. High drama was rarely performed before the public. Theater was primarily vaudeville, and its itinerant performers could hardly be called actors in the modern sense. The troupe typically consisted of acrobats, jugglers, and dancers whose repertory also happened to include a theatrical production. Usually, this was a low farce with heavy emphasis on the scatological and the erotic. To make matters worse, the actors' nomadic lifestyle, accompanied by a reputation for easy virtue, caused the profession to be held in contempt. Indeed, actors were often forbidden entrance into a city and had to perform outside the walls.

Such was the situation when Gottsched and Neuber launched their reforms. First, they improved the quality of theatrical production. To supply the company with suitable material, Gottsched compiled a repertory consisting of classical, French, and English dramas—as well as German pieces—which corresponded to the new standards. Next, they raised the respectability of the acting profession. Henceforth, members of the company were required to live socially acceptable lives. Eventually, Gottsched succeeded in attracting a number of young writers to Leipzig who accepted him as their leader. This group, now known as the Gottsched school, reached its peak in the 1740's.

Rebellion against Gottsched's rules

Although Gottsched made important contributions to the development of theater, his theory of dramatic composition proved to have a serious flaw. He sought to reform literature externally, by imposing rules on it. He had little use for imagination, which he, like many of his contemporaries, regarded as a recollective or reproductive faculty rather than a creative one. Furthermore, his efforts to create a German drama modeled on the French did not reflect the national taste. In the 1740's his views were challenged by two Swiss theoreticians, Johann Jakob Bodmer and Johann Jakob Breitinger. Both agreed that drama needed to be reformed, but, unlike their opponent, they sought to accomplish the task from within. They pointed out that great works are not the product of rules but that the rules arise from the product. Each work of art is a self-contained entity, a law unto itself. Hence, they called for more flexibility in form and for more freedom in the exercise of the imagination. As more writers sided with Bodmer and Breitinger, Gottsched's influence declined. His more talented disciples fell away and struck out on their own. The most gifted of them was Johann Elias Schlegel. Instead of imitating the French, he chose ancient Greek tragedy as his model. His tragedies *Hermann* (pb. 1743) and *Canut* (pb. 1746) reflect the more liberal trend in the judicious use of imagination and feeling. He also wrote two comedies, *Die stumme Schönheit* (pb. 1747; silent beauty) and *Der Triumph der guten Frauen* (pb. 1748; the triumph of the good women), whose originality further served to weaken the Gottsched school.

Unlike Enlightenment tragedy, which was burdened by rigid criteria, the theoreticians virtually ignored comedy. Before long, authors discovered that comedy and satire were better suited than any other literary form for expressing the tenor of the age. A great number of satiric dramas were produced that mocked attitudes, values, and behavior inconsistent with the Enlightenment's emphasis on reason. By means of ridicule, the writers of comedy hoped to institute change. Such moral didacticism is particularly evident in the pieces of Christian Fürchtegott Gellert, the most popular figure of the Enlightenment. In *Die Betschwester* (pb. 1745; bed sisters), he satirizes hypocrisy, while *Das Loos in der Lotterie* (pb. 1746; the lottery ticket) holds up materialism to laughter. He strikes a new note with *Die zärtlichen Schwestern* (pb. 1747; *Tender Sisters*, 1805), a tragicomedy concerning the integrity of feeling. Gellert's choice of contemporary topics and his innovative use of everyday language influenced the development of comedy through Gotthold Ephraim Lessing, the dominant figure of the later Enlightenment.

GOTTHOLD EPHRAIM LESSING

Both a dramatist and a critic, Lessing had a decisive influence on the development of German drama. Lessing joined those opposing the more restrictive canons of the Gottsched school in calling for greater freedom in the choice of subject matter and greater flexibility in form. He also insisted that tragedy need not deal with kings, princes, or heroes to be tragic. He then illustrated his point by writing *Miss Sara Sampson* (pr. 1755; English translation, 1933), a play about the seduction of a young woman of the middle class by an aristocrat. The drama marks the beginning of a new genre, the *bürgerliches Trauerspiel* (middle-

class, or bourgeois, tragedy). Here Lessing breaks with tradition not only in the choice of subject matter but also in the use of everyday language instead of the Alexandrines favored by the Gottsched school. He maintained this novel practice for *Emilia Galotti* (pr. 1772; English translation, 1786). For the rest of the century, the possibilities of this genre were successfully exploited by many authors. Its influence is recognizable in the nineteenth century in Friedrich Hebbel's prose tragedies, the social dramas of Henrik Ibsen and Gerhart Hauptmann, and, in modified form, in the mass-man dramas of the 1890's.

Lessing made two other lasting contributions. The first concerns his introduction of blank verse for tragedy, first employed for *Nathan der Weise* (pr. 1783; *Nathan the Wise*, 1781). Blank verse caught on quickly, and after Johann Wolfgang von Goethe had demonstrated its potential in *Iphigenie auf Tauris* (pb. 1779; *Iphigenia in Tauris*, 1793), it became the standard form for tragedy. Lessing's second major contribution is to be found in the critical essays of his *Hamburgische Dramaturgie* (1767-1768; *Hamburg Dramaturgy*, 1879). Through analysis of specific plays combined with his reinterpretation of Aristotle's *De poetica* (c. 334-323 B.C.E.; *Poetics*, 1705), he was able to free his contemporaries from the domination of Gottsched's theories and the rules of French tragedy while at the same time providing them with more liberal guidelines. In so doing, Lessing supplied the ammunition the next generation of writers needed to revolutionize drama.

STURM UND DRANG

As is the case with so many literary movements, the Sturm und Drang (Storm and Stress) movement was a revolt against the ideas and standards of the preceding generation. The young writers of this group assaulted the tyranny of reason, advocating the cultivation of the emotions and the imagination and calling for their expression in drama. Instinct and intuition should be trusted, they proclaimed, for humanity's true nature is to be found in the irrational depths of the heart. Whatever the mind failed to grasp, the imagination would. Next, they rejected the Enlightenment tenet that great art results from following rules. Hence, they denounced all traditional standards of dramatic composition—standards that, in their view, suffocate the creative spirit. They called on the authority of Lessing, who had written that the creative genius is a law unto himself. As their model they chose William Shakespeare, whose poetry and drama, they pointed out, broke every law in the book.

In the social sphere, these writers demanded equality and raised their voices against the privileges of the nobility. Individuals, they held, have the right and the duty to realize their potential, which they can only do if they are unrestricted by the class system. On another level, they claimed that people endowed with the strength and the talent to achieve greatness are not subject to the same standards of conduct as average people, who order their lives according to the prevailing values of the day. The only guide for extraordinary individuals is their own consciences.

Technically, the Sturm und Drang began with Johann Wolfgang von Goethe's *Götz von Berlichingen mit der eisernen Hand* (pr. 1774; *Götz von Berlichingen with the Iron Hand*, 1799) and ended with Friedrich Schiller's *Die Räuber* (pb. 1781; *The Robbers*, 1792). Typical of the period, Goethe's play is an account of a strong, independent man who is destroyed by the plotting of courtiers. The play was an overwhelming success and served as the model for the entire movement.

Criticism of contemporary society and the celebration of the vigorous personality are also the salient features of Goethe's contemporary, Friedrich Maximilian Klinger. His first effort, *Otto* (pb. 1775), resembles *Götz von Berlichingen with the Iron Hand* but with family strife complicating the plot. Rebellion against the law of primogeniture (the rights of the first-born son) is the subject of *Die Zwillinge* (pr. 1776; the twins), equality and the struggle against tyranny that of *Die neue Arria* (1776; *The Modern Arria*, 1795). Klinger's play *Sturm und Drang* (pb. 1776; *Storm and Stress*, 1978), which gave the movement its name, is set in the United States during the Revolutionary War and celebrates the triumph of freedom over oppression.

Another favorite theme of Sturm und Drang dramatists was the aristocracy's often unscrupulous treatment of the other classes. *Die Soldaten* (pb. 1776; *The Soldiers*, 1972), by Jakob Michael Reinhold Lenz, dramatizes the seduction of the daughter of a middle-class merchant by a caddish, ruthless officer and his later abandonment of her. Heinrich Leopold Wagner's *Die Reue nach der Tat* (1775; remorse after the deed), Schiller's *Kabale und Liebe* (pr. 1784; *Cabal and Love*, 1795), and Goethe's *Faust: Ein Fragment* (*Faust: A Fragment*, 1980) of 1790 all deal with different aspects of this theme.

Although many writers of the Sturm und Drang were active well into the 1790's, the vitality of the movement had spent itself by about 1780. Several factors contributed to the decline. Many of the playwrights went too far in scorning the laws of measure and restraint. Their taste for extravagant language and for incidents surcharged with passion and violence became excessive. Most important, the movement's two most gifted men, Schiller and Goethe, abandoned it. Yet despite the relatively short life of the Sturm und Drang and its obvious deficiencies, it prepared the ground for the Romantic movement.

CLASSICISM

The spirit of Athens and Rome that entered German drama in the late eighteenth century was the culmination of a trend in aesthetics that had its beginning in the work of Johann Joachim Winckelmann. In his influential *Geschichte der Kunst des Alterthums* (1764; *History of the Art of Antiquity*, 1849-1873), he had maintained that the only way a society could achieve greatness was to imitate the Greeks. His ideas caught on quickly and served as the basis for the introduction of the Greek ideal into education and art. Through Lessing, Winckelmann's ideas found their way into drama. Winckelmann's often quoted definition of the Greek ideal as "noble simplicity and quiet grandeur" also held great attraction for Schiller and Goethe, who had grown weary of the excesses of the Sturm und Drang.

JOHANN WOLFGANG VON GOETHE

Johann Wolfgang von Goethe's classical period covers the years between 1779 and 1810. His first piece of that period, *Iphigenia in Tauris*, underwent three revisions, in which his transition to classicism is evident. His turn from the Sturm und Drang became decisive after two years in Italy (1786-1788), where he was able to study antiquity at first hand. In Italy, he recast the prose of the first two versions of *Iphigenia in Tauris* into an elevated blank verse that ultimately became the standard form for German tragedy for more than a century. Inspired by Sophocles and Aristotle's *Poetics*, he incorporated features characteristic of Athenian tragedy. By exploiting the possibilities offered by recognition-reversal, tragic error, and catharsis, he achieved in his classical pieces a cohesiveness and economy of form unique in German drama. Goethe next wrote *Torquato Tasso* (pr. 1807; English translation, 1827) in the classical form. In this thinly veiled account of Goethe's own experiences at the Weimar court, Tasso is portrayed as a gifted poet who, like Goethe, aspires to a social position to which his talent alone does not entitle him. Following his inevitable humiliation, he regains his dignity and personal integrity by striking out on his own.

Goethe's two other classical dramas are *Die natürliche Tochter* (pr. 1803; *The Natural Daughter*, 1885) and his masterpiece, *Faust* (1790, 1833). The latter work occupied Goethe for sixty years. First conceived in the 1770's, it went through many revisions: the 1790 *Faust: A Fragment*; *Faust: Eine Tragödie* (pb. 1808; *The Tragedy of Faust*, 1823); *Faust: Eine Tragödie, zweiter Teil* (pb. 1833; *The Tragedy of Faust, Part Two*, 1838). Faust has been an archetypal figure in the imagination and literature of the West since the Middle Ages. In its traditional form, the legend tells of a man who sells his soul to the devil in exchange for supernatural powers and the enjoyment of earthly pleasures. Goethe reworked the legend, making it an investigation into the human condition, with Faust serving as the representative of humanity.

In Goethe's final version, Faust has become the object of a wager between God and Mephistopheles, the devil. The play begins with a "Prologue in Heaven" in which God praises Faust as his faithful servant and as a fine example of humankind. Mephistopheles wagers that he can easily divert Faust from the Lord's service and induce him to give up his striving for higher things (*Streben*), which the Lord has identified as the fundamental force governing all existence. Subsequently, Mephistopheles visits Faust in his study, and they come to an agreement: In return for services rendered, Mephistopheles may try to get Faust to abandon his striving. For his part, Faust is uninterested in the traditional inducements of earthly pleasure. He demands nothing less than to undergo the totality of human experience. He wants to feel everything of which a human being is capable; every pain and every joy from the highest to the lowest, so that his own experience will be commensurate with that of all humankind. Even though Mephistopheles' failure to win the bet and Faust's salvation are clearly foreshadowed in the "Prologue in Heaven," Goethe sustains the audience's interest through a multitude of incidents, scenes, and characters ranging from his present back to classical Greece, involving crime, temptation, sin, and ultimately purification and salvation. The matchless lyric poetry also serves as Goethe's contribution to the development of the German language as a means of literary expression: During the eighteenth century, there had been serious debate over whether German was an adequate vehicle for expressing lofty sentiments. Goethe laid these doubts permanently to rest.

FRIEDRICH SCHILLER

An even greater contribution to German drama was made by Friedrich Schiller, one of Germany's foremost dramatists. A lyric poet in his own right, a theoretician and philosopher of renown, he brought to drama a combination of philosophical insight, poetic power, and regularity of form that has perhaps never been exceeded.

Schiller began his career as a playwright when still an unwilling cadet at the military academy founded by the unimaginative despot Karl Eugen of Württemberg. Schiller wrote his first play, *The Robbers*, in secret because the explosive subject matter was sure to incur the duke's displeasure. For the same reason, he published it outside the duchy under a pseudonym. The play soon caught the attention of Wolfgang Heribert Dalberg, director of the Mannheim National Theatre in the neighboring state of Hesse. Dalberg produced the play in 1781. The premiere, attended secretly by the author, was a phenomenal success and soon brought him fame throughout Germany. When the duke, who took a personal interest in the lives of his subjects, learned of Schiller's clandestine visits to Mannheim, he forbade him to write any more "comedies" on pain of imprisonment. Having long since decided to live as a playwright, Schiller deserted his post as regimental surgeon and went into hiding at the country estate of an acquaintance in Thuringia. There, he completed *Die Verschwörung des Fiesko zu Genua* (pr. 1783; *Fiesko: Or, the Genoese Conspiracy*, 1796). Based loosely on Count Fiesko's revolt against Andrea Doria in 1587, it dramatizes the transformation of an idealistic political reformer into an egotist hungry for power.

Next, Schiller wrote his only middle-class tragedy, *Cabal and Love*. In this play, political intrigue is brought into conflict with basic human dignity. Schiller's next play, *Don Carlos, Infant von Spanien* (pr. 1787; *Don Carlos, Infante of Spain*, 1798), marks the transition to his classical phase. Set in sixteenth century Spain, it is an impassioned plea for freedom and basic human rights. Although the play was well received, it suffers from serious flaws in technique and organization, limitations of which Schiller himself was only too well aware. He abandoned drama for the next ten years. During this time, he made a careful study of ancient and modern tragedy and wrote several essays on the subject. Of particular importance are *Über die tragische Kunst* (1790; *On Tragic Art*, 1844), *Über das Erhabene* (1801; *On the Sublime*, 1844), and *Über das Pathetische* (1793; *On the Pathetic*, 1845).

Schiller's first drama after ten years of silence is the historical tragedy *Wallensteins Lager* (pr. 1798; *The Camp of Wallenstein*, 1846), generally considered to be his finest achievement. The play, a vast panorama of the Thirty Years' War, depicts the rise and fall of one of the dominant figures of that period, Albrecht von Wallenstein. Here Schiller explores the transitory nature of fame and achievement, the weaknesses in human nature, the fall of a great man brought low by schemers. In the manner of Athenian tragedy, he emphasizes chance and circumstance as well as individual shortcomings in motivating the hero's fall.

Following *The Camp of Wallenstein*, Schiller wrote outstanding plays at the rate of one a year until his death at the age of forty-six. In *Maria Stuart* (pr. 1800; *Mary Stuart*, 1801) and *Die Jungfrau von Orleans* (pr. 1801; *The Maid of Orleans*, 1835), he presents figures who bring about their destruction by committing a fatal error but who atone for their mistake through voluntary self-punishment. Schiller takes a different tack with *Die Braut von Messina: Oder, Die feindlichen Brüder* (pr. 1803; *The Bride of Messina*, 1837). The plot is structured along the lines of Athenian tragedy, and the action concerns the fulfillment of an ancient family curse and certain prophecies. Much like Sophocles' play *Oidipous Tyrannos* (c. 429 B.C.E.; *Oedipus Tyrannus*, 1715), it is precisely the effort to avoid the prophecy that causes it to be fulfilled.

Schiller's best-known play outside Germany is *Wilhelm Tell* (pr. 1804; *William Tell*, 1841). It concerns the successful revolt of the Swiss cantons against their Austrian oppressors. The piece was topical in that it was written in the shadow of the French Revolution and the Napoleonic Empire. In some ways, the play also functions as his answer to certain critics who had complained that his ideas about freedom and political reform did not allow the citizen to redress grievances by force. *William Tell* is Schiller's most popular play; it is still performed in Germany and Switzerland. During the Third Reich, it even had the honor of being banned as "provocative."

HEINRICH VON KLEIST

Next to Schiller and Goethe, the other leading dramatist of the period is Heinrich von Kleist. Active during the classical and the Romantic periods, he does not stand in the mainstream of either, yet he displays characteristics of both. The most striking feature underlying his early pieces is the notion that humans have little power to determine their destiny. According to him, human beings are subject to the workings of mysterious, and often malevolent forces. This feature is manifest in *Die Familie Schroffenstein* (pr. 1804; *The Schroffenstein Family*, 1916), in *Penthe-silea* (pb. 1808; English translation, 1959), and in his two comedies *Amphitryon* (pb. 1807; English transla-tion, 1962) and *Der zerbrochene Krug* (pr. 1808; *The Broken Jug*, 1930).

In his last, and finest, drama, *Prinz Friedrich von Homburg* (pr. 1821; *The Prince of Homburg*, 1875), he abandons the influence of external forces in favor of psychological motivation. The plot is based on a historical incident. In 1675, the Prince of Homburg defeated the Swedish army at Fehrbellin, but only by disobeying a direct order from the elector of Bran-denburg to hold his forces in reserve. In Kleist's ver-sion, Homburg is then court-martialled for insubordi-nation and sentenced to die. At first, he is gripped by the fear of death and pleads for mercy. The elector turns a deaf ear to him and to all who intercede on his behalf, including the entire army. Eventually, the elector puts the decision into the prince's own hands: If he thinks that his sentence is truly unjust, he may go free. This precipitates a reversal in Friedrich's atti-tude. He recognizes the ethical basis of the verdict and prepares for his execution. When the elector per-ceives that Friedrich has understood the deeper jus-tice of his sentence, he is able to pardon him.

ROMANTICISM

The Romantic movement is best viewed as a con-tinuation of the revolt against the Enlightenment initi-ated by the Sturm und Drang. The two movements are similar in that both stand in opposition to the overemphasis on reason and to the procrustean, limit-ing laws governing dramatic composition. Both movements advocated the cultivation of humanity's emotional side. The difference between the two is one of degree. The Sturm und Drang frequently went too far in its categorical rejection of all rules and of-ten carried the depiction of emotion to excess. The Romantics, by contrast, sought to strike a balance be-tween intellect and emotion, adherence to rules and freedom to experiment. In order to curb emotional excess, the concept of Romantic irony was devel-oped. The chief theoretician of the period, August Wilhelm von Schlegel, defined Romantic irony as the writer's ability to look at his work from a distance, as something outside of the writer's self. Romantic irony assigns the intellect the task of restraining feel-ing and keeping the enthusiasm within limits. Properly employed, it stands for clearness of vision, presence of mind, and calm judgment while at the same time permitting the writer to express the entire range of emotion.

In their efforts to break away from what they con-sidered to be the coldness of Enlightenment dramas, the Romantics concentrated on the role uncontrolla-ble forces play in life. Whereas, in classical tragedy, the hero's misfortune usually results from his tragic error, the Romantics explored the role of fate. The *Schicksalstragödie* (fate tragedy), which the new genre came to be called, reached its peak with Zacharias Werner's *Der vierundzwanzigste Februar* (pr. 1810; *The Twenty-fourth of February*, 1844). The play is set in a remote Swiss valley. Long before the action be-gins, Kunz Kuruth had, in a moment of anger, thrown a knife at his father, who then laid a curse on his son. Later, Kunz's own son kills his sister with the same weapon. The son leaves home, amasses a fortune, and, after many years, returns home incognito. Kunz, in serious financial trouble and tempted by the stranger's wealth, murders his son with the same knife. All these events occur on the same day, February 24. The fate tragedy found many imitators. Adolf Müll-ner followed with *Der neunundzwanzigste Februar* (pr. 1812; *The Twenty-ninth of February*, 1820) and *Die Schuld* (pr. 1813; *Guilt*, 1819). Franz Grillparzer contributed *Die Ahnfrau* (pr. 1817; *The Ancestress*, 1838), considered the finest example of the genre.

Despite the masterpieces of Schiller, Kleist, Goe-the, and the accomplishments of the Romantics, the playwright who dominated the German stage from 1789 to about 1830, and who enjoyed immense popu-larity throughout Europe, was August von Kotzebue. He had a keen sense for what the public wanted to see: sentimental domestic dramas and light comedy, all with a happy ending. Interestingly, although he wrote nearly two hundred dramas, they are now nearly forgotten. His significance resides in his influ-ence on the development of drama in general. The techniques, themes, moods, and effects that he intro-duced were major innovations for his day. Throughout Europe and the United States, his example encouraged the emergence of the sentimental drama, which has come to occupy such a conspicuous position in motion pictures, television, and on the contemporary stage.

BIEDERMEIER AND YOUNG GERMANY

German drama between 1820 and 1850 was in many ways a drama in transition. The Romantic movement was waning, and the new approach to come, realism, was yet undefined. The two movements filling the gap were Biedermeier and the Junge Deutschland (Young Germany) movement. Both represent a specific orientation to the reactionary political climate that set in after Napoleon Bonaparte was defeated in 1815. Biedermeier, predominantly middle class, reflects the widespread acceptance of established authority. The Young Germany movement, by contrast, attacked the establishment and clamored for political reforms. It called for universal suffrage and agitated for the unification of the German states into one nation. The Biedermeier produced no dramatists of distinction. Ernst Raupach specialized in gloomy historical pieces such as *Der Nibelungenhort* (pr. 1834; *The Nibelungen Treasure*, 1847), which have long been forgotten. Other playwrights, among them Michael Beer and Eduard von Schenk, contented themselves with providing entertainment that never rose above the commonplace.

Unlike Biedermeier fare, many of the dramas of the Young Germans have outlived their time. Georg Büchner's *Dantons Tod* (pb. 1835; *Danton's Death*, 1927), set in the first years of the French Revolution, depicts Danton's growing sense of futility in trying to translate the ideals of the Revolution into practice. He loses faith in his mission. Finally, he criticizes Maximilien Robespierre for the excesses of the Reign of Terror, which proves to be a fatal mistake; Robespierre engineers Danton's downfall and execution. Büchner's masterpiece is *Woyzeck* (pr. 1836; English translation, 1927), a psychological study of a simple soldier whose mind disintegrates when the woman he loves betrays him.

The most influential writer of Young Germany is Karl Ferdinand Gutzkow. His plays were well re-

ceived in part because they dealt with current issues. Religious toleration underlies *Uriel Acosta* (pr. 1846; English translation, 1860), Prussian militarism is criticized in *Zopf und Schwert* (pr. 1844; *Queue and Sword*, 1913), and the repression of the Young Germany movement by the authorities is the topic of *König Saul* (pr. 1834; King Saul).

AUSTRIAN DRAMA OF THE 1800's

With the untimely death of North Germany's most gifted dramatists—Schiller, Kleist, and Büchner—the center of dramatic activity shifted to Vienna. The capital of Austria had a dramatic tradition extending back some two hundred years. There, Italian Renaissance opera and the *commedia dell'arte* had flourished. The religious drama of the Jesuits had found an audience, and so had the works of the masters of the Spanish Baroque, Pedro Calderón de la Barca and Lope de Vega Carpio. The inheritor of this long tradition was Austria's most talented dramatist, Franz Grillparzer.

Grillparzer was born in Vienna and spent most of his life there. His first successful drama was *The Ancestress*. This fate tragedy is about a ghostly ancestress who watches over her family, the Borotins, until Jaromir, the last of the line, is executed for parricide. Another successful play takes its material from classical antiquity. *Sappho* (pr. 1818; English translation, 1820) retells the tragedy of the Greek poetess who loves the handsome Phaon but is not loved in return. Humiliated when he becomes infatuated with a pretty servant woman, she jumps from a cliff in despair.

After an unsuccessful trilogy on the Medea theme, Grillparzer turned to the history of his own country for the subject of *König Ottokars Glück und Ende* (pr. 1825; *King Otakar's Rise and Fall*, 1830). It dramatizes the triumph of the rightful emperor, Rudolf von Habsburg, over his rival, King Otakar of Bohemia. Following this, Grillparzer produced two outstanding plays, *Des Meeres und der Liebe Wellen* (pr. 1831; *Hero and Leander*, 1938), a love tragedy based on the Greek poem *Hero and Leander*, by Musaeus Grammaticus (fifth or sixth century C.E.), and *Der Traum ein Leben* (pr. 1834; *A Dream Is Life*, 1946). The latter is his greatest stage success. It dramatizes the fortunes of a country lad, Rustan, who longs for a life of excitement and adventure. The night before he is to embark on his quest, he has a vivid dream, the events of which are the action of the drama. The dream begins with a crime. Rustan kills the man who saves the life of the king of Samarkand and takes the credit for himself. In a cause-and-effect relationship, the initial falsehood leads him ever further into mendacity and lawbreaking. When the truth finally emerges, he is forced to flee for his life. Just as his pursuers are about to capture him, he jumps from a bridge into a raging torrent, at which point he awakens. Sobered, Rustan renounces adventure and settles down to a life of rustic tranquillity.

Grillparzer turned next to comedy, producing the masterpiece *Weh' dem, der lügt* (pr. 1838; *Thou Shalt Not Lie!*, 1939). The public rejected it, at first, and this reaction wounded him deeply; he became so discouraged that he almost gave up writing. Over the next thirty-five years, he wrote only three plays, and even these he retained in his desk. In the 1850's, Austria finally began to recognize Grillparzer's genius. His plays were revived, and he received honors from crown and state and recognition from critics. Yet on the occasion of the celebration of his eightieth birthday, he responded with the embittered "zu spät" (too late).

In addition to Grillparzer, there are other Austrian dramatists of note in the 1800's. Ferdinand Raimund specialized in fairytale comedies, a subgenre that flourished during the first decades of the nineteenth century. In his talented hands, it attained literary respectability. He is at his best depicting humor laced with pain and misfortune, such as the problems of growing old in *Das Mädchen aus der Feenwelt: Oder, Der Bauer als Millionär* (pr. 1826; *The Maid from Fairyland: Or, The Peasant as Millionaire*, 1962) and generosity and ingratitude in *Der Verschwender* (pr. 1834; *The Spendthrift*, 1949).

Raimund's contemporary and rival for the favor of the often fickle Viennese public was Johann Nestroy. A brilliant writer of farce and a master of dialogue, his pieces are appreciated for their wit and cynicism, local color, and characterization. Of his eighty-three productions, the best known and most enduring is

Einen Jux will er sich machen (pr. 1842; *The Matchmaker*, 1957), about an elderly man who goes to Vienna to have a good time and finds himself a second wife. The play served as the basis for Thornton Wilder's *The Matchmaker* (pr. 1954) and the musical comedy *Hello, Dolly!* (pr. 1964).

After the death of Grillparzer, the distinction as Austria's greatest dramatist fell to Ludwig Anzengruber. Anzengruber excelled in the representation of average people. Furthermore, because he believed that the purpose of literature is to instruct, a strong didactic vein runs through his work. This is apparent in *Der Meineidbauer* (pr. 1871; *The Farmer Forsworn*, 1914), which concerns the just retribution that is visited on a farmer who perjured himself to gain wealth. *Der Pfarrer von Kirchfeld* (pr. 1870; the priest of Kirchfeld) reflected the bitter controversy that erupted after the pope's proclamation of the doctrine of infallibility. Of all his work, the most enduring is *Das vierte Gebot* (pr. 1877; *The Fourth Commandment*, 1930). In it, he contrasts the ideal relationship between parents and children based on love and confidence with its opposite: the destructive effect of tyrannical control. The play caused an uproar. The Church accused him of undermining the Fourth Commandment ("Honor thy father and thy mother") and called down the wrath of God on him. The liberal community applauded him just as enthusiastically. This was Anzengruber's last success. The Viennese public, long known for its capricious and sudden changes in taste and fashion, began flocking to the operettas of Jacques Offenbach and the salon plays of Alexandre Dumas, *fils*.

REALISM

Although fiction was the preferred literary form during the period between the 1840's and the 1880's, three eminent dramatists, Friedrich Hebbel, Otto Ludwig, and Richard Wagner, were active during these years. Hebbel is known for his novel conception of tragedy. He rejects the traditional idea that misfortune is the result of a specific error or moral deficiency on the part of the hero. Rather, it is the result of an individual's exerting his or her will. Hebbel conceived of the world as governed by universal forces, which he sometimes calls the Idea, sometimes the Whole. It may manifest itself as custom, tradition, or simply the status quo. When people assert their will against the Whole, they separate themselves from it. In so doing, they withdraw a certain amount of energy. When the energy is finally consumed, the individual is reabsorbed into the Whole, a process that is invariably tragic. Hebbel saw it as his duty as a dramatist to clarify humanity's and the world's relation to the Whole.

In translating his ideas into practice, Hebbel often depicted the individual in conflict with tradition. This is the subject of *Maria Magdalena* (pr. 1844; English translation, 1935). It shows how a father's exaggerated sense of rectitude and honor, characteristic of his generation, drives his unwed, pregnant daughter to suicide. In *Agnes Bernauer* (pr. 1852; English translation, 1904), on the other hand, the plot involves the conflict between the prince's personal choice of a wife and his political obligations to the dukedom he is to inherit. Underlying the surface action of *Herodes und Mariamne* (pr. 1849; *Herod and Mariamne*, 1930) is the conflict between paganism and Christianity. In *Gyges und sein Ring* (pr. 1889; *Gyges and His Ring*, 1914), considered his finest achievement, the disaster is caused through the violation of custom. King Kandaules of Lydia is proud of the extraordinary beauty of his wife, Rhodope. Yet her native custom mandates seclusion from any man except her husband. Wishing to hear the praise of his friend Gyges, he secretly arranges for him to watch her disrobe. Rhodope, however, learns of the deceit. To restore her lost honor, she persuades Gyges to kill Kandaules and marry her. Gyges does so, but, after the wedding, she kills herself.

As a representative of the trends in German drama at this time, Hebbel's name is usually linked with that of Ludwig. Though Ludwig is best remembered for his fiction, he wrote a powerful tragedy in the new idiom, *Der Erbförster* (pr. 1850; *The Hereditary Forester*, 1913). In the play, Christian Ulrich regards himself as the hereditary forester of a large estate and therefore immune to dismissal. When the new owner removes him for disobeying a direct order, Christian seeks revenge. At the climax of the play, he shoots his own daughter in error, having mistaken her for the new master's son. Ludwig's only other tragedy, *Die Makkabäer* (pr. 1853; the Maccabees), a story based on material taken from the *Apocrypha*, is almost forgotten, as are his four comedies.

Although Hebbel and Ludwig produced excellent work, their fame is largely restricted to Germany and Austria. The only dramatist of the period to gain worldwide renown is Wagner. Wagner's achievement and influence reside in his creation of a new dramatic form, which he called the "music drama," as opposed to opera, which he repudiated as too burdened by tradition. In his view, music would be an integral part of the drama. It would aid in the interpretation of the action, it would evoke the appropriate feelings, and it would enhance the understanding. These ideas find their fullest expression in the trilogy *Der Ring der Nibelungen* (pb. 1853; *The Ring of the Nibelungs*, 1877). The plot is based on the ancient Germanic Siegfried myth. The central theme is the quest for power and wealth, symbolized first by the Nibelungs' store of gold and then by the fabulous ring into which it is transformed. On another level, Wagner anticipates problems that were soon taken up by the emerging science of psychoanalysis, such as the role of unconscious drives in the life of the individual.

In the tragedy *Tristan und Isolde* (pr. 1859; *Tristan and Isolde*, 1882) the themes range from Arthur Schopenhauer's denunciation of life as an evil illusion to the relation between eroticism and the death wish. Wagner's last work, *Parsifal* (pr. 1877; English translation, 1879), did not evoke the same enthusiasm from the public as his earlier pieces. The theme of infidelity and remorse did not reflect the prevailing intellectual climate.

NATURALISM

Naturalism was in large measure a literary response to social conditions of that time. When the German states were at last welded into a single nation in 1871, the new country embarked on a concerted program of rapid industrialization. An unfortunate side effect was the emergence of a proletarian underclass, whose welfare the industrial barons ignored. Safety conditions were appalling, and workers' rights were yet to be formulated. Most people of this class lived in poverty and squalor. A number of writers and intellectuals of the 1870's and 1880's addressed this problem in newspapers and pamphlets. As spokespeople for the oppressed, they denounced the incongruity between the stark realities of everyday life and a world of literature, art, and music which had become detached, self-indulgent, and irrelevant by comparison. In Berlin, several of these critics organized into a group and adopted a socially conscious stance. They were determined to expose the problems that society was ignoring: namely, the plight of the impoverished masses in general and the status of women in particular. The leading figures of the Berlin circle were the brothers Heinrich and Julius Hart, Arno Holz, Johannes Schlaf, Hermann Conradi, Karl Henckell, and above all Gerhart Hauptmann.

As a dramatic movement, naturalism began with Hauptmann's *Vor Sonnenaufgang* (pr. 1889; *Before Dawn*, 1909). This play sets the tone for the dramas that soon dominated the German stage. Its author aimed at a photographic representation of life. He wanted the audience to see, to touch, to smell, and to taste the misery of poverty. In addition, his slice-of-life depictions extend into speech. Hauptmann aimed at the phonographic reproduction of language: His characters often are inarticulate, speaking in fragmented, incoherent sentences and even mumbling and stuttering. These innovations were so radical that they caused a riot at the premiere of *Before Dawn* in Berlin. Nevertheless, the play established him as the undisputed leader of the movement.

Perhaps the most representative play of naturalism is Hauptmann's *Die Weber* (pr. 1893; *The Weavers*, 1899). The subject of this famous drama, originally written in the Silesian dialect, concerns the brutal repression of an uprising of the Silesian cottage weavers in 1844. There is no hero in the traditional sense; the entire weaving population is the collective protagonist, which is represented by colorfully drawn types. There is also no plot in the usual sense; each of the five acts has a different setting that illuminates the plight of the weavers from a different viewpoint— that of the rich industrialist, of government officials,

of the weavers themselves. The action is carried forward by the gradual formation of the weavers into a violent mob.

The Weavers also represents the naturalists' conception of tragedy. The naturalists rejected the Aristotelian view that misery and misfortune, as depicted in drama, should be the result of some mistake, however slight, on the part of the hero. Aristotle had pointed out that the spectacle of a perfectly innocent man suffering disaster should be avoided because it violates the spectator's sense of justice. This violation, by contrast, is exactly what the naturalists wanted to achieve. In their view, the more unjustified the misery that overtakes the hero, the greater the drama as a work of art. In *The Weavers*, for example, there is a figure called Old Hilse, who declines to participate in the uprising. He is a good man who wins the sympathy of the audience through the humble acceptance of his fate. When the soldiers arrive to crush the rebellion, he sits impassively in his hovel. Yet he is struck by a ricocheting bullet and killed. The audience leaves the theater with a sense of outrage at this injustice. In turn, this feeling may set in motion social forces directed at the improvement of conditions.

In addition to Hauptmann, there were other notable authors of this movement. Holz and Schlaf collaborated on *Die Familie Selicke* (pr. 1890; the Selickes); Hermann Sudermann brought out *Die Ehre* (pr. 1889; *Honor*, 1915). Among the more conspicuous authors is Frank Wedekind. He had a taste for the grotesque and the bizarre that is most clearly seen in his "Lulu" dramas: *Der Erdgeist* (pb. 1895; *Earth Spirit*, 1914), *Die Büchse der Pandora* (pr. 1904; *Pandora's Box*, 1918), and *Hidalla: Oder, Karl Hetmann der Zwergriese* (pb. 1904). The action concerns the adventures of a young woman, Lulu, an unprincipled opportunist who exploits the men who love her. Finally, she meets her fate in London at the hands of Jack the Ripper.

Shortly after the turn of the twentieth century the naturalists discovered the limitations inherent in the movement. They realized that photographic reproduction of the external world was, in fact, a reproduction of the impression that world made on them. Furthermore, the requirement to deal with the misery of the disadvantaged limited their subject matter. Interestingly, the most representative figure of naturalism was the first to leave it.

NEO-ROMANTICISM AND NEOCLASSICISM

Although Hauptmann was the foremost dramatist of naturalism, he was well aware of its limitations from the outset. As early as 1893, he digressed to write a neo-Romantic drama, *Hanneles Himmelfahrt* (pr. 1893; *The Assumption of Hannele*, 1894). Hannele, the child of a drunken bricklayer, tries to drown herself. She is pulled from the water and taken to a hospice for derelicts. Dying, she has a series of hallucinations that she takes for reality. The hallucinations, which are presented to the audience, show what her life might have been in better circumstances. The play derives its power from the juxtaposition of scenes of abject poverty with dream images of an idyllic life. In a similar neo-Romantic vein is *Die versunkene Glocke* (pr. 1896; *The Sunken Bell*, 1898), an allegorical fairytale drama with emphasis on the supernatural. After writing several more neo-Romantic pieces, Hauptmann developed an interest in the literature of classical antiquity, whereupon he entered his neoclassical period. These dramas are written in the classical form and take their subject matter from antiquity. Of note are *Iphigenie in Aulis* (pr. 1943), and *Agamemnons Tod* (pr. 1946).

Another important writer of neoclassicism is the Austrian Hugo von Hofmannsthal. He wrote several short plays distinguished for their lyric quality, most notably *Der Tor und der Tod* (pr. 1898; *Death and the Fool*, 1913). He also made an attempt to rekindle interest in Greek drama with *Elektra* (pr. 1903; *Electra*, 1908) and *Ödipus und die Sphinx* (pr. 1906; *Oedipus and the Sphinx*, 1968). Another Austrian writer of this period is Arthur Schnitzler. His greatest talent resides in his ability to create finely chiseled dialogue and suspense as in *Liebelei* (pr. 1895; *Light-o'-Love*, 1912), *Der grüne Kakadu* (pr. 1899; *The Green Cockatoo*, 1913), and *Professor Bernhardi* (pr. 1912; English translation, 1913). The other major representative of neoclassicism is Paul Ernst (1866-1933), author of several carefully constructed dramas in the classical form such as *Canossa* (pr. 1918) and *Yorck*

(pr. 1933). The further development of neo-Romanticism and neoclassicism was cut short by World War I, which, for the first time, brought humankind face-to-face with the question of its very survival.

EXPRESSIONISM

The primary concern of the expressionists was the fate of humanity in a world that has gone awry. Western society, they said, is rushing toward its destruction, and if nothing is done it will not survive. They placed the blame for this situation on industrialization, which, in their view, transformed the individual into a faceless, machine-tending robot. In an industrial society, enjoyment is divorced from labor, means from end, effort from reward. Consequently, the expressionists did not clamor for social reforms or agitate for the improvement of conditions in the workplace. They called for nothing less than a regeneration of the whole human race, a transformation and purification of character that would emancipate humanity from its evil environment. In short, they dreamed of a new society which, for its own survival, would return to preindustrial life.

Expressionism covers the years between 1910 and 1924. Notable authors are Ernst Barlach, Walter Hasenclever, Ernst Toller, and Fritz von Unruh. Among the most prominent representatives of the movement in both ideas and technique is Georg Kaiser, who rose to prominence with the phenomenal success of an early play, *Die Bürger von Calais* (pr. 1917; *The Citizens of Calais*, 1946), which premiered at Frankfurt in 1917. In presenting the sacrifice of self for the common good, he articulates the spirit and the religious fervor of the expressionists. The play that perhaps best captures the conceptions of the movement is his Gas trilogy, *Die Koralle* (pr. 1917; *The Coral*, 1929), *Gas* (pr. 1918; English translation, 1924), and *Gas: Zweiter Teil* (pr. 1920; *Gas II*, 1924). Set in the future, it shows what people will be like if current trends continue. In the play, machinery reigns supreme, and human beings are its faithful servants. To focus attention on the dehumanization that has occurred, the characters are not given names but designations such as the Father, the Daughter, Son, Worker, Secretary, Blue Figure, Yellow Figure. The symmetry of the dramas' structure, the parallelism, and the antithesis are designed to make the protagonists seem like machines themselves. The unreal effect is reinforced by the diction. Previously, Kaiser and a number of expressionists had adapted the principle of cubism to language and produced what is called the "telegrammatic style." They had rejected as unnecessary such parts of speech as adjectives, adverbs, prepositions, and definite and indefinite articles. In the Gas trilogy, the compressed speech achieves the rhythmic pattern of a machine.

As expressionism drew to a close in the mid-1920's, an ingenious new dramatist rose to prominence, Bertolt Brecht, probably one of Germany's most influential playwrights of the twentieth century. Although he had written a few plays of some merit in the early 1920's, his true genius did not emerge until he authored *Die Dreigroschenoper* (pr. 1928; *The Threepenny Opera*, 1949). First performed in Berlin, the production gained for him international recognition. Loosely based on John Gay's *The Beggar's Opera* (pr. 1728), Brecht's version is a scathing satire of middle-class society from the Marxist viewpoint. Brecht invented for this play a new form of drama, which he called "epic theater." It represents a radical break with theatrical tradition. Instead of a tightly knit plot, he presents a series of loosely connected scenes, each beginning with a didactic song or ballad.

Moral didacticism characterizes virtually all of Brecht's dramas. For him, literature is not entertainment; it is a means for educating and improving society. For this reason, he sought to keep the audience from becoming involved with the action on the stage. The spectators should maintain a critical distance at all times so that they could reflect on the subject matter while it was presented on the stage. So in order to keep the audience's critical faculties alert, he developed his now famous *Verfremdungseffekt* (alienation effect). During the course of the performance, for example, an actor might step out of character to convey to the audience an opinion of the character being portrayed. Brecht also used the technique of interrupting the action with film projections, tape recorded material, and music—all designed to break the illusion.

Following the phenomenal success of *The Threepenny Opera*, Brecht's future as a playwright seemed assured. All this changed when the National Socialist Party rose to power in 1933. Brecht, no favorite of the Nazis and thus fearing for his safety, was compelled to flee. After a lengthy odyssey, he came to the United States, where he settled in Hollywood, California. There, he composed his masterpieces *Leben des Galilei* (pr. 1943; *Life of Galileo*, 1947), *Mutter Courage und ihre Kinder* (pr. 1941; *Mother Courage and Her Children*, 1941), *Der gute Mensch von Sezuan* (pr. 1943; *The Good Woman of Setzuan*, 1948), and *Der kaukasische Kreidekreis* (pr. 1948; *The Caucasian Chalk Circle*, 1948). After the war, he returned to East Berlin, where he established the Berliner Ensemble, an acting company that produced plays in the Brechtian idiom. Despite his disillusionment with the communist regime after Soviet tanks crushed the failed popular uprising of the East Germans in June, 1953, Brecht still chose to remain in the East until his death three years later.

BLUT UND BODEN

Adolf Hitler's rise to power in January, 1933, reversed the literary and intellectual currents in Germany within a matter of months. Literary activity was brought into line with National Socialist dogma. Many eminent writers, fearing for their lives, fled into exile. Those who remained and refused to cooperate were forbidden to publish. The few who openly defied the authorities, such as Ernst Wiechert, were sent to concentration camps. Henceforth, the only type of literature acceptable was that which promoted the Nazi viewpoint. Plays glorified German power and Aryan superiority and vilified everything Jewish. These efforts are summed up in the epithet *Blut und Boden* (blood and soil) in that Aryan blood and German soil were hailed as the source of the nation's life and strength. Because nothing of lasting value was produced during this period, it is often referred to by the contemptuous contraction "Blubo" literature.

The most popular plays during the Third Reich were historical dramas dealing either with events from the Middle Ages or with the ascendancy of Prussia from the reign of the Great Elector to that of

Frederick the Great. The cycle of five plays by Hans Rehberg on this subject is representative. Another playwright who gained the favor of the authorities is Eberhard Wolfgang Möller. He earned approval with his anti-Semitic *Rothschild siegt bei Waterloo* (pr. 1934; Rothschild wins at Waterloo). Knowing of the battle in advance, the conniving Jewish banker enriches himself on the London stock exchange at the expense of both the French and his own English countrymen. Hanns Johst dedicated his play *Schlageter* (pr. 1933) to Hitler. It is a romanticized version of the life and death of Albert Leo Schlageter, a National Socialist "martyr" fighting the French to his death during their occupation of Germany's Rhineland. Yet another type of play popular at the time was the crude farce. Typical is August Hinrichs's *Krach um Jolanthe* (pr. 1931; row about Jolanthe), which features a hog in the title role. That this piece was extremely popular and enjoyed a long run says something about the prevailing taste. Theatrical production in Germany ceased in late 1944, when all theaters that had survived the firebombing of German cities were closed because of the war.

THE IMMEDIATE POSTWAR ERA

The collapse of the Third Reich was accompanied by the permanent eclipse of most of the playwrights who had cast their lot with it. Although many lived on for years, they all found it difficult, if not impossible, to make the transition to the postwar climate. Of the older generation that had fled into exile, a significant few lived to return. Chief among those who did were Brecht and Carl Zuckmayer. When Zuckmayer arrived in 1946, he brought a new play, *Des Teufels General* (pr. 1946; *The Devil's General*, 1962). Set in Germany during the early years of World War II, it dramatizes the life and suicide crash of the Luftwaffe test pilot Erich Udet, called "Harras" in the play. It examines the question of collective guilt with the object of demonstrating that there are no simple answers if everyone is implicated in the crimes. In part because of the play's topicality, it was an overwhelming success.

Plays dealing with various aspects of the Nazi past have been consistently present on the postwar German stage. Of particular note is Wolfgang Borchert. Returning from the Russian front fatally ill, he completed only one play before his death at age twenty-six, *Draussen vor der Tür* (pr. 1947; *The Man Outside*, 1952). This play, which portrays a young soldier who returns from the war and finds that he is unable to adjust, that he is unwanted and a misfit, is filled with the despair characteristic of the immediate postwar period. Another drama that attracted considerable attention is *Der Stellvertreter: Ein Christliches Trauerspiel* (pr. 1963; *The Representative*, 1963; also known as *The Deputy*) by Rolf Hochhuth. The play implicates Pius XII in the extermination of the Jews. In the play, the pope, instead of bringing the moral authority of the Church to bear on the Nazis, chose to remain silent because he did not want to weaken Germany's efforts to destroy the communists. Hochhuth's play involved Germany in a major controversy about the Nazi past.

SWISS PLAYWRIGHTS

While Germany was coming to terms with its past, there emerged two Swiss dramatists of considerable talent, Max Frisch and Friedrich Dürrenmatt, the first playwrights from that country ever to achieve international fame. Both authors have viewed the theater as a didactic institution, a vantage point from which to approach political and social problems. In their view, the purposes of theater are to expose and to educate. Perhaps both profited from the influx of German theatrical talent to Switzerland during the Nazi years. With its German-speaking audience, the Zürich Schauspielhaus provided a rare haven for non-Nazi plays to be produced, and exiled Germans found a creative outlet there.

Although Frisch had written plays of some merit in the 1940's, it was not until *Biedermann und die Brandstifter* (pr. 1958; *The Firebugs*, 1961), which was first produced in 1953 as a radio play, that he rose to international prominence. A morality play, it shows the inevitable results of man's preference to compromise with evil rather than to oppose it. His next drama, *Andorra* (pr. 1961; English translation, 1963), is a parable about the evils of anti-Semitism. After devoting several years to fiction, he returned to playwriting with *Triptychon: Drei szenische Bilder* (pb. 1978; *Triptych*, 1981), a grim statement about the problematic nature of human relationships and the repetitiveness of life. In the play, the protagonists have died and find themselves in an afterlife, not Heaven, not Hell, not Purgatory, but in the same surroundings familiar to them in life. There is no hope, no fear, nothing new, no future. There is nothing but infinite sameness. The men and women are strictly bound to the patterns established when alive and no change is permitted. A criminal, for example, tries to develop a relationship with his victim, who is unaware of his efforts because he had never known him in life and cannot now. Frisch's message to the reader is to lead life more fully, more thoughtfully, because the life one lives will be waiting to be lived again in the hereafter.

In 1989, Frisch adapted his polemic essay, *Schweiz ohne Armee? Ein Palaver* (1989; Switzerland without an army? A discussion), for the stage as *Jonas und sein Veteran* (pr. 1989; Jonas and his veteran). The essay and play were written on the occasion of a controversial people's referendum to abolish the Swiss army. Frisch's support for the referendum, which was ultimately rejected by a wide margin, once again made him enter the political arena as a dramatist. Performed to an appreciative, if critical, audience at the Zürich Schauspielhaus, the play offers an iconoclastic attack on Swiss pride in its popular army, which is seen as an irrelevant relict in the age of nuclear warfare.

Unlike Frisch's straightforward approach to problems, Dürrenmatt preferred satire. His first play, *Es steht geschrieben* (pr. 1947; *The Anabaptists*, 1967), concerns the rise and fall of the Anabaptists in Münster during Germany's Thirty Years' War. The theme is characteristic for Dürrenmatt in that it concerns the subversion of lofty ideals to personal gain. *Romulus der Grosse* (pr. 1949; *Romulus the Great*, 1961) centers on the final days of Rome's last emperor. In this play, Romulus is not presented as the traditional heroic figure. Instead, Dürrenmatt portrays a man totally indifferent to current events who, ironically, prefers to look after his chicken farm than to worry about the fall of an empire, which he real-

izes is inevitable. In accepting his fate and the fate of Rome as inevitable, he maintains his personal integrity.

The idea that a person can transcend his fate by accepting it is a theme in many of Dürrenmatt's plays, as for example in *Der Besuch der alten Dame* (pr. 1956; *The Visit*, 1958), a play that secured for him worldwide recognition. The drama is a step-by-step demonstration of how greed leads to the moral disintegration of an entire town. The plot concerns the fabulously wealthy Claire Zachanassian, now an old woman, who returns to her impoverished native village, Güllen, to seek revenge for a past wrong: In her youth, she had loved Alfred Ill and had become pregnant by him. When he refused to marry her, she brought him to court. Ill bribed two men to swear that they, too, had been Claire's lovers. She lost the case and, humiliated, was forced to leave town. Impoverished, she became a prostitute. After a few years, she married a billionaire and later inherited his wealth. At this point, she returns to Güllen and promises the citizens a billion dollars on the condition that they kill her former lover, Alfred. The offer is refused at first, but the prospect of virtually unlimited funds begins to erode the citizens' moral scruples until they carry out the deed. Thus, her dual revenge involves destroying Ill as well as the honesty of the town. The only person who retains his integrity throughout the ordeal is, strangely, Ill. As events unfold, he recognizes his culpability and accepts the inevitability of his fate. In so doing, he transcends it.

In addition to *The Visit*, Dürrenmatt has authored a number of outstanding plays. Notable is *Die Physiker* (pr. 1962; *The Physicists*, 1963), which explores the moral responsibility of nuclear scientists. In *Porträt eines Planeten* (pr. 1970; *Portrait of a Planet*, 1973) he makes a statement about the indifference of the godhead to the existence of humankind. One of his most frequently performed plays is *Play Strindberg: Totentanz nach August Strindberg* (pr. 1969; *Play Strindberg: The Dance of Death*, 1971). Its effectiveness is as much a result of the theatrical innovations as of the subject matter. Dürrenmatt's concern in the play is, to paraphrase his own words, to see what happens when certain ideas collide with people. To this end, he dispenses with the traditional stage: There are no sets, only an empty area lit from above by a battery of lights, like a boxing ring. Instead of scenes, there are twelve "rounds," each beginning with a gong. The play ends when the people and the ideas have been "knocked out."

Dürrenmatt's *Der Mittmacher* (pr. 1973; *The Conformer*, 1975), a deeply sarcastic play about lethal corruption among public officials from the bottom to the top of social hierarchy, met with widespread Swiss popular rejection. His last drama, *Achterloo IV* (pr. 1983), is a play within a play staged in a mental hospital. It is full of absurdities and chronicles the full range of the follies of human existence.

1960's: DOCUMENTARY DRAMA

In the 1960's, there emerged a generation of German playwrights relatively unburdened by the Nazi past and deeply involved in the political and social issues of the day. Their favorite genre became the documentary drama, which strove to dramatize real-life conflicts. Their political attitudes tended to lean toward the Left. Of note is Heiner Kipphardt, whose most important work is *In der Sache J. Robert Oppenheimer* (pr. 1964; *In the Matter of J. Robert Oppenheimer*, 1967). The play examines the events leading up to the cancellation of J. Robert Oppenheimer's security clearance because he was suspected of harboring communist sympathies.

One of the few playwrights of the 1960's to attract international attention was Peter Weiss, with his *Die Verfolgung und Ermordung Jean-Paul Marats, dargestellt durch die Schauspielgruppe des Hospizes zu Charenton unter der Anleitung des Herrn de Sade* (pr. 1964; *The Persecution and Assassination of Jean-Paul Marat as Performed by the Immates of the Asylum of Charenton under the Direction of the Marquis de Sade*, 1965); this lengthy title is usually contracted to *Marat/Sade*. Though set during the Napoleonic era, it deals with political issues of the 1960's. In contrasting the socialist-revolutionary ideas of Marat with the uncompromising individualism of de Sade, Weiss draws parallels between Marxism and democracy, favoring the former. Weiss died before the fall of the Berlin Wall in 1989. In spite of his politics, he remains one of the most influential dramatists of the 1960's.

LATER TWENTIETH CENTURY

The author whose pieces were most often performed during the 1970's and 1980's was Franz Xaver Kroetz, who believes that the world's basic problems can be comprehended and presented on the stage in order to bring about social improvement. Taking as his subject people from society's substratum, or underclass, Kroetz has contrasted their attitude to that of traditional morality on such matters as murder, infanticide, abortion, and rape. The matter-of-fact manner in which these deeds are staged make them appear as part of life's routine, no more worthy of note than eating and drinking. In this way, the author is able to illuminate how the pressures of modern society erode traditional values. Representative of his view are *Stallerhof* (pr. 1972; *Farmyard*, 1976) and *Geisterbahn* (pr. 1975; ghost train). In other plays, such as *Die Wahl fürs Leben* (pr. 1980, first produced in 1973 as a radio play), the playwright encourages people to cultivate pacifism. In it, a young man with a degree in engineering refuses a job in a munitions factory because it would mean contributing to the arms race. His working-class parents try to change his mind at first, but in the end, they recognize the truth of his argument and acquiesce.

Kroetz's political antics have at times alienated him from some German audiences. In 1972, he joined the West German Communist party. For a time his plays suffered from overt political propaganda, which reduced his characters to mere mouthpieces for political slogans. After leaving the Communist party in 1982, Kroetz continued to write plays critical of German democracy. *Furcht und Hoffnung der BRD* (pr. 1984, co-written with Alexandra Weinert-Purucker; fear and hope of the FRG) features dramatic monologues by unemployed workers and artists seeking a way out of a situation described as hopeless. *Bauern Sterben* (pr. 1985; farmers die) is a play reminiscent of expressionism in its rejection of modern technology and ironically echoes National Socialist glorification of German farmers. Even after the reunification of Germany in 1989, Kroetz remained critical of German society. His play *Ich bin das Volk* (pr. 1994; I am the people) satirizes the revolutionary slogan of the East Germans driving out their communist rulers, chanting "We Are the People." By 2002, Kroetz, though widely respected in dramatic circles, generally remained alienated from mainstream Germany.

The name most frequently associated with the analysis of language is that of Austrian Peter Handke, the postwar playwright with controversial theories. He rose to fame with *Publikumsbeschimpfung und andere Sprechstücke* (pr. 1966; *Offending the Audience*, 1969). *Offending the Audience* is a play true to its title: It consists of long tirades harassing the audience with profane expletives directed at their presumed stupidity, theoretically breaking down theater's fourth wall by directly involving a startled audience. *Kaspar* (pr. 1968; English translation, 1972) and *Der Ritt über den Bodensee* (pr. 1971; *The Ride Across Lake Constance*, 1972) call attention to how set patterns of speech are, in fact, set patterns of thinking and, in turn, set patterns of action. Language, Handke says, is a form of brainwashing in that linguistic conformity ensures automatic obedience. Handke has also written on a number of other social and political issues. In *Über die Dörfer* (pr. 1982; *Among the Villages*, 1984), for example, he examines the eroding effect of social and economic pressures on the creative individual.

In his native Austria, Handke's plays opened to generally favorable audiences in the 1990's. *Die Stunde da wir nichts voneinander wussten* (pr. 1992; *The Hour We Knew Nothing of Each Other*, 1996) is a completely silent play, taking to its logical end point Handke's suspicion of language. *Zurüstungen zur Unsterblichkeit: Ein Königsdrama* (pr. 1997; preparations for immortality) offers a dark vision of humanity. *Die Fahrt im Einbaum: Oder, Das Stück zum Film vom Krieg* (pr. 1999; journey in the dug-out canoe) offers a postmodern journey into the dark recesses of the human soul. In 1999, Handke stirred public controversy when he returned his 1973 Georg Büchner Prize and left the Catholic Church in protest of the Allied bombing of Belgrade as a means to end Serbian oppression of Kosovo's Albanians.

EAST GERMANY, 1945-1990

When the victorious Red Army occupied East Germany at the end of World War II, the Soviet Union mandated the establishment of a Marxist theater. Playwrights and directors who were willing to work under this regime were welcome to return, and theaters were quickly rebuilt to house revivals of socialist realist productions and plays agreeable to the Soviet agenda. Brecht and his wife, actress Helene Weigel, whom contemporary critics credit with much previously unacknowledged creative help for her husband's plays, founded the Berliner Ensemble in 1949. Led by Weigel after Brecht's death in 1956, it became the most influential East German theater in the 1950's and 1960's.

After the foundation of the German Democratic Republic (GDR) in 1949, which lasted until its dissolution on October 3, 1990, playwrights in East Germany struggled between the demands for Soviet-style, Stalinist socialist realist plays and a desire for more modern, artistically advanced forms. The crushed 1953 popular uprising brought with it ensuing repression and censorship. Yet the late 1950's saw a careful reemergence of plays somewhat critical of the state. After the Berlin Wall was built in 1961, the communist regime felt a bit more secure and allowed the production of critical plays that could be interpreted as being constructive and dedicated to a betterment of socialist society.

Volker Braun began as a proletarian playwright attempting to rectify existing problems in his society through a renewed commitment to the ideals of socialism. His *Die Kipper* (pr. 1972; the tippers) exemplifies the need of the workers to be involved in top-level management decisions if production methods are to be improved. Later, he became somewhat disillusioned with his society. His play *Die Übergangsgesellschaft* (pr. 1987; the transitory society) incorporates criticism of the GDR's environmental record and voices doubts that history has to develop with Marxist laws predicting the eventual victory of a classless society. Troubled by the end of the GDR tenure, Braun's *Iphigenie in Freiheit* (pr. 1992; Iphigenia in freedom) muses on what has been lost and what has been won after the demise of East Germany.

In contrast to Braun, whose nostalgia for socialism had alienated him from the critical young East German audiences by the 1970's and 1980's, Ulrich Plenzdorf was one of the rare popular playwrights whose poignant criticism was allowed to be performed, in turn winning him widespread acclaim. Most notably, *Die neuen Leiden des jungen W.* (pr. 1972; the new sorrows of the young W.) reimagined Goethe's novel about a troubled young man in love with an older married woman; he finally commits suicide. The play, which captured the authentic slang of East German teenagers of the time, was widely successful in East and West Germany. As one of the few East German dramatists who managed to keep a successful career after 1990, Plenzdorf became a famous writer of television plays. *Vater Mutter Mörderkind* (pr. 1993; father, mother, child of a murderer) was first staged in the Eastern town of Halle. It deals with the conflicts faced by the adoptive child of a West German terrorist who escaped to the East, where he lived quietly until the fall of the Berlin Wall. Arrested for his terrorist activities, the father leaves his child wondering about the new future. Based on the reality of former West German terrorists living quiet lives in the East, the play again touched a nerve with audiences in reunified Germany.

Heiner Müller was one of the most critical of East Germany's playwrights. His plays were often banned and could not be performed until after 1989. Müller was also a formalist and theoretical innovator. His *Hamletmaschine* (pr. 1979; *Hamletmachine*, 1984) won international acclaim for its stark musings on global human misery and humanity's capacity for destruction. Müller's plays won almost every literary prize in East and West Germany. His focus on the dark aspects of German history, from Prussia to Hitler to the East German uprising of 1953, characterized his plays until the end. *Germania 3: Gespenster am toten Mann* (pr. 1995; Germania 3: ghosts around the dead man) represents a reckoning with the East German party bureaucracy, whom Müller blamed for the betrayal of true socialism.

POLITICAL DRAMA AFTER REUNIFICATION

The mid-1990's saw the powerful emergence of new playwrights whose dramas were explicitly about Germany. Klaus Pohl's *Die schöne Fremde* (pr. 1991; *The Beautiful Stranger*, 1996) deals with the issue of xenophobia. In the play, after witnessing the racially motivated murder of a Polish man and suffering a sexual assault herself in a small town in the middle of Germany, a Jewish American woman, the beautiful stranger of the play, returns to exact her revenge. Pohl's *Wartesaal Deutschland: Stimmenreich* (pr. 1995; *Waiting Room Germany*, 1997) is a play manufactured entirely out of the real-life conversations overheard by the playwright while traveling through reunified Germany on an unrelated journalistic engagement.

Indicative of plays with a topical political focus, Dea Loher's *Fremdes Haus* (pr. 1995; *Stranger's House*, 1997) enacts the struggle of Yanne, a Macedonian refugee in Germany, who marries a German woman whom he does not love in order to get a permanent residency permit. The play transcends its political concerns with the civil war in the Balkans and the influx of refugees to countries like Germany, while offering a multidimensional portrayal of jealousy, erotic tension, and betrayal.

Topical politics also concern many of the new plays by Anna Langhoff, the granddaughter of Wolfgang Langhoff, director of East Berlin's Deutsches Theater from 1946 to 1963. Her *Transit Heimat: Der gedeckte Tisch* (pr. 1994; *The Table Laid*, 1997) takes place in the kitchen of a German shelter for Eastern European asylum seekers. People from the various countries distrust each other and, most of all, the German bureaucracy represented by the social worker, Frau Mertel. In the original German and the first British production of the play, cast members playing the refugee families cooked an actual ethnic meal on the stage, trying to involve the audience's senses of smell and taste.

THE PRIVATE, THE PSYCHOLOGICAL, AND THE INTERNATIONAL

German drama of the 1990's and the early twenty-first century encompassed more than political drama. Tankred Dorst, who as a teenager got kicked out of a Hitler Youth Camp for reading drama while on guard duty, started out as a puppeteer and always disdained documentary or political drama. Politics enters as an outside force in the richly imagined and detailed private lives of his characters. Beginning in 1972, he and his dramatist wife Ursula Ehler wrote many well-received plays examining the intricate inner worlds of an amazing variety of imagined people. The question of what constitutes truth is a recurrent theme in Dorst and Ehler's plays. Their witty *Fernando Krapp hat mir diesen Brief geschrieben: Ein Versuch über die Wahrheit* (pr. 1992; *Fernando Krapp Wrote Me This Letter: An Assaying of Truth*, 1996) showcases a con artist who tries to use his imagination to shape the world and the lives of his friends according to his wishes. Yet, he ends up destroying everything in the course of his adventure. *Wegen Reichtum geschlossen: Eine metaphysische Komödie* (pr. 1998; closed due to wealth: a metaphysical comedy) is Dorst and Ehler's funny treatment of the old fallacy that material wealth will bring automatic happiness.

The lasting popularity and influence of Austrian playwright Elfriede Jelinek is based on her ability to create psychologically complex and deep characters. Even though Jelinek was a member of Austria's communist party from 1974 until 1991 (when she left the party in disgust), politics remains secondary to her exploration of the inner mindscape of her richly envisioned characters. Her dark *Totenauberg* (pr. 1992; *Death/Valley/Summit*, 1996) imagines a fictional meeting of the real-life German philosophers and lovers Hannah Arendt and Martin Heidegger at Heidegger's mountain retreat in the Black Forest. Through intricate wordplay and wild punning, the characters try to assess their differences as a Jewish woman exiled from Nazi Germany and a German man interested in the philosophy of the self. The production also includes short film scenes, ideally shot by the play's director in amateur fashion, to further examine the interplay of mixed media and memory. Jelinek received the Berlin Theaterpreis (theater prize) in 2002, while working on a cycle of plays called *Der Tod und das mädchen* (death and the maiden). Two of these related plays, *Der Tod und das mädchen IV: Jackie* (part IV: Jackie) and *Der Tod und das mädchen V: Die Wand* (part V: the wall), were performed in 2002.

The German-language plays of Japan-born playwright Yoko Tawada represent the growing internationalism of German drama. Tawada moved to Hamburg in 1982. Her plays live from their dual grounding in German and Japanese dramatic traditions. Her haunting *Die Kranichmaske, die bei Nacht strahlt* (pr. 1993; the crane mask that beams at night) is a surreal wake for a dead woman, whose body on the stage is covered by large, cut-out letters of the alphabet that form her shroud. She is mourned by four characters, Sister, Brother, Translator, and Neighbor, who themselves rise out of the four coffins at the beginning of the play and to which they return at its end. Their fragmentary dialogue reflects their relationship with the dead woman and contains an intellectual discourse on the dramatic theories of German playwright Heiner Müller and musings about Japanese Nō theater by Zeami Motokiyo (1363-1432). Tawada's third play, *Till* (pr. 1998), features a contemporary group of Japanese tourists who happen on a German town inhabited by people who resemble characters out of the life of the medieval joker Till Eulenspiegel. With its juxtaposition of Japanese language spoken by the tourists, and the German of the townsfolk, the play challenges a monolingual audience to overcome language barriers by focusing on the performance of the cast instead of on language alone.

GERMAN DRAMA SINCE 2000

In the early twenty-first century, contemporary German playwrights faced certain difficulties in getting their plays produced. Of all the plays put on the regular stage, half are foreign translations, and only a fraction of all major productions are by original playwrights from Germany, Austria, or German-speaking Switzerland. There also is the temptation to write plays for television or to write for experimental, nonmainstream outlets like university, amateur, or prison productions. Cutbacks of once very generous budgets for local theaters further challenge dramatists to create plays that can draw audiences and carry a serious message.

Among the established dramatists, Botho Strauss is considered one of reunified Germany's foremost playwrights. With twenty plays to his credit by 2002, he is one of the most produced authors. Strauss, who in 2001 won the Lessing Prize, bestowed every four years to a German intellectual dedicated to the ideas of the Enlightenment, exemplifies the theater of a newly reconstituted Germany looking into the new millennium. *Der Kuss des Vergessens* (pr. 1998; the kiss of forgetting), and *Die Ähnlichen* (pr. 1998; the similar ones) both share an interest in the psychological makeup of characters drawn from society. *Der Narr und seine Frau heute abend in Pancomedia* (pr., pb. 2001; the fool and his wife tonight at Pancomedia) is a postmodern comedy encompassing nearly one hundred different characters set in the Hotel Confidence. Against a backdrop of real, surreal, and bizarre characters—ranging from a man impersonating a bellhop to ghosts, angels, and clowns—there is the tender love story of the writer Sylvia Kessel and the small-time publisher Zacharias Werner. Perhaps indicative of the trend in German drama to produce plays that examine the very act of writing and performing, the professions of the lovers ground them in the literary scene. *Unerwartete Rückkehr* (pr. 2002; unexpected return) is another of Strauss's popular plays combining psychology, postmodernism, and a keen sense of theater.

German playwrights since 1945 are imbued with the necessity of being directly involved with the pressing political and social issues of the day as well as writing personal, psychologically sophisticated plays. They often see as their mission not simply to describe the world but to change it. In their efforts to expose, to instruct, and to enlighten, these authors have created a rich and diverse body of drama. In the early twenty-first century, the German stage attempted to regain the international respect that it enjoyed before 1933.

BIBLIOGRAPHY

Bennett, Benjamin. *Modern Drama and German Classicism: Renaissance from Lessing to Brecht.* Ithaca, N.Y.: Cornell University Press, 1979. Still a valuable, comprehensive guide to German drama up to the middle of the twentieth century. Bibliography, index.

Berghaus, Gunter, ed. *Fascism and Theatre: Comparative Studies on the Aesthetics and Politics of Performance in Europe, 1925-1945.* Providence, R.I.: Berghahn Press, 1996. Contains good essays on the Nazi impact on theater in Germany and the staging of Nazi party rallies as a form of theatrical spectacle. Bibliography.

Brandt, George W., ed. *German and Dutch Theatre, 1600-1848.* Cambridge, England: Cambridge University Press, 1993. Exhaustive, scholarly survey of German drama of the period, ending with the failed 1848 liberal revolution. Substantial discussion of major playwrights, major plays, and major dramatic movements and events.

Case, Sue-Ellen, ed. *The Divided Home/Land: Contemporary German Women's Plays.* Ann Arbor: University of Michigan Press, 1992. In addition to the texts of seven plays, Case offers a collection of interviews with living women playwrights that provide perceptive information on their works.

Cicora, Mary A. *Wagner's Ring and German Drama.* Westport, Conn.: Greenwood Press, 1999. Critical study of the place of Wagner's musical drama masterpiece against the backdrop of dramatic trends in late 1800's German drama.

Dodgson, Elyse, ed. *German Plays: Plays from a Changing Country.* London: Nick Hern Books, 1997. Features the texts of four plays from the 1990's and provides a useful general introduction and comments on the works of each playwright.

Haymes, Edward R. *Theatrum Mundum: Essays on German Drama and German Literature.* Munich, Germany: Fink Verlag, 1980. Excellent collection of a rich variety of individual essays covering major playwrights from all eras of German drama after 1600.

James, Dorothy, and Ranawake, Sylvia, eds. *Patterns of Change: German Drama and the European Tradition.* New York: Peter Lang, 1990. Fine collection of individual essays ranging from reflections on Richard Wagner's theories of drama to the influence of Samuel Beckett on Peter Handke.

Lederer, Herbert. *Handbook of East German Drama, 1945-1985.* New York: Peter Lang, 1991. Excellent source on East German drama. Perceptive view of the artistic and ideological battles fought among dramatists, party officials, and intellectuals. Good discussion of the major plays and productions of the time covered.

Osborne, John. *The Naturalist Drama in Germany.* Totowa, N.J.: Rowman and Littlefield, 1971. Still useful, detailed study of the epoch. Bibliography.

Rigby, Catherine E. *Transgressions of the Feminine: Tragedy, Enlightenment and the Figure of Woman in Classical German Drama.* Heidelberg, Germany: Winter Verlag, 1996. Scholarly but accessible study of the treatment of women in the German plays of the Enlightenment era. Bibliography, index.

Ritchie, J. M. *German Expressionist Drama.* Boston: Twayne, 1976. Useful study of the major playwrights and works of the movement. Illustrated; bibliography and index.

Sebald, W. G., ed. *A Radical Stage: Theatre in Germany in the 1970's and 1980's.* New York: St. Martin's Press, 1988. Valid, informative assessment of the impact of political theories on the West German stage during the period.

Sieg, Katrin. *Exiles, Eccentrics, Activists: Women in Contemporary German Theater.* Ann Arbor: Michigan University Press, 1994. Excellent, groundbreaking academic study of the work of German women playwrights in the twentieth century.

John D. Simons,
updated by R. C. Lutz

Italian Drama Since the 1600's

The foundations of contemporary Western theater are undoubtedly to be sought in the theater of Renaissance Italy both from the viewpoint of theatrical practices and from that of dramatic theory and the formation and evolution of dramatic genres. Yet its coming into this role of preeminence was not sudden, and many and varied factors contributed to it.

Aside from some manifestations of popular *contrasti* such as "Rosa fresca aulentissima" (oh fresh and most fragrant rose) by Ciullo d'Alcamo, which exploits the eternal theme of the lover who tries to prevail over the ever weaker protestations of the damsel with whom he has fallen in love—the girl finally consenting and exhorting her lover with an explicit "*a lo letto ne gimo, alla bon'ora!*" (It's time to go to bed!)—or the secular divertissements provided by itinerant minstrels, university students, and occasional comedians, the European theater of the Middle Ages had been essentially a religious one. Later, this type of theater gradually acquired a more literary and professional quality, especially in Florence, where, from the late fourteenth century to the second half of the fifteenth century, the *sacra rappresentazione* began to be written out and performed by famous troupes, such as the Compagnia del Vangelista, while at the same time incorporating increasingly elaborate forms of staging and choreography.

With the advent of humanism and the rediscovery of the classical past, the fifteenth century began to see also the rebirth of erudite imitative creations, especially in the manner of Terence and Plautus.

In January, 1486, the erudite vernacular drama was born. On the occasion of a visit by the duke of Mantua to his future bride, Isabella d'Este, the duke of Ferrara ordered a memorable performance of Plautus's *Menæchmi*. Its success prompted many fifteenth century poets to try their hand at playwriting, and among the earliest examples of original secular plays written in the vernacular are a play in verse by Matteo Maria Boiardo, *Timone* (c. 1492), written in terza rima and translated from a dialogue by Lucian; *Cefalo* (1487), by Niccolò da Correggio; and the enormously more important *Orfeo* (pr. c. 1480; English translation, 1879), by Poliziano (Angelo Ambrogini). As a direct adaptation of a secular theme to the form of the Florentine *sacra rappresentazione*, Orfeo can rightly be considered the first fully original contribution to a genre that would continue well into the seventeenth century and inspire such playwrights as Torquato Tasso and Battista Guarini.

During much of the sixteenth century, experiments were conducted in finding ways to produce the plays of the great classical authors or new pieces written in imitation of the ancients. These productions were mounted in large halls of palaces belonging to ruling princes and dukes or to the newly formed academies of learned gentlemen. The halls had to be adapted for use as theaters by placing a platform at one end of the hall and seating around the other three walls, often allowing for a dais for the prince in the middle. In time, false perspective scenery was developed, eventually framed by a proscenium arch that opened on the scene and hid machinery used to shift scenery on and off. Early efforts in this direction took place in the 1540's in Vicenza by Sabastiano Serlio, who published the first treatise on theater buildings and scenery in 1545. The Accademia Olimpica, also in Vicenza, constructed a permanent theater in 1585, the Teatro Olimpico, designed by Andrea Palladio after the model of an ancient Roman theater but provided with false perspective street scenes designed by Vincenzo Scamozzi. It still exists today. In the Medici court, such designers as Bernardo Buontalenti and Giorgio Vasari developed elaborate temporary theaters with proscenium arches. By the early seventeenth century permanent theater structures were being built with changeable scenery and proscenium arches, including the Teatro degli Intrepidi in Ferrara built in 1609 on designs by Giambattista Aleotti, who also designed the similar Teatro Farnese for the ruling family of Parma in 1618. The latter theater also exists to this day, although it was nearly destroyed in World War II.

More important, Italy also began to take the lead in the development of dramatic theory and criticism, with particular emphasis on the precepts of the then newly rediscovered *De poetica* (c. 334-323 B.C.E.; *Poetics*, 1705) by Aristotle, which first appeared in print at this time. The thorough examination of this and other surviving theoretical treatises dealing with the nature and purposes of dramatic representation, especially of tragedy, and the many ensuing debates deriving from their interpretation, in particular on the question of the "three unities" and of "catharsis," made it possible to pass on to the rest of Europe an invaluable, although often stifling, body of theoretical interpretation, which remained substantially unchallenged until the end of the eighteenth century.

The sixteenth century saw also the birth of the regular Italian comedy, a genre much more akin to Italian sentiments, and to which Italian playwrights made a more lasting and original contribution. In a sense, Italian sixteenth century comedy can be considered a true national theater, as its content, more than that of tragedy, reflected and magnified societal mores and morality, and the preoccupations with the cultural, economic, religious, and political factors prevailing at the time. Early in the sixteenth century, great poets such as Ludovico Ariosto began trying their hand at writing comedy. Ariosto's *La cassaria* (pr. 1508; *The Coffer*, 1975), *I suppositi* (pr. 1509; *The Pretenders*, 1566), *Il negromante* (wr. 1520; *The Necromancer*, 1975), and two other comedies established the parameters of the written comedy, or *commedia erudita* (erudite, or learned, comedy), which was to live successfully alongside the truly innovative and popular *commedia dell'arte o all'improvviso* (improvised comedy).

COMMEDIA DELL'ARTE

Despite the importance and richness of the written erudite theater, Italy's most enduring and glorious contribution to the history of drama remains unquestionably the unwritten theater of the streets and marketplaces, the *commedia dell'arte*, which had its greatest success from 1560 to 1650.

Unlike the written erudite theater of poets and men of letters, which depended heavily on the patronage of courts and academies and was often brought to the stage by refined *dilettanti* and courtiers, the chief characteristics of the *commedia dell'arte* were improvisation, a brash and energetic acting style that feigned spontaneity, sudden gags and bawdy jokes known as *lazzi*, and stock characters, usually masked and immediately recognizable by their garb, played by professional actors.

Although not written, the plays had completely developed plots or scenarios known as *canovacci*, and each actor, usually specializing in a given role or mask, was expected to "improvise" a dialogue or speech, according to a precise situation or scene called for in the plot, by relying on his experience and on a repertoire of set expressions, proverbs, witticisms, jokes, and brilliant conceits. Often the actors would adroitly adjust their performance to satisfy the mood and temperament of the audience, or introduce *lazzi* of particular significance to a particular time or place.

From the era that *commedia dell'arte* thrived, well over one thousand *canovacci* have survived, the most important being those published in 1611 by Flaminio Scala, the leader of the Confidenti; those of Basilio Locatelli, dating about 1620; and those of Domenico Biancolelli, a famous Arlecchino (Harlequin) who achieved great popularity in Paris.

The mask (which often covered only the upper part of the face, leaving free the mouth), the accompanying costume, and the performer's body gestures and tone of voice functioned as immediate signs to the spectators of what to expect in terms of the disposition and likely behavior of a given character. Indeed, gestures and particular antics or pantomime must have accounted greatly for the enormous success that companies of Italian *commedianti* enjoyed throughout Europe. Thus, masks such as those of the old men, the doctor or Pantalone, the swaggering coward Captain, the clownish servants Brighella and Arlecchino, the unmistakable hook-nosed and humpbacked Pulcinella, and the fast-acting Scaramuccia became fixed in the iconography of sixteenth century dramatic arts and in the popular consciousness, making it possible for the *commedia dell'arte* to continue vigorously well into the eighteenth century.

Traveling troupes of professional actors known as *compagnie*, such as the Gelosi (the zealous ones) under the leadership of Francesco and Isabella Andreini, the Confidenti (confident in their success), and the Accesi (the ardent ones), whose premier actor, Tristano Martinelli, popularized the mask of Arlecchino, became so popular that they were often called by princes and kings to perform at their palaces. The French kings, especially, became so fond of this kind of theater that a troupe of *commedianti* was asked in 1660 to remain permanently in France, sharing from then on the Parisian stages with Molière and the Comédie-Française.

In 1699, Andrea Perrucci published an important theoretical document titled *Dell'arte rappresentativa, premeditata e all'improvviso* (on the representative art, premeditated or improvised), in which he analyzed and clearly described the distinguishing features of this genre, the tradition from which it had drawn, and that which it had helped to create. The influence of the *commedia dell'arte* on the development of European theater cannot be underestimated. Certain masks and particular situations developed by these highly skilled actors or by their *corago* (director) influenced many actors throughout the years, surviving in the acting of such modern masters as Marcel Marceau or Charles Chaplin. More important, it persisted, too, in the dramatic writings of some of the best playwrights of Western civilization: William Shakespeare, Molière, Lope de Vega Carpio, Marivaux, and Carlo Goldoni, up to the hauntingly emblematic Pirandellian characters of the twentieth century.

THE PASTORAL AND THE BIRTH OF MELODRAMA

The second half of the sixteenth century saw, besides the sudden appearance of the *commedia dell' arte*, the birth of a new dramatic genre: the pastoral play. Already in the Middle Ages and in the first half of the fifteenth century, imitation of the Virgilian bucolic eclogue had reached a sophisticated poetic level, but the real point of departure for the theatrical version had been Poliziano's *Orfeo*. The genre next reached a pinnacle in 1573 with a masterpiece by the poet Torquato Tasso.

When Tasso's *Aminta* (pr. 1573; English translation, 1591) was first performed, during the summer of 1573 in the idyllic setting of the island of Belvedere in the Po, Tasso had, like his great youthful predecessor Poliziano a century earlier, miraculously succeeded in creating an unsurpassable example in this genre, a model that was to remain for decades the source of inspiration for countless poets and playwrights all over Europe. The only other Italian play of this genre that can claim comparison with Tasso's masterpiece is the work of another Ferrarese poet: *Il pastor fido* (pr. 1596; *The Faithful Shepherd*, 1602) by Battista Guarini. Wrought in exquisite lyric verses, Guarini's play attempted to improve on the Tassian model by applying some innovations theorized by its author. Although following to a certain extent the classical models, the studied quintessential musicality of its rhymes and the all-pervading lyric tones made it evolve toward a more melodramatic genre by introducing a subtle mixture of tragic and lighter elements. Soon, by deemphasizing the complexity of human pathos and by stressing the romantic novelistic element of the story, this genre would quickly move toward a new theatrical form in the seventeenth century. With the addition of a musical accompaniment, at the waning of the sixteenth century the first step was taken toward what centuries later was destined to become the grand opera. Thus, the pastoral, and Guarini's innovations, proved an important milestone in bridging sixteenth and seventeenth century dramatic sensibilities.

After Tasso and Guarini, writers who excelled in this genre were Ridolfo Campeggi, with his *Philaminde*, and the then famous Guidobaldo Bonarelli, who produced the most important seventeenth century pastoral, *Filli di Sciro* (pb. 1607; English translation, 1655). The popularity of the genre was also attested by the countless manuscripts and published versions of pastorals, which continued to be produced until the end of the seventeenth century and well beyond. Thus, the pastoral as a poetic and dramatic genre did not die a sudden death, and both in Italy and abroad it continued to survive until the first half of the eighteenth century, when it experienced a last surge in popularity during the neoclassical period.

THE RISE OF MUSICAL THEATER

The time was ripe for further innovations, and when, toward the end of the sixteenth century, a group of gifted musicians under the leadership of Giovanni Bardi, Count del Verino, and the gifted theorist Vincenzo Galileo, father of the famous astronomer and scientist, formed the Camerata, they found in the musical verses and elegiac plots of the pastoral a ready-made medium for their musical experiments.

Galileo, and his fellow musicians Giulio Caccini, Emilio de' Cavalieri, and Jacopo Peri, together with the poet Ottavio Rinuccini, had maintained that music should be a mere accompaniment to the verses of the poet and should only complement their emotional expressivity without overpowering them; that is, music and words were to remain, as far as possible, equally important.

Adhering to these concepts, and under the leadership of Jacopo Corsi, who had succeeded Bardi, the Camerata artists produced in 1598 the very first opera, *Dafne*, a pastoral play written by Rinuccini and set to music by Peri. This first opera enjoyed great success and in 1600 was followed by a second one, *Euridice*, first staged during the celebrations of the marriage of Maria de' Medici to Henri IV of France. The libretto was again by Rinuccini, while the music was by Peri and Caccini, the former also singing the role of Orpheus.

Other operas followed, notably one with music composed by de' Cavalieri, but Florence suddenly lost her preeminence with the emergence, in Mantua, of one who was to prove the musical genius of the era: Claudio Monteverdi. In 1607, Monteverdi composed his *L'Orfeo* (pr. 1607; *Orfeo*, 1949; with a libretto by Alessandro Striggio), and the following year the moving *Arianna*, with a libretto by Rinuccini. Other important works by Monteverdi were *Il ritorno di Ulisse in patria* (pr. 1641; English translation, 1942), and *L'incoronazione di Poppea* (pr. 1642; *The Coronation of Poppea*, 1927). With Monteverdi, opera took a new direction, music gradually beginning to assert itself and claim the role of importance formerly held by the text, and the other scenic elements gradually acquiring a more spectacular function. Unlike the earlier operas of Peri and Caccini, with their monodic recita-tives and the subdued role of the music, Monteverdi's works disregarded the theories of the Camerata and stressed, instead, the more intense psychological and dramatic development of the characters, a more complex and richer musical framework, and, most important, a more prominent place for music.

ZENO AND METASTASIO

The musical theater continued its progress toward modern opera by compounding new romantic elements with classical themes and devices while poets and musicians worked ever more closely and combined their skills in perfecting stagecraft and verse-harmony. Toward the second half of the seventeenth century, however, the creative impulses of melodramatic poets in Italy seemingly began to dry up, and the plots became increasingly complicated and full of eccentric and highly improbable situations. The exceedingly rhetorical declamations of actors added a further note of imbalance. The time was ripe for reform, and the Venetian Apostolo Zeno, for more than ten years "Poeta Cesareo" at the imperial court in Vienna, was the first playwright of note to attempt it.

To return Italian melodrama to its original dignity and simplicity, Zeno went back to classical subjects shorn of absurd mixtures of pagan and Christian elements and unnecessary musical "embellishments" or to historical themes carefully researched, with the word gradually regaining its place of preeminence. Noteworthy examples among Zeno's production of more than sixty dramas are *Ifigenia in Aulide* (pr. 1718), *Andromaca* (pr. 1724), and *Scipione nelle Spagne* (pr. 1722). He introduced some technical innovations, such as the division between the *recitativo* and the *aria*, and also added the popular *strofetta* at the end of each scene. With Zeno, other consummate writers of melodramas and tragedies of the time were Giulio Agosti and the prolific Pier Antonio Bernardoni, who to a considerable extent anticipated Zeno's attempts toward a more natural and simpler dramatic production.

When, in 1728, honored and recognized throughout Europe, Zeno retired from the Viennese court to return to his native Italy, he suggested as his successor a poet who, in his opinion, was the best among the living Italian poets: Pietro Metastasio.

Pietro Trapassi, who took the pen name of Metastasio (a rough Greek translation of Trapassi meaning "steps beyond"), had been a child prodigy who at the age of ten was adopted and educated by the famous critic and dramatic theorist Gianvincenzo Gravina, became the undisputed master of Italian melodrama and justly deserves to be ranked among Italy's finest dramatists. Although his most intense period of activity coincided with the first decade in Vienna (where he remained until his death as "Poeta Cesareo"), he had already made a name for himself in 1724 with his *Didone abbandonata* (pr. 1724; *Dido Forsaken*, 1952), which anticipated the themes of many of his other melodramas. In this and other works, such as *Artaserse* (pr. 1730; *Artaxerxes*, 1761), *Adriano in Siria* (pr. 1731; *Adrian in Syria*, 1767), *La clemenza di Tito* (pr. 1734; *The Mercy of Titus*, pb. 1767), *Temistocle* (pr. 1736; *Themistocles*, 1767), and *Attilio Regolo* (pr. 1750; *Atilius Regulus*, pb. 1767), Metastasio grappled with the elemental human passions and conflicts of love and duty, sentimental gratitude, and patriotic ideals. These themes, Metastasio's powerfully sculpted characters, and the recurrent happy ending constituted, with or without music—as the eighteenth century critic Ranieri de' Calzabigi wrote— "perfect, precious tragedies." It is not surprising, therefore, that almost all the composers of the time, including Giovanni Battista Pergolesi, Wolfgang Amadeus Mozart, George Friedrich Handel, Domenico Cimarosa, and Maria Luigi Cherubini, set to music Metastasio's melodic verses, with *Artaserse* reaching more than 107 musical versions.

As for the genre in which he truly excelled, it can be said that Metastasio was successful in restoring literary dignity to the melodrama by completing the reform that had been initiated by Zeno and by establishing a fixed, albeit stylized, scheme to the dramatic action. "Many," wrote Carlo Goldoni of Metastasio, "have proved themselves after him both valorous and learned; but the ear accustomed to those verses, to those gentle thoughts, to that brilliant manner of scenic representation of the worthy poet, has not yet found anything which is worthy of comparison with him."

THE VENETIAN THEATER AND GOLDONI

When Carlo Goldoni was born in 1707, the opera was securely established, the Neapolitan *opera buffa* had become to comedy what melodrama and opera were to tragedy, and the stock themes of the *commedia dell'arte* were still going strong. Unlike other European nations, however, and aside from some occasional academic dramatic pieces intended more for reading than for performing, Italy had fallen well behind in the production of a national repertoire of spoken drama.

Perhaps not entirely by chance, Goldoni was born in Venice, a city that in those years was still basking in the warm light of its splendid culture and the richness of its slowly diminishing power. Although almost everywhere in Europe, social and economic unrest loomed ominously over ancient governments, in its declining years, Venice still appeared as an oasis of refined tranquillity and aristocratic traditions, seemingly oblivious to all impending changes. Life— that of the old ruling aristocracy, that of the emerging bourgeoisie, and that of the common classes—was gaily lived, almost in a theatrical fashion, in the crowded piazzas and on the bridges delicately arching over the canals, against a backdrop of architectural ornaments and of gondolas slowly gliding over the green lagoon. It was a city at peace with itself, conscious of what was and had been, and enriched by the presence of many great artists such as Antonio Canaletto, Francesco Guardi, Giovanni Battista Tiepolo, Baldassare Galuppi, and Antonio Vivaldi. It was, above all, a city of a vivacious new middle class whose main aspiration was to inherit, in orderly fashion, the privileges and power previously enjoyed only by the nobility. Goldoni's best theater reflected these aspirations and nodded understandingly at the changing order.

Goldoni's dramatic output includes more than two hundred titles, a number of them produced in Paris, where he spent the last thirty years of his life and where he died. After some attempts, some of which were well received, in the tragic and melodramatic genre, Goldoni found his true inspiration in the writing of comedies, a genre in which he was to excel and which he restored to literary dignity. Goldoni's crowning achievement, however, was to "reform" Italian comedy, which had become imprisoned by the passé and sterile stock formulas of the *commedia dell'arte*, by gradually introducing new realistic language, themes, and characters and by finally reclaiming for the playwright the traditional dominance that had been lost to the artists and directors of the *commedia all'improvviso*.

The initial stages of Goldoni's reforms were achieved with two comedies. In the first, *Momolo cortesan: O, L'uomo di mundo* (Momolo, man of the world), performed in 1738, only the part of the protagonist was entirely written out; the other parts were "improvised" in the fashion of the *commedia dell' arte*. The second, *La donna di garbo* (the good-mannered lady), was performed in 1743 and was Goldoni's first comedy to be entirely written out.

After important plays such as his *La vedova scaltra* (pr. 1748; *The Artful Widow*, 1968) and *La famiglia dell'antiquario* (pr. 1750; the antique collector's family), Goldoni promised to his public a new theatrical season during which he would write sixteen new comedies. Taxing himself to the extreme, he kept the promise by producing, among others, such favorites as *La bottega del caffé* (pr. 1750; *The Coffee-house*, 1925) and *I pettegolezzi delle donne* (pr. 1751; women's gossip). The first of these sixteen comedies, *Il teatro comico* (pr. 1750; *The Comic Theatre*, 1969), Goldoni wrote as a manifesto of his theatrical reform. In it, using the device of a play-within-a-play, Goldoni voiced through one of the characters his objections to the *commedia dell'arte*—"People are bored. . . . The audience knows what Harlequin will say before he opens his mouth"—and maintained that comedy had merely become ridiculous and could no longer be taken seriously, having lost its original purpose of correcting vice and satirizing bad customs. Goldoni advocated bringing onstage realistic situations and well-developed characters whom the public could appreciate and with whom they could identify.

With *La locandiera* (pr. 1753; *The Mistress of the Inn*, 1912), Goldoni skillfully applied the canons of his new theater, interpreting the new social expectations of women and of the working class in general while caricaturing the pretentious, boorish manner of the petty, idle representatives of Venetian aristocracy.

Goldoni's attempt at dramatic and social reforms did not go unchallenged. Two men especially, both famous in Venetian theater circles, tried to oppose Goldoni with a theater of their own: the Jesuit Pietro Chiari and the aristocrat Count Carlo Gozzi. Both of them achieved a considerable measure of popular success, but of the two, Gozzi fought a more acrimonious and unrelenting battle on behalf of the traditional and conservative social values represented by his class and in defense of the purity of the Italian language. He even challenged Goldoni's popularity by beginning, in pique, to write for the theater, and in 1760 he created the first and most famous of his fables, *L'amore delle tre melarance* (pr. 1761; *The Love of the Three Oranges*, 1921). This work, as well as three others that soon followed, *Il corvo* (pr. 1761; *The Raven*, 1989), *Il re cervo* (pr. 1762; *The King Stag*, 1958), and *Turandot* (pr. 1762; English translation, 1913), were fantastic fanciful stories, devoid of any social implication and bent on escapism. Yet they proved so popular that Chiari, after 1762, gave up writing comedies in the new style; their popularity was probably also a factor in Goldoni's decision to leave Venice and to go to Paris under contract to the Comédie-Italienne.

Before leaving for Paris, Goldoni bade farewell to his Venetian public by producing, in 1762, the play *Una delle ultime sere di carnovale* (one of the last evenings of carnival). In Paris, after encountering some problems in adapting his new comedy to the habits of the actors and the taste of the French audience, which expected the Comédie-Italienne to conform to the traditional Italianate theatrics of the *commedia dell'arte*, he wrote the stylistically mature *Il ventaglio* (pr. 1763; *The Fan*, 1892) and met with great success with some comedies in French, such as *Le Bourru bienfaisant* (pr. 1771; *The Beneficent Bear*, 1892), produced, after the death of Molière, for the Comédie-Française.

THE PRE-ROMANTIC TRAGEDY

The crisis of Italian tragedy, specifically of the *tragedia erudita*, continued in the second half of the eighteenth century despite the various attempts made to revive it. With the exception of the verse tragedy *La Merope* (pr. 1713; English translation, 1740), by Francesco Scipione Maffei, which was repeatedly performed and whose subject was later imitated by Voltaire and Vittorio Alfieri, the first half of the century had produced no serious drama of lasting significance. Minor tragedians had succeeded only in imitating the external aspects of the French classical theater, producing a congeries of redundant neoclassical pastiches, largely devoid of any artistic merit.

Consistent with their traditional interest in serious theater as a tool of moral edification, a more sustained effort in this genre was made at this time by Jesuit playwrights. Although permeated with moral vigor, the works of such authors as Alfonso Varano, who wrote some five tragedies, Giovanni Granelli, and the prolific Saverio Bettinelli, best known for his theoretical pronouncements contained in his *Discorso sul teatro italiano* (1771; discourse on the Italian theater), did little to raise the standards of the genre in Italy.

The second half of the century witnessed also a renewed interest in Shakespearean models, which resulted, however, in a still unresolved mixture of preromantic and classical elements and, often, in ponderous theatrical productions of dubious merit. Dignified and, at times, vigorous efforts were made by literati such as Alessandro Verri, the author of historical, anti-Aristotelian dramas; by Ippolito Pindemonte, who wrote several gothic, pre-Romantic works; and especially by Giovanni Pindemonte, who combined a strong interest in theatricality and a keen espousal of liberal political and social views. Yet the task of becoming the premier tragic writer of the age and of attempting a reform similar to what Goldoni had done for comedy would be left to Vittorio Alfieri.

Born to an aristocratic Piedmontese family in 1749, Alfieri, a passionate child of those troubled yet exciting times, instinctively filled the gap between the neoclassical tradition and the pre-Romantic mood while, at the same time, he succeeded in modernizing the centuries-worn genre of tragedy. After many travels and amorous adventures, Alfieri turned finally, albeit momentarily, to more intellectual pursuits and in 1775 wrote the first of his twenty-one

tragedies, *Antonio e Cleopatra* (pr. 1775; *Antony and Cleopatra*, 1876), which was successfully performed that same year in Turin. Encouraged, he continued to devote time to play writing, and other published works soon followed (produced at later dates), such as *Filippo* (pr. 1825; *Phillip II*, 1815), *Agamennone* (pr. 1842; *Agamemnon*, 1815), *Merope* (pb. 1784; English translation, 1815), *Polinice* (pr. 1824; *Polynice*, 1815), and the two masterpieces *Saul* (pr. 1794; English translation, 1815) and *Mirra* (pr. 1819; *Myrrha*, 1815).

In *Phillip II*, the struggle between the cruel Spanish king and his noble son Carlo symbolizes the struggle between tyranny and liberty and is compounded by the father's jealousy toward his son, who loves his former betrothed, now his stepmother. Thus political passions intermingle with strong human passions, which are the very essence of tragedy. *Saul*, which is said to have had more performances in Italy than any other tragedy, deals with the biblical story of Saul, the ancient king of Israel, who, abandoned by God, is tormented by remorse and driven to madness by his fear and hatred for David, his rival and successor. Saul's terror, which reaches the deepest levels of pathos, adds to the twofold despair of a man struggling with God and with himself. The protagonist, the first powerful prototype of tragic Romantic man, finally succumbs to distrust, madness, and fury and becomes the vacillating victim of his own distorted, overwhelming ego.

Typical of his fiery temperament, rather than follow the plots or the psychological development of his characters (which in most of his other tragedies appear stylized and fixed by the classical models), Alfieri often let his Romantic sentiments and emotions prevail: his hatred for tyranny, his patriotic longing for political freedom and Italian unity, his mistrust of the French role in the affairs of Italy, and his individualism. Yet despite these shortcomings, Alfieri's tragedies were remarkably new and innovative in their poetic form: Unlike the tragedies that had preceded them, they were written in unpolished blank verse, contained relatively few characters, and dealt with a simple, straightforward action. These qualities, and the grandeur of Alfieri's intensely felt political ideals, soon found a responsive echo in Italy and inspired many to follow in his steps, thus earning for Alfieri an important place in the theatrical and political history of Italy.

THE ROAD TO MANZONI AND THE RISORGIMENTO

At the end of the eighteenth century, the French troops of Napoleon invaded Italy, and the hopes of Italians for freedom from a foreign yoke and for political unity were shattered. It was inevitable that this bitter disappointment would be reflected in the works of the poets of the time and echoed in the plays written by the playwrights of the post-Alfierian generations.

Perhaps the most representative of the first generation of writers to be inspired by Alfieri was Vincenzo Monti, who had met Alfieri in Rome in 1781. In 1786, Monti's first tragedy, *Aristodemo* (Aristodemus, 1809), which was deeply rooted in the classical tradition and whose protagonist, the king of Messena, showed flashes of a Shakespearean or Alfierian quality, met with great popular success. Another of his tragedies, *Caio Gracco*, performed in 1802, proved equally successful, largely because the patriotic speeches of Gracchus against the tyrant Opimio struck a popular patriotic chord.

The great poet Ugo Foscolo was a follower of Monti and, above all, of Alfieri. His three imitative Alfierian plays, *Tieste* (pr. 1797), *Aiace* (pr. 1811), and *Ricciarda* (pr. 1813), give only a somewhat reduced manifestation of his creative powers. Foscolo dedicated *Tieste* to Alfieri for providing him with the only possible stylistic model to be followed, and it, too, abounds in lofty speeches against tyranny and in praise of liberty and justice. *Aiace*, although meeting with the disfavor of the public when first staged in 1811 in Milan, remains the best of Foscolo's productions and has been favorably compared to Alfieri's masterpiece *Saul*. Despite beautiful poetic lines and stirring speeches, however, it suffers from a lack of dramatic action on the stage, and it has contributed more to Foscolo's reputation as a poet than to his reputation as a playwright.

The most important of the anticlassicist writers to emerge in Italy in the first half of the nineteenth century was the Milanese Alessandro Manzoni, the author of the literary masterpiece *I promessi sposi* (1827; *The Betrothed*, 1951).

In the preface of the first of his two tragedies, *Il conte di Carmagnola* (pb. 1820; the count of Carmagnola) and in the subsequent treatise-like *Lettre à M. C[hauvet] sur l'unité de temps et de lieu dans la tragédie* (1823; letter to Mr. Chauvet on the unities of time and place in tragedy), Manzoni denounced as constricting and artificial the traditional observances of the so-called Aristotelian unities, especially those of time and space. Furthermore, variously influenced by the dramatic theories of Friedrich and August Wilhelm von Schlegel, Johann Wolfgang von Goethe, and "that barbarian of genius," as he defined William Shakespeare, and true to his own interpretation of Romanticism, which he saw as more Christian than classicism, he defended "dramatic poetry" as a deeply moral genre. The representation of tragic real life and historical events could be used to inspire the spectators to meditate on the frailty of man's existence and on their ultimate destiny, and thus he laid the groundwork for one of the fundamental tenets of his art, the reconciliation of morality and aesthetics.

A careful reading of some of Shakespeare's works, especially of *Richard II* (pr. c. 1595-1596), had convinced Manzoni that it was indeed possible to write a tragedy befitting his definition of Romanticism based both on Christian principles and on true historical events. The carefully researched action of *Il conte di Carmagnola* focuses on the events leading to the death of Francesco Bussone, count of Carmagnola, a mercenary captain who, after having honorably served the duke of Milan, offered his services to Milan's enemies, the Venetians, in order to seek revenge against Filippo Visconti, who had tried to kill the count and deprive him of his possessions. After winning a decisive battle for the Venetians, in an act of magnanimity he frees all the prisoners taken, incurring the suspicion of some powerful noblemen, who lure the count back to Venice and manage to have him tried for treason. After a noble stand, Carmagnola is finally convicted and dies still proudly proclaiming his innocence.

The second of his tragedies, *Adelchi* (pr. 1822), deals with the end of the Longobard rule in Italy at the hands of the Frankish king, Charlemagne, and, indirectly, with Italy's political woes and the failures up to that point to achieve national political unification. More important, it reflects once more Manzoni's concerns with moral choices. Adelchi is a Hamlet-like tragic hero who, despite his moral and religious feelings, is forced by filial duty to fight in a war that is to him ethically repugnant. Adelchi's fatalism finds its counterpart in the resignation of his saintly sister Ermengarda, who, in the face of misfortune and repudiation by her husband, does not seek revenge and accepts her tragic life with a sense of Christian resignation and moral duty.

The plays—which are divided into the traditional five acts and feature some beautiful choruses that the poet used to provide lyric relief and to express his own metahistorical moral comment—rely more on a dynamic of words than of action and therefore lack sufficient dramatic force to have made a lasting impact on the tragic genre. Dramatically weak, they have in fact rarely been performed and have often been judged as more suitable for reading than for staging.

Manzoni's contemporaries espoused Romanticism with the passion one would give a political credo, and their dramatic production invariably presents a mixture of patriotic and Romantic ideals. For example, Silvio Pellico, whose *Le mie prigioni* (pr. 1832; *My Prisons*, 1833) rivaled in popularity Manzoni's *The Betrothed*, shared also his Christian religiosity but instilled in his many works such vehement, unadulterated patriotism that his tragedies, such as *Francesca da Rimini* (pr. 1815; English translation, 1851), despite some severe shortcomings, were greeted with tremendous popular acclaim. Another of Pellico's historical plays, *Eufemio di Messina* (pr. 1820; *Eufemio of Messina*, 1934), introduced significant innovations to the development of the historical Romantic drama, especially in staging techniques. Like most tragedies produced at this time, however, it suffers from a too shallow, one-dimensional portrayal of characters and from lack of true tragic tension.

Like Pellico and Manzoni, Giovanni Battista Niccolini was a great patriot, and his many tragedies became powerful vehicles for his democratic, republican ideas and for his hatred of the Papacy and of the foreign rulers who perpetuated Italy's lack of unity. His first tragedies dealt with the common historical and Romantic themes of the time and with lofty, uncompromising patriotic ideals. His famous *Giovanni da Procida* (pr. 1830; Giovanni of Procida), for example, dealt with the "Sicilian Vespers," the Sicilian uprising against the French occupying forces in 1282. More controversial, and immensely more popular, although it was banned almost everywhere, was his masterpiece, *Arnaldo da Brescia* (pb. 1843; *Arnaldo of Brescia: A Tragedy*, 1846), about the twelfth century religious reformer who rejected both the temporal power of the Church and the political interference of imperial forces.

Other playwrights of some note of this period were Carlo Marenco, who tried to follow the lead of Manzoni and Pellico; Paolo Ferrari; and Pietro Cossa, whose plays dealt with the emerging interest in social problems.

THE BOURGEOIS THEATER AND VERISMO

The first attempts at a post-Risorgimento, socially oriented theater were largely devoid of profound political tensions or sentiments and were voiced by Achille Torelli. With *I mariti* (pr. 1867; the husbands), Torelli interpreted the desires of the emerging social class, the bourgeoisie, for a social order made of solid values and sane, middle-class moral principles. His somewhat less traditional technique and his fresh approach to new dramatic contents aroused enormous public interest and met with the approval of some of the most important critics of the time, including that of the aging Manzoni. Torelli, however, in his other works rarely achieved again the harmonious, realistic effects of *I mariti*, and he ended up by producing a number of uneven, often contrived works of inferior merit. Other writers who found inspiration in a realistic yet critical representation of the bourgeois milieu of the new Italy were Gerolamo Rovetta, whose *La trilogia di Dorina* (pr. 1889; Dorina's trilogy) was widely acclaimed; and Giacinto Gallina, who achieved great notoriety for his comedies depicting Venetian popular and middle-class life. Interesting dramatic works were also produced by two other playwrights of the time: Giovanni Bovio and Giuseppe Giacosa. With *San Paolo* (pr. 1895; Saint Paul), *Il millennio* (pr. 1895; the millennium), and *Leviatano* (pb. 1899; Leviathan), Bovio tried to create a different and more philosophical drama by permeating his work with his own fervent secular creed. Giacosa, on the other hand, evolved from medievally inspired light dramas in verse such as *Un partita a scacchi* (pr. 1873; *The Wager*, 1914), which long remained the most popular of his early works, to a masterfully realistic depiction and psychological analysis of the bourgeois world in *Tristi amori* (pr. 1887; *Unhappy Love*, 1916) and *Come le foglie* (pr. 1900; *Like Falling Leaves*, 1904), which is still performed today.

By the late nineteenth century, the time had become ripe for a codification of the new aesthetic principles that many of these playwrights had, albeit confusedly and instinctively, propounded in their works. The unification of Italy, finally accomplished in 1870, provided the necessary impulse for this assessment while exerting an immediate and profound influence on Italian letters and on the Italian stage. Preoccupation with Italy's new reality and with its collective moral and psychological soul induced many writers to turn their attention to contemporary issues and to shun the trite and frequently irrelevant historical and mythological themes that had become a mannered and idealized commonplace in the theater.

The theorist of the new movement of *verismo*, or Verism, a sophisticated form of realism, was Luigi Capuana, who, after reading and studying European literature, especially contemporary French authors, and writing a number of theatrical reviews that he collected and published as *Il teatro contemporaneo* (1872; the contemporary theater), decided to devote his attention to the short story and the novel. In 1888, however, he wrote a drama titled *Giacinta* (pr. 1888; based on his novel of the same title, published in 1879), in which he tried to react against the falsehoods of conventional theater and traditional conformism by interjecting regional motifs and by having the characters speak in a language born out of their personal experience and condition, rather than simply functioning as mouthpieces for the author's

literary vagaries. To get closer to the reality that he knew best, he wrote eleven works in Sicilian dialect, among which is the important *Malìa* (pr. 1895; spell).

Capuana's theses and his proposition that a truly national Italian theater could be achieved only by passing through the stage of a regional theater found many followers, among them Federico de Roberto, whose best-known dramatic work is *Il rosario* (pr. 1913; the rosary), and the greatest novelist of the second half of the nineteenth century and the most representative author of Verism, Giovanni Verga.

When Giovanni Verga began to write for the theater, he had already written the first of his two literary masterpieces, *I malavoglia* (1881; *The House by the Medlar Tree*, 1890). In 1883, however, anticipating by five years Capuana's own successful application of the principles of Verism to a dramatic work, and over the skepticism of many experts who thought that the public would reject this as a too naturalistic, untheatrical representation, he adapted for the stage one of his novels: *Cavalleria rusticana* (pr. 1884; *Cavalleria Rusticana: Nine Scenes from the Life of the People*, 1893). This simple, tragically fatalistic Sicilian tale of seduction, love, jealousy, and death met with surprising success, was later used by Pietro Mascagni as a libretto for one of his most successful operas, and became a major influence in the development of modern Italian theater.

Of Verga's other plays, worthy of mention are the frequently performed *La lupa* (pr. 1896; the she-wolf), which deals with the doomed, insane passion of a woman for her daughter's husband, and *Dal tuo al mio* (pr. 1903; from thine to mine), which explores the social conflicts taking place in Sicily between the emerging bourgeoisie and the old aristocracy. Despite his relatively meager dramatic production, Verga played a larger-than-life role in the rebirth of modern Italian tragic theater, and his influence can be traced through the theater of Annibale Butti and Gabriele D'Annunzio up to the masterly cinematic adaptation of *I malavoglia* by Luchino Visconti in 1948, *La terra trema*.

Following on the heels of Capuana's and Verga's venture into realism were the works of two significant playwrights, both of them realists but very different from one another in other respects. One was Marco Praga, a Milanese critic and writer, who explored with plays such as *Le vergine* (pr. 1889; the virgins) and *La porta chiusa* (pr. 1913; *The Closed Door*, 1923) the psychologically distorted and morally decadent world of the emerging bourgeois class. The other was Roberto Bracco, who has been called the "Italian Ibsen" for his adoption of social issues, especially women's issues, in his realistic plays set in his own Naples. His "women's" plays include *Don Pietro Caruso* (pr. 1895; English translation, 1912), dealing with a man's efforts to protect his daughter only to find her the mistress of his close friend, and *Nellina* (pr. 1908; English translation, 1908), portraying a prostitute intent on hiding her profession from her daughter, who she later discovers is also a prostitute.

TWENTIETH CENTURY ITALIAN THEATER

Drama in the last part of the nineteenth century in general set aside patriotic themes in favor of a more realistic depiction of Italian society and of the socio-economic tendencies and implications that were then prevalent. Italian realism, or Verism, was receiving continuous support from the regional theater and from the dialect theater, which had become increasingly popular. Only the success of some of Gerolamo Rovetta's idealist drama, with its classical and Romantic undertones, seemed to offer an alternative to the prevailing popularity of realistic theater. The playwright on whose shoulders fell the task of leading Italian theater in a new direction was the flamboyant and brilliant poet Gabriele D'Annunzio.

Instrumental in D'Annunzio's turning to the theater was a passionate encounter with Italy's greatest actress of the time, Eleonora Duse. For her he wrote in 1897 *Sogno di un mattino di primavera* (pr. 1897; *The Dream of a Spring Morning*, 1902) and, the following year, *Sogno di un tramonto d'autunno* (pr. 1905; *The Dream of an Autumn Sunset*, 1904), two highly unusual, nondramatic, symbolic compositions much in the tradition of decadent poetry. His best theater, however, was yet to come: *La città morta* (pr. 1898; *The Dead City*, 1900), for Sarah Bernhardt, *La Gioconda* (pr. 1899; English translation, 1902),

which he dedicated to Duse; and *La gloria* (pr. 1899; the glory), in which the poet dealt with the Nietzschean concept of the superman divided between his love for a woman and his glorious political destiny. One of D'Annunzio's finest tragedies, *Francesca da Rimini* (pr. 1901; English translation, 1902), a historical drama of unromantic, gruesome realism, became a tremendous popular success and encouraged the poet to continue writing for the theater. In 1904, he produced the most successful of his plays, *La figlia di Jorio* (*The Daughter of Jorio*, 1907), a drama permeated by the primitive violence of the shepherds of D'Annunzio's native Abruzzi and by the evocation of their naturalistic, quasi-pagan mysticism, and which might have been inspired by the popular realism of Verga's *Cavalleria rusticana*. In 1905, on the same theme, D'Annunzio produced the powerful and well received *La fiaccola sotto il moggio* (the torch under the bushel). Later works include *La nave* (pr. 1908; the ship), a sinister vision of the impending cataclysm in Europe; *Fedra* (pr. 1909; Phaedra), imbued with sensual flames of incestuous passions; and a few others written directly in French verse, among which the most significant remains the pseudomystical *Le Martyre de Saint Sébastien* (pr. 1911; the martyrdom of Saint Sebastian), which was set to music by Claude Debussy.

When World War I began, D'Annunzio's energies became absorbed in the war effort, and in 1919, when the Paris Peace Conference had denied to Italy the Italian-speaking territories on the Dalmatian coast, he daringly occupied Fiume, putting into effect the political ideas already expressed in *La gloria*. With the war over, D'Annunzio returned to literature, and although some twenty films were made from his works, he never chose to write again for the stage. With the exception of a few imitators, the best of whom is considered to be Sem Benelli, D'Annunzio left no school or lasting impact on the modern Italian stage.

At the beginning of the twentieth century, the reaction against the theater of realism was also expressed by the curious, uneventful application of the principles of the *Manifesto del teatro futurista* (manifesto of futurist theater) that called for a noisy, atechnical, alogical, sensory theater.

After D'Annunzio, the Italian stage was dominated by the genius of Luigi Pirandello, a twentieth century master of undisputed international stature who combined prolific activity as a poet and essayist with a continuous and sustained interest in the narrative genre. Pirandello was prodded into writing his first work for the theater by the actor and fellow-Sicilian Nino Martoglio, who suggested that he rewrite for the stage one of his short stories, "La morsa" (the vise). This was soon followed by other similar works, such as *Lumìe di Sicilia* (pr. 1910; *Sicilian Limes*, 1921), *Liolà* (pr. 1916; English translation, 1952), *Pensaci, Giacomino!* (pr. 1916; think about it, Jimmy), in which the world of the Sicilian peasants and petite bourgeoisie is sarcastically explored in its naturalistic, often grotesque, social contradictions. Other plays, such as *Vestire gli ignudi* (pr. 1922; *Naked*, 1924) and *La vita che ti diedi* (pr. 1923; *The Life I Gave You*, 1959), deal with the same ideological implication of humankind's sorrowful existence brought to the level of a universal predicament. Yet starting with *Così è (se vi pare)* (pr. 1917; *Right You Are [If You Think So]*, 1952), one can perceive the first signs of Pirandello's greatest dramatic season, which includes *Sei personaggi in cerca d'autore* (pr. 1921; *Six Characters in Search of an Author*, 1922), *Ciascuno a suo modo* (pb. 1923; *Each in His Own Way*, 1923), and *Questa sera si recita a soggetto* (pr. 1930; *Tonight We Improvise*, 1932).

In these works, Pirandello explores the painful contradictions of people's lives: the vanity and therapeutic quality of the logical reasoning with which people try to explain their unchangeable, fatalistic existence, the irrationality of humankind's history, feelings, and personality, the illusion and relativity of all cognitive reality, and the tragic problem of the inability of human beings to communicate. To paraphrase the title of one of Pirandello's best-known novels, each man is one person, is no one, or is one hundred thousand people, according to how he feels at a given moment, how he is seen by others, or how others act toward him on that particular occasion.

Pirandello's best-known play, *Six Characters in Search of an Author*, deals with the theme of theater-within-theater; the function of authors, characters, actors, directors, and spectators; the nature and role of the theater as an art; and the central aesthetic problem of the conflict between art and life. The six characters who have been created as immutable masks demand to "relive" on the stage their ever immutable drama, but their illusion is shattered when it becomes clear that life is a continuous, unpredictable, and undefinable flow, which can never be frozen or defined in a recognizable form.

The Pirandellian theater with its fatalistic and surrealistic depiction of humankind's absurd and irreconcilable existence, and the revolutionary dramatic techniques with which Pirandello tried to eviscerate the exemplary artistic role of this theater of the irrational, have left a profound mark on the modern consciousness and on the very essence of the dramatic arts as they are perceived today. While D'Annunzio's example has left little that can easily be discerned and traced to him in contemporary Italian drama, Pirandello's legacy is still vital, and his influence can be seen everywhere.

CONTEMPORARY ITALIAN THEATER

After more than twenty years of Fascism, and in the aftermath of World War II, a curious yet understandable phenomenon took place. After years of censorship and cultural self-sufficiency, Italian producers begin to turn to the forbidden fruit of foreign scripts and ignored, for a while at least, Italian plays. Nevertheless, distinguished Italian dramatists, from Ugo Betti, Diego Fabbri, Eduardo De Filippo, and Dario Fo, undaunted, kept writing plays of significant social value and dramatic vigor. They had not forgotten Pirandello's lesson, although now the emphasis was placed on an immediate and contingent moral, rather than philosophical level, be it of religious or historical and ideological nature.

Ugo Betti, a poet and playwright who found his inspiration in the "human cases" that he witnessed as a judge and magistrate, achieved the best results with *Frana allo scalo nord* (pr. 1936; *Landslide*, 1964), *Delitto all'isola delle capre* (pr. 1950; *Crime on Goat Island*, 1955), and especially the often performed *Corruzione al palazzo di giustizia* (pr. 1949; *Corruption in the Palace of Justice*, 1962). In these plays, behind the corruption and violence of which humans are capable, one can perceive the moral theme of guilt and lost purity, with all the metaphysical anguish and burdensome intensity that accompany it.

A more openly problematic religious theme, exploring the equivocal relationship between God and humankind, has been the main inspiration of Diego Fabbri. After starting with some psychological plays that dealt with more recognizable moral and social conflicts, among which *Paludi* (pr. 1942; marshes) and *La libreria del sole* (pr. 1943; the bookstore of the sun) are noteworthy, Fabbri quickly progressed toward a more cogent and religiously severe discussion of humankind's often unclear existential and metaphysical awareness of the self and of human beings' relationship with God. *Processo di famiglia* (1953; family trial), *Inquisizione* (pr. 1950; inquisition), and above all *Processo a Gesú* (pr. 1955; *Between Two Thieves*, 1959) and *Veglia d'armi* (pr. 1956; armed watch) have received wide critical acclaim and have been performed often in Italy and abroad. Another important vein in Fabbri's playwriting, one that reflects his own personality, has been a kind of humorous comedy of manners, with *Il seduttore* (pr. 1951; the seducer) and *La bugiarda* (pr. 1956; the liar) being the most successful examples.

Eduardo De Filippo is the playwright who, after Pirandello, has enjoyed the most continued and undivided public support. In his plays, De Filippo has managed to produce with surprising continuity an impressive array of themes that combine various indigenous theatrical elements, from those of the *commedia dell'arte* to those of immediate regional inspiration, from Pirandellian rationality to an ideologically committed interpretation of contemporary society's crises. Among his most articulate works, in which can be seen a "poetics of the poor" and a subtle yet bitter picture of prejudices existing in Italy's postwar reality, are *Questi fantasmi* (pr. 1946; *Oh, These Ghosts!*, 1964), *Napoli milionaria!* (pr. 1945; English translation, 1996), *Le voci di dentro* (pr. 1948; *Inner Voices*, 1983), *De Pretore Vincenzo* (pr. 1957; on Pretore Vincenzo), *Filumena Marturano* (pr. 1946; *The Best House in Naples*, 1956), and *Sabato, domenica e lunedì* (pr. 1959; *Saturday, Sunday, Monday*, 1973). De Filippo's consummate artistry as an actor, director, and playwright, and his recurrent use of Neapolitan settings and of the literary Neapolitan language in a manner that transcends their immediate source of inspiration, have all in some ways contributed to the worldwide renown of this author and his work.

The inspiration for the satirical and farcical productions of Dario Fo, with their biting ideological criticism, can be traced back to the medieval *jongleur* tradition and the histrionics of the *commedia dell'arte*. A skillful actor as well as a playwright, Fo has achieved his best results in often controversial plays with suggestive surrealistic titles: *Gli arcangeli non giocano al flipper* (pr. 1959; *Archangels Don't Play Pinball*, 1987), *Aveva due pistole con gli occhi bianchi e neri* (pr. 1960; he had two pistols with white and black eyes), *La signora è da buttare* (pr. 1967; the lady should be discarded), and the politically polemic *Morte accidentale di un anarchico* (pr. 1970; *Accidental Death of an Anarchist*, 1979), which openly express the "New Left" criticism of capitalist society. Fo, who is clown, serious actor, director, designer, and playwright has worked closely with his wife, Franca Rame, both of them acting in plays, almost all of them written by one or the other or both of them. Their work is closely associated with the tradition of the *commedia dell'arte*, but updated to engage with contemporary audiences on issues of immediate relevance.

After 1969, most of their plays were performed in found spaces: in factories, on farms, in public squares, and always with a minimum of scenery. They include such plays as *Mistero Buffo: Giullarata popolare* (pr. 1969; *Mistero Buffo: Comic Mysteries*, 1983), *Clacson, trombette e pernacche* (pr. 1981, *Trumpets and Raspberries*, 1983), *Johann Padan a la descoverta de le Americhe* (pr. 1991; Johann and the discovery of the Americas), and *Lu Santo Jullare Francesco* (pr. 1997; the Holy Fool Saint Francis). In 1997, Fo won the Nobel Prize in literature. His acceptance speech was itself a performance. His winning the Nobel Prize was highly controversial as it was the first time the prize had ever been awarded to a performer, and yet it was based on Fo's commitment to a form of theater that addressed serious social issues in vibrant and comic ways.

Despite a perhaps distracting presence of a very active cinema and of the television industry, many other eloquent contributions to the Italian theater have been made by important literary authors and playwrights in the late twentieth century. A brief mention should be made at least of the still underrated theater of Vitaliano Brancati, with the highly erotic themes of his later production; of the existentially meaningful *Un caso clinico* (pb. 1953; a clinical case) and *L'uomo che andrà in America* (pb. 1968; the man who will go to America), by Dino Buzzati; of the mystical and, at the same time, religiously modern *L'avventura di un povero cristiano* (pb. 1968; *The Story of a Humble Christian*, 1971), by Ignazio Silone; and of the five controversial political tragedies by Pier Paolo Pasolini, in which he uses the representation of sexual extremes and physical violence in order to condemn all forms of violence.

Among other late twentieth century playwrights of note, one must include Alberto Moravia, who has adapted some of his narrative works for the theater and has, in addition, written some of the most important and stimulating plays of the postwar period, including *Il mondo è quello che è* (pr. 1966; the world is what it is), *Il dio Kurt* (pb. 1968; God Kurt), and *La vita è gioco* (pb. 1969; life is a game); Giuseppe Patroni Griffi, with his pessimistic ironic outlook in plays such as *D'amore si muore* (pr. 1958; one can die of love) and *Anima nera* (pr. 1960; black soul); Natalia Ginzburg, with the extremely successful *Ti ho sposato per allegria* (pr. 1966; I married you for fun) and *L'inserzione* (pb. 1967; *The Advertisement*, 1969); Dacia Maraini, with her strong ideological commitment and assertive feminist poetics in plays such as *Manifesto dal carcere* (pr. 1971; manifesto from the prisons) and *La donna perfetta* (pr. 1974; the perfect woman); and Carmelo Bene, an author, actor, and director who sought new directions in staging and representative techniques and who, with plays such as *Salomé* (pr. 1963), *Faust o Margherita* (pr. 1965), and *Nostra signora dei Turchi* (pr. 1966; our lady of the Turks), probed creatively into the realm of experimental theater.

In the postwar era, an important change came with the establishment of several theaters with fixed homes, resident companies, and strong modern directors who developed more ambitious and meaningful repertories. This was a development that the critic Silvio d'Amico had urged and campaigned for beginning in the 1920's. The new enterprises included the Piccolo Teatro of Milan founded in 1947 by Paolo Grassi and Giorgio Strehler, the Piccolo Teatro of Rome created by Orazio Costa in 1948, the Teatro Stabile of Genoa established by Luigi Squarzina in 1952, and the Teatro Stabile of Turin led by Gianfanco de Bosio. Of these the most important and enduring has been the Piccolo Teatro of Milan, an institution that contributed greatly to the development of drama in Italy in the second half of the twentieth century. It was founded in the immediate aftermath of World War II. Strehler has been among the most prominent directors in Italy responsible for some of the finest productions and for encouraging the work of emerging dramatists. The Piccolo was indeed little, housed in a former movie theater that had been used by the Nazis as a prison and interrogation house. It was an apt transformation, turning the facility into an instrument of civilized culture. It eventually outgrew the small theater, though never abandoned it. A newer theater was created by altering a box pit-and-gallery theater into a corrale style theater (the Teatro Studio) and, in 1998, a new large facility opened after nearly twenty years in construction. Unfortunately, Strehler died in 1998, just prior to the opening of the theater for which he had campaigned so long.

These new institutions and others like them have exerted strong influence on the development of playwrights in Italy. No longer do playwrights feel the impulse to send their plays elsewhere, as Pirandello did up to the time he created his own company.

BIBLIOGRAPHY

Carlson, Marvin. *The Italian Stage from Goldoni to D'Annunzio*. Jefferson, N.C.: McFarland, 1981. A very thorough and useful account of the dramatic literature and production practices in Italy from the eighteenth century to the early twentieth century.

Cope, Jackson I. *Secret Sharers in Italian Comedy: From Machiavelli to Goldoni*. Durham, N.C.: Duke University Press, 1996. Cope isolates particular comic qualities inherent in Italian comedies from the Renaissance through the eighteenth century.

Di Gaetani, John Louis. *Carlo Gozzi: A Life in the Eighteenth Century Venetian Theater, an Afterlife in Opera*. Jefferson, N.C.: McFarland, 2000. A portrait of the life of Carlo Gozzi, with contextual information about the era in which he lived.

Duchartre, Pierre L. *The Italian Comedy: The Improvisation, Scenarios, Lives, Attributes, Portraits, and Masks of the Illustrious Characters of the Commedia dell'Arte*. Translated by R. T. Weaver. New York: Dover, 1929. An old but very useful standby in the scholarship on the *commedia*.

House, Jane, and Antonio Attisani, eds. *Twentieth Century Italian Drama*. New York: Columbia University Press, 1995. A broad collection of Italian plays translated in English from the first half of the twentieth century.

MacClintock, Lander. *The Age of Pirandello*. Bloomington: University of Indiana Press, 1951. A study of Italian playwrights from the first three decades of the twentieth century.

Oreglia, G. *The Commedia dell'Arte*. New York, 1968. One the most readable accounts of the nature and development of the *commedia dell'arte*.

Roberto Severino,
updated by Stanley Longman

RUSSIAN DRAMA SINCE THE 1600'S

Russian drama sprang from universal human impulses to imitate, mime, playact, dance, sing, jest, and celebrate nature's cycles. Like Egyptians, Greeks, Romans, Germans, and many other peoples, ancient Slavs had pagan ceremonies to celebrate the death of winter and birth of spring. Later, when Christianized, they dramatized the festivals of Christmas and Easter, or mixed cultural rituals in carnival rites, reminiscent of Greek Dionysian festivals, which featured *skomorokhi* ("merry men") who played flutes and gamboled.

By the sixteenth century, the conservative Russian Orthodox Church began to persecute groups of nomadic *skomorokhi* because their puppet shows often featured satirical, anticlerical themes. In riposte, Czar Ivan IV ("Ivan the Terrible," reigned 1533-1584) baited the Novgorod bishopric by costuming a street clown as Archbishop Pimen and using jesters and dancing bears at royal weddings. The Church did introduce some morality plays closely tied to the liturgy, but their quality was inferior to imported Western morality plays, which popularized religious and moral concepts in the vernacular. These works inspired Russia's first noted playwright, Saint Dmitry Rostovsky, to compose religious plays. They were performed for many decades by itinerant actors in the houses of landed gentry, who paid the troupes in food, drink, and clothing.

Czar Alexis I (reigned 1645-1676), influenced by European advisers, had an imperial theater built in his residence, sent emissaries to Germany to recruit actors, and authorized Johann Gregory, a minister of Moscow's Lutheran Church, to found a theatrical school in 1673, wholly financed by the czar's treasury. This patronage began a long tradition of dependency on the throne for the Russian state theater, with all theatrical workers considered government employees, and playwrights expected to accede to monarchical mandates. Even provincial theaters, which began to burgeon in the eighteenth century, were controlled by local imperial bureaucrats and subject to the authority of censorship as well as the comfort of subsidy.

Czar Peter I ("The Great," reigned 1682-1725) had the imperial theater moved to the new Russian capital he built, St. Petersburg, in 1709. As a determined westernizer, he welcomed the immigration of a German theatrical company headed by Johann Kunst, and he encouraged Kunst and his successor, Otto Furst, to train Russian ensembles that would glorify his military triumphs and domestic reforms. Moreover, when the czar replaced his plain empress with a pretty German princess, he ordered a revision of a play depicting the biblical story of *Esther* so that the play's king would now be shown as noble in his decision to separate from his wife and unite with a beautiful foreigner.

The German domination of the official court theater was challenged during the reign of Empress Anna (reigned 1730-1740) by the influx of a group of Italian actors, singers, and mimes directed by a Neapolitan composer, Francesco Araia, who introduced Russians to the improvised techniques of the Italian form of *commedia dell'arte* and also inaugurated opera in St. Petersburg. At the same time, Antonio Fusano organized the first ballet performances, only to be soon replaced by Jean Baptiste Landet, usually called the father of Russian ballet.

Anna's successor, Elizabeth Petrovna (reigned 1741-1762), issued a decree in 1750 authorizing theatrical performances in private houses. This attracted a number of foreign companies, most of them French, which performed the plays of Molière, Jean Racine, and Pierre Corneille. The edict also encouraged Russia's first great dramatist, Aleksandr Petrovich Sumarokov, the first nobleman to choose literature as a profession. Sumarokov wrote literary criticism, poetry, and journalistic articles, but his reputation rests principally on his plays. His tragedy *Khorev* (pr. 1750; English translation, 1970) is the fountainhead of Russian classical drama. It follows the French unities of time, place, and action; parades elevated themes in elevated language; and concentrates on royal characters. It is not surprising that Sumarokov—even though seven of his nine tragedies deal with his native land's history—was called the "Russian Racine."

Sumarokov was delighted to cast in his plays the first great Russian actor, Fyodor Volkov. Together they founded the first professional Russian theatrical company in 1756, with the dramatist its first director, Volkov its leading actor, and Empress Elizabeth Petrovna an enthusiastic patron. The institution's imperial subsidy was, however, comparatively meager: In its first year it received five thousand rubles, the French, twenty thousand, and the Italians, thirty thousand. After Catherine II ("The Great," reigned 1762-1796) assumed the throne, the theater flourished, with the empress herself composing (with considerable help) three dramas, eleven comedies, and five operas—all quite forgettable. In 1779, Catherine authorized the Imperial Theater School for the training of actors, singers, and dancers, commonly called the Bolshoi Theater. She established the Administration of Theaters, which tightly controlled the policies and finances of all state companies but had no jurisdiction over the private theaters owned by boyars (noblemen) and rich landowners. Many of the gentry imitated the imperial court by establishing their own theatrical troupes, recruited from their serfs; hence, these were termed "serf theaters."

Fancying themselves miniature czars, members of the upper class staged lavish theatrical extravagances. Prince Yusupov had a whole corps de ballet on his estate, as well as dramatic and operatic companies; Count Kamensky spent thirty thousand rubles on one performance of an opera. Because all performers were serfs, they were subject to the caprices of their masters, who could and would sell them, send them to Siberia, birch them, or bed them. The serf theater with the highest dramatic standards belonged to Count Peter Shevemetyev, who trained and treated his troupe well, entertained visiting foreign monarchs, and married his leading actress. In the nineteenth century, many estate owners found their affluence declining because they could not compete successfully with their European peers, who employed more progressive agricultural techniques. They therefore disbanded their theaters as an unaffordable luxury, but not before a large number of actors had honed their skills in them.

Sumarokov's successor as a distinguished dramatist was Denis Ivanovich Fonvizin, the father of Rus-

sian comedy. His masterpiece, *Nedorosl* (pr. 1782; *The Minor*, 1933), presents a grimly satiric portrait of the brutality and duplicity endemic in the landed gentry, yet is also witty and sharply realistic in language and characterization, and comprehensive in its portrayal of secondary characters. Fonvizin is the talented forerunner of the realistic school of Russian drama, to be graced by Alexander Griboyedov, Nikolai Gogol, Alexander Ostrovsky, and Anton Chekhov.

NINETEENTH CENTURY

Czar Alexander I (reigned 1801-1825) promoted a relatively benign and liberal policy toward the performing arts, slanted only by his marked preference for foreign achievements: Of the 135 operas presented during his reign, only 45 were Russian, and the music and librettos of the latter were seldom by native composers. At court, persons of culture spoke French or German; Russian was for the rabble. Nevertheless, a growing intelligentsia and middle class showed increasing interest in a Russian repertory. In 1824, the Moscow Maly (or "small") Theater became a national center for drama, while St. Petersburg's Bolshoi (or "big") Theater concentrated on ballet and opera. The Maly was soon rivaled by St. Petersburg's Alexandrinsky Theater, finished in 1832, which boasted a gifted galaxy of actors headed by Vasily Karatygin, the leading tragedian of his era. Karatygin was famous for the studied care that he applied to his roles, the subtle restraint of his technique, and the polished sonority of his voice. His most popular counterpart was Pavel Mochalov, the son of a serf actor, whose spontaneous temperament and intuitive style put him at polar odds with Karatygin's highly calculated method. One Russian critic compared Mochalov to the English Romantic actor Edmund Kean, calling the former a forest while Karatygin resembled a well-kept garden.

A third great actor was Mikhail Shchepkin, also the son of a serf, whose brilliant performances illuminated the Maly Theater after his freedom had been expensively bought in 1823. The most influential Russian critic of the era, Vissarion Belinsky, judged Shchepkin's skills a synthesis of Mochalov's passion and Karatygin's technical prowess. Shchepkin emphasized the dignity of his profession and founded a school of acting, the disciples of which excelled in the plays of Ostrovsky, Chekhov, and Maxim Gorky.

Among actresses, the most intense competition was international: Mlle Marguerite George acted with a French company in Russia for five triumphant years. Her rival was Ekaterina Semenova, the daughter of a landowner and a serf mother. Both women excelled in tragic roles and attracted fanatic followings; after one heroic performance, Semenova was given a diamond diadem valued at 100,000 rubles.

Among dramatists of the early nineteenth century, the most popular was Ivan Krylov. Basically a writer of fables, he was read and quoted everywhere. His comedies, such as *Modnaya Lavka* (pb. 1807; the fashion shop), mock Gallomania, sentimentality, vanity, hypocrisy—all good targets for an acerbic satirist. A better though less influential comic playwright was Alexander Griboyedov. His best play, *Gore ot uma* (pr. 1831; *The Mischief of Being Clever*, 1857), is a powerful protest against the corruption and complacency of czarist society and has remained in the canon of notable Russian reformist dramas. The role of its vehement protagonist, Chatsky, is prized by young Russian actors as a formidable challenge.

Russia's greatest poet, Alexander Pushkin, wrote his monumental political drama *Boris Godunov* (wr. 1824-1825; English translation, 1918) under the inspiration of William Shakespeare and George Gordon, Lord Byron. Denied production by contemporaneous censors, it was not staged until 1870; it was then adapted by Modest Mussorgsky for his towering 1873 opera. Pushkin's main contribution to Russian drama was to shape the Russian language into a fusion of upper-class elegance and popular parlance that made it a literary language serviceable for his successors. His friend and follower, Mikhail Lermontov, met with kindred frustration from the censors: His plays were also suppressed as too inflammatory. He wrote his greatest work, *Maskarad* (pb. 1842; *Masquerade*, 1973), in 1834-1835; it was not produced in a faithful version until 1917, becoming the last drama mounted at the Alexandrinsky Theater before the October Revolution.

The year 1836 was a watershed for Russian performance art: Mikhail Glinka wrote and saw performed his opera *Zhiznza tsarya* (life for the czar), which was a native achievement comparable to the best European compositions, and Nikolai Gogol wrote *Revizor* (pr. 1836; *The Inspector General*, 1890), commonly regarded as the foremost Russian comedy. These two works engaged a broader audience than any previous Russian art. Whether Gogol's play is interpreted as realistic or grotesque, as naturalistic or symbolic, matters less than that it constitutes a deeply native contribution, one at once terrifyingly honest and cunningly adroit in exposing the moral bankruptcy of Russian officialdom.

Gogol's comedies were unique in their explosions of abrasive malice and grotesque hilarity. Ivan Turgenev tried to pursue their mode in ten plays, which he wrote between 1843 and 1852, but he instead succumbed to the more prevalent influence of sentimental melodramas. One play, however, his *Mesyats v derevne* (pb. 1855; *A Month in the Country*, 1924), constitutes an original achievement as the Russian theater's first psychological drama, stressing the internal conflicts of its leading characters. Its emphasis on the attrition of the soul and wistful resolution in sadness and stalemate anticipate Chekhov's masterpieces of renunciation.

The only playwright who directly continued some aspects of the Gogolian manner was Alexander Sukhovo-Kobylin, who knew and admired Gogol. Sukhovo-Kobylin's life provided the substance for his three caustic comedies: In 1850, he was accused of having murdered his French mistress and was hounded by the authorities for seven years until the czar pardoned him. In consequence, his comedic trilogy, comprising *Svadba Krechinskogo* (pr. 1855; *Krechinsky's Wedding*, 1961), *Delo* (pb. 1861; *The Case*, 1969), and *Smert Tarlinka* (pb. 1869; *The Death of Tarelkin*, 1969), stresses individual helplessness against the state's sinister power, bridging the gap between Gogol and Franz Kafka.

Russia's first professional playwright, Alexander Ostrovsky, was also its most prolific, composing some eighty plays in thirty years. As the son of a shop clerk and minor bureaucrat in the Moscow Commercial Court, Ostrovsky gained intimate knowledge of the self-contained society of the middle and lower classes: merchants, artisans, petty officials, small farmers. In his most popular play, *Groza* (pr. 1859; *The Storm*, 1899), he wrote a searing tragedy of victimization with a pure-hearted young wife driven to commit suicide by a sadistic mother-in-law, spineless husband, and harshly unforgiving community. Despite having to battle censorship throughout his career, Ostrovsky was appointed, late in his life, director of the artistic department of the Moscow imperial theaters—the first professional given the post. His plays proved immensely popular, receiving almost eight hundred performances between 1854 and 1872.

Two peasant tragedies had a powerful impact in the second half of the nineteenth century. One, by Alexey Pisemsky, *Gorkaya Sudbina* (pb. 1859; *A Bitter Fate*, 1933), was a grim work dealing with a married peasant woman who becomes her master's mistress during her husband's absence, begets a child by the master, and is mistreated by the husband, who then murders the infant. *Vlast tmy* (pb. 1888; *The Power of Darkness*, 1888), by Leo Tolstoy, has a parallel plot, with the peasant Nikita killing the baby his mistress has had, then confessing his crime in the midst of the young woman's engagement party. Despite Tolstoy's fame, the censor found his drama too bleak in its portrayal of rural life; its first performance was therefore staged in Paris at André Antoine's pioneering Théâtre Libre.

In this era, the most important Russian theater was Moscow's Maly, frequently called "Moscow's second university." The Maly resembled the Comédie-Française in harmonizing a standard classical repertory with current native drama such as Ostrovsky's. Konstantin Stanislavsky's memoirs recount how he and student friends trained for a Maly evening: They first read the play's text, then secondary literature about it, then met to discuss it, and sometimes even invited a lecturer to address them on its merits. Known as "the house of the actor," the Maly featured such outstanding performers that audiences usually overlooked glaring deficiencies in the costumes, makeup, and other aspects of the *mise en scène*. The theater's outstanding performer in the late nineteenth century was the tragedienne Maria Yermolova, whom Stanislavsky admired as the greatest actress he had known. When she played a revolutionary in a Lope de Vega Carpio drama, she stirred a political demonstration by the audience, which in turn caused the authorities to ban the production.

A brief note on ballet is appropriate here: A Frenchman, Marius Petipa, became ballet master of the Imperial Ballet School in 1862 and dominated Russian choreographic art for four decades. By the 1880's, Russian ballet companies had become internationally famous, with Petipa creating more than seventy main ballets and thirty divertissements while he shaped the form and style of hundreds of dancers.

THE SILVER AGE

At the turn of the twentieth century, a revolution in stage production swept over Russia in what was called the "Silver Age" of the arts. Two European theatrical companies provoked enormous interest: The Théâtre Libre, founded by André Antoine in 1887, specializing in the new plays of Henrik Ibsen, August Strindberg, and Gerhart Hauptmann, and inaugurating innovations in acting styles and scenic design; and the Meiningen Players, formed by the theater-loving George II, duke of Saxe-Meiningen, in 1874, and integrating every detail of a performance into a unified ensemble. The Meiningen Players stressed a high level of discipline, with every company member contributing to the overall effect of period accuracy, superb crowd scenes, and unified purpose. They toured Russia in 1890 and made a sensational impression on such aspiring directors as Stanislavsky and Vladimir Nemirovich-Danchenko.

Stanislavsky was the son of a rich industrialist who had him trained in singing, acting, and dancing; at one time, Stanislavsky dreamed of becoming an opera performer. As a young man he went to Paris, saw two plays daily, acted in amateur companies, and then began his career as a Russian director at Moscow's Hunters' Club, staging both naturalistic and Symbolist works from 1888 to 1896. In June, 1898, he had a fateful meeting, lasting eighteen hours, with nobleman Nemirovich-Danchenko, whose 1896 play,

Tsena zhizni (the worth of life), had been the hit of the season. These two visionaries agreed to found the Moscow Art Theatre, soon Russia's foremost theatrical company, which became one of the world's most illustrious stage enterprises.

The Moscow Art Theatre was a highly idealistic, cooperative venture, issuing shares to its patrons and encouraging company members to live in groups as they rehearsed with strenuous energy, fierce dedication, and remarkable fondness for one another. Nemirovich-Danchenko was primarily responsible for the literary and administrative aspects of the organization, while Stanislavsky concentrated on directing but also often acted in such roles as Astrov in Chekhov's *Dyadya Vanya* (pr. 1899; *Uncle Vanya*, 1914) and as Vershinin in *Tri sestry* (pr. 1901; *The Three Sisters*, 1920). They had mutual veto rights but seldom exercised them. Both agreed on the dramaturgic premise that the director had absolute authority over a production, conceiving and shaping it as an integration of verbal, pictorial, and musical components; each actor therefore had to fit into the organic unity of the presentation: "There are no small parts, only small actors"; the star system and sentimental, affected, declamatory acting styles were forbidden; each play was thoroughly discussed by company members before parts were assigned; each actor was urged to catch from closely observed life experiences the characteristic motives and meaning of his or her role; the actors onstage were encouraged to forget about the audience and react to another, sometimes turning their backs to the public; and the *mise en scène* of settings, sounds, and costumes was carefully coordinated with the play's text and tone.

In October, 1898, the Moscow Art Theatre began a new era for the Russian theater with its premier production: *Tsar Fyodor Ioannovich* (pr. 1868; *Tsar Fyodor Ivanovich*, 1923), a play by Alexei Tolstoy about Ivan the Terrible's pathetic son. The spectators were astounded to see onstage an exact replica of the czar's quarters in the Kremlin; all costumes, furnishings, and weapons were museum pieces; acting was unaffected and verisimilar; makeup was natural rather than exaggerated. The response was enthusiastic acclaim, which only intensified when, in succeed-

ing productions, Roman streets were accurately reproduced for Shakespeare's *Julius Caesar* (pr. c. 1599-1600) and Norwegian furniture imported for Ibsen's *Hedda Gabler* (pr. 1891; English translation, 1891). When enacting *Na dne* (pr. 1902; *The Lower Depths*, 1912), by Gorky, the players wore real rags and filthy, broken-down shoes.

The Moscow Art Theatre's greatest triumphs were productions of the four major plays of Chekhov. By 1898, Chekhov had already become recognized as his country's finest writer of short stories; however, his one-act dramas had attracted little attention. In 1896, his full-length play *Chayka* (*The Seagull*, 1909) was given an indifferent production by the Alexandrinsky Theater and became, as a contemporaneous joke had it, a dead duck. Nemirovich-Danchenko, however, admired the work and insisted, over the initially strong opposition of Stanislavsky, on staging it. He stressed the subordination of all gestures and diction to the drama's central mood and tone of wistful, subtly nuanced sadness and melancholy frustration. The production became an overwhelming success, with the Moscow Art Theatre later adopting the seagull as its emblem and becoming famous as the Theater of Chekhov—a far more honorable name than that of Gorky Theater, which the Soviet government decided to call it after the 1917 Revolution. Chekhov's *Uncle Vanya* proved an equally resounding triumph in an 1899 production, followed by *Three Sisters* in 1901 and *Vishnyovy sad* (*The Cherry Orchard*, 1908) in 1904. Even though Stanislavsky and Chekhov occasionally had passionate artistic arguments, with the former pressing the dictatorship of the regisseur while the latter insisted on the primacy of authorial intent, their collaboration established the Moscow Art Theatre as an unequaled home for psychological drama and Chekhov as Russia's greatest playwright.

Chekhov introduced Nemirovich-Danchenko and Stanislavsky to Gorky, whose ruthlessly grim naturalism was in polar opposition to Chekhov's intricately laced undercurrents of resignation. Nevertheless, Stanislavsky gave Gorky's proletarian masterpiece *The Lower Depths* a sharp, full-blooded production that ran for five hundred consecutive performances with Stanislavsky himself triumphing as Satine, the only character clear-sighted enough to dispense with the crutch of self-delusions. Still, crudely delineated Socialist Realism was not the Moscow Art Theatre's preferred mode. Stanislavsky was far more attracted to the Symbolist drama of one of Gorky's many protégés, Leonid Andreyev. In 1907, Stanislavsky interpreted *Zhizn cheloveka* (pr. 1907; *The Life of Man*, 1908) as an abstract-expressionist allegory, the bleak pessimism of which he underscored by having the actors sound hollow and coating the settings in black, until, at the end, all the nameless figures disappeared in a black mist out of which "Someone in Gray" pronounced the misery of humanity's absurd existence.

The period before the Revolution saw new currents of culture bringing electrifying energy into all the arts. In poetry, the new Symbolism yielded to Futurism, Acmeism, Imagism, and a diversity of unclassifiable styles. In fiction, not only Gorky and Andreyev but also Vladimir Korolenko, Ivan Bunin, Alexey Remizov, and Fyodor Sologub ventured important experiments. In music, Igor Stravinsky with his *The Rite of Spring* (1913) killed romantic melodic clichés. In painting, Wasily Kandinsky and Kazimir Malevich became abstract expressionists and Suprematists. All the arts shared a revulsion against social and moralistic messages and a preference for aesthetic formalism.

In ballet, the leaps of achievement were prodigious: The choreographer-dancer Michel Fokine rejected the conservative techniques of the imperial ballet schools in favor of dramatic integration of the corps de ballet with the plot. He was championed by Sergey Diaghilev, the editor of the era's most influential periodical, *Mir Iskusstva* (the world of art). Diaghilev became the twentieth century's greatest impresario, touring the world with his opera company and Ballets Russes from 1909 to 1929 and profoundly shaping the West's cultural life. In addition to Fokine, his company included two of ballet's greatest legends, Anna Pavlova and Vaslav Nijinsky. Diaghilev used Pablo Picasso, Henri Matisse, and Georges Braque on his international staff of painters and costume designers and commissioned compositions by Stravinsky, Sergey Prokofiev, Maurice Ravel, and Paul Hindemith. After the Revolution, his company exiled itself from the Soviet Union, enriching Europe and the United States while impoverishing Russia.

The leading Symbolist poet, Aleksandr Blok, made significant contributions to Russian drama at the beginning of the twentieth century. His plays, *Balaganchik* (pr. 1906; *The Puppet Show*, 1963), *Neznakomka* (pr. 1913; *The Unknown Woman*, 1927), *Korol' na ploshchadi* (pr. 1923; *The King in the Square*, 1934), and *Roza i Krest* (pr. 1921; *The Rose and the Cross*, 1936), reflect the spirit of the time, when the idealistic, unrealistic attitudes prevailed over the mundane and naturalistic ones. They were all successfully staged by Vsevolod Meyerhold.

On the stage, the spirited ensemble work of the Moscow Art Theatre declined after 1917 as it tried to adapt to the mandates of the Soviet regime. It did remain the unchallenged interpreter of Chekhov, with his widow, Olga Knipper, playing Madame Ranevskaya in both the premiere of *The Cherry Orchard* and its three hundredth performance in 1943, but it became increasingly a dramatic conservatory, decreasingly an experimental workshop.

Meyerhold displaced Stanislavsky as Russia's boldest innovator in directing. He dominated the avant-garde stage for a generation beginning in 1905, when Stanislavsky made him head of a newly formed studio theater for the training of actors. Although Meyerhold admired Stanislavsky, he soon came to oppose most of his sponsor's methods. Whereas Stanislavsky sought to immerse the spectators in the atmosphere and action of the play, Meyerhold wanted the audience always to be conscious of the stage's artifice and the actor's art. Although Stanislavsky decried such stock character classifications as "ingenue," "romantic lead," and "noble father," Meyerhold defended the notion of such fixed *emploi*, placing the actor's contribution on a level no higher than those of other means of stage presentation—indeed, often regarding him as a supermarionette. Meyerhold was essentially an antirealist and antinaturalist who loved to experiment with Symbolist stylization. "The time has come," he repeatedly declared, "to attempt to stage the unreal, to render life as perceived in fantasy and visions." Stanislavsky came to regard Meyerhold's dramaturgy as dehumanizing and closed the training studio in 1907.

Meyerhold was soon invited to join the theatrical company headed by the actress Vera Komissar-zhevskaya, who had been converted to the aesthetics of Symbolism. She at first gave him his head, and he staged a series of hotly disputed productions. In a performance of *Hedda Gabler*, each character had his own color and fixed set of gestures, with Hedda attired in a seawatery green dress; the furniture was white, the carpet greenish blue, the stage walls covered with silver lace. Although Meyerhold's experiments interested the critics, they were too abstract to please the general public, which was largely puzzled by his reduction of acting skills to strictly confined patterns of diction and movement. When Meyerhold found no role for Komissarzhevskaya in several successive stagings, she dismissed him. Thereafter he worked for many other companies and during the 1920's was given his own theater workshop, where he developed a system of training for actors, "biomechanics," intended to produce a nearly acrobatic control of the body while reducing the actor to little more than a director's puppet.

Meyerhold's replacement in 1909 at the Komissarzhevskaya Theater was the dramatist-actor-director Nikolai Evreinov. He, too, was a determined opponent of naturalism. He was an enthusiastic, witty free spirit who preferred improvisation to planning and saw all life as a constantly changing stage, with people presenting themselves in diverse roles every waking minute. Hence every spectator recognizes and identifies himself with the actor onstage, who is his double—or vice versa.

THE REVOLUTION

When the Bolsheviks seized power from Aleksandr Kerensky's six-month republican administration in October, 1917, most theatrical professionals adopted a "wait-and-see" attitude, while a few, such as Meyerhold and many Symbolist writers, enthusiastically welcomed the replacement of the Whites by the Reds. Evreinov produced an extraordinary pageant on November 7, 1920: *Vzyatiye zimnego dvortsa*

(pr. 1920; the storming of the Winter Palace). He used eight thousand actors and the cruiser *Aurora* to restage, in the very square in front of the Winter Palace, where the event had occurred, the Bolshevik attack on the headquarters of Kerensky's provisional government. An audience of 100,000 sang the "Internationale," an orchestra of five hundred played revolutionary tunes, the *Aurora* fired her battle guns, a colossal red flag was again hoisted, and the director received a fur coat for his fee.

Another sample of massive morality theater was Meyerhold's 1918 mounting of *Misteriya-buff* (pr. 1918; *Mystery-Bouffe*, 1933), by the Futurist poet-playwright Vladimir Mayakovsky. This was a wild extravaganza, parodying the Old Testament by imagining a new Flood and new Ark, with previously exploited proletarians throwing their oppressive rulers overboard, then sailing to a promised land of communist utopianism. Meyerhold, a natural radical who even became a party commissar, restaged this work in revised form in 1921, although critics berated its posterlike crudeness and conceptual vulgarity.

Nevertheless, the first decade of the Bolshevik Revolution became an era of relative freedom and creativity. Under Anatoli Lunacharsky, the regime's first commissar for education and himself a playwright, the theaters received generous state subsidies. The revolution's first years were a time of new beginnings, hard work, reconstruction, and renewed hopes, even though living conditions were austere; the government gave mixed signals. On the one hand it unified, by a decree signed August 26, 1919, all theaters under a Central Theatrical Committee with power not only to administer them but also to approve their repertory. Theaters were divided into two categories: "politically mature" companies, which were usually well-established and which were left largely autonomous; and private theaters, which were to be far more strictly supervised. On the other hand, new audiences were encouraged to attend the theater through the distribution of free tickets to soldiers and laborers. Thousands of new theaters were founded; amateur troupes and dramatic schools flourished; in the cities, crowds jammed the auditoriums; in the towns and country, the residents clamored for visits from urban companies. Although the Bolsheviks fully appreciated the power of the theater as a propaganda weapon, they were too preoccupied with the ravages of the civil war and the reforms of the New Economic Policy (NEP, existing between 1922 and 1928) to tighten the levers of control. The avant-garde therefore had a heyday until the late 1920's, with Meyerhold riding high by producing and directing a series of stirring performances.

Perhaps the most provocative was Meyerhold's 1925 staging of *Mandat* (pr. 1925; *The Mandate*, 1975) by the gifted Nikolai Erdman. Its protagonist is Pavlusha Guliashkin, a Soviet version of *The Inspector General*'s rogue, who spreads a rumor among Muscovites that he has a "warrant," with duly affixed seals and signatures, enabling him to do and obtain anything and everything. A hive of "former people" swarm about Guliashkin, fancying a return to their former status. At the play's climax, he is exposed as a liar and crook: His "warrant" is a worthless slip of paper. Erdman's satire is double-edged, directed against both the philistines covertly awaiting restoration of their lost privileges and the Soviet regime filled with scoundrels claiming "warrants" for terrorizing the nation. Some of the spectators shouted "Down with bureaucracy" and "Down with Stalin" on opening night. As a result, Erdman's second play, *Samoubiitsa* (pr. 1928; *The Suicide*, 1975), was banned by the Communist Party Central Committee. During the purges of the 1930's, he was arrested and sent to a Siberian concentration camp, with his end unknown.

In 1927, the year in which Joseph Stalin had his rival Leon Trotsky expelled from the party, the agitprop department of the Central Committee set up "artistic counsels" within theaters to select orthodox plays. In 1928, Stalin exiled Trotsky from the Soviet Union; in 1929, he authorized a Chief Repertory Committee with authority to censor and "filter" plays— that is, return the manuscripts to their authors for line-by-line conformity to official doctrine. Somehow, Mayakovsky was able to evade this policy by having his devastating satire on Soviet bureaucracy, *Banya* (*The Bathhouse*, 1963), produced for the first time by Meyerhold in March, 1930. Soviet critics, and Stalin himself, reacted with fury to this work as

well as to a previous Meyerhold-Mayakovsky collaboration, *Klop* (pr. 1929; *The Bedbug*, 1931). Both men were summoned for denunciation by the Russian Association of Proletarian Writers, commonly called by its Russian initials, RAPP. The hypersensitive Mayakovsky, who had once acclaimed the revolution, committed suicide in April, 1930.

Meyerhold's position in the party eroded seriously from the early 1930's on. Many of his previously influential party friends were accused of Trotskyism or other "idealogical errors." RAPP and other official agencies accused him over and over again of "formalism" and of holding an "inimical attitude toward Socialist Realism." His 1934 production of Alexandre Dumas, *fils' La Dame aux camélias* (pr. 1852; *Camille*, 1856) was howled down by party critics as emphasizing "lyric treatment" rather than the "social and tragic clash of the characters in its social content." In 1936, the government began a ruthless purge of "hostile elements" in literature, music, painting, and drama, and *Pravda* scorned Meyerhold as a "class alien" director who slandered the Soviet way of life. In January, 1938, the Committee on the Arts ordered his theater closed. At this critical turn in his life, his aesthetic adversary, Stanislavsky, offered him a post in the Moscow Art Theatre Studios, but Stanislavsky died that same year. In June, 1939, Meyerhold attended the All-Union Congress of Directors, hearing a keynote address given by the Soviet Union's notorious attorney general, Andrey Vyshinsky. Meyerhold then made an audacious speech defending his artistic aims and lashing at the regime's persecution of artistic creativity. "In my heart," he said, "I consider what is now taking place in our theaters frightful and pitiful. . . . In hunting formalism, you have eliminated art!"

The next day, Meyerhold was arrested. Whether he died in a prison camp or committed suicide after his prison release is unknown. Several days after his arrest, his actress wife, Zinaida Raikh, was found brutally murdered in her apartment. Police authorities blamed the deed on an unknown tramp.

The humiliation of the free writer or director and the systematic pollution of independent sensibility in the long winter of Stalinism drained Russian drama of its blood and substance throughout the twentieth century. Yevgeny Zamyatin, a brilliant satiric novelist and playwright, sought to preserve the Russian literary heritage by inspiring the Serapion Brotherhood, which asked that art be allowed to exist independently of ideology or party. By 1929, he was violently attacked by RAPP as an enemy of the Revolution and was fortunate to be permitted to emigrate to Paris in 1932—after a direct appeal to Stalin.

Zamyatin's plays include *Ogni svyatogo Dominika* (wr. 1920; *The Fires of St. Dominic*, 1971), *Blokha* (pr. 1925; *The Flea*, 1971), and *Obshchestvo pochetnikh zvonarei* (pr. 1925; *The Society of Honorary Bell Ringers*, 1971). Most of his plays are set outside of Russia, underscoring his ability to transcend the local milieu and to lend his plays universal meanings, while at the same time alluding to domestic issues.

The dictator made a significant phone call to another talented novelist-dramatist on April 18, 1930. Stalin phoned Mikhail Bulgakov after the writer's plays had been banned in 1929. In March, 1930, Bulgakov wrote a courageous letter to the Chief Repertory Committee, requesting that the Soviet government either allow him to leave Russia or give him the opportunity to work creatively. Stalin, who had inexplicably liked Bulgakov's play *Dni Turbinykh* (pr. 1926; *Days of the Turbins*, 1934), dealing with the last days of the civil war between the Whites and the Reds, thereupon responded to Bulgakov's appeal. According to Ellendea Proffer's 1984 critical biography, Stalin informed Bulgakov that his letter would "have a pleasing answer" and secured his appointment as an assistant director of the Moscow Art Theatre. Allowed to work in the Soviet Union though not to publish, Bulgakov lived another decade, spending much of it composing his acclaimed novel *Master i Margarita* (1966; *The Master and Margarita*, 1967).

Not so "fortunate" was Isaac Babel, one of the Soviet Union's greatest short-story writers and also the author of at least two fine plays, *Zakat* (pb. 1928; *Sunset*, 1960) and *Mariia* (pb. 1935; *Maria*, 1966). The first drama describes the sunset of the career of a legendary Jewish bandit, Mendel Krik, who is brought low in Lear-like fashion by his children. The second is a more ambitious work, describing the dis-

solution of prerevolutionary Russia's middle-class intelligentsia in the chaotic civil war year of 1920. In 1935, Babel's powerful protector Gorky died, and Babel, though publishing nothing more thereafter, was arrested on May 15, 1939, tried on undisclosed charges on January 26, 1940, and announced as dead on March 17, 1941. On December 18, 1954, the supreme court of the Soviet Union reviewed his case and revoked his sentence "in the absence of elements of a crime."

Several other writers exploited the theme of the civil war and rewrote their successful novels into plays. Leonid Leonov dramatized his *Barsuki* (pr. 1927; the badgers), Vsevolod Ivanov rewrote *Bronepoezd 14-16* (pr. 1927; *Armored Train 14-69*, 1933), Boris Lavrenyov dramatized *Razlom* (pr. 1927; the breakup), and others. They all offer their own vision of the revolution that often deviates from the official view, which was possible during the period of the NEP.

Perhaps the safest path for a nonconformist writer in Soviet society was that taken by Yevgeny Shvarts, who lived longer than most of his colleagues. Shvarts spent most of his career as a writer of children's stories and plays. His nearly one dozen plays are united by two themes. The first is innocuous: Love is life's most powerful and magical experience. The second is dangerous: Though despots are charlatans, most people accept them, preferring the security of despotism to the dreadful burden imposed by liberty. This pessimistic thesis, parallel to Fyodor Dostoevski's "Legend of the Grand Inquisitor," in *The Brothers Karamazov* (1879-1880), is cloaked with fantasy and absurdist humor in Shvarts's best play, *Drakon* (pr. 1944; *The Dragon*, 1966). Lancelot, the good knight who kills the dragon, states at the play's end that he must also slay the dragon in each person before the town will be safe from tyranny. Why does he undertake this task? "My friends, I love you all. . . . And if I love you, everything will be wonderful." *The Dragon* had only a single performance each in Leningrad and Moscow in 1944, was briefly revived in 1962, and has not appeared since then in the Soviet repertory.

Russian drama after the revolution, therefore, was dictated for several decades by external events and developments and by political and ideological edicts. Some playwrights, such as Mayakovsky and scores of lesser names, wholeheartedly embraced the revolution and wrote plays expressing their allegiance. Some, including Babel and Shvarts, tried to accommodate while at the same time endeavoring to preserve their artistic freedom. Also, some never accepted the outcome of the revolution and either fell silent or emigrated. The NEP era allowed certain freedom of expression because the country, coming out of the ruins of the world war, revolution, and civil war, needed time to bounce back. During this period, some of the best plays were written by Babel, Bulgakov, and Yury Olesha, to name a few, and bold experimental and innovating strides were made in dramaturgy, led by Meyerhold. Olesha's plays *Zagovor chuvstv* (pr. 1929; *The Conspiracy of Feelings*, 1976) and *Spisok blagodeyaniy* (pr. 1931; *A List of Blessings*, 1960), carried on a unique "dialogue with the epoch," in which Olesha defended his rights as an individual and as an artist. Even his *Tri tolstyaka* (pr. 1930; *The Three Fat Men*, 1983), although ostensibly written as a fairy tale for children (and rewritten into a play), has a thinly veiled message for the adults forced to live in a totalitarian society.

NEP ended in 1928 and was replaced by the First Five-Year Plan, stressing the industrialization of the country and collectivization of the villages as its prime goals. Scores of plays were written extolling the efforts of the state in achieving these goals; however, most, if not all, of them were inferior propaganda tools, now completely forgotten. This period was replaced by an ominous intrusion of the authorities into cultural matters, demanding that the writers follow the officially sanctioned method of Socialist Realism. This blatant abolition of artistic freedom was a prelude to a brutal reign of terror in the late 1930's, during which numerous writers, including playwrights, perished in jails or concentration camps. The reign of terror did not end until World War II. As expected, the plays during the war and afterward were written in support of the war efforts, extolling the heroic struggle of the Russian people against the invader. Though received well by the public, most of these plays now have only historical value.

POST-WORLD WAR II

At the end of the war, the repressive policy concerning literature continued until the death of Stalin in March, 1953. A gradual thaw ensued that did not reach its climax until several years later. Two playwrights, Alexey Arbuzov and Viktor Rozov, wrote several successful plays each. Arbuzov wrote *Irkutskaya istoriya* (pr. 1959; *The Irkutsk Story*, 1961) and *Moi bedny Marat* (pr. 1964; *The Promise*, 1967), and Rozov wrote *Vechno zhivyo* (pr. 1956; *Alive Forever*, 1968). Many playwrights who were ostracized during the previous decades were rediscovered. Even Mayakovsky's plays were staged again, some thirty years after their premieres. Noteworthy also is Alexandr Solzhenitsyn's drama, *Olen' i shalashovka* (pr. 1968; *The Love Girl and the Innocent*, 1969). Banned after it was accepted for staging, the play depicts a love story of two prisoners in a Stalinist slave-labor camp and their struggle to preserve their integrity by refusing to compromise.

After the demise of communism and gradual rebirth of Russia in the 1990's, playwrights tried to cope with the increasing freedom to express themselves. Some of the older playwrights continued to write plays, and new notable names also arose. One of the most powerful among them is Vassily Aksyonov, with his comedies, *Vsegda v prodazhe* (pr. 1965; always on sale) and *Vash ubiytsa* (pr. 1975; *Your Murderer*, 2000).

BIBLIOGRAPHY

Karlinsky, Simon. *Russian Drama from Its Beginnings to the Age of Pushkin*. Berkeley: University of California Press, 1985. Studious analysis of Russian drama before Pushkin, from the religious beginnings and the secular drama and into the nineteenth century. Treats with equal attention tragedy, comedy, verse drama, and the relationship between drama and opera. One of the best studies of the subject.

Leach, Robert, and Victor Borovsky. *A History of Russian Theatre*. Cambridge, England: Cambridge University Press, 1999. One of the most comprehensive histories of Russian drama and theater. Covers all the important playwrights, their plays, and all matters concerning the theater.

Russel, Roberts. *Russian Drama of the Revolutionary Period*. Totowa, N.J.: Barnes and Noble Books, 1988. Starts with the prerevolutionary drama and follows Soviet drama from 1917 to 1921. Emphasizes the depiction of the civil war, as in Bulgakov's plays, but also discusses Mayakovski, Olesha, and Erdman, among many others. Competent introduction to this period and good bibliography.

Segel, Harold B. *Twentieth Century Russian Drama from Gorky to the Present*. Rev. ed. Baltimore, Md.: John Hopkins University Press, 1993. Valuable survey of Russian drama from Gorky's prerevolutionary plays into the 1990's. Analyzes both the plays and the relevant background material impacting them, especially political and ideological factors. The updated edition has a chapter on the drama from the late 1970's to the collapse of the Soviet Union in 1991. Generous bibliography.

Slonim, Marc. *Russian Theater from the Empire to the Soviets*. Cleveland, Ohio: World, 1961. A historical presentation of Russian drama and theater from the beginnings to the 1950's. Thorough analysis of the plays and theater in general, with pertinent observations about nonliterary factors. Pays special attention to connections between Russian and foreign dramas.

Varnecke, B. V. *History of the Russian Theatre*. New York: Hafner, 1971. A thorough study of the Russian theater by a leading Russian scholar, covering playwrights and their plays as well as the development of Russian dramaturgy from the seventeenth through the nineteenth centuries. The original appeared in 1939, but it is still a standard work in its field.

Welsh, David. *Russian Comedy, 1765-1823*. The Hague: Mouton, 1966. Limited in scope but a penetrating study of themes, characters, genre, and structure of the fifty years of Russian comedy from the last quarter of the eighteenth to the first quarter of the nineteenth century. Emphasizes the representative comedies and the influence of foreign comedy, especially French.

Gerhard Brand,
updated by Vasa D. Mihailovich

SCANDINAVIAN DRAMA SINCE THE 1600'S

The Scandinavian countries have been heavily influenced by and have heavily borrowed from one another throughout their dramatic histories. At the same time, these Nordic countries—notably Norway, Denmark, and Sweden—have been influenced by European humanist literary trends that have played a major role in enhancing Scandinavian drama. Under Swedish control until 1809, Finland did not produce much literature until the late nineteenth century, when a ban was lifted to allow original productions as well as numerous translations of literature. Isolated from the other Scandinavian countries and economically dependent on Norway and then Denmark, Iceland did not acquire complete independence until 1944. Iceland produced thirteenth century sagas, lyric poetry, and histories, but no drama until the late nineteenth century.

From the thirteenth to the seventeenth centuries, Norwegian folk literature was the main form of literary production. A few royal documents, Danish bibles, poems, and ballads also were produced. The dramatic history of Norway was largely affected by and dependent on the country's union with Denmark in the late fourteenth century, by its subsequent assimilation of the Danish language, and by its remaining under Danish control until 1814, when it created its own constitution.

Scandinavian drama in the first half of the sixteenth century was significantly affected by the Reformation, which seemed to sterilize literary production in all the Scandinavian countries. Because the Epiphany plays and gospel reenactments—which were influenced by European drama—were disallowed in the churches, the students of the Latin schools began to perform these religious ceremonies by marching in procession from house to house. In Sweden, the addition of folk figures and audience participation enhanced the processionals.

Soon, school drama, a pedagogical, moralistic type of play, was performed by students and greatly encouraged the development of professional drama. Particularly popular in both European and Scandinavian countries during the Reformation, school drama borrowed from both classical tragedy and comedy, from medieval drama and morality plays, and adapted these forms to the native drama.

The school dramas of sixteenth century Danish writer Hieronymus Justesen Ranch serve as one example of this early development. *Karrig Niding* (stingy miser), performed in 1606, printed in 1633, ridicules the habits of a miser. *Samsons Fængsel* (pr. c. 1599; Samson's prison), usually considered Denmark's first operetta and a prototype of the later elaborate Renaissance drama, is a reenactment of the singing chorus of classical tragedy. Christiern Hansen's *Den utro Hustru* (pr. c. 1531; the unfaithful wife), a short, one-act medieval farce, and the anonymous *Ludus de Sancto Kanuto Duce* (pr. 1530) rely on Danish rather than Continental sources.

The earliest extant Swedish drama, *Tobie comedia* (pb. 1550), generally attributed to Olaus Petri, combines Christian moral teaching with the vernacular. Johannes Messenius sought to incorporate Swedish saga and history into the religious drama of the age and to instill national pride in his audiences. Four plays were printed and performed by his students from 1611 to 1614. Although immature, these plays are, nevertheless, the first original plays in Swedish on secular subjects.

King Gustav II added a professional troupe of players to his court orchestra in 1628; later monarchs provided quarters for private, resplendent playhouses within the palace, where ballet, opera, and drama were performed. A troupe of professional players arrived from France to introduce the French drama of Jean Racine, Voltaire, and Molière. The court was particularly fond of the new French masque and an imitation of it in Swedish by Georg Stiernhielm. Swedish writer Jacobus Petri Rondeletius's *Judas Redivivus* (pr. 1614), a Christian tragicomedy about Judas Iscariot, is broadly imitative but serves as a precursor to later native drama. An adaptation of *Rosimunda* (pr. 1665), written by Urban Hiärne and in unrhymed dactyls, is simply an extension of school drama without the elements of didacticism so common during the Reformation. *Rosimunda* adopts Senecan tragedy and its themes of single-minded bloody revenge. The 1660's witnessed the first Swedish company of actors, a student group whose activities were to enhance the development of theater in Scandinavia.

1600's AND 1700's

Many factors contributed to the growth of Scandinavian theater in the seventeenth and eighteenth centuries: the opening of the opera house in Copenhagen in 1703 (the 1689 edifice burned after the second performance), the opening of the court stage in Copenhagen in 1712, the opening of Denmark's first national theater in 1722, and the later temporary Danish Royal Theater of 1747 and permanent theater of 1748. The introduction of the Royal Swedish Stage in 1737 led to the opening of the Royal Dramatic Theatre in Stockholm at the end of the eighteenth century. These theaters introduced the tradition of regular performances to the general public rather than to an exclusively royal attendance, established the native comedies of Ludvig Holberg, and encouraged both French drama and sentimental drama. By the eighteenth century in Scandinavia, court entertainment and strolling players—many from England and France—gradually replaced the schools as the primary advocator of school drama.

Largely influenced by the Enlightenment and its attendant belief in wit, common sense, and rationalism, Dano-Norwegian Ludvig Holberg, the first comic theorist in Scandinavia, theorized that comedy must make people laugh and must instruct when performed. To achieve this aim, Holberg utilized the techniques and styles of previous comedy, combining the classics, in particular Plautus, with Molière's plays and fusing these with native materials and stock characters in a comic yet realistic manner that ultimately allowed Danes to witness for the first time their own social manners, customs, and frequently objectionable habits. His comedies largely replaced school drama and restored the Danish language and Danish themes.

On the strength of his successful *Peder Paars* (1722; English translation, 1962), a mock-heroic epic

poem, Holberg was appointed director of the newly opened Danish Theater in Copenhagen in 1722, a post that provided an opportunity for him to alternate his Danish comedy with translations of French plays. His first comedy, *Den Vægelsindede* (pr. 1722; *The Weathercock*, 1912), portrays a capricious character exposed to ridicule. The most important of Holberg's comedies, perhaps, are *Den politiske kandestøber* (pr. 1722; *The Political Tinker*, 1914), which opened at the temporary Danish Royal Theatre in 1747; *Jeppe paa Bjerget* (pr. 1722; *Jeppe of the Hill*, 1906); and *Erasmus Montanus* (wr. 1723; English translation, 1885). In *The Political Tinker*, Holberg satirizes a political college, a mock city council, which, in examining the status of the world, exposes hypocrisy, self-interest, intolerance, irresponsibility, and stupidity. A more realistic and serious play, *Jeppe of the Hill* examines the human degradation of the oppressed Danish peasant, a man unable to control his life and who must be intimidated by responsible people. In *Erasmus Montanus*, one of his greatest comedies of character, Holberg satirizes fragmented learning and useless knowledge. His thirty-three comedies have been collected in three volumes under his pseudonym: *Comedies Written for the Newly Founded Danish Stage by Hans Mickelsen* (1723-1725), later increased to five volumes and called *The Danish Stage* (1731).

Scandinavians, however, soon became more interested in English works, elaborate Rococo drama, and sentimental comedy—all of which altered the style of Danish drama—than in the indigenous comedies of Holberg.

When Pietist king Christian VI ascended the throne, he stifled theatrical activity in both Denmark and Norway. In 1738, he decreed that no actors or their plays be found in Norway or Denmark. Only with the accession of Frederick V was the theater reopened in 1748. With no skilled actors and with a still undeveloped language, however, many Danes watched German and French rather than Scandinavian drama.

Sweden had few native dramas from which to choose, had royalty that still favored imported drama until the 1771 ascension of Gustav III, and lacked a theater until 1737, at which time Carl Gyllenborg opened the Royal Swedish Theater with his five-act satiric comedy *Den Svenska Sprätthöken* (the Swedish fop).

Olof von Dalin is the most eminent Swedish writer of the Enlightenment. Leaning heavily on French tragedy, Molière, Holberg, and English writers, Dalin wrote the comedy *Den avundsjuke* (pr. 1738; *Envy*, 1876) and the tragedy *Brynhilda* (pr. 1738). Johan Henrik Kellgren assisted the king and also assisted the playwright Karl Gustaf af Leopold.

Many important literary events took place during King Gustav's reign, which began in 1771: the founding of the Royal Opera in 1773 to continue the lavish court ballets, the founding in the 1780's of the Society for the Improvement of the Swedish Language, the establishment of the Swedish Academy in 1786, and the opening of the Royal Swedish Dramatic Theatre in 1788 to serve both French and Swedish companies and to produce exclusively original works rather than translations, a prohibition dropped in 1789. Because he believed in recruiting the best possible dramatists and actors, because he fostered an atmosphere of literary enlightenment and encouraged a native Swedish drama based on national themes, and because he provided the stage on which these plays could be viewed, King Gustav established a solid dramatic tradition.

The mid-eighteenth century fostered playwrights who anticipated Romantic drama: Johannes Ewald, Norwegian-born Johan Herman Wessel, and Ole Johan Samsøe. A well-known lyric poet, Ewald wrote *Adam og Ewa* (Adam and Eve) in 1769, a dramatic poem in the style of French tragedy. The blank verse drama *Balders Død* (pr. 1773; *The Death of Balder*, 1889), however, established Nordic tragedy on the stage. His last play, an eleven-syllable verse form, *Fiskerne* (pr. 1779; the fishermen), explores the heroism of the common person. A song from this play (translated into English by Henry Wadsworth Longfellow as "King Christian Stood by the Lofty Mast") has become the Danish royal anthem. Wessel wrote a parody tragedy *Kierlighed uden Strømper* (pr. 1772; love without stockings), and in 1776 he wrote *Lykken bedre end Forstanden* (more lucky than

wise), a mock-heroic drama that ridicules the bad imitations of French classicism. Whereas Ewald and Wessel were precursors of Romanticism, Samsøe's national tragedy *Dyveke* (pr. 1796) announced the Romantic Age. This gothic drama features an innocent person who is ruined in the courtly environment in which she is forced to live.

By the end of the eighteenth century in Norway, dramatic performances solely for royalty lapsed, Swedish and Danish performers replaced foreign troupes, and actors expanded their repertoires. Stage managers improved their equipment, their scenery, and their lighting; playwrights became more abundant. All this interest led to the 1800 opening of Norway's first permanent theater.

THE ROMANTIC AND GOLDEN AGES

The early nineteenth century witnessed the first fruits of the Romantic Age in Scandinavia and intensified Denmark's Golden Age. Danish poet and playwright Adam Gottlob Oehlenschläger, influenced by Friedrich Schiller and by German Romanticism, adopted Nordic mythology and history to create Romantic works. An early play, *Hakon Jarl hin Rige* (pr. 1807; *Earl Hakon the Mighty*, 1857), evokes Hakon's adversary Olaf Tryggvesøn, who wishes to convert Norway to Christianity and to destroy Hakon's power. Hakon sacrifices his son to gain Odin's favor and is in turn sacrificed. His next tragedy, *Palnatoke* (pr. 1809; English translation, 1855), again details a doomed struggle against Christianity. The tragedy *Corregio* (pr. 1811; English translation. 1846), originally written in German, dramatizes the life of the Italian painter. Heavily influenced by French classical tragedy, he wrote *Axel og Valborg* (pr. 1810; *Axel and Valborg*, 1851), a more controlled drama that treats a twelfth century tragedy of love and duty. *Staerkodder* (pr. 1811) involves the repentance of Staerkodder, who slew King Olaf. *Hagbarth og Signe* (pr. 1816), also influenced by French classicism, reveals two lovers who are parted and finally joined in death.

Various Shakespearean productions in Denmark fostered a greater attention to costumes, settings, and lighting. The ability to mount three settings at once reduced the need for partial scene shifts. Then, too, the stage was expanded, footlights were made longer, and, in 1819, oil-burning lamps replaced candles.

Whereas Oehlenschläger was interested in tragedy, Johan Ludvig Heiberg wrote comedy, introduced Georg Wilhelm Friedrich Hegel's philosophy to Denmark, and was a leading literary critic. He categorized drama by genre ranging from speculative drama—a synthesis of the lyric drama of Pedro Calderón de la Barca—to the vaudeville of Eugène Scribe. He domesticated Scribean vaudeville, a type of cleverly plotted and subplotted musical play in which songs are set to recognizable melodies and interspersed with the dialogue. An imitator of French vaudevilles and a classicist, he also wrote serious drama and gradually surpassed Oehlenschläger. Heiberg influenced the work of Søren Kierkegaard, Henrik Ibsen, Hans Christian Andersen, and Georg Brandes. In 1813, he wrote the comedies for marionettes *Don Juan*, an adaptation from Molière, and *Pottemager Walter* (Walter the potter). *Kong Salomon og Jørgen Hattemager* (pr. 1825; King Solomon and George the hatter), a vaudevillian play, depicts the theme of mistaken identity. In his *Om Vaudevillen som dramatisk Digtart* (1826; on the vaudeville as a dramatic genre), he lauds vaudeville as a genre; thirty years later the work impressed even the great Norwegian dramatist Ibsen. Heiberg's vaudevilles were quite successful on the stage, helped, in part, by his wife, the famous actress and director Johanne Luise Heiberg.

Hans Christian Andersen, the writer of fairy tales, wrote a dramatic parody, *Kjærlighed paa Nicolai Taarn: Elle, Hvad siger Parterret* (pr. 1829; love on St. Nicholas tower). In the play *Mulatten: Romantisk drama i fem acter* (pr. 1840; the mulatto), he portrays the reckless passion of a French countess for a racial outcast that makes the work a revolutionary exception in nineteenth century Scandinavian drama. He also wrote fairy-tale plays that combined drama, ballet, and opera. Thomas Overskou, a drama critic and historian, wrote his best-known play, *Capriciosa*, in 1846, in which supernatural beings intervene as in the Viennese plays by Ferdinand Raimund and Johann Nestroy, which served as models for Overskou, as well as for Andersen's fairy-tale plays.

Two other playwrights interested in Heiberg's type of vaudevillian drama were Henrik Hertz and Jens Christian Hostrup. Besides being interested in Heibergian vaudeville, Hertz was influenced by the character comedy of Holberg. In 1827, Hertz produced his five-act satire *Herr Burchardt og hans Familie* (Mr. Burchardt and his family). His best comedy is *Sparekassen* (pr. 1836; the savings bank), in which a family mistakenly believes that they have won the lottery.

MOVEMENT TOWARD REALISM

In Sweden during the early nineteenth century, poetry and then the novel predominated. Although Per Daniel Amadeus Atterbom and Erik Johan Stagnelius wrote drama, they are mainly known for their Romantic poetry. Gradually, Sweden leaned toward realism and away from the subjective German philosophy of Schelling. Romanticism persisted mainly in the gothic and Platonic trends.

Carl Jonas Love Almqvist, a transitional Swedish figure, wrote in many genres, publishing his work in successive volumes of *Törnrosens bok* (1832-1851; the book of the briar rose). Johan Ludvig Runeberg, author of the Finnish national anthem, was another transitional figure; his *Kungarne på Salamis* (pr. 1863; kings on Salamis) is a classical tragedy influenced by William Shakespeare. A more important work, *Kung Fjalar* (pr. 1844; *King Fjalar: A Poem in Five Songs*, 1904), blends narrative and dramatic elements to achieve an approximation of Greek tragedy.

Another Swedish dramatist, August Blanche, imitated both Heiberg and Scribe. Blanche's drama *Läkaren* (pr. 1845; the doctor) represents an early attempt at serious drama.

Nordahl Brun produced his tragedy *Zarine* (pr. 1722), and later *Einer Tambeskielver* (pr. 1772), the first Norwegian saga play. Henrik Anker Bjerregaard wrote a musical play, *Fjeldeventyret* (pr. 1824; the adventure on the mountain); Andreas Munch, an imitator of Oehlenschläger, wrote his prizewinning *Kong Sverres Ungdom* (pr. 1837; King Sverre's youth) but is primarily known for his poetry. Primarily a poet, Ivar Aasen produced *Ervingen* (pr. 1855; the heir), a popular but weak musical play. Attempting to create a language with its roots in the native tradition, Aasen created *Landsmål*, or New Norse, the rural rather than official language.

Although primarily a poet, Henrik Wergeland attempted to make Norwegian drama a native drama. He wrote many now-forgotten plays and championed the Jewish cause. Mauritz Hansen based his dramas on Norwegian sagas.

Toward the end of the nineteenth century, three Norwegians bridged the gap between Romanticism and realism: Jonas Lie, Alexander Kielland, and Arne Garborg. Known more for his novels than his plays, Lie nevertheless received recognition for a three-act play, *Grabows Kat* (pr. 1880; Grabow's cat), which discusses conflicts between old and young; for *Lindelin* (pr. 1897), a four-act play; and for *Lystige Koner* (pr. 1894; merry wives), a three-act social comedy that deals with society women, frivolous lives, and adulterous affairs.

Largely influenced by Kierkegaard, Heinrich Heine, and Danish radical critic Georg Brandes, novelist Kielland wrote *For Scenen* (for the stage), which consists of three short plays: *Paa Hjemveien* (pr. 1878; homewards), which deals with business morality; *Hans Majestæts Foged* (pr. 1880; his majesty's sheriff), a two-act play about a sheriff who becomes a laborer; and *Det hele er ingenting* (pr. 1880; it is all nothing), a one-act play about a man who cannot take life seriously or find love. *Professoren* (pr. 1888; the professor) shows a professor who sacrifices his daughter's honor to attack his adversary, the man his daughter loves.

Garborg's *Uforsonlige* (pr. 1888; irreconcilables) deals with the peasants' social problems, his *Læraren* (pr. 1896; the teacher) is a five-act play about a theologian forced to leave the university because of his unchristian life, and *Den burtkomme Faderen* (pr. 1899; *The Lost Father*, 1920) details the perils of egotism. Interested in Norwegian peasantry and in a religion free from dogmatism, Garborg anticipated Symbolism.

Ibsen and Bjørnson

In 1850, the Norwegian Theater began to cater to professional performers and Norwegian drama and stage design rather than to Danish drama. This interest provided the impetus for the plays of both Bjørnstjerne Bjørnson and his contemporary Ibsen, both of whom abandoned the well-made play and revolutionized Norwegian thought.

Known as the "Father of Modern Drama," Ibsen showed promise with his first play, *Catalina* (pb. 1850; *Cataline*, 1921), the first Norwegian play published in years. Performed in Sweden in 1881, *Cataline* introduced the rebelliousness that was later to characterize most of Ibsen's plays and also revealed his gift for psychological insight. Ibsen's early plays lean toward Oehlenschläger, reveal romantic characteristics, and detail Norwegian culture.

While stage director of Bergen's Norse Theater, Ibsen visited Copenhagen's Danish Royal Theater, headed by Heiberg and directed by Overskou, and studied the stage in Germany. On his tour he was impressed with the plays of Scribe, Shakespeare, Holberg, Oehlenschläger, Heiberg, and Hertz. This directing experience provided him with a remarkable capacity to portray the psychological states of his characters and to use moods, lighting, and settings to enhance the action of the play. Hermann Hettner's *Das Moderne Drama* (1852) and Danish critic Georg Brandes's *Hovedstrømninger* (1872-1890; *Main Currents in Nineteenth-Century Literature*, 1906) also influenced Ibsen. The latter discussed modernism, espousing social, sexual, and religious themes and the new naturalism promulgated by Émile Zola. Moreover, Brandes's astute criticism of Ibsen's technique led to Ibsen developing a more realistic dramaturgy.

After he, his wife, and their son left Norway in 1864 for twenty-seven years of self-imposed exile, Ibsen wrote the poetic drama *Brand* (pr. 1885; English translation, 1891) and the celebrated *Peer Gynt* (pb. 1867; English translation, 1892). *Brand*, a play that reveals Kierkegaardian thought and depicts an uncompromising, idealistic religious crusader, established Ibsen as the pioneer of revolt against tradition, compromise, and hypocrisy.

Ibsen's middle plays, written from about 1877 to 1887, are primarily sociopolitical and moral dramas. Many of them reveal Ibsen's radical politics, and many champion the cause of women: *Samfundets støtter* (pr. 1877; *The Pillars of Society*, 1880); *Et dukkehjem* (pr. 1879; *A Doll's House*, 1880), his first successful social play; *Gengangere* (pr. 1882; *Ghosts*, 1885), the last Ibsen play to use the first-person pronoun; *En folkefiende* (pr. 1883; *An Enemy of the People*, 1890); *Vildanden* (pr. 1885; *The Wild Duck*, 1891); and *Hedda Gabler* (pr. 1891; English translation, 1891).

These plays, perhaps his finest, mark a transition to Ibsen's final phase of development, in which he continues to analyze marital relationships and to provide keen psychological insight into his characters. A favorite technique is to use the retrospective method of exposition rather than to present scenes chronologically on the stage as they occur. Many of these plays open in a calm atmosphere, then suddenly an outsider appears, one whose reminiscences create bitter memories. The plays usually end in catastrophe. *The Pillars of Society*, a relentlessly realistic social play, indicts a particular type of bourgeois figure, analyzes specific evils, and applauds those who free themselves from lies and conventional morality. *Ghosts* may be viewed on two levels: as depicting ghosts of the past, the sins of the fathers irrationally visited on the son, or as symbolizing dead beliefs that infiltrate society. *An Enemy of the People*, a psychological and metaphysical play, retaliates against those who had attacked Ibsen because of *Ghosts*. (In 1951, *An Enemy of the People* was successfully adapted by American playwright Arthur Miller.)

Ibsen's next plays concern the conflict within the individual between happiness and the demands of conscience, between age and youth. *The Wild Duck* concludes that people are too weak to bear the truth and need lies and dreams to make existence bearable. Here Ibsen consciously alters his technique toward mysticism, a tendency prevalent in Norwegian writing of the 1890's.

During his last phase, Ibsen became more mystical with such plays as *Rosmersholm* (pr. 1887; English translation, 1889), *Bygmester Solness* (pr. 1893; *The Master Builder*, 1893), *John Gabriel Borkman* (pr. 1897; English translation, 1897), and *Naar vi døde vaagner* (pr. 1900; *When We Dead Awaken*, 1900).

In *Quintessence of Ibsenism* (1891, 1913), George Bernard Shaw states that Ibsen's concern with current abuses was his most obvious achievement. In his canon, Ibsen chooses to ask searching questions, never to answer them, to focus on incompatible family relationships, to celebrate individuality, to explore sexual relationships, and to probe psychological motivation, idealism, and illusion.

Nobel Prize winner Bjørnson, like his contemporaries Ibsen and August Strindberg, propelled Scandinavian drama to a position of worldwide prominence. Like Ibsen, Bjørnson began writing in the romantic/historical mode, but he employs different themes. Ibsen strongly endorses individualism whereas Bjørnson favors the family; Ibsen is often pessimistic while Bjørnson foresees a perfected humanity. Although Bjørnson explored social/moral problems before Ibsen did, Ibsen's work is stronger, more imaginative, of better quality, and more universal than Bjørnson's.

Bjørnson's work may be roughly divided into three periods. The first period (1854-1860) includes his directorship of the Bergen Theater, where, in addition to his own plays, Bjørnson produced Richard Brinsley Sheridan's *The School for Scandal* (pr. 1777). Bjørnson stated that dramatists should be more contemporary and more interested in probing human nature but less romantic and less inclined to fit drama into the neat patterns of the well-made play.

Much of his early work, however, focuses on the Romantic themes of folklore, history, and patriotism. The list includes *Mellem Slagene* (pr. 1857; *Between the Battles*, 1948), a one-act play set in the twelfth century; *Halte Hulda* (pr. 1858; limping Hulda); *Kong Sverre* (pr. 1861; King Sverre); *Sigurd Slembe* (pr. 1863; Sigurd the boisterous, 1888), taken from the history of Norway and usually considered his best saga drama; and *Maria Stuart i Skotland* (pr. 1867; *Mary Queen of Scots*, 1912). His basic theme during this period was that suffering was inevitable in order to overcome weakness of character or difficult situations. *Kong Sverre* examines the story of a king who must overcome great odds to establish his power; once he conquers the last opposition, he dies.

From 1865 to 1867, Bjørnson directed the Christiania Theater, as had Ibsen before him. There he presented contemporary Danish and Norwegian drama, including Ibsen's, as well as French drama and Shakespeare's plays, and boldly experimented with theatrical techniques.

His second period includes realistic social dramas similar in theme to those of Ibsen's second period: *De nygifte* (pr. 1865; *The Newlyweds*, 1885), *Redaktøren* (pr. 1875; *The Editor*, 1914), *En Fallit* (pr. 1875; *The Bankrupt*, 1914), *Kongen* (pb. 1877; *The King*, 1914), *Leonarda* (pr. 1879; English translation, 1911), and *Det ny System* (pr. 1878; *The New System*, 1913). After a one-year period of lecturing in the United States from 1880 to 1881, he wrote *En handske* (pr. 1883; *A Gauntlet*, 1886) and *Over ævne, første stykke* (pr. 1886; *Pastor Sang*, 1893; also known as *Beyond Our Power*, 1913), which was originally intended as a series of plays. *The Bankrupt* introduces a new theme in Scandinavia—the theme of money, bankruptcy, and honor.

During his last phase, he wrote *Over ævne annet stykke* (pr. 1895; *Beyond Our Might*, 1914), *Paul Lange og Tora Parsberg* (pr. 1901; *Paul Lange and Tora Parsberg*, 1899), *Daglannet* (pr. 1905; dayland farm), and *Når den ny vin blomstrer* (pr. 1909; *When the New Vine Blooms*, 1911).

Generally considered to his best work, *Pastor Sang*, or "beyond one's power," reveals Bjørnson's interest in spiritual rather than social problems and his interest in the danger of overextending oneself. One of his finest dramas, it demonstrates the regenerative power of prayer.

LATE 1800's: DANISH, FINNISH, AND ICELANDIC DRAMA

Reacting to the realism and naturalism of the 1870's and 1880's, Norway's Sigbjørn Obstfelder wrote three plays but is mainly known for his poetry. Like other Symbolist dramatists, he wrote "static" drama, a largely obscure form that communicates via suggestion and mood.

Compared with Norway's prestigious output, Denmark's creativity was meager during the late nineteenth century. Noteworthy is Holger Drachman, poet and playwright, who wrote *Der var engang* (pr. 1885; once upon a time), a fairy-tale comedy, and *Vølund*

Smed (pr. 1894; Wayland the smith), a lyric drama. His plays adhere to poetic and lyric forms rather than structural forms.

Although overshadowed by Ibsen, Finland could boast of a few dramatists who wrote in Swedish: Josef Julius Wecksell wrote the tragedy *Daniel Hjort* (pr. 1862); Mikael Lybeck used classic restraint, realism, and Symbolism in his works; Arvid Mörne wrote poems, novels, and plays; and Runar Schildt used psychological penetration and sympathy in his works.

Other Finnish dramatists used their own language, among them Aleksis Kivi, Kaarlo Bergbom, Juhana Henrik Erkko, Minna Canth, and Hella Wuolijoki. A playwright of imagination and wonderful style, Kivi authored the first important drama in the Finnish language, the comedy of peasant life, *Nummisuutarit* (pr. 1865; the parish cobblers). Kivi's death marked a stagnation of literary activity in Finland until 1880, when naturalism arose with its various themes of oppression.

As in Finland, most Icelandic writers of the 1890's were poets; many emigrated to North America because of famine and heavy polar ice drift in 1881. Iceland's home rule, achieved in 1904, and subsequent full independence, granted in 1918, encouraged the revival of nationalism. Jóhann Sigurjónsson lived in Denmark but frequently used Icelandic themes and settings to depict possessive love. His plays include *Bóndinn á Hrauni* (pr. 1908; *The Hraun Farm*, 1916), *Bjærg-Ejvind og Hans Hustru* (pr. 1911; *Eyvind of the Hills*, 1916), and *Løgneren* (pr. 1917; the liar), which uses a theme from the Njáls Saga.

Known for his poetry, Matthías Jochumsson wrote the first romantic play in Iceland, *Útilegumennirnir* (pr. 1864; the outlaws—the title was later changed to *Skugga-Sveinn* in 1898), based on an Icelandic folktale. Influenced by Shakespeare, he also wrote the historical play *Jón Arason* (pr. 1900). A writer known for his translations and his plays, Indriði Einarsson, a romantic, wrote *Nýjársnóttin* (pr. 1872; revised 1907; new year's night), a romantic, lyric play. Influenced by Ibsen, his more realistic problem drama *Skipið sekkur* (pr. 1902; the ship is sinking) depicts contemporary rural life. He later turned to romantic historical and folklore themes, notably the drama *Sverð og*

Bagall (pr. 1899; *Sword and Crozier*, 1912), a depiction of heathen versus Christian ideas based on an episode from the Sturlunga saga. Another play, *Dansinn í Hruna* (pr. 1921; the dance at Hruni), has a Faustian theme and is written in blank verse.

AUGUST STRINDBERG

August Strindberg—subjective, confessional, and misogynist—became Sweden's greatest dramatist. A complex pioneer of reform, his dark, visionary mysticism added a new dimension to drama. Moving from realism to naturalism to mystical expressionism, he was the first to stage a psychological dreamworld and to explore abnormal behavior. Throughout his career, he incessantly searched for his own innovative literary forms, gradually rejecting nineteenth century staging conventions because they could not express his visionary concepts. Combining stylistic variety with economy of phrasing, his plays are compellingly direct. His sixty-two plays have profoundly influenced subsequent dramatists. His work may be divided into two periods: those works before 1892 and those after 1892.

Strindberg's early plays—historical and realistic-naturalistic—show an indebtedness to Shakespeare; George Gordon, Lord Byron; Schiller; Oehlenschläger; Ibsen; Bjørnson; and Kierkegaard. Critic Brandes's analysis of Shakespeare and Heiberg's Danish comedies influenced Strindberg's best pre-1894 history play, *Mäster Olof* (pb. 1878; *Master Olof*, 1915), a five-act drama. His historical dramas attempt to dramatize the history of Sweden from the middle of the thirteenth century to the beginning of the nineteenth century. His realistic plays analyze the basic tendencies of human nature. Strindberg's basic technique is to create a three-dimensional stage environment whereby he can present his central characters from myriad points of view and multiple situations to see how they respond to their world.

Strindberg gained worldwide recognition as a dramatist with his naturalistic works: *Fadren* (pr. 1887; *The Father*, 1899); *Fröken Julie* (pr. 1889; *Miss Julie*, 1912), performed in Sweden in 1906, written under Friedrich Nietzsche's influence; and *Fordringsägare* (pr. 1889; *Creditors*, 1910). These plays eliminate nonessential detail and concentrate on the action. Strindberg termed *Miss Julie*, his first chamber play, the first naturalistic tragedy in Swedish drama. In the preface, Strindberg discusses musical themes and structures and promotes the aims of Zola's naturalistic tenets: the belief that people are products of their heredity and their environment, the belief in determinism, and the belief in Charles Darwin's theories of survival of the fittest; he did not, however, promote scientific objectivity. Instead, he advocated asymmetrical, nonsequential, impressionistically arranged dialogue that copies the haphazardness of life.

In his 1889 article "On Modern Drama and Modern Theatre," Strindberg terms naturalism "the great style, the deep probing of the human soul." This naturalism "delights in the struggle between natural forces" and is concerned with motive and conflict, a view echoed in his expressionistic plays. Creating an external illusion, he maintained, was simply a way to intensify dramatic mood and conflict.

From 1894 to 1897, Strindberg suffered from his "Inferno Crisis," a period of mental breakdown and stasis following two divorces. He largely overcame his frustrations and his feelings of persecution, however, and the twenty-nine plays that emerged following his crisis include many of his finest works.

Brott och brott (pr. 1900; *Crimes and Crimes*, 1913), a transitional play written just before Strindberg's final phase, looks backward to his realistic period and anticipates his expressionist period. His post-Inferno plays are either historical or expressionistic, with the expressionistic plays probing the unexplored recesses, obsessions, and impulses of the human mind and the fifteen historical dramas focusing on specific moments and themes. These frequently autobiographical plays generally deal with morality or with the problem of evil and include the dramatic trilogy *Till Damaskus* (pb. 1898-1904; *To Damaskus I-III*, 1913), a radical departure from previous stage techniques that indicates his postnaturalistic interest in Nietzschean idealism, in mysticism, and in archetypal figures; and the chamber plays *Ett drömspel* (pb. 1902; *A Dream Play*, 1912) and *Spöksonaten* (pr. 1908; *The Ghost Sonata*, 1916). One of his dream plays from this late period, *The Ghost Sonata* reveals

Strindberg's interest in the psychic and the occult and also anticipates the Theater of the Absurd. Using the theme of appearance versus reality as he does in all of his chamber plays, this play is written in the form of a sonata. To Strindberg, reality is redefined to indicate the irrational behavior, the fragmentary thinking, and the exaltation and ecstasy of modern visionaries.

In the introduction to *A Dream Play*, a highly original play, Strindberg states that he has sought to reproduce the "disconnected but apparently logical form of a dream" where everything is possible and where chronology does not exist.

1900'S: INTERWAR ERA

The most important of the neo-Romantic Norwegian dramatists writing between the wars were the aristocratic individualist Gunnar Heiberg, Knut Hamsun, Hans E. Kinck, and Nils Kjær. Heiberg's *Balkonen* (pr. 1894; *The Balcony*, 1922) and *Kjærlighetens tragedie* (pr. 1904; *The Tragedy of Love*, 1921) are excellent character portrayals. The latter exposes the conflict between a woman's love and a man's work, insists on a new psychological emphasis, and owes much to Ibsen. Primarily a novelist, Hamsun wrote the dramatic trilogy that includes *Ved rigets port* (pb. 1895; at the gate of the kingdom), *Livets spil* (pb. 1896; the play of life), and *Aftenrøde* (pb. 1898; afterglow). These plays attack prevalent conceptions of life and love, but the characters lack dramatic essence. Using language that is more concentrated than the lyric language of Hamsun, the neo-Romantic Kinck's chief works are verse dramas that synthesize his themes of Norwegian folk psychology and nature. Kjær's plays dramatize political and religious problems. He reacts not only to neo-Romanticism but also to much of the optimism of the preceding generation.

ANTINATURALISM, ANTIREALISM, AND EXPRESSIONISM

Following Strindberg's death, a new generation of Swedish dramatists and directors emerged who were concerned both with modernism and its attendant forms of expressionism and with proletarian drama. One important director, Per Lindberg, brought to the theater modernistic views of acting and staging that he had learned in Berlin. Seeking to revolutionize dramatic structure, playwrights often presented fantasies, hallucinations, nightmares, and other subjective experiences. In addition, they developed new lighting and staging techniques—particularly the turntable stage—that portrayed myriad moods rather than a single mood, and they excluded irrelevancy. Influenced by German expressionism, Symbolism, and Sigmund Freud, many of these playwrights were antinaturalistic.

In his important manifesto, *Modern teater: Synpunkter och angrepp* (1918; *Modern Theatre: Points of View and Attack*, 1966), the Nobel Prize-winning writer of fiction, poetry, and essays Pär Lagerkvist attacked naturalism, embraced expressionism as espoused by Strindberg, and lauded antirealism as espoused by Hjalmar Bergman. Although he attacked realistic and naturalistic plays such as Ibsen's one-wall-away drama with its limited perspectives, he praised Ibsen's dramatic intensity. The playwright, Lagerkvist argued, must exclude irrelevancies and must create freely to make full use of "all the possibilities of the modern stage."

Lagerkvist's first expressionistic play, *Sista mänskan* (pb. 1917; *The Last Man*, 1989), uses short, abrupt phrases to portray a city's last survivors desperately struggling for existence. *Himlens hemlighet* (pr. 1921; *The Secret of Heaven*, 1966) re-creates a ghastly vision of life on Earth. On the stage, the audience sees emaciated, listless humans who are watched by God, a helpless, passive old man.

As their author matured, Lagerkvist's plays became less visionary and obscure and simpler in form, although he was always preoccupied with the theme of good and evil. *Han som fick leva om sitt liv* (pr. 1928; *The Man Who Lived His Life Over*, 1971) marked a turning point in that the dramatist abandoned many of his symbolic methods in favor of more concreteness.

In the 1930's, Lagerkvist became interested in European political developments. Two plays that depict his indignation with fascism and Nazism are the dramatized version of the short novel *Bödelyn* as *Bödeln* (pr. 1934; *The Hangman*, 1966), written to be performed without interruption, and *Mannen utan själ* (pr. 1938; *The Man Without a Soul*, 1944). The first, a polemic against racism and Nazism, represents Lagerkvist's visionary techniques, and the latter is heightened, suggestive realism—subtle and bare in outline—concerned with the consequences of a recently committed political murder. *The Hangman*, consisting of two scenes with no pauses between them, uses startling lighting effects and depicts good coming out of evil, violence, and bloodshed.

In the 1940's, Lagerkvist returned to many of the tenets established in his *Modern Theatre*, particularly freedom of form. *De vises sten* (pr. 1948; *The Philosopher's Stone*, 1966), *Midsommardröm i fattighuset* (pr. 1941; *Midsummer Dream in the Workhouse*, 1953), and *Låt människan leva* (pr. 1949; *Let Man Live*, 1951) generally focus on Sweden's wartime affinity to Western traditions with their insistence on freedom of thought and expression. They also show a continuing interest in universal morality, in the significance of life, and in dramatic experimentation. The first play is concerned with the implications of the atom bomb; the second blends dream elements with realism to produce a dramatic fantasy. The theme exposes those who judge others. The third play shows martyrs from various historical periods; a musical technique develops the theme. Many of Lagerkvist's plays were directed by Lindberg and his brother-in-law Bergman.

Like Lagerkvist, Bergman understood the meaningless brutalities of life and sympathized with the victims ensnared by life's bitter trap. Both men used many of Strindberg's dramatic forms and techniques; both were pessimistic. In his plays, Bergman fills his dialogue with unexpected phraseology, delineates the destructive forces of life, and reveals tendencies toward fatalism.

Bergman's "Marionette Plays"—*Dödens Arlekin* (pr. 1917; death's harlequin), *En skugga* (pr. 1917; a shadow), and *Herr Sleeman kommer* (pr. 1919; *Mr. Sleeman Is Coming*, 1944)—are absorbing experimental dramas in which people are marionettes, directed by a higher power. His plays indicate a complex, disturbing, tragic form of art. *Mr. Sleeman Is Coming* offers fatalistic meditations over whether human destiny is determined by irrational and darkly evil forces that control humans in a marionette-like manner.

Bergman's successful comedy *Swedenhielms* (pr. 1925; *The Swedenhielms*, 1951) departed from his earlier style to incorporate plot complications, brilliant dialogue, and swift transitions in mood. In addition, the play served as a response to criticism of his preceding work for being too symbolic, gloomy, and obscure.

Other Swedish writers include Rudolf Värnlund, Karl Ragnar Gierow, and Ragnar Josephson. Värnlund's interest in German expressionism and constructivism became a vehicle for his proletarian dramas: For example, *Den heliga familjen* (pr. 1932; the holy family) pictures a worker's home and a Swedish labor movement beset by a strike. Both Josephson and Gierow were appointed chiefs of the Royal Dramatic Theater. In his plays, Gierow uses historical and legendary disguises to treat modern problems while describing tragic views of human destiny and appearing obsessively preoccupied with human cruelty. A more sophisticated writer than Gierow, Josephson probes the human psyche without offering judgments. His successful *Kanske en diktare* (pr. 1932; *Perhaps a Poet*, 1944) describes a man whom life has passed by and who must, of necessity, create his own life until he realizes that this imaginary life is but an illusion and commits suicide.

Ingmar Bergman, who has written and directed some of the world's greatest films, has also been a brilliant dramatist, theater director, and interpreter of the classic repertory. As a director, he coordinated design elements, was sensitive to mood and rhythm, and always maintained a close contact between actor and audience through various visual and physical techniques (sometimes called stage tricks). His most interesting plays are *Mig till skräck* (pr. 1947; dread unto me), *Dagen slutar tidigt* (pr. 1947; the day closes early), and *Mordet i Barjärna* (pr. 1952; the murder at Barjärna), bizarre morality plays reminiscent of the post-1892 Strindberg.

The Danish Helge Rode, a lyric meditative dramatist, and Hjalmar Bergstrøm are closely aligned to Ibsen in thematic aspects; Gustav Wied, a cynical satirist, is closely affiliated with Strindbergian technique.

Among these Danish writers, many of whom were implementing the techniques of expressionism, Kaj Munk and Kjeld Abell are better known.

In his plays, Danish minister Munk, who first lauded the superman and then the little man, portrayed violent conflicts and used the conventions of heroic drama. He attempted to invigorate modern theater vis-à-vis a return to gaudy ornaments, to violent terror, and to worldly struggles juxtaposed against religious exaltation. A controversial writer, Munk rebelled against the psychological play and its narrow "hour-long soul dissections" where nothing takes place. Instead, he believed, playwrights must affirm life despite existing terrors. Largely opposed to naturalistic tenets, Munk did not entirely abandon them. The most frequently performed Scandinavian playwright of the 1930's and 1940's, Munk became known for his historical play *Cant* (pr. 1931; English translation, 1953), a free-verse denunciation of self-righteous hypocrisy. Another historical play, *Ordet* (pr. 1932; *The Word*, 1953), is concerned with the conflict between faith and doubt in Christianity. The protagonist, a man who believes that he is Christ, "raises" his sister-in-law from the dead. The resistance play *Niels Ebbesen* (pr. 1943; English translation, 1944) pictures Munk's opposition to Nazi infiltration, a belief that later cost Munk his life. Filled with the final judgment of God, the play is imbued with bloody action and idealistic deeds of violence.

In his eighteen plays, Abell, unlike Munk, embraced experimentation and disdained realism and naturalism. He believed that audiences should participate in the theatrical experience rather than passively view it. *Melodien, der blev væk* (pr. 1935; *The Melody That Got Lost*, 1939) satirizes contemporary society and its conventionality and makes use of innovative expressionistic techniques such as curtains with bodies painted on them and mannequins acting as characters. Abell allows intrusions from the audience and incorporates elements of ballet (which he learned as a ballet set designer) and pantomime. A common theme in Abell's canon is the "melody that got lost"—that is, the youthful sense of life that adults, constrained by conventionality and complacency, frequently lose. *Eva aftjener sin barnepligt*

(pr. 1936; Eve serves her childhood) is a satiric antinaturalistic burlesque. His canon ends with *Skriget* (pr. 1961; the scream), a mystical play that works on several interrelated levels at once.

The Danish playwright Hans Christian Branner frequently depicted the transformational power of love and the inadequacy of language as he gradually moved from realism to more psychological forms. Of note are his experimental radio plays: *Jeg elsker dig* (1956; I love you) and *Et spil om Kaerligheden og døden* (1960; a play on love and death). Branner triumphed as a dramatist with *Søskende* (pr. 1952; *The Judge*, 1955), a play about three siblings who are incapable of freeing themselves from the past, and *Thermopylæ* (pr. 1958; *Thermopylae*, 1973), a pessimistic drama of ideas in which Branner seriously analyzes the concept of humanism. *Jeg elsker dig* is a lyric play about a couple who wish to leave their respective spouses but who discover that they cannot escape their guilty consciences.

REALISM AND FOREIGN INFLUENCE

After 1920, Icelandic literature became more realistic and more receptive to foreign influences. Kristín Sigfússdóttir interprets Icelandic rural life. Gudmundur Kamban depicts modern Icelandic life and, like Sigurjónsson, depicts possessive love. *Vi mordere* (pr. 1920; *We Murderers*, 1970), the first in a series of plays on marriage, written after his return from the United States, and *Örkenens Stjerner* (1925; the stars of the desert) are realistic plays critical of modern society. His last play, *Komplekser* (pr. 1941; complexes), satirizes the effects of Freudian complexes on marriage. Incorrectly believing that he was a Nazi sympathizer, Danish patriots shot Kamban.

The Norwegian writers Helge Krog and Nordahl Grieg are particularly noteworthy. A writer of social and psychological drama, Krog is best known for the play *Opbrudd* (pr. 1936; *Break-up*, 1939), which emphasizes dialogue and analyzes the love triangle. Like Ibsen, Krog depicts women as the stronger and more independent of the sexes. Perhaps Grieg's death in an Allied plane over Berlin in 1943 has made him a more celebrated figure than his plays warrant; a most interesting play, however, *Vår ære og vår makt* (pr. 1935; our honor and our power), is a war play that owes much to Russian experimental theater, in that Grieg is concerned with sharp dramatic contrasts and effective sound and lighting effects to expose groups against groups rather than groups against individuals. Grieg chastises a merchant fleet's owners for their exploitation of seamen and for their blatant disregard of human life in order to make money.

POST-WORLD WAR II

During World War II, only Sweden was able to maintain its neutrality. Denmark and Norway were occupied by German troops, Iceland by Allied forces, and Finland became involved in a bloody war against the Soviet Union. Following the brutality and destructiveness of the war, the quest for a meaningful and existential basis of life became a driving force in Scandinavian literature. It found its expression primarily in a poetry initially permeated with feelings of impotence and fear but increasingly by a spiritual or metaphysical search for meaning. In the middle of the 1950's, however, a gradual focusing on social and political reality became perceptible, primarily in prose works. In the 1960's and early 1970's, this trend was manifest in an extroverted, experimental poetry. At the same time, an increased interest in drama written for the stage as well as for television was apparent, with women becoming increasingly important as playwrights. One also finds among playwrights a predilection for writing film scripts and using the more intimate cabaret genre, which includes music and song.

In the last decades of the twentieth century, the ideological approach to literature receded in favor of a more playful and experimental way of writing: Reality became mixed with fantasy, the absurd aspects of human life were shown onstage, and there was a return to a more romantic use of the past, with historical topics or portrayals of former literary and historical personalities taking a central role.

In Denmark, the new postwar drama was initiated by Marxist poet Erik Knudsen's satiric revue *Frihed, det bedste guld* (pr. 1961; freedom, the best gold), a socialist critique of bourgeois society and culture. The prolific novelist Leif Panduro, in a series of immensely popular television plays, focused on the contrast between established society and revolutionary youth, as well as people's everyday problems and insecurity during the Cold War period. *Farvel, Thomas* (pr. 1968; good-bye, Thomas), *I Adams verden* (1973; in Adam's world), and *Louises hus* (pr. 1977; Louise's house) became, in their skillful analyses of conflicts set in recognizable, everyday situations, culminations of Scandinavian television drama. The greatest success was enjoyed, however, by Ernst Bruun Olsen. His plays combine realism with fantasy and deal with contemporary trends. *Teenagerlove* (1962) satirizes the cult of pop music, *Bal i den Borgerlige* (pr. 1966; middle-class ball) constitutes a political criticism of half-hearted socialism, and *Hvor gik Nora hen, da hun gik ud?* (pr. 1968; where did Nora go, when she left?) combines—with Ibsen's famous *A Doll's House* as a point of departure—a discussion of gender roles with a socialist outlook.

However, of greater artistic importance were the dramas for stage, radio, and television by Leif Petersen, which focused on human isolation behind the facade of the welfare state. This theme is presented, in particular, in Petersen's plays of the 1970's: *Fremad* (pr. 1974; forward) and *Nix pille* (pr. 1976; don't touch).

In Danish literature more than in that of other Scandinavian countries, women found their own voice on the stage. Since 1971 Ulla Ryum has written more than two dozen dramas, most of which are set in a future world in which imagination and poetry are contrasted against the representatives of a brutal, militarized world. *Og fuglene synger igen* (pr. 1980; and the birds sing again), a representative title of Ryum's plays, simultaneously shows various sequences of the plot unchronologically and uses a highly stylized milieu.

Two prominent playwrights are Bohr Hansen and Astrid Saalbach, whose plays have developed from a more traditional form toward increased experimentation, as evidenced by Saalbach's *Morgen og aften* (pr. 1993; *Morning and Evening*, 1996) and *Aske til aske, støv til støv* (pr. 1998; ashes to ashes, dust to dust), in which several authorial voices are employed to reshuffle the concepts of time and place. Thematically, however, she holds on to her original topic: psychological analyses of human behavior and attitudes that are guided by misunderstandings and lies. While the same topic is treated by Hansen in plays such as *Verden bag væggen* (2001; the world behind the wall), about children's fear and the adult's powerlessness, Hansen nonetheless has chosen humor and irony to express his concern about human loneliness and isolation in contemporary Denmark.

During the 1960's, a political radicalization began to be noticeable in the postwar literatures of the other Scandinavian countries. In Iceland it was initially voiced in poetry and prose, with Halldór Laxness perhaps the most prolific representative. However, influenced by the Eastern philosophy of Daoism, in the 1960's he increasingly rejected the concepts of class struggle and materialism, a theme that he expressed in the comedy *Dúfnaveislan* (pr. 1966; *The Pigeon Banquet*, 1973). The novelist Vésteinn Luðviksson continued this political theme with his satirical play *Stalin er ekki hérna* (pr. 1974; Stalin is not here). In the later 1960's, a resurgence of drama was perceptible, initiated with the founding of an experimental stage in the capital of Reykjavík in 1960. The most prolific playwright of the period was Jökull Jakobsson, who wrote more than thirty plays between 1960 and 1978 dealing with the generational gap and the changing social conditions after World War II. Jakobsson employed satire and, under the influence of Eugène Ionesco, features of the absurdist theater. Contemporary Icelandic drama is a flourishing genre with names such as Kristín Ómarsdóttir, Kristján Kristjánsson, and Hallgrímur Helgason.

Swedish postwar drama is dominated by Lars Forssell and Sandro Key-Åberg. In his first play, *Kröningen* (pr. 1956; *The Coronation*, 1964), Forssell provides a hero who actually dares to be afraid: Such antiheroes play an important role in his dramas. One example is King Gustav IV in the Bertolt Brecht-inspired *Galenpannan* (pr. 1964; *The Madcap*, 1973), who serves as a mirror to humankind and demonstrates emptiness and pettiness. Another superb play is *Christina Alexandra* (pr. 1968), a psychological analysis of the seventeenth century Swedish princess. Key-Åberg shows an infallible ear for dialogue in a series of short satirical sketches (such as *O*, pr. 1965;

English translation, 1970), which were presented in several European theaters. These texts provide no stage directions but merely identify different voices. Some of Key-Åberg's later plays are more conventional, even melodramatic. In 1975, Swedish novelist Per Olov Enqvist made his dramatic debut with *Tribadernas natt* (*The Night of the Tribades*, 1977), delineating the struggle between August Strindberg and his wife, Siri von Essen, during the rehearsal of a play that is based on their lives. The play became an immediate international success and Enqvist brought forth a related play, *Från regnormarnas liv* (1981; *The Rain Snakes*, 1984), in which one of the main characters is the Danish fairy-tale writer Hans Christian Andersen. In both plays, questions of identity and integrity are central. Conflicts and emotions are likewise present in the plays of prominent Swedish playwright Lars Norén. Virtually all of his plays revolve around traumatic parent-child relations.

The most important influence on postwar Norwegian drama came from Brecht. This is, above all, the case with Jens Bjørneboe's *Fugleelskerne* (1966; *The Bird Lovers*, 1994). Arguably Bjørneboe's finest play, *Fugleelskerne* is set in Italy, where a group of German bird lovers, whose leaders are former criminals, are about to establish a bird refuge. A battle between the locals and the intruders is won by the latter, who have money and thus power. One of the pioneers within the teleplay, both as a director and a script writer, was Sverre Udnæs. Among his most interesting plays, particularly because of their artful dialogues, are *Symptomer* (pr. 1971, symptoms) and *Kollisjonen* (pr. 1978; the collision). During the same period, Peder W. Cappelen chose an entirely different approach to his drama, writing plays consisting of allegories based either on folktales and legends (*Tornerose*, pr. 1968; briar rose; *Hvittenland*, pr. 1975; *Whittenland*, pr. 1989) or on myth, saga, and history (*Sverre: Berget og ordet*, pr. 1977; Sverre: The mountain and the word). Feminist concerns were brought to the stage by Bjørg Vik, whose *To akter for fem kvinner* (1974; two acts for five women) consists of a discussion among women who represent different attitudes regarding their placement in society and whose *Sorgenfri* (pr. 1978; free from sorrow) tells about love relationships in three generations.

Two of the most unconventional playwrights of the younger generation in Norway are Edvard Hoem and Cecilie Løveid. Hoem is a politically oriented novelist and playwright. His most successful drama, *God natt, Europa* (pr. 1982; *Good Night, Europe*, 1989), portrays an old politician and war hero who tries to come to terms with his past, which turns out to be not heroic at all. Løveid has worked directly with a major theater in the western Norwegian town of Bergen on several of her dramas, including *Vinteren revner* (pr. 1983; the winter cracks) and *Balansedame* (pr. 1986; tightrope walker). In her works in the 1990's, Løveid moved her plots back to the seventeenth and eighteenth centuries, employing a series of historical characters.

The most discussed theatrical text in postwar Finland was *Lapualaisooppera* (pr. 1966; the Lapua opera) by Arvo Salo, a Brechtian portrayal—with music—of the semi-fascist Finnish movement of the 1930's. His subsequent stage works were similarly oriented toward an antagonistic view of Finland's past, such as *Yks perkele, yks enkeli* (pr. 1985; a devil, an angel), about the great names of Finnish Romanticism. Jussi Kylätasku writes for the stage, film, and radio. In the 1970's, he wrote two farces for the stage that dealt with traffic and military issues; for director Risto Jarva, he wrote several screenplays; and among his best works are a series of radio plays, all of which deal with the issue of crime. The stage work *Haapoja* (pr. 1989) describes a stereotypical Finnish killer who confronts a reformer of prisons. Like Salo before him, Jouko Turkka was able to upset theatergoers: In *Lihaa ja rakkautta* (pr. 1987; meat and love), the central twist of the plot is a meat-plant owner who mixes diced vagrants, imbibed with alcohol, into his sausages.

Contemporary Scandinavian drama shares the vitality and eagerness to experiment, characteristics shared by other Scandinavian genres, including poetry and prose. Although the classics by Holberg, Ibsen, and Strindberg continue to be performed primarily at the larger theaters, a great number of smaller, mostly state-subsidized experimental stages have opened, presenting innumerable plays before large audiences. Scandinavian drama, much as it did during the time of Ibsen and Strindberg, earns international acclaim with playwrights such as Enqvist, Norén, and the Norwegian Jon Fosse, whose somber and pessimistic postmodern plays about loneliness and longing for love have made a definitive mark in the theatrical world.

BIBLIOGRAPHY

Gunnell, Terry. *The Origins of Drama in Scandinavia.* New York: D. S. Brewer, 1995. Traces twelfth and thirteenth century influences on the dramatic tradition in Scandinavia, including the dialogic poems of the Poetic Edda and folk use of mask and costumes.

Marker, Frederick J., and Lise-Lone Marker. *A History of Scandinavian Theatre.* Cambridge, England: Cambridge University Press, 1996. A thorough study of the history and development of Danish, Norwegian, and Swedish drama from the Middle Ages to the 1990's. Focuses on major styles and trends. Special attention is paid to the interaction with European theater. Provides a select list of secondary works.

Rossel, Sven H. *A History of Scandinavian Literature, 1870-1980.* Translated by Anne C. Ulmer. Minneapolis: University of Minnesota Press, 1982. A survey of all five Scandinavian literatures, including Finland and Iceland. Discusses not only standard works and well-established writers but also those who, undeservedly, have remained unknown to a larger audience.

Rossel, Sven H., ed. *A History of Scandinavian Literatures.* Vols. 1-5. Lincoln: University of Nebraska Press, 1992-2003. All five volumes present Scandinavian literature from its beginning until the late twentieth century. Also includes social and cultural history. The volumes are provided with indexes and extensive, reliable bibliographies focusing on secondary sources in English.

Zuck, Virpi, ed. *Dictionary of Scandinavian Literature.* Westport, Conn.: Greenwood Press, 1990. A reference work with brief presentations and precise characteristics. With bibliography and index.

Bette Adams Reagan,
updated by Sven H. Rossel

Spanish Drama Since the 1600's

Spanish theater of the Renaissance begins with startling suddenness given the fact that there is an inexplicable absence of dramatic texts before the sixteenth century. Castilian literature, unlike Catalan literature, where the presence of mystery plays is well documented, offers only a few examples of dramatic works in the Middle Ages. The earliest extant work, *Auto de los Reyes Magos* (the play of the Magi), is a twelfth century fragment dealing with the search for Jesus by the Three Wise Men. More than three hundred years elapse before one finds another mystery play, Gómez Manrique's *Representación del nacimiento de Nuestro Señor* (wr. 1467-1481; Nativity play). Curiously, the earlier play is considered to be much more advanced dramatically than the latter work.

Research into the absence of medieval plays has not resolved the issue, although it is accepted that Catholic liturgy and festivals had a considerable impact on the nature of all early plays. Of these liturgical performances, only those that celebrated the Eucharist prospered sufficiently to continue to be performed. These representations, which came to be called *autos sacramentales*, or sacramental plays, and which were performed at the feast of Corpus Christi, did not reach full maturity until the last part of the sixteenth century. They were originally presented on carts; later, they took place in the streets of the city and retained their popular religious flavor. The strong theological framework that characterizes them was not established until the seventeenth century.

The use of religious matter informs all plays of the early Renaissance. The purpose of these works was to dramatize sacred events as well as to render more immediate religious experience. Just as the Mass revealed its mystery, so did the plays project the deeper significance that underlay the physical occurrence. At the same time, numerous short plays were produced either as court entertainment or to celebrate extraordinary events such as military victories, betrothals, weddings, or the entrance of the monarch into a city. Perhaps the influence of the pastoral eclogue on this early theater is responsible for the persistent use of verse rather than prose, an element that was to dominate in Spanish theater throughout the sixteenth and seventeenth centuries. Finally, it is important to name the pervasive influence of Fernando de Rojas's *Comedia de Calisto y Melibea* (1499, rev. ed. 1502 as *Tragicomedia de Calisto y Melibea*; commonly known as *La Celestina*; *Celestina*, 1631), a work whose theme and effective dialogue reverberate in a variety of subsequent works.

Sixteenth century periods

Sixteenth century drama can be divided into three uneven periods. The first, roughly from the beginning of the century to the middle, includes the primitive dramatic writers whose efforts laid the groundwork for later developments. The second period includes playwrights who were influenced by humanist writings and by the Aristotelian commentaries that dominated critical discourse from the middle of the sixteenth century onward. Some of these writers wrote for universities or small circles of friends, while others had a wider audience. Neither of these groups had a great impact on the development of drama, but their works represent a serious, if failed, attempt to introduce high tragedy into Spanish theater. The last two decades of the century are characterized by the arrival of the Valencian School of dramatists and of Lope de Vega Carpio, thus setting the stage for the entrance of the new comedy, a dramatic form that extended over the entire seventeenth century.

Early Spanish drama is dominated by three figures—Juan del Encina, Bartolomé de Torres Naharro, and Lope de Rueda—but includes other playwrights whose works made telling contributions to the development of an indigenous tradition.

Juan del Encina has long been considered the initiator of Spanish drama because it was his Nativity play in the last years of the fifteenth century that began the uninterrupted development of the genre. He wrote fourteen eclogues, a term that he introduced to define his production. His plays show a certain progression from purely liturgically influenced material to a secular view of the world. This tendency is best represented by his *Egloga de Plácida y Vitoriana* (XIV; pr. 1513), in which a suicide caused by love is contemplated, and is perhaps a consequence of his being exposed during his voyage to Italy to Italian literary tastes, in particular the pastoral mode, which reigned supreme among all other literary forms. Encina's works are characterized by the presence of rustics who speak a dialect called *sayagués*, a convention that was to be widely imitated by subsequent writers, and by the use of the plot summary, with which the spectators were aided in the comprehension of the play.

Several important dramatists belong to this period and either continued or developed the material and devices introduced by Encina. Gil Vicente was a Portuguese who wrote many of his forty-two works in Spanish. He prepared many pieces for various occasions. Outstanding among them are *Tragicomédia de dom Duardos* (pr. 1525; English translation, 1942), a lyric rendering of a chivalric romance, and *Auto da sibila Cassandra* (pr. 1513; *The Play of the Sibyl Cassandra*, 1921), an allegorical reworking of a Nativity play. Another contemporary was Lucas Fernández, who continued the interest in eclogues and Nativity plays. Diego Sánchez de Badajoz, whose morality plays contributed heavily to the development of the sacramental plays, is also worthy of note.

Although he had scant exposure in Spain during his lifetime, Bartolomé de Torres Naharro is important to the history of the theater because he made several significant contributions. His collected works, titled *Propalladia* (English translation, 1943), published in Naples in 1517, reveal his strong connection with the Italian humanist milieu in which he lived. In his introduction, he theorizes on the nature of comedy and tragedy, on the number of actors and acts in a play, and on the need for dramatic decorum. He also sets up a classification for comedy, suggesting that there should be two types. The first type is a comedy of observation that describes social customs with some realism: *Comedia tinellaria* (pr. 1516; *The Buttery*, 1964) exposes domestic malpractices in the kitchen of a Roman cardinal, and *Comedia solda-* desca (wr. 1510; the soldiers' comedy) deals with army life in Renaissance Italy. The second type is a comedy based on fantasy—that is, a realistic depiction of imaginary events. His *Comedia Himenea* (pr. 1516; *Hymen*, 1903) and *Comedia seraphina* (wr. c. 1508) exemplify this kind of play, which introduced into Spanish theater the use of plot complications based on confusion of incidents.

Among Torres Naharro's other contributions to Spanish theater were the introduction of the honor theme and the development of a full-length play. He was the first to use the term *jornada* to indicate "act" as well as the first to introduce dramatic devices that were to be used frequently by later dramatists.

The last significant writer of this period was Lope de Rueda, the first man to write plays that were presented by his own theatrical troupe. Unlike the plays of Torres Naharro, those of Lope de Rueda were meant to be performed: They were staged in city squares. Lope de Rueda was largely responsible for the development of the interlude, or *paso*, a genre deeply indebted to the Italian *commedia dell'arte*. These short plays, written in prose, are based on everyday situations and are mostly comic in nature. Miguel de Cervantes, as an old man, remembered this playwright and remarked that the scenery and costumes of the period could all fit in one sack. Theatrical effects, as a matter of fact, did not improve for a long time, because Cervantes himself, in one of his plays, directs that thunder and lightning be reproduced by making noise under the stage with a barrel full of stones and by the discharge of a rocket. To Lope de Rueda is also given the credit of introducing the figure of a comic type that was later to develop into the *gracioso*, the comic servant whose quick wit and realistic view of life enliven classic Spanish theater. Rueda's best-known *pasos* are *El convidado* (pb. 1567; the guest), *La carátula* (pb. 1567; *The Mask*, 1964), and *Las aceitunas* (pb. 1567; *The Olives*, 1846).

SERIOUS DRAMATIC EXPRESSION

Straddling the first half of the century and the arrival of the new comedy were the efforts of men of letters who, under the influence of the great controversy over the interpretation of Aristotle's *De poetica* (c. 334-323 B.C.E.; *Poetics*, 1705), sought to promote a more serious dramatic expression. University-based writers tried to introduce classical tragedy into Spain. The audience for this kind of theater was not yet developed, however, and these plays remained a theater for a select minority of closet dramas that had relatively little influence on future playwrights.

The most important of these dramatists are Fernán Pérez de Oliva, who adapted prose tragedies of Sophocles and Euripides to Spanish; Micael de Carvajal, best known for the religious tragedy *Tragedia Josefina* (pb. 1535; *The Josephine Tragedy*, 1998); Jerónimo Bermúdez, who left two works, *Nise lastimosa* (pb. 1577; Nise the pitiful) and *Nise laureada* (pb. 1577; Nise crowned), closely related to a play by António Ferreira dealing with the topic of the tragic Portuguese figure of Inés de Castro; Andrés Rey de Artieda, whose best work is *Los amantes* (pb. 1581; the lovers), a story of two lovers whose destiny leads to tragedy; Cristóbal de Virués, who produced five plays and moved slowly away from imitation of Greek tragedies, including the observance of the unities, and toward a more popular genre closely related to the romantic comedy that Lope de Vega was later to develop; and Juan de la Cueva, who is perhaps the most notable dramatist of this group. He tried to direct tragedy away from imitations of Greek works and toward a more nationalist conception of the genre. His best-known plays are *Los siete infantes de Lara* (pr. 1579; the seven princes of Lara), the theme of which is taken from medieval epic literature, and *Tragedia del príncipe tirano* (pb. 1588; the tragedy of the tyrant prince), which deals with the nature of proper government, a theme of great interest in the sixteenth century. Cueva's importance rests principally on his introduction of Spanish themes from history and literature, although it seems he was unable to accommodate his material within the limits imposed by theatrical exigencies. Lupercio Leonardo de Argensola is remembered as a dedicated classicist who strongly criticized the new comedy proposed by Lope de Vega. His two extant plays, *Alejandra* and *Isabela* (pr. 1585), are Christian tragedies with a strong moralistic tone.

The last member of this generation was Miguel de Cervantes. What is known about his theater is based on the introduction to his *Ocho comedias y ocho entremeses nuevos* (pb. 1615; eight comedies and eight interludes). Cervantes states that he had written nearly thirty plays in his early years and that he had reasonable success with them, but only two plays from this period (the 1580's) are extant. Cervantes also reveals that when he tried to perform his works, he had no takers. Lope de Vega had come on the scene, and the older genre that Cervantes represented held no interest for the public. Cervantes's most famous play is *El cerco de Numancia* (wr. 1585; *The Siege of Numantia*, 1870), which is based on the siege by the Romans of the Celtiberic city of Numantia. The siege, which lasted many years, finally ended with the death of the last inhabitant, who preferred to die by suicide rather than become a slave. The play mixes history and legend and seeks to establish that the victorious expansion of the Spanish Empire in the sixteenth century was but the fulfillment of that courageous resolve. The author of *El ingenioso hidalgo don Quixote de la Mancha* (1605, 1615; *The History of the Valorous and Wittie Knight-Errant, Don Quixote of the Mancha*, 1612-1620; better known as *Don Quixote de la Mancha*) contributed to the Spanish theater a strong preoccupation with personal experience. Cervantes made use of his adventures as a captive slave in Algiers to write several plays and such lively interludes as *El juez de los divorcios* (pb. 1615; *The Divorce Court Judge*, 1919) and *El retablo de las maravillas* (pb. 1615; *The Wonder Show*, 1948), which sparkle with wit and social criticism.

RISE OF PERMANENT THEATERS

The next development of the Spanish theater was largely the result of a much-needed reform. Performances had taken place in city squares and in palaces but always on a movable stage with no possibility of making technical improvements. The opportunity to do so came with the establishment of fixed places of performance in Madrid, Valencia, and Seville. The theater of the Golden Age owes its existence to a confluence of seemingly contradictory forces. Religious confraternities in need of money for their charitable works decided that the popularity of theatrical performances afforded them the best source of revenue. They leased *corrales*, courtyards surrounded by houses, and had an administrator take care of the arrangements. At first, these organizations received a part of the daily income, but eventually, after the city governments took control of the theaters, they received an annual subsidy. This unlikely connection is important because it explains the capacity of the theater to withstand a barrage of criticism against its alleged immorality. Because the institutions needed the funds for worthwhile works, the theater was not only tolerated but also protected. In fact, performances that were initially permitted only on Sunday came to be more and more frequent, until nearly all restrictions were removed.

The courtyards, the most important in Madrid being the Corral de la Cruz (1579) and the Corral del Príncipe (1582), were bordered on either side by houses whose windows served as lodges and were occupied by important personages. The back had a balcony that was reserved for women, who used a separate door. The sides below the windows had rows of seats, and the middle ground was left empty and was used by the humblest element of the audience. The stage, which occupied the side opposite the ladies' balcony, was an elevated platform with a curtain that permitted exits and entrances. There were no stage props other than a gallery above the stage that served variously as the balcony of a building, the ramparts of a castle, or any other high place. Influential at this juncture was the presence of Italian troupes, especially that of Alberto Naseli, known as Ganassa, who contributed money to the building of the first Spanish theater and who, with other Italians, was responsible for the introduction of new scenic techniques as well as stage machinery. Performances took place during the day, and, because there was no scenery, the text itself had to supply information regarding place, time, and circumstances.

VALENCIA VERSUS MADRID

The development of Spanish drama in the seventeenth century took its impetus from the titanic output of Lope de Vega Carpio. Modern research, however, has advanced the idea that the honor of first having a fixed theater belongs to Valencia rather than to Madrid. It was believed that the Valencian dramatists owed their development to the presence of Lope de Vega, who went there in 1588 after being banished from Madrid for having libeled an actress. It is quite possible, however, that it was Lope de Vega who profited from his stay in Valencia by learning from the older and more experienced playwrights of the previous period. Among them were Francisco Augustin Tarregá, author of *El prado de Valencia* (pr. 1600; the meadow of Valencia) and *La duquesa constante* (pr. 1608; the constant duchess), two works that include many elements that became the characteristics of the Golden Age, such as local atmosphere, love complications, conceptual language, and multiple metric forms, among others; Rey de Artieda, the author of *Los amantes*, which depicted the legend of the star-crossed lovers that was also used by later playwrights; and Gaspar de Aguilar, known particularly for his *El mercader amante* (pr. c. 1600; *The Merchant Lover*, 1849), a play in which the character of two women in love is tested.

The most significant member of this group was Guillén de Castro y Bellvís, whose plays *El amor constante* (pr. 1596-1599; the constant love) and *Los mal casados de Valencia* (pr. 1595-1604; the unhappy marrieds of Valencia) show strong local flavor. He took the themes of his plays from Cervantes, using mythology as well as medieval ballads. It was precisely from this source that he took the inspiration for his best-known play, *La mocedades del Cid* (1618; *The Youthful Adventures of the Cid*, 1939), in two parts. This play, which contributed substantially to Pierre Corneille's *Le Cid* (pr. 1637; *The Cid*, 1637), vibrates with passion and energy and is a fitting representation of the national hero of Spain as a young man.

The main historical problem here is whether it was Lope de Vega who during his exile introduced his vision of the new comedy or whether, on the contrary, the young Lope de Vega, then aged twenty-six, was influenced by these writers and then built on this experience to develop the drama of the Golden Age.

GOLDEN AGE COMEDIA

This drama, which is known collectively as the *comedia*, without distinction among comedies, tragedies, and dramas, is a vast body of plays that at one time numbered in the thousands—a plenitude attributable not only to the astonishing prolificacy of the writers but also to the fact that, given the smallness of the total audience, plays had to be replaced after one or two performances; playwrights often refer to the Spaniards' impatience and desire for novelty. Lope de Vega alone, according to best estimates, wrote nearly five hundred plays, more than three hundred of which are still in existence. This huge number of works has not been completely analyzed or classified. As a consequence, an authoritative, all-encompassing view is not possible. Lope de Vega's canon draws on a bewildering number of sources for its plots: Spanish history, medieval ballads, chronicles, mythology, Italian novellas, Roman history, the Bible, chivalric novels, hagiography, and everyday events. There are, however, some general characteristics that can be pointed out as guideposts for Lope de Vega's readers.

The *comedia* is a three-act play, written in verse, with each act numbering roughly one thousand lines. It is a polymetric genre that uses traditional Spanish verse forms, the most common of which is the *romance*, the Spanish ballad form, featuring eight-syllable lines and assonant rhyme; the Italian-influenced seven-syllable and eleven-syllable lines are also frequently employed in various stanzaic forms. These forms are used with reliable idiosyncrasy by the various dramatists, and it is possible to determine the chronology of their production by the preference that they accord to the various verse forms at a particular time. Lope de Vega in his *El arte nuevo de hacer comedias en este tiempo* (1609; *The New Art of Writing Plays*, 1914) suggests under which dramatic situations these verse forms should be used. Each act is divided not into scenes but into action blocks, of which there are usually three. As indicated above, the stage had no set decoration and no costumes that were chronologically appropriate. They did, however, have costumes to indicate the different social classes, and some were extremely costly. Reliable stage machinery was introduced very slowly until Italian ex-

perts were imported for the preparation of court plays. After that, stage machinery was used with increasing skill and effectiveness, mostly to provide thrills and amazement for noble spectators.

The *comedia* sees events and human behavior from a preconceived point of view. Its basic preoccupation is not to investigate a human, ontological, or theological problem in order to uncover new perspectives or attitudes, but to reaffirm established truths. Rarely are the spectators challenged in their values; rather, they are presented with illustrations of proper behavior, provided with moral direction, or given arguments for existing personal and social values. A favorite metaphor of this theater is the crucible, in which the dross is divided from pure matter. The *comedia* takes individuals, places them in a stressful situation, and observes whether they are as whole in character or intention as they presented themselves to be at the beginning. This experience, however, rarely produces a change in the individual; the main purpose is to reveal his essential merits or faults. Usually, there is no epiphany, no personal or moral reorientation, except in those plays that deal with religious conversion, or in the moment of death, when the character, however evil he may have been, seeks reconciliation with God. The providential view of the world, the importance of loyalty, the necessity to be faithful in love, the duty to defend one's honor, and the need to be generous and courteous, courageous and modest, steadfast and prudent are never questioned. As a consequence, there is available a limited range of conflictive situations, which makes for repetition of themes and solutions.

This uniformity of values from period to period and from author to author, in spite of personal differences that are at times considerable, suggests to critics that Spanish society was either frightfully closed within itself or functioned as a community in which there was very little difference of opinion. Neither of these hypotheses seems to fit the historical circumstances. Spain, in spite of its increasing decadence as a world power, continued to maintain close relations with Europe. Meanwhile, the social and economic conflicts that had surfaced at the beginning of the Renaissance still existed. The fact that the theater was, to a great extent, a product of the capital, performed in the presence of kings and nobles, high prelates, and rich bourgeois, may have caused it to serve as an artificial preserver of a worldview that did not correspond to reality. There are more recent points of view that charge the *comedia* with having become the propaganda arm of the establishment, for this reason refusing to advance a more realistic and critical view of society.

The basic values of the *comedia* are religion, duty to king or collective authority, honor, and love. Religion is never challenged unless it be on the part of an infidel or a sinner who will either convert or be summarily punished. The remaining three secular values are often pitted against one another to create the necessary conflict that propels the drama. Love, although it is presented in nearly every play and although it is often the mover of the action, is never judged to be on an equal standing with loyalty to liege lord or honor. In nearly every case, love must cede to other pressures. There is, however, a delightfully subversive play by Lope de Vega, often called the great conformist, *El perro del hortelano* (pb. 1618; *The Gardener's Dog*, 1903), in which a noblewoman knowingly consents to a false arrangement so that she can marry her commoner secretary.

The great dramatic conflict of the *comedia* is the opposition between one's honor and one's loyalty to a higher authority—a liege lord or, more often, the ruling prince. This situation pits two basic values of the individual, values that make up the very nature of the nobleman. This conflict has often been misunderstood, and claims have been made that the overriding importance of kingship or the propagandistic purpose of the Golden Age drama obliged dramatists to put obedience to the king above even personal honor. This position cannot be sustained, however, because there is no play in which honor is placed below obedience. Indeed, in the case of the conflict between honor and king, it is impossible to make a clear choice, because both elements are considered to be basic components of the culture. An individual cannot cease to be what he is by surrendering his honor. If he does that, he forgoes any other rights that he may have. In *La mocedades del Cid* of Castro y

Bellvís, Rodrigo must take vengeance on his fiancée's father, who has offended Rodrigo's father, because otherwise Rodrigo would not, as a dishonored man, be worthy of his fiancée's love. At the same time, his fiancée, Jimena, cannot avoid seeking vengeance against the man she loves, Rodrigo, without forgoing her own standing and her own self-esteem. Yet at the same time, the individual cannot forget that he belongs to a social group that is represented by the lord, prince, or king. If he acts against his ruler, he is acting against the collectivity that creates the social structure of which he is a member and which, indeed, gives him a reason for being. To challenge the representative of the group is to deny the group itself. As a consequence, neither choice is acceptable, and the dramatists of the Golden Age preferred to find an accommodation, however fragile though it might be, rather than create chaos. This unwillingness to choose between two equal values and the unwavering belief in a providential God prevent the *comedia* from developing a genuinely tragic sense of life.

On a dramatic level, this theater presents some unique characteristics. To begin with, although there were acrimonious controversies on the subject, the *comedia* refused steadfastly to adopt the concept of the unities that the learned commentators on Aristotle sought to impose. Perhaps in part because the *comedia* was performed for the common people rather than for erudite scholars, playwrights did not feel obliged to obey literary authorities. The *comedia* is a freewheeling form, in which years may pass between acts, in which actions can take place in different countries, in which plots and subplots are often the staples of the play, and in which tragic and comic strands are mixed together. The seventeenth century partisans of the *comedia* were quite certain that the genius of Lope de Vega was as great as that of any dramatist who had ever lived, and that he therefore had the right to establish his own school. This freedom from literary tradition, so clearly enunciated, was admired fervently by the German Romantics, who made Pedro Calderón de la Barca a symbol of their literary rebellion. Yet, while the dramatists were proclaiming their independence from dramatic rules, the literature of the period was in fact very traditional in its observance of accepted norms.

GOLDEN AGE PLAYWRIGHTS

Lope de Vega, the recognized father of the new drama, is admired for his great facility as a poet and for his unerring dramatic sense. He is more lyric than philosophical or moralistic, adjectives that can be used for the other two great dramatists of the period, Pedro Calderón de la Barca and Tirso de Molina. There are many plays by Lope de Vega that fail in their dramatic intent because of hurried construction or thinness of material, but his great and even good plays are developed with remarkable assurance. Especially notable is the liveliness of dialogue, the handling of tempo, and the swift change from dramatic to lyric situations. Only a few of his best plays can be mentioned here: *El caballero de Olmedo* (pb. 1641; *The Knight from Olmedo*, 1961), a drama that moves from initial comedy to a steadily increasing conflict of jealousy and an intimation of tragedy, until love and inevitable death meet on a dark night; *Peribáñez y el comendador de Ocaña* (pb. 1614; *Peribáñez*, 1936), a tightly developed drama in which the honor of the peasant Peribáñez is threatened by his liege lord, developed on the brilliant opposition of the country-city duality so beloved by writers of the period, which reflected the influence of the Horatian theme of the *Beatus ille*; and *El castigo sin venganza* (pb. 1635; *Justice Without Revenge*, 1936), a dark play of infidelity, near-incest, and death taken from an Italian novella. In the latter play, the lecherous duke of Ferrara, forced to marry for dynastic reasons, abandons his young wife to go to war. She and his young bastard son fall in love, consummate their love, and are finally denounced to the returning duke, who causes them to be killed while keeping secret the reason for their death. Lope de Vega's most famous play, however, is *Fuenteovejuna* (pb. 1619; *The Sheep Well*, 1936). The drama is based on a peasant rebellion against a cruel and tyrannical overlord. The play has a complex development in which the concept of the harmony between the microcosm and the macrocosm is the determining structure. Lope de Vega establishes four different types of conflicts: the war be-

tween Portugal and Spain for the succession to the Castilian throne, the uprising of the comendador of Fuenteovejuna against his Castilian monarchs, the struggle between him and his peasants, and the lack of agreement among the peasants on the meaning of love. Lope de Vega unfolds these themes and then resolves them, going from the personal to the national level. In the process, he establishes the overpowering force of love, which not only unites people but also leads to an imposition of this unity on the disturbing element of society. Thus, the brutal death of the comendador is transformed into an act of social and, by implication, world harmony.

An equally important playwright is the Mercedarian monk, Gabriel Téllez, known as Tirso de Molina. Given his vocation, it is not surprising to find among his works many religious plays. The most important of these is *El condenado por desconfiado* (pb. 1634; *The Saint and the Sinner*, 1952; also known as *Damned for Despair*, 1986), more for the important topic of predestination and free will than for its dramatic coherence. Among the historical plays, *La prudencia en la mujer* (pb. 1634; *Prudence in Woman*, 1964) is noted for its successful presentation of the Queen-Regent Maria de Molina and for its undoubted reference to contemporary political events. The playwright was also capable of writing brilliant farces, such as *Don Gil de la calzas verdes* (pb. 1635; *Don Gil of the Breeches Green*, 1991), in which a woman who has been abandoned by her lover disguises herself as a man dressed in green, producing an unexpected number of suitors who take up the disguise, thus creating a confusion of events that seems unlikely to be unraveled. Tirso's most famous play, however, is *El burlador de Sevilla* (pb. 1630; *The Trickster of Seville*, 1923). This work, the earliest literary treatment of the Don Juan myth, sprang from a variety of disparate elements, none of which pointed, in any way, to the formation of a figure that was to reverberate through the centuries. Tirso's Don Juan is not a heroic figure; the playwright means to portray him and his friends as young profligates who take advantage of their influence at court to behave immorally and illegally. Don Juan has not yet become the overwhelming seducer to be found in later works. He is, rather, a trickster, who comes to possess women either through disguise or trickery; it is not his charm that conquers them. Yet within this reductionist view of the character, there are several elements that point toward his future development: He is fearless, disdainful of power and social conditions, and a manipulator of other people's unspoken feelings.

Associated with these playwrights, at least chronologically, are Juan Ruiz de Alarcón , Luis Vélez de Guevara, and Antonio Mira de Amescua. Ruiz de Alarcón is known for his preoccupation with social manners and for his calm, reasoned approach to drama. There is none of the exuberance and passion of Lope de Vega nor the interest in personality evident in Tirso de Molina. The Mexican-born playwright, who had a physical deformity, works within the theme of social relationships in measured tones and carefully crafted pieces. His best-known plays are *La verdad sospechosa* (pb. 1630; *The Truth Suspected*, 1927) and *Las paredes oyen* (pr. 1617; *The Walls Have Ears*, 1942). The first deals with the complications brought about by a pathological liar, while the second explores the consequences of gossip in society. Vélez de Guevara, a writer of considerable talent, is known for his propensity for verbal embroidery. His best play is *Reinar después de morir* (pr. 1653; rule after death), which repeats the story of the love of Inés de Castro and Prince Pedro of Portugal. The unauthorized marriage of the two young people provokes the king into ordering the death of Inés. When Pedro finally becomes king, he crowns the dead Inés queen and orders that obeisance be paid to her enthroned body. Mira de Amescua is known for intensifying the general lines of Lope de Vega's formula. He complicated the action, often losing himself in incidental events. He sought to amaze his spectators with sudden changes, brilliant set pieces, or surprises in the plot, thus losing track of the structure of his dramas. His best-known work is *El esclavo del demonio* (pr. c. 1608; *The Devil's Slave*, 1939), which belongs to a category of plays known as *comedias de santo*, plays that deal with sin and repentance and with the problem of predestination and free will, a topic of great theological interest during this time. In this play, a friar known for his devotion falls into

temptation and, together with a woman, dedicates himself to crime and to the pleasures of the flesh. He makes a pact with the Devil, but the reward for the friar is only a simulacrum of a woman, which turns into a skeleton while in his arms. This image exemplifies the concept of disabusement (*desengaño*), which was so prevalent in the period and which is best seen in the dramas of Calderón. Having finally recognized the insignificance of human life and its pleasures, the friar is moved to repentance.

It was up to Calderón de la Barca to develop to their full extent some of the great themes of the *comedia*. Born at the beginning of the century, he began to write plays at a time when Lope de Vega, although still vigorously active, was reaching the end of his life, and the *comedia* seemed to be entering a phase of settling down rather than of innovation. The Jesuit-trained Calderón de la Barca brought to his drama an organization of thought, a severity of mind and principles, and a manner of arguing and development of action that reflected both his intellectual background and his strong moral sense. The open, spontaneous outpourings of Lope de Vega were replaced by a rhetorical style, a rigidity of thought, and even a mechanistic production of images. Although Calderón de la Barca's production extends from mere plays of intrigue to mythological plays in which the full theatrical resources of palace productions were employed, he is best known for his honor plays and for his plays on the transitoriness of life on this earth. His honor dramas include *El alcalde de Zalamea* (pr. 1643; *The Mayor of Zalamea*, 1853), *El médico de su honra* (pb. 1637; *The Surgeon of His Honor*, 1853), *A secreto agravio, secreta venganza* (pb. 1637; *Secret Vengeance for Secret Insult*, 1961), and *El pintor de su deshonra* (pb. 1650; *The Painter of His Dishonor*, 1853). The last three deal with murder of the wife in order to avenge one's honor and are uncompromising in their affirmation of this right. There exists much controversy regarding the interpretation of these plays. Critical opinion has gone from condemnation of the playwright for maintaining such an unchristian attitude to claims that Calderón was, without taking sides, merely reflecting contemporary attitudes to the idea that Calderón was really criticizing the perversion of Christian morals represented by the murders, to the suggestion that he used these effective dramatic situations to compel a reflection on the right of the individual to self-respect and social dignity. Calderón in these plays gives a variety of hints that are difficult to coalesce into one coherent viewpoint.

The one play of Calderón that is known worldwide is *La vida es sueño* (pr. 1635; *Life Is a Dream*, 1830). Its point of departure is that life is to eternity what a dream is to life: Both life and dreams seem real while one experiences them but are nothing but a passing moment when compared with their corresponding realities. Segismundo is an Everyman who in his pride considers himself fit to challenge authority both terrestrial and divine. When placed momentarily in a position of power, he abuses it violently, thus proving his incapacity to check his arrogance and his passions. When he is returned to the prison from which he had been taken while drugged, he cannot ascertain whether that moment of power was real or was merely a dream. He decides that man does not have the capacity to find orientation by himself in this world and chooses divine guidance. The recognition of his dependence is the signal that he has comprehended the limitations of life, and this disabusement leads him to the acceptance of God and the pursuit of the good.

Another facet of Calderón's genius is to be found in his *autos sacramentales*. He became the most important author of these circumstantial religious pieces, which were commissioned by the city of Madrid; his place was so unchallenged that he was their sole producer for the last three decades of his life. The thematic vehicles that he used were taken mostly from the Bible and from mythology, and their purpose was to dramatize in the form of allegory the significance of the Sacraments. Although Calderón is considered the greatest practitioner of this genre, the tradition, as indicated, goes back to the Middle Ages and was built on the contributions of many writers. The *autos* become particularly important as a means of fighting heresies and enemies of the Catholic faith, and they were used not only as a means of celebration but also as a way of teaching Christian doctrine to the masses.

End of the Golden Age

Francisco de Rojas Zorrilla and Agustín Moreto y Cabaña are the last of the major dramatists of the period. They are considered to be thematically derivative writers, but each has a particular approach to his task. Rojas Zorrilla, who wrote serious as well as comic plays, displays a more understanding attitude toward women and the question of honor, as evidenced in the humane endings of his plays. His *Del rey abajo, ninguno* (pb. 1650; *None Beneath the King*, 1924) rejects the immolation of women in the defense of honor, although it does not renounce man's right to take revenge on the offending man. Moreto y Cabaña, on the other hand, is described by critics as a man of measure and order. His two best-known plays are seen as examples of a comic spirit in which his tolerance of human frailty is evidenced. *El lindo don Diego* (pb. 1662; the dandy Don Diego) treats the topic of the self-centered dandy with great success, while *El desdén con el desdén* (pb. 1654; *Love's Victory: Or, The School for Pride*, 1825) deals with a woman who vainly challenges the traditional view of her sex, according to which her life is supposed to center on love and marriage. Moreto y Cabaña, as did Molière, rejects the woman's stance as contrary to nature; the protagonist eventually relents by falling in love, thus reaffirming the established order.

Public theater, together with other literary forms, suffered a decline in the middle of the seventeenth century. The closure of the theaters for more than five years, except for a brief interval, provoked a disbanding of troupes and a general decline. At the same time that this was happening, the existence of a theater called Coliseo, ostensibly public but given to royal performances, further contributed to the demise of the *corrales*. This theater had a proscenium arch, painted scenery, and sophisticated stage machinery that was introduced by Italian technicians. The movement from popular to court theater, which included spectacular stagings in the royal gardens of the Retiro, along with other circumstances, brought to a close the creative phase of the *comedia*. Although Golden Age plays continued to be written, they were largely tired imitations of earlier efforts. Antonio de

Zamora and José de Cañizares, the epigones of this theater, although good technicians, failed to produce a single work of note. Indeed, it was in the French theater that reworkings of Spanish plays acquired new dramatic vitality.

EIGHTEENTH CENTURY

With the death of Charles II in 1700, the Habsburg line came to an end in Spain and was replaced by the French Bourbons. Philip V, a grandson of Louis XIV, and his Italian wife began a long line of rulers who sought to bring the country in line with the predominant French culture of the eighteenth century. Among the reforms that were effected were the suppression of the *autos sacramentales*, the banning of the Jesuit order, and the modernization of the theaters. The overall results were not entirely satisfactory, because Spain finished the century only partially incorporated into European society.

As far as the theater is concerned, the battleground was the introduction of the neoclassical tragedy, a genre whose earlier form had not had success in Spain and that required a complete reordering of aesthetic values for the Spanish public. The individuals who sought to promote neoclassical tragedy were not talented and trained playwrights but rather members of an educated elite whose tastes and ethical preoccupations were not in harmony with the public that they sought to influence. The resulting standoff between reformers and traditionalists made possible the entrance into Spain of a large number of translations from the French and the Italian as well as operatic performances, which were beginning to acquire great popularity. The first Spanish play that is worth noting from this period is *La Hormesinda* (pr. 1770), by Nicolás Fernández de Moratín, a play that deals with Pelayo, the hero of the first battle for the Reconquest of Spain. This showpiece of the reformist movement failed as a neoclassical work, however, not only because of its exaggerated nationalism (which overwhelmed the nuances necessary for tragic situations) but also because of its intense and meaningless rhetoric, a regrettable element of Spanish theater that persisted well into the twentieth century. Other writers who tried their hand at introducing high tragedy were

José Cadalso y Vazquez with his *Don Sancho García* (pr. 1771), Gaspar Melchor de Jovellanos with *El Pelayo* (pr. 1769), and Ignacio López de Ayala with *Numancia destruída* (pb. 1775; the destruction of Numantia).

Few writers of the eighteenth century merit particular attention. One is Ramón de la Cruz, who specialized in a short comic piece known as *sainete*. This genre is actually the continuation of the interludes of the sixteenth century, and it depends for its entertainment value on popular customs and characters as well as on satire and topical allusions. Ramón de la Cruz wrote more than one hundred of these short plays, and they are prized as lively documents of Spanish society of the period. Another playwright of note during this period is Vicente Garcia de la Huerta, whose tragedy *Raquel* (pr. 1778) is the only eighteenth century play that can still be appreciated. It is based on a play by Lope de Vega and dramatizes the love of King Alfonso VIII for the Jewess Rachel. The play sets up the duality of love versus duty to nation, and although it is not able to forgo completely its dependence on nationalistic fervor, it manages to introduce genuine human sentiments and, therefore, rescue itself from the failure to which previous efforts were condemned. Little was learned from the implicit lessons of this work, however, and neoclassical tragedy played out its string with *Pelayo* (pr. 1805), by Manuel José Quintana, another variant on the theme that had been treated by others earlier.

The only writer of this epoch who managed to achieve both popular and artistic success is Leandro Fernández de Moratín. Unlike his self-conscious father, Leandro dedicated himself to comedy. The moralistic preoccupation of the eighteenth century is not missing in his works, but his critical view of society and its foibles is both charmingly and effectively presented. He understood the goal of comedy to be the revelation of the vices and errors that are common in society and the affirmation of truth and virtue. His success results from his ability to present a critical viewpoint while not ignoring the sentimental side of the plot. His plays include *El viejo y la niña* (pr. 1790; the old man and the young girl), *La comedia nueva: O, El café* (pr. 1792; the new comedy), and his most famous work, *El sí de las niñas* (pr. 1806; *When a Girl Says Yes*, 1929). This play observes fairly rigorously the unities of time, space, and action; yet, in spite of these limitations, it unfolds with great naturalness both in its action and in its language. The play deals with the arranged marriage of an old gentleman and a young girl who is in love with the old man's nephew. The self-interest of the mother, who pushes the young girl to an inappropriate marriage; the young girl's inability to speak her mind; and the old man's self-deception about the feasibility of such a union are revealed with wit and feeling.

NINETEENTH CENTURY

Spain underwent great turmoil with the beginning of the new century. The Napoleonic invasion, the rebellion of the Spaniards against the French, the various events connected with the restoration of the Bourbon monarchy, and the liberals' efforts to establish a constitutional monarchy impeded the normal development of cultural life. Indeed, the dominant cultural events of this period were the flight of those Spaniards who had supported French rule in the hope of bringing about a reform in Spanish society and, later, the exile of the liberals who had sought in vain to obtain constitutional guarantees from Ferdinand VII when he was restored to the throne. Romanticism came late to Spain when these liberals returned at the death of Ferdinand VII (1835), and it had, therefore, the flavor of a fashion rather than the force of an idea. Moreover, because Spanish theater never embraced neoclassicism fully, the Romantic rebellion did not have the function of a renovating force, as it had in France.

The general situation of Spanish theater had not changed much in two centuries. There were still only two theaters in Madrid, the Corral de Príncipe and the Corral de la Cruz, although they were different structures. It was at this time that the traditional separation in the seating of men and women finally came to an end. The theatergoing public was still so limited in number that impresarios were obliged to change the billing every few days. The great theatrical triumphs of the Romantic period can therefore claim performances that ranged in number from only seven to fifteen.

The Romantic period began in 1834 with the performances of *La conjuración de Venecia año de 1310* (the conspiracy of Venice) by Francisco Martínez de la Rosa and *Macías* by Mariano José de Larra, the first of which, symbolically enough, was written during the author's exile in France. The first Romantic play to enjoy great success was *Don Álvaro: O, La fuerza del sino* (pr. 1835; *Don Álvaro: Or, The Force of Destiny*, 1964) by Ángel de Saavedra, also known as the duke of Rivas. Spanish Romantic drama leans heavily on historical plots; uses passionate, absolute love as a vehicle; and has fatality as its major theme. The Romantic conflict occurs between the individual and an uncomprehending order that causes the death of the protagonist. The year 1835 marks the apogee of Romantic drama with the performance of *Don Álvaro*. The protagonist is a man of obscure origin but of great merit. His valor, courtesy, and tenderness, however, are all negated by an adverse fate that pursues him tenaciously, even seeking him out when he retires from the world by becoming a monk. In the end, unable to control or understand this cosmic persecution, he commits suicide.

Following immediately on the heels of the duke of Rivas was Antonio García Gutiérrez. Although the author of many dramas, such as *Simón Bocanegra* (pr. 1843), *Juan Lorenzo* (pr. 1865), and *Venganza Catalana* (1864; Catalan vengeance), he is best known for his *El trovador* (pr. 1836; the troubadour), another play of love and fatality. Also writing around this time were Manuel Bretón de los Herreros, a comic writer whose best-known play is *Muérete y verás!* (pr. 1837; *Die and You Will See!*, 1935), and Juan Eugenio de Hartzenbusch y Martínez, who retells the story of the unhappy lovers of Teruel in *Los amantes de Teruel* (pb. 1837; *The Lovers of Teruel*, 1938), leaning heavily on the fatality theme. The last of the Romantic dramatists was José Zorrilla y Moral, who resurrected another play from the Golden Age with his *Don Juan Tenorio* (pr. 1844; English translation, 1944). Zorrilla y Moral continued the figure that had gained momentum with Molière and with Lorenzo da Ponte's libretto for Mozart's opera. The play is divided into two parts, one dealing with the libertinage of Don Juan, the other with his slow movement toward repentance, culminating in divine forgiveness as a consequence of the pure and self-sacrificing love of the heroine. The change in the denouement shows a telling difference in ideology between the Romantic play and the work of Tirso de Molina written two centuries earlier.

Zorrilla y Moral brought to close the short period of Romantic drama, which was followed by a more realistic genre known as "high comedy." Abandoning the destiny theme and the violent passions so prevalent in the previous period, the playwrights of this era focused on the mainsprings of society and its individuals. They sought to uncover the real motivations, both psychological and cultural, of their characters, eschewing the highly charged scenes of the Romantic period and concentrating on physical circumstances rather than emotions. One can trace in this new drama a slow movement toward melodrama.

Ventura de la Vega, regarded as the precursor of this group, anticipates their concerns most clearly in *El hombre del mundo* (pr. 1845; *The Man of the World*, 1935). The wide world of the Romantic period is now restricted to the narrow confines of the bourgeoisie. Less emphasis is placed on the power of the word to sway the public, while more dramatic weight is carried by the situation, thus making for better-integrated plays. The representatives of this new drama, playwrights who were brought up during the Romantic period, are Adelardo López de Ayala y Herrera and Manuel Tamayo y Baus. López de Ayala provides an interesting mixture of the Romantics' identification with the people and a neoclassical preoccupation with reforming society. In his best-known play, *El tanto por ciento* (pr. 1861; the percentage cut), the self-interest of people leads them to prey on a man and a woman of noble spirit who are guided solely by honor, loyalty, and love. The play is marred by a sentimental denouement in which the noble pair emerge victorious from the intrigue. Perhaps as a consequence of the commercial and industrial development of the nineteenth century, the predominant themes of this theater are the conflicts created by the opposition of two distinct types: the individual whose obsessive quest for wealth overrides all other personal and social concerns, and the traditional, value-directed person, often represented by a true, unselfish lover, unconcerned about money and therefore easy prey for the unscrupulous. In *Consuelo* (pr. 1878; English translation, 1935), López de Ayala returns to the theme of economic and social interest over true love. The protagonist prefers a rich, unscrupulous man over a dedicated and poor one. Her unhappy marriage eventually leads to the loss of her husband, the death of her mother, and the disdain of the former true lover.

Manuel Tamayo y Baus shared with López de Ayala the public's admiration. He wrote a great variety of plays, from historical dramas to thesis plays, but is best remembered for his *La locura de amor* (pr. 1855; love madness) and *Un drama nuevo* (pr. 1867; *A New Drama*, 1915). He preferred prose to verse, because of its greater naturalness, and he was particularly interested in uncovering the moral reasons for his protagonists' behavior. *La locura de amor* treats the tragic fate of Queen Juana of Spain, whose intense love and jealousy toward her husband, Philip, cause her to become mad. *A New Drama* develops with some success, but with exaggerated theatrical effects, the theme of the play-within-a-play. The central character, a comic actor, insists on playing the role of a husband deceived by his young wife. The situation, ironically, parallels the real circumstances of the actor, who, when he discovers, while acting, the infidelity of his wife, kills the man who in real life as well as on the stage has seduced his wife. With Tamayo y Baus, the so-called realistic theater came to an end, and the stage was occupied until the end of the nineteenth century by the controversial figure of José Echegaray y Eizaguirre.

Echegaray enjoyed a long and productive career, winning the Nobel Prize in Literature in 1904. Yet in spite of the undoubted success and international prestige that crowned Echegaray's career, modern critics have been harsh in their judgment of his works. In particular, they have seen falsity in the grandiloquence of his expression, in the psychological exaggeration of the situations, and in the derivativeness of his dramatic art. He fuses the grandstanding of the Romantic writers with the social and moral preoccupations of the writers of "high comedy." In the process, he creates a kind of melodrama in which emotional responses take precedence over reason and naturalness of content. In *O locura o santidad* (pr. 1877; *Folly or Saintliness*, 1895), the protagonist, a respected and wise man whose daughter is about to be engaged to a duke, goes mad and is eventually taken to an insane asylum when he finds out that he is not the respected son of a bourgeois family but the illegitimate son of a maid. Echegaray's masterpiece, *El gran Galeoto* (pr. 1891; *The Great Galeoto*, 1895), develops the thesis that society with its gossip and propensity for evil is the cause of the destruction of a noble union. Insinuations that a young man protected by a generous friend is the lover of the latter's wife provoke a series of reactions that lead to a duel, death, social condemnation, and, eventually, like the book on Galahad that brought Paolo and Francesca to their adulterous union, to the realization of something that originally did not exist.

Drama of Social Commitment

Echegaray dominated Spanish theater for the last twenty years of the nineteenth century. The only antidote to his drama was supplied by two socially committed writers who made their appearance toward the end of the century, novelist and dramatist Joaquín Dicenta y Benedicto and the novelist Benito Pérez Galdós. Dicenta's early work was very conventional and was influenced by the dominant post-Romantic mode of the period. In 1895, however, his *Juan José* was performed to unexpected success. Spanish theater was not accustomed to treating the lower classes as individuals whose problems deserved to be taken seriously. Dicenta adapted the old theme of honor and jealousy to a proletarian setting; while there are references to social conditions, and although the motive that propels the final tragedy is physical deprivation, the drama is essentially one of honor. In the process, however, the lower classes are presented, for the first time since Golden Age drama, as having dignity and a sense of self-value.

Although he wrote some pieces directly for the stage, Pérez Galdós owes his reputation as a playwright to adaptations of his novels. What he contributed to the stage was a concern for the reality of hu-

man emotions and situations rather than a renovation of dramatic techniques. Pérez Galdós was interested in the opposition between two visions of life and society: that of individuals who are paralyzed in their attitudes and feelings by the weight of tradition and customs and that of individuals who seek the truth about people and events and are, therefore, willing to challenge established views. In *Realidad* (pr. 1892; reality), the old problem of adultery is not treated with the automatic responses that countless other plays present but is seen from a new perspective when the husband realizes that his values are closer to those of the seducer than to the values of his wife. *El abuelo* (pr. 1904; *The Grandfather*, 1910) upsets another well-worn convention. An old count has come to visit his daughter-in-law, now widowed, to discover which of his two granddaughters is the "real" one. His preoccupation with the legitimacy of his proud and noble line, however, is brought to an end when he discovers that the girl to whom he responds and who is devoted to him is the illegitimate granddaughter.

The Twentieth Century

The earnest but essentially nondramatic efforts of Pérez Galdós were replaced by the bourgeois theater of Jacinto Benavente y Martínez. The considerable production of this Nobel Prize winner includes a variety of plays, ranging from rural dramas to plays for children. In spite of this, his theater is easily identifiable by its characteristic preoccupations and dramatic techniques. Interestingly, although Benavente y Martínez was reputed to know every detail of dramatic construction, his theater depends heavily on narration to develop the action, while dialogue is relegated to a secondary role. He was reluctant to deal seriously with the central issues of his society, preferring to maintain an aloof, skeptical attitude. In spite of his large and varied production, Benavente y Martínez is invariably connected with a high bourgeois world of elegant salons and of individuals bored with life. Thematically, Benavente y Martínez deals with the same material that served the "high comedy" writers: the tyranny of social conventions, hypocrisy, and falseness. What he removed from his plays was the high-blown rhetorical style, the charged words, and the empty passion. Pleasant as is his theater and smooth as is his technique, one leaves his plays with a sense of insubstantiality.

Two of his works, however, escape the ironic indifference that dominates the rest of his production: *La malquerida* (pr. 1913; *The Passion Flower*, 1917) and *Los intereses creados* (pr. 1907; *The Bonds of Interest*, 1915). *The Passion Flower*, set against a rural backdrop, presents the theme of the power of passion, which in this case is incest. Esteban is in love with his stepdaughter, whose fiancé has been killed. The investigation into the death of the young man leads to the discovery of the culpable love of Esteban, to the horror of the mother. When it seems that the father repents his error and the mother is willing to forgive, the stepdaughter's passionate love for her stepfather is revealed, and the mother, unwilling to see the daughter commit the ultimate sin, kills her husband.

The Bonds of Interest employs *commedia dell'arte* characters to make clear in a devastating way that there exists an unavoidable connection between idealism and materialism and that the very existence of one depends on the other. Although Benavente y Martínez continued to write for many years after he first achieved international success, nothing in his later production added to his fame. Although he was instrumental in removing from the stage the rhetoric and verbal fireworks of late nineteenth century, he did not bequeath to Spanish drama a more critical attitude toward the reality of human life.

A contemporary of Benavente y Martínez, Carlos Arniches continued the tradition of Lope de Rueda, Cervantes, and Ramón de la Cruz with a modern version of the *sainete*, a one-act play. Arniches and others made use of the considerable cultural differences in Spanish regions and types to stimulate a popular, optimistic view of life. Arniches specialized in portraying the people of Madrid—those who lived in the old, traditional neighborhoods. Normally, the *sainete* utilizes a love triangle composed of two men who court a young girl. Although at one point, she is usually bedazzled by the fast-talking, self-important, nearly delinquent young man, eventually she comes to marry his hardworking, well-intentioned, and seri-

ous rival. The genre lends itself to a folkloric representation of life rather than to critical analysis and is distinguished by a lively, humorous, colloquial speech whose intentional distortions are used for comic effects. Equally popular were the brothers Serafín Álvarez Quintero and Joaquín Álvarez Quintero. They concentrated on the Andalusian milieu and contributed to the continuation of the stereotypical image of Andalusia as a land of sun, song, and smiles. They ignored all the problems that beset that region to depict a near patriarchal society, perhaps as an antidote to the raging poverty that has characterized its history.

A group of minor dramatists contributed to Spanish theatrical life during this time: Manuel Linares Rivas y Astray, a follower of Benavente y Martínez without the latter's sense of irony; Eduardo Marquina, who reintroduced poetic drama and whose *En Flandes se ha puesto el sol* (pr. 1909; the sun has set in Flanders) recalls nostalgically the lost glory and traditions of Spain; Gregorio Martínez Sierra, best known for his *Canción de cuna* (pr. 1911; *The Cradle Song*, 1917), whose idealization of womanhood is his defining characteristic; and Pedro Muñoz Seca, who wrote comic plays featuring outrageous situations and verbal high jinks. He is best known for *La venganza de don Mendo* (pr. 1918; the vengeance of Don Mendo), a highly successful parody of the history plays of the Romantic period. There are also plays of a strikingly different mood by Miguel de Unamuno y Jugo, whose ontological preoccupations leave behind the narrow social problems treated by his contemporaries. His conception of drama was to present a schematic action reduced to its essence, allowing for only the most relevant of passions to enter a play. It is logical that he should rely on myths as the vehicles for the basic nature of his concerns. The philosopher Unamuno, however, was no more able to dramatize his themes than he was able to novelize them. The nondramatic quality of his works has, therefore, relegated them to closet dramas.

The only real innovator of Spanish theater during this period was Ramón María del Valle-Inclán. He was so far removed from the thematic and dramatic sensibility of his time that he had considerable difficulty not only in being performed but also in being recognized as a dramatic author. His absence from the theater—first, because of his vision of what constituted theater, and second, because of political considerations—has been reevaluated by modern scholars, and he is now considered to be among the most modern of Spanish playwrights. The basic reforms of Valle-Inclán's theater are the abandonment of the conflictive situation as the motivating force of the play; the use of a cinematographic technique requiring multiple actions or fast, sequential actions; the rejection of bourgeois values, which are seen to be nothing but a control mechanism; and the use of setting as an active participant in the dramatic situation. Valle-Inclán also abandoned the use of plot as a symbolic ordering for the theme of the work. Valle-Inclán's dramatic development can be traced from an early, decadent phase to a transitional period and, finally, after a break, to an explosion of originality with his *esperpentos*, a genre that he originated. The *comedias bárbaras* (barbaric comedies) constitute a trilogy that presents a primitive world of emotions in nineteenth century Galicia.

To take the place of the conflictive situation, Valle-Inclán introduced the principle of duality of response. His earlier plays employ the duality of heroism and absurdity; later, especially in the *esperpentos*, he juxtaposed the tragic and the grotesque. The transitional theater of Valle-Inclán came to fruition with *Divinas palabras* (pb. 1920; *Divine Words*, 1968). The play continues the world of the barbaric trilogy while opening the door to a later theater. The plot concerns a deformed child who is the center of a struggle between two women who seek to exploit his condition to display him in country fairs. Mari-Gaila wins, and she goes from fair to fair, pleased with the freedom that this entails. This desire for freedom leads her to a sexual liaison with a darkly compelling figure. When she is found by the villagers making love to him, she is dragged to the village and presented to her weak husband for punishment. He tries to calm them by uttering the words of Christ regarding casting the first stone, but they react in anger. He then repeats the words in Latin. The incantation of the mysterious words arouses their fears and superstitions, and they quickly dissolve. The ambiguity of the plot and the difficulty in focusing on a discernible theme are offset by the powerful presence of the cultural background and the landscape. The tension of the play is created by the opposition between the primitive, pagan view of life and the implicit Christian context.

For Valle-Inclán, contemporary Spain is a grotesque variant of European civilization. For this reason, it is not possible to look at it with normal vision, but only through eyes that systematically deform its reality. Tragic emotions are to be counterbalanced by the grotesque elements that surround the individual. The artist must remain impassive before the human farce played out by poseurs. Yet, the dramatic reality of Valle-Inclán's two major *esperpentos, Luces de bohemia* (pb. 1920; *Bohemian Lights*, 1967) and *Los cuernos de don Friolera* (pb. 1921; *The Grotesque Farce of Mr. Punch the Cuckold*, 1991), attest not an indifference to the human condition but a cold anger at the depravity of society. *The Grotesque Farce of Mr. Punch the Cuckold* is particularly meaningful because it destroys the traditional myth of sexual honor so much discussed in Spanish theater through the centuries.

The desire to reform Spanish theater and to bring to an end its dependence on realistic representation was shared by Jacinto Grau Delgado. Like Valle-Inclán, he was ignored by both critics and public, and like his contemporary he refused to adapt himself to the dominant mode. His production moved from tragedy to farce. *El conde Alarcos* (pr. 1917; the Count Alarcos) is a dark and uncompromising tragedy based on a medieval ballad that fails in the author's intent to avoid the clichés of earlier historical plays; more successful is *El señor de Pigmalión* (pr. 1923; Mr. Pygmalion), a tragic farce in which the creator of a group of puppets is attacked and finally killed by his own creations.

The most successful playwright of the first part of the twentieth century and the only one to have acquired undoubted international standing is Federico García Lorca. His theater is based on poetry and feeling as expressive vehicles, and his major theme, presented under different guises, is the stifling of human emotions and of freedom by nature and circumstances. This inevitable defeat of man and his passions is conveyed through a carefully wrought poetic language based on myth and history, nature and literature. Instinct is destroyed by authority, love is rendered impossible by one's nature or by the intervention of others. The central images have a strong telluric force that gives his theater a mythic quality. Although strongly aware of the social conditions of Spain, García Lorca does not enter fully into this arena. His death gave him a political symbolism that was not warranted by his life. It is true that he was moving toward a more politically aware position, but his early death prevented him from realizing this process.

García Lorca's first works are essentially poetic. Even the protagonist of *Mariana Pineda* (pr. 1927; English translation, 1950), whose heroine is the legendary figure who was executed for her connection with liberals, becomes, in the hands of García Lorca, a delicate flower trembling with passion rather than the symbol of political freedom. García Lorca's characters, although firmly fixed within Spanish culture, must be seen as generic types. Their circumstances may be Andalusian, but their aspirations and emotions have a universal application. There is, then, a full rejection of the social mores that dominated the theater of the period. García Lorca's earlier theater is influenced by Symbolism, to which the earlier Valle-Inclán was also indebted, and his later work by Surrealism, which for a variety of reasons achieved little penetration in Spain. The avant-garde, experimental work *Así que pasan cinco años* (wr. 1931; *When Five Years Pass*, 1941) and two incomplete plays represent a less well recognized side of his dramaturgy, as does the Chekhovian *Doña Rosita la soltera: O, El lenguaje de las flores* (pr. 1935; *Doña Rosita the Spinster: Or, The Language of the Flowers*, 1941).

García Lorca's best-known theater is represented by the trilogy of rural tragedies, each unfolding the essentially tragic condition of man as a being unable to find fulfillment: *Bodas de sangre* (pr. 1933; *Blood Wedding*, 1939), *Yerma* (pr. 1934; English translation, 1941), and *La casa de Bernarda Alba* (wr. 1936; *The House of Bernarda Alba*, 1947). All three deal with

sexual frustration as a symbol of unfulfillment. Failure is inevitable, no matter what actions people take. In *Blood Wedding*, the escape of the lovers from their families leads to tragedy; in *Yerma*, the unwillingness of the unhappily married heroine to give herself to the man she loves similarly leads to death; and in *The House of Bernarda Alba*, both those who conform to their circumstances and those who fight against them encounter disaster. The failure cannot be ascribed to personal weaknesses, because both passivity and activity lead to the same end. Moreover, the poetic world of García Lorca, which places these characters within the setting of seasons and crops, water and animals, astral bodies and vegetal cycles, impels the audience to consider events not personally or circumstantially, but as part of the natural order of things.

SPANISH CIVIL WAR

The Spanish Civil War not only cut off an important new direction of Spanish theater but also brought about the emigration of many intellectuals and writers. The best Spanish theater was produced by three dramatists in exile, Rafael Alberti, Alejandro Casona, and Max Aub. Alberti is the most political of the group. Influenced by expressionism and by his political convictions, he has sought systematically to reform Spanish theater. A painter and a poet before a dramatist, Alberti constructed a dramaturgy characterized by a sense of movement and form. *El adefesio* (pb. 1944; the absurdity) unites both his social and his artistic concerns in his denunciation of his narrow, superstitious society. The play uses a schematic plot and symbolic, caricatured personages to effect a criticism of blind authority and social hypocrisy.

Casona's theater, written mostly in exile, was introduced into Spain late, and at a time when Spain was unreceptive to Casona's moral and psychological preoccupations. Yet Casona's work, to the degree that it represented a departure from the realistic theater that continued to be in vogue in Spain up to the 1960's, must be classified as an innovative force. *Prohibido suicidarse en primavera* (pr. 1937; *No Suicide Allowed in Spring*, 1950) and *Los árboles mueren de pie* (pr. 1949; trees die standing up) unfold the central theme of Casona's work, the struggle between illusion and reality. Illusion is the refuge of those who cannot fight successfully against adversity, but only an acceptance of reality can bring about an acceptable resolution.

Aub began with an antinaturalist theater, moved to an activist phase during the Civil War, and wrote his best plays in exile. These plays are a reflection on the bitterness of war and suffering: *San Juan* (pr. 1942) narrates the plight of exiled Jews, *Morir por cerrar los ojos* (pr. 1944; to die for shutting one's eyes) chronicles the surrender and defeat of France, and *El rapto de Europa* (pr. 1943; the rape of Europe) repeats the theme of exiles in flight from the Nazis, but this time it includes a woman whose dedication to aiding the afflicted represents the humanitarianism that Aub found missing during his own experiences.

One important comic playwright was Enrique Jardiel Poncela. His comedy rejected the traditional formula of puns and exaggerated situations and was based on the whimsical and the unreal. *Eloisa está debajo de un almendro* (pr. 1940; Eloise is under an almond tree) and *Los ladrones somos genta honrada* (pr. 1942; we thieves are honorable people) are good examples of Jardiel Poncela's application of logic to absurd situations, thus creating comedies that require an intellectual approach to enjoyment.

A similar attraction to the logic of the absurd is to be found in Miguel Mihura Santos. Mihura was a comic genius whose best work, *Tres sombreros de copa* (pr. 1952; *Three Top Hats*, 1968), written in 1932, was performed twenty years later because, like many other playwrights before him, he could not convince impresarios to stage a play that was so far removed from dominant tastes. The revolution that Mihura proposes in the play—the importance of irrationality, rebellion against verbal forms, the clash between the dull world of the bourgeois mentality and the aspirations of free spirits—represents the unrealized revitalization of the Spanish theater.

THE FRANCO YEARS

The civil war distorted the development of Spanish drama. During and after the conflict, plays were staged for their propaganda value. After his victory, Francisco Franco imposed strict censorship, which

was relaxed slowly over the thirty-five years of his dictatorship but which was still in effect at his death in 1975. Most of the theater of the 1950's and 1960's was self-absorbed and withdrawn, both theatrically and thematically. Although before the war the conservative taste of the middle class and the financial interests of the impresario determined the fate of plays, after the war, political considerations became equally important. The postwar theater concentrated on entertainment, some inoffensive social criticism, and occasional moral issues. Little drama dealt with the lower classes or with their problems. Some of the dramatists of this period are Juan Ignacio Luca de Tena, José María Pemán, José López-Rubio, Joaquín Calvo Sotelo, and Víctor Ruiz Iriarte.

A new epoch in Spanish drama began with the staging of Antonio Buero Vallejo's *Historia de una escalera* (pr. 1949; *Story of a Staircase*, 1955). From the very beginning of his career, Buero Vallejo viewed Spanish society with intense, serious eyes, seeing the lack of social concern, the self-imposed blindness of the people to avoid a recognition of their condition, the moral ambiguity, the selfishness, the lack of freedom. He accomplished for nearly thirty years the impossible task of criticizing Spain without incurring political difficulties. He was able to achieve this not only because of his undoubted moral sincerity but also because he developed an oblique way of dealing with social problems. His characters are often historical—such as Velázquez in *Las meninas* (pr. 1960; English translation, 1987), Goya in *El sueño de la razón* (pr. 1970; *The Sleep of Reason*, 1985), and Larra in *La detonación* (1977; *The Shot*, 1989)—who lived in critical moments of Spanish history and who had to confront the same moral and political problems that were present during Franco's regime. Buero Vallejo has constantly renewed his dramatic structure and made use of an "immersion" technique, a device in which the spectator is forced to confront the same problems that face the dramatic personage. He was the first to deal with the traumatic effects of the Civil War in *El tragaluz* (pr. 1967; the skylight). It is a measure of the forces that controlled Spanish theater that a reflection on the event that shook modern Spain could be staged only thirty years after that event took place. Not even Buero Vallejo, however, was able to get his play dealing with police torture, *La doble historia del doctor Valmy* (pb. 1967; *The Double Case History of Doctor Valmy*, 1967), staged during Franco's life.

Although Buero Vallejo was successful in maintaining a dialogue with fellow Spaniards, Alfonso Sastre, with his more direct, uncompromising attack on Franco's Spain, was unable to get his work performed. His plays either were completely censored or were allowed to be performed for one night by student groups. In his articles as well as in his works, he maintains the unavoidable social responsibility of the writer, the need to keep alive the cry of freedom. *Escuadra hacia la muerte* (pr. 1953; *The Condemned Squad*, 1961), in which individuals assume an existentialist attitude in spite of their limitations; *La mordaza* (1954; the gag), in which he transposes tyranny from a national to a familial setting; *Guillermo Tell tiene los ojos tristes* (pr. 1960; *Sad Are the Eyes of William Tell*, 1970), a direct attack on dictatorship; and *La sangre y la ceniza* (pr. 1965; blood and ashes), a play about intolerance, all form a testimony to his untiring struggle.

The 1960's saw the emergence of a large number of younger playwrights who became known collectively as the "realistic generation." Their interest in the sociopolitical problems of Spain drew them together, as did their constant struggle to be allowed to perform and be performed. Their theater, in large measure, was one of protest. Their fight against Franco absorbed their creative energy, and some of their plays lost considerable relevance with the change in the circumstances of the country. Lauro Olmo, José Martín Recuerda, José María Rodríguez Méndez, Carlos Muñiz, and Antonio Gala formed part of this generation.

THE POST-FRANCO PERIOD

The death of Franco and the reestablishment of democracy and political freedoms provoked an explosion in the theater. Plays that could not be performed before were staged, and performances ranged from the traditional to the determinedly avant-garde. The plays of many dramatists who were born in the

1930's, 1940's, and 1950's were staged only after Franco's death. Two playwrights, José Ruibal and Francisco Nieva, distinguished themselves by portraying the irrationality of modern life, which led them to develop a correspondingly hallucinatory dramatic art. Finally, mention should be made of Fernando Arrabal, whose debut in Spain in 1958 was discouragingly received by the Spanish public and whose temporary emigration to France constituted, for a while, the loss of a renovating force in Spanish theater.

After the initial flurry of plays that finally saw production in Spain after the death of Franco, audience interests quickly shifted to new tastes by the early 1980's. The political critique of the fascist regime, which was at the core of most of the previously suppressed and forbidden works, appeared suddenly dated, even though audiences shared its message. There was a general desire to move out of the fascist past, and theatergoers looked for fresh plays that did not dwell on previous problems.

This audience rejection of plays that centered on social criticism and advocated an often radical social agenda went hand in hand with a desire for entertainment and, ironically so, if compared to the tastes of contemporary American audiences, a thirst for experimental theater and absurdist plays. Caught off guard, some of the older playwrights began to revise their dramatic output to reflect these changes. Arrabal's plays, for example, became less political and more avant-garde in their experimentation. Although his *Inquisición* (pr. 1980; inquisition) still concerns itself with Spain and its troubled history, it also includes more experimental approaches than those typical of the social realism of his earlier work.

With new political freedom, the old antagonism of the *posibilistas* like Buero Vallejo, who managed to get produced under Franco, and the *imposibilistas* like Sastre, whose works rarely saw the light of day, suddenly disappeared. With it, a new heated struggle for fame, recognition, public success, and acceptance broke out among the established dramatists. No longer did the notion of political persecution serve as a moral counterweight to a lack of popular and institutional acclaim. Understandably, most dramatists tried to capture the interests of a somewhat hedonistic audience who hungered for entertaining fare and also desired intellectual experimentation and avant-garde plays, rather than a play concerned with traditional social issues.

Buero Vallejo captured the new wave with plays like *Lázaro en el laberinto* (pr. 1986; *Lazarus in the Labyrinth*, 1992), which combined his political interests in revisiting the past of Franco's dictatorship with a highly stylized treatment of the subjective and fragile nature of memory. While the main character tries to remember whether or not he actually saved his student lover, the young woman Amparo, from fascist thugs back in 1964, an invisible telephone rings in his mind (and in the theater), trying to force him to acknowledge the truth that he abandoned his lover to a certain death. At the time of his death in 2000, Buero Vallejo had become a widely studied and acclaimed Spanish dramatist.

Sastre had to wait longer until his move toward more popular plays paid off in terms of public and official acclaim. His *La taberna fantástica* (pr. 1990; the fantastic tavern), which concerned itself with Madrid's rowdy and bawdy underworld, played to sold-out audiences in the capital and became an international hit. He won the Premio Nacional de Teatro, Spain's foremost theatrical honor, for it, and this play became the basis of his ongoing fame and critical success.

SOCIALIST THEATER SPONSORSHIP

The election victory of the Socialist Party in 1982 translated into the foundation of government sponsorship for Spanish theater. Dramatists found themselves competing for government grants, and many felt that a new era of intense personal rivalry had begun. Paloma Pedrero, a former actress turned successful playwright, stunned audiences with her angry play *La llamada de Lauren* (pr. 1985; the call of Laura), which challenged traditional gender roles in Spanish society. The topic is central to her other masterpieces such as *El color de agosto* (pr. 1988; *The Color of August*, 1994). Yet in 1995, Pedrero caused great controversy when she turned against the system of state sponsorship. She accused fellow playwrights of inane

personal infighting and self-censorship in order to please the government bureaucrats who decide on the disbursement of grants.

In Pedrero's view, the democratic government had become as much of a censor of the theater as Franco's government, with money instead of police and prison the enforcement tools of the regime. She felt that competition for limited state sponsorship inhibited creativity and hastened the move toward commercialization of theater.

However, in spite of state sponsorship, economic problems persisted at Spanish theaters. Audiences were increasingly attracted to lavishly produced foreign plays. Among Spanish playwrights, the desire for artistic and material triumph led to what some critics saw as a pandering to the lowest of audience interests. If social themes were featured in the plays, they were lurid ones of drug abuse and sexual transgressions, including prostitution and sexual exploitation. Spanish theater had become erotically intense, but some of the plays were using these themes gratuitously.

In the overall crisis, there were exceptions. Ana Diosdado is one of the few important playwrights whose drama has maintained an enormous economic success. Her *Los ochenta son nuestros* (pr. 1988; the eighties are ours) won popular acclaim in Madrid as well as the rest of Spain, and *Trescientos veintiuno, trescientos veintidos* (pr. 1993; three twenty-one, three twenty-two) was an instant success with fascinated audiences. The latter play is a witty comedy of manners concerning two couples in adjacent hotel rooms, hence the name of the play that puns on the room numbers. Two newlyweds room next to a strange couple, a politician and his call girl, who is really an investigative journalist. The ensuing comic complications nevertheless cast some light on contemporary Spanish cultural conflicts, thus helping to distinguish Diosdado's work as uniquely Spanish. Her plays stand out in a sea of commercially successful plays that nevertheless lack any specific connection to Spain.

EARLY TWENTY-FIRST CENTURY ISSUES

Curiously, one response to the perceived crisis in Spanish drama has been a turn to experimental theater. This trend enjoys considerable success and is acclaimed by its urbane audience. Sergi Belbel best exemplifies this trend. His first play, *Minimmal Show* (with Miquel Górriz, pb. 1992; minimal show), set the direction for these minimalist, experimental plays, usually staged at small, out of the way, but critically influential art house theaters. Consisting of very little verbal dialogue, with almost no discernible sets or decorations and only occasional stage action, his plays focus on the postmodern topics of failure of communication and the inherent artificiality of all existence. *Talem* (pr. 1990; *Fourplay*, 2000) literally circles around a bed, the only prop on an otherwise barren stage. Two couples each try to persuade the other to make use of this bed, and in thirty-eight scenes all possible permutations among the characters, who use trickery and charade in order to accomplish this goal, are explored. As such, *Talem* is representative of the minimalist plays that have sprung up as a relatively inexpensive alternative to the obstacles of getting an original Spanish play staged at the major playhouses.

This turn toward the experimental, abstract play for a rarefied yet intellectually influential audience has not been without its critics. Since the 1980's, Spanish plays that are performed have become less political and socially engaged, and the near worldwide collapse of Marxism has further undermined traditionally left-wing dramatic themes and approaches. Audiences seem to favor either lavish foreign productions or plays that emphasize performance and production values over the written text. Ironically, the experimental plays performed at *los alternativos*, the small art houses, contribute toward the trend of extra-linguistic spectacle and multimedia approaches, to the detriment of text-based drama. With little emphasis on meaningful dialogue and an understanding that verbal discourse is inherently artificial, the plays of Belbel and his circle are perceived as yet another threat to the demanding, text-based Spanish play.

Exemplary of this threat is the situation of Concha Romero. She has seen the commercial production of only her first play, *Un color a ambar* (pb. 1983; the color of amber), which features the semi-comical struggle for the remains of Santa Teresa de Jesus in

sixteenth century Spain. A witty and crafty allegory on the multiple demands placed on women in Spanish society, which ends with the literal dismemberment of the corpse of the female saint, the play was widely acclaimed. Yet Romero's subsequent plays have not seen any performance apart from small university productions and have failed to find a viable audience. In turn, Romero has moved toward writing movies, scripting television series, and teaching.

The movement to outlets beyond the theater has been typical for many contemporary Spanish playwrights. Many intellectually ambitious dramatists of the generation born between 1960 and 1970, like Luisa Canille, Juan Mayorga, Antonio Onetti, Itziar Pascual Sanchez, and Margarita Sanchez Roldan, have also worked in film or television, or doubled as critics or lecturers. Yet many of the plays that are performed in Spain are deemed undemanding in terms of time and cost spent toward their production: They have often lost any Spanish flavor in the obvious attempt to make them more palatable to a lucrative global audience.

By 2002, many critics of Spanish theater longed for a return to the intellectually distinguished, dialogue-based drama that relied less on spectacle, performance, and special multimedia effects. What is desired is the work of serious, professional playwrights who need a venue for their productions and an audience to sustain them. If audiences return to such productions, the longed-for revival of Spanish drama might happen.

BIBLIOGRAPHY

Brown, J., ed. *Women Writers of Contemporary Spain: Exiles in the Homeland.* Cranbury, N.J.: Associated University Press, 1991. Contains brief entries on major women dramatists of the twentieth century, with good overviews of their lives and creative output.

Bryan, T. Avril. *Censorship and Social Conflict in the Spanish Theater.* Washington, D.C.: University Press of America, 1982. Detailed description of the conflict between the *posibilistas* and *imposibilistas* and their divergent attitude toward state censorship during the Franco regime. While focused primarily on Alfonso Sastre, the book is valuable for its discussion of the general conflict between theater and government under fascism.

Cook, John A. *Neoclassical Drama in Spain*. Dallas: Southern Methodist University Press, 1974. Still one of the best and most thorough studies of Spanish drama under the Bourbon monarchy, who tried to reshape Spanish theatrical tastes to their own liking. Good overview of the actual practice of performing plays during this period.

Edwards, Gwynne. *Dramatists in Perspective: Spanish Theater in the Twentieth Century*. New York: St. Martin's Press, 1985. Still useful, especially for the earlier parts of the 1900's. Accessible overview featuring the lives and works of major dramatists. Also provides background of the social, historical, and intellectual forces shaping Spanish theater up to the first decade after Franco's death.

Ganelin, Charles. *Rewriting Theatre: The Comedia and the Nineteenth-Century "Refundiciones."* Lewisburg, Pa.: Bucknell University Press, 1994. Close look at the adaptations of the theater plays of the Golden Age in the 1800's. Also talks about the general problems of revitalizing a national theater through a return to its best previous works. Overall sympathetic review of the issue, with good discussions of individual plays.

Gies, David Thatcher. *Theater and Politics in Nineteenth Century Spain*. Cambridge, England: Cambridge University Press, 1988. Revealing look at the interplay of political issues and dramatic responses. Focus is on Juan Grimaldi, who worked as both a theater manager and a government agent.

_____. *Theater in Nineteenth-Century Spain*. Cambridge, England: Cambridge University Press, 1994. Comprehensive study of the era, with many useful discussions of individual dramatists and their most important works. Scholarly, with superb references.

Halsey, Martha T. *From Dictatorship to Democracy: The Recent Plays of Buero Vallejo*. Ottawa, Ont.: Dovehouse Editions Canada, 1994. Thoughtful discussion of the life and work of this crucial dramatist who managed to have his plays performed under Franco by hiding some of his radicalism, and who remained a celebrated playwright once Spanish theater tastes shifted in the post-Franco democracy. Also mentions actions and fates of other playwrights.

Halsey, Martha T., and Phyllis Zatlin, eds. *The Contemporary Spanish Theater: A Collection of Critical Essays*. Lanham, Md.: University Press of America, 1988. Contains many specialized essays dealing with individual playwrights, plays, or theater movements and issues.

McClelland, Ivy Lilian. *Spanish Drama of Pathos, 1750-1808*. 2 vols. Toronto, Ont.: University of Toronto Press, 1970. Long considered the standard work on the time period. Ends with the Napoleonic conquest of Spain, which also altered dramatic sensibilities.

Martin Gaite, Carmen. *Love Customs in Eighteenth Century Spain*. Translated by Maria C. Tomsich. Berkeley: University of California Press, 1991. Includes a perceptive discussion of the theme of love in Spanish plays of the period. Occasionally a bit theoretical, but excellent on the subject.

Parker, Mary, ed. *Modern Spanish Dramatists*. Westport, Conn.: Greenwood Press, 2002. Comprehensive portraits of thirty-three playwrights, with full bibliography of their work, and a useful introduction to Spanish theater in the modern period.

Peak, J. Hunter. *Social Drama in Nineteenth Century Spain*. Chapel Hill: University of North Carolina Press, 1964. Still one of the best works in English on this period. Study of individual playwrights and their output. Credits the Romantic period with bringing social issues to the stage and focuses on the rebellious attitude of the High Comedy dramatists.

Zatlin-Boring, Phyllis. *Cross-Cultural Approaches to Theatre: The Spanish-French Connection*. Metuchen, N.J.: Scarecrow Press, 1994. Excellent discussion of the fate and impact of the Spanish dramatists who, like Fernando Arrabal, chose French exile over life under Franco. Also discusses the staging of forbidden Spanish plays in France and their cultural impact there and internationally.

Frank P. Casa,
updated by R. C. Lutz

WORLD
DRAMA

PRIMITIVE DRAMA

In virtually every culture, drama—both Western and non-Western—seems to have evolved from religious practice. However, because primitive drama came into being during prehistory, its precise forms are not well documented and must be studied through the anecdotes and legends that eventually led to each society's transcribed literary history.

Drama, even the secular drama of the present day, resembles a religious ceremony in a number of ways. Both the religious service and the play are ritualistic. The communicants participate in the service largely through the performance of an intermediary, a priest or preacher. The members of the audience also participate in the play through the performance of intermediaries, the actors. As the service features music, so the play often features music (song and dance appear to have provided the bulk of most primitive drama). Finally, the play demands of the playgoers a certain act of faith. The audience knows that what they are seeing on the stage is not literally true but they willingly suspend their disbelief for the duration of the performance to experience whatever intellectual or emotional pleasure the play provides.

It is interesting to note that when the Roman Empire collapsed in the fifth century C.E., the highly developed, sophisticated drama produced by the Greeks and Romans utterly disappeared. When, after an absence of nearly five hundred years, a crude drama gradually reappeared in Europe, it was in the liturgy of the medieval church.

GREEK DRAMA

The infancy of Greek drama can be traced to the sixth century B.C.E, perhaps earlier. The Greeks chose to honor the god Dionysus, also known as Bacchus and Iacchos, by establishing an annual festival dedicated to his worship. This Greater Dionysia was celebrated in March and was eventually followed by a second festival in Dionysus's honor, the Lenaea ("wine press"), held in the winter. The popularity of this "God of many names" among the ancient Greeks is understandable. His mother was Semele, a mortal princess seduced by Zeus. He was associated especially with wine and fecundity. It is believed that huge phalli were prominently featured at the Dionysia. Maenads (sometimes called bacchantes), female devotees of Dionysus, danced frantically at the god's feasts. According to legend, these priestesses would race over the countryside in a sexual frenzy, even snatching up and biting the heads off small animals.

The earliest festivals featured a large chorus of singers and dancers. The term "orchestra" is derived from a Greek word that means "dancing place." The first evolution of the chorus produced a leader. An exchange of speech, song, or chanting between leader and chorus was then possible. The chorus dressed as goats (an animal believed sacred to Dionysus) or as satyrs (a mischievous, lecherous mythical half-goat, half-human companion of the god). In fact, the word "tragedy"—a dramatic form central to the Dionysia—is derived from the Greek word *tragos*, meaning "goat." The wild and emotional choric hymn, composed in an elevated style and sung to the music of the flute, was called a dithyramb.

In 534 B.C.E (some scholars argue for a later date, 501 B.C.E.), tragedies were introduced as a part of the Greater Dionysia. Credit for the creation of the first truly dramatic production has been attributed to Thespis, who may have been a real person or may be purely legendary. The little that is known of Thespis is found in the accounts of others, perhaps unreliable. He, or someone, conceived of a performer existing apart from the chorus and its leader. This performer could pose questions for the members of the chorus, could be questioned by them, and could perhaps challenge assertions made in their lyrics. The appearance of this performer in the orchestra along with the chorus created the first absolute dramatic form in the Dionysian festivals. Thespis, whose name comes from a word meaning "divinely speaking" or from a similar word meaning "divinely singing," is honored as the first writer-director-composer-choreographer-actor in Greek drama. With the introduction of the first actor, the primitive period of Greek drama concluded and the era of high drama began. It is fitting that actors are still called "thespians" in honor of the first true Western dramatist.

EGYPTIAN DRAMA

The cult of Osiris and Isis proved important in the development of early Egyptian drama occurring around 2000 B.C.E. The first Greek historian, Herodotus, who traveled widely throughout the Middle East during his lifetime (c. 484-425 B.C.E.), wrote that Isis, goddess of the Moon, and Osiris, god of the Sun, were the only gods worshiped by all the Egyptians. Because a common practice of the Greeks and Romans was to identify the gods of other peoples with their own, Herodotus referred to Isis as Selene (one name for the Greek goddess of the Moon) and her husband as Osiris Dionysus. Herodotus also associated Isis with Demeter, Greek goddess of agriculture and fertility, because swine were sacrificed to both. He particularly identified Osiris with Dionysus because their festivals agreed exactly, except for the matter of choruses and the substitution of eighteen- to twenty-two-inch-long sex toys for the huge Dionysian phalli. Herodotus appeared to suggest that Osiris and Isis were once human rulers of Egypt; that Osiris was slain by Seth, Egyptian god of evil; that his widow and son, Horus, eventually avenged his death and secured the throne of Egypt; that the virtues and sufferings of Osiris and Isis changed them into gods; and that Osiris rose from the dead.

Greek authors allude to dramatic performances in honor of Osiris but give little detailed information. Fortunately, a recovered ancient stele, an engraved stone pillar, bears an inscription giving a brief account of the world's first recorded "passion play" as performed annually at Abydos, the city in which Osiris was entombed and to which Egyptians made pilgrimages, thus creating a cult of the deified king. Ikhernofret, a royal representative, was apparently responsible for organizing the performance, and he listed the parts he himself acted, some thirteen in number, on the stele. The play dramatizes at length the saga of Osiris in many elaborate scenes performed during a long progress to the symbolic tomb

from which the man-god would arise. Whereas the Greek plays lasted hours at most, Ikhernofret's description suggests that the passion play extended through several weeks. Some version of the passion plays continued to be performed until sometime around 500 B.C.E. The stele inscription is proof that more than forty centuries ago, the passion plays of Abydos were a vibrant part of Egyptian life.

INDIAN DRAMA

The tradition of Indian drama is ancient and has mythical origins. Bharata Muni's *Nāṭya-śāstra* (between 200 and 300 C.E.; *The Nāṭya shāstra*, 1950) describes the legendary ancient creation of theater. The text notes that when the world passed from the Golden Age to the Silver Age, people began to lose their innocence and develop vicious practices. The Hindu god Indra asked Brahmā, the creator of the universe, to give all the people a diversion from their vices. The four Vedas, the sacred books of Hinduism, were forbidden to the lower caste, so Brahmā fashioned another Veda from the elements of speech, song, mime, and sentiment. This Veda was the *Nāṭyaveda*. When Indra reported that no god possessed the requisite dramatic skill to use the holy book effectively, Brahmā taught the art of dramaturgy to the great sage Bharata so that he might popularize the Veda. He, in turn, taught it to his hundred sons. Thus, tradition has it that the celestial *Nāṭyaveda* was brought from heaven to earth for the moral improvement of the people.

In *The Nāṭya shāstra*, Bharata consolidated and codified earlier traditions in dance, mime, and drama. No other ancient book matches the comprehensive study of dramaturgy found in Bharata's work. The treatise provides exhaustive notes on production and direction. It furnishes every conceivable detail of makeup, costumes, colors, and jewelry. It directs the players' body postures, styles of gait, and movements of the neck, breast, and eyeballs. It states a theory of aesthetics and analyzes how various sentiments should be portrayed.

As in Greek drama, the playwright, the director, and the actor were inseparable in Hindu drama. However, the two forms of theater differed both physically and temperamentally. Whereas an audience of twenty thousand might witness a play in the Athenian amphitheater, the Hindu theater barely accommodated four hundred spectators. The unities of time, place, and action—developed rather early in Greek drama—were unknown in Hindu drama. Unknown also was the concept of tragedy, for the hero of a Hindu play triumphs over all obstacles. The plays were a mixture of prose and verse and were performed in Sanskrit, the classical literary language of India, except for characters of low birth who spoke Prakrit, a vernacular tongue. Sanskrit plays open with the *nandi*, a few lines of verse in praise of the gods. Then the Sutradhara and his wife enter. He serves as a sort of commentator on the place and action, analogous to the Greek chorus. Greek influence filtered into India during the third century B.C.E., but the Hindu drama was already highly evolved by that time.

CHINESE AND JAPANESE DRAMA

Evidence is found in the earliest Chinese history of the mimetic art of shamans, important precursors to Chinese theater. A shaman was a priest or intermediary who could, so it was believed, invoke and communicate with spirits and gods. His special powers were revealed through a performance combining singing, dance, gesture, posture, and costume. According to Confucius (551-479 B.C.E.), shamans were practicing in China as early as the third millennium B.C.E. During the Tang dynasty (618-907 C.E.)—an era known for the flourishing of the arts—Emperor Ming Huang (685-762 C.E.) founded imperial music and drama academies, where several hundred boys and girls were trained to sing and play instruments for the amusement of the court. The emperor was said to have tutored the young performers himself in the Pear Garden of the Imperial Park at Changan (later Xian). Acrobatics became as much a part of the performance as costume and makeup. More mature Chinese dramas did not arise until the thirteenth century. However, most traditional Chinese drama could be called opera, for not until the twentieth century would a Chinese audience consider a piece to be theater without music or singing of some kind.

The origins of Japanese drama lie in the sacred dances, religious ceremonials, and folk dances of an-

cient times. The oldest of these dances was *kagura*, associated with the legend of the Japanese sun goddess. In the seventh century, *gigaku*, a processional dance play in which masks were used, was adapted from a Chinese dance form. As the twelfth century approached, *bugaku*, of Chinese, Hindu, and Korean origins, superseded *gigaku* as a popular court entertainment and as a Buddhist ritual dance. It was replaced, in turn, by the *dengaku*, a simpler and more acrobatic form of entertainment favored by the general public. Arising at the same time was the *sarugaku*, which began as a comic, mimic dance, then developed into more serious forms. These dances eventually resolved themselves into separate techniques. For example, the *sarugaku* was refined in such a way that it became the basis of the Nō drama, which was perfected by the fourteenth century Buddhist priest Kan'ami Motokiyo and his son Zeami Motokiyo. The perfection of the Nō theater laid a solid foundation for the eventual development of the highly stylized Kabuki, which arose in the early seventeenth century.

BIBLIOGRAPHY

Arlington, L. C. *The Chinese Drama from the Earliest Times Until Today.* 1930. Reprint. Bronx, N.Y.: Benjamin Blom, 1966. Arlington traces the origins of drama in China. He describes its actors (in both male and female roles), the costumes and makeup, superstitions and stage slang, and accompanying music and musical instruments.

Fey, Faye Chunfang. *Chinese Theories of Theater and Performance from Confucius to the Present.* Ann Arbor: University of Michigan Press, 1999. Provides a historical overview of four major periods in Chinese theatrical history, starting with antiquity and ending with the twentieth century. Much of the analysis is presented in English for the first time.

Gargi, Balwant. *Theatre in India.* New York: Theatre Arts Books, 1962. The first two chapters, "The Birth of Theatre" and "Greek and Hindu Theatre," are the most valuable for understanding early theater. The chapters "Classical Dance" and "Folk Dance" are also of some interest.

Ley, Graham. *A Short Introduction to the Ancient Greek Theater.* Chicago: University of Chicago Press, 1993. Explores the original conditions of production for tragedies, comedies, and satyr plays in ancient Greece and provides observations on all aspects of performance.

Mackerras, Colin, ed. *Chinese Theater from Its Origins to the Present Day.* Honolulu: University of Hawaii Press, 1995. Examines the documented performances associated with shamanism as early as the third millennium B.C.E.

Mehta, Tarla. *Sanskrit Play Production in Ancient India.* Columbia, Mo.: South Asia Books, 1995. Provides a good introduction to the history of Sanskrit drama in India.

Pickard-Cambridge, Sir Arthur Wallace. *Dithyramb, Tragedy, and Comedy.* Special ed. Oxford, England: Clarendon Press, 1997. Reissue of a valuable work that traces the choric component of Greek drama from the dithyramb, the wildly emotional hymn in honor of Dionysus.

Ridgeway, William. *The Dramas and Dramatic Dances of Non-European Races in Special Reference to the Origin of Greek Tragedy, with an Appendix on the Origin of Greek Comedy.* Cambridge, England: Cambridge University Press, 1915. Reprint. New York: Benjamin Blom, 1964. Although this scholarship is obviously not recent, it is impeccably thorough. Ridgeway chronicles the origins of drama in Greece, Western Asia, ancient Egypt, Java, Burma, the Malay Peninsula, Cambodia, China, Japan, the Indian and Pacific Oceans, Australia, Africa, and America.

Scott, A. C. *The Kabuki Theatre of Japan.* London: George Allen & Unwin, 1955. Although Scott focuses on Kabuki rather than primitive drama, in one chapter, he outlines the origins of Japanese drama and describes similarities to the origins of Chinese drama.

Wiles, David. *Tragedy in Athens: Performance Space and Theatrical Meaning.* New York: Cambridge University Press, 1999. A study of the development of the orchestra, the *skene*, and other constituent parts of the Greek theater.

Wise, Jennifer. *Dionysus Writes: The Invention of Theatre in Ancient Greece.* Ithaca, N.Y.: Cornell University Press, 1998. Examines sixth century B.C.E. Greek theater and traces the roots of modern Western theater to this era.

Zimmerman, Bernhard. *Greek Tragedy: An Introduction.* Baltimore, Md.: Johns Hopkins University Press, 1991. A primer that is well characterized by its title.

Patrick Adcock

POSTCOLONIAL THEATER

Postcolonial theater is drama that focuses on issues surrounding oppressed peoples. A major current of mid- to late twentieth century history was the decolonization of English, French, Dutch, and British empires, and the emergence of talented and exciting playwrights from these cultures has been significant. Postcolonial literature and theater deal with the question of the "subaltern" finding his voice. A subaltern is a person in a subordinate position, and the term has come to refer to anyone who fights the process and results of colonialism. In examining many different postcolonial voices, one can see many of the difficult issues raised—including the intersections of nationalism, identity, and race—and discern the ways in which many of the leading postcolonial playwrights have chosen to deal with these issues.

RECLAIMING IDENTITY AND CULTURE

One of the main actions of the colonial powers was the disruption and replacement of indigenous culture. Frantz Fanon, the great postcolonial theorist and "freedom fighter" in the Algerian independence movement in the 1950's, felt that the goal of French colonization was the creation of "black Frenchmen" who were one step lower on the social scale than whites. For example, Fanon describes how, growing up in the French colony of Martinique (he later moved to Algeria), he never heard of writers such as Martinique's poet and playwright Aimé Césaire but studied and learned all the French classics and spoke only French, thus participating in an educational system that slowly and effectively marginalized African cultural references. This pattern of acculturation was repeated throughout the colonized world, from Australia to India and Africa.

Postcolonial playwrights, therefore, have served not only as playwrights of protest but also as figures resisting the colonization of their native cultures. In some cases, where the process of acculturation has been thorough, postcolonial plays have revealed elements of culture destroyed by the colonizers. Cultural revival serves as a powerful force in the establishment and creation of independent nationhood. By exploring the indigenous myths of a place and people before the arrival of Western culture, postcolonial playwrights have attempted to aid in the reclamation of cultural memory and to assert the colonized peoples as legitimate and historical communities, that is, as true nations.

A sense of nationhood is also deeply connected to the idea of racial identity. In many instances of colonialism, issues of race are pushed to the forefront and used as a tool of subjugation by the colonizers. For some playwrights and theorists, the quest for their own racial and cultural identity supersedes the quest for nationhood. For these writers, the desire to assert their humanity after decades of oppression becomes one of the dominant themes in their work. Nonwhite playwrights might feel that they must prove their worth to the world, which often tends to identify them as less important than their counterparts of European ancestry.

REINVENTING THEATRICAL CONVENTIONS

The emergence of playwrights from formerly colonized countries has introduced a host of issues to the theatrical world. For one thing, playwrights have been forced to choose whether or not they will write in their indigenous language or in the language of the colonizer. This has been a sensitive topic because some postcolonial playwrights insist that to write in the language of the colonizer is implicitly to endorse the actions of colonization. Others, having trained in the language of the colonizer, find its use revolutionary. They claim that writing in the language of the oppressors liberates the language and allows their message to spread beyond a localized audience.

These playwrights have also had to wrestle with issues of performance and style. Many postcolonial authors have chosen to reject the realistic or conventional play format of the colonizer and have instead turned to ancient or indigenous performance forms such as dance (either tribal or religious), religious ritual, song, puppetry, and mime. In addition, they avoid the dominant two- or three-act structure. Often, their plays can take the form of performance pieces with audience interaction or short staccato scenes depicting colonized life. Many postcolonial authors use the colonizer's forms of drama to turn the work back on the oppressor. Many playwrights also use ancient myths of their people and incorporate them into drama, to comment on a current political situation. Still other playwrights, such as Césaire, use Western classics such as those by the Greeks or by William Shakespeare. They transform the plays or recast them in order to make direct political commentaries. In addition, the transformation of Western classics allows the playwright to show how his or her country has been transformed through Western acculturation.

Finally, one of the key issues that postcolonial playwrights have to deal with is the issue of audience. When the struggle for decolonization is going on, many playwrights write work that is directly political in nature, and many write agitprop dramas to rally support for the political cause. However, once liberation has been achieved, questions can arise regarding the playwright's intended audience. Some have faced claims that they are too exclusionary, writing only for their own people, while other playwrights have faced charges that they have "sold out" their own culture for the consumption of the rest of the world.

THE AFRICAN EXPERIENCE

The Berlin Conference of 1884-1885 carved up the African continent (with the notable exceptions of Ethiopia and Liberia) among the European powers. After World War II, independence swept the continent as colonizers relinquished their control. New nations emerged, albeit with the old colonial boundaries. These countries sometimes combined different mutually antagonizing societies under the control of one government, creating tremendous instability and violence. Out of these newly formed and struggling nations emerged several leading playwrights.

In South Africa, in particular, the birth of nationhood did not end the oppression of the indigenous peoples. The state system of apartheid disenfranchised the nonwhite majority in favor of a ruling white minority. Many white South Africans joined the black majority in protest of this system. Playwrights also joined in this effort. Among the best known is Athol Fugard, a white South African who was censored for working with the Circle Players, a mixed-race theater company, as well as with the black South African actors John Kani and Winston Ntshona. Fugard's popularity grew until he was known worldwide, and many view him as the dominant anti-apartheid theatrical voice in South Africa. Some of his best-known plays include *Sizwe Bansai Is Dead* (pr. 1972), *The Island* (pr. 1973), *"MASTER HAROLD" . . . and the Boys* (pr. 1982), and *My Children! My Africa!* (pr. 1990).

Another South African postcolonial playwright of note is Maishe Maponya, who was born in the Johannesburg township of Alexandra in 1951. Maponya, a black South African, began his writing career while working as a clerk and then became involved with the Medupi Writers Association. After the government in 1977 banned the Writers Association, Mapoyna formed the Bahumutsi Drama Group, which produced many of his plays but also endured forms of censorship from the government. Maponya's works are heavily influenced by Bertolt Brecht's theories of social drama and tend to be more overtly political than those of Fugard. His best-known works include *Dirty Work* (pr. 1985), *Gangsters* (pr. 1985), and *The Valley of the Blind* (pr. 1987).

Another African nation whose drama flourished after independence was Nigeria. After Nigeria gained its independence from Great Britain in 1960, many of its native writers turned to the ancient rituals and performance rites of the indigenous Yoruban culture to inform their writings. One playwright who did so is Wole Soyinka, who writes about the collision between modern and traditional cultures. Some of his best-known works are *Lion and the Jewel* (pr. 1959) and *Death and the King's Horseman* (pr. 1976), and he was awarded the Nobel Prize in Literature in 1986. Another popular and critically praised Nigerian writer is Femi Osofisan, who has written plays that deal directly with the effects of colonization upon local culture and history.

ASIA

Asia, as a vast continent, consists of many different cultures and countries. Despite the presence of Asian indigenous performance forms since classical times, many Asian cultures were nonetheless conquered and subsumed by Western colonialism. Although colonial experiences and circumstances vary widely in South and Southeast Asia, the Philippines, and China, these areas all share similar concerns regarding the influence of Western imperialism on Eastern culture.

India has taken the lead in producing colonial and postcolonial drama that is critical of its colonizers. Before being colonized, India had numerous performance forms, including Sanskrit performance and *kathākali* dance drama. After the removal of British rule in the mid-twentieth century, Indians had to confront the way in which imperialism had blended a widely diverse population of the subcontinent into one single nation. One of the leading playwrights who deals with these issues is Girish Karnad. Karnad's early work was derived from ancient stories in Indian classics such as the *Mahābhārata* (c. 400 B.C.E.-400 C.E.; *The Mahabharata of Krishna-Dwaipayana Vyasa*, 1887-1896; also known as *The Mahabharata*), which he transformed to comment on the modern political climate. His work continues to explore the intersections of ancient Indian culture and the modern world. One of his best-known plays is *Hayavadana* (pr. 1972), which incorporates an ancient Indian form of theater known as *yakshagana* and brings forth intertwined plots to comment on the nature of reality and questions of identity.

NORTH AMERICA

North American postcolonial expression can be found in the work of the indigenous peoples displaced by European settlers moving across the continent. These writers address issues such as complete acculturation and the loss of land that they and their ancestors endured. Like many oppressed people, these writers face issues of assimilation versus acceptance of the dominant settler culture. In Canada, Tomson Highway has emerged as a strong voice for the First Peoples population with plays such as *The*

Rez Sisters (pr. 1986) and *Dry Lips Oughta Move to Kapuskasing* (pr. 1989). These plays explore the troubles and triumphs of life on government reservations and often use indigenous spirits as characters to further the plots.

AUSTRALIA

Like Highway, Jack Davis, a Western Australian-born Aborigine, was concerned with issues of assimilation among the Aborigines of Australia, whose story of land loss and cultural destruction mirrors those of the indigenous peoples of North America. Davis taught himself to read and write while growing up outside Perth, Australia, in the 1920's. He was both a political and a literary figure and known for his poetry as well as his drama. His most famous work, *No Sugar* (pr. 1985), dramatizes his personal recollections of the forced movement of his Aboriginal community to the Moore River Native Settlement and how these resettlements contribute to the destruction of Aboriginal culture.

SOUTH AMERICA AND THE CARIBBEAN

Postcolonial work in South America is often written not only in response to conventional Western imperialism but also against repressive political regimes, often instituted with the help of Western countries, and as such, considered by some as "neocolonial" tools to propagate Western power. Writers such as Griselda Gambaro of Argentina chronicle South America's unfortunate history of political repression and its effects. In her play *Información para extranjeros* (wr. 1971; *Information for Foreigners*, 1992), Gambaro uses environmental theater techniques to engage her audience members individually with the process and isolation of state terror.

Writers in the Caribbean had many of the same concerns as postcolonial writers in Africa and Asia. Specifically, writers such as Césaire and the West Indian playwright Derek Walcott have blended island culture with Western literature and stories.

EUROPE

Although many would claim that Europe has been the colonizer and not the colonized, several oppressed cultures in Europe have developed their own playwrights with unique voices. Many scholars contend that the work of Irish and Eastern European playwrights can be examined under the lens of postcolonial theory.

The island of Ireland has a long history of oppression from its British neighbors. Although the differences and tensions between the British and Irish have been the subject of many plays, the mid- to late twentieth century explosion of the "troubles" in Northern Ireland led to a great deal of reactionary and revolutionary writing. Notable among these contributions are those of Brian Friel, who founded the Field Day Theatre Company in 1980 with writer Seamus Heaney and actor Stephen Rea, among others. Friel's plays are concerned with the disruption and dissolution of Irish identity in the face of English acculturation and the transformation of that culture in the modern world. Among his best-known works are *Translations* (pr. 1980) and *Dancing at Lughnasa* (pr. 1990).

As the Irish have been oppressed with the troubles in Northern Ireland, so too have the people of Eastern Europe suffered under the yoke of communist totalitarianism during the latter half of the twentieth century. Out of this situation emerged playwrights of resistance such as Czechoslovakia's Václav Havel and Poland's Sławomir Mrożek. Although these writers emerged from different cultures and have different styles, their work reflects a shared concern over the effects of political domination on an individual's psyche and identity.

BIBLIOGRAPHY

Ashcroft, Bill, Gareth Griffiths, and Helen Tiffin, eds. *The Post-Colonial Studies Reader.* London: Routledge, 1995. Complete and thorough collection of essays dealing with a host of issues surrounding postcolonial theory. Essays by almost every major postcolonial literary theorist. The book has sections dealing with topics such as identity, hybridity, history, and language. Amazingly useful and complete, this is a wonderful resource for anyone interested in the basic texts of postcolonial literary theory.

Fanon, Frantz. *The Wretched of the Earth.* Translated by Constance Farrington. New York: Grove Press, 1963. A seminal postcolonial text, this book applies concepts such as materialism, identity construction, colonialism, and racism to the decolonization of Africa. Fanon stresses the need to replace the false identities of colonialism with new structures of nationhood.

Gandhi, Leela. *Postcolonial Theory: A Critical Introduction.* New York: Columbia University Press, 1998. Broad overview of the structures, ideas, and contexts of postcolonial theory, with extensive discussions of such influential writers as Edward Said, Homi Bhabha, and Frantz Fanon. The book has several sections on relationships between postcolonialism and other literary theories such as feminism, poststructuralism, and Marxism.

Gilbert, Helen, ed. *Postcolonial Plays: An Anthology.* London: Routledge, 2001. Excellent anthology containing several well- and lesser-known dramas, with selections from such playwrights as Femi Osofian, Derek Walcott, and Girish Karnad. Plays range from Argentinian to Canadian to South African, and each play is marked by a discussion of both the dramatic work and the political situation in the author's homeland.

Said, Edward. *Orientalism.* New York: Vintage Books, 1979. Another seminal text from the postcolonial canon, this book explores how the West has created and marketed a fictionalized "Orient" for its own consumption. Said illustrates how this desire to control the "Exotic East" has led to the political and cultural clashes facing the world today.

David Jortner

Movements in Modern Drama

Before the remarkably sudden transformation of Western theater in the middle of the nineteenth century, the basic architectural and economic structures of theatrical entertainments had been securely in place for two hundred years. After the European patronage theater of the seventeenth century, theater operated for the pleasure of the elite and the middle class, surviving by gradually refining the Aristotelian laws, filtered through the common desire for fantasy and romance, until the well-made play dominated the stage and overpowered the creativity of theater artists.

Experimental theater was a reflection of a much larger revolution, articulated by political theorist Karl Marx, philosopher Friedrich Nietzsche, psychological pioneer Sigmund Freud, and evolutionary theorist Charles Darwin and manifested in the industrial and technological explosion of the mid-nineteenth century and in the accelerated social interchange brought on by modernized communications and transportation. As part of that revolution, theater artists moved away from the stale entertainments designed to please the masses toward an examination of large ideas and new theatrical forms with which to dramatize humanity's relationship to itself, to God, and to the natural world.

Naturalism

At first glance, naturalism appears to be not the experiment but the long-reigning tradition from which other kinds of experimentation departed. In fact, naturalism itself was probably the most innovative and daring movement ever to bring traditional Western art to its knees. Until the 1860's (except for the work of a few geniuses ahead of their time), theater was an artificial recitation of lines of usually poetic or overblown dialogue, staged with a minimum of attention to detail, in front of a generally flat series of paintings representing scenic elements of a universal nature: mansions, streets, hills, and forests only vaguely identified with the location of the play itself. It was as though humanity had never really looked at itself carefully, satisfied instead with the simplistic portraits drawn by religious leaders and monarchs in

their own self-interest. When Darwin and his contemporaries suggested that humans were part of a natural universe (hence the word "naturalism"), artists began to seek in their art the actual objects and ideas of the world around them. The abstractions of centuries gave way to the realistic appraisal of human choices limited only by physical laws. Working in tandem with developments in photography, art took on the elements of scientific inquiry: close attention to minute detail; categorization and cataloging of what is, rather than what should be; and an insistence on showing the real rather than the merely beautiful. Dramatically, this trend toward naturalism evolved into the presentation of everyday events, such as family gatherings; struggles for survival; typical days in the lives of normal, recognizable human beings; and the balanced discussion of social imperfections.

The latter tendency—discussion of social problems—earned for Henrik Ibsen the title "Father of Modern Drama." Ibsen, along with Anton Chekhov in Russia, August Strindberg in Sweden, and other leading playwrights, astounded the theatrical world with the controversial notion that real life, in all its tawdry detail, was worthy of theatrical exploration. Although in his early years Ibsen wrote his share of romantic and patriotic fantasy dramas, in his middle plays, he explored the dramatic possibilities of such socially volatile issues as women's rights, venereal disease, corruption in private enterprise, and the conflicts between scientific truth and the economic well-being of communities.

Stage design and technology, to accommodate the new drama, abandoned the perspective illusion of the wing-and-drop set in favor of the three-dimensional box set with realistic details of furniture and accessories. Thomas William Robertson, who introduced these revolutionary ideas to England, gave the name cup-and-saucer drama to his theater because he used real cups and saucers in his plays, such as *Caste* (pr. 1867). Realistic subject matter, steeped in natural, believable settings of everyday life, with believable dialogue accompanied by appropriate gestures and such paralinguistic supports as pauses and inflection, rather than the flamboyant gesticulation of the traditional stage—such innovations do not seem very experimental or revolutionary today, but in their time, they were considered to be the explosive destroyer of centuries of theatrical tradition.

Just as a new stagecraft was needed to bring the new drama to life, so a new acting style was required, one which examined the internal life of the characters in the same careful detail. Inroads were made by George II, duke of Saxe-Meiningen, and the Meiningen Players, who introduced the bold new ideas of ensemble playing, rehearsing in characters, and the organization of the aesthetic whole by a "director," who replaced the actor-manager, once the mainstay of the star system of popular theater. The Meiningen Players' tour of Europe (1874-1890) influenced all modern drama. Even more significant was the contribution of Konstantin Stanislavsky, whose work with the Moscow Art Theatre is regarded as the origin of modern acting styles. Using the full-length portraits of decadent Russian aristocracy as depicted in the work of Chekhov, Stanislavsky's students probed the depths of human actions and reactions, building from the inside out the three-dimensional and complex characters that now stand at the pinnacle of great modern drama: Uncle Vanya, Trigorin, the Sisters Prozorov, and all the others.

SYMBOLISM AND DADA

Naturalism, however, was not without its detractors. Very early, in fact within a few years of Ibsen's successes with realistic drama, other artists saw its limitations and proposed several variations and departures from the purely photographic replication of life. The first objection came from the Symbolists, who maintained that another reality, universal and eternal, resided in common symbols—such as the rose, whiteness, and the sea—and could be revealed on the stage by the careful manipulation of the collective unconscious through the interweaving of the objective correlatives to abstract experience. In other words, Symbolist dramatists, like Symbolist poets, tried to speak of a higher existence than the temporal one, by dramatizing certain moments in human life

when universal experiences were recognized and shared. Maurice Maeterlinck, a Belgian playwright, wrote _Intérieur_ (pr. 1895; _Interior_, 1896), _L'Intruse_ (pr. 1891; _The Intruder_, 1891), and other short plays in which the moment of death was held transfixed on the stage long enough for the audience to recognize the common bond implied in their own mortality. In _Les Aveugles_ (pr. 1891; _Blind_, 1891), Maeterlinck showed how all humanity shares the failure to see or comprehend its purpose in the universe; the play deals with twelve blind persons lost in a forest, seeking a guide who does not appear.

Because by definition Symbolism was not interested in everyday life, it was a short-lived theatrical movement, although echoes of the philosophy can be heard in much of the subsequent realistic drama. Another short-lived but important experiment in the capacity of the stage to present something other than familiar reality was Dada, a movement that began as a cabaret experiment in Switzerland. The guiding spirit of Dada was the Romanian poet Tristan Tzara, who, in his 1924 manifesto, asserted that the first order of business for the new artist was to raze all existing structures, including logic itself, in order for a new world to be built on cleared ground. Consequently, the Dadas looked at reason and logic and proceeded to apply the direct opposite: If it was logical for a poet to read his work in a lecture hall, the Dada poet had his work read in a bathroom; if it was logical to choose a name for the movement that made sense, the Dadas chose their name at random and made up several stories about it. The essence of Dada's refusal to be logical is summed up in Tzara's manifesto: "In principle I'm against manifestoes, as I am also against principle." Besides Tzara's _Le Coeur à gaz_ (wr. 1921; _The Gas Heart_, 1964), other examples of these odd pieces are Guillaume Apollinaire's _Les Mamelles de Tirésias_ (pr. 1917; _The Breasts of Tiresias_, 1964) and Jean Cocteau's _Les Mâriés de la Tour Eiffel_ (pr. 1923; _The Wedding on the Eiffel Tower_, 1937).

SURREALISM AND FUTURISM

Emerging at approximately the same time as the Dada movement was Surrealism, born from the same artistic impulse to express something more than naturalism but founded in a more coherent manifesto, written by André Breton in 1924. Surrealism, as its name suggests, deals with a reality above the everyday and is closely associated with the peculiar logic of dreams. The Surrealists maintained that dreams are written in a higher language, one obfuscated by the five senses but allowed to emerge during sleep. The plays of Antonin Artaud, notably *Le Jet de sang* (pb. 1924; *The Jet of Blood*, 1963), are not simply nonlogical constructions but are rather attempts to rephrase the logic of the dream onstage. On the surface sharing much of Dada's disregard for concatenative, traditional plot and meaning, Surrealist theater has an order of its own, not always obvious to the viewer but based on a series of connections in the mind of the dreamer-playwright and expressed through the limitations of stage presentations. Thus, Artaud's play calls for hurricanes, crashing stars, pieces of human bodies, and an army of scorpions; Roger Vitrac's *Les Mystères de l'amour* (pr. 1927; *The Mysteries of Love*, 1964) includes beatings, shouts, gunshots, bloodstained clothes, and pieces of human flesh in a dresser drawer. Drawing their inspiration from Strindberg's *Ett drömspel* (pr. 1907; *A Dream Play*, 1912), which Strindberg wrote after his more realistic period of *Fadren* (pr. 1887; *The Father*, 1889) and *Dödsdansen, första delen* (pr. 1905; *The Dance of Death I*, 1912), the Surrealists did what they could to transform into reality the disjointed but strangely logical sequences of dreams.

One other brief but important experiment in the theater occurred soon after Chekhov's successes with naturalist drama: The Futurists of Italy, like their Dada counterparts, used the cabaret format to present very short, deliberately meaningless pieces with no unifying feature except the praise of technological innovation. The Italian movement, led by Filippo Tommaso Marinetti and his colleagues, is notable primarily because it foresaw the sweeping changes that such inventions as the airplane and electricity would have on art as well as on society.

EXPRESSIONISM

By far the most influential and long-reaching experimental variation on naturalism was the German

aesthetic known as expressionism. Here, the reality depicted is underneath the ordinary everyday; it is a reality seething with emotion and subjective responses just below the surface of social decency. The name, borrowed again from fine art, refers to the explosion, or expression, of something under pressure; in the artist's case, it is the sublimated id of Sigmund Freud and the suppressed passions of the masses held down by the elite.

Expressionism was the most successful stage development to compete with naturalism, because its physical manifestations were more direct and theatrical. The German playwrights Georg Kaiser and Ernst Toller developed the form into its most effective state: short, episodic structure and long monologues of internalized tension, followed by staccato half-sentences of dialogue that left a rhythm of broken order and chaos. Often, as with Kaiser's Gas trilogy (1917-1920), the "evil" force is represented by a piece of machinery, in this case a gas-manufacturing plant, which is destroyed in the process of the fight for liberation and freedom. The protagonists are presented as individuals in an otherwise regimented and suppressed society of stereotypes—the characters are usually named for their occupation or social status—who free themselves from the chains of conformity and precipitously destroy everything in the path of individuality.

Some early work of Bertolt Brecht is in the expressionist mold, notably *Baal* (pr. 1923; English translation, 1963), but his later work developed as an experimental excursion into the epic form, normally reserved for the novel and the saga. By "epic theater," Brecht meant a theater that presented itself as such, without attempting illusion, and that chronicled the ongoing struggle of the human race against those who would enslave it in a noncommunist state.

NEW IDEAS FOR SETS AND LIGHTING

European theater experimentation in scenography did not stop with the box set. Two visionaries in lighting and stagecraft transformed the stage into a sculpture of light and space: Adolphe Appia the theorist and Edward Gordon Craig the practitioner. Appia, a Swiss musician impressed with the new operas of Richard Wagner, published *La Mise en scène du drame Wagnérien* (1895; *Staging Wagnerian Drama*, 1982) and a number of other works, which set forth the artistic notion that the actor, the scenery, and the stage itself formed a painting of vertical and horizontal shapes. Lighting, according to Appia, fused the elements into a nonillusionistic series of moods, emotions, and action that could be manipulated, even orchestrated. Yet most of Appia's ideas remained in the theoretical stage, in notebooks, sketches, and drawings. Craig, who came from a theatrical family, worked independently of Appia and published *The Art of the Theatre* (1905) as an expression of his work for the stage in the first years of the twentieth century. His sets and lights helped popularize Eleonora Duse in Italy, and in 1912 he worked with the Moscow Art Theatre. Craig agreed with many of Appia's ideas but maintained that scenography was an art in itself, because the public went to see and not to hear a play. He advocated the *Übermarionette* approach to theatrical art, in which the actor was merely a puppet in the hands of the grand artist.

In Russia at about the same time, a student of Stanislavsky named Vsevolod Meyerhold began to depart from naturalism to seek more theatrical stage forms. In 1911, for example, in his staging of Molière's *Dom Juan: Ou, Le Festin de Pierre* (pr. 1665; *Don Juan*, 1755), Meyerhold deliberately exposed the scenic elements of the stage, removing the curtain, leaving the houselights on (as in the eighteenth century), and revealing the machinery of production to the audience. His approach to stagecraft, called Constructivism, featured the skeletons of the engineered set, with ramps, supports, railings, beams, and machinery visible as part of the formal statement of his art. Eventually condemned by the revolutionary government and banished from the theater, Meyerhold died in obscurity but left behind the challenge to naturalism that remains today in contemporary experimental theater in Europe and the United States.

Another experimental philosophy with long-lasting effects was the aesthetic statement of Artaud, whose Surrealist works were followed by a remarkable book titled *Le Théâtre et son double* (*The Theater and Its Double*, 1958), actually written in the 1920's but collected and published in 1938. Stemming from Surrealist ideas but combining Constructivism and expressionism at the same time, Artaud's stagecraft called for wildly innovative audience-stage arrangements, including one performance envisioned with the audience in the middle of a circular stage on which the action took place all around the audience. In 1914, such a performance was actually staged in a gymnasium of Columbia University. Artaud's ideas were never realized in his lifetime but influenced all the subsequent nonrealistic theater and film to follow.

THEATER OF THE ABSURD

After World War II, and partly in response to the devastation of modern weaponry, the philosophical notion of existentialism found its theatrical form in the Theater of the Absurd. More an experiment in the meaninglessness of art and life than a revolution in staging practice, Theater of the Absurd sought either to express or represent (or both) the chaos resulting from a belief in the absence of God and order. The existential philosophers Jean-Paul Sartre and Albert Camus wrote plays that were formally nonexperimental but whose characters faced existential and ontological conclusions.

More important to experimental theater were the playwrights Samuel Beckett and Eugène Ionesco, who found a theatrical equivalent to meaningless. In Beckett's *En attendant Godot* (pr. 1953; *Waiting for Godot*, 1954), two derelicts confront the pointlessness of their lives in a barren region visited only by a circuslike master and slave, and a small boy with a cryptic message that the derelicts should wait another day. Ionesco's *La Cantatrice chauve* (pr. 1950; *The Bald Soprano*, 1958) dramatizes the emptiness of language and the failure of humans to communicate given the loss of center and purpose in the existential world. Other absurdist writers, such as Arthur Adamov, Friedrich Dürrenmatt, and Fernando Arrabal, continued the exploration into the expression of meaninglessness, giving the stage its first real taste of postmodern, self-exposing theater.

GROTOWSKI'S "POOR THEATER"

After the absurdists, European experimental theater turned to a self-conscious theatricality in which every element of the actor-audience relationship was examined piece by piece in an effort to discover the center of the theatrical experience. During this period of cultural exchange between Europe and the United States, the single most important figure was Jerzy Grotowski, a Polish director and leader of the Polish Laboratory Theatre. Grotowski worked with his actors in a unique way: Drawing from the innocence and spontaneity of childhood, relying less on a script than on the natural improvisational imagination of the individual actor, Grotowski taught his actors to release the potential of their bodies and faces and voices, moving past the boundaries of simple representation into the masklike and almost grotesque "incorporation" of the character into the entire body. The extreme physicalization of the character, which required extensive training over a period of years, was a feature adopted by several other acting schools, and Grotowski's book *Możliwość teatru* (1962; *Towards a Poor Theatre*, 1968) became the acting and directing text for many experimental theaters in the United States and abroad. The term "poor theater" reflects Grotowski's belief that the actor-audience relationship does not require expensive and elaborate sets, lighting, makeup, or costuming, but that the actor alone, in an almost religious transformation, breathes in the life of the character and drama and guides the audience into it. The Polish Laboratory Theatre's *Akropolis* (pr. 1968; based on scenes from the play by Stanisław Wyspiański, pr. 1916) made use of Grotowski's theories and served as a model for experimental theaters, notably Peter Brook's company in England and the Open Theatre in the United States.

EUROPEAN AVANT-GARDE

European avant-garde theater in the 1970's and 1980's can be summed up in one major idea: the reexamination of theater forms by scrutinizing all aspects of the theatrical experience, from the actor-audience relationship, to the value of the text to performance, to the balance of presentational to representational action, to the incorporation of new technology in the theater versus bare-bones theater. Michael Kirby as editor of *The Drama Review* has gathered performance documentation from Europe and the United States in his book *The New Theatre* (1974).

Typical of the nonplotted theatrical presentation is the work of the Théâtre Laboratoire Vicinal of Brussels, an experimental company strongly influenced by Grotowski's Polish Laboratory Theatre. The pieces produced by this company require great physical strength and flexibility on the part of the players; in *Real Reel*, for example, an actor rolls with a large industrial spool and must contort his backbone to fit around the core of the spool. While the pieces are partially scripted and have some larger thematic reference, they find their theatricality in the "impersonal energy bordering on delirium" that the actors bring to each performance. The "props" of this kind of theatrical experiment are pipes, wheelbarrows, wheeled tables, and other products of a technological society that are rehumanized by the actors' presence and by the improvisational creativity that goes into their use. In environmental theater, real spaces are used as theatrical spaces, often transformed by huge ramps and scaffolds, reminiscent of Meyerhold's Constructivism; sometimes the audience is asked to move from room to room, as in Luca Ronconi's *XX* (pr. 1972) at the Théâtre de l'Odéon in Paris. Common to all experimental theater of the period was an essential disregard of the storytelling elements of theater in favor of the performance-dance aspect of the actor presenting himself or herself in the act of art.

Western European theater experiment can no longer be separated from a more universal artistic movement finding its voice in South America and the United States as well as in Eastern Europe and Asia. Modern-day experimenters have found an audience and a market of their own, no longer directly competing with the commercial theater or even the professional nonprofit regional theater. They have joined hands with the art of dance, and with the fine arts, so as to be almost indistinguishable, and they have toured other countries, exchanging ideas and methods freely. Peter Handke's experiments, such as *Der Ritt über den Bodensee* (pr. 1971; *The Ride Across Lake Constance*, 1972), marked a new direction for the experimental theater, because the script in essence was an experiment in "deconstruction," in which the language of the stage is examined for its parts and removed from its semantic and semiotic functions.

REEMERGENCE OF CHINESE THEATER

When Jiang Qing, wife of communist leader Mao Zedong, helped launch the Cultural Revolution in the People's Republic of China in 1966 (lasting until Mao's death in 1976), three thousand years of Chinese dramatic history were officially abolished. The one billion people of China were allowed to view only eight revolutionary Maoist model plays and attend Jiang's state-sponsored revolutionary operas. All other dramatic activity was banned, most theatrical companies were dissolved, and people involved in the theater were physically and psychologically humiliated, punished, subjected to harsh labor, jailed, and occasionally killed. Cultural life all but came to a standstill. A decade later, only the murderous Khmer Rouge of Pol Pot's Cambodia went further in its complete eradication of theater from the new communist society. From April, 1975, to January, 1979, under Khmer communist leader Pol Pot, all theatrical activity was forbidden in the country, and many performers, dramatists, and directors were among the more than one million victims of Cambodia's "killing fields."

After Jiang Qing's fall from power in October, 1976, theater began to revive in China. New theater companies attracted old talent who had managed to survive the revolution, and young people felt drawn to drama. Dramatic arts were taught at the universities again, and traditional forms, such as Beijing Opera, were revived with great success. New tragedies and comedies appeared, which were often set in the distant past but clearly reflected the Mao years. By the 1980's and 1990's, China's increasing openness to the West—which has enabled Chinese playwrights, performers, and theatrical staff to encounter European and American theater in theoretical and practical form—began to affect the production of traditional plays, indicating a cultural fusion. For example, Wei Minglun's *Pan Jinlian* (pr. 1986; English translation, 1993) has been called one of China's first absurdist plays. Combining the traditional form of

Sichuan opera and the traditional story of evil Jinlian with a modernist reinterpretation of her character as a victim of patriarchy, Wei's play crosses from China's imperial past to the communist present and includes the title character from Leo Tolstoy's *Anna Karenina* (1875-1877). Cultural fusion in drama sometimes produces strange ironies. In 1998, while Indian conductor Zubin Mehta directed Giacomo Puccini's opera *Turandot* (pr. 1926; English translation, 1926) to a Chinese elite in Bejing at ticket prices of $1,250, Wei Minglun's Zigong Chuanju (Sichuan Opera Troupe) performed his adaptation of the play, at $2 to $4 a ticket, at Zheng Xie Hall in the same city.

The fate of Gao Xingjian, the 2000 winner of the Nobel Prize in Literature, shows that life for dramatists in the Asian countries that have nominally remained communist continues to be uncertain. Although his *Chezan* (pr. 1983; *Bus Stop*, 1996), in which characters wait for ten years for a bus that never arrives, was lauded as China's answer to Samuel Beckett, *Bj' an* (wr. 1986, pr. 1989; *The Other Shore*, 1999) was forbidden to be performed in the People's Republic. Gao left China for France in 1987. After the Tiananmen Square massacre in 1989, he renounced his membership in the Communist Party and wrote a poignant play about the event, *Taowang* (pr. 1990; *Fugitives*, 1993). When the play was staged in Germany, the set depicted the Nazi era to make the point that political repression and totalitarianism are enemies of humanity everywhere.

THEATER AFTER THE SOVIET UNION'S FALL

The momentous events of 1989, which saw the fall of the Berlin Wall and the liberation of Eastern Europe from communist dictatorships, and those of 1991, which saw the formal dissolution of the Soviet Union, have dramatically affected the movement and direction of drama in the nations undergoing these drastic changes. Beginning in 1985, Soviet president Mikhail Gorbachev's policy of *glasnost*, or openness, allowed for a gradual easing of state censorship of culture, including drama. New plays critiquing the stagnant and repressive regimes in the East had managed to be produced. Drama reflected the popular dissatisfaction with socialist society. Yet while Gorbachev and other communist leaders had hoped for a gradual reform, the pent-up creative energies helped to sweep away the very regimes that had attempted to reduce repression. When the British rock group Pink Floyd performed *The Wall* in reunified Berlin in 1990, the atmosphere was that of a genuine people's theater.

After Eastern European and Russian theater's active participation of the events of 1989 and 1991, new challenges created seismic shifts in the theatrical landscape of these nations that would emerge by the early twenty-first century. The old system of generous public funding of state-approved cultural and theatrical activities has moved in the direction of a market economy, placing at least some burden on theater to contribute to its own economic viability. State budget cuts have threatened the survival of previously maintained theaters and professional companies. Theater management has had to change its production schedule away from a revival of old, political plays in the vein of Social Realism. If Eastern European and Russian playwrights and theatrical companies want to draw audiences for national plays, rather than relying on international revivals, they have to create works that contain local relevancy, have certain production values, and include some form of entertainment. In Russia, there has been the temptation to yield on the drawing power of the precommunist classics, in particular the plays of Chekhov. Yet the challenge to produce relevant contemporary plays attractive to the fresh tastes of a newly demanding audience remains significant.

THEATER FOR DEVELOPMENT

The 1990's and early 2000's saw a strong interest in using theater to help foster economic development, promote physical health, and facilitate social change in many areas of the developing world. In most areas, there was a shift away from the top-down political propaganda initially associated with this form in the 1970's. The new emphasis is on grassroots theater, which seeks to connect to real-life issues of an often rural or poor urban audience. Its proponents try to draw subject material, cast, and staff from the population whose issues the plays seek to address.

Although often funded by outside agencies such as those of the United Nations or nongovernmental agencies such as Medicines Sans Frontiers (Doctors Without Borders), the new theater for development stresses the involvement of local talent at all levels of creation, production, and performance of the plays. Although outside agents may foster and mentor local people, the ultimate decisions as to subject, script, and performance of the play rest with those who come from its intended audience. International and national professionals may invite local leaders and artists to share their ideas at workshops and discussion groups, identifying the need for professional training and assistance and assessing existing local resources and skill levels. Often, training a core of local talent works as a catalyst for the transmission of their new knowledge of dramatic skills, and their new perspectives and insights gained, back to other members of their community. The approach stresses the ideals of collective theater because it seeks to involve the whole community to create a theater genuinely emerging from grassroots concerns.

In Latin America, theater for development seeks to embrace dispossessed and rootless *campesinos*, or peasants, for example. Members of indigenous groups have used theater for development and popular theater to identify areas for improvement in their lives and to raise global awareness of the issues affecting them. Theater for development schemes have also been used in various coca-eradication programs, with mixed results. The Caribbean has long enjoyed the performances put on by the theatrical grassroots company Sistren, traditionally made up of working-class women. Sistren has toured North America and Britain, and its plays have influenced women of African descent in both areas.

By the early twenty-first century, one of the most important topics of African theater for development was national health in the light of the devastating HIV-AIDS epidemic. From Uganda to southern Africa, international health officials aid professional and amateur theatrical troupes to produce plays that seek to educate audiences about the risks of certain behaviors and to encourage responsible sexual practices. Health awareness plays are performed at local hospitals, village centers, converted cinemas, or open-air spaces supportive of a dramatic event, such as the hill country of Uganda. Many of these plays also seek to incorporate child players or puppetry to reach audiences of all ages.

Theater for development in Southeast Asia often focuses on environmental and economic issues. The early twenty-first century witnessed many developing countries, which recognized the dangers posed by unstopped environmental degradation, using drama to create a stronger ecological awareness among their communities. The huge wildfires covering parts of Malaysia and Indonesia in 2001 and the persistence of a "brown cloud" polluting the air over a huge area of Asia in the summers of the early twenty-first century motivated funding for plays and programs that promote alternative, less environmentally damaging behavior than the burning of forests for planting or the use of inefficient cooking fuel such as cow dung in India. In India, popular theater is also used by the underprivileged members of society, such as the former pariahs, or "untouchable" caste members of the state of Tamil Nadu, who have formed their own Association for the Rural Poor that regularly enacts plays concerning issues facing them in daily life.

THEATER IN THE ROUND

One of the most fundamental challenges to the actual performance of formal Western-style plays has been the emergence of theaters in the round, primarily in the United Kingdom. Based on an actual 1914 production at Columbia University and the theories of Artaud, theater in the round places audience members in a complete 360-degree circle around a central stage. Its proponents, such as Stephen Joseph, Alan Ayckbourn, and Peter Cheeseman in England, testify that this design allows for a more intimate relationship between the audience and the actors. In the early twenty-first century, there were several British professional theaters built to this design, including those at Scarborough, Manchester, Richmond, and Newcastle-under-Lyme, while many famous venues like London's Barbican Pit can be adapted to a "round" production.

Theater in the round does provide close seating for a large audience: The New Victoria at Newcastle-under-Lyme seats six hundred, for example and no seat is further than twenty-five feet away from the stage, compared with the huge distance of the remote seats at some of the United States' and Europe's largest professional theaters. The challenge is for the cast to act in the full space of the stage, sometimes with their backs to a significant part of the audience. Yet technological developments in sound and acoustics seem to have solved the sonic problems associated with such a performance to the satisfaction of British theatergoers. Sets do not have to be as minimal as the absence of a curtain and the need not to obstruct 360-degree views might indicate. By the late 1990's, Cheeseman had designed productions that included tennis courts and rivers on the "round" stage. Faced with the full challenges of technologically mediated forms of entertainment, from movies to television, rock concerts, and sports events, the theater in the round may prove itself as an innovative approach to highlight one of the persisting strengths of live theater, the close contact of the live human audience with individual people performing on a live stage.

BIBLIOGRAPHY

Barter, Enoch, and Ruby Cohn, eds. *Around the Absurd: Essays on Modern and Postmodern Drama.* Ann Arbor: University of Michigan Press, 1990. Useful collection of scholarly essays covering most aspects of the absurdist movement in Europe and America. Focus is often on theory and actual performance of absurd plays. Bibliography and index.

Byam, L. Dale. *Community in Motion: Theatre for Development in Africa.* Westport, Conn.: Bergin and Garvey, 1999. Excellent overview of theory and practice of this dramatic movement. Includes a perceptive foreword by Kenya's exiled playwright Ngugi wa Tiong'o, who tells of his firsthand experience. Bibliography and index.

Chen, Xiaomei. *Acting the Right Part: Political Theater and Popular Drama in Contemporary China.* Honolulu: University of Hawaii Press, 2002. Brilliant study of Chinese drama in the post-Mao era.

Strong focus on Chinese dramatic traditions, popular drama, and the role of the community in drama. Bibliography and index.

Davis, Tony. *Stage Design*. Crans-Pres-Celigny, France: Hove Roto Vision, 2001. Survey of international stage design solutions, with focus on individual designers. Richly illustrated. Index.

Gaensbauer, Deborah B. *The French Theater of the Absurd*. Boston: Twayne, 1991. Comprehensive survey of the major playwrights and their most important work, and the impact of their theories and plays on drama. Bibliography and index.

Grace, Sherrill. *Regression and Apocalypse: Studies in North American Literary Expressionism*. Toronto, Ont.: University of Toronto Press, 1989. Excellent, lavishly illustrated study of the expressionist movement in North America and its impact on the American stage.

Innes, Christopher, ed. *A Sourcebook on Naturalist Theatre*. London: Routledge, 2000. Excellent collection of sources for the works of Ibsen, Chekhov, and Shaw, the three playwrights who shaped naturalism. Includes an overview of history and criticism of naturalism. Bibliography and index.

Izenour, George C. *Theater Design*. 2d ed. New Haven, Conn.: Yale University Press, 1996. Deals with all aspects of modern theater design solutions and discusses practical examples. Includes two essays by other authors on the acoustics of multiroom facilities such as London's Barbican Pit. Illustrated. Bibliography and index.

Jackson, Nagle. *The Quick-Change Room: Scenes from a Revolution*. New York: Dramatists Play Service, 1997. Perceptive analysis of the changing role, nature, and function of theater in post-communist Russian society. Illustrated.

Kuhns, David F. *German Expressionist Theatre: The Actor and the Stage*. Cambridge, England: Cambridge University Press, 1997. Substantial overview of the history of the movement in Germany and its impact on styles of acting and set design. Bibliography and index.

Orban, Clara Elizabeth. *The Culture of Fragments: Words and Images in Futurism and Surrealism*. Atlanta, Ga.: Rodophi, 1997. Perceptive overview of the key elements in both movements, from a literary-dramatic and a visual arts perspective. Bibliography and index.

Sheppard, Richard. *Modernism-Dada-postmodernism*. Evanston, Ill.: Northwestern University Press, 2000. Places Dada in the context of modernism and analyzes its impact on postmodernism. Relevant plays are discussed, as well as the theories of the movement and its impact in other literary fields and the visual arts.

Van Erven, Eugene. *Community Theatre: Global Perspectives*. London: Routledge, 2001. Comprehensive survey of global applications of the theater for development approach, with a clear emphasis on community-oriented projects. Bibliography and index.

Wolford, Lisa, and Richard Schechner, eds. *The Grotowski Sourcebook*. London and New York: Routledge, 2001. Has plenty of criticism and interpretation of the life and work of the founder of "poor theater." Illustrated. Bibliography and index.

Thomas J. Taylor,
updated by R. C. Lutz

ENGLISH-LANGUAGE AFRICAN DRAMA

English-language countries in sub-Saharan Africa include Nigeria, Ghana, Sierra Leone, Gambia, and Liberia in the west; Uganda, Kenya, and Tanzania in the east; Malawi, Zambia, and Zimbabwe in the center; and Namibia, South Africa, Swaziland, Botswana, and Lesotho in the south. Several of these countries have produced a considerable body of drama and can serve as representatives of the activity that is taking place in Anglophone countries throughout Africa.

In all these countries, scripted drama in English developed even later than other written forms, perhaps because, as Cosmo Pieterse—one of the most prominent figures in the African theater—and others have suggested, traditional community life still satisfied the dramatic instinct through rituals involving music and dance and through oral narrative—both forms in which the audience was not only spectator but also participant. The potential of African drama, once established, stemmed from its ritual character and became evident soon after independence (mostly around 1960). African plays, in capitalizing on the ritual element, usually go beyond the need for mere entertainment in the search for cultural identity and social cohesion.

African plays fall generally into two categories: those that are immediately accessible to Western audiences because they rely primarily on dialogue and a tightly knit structure, with personal conflict, rising action, climax, and denouement, and those that show the influence of such structures but return to forms of community ritual. The first group seems intended partially for audiences beyond Africa, with an eye on publication by foreign presses. One effect, if not motive, of such drama is to make Africa a part of the international community. The other group often disparages such concerns and focuses attention solely on an African audience, on the education, self-awareness, and cohesion of the African community. Many such plays therefore use the local idiom and unless translated are inaccessible not only to the outside world but also to other Africans. Still, a large body of drama, even in the second group, relies on English—with only scattered uses of local language for song or intimate dialogue—because dramatists need English to reach beyond their own ethnic groups. One must insist, however, that no English-language play has the integrative quality of traditional drama, religious or secular. Cut off from the ceremonial, ritual life of the people, it is not "African" in that fundamental sense.

Some permanent theater sites exist, most notably at large universities in urban areas, but traveling companies attempt to reach the people directly. One alternative has been to encourage high schools to establish acting groups. A popular form of contemporary drama is the radio play. The British Broadcasting Corporation's African Theatre Series has sponsored competitions, the second one in 1971-1972, to encourage the writing and production of plays by Africans. Such plays, written for radio, were necessarily short, designed as thirty-minute programs. Brevity has been characteristic of other African plays as well. They are frequently one-acts, simple in outline and action, often using between two and five characters. The plays can be subtle, even ambiguous, in their statements. A play of simple dialogue can have far-reaching symbolic overtones. What appears to be a direct statement about a social or political situation contains nuances that one should perhaps expect from a culture accustomed to proverbial and ritualistic speech. The brevity of the plays may have something to do with their appeal to a broad audience, but it does not imply any absence of subtlety or sophistication in dealing with personal or social issues. Further, even in the short, well-made plays, the characters are not so much individuals as "ritual" representations. They invite the audience to be participants rather than spectators. African plays, at their best, have suggestions of communal experience.

EAST AFRICA: UGANDA

In East Africa, Kenya and Uganda have been the most active dramatically. Makerere University in Uganda, with its own traveling theater company, has had a tremendous impact. The plays that have come out of this region, despite considerable diversity, have common, identifiable features. For the most part, they are well made. With the exception of Ngugi wa Thiong'o (who wrote as James T. Ngugi until 1970), the dramatists rely on simple, intimate situations, choosing to reveal the larger social setting within the microcosm of a small group. Even when the setting is a traditional village, either in the past or in contemporary times, with one or two exceptions the complicating features of song, dance, and ritual are absent. In addition, a pervasive motif preoccupies dramatists, whether they are speaking of the traditional life of the people or the modern conflict between African and non-African, both European and otherwise: On the most basic level, the motif is self-aggrandizement, an imposition of the self on others. In Ugandan plays, especially, self-aggrandizement frequently leads to self-destruction as well.

Nuwa Sentongo's *The Invisible Bond* (pb. 1975) is a paradigm of this theme. Kibaate murders his wife's beloved only to have the corpse return to haunt him. While he slowly becomes a slave to this dead master, his wife is killed and joins her lover, Damulira, in death. In the background of the personal conflict, night-walkers (cannibals), acting as a chorus of dancers, stalk the dead, first calling up Damulira, then Kibaate's wife, as food for their tables. The feeding of one on another attains a level of ritual condemnation. Elvania Namukwaya Zirimu in *Family Spear* (pr. 1972; radio play) and Tom Omara in *The Exodus* (pr. 1965) call into question the role of tradition in sanctioning such behavior. In both plays, the ancestral spear, the symbol of authority, signifies the continuing power of tradition to prevent a sensitive response to the human needs of the present.

Several Ugandan and Kenyan dramatists are of Asian (Indian or Pakistani) ancestry. Their special situation within the African setting raises issues of race, belonging, and patriotism. Significantly, however, the theme of self-aggrandizement remains the key concern. Jagjit Singh's *Sweet Scum of Freedom* (pr. 1972; radio play) ennobles the "scum," or victims, of society (the heroine is a prostitute) and suggests strongly a desire for self-destruction in those who ex-

ploit them. Ganesh Bagchi shows, in *Of Malice and Men* (pb. 1968), the difficulty an Indian, Sudhin, and an Englishman, Michael Knight, have in getting outside their ideologies to establish a personal relationship with a young Indian woman, Sona. One sees them both impose their ideologies on themselves and on her. What constitutes a modern African state; what responsibilities individuals have to themselves and to their country; what race, ideology, and tradition have to do with identity within the state; and most specifically, what happens to individuals who fail to acknowledge the rights of others within the society— these were the concerns of Ugandan drama of the 1960's and 1970's.

The years of the dictatorship of Idi Amin (1971-1979) and the following civil war-like atmosphere until the reestablishment of a stable democracy in 1986 effected their toll on the theater. Prominent playwright Byron Kawadwa, who wrote like many Ugandan dramatists in the Luganda language, was murdered for his satire *Oluimba Iwa Wankoko* (pr. 1971; *The Song of Mr. Cock*, 1971), which criticized unlawful government actions. As a result of this repression, others like the influential playwright and producer Robert Serumaga chose exile during the final years of Amin's terror-inflicting rule. Serumaga founded the popular Abafumi Players, who had come to him from other theater venues, and formed a closely knit group of actors and theater workers. Serumaga fled Uganda for Kenya from 1977 to 1979, taking his Abafumi Players with him, and died in Nairobi in 1980 after a brief return to post-Amin Uganda.

Since 1986, peace has brought a renewed flourishing of Ugandan theater. Audience appetite for drama, dance, and musicals is very high. In the capital of Kampala, the national theater is an insufficient outlet to satisfy demand, and theater companies are often forced to perform in cinemas, in large halls, and outdoors. Traveling troupes always find sold-out audiences in the countryside, where moderate weather and gentle running hills provide good conditions for the many open-air performances.

Social criticism has become possible again in plays such as those by Cliff Lubwa p'Chong. His

Kinsmen and Kinswomen (pr. 1986) focuses on often intricate family relationships, which can be both source of progress or barriers of social change. From 1988 until his departure for the United States in the 1990's, Jimmy Katumba's troupe, the Ebonies, were very active in performing detective plays with a strong social message. Typically improvising heavily, the Ebonies staged John W. Katunde's plays *The Dollar* (pr. 1988) and *The Inspector* (pr. 1990) in an abandoned school in Kampala. The plays, which criticize greed, corruption, and mismanagement, derived a substantial amount of their popularity from the musical numbers they incorporated. Although the Ebonies have become less active without Katumba, other producers have followed the successful model of combining music, satire, and criticism.

Ugandan audiences savor theater as entertainment. The appetite for farce, comedy, and dance drama runs high, often satisfied by touring theater groups who use movement, dance, and music to overcome barriers posed by local languages and dialects. Their performances are very popular, but critics in the capital frown at their somewhat amateurish standards. Playwrights such as Alex Mukulu, who started as an actor himself, try to raise the professional standards for scripting and performance. His *Wounds of Africa* (pr. 1990) and *Thirty Years of Bananas* (pr. 1993) have a satirical message about Uganda's problems. The production values of their music, mime, and dialogue are high, and Mukulu likes to use his own star performance to set the standards for the rest of the talent.

As elsewhere in Africa, in Uganda theater has also been used as an educational tool. Under the leadership of academic playwrights such as Rose Mbowa, brief plays are performed, aimed at coating their serious message with entertaining songs, dance, and witty dialogue. Mbowa's *Mother Uganda and Her Children* (pr. 1987) strove to reunify the country. In 2002, the Global Lutheran World Federation Campaign against HIV/AIDS enlisted the creative services of Uganda's TASO drama group to disseminate information about the disease through mini-plays performed at hospitals and community centers in Uganda.

KENYA

Kenya's dramatists Kuldip Sondhi and Ngugi wa Thiong'o face a situation similar to that of the Ugandan dramatists. Although he was educated in Kenya, Sondhi was born in West Pakistan and thus is sensitive to the social ostracism that characterizes the modern African state. In his plays, this emerges as an imposition of one's culture or personal values or prejudices on another. In *The Magic Pool* (pb. 1972), it is the social rejection of a hunchback; in the radio play *Sunil's Dilemma* (pr. 1970), it is the invasion of an Asian's home by Africans identified as both thieves and police. *With Strings* (pb. 1968) warns of the imposition of the past on the present. When a wealthy uncle, who, for whatever motive, uses a promise of money to influence critical decisions in the lives of the younger generation, suddenly dies of a heart attack, the hand of the past releases its grip. The young Indian man and African woman who are the play's focus can make their decision about marriage without prejudice, and, it would seem, the two races can merge, albeit with some difficulty.

In *Undesignated* (pb. 1968), Sondhi explores what appears to be a personal dilemma (he is both engineer and writer). The main character, an African named Solomon, is tempted to become the head of a department in an engineering firm so that he can have wealth and influence, motives that are ultimately self-destructive. Because another is chosen for the position, however, he is forced to use his talents as an artist instead, to the benefit of both himself and his country. Sondhi's play *Encounter* (pb. 1968) not only reiterates this theme but also does so in a context that is more common to the work of Ngugi wa Thiong'o. Two encounters, one between a British lieutenant and a fellow officer, the other between the lieutenant and a rebel, General Nyati, reveal the power of ideology and cultural loyalties. Both the lieutenant and the general are idealists, but the force of the general's personality prevails because it is ultimately in the service of freedom and not of exploitation. In the early twenty-first century, to survive financially, Sondhi increasingly concentrated his energies on the Mombasa and Coast Tourist Association, winning an award in

June of 2002 for his efforts on behalf of Kenya's tourism industry.

Ngugi wa Thiong'o, as the most prominent figure in East African literature, is mainly known as a novelist and a critic of Western exploitation. His plays are not as powerful as his novels, but they explore the same themes and allow him to speak his political views directly to the people. Ngugi combines in a more complex way than the other East African dramatists the three common elements in African drama: the sociopolitical context, traditional modes of performance (song, dance, and oral narrative), and personal dialogue that captures with intimacy the consequences of forces at work in contemporary Africa. *This Time Tomorrow: Three Plays* (pb. 1970) contrasts a narrator-journalist, whose view of the slums in Nairobi is rhetorical, insensitive, and exploitive, and a stranger, who enters the slums just before their removal in order to incite the people against the government. When the stranger is arrested, the people fail to support him. The play ends with a young woman leaving her homeless mother to marry into wealth. This pattern of the seduced woman recurs in Ngugi's work. In *I Will Marry When I Want* (pr. 1982; with Ngugi wa Mirii), first produced in the Gikuyu language in 1977, the beautiful daughter of a poor, exploited family is seduced by the son of the family's exploiter. The family sees its condition deteriorate, partly through its own lapse of will, as even the one piece of land left to it is cleverly bargained away.

The most powerful and innovative of Ngugi's plays is *The Trial of Dedan Kimathi* (pr. 1974; with Micere Githae-Mugo). Using a variety of juxtaposed scenes, it captures the trial of this famous rebel leader, the children who grow up amid the injustices of the British system, and the seduced young woman who has recovered her identity and become a part of the rebel movement. The final act is a positive, courageous gesture of the two children, motivated by the woman's persuasive presence, to attempt to save Kimathi during the sentencing. Ngugi applies the theme of exploitation to a cultural attack against the exploiter. His concern, evident in the theme and in the form, is not primarily the self-destructiveness of the victimizer but rather the effects on the victims and the need for revolutionary change in the social structure: a return to communal values and traditional attitudes toward property and personal worth.

After his exile from Kenya in 1978, Ngugi settled in London, later moving to the United States for a professorship in the department of comparative literature at New York University. Although he became less active in the theater, his novels *Caitaani Mutharaba-Ini* (1980; *Devil on the Cross*, 1982) and *Matigari ma Njiruungi* (1986; *Matigari*, 1989) and his political commentary *Decolonising the Mind: The Politics of Language in African Literature* (1986) have kept him in the public eye. Since his 1986 book, Ngugi has returned to write literary criticism in English. *Penpoints, Gunpoints, and Dreams* (1998), the collection of his Clarendon Lectures in England, also focuses on dramatic issues.

During the 1990's, drama in Kenya suffered from political repression. Prominent playwrights such as Ngugi and Mugo had gone into exile. To get a permit to produce a play, whether by a Kenyan or an international playwright, the theater company had to submit the script to a government agency for approval. The production companies, such as Sarasaki Limited or the Miujiza Players of the Phoenix Players repertory company, were subjected to intense political checks. Nairobi's National Theatre has tried with varying success to run a middle course between standard, inoffensive fare and more politically challenging productions, some of which were at least diluted by government intervention.

TANZANIA, MALAWI, AND ZAMBIA

Because of the ideological commitment to Swahili as the official language of Tanzania by its first post-independence ruler, Julius Nyerere, Kenya's neighboring country to the south has not experienced much dramatic output in English. In the early twenty-first century, foreign plays were performed in English by two companies in the capital, the Dar es Salaam Players and the Arusha Little Theatre. Some works by Tanzania's playwrights such as Ebrahim Hussein have been translated into English.

Most of Malawi's dramatic output is in the local language of Chichewa. The 1990's saw a continuous rise in the popularity of the radio programs featuring English-language plays that were broadcast on Saturday evenings, such as *Theatre on the Air* by the Malawi Broadcasting Corporation. The end of that decade saw the publication of many of Du Chisiza, Jr.'s plays, such as *De Summer Blow . . . And Other Plays* (1998) and *Democracy Boulevard and Other Plays* (1998), which focus on the daily struggles of the Malawi people in the cities and the countryside.

In the early twenty-first century, Zambia's capital of Lusaka possessed two major theatrical venues, the Lusaka Playhouse and the Tikwiza Theatre, which staged impressive production schedules based on Zambian and international plays in English. At the Lusaka Playhouse during this period, Zambia's first privately organized theater festival combined performances with special workshops aimed at improving artistic standards; more than 120 performers from Zambia and southern Africa participated. Zambian playwrights working in English often focus on the issues of the urban society and other local problems. The country also had a tradition of traveling theater groups, one that had begun in 1971 when the Chikwakwa Theater started to tour the country, and remained in groups such as the Zhaninge Travelling Theatre Group, founded in 1984.

ZIMBABWE

Theater got off to a successful start when Zimbabwe became a new nation in 1980. The government was interested in supporting community-based theater movements and embraced the idea of theater-for-development, using short plays and dramatic performances to highlight the need for positive changes. Under the guidance of playwright Stephen Chifunyise, who became a minister of education, sport, and culture, many performance groups were founded and theater was widely supported. In 1984, the University of Zimbabwe began offering classes in dramatic arts and staged local plays.

By 1996, more than one hundred theater troupes existed in Zimbabwe, and the National Theatre Organisation, located in Harare, had been invigorated by the influx of local playwrights writing for its production schedule. Zimbabwe offered a flourishing pa-

tronage for theater, as well as excellent theaters for successful productions. International theater festivals were organized and brought global talent in touch with Zimbabwean playwrights, producers, and performers. Zimbabwean, British, and African dramatic heritages started to fuse to create an exciting new national theater. Amakhosi Productions of Bulawayo drew its material from the popular concerns of the urban and rural people and invigorated traditional folk theater. International and domestic organizations sought to ameliorate the issue of homeless teenagers by integrating them in well-funded production companies.

Yet, by 2002, the economic and political crisis in Zimbabwe hit the world of theater as well. The Harare International Festival of the Arts, which had been a great success since its start in 1999, was cancelled by the government. Scheduled to run just before the March, 2002, elections—which saw an arguably fraudulent reelection of Robert Mugabe, who has ruled the country since independence—the government felt unable to ensure a safe stage. Playwrights, actors, and producers, however, refused to be intimidated by increasingly violent government repression. Daves Guzha's Rooftop Promotions completed its production of *Dare/Enkundleni* (pr. 2001), which saw actors from all of Zimbabwe's provinces in the country's largest theatrical production to date. The play attacked government regulations, including its monopoly on the sale of maize, a stable crop, which forces farmers to sell their products to the government at an economic loss to themselves. This arrangement jeopardizes the farmers' ability to feed an increasingly hungry nation because they lack the funds to buy new seed. During several productions of *Dare/Enkundleni*, radicals voicing support for the government ran on the stage and beat actors.

In Zimbabwe's cultural capital of Bulawayo, also a stronghold of anti-Mugabe opposition, Collin Sibanda's theater organization, Artists Against Violence International (AAVI), has been threatened with physical violence. Government-supported radicals, unhappy with the group's dramatic readings of poetry that are critical of the ruling party, unsuccessfully tried to interrupt performances in schools. Chifunyise was one of the few dramatists who, after the events of early 2002, still defended the repressive government. Artists such as Guzha feared that Mugabe's power to forbid any unapproved public gathering could be used to forbid the staging of critical plays.

NAMIBIA, BOTSWANA, LESOTHO, AND SWAZILAND

Theater in the southern African nations of Namibia, Botswana, Lesotho, and Swaziland is often based on traditional African forms and performed in local languages. Local dramatists who write in English generally produce plays that are appreciated mostly by an urban audience. Local playwrights commonly work together with theater-for-development projects funded in part by the United Nations and write scripts for educational plays performed by traveling troupes or amateur actors.

In Namibia, the National Theatre in the capital of Windhoek offers formal drama, musicals, and ballet based on Western models and revivals of Western plays. The Warehouse Theatre in Windhoek, to the contrary, focuses on informal theater, experimental theater, and one-person shows. Drama has also taken an active role in combating one of southern Africa's most pressing health problems. For example, two drama groups, Puppets Against AIDS (PAAN) and Yatala, offered Dramas For Health workshops on a nationwide tour. The presentations highlighted the health and social implications of HIV/AIDS and offered clear HIV-prevention messages. For performance in the countryside, the Caprivi Drama Group has put together educational theater such as its Fire Drama Play, which transmits through its drama strategies for fire prevention and fire fighting techniques.

Although traditional African drama and dance forms were flourishing in Botswana by 2002, the capital Gaborone lacked a formal theater but could claim the Okava Theatre Production company supported by the Alliance Francaise de Gaborone. On President's Day (July 16), traditional dances are performed in the capital. Most people in Botswana prefer traditional, informal theater, which often draws its actors directly from the audience, and state support for theater is rather limited.

The vast majority of plays written and performed in Lesotho exists in the Sesotho language. A promi-

nent exception is the work of South Africa-born playwright Zakes Mda, who emigrated to Lesotho in 1963. Mda has written political plays in English, such as *Dead End* (pr. 1979), which deals with connections between prostitution and the former apartheid system, and *The Road* (pr. 1982), which focuses on labor issues. His characters are heavily influenced by the political situation in which they are forced to act, and Mda favors situational drama over straightforward political agitation. Moving into the field of criticism, he wrote *When People Play People: Development Communication Through Theatre* (1993) about his experience with theater-for-development projects, to which he was devoting most of his energy by the dawn of the twenty-first century. His Marotholi Travelling Theater company's goal is to bring educational theater to all levels of Lesotho's primarily rural and migrant labor society, and it also has toured abroad. Launched in 1999, the Morija Arts and Culture Festival includes local drama performances, one of Lesotho's relatively few formally organized outlets for theatrical performances.

Indigenous theater in Swaziland remained underdeveloped in the early twenty-first century. Swazi audiences typically prefer South African productions and have been known to throw beer cans at their own local talent, driving them off stage in favor of South African performers. The Siyavuka! Swaziland National Arts Festival was started in December of 2000 to change this situation by featuring and promoting local drama productions. The organizers welcomed all local talent to perform on its stage, and the event proved successful.

SOUTH AFRICA

The Republic of South Africa offers a variety of plays written in English. The least compelling of them seem carbon copies of plays from other countries in Africa. They are not uninteresting, but they do not seem to arise from the particular complex of issues in the South African setting. Alfred Hutchinson's *Fusane's Trial* (pb. 1968), for example, deals with a typical conflict between the old and new cultures. A young girl, Fusane, refuses to become the fourth wife of an old man. Before the actual marriage ceremony, he forces himself on her. In defending herself against rape, she kills him. When the court finds her innocent, her family is both penitent and joyous. New concepts of love and marriage win over the old. Arthur Maimane's *The Opportunity* (pb. 1968) deals with the ironies of a domestic situation in which a former leader in the rebel cause must divorce his wife and marry an educated woman in order to be eligible for a post as ambassador to the United Nations. The authority he wields according to custom makes it easy to take this symbolic step into the modern world.

In other plays, technical experimentation is at least as important as the conflict itself. Namibian-born Cosmo Pieterse, an editor of numerous texts and an actor as well as a dramatist, has attempted poetic drama in his *Ballad of the Cells* (pb. 1972). In Credo V. Mutwa's intriguing *uNosilimela* (pb. 1981), the "experimentation"—if that is what it should be called—is an incorporation of traditional modes. *uNosilimela* is an epic tracing of uNosilimela's journey from mythical origins to her experiences in modern South African settings—her fall from grace, sufferings, abuse, and eventual return to the family. The final act is accompanied by the Apocalypse: the end of the white regime, the end of apartheid, and the attainment of Eden for South African blacks. The play uses allegory, myth, dream, music, dance, and ritual. It is not a well-made play, nor does it appeal primarily to an international audience. It is an indigenous play written for the people. Though the predominant language is English, some conversation and the songs and ritual portions are conducted in local languages.

The one playwright who has most clearly spoken for the creative potential of South Africa and the entire African experience is Athol Fugard, considered South Africa's premier and most contentious playwright. Fugard, who has directed and appeared in several of his own works, has built his reputation on four seminal but highly theatrical works: *The Blood Knot* (pr. 1961), *Boesman and Lena* (pr. 1969), *A Lesson from Aloes* (pr. 1978), and *"MASTER HAROLD" . . . and the Boys* (pr. 1982). His dramatic output of the late twentieth century includes *A Place with the Pigs* (pr. 1987), *My Children! My Africa!* (pr. 1990), *My Life* (pr. 1994), and *The Captain's Tiger*

(pr. 1997). *Playland* (pr. 1992) anticipates the end of the apartheid system, which happened in 1994, with its careful exploration of a productive dialogue between white and black South Africans.

Valley Song (pr. 1995) is Fugard's postmodern play about the role of intergenerational conflict. It contains a strong vision to sustain the new, democratic and multiracial South Africa. In the South African production of his play, Fugard starred himself in the double role of Author and Buks, a "colored" (mixed-race) farmer trying to hand down his rural values to his city-bent granddaughter Veronica. The character of the Author introduces the play by sowing his field, which the stage has become, talking of spring and rebirth, two themes the local audience readily perceived as metaphors for the politics of their nation. Fugard then assumed the role of Buks, occasionally slipping back into his Author character, and reflected on a former harsh, but meaningful, life as farmer. His spunky granddaughter, who dances and swirls around the stage, tells Buks of her plans for a sparkling city life. She is modeled as a representative of South Africa's youth, yet she also shares some quiet, tender moments with her grandfather, whom she clearly loves.

Until the end of apartheid in 1994, plays that were most interesting to an international audience, perhaps, were those that dealt directly with the apartheid system. They were inevitably critical of the system, but with varying degrees of intensity and subtlety. The approach is generally that of most African writers, with the exception of Ngugi: a concentration on a particularized and limited situation that reflects the social setting rather than a broad social and political attack. Harold Kimmel's two-act play *The Cell* (pb. 1972) focuses on two prisoners in the same cell, a Boer extremist and a Jewish liberal. In act 1, Peter reduces Levine to the status of a black in an apartheid state; in the second act, Levine uses the leverage of truth about Peter's activities and motives to create a socialist state. Richard Rive, in *Resurrection* (pb. 1972), attacks racism directly, and in his radio play *Make Like Slaves* (pb. 1972), he suggests more subtly the difficulty of crossing the racial line. An aggressive white woman and a "colored" man not only have some difficulty understanding each other but also find no way to enter a third world, that of the blacks. David Lytton's *Episodes of an Easter Rising* (pb. 1972) is a sensitive treatment of two older white women who take up residence in an isolated region because racial conflict takes up too much time from the act of living. They are thrown into the conflict, however, when they humanely and instinctively befriend a revolutionary leader, "the man," and protect him from the police. They eventually realize their involvement and at the end confirm their commitment by taking in the family of a black man who has died in a seditious act. Lytton thus suggests that the line between the races is not an unsurmountable barrier.

After 1994, the postapartheid era saw an upswing in theatrical productions. New creative energies were bestowed on the writing and the production of plays that reflected the new, democratic South Africa. Civic and commercial theaters were integrated, with black, white, Indian, and mixed-race talent performing together for multiracial audiences. When Fugard, of white Afrikaaner origin, played the "colored" farmer Buks in *Valley Song*, many South Africans felt that an important creative barrier had been overcome. Black writers, directors, and producers have become very influential in shaping the artistic identity of formerly segregated cultural institutions and theater companies. Experimental theater enjoyed commercial success by the early twenty-first century, and South Africa's university system aids in the development of a genuine South African theater that encompasses members of all races.

WEST AFRICA

The plays of West Africa are distinctly different from those of the east and south. Because Europeans did not settle there and take away the land, racial conflict and demands for the recovery of economic and political rights are not major themes. It is not the residual colonial presence, or ideology, or patriotism that primarily motivates West African drama. Plays from this region tend to be exposés of political, social, or economic chaos, or of the corruption among the high and low officials who have replaced the white bureaucracy. Some of the plays attempt to deal

with the conflict of values between the old and new cultures; they often broach such topics with detachment and even with a comic spirit. These plays of West Africa are typically busier than their counterparts elsewhere on the continent, as though their purpose were to capture the fullness of life, especially in the modern urban centers and marketplaces, through local color, dialect, and a wide variety of characterization and mood.

NIGERIA

Sanya Dosunmu's *God's Deputy* (pb. 1972) is a Cinderella story set in Nigeria in the late nineteenth century. The divine right of a local king is enough to overcome all obstacles to permit him to marry the beautiful princess, the daughter of a village chief. The play incorporates the paraphernalia of traditional customs—children's games, a festival, the Egungun dance, symbols of various gods such as Ogun and Esu—but it is, in the final analysis, a light piece of entertainment, a musical. Kofi Awoonor's *Ancestral Power* (pb. 1972) is a dialogue between a proponent of the past and a man of the new age. The traditionalist claims to possess powers from his dead ancestors, only to be abruptly exposed as a braggart and coward. His exposure raises questions about the tradition itself and suggests the necessity of entering reasonably into the twentieth century, yet the twist at the end is more cleverness than dramatic peripeteia. Gordon Tialobi attempts Kafkaesque nightmare in his radio play *Full-Cycle* (pr. 1971). General Maga is arrested by revolutionaries, tried, sentenced, and executed. He wakes up to find that it was all a dream but then experiences the same thing again as either another nightmare or reality. The clever ambiguity and the surrealistic mode detach the audience from the psychological and political theme. Ngugi would not dissipate the force of his attack by such dramatic devices.

A popular vein in West African drama is the largely comic treatment of bribery, corruption, and business dealings in the modern city. Imme Ikiddeh in *Blind Cyclos* (pb. 1968) applies poetic justice to Olemu, the minister of housing, who uses his position to demand "kola" or bribery for his special favors. A local medicine man, also seen as a prophet, turns the tables by casting a spell on him. Not only does he charge him an enormous fee for his services, but he also puts into motion a series of events that lead to Olemu's arrest and exposure. Femi Euba's *The Game* (pb. 1968) turns the old society upside down as a wealthy businessperson's second wife takes a lover (polygamy reversed), and a beggar takes advantage of the situation through deceit, bribery, and the selling of information to enter the world of high finance. There is no difference between the beggar and the businessperson whom he is exploiting.

Wole Soyinka, who gives an especially sensitive reading of *Song of a Goat* in his book *Myth, Literature, and the African World* (1976), is the one figure of West African drama who not only represents the qualities already mentioned but also, as an accomplished and gifted writer, has realized their potential. He has attempted practically every mode of drama, from farce to Swiftian satire and tragedy, sometimes mixing modes in one play. He has received criticism for not using his talent in more patriotic ways—for being too much the artist, not enough the social critic—but a Western reader is likely to view this "fault" as a virtue. Soyinka's successful merger of psychological realism, dramatic form, and mythical substructure gives historical continuity to a specific situation and raises drama to a ritual level. Soyinka, who won the Nobel Prize in Literature in 1986, has moved away from the dramatic genre to concentrate on poetry and essays. His plays in the 1980's included *A Play of Giants* (pr. 1984) and *Requiem for a Futurologist* (pb. 1985).

Soyinka's *A Scourge of Hyacinths* (pr. 1991) was a successful radio play aired by the British Broadcasting Company (BBC). *The Beautification of Area Boy: A Lagosian Kaleidoscope* (pr. 1996) was first performed in Leeds, England, because of the increasing political oppression under Nigeria's former military dictatorship. In 1994, the former dictator Sani Abacha had sentenced Soyinka to death in Nigeria, and the playwright had to flee his country to save his life. In 1998, with democracy restored in Nigeria, Soyinka returned home. His fellow Nigerian playwright and writer, Ken Saro-Wiwa, was not as fortunate. On November 10, 1995, Saro-Wiwa was hanged

for his writings, which include *Four Farcical Plays* (pb. 1989), because they expressed political opposition to the oppression of his Ogoni people.

The dark years of the Abacha regime negatively affected Nigerian drama. Concern for personal safety discouraged audiences from attending plays. Many dramatists and performers left the country. Ola Rotimi stayed until 1995. The influential playwright had tried in vain to lead the African Cradle Theatre, a company dedicated to the development of professional standards and high artistic talent. When economic mismanagement at the hands of the military dictatorship destroyed all possible funding for the arts, even the huge success of his satirical play *Man Talk, Woman Talk* (pr. 1995) could not provide the resources he deemed necessary for professional theater. In 1995, Rotimi left for a professorship in the United States. Like Soyinka, Rotimi returned in 1998, but he died before fulfilling his final dream of a huge play with hundreds of extras.

The return to democracy ushered in a revival of Nigerian theater, yet playwrights, actors, and producers still face huge economic problems. By the early twenty-first century, ongoing civil strife among Nigeria's many ethnic and religious groups threatened a peaceful and just coexistence, as envisioned by artists such as the executed Saro-Wiwa.

GHANA

Immediately after independence in 1957, Ghanaian playwrights were invited to play an active role in supporting the new government. Efua Sutherland established the Ghana Drama Studio in Accra in that year, and her plays fused Western and African ideas as well as mixed media. Ama Ata Aidoo built her pan-African fame with her play *The Dilemma of a Ghost* (pr. 1964), which tells of the conflicts between a Ghanaian husband and an African American wife. She was appointed minister of education in 1982, but disillusioned with Ghana's continuing slide into economic depression during the 1980's and 1990's, she left for exile in Zimbabwe in 1983, focusing there on novel writing.

Economic decline saw the departure of many other Ghanaian dramatists. Formal and English language theater has become popular only among relatively small urban audiences. Traditional Ghanaian theater typically uses indigenous languages and is based on performance, dance, and music. It is performed during so-called concert parties along Ghana's coast and is hugely popular with large local audiences. Yet, there also have been Ghanaian dramatists working in English, often enduring economic hardship and a persistent lack of public funding.

The Ghanaian dramatist Patience Henaku Addo, in a typical portrait of city life, *Company Pot* (pr. 1972; radio play), traces the education of a young girl in the ways of the city; she has to face seduction, con games, drugs, and prostitution, but survives a wiser woman.

This mixture of romance, comedy, and satire, however, is not the whole picture. In Derlene Clems's indictment of Ghanaian bureaucracy in *The Prisoner, the Judge, and the Jailor*, first broadcast in 1971, the ingratiating hand of friendship and fellow suffering quickly becomes the grip of the law. The artistry of the play reinforces rather than dissipates emotional effect. Jacob Hevi, in his play *Amavi* (pb. 1975), traces a Ghanaian peasant woman's life to show how, for twenty years, she has been exploited. Among the most famous of the West African dramatists is John Pepper Clark-Bekederemo. His play *Song of a Goat* (pr., pb. 1961) makes sexual impotence a tragic event. It attempts to capture and preserve a way of life that modern audiences, even in regarding that particular play, find hard to appreciate.

In the late 1990's, democratic reforms and a degree of economic relief has fostered a resurgence of formal Ghanaian theater. Playwright Efo Kodjo Mawugbe has written works dealing with family relationships and the conflict between traditional and modern, global ways of thinking. There is renewed interest in obtaining funding for theater to ensure the production of professionally staged plays.

Gambia

The small West African nation Gambia, along the Gambia river, has struggled to maintain a viable live theater. In the 1960's, troupes such as the Dimbalanteh Company performed to enthusiastic audiences. In the 1970's and 1980's, plays about Gambia's history and contemporary social issues still found spectators, and Gambia's Association Dramatique Nationale represented the country at international theater festivals. By the late 1990's, live theater experienced a steady decline in Gambia. Radio plays survived, but audience interest had waned. In the early twenty-first century, Gambia lacked a permanent theater.

Liberia and Sierra Leone

In Sierra Leone, plays in the local Krio language, which has its roots in English, were popular after independence in 1961. Dele Charley staged the popular dance-drama *Fatmata* (pr. 1977), which founded a new genre. Yulisa Amadu Maddy produced *Big Berin* in the early 1970's, which was highly critical of the government's attitudes toward the urban poor. Imprisoned and forced into exile by the late 1970's, Maddy tried sporadically to return to Sierra Leone in the 1980's and 1990's to revive its theater. From 1978 to 1986, plays in Krio and English were performed in the capital's new city hall, which could house one thousand spectators, before it was closed to theater. The lengthy and brutal civil war that began in 1992 effectively ended most organized performances, as the capital of Freetown was plagued by looting marauders who burned down many large structures suitable for theater, causing utter social fear and instability.

The situation in neighboring Liberia has been equally unfortunate for theater. Relatively calm until the 1980's, a brutal civil war ravished the country and continued into the early years of the twenty-first century. Possible sites for theatrical productions were plundered and burned to the ground. A climate of violence and fear discouraged any large public gathering. However, on the village level, local and traveling theatrical companies managed to survive. The peace-promoting efforts of one of such group, the Flomo Theater Production Company, were praised by the American ambassador to Liberia in July, 2002.

Outlook

Scripted African drama in the English language, with the exception of the situation in South Africa, is still in its development phase, but dramatic activity is extensive. For various reasons—political, cultural, aesthetic—the commitment to the form is real. Where peace, stability, and democracy have been established, formal theater has flourished and traditional dramatic forms reached large, widespread, and appreciative audiences. Political freedom also encouraged playwrights, actors, and producers to give free reign to their remarkable creativity. The steady presence of African plays in English at international theater festivals is a positive indicator for the intense vitality and viability of the form.

BIBLIOGRAPHY

Brown, Lloyd W. *Women Writers in Black Africa.* Westport, Conn.: Greenwood Press, 1981. Still a groundbreaking study of the development of African women writers, among whom the Ghanaian dramatists Efua Sutherland and Ama Ata Aidoo are discussed in detailed chapters of their own. Notes, bibliography, and index.

Etherton, Michael. *The Development of African Drama.* New York: Africana, 1982. An excellent work on the origins and development of traditional and contemporary African drama. Unsurpassed in its cogent analysis of the roots of African drama and the effect of the European dramatic influence on modern African drama. In-depth analysis of three plays from Ghana and Wole Soyinka's protest plays, among others. Illustrated glossary of dramatic terms and their applicability to the African context. Bibliography and index.

Kerr, David. *African Popular Theatre: From Pre-Colonial Times to the Present Day.* London: James Currey, 1995. Accessible study of the roots and development of African theater as enjoyed by the majority of sub-Saharan Africans. Includes discussion of formal theater, folk rituals, and folk theater. Good overview of the coexistence between traditional and European-inspired forms. Bibliography.

Larlham, Peter. *Black Theater, Dance, and Ritual in South Africa.* Ann Arbor, Mich.: University Microfilms International Research Press, 1985. Although somewhat dated by the end of the apartheid system in 1994, the book still provides a useful, exemplary study of the interconnections between indigenous theatrical and dramatic traditions and their contact with European forms. Provides a good discussion of theater's relationship to society and politics.

Muhando Mlama, Penina. *Culture and Development: The Popular Theater Approach on Africa.* Uppsala, Sweden: Scandinavian Institute of African Studies, 1991. Persuasive study of the uses of popular African theater to aid the development of culture and society. Covers such aspects as the use of drama, occasionally by amateur performers, to transmit social messages.

Ndumbe Eyoh, Hansel. *Beyond Theatre.* Bonn, Germany: German Foundation for International Development, 1991. Interview of Africans involved in writing, production, and performance of popular theater. Excellent background on the ideas of people actively involved in shaping popular theater in Africa.

Wertheim, Albert. *The Dramatic Art of Athol Fugard.* Bloomington: Indiana University Press, 2000. Perceptive critical assessment of the work of one of Africa's most recognized and internationally famous playwrights. Especially good for its discussion of Fugard's use of specific African themes and his international reception. Bibliography and index.

Wright, Derek. *Wole Soyinka Revisited.* New York: Twayne, 1993. Extensively revised, covers all aspects of Soyinka's dramatic work, including his roots in the Yoruba folk theater traditions and his development of his dramatic theories. Thorough discussions of individual plays. Rich bibliography.

Thomas Banks, updated by Thomas J. Taylor and R. C. Lutz

FRENCH-LANGUAGE AFRICAN DRAMA

African drama written in French has been as much a part of the literary tradition as that established by French-language African poetry and the novel. Yet, this genre of African literature seems to exist to a large extent in the shadow of the latter two. This is somewhat surprising, since francophone theater enjoys, on the whole, greater cultural and literary credibility. That is to say, the authenticity of this particular genre is regarded with a less incredulous eye because it is possible to confirm the existence of drama within the oral tradition. This criterion is not enough, however, to upgrade the literary status of francophone theater, which seems thus far to have been less successful, with the exception of a few select playwrights, both on the continent and abroad.

The francophone theater in this article consists of dramatic works, published and unpublished, that have been written by Africans using French as their vehicle of linguistic expression. There are several factors that have had a significant influence on both the content and the form of literary African drama. A brief summary of its origins will help shed some light on the artistic features characteristic of francophone African plays and their playwrights.

ORAL TRADITION

Without delving profoundly into early oral tradition of French West Africa, which is as varied and complex as the many ethnic groups that inhabit this region, it suffices to mention the important role of rites, ritual, and traditional ceremonies in the daily life of precolonial Africans. Although rites and rituals were generally connected with religious practices, they were often accompanied by music, dance, and, in many cases, formal expressions and gestures. The special masks and attire worn for such occasions were also reminiscent of drama. Although many of the traditional African ceremonies represented solemn occasions enacted to pay homage to the ancestral gods or to celebrate rites of passage, there were those that also served as a source of entertainment, such as the ceremonies associated with the celebra-

tion of the harvest, hunting, marriages, and births. In a less elaborate form, elements of drama were also present in traditional storytelling. The storyteller, often the village griot (musician-entertainer), brought to life numerous characters through his dramatic impersonation of the various personalities in folktales, legends, and epics.

COLONIAL INFLUENCE

Africans were introduced to the European concept of theater for the most part during the colonial era, as a result of the establishment of the missionary schools. On one hand, the missionaries introduced drama to their young catechumens as a source of entertainment. On the other hand, the plays they performed were usually based on the lives of different saints and coincided with the celebration of certain religious holidays. One immediately recognizes the similarity between the African traditional ceremonies honoring the ancestors and the tribute paid to saints through dramatic productions, both of which underscored some religious practice or event. The missionaries succeeded in using this rather uninspiring form of drama to inculcate and reinforce Christian values among the would-be catechumens. Thus, this period represented a pseudo-beginning of African drama performed in French, albeit in a European context.

ÉCOLE NORMALE WILLIAM PONTY

Another important factor affecting the development of African drama written in French was the École Normale William Ponty in Senegal, which opened in 1913 as a training center for African teachers and officials. By the 1930's, this school was taking the lead in the study of indigenous African traditions, and as such it became the catalyst that gave the greatest impetus to the growth of French African drama. It is not surprising that Senegal became the first country to enjoy a modest flourishing of dramatic art; it was a major academic and artistic center during the colonial era and, for some years thereafter, for all of French West Africa.

The amateur performances presented by the students at the École Normale William Ponty represented only a part of the institution's contributions to the growth of francophone theater. The students were encouraged to research, translate, and stage a major theatrical production derived from their African folklore tradition. There was a coming together, therefore, of scholarly pursuits and artistic creativity. The various plays produced during the years when this dramatic activity flourished were inspired by the folklore of Senegal, Dahomey, and the Ivory Coast, to name only a few regions. Although the European influence still overshadowed both endeavors, it was nevertheless an important time, because now the students were drawing on their own cultural and literary heritage for intellectual and artistic inspiration. The result of this cultural diversity was that, while the Europeans were exposed to African culture and values, the African students underwent a similar experience, and each group came into contact with the folkloric traditions originating outside its homeland.

The importance of the dramatic performances produced by the students went beyond the walls of the École Normale William Ponty. As Bakary Traoré notes in *The Black African Theatre and Its Social Functions* (1972; originally published in French in 1958), the number of plays performed by the students in a few major cities throughout French West Africa, as well as a celebrated performance before a French audience during the Colonial Exposition in Paris, testifies to the popularity of the students' dramatic productions. There were even a few leading African artists who were former students of the École Normale William Ponty, such as Keita Fodéba, noted primarily for his theatrical productions, and Bernard Badié, who translated African folklore and wrote poetry, novels, and plays. In spite of the success of the plays, there were some drawbacks, the single most important one of which was language. French was the primary language used in all theatrical productions because it was the language of instruction and daily communication for the students. Problems of translation from the vernacular languages to French abounded. Moreover, the students' audience was most often made up of the European and African elite. Despite these obstacles, the École Normale William Ponty theater clearly marked the emergence of francophone theater in Africa.

PERFORMANCE AND PUBLISHING

Following the decline of the École Normale William Ponty theater in the late 1940's, African drama enjoyed varying degrees of popularity and success. For example, many playwrights did not get an opportunity to stage their dramatic works. Unlike other genres, which need only to bring together reader and written text, plays are written to be performed; performers, costumes, technical arrangements, and rehearsals must all be coordinated and financed. The problem is compounded further when one recognizes there were many plays that were performed but were never published. Thus, the task of how to increase the theatrical production of French African plays remained, in general, a difficult one for African playwrights. Moreover, the vast majority of plays that were performed did not open in theaters outside the continent, inhibiting worldwide recognition of African drama, playwrights, and actors.

Nevertheless, some progress was made. The creation of publishing companies interested in the publication of French African plays (for example, Présence Africaine, in Paris, and the African companies P. J. Oswald and the Cameroon-based CLE) helped to increase the number of dramatic works that appeared in print and to make them available to a larger African and foreign readership. Although there were fewer opportunities to see a theatrical production of an African play in French than to read one, plays were performed in African cities, villages, and, occasionally, abroad. The establishment of national theaters, such as the Daniel-Sorano Theatre in Dakar, Senegal, brought about the gradual institutionalization of francophone theater. Television and especially radio quickly became media through which African playwrights were able to produce their plays. As a result, African playwrights were no longer limited to producing their works mostly for a theatergoing elite.

If African playwrights were successful in their artistic treatment of content and form, language posed a far greater challenge. No matter how acclaimed a literary work was, no matter how well an African writer translated, transliterated, superimposed, or interjected African languages into his or her work, the continued use of the colonial language somehow always raised questions regarding the authenticity and linguistic merit of African creative writing. African plays written in French are no exception. In general, the use of French as the vehicle of linguistic expression seemed to suggest that African playwrights created works for a predominantly European and educated African audience.

The performance aspect of drama made it possible for playwrights to overcome in some measure the concern about language. In addition to body expressions and gestures, which are always part of a theatrical production, African dramatists made great use of music and dance. The latter were undoubtedly a carry-over from traditional art, and so their inclusion in drama served to create a familiar cultural setting despite the linguistic barrier for the nonspeaker of French, in particular the illiterate population in Africa.

INTEGRATION OF GENRES

The inclusion of music and dance in drama is one of the major features of francophone African plays. It is not uncommon for African playwrights to make use of the vast repertoire of traditional songs and dances. The African playwrights' techniques in using song and dance in plays may be similar or differ significantly depending on the extent of their integration into the dramatic works. At the beginning of a performance, the playing of the tam-tam captured the audience's attention and announced the start of the play. Song and dance were often used in the re-creation of a traditional African setting to highlight important moments as the action progressed or to bring the performance to a close. In Guillaume Oyono-Mbia's *Trois prétendants . . . un mari* (pr. 1960; *Three Suitors One Husband Until Further Notice*, 1968), the action in the play culminates in a fanfare of music and dance in which both the actors and the spectators take part. Such a finale places emphasis on the role of the African play as a collective experience.

Other traditional elements that originated from the playwrights' African heritage served to give francophone drama its African flavor. The overlapping of different genres, another identifiable characteristic of African creative writing, offered the playwrights an excellent opportunity to experiment with content and form. The importance of this particular aspect of African aesthetics was stressed by the Senegalese poet Léopold Senghor, who rightly noted that a fine line distinguishes the different genres, among which African artists move uninhibited.

The Senegalese dramatist Abdou Anta Kâ, for example, used an interesting combination of drama and legend in *La Fille des dieux*, which was first performed in 1957. The play is based on a popular song whose hero, Awa, reappears in the dramatic version. The setting is somewhat vague, perhaps a deliberate act on the part of the author to create a sense of remoteness in time. More interesting, the playwright has Awa narrate intermittently a creation story, the events of which parallel certain ones in the play. Like the moon and Massassi, the first man and woman who were sent away to earth, Awa and Madhi were forced to leave their native village to seek refuge in the forest. In a similar fashion, the hunter recounts the legend of Arissâ, a young girl of sixteen who gave up her life to save her village. Through the telling of this legend, the hunter convinces Awa, who identifies with the character of Arissâ, to sacrifice her life to save the village that was responsible for her exile. The notion of legend takes on a dual meaning in the play, that of both story and history. It is clear that Kâ makes use of this particular aspect of oral tradition to underscore the dramatic quality of his play.

Verbal communication in proverbs, a technique that has been popularized by African novelists, is not an unusual occurrence in African plays. In Bernard Dadié's *Béatrice du Congo* (pr. 1969), much of the dramatic discourse of the African characters includes proverbial expressions that serve indirectly as philosophical commentary on the events in the play. The character Niambali takes on the role of the African griot in Cheik Aliou Ndao's *Du sang pour un trône* (pb. 1983). In the past, the griot was the repository for the safeguarding and preservation of the history of the community. He was also considered to be a skillful and creative storyteller. Niambali is invested with both of the functions of the traditional griot. It is he who sets the tone for the spectators. In his monologue, which marks the beginning of the play, Niambali describes briefly the historical setting of the events that are about to occur. He addresses the spectators directly to show that they participate actively in the play. Niambali's brief monologue also accentuates the element of storytelling that is conveyed by his presence and later through the dialogue.

The adaptation of traditional artistic forms for dramatic works provided, therefore, a means by which the African playwright could mediate the problem of language. Furthermore, although traditional material stands out because it is embedded in a non-African language, this kind of imaginative use of literature would still be found in literary texts written entirely in the vernacular.

It is most often on the level of language, setting, and dramatic presentation that the African playwright diverges from the European notion of drama. In terms of structure, however, most plays seem to follow a standard organization that divides a play into several acts and scenes. Ndao breaks with tradition in *Du sang pour un trône*. The entire play is considered to be a single act, which suggests a certain notion of uninterrupted action. The nine so-called "ruptures" could be viewed as a compromise with the conventional structure of European drama, but it is also apparent from the example of Ndao's play that French-language playwrights in Africa had begun to look for more imaginative ways to approach the various aspects of drama.

An essential characteristic of francophone theater that has been mentioned repeatedly is that it represents a form of entertainment. In the preface to his play *Three Suitors One Husband Until Further Notice*, Oyono-Mbia reiterates this idea by pointing out that the *raison d'être* for his creative writing is to entertain, not simply to moralize, although he does not deny the didactic quality of his plays. Francophone theater in general seeks, through entertainment, to educate and to inform its audience. A look at the recurrent themes treated in French-language plays reveals

how African playwrights dealt with the relationship between the medium and the message.

THEMES AND GENRES

Historical plays constituted a large number of the dramatic works that made up the francophone theater. There were several reasons for the popularity of this kind of play. On one hand, the themes found in the historical plays represented a carryover from the negritude movement, which emphasized the importance of the revalorization of the African past, people, and culture. A dramatic performance was perhaps the most poignant way to reveal the importance of African civilization. Besides this fact, there was also a wealth of traditional material that could serve as a source of creative inspiration for African playwrights.

Kâ's *Les Amazoulous* (pr. 1968) is an example of the historical play. This dramatic work is based on the life of the legendary figure Shaka, the subject of numerous literary works and history texts. In his play, Kâ presents Shaka the man, as well as the warrior whose heroism has reached epic proportions. As a result, the author relates Shaka's life to the issues affecting the quality of life of Africans and at the same time immortalizes the past of an important African figure. In like manner, Ndao, in his historical play *Du sang pour un trône*, dramatizes the struggle for power between Macodou Fall, the father, and Samba Lawbe, his son. Through the character of Niambali, he also alludes to the power struggle that exists in real life. Thus, Ndao establishes a symbolic relationship between the events of the play and the sociopolitical climate in Africa.

Béatrice du Congo, another historical play, deals with the question of assimilation. This was an important part of the French civilizing mission in Africa. Dadié's humorous portrayal of the Congolese king who sought to imitate European values criticizes this policy of assimilation. This is indeed a play that attempts to raise the political consciousness of the spectator by dramatizing the adverse effects of colonialism on Africa and Africans.

The initial appeal of the historical plays, based on the use of legendary figures as the central and dramatic focus, gave way to the dramatic realization of modern issues. Historical plays have been classified among the most successful literary accomplishments in francophone African drama, yet the political message that they have evoked has been interpreted by some as a promotion of a unifying national identity or the perpetuation of elitist politics. One critic, John Conteh-Morgan, remarked that works by such playwrights as Dadié, Aimé Césaire, Felix Tchikaya U'Tamsi, and Maxime N'Débéka, although few in number, represented nonetheless a "powerful minority" within the impressive body of plays in francophone Africa. In light of this, there has been a move to revisit the importance of historical plays in the process of evaluating the evolution of African drama.

The subgenres that have followed the historical genre reveal a shift in vision and thematic preoccupation. The daily concerns of surviving in the complex world of modern Africa have become a new source of inspiration and are being combined with traditional dramatic modes in innovative ways. Ancient and outmoded aspects of traditional art are gradually fading from prominence, but aspects of it continue to coexist with modern African performance.

Another category of plays deals primarily with the theme of modernism versus tradition. These plays dramatize the problems produced by a society in transition. Oyono-Mbia's *Three Suitors One Husband Until Further Notice* focuses on the changing attitudes of the young, who want greater control over their lives but do not quite succeed in attaining it. The characters Abessolo and Atangana are constantly alarmed by the lack of regard for tradition. There is, for example, the problem of the young people who eat the meat of animals that are taboo. Oyono-Mbia also emphasizes the generation gap through the main character, Juliette. The primary action revolves around the members of the heroine's family, who attempt to find a husband for her. Juliette becomes a victim of the whims of her family and the villagers, who all look to benefit from the dowry and arranged marriage. Oyono-Mbia's play criticizes in a humorous fashion the practice of the dowry and the lack of meaningful communication between the older and the younger generations.

Rabiatou Njoya's *La Dernière aimée* (pb. 1980) is mentioned here primarily because it is a play written by a woman. On the whole, female writers represent a small minority in French-speaking Africa. Their creative works are important especially because they provide a woman's point of view. Through her female characters, Njoya explores the effects of polygamy on the African woman's life. For the most part, the female characters are portrayed as victims who have little or no control over their lives. Although the theme is not a new one, its treatment in the play reveals the growing interest in sociocultural problems of the Africans.

MODERN INNOVATIONS

Given the modest, yet noteworthy, beginnings of literary drama in francophone Africa, the creative productivity continued to increase, confirming its important place as a genre in modern African society. This growth compelled more critics of African literature, in general, to take a look at its content and form in order to reexamine issues of authenticity, traditional aesthetic influences, and artistic uniqueness (that is, as the features distinguishing French-language drama from its Western counterpart), and to study dramatic works conceived and performed exclusively in the African languages. Moreover, the search for verbal and cultural authenticity served again to catalyze other significant approaches to creating African plays.

Studies have revealed the inspiring efforts of acclaimed playwrights, amateur dramatists, and actors who have experimented with genres, the end result of which has been the diversification of dramatic form and content. This kind of innovative exploration has ranged from the use of pidgin French, to draw on local and popular language usage in an attempt to minimize immediate association with the parent language of France, to developing plays characterized by a more complex intermixing of traditional genres such as music, dance, mime, masks, and ritual.

One example of the appearance of new forms was the notion of "total theater," which characterized the plays of the Cameroonian playwrights who promoted this type of drama. The emphasis was placed on the production of plays that had an aesthetic relevance to the modern African audience. There was a desire to creatively validate the existence of distinct dramatic forms in Africa. In particular, experimentation with space maximized the union between actors and audience. The plays incorporated moments when members of the audience were spontaneously sought out to take on a role in the performance, finding themselves therefore transformed from spectator to actor. In a very different mode, Were Liking's "ritual theater," which explores the manifestation of spirituality and religion in the context of drama, is regarded a significant literary contribution by a Cameroonian female dramatist.

ADVANCEMENTS AND DETRACTIONS

It has already been noted that the presence of École Normale William Ponty was a historic milestone in the arts, its tenure designating the official period of the appearance of French-language drama. This era has been followed by the establishment of national theaters, the financial support of the French government as part of a campaign to promote its language in other French-speaking countries, the creation of theaters abroad interested in presenting the plays of African playwrights, and the organization of theater troupes and programs to provide avenues for increasing the number of professional actors.

Festivals, conferences, and radio broadcasts are some of the venues that have made it possible for African dramatists to acquire a larger theater audience. Important collaborations with experts in the field of theater, as well as staged performances of African plays abroad, have given rise to an international presence.

The portable nature of African theater has also facilitated its sustained popularity, especially with local dramatic forms, which are less reliant on costly stage and costume production, and on the technologically equipped theaters found in Western society. The participatory nature of drama in Africa, determined by the interactive role of the onstage griot as interlocutor or the inclusion of audience as actor, has also reinforced the importance and popularity of drama as a vital artistic expression for both the purpose of enter-

tainment and the valorization of the collective human experience in Africa.

Although these factors highlight the advancements and growth of francophone African drama, other situations have hindered its development, notably the scarcity of professional theater troupes and actors, and government policies in certain countries that have defined the parameters of artistic expression of dramatists, who in turn have to be cautious to avoid obvious criticism of the government in their plays. In some cases, this has resulted in the creation of plays written and performed in exile.

Furthermore, cultural neocolonialism is reinforced by the ongoing promotion and primacy of French verbal dramatic expression by institutions and social structures, whether the play is written in French or not. For example, the policy regarding submissions to a dramatic competition sponsored by France illustrates this issue. New plays submitted to the Inter-African Radio Drama Competition, established by the French Office de la Coopération Radiophonique, encouraged freedom of artistic expression, yet all plays had to be in French. However, the favoring of French language did not appear to stop the flow of African playwrights submitting their work and seeking an outlet for the production of their plays. Presumably, in the face of circumstances arising from the language issue, French-language dramatists of Africa remain conscious, but perhaps not self-conscious, about the implications of cultural neocolonialism for their literary works.

As the twentieth century drew to a close and most countries of the African continent grappled with some combination of economic, political, and social problems, unsurprisingly, the development of the arts, and African drama in particular, was not necessarily a high priority. Yet, the situation of drama in francophone Africa is similar to the ebb and flow of its Western counterpart, which enjoys periods of heightened output when the arts flourish because of public interest, accomplished playwrights emerge, and stable private or public financial support is provided. Although such imperatives in forging a fertile terrain from which drama can flourish are less certain in francophone Africa, the persistence of those writing, performing, and promoting drama continues to bear fruit. There has been a rapid increase in the study of African drama, and some suggest that it is only a matter of time until, given the right social and political conditions, African drama, and its playwrights and actors become household names among French-language audiences.

BIBLIOGRAPHY

Banham, Martin, and Clive Wake. *African Theater Today.* London: Pitman, 1976. Provides history and criticism on African drama and theater. Good source for identifying important literary preoccupations before the 1980's. Includes an extensive bibliography and index.

Bjornson, Richard. *The African Quest for Freedom and Identity: Cameroonian Writing and the National Experience.* Bloomington: Indiana University Press, 1991. Collection of articles focusing on critical discussion of literary developments in Cameroon. One article is devoted exclusively to major playwrights' impact on Cameroonian theater and drama. Also has comprehensive end notes and index.

Conteh-Morgan, John. *Theater and Drama in Francophone Africa: A Critical Introduction.* Cambridge, England: Cambridge University Press, 1994. In-depth analytical study of French-language drama and its evolution. Provides a history and discussion of published and unpublished dramatic works. Includes significant bibliographical references and index listing playwrights, theaters, theater companies, groups, and festivals.

Kerr, David. *African Popular Theatre: From Pre-Colonial Times to the Present.* London: James Currey, 1995. Detailed discussion of the evolution of traditional drama, and anglophone and francophone drama. Bibliography and index included.

Owomoyela, Oyekan, ed. *A History of Twentieth Century African Literatures.* Lincoln: University of Nebraska Press, 1993. Devotes a number of critical articles to the three dominant genres of English-language and French-language African writers: poetry, fiction, and drama. Other articles focus on issues related to African women writers, problems of language, and publishing. Also includes a lengthy index.

Rubin, Don, ed. *The World Encyclopedia of Contemporary Theatre.* Vol. 3. London: Routledge, 1997. Contains brief profiles of all the nations of Africa followed by descriptive summaries of key moments in the historical development of their theater. Identifies important African theaters, playwrights, actors, and performances. Very useful bibliographies and cumulative index are also provided.

Traoré, Bakary. *The Black African Theatre and Its Social Functions.* Translated and with a preface by Dapo Adelugba. Ibadan, Nigeria: Ibadan University Press, 1972. Historical perspective provided by one of the first important comprehensive studies of the emergence of francophone drama and its influences. Informative study of early criticism. Includes bibliography.

Cherie Maiden

Asian Drama

Except for modern spoken drama, which was a new Western-oriented theater type introduced and created in the twentieth century, dramatic arts in Asian countries are highly developed. They are ancient, diverse, and rich in religious, cultural, social, and traditional heritage and share theatrical influences from neighboring countries. The countries of Central Asia, until the dissolution of the Soviet Union in 1991, were saddled with dual Russian and Soviet dramatic traditions, which consisted almost exclusively of plays that glorified czarist governments and Soviet communism. East Asian countries boast well-developed theatrical traditions based on shared Confucian ethics, Buddhism, and past systems of imperial rule. Pacific Island nations in Melanesia, Micronesia, and Polynesia are part of Oceania and share theatrical traditions based on religion, a common ancestral history, and ancient dances. South Asian countries are rich in theatrical tradition, fertile in Hindu and Buddhist themes with baroque, emotional, and colorful theatrical displays and dance forms. The countries of Southeast Asia accepted and developed literature, dance, and religious traditions from both South and East Asia and melded them with their own indigenous theatrical forms, assimilating several influences into their own theatrical styles.

CENTRAL ASIAN REPUBLICS

Kazakhstan, Kyrgyzstan, Tajikistan, Turkmenistan, and Uzbekistan are countries with many shared features. They were all incorporated into the Mongol Empire of Genghis Khan in the thirteenth century, subjugated into czarist rule in the nineteenth century, and subjugated into Soviet republics under the Soviet Union until its breakup in 1991. These nations have a history of their own theatrical traditions. However, with Russianization before and Sovietization after 1917, their dramatic practices and theatrical aesthetics were heavily (and still are to some degree) influenced and forced by Russian classics and socialist-communist propaganda of the Soviet Union.

Kazakhstan had relatively no written literature; however, poetic and musical folklore flourished for many centuries under the country's traditional feudal and nomadic life, becoming an indigenous cultural heritage through oral preservation. Because of intense eighteenth and nineteenth century colonization, Europeanization and Russianization penetrated all spheres of Kazakh life. Kazakhstan was turned into a Soviet Republic in 1936, after which Soviet literature and performing arts became endemic, and traditional art forms were discouraged and suppressed. Kazakh-Soviet dramatic art heavily reflected politically communist agendas, notably plays praising Soviet power, socialism, and the collectivization of Kazakh culture and the industrialization of the country, even after World War II. In the mid 1950's, Kazakh theater experienced some relaxation in censorship as it tried to update its dramatic repertoire. The 1960's ushered in a taste for Kazakh comedy, which developed into a rich new blend of Kazakh modern drama. Kazakhstan's Lermontov State Academic Russian Drama Theatre, with a repertoire of Soviet propaganda, staged plays about Soviet power and socialism and flourished during the 1970's. Toward the end of 1980's, some improvements in Kazakh theater included objective theater criticism, changes in theater structures, and a growing openness toward new and gifted stage directors and playwrights. In the late 1990's, typically only the theatrical work of small ethnic theaters in Kazakhstan were able to consistently produce plays because, since independence in 1991, major Kazakh theaters have experienced economic difficulties. The few theaters that have survived have attempted to revive dramatic art that would critically reflect the varied cultural and social climate of the country.

Kyrgyzstan's early theatrical arts consisted primarily of singing, improvisation, and storytelling of national epics, along with a primitive form of comedy. In 1917, with Russian and Soviet influences, Kyrgyz Soviet dramas were given in Russian; as a result, Kyrgyzstan was under severe political and cultural repression in the late 1920's. The Kyrgyz Studio, the country's first state theater, produced both Kyrgyz and Russian plays, forging an awareness of social issues and developing a new theatrical sophistication. The Kyrgyz State Drama Theatre, established in 1941, produced thematic war plays that supported the Soviet Union's involvement in World War II—or, as it was called, the Great Patriotic War—as well as plays heavily influenced by Kyrgyzstan's historical past and its struggle against foreign hegemony. In the mid-1940's, theaters and dramatic art were regulated carefully by the state and required to produce repertoires validating the advantage of socialism and communism, becoming the official dramatic style and form until the mid-1980's. During the war years, adaptations of Western classics, notably William Shakespeare's works, were also quite popular as mass entertainment at the expense of weakened indigenous and national playwriting. Decades later, despite the ongoing economic crises of the 1980's and 1990's, the Kyrgyzstan Russian Drama Theatre was one of few successful companies because of a large Russian diaspora in Kyrgyzstan during this time. In the early twenty-first century, theater and dramatic training take place at the Kyrgyz State Arts Institute in Bishkek, the current capital and largest city.

Stemming from the Hellenic period, Tajikistan boasts centuries-old traditions in national arts, consisting of comic sketches, pantomimes, humorous stories, fantasies, fairy tales, festival songs, and certain theatrical elements derived from Muslim holidays. Present-day Tajikistan has been invaded by Persians, Macedonians, Arabs, Mongols, and Russians. Tajik and Uzbek share many theatrical and dramatic traditions since Uzbeks consist of the largest minority group in Tajikistan. This rich history was largely curbed however, when, like all other Central Asian Soviet republics during the twentieth century, Tajikistan found itself complying with the Soviet mandate to stage plays glorifying Soviet power and communism. However, comedy rooted in *maskharoboz* (buffoonery) was able to prevail because it was truer to Tajik theatrical form than Soviet realism. The 1950's saw some attempt at reflecting contemporary Tajik life in national plays; however, such plays met with harsh Soviet criticism. During the 1960's, some improvement to restore Tajik national identity and its own dramatic art was successful because of the lessening of Soviet censorship. With the dissolution of the Soviet Union in 1991, economic and political crises were staggering. Remarkably, however, Tajikistan was a center of unique theatrical and dramatic experiments, a surprising paradox because the more politically and economically unstable the country became, the more sophisticated and interesting were Tajikistan's drama works. Tajik theater did suffer financially and otherwise during the 1990's, however, because of a prolonged civil war and several government coups.

Turkmenistan, made up mostly of Turkmen-speaking people of Sunni Muslim religion, has centuries-old rich theatrical forms of poetry and music performed by itinerant singers and folk storytellers. After its incorporation as a Soviet Republic in 1925, Turkmenistan was forced to stage plays of Russian and Soviet agendas until the dissolution of the Soviet Union in 1991. Yet, unlike other Central Asian countries, it still has a repressive political system, closely resembling the no-opposition politics of the Soviet era. Influences of socialist realism remained in Turkmen dramaturgy up through the 1980's. The 1990's finally enjoyed an updated and reenergized dramatic repertoire in Turkmenistan, notably evidenced with the production of a Yugoslavian play called *Sheherezada* (pr. 1991) based on *Alf layla wa-layla* (15 C.E.; *The Arabian Nights' Entertainment*, 1706-1708), an Oriental epic tale. Despite Turkmenistan's heavy-handed government, a new era of contemporary consciousness of Turkmen national identity and cultural issues seemed to emerge in the early twenty-first century, providing the first steps in the revitalization of the country's dramaturgy.

Uzbekistan—landlocked and a populous Central Asian country, because of its geographical location on the ancient Silk Road with great influences from Arab, Chinese, Greek, Persian, Turkic, and Hindu cultures through trade, invasion, and pilgrimage—boasts a long tradition of exemplary scientific achievements and great individuals from the medieval period. As in Tajikistan, Uzbek indigenous performances are full of theatrical elements that encompass puppetry, storytelling of legends and tales, *askias* (humor competition with joke improvisations), and *maskharoboz* (buffoonery). These theatrical forms were often performed outdoor in courtyards and bazaars.

Unlike other Central Asian republics, Uzbekistan had its own amateur theater beginning in the nineteenth century that staged plays promoting moral behavior in Uzbek Islamic culture. The theater was led by the Jadid movement, an educational reformist group. Even before the Jadid movement, nondramatic writing existed in Uzbekistan. However, after 1925, Uzbek Soviet theatrical and dramatic practices, as in other Soviet republics, were state subsidized to propagandize the agenda of the Communist Party.

Uzbekistan has a history of a wide range of artistic genres and forms in its dramaturgy. These include drama, ballet and opera, satire, theater for the young, operetta, puppetry, comedy, musical, and experimental theater, all operating in professional theater companies. Western influences are seen in the youth activities of ballroom dancing, aerobics, break dancing, and especially hip-hop. Today Uzbekistan fares better in its artistic heritage and preservation than its Central Asian neighbors as its theater and dramaturgy are more structured and sophisticated because of a greater investment in high-tech theatrical space and actor training. The Khamza Fine Arts Institute in Tashkent, the capital and cultural center of Uzbekistan, boasts itself as a major artistic and cultural research center for all of Central Asia.

EAST ASIA

China's artistic and theatrical heritage finds its place in the country's very early history. Highly developed, and rich and extensive with a wide range of genres and periods, Chinese traditional theater, in its fundamental structure, is choreographically secular, presentational, and musical. Chinese theater and drama changed, adapted, and developed along with the country's long history and its political, cultural, and social upheavals.

Theater in Hong Kong is sometimes seen as inferior to theater in mainland China; however, on closer

examination, it is innovative it its own way while still retaining the theatrical sophistication and richness of Chinese theater, from which it is borrowed. Cantonese opera, or *Yueju*, made its way to Hong Kong from South China with the basic styles and structure borrowed from the more refined and renowned Beijing Opera. Western-oriented modern spoken Chinese drama (*Huaju*), performed either in English or Cantonese, continues to thrive in Hong Kong, probably because of its former status as a British colony. *Gozai Xi*, or Taiwanese opera, is derived from Chinese drama that came from the Fujian province in southeastern China. Although musically different from Beijing Opera, *Gozai Xi* shares with it the basic movement, costumes, makeup, and staging accompaniment.

Like many other Asian nations, Japan sees traditional and sophisticated theater as an open-ended art form, in which many elements of song, music, dialogue, elocution, and props are blended. Unlike the Western emphasis on spoken drama, with its heavy concentration on content and meaning, the Japanese value theater as a complete performing art: Spoken drama and theater are considered a separate art distinct from written literature.

North and South Korea boast a long history of theatrical tradition, especially in mask dance drama and puppetry. Because of the division of the country in 1948, traditional theater in North Korea was subjugated in favor of modern, Western-influenced spoken drama that idealized communism and the state. In South Korea, preservation of traditional theater was encouraged and coexisted with modern spoken drama based on Western and European models.

OCEANIA

Though divided into three geographical regions based on cultural, ethnic, and linguistic differences, Melanesia, Micronesia, and Polynesia share three common theatrical features. The first feature includes theatrical performances that take place in the forms of festivals, communal feasts, and life-cycle rituals to celebrate social life and the community. The second feature includes comic skits that are traditionally enmeshed in music, poetry, and dance. These comic skits are with actors but they do not portray other personas in a structured narrative (as in Western spoken drama). The third feature stresses the importance of professional specialists and expertise performance in these traditional art forms. Social, cultural, and political changes were inevitable because of Western colonialization and Christianization in the nineteenth and early twentieth centuries, and Oceania's theatrical tradition was not immune to the change, finding itself increasingly based on Western models.

Melanesia is known for dance mimes, the use of masks with a dramatic bent. These mimetic dances are performed from the perspective of the prey in reenactments of fishing and hunting and serve social and cultural functions, in comparison with Micronesia and Polynesia, where dances of hunting and fishing are performed from a human perspective. In Micronesian theatrical performances, song texts are very central and choreographical gestures are abstract, whereas mimetic role play is not emphasized (although it exists). Micronesian dances are much more decorative than Polynesian dances, which are more metaphorical and use poetic texts as intrinsic elements. Western-influenced modern spoken drama is found in Melanesia and Polynesia, and it often criticizes Western influences or reflects each region's culture. Despite the pervasiveness of modern film and television, theatrical traditions and drama seem to keep pace with the times and continue to be a vital tradition to the people of these three regions.

SOUTH ASIA

India has a long and very rich, highly developed history in theater, in both its structures and sophistication. Indian theatrical style is often baroque, colorful, corporeal, emotional, and not at all restrained like East Asian theater. Because of the nation's multicultural population, Indian theater is vast and quite extensive, with varying influences on its nearby neighbors, Bangladesh and Pakistan, as well as other South Asian countries.

Bangladesh and Pakistan have theatrical traditions related to each other and to India. To understand these commonalities, geographical, historical, and political facts need to be considered. The people of

Bangladesh, which became independent in 1971 from West Pakistan, are predominantly Muslim, like the Pakistanis, but linguistically and ethnically Bengali, like the people in northeastern India. Therefore, Bangladeshi theater is directly related to Bengali theatrical history and tradition. In Bangladesh, *jatra*—a regional theater form dating to the sixteenth century as part of the Vaishnava religious movement in which dances, songs, and plays are fundamental elements— is very popular because it originated from the rural areas of Bengal and is performed in Bengali language. Modern drama, thematic in the struggle for independence and against repression of the Bengali people, was popular in the 1960's.

The current borders of Pakistan and India were created in 1947. Historically, Pakistani theater came into existence in 1853 from the city of Lucknow in north central India. However, because Pakistan, is Muslim. theater and drama are not encouraged or even condoned for religious reasons. In essence, theater in Pakistan is slow in developing, and little has been written or researched on the subject of its theater.

Nepal has a colorful and popular form of dance drama called *mani-rimdu*. It is performed by Buddhist monks who wear large masks in a seasonal nine-day ceremony in open-air monasteries to celebrate traditional devotion and Buddhist beliefs and to assert Buddhist superiority over the Bon religion. Modern urban theater is really performed only in the country's capital of Kathmandu. Very little research and written work have been done on the subject of modern Nepalese theater.

Sri Lanka, an island country, is inhabited by Buddhist Sinhalese and Hindu Tamils, the country's minority group originally from India. Sri Lanka has no classical Sinhalese theatrical tradition—except one provided by the Sanskrit tradition—because in ancient times Buddhist monks considered drama and theater taboo. Instead of writing about drama and theatrical arts, they concentrated on poetry and narrative stories. Folk theater includes various genres including *kolam*, a masked folk theater in which comic elements are exaggerated to provoke laughter and general entertainment. Modern drama began in the late nineteenth century with Western influences, dealing primarily with urban and social issues.

SOUTHEAST ASIA

Traditional theater in Southeast Asia—Myanmar, Cambodia, Indonesia, Laos, Malaysia, the Philippines, Singapore, Thailand, and Vietnam—is more than one thousand years old and has roots in dance, literature, and the religions of both South and East Asia, regions that hold their own rich performance traditions. Western-oriented modern spoken drama is also popular in these countries. Because these nations had international contacts along with their own indigenous performance history, they are well endowed with a highly developed theatrical heritage with influences from both South and East Asia. Myanmar, Cambodia, Malaysia, and especially Indonesia are well influenced by Indian theatricality. Vietnam is heavily influenced by Chinese theater because of its centuries-long domination by China. Each country still maintains its own distinct dramatic forms despite the fact that theatrical similarities are inevitable because of geographic proximity and historical and political similarities. Southeast Asian drama gives priority to performance instead of sustained narratives like Western drama, but it is not at all less intellectual than Western theater or drama tradition. The understanding of Southeast Asian theater requires the knowledge of the whole genre and form and not just individual plays.

BIBLIOGRAPHY

Brandon, James R. *Brandon's Guide to Theatre in Asia*. Honolulu: University Press of Hawaii, 1976. A guide to theater models and trends in Asia.

Brandon, James R., and Martin Banham, eds. *The Cambridge Guide to Asian Theatre*. Cambridge, England: Cambridge University Press, 2000. Includes entries on individual Asian countries and their respective theatrical developments and history, with comprehensive listing of the most important aspects of each country's dramatic genres and styles.

Brandon, James R., and Elizabeth Wichmann, eds. *Asian Theatre: A Study Guide and Annotated Bibliography*. Washington, D.C.: University and College Theatre Association, 1980. A study guide with comprehensive bibliography on Asian theater.

Mohd, Taib Osman, ed. *Traditional Drama and Music of Southeast Asia*. Kuala Lumpur: Dewan Bahasa dan Pustaka, Kementerian Pelajaran Malaysia, 1974. Contains a collection of papers presented at the International Conference on Traditional Drama and Music of Southeast Asia, Kuala Lumpur, in 1969, with entries by scholars and experts.

Obeyesekere, Ranjini. *Sri Lankan Theater in a Time of Terror: Political Satire on a Permitted Space*. Thousand Oaks, Calif.: Sage, 1999. Examines Sri Lankan socially critical theater of the 1980's, including extracts and descriptions of several plays, interviews, and a history of one theater company.

Rubin, Don, ed. *The World Encyclopedia of Contemporary Theatre*. London: Routledge, 1994. Volume is concentrated on theater and dramatic history and development in almost all Asian countries, notably those of Central Asia.

Hanh N. Nguyen

CHINESE DRAMA

Although from early times Chinese of all classes have always displayed a love for theatrical entertainments of all kinds, orthodox literary criticism generally rejected the text of a play as a legitimate branch of literature primarily because of the divorce that had taken place between *wenyan*, or classical Chinese, and *baihua*, or plain speech. Because all serious literature was the exclusive province of classical Chinese and drama was predominantly a vernacular medium so far as linguistic expression was concerned, the play enjoyed no respectable literary status.

Moreover, Chinese society relegated actors and actresses to the fifth and lowest rung of the social ladder, ranking them together with prostitutes, slaves, paid servants, barbers, jugglers, and beggars. Thus, actors suffered the legal discrimination of the other members of this class, for example, being prohibited, together with their families, from sitting for the official examinations, the normal entry into Chinese official life. Actors and actresses were considered to have low moral standards. Homosexuality was widespread among actors, and actresses were normally prostitutes because the ability to dance and sing was a necessary qualification of a good courtesan. In short, there were social and moral objections to the theater, and during the Ming and the Qing Dynasties the government issued various decrees directed against both players and plays.

Also, the text of a Chinese drama was but an occasion and guide to its theatrical performance, which involved much more than plot, the presentation of characters, and dialogue. Chinese drama was predominantly musical and operatic, with verse and song occupying a large proportion of a play's script. Hence the quality of the singing as well as of the instrumental musical accompaniment was of first importance. Moreover, Chinese dramaturgy also involved dancing, symbolic costumes, masks or painted masklike faces, symbolic acting techniques, and symbolic stage props. In military plays, skill in the martial arts (*wu shu*), which included *kung fu*; use of weapons such as cudgel, sword, and spear; and acrobatics,

were important features. There was no scenery and only a minimum of stage props. The script of a Chinese play, therefore, was a dynamic rather than a static and dogmatic element, subject to interpretation and revision by the performers, and merely one element in a complicated, harmonious dramatic process.

RISE OF CHINESE DRAMA

Some historians have given the impression that the rise of the Chinese drama to full maturity during the Yuan Dynasty (1279-1368) was both meteoric and *ex nihilo*. Actually, the drama began to emerge in popular religious ceremonies, ritualistic practices, and festival celebrations as early as the Shang Dynasty (1600-1066 B.C.E.). This can be seen in the practices of shamanism. Shamans, or priests, termed *wu* if female and *xi* if male, acted as mediums between the spirits and the rest of humankind. They would recite incantations, dance, and otherwise posture in an effort to induce the spirits to descend into their bodies. When the spirits had apparently entered into them, they would impersonate them and communicate their thoughts to the audience.

Under the Zhou Dynasty (1066-256 B.C.E.), ritualism developed into a fine art. All ritual was governed by strict rules of etiquette (*li*), respecting dress, speech, and action. Confucius, the greatest Chinese philosopher of this era, stressed *li*, the rules of proper conduct, together with *ren*, the duty of one person to another, in his system of ethics. He legislated on funeral practices, ancestor worship, and filial piety (*xiao*). At funerals, puppet shows were shown to relieve the grief of the mourners. In the ceremony in which descendants showed reverence to a departed ancestor, it was customary to choose a member of the family, usually a minor, to impersonate the dead ancestor at the sacrifice. This person, termed the *shi*, assumed the garb of the deceased and seated himself at the sacrificial table to accept the offerings of food and drink and the kowtows of the family members. Filial piety included the proper reciprocal relationship between the citizen and the chief of state.

Early monarchs employed court fools or jesters to entertain them. Known as *pai you*, these actors sometimes performed useful services by facetious criticism of public policies or in emotionally supportive roles. For example, it is recorded that when a very meritorious prime minister of the state of Zhu died in office, his prince missed him so much that he ordered an actor-entertainer named Meng to dress in the deceased minister's clothing and impersonate him in memorable episodes from his life. So effective was Meng's impersonation that the prince appointed him prime minister. As a result of this occurrence, there came into Chinese usage the phrase *you Meng yi guan*, literally meaning "the garments of the actor Meng" but used as a verbal idiom meaning simply "to dress up." Such *pai you* as Meng sang, danced, and gave impersonations, but at this time they did not yet tell a sustained story. Such a development did not take place until the Han Dynasty (206 B.C.E.-220 C.E.).

During the Han, the term *you ren* applied to the majority of professional entertainers and could mean minstrel, dancer, juggler, acrobat, actor, or jester. The most vital element that the Han contributed to early Chinese drama, however, was the story-sketch or simple playlet. A sketch of this kind was *Donghai Huanggong* (Mr. Huang of the eastern ocean). Mr. Huang was a magician who in his youth loved hunting. He killed tigers and other dangerous creatures with his sword after charming them with his magic spells. As he grew older, he grew exceedingly fond of drinking wine. One day he heard of a fierce tiger in his neighborhood. He sallied forth wearing a red turban on his head and gripping a sword in his hand. When he came face-to-face with the tiger, he attempted to charm it with his magic spells. Because his excessive wine drinking had rendered him impotent, however, his spells failed to achieve the desired result, and the tiger devoured him forthwith. The Han emperor Wudi made this skit into a "horn-butting" (*jiu-di*) game or sport (*hsi*). In such contests, two opponents vied for supremacy. The Han emperor included this contest between man and tiger among the Hundred Games (*baixi*), which were entertainments of a circus or fairground nature. Outside the western gate of the capital of Luoyang, there was a fairground

where pantomimes, dances, acrobatic performances, magic acts, juggling, sword-swallowing, fire-eating, and the like amazed both emperor and peasant. As a result of the character of Mr. Huang, the Chinese language adopted the curious phrase *huang wang*, meaning "wild and lost." This idiom contains both a pun and two lacunae, for "Mr. Huang" means "Mr. Wild," who was both "wild" (with the excessive love of hunting) and "lost" (through the excessive drinking of wine).

SONG AND DANCE SKITS

A long period of disunity followed the downfall of the Han Dynasty. With political power decentralized, invasions by non-Chinese peoples from Central Asia, war and internecine strife, and foreign influences of various kinds affected the Chinese. A minor influence during the Han Dynasty, Buddhism, was by the sixth century one of the three major religions of China. With Buddhism may have come some knowledge of Sanskrit drama, but no specific evidence suggests that it figured in the development of Chinese drama. The Central Asian frontier, however, did make signal contributions not simply to music and song but also to dance and storytelling, in musical skits known as *kewu ji* (literally, "song-dance art").

In the northwest corner of China of the sixth century, the Northern Qi kingdom was ruled by the Topas, a Tungusic-speaking family. Prince Lan Ling was a Qi warrior who, though a skilled and valiant fighter, labored under the handicap of being handsome to an almost effeminate degree. Hence, for close combat he wore a fierce-looking mask to disguise his beauty and to put fear and respect into the minds of his opponents. Thus arrayed, he scored victory after victory until he gained the admiration of his people, to whom he appeared a great hero. Wishing to honor him by celebrating his heroic deeds, they devised a song-and-dance routine in which actors wore *dai mian* (literally, "substitute faces") and impersonated him and his opponents in rousing combat.

In Qi there also was a layman named Su Baobi, a common man (indicated by his surname Su) and a failure and a drunkard with a pimply nose (indicated by his personal name Baobi). He was in the habit of attiring himself in the dress of a high official and parading to the local wine shop, where he indulged his fondness for drinking. Returning home drunk, he would quarrel with his wife and beat her unmercifully. She would then bemoan her hard lot to all who would listen to her woes. Amused by this repeated incident, the people invented a song-and-dance routine in which two male actors portrayed this quarrel between Mr. and Mrs. Everyman. The doleful singing of Su's wife is said to have elicited the participation of the audience.

During the Tang Dynasty (618-907), both these song-and-dance skits became particularly popular. The Prince Lan Ling story was given the title *Lanling Wang ru zhen qu* (melody of the Prince of Orchid Mound's going into battle). It is said to have involved the marshaling of troops, personal combat, and the wearing of the mask. The sketch about the Su couple became known as *Dayao niang* (stepping and singing woman). The title of government secretary that the husband had assumed was changed simply to Uncle Ah. The wife's part came to be played by a woman instead of by a male actor. The husband wore a hat and was dressed in red clothes; his face was painted red (or he wore a red mask) to emphasize his commitment to drinking wine. Apparently a third character, a treasurer or stockman, was added to the cast, thus considerably altering the original skit.

ADJUTANT PLAY

Another kind of skit, known as the adjutant play (*canjun xi*), became very popular during the Tang. The skit was based on the story of a mandarin and an adjutant found guilty of crookedness who, while still retained by the emperor because he valued his services, was yet required to suffer the punishment of being publicly ridiculed by actors at courtly feasts forever afterward. Some say that the character of the adjutant was based on the Han Dynasty magistrate Xi Dan, who, found guilty of accepting bribes, was punished in this way; others say that the adjutant came from a Six Dynasties mandarin, Zhou Yan, who was convicted of "squeezing" thousands of rolls of government silk and was punished in the same way as Xi Dan. At any rate, the adjutant play proved so popular

that it was still being played during the Five Dynasties period (907-960). By this time, the adjutant was referred to as the Pillar (*Zhu*), and his companion and servant was called Gray (or Green) Hawk (*Cang gu*), no doubt because he wore a gray or green hat.

The Pillar or Post (*Zhu*), the adjutant, and "false official" was the "prey" and "mark" swooped down on and attacked by the Gray Hawk. The Chinese have a saying: *Gu fa bi zhong*, "When the hawk swoops it always hits its mark." The later Jin Dynasty (936-946) is famous for its farcical playlets known as *yuanben* (literally, "brothel scripts"). In them, the Pillar and the Gray Hawk are termed respectively *fujing* and *fumo*. The former was a clown with a painted face (*lianpu choujiu*) who was the main comic attraction. The latter was the clown's assistant and his victimizer; in short, he was the "straight man," to use the argot of the Western theater. By the early Ming Dynasty (1368-1644), two other characters had been added to the *fujing* and the *fumo*; they were the *moni* and the *jieji*. The *jieji* was a sort of master of ceremonies with introductory functions, and the *moni* was a sort of stage manager also functioning as a kind of master of ceremonies. The *fumo* carried a *kegua* (literally, "knocking gourd"), some sort of soft club with which the *fumo* habitually struck the *fujing* whenever the latter did or said something silly or foolish.

MING HUANG

The significance of all this was not only that a kind of narrative structure was being developed but also that stage roles were being categorized. Stereotyped roles, each distinctively different from the others in facial appearance, costuming, voice quality, gestures. and movements, were to become a dominant feature of the later, more mature Chinese drama. During the reign of Emperor Ming Huang, the comical adjutant play of *canjun xi* rivaled in popularity the musical skit or *kewu ji*, and it survived into the Song Dynasty (960-1279). Also, by the end of the Tang Dynasty. a drama with a more extended story is known to have been performed at the court of Emperor Zhao Zong. In 901, the emperor composed and had performed at an imperial dinner a historical drama titled *Fan Guai pai chun nan* (Fan Guai rescues his monarch from distress), based on an assassination plot directed against the first emperor of the Han Dynasty. It appears that this play was acted rather than merely sung and danced.

Emperor Ming Huang was very fond of music and song and of theatrical entertainment generally. He had puppet shows performed at court by the Imperial Academy of Music (Jiao Fangsi), and he composed a poem in which he compared himself to a puppet. He also established the Pear Garden Conservatory (Li Yuan) for the training of men and women entertainers, although they were mainly singers and musicians rather than stage actors. Nevertheless, he has always been honored by the acting profession as the founding father of Chinese drama, and Chinese actors have been called, and have called themselves, "Disciples of the Pear Garden." Certain developments in literature, too, during the Tang had consequences for later drama. The Buddhist "popular sermon," or *sujiang*, was represented by a written text called the *bianwen*, a term referring to a "transformation" or "the text of a scene." Written in the vernacular mixed with literary Chinese, this form used Buddhist fables that were paraphrases of the *sutras* (*jiangjing wo*) and were written in prose, song, and verse. Such a *bianwen* was *Da Mujianlian mingjian jiumu bian wen* (great Mandalyāyana saves his mother from the underworld). In the realm of classical literature, the literati began composing short stories called *chuanqi* (literally, "transmission of the strange"). Written in the literary language, they were composed as practice exercises in preparation for the civil service examinations and also simply for entertainment. These stories, however, later served as the basis of plots for many dramas.

ZAJU AND XIWEN

With the advent of the Song Dynasty, all the basic elements of drama were in existence, but they had not yet been combined into a distinctive dramatic shape having a sustained story given logical development in support of some theme. The beginning of such a coalescence, however, occurred during the Song and the Jin Dynasties.

The Song divided itself into the Northern and Southern Song Dynasties. The Northern Song (960-1127) had its capital at Bianliang (modern Kaifeng) in northern China. The dynasty ended when the non-Chinese Jurchens (Ruzhens), the ancestors of the Manchu, who had established the Jin Dynasty (1115-1234), overcame the Song. In 1126, the Jurchens captured the Song capital, abducted the emperor and his father, and made what is now Beijing one of their capitals. The Song court fled southward and established the Southern Song Dynasty (1127-1279), ruling middle and southern China from a new capital at Hangzhou in mid-southeast China.

During this period, when the Jin and the Southern Song Dynasties controlled most of China between them, drama made strides that brought it to the forefront in the succeeding Yuan (Mongol) Dynasty to make it the age of drama. These strides consisted primarily in the appearance of some new dramatic forms. In the north appeared the Song *zaju* (literally, "variety show"), also called the *beiqu* ("northern musical"), and the Jin *yuanben*. Both these new dramatic forms were originally much the same and may have been different names for roughly the same thing. In the south there appeared the *xiwen* (literally "play script"), also called the *nanxi* ("southern drama").

Although the *zaju* began its development under the Northern Song Dynasty, it did not become popular until after the establishment of the Southern Song. The early *zaju* appears to have been simply a mixture of music and comedy that came in a variety of forms: the *kui zaju* (wooden puppet show), the *ya zaju* (dumb show), the *da zaju* (big variety show), and the *xiao zaju* (little variety show). In these forms, there were bawdy skits (*huxi*), ghost skits (*guixi*), military skits (*wuxi*), and civil skits (*wenxi*).

The early *zaju* were short performances used as introductions or interludes in larger entertainments featuring music, dancing, and sword or spear fighting. Such performances as the Official Varieties (*guanben zaju*) and the Wenzhou Varieties (Wenzhou *zaju*) were apparently "acted-out" stories. The Wenzhou Varieties are believed to have been more story-oriented and lengthier than the Official Varieties. By the Southern Song period, the shorter variety was strictly referred to as *zaju*, and the lengthier type became known as *xiwen* to distinguish them. By the

Yuan Dynasty, both terms applied to musical dramas of full play length, but the *xiwen* remained far lengthier than the *zaju*. After the collapse of the Song in 1279, the *zaju* was replaced by the *xiwen*. Nevertheless, the former penetrated the south and influenced the latter, effectively, over time, replacing it: Far more *zaju* were produced than *xiwen*, and many more have been preserved. About 733 *zaju* are known to have been written and about 162 preserved, but only about 150 *xiwen* were written and only 3 or 4 preserved.

YUANBEN

While the *zaju* and the *xiwen* were developing under the Song, the *yuanben*, or short, comic sketch, was developing under the Jin Dynasty. Although no texts of the Jin *yuanben* remain, the popularity of the form is attested by the numerous titles recorded in contemporary sources. Some titles are the same as those of the Official Varieties and thus are indicative of the close identity between the Jin *yuanben* and the Song *zaju* in their original forms.

Two extant poems of the late thirteenth century briefly describe *yuanben* performances. Each describes a visit to a *koulan*, a theater situated in a *wazi*, or city amusement center that included the prostitutes' quarter. ("Prostitutes' quarter" is another meaning of *koulan*.) The earlier of the two accounts, a poem written by Du Renjie, is *Zhuangjia bushi goulan* (a farmer takes a look at the theater). In the poem, a farmer visits the theater for the first time and witnesses a *yuanben*, which introduces the entertainment program. It is a comic skit that portrays the attempt of a rich man to seduce a pretty girl into marriage by false promises made to her by a waiter whom the suitor employs as a go-between. Her sharp remarks and the exasperation of the suitor convulse the audience, including the farmer, into gales of laughter. Made to retire from the theater by the pressure on his bladder, the farmer misses the conclusion of the humorous skit.

The later account is a poem written by Gao Andao in the late thirteenth or early fourteenth century. It describes the employees, the audience, the musicians, and the entertainers and actors in the theater as well as the entire program, which includes a *yuanben*.

There is a tough-looking doorkeeper who is also the bouncer, a peppermint vendor, and a flutist and drummer of unsavory appearance. The women musicians are unattractive prostitutes who leer at the hoodlum audience in search of prospective customers. The program is introduced by singing, after which come successive acts of clodhopping dancing, acrobatics, stilt-walking, back-flipping, and the antics of demons. Following these mixed specialty acts (reminiscent of Western vaudeville), a *yuanben* introduces a larger *zaju* drama. The program is concluded by a *sanduan* (literally, "dispersal section"), which typically consisted of a *zaban*, or "joke-telling" act. The "vaudeville" section of the program is described as woefully incompetent, the demon act in particular being a complete flop. The *yuanben* performance is described as tasteless, and the *zaju* actors are said to have murdered the drama. How just this criticism may be is undeterminable; no doubt the poet indulged in some poetic license. At any rate, some rough idea of the nature and the role of the Jin *yuanben* and its relationship to the Song *zaju* can be gained from these two poetic descriptions.

Although the traditional *yuanben* originated in the north, it was incorporated into the *nanxi*, or southern drama, as well as into the *zaju*, or northern drama. The few *yuanben* that survive are of late date—from the fourteenth to the sixteenth centuries—some as parts of *zaju* or *nanxi* and others as independent entities. For example, a *yuanben* appears in an early Ming *zaju* written by the imperial prince Zhu Yudun. The *zaju*, titled *Shenxian hui* (meeting of Immortals), relates the story of the Goddess of Immortality. Having transgressed the laws of Heaven, she was banished to Earth, where she was incarnated as a courtesan. The *yuanben* inserted into the larger drama has to do with the goddess's birthday. On this occasion, four gods, sent to earth disguised as men to assist her, decide to present her with gifts and wishes for a long life. Acting the parts of Star Gods of Longevity, they play functional roles assigned to them by the text: *fumo*, *ching*, *moni*, and *jieji*. Whether this early Ming skit is typical of the Jin or Yuan *yuanben*, however, is unknown. Further, the Ming developed a new kind of short, literary type of play that was also called the *yuanben* but which departed sufficiently from the form and spirit of the traditional type to constitute a new genre. This literary type of *yuanben* is typified by the one-act play written in the sixteenth century by Wang Jiusi titled *Zhongshan long* (wolf of Central Mountain).

ZI AND ZHU

Because traditional Chinese drama is operatic, its development was intimately associated with both speech and music, and therefore with *shouchang wenxue*, or "literature to be narrated or sung." Under the Tang, the *bianwen* originated as a popularized Buddhist sermon in verse and prose featuring examples from Buddhist legend that became secularized. There was also the *huaben* (literally, "story root"), the vernacular short story narrated by professional storytellers to entertain people in the big cities, which became a popular written form during the Song Dynasty. Apart from the adjutant play, or *canjun xi*, and the musical skit called the *kewu ji*, the Tang originated the lyric meter called the *zi* (literally, "song-words"), in which the poet invented words to fit an existing tune, being bound by the formal structure of the whole tune. The *zi* became the dominant vehicle for lyric poetry during the Song Dynasty.

Under the Jin Dynasty, the *zhu* (literally, "song"), or "dramatic verse," originated. The *zhu* is related to the long-short verse style called *changduanzhu* and also to the *zi*, which it replaced as the major poetic vehicle during the Yuan Dynasty. The origins of the *zhu* are apparently connected with its use in the dramatic medley called the *zhugongdiao*, the popular Jin narrative poem employing musical tunes in various modes. Only one complete example survives, the *Xixiang ji chi zhugongdiao* (medley of the story of the western chamber), written by Dong Jieyuan, who based his ballad on the famous Tang *chuanqi* (or classical short story) *Yingying zhuan* (also known as *Hui zhen ji*; the story of Yingying), the work of the ninth century literatus Yuan Zhen. Although there may be a connection between the *zhugongdiao* and the *yuanben*, the exact nature is unknown.

Other ballad types of the period also contributed to the development of the drama, from the "big song" (*da qu*), made of a series of *zi*; through the "turn" (*zhuanta*), of alternating *zi* and *shi* stanzas; to the "drum song" (*guzi ci*), whose musical accompaniment was a small drum. The best-known drum song, *Shengdiao dielianhua* (the tune "The Butterfly Loves Flowers" in the Shangdiao mode), was also based on Yuan Zhen's prose tale *Yingying zhuan*. This drum song was constructed around ten stanzas of a *zi* written to the tune "The Butterfly Loves Flowers," a widely sung aria of the Song Dynasty.

Apart from the role of the *yuanben*, therefore, the chief narrative elements of the Yuan drama were derived from the dramatic *zhu* as used in the *zhugongdiao*, and the main lyric elements came from the shorter song form of the *sanqu* in suite form. This meant grouping tunes belonging to the same mode and arranging them in a "suite" (*taoshu*) to make a musical composition to which words might be applied. Although the *zhu* was divisible into two separate schools, the northern (*beiqu*) and the southern (*nanqu*), the term normally refers to the dramatic arias written for the stage (*xi qu*) and the lyric verse forms (*sanqu*), especially the northern suite style (*taoshu*).

THE MONGOLIAN INFLUENCE

After peace was concluded between the Jin and the Southern Song in 1141, there followed a period of coexistence and cooperation that extended for seventy-three years, during which time considerable cultural exchange took place. This period came to an end in 1214-1215 when Mongol Genghis Khan launched his attacks. By 1234, the Mongols had annihilated the Jin empire. The complete conquest of China, however, was left to Genghis's grandson, Kublai Khan, who sent his armies eastward down the Yangzi (Yangtze) River toward Hangzhou. They captured the young Chinese emperor, Kung Ti, in 1276. Although Song resistance continued, it ended with the fall of Canton and the defeat of the Chinese fleet off Yaishan Island in 1279. Kublai had already proclaimed the establishment of the Yuan Dynasty in 1271. Now he actually ruled all China, and it was as the Chinese emperor rather than as the Great Khan that he asserted his authority over the Chinese people.

With China in the hand of the Mongols, further cultural and political changes took place that had the effect of promoting the development of drama and other arts quite accidentally. The Chinese language underwent drastic change, owing to the difficulties the Mongol conquerors experienced with Chinese intonation and pronunciation. The result was a simplification of the spoken language, with the number of tones being reduced from five or more to four; final *k*'s, *t*'s, and *p*'s being dropped; and final *m*'s becoming *n*'s. This reduction and change in the number of phonemes gave the north a language generally understood by everybody. As a result, southern as well as northern playwrights had at their disposal what amounted to a national tongue, a standardized stage language. To keep the playwrights straight on the matter of the phonological system of the Beijing dialect, thirteenth century Zhou Deqing wrote his *Zhong-yuan yinyun* (1324; sounds and rhymes of the central plain), a prescriptive effort to establish a standard usage for *zaju* plays.

A drastic change in the political circumstances of the Chinese literati also had the accidental effect of promoting the drama and other arts. Chinese scholars normally expected an official career, which they generally entered after demonstrating their understanding of the Confucian classics and their skill in classical composition in the civil service examinations. To the Mongol leaders, however, the Chinese literati had been responsible for Chinese resistance during their effort to conquer China, and hence to them they were *personae non gratae*. The Mongols preferred Mongols, non-Chinese Asiatics, and even Europeans in the administration of government to any Chinese. The Mongols therefore held the traditional civil service examinations once, in 1237, and then not for three-quarters of a century. When they were resumed in 1313, the requirements had been changed to disfavor the Chinese. When Chinese were admitted to government service, they were generally obliged to accept positions at levels much below their capabilities.

Many Chinese literati preferred not to cooperate with the Mongols at all. Instead, they "retired" and went into seclusion, often seeking a creative outlet for their talents in "scholar's painting" (*wenrenhua*), a combination of drawing, poetry, and calligraphy. Many other scholars needed employment of some profitable kind to earn a livelihood. The less creative became tradesmen of some kind, such as shopkeepers or butchers. Some practiced medicine or engineering. The more creative adopted the trade of writing songs and plays or popular prose fiction, especially novels. For the first time, the commercial production of plays and prose fiction took place on a wide scale, and many hands were busy at popular vernacular literature. Such activity fostered the rapid rise of drama and novels during the Yuan Dynasty. Released from the grip of classical literature, the entire populace developed an avid interest in plays and other popular literary forms. What formerly had been disapproved of was now approved, even by numerous literati.

YUAN ZAJU

The *zaju* reached its apogee during the Yuan period, making it the age of drama. A great number of *zaju* were written at this time, and many of them survive, particularly in Ming editions. They continued during most of the Ming Dynasty but eventually gave way to the more popular Ming *chuanqi* dramas.

With the onset of the Yuan, the *zaju* became a sophisticated musical drama that featured narrative action, dialogue, recitation, the singing of arias and other songs, and musical accompaniment. These features were integrated into a unified and sustained theatrical performance with a beginning, a middle, and an end. The narrative action included not only the acting out of emotions in the context of social interaction but also ritual, dancing, and demonstrations of martial arts (*wu shu*) such as *kung fu*, swordsmanship, staff or cudgel fighting, and other acrobatic feats. These actions were performed in a symbolic rather than a realistic manner, pantomime often being employed. In addition to singing, dancing, dialogue, recitation, display of martial skills, and acrobatics, *yuanben* or comic interludes were often included in *zaju* performances.

The format of a *zaju* drama normally consisted of four acts (rarely five), called *zhe*. Optionally, a demiact (rarely two), called *xiezi* (literally, "wedge"), might be included. A *zhe* was defined musically rather than dramatically. It meant a "suite" (*tao zhu*), that is, a string of arias and of cluster arias belonging to a single "mode" (*gongdiao*) together with the accompanying dialogue and dramatic machinery. The arias (*qu* or *xi qu*) in an act were arranged according to a conventional sequence, the act beginning with a certain melody or *zhu* "tune" and ending with a certain coda form. The suite had to conform to a single rhyme and be sung by a single character, there being only one singing role in any one act. The same performer, however, might play the male lead in one act and then the female lead in another act. If the male and female leads were played by different persons, the two might appear together in the same act, but only one lead would sing. In some plays only one lead would sing throughout the drama, but in others there would be different leads for different acts. Both men and women performed in the Yuan *zaju*, but some individuals played both male and female roles.

The idea of role-types (*tai zhi*, literally, "pillars of the stage") was an important dramatic convention of the Yuan *zaju*. No matter what the plot, the theme, or the individual being portrayed, each character was assigned a role-type, and it was his or her main mark of identification. There were but two main role-types: the *zhengmo* (abbreviated as *mo*), or leading male character, and the *zhengdan* (abbreviated as *dan*), or leading female character. *Mo* roles included both young and old men, usually of a serious and dignified type: scholar, general, hermit, monk, judge, and shopkeeper, although occasionally the character was comical. *Dan* roles were usually fairly young or middle-aged women ranging from noble or otherwise dignified lady to singsong girl and maidservant. The secondary roles were prefixed by the word *wai* (secondary), but if elderly by *lao* (old), and if very young by *xiao* (little). The *jing* was clownish or villainous, sometimes both, and included the dishonest or harsh official, the vagabond knight-errant, the rascally monk or bricklayer, and the Machiavellian general. The subtype-roles included the bad female (*cha dan*) and the genuine clown (*chou*). These role-types had a direct bearing on the costumes and face makeup that the performers assumed in playing such role-types.

MUSIC IN YUAN DRAMA

Music was vital to Yuan drama, but no musical scores are extant; only the texts of lyrics are available. Little is known, therefore, about the exact character of the music accompanying the dramatic *zhu*. Northern music employed the heptatonic scale, southern the pentatonic, Chinese scales not being tempered. Northern music was modal in its organization, whereas southern ignored modes in favor of ordering the sequence of songs. Southern music had no modal rules. On the other hand, northern required that the tunes of a suite (*tao shu*) be arranged not only in sets but also in but one modality for any particular dramatic act (*zhe*). Northern music employed nine modes (*gongdiao*) derived from five scales (*di se*). The moods evoked by the modes are known only through descriptions given by the Yuan critic Ji An, in his *Changlu* (discourse of singing). There, for instance, he describes the *xianlu gong* mode as "refreshing and soft." From other evidence, it is clear that a distinct correlation exists between the mode and the dramatic content of the act.

Vocalization in the Yuan theater was apparently predominantly nasal, the tongue, teeth, and lips seldom employed except for labial enunciation. In the *zaju*, however, the word took precedence over the tune, one or more syllables being sung to the note. Thus the singing was not far from recitative. On the other hand, in southern singing, tune dominated word. Southern singing was melismatic, several notes dwelling on a single syllable that was frequently extended. Northern drama emphasized understanding, southern emotional appeal. As for the dramatic orchestra, it occupied a place on the stage called the *yuechuan* (music bench). The orchestral instruments were commonly the drum (*gu*), the gong (*luo*), wooden or ivory clappers (*ban*), and the flute (*dizi*). The flute provided the melodic lineaments, while the drum, gong, and clappers reinforced them. Sometimes characters in a drama appeared onstage with musical instruments to accompany their own singing.

An important aspect of the Yuan drama was that the musical structure of the dramatic *zhu* directly reflected the linguistic structure of Chinese speech. The arias incorporated elements of the spoken language as one necessary element. Apart from the arias and the independent songs, the drama included prose speeches. The entrance speeches, written in six-four ornamental prose, were rendered in recitative style. In these speeches, the characters introduced themselves, explained their circumstances, and sometimes recited *shi* poems. The dramatic dialogue, on the other hand, was very colloquial, even racy at times. If not addressed to other characters in the drama, dialogue was addressed to the audience; there was little monologue except in terms of an occasional aside. The important ingredient in Chinese speech from a musical standpoint is that it incorporates the aspect of *sheng*—usually translated as "tones." *Sheng* involve the level, rising, and falling elements of the spoken language, and they not only affect the actual meaning of the words but also act as an independent basis for musical composition, a "melodic movement." The *zhu* music, therefore, was more closely related to the syntax of the lyrics than is the case with Western opera. Because of the emphasis on modality and sequential organization found in the *zaju*, the aria sequence in the suite was tied to the progression of the plot to a large degree. The music of the Yuan drama, however, was not "composed" in the usual sense, since *zhu* were set to already existing tunes. The rule was *Zhao bu tian ci*: "Fill in the words according to the musical pattern."

YUAN DRAMATISTS

In 1215, the Mongol armies of Genghis Khan swept across the north and left the Jin capital at what is now Beijing in ruins. In 1234, a combined Chinese and Mongol force defeated the Jin emperor. Genghis's grandson, Kublai Khan, assumed power in 1260 and immediately began reconstruction of the former Jin capital, which he renamed Dadu in Chinese and Cambaluc or Khambaligh in Mongolian, designating it his western capital. Under Mongol rule, Dadu became again what it had been under the Jurchens—the center of Chinese drama. Although the Mongols ruled over northern China, they were unable to conquer the Song Empire in the south until 1279.

Although the Yuan Dynasty is usually dated 1279-1368, the history of Yuan drama begins earlier and is actually divisible into two periods. In the early period, 1234-1279, the outstanding dramatists were predominantly northerners who were either natives or residents of Dadu. Few southerners resided there. During the second or late period, 1280-1367, most of the major playwrights were southerners who were either natives or residents of Hangzhou. Even a number of northern writers had intimate connections with this southern city, mainly by virtue of residence there during their service in government posts. The justification of this periodization comes particularly from a curious book compiled in 1330 by Zhong Sicheng. Titled *Lu guibu*, meaning "a record of deceased personages in the theatrical profession," this work lists the names of playwrights who died before 1330 as well as those who were the author's contemporaries.

Chinese drama advanced rapidly in the north in and around Dadu between 1234 and 1279. Four outstanding dramatists emerged who became designated the Four Great Men (*si weiren*) of the Yuan *zaju* drama. The leader of this group, often considered the real founder of the Chinese drama, was Guan Hanqing. A native of Dadu, he was for a time a member of the Academy of Emperial Physicians. A Jin sympathizer (he had served at the Jin court before 1234), he became an actor-manager and playwright. He wrote more than sixty plays, only fourteen of which survive.

His dramatic masterpiece is generally considered *Dou O yuan* (*The Injustice Done to Tou Ngo*, 1972). In this play, a young widow, Dou O, is wrongfully accused of murder and is sentenced to be beheaded. Kneeling before her judge and executioners, she predicts that following her death heaven will testify to her innocence by perpetrating three miracles, including the falling of snow in the summertime. Her prediction proves true, and justice triumphs. Dou O appears as a ghost in the last act of the drama. This play has been praised for its heartrending emotion, its delineation of the female character, and its moral idealism.

Other noteworthy plays by Guan are *Jiu fengchen* (*Rescued by a Coquette*, 1958), *Wang jiangting* (the riverside pavilion), *Hudie meng* (*The Butterfly's Dream*, 1937), *Jiequai dan* (slicing fish), *Baiyue ting* (moon prayer pavilion), *Shuangfu meng* (dream of two on a journey), *Dandao hui* (single-sword meeting), and *Wu hou yan* (the banquet of five lords). A collection of Guan's plays translated into English was published by Beijing's Foreign Languages Press in 1958. Guan apparently ended his career in Hankou. Besides writing plays, he was noted for the excellence of his lyric *zhu*. He was a friend of the poet Wang Heging and of the beautiful courtesan Zhu Lianxiu (Peal Curtain Beauty).

Bo Pu (also known as Bo Renfu) was a native of Zhengding (modern Shijia Zhuang), about one hundred miles southwest of Dadu. He was from an official family connected with the Jin government. He was about seven years old when the Mongols occupied the region. His father was a man of literary interests who was a close friend of the distinguished poet Yuan Haowen. The latter tutored the young Bo in learning and literature. About 1280, Bo moved southward to Nanjing. He was fond of writing *zi* and *zhu* as well as dramas. Of the sixteen plays credited to him, only three are preserved. He is remembered particularly for his drama *Wu tongyou* (rain on the paulownia tree), which tells of the tragic love between the Tang emperor Ming Huang and his favorite concubine, the beautiful femme fatale named Yang Guifei. Bo's other extant plays are *Qiang tou ma shang* and *Dong qiang ji*.

Ma Zhiyuan was a native of Dadu, where he spent his youth and early adulthood. About 1285, however, he removed himself to Hangkou. A minor official, he resigned his post to live the life of a recluse. Of his sixteen plays, seven survive. His masterpiece is *Hang gong qiu* (*The Sorrows of Han*, 1829), the story of a Han emperor's tragic love for a ravishing concubine, Wang Zhaozhu (Lady Splendor Wang), whom he was forced to relinquish into the hands of a Xiongnu tribal chief who demanded her for his wife. After their sad parting, the emperor again experiences the pains of their separation in a horrible dream. Later he learns that the young lady drowned herself in the Amur River rather than submit to a barbarian husband. This sad ending is an exception in Chinese drama. Most plays are comedies or contain humorous incidents. Other notable dramas by Ma are *Qing shan lei* (green

smock tears) and *Jie fu bei*, which feature immortals and recluses living in the mountains, and *Yue Yang lou*, *Ren feng zi*, and *Chen Tuan go wo*, all of which emphasize disillusionment with men and society. Of these, perhaps the *Qing shan lei* is the most interesting. It tells of the love of the Tang poet Bo Quyi for the beautiful courtesan Pei Xingnu, his dismissal from official life and exile, the false report of his death and her marriage to another, and the reunion, elopement, and vindication of the poet and the woman.

The fourth of the Four Great Men, Zheng Guangzhu, was a Confucian-educated northerner who held a minor official post in Hangzhou and also wrote for the theater. He himself was a great favorite with people in the theatrical profession. Of his sixteen plays, many survive in some form. He became famous particularly for his *Zhougong shezheng* (regency of the duke of Zhou), a story of one of China's political saints, Ji Dan, the epitome of selfless loyalty to one's monarch. Other notable plays by Zheng are *Hanlin fengyue* (romance of the Hanlin academician) and *Wang Can denglou* (Wang Can ascends the throne).

Perhaps the most famous Chinese play of all was composed by Wang Shifu, a native of Dadu who was of the younger generation. This celebrated play was *Xixiang ji* (*The Romance of the Western Chamber*, 1935), a very long *zaju* in five acts (actually five *zaju*, each of them in four acts) telling one of China's great love stories, the romance of a handsome and gifted young scholar (*caizi*) and a beautiful and gifted maiden (*jiaren*). Although the romance of the scholar and the beauty was originally told by the Tang writer and poet Yuan Zhen in his classical short story *Yingying zhuan*, the actual model for Wang's *zaju* was the *Xixiang ji chi zhugongdiao*, composed by the Jin poet Dong Jieyuan. As popular writers using the colloquial language to address commoners rather than literati, both Dong and Wang altered the plot of Yuan's *chuanqi* to provide a happy ending, thus eliminating the original story's irony and cynicism.

XIWEN

Production of *xiwen* was curtailed in the north when the Mongol armies moved in and ravaged the

Song capital. When the Song court retreated southward and established the Southern Song Dynasty in 1127, with its capital at Hangkou, many displaced theatrical troupes followed it and took up residence at Hangkou and at other sites in the southern provinces. Some of these locations, such as Haiyan, Youyao, Ningbo, and Wenzhou, were also in Chekiang Province. Others were in other provinces: Yiyang in Jiangxi and Kunshan in Jiangsu, for example. During the interim lasting more than fifty years before the Mongols were able to crush the Southern Song Dynasty in 1279, a drama that was largely Chinese flourished in the south. At first referred to as the Wenzhou *zaju*, or Wenzhou Varieties, this southern style came to be called *xiwen* to distinguish it from the style termed Official Varieties (*guanben zaju*). After the collapse of the Song and the reunification of China, the *zaju* penetrated the south and largely replaced the *xiwen*, which, however, continued to be produced. Some performers acted in both *zaju* and *xiwen*, and some playwrights wrote both kinds of drama.

The formal properties of the *xiwen* differed considerably from those of the *zaju*. First, the number of acts in the *xiwen* was not fixed; there could be many acts as well as multiple changes of scene, as many as forty or fifty. The acts could also vary in length from very short to very long. A prologue invariably preceded the main body of the play but was an integral part of the whole. There was no "wedge" and no epilogue.

Second, the *xiwen* permitted multiple singing roles, and sometimes the singing was done in unison. The singing could be assigned to any character and to any number of characters. The role categories also differed from those in the *zaju* and were more expansive. There were four main role categories: *sheng*, *dan*, *jing*, and *chou*. The *sheng* was the leading male character and the *dan* the leading female. The *sheng*, however, was not the same as the *zhengmo* in the *zaju*. It did not include martial types and usually consisted of Confucian scholars or young students. The *jing* and *chou* were much the same, both consisting of some comical types. In addition to the main roles, there were secondary role categories. The *mo* was the secondary male role and the *wai*, though usually

male, could also be the secondary female role, while the *tie* was always the secondary female role.

Third, the music of the southern drama was closer to traditional Chinese music than that of the northern style. Southern music stuck to the traditional Chinese scale (pentatonic, with five full tones and two semitones, one semitone appearing between the fourth and fifth degrees), whereas northern music employed a modified scale introduced by Kublai Khan (heptatonic, with seven full tones and two semitones, one semitone being between the fifth and sixth degrees). The Mongols also devised a new system of musical notation. Southern music was fitted to the *gu* (drum) and the *paiban* (wooden clappers, or "castanets"), whereas northern music was fitted to the *pipa* (four-stringed lute) and the *dizi* (horizontal flute). The *pipa*, however, was usually reserved for the singing of nondramatic *zhu*. The *xiwen* derived more tunes from Tang and Song *zi* than did the *zaju*, the latter adopting many tunes from the folk music of Central Asia. Although there were modes in southern as well as northern music, mode was not a measure of the aria melodies of the *xiwen*. Rather, the songs were organized on the basis of a series of different tunes or of sequences based on transposition or ornamental variation without regard to modal relationship.

Fourth, the prosody of southern *zhu* employed fewer "padding words" (*chenzi*) than northern, sometimes none at all. The rhyme, too, could be shifted. Southern pronunciation was used in the singing and recitation parts of the *xiwen* so that its melodic structure differed from that of the *zaju*, in which northern pronunciation was employed. Northern pronunciation had dropped the *rusheng*, or "entering tone," to have but three pitch levels, whereas southern pronunciation had retained it to have four pitch levels. After the reunification of China, some critics objected strongly to the stylistic "faults" of southern playwrights and championed the "purity" of northern speech. One such critic was Zhou Deqing. In his prescriptive manual, *Zhong-yuan yinyun*, Zhou describes the phonological system of the Beijing dialect for use in northern plays and songs. Southerners were advised to adopt the Beijing dialect as the standard language to be used in their plays and songs as well.

Fifth, the southerners preferred romantic themes in their dramas to the military themes of which northerners were fond. Generally in Chinese drama, plays were divided into two main categories, civil plays (*wenxi*) and military plays (*wuxi*), rather than into the two main categories characteristic of Western drama, namely, comedy and tragedy. The *xiwen* (or *nanxi*) was more of a "pop" product than was the *zaju* (or *beixi*). The *xiwen* was more "baroque" than "classical" and more spectacular than "natural and genuine" in audience appeal. Hence, in respect to the principal difference between northern and southern audiences, it was said: "beiren tingting, nanren kankan" ("northerners listen, southerners watch").

The social status of the authors of the two kinds of drama also differed generally. The authors of *zaju* were often renowned scholars (*mingjia*) apart from their theatrical writings or prominent actor-playwrights (*hangjia*). On the other hand, the authors of *xiwen* tended to be obscure writers operating in the shadows of the literary and theatrical worlds. Their works have not been preserved, and their names are not known. Although more than one hundred seventy *xiwen* dramas were written—far less than the *zaju*, with more than seven hundred—only four genuine and complete texts have been preserved. Three of these were found preserved in chapter 13,991 of an imperial encyclopedia, *Yongle dadian* (1403-1408; grand repository of eternal joy). Dating from the late thirteenth century, the three plays are as follows: *Xiang Sunzi* (little butcher sun), *Zhang Xie zhuangyuan* (top graduate Zhang Xie), and *Huanmen zidi cuo lishen* (mistakes of an official's son, sometimes rendered as "in the wrong career"). The fourth extant text, preserved by virtue of its quality and popularity, is Gao Ming's masterpiece, *Pipa ji* (pr. c. 1367; *The Lute*, 1980). On the other hand, many *zaju* survive, especially in Ming editions, and are available today principally in three collections: Zang Mouxun's *Yuanqu xuan* (anthology of Yuan music dramas), published in 1615 or 1616 (reprinted in four volumes in 1958), which contains a hundred plays; Sui Shushen's *Yuanqu xuan waibian* (supplement to the anthology of Yuan music dramas), published in 1959, which contains sixty-two additional plays; and Yang

Jialuo's thirty-two-volume *Chuan Yuan zaju* (the complete Yuan music dramas), published in 1963, which contains the major editions of the Yuan dramas published during the fifteenth and sixteenth centuries, the basic material of Zang's research.

Gao Ming, the scholar and playwright, was a native of Rui-an, near Wenzhou. He became an official and was apparently forced to serve the Mongols against his will. After leaving office, he turned to writing. His famous *xiwen*, *The Lute*, is in forty-two scenes and was apparently derived from a Wenzhou *zaju*. It has a prologue for the *fumo*, singing and spoken parts, and a large cast of characters. Its theme has to do with the moral dilemma of choosing between loyalty and filial piety, a choice that is presented to the hero, a successful scholar who wins high office. The character of this *xiwen*'s hero is based on that of historical personage, the great writer Cai Yong of the Han Dynasty. The hero's first dilemma is his having to choose whether to leave his aged parents to go to the capital to compete in the imperial examination. Leaving the affairs of his family in the hands of a respected neighbor, he leaves his new bride and journeys to the capital, where he takes the top position in the examination. Impressed by his abilities, the emperor orders his prime minister to confer his daughter in marriage on the successful candidate. At first, Cai declines the honor, pleading that he must care for his parents and has a wife at home. The anger of the minister and his colleagues at court, however, forces Cai to reverse his decision, and he accepts the offer of a second wife. Meanwhile, at home his first wife tries her best to care for his parents, but despite her efforts, they die. Following their burial, the first wife travels to Luoyang in an attempt to locate her husband, supporting herself on the journey by playing the *pipa*. Learning that her husband resides in a mansion in town, she visits it to discover his condition. Because Cai's second, very rich wife needs a maidservant, she employs the first wife in that capacity. When she discovers the identity of her new maidservant, she is struck by the loyalty and devotion the first wife displayed toward her parents-in-law and husband. Because Chinese law then sanctioned polygamy, the three are happily united, and Cai and his two wives visit his parents' grave. The play is noted for the skill displayed by Gao in successfully combining the plainness of folk speech with the elegance of refined rhetoric.

MING DYNASTY DRAMA

By the middle of the fourteenth century, the Chinese people were becoming restless, even rebellious, under Mongol rule. Disorders began occurring in southern and central China and on the seacoast as well as in the river valleys. Finally, a rebel leader emerged who was fiercer, more intelligent, craftier, and more ruthless than any other. A native of what became modern Anhui Province, he was a born leader and fighter. Strong and grossly ugly, his countenance was said to resemble that of a pig. A Chan Buddhist monk of humble origin, trained in meditation and the martial arts at the Huangque Temple near Fengyang, his birthplace, his name was Zhu Yuanzhang. He demanded that other rebel leaders join with him. Those who refused, Zhu killed. With his forces increased, he took Nanjing in 1356. With his capture of Beijing in 1368, he declared himself emperor of a new Chinese dynasty, the Ming, ruling as Emperor Hong Wu. He repulsed every effort of the Mongols to regain power and drove them completely from China proper by 1371, and out of Yunnan by 1382. Ruling for thirty years, from 1368 to 1398, he revivified Chinese society and culture. Fathering twenty-four sons by four wives (a first wife and three concubines), he placed his grandson on the throne shortly before he died, declaring that none of his sons was competent to rule over the Ming empire.

With the establishment of the Ming Dynasty in 1368, the Chinese were once more the arbiters of their own destiny. Hong Wu immediately set about organizing the new government by inaugurating the provincial system. He published a new penal code, abolishing punishment by mutilation. He reformed the tax and the monetary systems, fixing the value of money. He reestablished the time-honored civil service examination system, instituting a new and rigid form of essay called the *bagu wenzhang* (eight-legged essay). The Chinese people had begun to react strongly against all foreign ways and things, so the emperor led the way by adopting a pro-Chinese policy. Emphasizing agricultural pursuits, Hong Wu revived the annual planting ceremony. He fostered the planting of crops and of silk culture. He revived the annual ceremonies of the seasons. He restored Tang dress, forbade eunuchs to hold public office, and made Buddhism and Daoism state religions on a par with Confucianism. He became a patron of the arts. Because he himself was a man of the people, he knew the delight they took in the popular drama. He again led the way, collecting hundreds of volumes of songs and plays, promoting both northern and southern drama at his court.

Before Hong Wu had ascended his throne, he had witnessed performances of Gao's *xiwen*, *The Lute*, and had been delighted by it. When he became emperor, so great was his admiration for Gao that he sought to employ him at his court. Only by feigning insanity was the playwright able to escape this responsibility. Hong Wu commanded his court actors to perform the play daily. Soon, however, he became troubled by the lack of string accompaniment and ordered the Music Academy to compose new musical arrangements, with northern tunes substituted for the southern lyrics, thus allowing accompaniment by the *pipa* (the four-stringed lute) and the *zheng* (the fourteen-stringed zither, with the strings elevated on movable bridges). According to the sixteenth century scholar-playwright Xu Wei (or Xu Wenchang), when a copy of the play was presented to Hong Wu, he remarked that it was more precious than the Five Classics and the Four Books, which every household possessed, and *The Lute* was a rare delicacy that no noble household should be without. Indeed, Gao's play remained a favorite with the Chinese for centuries. It was viewed as the model for southern drama, which during the Ming Dynasty came to be designated *chuanqi* (literally, "strange tales"). The term had formerly been used to refer to the classical short stories written by the literati during the Tang Dynasty, but during the Ming Dynasty it meant the epic-lyrical type of southern drama previously called the *xiwen* or *nanxi*. The *chuanqi* drama largely replaced the Yuan *zaju* in popularity throughout the Ming and most of the Qing Dynasties. The musical accompaniment provided by the Music Academy by imperial order for Gao's play, called the *xiangsi guanqiang* (official stringed-music style), soon became common for other *chuanqi*. The style of the musical accompaniment directly affected that of the singing, so that identifying terms embraced both of these musical features.

Gradually, the "official stringed-music style" was replaced by various local styles of music, especially the Haiyan *qiang*, Youyao *qiang*, and Yiyang *qiang*, and finally these were replaced by the most enduring style of all, the Kunshan *qiang*. Haiyan, in northeastern Zhejiang Province, was near Hangzhou. This music was accompanied by the *pipa*, the *yue yang lou* (four-stringed moon guitar), and the *zheng*. The *xiangban* ("castanets," or clapper) was used to mark the rhythm in the singing. The Haiyan *qiang* style was prevalent in Wenzhou, Jiaxing, Huzhou, and Taizhou. Youyao was also near Hangzhou, and the Youyao *qiang* style prevailed in Zhejiang and Jiangsu provinces. Yiyang *qiang* originated in Yiyang in Jiangxi Province. This style employed the *dan pi gu* (small drum) and *po* (cymbals) to maintain the rhythm. Another characteristic of this system was the use of the *bangqiang* (helping chorus), in which a single person would begin the singing and then be joined by several others. Popular in Jiangxi, this style spread to Beijing and Nanjing as well as to Hunan, Fujian, and Guangdong Provinces. Haiyan *qiang*, Youyao *qiang*, and Yiyang *qiang* were in prominent circulation from the late fifteenth through the early sixteenth centuries until they were practically supplanted by Kunshan *qiang* music (also referred to as *Kunqu*), which takes its name from its place of origin, Kunshan, in Jiangsu Province, not far from Suzhou. Thus, after about 1500, the history of Chinese drama becomes more a history of musical styles than a history of dramatic genres.

The Ming Dynasty also saw a change in the musical scale. The Mongols had brought with them a different scale and a different notation from those of the Chinese. The ancient Chinese scale, like the Western diatonic scale, was composed of five full tones and two semitones, but the Chinese scale differed from the Western in that one of the semitones appeared between the fourth and fifth degrees instead of the third and fourth degrees, as in the Western scale. Although untempered, it was a pentatonic scale. In Western notation, the Chinese scale amounted to C, D, E, E-sharp, G, A, B, C-flat (or, in Chinese notation, *gong*, *shang*, *jiao*, *bianzhi*, *chi*, *yu*, *biangong*, *gong*). On the other hand, the Mongol scale in Western notation amounted to C, D, E, F, G, A, B, G-flat, D-flat (or, in the new Chinese notation, *he*, *si*, *yi*, *shang*, *chi*, *gong*, *fan*, *liu*, *wu*). Under Chinese pressure, however, Kublai Khan, always willing to pay deference to Chinese tradition, attempted to reconcile the Mongol scale with the Chinese scale by introducing F-sharp under the name of *kou*. This modified scale in Western notation amounted to C, D, E, F, F-sharp, G, A, B, C-flat, D-flat (or, in Chinese notation, *he*, *si*, *yi*, *shang*, *kou*, *chi*, *gong*, *fan*, *liu*, *wu*). This was a heptatonic scale, and it became the dominant scale used during the Yuan Dynasty. During the fifteenth century, the Ming adopted the Yuan gamut but excluded all the semitones, thus returning to a pentatonic scale. In Western notation, the new Ming scale amounted to C, D, F, G, A, C-flat, D-flat (or, in Chinese notation, *he*, *si*, *shang*, *chi*, *gong*, *liu*, *wu*).

MING CHUANQI AND KUNQU

The development of the Ming *chuanqi* roughly falls into three periods that may be termed Early Period (1368-1500), Middle Period (1500-1580), and Late Period (1580-1644). The Early Period marks the revitalization and the rise of *chuanqi* drama. Representative dramas of this period include *Baiyue ting* (moon prayer pavilion), attributed to Shih Hui (or Shi Junmei) and not to be confused with the play of the same name by Guan Hanqing; *Sha gou ji* (story of the slain dog), by Xu Zhen (or Xu Ji); *Jingchai ji* (story of the thorn hairpin), by Ko Dancui; and *Xiangnang ji* (story of the perfumed sachet), by Shao Gan.

During the Middle Period (1500-1580), *chuanqi* drama arrived at maturity to become a highly sophisticated art form. Regular *chuanqi* were long (running from twenty to fifty or more acts), intricate (with double plots in parallel development that sometimes overlapped), and complex (combining recitation, narrative action, dialogue, singing—with the songs sung by a variety of characters, sometimes chorally, and with the modality of the songs changeable within any scene—and orchestral accompaniment). Other developments included the writing of short plays that had but four or five changes of scene and only ten or twelve musical tunes. To distinguish these short dramas from the standard-length *chuanqi*, with their numerous acts, they were called *zaju*. These Ming *zaju*, therefore, must not be confused with the Yuan *zaju*. In addition, another development was the merging of southern with northern dramatic techniques, as seen particularly in the dramas of Xu Wei. The most significant development of this period, however, was the emergence and rise of that very lyrical form of Ming drama called the *kunqu*. Beginning as a local regional style in the Kunshan area (not far from modern Shanghai), the Kunshan *qiang* spread to the then theatrically vibrant city of Suzhou by 1580, where it flourished to become a national favorite. It became the theater of the literati, patronized by scholars and the court, and was regarded as a classical art.

Those most responsible for the rise of *kunqu* drama were the actor and singing-master Wei Lingfu, the playwright Liang Chenyu (also known as Liang Bolung), and two flutists, Chang Meiku and Hsieh Linchuan, all of whom were friends and colleagues. During the 1550's, Liang provided the finished texts that carried out the musical ideas of the actor-singer and the two flutists. The singing, which was based on the Suzhou dialect, was characterized by lengthy sustained notes and elaborate ornamentation requiring a display of bravura on the part of the performer. At the same time, the soft and supple notes of the flute gave the *kunqu* music a generally plaintive quality. The play Liang provided for this movement, *Huan sha ji* (the washing of the silk stole), has no particularly stirring plot and was admired mostly for its elegant songs and adroit language.

Other playwrights and plays of the second period worth mentioning are Li Kaixiang for his *Baoqian ji* (story of the precious sword) and Wang Shicheng for his *Meng feng ji* (story of the singing phoenix). Li Kaixiang wrote both *zaju* (*beixi* in the Yuan manner) and *chuanqi* drama. He was more admired, however, for the latter rather than for the former, especially for

his *Baoqian ji*. Nevertheless, his work pioneered the Ming effort to produce a synthesis of northern and southern drama to make something new.

It was left to Xu Wei to epitomize more fully the successful merger of these diverse dramatic techniques. Xu Wei's accomplishment is seen in his dramatic tetralogy *Si sheng yuan* (the four shrieks of the monkey), of which the fourth play, *Nü Zhuang Yuan* (a woman named Zhuang Yuan), is perhaps the most noteworthy. He wrote only *zaju* but varied the acts and freely mixed northern and southern *zhu*. This fourth play not only is technically brilliant but also introduces the unusual, feminist theme that a woman is not necessarily inferior to a man. It relates how the heroine, a gifted scholar and writer named Huan Conghu, was fond of wearing male attire. Thus disguised as a man named Zhuang Yuan, she submits herself to the imperial examination, from which she emerges the top graduate. Employing puns, jokes, and humorous dialogue to support his argument, Xu manages to tell his story with disarming charm and good humor.

In his *Meng feng ji*, Wang Shicheng also presented a new trend, introducing a political theme based on current rather than on past history. His play is a bitter protest against the injustices perpetrated by a powerful prime minister named Yan Song, who had been responsible for falsely incriminating Wang's own father, who consequently suffered execution. This bold and daring effort to present a national political issue that was then current contrasted sharply with the love dramas, which were the usual Ming stage fare in Wang's day. His play also represented a break with past tradition because previous historical or military plays were inevitably set in the remote past.

Another dramatic departure of this second period was the creation of short Ming plays that received the designation of *zaju* to distinguish them from the longer and more elaborate *chuanqi*. The chief writers of such *zaju* were Xu Wei, Huang Fangyu, and Yang Shen, noted for his short drama *Lu Ling chun* (the spring in Luling), which depicts a Utopian society. The short *zaju* of the Ming Dynasty must be distinguished from the Yuan *zaju*, as well as from the imitations of Yuan *zaju* written during the Ming period.

The Late Period (1580-1644) was one of adaptation, divergence, and consolidation. Interest was revived and intensified in the old Yuan *zaju*. Playwrights, editors, and bibliophiles assembled texts from palace and privately owned editions and preserved them for posterity by placing them in their own libraries or by printing and publishing them. An important result of this interest was the publication in 1615 or 1616 of Zang Mouxun's *Yuanqu xuan*, an anthology of one hundred plays. Another important phenomenon of the late Ming was the competition that took place among various regional musical styles. Though favored by the educated class as "refined music," Kunshan *qiang* was not to the liking of everyone. Many dramas of the period were performed in Yiyang *qiang* or some variant of it, even though they did not enjoy the literary prestige of the *kunqu* dramas. A popular variant of Kunshan *qiang* was Jingyang *qiang*, which hailed from Anhui Province. In short, Kunshan *qiang* was not unchallenged. Local and national styles of music were merged and adapted to suit the changing tastes of the time. Many dramas designed for one musical style were adapted to suit another style. A popular method of such adaptation was the use of *jiagun* (literally, "added roll") or *gundiao* (literally "rolling tune"), which meant the addition of speech or verse between the lines of the original text. This was necessary to make the *kunqu* texts understandable to the masses in the popular theater. Finally, another significant development in this third period was the divergant path that *kunqu* drama took under the influence of the two outstanding playwrights of the era, Tang Xianzu and Shen Jing, the former leading the drama in the direction of literature, to the detriment of the music, and the latter emphasizing the musical qualities while remaining relatively unconcerned about the drama as literature.

Tang Xianzu was a native of Linchuan in Jiangxi Province. He entered on an official career and held several important posts, but after a time he apparently disliked official life and maneuvered his retirement to devote himself to writing. He wrote four *chuanqi* reflecting his personal views of life. His most celebrated play is *Maodan ting* (*Peony Pavilion*, 1972). In an intricate style studded with classical allusions and quotations, the play is the love story of a pretty maiden, the daughter of an important official, and a handsome and brilliant young scholar, based on a dream fantasy and the miraculous return of the young lady from the world of the dead to be reunited with her lover. A number of Ming dramatists admired Tang's style and became his followers, forming the Linchuan school of playwrights, including Wu Bing, Chengshan, and Ruan Dacheng, all of whom flourished in the 1640's.

Shen Jing was a native of Wuzhong in Jiangsu Province. He entered on an official career but eventually retired because of ill health, devoting the rest of his life to writing. He wrote not only plays (both *zaju* and *chuanqi*) and *zhu* poetry but also treatises on poetic and musical form. A musical theorist, he was a sharp critic of the plays of Tang, which he thought were deficient in their music. His own plays show a nice correspondence between the prosody and the musical structure, but he was criticized for his concern over musical precision. His work, too, attracted followers, who formed the Wuzhong school of drama.

QING DRAMATISTS

Drama continued to flourish during the Qing Dynasty (1644-1911), although the Chinese were again conquered by a foreign people, the Manchu, a tribe of the same ancestry as the Jurchen of the Jin Dynasty and who were aided in their conquest by Ming corruption and inefficiency, internal disputes, and traitorous officials and generals as well as renegade literati. The Manchu emperors, especially Kangxi (reigned 1662-1722; also known as Sheng Zu) and Qianlong (reigned 1736-1795; also known as Gao Zong), paradoxically both patronized and supported drama and sought to censor and control it in its popular form. In the early Qing, most of the playwrights and actors continued to come from Jiangsu Province, the original home of Kunshan *qiang*, and *kunqu* drama predominated. Competing musical styles, however, especially Yiyang *qiang* and Jingyang *qiang*, more popular with the masses, gained ground until it appeared that *kunqu* might become strictly an esoteric form exclusive to the intelligentsia. Meanwhile, a number of playwrights made important contributions to the drama during the 1640's and 1650's, including Li Yu, Zhu Cuchao, Ye Jifei, Qiu Yuan, Chang Tafu, Wu Weiye (also known as Wu Mei Cun), Li Liweng (also known as Li Yu), You Tuan, and Zhu Hao (also known as Zhu Sichen), author of the popular play *Shi wu guan* (*Fifteen Strings of Cash*, 1957). Before 1700, however, two masterly *kunqu* dramas had appeared that would unexpectedly revive the drooping fortunes of the genre. These were Hong Sheng's *Zhangsheng dian* (pr. 1687/1688; *The Palace of Eternal Youth*, 1955) and Kong Shangren's *Taohua shan* (pr. 1699; *The Peach Blossom Fan*, 1946).

Hong Sheng, a native of Zhejiang Province, was a scholarly man who was an accomplished *shi* poet and essayist as well as a writer of plays. In attendance at the Imperial Academy in Beijing for several years, he completed *The Palace of Eternal Youth* in 1687 or 1688. It was promptly staged by a Kunshan *qiang* troupe of actors and met with instant success. It received high praise from the Kangxi emperor. Unfortunately, Hong's career was soon abruptly cut short by the malicious machinations of a scholar-official whom the playwright had, perhaps accidently, offended.

The Palace of Eternal Youth, based on Bo Quyi's famous poem *Chang hen ge* (the everlasting sorrow) and a *chuanqi* short story by a contemporary, Chen Hong, presents the love that the Tang emperor Ming Huang bore for his favorite concubine, the beautiful Yang Guifei. In fifty acts, the play is much longer than Bo Pu's Yuan drama on the same subject, *Wu Tongyou*, not being limited by the death of Yang Guifei. In *The Palace of Eternal Youth*, she appears frequently in spirit form following her death. At the conclusion of the play, a Daoist priest, a spiritualist and magician, arranges a meeting between the two lovers by providing a bridge to the moon that enables the emperor to rejoin his beloved. The play as a whole amounts to a litany of love. It has been praised for the perfect correspondence it shows between its prosody and its musical structure. It is a highly imaginative as well as an emotionally sensitive work. Despite its standard happy ending, the progress of its plot reveals the depth of the personal as well as the

political tragedy that Ming Huang experienced during his lifetime.

Kong Shangren, a native of Shantung Province, was a direct descendant of Confucius. He was a profound student of the ancient classics and a teacher of rites and music. Indeed, for his accomplishments the Kangxi emperor appointed him a doctor in the Imperial Academy. During his career, he held several important official posts. He was also an art collector and a distinguished calligraphist as well as a famous playwright.

Kong's famous play, *The Peach Blossom Fan*, was begun around 1689. He kept writing and rewriting it for some ten years, completing it in 1699. It was performed at the imperial palace in the same year and proved an immediate success. It soon became widely popular. A long play with forty-four acts, it has an involved plot that deals with current instead of past history—the recent downfall of the Ming Dynasty. All the leading characters in the play represent real historical persons. Furthermore, the plot is built around the central symbol of the peach blossom fan, originally a present from the hero, the young poet-scholar Hou Fangyou, to his mistress, the beautiful courtesan Li Xiangzhun, the heroine of the drama. Seeing herself being forced by an enemy of Hou to marry another man, in her despair she tries suicide by banging her head against a wall and thus splatters her fan with her own blood, but she is otherwise unsuccessful in her attempt to kill herself. Later a famous artist paints the blood spots into a picture of peach blossoms. At the conclusion of the play, the hero arranges a rendezvous with his mistress at a Daoist temple. There, a diligent priest succeeds in persuading the lovers to abandon the folly of mortal love and sex to follow a life of reclusion and meditation. As a result, the lovers decide to part forever.

The play abounds in excellent characterization. Its plot is also intricately constructed, with the difficulties of the lovers played out against the backdrop of the conflict between the corrupt southern Ming Dynasty and the neo-Confucian scholars, who severely disapprove of the degenerate morals of the court. The hero, Hou Fangyou, is a member of the neo-Confucianist Reform Society, or Fushe. Either directly or indirectly, the plot touches on the peasant revolt, the threat of the Manchu invasion, and the conflicts between certain Ming generals. The play has been criticized on the grounds that its prosody does not fit exactly the aria melodies. The play does display two innovations on the part of Kong: He uses the *fumo* actor not only to introduce the play but also to take an active role in the rest of the drama, and he rejects the standard happy ending.

QING COURT DRAMA

The Manchu emperors remained patrons of court drama all through the Qing period, and they maintained their own court players. The Kangxi emperor admired the plays of You Tuan and had them set to music for performance by his players. The Qianlong emperor commissioned plays for his acting troupe from the playwright Zhang Zhao. He also had him make a great collection of extant plays for preservation. The nineteenth century ill-starred empress-dowager Zi Xi enjoyed theatrical entertainments so much that she sometimes neglected the affairs of state to witness them.

At the same time, however, the Manchu rulers remained continually suspicious of the drama in its popular form, fearing that it might foster sedition or contribute to the moral delinquency of the masses. Hence they frequently issued edicts banning theatrical performances. The Yongzheng emperor (reigned 1722-1735; also known as Yinzhen) maintained a spy system to keep him informed about performances in the theater. The Qianlong emperor conducted a thorough literary inquisition during the years 1774-1782. During this time, numerous books were burned and severe punishments were enacted against offending authors. In accordance with the sentiment in the central government, many provincial and local officials attempted to control or suppress popular play acting.

At the same time, palace plays were regularly produced. Often they were specially commissioned of playwrights by the Manchu emperors and presented themes that suited both the entertainment and the propaganda needs of the court. Zhang Zhao composed or adapted many plays for the Qianlong emperor. He

wrote five "bumper" plays (*zhengben daxi*, literally, "really big plays") for him. The standard length of a "bumper" play consisted of ten parts, each of twenty-four acts, or 240 acts in the whole drama. One such play by Zhang was called *Chuan shanjin ke* (golden carvings for teaching virtue), and it aimed at promoting loyalty. Other noted playwrights connected with palace performances were Zhang Jian; Dong Reng, who wrote a play about two famous women generals; Yan Zhaoguan, who was particularly famous for his one-act plays such as *Bayan* (stopping the feast); Jiang Shiquan, perhaps the most famous playwright of his time; and Shen Qifeng, who was particularly respected by the acting profession.

Most of the Manchu court actors were eunuchs until *kunqu* actors from the Jiangsu-Anhui region began moving into the capital to constitute a separate body of court actors. Palace plays of the eighteenth century used only Kunshan *qiang*, Yiyang *qiang*, and Qingyang *qiang* music. Kunshan *qiang* was used for romantic and other delicate scenes, whereas Yiyang *qiang* or Qingyang *qiang* was used for rowdy or violent action, such as fighting in the military plays. In the palace plays, the costumes were unusually resplendent and stage properties were abundant.

Despite the revival of *kunqu* drama following the successes of Hong and Kong, this notable style had begun to wane by the 1790's. This was true not only in Beijing but also in Suzhou, its original home. More popular styles that featured more raucous music and more vulgar language dominated the theatrical scene and flourished to such a wide extent that an imperial edict was issued against them in 1798. The leaders of this "pop movement" were mostly actors from Anhui Province, who began arriving in Beijing in large numbers during the 1790's. They brought with them two new modal styles, Qin *qiang* (otherwise known as Bangzi *qiang*, or "clapper opera") and Erhuang *diao*. The latter is thought to have originated in Jiangxi Province. At first these popular drama featured the *dizi* (flute), but after reaching Beijing they also employed the *huqin* (violin). The imperial edict against the popular drama proved quite ineffective, as both these styles of music were much in evidence in Beijing by 1810, and actors were increasingly coming to the capital from Anhui rather than from Jiangsu Province. Actors from Hubei Province also began arriving in Beijing to establish reputations for their performances of the "new music." In 1827, the leading Suzhou *kunqu* troupe disbanded, its performers evidently convinced by this time that the masses preferred more elaborate, noisy, and costumed plays than they provided, wanting, too, more painted faces. With the destruction of the city of Suzhou in the course of the Taiping Rebellion (1851-1864), the *kunqu* drama almost ceased to exist. Although some revivals occurred between about 1864 and the Chinese Revolution of 1911, with the establishment of the republic, *kunqu* appeared doomed to extinction. It was saved from this fate only when a group of enthusiasts established the Institute for the Teaching of *kunqu* in Suzhou around 1921, and somewhat later a *kunqu* troupe was established in Beijing.

BEIJING OPERA

If the first important event in the history of Qing drama was the revival of *kunqu* drama from the 1690's to the 1780's, the second important event was the decline of *kunqu* and the concurrent rise of the popular drama during the 1790's, extending into the 1830's. The third important event was the creation of a new style of drama known as *jingju*, commonly called Beijing Opera, by Anhui actors sometime in the 1830's, when two modes of music, Erhuang *diao* and Xipi *diao* (a variety of Qin *qiang*), were brought together. By the 1870's, it had become the predominant form of Chinese drama. The Erhuang *diao* apparently originated in Jiangxi, and the Xipi *diao* evidently came from Hubei. In Hubei, according to the scholar Ouyang Yuqian, "singing" was called *pi* (skin), a section of song was referred to as "a stretch of skin," and the term *xipi* was used to refer to the method of singing popular in the *xi* (west), meaning Shaanxi. Beijing Opera is often referred to as *pihuangqu*, a word derived from these two modes. Actually, the repeitore of Beijing Opera troupes also includes other kinds of music. With the devising of these two modal styles, other modes were absorbed and embraced. Altogether, about thirty aria types of mixed melodies were called by such names as

erhuang, *xipi*, *fan xipi*, or *fanerhuang*. Folk tunes were also absorbed.

The principal modes of Beijing Opera, *erhuang* and *xipi*, have characteristic uses that contrast with each other. The former, solemn in tone, is used for tragic or sad scenes. The latter, lively in tone, is used for exciting or joyous actions. The musical accompaniment is dominated by percussion instruments—drums (small and large), clappers, and gongs (small and large)—to signal the stage movements and to mark the principal steps in the progress of the plot of the drama. Stringed instruments consisting of the *huqin*, the *jing erhu* (southern violin), the *yueqin* (moon guitar), the *sanxian* (three-stringed guitar), and the *pipa* carry the melodies. At first the principal instrument in Beijing Opera was the *dizi* (horizontal flute), but it was replaced in this role during the 1870's by the *huqin*. Sometimes the raucous *suona* (trumpet) is used to complement the stringed instruments.

The prosody of the lyrics in Beijing Opera also has its own characteristics. The lines of the lyrics are of even length (unlike those in Yuan *zaju*, *nanxi*, and *kunqu*) and are generally between ten and twelve syllables long. They are divisible in both sense and rhythm into 3-3:2-2 and 2-2:3 respectively, the music closely following the semantic divisions of the lyrics as well as the rhythmic pattern. Sometimes *chenzi*, or "padded words," are added to the lyrics. They are less prominent, however, than in the case of *zhu*, and in the singing they are treated very casually. The rhymes are divided into thirteen groups. Any particular passage of singing must keep the same rhyme sound. The language of Beijing Opera consists of a mixture of Mandarin dialects, southwestern, southern, and northern (Szechwan, Hubei, Anhui, and Hebei provinces). Actors playing *chou* roles use Beijing colloquial. This mixture of the variations of the Mandarin dialect gives Beijing Opera a certain linguistic character of its own. Most of the Beijing Opera texts, however, are so thin in their diction that they amount to very little as literature and depend on the acting and singing for their effect. Thus, they are in sharp contrast to the Yuan *zaju*, the *chuanqi*, and the *kunqu*, which not only were eminently performable but also were sufficiently rich in their linguistic texture to make excellent reading.

Nevertheless, Beijing Opera is such a complex theatrical style that it merits a much more detailed exposition than is possible in this space. It should be said, however, that it has four main role categories, *sheng*, *dan*, *jing*, and *chou*, but each one of these has many subdivisions. The *jing* (villain) roles employ painted faces that come in an astonishing variety of designs, or *lianbu* (face characteristics), each of which symbolizes some character type, or personality. For example, a villain is indicated by flat white makeup over most of the face, with some lines of black and gray. The *chou*, or "clown," wears white makeup only around the eyes and nose. The *laodan* (old woman) wears no makeup at all. The *dan* (woman) wears heavy red makeup around the eyes, which fades to pale pink on the cheeks and chin, red lips, and black-penciled eyebrows, with the bridge of the nose and the forehead left white. Beijing Opera employs a wide variety of costumes and headdresses, but no naturalistic scenery was used until modern times, and the stage properties are very sparse, with little except some tables and chairs, although these few properties are employed imaginatively. Finally, stylized gestures, miming, and symbolism are prominent features of Beijing Opera.

ACTORS' DOMINANCE

The fourth important event in the history of Chinese drama to occur during the Qing Dynasty was the loss in status of literary playwrights, given the establishment of Beijing Opera as an independent style of drama and its predominance over all other theatrical styles. Literary playwrights with distinctive identities were replaced by actors with distinctive identities, audiences being attracted by plays acted by a particular actor instead of by plays written by a particular dramatist. By the 1840's, it became common practice in the production of Beijing Opera for actors to adapt and devise their own plays for the exercise of their particular talents, and actors rather than playwrights became the focus of audience attention. The names of actors, therefore, instead of the names of playwrights, became dominant in the history of Beijing Opera,

while the texts of the plays became mere scenarios to guide the actor in his performance, allowing him almost complete freedom to invent stage business, to improvise, and to embellish his performance.

The first actors to achieve "stardom" in the first half of the nineteenth century played *laosheng* (older male) roles. They included Yu Sanshen, from Hubei; Zhang Erkui, from Zhejiang; and Cheng Zhanggeng, from Anhui, considered by some to be the father of Beijing Opera. All became famous acting in Beijing. In the second half of the century, the most prominent actors also favored *laosheng* roles, except for one, Mei Caoling (the grandfather of the twentieth century actor, Mei Lanfang), who played *dan* roles. The others were Sun Quxian, from Tientsin; Dan Xinpei, from Hubei; and Wang Guifen, from Hubei. All became famous in Beijing.

Although there were playwrights who were active during the late eighteenth and early nineteenth centuries whose names are worth mentioning, they wrote either *saqu* or *chuanqi*. The best known of these were Shu Wei, from Jiangsu; Liang Tingnan, from Guangdong; Zhou Leqing, from Zhejiang; Yan Tingzhong, from Yunnan; Huang Xieqing, from Zhejiang; and Chen Lang. By the time of Chen, it was already the era of the actor, which also meant the era of the actor-playwright, or of the anonymous dramatist, as well as of the *erhuang* and the *xipi* drama.

In preparing their dramas, the Beijing Opera playwrights drew on a great variety of sources: Yuan *zaju*, Ming *chuanqi* and *kunqu*, Tang *chuanqi* stories, the popular vernacular novels, incidents from Chinese history, Buddhist tales, Chinese myths, fairy tales, and folklore. The most popular sources, however, were the stories of Mandalyāyana (Mulien) and military romances such as *Sanguo zhi yanyi* (fourteenth century; *Romance of the Three Kingdoms*, 1925), attributed to Luo Guanzhong, and *Shuihu zhuan* (possibly the fourteenth century; *All Men Are Brothers*, 1933; also known as *Water Margin*, 1937), by Shi Naian. Beijing Opera playwrights also drew on the popular novels *Xiyou ji* (pb. 1592; also known as *Hsi-yu chi*; partial trans., *Monkey*, 1942; *The Journey to the West*, 1977-1983), by Wu Chengen; *Jin Ping Mei* (c. 1610; *The Golden Lotus*, 1939), author unknown;

and *Hongloumeng* (1792; *Dream of the Red Chamber*, 1958), by Cao Xueqin. The extent and richness of all this source material produced an abundance of Beijing Opera plays, with modern estimates placing the number of titles at well over three thousand and some fourteen hundred still available for performance.

HUAJU AND XINGEJU

The Qing Dynasty came to an end in 1911 when a revolution led by Sun Yat-sen was successful because of the consent of the regime's military commander, General Yuan Shih-k'ai, who then dominated the scene as the first president of the new republic. By this time, Western influences had come to the fore, the Chinese people having realized that they needed to absorb large amounts of Western knowledge if they were to defend themselves against foreign aggression and domination. Hence, translations of Western literature of all kinds, artistic as well as technical, began to be issued by Chinese presses. Such translations included the plays of William Shakespeare, Molière, Friedrich Schiller, Henrik Ibsen, Anton Chekhov, Oscar Wilde, and others. First to appear were reformist Chinese plays, *xinxi* (new drama), which featured Western themes but were in the form of Yuan *zaju* or Ming *chuanqi*. Then, reformist plays appeared that were either translations of Western plays or imitations of Western-style Japanese plays. These plays were called *huaju* (spoken drama), because like Western plays, they excluded singing. They excluded, therefore, classical Chinese, or *guwen*, the linguistic medium of the major portion of the musical drama, and used *baihua* (colloquial speech) entirely. Shanghai became the center of the *huaju* movement to turn Chinese drama into a "spoken drama" like that of the West. In the early *huaju* movement, Japanese influence was particularly strong.

By the end of World War I, thousands of Chinese had become acquainted with Europe and the United States. In 1916, a young Chinese scholar who had studied in the United States advanced the notion that the colloquial language was the only practical instrument for all literature in China. Although this notion was strongly opposed by conservatives, it gradually gained ground and became victorious when the May Fourth Movement of 1919 lit the fires of revolt. The general literary reform movement, therefore, favored the *huaju* movement in drama and the writing and production of what came to be called *wenmingxi xinxi* (civilized new plays).

By the 1930's, the Nationalist government became alarmed at the seditious emotions generated by the new *huaju* plays and took steps to suppress them. A number of actors and dramatists were arrested in 1932. Of the many new *huaju* playwrights of this period, Cao Yu, author of the play *Leiyu* (*Thunderstorm*, 1958), written in 1933, is perhaps the most noteworthy. With the Japanese invasion of China in 1937 and the long war that followed, drama was employed by both Nationalists and Communists as a propaganda vehicle.

The late years of the war period, however, produced a new form of drama in which *huaju* and traditional Chinese drama were brought together. Called *xingeju* (new opera), it dealt with contemporary themes and contained large sections of plain speech together with song and poetic matter. The first important play of this kind was produced in 1944 by Ting I and He Jingzhi, both communist writers. Produced at the Lu Xun Art Academy in Yennan in 1944, the play was called *Baimo nü* (*The White-Haired Girl*, 1954) and was considered an artistic triumph by the communists. It is the story of the persecution of a tenant's daughter by a cruel and ruthless landlord.

BEIJING OPERA AND OTHER TRADITIONAL FORMS

Although Western-style drama had clearly taken hold in China, the authorities adhered to a policy of preserving Beijing Opera. From the founding of the republic until the Japanese invasion in 1937, Beijing Opera flourished, and it remained the major force in twentieth century Chinese theater. As before, actors rather than playwrights continued to be the major force in this traditional genre. The most influential as well as the most famous Chinese actor of the twentieth century was the great master of *dan* roles, Mei Lanfang. His performances in major cities all over China made him an object of adulation to Chinese audiences. He also made highly successful tours abroad, including tours of Japan, the United States, and Russia. Much of his dramatic success, however, depended on his collaboration with the scholar-dramatist Qi Rushan, who joined Mei in 1914. Their partnership lasted until 1931, during which time Qi wrote or revised twenty plays for Mei. They include the early twentieth century plays *Zhang E penyue* (Zhang E flies to the moon) and *Guifei zhuijiu* (the drunken concubine). Besides Mei, there were other actors of high repute during his time, such as the *dan* actor Cheng Yanqiu and the *sheng* actors Ma Lianliang and Yu Zhenfei. During the 1920's, social disapproval of male actors playing female parts mounted until, by 1928, men and women appeared in Beijing Opera together. Women actors such as Xue Yanjin, who had been a pupil of Mei, began to acquire high reputations. Some of the women even moved from playing female roles to playing male roles.

Although Beijing Opera has dominated the modern period, many other regional styles are also popular. *Kunqu* operas are performed and respected. In Shansi and Hebei Bangzi opera, the orchestra keeps time by beating a wooden block with a wooden stick, and the stringed instrument called the *banhu* is used instead of the *huqin*. Also, the singing voice is produced from the diaphragm instead of from the chest and throat. *Pingxi* opera, which originated in Manchuria, depends on classical stories, especially material from the novel *Dream of the Red Chamber*, and indulges in no acrobatics. Its main instrument is the *banhu* (no *huqin* is used), and it employs a large bass instrument not used on other operas. It has been promoted mostly since the start of the communist regime in China. *Yueju* opera features an entirely female cast. Its plays are mostly love stories, especially material from *Dream of the Red Chamber*, and it uses no *huqin*. *Chuanju* opera from Szechwan emphasizes singing and features a soft poetic style using a small gong and a *muqin*. The singer is accompanied only by percussion sounds and sings in a more natural style than the constrained voice of Beijing Opera. Considerable attention is paid, however, to the quality of the acting. *Wuju* opera focuses on dance movements, and its singing is done in a natural voice and in a soft, melodious fashion. It uses a small gong and a *muqin*. Although these local styles of drama are performed mostly in rural areas, they are also performed in the capital city.

BEFORE THE CULTURAL REVOLUTION

With the end of the Japanese conflict in 1945, full-scale civil war broke out between the Nationalists and the Communists. The Nationalists, under the leadership of Chiang Kai-Shek, were defeated in 1949 and fled from the mainland to the island of Taiwan, where they established the Republic of China. The Communists on the mainland, under the leadership of Mao Zedong (Mao Tse-tung), established in the same year the People's Republic of China.

Practically all the prominent playwrights remained on the mainland and took an active role in theatrical affairs. They included Cao Yu, Hong Shen, Tian Han, Ouyang Yuqian, Xia Yan, Guo Moruo (Kuo Mo-jo), and Lao She. All except Guo Moruo and Lao She were the best-known *huaju* playwrights before the war with Japan. Guo Moruo and Lao She became known as dramatists during the war, and under the Communist regime they contributed to the development of the spoken drama. Mei Lanfang and other famous actors also remained on the mainland after the Communists came to power, continuing to act on the stage.

At first, the Communist regime became a patron of Beijing and other types of opera but showed less interest in the modern spoken drama. Indeed, it seemed favorably disposed to allowing a variety of dramatic approaches to flourish. Soon, however, the Communist hierarchy began to exert pressure on the playwrights and actors to bring their work more in line with Communist ideology and the official party line. Between 1950 and 1952, the Ministry of Culture banned twenty-six plays, including fifteen Beijing Operas, two *chuanju*, and seven *pingxi* (formerly *pingqu*). The Communists objected to plays with supernatural elements (including the presence of ghosts and demons); to feudal elements, superstitions, and fatalism; to brutality and violence; to sexual spice and lewdness; and to evidence of bourgeois mentality. Communist officials made constant attempts to change the mentality of playwrights and to "reeducate" them along Marxist-Leninist ideological lines. They pointed to Xia Yan's 1954 play *Shilian* (*The Test*, 1955), whose setting was in an electrical machinery factory, as a model to be followed. At the same time, however, there was some interest shown in the past. In 1956, a drastically revised version of the Qing author Zhu Hao's *Fifteen Strings of Cash* was performed by a *kunqu* company, and there were critical discussions of Gao Ming's *The Lute*. Then Tian Han wrote a play, *Guan Hanqing* (English translation, 1961), based on *chuanqi* form, to celebrate the 340th anniversary of the great Yuan dramatist's death.

In 1966, Mao launched the Cultural Revolution, supported by the Red Guards. As adviser on cultural work to the army, Mao's third wife, Qiang Qing, a former Shanghai film actress, was able to give direct orders to playwrights and opera companies, and she became the leader of a "new drama" (*xinxi*) movement. Heavy criticisms were directed at two recent plays, Yao Xinnong's *Qinggong yuan* (*The Malice of Empire*, 1970) and Wu Han's *Hai Rui baguan* (*Hai Rui's Dismissal*, 1971). Traditional and *huaju* dramas were attacked as "feudalistic." Wu, Tian, and other playwrights were arrested. It was rumored that Lao's death was a suicide. Of the leading playwrights, only Guo endured. The Communist regime proposed that in the future, eight cultural models be followed in theatrical entertainment. Of these "eight models," five were "revolutionary Beijing Operas" (*geming xiedai jingju*), two were "revolutionary modern ballets" (*geming xiedai wu-zhu*), and one was a symphonic performance. The five Beijing Operas, in which the emphasis is on action, all appeared around 1964 and included the following: *Ji chu wei hu shan* (*Taking Tiger Mountain by Strategy*, 1969), an account of the taking of a bandit's hideout by a Red Army unit in 1946; *Hai-kang* (*Sea Battle at Night*, 1968), a story of the defeat of a saboteur on the dock of a seaport in 1963; *Qixi Baihutuan* (*Raid on the White Tiger Regiment*, 1967), an account of a raid by a Red Army unit on the headquarters of a South Korean regiment in 1953; *Shajiabang* (English translation, 1967), an account of a Red Army unit's destruction of Japanese soldiers and their Chinese collaborators in the town of Shajiabang; and *Hongteng ji* (*The Red Lantern*, 1970), the story of how a railway switchman and his family fought the Japanese, with vigorous piano accompaniment to the Beijing Opera singing. The two ballets were *Hong se niang ji zhun* (*Red Detachment of Women*, 1971) and *Baimo nü* (rendered as a film, *The White-Haired Girl*, in 1970), based on the play by Ting I and He Jingzhi. The symphony was *Shajiabang* and was based on the play of the same title. These new dramas were a radical departure from previous types. Costumes and setting were fairly realistic but stylized. The Communist heroes were presented in an idealized manner and their characters kept simple, in contrast to the complicated characters of traditional Chinese heroes. Modern uniforms and weapons were prominent features of four of the five plays. The singing was based on traditional Chinese style but produced an overall effect that was completely different.

AFTER THE CULTURAL REVOLUTION

The rampage of Mao's cultural revolution eventually came to an end with his death in 1976 and the subsequent fall of the "Gang of Four," headed by his wife. The ruling party admitted that the political turmoil of the past ten years had been a disaster for the whole country and began to take a series of measures to rescue the country from the brink of total collapse. In the dramatists' circle, all the artists victimized by Mao's constant purges were reaccepted one after another, though some of them, such as Lao and Tian, did not live to see their names cleared. Dramatists' associations at various levels resumed their operation. Regional schools of opera began to recover along with Beijing Opera and *huaju*, the two most influential of all dramatic genres. Dramatic works once condemned by the Gang of Four reappeared on the stage throughout the country. Dramatic characters disdainfully labeled by Mao as "emperors and kings, generals and ministers, scholars and beauties" came back with a vengeance to retake the center stage from his "revolutionary heroes." New plays began to emerge, many not necessarily created according to Mao's theories on art and literature.

Members of the dramatists' associations throughout China used to be *ganbu* (cadres) working for the government with fixed salaries. After the government's shift in 1979 from a planned economy to a market economy, freelancers and collectively or privately owned troupes of various dramatic genres began to appear and many non-*ganbu* artists joined the dramatists' associations. In 2001, the Chinese Dramatists Association in Beijing had twelve thousand members, representing not only *huaju* and Beijing Opera but also about two hundred regional or local *juzhong* (schools of opera).

Each of the regional operatic schools has a history of its own as well as a unique repertoire. Each employs a dialect as a medium of communication and uses the style of an easily identifiable geographical area. From North China are Pingju, Yuju, Hebei Bangzi, and Henan Bangzi, to name but a few. Pingju (Ping Opera) is most popular in Beijing and Tianjin, with its best-known pieces being *Xiao nuxu* (child husband), *Jiemei huanghou* (empresses), and *Hua wei mei* (flowers as the keepsake), all from the twentieth century. Yuju (Yu Opera) is a major local opera in Henan Province with a repertoire of more than six hundred traditional plays such as *Tang zhixian shen Gao Ming* (clever magistrate), *Fuliu nuren* (modern woman), and *Fengliu caizi* (romantic scholar). Hebei Bangzi is one of the major forms of local opera in Hebei Province, offering more than five hundred traditional and two hundred contemporary plays such as *Hudie bei* (butterfly cup), Baoliandeng (magic lotus lantern), and *Chen sanliang* (unwilling concubine). From South China is Yueju (Yue Opera), more commonly called Guangdongxi. It is the predominant dramatic genre in Guangdong, Guangxi, Hong Kong, and Macao, with a huge repertoire of five to six thousand traditional pieces such as *Diaoman gongzhu* (crafty princess), Guan hanqing (fatal opera), and *Sou shuyuan* (search the school).

From East China are such schools as Huangmeiju, Yueju, and Chaoju. Huangmeiju (Huangmei Opera) thrives in south Anhui Province and some regions of adjacent Jiangxi and Hubei Provinces. Among its most frequently staged pieces are *Nu fuma* (emperor's female son-in-law), *Niulang zhinu* (fallen stars), and *Tianxian pei* (goddess's marriage). Yueju (Yue Opera), often called Shaoxingxi, prevails in

Zhejiang Province. All its performers used to be women. Its eighty-year-old repertoire includes *Liang shanbo yu zhu yingtai* (butterfly lovers), Qing tan (jade fan pendant), and *Pan fu* (truth revealed). Chaoju (Chao Opera or Chaozou Opera), a regional opera deeply influenced by *nanxi*, has a large following in the Chao'an and Shantou regions of Guangdong Province and in the areas of Fujian Province and Taiwan Province where Chaozhou dialect is spoken. Among its masterpieces are *Meiren lei* (beauty's tears), *Chi meng* (idiot's dream), and *Tou shi* (stealing a poem).

From West China are, among others, Zangju and Chuanju. Zangju (Tibetan Opera) has a history of several hundred years and a repertoire containing thirteen masterpieces of a religious nature, including *Wencheng gongzhu* (Princess Wencheng) and *Yuncheng wangzi* (Prince Yuncheng). It is the most popular and influential in the Autonomous Region of Tibet and part of Sichuan Province, Gansu Province, and Qinghai Province. Chuanju (Chuan Opera), a relatively young school with a history of more than seventy years, dominates in Sichuan Province and some regions of Yunnan and Guizhou Provinces. Among its best-known pieces are *Bashan xiucai* (Dongxiang massacre), *Fuqi qia* (husband-wife bridge), *Dajiao furen* (madame big feet), and *Funu zhuan* (profile of Tao Furu).

As a rule, regional schools of opera do not cross a major geographical divide like the Yangzi (Yangtze) River; however, there is one exception, namely Nankun (southern Kun Opera). Nankun originated from Suzhou in Jiangsu Province south of the Yangzi River, but it has its derivative Beikun (northern Kun Opera) in faraway places north of the river. Together they are named Kunju (Kun Opera), with their most famous pieces being *Shi wu guan* (fifteen strings of coins), *Qianli song Jingniang* (escorting Jingniang home), and *Qiang tou ma shang* (love at first sight).

Along with the restaging of old plays came the creation of new ones. Some of the new creations attempted to make use of modern stage techniques and the old method of combining realism and romanticism to convey political and ideological messages. One of these politically oriented creations is a spoken play titled *Huaihai zhanyi* (pr. 1987; Huaihai campaign). Written and staged by the Modern Drama Troupe affiliated with the General Political Department of the People's Liberation Army, it portrayed Deng Xiaoping as a Communist Party leader during the Chinese Civil War right after the Japanese were driven out of China in 1945. Another example is a Beijing Opera work titled *Hua ziliang* (pr. 2001) by Wei Zhong and Da Ming, glorifying the "heroic sacrifices" of Communist Party members in their struggle against the Nationalists in the 1940's.

Many of the new dramatic works, however, focused on the inevitable social issues and changes brought about by the policies of "opening up to the world," the market-oriented economy that the government began to implement in 1979. For instance, on the *huaju* stage, Le Meiqin's *Liushou nushi* (pr. 1991; woman who is left behind) explored the complex feelings and emotions of young men and women whose spouses have left China to seek adventure in Japan, Australia, Canada, and the United States. Sha Yexin's *Yesu, Kongzi, Pitoushi Lienong* (pr. 1988; Jesus, Confucius and John Lennon) exposed some of the social absurdities witnessed by Christ, Confucius, and Beatles member Lennon during their travels together on Earth as well as on the moon.

BIBLIOGRAPHY

Idema, Wilt, and Lloyd Haft. *A Guide to Chinese Literature.* Amsterdam: Amsterdam University Press, 1996. Translated by the Center for Chinese Studies, University of Michigan, 1997. An up-to-date guide to Chinese literature, it covers Chinese drama up to the early 1990's, with all the literary titles and authors' names given in pinyin. It contains a 103-page bibliography, a glossary, and an index of major works and authors in both Chinese characters and pinyin.

Leung, Laifong. *Morning Sun: Interview of Chinese Writers of the Lost Generation.* Armonk, N.Y.: M. E. Sharp, 1994. A valuable reference for plays focusing on social issues in the 1990's by writers of the so-called *zhiqing* generation, namely those who participated in Mao's Cultural Revolution, were exiled to the countryside, and, finally, after Mao's death, came back to cities to face a rapidly changing society driven by a market economy.

Lopez, Manuel D. *Chinese Drama.* Metuchen, N.J.: Scarecrow Press, 1991. An annotated bibliography of commentary, criticism, and plays in English translation, it consists of two parts. The first part covers the background and development of Chinese drama from before the Han Dynasty to after the Cultural Revolution, and the second part covers individual plays, anthologies, and collections.

McDougall, Bonnie S. *Mao Zedong's "Talks at the Yan'an Conference on Literature and Art": A Translation of the 1943 Text with Commentary.* Ann Arbor: University of Michigan Press, 1980. The 1943 text is a must for anyone interested in understanding the theory behind the party policy on art and literature and the reason for artists' resistance to the party policy between 1949 and 1976.

McDougall, Bonnie S., and Kam Louie. *The Literature of China in the Twentieth Century.* New York: Columbia University Press, 1997. Contains a section titled "Drama: Writing Performance," introducing some of the most influential dramatists in the first three-quarters of the twentieth century who fought for a new, strong China free from corruption, injustice, and foreign domination.

Scott, A. C. *The Classical Theatre of China.* Reprint. Westport, Conn.: Greenwood Press, 1978. Chronicles the development, themes, and performances of classical theater.

Shih, Chung-Wen. *The Golden Age of Chinese Drama: Yuan Tas-chu (Yuan Zaju).* Princeton, N.J.: Princeton University Press, 1976. A rigorous discussion of various aspects of the plays in the Yuan Dynasty, including their historical background and social milieu, convention and structure, characterization and themes, and language and music.

Richard P. Benton,
updated by Chenliang Sheng

INDIAN DRAMA

Ancient and varied as the country that produced it, Indian theater had its beginnings centuries before the Christian era. How it turned from performances of wandering singers, magicians, puppeteers, and dancers into formal theater remains uncertain. There is a myth telling how the gods invented drama, the highest of the arts, and at first kept it only for themselves. Then one day during a celestial performance, the talented actress Urvasi allowed her thoughts to dwell on her earthly lover and stumbled in her dialogue. Expelled from Paradise for her misbehavior and destined to wander on Earth, Urvasi taught the theatrical arts to mortals. Thus it is said that drama, as a fully realized artistic form, came to the ancient Indians as an accidental gift from the gods.

THE TRIVANDRUM PLAYS

Although dramatic dialogues appear in the *Rigveda*, composed around 1500 B.C.E., the oldest complete plays extant are attributed to Bhāsa, a dramatist thought to have lived in the second or third century C.E. Even though later Sanskrit playwrights and critics referred to him and quoted his work, the plays vanished at some point. In 1917, an Indian scholar discovered in a South Indian library a manuscript, now called the Trivandrum plays, which contained thirteen intact works written in Sanskrit. Admitting that the authorship may be subject to dispute, most scholars agree that Bhāsa wrote the plays and that they remain unchanged from their original form. Six of the pieces, all short, take their subject matter from an Indian epic, the *Mahābhārata* (c. 400 B.C.E.-400 C.E.; *The Mahabharata of Krishna-Dwaipayana Vyasa*, 1887-1896; also known as *The Mahabharata*). Although lacking continuity, these plays still may have been performed together as a cluster of stories from the epic. *Pratimā-Nāṭaka* (second or third century C.E.; English translation, 1930-1931), one of the most fully realized, recounts much of another epic, the *Rāmāyana* (c. 500 B.C.E.; English translation, 1870-1889). The best known and the most advanced in dramatic structure is *Svapna-vāsava-datta* (second or third century C.E.; English translation, 1930-1931), which tells the story of two women who are potential rivals, yet through their goodness they overcome the temptation to act in the evil way that such a situation warrants. The king completes the triangle, married to the one, still haunted by the other, whom he believes dead. Tangled court intrigue brings about the ironic circumstance in which the former queen becomes the lady-in-waiting to her successor. One of the most noted episodes in the drama occurs when the king believes that he beholds his former wife in a vision, while in actuality, he has unknowingly met her in the flesh.

In addition to their theatrical soundness, the Trivandrum plays hold a significant place in the history of Indian drama. They did not spring fully developed in the second or third century but obviously represent several hundred years of dramatic tradition, therefore establishing how advanced the theater was when Bhāsa began to write. Unfortunately, those works preceding the Trivandrum plays have been lost.

SANSKRIT DRAMA OF THE CLASSIC PERIOD

Bhāsa's writing, sophisticated and courtly, foreshadowed the golden age of drama written in Sanskrit. The Classic Period, as it is generally called, lasted from about 300 C.E. to 800 C.E. Considered the highest achievement of Indian literature, the Sanskrit drama drew its support and audience from the courts that flourished until the Muslim invasions eventually destroyed them between 1000 and 1300.

Because the plays aim to be both pleasing and instructive, they contain a mixture of the worldly and the unworldly, an approach that characterizes much of Hindu art. Further, the drama reflects, specifically, Hindu thought. The loftiest plays, called *nātaka* (heroic drama), draw from the same repositories of Hindu mythology as Bhāsa's work does. Devotional stories, in one sense, their action often revolves around the exploits of the gods Vishnu and Śiva. Suffering or disaster never befalls these heroic characters, be they gods or kings, because it was unthinkable that such personages could meet defeat and death. This requirement, to which playwrights adhered faithfully, explains the absence of tragedy in Indian theater. Other plays, equally popular, are those called *prakarana* (social or bourgeois drama), which re-create domestic life and stress the ideal of family. A subtle eroticism pervades these works to heighten the Hindu emphasis on fertility and reproduction.

Considering their twofold aim, to delight and to instruct, both kinds of plays employ a mixture of comedy, pathos, spectacle, and elegant language to make the lesson palatable. Whereas the comedy usually focuses on human foibles, the pathos most often arises from sentimental scenes, such as a great favorite among audiences: the reunion of long-separated family members, friends, or lovers. Music, an essential part of the play's structure, adds to the spectacle provided by elaborate costumes, set pieces, and, sometimes, the design of the theater itself, which was treated as an important element. Although decorative, Sanskrit staging prefers to permit unhampered movement of time and place. Above all, the language reigns, with poetry assigned to the gods and kings, prose to the women and lesser male characters.

The dramas also follow a strict code of decorum; for example, eating or kissing never takes place onstage, because such actions are considered not only vulgar but also offensive to the gods. Neither do the plays rely heavily on conflict or suspense, but more on an unfolding of events that appears endless, the past melding into the present, the present into the future. As Western critics familiar with Sanskrit drama often point out, the plays resemble their Western counterparts to the point that they can be understood and appreciated by Westerners, even in translation, but only on one level—for the dramas remain firmly rooted in the Hindu view of the world, a view dominated by a concept of reality and unreality rarely grasped by the Western mind. No matter how worldly, how farcical, or how political the play's action, the intent is ultimately metaphysical and religious. It is noteworthy that each performance begins and closes with a prayer to the gods.

THE LITTLE CLAY CART

Numerous Sanskrit plays are extant; in fact, they far outnumber those surviving from the golden age of Greek drama. Several of these dramas have established themselves in theatrical repertory, being performed currently both in India and in the West. The resurgence after independence in 1947 of Indian culture at home and abroad accounts for the renewed interest in Sanskrit theater. Two of the most widely read and performed dramas are *Mṛcchakaṭikā* (c. 300-600 C.E.; *Mrchhakatika*, 1898, also known as *The Little Clay Cart*) and *Abhijñānaśākuntala* (c. 45 B.C.E. or c. 395 C.E.; *Śakuntalā: Or, The Lost Ring*, 1789).

Although attributed to King Śūdraka, the authorship of *The Little Clay Cart* remains unknown. For that matter, so does historical evidence to prove the existence of an actual King Śūdraka. The real author, it is generally assumed, hid behind the probably fictitious king to maintain his anonymity. The play's date, too, is speculative; sources vary widely. Regardless of such uncertainties, the play is indisputably the work of a master and stands as one of the classics of world theater. India at its most exotic emerges through the author's evocation of the atmosphere of a large fifth century Indian city. The manners, customs, sights, smells, and sounds come to life, delineating not only the India of the past but also the timeless aspects of modern India. More important, the characters in their human struggle spark a recognition that makes them and their actions universal.

The plot revolves around Cārudata, who belongs to the highest of the castes, the Brahman. Noted for his goodness, Cārudata long ago gave away his riches to the poor and now lives, almost friendless, in a kind of genteel poverty. As the play opens, he has unknowingly become the object of the courtesan Vasanthasenā's affections. "Lovely as the springtide," the director of the theater describes her in the customary prologue; Vasanthasenā so admires Cārudata's character that she sets out to gain his attention. This exposition established, the scenes unfold in a leisurely manner. Melodramatic devices such as mistaken identity, a false murder, court intrigue, lust, a woman in distress at the hands of a villain, and a last-minute reprieve before an execution carry the plot to its denouement. Comedy, directed for the most part toward human weakness and pretensions, gives relief to these grim devices and sets a mood to assure the audience that the near catastrophes will be avoided and that all will be resolved as it should in an orderly universe. Still, even when Vasanthasenā makes her love for Cārudata known and he responds, they do not live happily ever after in the Western sense, for Sanskrit drama shies away from such conclusiveness in human matters. That Cārudata already has a wife presents no problems or conflicts: The wife represents the ideal of home, the courtesan the erotic side of sexual nature.

The Little Clay Cart, while abundant in action, suspense, and comedy—elements that many Sanskrit plays lack—still takes seriously its instructive purposes. A look at the significance of the title will help to explain the intended message. Cārudata's son has but a single toy, a little clay cart. Once he receives from the wealthy courtesan his great wish, a little cart made of gold, he still owns only a toy. The cart, made first of the humblest material, then of the richest, represents the Hindu attitude toward poverty and wealth. Both are toys, hence only playthings in true reality, where substance—be it clay or gold, the street or the palace, fine garments or rags—plays no valid part in human experience. This sense of a higher order is expressed by Cārudata in the speech that concludes the ten-act play:

> May the cows never cease to give abundance of milk; may the earth bring forth rich harvests; may Indra's rain seasonally descend upon the fields; may the breath of the pure winds refresh the hearts of men; may all living things enjoy unchanging happiness; may the Brahmanas be worthy of the veneration that is accorded them; may the kings, vanquishing their enemies and always mindful of their duties, rule gloriously over the world.

ŚAKUNTALĀ

Śakuntalā, another of the major Sanskrit plays, contains a finely wrought language and a level of thought characteristic of its author, Kālidāsa, known not only for his three extant dramas but for his sublime elegiac poems as well. Less grounded in the real world than the author of *The Little Clay Cart*, Kālidāsa in *Śakuntalā* relies on myth and symbol to set forth a philosophy in which people and nature exist in harmony, equating as he does seasons in nature and fertility in human life. Through his exquisite language, he celebrates nature and its beauty as it moves from one season to another, from life to death to life, endlessly. In the same spirit, he praises human sexuality, which he treats both biologically as the source of life and idealistically as the erotic impetus of love.

While drawing his plot from *The Mahabharata*, Kālidāsa takes some liberties with his source in tracing the trials and triumphs of the lovely Śakuntalā, reared in the forest by a hermit and discovered by the powerful and handsome King Dushyanta, who falls in love with her. She in turn pledges her love to him. Dushyanta promises to return and leaves his ring as a symbol of his fidelity. Soon after his departure, misfortune strikes Śakuntalā when she falls under a curse, which will cause her beloved Dushyanta to be unable to recognize her unless he sees the ring. The pregnant Śakuntalā loses the ring on her way to meet her lover, and only after extended uncertainty and agony on the part of the separated pair does a fisherman finally find the ring inside a fish. Once returned and identified, the ring unleashes in the king recollections of Śakuntalā, whom he had earlier denied and who now lives in exile with their son. Before long the two reunite; order is reestablished, family idealized, and love triumphant.

Throughout the unraveling of this preposterous but charming story, Kālidāsa provides magnificent evocation of nature's beauty, celebrates the physical and idealistic realms of love, and comments on the frailty and absurdity of the human condition; indeed, he interweaves into the narrative all the strands that form the tapestry of the Hindu worldview.

From 800 to 1000, Sanskrit drama continued to flourish but never again reached the heights of the Classic Period. A period of decline set in from 1000 to 1300, with the plays patterned after those of the golden age but increasingly marred by their artificiality, sterility, tedium, pretentious language, and threadbare plots. This decline coincided with the Muslim invasions, which changed the face of the country and destroyed the Hindu courts that had supported the theater. Even though the conquerors could have inherited such a rich theatrical tradition, drama was not among Muslim artistic pursuits, which lay more in painting, music, nondramatic literature, and architecture. To an extent, the invaders absorbed the other Hindu arts into their own, but the glorious Sanskrit theater died for lack of interest and support, its grandeur lost until its rebirth in the twentieth century.

THE EUROPEAN INVASION

By the seventeenth century another invader had arrived: the Europeans. Far more foreign and subtle than the Muslims, the new conquerors tended to superimpose their own culture on things Indian instead of absorbing them. Although the Europeans launched their struggle to gain supremacy in India during the 1600's, not until the nineteenth century did the Europeans, especially the British, fully accomplish their goals. Between 1853 and 1919, most of William Shakespeare's plays were translated into Indian languages—*The Merchant of Venice* (pr. c. 1596-1597) alone appeared in nine different languages, and by the mid-1900's, Shakespeare had begun to occupy the stage long left dark by the Sanskrit dramatists.

Another kind of theater prevalent in the late 1800's and early 1900's grew from melodramatic renditions of thrilling episodes lifted out of English novels, which had been translated into Indian languages and made available in the bookstalls. Adapted to the tastes and languages of their Indian audiences, these plays, written by hack writers, bore no resemblance to the elegant Sanskrit drama of the Classic Period.

Under the new foreign rulers, Calcutta, the cosmopolitan city on the eastern coast, developed into the major cultural center. By the mid-1800's, attempts to rebuild an authentic Indian theater were under way, with dramatists such as Pandit Ramnarayan, Michael Madhusudan Dutt, Dinabandhu Mitra, Girish Chandra Ghosh, and Dwijendra Lal Roy writing plays for the next half century but failing to strike the right chord. Not until Rabindranath Tagore appeared did modern drama come to India. Better known for his poetry, for which he won the Nobel Prize in 1913, Tagore wrote about forty plays, among

which *Chitrāngadā* (pb. 1892; *Chitra*, 1913), *Rājā* (pb. 1910; *The King of the Dark Chamber*, 1914), and *Dakghar* (pb. 1912; *The Post Office*, 1914) are the most widely known and performed. Lyric, symbolic, and static, Tagore's plays often rely on dreams, ancient myth, and the mystical.

TWENTIETH CENTURY DRAMA

In some respects, a history of Indian theater could begin and conclude with a study of Sanskrit drama, which started its decline around 800 and eventually lay dormant for several centuries. Although rediscovered in the twentieth century, partly through the efforts of British and German scholars, it has failed to regain its supremacy. The Sanskrit language alone sets up barriers, so that even many Indians must see their classic plays performed in translation, either in English or in one of the many other official Indian languages. After a hundred or more years of European plays, including ones by Shakespeare, Henrik Ibsen, August Strindberg, and George Bernard Shaw, Indian theatergoers have become so accustomed to tragedy, conclusive endings, specific characterization, and other conventions of Western drama that the form of a Sanskrit drama might seem foreign even to them.

The revival of the classic drama actually remains somewhat limited in its scope, confined often to the studies of scholars and to the provinces of those devoted to the restoration of a pure Indian culture divorced from Western influences. The promotion of the latter attitude, some Indian critics argue, hampers the establishment of a vital modern theater that would combine that which is typically Indian with the inevitable inheritance from the West.

Throughout much of the twentieth century, Indian playwrights, often against heavy odds, have attempted to meld the two traditions and thereby establish a drama that honestly could be called modern Indian theater. Though not altogether rejecting the unworldly quality of their Sanskrit heritage, the dramatists have still focused on worldly matters, for the major thrust in modern drama has been in the realm of protest theater. At times naturalistic, even brutal, in their depiction of social ills, these playwrights often turn to myth and mysticism for solutions, the essence of the Indian apprehension of the universe.

COLONIAL PROTEST THEATER

Protest in Indian theater is not a twentieth century invention. For example, Mitra's *Nil Darpan* (pr. 1860; English translation, 1861) exposed the atrocities carried out against Indian workers by British indigo planters. At the end of the century, a strong theater of purpose, especially in the Marathi and Bengali languages, had risen, taking up such social concerns as child marriage practices, the consequences of alcoholism, purdah, and the treatment of widows.

Although none of these plays was exceptional, they did foreshadow the first wave of twentieth century drama, which found its voice in expressing the anti-British feeling engendered by Mahatma Gandhi's successful efforts to raise the consciousness of his fellow Indians living under the inequities and humiliation of imperialism. Once the national movement had gained strength, the playwrights added their voices to the protests. Some of them retold episodes from *The Mahabharata*, but their allegorical satires were so thinly disguised that even the British understood them and took legal steps to quell this new enemy of the empire. At the height of the Gandhian years in the 1930's, the British had silenced the playwrights, along with novelists and poets, who criticized foreign rule. Therefore, purpose in theater vanished and only escapist drama survived. During this time, yet another blow from the West struck the stage—that is, the cinema. Before long, live theaters were transformed into motion picture houses, and the most talented of the writers and performers deserted the stage for the more lucrative film business. The cinema currently remains immensely popular in India and stands as a major hindrance to the establishment of a vital and widespread living theater. Another problem stems from the multiplicity of official Indian languages, ten or so, including English.

Yet even in the face of these difficulties, modern playwrights have never despaired altogether. Just before independence in 1947, the protest theater reemerged again, and it has continued its growth steadily. When World War II ended, the British finally realized that they must leave India; thus they set into motion the machinery to grant independence to the country they had long ruled. However, soon the machinery threatened to cut the country into parts. That India might be carved up to create Pakistan affected many Indians deeply, especially in view of their mystical idea of a Mother India. One such person, Prithviraj Kapoor, a wealthy film actor, believed so strongly that the theater could help prevent the tragedy that he formed the Prithvi Theatre, a company of able performers that crisscrossed India to perform plays against partition. Two of the most popular, written by Kapoor and Inder Raj Anand, are *Deewar* (pr. 1945), which told of a wall built between two brothers by a foreign seductress, and *Pathan* (pr. 1945), which showed how unity between Hindus and Muslims might be brought about by blood sacrifice. Melodramatic and propagandistic, the Prithvi plays never pretended to be great theater, and soon after 1947 they were forgotten. While they failed to prevent partition, the plays, however poor, helped to revive the theater of purpose, which was to thrive in the years to come.

POST-INDEPENDENCE DRAMA

The protest theater that ensued no longer focused on British rule but on the corruption and ineptitude writers saw in their own government. A playwright in the forefront of this movement was Bidal Sircar, who wrote in Bengali and whose work was translated into English. In his plays, he explored the social, economic, and historical forces that affect and disrupt Indian society. One of the most powerful expressions of these concerns, *Michhil* (1978; *Procession*, 1983), contains a series of scenes that shows one man's repeated death, each time the result of the social ills afflicting the individual citizen. Throughout the play, the actors stage processions into and out of the audience, and at the end they ask the audience to join them in a final procession of dreams that represents the hopes that endure despite the false processions ending only in death. Encouraged to join this procession, which promises "to show us a way, the way home," one of the characters tiredly responds: "I've seen so many processions. They never show you a way." Nevertheless, once convinced that the procession of "men's dreams" is "real," he joins. The play, in spite of its graphic portrayal of Calcutta, which Sircar called "a monster of a city," ends on a mystical note. Significantly, to his description of Calcutta as a "monster," Sircar added, "But a monster that is alive, throbbing with vitality and viciousness, maybe vision too." *Procession* exemplifies how modern Indian drama at its best has wedded its own traditions to those inherited from the West.

One story that postindependence theater has largely ignored is that of Gandhi's life and work, a subject that literally hundreds of poems, novels, and biographies have taken up in all of India's languages. Perhaps portraying the Mahatma as a flesh-and-blood character on the stage offends many Indians. In *Gandhi: A Play* (1983), written in English, Indian humorist V. D. Trivadi treats his subject satirically, stressing what he sees as Gandhi's thirst for martyrdom. At the time of the play's publication, before it was performed, one reviewer hoped the play would escape censorship. A daring work, this play, more than anything else, questions the pompous way many writers have approached Gandhi. Trivadi's treatment of so revered a subject does indicate the theater's growing maturity after independence.

FOLK THEATER

Yet another kind of theater continues to flourish throughout India, both in the country and in the cities: the folk theater. It flourished centuries before the Christian era and continued to do so outside the courts where the elite watched Sanskrit plays. The folk theater outlived these works and carried on during the centuries in which the classic drama lay buried waiting for revival. Unaffected by the comings and goings of conquerors, even by the advent of film, the folk theater adapted and has survived.

Folk theater employs dance, song, mime, and improvisation. Dialogue, in the people's dialect, is sometimes included but seldom written down, for the presentations rely less on language than they do on movement. Those forms that borrow from the religious epics relate the myths surrounding the multiple Hindu deities, and the productions often make up part

of the temple activities during religious festivals. Other folk forms have no such high aims—their stories are bawdy and ribald, full of sexual innuendos.

In some performances, the entire village is involved. At times, a traveling troupe, even a single storyteller or mime, is engaged to entertain, perhaps at a celebration such as a wedding. Animals—namely, elephants and monkeys—well trained and often costumed, also take part. Usually transvestites play the women's roles, because folk theater at its most vulgar is thought improper for women, either to act in or to see. Lively, varied, and enduring, the folk theater does have one threat: the spread of television. Yet it is not likely that television will destroy a tradition that has already withstood countless invasions, religious wars, natural disasters, famine, political upheavals, and partitioning of the land.

CONTEMPORARY THEATER

In a country in which illiteracy still dominates, a strict class structure prevails, and rural people far outnumber urban, the formal, written theater continues to be restricted. Nor have contemporary Indian plays, even those written in English, made an impact internationally. The drama has never gained the enthusiastic reception given overseas to Indian fiction in English. This is not say, however, that live theater in India is a disappearing art, even though it must compete with the immensely popular cinema and the expansion of television. The theaters are located in the large cities, such as Bombay, Calcutta, and New Delhi; and like the ancient Sanskrit drama, contemporary theater presents to an audience consisting only of the elite.

Competing with indigenous plays are those from the Western world, especially English-language drama, which is performed either in the original or in translation. Plays by the classic British dramatists, Shakespeare in particular, continue to be popular. Because many of these dramatic works, as well as Greek tragedies and European dramas, have been translated into the major Indian languages, they have been absorbed into Indian culture and are probably more familiar and perhaps more accessible to the educated Indian than classical Sanskrit drama. Therefore it would not be surprising in modern India to find productions of Shaw's plays, or those of Strindberg, Ibsen, Arthur Miller, Edward Albee, Neil Simon, and other Western playwrights. The well-traveled, English-speaking Indians would be especially at home with the staples of Western theater.

A survey of contemporary Indian plays shows that for the most part they have little relationship to traditional Indian drama but have become thoroughly Westernized, whether they are produced in English, Hindi, Gujarati, or Marathi—India's four major languages. Many of the plays tend to fall into familiar categories: sophisticated comedy, satire, protest plays, and dramas of family conflict; adaptations from Hindu mythology and historical plays also appear.

The English-language theater displays a fondness for sophisticated comedies, which are produced by companies appealing to what one advertisement calls the "large, upmarket and hip crowd." One such production, *A Fly in the Pizza* (pr. 2000), takes up the war between the sexes, and another, called *I Do, I Don't!* (pr. 2000), explores the pitfalls of marriage. A play with a feminist theme, *Once I Was Young . . . Now I Am Wonderful* (pr. 2002), addresses a society obsessed with youth and beauty. On another note, *It Happens Only in India* (pr. 2000) takes a satiric look at India's sociopolitical situation, castigating the country for its bumbling bureaucracy, corruption, and failure to live up to its ideals as "the world's largest democracy." Although these plays do not constitute great or lasting theater, they resemble much of what would be available at any given time on the London or Broadway stages.

The Hindi, Marathi, and Gujarati theaters also produce light comedies full of sexual innuendoes, which could be described as sophisticated versions of the ribald folk plays. Generally, though, the dramatists appear to be more serious than their English-speaking counterparts. For one thing, they consistently dramatize typical family conflicts in Indian society. For example, the Hindi play *Prayashchit*, by Sukant Panda (pr. 2001), probes arranged marriages and the accompanying dowry system, which in many cases cause women enormous anguish. As the drama unfolds, a young, educated bride suffers at the hands of her husband and his parents, who accuse her of being unable to conceive a child. Although the abused bride triumphs—unlike many of the real women involved in such situations, the play presents a forthright exploration of a delicate subject in Indian life. These plays, whether serious or comic, are usually set in the milieu of their middle- or upper-class audiences.

There still remains an audience, even among the elite, for renditions and adaptations of Hindu mythology. The English theater, however, is less likely to produce such dramas. When modern playwrights draw from these ancient and rich sources, they understand that most of their audience will already know the story, so they must reshape the familiar tales and make them relevant for the modern world. This theater undoubtedly stays closest to Indian dramatic tradition. Another development is the production of historical plays recounting events that took place during British rule, such as the Great Mutiny of 1857. It has been noted that these plays serve to forge a postcolonial identity by reminding the modern audience of the heroism and sacrifices made by those who fought against the English.

BIBLIOGRAPHY

Bhatia, Nandi. "Staging the 1857 Mutiny as 'The Great Rebellion.'" *Theatre Arts* 51 (May, 1999): 167-184. Examines how the contemporary staging of a historical event such as the 1857 mutiny against the British helps to foster an anticolonial identity in India.

Brandon, James R., and Rachel Van M. Baumer, eds. *Sanskrit Drama in Performance*. Honolulu: University Press of Hawaii, 1981. Traces the development of Sanskrit drama and provides analytical criticism of the genre.

Chattopadhyay, Siddheswar. *Theatre in Ancient India*. New Delhi: Manohar Publications, 1993. A thorough history of Sanskrit drama that includes material on staging, acting, and dramaturgy.

Garagi, Balawanti. *Theatre in India*. New York: Theatre Arts Books, 1962. Although not contemporary, it remains an authoritative historical source on the development of drama in India.

Reddy, P. Bayapa. *Studies in Indian Writing in English, with a Focus on Indian Drama.* New Delhi: Prestige Books, 1990. A helpful introduction to Indian fiction and poetry, along with a more detailed survey of Indian plays.

Richmond, Farley P., ed. *Indian Theatre: Traditions of Performance.* Honolulu: University of Hawaii Press, 1990. A varied collection of articles that stresses performance of Sanskrit and folk theater.

Robert Ross

ISLAMIC DRAMA

Islam began with the Prophet Muḥammad, born in Mecca in 570 C.E. Believed to be a descendant of the Jewish patriarch Abraham, the Prophet is said to have received visitations from the archangel Gabriel in 610 after becoming a successful merchant. During these sessions, Gabriel dictated the Muslim holy book, the Qur'an, and gave instructions on how the faith should be spread through the world. After the death of the Prophet, Islam began an electrifying expansion, usually but not always peaceful, which would eventually place Muslims in nearly every corner of the world. Muslim armies conquered Syria, the Persian Empire, and Egypt in the twelve years after the Prophet's death. Between the seventh and eighteenth centuries, Muslims had established cities, centers of Islamic thought, and powerful dynasties in Spain, much of France, Turkey, Central Asia, Austria, Hungary, eastern Europe, most of India, parts of China, Indonesia, Malaysia, the Philippines, southern Thailand, and much of Africa. Muslims have played a significant role in the histories of almost every country on earth, including the United States, where Muslims were first brought as African slaves but now play a prominent role in the cultural and political life of the nation.

Despite its global prevalence, Islam remains generally poorly understood in the West, even by many prominent intellectuals and leaders. There are many reasons for this lack of understanding, but not least among them seems to be unwillingness on the part of Westerners to inquire into Muslim history and belief. This has led to some tragic misunderstandings between cultures: Chief among these is the common misapprehension that Islam is composed of a single, monolithic ideology. In fact, Islam consists of many cultures, each with its own distinct history. Like Christianity, as Islam spread, it came into contact with many different artistic traditions: Some became part of the Islamic mainstream, some dwindled. Traditional theater historically has not fared well in Islamic culture for a variety of reasons, chiefly to do with the purpose of art in an Islamic society.

ISLAMIC ART

In Islam, art is considered best used when it serves to crystallize the most important aspects of the religion, such as harmony, clarity, and serenity. In addition, Muslims make art in order to enhance the ambience necessary for an Islamic life, that is, to reflect the presence of Allah in the everyday. A well-known *hadith* (proverb) asserts that "Allah is beautiful and He loves beauty" (*Allahu jamilun yuhibbu'l-jamal*). For this reason, among others, Islamic artists have tended to concentrate on decoration: the beautification of ordinary useful things. The greatest achievements of Muslim artists have been in the realms of architecture, calligraphy, and crafts such as pottery, clothes making, and carpet weaving.

Islamic art is also bounded by a proscription against iconic representations of men or animals. Representational art is considered to be a violation of the Second Commandment prohibiting idol worship. Theatrical performance, in which humans represent themselves as other creatures, other men, or gods, skates dangerously close to idolatry for some Muslims. Theater, along with the novel, is also considered by many Muslims to create a fanciful and fictitious world and to operate against an important Islamic principle to avoid forgetfulness of the reality of Allah. Therefore many Muslim scholars and artists do not, as a rule, pay much attention to dramatic expression.

Prejudice against theater as irreligious is, of course, not exclusively Islamic: Many centuries before the advent of Islam, the Latin church father Tertullian (c. 160-230) asserted in his *De spectaculis* (197; English translation, 1931; also known as *The Shows*) that theatrical performances, grounded as they were in pagan worship and focused on creating pleasurable false realities, were idolatrous and fundamental tools of the devil. The Christian prejudice against performances was powerful enough to all but annihilate official performances in Europe during the Dark Ages (c. 400-c. 900) and continued to influence European theater history through the Renaissance.

Neither the novel nor the play ever gained great standing in the early Islamic world, although literary arts in other forms, including poetry and the short story, flourished. Both poetry and short stories were designed to be recited publicly, especially at princely courts, and so may be construed as a type of drama. In addition, the general neglect of drama did not prevent the spread of many forms of performance, including sports such as *kirkpinar* (Turkish wrestling), *Varzesh-e Pahlavani* (Persian martial arts), and in Muslim India, displays of chariot racing, archery, and horsemanship. Nevertheless, traditional forms of playwriting did exist in the Muslim world and survived, however incomplete.

TA'ZIYEH PLAYS

For centuries, communities of Shiite Muslims in Arab countries such as India, Pakistan, and elsewhere have annually re-enacted a passion play called Karbalā' or Ta'ziyeh (sympathy), commemorating the martyrdom of Ḥusayn, grandson of the Prophet Muḥammad. According to tradition, the archangel Gabriel told the Prophet to name his son-in-law, 'Alī ibn Abī Ṭālib, as his successor to the caliphate, and when 'Alī died in 661, the caliphate passed to the eldest of his sons, Hassan, who abdicated in favor of Mu'āwiyah I, governor of Syria. Hassan was poisoned by one of his wives in 669. When Mu'āwiyah I died in 680, 'Alī's second son, Ḥusayn, stepped forward to become caliph, but Mu'āwiyah I's son Yazīd opposed him. The result was an internecine war in which the forces of Ḥusayn were slaughtered by Yazīd's vastly superior army in the desert of Karbalā'. After two days, only Ḥusayn remained alive, and he was wounded, captured, and beheaded. Yazīd further mutilated the head of his rival until he was reminded that the lips of the Prophet himself had often kissed that same head, because Ḥusayn was the Prophet's grandson.

During the month of Muharram some Shiite communities perform this sacred story in a powerful ritual involving a complicated procession and self-flagellation: the participants in the play slash their own heads with swords or flay themselves with knives-on-chains, and even babies receive one or two scratches on their heads. The procession includes bloody "living tableaux" of other martyrs who suffered terrible wounds. Following the procession, the Battle of Karbalā' is re-enacted with hundreds of actors bearing weapons, along with the symbolic burning of the tents of Ḥusayn's company and the taking of Ḥusayn's head by Yazīd's forces. Following this event, the spectators burst into tears and publicly display their grief by tearing their hair and beating on their chests. Participation in these ceremonies is held by Shiites to be a sacred and redemptive act that will earn the intercession of the martyr Ḥusayn at the Last Judgment. The whole performance is very similar to medieval and modern Christian passion plays, such as the Stations of the Cross, which also include public weeping and self-flagellation.

Hundreds of Ta'ziyeh scripts exist, but many scholars believe that Ta'ziyeh plays are the only form of drama developed entirely out of Islam. In other countries, however, preexisting dramatic forms were absorbed when the societies who practiced them became Islamic.

KARAGOZ

Ritual and religious performances in Turkey predate the advent of Islam by many thousands of years, even into prehistory. These took many forms, including *Meddah* (storytelling), as well as Greek-style traditional theater that survived in the Byzantine Empire until Constantinople fell to Islam in 1453. One of the varieties of ancient performance that merged well with Islamic ideals was the Karagoz, or shadow puppet theater.

Shadow puppetry gained prominence in Turkey after the fall of Byzantium. The puppets are elaborate and beautiful colored cutouts of translucent leather. The cutouts, whose arms, legs, and heads are jointed, are manipulated by the use of long sticks by an offstage puppeteer. The cutouts themselves are rarely seen: the shadows of the figures are projected by lamplight onto hanging sheets or screens to create a hauntingly beautiful, elegant, almost cinematic performance, complete with an illusion of depth and three-dimensional action. This projection, which has a surreal quality, does not seem to offend Islamic prohibitions against representation in art: The puppet figures are so stylized that they do not much resemble real humans.

The Karagoz feature the comic exploits of the farcical character, Karagoz, who according to legend was a real man, a laborer in Bursa whose hilarious antics on the work site delayed the completion of a mosque. The comedian was executed for this delay, but his comic routines were immortalized by a local puppeteer, Seyh Kusteri. The character Karagoz is working class, unemployed, uneducated, and always attempting some "get-rich-quick" scheme that never works. Like the European puppet character Punch, Karagoz often indulges in comic violence when his plans go awry, but he is also forthright and virtuous, a heroic Everyman figure. Other characters in this wacky world include a drunkard, an opium addict, a man-chasing woman, an Arab, a Jew, and a Persian. Although the Karagoz is mainly comic, it has been used by some performers to be satirically critical of Islamic society.

WAYANG KULIT

In Indonesia, Hinduism had been a dominant religious tradition for centuries before the introduction of Islam. Hinduism, an Indic religion rich with complex stories, is associated with many performance traditions that are thousands of years old, based on the stories of the *Mahābhārata* (c. 400 B.C.E.-400 C.E.; *The Mahabharata of Krishna-Dwaipayana Vyasa*, 1887-1896; also known as *The Mahabharata*) and the *Rāmāyana* (c. 500 B.C.E.; English translation, 1870-1889), ancient epic tales of the many divine god-heroes of Hindu religion. Although Muslims are encouraged to avoid participating in non-Islamic rituals, in some areas, established performance traditions blended with Islamic ideals, with varying degrees of success.

One performance tradition that appears to have merged well with Islam is the *wayang kulit* or shadow puppet theater of Java, which avoids the proscriptions against iconic representation much as the Turkish version of the tradition does. In the *wayang*, as in the Karagoz, colored translucent leather cutout puppets are manipulated by rods to cast shadows on a nearby

screen, although the audience may watch the performance from either side of the screen, switching if they choose. The puppeteer sings the tale along with musical accompaniment and may have hundreds of stories in his repertoire.

Unlike the Karagoz, the *wayang* is based on wholly non-Islamic religious stories from the polytheistic Hindu tradition. Muslim doctrine, like that of Jews and Christians, strictly prohibits the worship of multiple gods, but the *wayang* was gradually adapted to become more palatable to Muslim faith as Java became converted to Islam between the eleventh and sixteenth centuries. By the sixteenth century, the two traditions had so commingled that the genealogies of Javanese kings connected the biblical Adam and the Prophet Muḥammad with the divine heroes of *The Mahabharata*, and the *wayang* was considered part of Java's Islamic heritage. "The *wayang* show is indeed a [mirror]-image of the One, one can call it an image of the Law," said one of the *wali* (saints) who brought Islam to Java. "The *wayang* stands then for all mankind, [and] the *dhalang* (puppeteer) is to be compared with Allah, the creator of the Universe."

MODERN ISLAMIC DRAMA

In modern Islamic countries, Western-style drama has found a new role to play. Muslims sometimes use drama, as a Western artifact, to challenge Islamic traditions in their countries, sometimes to assert a national character. In nineteenth century Turkey, for example, the Turkish National Theatre was established and forged connections with Western theater artists. One key figure was Ahmet Vefik Pasa, who founded a theater in Bursa and translated and adapted the plays of Molière into Turkish. In the twentieth century, the Turkish government fostered the development of many native playwrights. In Egypt and Muslim Eastern Europe, drama has recently begun to reappear in many forms, from classical-style tragedies to experimental forms.

In countries that adhere to a more conservative version of Islamic law, such as Iran, Iraq, and Afghanistan, most public performances are strictly prohibited. In 1999, two Iranian students wrote a play satirizing a Messianic figure in Shiite Muslim belief,

Imam Zaman. This play, *Konkur: Vaqt-e zohur* (*University Entrance Exams: Time to Reappear*, 1999), circulated the world through the Internet and so outraged religious leaders that they called for the execution of the playwrights.

BIBLIOGRAPHY

Chelkowski, Peter, ed. *Ta'ziyeh: Ritual and Drama in Iran*. New York: New York University Press, 1979. Proceedings of an international conference on Ta'ziyeh dramas.

Dwight, H. G. *Persian Miniatures*. New York: Doubleday, Page, 1917. Dwight, an American "Orientalist," was a prejudiced but keen observer, and his writings remain valuable records of pre–World War I Persia, Turkey, and Egypt.

Geertz, Clifford. *Islam Observed*. Chicago: University of Chicago Press, 1968. A very comprehensive survey of cultural traditions in Islam from one of the world's leading anthropologists.

Nasr, Seyyed Hossein. *A Young Muslim's Guide to the Modern World*. Chicago: KAZI Publications, 1994. Written to provide a code for young Muslims living in the West, this book gives clear, thoughtful descriptions of the collision of Western art and Islamic values from an Islamic point of view.

Sears, Laurie J. *Shadows of Empire: Colonial Discourse, and Javanese Tales*. Durham, N.C.: Duke University Press, 1996. Demonstrates the complex relationship between the *wayang kulit* and Islamic thought, and how both changed as the Dutch colonized Java in the eighteenth century.

Michael M. Chemers

JAPANESE DRAMA

The Japanese theater began as a combination of music, dance, and drama. Early accounts explaining the origin of these basic elements are to be found in ancient legends that tell of the native deities who played crucial roles in the birth of the various performing arts. For example, *Kojiki* (712; *Records of Ancient Matters*, 1882), relates the story of Ame-no-Uzume-no-Mikoto, a young goddess who performed a spectacular dance intended to entice Amaterasu Ōmikami (the sun goddess) from a cave where she had secluded herself. The plan succeeded, and sunlight was restored to a world covered in total darkness. This episode traditionally marks both the beginning of Japanese dance and the origin of *kagura*, the ritualistic ceremony of Shintō, the native religion of Japan. Because dance and music dominated the early performing arts, a discussion of *kagura* and *dengaku* serves as an appropriate introduction to the Japanese theater.

KAGURA

From prehistoric times, through *kagura*, the Japanese paid homage to the native deities and offered comfort to the souls of the dead as part of the Shintō ritual. Traditionally, *kagura* was divided into *mikagura*, the performance held at the imperial palace, and *satokagura*, held at the various Shintō shrines. *Satokagura* has undergone significant changes during its growth and development, but *mikagura* has remained almost unchanged since its official formulation in the eleventh century. *Mikagura* is performed by the members of the Imperial court dance group. Its program consists of an introductory song, dances accompanied by song and music, a shamanistic ritual, a pantomimic performance, and more songs. Although the basic form of *kagura* is mime with song and music, even in earlier times it was affected by other performing arts. The more sophisticated masked plays in its repertory were likely borrowed from *gigaku* together with the lion dance. *Tanemaki* (seed planting dance) in *kagura* can be traced to *dengaku*, a native festivity related to rice growing. In

the thirteenth century, *kagura* included dramatic pieces anticipating the Nō theater, which developed later.

DENGAKU

Along with *kagura*, which was essentially a Shintō ceremony, *dengaku*, another native form of drama, developed in the rural areas of Japan, where rice growing was the main activity. *Dengaku* (rice paddy dance) was popular among farmers, who prayed to their local deities for abundant harvests. Even today, festivals related to rice farming are found in various parts of Japan. By the time *dengaku* emerged as a popular form of entertainment, it had already incorporated exotic elements from *gigaku* and *sangaku*. In short, *dengaku* had added to its repertory the lion dance, juggling, acrobatics, and other acts as well as Chinese gongs and drums. Although it started as a rather primitive and rustic entertainment, *dengaku* developed into a highly polished theater with elaborate dances and costumes. Eventually, *dengaku* developed its own prototype of the Nō theater, rivaling the similar efforts of *sarugaku*, which rose out of the *sangaku* tradition. After the emergence of Nō theater, however, *dengaku* rapidly lost popularity and retreated to the temples and shrines; by the end of the seventeenth century, it had all but disappeared as public entertainment.

BUGAKU

Although *kagura* and *dengaku* were the principal forms of early native theater, Japan was also the beneficiary of imported dramatic forms, especially from China by way of Korea. Among them, *bugaku* has had a long, uninterrupted tradition that goes back as far as the eighth century. At the time that *bugaku* arrived in Japan, it was a ceremonial dance performed during the Tang Dynasty (618-907) at the Chinese imperial court, where it was presented in splendid surroundings, with several teams of dancers accompanied by large string and woodwind sections. On reaching Japan, *bugaku* was also adopted as the dance for Japan's imperial court. With the rise of the samurai class and the decline of imperial power in the late twelfth century, *bugaku* lost its prestige and influence; up to the sixteenth century, only large shrines and temples could afford to subsidize its performances. During the Tokugawa period (1600-1867), the shogunate supported a *bugaku* troupe at Edo (now Tokyo) for ceremonial occasions. In 1890, more than two decades after the Meiji Restoration (1868), when Japan assumed the role of a modern nation, the imperial court again was in charge of *bugaku*. Today, certain temples and shrines in the ancient capitol of Nara also support *bugaku*.

In addition to elements imported from abroad, *bugaku* includes conventions subsequently added in Japan. The dancers in the native *bugaku* pieces wear no masks and perform to Japanese-style musical instruments including the koto—an instrument with numerous strings—and the flute. The *bugaku* dances are mostly of foreign origin: The dance of the left includes pieces generally from China and India, while the dance of the right derives from Korea and Manchuria. In the past, these two categories of dances were always performed alternately, but now, because of restrictions on time, this custom has been abandoned.

Gagaku, the musical component of *bugaku*, is played by several different instruments at a rather slow tempo. At the imperial court, *bugaku* is performed on a large, raised stage, about twenty-three feet square, on a platform somewhat smaller in size. The orchestra consists of woodwind instruments made of bamboo, two biwa—lutelike instruments—and the koto. The percussion section includes a variety of large and small drums and a bronze gong. Since these deliberate and graceful dances attempt to emphasize the pure dance forms rather than their dramatic elements, their execution consists of many symmetrical patterns. The dancers usually wear striking masks and dress in magnificent brocaded costumes.

The musicians who perform for *bugaku* can trace their ancestry back through many generations. In preparation for such a career, the candidate must begin his musical education around the age of twelve and become familiar with both Japanese and Western music.

GIGAKU

According to early records, *gigaku* arrived from Korea in 612. By the mid-eighth century, it was highly popular; by the twelfth century, however, its appeal had declined significantly. Although present knowledge about this ancient form is fragmentary, the extant masks, numbering about 250—many still preserved in Buddhist temples—permit some speculation as to its character. These comic masks suggest that *gigaku* performances were meant to amuse and to entertain. The facial features on the masks are neither Chinese nor Japanese, and their ultimate origin may have been beyond the Silk Road, which brought Near Eastern culture to ancient China. The *Kyō-kunshō* (1233), a highly reliable source on the history of early Japanese music, mentions that *gigaku* was performed within temple grounds. The performers first marched around in a circle carrying large masks to the accompaniment of flute, drums, cymbals, and a pair of small gongs. After a play with a religious message was performed, a group of mimic pieces was performed, followed by a joyous musical finale. The participants in the parade included the leader—a figure with a long-nosed mask—a company of musicians, a two-man lion dance, and a pair of performers dressed as lion cubs. While the lion is not found in Japan, the lion dance in *gigaku* became a familiar part of *kagura*, *dengaku*, Nō theater, Kabuki, puppet theater (Bunraku), and the Japanese dance tradition. Some of the musical instruments originally identified with *gigaku*—flute, cymbals, and drums—were later incorporated into *bugaku*.

SANGAKU

In Japan, *sangaku* arrived at about the same time as *bugaku*. Although the two forms were essentially the same, in China, *bugaku* belonged to the courtier class while *sangaku* was regarded as entertainment for the commoners; hence, the dances featured in *sangaku* were performed on a much smaller scale. In the beginning, *sangaku*, like *bugaku*, was given support by the imperial court, but by the late eighth century, it lost this privilege and was forced to carry on as public entertainment. The differences between the two were important for the growth and development of the Japanese theater. In addition to the dance component, *sangaku* also included a variety of acts such as comic sketches, mime pieces, acrobatics, juggling, magic tricks, puppetry, and trained birds and animals. Among these offerings, the dramatic elements found in the humorous pieces and pantomimes caught the immediate attention of the Japanese audience. These elements quickly found their way into *bugaku* and even into religious rituals held at shrines and temples. From its early arrival, the humble popular theater from China had an immediate impact in Japan and, through *sarugaku*, its successor, this popular theater continued to exert a powerful influence.

SARUGAKU

Although the difference between *bugaku* and *sangaku* is clear, in the case of *sangaku* and *sarugaku*, the distinction appears to be the degree of emphasis on the dramatic aspect of the theater as a performing art. Furthermore, this significant shift toward greater emphasis from *sangaku* to *sarugaku* also indicated a change in public attitude toward acting, "imitative art," as a profession. As early as the tenth century, *sarugaku* was a term applied to *sangaku* but in a pejorative sense. In this context, the "saru" in *sarugaku* was written with the Chinese character denoting "monkey," a reference to the age-old belief that this animal could humorously imitate human behavior. By implication, those who acted like a monkey in front of an audience were considered less than human; hence, their performances should be called *sarugaku* (monkey dance). Nevertheless, by the eleventh century, the dramatic aspect of *sarugaku* was drawing greater public attention. In short, *sarugaku* performers may be regarded as the dedicated practitioners of the *sangaku* tradition who actively cultivated that specific area involving comedic skits and pantomime, apart from the other popular acts identified with *sangaku*. *Sarugaku*, then, represented a growing tendency in the Japanese theater to redirect its attention away from the earlier preoccupation with dance and music and to show a deeper con-

cern for drama. From the mid-thirteenth century to the late fourteenth century, these *sarugaku* performers, who were attached to the shrines and temples, began organizing their own troupes and competing with one another, eventually helping to establish the Nō theater. Toward this effort, *dengaku* and *ennen* also tried to formulate their own prototypes of the Nō drama, but in the end, the *sarugaku* version prevailed.

ENNEN NŌ

By the end of the eleventh century, *ennen*, which was a ritualistic banquet held after Buddhist and Shintō services, had become popular. Dances, extemporaneous songs, and mimic performances were gradually added to this extension of a religious service, and *ennen* evolved into a recognized form of entertainment. By the thirteenth century, additional song and dance, humorous dialogue, and dramatized legends became part of this ever expanding repertory. The performances took place on the gallery of a religious building, on the lawn, or on a stage set up on the grounds. At such events, the performance of the *ennen* Nō came at the end. The players used masks for such roles as ghosts in these presentations. The rather formalized productions, which were filled with religious symbolism, used rather austere costumes. With the rise of the Nō theater, *ennen* declined rapidly as a theatrical activity.

DENGAKU NŌ

As a performing art, *dengaku* Nō developed slowly and did not gain public recognition until the fourteenth century. With the political rise of Shogun Ashikaga Takauji in 1338, however, *dengaku* Nō suddenly became the favored theater, and although it still bore a rustic quality reflecting its rural background, at one point *dengaku* Nō surpassed *sarugaku* Nō. Nevertheless, *dengaku* Nō could not readily discard its ritualistic pieces, such as acts on stilts, performances with *binzasara* (a bamboo rattle used in farm festivals), and sword-juggling acts. In comparison with Nō theater, masks were used sparingly. *Dengaku* Nō had a stage similar to that of the Nō theater, with the *hashigakari*, a familiar passageway, leading to the stage entrance. The subject matter of *dengaku* Nō was drawn primarily from Japanese literature, history, and legends and stories based on Buddhist tradition. Although at one time *dengaku* Nō may have rivaled *sarugaku* Nō, it failed to develop into a new form of drama because it was apparently unable to discard its agricultural tradition.

SARUGAKU NŌ

Though *sarugaku* performers were once treated as socially inferior to their colleagues in the other forms of theater, they were finally able to gain public recognition through their devotion to an artistic vision. They had set the stage for the next phase in the final establishment of the Nō theater. The standard program of *sarugaku* Nō began with the ceremonial Okina play, beseeching the deities for abundant harvests and longevity. This piece was followed by several Nō plays. By skillfully employing the well-known themes from folktales, legends, and Japanese classics and by interpolating passages from poetry and fiction into the play scripts, *sarugaku* Nō gained a distinct advantage over its rivals. The introduction of fresh, brilliant dance pieces also contributed to its success. By the first quarter of the fifteenth century, *sarugaku* Nō would achieve its goal of becoming a fully developed new theater.

From the twelfth to the fourteenth centuries, culminating in the establishment of the Nō theater, *sarugaku* served as the basis for encouraging other genres to cultivate *nō* (acting skill). Yet *sarugaku* Nō was also influenced by the *kusemai*, a minor form of entertainment from the Heian period (794-1185) which featured a female performer, dressed as a male, who danced and sang currently popular songs. These women often wore a ceremonial cap, used a Japanese folding fan in their dancing, and played on a drum tied to the waist. *Sarugaku* Nō was also indebted to *kōwaka-kusemai*, which rose out of this tradition. In *kōwaka-kusemai*, male performers accompanied by refined temple music render a melodic recitation of war tales such as the *Heike monogatari* (*The Heike Monogatari*, 1918; also as *The Tale of the Heike*, 1975, 1988), a literary classic from the twelfth century. The lyric narrative style employed by the *kōwaka-kusemai* performers was later adopted by the Nō theater and subsequently made a strong impact on *jōruri*, the narrative portion accompanying the puppet theater.

NŌ THEATER

The establishment of the Nō theater as an independent performing art can be credited largely to the brilliant leadership of Kan'ami Kiyotsugu, born in 1333, and Zeami Motokiyo, born in 1363. By their joint efforts, and particularly by the achievements of Zeami, Nō theater reached its peak. As *dengaku* Nō had gained the support of Ashikaga Takauji, the first shogun in this line of succession, both Kan'ami and Zeami were under the patronage of Ashikaga Yoshimitsu (1358-1404), the third Ashikaga shogun and a devoted patron of the arts. Kan'ami incorporated elements from the *kusemai* tradition and also from *dengaku* in order to establish the foundation for the Nō theater. His son Zeami successfully completed the work of his father and, in addition, distinguished himself as a performer, dramatist, and brilliant thinker who wrote extensively on the dramaturgy of the Nō theater; his *Kadensho* (1400-1402; English translation, 1968) is regarded as a definitive treatise on this subject. Throughout the Tokugawa period, the Nō theater continued to enjoy government support as the official entertainment of the samurai class. During the Tokugawa regime, five major schools of Nō were established: Komparu, Kongō, Kanze, Hōshō, and Kita. Later, the Umekawa school, an offshoot of the Kanze school, was formed after the Meiji period (1868-1912).

One element of the Nō theater that separates it from earlier performing arts of Japan is its readily accessible written texts; most of the plays still presented can be assigned to specific authors. For example, about fifteen are known to be the work of Kan'ami, including *Jinen Koji* and *Sotoba Komachi* (English translation, 1915). Zeami's plays number more than one hundred and include *Semimaru* (English translation, 1970) and *Ashikari* (*The Reed Cutter*, 1970).

Among the more than eight hundred extant plays, more than a quarter are performed regularly. The classification of these plays is commonly based on the main character of each piece: God, Man, Woman, Madman, and Devil. God plays are always presented at the start of each performance and contain words of felicitation. Man plays feature ghosts of dead warriors who seek assistance from an itinerant priest who can deliver them from spiritual torment and help them gain salvation. Woman plays often include heroines from the Japanese classics who suffer from unrequited love. Madman plays, though dealing with mentally deranged characters, also contain historical figures and themes from contemporary life. Devil plays are based on supernatural creatures from legends and literary works, both malicious and benign.

The three principal roles in Nō plays are *shite* (main character), *tsure* (companion), and *waki* (secondary character). The *tsure* may also have a companion called *waki-zure*. The progression of a Nō play takes place according to the concept of *jo* (introduction), *ha* (main theme), and *kyū* (finale). In this standard form, the tempo of the play builds up to the *ha*; at this point, its pace slows down, and the performance takes on refinement and complexity. The final phase serves the function of releasing the audience from the tension accumulated during the development of the play—a kind of catharsis.

The Nō stage is about eighteen feet square and has large pillars at its corners to guide the performers, who often wear masks that obscure their vision. The musicians sit upstage and play the flute and the three types of drums. An old pine tree, symbolizing longevity, is painted on the backdrop. The bamboo flute carries the melody, and the drums simply mark the beat. Extending from stage right, the *hashigakari*, a long passageway, leads to a curtained entrance for the performers. The three pine trees planted along this corridor are of diminishing size, with the tallest planted closest to the main stage. The idea of distance is conveyed by this arrangement.

The Nō masks are broadly classified into male, female, and supernatural beings. The human masks depict a wide range of characters ranging in age from youth to old age; others represent deities, devils, and animals. These masks, which are slightly smaller than life-size, are intended to cover up the unique features of the performers; those without masks display

no emotion on the stage. The movements of the performers are strictly controlled; there are more than two hundred different patterns of movement in this highly stylized theater. The act of weeping, for example, may be suggested by a slightly bowed head with a hand raised in front of the performer's eyes. In walking, the feet slide along the floor as the toes are raised slightly. The studied formalism of the Nō theater, reflected in the appearance of the stage, style of speech, movement, dancing, costume, and masks, suggests a theater dedicated to the reduction of dramatic experience to its purest abstraction.

KYŌGEN

The dramatic element in *kyōgen* can be traced to *sarugaku*, which gained wide popularity through its comedic sketches and mimic performances. Although the history of *kyōgen* is still uncertain, by the time that the Nō theater was established, *kyōgen* was already a mature drama. Although it is true that the Nō theater is traditionally treated with greater deference than is the *kyōgen*, the latter has had far more impact on the later development of the Japanese theater. During the Tokugawa period, when the townspeople's culture suddenly created the opportunity for the emergence of both the Kabuki theater and the puppet theater, the Nō theater remained relatively isolated under the patronage of the samurai class. On the other hand, *kyōgen* helped to raise Kabuki from a coarse public entertainment to one of the greatest theatrical traditions of Japan. In this process, the minor players from *kyōgen* who had attached themselves to the early Kabuki troupes made an inestimable contribution. Moreover, during the formative years of Kabuki, *kyōgen* plays were frequently borrowed to develop the Kabuki repertory.

The main schools of *kyōgen*, Ōkura, Sagi, and Izumi, were established in the mid-Muromachi period (1336-1573); they were all supported by the Tokugawa government. Since the beginning of the Meiji period, the Sagi school has been inactive.

The *kyōgen* plays are commonly classified according to the main character in each play: *Daimyō* (feudal lord), *Shōmyō* (petty landowner), *Muko* (son-in-law), *Oni-yamabushi* (devil-mountain priest),

Shukke-zatō (priest-blindman), and *Atsume* (miscellaneous). The authorship of these plays is unknown because they were, as a rule, performed extemporaneously. Further, the written scripts were considered secret and remained the exclusive property of the *kyōgen* schools. The Ōkura school recognizes 180 plays in its repertory, and the Izumi school, 254. Among the plays available in translation are *Bōshibari* (*Pinioned*, 1882), *Busu* (*Somebody-nothing*, 1921), and *Utsubozaru* (*The Quiver Monkey*, 1921). These plays can be found under slightly different titles in *Selected Plays of Kyōgen* (1968).

Depending on the theme, the content of the *kyōgen* plays may deal with various aspects of human frailty, such as greed, hypocrisy, jealousy, arrogance, and stupidity. The plays humorously expose familiar weaknesses and ridicule those who are blissfully unaware of their shortcomings. In *kyōgen*, two or more characters are at odds with one another; comic situations are generated as the result of these conflicts. The dialogue in a Nō play often consists of passages from classic sources in literature, history, philosophy, or religion. In *kyōgen*, the lines spoken by the characters are patterned after ordinary conversation. Although a legacy from a bygone era, the content is quite comprehensible to modern audiences.

The postures assumed by the *kyōgen* performer are basically similar to those in the Nō theater. To provide a firm stance on the stage, the performer's hip is thrust back from the waist and his chin is tucked in. When the performer gazes at an object or follows it with his eyes, convention dictates that the whole face must rigidly go through a similar motion. The *kyōgen* plays make some use of masks, but they are not regarded as having the same level of craftsmanship as the Nō masks. In *kyōgen*, supernatural creatures may be frequently personified. Also, animal masks with surprisingly human features often appear on the *kyōgen* stage. The artistic quality of the *kyōgen* masks is generally inferior to that of the masks in the Nō plays, but the unpretentious *kyōgen* masks have the warm, down-to-earth quality that characterizes this performing art. Whereas the costumes in the Nō are noted for their splendor and refinement, those used in *kyōgen* are simple, plain, and realistic. *Kyō-*gen plays rarely have musical accompaniment. About half of the stage properties and costumes used in the *kyōgen* plays come from the Nō theater. In some Nō plays, the *kyōgen* performers appear as members of the cast; at no time, however, do they play the roles of individuals in high authority.

Because *kyōgen* remained an integral part of the Nō theater, it could neither extend its dramatic potential beyond the limits of the Nō stage nor escape the stylistic demands imposed by the nature of the Nō theater. Although *kyōgen* inspired other theaters to further cultivate acting skill, the most important function of *kyōgen* was to serve as the unobtrusive, faithful companion of the Nō theater.

PUPPET THEATER

The puppet theater began around the late sixteenth century with the joining of three basic elements: *jōruri* (narrative chanting), the samisen (three-stringed musical instrument), and the puppet. The *jōruri* was preceded as popular entertainment by the Heike biwa, another form of narrative chanting from the thirteenth century. The Heike biwa was performed by blind musicians who recited episodes from *The Tale of the Heike*, the tale of the war between the Minamoto and the Taira. These musicians used the biwa, a lutelike instrument, in their performances. As a variation on this narrative tradition, *jōruri* included the romantic tale of Princess Jōruri and the young Ushiwakamaru, who later became Minamoto Yoshitsune, the victorious general in *The Tale of the Heike*. This narrative piece became so popular that the entire genre was called *jōruri*, the name of its beautiful heroine. At this time, the biwa was still the basic instrument for *jōruri*. In the mid-sixteenth century, the jamisen, the precursor of the samisen, reached Japan from the Ryūkyū islands (now Okinawa). The Japanese modified the jamisen to produce a milder, delicate sound; the combination of *jōruri* and the samisen was an overnight sensation. By the beginning of the seventeenth century, the puppet joined *jōruri* and samisen to create *ningyō-jōruri* (puppet-*jōruri* play), a new performing art.

Many centuries before, the *kutsugu-mawashi* (puppeteer-storyteller), who manipulated simple dolls inside a boxlike stage suspended from the operator's neck, arrived with *sangaku* from the Asiatic mainland. The puppet theater quickly enhanced its repertory by freely borrowing from traditional folktales, religious stories, and familiar legends. In the 1660's, another *jōruri*, depicting the amusing exploits of a somewhat naïve but good-hearted warrior, Kimpira, who had superhuman strength, gained popularity in Edo. Later, the celebrated story of this fearless, dashing hero was adopted by Ichikawa Danjūrō I as the *aragoto* (rough business), the acting style for his Kabuki performances. The *aragoto* became permanently identified with the illustrious line of Kabuki actors founded by Danjūrō I.

The next big stride in the development of the puppet theater was the collaboration between Takemoto Gidayū and Chikamatsu Monzaemon, the great Japanese playwright. Takemoto Gidayū had created *gidayū-bushi*, a *jōruri* style that still bears his name. In 1685, he recited *Shusse Kagekiyo* (pr. 1686; Kagekiyo is victorious), a Chikamatsu masterpiece, which became the decisive work separating the "old" and the "new" *jōruri* plays. This play raised the artistic level of the puppet play to an unprecedented height. Although Chikamatsu's early plays for the puppet theater were historical and portrayed the upper classes, in 1703, his *Sonezaki shinjū* (pr. 1703; *The Love Suicides at Sonezaki*, 1961) depicted the tragic romance between a clerk at a soy-sauce shop and a young prostitute, based on an actual occurrence in Osaka, which ended in a double suicide. This *shinjūmono* (love suicide play) was the forerunner of a series of plays on the same theme, focusing on the lives of the common people. The close association between Takemoto Gidayū and Chikamatsu lasted until the former's death in 1714.

Although Chikamatsu wrote independently for the puppet theater, his successors often engaged in producing cooperative works. Among these works, the following represent outstanding examples of collaborative writing: *Sugawara denju tenarai kagami* (pr. 1747; *The Secrets of Sugawara's Calligraphy*, 1921), *Yoshitsune senbonzakura* (pr. 1747; *The Thousand Cherry Blossoms of Yoshitsune*, 1915), and *Kanadehon chūshingura* (pr. 1748; *The Treasury of Loyal Retainers*, 1880). These plays, which were presented consecutively within a period of three years in the mid-eighteenth century, remain among the all-time favorites in both the puppet theater and the Kabuki theater.

The major categories of puppet plays are the *jidaimono* (historical plays) and the *sewamono* (domestic plays). The historical plays are more stylized and romantic, picturing the world of the nobles and the samurai, quite removed from the experience of the common people. In contrast, the *sewamono* treated themes often based on everyday occurrences, including the love suicides, which the audiences knew well.

In the puppet theater, the chanter communicates the thoughts and inner feelings of the characters and provides the descriptive passages that hold the entire story together. By modulating his voice according to the roles he takes, the chanter imitates the voices of the puppets on the stage. The samisen player establishes the mood and the tempo appropriate for the various scenes and provides the necessary dramatic tension by his carefully arranged use of the samisen. According to circumstances, the number of supporting musicians and chanters may vary.

The three-man puppet was first introduced in 1734; until then, each puppet operator manipulated a single doll. The operation of the three-man puppet is more complicated because it requires careful coordination for a smooth, effective manipulation. To create convincing, realistic movements, the specialists, who are in charge of the head and right arm, the left arm, or both feet, must act simultaneously with split-second precision. Years of dedicated training are required to develop this skill. In order to train for this work, the apprentice must begin with the feet, then work with the left arm, and finally become involved in the manipulation of the head and right arm.

The head, arms, legs, and torso of the puppets can be disassembled, and the parts exchanged. The height of the puppets ranges from four to four and a half feet, somewhat smaller than life-size. The puppets may carry out various movements with the eyes, eyebrows, mouth, and joints of the fingers and toes. Although props are usually scaled down to match the size of the puppets, swords, smoking pipes, writing brushes, and other implements of normal size may be manipulated by the operator to highlight a crucial scene. Ordinarily, the puppet operators are dressed in black and wear hoods over their faces; they are regarded as "invisible" to the audience. Outstanding operators may perform dressed in formal costume and with their faces uncovered. The operators wear specially elevated footwear so that they can manipulate the dolls in full view of the audience while moving in trenchlike spaces built within the performance area.

In the puppet plays, the most important issue raised invariably deals with the conflict between *giri* (duty) and *ninjo* (human feelings). Whether in the relationship between master and subject, husband and wife, parent and child, or young lovers, there are always higher duties that pit the individual against the demands made by the rest of society. In the *jidaimono* play, a samurai may have to sacrifice his son to protect the life of his master's son; a woman may be caught between her role as a mother and her role as a dutiful wife to a warrior husband. The same kind of choice awaits a love-smitten son who may have to disobey his parents' wishes in order to marry the girl whom he desperately adores. In the *sewamono* play, this kind of dilemma, which required the principal characters to weigh their own personal happiness against ethical and societal obligations, often brought the performance to a tragic ending by double suicide. Modern Japanese society no longer adheres to the rigid ethical standards once established by the samurai class. In this sense, the puppet theater in the modern world is the legacy of a bygone era.

KABUKI

Although the popular account of the Kabuki theater attributes its establishment to Okuni, the legendary vestal maiden of the Izumo Shrine who danced on the dry riverbed of the Kamo River in Kyoto in 1603, its actual development appears more obscure and uncertain. Around the late sixteenth century, when Japanese society was at last emerging from centuries of political and social unrest, many groups of itinerant entertainers—both male and female—were roving all over the country. Among these troupes, Okuni is said to have introduced *Kabuki-odori* (Kabuki dance), which quickly gained a nationwide following. The term "kabuki" meant something "outrageous," "shocking," "exotic," or "quite extraordinary," and Okuni's instant success was apparently the result of her clever management and showmanship. The accounts of her performances suggest that the most popular aspect of her show consisted of erotic dances and scenes with nudity. In all probability, Okuni's variety show had minimal artistic pretensions and was meant largely to attract customers for its performers, who also practiced prostitution. The public disorder resulting from their stage performances finally led the authorities to ban all women from the theater in 1629.

In the meantime, *wakashu* Kabuki (young boys' Kabuki) had also attracted wide attention. These performers, who had not yet reached adulthood (which was age fifteen), were involved, like the officially banned *onna* Kabuki (women's Kabuki), in using the stage show as a means of attracting customers to whom they would sell sexual favors. Thus, in 1652, *wakashu* Kabuki was also declared illegal. The government insisted that Kabuki become a serious theater styled after *kyōgen*, the realistic dialogue and acting skills of which were highly developed. The *yarō* Kabuki (young men's Kabuki), which replaced *wakashu* Kabuki, was placed under strict government control. The young men who became Kabuki performers were obliged to cut off their forelocks to show that they were of legal age. The position of the government was uncompromising; its impact on the *yarō* Kabuki was soon evident. In the 1660's, the forerunner of the *hanamichi*, the auxiliary stage for the performers' entrances and exits, quickly developed. In 1664, two theaters made use of the *hikimaku* (draw curtain), a sign that the plays were becoming longer and more complex. During this period, the *onnagata* (female impersonator) had assumed an important position in the further development of the Kabuki theater. Contrary to past practice, a female role was no longer meant to be only decorative, played by boys who merely displayed their youthful charms and physical beauty, dressed in feminine costumes.

The early Kabuki plays, which were simply borrowed from Nō, *kyōgen*, and early puppet theater, were supplemented by dramatic works written specifically for the Kabuki stage. By 1673, Ichikawa Danjūrō I had created his *aragoto* plays, inspired by the *jōruri* style of *Kimpira-bushi*, popularized by Takemoto Gidayū of the puppet theater. By the time Kabuki reached its first great epoch in the Genroku period (1688-1703), it had become firmly established as a performing art. After a period of relative inactivity during the first half of the eighteenth century, caused mainly by the dominance of the puppet theater, the Kabuki theater regained its popularity through the development of its own narrative musical style and through the spectacular growth of its dance pieces. Through these efforts, Kabuki achieved its second great flowering, which lasted from the late eighteenth century to the early nineteenth century. After the mid-eighteenth century, the center of activity for the Kabuki theater shifted completely from the Kyoto-Osaka area to Edo. Of the celebrated Kabuki plays, the longer pieces have not been translated into English. *Sukeroku Yukari no Edo zakura* (1713; *Sukeroku: Flower of Edo*, 1975) and *Narukami Fudo kitayama zakura* (1742; *Saint Narukami and the God Fudo*, 1975) may be read in their generally complete form in *Kabuki: Five Classic Plays* (1975). These two plays belong to the *aragoto* style of Ichikawa Danjūrō I and belong in the category of historical plays.

Kabuki plays, like puppet plays, are divided into *jidaimono* (historical plays) and *sewamono* (domestic plays). *Jidaimono* plays depict the aristocratic classes of pre-Tokugawa Japan. *Sewamono* plays show the lives of common people living in a contemporary Tokugawa setting. Although *jidaimono* plays tend to be highly stylized and romantic, *sewamono* dramas are more down-to-earth; dialogue is closer to ordinary speech, costumes and props are taken from daily life, and the movement of the performers tends to be natural and realistic. *Shosagoto* (dance plays) are shorter Kabuki pieces in which music and dance are the main components.

In the first half of the nineteenth century, the *sewamono* plays, which depicted the lives of the common people, reached the highest degree of realism. The *Tōkaidō Yotsuya kaidan* (the ghost story of Yotsuya), written in 1825 by Tsuruya Nanboku IV, is regarded as the greatest work in this genre. The trend toward more realistic presentation on the Kabuki stage led to the *kizewamono* ("raw" domestic plays), which carried violence, brutality, and eroticism to shocking extremes.

After the death of Namboku IV in 1829, the only other playwright of distinction was Kawatake Mokuami, a dramatist whose career spanned the fading feudal world of the Tokugawa era and the government-backed modernism of the new Meiji era. Representative of the new era were his "cropped hair plays" (*zangirimono*) in which men's long feudal locks were replaced by Western haircuts. Paradoxically, audiences preferred the more traditional Kabuki plays in which they found the comforting values of a familiar, if fading world. Although Mokuami repeatedly demonstrated his genius for incorporating the atmosphere and events of the modernizing world into his plays, Kabuki could not, finally, give expression to the reality of the new Japan. It gradually receded into the category of traditional theater, along with *bugaku*, Nō theater, *kyōgen*, and puppet theater.

Two distinctive features of the Kabuki stage deserve special mention. The *hanamichi*, a ramp that extends from stage right to the back of the theater through the audience, plays an essential role in creating a feeling of intimacy and involvement for the spectators. The appearance of actors on this auxiliary stage provoked audience response and helped to create a feeling of spectator involvement in the drama. The *mawari-butai* (revolving stage) is a Japanese invention created in the mid-eighteenth century by a Kabuki playwright. This device allows two or even three separate scenes to be staged at once by simply rotating the giant platform built into the main stage.

A familiar feature of the Kabuki theater is the *hikimaku* (draw curtain), which has green, tan, and black vertical stripes, once authorized to be used at only the major Kabuki theaters of the Tokugawa period. When the *hikimaku* is fully drawn, it can also create a special performance area in front of the curtain line. Then the activity on the apron stage can be coordinated with that occurring on the *hanamichi*, result-ing in a greater sense of involvement for the audience seated in the orchestra. With the main stage closed, this feeling of intimacy is heightened.

In a Kabuki performance, the elements of music, dance, and drama are often intermingled, even during scenes that are generally played in a realistic style. Certain lyric lines may be recited like an aria, with the soft melody of a samisen playing in the back-ground. Some stylized movements in a *jidaimono* play approach the studied gracefulness of a dance se-quence. The influence of the puppet theater after the mid-eighteenth century encouraged the use of *jōruri* and other vocal and musical accompaniment in the later Kabuki plays. More than half the plays in the present Kabuki repertory once belonged to the puppet theater.

The historical difference in the function of the script explains a good deal about differences between Kabuki and puppet theater. In the puppet theater, the written text formed the basis for the entire produc-tion; it clearly specified the functions of the chanter, the doll operator, musicians including the samisen player, the chorus, and the orchestra. Because the play script for the puppet theater was so important, even in the early seventeenth century, the authorship of specific plays was given on the published play scripts. In the case of the Kabuki theater, its growth and development did not follow the relatively smooth course pursued by the puppet theater. In the begin-ning, the distinction between the performer and the playwright was not crucial. The pieces were short and simple; the performances could be prepared easily with little practice and given almost extemporane-ously. During its early stages, Kabuki took its materi-als from the currently popular theaters as well as from oral and written traditions. The first profes-sional Kabuki dramatist did not appear until the Genroku period. Although Chikamatsu began his ca-reer as a Kabuki playwright, none of his plays in this genre remains except in rough outline, whereas his works for the puppet theater are readily available as complete texts.

Most writers for the Kabuki theater wrote in col-laboration, making the precise authorship of any one work almost impossible to determine. The head dra-matist of a Kabuki theater may have been solely re-sponsible for any given play; authorship was quite a different issue. Because play scripts were the exclu-sive property of the theater where the dramatist was employed, the issue of authorship never surfaced dur-ing the two hundred years of the Tokugawa period. The question of copyright finally came up as Japan went through modernization in the early Meiji peri-od, when Mokuami, the last playwright in the Tokugawa tradition, settled the issue in court in a suc-cessful suit against his publisher. After Mokuami, most of the plays for the Kabuki theater were written by novelists, dramatists, and journalists who had not served an apprenticeship as Kabuki writers. These newer plays are called *Shin-Kabuki* (New Kabuki Plays) to distinguish them from the older tradition, which quickly declined after the death of Mokuami.

MODERN THEATER

Kabuki was the most vibrant dramatic form at the beginning of the Meiji period as Japan began its Her-culean effort to transform itself into a modern nation. The limited realism of Mokuami's "cropped hair plays" and other *sewamono* plays was the most prom-ising dramatic resource to capture the emerging new world; after two decades, however, the *zangirimono* failed to turn into a contemporary theater and Kabuki came to represent the values of a fast fading feudal world. In an ironic twist of history, what had long been the theater of outcasts was, in its last years, em-braced and legitimized by a government keen to maintain a "national theater" on a par with those of European nations. The essentially feudal world of Kabuki, with its Confucian morality and samurai eth-ics, could not support stories centered on the individ-ual, and the well of modernism was nothing if not a font of individualism. As the government attempted to make Kabuki into something it had never been—a national literary theater—the eyes of Japanese intel-lectuals focused on tales of individuals struggling to be born to a larger freedom.

For the next sixty years, attempts to create a mod-ern Japanese theater were dominated by what many critics now see as an almost schizophrenic compulsion to ingest the literary drama of the West and produce an imitative Japanese version. Needless to say, the audience for bookish experiments in this vein was limited to educated intellectuals. Group after group took up the challenge of creating a new national drama that centered on the individual. Many groups disappeared or splintered into new formations with the death of the founder.

The first such group was the Shimpa (New Wave Theater), begun by political activists. Shimpa was a mutant form that preserved the energy of Kabuki as it appealed to nationalist sentiments. Some of the plays celebrated Japanese military victories in the years around the turn of the twentieth century. Early plays were thinly disguised propaganda in dramatic form. In some ways Shimpa was no more than an amateurish attempt to escape from the Kabuki tradition; it gained popularity with its realistic fight scenes, which went beyond the carefully choreographed action taking place on the Kabuki stage. The most important historical figure behind the Shimpa movement was Kawakami Otojiro, born in 1864. He and his wife, the actress Sada Yakko, went abroad with the Shimpa troupe and pleased audiences in Europe and the United States with the energy of Shimpa's spectacle. Kawakami adapted several European plays for the Japanese stage.

Tsubouchi Shōyō was preeminent among the Meiji literary scholars who were engaged in the problem of transforming the Japanese theater into something resembling that of the Europeans. He hoped that elements of both Japanese and Western traditions might be combined in a new theater for Japan. Tsubouchi spans the drama of two eras; he was the author of a Kabuki play, *Kirihitoha* (pr. 1904; a paulownia leaf) as well as the translator of the complete works of William Shakespeare. In 1906, he established the Bungei Kyōkai (literature and arts society), an acting school that accepted only amateurs with no previous training in Kabuki or Shimpa. Its students staged plays by Shakespeare and George Bernard Shaw, among other Western playwrights. Tsubouchi worked closely with Shimamura Hōgetsu, his former student and colleague at Waseda University in Tokyo. Later, Tsubouchi and Shimamura parted company, and the

latter formed the Geijutsuza (arts theater) and performed plays in translation by Henrik Ibsen, Anton Chekhov, Oscar Wilde, and others. In 1918, with the death of Shimamura, the group disbanded after six years of activity. The theater troupes founded by Tsubouchi and Shimamura, as well as the other groups discussed below, were part of Shingeki, Japanese for "modern theater."

Osanai Kaoru was another key figure in the early twentieth century development of Shingeki. He and Ichikawa Sadanji II, a Kabuki actor, founded the Jiyūgeki Kyōkai (free drama society), a study group, which emphasized the training of performers in Western acting techniques. Most of the members were Kabuki actors, and the group also included some actresses with training in the Kabuki tradition. They tended to perform translations of works by Western dramatists such as Chekhov, Ibsen, and August Strindberg. This group, which was most active before World War I, dissolved after ten years. Osanai then collaborated with Hijikata Yoshi, another of the key founders of the Shingeki movement, in the establishment of the Tsukiji Shōgekijō (Tsukiji Little Theater). This playhouse, with a capacity of about five hundred, was built specially for the performance of modern plays; its architecture conformed to the Western theatrical tradition. Osanai surprised playwrights before the opening of the theater in 1924 by declaring that no Japanese dramatist could live up to the artistic standards he had established, so for the time being no Japanese drama would be performed on the boards at Tsukiji. In his first forty-four consecutive programs, Osanai revealed his broad taste in Western drama by presenting some of the following playwrights: Shakespeare, Ibsen, Strindberg, Georg Kaiser, Eugene O'Neill, and Luigi Pirandello. Later, Osanai chose to stage plays written by Japanese novelists as well as plays written by himself. Besides directing plays, Hijikata managed the financial affairs of the new playhouse. This theater's most vital contribution to the development of the modern theater in Japan was its legacy of experienced performers and competent technical theater personnel. The sudden death of Osanai in December, 1928, led to the dispersal of the company.

After the dissolution of the Tsukiji Shōgekijō, Hijikata, who had leftist leanings, founded the Shin-Tsukiji Gekidan (New Tsukiji Theater Group), which served the proletarian movement by attracting the intelligentsia and members of the labor unions. The remaining members of the older company called themselves Gekidan Tsukiji Shōgekijō (Theater Group/ Little Tsukiji Theater) but disbanded two years later; in 1937, these members founded the Bungakuza (Literary Theater), which still performs today. In the meantime, the proletarian theater of Hijikata came increasingly under attack by the militarists and was forced to disband in 1940. During World War II, modern theaters were often required to mobilize their members to present propaganda plays. They suffered professionally under the harsh wartime conditions.

After September, 1945, most forms of artistic oppression disappeared, although the Americans, with their distrust of Kabuki's feudalistic powers, were not completely objective in their support of the theater arts. The proletarian theater movement, however, whose members were often imprisoned and harassed during the prewar years, enjoyed the sudden freedom. Hijikata had spent fours years in jail before being released at the end of the war.

The rising power of the militarists in the 1930's had resulted in stricter censorship over newspapers, motion pictures, and theaters. In this period, the free statement of ideas and the exercise of artistic creativity, especially along Western lines, was not readily tolerated by the government. Since travel abroad was still slow and costly, the opportunity for serious performers or dramatists to live or study abroad and actually attend performances of foreign plays was quite limited. There were exceptional cases, such as that of Kishida Kunio, who studied in France and tried to apply Western dramaturgy to Japanese needs, but even after much tireless effort, the results were not widely appreciated outside his own circle.

Shingeki enjoyed a boom in popularity after the war, and Japan again turned its eyes to the new drama of the West. Tennessee Williams's *A Streetcar Named Desire* (pr. 1947) was performed in translation in 1953. Works by Samuel Beckett, John Osborne, Jean-Paul Sartre, and Arthur Miller became as familiar as those written by contemporary Japanese authors. Postwar dramatists of note include Michio Kato, the author cf *Nayotake* (pr. 1946), a work based on an old Japanese legend; Junji Kinoshita, whose *Yūzuru* (pr. 1949; *Twilight Crane*, 1956) was performed internationally and Yukio Mishima, the internationally famous novelist and right-wing activist. During his brief but prolific career, Mishima wrote Kabuki plays in a classical style as well as modern Nō plays, which managed to capture the mysterious, otherworldly mood of the Nō drama in the contemporary idiom.

Kōbō Abe, like Mishima, is better known for his novels than for his plays. Abe grew up in Manchuria and returned to Japan as an adolescent in 1941; this fact is perhaps partially responsible for his startling objectivity in dealing with the social fabric of Japanese society. His play *Tomodachi* (pr. 1967; *Friends*, 1969) employs a surface realism to deconstruct the contemporary Japanese understanding of democracy. A young salaried worker's apartment is invaded by a family cf total strangers who insist that privacy and the single life are not good for him. Abe's use of realism is in stark contrast to that of decades of Shingeki dramatists who emulated the work of European dramatists. Another Abe play, *Omae ni mo tsumi ga aru* (pr. 1978; *You, Too, Are Guilty*, 1979) addresses issues of social responsibility through a confrontation between a young professional and a temporarily abandoned corpse.

For more than seventy years, Japanese theater had served as a vehicle for and a reflection of the modernization and Westernization of Japanese society. The neo-mysticism of the Nō theater and the celebratory spectacle of Kabuki had been abandoned in favor of the rational realism of late-nineteenth century European drama. In the late 1960's, however, social unrest surrounding the renewal of the Mutual Security Treaty with the United States cracked open the conservative middle-class values that had solidified during the postwar "economic miracle." In the chaotic atmosphere of the student movement, some young Japanese intellectuals saw the need to shed the constraints of logic-bound realism and reopen Japan's windows to the gods and spirits of the past. The movement that resulted was called the post-Shingeki or Angura (underground) movement. This movement was characterized by its greater spontaneity, its rejection of proscenium arch realism, an emphasis on performance rather than script, and an embrace of Japan's mythic past.

Among those in the Angura movement, Minoru Betsuyaku is an important figure. He began writing for the Waseda Shōgekijō (Waseda Little Theatre), which performed his iconoclastic *Zo* (pr. 1962; *The Elephant*, 1986). Betsuyaku not only detonated the hegemony of Shingeki orthodox realism but also took on the Japanese language itself, exploring the possibilities of a new idiom. Like Abe, Betsuyaku deals with the absurd, anxiety-ridden quality of life in the postmodern metropolis, and his language has the power to draw the audience into a dark, unfriendly world full of anxiety and mystery. Presented in 1973, his *Idō* (1971; *The Move*, 1979) sends a family on a desperate journey to nowhere; at the end of the play, a half-crazed woman with a dead baby on her back urges the husband to keep moving, although they have lost most of their family and personal possessions.

Other important writers of the post-Shingeki movement are Shuji Terayama, Makoto Sato, and Juro Kara. As is almost always the case in Japan's theatrical world, where a system of independent artists and producers has only recently begun to appear, these dramatists have been affiliated with their own theatrical organization. Terayama founded the Tenjo Sajiki ("Children of Heaven") group and managed to shock his middle-class audiences with great regularity. In a world dominated by the importance of one's academic career, he urged Japanese youth, in the title of a collection of dramatic readings, to "dump your books and get into the street" (*Sho wo Stueyō! Machi e Deyō!*,1969).

Sato was one of the influential figures behind the founding of the Kuro Tento (black tent) troupe in 1968. Sato's creation of a mythic, Robin Hood-like character in *Nezumi Kozō Jirokichi* (pr. 1969; *Nezumi Kozō: The Rat*, 1986) displayed his refusal of the modernist tradition. Sato's career in the last decades of the twentieth century was a barometer of the changing tastes in Japan's theater world. One thing that

Shingeki and post-Shingeki drama had in common was the seriousness of their themes. Dramatists in the late 1970's began to take a lighter tone and shy away from plays with political agendas. In 1976 the Kuro Tento group reorganized itself and proclaimed its intention to engage in lighter entertainment. In 1996, the group dissolved. Sato himself has turned in recent years away from drama and toward opera direction.

A member of the same generation, and an important innovator of performance technique, is Tadashi Suzuki, the internationally acclaimed director who pioneered the use of training exercises from Nō and Kabuki drama. Suzuki was one of the founders of the Waseda Sho-Gekijo; he started off directing plays by Betsuyaku and other post-Shingeki playwrights. He then turned to American drama but eventually tapped the kind of universality he was searching for in the premodern world of classical Greek drama. Suzuki finds ways to question the hegemony of modern common sense by emphasizing the physicality of the actors' stylized movement and by reopening and fusing the mystical spaces of ancient Greek and classical Nō drama.

Post-Shingeki plays mark a return to premodern drama not only in their openness to Japanese myth and their rejection of the conventions of realism; with hardly an exception post-Shingeki dramatists have emphasized the primacy of performance over fidelity to the script. Some eighty years after the Meiji government's determined efforts to tame the spontaneity of Kabuki and turn it into a national literary theater, the plays of the post-Shingeki dramatists went into the streets and parks of Tokyo unfettered by concern over the written word.

The twentieth century was a time of immense social upheaval in Japan. At the heart of these changes lies the reality of Japan's understanding of and response to modernism. Kabuki, which began with the dance of an outcast on a dry riverbed in Kyoto at the beginning of the seventeenth century and flourished for more than three hundred years, was eclipsed by the onslaught of modernism in the late nineteenth century. More than seventy years later, the post-Shingeki dramatists rejected that same modernism as being ossified and fruitless and tried to reopen the sacred spaces of earlier Japanese drama. In the last few decades of the twentieth century, dramatists turned to lighter themes as theater became more commercialized and young people lost their taste for political movements and avant-garde philosophy.

The traditional forms of drama continue to flourish in the twenty-first century, subsidized by the government. The post-Shingeki movement has splintered into the myriad troupes of the *shogekijo* (little theater) movement who aim to amuse their young followers with light, topical themes. As the final waves of modernization reach into the feudal strongholds of Japanese banking and education, social and financial crises loom large in the twenty-first century. No one can predict the shape or focus of the drama that will address these problems.

BIBLIOGRAPHY

Brazell, Karen, ed. *Traditional Japanese Theater: An Anthology of Plays*. New York: Columbia University Press, 1998. A collection of translations of traditional plays with an introduction, detailed stage directions, and extensive photographs.

Keene, Donald. *Twenty Plays of the Nō Theatre*. New York: Columbia University Press, 1970. This volume of translations by a noted scholar of Japanese literature has an excellent introduction to Nō drama. The translations are hauntingly beautiful and manage, in their poetry, to capture the mystery of Nō's spiritual journeys.

Leiter, Samuel L., ed. *A Kabuki Reader: History and Performance*. Armonk, N.Y.: M. E. Sharpe, 2002. This collection of scholarly essays deals with all aspects of Kabuki, from its early origins to government censorship and Meiji attempts to make Kabuki into a national theater. The volume includes fascinating work on "Communist Kabuki" as well as on gender issues.

Ortolani, Benito. *The Japanese Theater: From Shamanistic Ritual to Contemporary Pluralism*. Princeton, N.J.: Princeton University Press, 1995. Focuses on a historical range of performing traditions in comprehensive overviews and offers a history of Western scholarship on the topic and a thorough bibliography of sources in Western languages.

Rolf, Robert T., and John K. Gillespie, eds. *Alternative Japanese Drama: Ten Plays*. Honolulu: University of Hawaii Press, 1992. This work provides valuable information about the post-Shingeki movement of the 1960's and 1970's. Besides the excellent general introduction to the period by Takahashi Yasunari, introductions to each author's works are included before the translations. Makes work by writers such as Betsuyaku Minoru, Kara Juro, and Sato Makoto accessible in English for the first time.

Ted T. Takaya,
updated by Hideyuki Kasuga

KOREAN DRAMA

Traditional Korean theater, which encompasses different forms of mask-dance drama and puppet drama, and modern Korean theater, which consists of imitated Western melodrama and drama influenced by Western realism and naturalism, are increasingly embraced as part of the cultural and national heritage of North and South Korea. During the successive rule of three dynasties—Silla, Koguryŏ, and Choson (57 B.C.E.-1910 C.E.)—various forms of dance and mask-dance play were performed under the court's auspices and encouragement, with the exception of puppet drama, because its status was that of belonging to society's common class. Modern drama developed at the beginning of the twentieth century with many Western influences in the areas of theatrical themes and literary concepts.

FOLK THEATER

The history of traditional Korean theater dates back more than two thousand years, but its exact origin is unknown. Historians and scholars have theorized that its origin may be traced back to ancient religious rites, folk observances, shamanistic rituals, court performances, and general amusement both for the elite at court and for the commoners. Korean mask-dance drama is usually grouped into two types of drama: village-festival or ceremony plays known as *purakje* and court theatrical plays or performances known as *sandae-gŭk*. *Purakje* includes village drama in the genre of *pyŏlsin-gut* among various genres of village plays. *Sandae-gŭk* includes court drama with several variations driven by region or locale: *ogwangdae, pyŏlsandae, t'alch'um,* and *yaryu*.

People of all social classes were greatly entertained by the many forms of mask-dance drama and puppet theater in Korean society and culture until the beginning of the twentieth century. At this point, however, folk dramas were becoming obsolete because modern audiences found them antiquated and not relevant to contemporary issues. Moreover, in the first decade of the twentieth century, folk drama was censored and prohibited by the occupying Japanese

colonial administration, which wanted to eliminate Korean cultural heritage and force a Japanese acculturation; therefore, it banned mask-dance drama and puppet plays from 1930 to 1945. Between 1910 and 1930, Korean intellectuals and other dramatists were still able to produce modern plays that focused on Korean suffering at the hands of the Japanese occupation. However, these plays did not elicit the approval of the Japanese officials, and in turn, from 1930 to 1945, the Japanese eliminated the presentation of all Korean cultural heritage, which included theatrical productions. However, folk theater re-emerged during the 1970's, with a return to Korean roots via government and academic intervention and renewed interest from contemporary audiences.

Ogwangdae mask-dance drama was performed according to the lunar calendar on New Year's Eve, and unique to Pamm ri, a town situated on the bank of Naktong-kang River, Kyongsang-namdo Province, South Korea. Although its origin is unclear, one story suggests that the villagers found a casket floating along the bank near Pamm ri. They finally opened the basket to find the masks and instructions for enacting a mask-dance drama. The purposes of *ogwangdae* were to exorcize demons and evil spirits of the past year and to ensure prosperity for the next year, a good harvest, and an abundance of fish for the villagers. *Ogwangdae* means "five-clown play." The plays in this mask-dance drama usually consist of five scenes. No original masks, made of paulownia wood, from Pamm ri have survived because of a great fire in1909. Dance, music, and witty dialogue are fundamental elements of the production of *ogwangdae* drama. The dance, which used to be brisk and lively, has become more slow and languid over time.

The origin of *pyŏlsandae* is described in a legend of more than two hundred years ago. According to this legend, the townspeople of Yangju, about fifteen miles northeast of Seoul, began to put on a dance performance by making their own masks after court performers of *sandae-gŭk* (which encompasses most forms of Korean court mask-dance drama forms preserved through oral tradition) did not appear for the scheduled performance. After the unexpected success of this mask-dance drama, the townspeople called it Yangju *pyŏlsandae*. The word *pyŏlsandae* means "separate stage performance" because it is derived from *sandae-gŭk*. The *pyŏlsandae* mask-dance drama was performed several times a year for heaven worship and reverence to the gods, notably for autumn harvest, and Buddha's birthday on the eighth day of the fourth lunar month, with people dancing and singing in these ceremonies. Dance and music are very important in the *pyŏlsandae*, which uses most of the basic Korean mask-dance forms. The music in this drama derives from folk and shamanistic lamenting songs.

There are thirty-two masks in the *pyŏlsandae*, although only twenty-two masks are usually used for its performance; however, none of the original masks has survived. The masks for this mask-dance drama are made from dried gourds, paper, wood, and pine bark.

Until the early of part of the twentieth century, the *pyŏlsin-gut* mask-dance drama was a traditional ceremony, performed once every ten years in Hahoe Village, North Kyongsang Province, South Korea. The word *pyŏlsin* broadly means incantation, and *gut* means spectacle or show. Together, *pyŏlsin-gut* broadly means incantatious spectacle or show. The origin of this village mask-dance drama is not exact, although some experts suggest that it may have had its root in many forms of heaven or shamanistic ceremony practice by villagers in the Hahoe region. Hahoe villagers were not the only people partaking in the *pyŏlsin-gut*; the people of neighboring regions were also fond of this mask-dance drama. The purposes of *pyŏlsin-gut* were to ensure prosperity for the village, to exorcize evil spirits, and to provide amusement for the villagers.

The wooden masks of *pyŏlsin-gut* are very refined in their carving and age because they were not burned at the end of each performance, unlike other forms of Korean mask-dance drama. Only nine of the original twelve masks remain. Reasons for the disappearance of the other three masks are not known.

The word *t'alch'um* means "masked dance" and supposedly came from various regions in the western

and southeastern plains and coastal towns in present-day North Korea. Of the three regions, only *t'alch'um* from Pongsan of the western plains continues to be performed; other versions of *t'alch'um* are now obsolete. This mask-dance drama was performed during the Tano Festival, one of Korea's oldest holidays honoring village spirits and ancestors, an event that takes place outdoors. The *t'alch'um* was a satirical dance, used by local villagers to alienate their anger, sadness, and frustrations with life. This mask-dance drama is no longer performed in North Korea because it is considered backward and not revolutionary enough by the communist government. However, it is preserved in South Korea by those performers who escaped from North Korea during the Korean War (1950-1953).

The masks of *t'alch'um* are well known because of their grotesque and outlandish appearances. This mask-dance drama is especially noted for its poetry, music, beautiful dialogue, and puns. The masks used in *t'alch'um* are smaller than in other mask-dance dramas and are usually made of paper. Often these masks are considered demonic masks because of their grotesque appearance.

The word *yaryu* means "playground or field play" because this mask-dance drama was usually held outdoors in the market square. It is very short, with only four or five scenes. The *yaryu* was found in the region east of Naktong-kang River, Kyongsang-namdo Province, South Korea, though its origins are not certain. This mask-dance drama was often performed in sacrificial festivals for the gods as an exorcism and to ensure safety and an adequate harvest for the villagers.

There are eleven masks required for the performance of *yaryu* theater. Eight masks represent human characters, two masks represent animals, and one represents a character that is neither human nor animal. Because it was required that all the masks be burned to ensure the peace and prosperity of the village, no original masks exist today. These masks are made of dried gourds, paper, and bamboo.

PUPPET DRAMA

The word *kkoktu* means "puppet," and generally puppet drama is called *kkoktu kaksi*. Scholars have suggested that Korean puppetry may have come from

China or Asia Minor because of its linguistic roots. This puppet drama was highly popular among the commoners in Korean culture and society because of its subject matter and thematic relevance to the oppression of the lower classes. *Kkoktu kaksi* was performed for numerous purposes: religious worship, shamanistic rites, ancestral worship, ceremonial and military functions, and general amusement. For general entertainment, puppets of stock characters, such as corrupted officials, lustful monks, and other domestic characters, were greatly satirized, thereby serving popular amusement for the commoners. Historically, few attempts have been made to preserve *kkoktu kaksi*; scanty evidence implies that puppet plays were not considered to have literary or aesthetic value in ancient times. However, attempts by modern scholars and historians to restore this heritage began in the mid-twentieth century and continue in the contemporary period.

The construction of the puppets involves carved wood and papier-mâché with wooden frames. A puppet theater company is usually made up of six or seven performers, three or four puppeteers, and three musicians.

MODERN THEATER

When the popularity of folk drama began to decline at the beginning of the twentieth century, modern forms of drama began to emerge. This modern drama dealt with contemporary social issues that were deemed more relevant to Korean people than folk drama.

Shinp'a refers to a genre of modern drama, a popular commercial theater form emerging during the 1930's and influenced by Japanese modern theater and Western literary sources. *Shinp'a* is made up of three types of plays: domestic, military, and detective plays. Among these types, the domestic plays were most popular because they were melodramatic, dealing with love, and family separation and bankruptcy, evidenced notably in Pak Sung-hi's play *Arirang-goge* (pr. 1926; Arirang Pass). These themes likely arose in response to Japanese occupation and exploitation. In South Korea, the production of contemporary American plays by such playwrights as Arthur

Miller, Tennessee Williams, and William Inge was predominant in the *shinp'a* during the 1950's. The 1960's saw European authors such as Jean Anouilh, Max Frisch, and Samuel Beckett being introduced in the *shinp'a*. In the *shinp'a* genre of the early twenty-first century, surrealism and experimental techniques have been introduced, embraced by modern Korean audiences.

In 1948, Korea was divided into the Republic of Korea (South Korea) and the Democratic People's Republic of North Korea after the liberation from Japanese occupation at the end of World War II. In North Korea, under a communist regime, *shingŭk* arose as a dominant genre of realistic modern drama, dealing with left-wing interests and nationalist propaganda, evidenced in a play called *Kongsan ppalchisan* (communist guerrilla) in the 1950's, a spectacular modern vision of Korean struggle against Japanese domination led by General Kim Il Sung, the first leader of North Korea. Plays were also written to promote Kim's political propaganda and other nationalistic ideologies. *Shingŭk* remained isolated to North Korea because of its leftist nature and never emerged in South Korea, which favored the Western-influenced *shinp'a*.

Three types of *shingŭk* emerged in North Korea in the 1970's. Revolutionary opera, music and dance drama, and epic drama in music and dance were grand and spectacular productions on the stages of Pyongyang, the capital of North Korea. Recurring themes included the struggle against Japanese domination, war against American imperialism, and the glorification of Kim Il Sung. These themes continued to dominate in the last decade of the twentieth century despite the demise of communism in Eastern Europe and Russia (1989-1991).

In the last decades of the twentieth century, theaters in North and South Korea struggled to attract audiences and to create new works in Korean drama. Because a number of historical and political factors have worked toward the eradication of traditional Korean theater, the preservation of traditional and modern Korean drama as a cultural art and heritage is very important. Although new ideas and influences, especially from American and European playwrights and writers, are welcomed, historical elements of Korean theater and dance hold an important place in encouraging the success of modern-day Korean theater.

BIBLIOGRAPHY

Brandon, James R., and Martin Banham, eds. *The Cambridge Guide to Asian Theatre.* Cambridge, England: Cambridge University Press, 1997. The book has entries on individual Asian countries and their respective theatrical developments and history, with comprehensive listings of the most important aspects of each country's dramatic genres and styles.

Cho, Oh-kon. *Korean Puppet Theatre: Kkoktu Kaksi.* East Lansing: Michigan State University, 1979. Focuses on the whole history and development of Korean puppet theater, with details on the linguistics and origins of the puppet plays.

_____. *Traditional Korean Theatre.* Berkeley, Calif.: Asian Humanities Press, 1988. Provides a comprehensive and detailed history of the development, importance, influence, and aesthetics of each genre of mask-dance drama and puppet plays in Korean folk theater. Scholarly and expert information details the similarities and distinctions among the genres of mask-dance plays.

Kardos, John. *An Outline History of Korean Drama.* New York: Long Island University Press, 1966. Offers basic information on the historical importance of Korean drama and its development and cultural heritage up to the time of publication.

Schechner, Richard, and Willa Appel, eds. *By Means of Performance: Intercultural Studies of Theatre and Ritual.* Cambridge, England: Cambridge University Press, 1990. Discusses the importance and influences of Korean shamanistic rites and ceremonies and how this shamanistic tradition is portrayed in Korean folk drama.

Hanh N. Nguyen

Southeast Asian Drama

In Southeast Asia, traditional theater is more than one thousand years old and has roots in dance, literature, and the religions of both South and East Asia, which have their own indigenous performance traditions. Modern theater, especially spoken drama, has been influenced by the West. This indigenous performance history, enriched by contact with the West and outside traditions, creates a highly developed theatrical heritage. Dramatic similarities are inevitable in traditional theater because of geographic proximity and historical and political similarities, but each country still maintains its own distinct dramatic forms. Unlike Western drama, Southeast Asian drama gives priority to performance rather than sustained narratives. Yet this does not make it less intellectual. Understanding Southeast Asian theater requires a contextualized examination of the whole genre and form, not just individual plays.

BURMA

Modern-day Myanmar, a country once known as Burma, has a rich dramatic tradition. Burmese theater includes animistic performance, Buddhist theater, court dance drama, and popular theater. Dance and music are fundamental in traditional animistic performance, in which *nat* (spirits) of heroes and ancestors are invoked through trance manifestations during festivals or private séance sessions. Prescribed songs and dance numbers, with ancient, jerky movements, are used to summon thirty-seven specific *nat*.

Buddhist theater is primarily concerned with *jakata*, tales of Buddha and his prior lives. Court dance drama was greatly influenced by Siam (present-day Thailand) when Burmese King Hsinbyushin captured the Siam capital of Ayutthaya in 1767. Captured Thai dancers helped to refine the Burmese court theater. This fusion gave rise to a new literary art, with court dance drama performers accorded higher status than that of animistic *nat* performers.

Popular theater emerged when patronage of court dance drama diminished under British control in the 1800's. *Pya zat* (new plays) are modern comedies and dramas with texts by individual authors. *Pya zat* are popular because they address contemporary issues of modernization and urbanization, topics more appealing to modern audiences.

CAMBODIA

Cambodia's theatrical traditions are more than seventeen hundred years old, derived from the ethnic Khmer people of Cambodia, and include traditional village performance, court dance drama, and modern theater. Traditional village performance is multifunctional and simultaneous with spirit invocation, ritual functions, social integration, and general entertainment. Chanting, dancing, and music are found in a form of folk chanting (*ayay*) for entertainment and courting between men and women. Dancing and music are found in stag dance (*trott*), where performers impersonate a deer and hunters.

Lakon kabach boran (the dance of the palace ladies) was a highly refined and aesthetic genre in court dance drama, performed by well-trained royal harem women. This is known in the West as Royal Cambodian Ballet, performing *roeung* (epic dance drama) with Indian, Javanese, and Thai influences. It initially suffered under French colonial rule after 1867 when a lack of court patronage forced many female dancers to live by other means. During the 1930's, French support and a court renaissance of the *Lakon kabach boran* remarkably revived the genre. It managed to survive the murderous Pol Pot regime, which banished all forms of arts and entertainment and killed many of its most famous dancers from 1975 to 1979. In 2000, a guest tour in France of this ballet form was a spectacular success.

Modern theater is fused with indigenous Khmer performance and Thai, Malay, Chinese, and Vietnamese theatrical traditions. Modern spoken drama (*lakon niyey*) is influenced by French drama and is very popular with contemporary Cambodians, dealing with current and pressing urban issues.

INDONESIA

Indonesian theater consists of proto-theatrical forms,

court and folk theater, urban drama of the last hundred years, and modern drama. Proto-theatrical forms include epic recitation of tales from Indian traditions, poetic dialogue performances with Malay verse, and spirit invocation with trance and séance performances.

Court and folk theater arose between the seventh and thirteenth centuries with substantial influence from Indian Buddhist and Hindu religions. Indian-influenced female dance, mask dance, and shadow puppetry (*wayang*), which is also Chinese-influenced, were integral in spiritual and political empowerment of rulers. When Islam made inroads into Java in the thirteenth century, the Buddhist-Hindu ruling elite moved to Bali. *Gambuh* (ritual dance drama of Bali), with predictable story lines of tensions among ladies-in-waiting and the prince and his ministers, has declined since 1906. In Java, shadow puppetry and mask dance drama were redefined by Islamic influences. In Sunda, theatrical traditions occupy a middle ground between the frenzied aesthetics of Bali and the fluid aesthetics of Java.

Urban drama of the last one hundred years—with precedence of dialogue over dance and plots and story lines come with sustained narratives—was influenced by touring Malaysian troupes and was aimed at commercial entertainment. This form of urban drama is similar to the Italian *commedia dell'arte*. The urban dramatic tradition forces the audiences to confront the epic and classical worlds.

Modern drama is spoken drama that asks the contemporary audiences to confront current problems and issues of city life. Modern plays are typically written and performed in the modern Indonesian language. Rustam Effendi's 1926 verse drama *Bebasari*, about the abduction of Princess Bebasari (Indonesia) by Rawanda (Holland), was quickly banned by the Dutch colonial government. Even after Indonesian independence in 1945, the imprisonment of playwrights and widespread censorship continued. For that reason, ties between modern drama and politics remain significant.

Laos

Laotian theatrical traditions are directly influenced by Thai and Cambodian (Khmer) theater and

drama and fall into three categories: proto-theatrical and indigenous performance, court dance and theater (influenced by Khmer-Thai models), and modern drama derived from folk performance and popular Thai theater. Proto-theatrical and indigenous performance still serve a function as epic storytelling, courting, and curing. Now rare, *lum pun* (sung storytelling) was an ancient performance of *jataka*, executed by male chanters in the Lao language. *Pa-nyah* is a courting game in which men and women sing poetic dialogues, accompanied by music. *Lum pee fah* (sky spirit singing) is a curing performance executed only by women, who communicate with good spirits to chase away a disease.

Court dance and theater began in the fourteenth century when the Lao court wanted to emulate Khmer monarchs. Neither as rich as the Khmer nor possessing Thailand's sophisticated theatrical traditions, the Lao Kingdom created smaller versions of their court dance performances.

Modern drama, with spoken roles and a sustained narrative, emerged in the Lao-speaking region in Northern Thailand in the 1920's. It has been influenced by Thai dramatic troupes and adapted forms of *Nang Daloong*, the genre of Thai shadow theater. Before the communist takeover in 1975, the traditional forms of dance and court drama were preferred in Laos, whereas Lao people in Thailand prefer the popular modern drama. A lessening of communist repression in Laos has led to the open reemergence of traditional dances.

Malaysia

Malaysian theatrical traditions embrace the categories of proto-theatrical performance, Hindu-Muslim folk and court theater, urban theater, and modern drama evident since World War II. Proto-theatrical performance includes singing of epics (*penglipur lara*), spirit invocation, and poetry performances with roots in Malay customs. Hindu-Muslim folk and court theater shows influences from India, Indonesia (especially female dance theater), and Islamic sources. Urban theater emerged along the west coast of Malaysia. *Bangsawan* (a form of opera), the most successful commercial theater genre of the twentieth century, emerged in the late nineteenth century as a drama for urbanites with plays gradually drawn from Arabian, Chinese, Western, and Indian models. Modern drama emerged between 1940 and the 1960's after the decline of urban theater. *Purbawara*, plays about the glory of historical and mythical personages, were performed in the Malay sultanate as a form of protest against British colonial control, which ended in 1957. After World War II, Malay nationalism was infused with modern and urban considerations. Modern spoken drama (*drama moden*), pioneered by Mustapha Kamil Yassin in 1963, tries to mediate between past and present, asking Malay audiences to be critical of their culture and society.

PHILIPPINES

Filipino theatrical heritage includes proto-theatrical performance, Islamic dance, Hispanic-influenced theater, American-influenced theater, and modern drama. Proto-theatrical performance functioned as spirit communication, dance rituals, epic recitation, curing, courting, and rites-of-passage ceremonies and dates from before Christian and Muslim influences. Islamic dance is similar to the Muslim music and dance traditions of Malaysia and Indonesia.

Hispanic-influenced theater sees continuous popularity with religious performances, notably the *komedya* (genre of religious plays), written from the seventeenth century to the modern day. *Zarzuela*, Filipino operettas based on Spanish models, were popular from 1890 to 1930 and dealt with romantic love suffused with nationalism and realism. American-influenced theater includes *bodabil* or *vadavil* (vaudeville), which appeared around 1916 and gradually developed into burlesque.

Modern drama of the late twentieth and early twenty-first centuries was spawned from a century of colonial and nationalistic struggles. Some of the first scripted, spoken plays in all of Southeast Asia were written by the Filipino *Ilustrados* (elite) and dealt with guerrilla warfare against the United States (1909-1916). Even after independence in 1946, Filipinos still wrote plays in English because the American education system had introduced Broadway mu-

sicals and Western classics. Modern spoken dramas deal with the colonial past, indigenous heritage, the Philippines' own political corruption (notably the overthrow of the Ferdinand Marcos regime in the mid-1980's), and current urban issues.

SINGAPORE

Singapore has four concurrent theatrical traditions: English, Malay, Mandarin, and Tamil. Until Singapore's separation from Malaysia in 1965, Malay theater enjoyed an era of high literary prestige, led by the Sriwana theater company. Sriwana staged plays in *purbawara* and *drama moden*.

Tamil theater emerged in the 1950's with adaptations of reformist and realistic plays from traditional Tamil tales. The contemporary Tamil dramatic system has appeared to be in no hurry to change aesthetically or otherwise. Mandarin theater was interrupted by the Cultural Revolution in China (1966-1976), which inspired Kuo Pao Kun to write epic plays demystifying Mandarin dramas in Singapore. His professionalism, dramatic education, and vision for the revolutionary theater in Singapore popularized his work. In the 1980's, Kuo wrote several successful Mandarin-English plays that were less revolutionary and more reflective and expressionistic, notably *The Coffin Is Too Big for the Hole* (pr. 1985). Following 1986, Singapore's English dramas were performed extensively because the appeal of Asian dramatic forms among the younger Westernized generation is tenuous.

THAILAND

Thai theatrical traditions include village animistic performance, court dance drama, popular drama, and modern spoken drama. Village animistic performance is infused with Buddhist and Hindu influences from the Malay region in Southern Thailand, stemming from the fourteenth century. Present animistic dances are staged for entertainment in the context of temple rituals and spirit festivals.

Court dance drama includes *nang yai* (large leather puppets), a shadow and silhouette puppet theater with an Indian-influenced epic story; *khon* (masked-dance drama), performed by a male cast to a chanted narrative with musical accompaniment and dancers miming the actions of the text; and *lakon fai nai* (female dance drama), supposedly derived from Khmer court female dancers captured in the fifteenth century. The *lakon fai nai* is generally considered the most elegant, poetic, and graceful of all Thai dance dramas.

Popular drama serves as entertainment and is found in the genres of *nang talung* (shadow puppet theater) and *likay* (commercial theater created in the twentieth century). It mixes classical dance, costumes, songs, and music with melodramatic story lines. Modern spoken drama lacks mass appeal and remains an elitist art for a rarified royal, university-educated, and Westernized Thai audience.

VIETNAM

Vietnam, the only Southeast Asian nation in which Chinese influences are ubiquitous in dance and theater, has theatrical traditions that include folk performance, classical performance, popular theater, and spoken drama. Folk performance, with proto-theatrical influences, functioned in spirit incarnation, courting, storytelling, and other entertainment traditions. *Múa rôi nuôc* (water puppetry) is a unique folk tradition that has been preserved orally.

Classical performance was mostly court dance drama, which was heavily influenced by Chinese traditions because of China's thousand-year domination of Vietnam. *Hát bôi*, a genre of classical court opera theater, developed in the eleventh century.

Popular theater, which developed in the early twentieth century, is predominantly *cäi luong* (reformed theater), a highly popular genre of melodramatic theater with a foundation of singing. Its popularity was primarily in South Vietnam; elitist Northern Vietnamese theater patrons often evaluated it as having lower artistic merit.

Kòch nói (spoken drama) was a twentieth century development with French influences. This genre was undertaken by the literary elite privileged with a Western university education under French colonial rule. Vu Đình Long's *Chén thuôc óc* (a cup of poison) was the first Vietnamese spoken drama about a morally troubled civil servant and was performed in

1921 in Hanoi. Spoken drama has become a genre in which writers and literary figures reflect on the cultural, social, and political life introduced under communist rule and confront pressing modern and urban issues.

BIBLIOGRAPHY

Brandon, James R. *Brandon's Guide to Theatre in Asia*. Honolulu: University Press of Hawaii, 1976. Functions primarily as a guide to theater models and trends in Asia.

_____. *Theatre in Southeast Asia*. Cambridge, Mass.: Harvard University Press, 1967. Provides valuable basic facts and history of theatrical traditions of Southeast Asian countries.

Brandon, James R., and Martin Banham, eds. *The Cambridge Guide to Asian Theatre*. Cambridge, England: Cambridge University Press, 2000. Offers entries on individual Asian countries and their respective theatrical developments and history, with comprehensive listings of the most important aspects of each country's dramatic genres and styles.

Miettinen, Jukka O. *Classical Dance and Theatre in South-East Asia*. New York: Oxford University Press, 1992. Provides an overview of historical and traditional developments of dance and theatrical models for each Southeast Asian country. Pictures and color plates help reader visualize the rich theatrical forms of each country.

Mohd, Taib Osman, ed. *Traditional Drama and Music of Southeast Asia*. Kuala Lumpur: Dewan Bahasa dan Pustaka, Kementerian Pelajaran Malaysia, 1974. Provides a collection of papers presented at the International Conference on Traditional Drama and Music of Southeast Asia, in Kuala Lumpur, in 1969, with entries by scholars and experts.

Peterson, William. *Theater and the Politics of Culture in Contemporary Singapore*. Middleton, Conn.: Wesleyan University Press, 2001. Examines numerous facets of modern-day Singapore theater, including dramatic constructions of gender, its festival culture, "interculturalism," and the Singapore musical.

Sears, Laurie J. *Shadows of Empire: Colonial Discourse and Javanese Tales*. Durham, N.C.: Duke University Press, 1996. Explores Javanese shadow theater as a staging area for negotiations between colonial power and indigenous traditions; shows how the modern shadow theater must be understood as a hybrid of Javanese and Dutch ideas and interests, inseparable from a particular colonial moment.

Hanh N. Nguyen

AUSTRALIAN DRAMA

Although the beginnings of an identifiably Australian drama can be discerned in plays written during the 1930's, it was not until about 1960 that plays of lasting or literary merit were frequently printed or performed. For convenience, Ray Lawler's *Summer of the Seventeenth Doll* (pr. 1955) is often regarded as the precursor of modern Australian drama, yet in 1956, A. D. Hope, in a *Current Affairs Bulletin* article, "Standards in Australian Literature," published by the University of Sydney, noted that "there is not much to say about Australian drama," and Cecil Hadgraft, in *Australian Literature: A Critical Account to 1955* (1960), a highly regarded conspectus, wholly omitted any consideration of plays.

The late flowering of Australian drama is not readily explained. Though the national population has always been small, it has consistently been urban and relatively literate and affluent, sustaining almost all the other forms of culture, both popular and high. Paradoxically, both at home and abroad Australians have been keen theatergoers, and until the advent of television Australians were among the world's most frequent moviegoers, yet few local writers produced film scripts, although Australian-made and -directed films came into their own in the 1970's and 1980's.

EARLY ORIGINS

In June, 1789, only eighteen months after the arrival of the First Fleet, George Farquhar's *The Recruiting Officer* (pr. 1706) was performed in Sydney by a cast of convicts as a King's Birthday entertainment for an audience of sixty that included the colonial governor. Thereafter, musical entertainments as well as civil and religious spectacles and stage plays were commonplace; that is, theater became an integral part of the regional culture, and taking into account the educational background of some of the convicts, one might have expected original dramatic materials making use of the novel local milieu. Convicts, soldiers, settlers, and Aborigines isolated in a generally inhospitable and inaccessible environment would seem to have offered ample scope for plays on themes of expatriation, penitence, ambition, fortitude, and rivalry set in unusual, if not exotic, locales, but a deference to established, successful models; a reluctance to experiment; and minimal leisure combined to keep local drama imitative, derivative, and repetitious in structure, theme, and characters. These traits are to be found in the other genres also; it was some time before recognizably Australian characters, speech, and subjects were widely incorporated into Australian literature.

Literary reputations in Australia were traditionally based on achievement in poetry or fiction, while the dominance of comedy and musical comedy in commercial theaters (a reflection of British theater offerings) eliminated the stimulus to attempt serious plays and tragedies, which were relegated to little theaters—located in suburbs or in the insalubrious sections of the capital cities, in the main. A publishing industry that could rarely justify poetry, short stories, and novels commercially was understandably reluctant to print plays. The almost total absence of professional theater personnel militated against successful staging of plays by Australian authors.

Although most of these impediments have been removed and there are indications that drama—for stage, broadcast, film, and literary study—has attained the artistic level of Australian poetry and prose fiction, there is still no playwright of the international stature of South African Athol Fugard; there are, however, many of commendable achievements.

The first play written in Australia was *The Bushrangers* (pr. 1829), a typical nineteenth century melodrama set in Tasmania in 1825 and dealing with contemporary subject matter and characters. Its author was a Scots settler and editor of *The South Briton: Or, Tasmanian Literary Journal*, David Burn. In all, Burn wrote eight plays, some in prose, some in verse, that attempted most of the forms—melodrama, farce, blank-verse tragedy, and historical drama. They became the first plays published in Australia (1842). Curiously, the two plays set in Australia were never staged there.

The Bushrangers was produced in Edinburgh in 1829. In its episodic structure, satire of officialdom, social criticism, and juxtaposition of government and highwayman moralities it is reminiscent of John Gay's *The Beggar's Opera* (pr. 1728). Like Gay's ballad opera, *The Bushrangers* had its imitators: two of identical title were written by Henry Melville (pr. 1834) and Charles Harpur (wr. 1835), while a plethora of others used contemporary social antagonisms and issues as subjects. Some, such as Edward Geoghegan's *The Currency Lass* (pr. 1849), were original; others, such as Garnet Walch and Alfred Dampier's *Robbery Under Arms* (pr. 1891) and Thomas Somers and Dampier's *His Natural Life* (pr. 1886), were adaptations of successful Australian novels.

Throughout the nineteenth century, however, local playwrights tended to imitate the current London stage fare with melodramas, farces, and pantomimes or tableaux that made only minimal concessions to the location. When American plays were introduced, they, too, were imitated. J. C. Williamson and Maggie Williamson's *Struck Oil* (pr. 1874) had its replications in Francis R. C. Hopkins's *All for Gold* (pr. 1877), Dampier's *The Miner's Right* (pr. 1891), and his and Kenneth MacKay's *To the West* (pr. 1896). Some imaginative dramatists attempted to fuse British, American, and Australian elements, so that Euston Leigh and Cyril Clare's *The Duchess of Coolgardie* (pr. 1896), set in the Western Australian goldfields, could have an Aborigine's lines written in an approximation of South Carolinian Gullah dialect and an implausible cast and improbable plot. Yet the play was successful: It was performed in Drury Lane Theatre, printed in London, and imitated by George Darrell's *The King of Coolgardie* (pr. 1897).

RISE IN NATIONALIST DRAMA

The increasing nationalism at the close of the century became a feature of all forms of Australian culture. With federation in 1901, chauvinism became less strident yet no less apparent: Australia's participation in the Boer War, World War I, and the Versailles Peace Treaty sustained the sense of national identity. In drama, William Moore (who organized a

writers' theater) and Louis Esson, who had met William Butler Yeats and been advised by him to write "Australian plays," accepted responsibility for the encouragement of an Australian drama.

Esson's *Three Short Plays* (pb. 1911), which included *The Woman Tamer*, *Dead Timber*, and *The Sacred Place*, helped establish the one-act play as a national norm and influenced the choice of theme and characters. (The one-act play became the dramatic equivalent of the short story in Australian fiction; Esson's role was thus similar to that of Henry Lawson.) Esson redirected the play from the melodrama of his forerunners to social realism, represented both city and country issues, and included the attitudes, problems, and antipathies of the several social classes. Accordingly, some critics have noted the influence of Henrik Ibsen and George Bernard Shaw rather than of Yeats, John Millington Synge, or Lady Augusta Gregory. In *The Woman Tamer*, Esson explores interrelationships in a slum household; in *Dead Timber*, he reveals the monotonous struggle for existence and for love in the Outback; and *The Sacred Place* suggests that slum life has its own morality and that this is justified. Impressive as these plays are, they have not been as popular as *The Drovers* (pr. 1923), in which an injured drover is of necessity abandoned by his mates and cared for by an Aborigine whose eerie wails accompany the drover's death and enhance the pathos. In this play, the influence of Synge's *Riders to the Sea* (pb. 1903) seems obvious. Later plays, such as *Mother and Son* (pr. 1923), which reexamines the loneliness of bush life and the disconcerting effects of an inhospitable environment, and *The Bride of Gospel Place* (pr. 1926), a study of city violence, demonstrated that Esson was adept in the full-length dramatic form. His place in Australian drama is secure, though his plays are infrequently staged. His satiric, sardonic, yet sympathetic approach is largely representative of the national ethos, and his themes and subjects are at once historical and regional, continuing and universal.

Compared with Esson's plays, those of two of his contemporaries are inferior, yet they have earned a niche in Australian dramatic literature. Vance Palmer's *Hail Tomorrow* (pb. 1947), about the 1891 shearers' strike, uses characters and issues dear to the Australian heart, yet the play suffers from an inadequate comprehension of dramatic conventions. Like John Steinbeck, Palmer was a fine fiction writer but was unable to work with ease and conviction in drama. Sydney Tomholt's *Bleak Dawn* (pb. 1936) is a praiseworthy study of the divorced working-class woman living in a male-oriented society.

WOMEN PLAYWRIGHTS

The role of women in Australia, which has increasingly become the focus of sociological studies, has been explored with understanding and feeling by several competent dramatists, among them Katharine Susannah Prichard, Betty Roland, and Dymphna Cusack. Prichard, author of twenty-four published novels, also wrote seventeen plays, eleven of which were produced in Australian little theaters. Only one, *Brumby Innes*, which won a drama contest run by *The Triad* magazine in 1927, was published (1940); it remained unproduced until 1972, possibly because it had been expanded into the very successful novel *Coonardoo* (1929). Set in the Outback, *Brumby Innes* is a mature investigation of black-white and male-female interrelationships, which, it suggests, follow a course from affection and accommodation to sensuality, dominance, and brutal imperiousness. *Brumby Innes*, in its analysis of alienation, self-doubt, domination, and denigration, perhaps reflects the influence of Eugene O'Neill.

Roland's *The Touch of Silk* (pr. 1928) has continued to hold a unique position in Australian drama: It was published by a university press and continues to enjoy readership and discussion, unlike Roland's later, more propagandist plays, the best known of which is probably *Are You Ready, Comrade?* (pr. 1938). *The Touch of Silk* is a study of the difficulties of a sensitive young French woman, Jeanne, in adapting to the cultureless and unaesthetic Outback, with its materialism, crudities, and primitive possessiveness, predicated on the unequal roles and status of men and women and resulting in the very denial of love. After Jeanne buys lingerie from a traveling salesman and goes to a dance with him, she pretends that she has had an affair: The illusion is a necessary balance for a loveless life in an unbeautiful and isolated environment.

Cusack's full-length plays *Red Sun at Morning* (pb. 1942) and *Morning Sacrifice* (pb. 1943) deserve greater recognition than they have gained. The first has as subject matter the flight of a mistress from an overbearing military officer and so treats a continuing Australian phenomenon, the pervasive authoritarianism in society, while also examining interpersonal relationships outside marriage. The play's historical setting (1812), however, and the improbability of the means of escape militate against its success. *Morning Sacrifice* has a wider appeal. It is set in a girls' school, where the students are conditioned "to accept all, question nothing and grow into nice, well-behaved yes-girls": The indictment of the national educational-social outlook is forceful, the examination of teacher-supervisor roles is perspicacious, and individual weaknesses and ambitions are carefully scrutinized. The simulated sincerity, frustrations, jealousies, and ambitions of the teachers become paradigmatic of society; the badinage and ripostes suggest the depth of animosity that underlies surface compatibility. The minuscule society of the school tragedy is a metaphor for life itself.

MID-TWENTIETH CENTURY DRAMA

During the 1940's, other dramatists developed their art. Max Afford wrote and adapted plays for radio: His *Lady in Danger* (pr. 1944), a well-constructed, popular comedy-thriller, has retained its enthusiasts, though it is subliterary. Sumner Locke Elliott, author of *Interval* (pr. 1942), a sophisticated piece set in London that demonstrated his mastery of dramaturgy, achieved fame with *Rusty Bugles* (pr. 1948), "a play of inaction" as one critic termed it, which has no principal characters, includes the coarse language characteristic of soldiers stationed in an isolated ordnance camp, and engages its characters in antiwar discussions. After the success of *Rusty Bugles*, the playwright moved to New York, where he regularly wrote and adapted plays for *Studio One*, *Sunday Night Playhouse*, and other broadcast series. He adapted his first novel, *Careful, He Might Hear You*, into a successful film in 1984.

The radio dramas and verse plays of New Zealand-born Douglas Stewart gave indications that he was properly to be compared with Louis MacNeice and Christopher Isherwood as a major dramatist in these forms, but the virtual eclipse of radio drama after World War II, the growth of theatergoing, and the demise of verse drama combined to deflect attention from Stewart's very remarkable plays. In an environment in which even standard English was a rarity, Stewart's language (with its finely turned phrases and impeccable nuances of diction) clearly created an impression, but where the predisposition of the public was for musical comedy, operetta, and the domestic comedy, his expressed interest in the creation of national myths from legendary individuals established barriers to the realization of his goals. It is therefore noteworthy that he continued his course and gained wide popularity.

Stewart's principal dramas are *Ned Kelly* (pr. 1942), written in both stage and radio versions, a study of the legendary bushranger and archetypal antihero; *The Fire on the Snow* (pr. 1941), a moving radio play treating the unsuccessful polar expedition of Robert Falcon Scott in 1912; and *Shipwreck* (pr. 1947), another historical play, which treats the 1629 massacre of a majority of the passengers of the *Batavia* while the captain, Pelsart, was in search of help. In each of these plays, Stewart reexamines the popular concept of the dreamer, the visionary, the leader, with his illusions of invincibility, showing also the relationship between national legends and cultural archetypes.

Considerable attention has been given in histories of Australian literature to Lawler's *Summer of the Seventeenth Doll*, which was staged in London and New York to critical acclaim. There is a consensus that this overseas recognition resulted in a resurgence of playwriting in Australia. Certainly it provided a helpful fillip, but it should be remembered that the themes of alienation, physical isolation, mateship, and country-city and man-woman interrelationships had long been the very substance of the national drama. Yet *Summer of the Seventeenth Doll* did add dimensions to established materials: It explored with understanding the inevitable disillusionments of mid-

dle life, the disintegration of friendships, and the decreasing importance of hollow ritual and token remembrances. It played an equivalent role in Australian drama to the role John Osborne's *Look Back in Anger* (pr. 1956) did in British drama, in that despite possessing only moderate artistic merit, it opened up new possibilities and alternatives for subsequent playwrights and for the field of drama as a whole, while also permitting the expression of a wider range of feeling and behavior onstage. Lawler's subsequent play, *The Piccadilly Bushman* (pr. 1959), examined the reactions to and of a returning expatriate (a common Australian experience, treated most memorably by Henry Handel Richardson in *The Fortunes of Richard Mahony*, one of the classic Australian novels, in 1917).

Richard Beynon's *The Shifting Heart* (pr. 1957) is yet another treatment of the perennial Australian confrontation with nonnatives, whether they be Aborigines or Europeans. Better than most of its genre, it shows the depth and suggests the causes of this xenophobia, exclusiveness, and even small-mindedness that is finally disappearing. Alan Seymour's *The One Day of the Year* (pr. 1961) used the artificial camaraderie of Anzac Day (the national veterans' holiday) to deflate myths, to explore the concept of mateship, and to show the irrelevance of some myths when seen across the generation gap. This play was a timely reassessment of subjects of national importance.

CONTEMPORARY DRAMA

After 1960, Australian dramatists attempted most of the modern techniques of the theater and wrote in other than realist terms. The influences of absurdism, expressionism, and symbolism could be noted. Bertolt Brecht and Friedrich Dürrenmatt became as influential as Shaw and Ibsen, Arthur Miller and Tennessee Williams, and Eugène Ionesco and Samuel Beckett. As a consequence, a narrowly nationalistic and dominantly realist drama became cosmopolitan in the widest sense. The transformation was aided by the establishment of drama schools and professional theaters, extended university education, overseas travel, and the surcease of blind adherence to outdated and overused dramatic modes. Among the important new playwrights to develop were David Williamson, Alexander Buzo, Jack Hibberd, Ric Throssell, Dorothy Hewett, and Patrick White.

With four plays produced between 1961 and 1964, White—best known as a novelist—established himself as a dramatist of some stature. *The Ham Funeral* (pr. 1961), which is informed by Ibsen's theory that illusion is essential for equanimity, shows that there is poetry in even circumscribed, dreary lives. *The Season at Sarsaparilla* (pr. 1962), a patently expressionist play subtitled *A Charade of Suburbia*, is a devastating comedy of conformism. The main characters lead lives not quite of quiet desperation but ones in which "there's practically no end to the variations of monotony." *A Cheery Soul* (pr. 1963)—based on one of White's own short stories—explores the artificiality of a voluble, self-satisfied suburban do-gooder, while *Night on Bald Mountain* (pr. 1963), a darker play, subsumes all the themes and essential character-types of the author's earlier work to stress the sterility of the proud, the detached, and the intellectual. Toward the end of the play, Professor Sword says, "You and I are here on the edge of the world, and might so easily slip over, into this merciless morning light . . . along with the illusions of importance and grandeur that we had." The theme of the play is summed up in Sword's later aphorism, "Failure is sometimes the beginnings of success."

Williamson's *Don's Party* (pr. 1971) and *The Removalists* (pr. 1971), Hibberd's *A Stretch of the Imagination* (pr. 1972) and *A Toast to Melba* (pr. 1976), and the several plays of the prolific Buzo are among the more inventive, substantial, and likely to survive as both literature and theater. Buzo's *Norm and Ahmed* (pr. 1968) is one of the most affecting treatments of xenophobia; *The Front Room Boys* (pr. 1969) lays bare the sterile life of the office worker confined to the routines of the large corporation. In both, there is the sure touch of the playwright who has an ear for the speech and interests of the common person and the analytic methodology of the sociologist. Williamson's output has been astonishing, as have been his range and his development over three decades. *The Removalists* is an excavation of the "ocker" stereotype, what in the Untied States would

be called the "redneck"—the ill-mannered, often violent working-class male. *Don's Party* is a depiction of the social and sexual turbulence of the early 1970's middle class, which also takes a serious look at Australian political immaturity. *Travelling North* (pr. 1979) is a moving depiction of an older couple who have devoted their lives to a misplaced commitment to hardline communism. *Dead White Males* (pr. 1995) satirized "political correctness" in academia, whereas *Heretic* (pr. 1996) took on anthropology's romanticization of Pacific Islands peoples. However, it is a mistake to see Williamson as merely a topical or thematic dramatist. *Emerald City* (pr. 1987), about an younger man's love for an older woman, a father's love for his son, and the corrupting effects of widespread wealth in the new "Yuppie" leisure class, assays perennial questions in a resonant fashion. By the end of the twentieth century Williamson had become the best-known Australian dramatist worldwide, and his plays became a collective social and cultural record of the Australia of his time.

Hibberd's outrageous inventiveness, formal unconventionality, and sheer Australianness have led to his prominence on the Australian stage. His wedding farce *Dimboola* (pr. 1969) became a staple of performance in Australia, not only for its rowdy display of bad behavior but also for its subtle insight into social behavior patterns. It is one of the most frequently performed plays in Australia, and its rendering of the wedding reception of Morrie and Reen McAdam has become beloved despite its side-splitting critique of Australian suburban society. *A Stretch of the Imagination* is a monodrama whose protagonist, Monk O'Neill, is at the end of his rope both physically and cognitively, but whose struggle to achieve a genuine sense of life is tremendously moving.

By the mid-1970's, professional theaters could present local texts without suffering at the box office; an annual National Playwrights' Conference, first held in Canberra in 1971, established a link between the development of solicited works and commercial production; and the fledgling film industry achieved international success with films such as *Gallipoli* (1980), *Breaker Morant* (1980), *My Brilliant Career* (1979), and *Picnic at Hanging Rock* (1981).

The demand for published plays, stimulated by their inclusion in academic drama courses, was met by a new company, Currency Press, founded by Katherine Brisbane, which was associated with the established publisher Methuen in 1982. The women's movement, the development of Aboriginal scripts, and the emergence of a new and vigorous community spirit—giving voice to the workplace and specific geographical areas—have challenged the beliefs and practices of established theaters. Chief among the new playwrights are Alma De Groen, whose *Rivers of China* (pr. 1990) challenged the way people at the margins attempt to speak at the center; Michael Gow, who in *Away* (pr. 1987) examines the coming-of-age of his teenage protagonists and deals with a 1960's society on the verge of political and social self-realization; and Stephen Sewell, who explores the domestic turmoil of a fascist politician new to the Australian order in *Hate* (pr. 1988). Gow's drama has become a staple of contemporary Australian theater, with his later work exploring his place within Australian gay male writing. Sewell has become a leading politician playwright, and his *Dreams of an Empty City* (pb. 1986) foreshadowed the themes of globalization and economic rationalism that were to become predominant in Australian culture in the 1990's.

Louis Nowra's extraordinarily various and resourceful talents of imagination are a major asset for the contemporary Australian theater. Nowra's masterpiece is *The Golden Age* (pr. 1985), concerning a tribe of isolated whites in Tasmania, long lost to the outside world, who take on contours of Aboriginality. Nowra explores contrasts between the civilized and the primitive, the cultured and the earthy, nostalgia and perseverance. *Inner Voices* (pr. 1977) concerns the Russian czar Ivan VI, deposed at the age of two and imprisoned for the rest of his life. Nowra is less interested in the historical details of Ivan's life than the dilemmas and refractions of consciousness that ensue from his predicament, especially the flawed tutelage he has imbued from his malevolent instructor, Mirovich. *The Temple* (pr. 1993) examines the effervescent entrepreneur, and *The Incorruptible* (pr. 1995) scrutinizes the other side of the Australian social coin, the working-class charismatic politician.

Così (pr. 1992) concerns issues of insanity and the imagination as it posits a young director staging a play in a mental institution in 1970, and *Radiance* (pr. 1993), concerning three Aboriginal women in the aftermath of their mother's death, continues Nowra's rare insight into various states of social being and consciousness; it was adapted into a film in 1998 by the Aboriginal director Rachel Perkins. *The Language of the Gods* (pr. 2000) examines the disintegration of Dutch colonialism in Indonesia.

Drama by women, and drama with explicitly feminist concerns, became far better known in the 1980's and 1990's. Dorothy Hewett's *The Chapel Perilous* (pr. 1971), concerning the quest of an unconventional woman to realize her potential, notwithstanding the obstacles placed in her way by social accretions and male authority figures, was already a classic (though it was banned for decades in the author's native state of Western Australia for fear of libel). In later decades of the twentieth century, Hewett continued to produce buoyantly, *Golden Valley* (pr. 1981) and *Song of the Seals* (pr. 1983) being good examples. De Groen's *Rivers of China*, about the life of the New Zealand short-story writer Katherine Mansfield, became the touchstone for feminist drama at the end of the twentieth century. Sandra Shotlander's work depicted affirmative images of lesbian identity in an experimental mode; *Is That You, Nancy?* (pr. 1991) is considered her major work. A more conventional, but very interesting, dramatist is Hannie Rayson, whose *Life After George* (pb. 2000) concerned the death of a veteran leftist politician in a plane crash and the way his image lingers in the perspectives of those who knew and loved him. In 2002, the play was produced in London to positive reviews.

Another growing area of Australian drama in this era was plays by writers of migrant background. Ron Elisha's *Two* (pr. 1983) concerns the partition of Palestine between the Arabs and the Jews in 1948 as a sounding board for illustrating general motifs of division and duality. Work that exploded the boundaries between drama, poetry, and dance also proliferated, with the collaborations of Richard James Allen with his wife, the American Karne Pearlman, serving as but one example.

An interesting aspect of contemporary Australian theater is a maturity of vision that gives recognition to the work of Aboriginal dramatists, in particular Jack Davis (*No Sugar*, pr. 1985; *Honey Spot*, pr. 1985) and Robert Merritt (*The Cakeman*, pr. 1988; *Women of the Sun*, pr. 1989, a television series). They have pioneered a drama seemingly free of colonial and imperialist thought.

Wesley Enoch and Deborah Mailman co-wrote *The Seven Stages of Grieving* (pr. 1995), which is a collaborative work incorporating traditional Aboriginal devices. *The Seven Stages of Grieving* veers away from the idea of dramatizing the problem of "race" for a privileged, white-liberal audience. Questions of Aboriginal identity and Aboriginal land rights have moved to the forefront of Australian cultural discourse in the modern era, and in contemporary accounts of Australian drama, Aboriginal works are increasingly finding substantial discussion and analysis.

BIBLIOGRAPHY

Carroll, Dennis. *Australian Contemporary Drama.* Sydney, Australia: Currency Press, 1995. A lucid and accessible survey of figures in late twentieth century Australian drama.

Gilbert, Helen. *Sightlines*. Ann Arbor: University of Michigan Press, 1998. Occasionally dense writing, but a good overview of major figures and trends in Australian drama of the 1980's and 1990's.

Kelly, Veronica. *The Theatre of Louis Nowra*. Sydney, Australia: Currency Press, 2000. Thorough account of Nowra's dazzling career.

Tate, Peta, and Elizabeth Schafer, eds. *Australian Women's Drama: Texts and Feminism*. Sydney, Australia: Currency Press, 1997. Traces the evolution of women's drama and examines the way in which it reflects emerging feminist theory.

Vandenbroucke, Russell, ed. *Contemporary Australian Plays*. London: Methuen, 2001. This anthology of 1990's plays includes a long and useful introduction to the subject by an American critic.

Webby, Elizabeth, ed. *The Cambridge Companion to Australian Literature*. New York: Cambridge University Press, 2001. Includes two thorough and comprehensive chapters on Australian drama.

Alan L. McLeod,
updated by Nicholas Birns

CANADIAN DRAMA

Until the late twentieth century, almost all Canadian literature appeared to be self-restricted to a severely circumscribed range of subjects and themes, forms, and language. The daring and inventiveness of such fiction writers as Alice Munro, Margaret Laurence, Mordecai Richler, and Margaret Atwood, however, have helped Canadian literature, including drama, achieve a new level of mature confidence.

THE BEGINNINGS TO 1900

Historically, the dominant metaphor in the study of Canadian literature has been Northrop Frye's "garrison mentality," which he described as an unthinking herd mind that resulted in the suppression of individualism and the maintenance of the cultural status quo. Canadian drama has been particularly vulnerable to this criticism: Its themes for too long concentrated on the struggle of the settler with an intimidating and almost overwhelming natural environment (including the Native peoples) and the struggle of the individual against the formidable powers of conformity or cultural imperialism. Furthermore, Canadian dramatists have often observed the methods of established, mainline American and European playwrights, rather than those of the avant-garde. The explanation for this situation might be found in a pervasive sense of cultural colonialism, the feeling that the theater—whether in text or in performance—is fundamentally an art form that has been developed elsewhere (New York, Paris, London) and is only to be imitated in Canada.

It is generally believed that the earliest stage piece produced in Canada (then New France) was *Le Théâtre de Neptune en la Nouvelle France* (pr. 1606; *The Theater of Neptune*, 1927), which was written by Marc Lescarbot to celebrate the return to Port Royal, Nova Scotia, of Sieur de Poutrincourt from a journey of exploration. Unfortunately, this pioneering work seems not to have created any demand for theater, because thirty years passed before there was mention of another play—Pierre Corneille's *Le Cid* (pr., pb. 1637; *The Cid*, 1637). In 1694, an episcopal decree

suspended performances of Molière's *Tartuffe: Ou, L'Imposteur* (pr. 1664, rev. pr. 1667; *Tartuffe*, 1732) in Quebec, and both the drama and theater in French Canada remained moribund until the late nineteenth century.

By contrast, the British Canadian authorities encouraged the theater, both literary (Elizabethan and contemporary eighteenth century authors) and popular (farces, topical sketches, and pantomimes). Moreover, long before English-language plays were written in Canada, the country was the subject of *Liberty Asserted* (pr. 1704), a tragedy by the British literary critic John Dennis. In his play, Dennis treats the French-Iroquois wars, the beneficence of the English, and the consequences of conquest, miscegenation, and cultural pluralism. Notwithstanding his identification of several issues of lasting concern in Canada, however, Dennis's work appears to have had no discernible effect in the stimulation of playwriting in the country. In fact, for more than 150 years no play or dramatist of note appeared.

In the nineteenth century, in contrast, plays seemed to be as common as volumes of poems. Despite their number, however, only a few Canadian plays of the nineteenth century had any lasting interest or true merit. Many were closet dramas; some were intended for theater production but were neither staged nor published; a few enjoyed brief runs. In the tradition of the era, many plays incorporated songs for diversion; most contained political subject matter or allusions—often local or regional—that restricted their interest. Such is *The Female Consistory of Brockville* (pb. 1856), by the pseudonymous Caroli Candidus; the play centers on the efforts of the female members of a Presbyterian congregation to bring about the dismissal of their pastor. Another is Nicholas Flood Davin's *The Fair Grit* (pr. 1876), built around the dilemma of lovers thwarted by the political affiliations of their parents. Somewhat more imaginative is Thomas Bush's *Santiago* (pr. 1866), which explores the evil that pervades a South American country and in the process uses songs, Elizabethan and biblical language, grand melodrama, divine intervention, and exotic scenes and characters. Clearly, it is more a potpourri than a play.

Of a somewhat different character is W. H. Fuller's *H.M.S. Parliament*, popular immediately upon its performance in 1880 and for many years later. While it parodied W. S. Gilbert and Sir Arthur Sullivan's *H.M.S. Pinafore* (pr. 1878), it added topical satire and local characters and allusions and thus suggested a line of development that was not resumed until the plays of Robertson Davies.

Charles Heavysege, who migrated from England to Montreal in 1853, contributed to Canadian literature through his journalism, poetry, and drama. Indebted to the Bible and to John Milton in particular, Heavysege gave expression to a pessimistic worldview according to which God is a rather capricious and even vindictive force who dispenses injustice. This outlook can be discerned in *Saul* (pb. 1857), a closet drama of 135 scenes, and in *Count Filippo: Or, The Unequal Marriage* (pb. 1860), a five-act tragedy of love and intrigue. Although Coventry Patmore declared *Saul* to be the greatest poem in English published outside Britain, and Henry Wadsworth Longfellow judged Heavysege the greatest dramatist since William Shakespeare, today he is unread except by literary historians.

Charles Mair, who was associated with the ultra-nationalist "Canada First" movement, made tentative steps toward a national authenticity but stopped short of stellar achievement. His *Tecumseh* (pb. 1886), yet another blank-verse closet drama, remains a curiosity despite its potential: It retains the fustian and bombast of late Restoration tragedy and has its natives orate in stylized, rhetorical diction, although the play also contains powerful evocations of the frontier landscape.

A bibliography of Canadian drama in English compiled by Geraldine Anthony and Tina Usmiani lists more than two hundred women dramatists. Most were active during the nineteenth century, but not many had their plays published and fewer saw them on the stage. Almost all remain footnotes in Canadian literary and theatrical history. Nevertheless, their range can be inferred from a listing of representative examples: *Esther: A Sacred Drama* (pb. 1840), and *The Intercepted Letter* (pb. 1845), by Eliza L. Cushing; *The Secret* (pb. 1865) and *The Talisman* (pb. 1863), by Mary Anne Sadleir; and *Laura Secord, the Heroine of 1812* (pb. 1887), by Sarah Anne Curzon.

After 1875, a gradual revival of French-Canadian drama occurred, with comedy and melodrama predominating. Plays such as Félix-Gabriel Marchand's *Les faux brillants* (pr. 1885; the false jewels) and Régis Roy's *Nous divorçons* (pr. 1897; we're getting divorced), both light comedies, and numerous historical epics set in Quebec's eventful past were often commercially successful but seldom merited serious literary consideration. This situation continued for most of the first half of the twentieth century, with a slowly increasing number of theatrical productions unaccompanied by any discernable improvement in intrinsic quality.

1900 TO 1967

The founding of the Hart House Theatre in 1919 brought attention to the plays of Merrill Denison and gave a boost to English-language Canadian playwriting, for a little theater in Toronto and another in Montreal (the Community Players) seemed to offer vastly improved chances of production in major urban centers. These theaters, however, and with them the Drama League Theatre in Ottawa, could not make an exclusive commitment to Canadian drama and remain solvent. Besides, the plays that were written in the 1920's and 1930's were mainly one-act pieces, light and "popular" in the pejorative sense; some, such as Marjorie Pickthall's *The Woodcarver's Wife* (pb. 1922), reverted to an earlier mode of verse drama, dealt with tragic love feuds, and used overblown diction.

In some ways an iconoclast, Denison nevertheless made a name for himself with short, ironic plays that explored the accepted mythology of the heroic Northland, national patriotism and sovereignty, and Puritan industry and frugality. His most popular plays were collected in 1923 as *The Unheroic North*. One of them, *Marsh Hay*, has been compared in its intensity of mood with Eugene O'Neill's *Desire Under the Elms* (pr. 1924). It depicts the moral decadence of Canada's isolated communities and questions the premise that the urban environment is the least congenial to nobility, neighborliness, and morality. Within a decade, Denison left Canada for the United States, however, and the stimulus that he helped provide was soon lost, though plays in this realm continued to be written, staged, and published.

Among other plays of the 1920's, Mazo De la Roche's four slight comedies, published as *Low Life and Other Plays* in 1929, reveal a proclivity for farce; Duncan Campbell Scott's Pierre (pr. 1923), a domestic tragedy set in Quebec, deals with a prodigal's return and departure with the family savings, even as he is being extolled by his mother; and L. A. MacKay's *The Freedom of Jean Guichet* (pr. 1925), offers a melodramatic mélange of characters and themes. In the following decade, Alice Chadwicke gained momentary fame with her 1937 adaptation of L. M. Montgomery's *Anne of Green Gables* (1908). All now seem dated and of little permanent cultural value.

Of the more than four hundred plays written between the world wars, fewer than half were ever staged, and of these, perhaps no more than half were ever published in any format. According to Terence Goldie's analysis of this great mass of theatrical material, the primary thematic interests are the terrain, politics, history, and religious concerns of Canada. Melodrama and comedies prevail, and they are superficially about contemporary society—particularly about the difficulties of romantic affection—but the playwrights devote most of their energies to the manipulation of dramatic devices rather than to the exploration and elucidation of their subjects and themes. Those who seem to have the greatest potential and proficiency concentrate on characteristically Canadian materials. The plays that deal with the terrain are superior to those that deal with politics, and these, in turn, seem superior to the remainder. Because more than four hundred plays were written during these two decades, there is adequate evidence of writers' interest in dramatic composition and theatrical presentation.

During the 1940's, the Canadian Broadcasting Corporation's support of radio drama, under the en-

thusiastic leadership of Andrew Allan, helped playwrights such as Gwen Pharis Ringwood, John Coulter, and Robertson Davies to attain stature as dramatists and to influence the development of an identifiably Canadian drama. Naturally, they were not alone. Dorothy Livesay, in *Call My People Home* (pr. 1950), wrote a documentary verse drama for radio about the expulsion of ethnic Japanese from the West Coast after 1941; Patricia Joudry, in *Teach Me How to Cry* (pr. 1955), wrote a play that (in her own words), "tells the story of a troubled teenage girl who is steered away from a hazardous life of escapism by the love of a boy who has himself learned to face reality." *Teach Me How to Cry* is therefore in the tradition of Henrik Ibsen and Tennessee Williams in its juxtaposition of reality and illusion in contemporary life, but it lacks deftness in dialogue, dramatic intensity, and individualization of characters. Notwithstanding, it achieved some acclaim when staged in both New York and London.

The best of Gwen Pharis Ringwood's several plays, the one-act *Still Stands the House* (pr. 1938), and *Dark Harvest* (pr. 1945), are somewhat melodramatic studies of family relationships in farming communities during the Great Depression, but the attachment to farmhouse, family, and the infertile land is explored with great sensitivity, so that one senses the depth of the drama when a choice has to be made. Local color, despair, and the contrasted feelings for sibling and spouse are handled with unusual skill. Among Ringwood's other plays, only *The Courting of Marie Jenvrin* (pr. 1942), set in the Northwest Territories, and *Mirages* (pr. 1979), which takes place in Saskatchewan, deal with life outside Alberta. Clearly, Ringwood has the same attachment to place, and the same insights into the human condition of life on the land, that distinguishes the Nebraskan stories of Willa Cather.

John Coulter migrated from Ireland, and many of his plays, such as *The House in the Quiet Glen* (pr. 1937), and *The Family Portrait* (pr. 1937), are set there; they suggest, in many ways, the depth of his indebtedness to playwrights of the Irish Literary Revival such as William Butler Yeats, Lady Augusta Gregory, and John Millington Synge. In 1962, however, Coulter produced a clearly Canadian drama, *Riel*, which deals with the Northwest Rebellions of 1869-1885 in the Red River settlements. These were led by Louis Riel, a Manitoban of mixed Native and French—or "Metis," as this ethnic group is known in Canadian—heritage. The drama presents the protagonist as an enigmatic, charismatic, yet ruthless fanatic whose defense of Metis land rights resulted in his being tried and hanged for treason. The play is doubtless an advance on Mair's *Tecumseh*, and helps to create a new Canadian mythology through its revisionist interpretation of the consequences of the dissolution of the hegemony of the Hudson's Bay Company and the advent of Confederation.

Robertson Davies, better known for his novels than his plays, nonetheless made a definite contribution to Canadian drama with deft, short pieces of amusing and inconsequential substance such as *Eros at Breakfast* (pr. 1948) and the more serious *Fortune, My Foe* (pr. 1948), an examination of the dilemma of contemporary Canadian intellectuals and his first full-length play. *At My Heart's Core* (pr. 1950), set during the Upper Canada Rebellion of 1837, and *Question Time* (pr. 1975), in which a Canadian prime minister's psychological problems are examined in a way that reflects Davies' deep involvement with the theories of Carl G. Jung, also deserve mention.

French Canadian drama experienced a gradual revival after World War II, with playwrights such as Gratien Gélinas and Félix Leclerc breaking away from European trends and examining the workings of Quebec society. Gélinas's *Tit-Coq* (pr. 1948; English translation, 1967), in which a French Canadian Everyman fails in his quest for a meaningful family life, and Leclerc's *Le p'tit bonheur* (pr. 1959; a little happiness), an affecting portrait of rural Quebec's working class, represent the tone of serious engagement with their own culture that would dominate subsequent French Canadian drama.

In the late 1950's and 1960's, a new generation of playwrights including George Ryga, Norman Williams, John Reeves, and James Reaney came to the fore in English Canada. Ryga's *The Ecstasy of Rita Joe* (pr. 1967) drew attention to the plight of Canada's indigenous peoples and has had several international productions while becoming a repertory piece in many Canadian theaters. Williams demonstrated his skill in the one-act play form with *Worlds Apart: Six Prize-winning Plays* (pb. 1956), an anthology of six of his plays, and Reeves's *A Beach of Strangers: An Excursion* (pr. 1959) adapted the techniques of radio drama to the stage in a play that owes much to Dylan Thomas's *Under Milk Wood* (pr. 1953), but has its own distinctive vitality. Reaney has worked in myriad forms with varying success. His trilogy *The Donnellys*, written between 1968 and 1974 and consisting of *Sticks and Stones* (pr. 1973), *St. Nicholas Hotel Wm. Donnelly, Prop.* (pr. 1974), and *Handcuffs* (pr. 1975), is a stark saga of an Irish immigrant family's murder by their neighbors, and is unquestionably one of the period's major dramatic achievements.

FROM 1967 ON

Canada celebrated its centennial year in 1967, the one-hundredth anniversary of the establishment of the Dominion of Canada. Buoyed by an effervescence of nationalistic sentiment as well as major increases in funding by governmental cultural agencies, artists in every field experienced an unprecedented demand for—as well as interest in—their work. In drama as elsewhere, 1967 is considered a watershed year that marks the emergence of a distinctly Canadian identity.

In the late 1960's and early 1970's, small theater companies such as Theatre Passe Muraille, Factory Theatre Lab, Toronto Free Theatre, and Tarragon Theatre made Toronto a hotbed of dramatic production. St. John's, Newfoundland, spawned the Mummers Troupe and Codco; in the west, Saskatoon's Twenty-Fifth Street Theatre, Calgary's Alberta Theatre Projects, and Edmonton's Theatre Network were also lively centers featuring new Canadian plays and productions. The much improved theatrical climate saw the emergence of many young and talented playwrights in the years that followed, with women and multicultural writers playing a much more important part than had previously been the case.

This period also saw the emergence of Quebec's most prominent contemporary dramatist, Michel

Tremblay, whose first play, the streetwise tale of Montreal slum life *Les Belles-sœurs* (pr. 1968; English translation, 1973), was a popular as well as critical success. Many further dramas of note, including *Hosanna* (pr. 1973; English translation, 1974), *Les anciennes odeurs* (pr. 1981; *Remember Me*, 1984), *Albertine en cinq temps* (pr. 1985; *Albertine in Five Times*, 1986), and *Encore une fois, si vous le permettez* (pr. 1998; *For the Pleasure of Seeing You Again*, 1998) followed. Tremblay's work has received many international productions, and he is arguably Canada's best-known, as well as most prodigiously talented, writer for the stage.

Quebec's Robert Lepage has also made his mark on the international scene as a playwright, producer, actor, and, especially in the 1990's, film director. His first play, *Circulations* (pr. 1984; circulations), was primarily written in French, but aroused controversy in Quebec because it made substantial use of English in recounting a young woman's travels through the Northeastern United States. To his credit, Lepage has continued to insist that his art requires a multilingual as well as multidisciplinary presentation. *Aigulles et l'opium* (pr. 1992; *Needles and Opium*, 1992), which dealt with the attraction that drugs hold for some creative artists, *Le polygraphe* (pr. 1987; *The Polygraph*, 1997), a Hitchcock-like thriller about a murderer who cannot remember his crime, and *Les Sept branches de la riviere Ota* (pr. 1996; *The Seven Branches of the River Ota*, 1996), a spectacular seven-hour homage to the destruction of Hiroshima that has had several United States and European productions, stand out among his many notable accomplishments.

Although English Canada has not produced anyone of either Tremblay's or Lepage's stature, its post-1967 theater scene has been an active and productive one. For the first time in the history of the country's drama, women playwrights were as prominent as their male counterparts: Carol Bolt, Margaret Hollingsworth, Sharon Pollock, and Judith Thompson all embarked on successful careers, and male playwrights such as George F. Walker, David Fennario, Michael Cook, and John Krizanc also made particularly strong impressions during this period.

Bolt scored two early successes with plays that made interesting use of the Canadian past. *Gabe* (pr. 1973), took the revisionist view that Louis Riel's struggle for his people's rights meant little to contemporary Metis youth; *Red Emma*, (pr. 1974) re-created the life of the American anarchist Emma Goldman in fashioning a drama about the relationship between feminism and radical politics. The thriller *One Night Stand* (pr. 1977), in which a lonely young woman is terrorized by a psychotic drifter, was given a prime-time television production by the Canadian Broadcasting Corporation and has become one of the country's most popular plays. Bolt spent most of her subsequent career working with younger dramatists before she passed away in 2000.

Walker has created a notable body of work in which grotesque, surreal, and absurd elements have come to predominate. Earlier plays such as *Sacktown Rag* (pr. 1972), and *Bagdad Saloon* (pr. 1973), express this through the medium of, respectively, cartoon characters and B-movie plots; soon, however, Walker's drama blossomed into the spectacular otherworldliness of *Zastrozzi: The Master of Discipline* (pr. 1977), which blends gothic melodrama, a psychological study of obsession, and swashbuckling swordplay into a remarkable theatrical entertainment. Subsequent highlights of his prolific and productive career include: *Criminals in Love* (pr. 1984), a blackly humorous tale of small-time losers bumbling through life; *Nothing Sacred* (pr. 1988), a sharp-tongued comedy based on Ivan Turgenev's novel *Ottsy i deti* (1862; *Fathers and Sons*, 1867); and a six-play cycle of contemporary urban dysfunction, *Suburban Motel* (pr. 1997).

Operators (pr. 1974), a portrait of the complex friendship between two factory workers, inaugurated Hollingsworth's characteristic concern with relationships between women. Her *Ever Loving* (pr. 1980), a nonlinear evocation of the experiences of three war brides in post-1945 Canada, and *Poppycock* (pr. 1995), an exploration of feminist experience through innovative production techniques, stand out among her many varied treatments of this theme. *Commonwealth Games* (pr. 1998), an autobiographically based examination of what it means to be an English immigrant in Canada, demonstrated Hollingsworth's ability to find new slants on her chosen material.

Fennario has written several realistic, politically engaged dramas about Montreal's working class. *On the Job* (pr. 1975), deals with an unsuccessful factory-workers' strike from a Marxist perspective; *Balconville* (pr. 1979), a bilingual play that depicts unemployed inner-city residents acting out Canada's French and English divisions with humor as well as bitterness, has become a repertory staple; *The Death of Rene Lévesque* (pr. 1990), which some French Canadian critics found offensive in its treatment of one of Quebec's most popular political figures, continued Fennario's willingness to examine subjects that most other Canadian playwrights have eschewed. In the 1990's, Fennario chose to end his association with commercial theater and concentrate on community-based drama that would express the need for fundamental social and political change.

Pollock's career took off with the success of *The Komagata Maru Incident* (pr. 1976), based on the true story of Sikh immigrants whose ship was denied entry to Canada in 1914. Her widely admired *Blood Relations* (pr. 1980), a sympathetic treatment of Lizzie Borden and her trial for murder, as well as the harrowingly autobiographical revelations of *Doc* (pr. 1984), confirmed her status as one of the nation's major playwrights. *End Dream* (pr. 2000), in which a Scottish nanny's 1924 murder goes unsolved, and *Angel's Trumpet* (pr. 2001), a drama of Zelda Fitzgerald's attempt to maintain her sanity in an apparently insane milieu, struck a new note of postmodern ambiguity while continuing Pollock's established interest in the fortunes of the downtrodden.

Newfoundland's Cook made himself the voice of his province's past in historically based plays such as *The Head, Guts, and Sound Bone Dance* (pr. 1973), *Jacob's Wake* (pr. 1974), and *The Gayden Chronicles* (pr. 1980), before passing away in 1994. In many respects a thoroughly realistic dramatist—*The Head, Guts and Sound Bone Dance* features the gutting of codfish onstage—Cook also strove for emotional, at times melodramatic effects that would shock audiences out of their comfortable assumptions about Canada's least economically developed province. His

work constitutes an enduring and artistically powerful tribute to a region that remains somewhat apart from the Canadian mainstream.

Thompson has concentrated on violent and often surreal depictions of the lower depths of Canada's cities in plays such as *Crackwalker* (pr. 1980), whose alcoholic, mentally subnormal characters count another day survived as a victory, and *White Biting Dog* (pr. 1984), where slightly higher social status is no guarantee against a downward spiral of suffering and death. *Perfect Pie* (pr. 2000), features a successful film star who reexperiences her difficult youth in circumstances that remain tantalizingly unclear, not least because of our uncertainty as to whether she is dead or alive.

Krizanc's *Tamara* (pr. 1981), in which the audience follows the actors from room to room during a melodrama set in an old mansion, is a great audience favorite that continues to receive domestic as well as international revivals. His Governor-General's Award-winning *Prague* (pr. 1984), a blackly humorous as well as deadly serious story about producing a play in Czechoslovakia, and *The Half of It* (pr. 1989), in which capitalism and environmentalism collide with chaotic results, solidified his status as an important figure in contemporary Canadian theater.

Native Canadians and playwrights from multicultural backgrounds have also produced many interesting works. The establishment of the Native Theatre School, now the Center for Indigenous Theatre, in Toronto in 1974 enabled its students to participate in Canadian professional drama while maintaining roots in their own cultures. Tomson Highway, of Cree descent, has written two very successful plays about reservation life, *The Rez Sisters* (pr. 1987), and *Dry Lips Oughta Move to Kapuskasing* (pr. 1989), and in 1994 became the first aboriginal writer to be inducted into the Order of Canada. Drew Hayden Taylor, an Ojibway, takes a similarly unapologetic and refreshingly forthright approach to Native culture in *Someday* (pr. 1992) and *Only Drunks and Children Tell the Truth* (pr. 1996).

Two notable playwrights of African Canadian origin are George Elliott Clarke, author of the two lyrical verse-plays *Whylah Falls* and *Beatrice Chancey*, both published in 1999, and Djanet Sears, whose *Afrika Solo* (pr. 1989) and *Harlem Duet* (pr. 1997), have proven popular with audiences of all varieties. Marty Chan's Chinese heritage is the basis for his hit comedy *Mom, Dad, I'm Living with a White Girl* (pr. 1995), and Rahul Varma makes his native India the setting for the docudrama *Bhopal* (pr. 2001), which examines the consequences of a disastrous accident at an Indian chemical plant in the 1980's.

The emergence of new playwrights has been accompanied by a corresponding growth in new theatrical venues. At the beginning of the twenty-first century, Toronto's traditional dominance of English-language production was reflected in the work of such lively alternative companies as the feminist collective Nightwood Theatre, the da da Kamera company and its commitment to exploring the emotional implications of time and space, and the gay- and lesbian-oriented plays of the Buddies in Bad Times Theatre. Montreal kept pace with the French-language Carbone 14, whose multimedia exercises in social commentary were warmly greeted, and Théâtre Ubu, notable for its stylized, starkly lit interpretations. The success of The Other Theatre, a company whose radical deconstructions of contemporary media were staged in both French and English, may presage a greater degree of interaction between Canada's two founding languages. The Winnipeg Jewish Theatre opened its doors in 1987 with productions dedicated to preserving and maintaining another important strand of Canada's multicultural identity, while Calgary's One Yellow Rabbit and Vancouver's Rumble Productions concentrated on multimedia and multidisciplinary work; the latter's *A Concise History of Drumming* (pr. 1993), is a fine example of the creative integration of drama and music.

Whereas a 1960's observer of the Canadian theater scene might legitimately have discounted its significance, the remainder of the twentieth century was marked by spectacular growth in both number and quality of domestic performances. Once little more than a colonial outpost where foreign influences were slavishly and not necessarily competently emulated, Canada has now joined the mainstream of contemporary theatrical activity and appears headed for a distinguished as well as productive future.

BIBLIOGRAPHY

Ball, John, and Richard Plant. *Bibliography of Theatre History in Canada: The Beginnings Through 1984*. Toronto, Ont.: ECW Press, 1993. An exhaustive bibliography of noted playwrights and movements of Canadian theater.

Benson, Eugene, and L. W. Conolly, eds. *The Oxford Companion to Canadian Theatre*. Toronto, Ont.: Oxford University Press, 1989. This authoritative, accurate, and on the whole indispensable guide is the outstanding work of general reference in the field.

Brask, Per, ed. *Contemporary Issues in Canadian Drama*. Winnipeg, Man.: Blizzard, 1995. Each of the book's fifteen essays concentrates on a specific aspect of recent developments in theater, and together they succeed in presenting a remarkably complete overview of their subject.

Rubin, Don, ed. *Canadian Theatre History: Selected Readings*. Toronto, Ont.: Copp Clark, 1996. This most recent, and most useful, collection of original source materials covers developments from the early 1800's to the 1990's.

Rudakoff, Judith, and Rita Much. *Fair Play: Twelve Women Speak*. Toronto, Ont.: Simon & Pierre, 1990. Carol Bolt, Margaret Hollingsworth, and Sharon Pollock are among the dramatists interviewed, while play excerpts, biographies, and bibliographies are also included.

Usmiani, Renate. *Second Stage: The Alternative Theatre Movement in Canada*. Vancouver.: University of British Columbia Press, 1983. Usmiani's once-controversial thesis that 1970's experimental theater set the tone for subsequent Canadian drama is now the standard view, and her book also abounds with insightful analyses of important productions.

Wagner, A., ed. *Establishing Our Boundaries: English-Canadian Theatre Criticism*. Toronto, Ont.: University of Toronto Press, 1999. A collection of scholarly essays on the country's drama critics that ranges from 1829 to 1998, thus filling a major gap in Canadian theater history.

Alan L. McLeod
updated by Paul Stuewe

LATIN AMERICAN DRAMA

A brief survey of Latin American drama cannot do justice to the more than five-hundred-year history of such a vast continent, even if a skeptic might make short shrift of much of the dramatic literature of Latin America. From the Southern Cone to the Latino communities of North America, from the earliest mystery plays used by the Spaniards to convert and assimilate the indigenous peoples to the drawing-room comedies that have plagued serious critics and enthralled huge audiences throughout the past century, from the derivative experimentalism of arcane ensembles to the educational and agitprop methods of hundreds of revolutionary groups—all have made an impressive mark on theatrical performance.

Because of the historical importance of unscripted work (such as pre-Columbian religious rituals, colonial pageants, and "folk" theater) and of unpublished works of which only the gist and impact have been recorded, many recent scholars of Latin American theater study more than just texts that have been preserved as dramatic scripts and take into account a great deal of anthropological and even archaeological evidence to describe this complex and multifaceted history. Despite the undeniable importance of factual compilations, one must recognize the difficulty of summarizing trends and quoting names and examples too selectively, to the exclusion of many, and it is this challenge that is undertaken in this limited essay.

This summary includes only the theater of Spanish-speaking countries in the Americas, to the exclusion of Brazil and of the French- or English-speaking areas of the continent that are now considered part of Latin America. The Hispanic theater of the United States, however, is included, as a part of the historical continuum of the same linguistic and cultural area.

AZTEC PRECEDENTS

Although many civilizations flourished in Central and South America thousands of years before the coming of the Spanish *conquistadores*, the history of pre-Columbian theater is very poorly understood. There are many reasons for this gap, including the fact that few records from the ancient Mayan, Olmec, and Aztec civilizations survive, and those that do exist are difficult for modern scholars to interpret. The main records of the Aztec civilization come from Spanish monks who arrived in the New World to convert the Aztecs to Christianity: Naturally, these records are very biased in favor of European civilization.

Performance art for the Aztecs was basically religious, and demonstrated the central focus of Aztec theology: the great interconnectedness between humanity and the gods. The Aztec calendar had eighteen months, and each month was marked with a major festival paying homage to the gods: Many of these festivals involved spectacular dances of numbers of performers wearing elaborate and beautiful costumes honoring, for instance, the Aztec god of rain and wind, Quetzalcoatl. This is probably the origin of the traditional *quetzal* dance still performed annually in Mexico, in which dancers wear headgear of paper, silk, and feathers measuring up to 5 feet (1.5 meters) in diameter.

A major component of Aztec performance ritual was human sacrifice: For the Aztecs, this sacrifice demonstrated their connection to the divine, and sacrificial victims were thought to enjoy special privileges in the afterlife. One great theatrical ritual of the Aztecs was the ritual honoring the god Xipe Totec in the second month. In this ritual, prisoners reenacted sacred battles with Aztec warriors, similar to the Ta'ziyeh plays still performed in Arab countries. At the end of the battle, the prisoners were shot with arrows or had their hearts removed with flint knives. Their limbs were then eaten in a ceremonial stew at a special meal. In the fifth month ceremony, a young man who had spent a year spiritually impersonating the god Tezcatlipoca started a ritual of singing and dancing, and playing sacred instruments. At the end of the ceremony, he would climb the steps of a temple, breaking the instruments, and was seized by priests who swiftly removed his heart and head. In the eleventh month, the mother-goddess was honored by an old woman who impersonated the goddess by ritually reenacting spiritual events. Finally, she was decapitated and her flayed skin was worn by a male priest to demonstrate the unity of male and female in the divine plan.

Colonial Era

The Spanish conquest of the New World began in the 1490's, when the Aztec capital city of Tenochtitlan (now Mexico City) was one of the largest cities in the world. The Spaniards were impressed with the Aztec accomplishments: Cortes wrote to his king that the palaces of King Moctezuma were grander than anything in Spain, and the Spanish soldiers believed the marketplaces of the city to be greater than those of Rome or Constantinople. However, the conquering Spaniards saw the indigenous Americans only as misguided savages despite their ancient and complex culture and their great achievements in architecture, art, weaving, and metalwork. To Spanish monks, the great Aztec gods were merely the devil in disguise, and converting the Aztecs and destroying their culture became a primary mission of the conquering Spaniards.

Theater was one of the chief forms of entertainment of these newcomers, who often performed *actos*, *entreméses*, or even dramas to fill their leisure time. Thus in the explorers' chronicles there are reports that soldiers acted for fun in the late sixteenth century, in Northwestern outposts that are now part of the southwestern United States, and in the 1760's, shortly after Spain acquired the Falkland Islands, off the coast of modern-day Argentina, from France, the local garrison put on a three-day festivity that included dramatic performances, with props and materials provided by the military governor.

Theater was from the beginning a proselytizing tool. Some of the earliest attempts by Spanish missionaries to convert the natives involved the Spanish equivalent of the Passion plays and miracle plays of Western Europe. The evangelical zeal of the conquerors went to extraordinary lengths, as evidenced by the willingness of the friars to learn native languages and to present religious doctrine (often through drama) in those languages, and by the cultural syncretism between Catholicism and Indian beliefs that appears

even as late as the mid-seventeenth century, in an allegorical play by the famous Mexican writer Sor Juana Inés de la Cruz.

Plays brought as instruments of ideological control and religious persuasion became part of the heritage of the common people. Miracle plays can still be seen in Mexico (and in the former Mexican territories of the southwestern United States); villagewide reenactments of the Passion plays are still common at Easter in many parts of Mexico and Central America, and the quasi-ritualistic *Moros y cristianos* plays keep alive the allegorical struggle between Christians and the Moors, in mock battles and in full costume, throughout Latin America and even in the Philippines. Yet these traditional forms of Spanish theater survive primarily only at the level of folk theater, and it was only in the late twentieth century that professional theater groups returned to them as sources of material and artistic expression, integrating them into a theater with a much wider audience.

Theater has served as a medium for satire or social protest in Latin America since the sixteenth century, but this was not a radical departure from one of the traditional functions of theater throughout the Middle Ages either. The earliest recorded case of a playwright being punished for writing such material was that of Cristóbal de Llerena, who in 1588 was banished to the Caribbean coast of South America from Santo Domingo for having published an *entremés* that satirized corruption and poor government in the colony.

Throughout the history of the colonies, theater played an important part in community entertainment, mainly at public holidays (such as the king's birthday) or in pageants and festivities welcoming a new viceroy or other dignitaries. There could be private performances of the latest plays from Spain, or of works by native authors, in the courtyards or ballrooms of distinguished residents, while in streets and plazas one often found plays presented by guilds and brotherhoods and performances by Indians or blacks that reflected the variety of ethnic influences already present in the colonies. Within the first half-century of Spanish rule, religious plays were being performed in colleges, and occasionally the students and scholars would introduce a secular play that might merit censorship because of its content.

The development of theatrical activity in the different colonies depended on the degree of encouragement or repression offered by the representatives of the crown and by the Church hierarchy. In some cases, an enlightened viceroy or captain-general would strike a deal with the bishop, by which the Church would lift its ban on theatrical performances, and box-office returns would go to a needy institution (such as an orphanage, a women's hostel, or a hospital).

Theater was usually presented in improvised public spaces or in a *corral* owned by an entrepreneur, but by the end of the eighteenth century, most principal cities of the Spanish colonies had theater houses to cater to the Mestiza elite and a rising bourgeoisie. Entertainment was not necessarily the priority only of liberal governments: One of the most impressive theaters was built in Havana by Captain-General Miguel de Tacón, who headed a very repressive government during the Cuban War of Independence; the Paraguayan dictator José Gaspar Rodriguez Francia, who virtually sealed his country from the outside world, was a devotee of culture and built a beautiful theater.

THE ERA OF INDEPENDENCE

Drama and theatrical activity played a minor albeit interesting role in the transition to independence and in nation building. The end of the eighteenth century brought the success of the *sainete* (a genre made popular in Spain by Ramón de la Cruz), the characters of which were drawn from everyday contemporary society and were often social types; these characters reflected the particular social makeup of a given colony, and in the unique ethnic origins, opinions, and speech patterns presented onstage, the colonized could begin to see their own distinctive national identity.

The patriotic theme was the subject of a few plays throughout Latin America, beginning in Chile, Peru, and Argentina between 1812 and 1820, then in Mexico around 1820 and eventually Cuba and Puerto Rico beginning around mid-nineteenth century. *Abdala* (pb. 1869), by the Cuban patriot José Martí, is an allegory of independence with an African hero,

an early attack on colonialism, specifically Spanish domination of Cuba.

In Argentina, on the eve of independence, one could find some rural comedies and satires of Spanish theater. In Cuba, after the remainder of Latin America was free and long before Cuba's wars of independence (1868-1900), comedy developed through the fifty-year career of a brilliant actor and impresario, Francisco Covarrubias, the author of several dozen comedies that laid the foundation of Cuban theater. (The texts were lost; only records of the performances remain.) *Costumbrismo* (comedy and drama that depict social types and customs) dominated the scene in most countries, and elements of it resurfaced even in the naturalist theater of the early twentieth century.

Romanticism flourished in the nineteenth century with several distinguished playwrights, such as Francisco Javier of the Dominican Republic, Alejandro Tapia y Rivera of Puerto Rico, Joaquín Lorenzo Luaces and Gertrudis Gómez de Avellaneda of Cuba, and Carlos Bello of Chile. A theater of ideas or for social or political protest appeared occasionally: Juan Bautista Alberdi wrote his dramatic satire while in exile from Argentine dictator Juan Manuel de Rosas between 1838 and 1879, and Alberto Bianchi was jailed in Mexico in 1876 for criticizing the draft in *Los martirios del pueblo* (pr. 1876; the people's martyrdom).

The *teatro bufo* of Cuba, with its stock characters, spanned a quarter-century and had its counterparts in Puerto Rico and the Dominican Republic. It, too, was an important spawning ground for impresarios, actors, musicians, and playwrights. It is interesting to note that although many of the plays elicited sympathetic responses from patriotic (anti-Spanish) audiences, many of the playwrights were opposed to independence, and that the early *teatro bufo*, with its comic sketches of unique freshness, gave way after independence (1900-1920) to burlesque and vaudeville similar to those of the United States.

TWENTIETH CENTURY DRAMA

As the independent republics became relatively stable democracies with increasing industrialization and European immigration, the theater continued to develop along two main lines: "serious" drama that addressed grave questions and moral issues or the human condition, in a fairly traditional, formal structure; and popular theater that broached topical issues or questions of morality, lightly at best, in a satiric vein.

The first sophisticated social drama emerged in the early twentieth century, with the theme of national identity still prominent, either in response to a changing historical and political reality or as a new perspective on the same old problems of race and class. Historically, playwrights, like other Latin American artists and intellectuals, have been committed to their role as critics and are often involved, through their main profession (as teachers, journalists, and diplomats), in the affairs of their country. Many have used drama as a medium for expressing their commitment; a few good writers have made the stage a powerful forum for debates by characters that are often allegorical or stereotypical yet manage to move an audience and to challenge prejudice, outmoded behavior, and destructive systems.

José Antonio Ramos, a leading Cuban intellectual and a diplomat, analyzed his country's most basic conflicts, embodied in different family members whose future is tied to their large estate in his play *Tembladera* (pr. 1917). The play explores intergenerational conflict and the roots of Cuba's economic crisis; American penetration of Cuba, especially after the Spanish-American War, and the remnants of loyalty to Spanish tradition; and the contradictions inherent both in cultural tradition and in progress.

Between 1903 and 1906, Florencio Sánchez in a similar naturalist vein attacked the prevailing assumptions about national identity and immigration in Argentina and Uruguay. His *Barranca abajo* (pr. 1905; down the precipice) exposes the real condition of an old peasant: Changes in economic relations and control of the land strip him of his property and his dignity, leading him to suicide. *La gringa* (1904; *The Foreign Girl*, 1971) is about the daughter of Italian immigrants: Her marriage to a local youth promises a solution to the conflict between the value systems of

the "old," rural Argentina (or Uruguay) and the different austerity imposed by the newcomers.

Antonio Acevedo Hernández, who was influenced by Florencio Sánchez and Russian author Maxim Gorky and by Pyotr Kropotkin's ideas, detailed in a fairly brutal manner the degradation of the rural poor in Chile. He won the national theater prize four times in forty years with such plays as *Almas perdidas* (pr. 1917; lost souls, a play about the slums of Santiago), *La canción rota* (pr. 1921; the pauper song, about the indentured farm laborer), and *El arbol viejo* (pr. 1928; the old tree, about young people leaving their roots and their father to go to the city).

In Mexico, some of the strongest naturalist drama of the years before the revolution of 1910 was written by Federico Gamboa, who is better known as a novelist. *La Venganza de la gleba* (pb. 1907; the revenge of the soil) is considered to be the first weighty criticism of the system that was crushing the Mexican peasant.

Historical drama finds its best voice, perhaps, in Rodolfo Usigli, who in a famous "antihistorical" trilogy challenges three historical myths of Mexico: the apparition of the Virgin of Guadalupe in *Corona de luz: La virgen* (pr. 1963; *Crown of Light*, 1971); the role of Doña Marina in Hernán Cortés's conquest of Mexico and the martyrdom of chief Cuauhtémoc in *Corona de fuego* (pr. 1960; crown of fire); and the madness of Carlota, after the execution, by a Mexican firing squad, of her husband, Emperor Maximilian, in *Corona de sombra* (pr. 1943; *Crown of Shadows*, 1946). In each of the dramas, the historical characters are at once fictionalized and humanized, thus becoming keys for a new, critical understanding of three crucial periods in the formation of the modern Mexican nation: the conquest and domination of the indigenous peoples; the merging of cultures; and the emergence of the liberal republic under Benito Juárez (the historical antecedent of the revolution of 1910).

An equally celebrated play of Usigli is *El gesticulador* (pr. 1947; the impostor), one of the earliest critiques of the political system that was established after the revolution. The play's protagonist, a history professor, enters politics by assuming the identity of César Rubio, a revolutionary hero who disappeared during the war, but the protagonist finds that he has entered a labyrinth of lies. The protagonist is murdered by the rival candidate, a corrupt politician who was responsible for the death of the original César Rubio, and the protagonist's death (blamed on a fanatic enemy of the revolutionary party) becomes the killer's ticket to victory. The analogy to Julius Caesar is obvious, as Usigli takes a historical referent that to this day epitomizes the ambiguity of power and of human motivation, adapting it to illustrate also the ambiguities of contemporary events. Usigli's younger contemporary Wilberto Cantón looks very critically at a turning point in the revolution in *Nosotros somos dios* (pr. 1965; we are God).

CONTEMPORARY DRAMA

The final four decades of the twentieth century saw terrible upheavals in Latin America: poverty, disease, hunger, natural disasters, guerrilla fighting, oppression, torture, kidnappings, hijackings, strikes, riots, wars, and the appearance of death squads, drug cartels, and massacres of indigenous peoples, all of which incited a more widespread feeling of discontent with government across the continent. Social protest and dissent met with repression, including assassinations and disappearances. Playwrights and other theater artists have come to figure prominently as agents of social and political protest, combining aesthetics with what Paulo Friere called *conscientizaçao*, or "conscienticization." Building on the political theater writings of Bertolt Brecht, certain playwrights led a movement collectively known as "Theatre of Revolt." So effective has this movement been in challenging oppression that theater has become the art form of those most frequently harassed by military governments. Playwrights have been censored, arrested, and tortured; theaters have been closed or even burned down by government forces. Around 1973, the year of the military coup in Chile and widespread continental unrest, theater in Latin America suffered a near-paralysis, which in some places persisted for years. Yet certain playwrights' works have managed to persist in these horrifying periods.

Socially conscious theater has flourished in Chile since the 1970's in the work of several outstanding playwrights. Among the forerunners in this century

are María Asunción Requena and Isidora Aguirre, who have written about women's struggles, of relations between whites and Indians, and of class conflict; and the poet Pablo Neruda, with his *Fulgor y muerte de Joaquín Murieta* (pr. 1967; *Splendor and Death of Joaquin Murieta*, 1972), a re-creation of the tragic life of Chilean prospectors in the California gold rush. Since the 1950's, audiences have seen Egon Raúl Wolff's carefully choreographed invasions of the bourgeoisie's comfortable space by threatening creatures from the wrong side of town in *Los invasores* (pr. 1964; the invaders) and in *Flores de papel* (pr. 1970; *Paper Flowers*, 1971); Jorge Díaz Gutiérrez's neoexistentialist critiques of modern alienation, such as *Réquiem para una girasol* (pr. 1961; requiem for a sunflower), followed by a powerful piece on the miners of Chile, *El nudo ciego* (pr. 1965; the blind knot), and by the ferocious satire *Topografía de un desnudo* (pr. 1967; the topography of a nude), about the 1963 massacre of Brazilian peasants; and Alejandro Sievking's critical view of political oppression in Chile in *Pequeños animales abatidos* (pr. 1975; small downcast animals).

Social and political themes have been presented by equally sophisticated writers in other countries, especially in Argentina, which has produced some of the continent's leading playwrights. Three excellent examples are Osvaldo Dragún, Andrés Lizárraga, and Griselda Gambaro, whose works are proof of the possibility of achieving universal appeal along with very specific messages about history, social relations, and economic questions.

Dragún, active since the mid-1950's in popular theater, has dealt with some of his country's (and Latin America's) most difficult themes: class relations and the malaise of youth in *Y nos dijeron que éramos inmortales* (pb. 1962; and they told us we were immortal); the tendency to rely on formulaic ideas to solve problems that require an original, native solution in *Heroica de Buenos Aires* (pr. 1966); and the power of economic pressures that can turn one into a watchdog for hire, let one die of an abscessed tooth, or kill hundreds of Africans with tainted meat for the sake of a multinational corporation's profits in *Historias para ser contadas* (pr.

1957; *Stories for the Theatre*, 1976). Dragún has also handled a historical figure that has become a favorite of the Latin American stage, the Inca Tupac Amaru, who led a major rebellion against the Spaniards in the eighteenth century; in *Tupac Amaru* (pr. 1957), the tormentor is ultimately driven mad by the spiritual resistance of the physically broken and defeated hero.

Lizárraga has criticized the narrowness of provincial life, the hypocrisy of Argentina's social system, and the sentimentalization of history as a tool of social control. Some of his best work is contained in his trilogy about the wars of independence; one play in this trilogy, *Santa Juana de América* (pr. 1960), is an award-winning portrait of a female revolutionary figure, presented in a Brechtian style.

Griselda Gambaro's work is sometimes labeled Theater of Cruelty or Theater of the Absurd, because of its formal and structural similarity to European and North American works of those genres. Yet it is profoundly rooted in Argentine reality, and despite its possibilities as an art that dissects the most perverse aspects of human relationships, it points to the larger picture: that of a society whose collective psyche was already torn, by the mid-1960's, between "Cains," who took pleasure in asserting their power and their cruelty, and "Abels," who suffered passively, and sometimes foolishly, through deceit and betrayal. A good example is her *Los siameses* (pr. 1967; *The Siamese Twins*, 1967).

In *El campo* (pr. 1968; *The Camp*, 1970), Gambaro creates a brilliant piece of ambiguity (despite its almost mechanical workings): The title translates as "the countryside" (where the main protagonist, who controls the events, insists that the action is taking place) or as "the camp," that is, a military camp or a concentration camp, an interpretation suggested by most of the signs (the physical appearance of the main character in his uniform, the brutal behavior by guards toward the "guests," and the cries of pain). The irony of the play is that while its main referent is the Nazi experience of the 1930's and 1940's (with its possible relevance to Argentina, where so many Nazis fled after the war), its ideological structure is not entirely alien to Argentina: The climate of the "liberal democracy" shifted radically in the 1960's, and

the polarization resulted in the excesses of the 1970's, when such concentration camps became a reality, and when the entire society began to function in ambiguous codes—the authorities denying their actions (much like the play's protagonist), and the victims (society at large) accepting the authorities' definition of reality.

In 1977 Gambaro's novel *Ganarse la muerte* (to earn one's death) was banned and Gambaro left Argentina to live in Spain and France, returning in 1980 and continuing her work as a playwright. Gambaro received a great deal of global attention with her 1973 play *Información para extranjeros* (wr. 1971; *Information for Foreigners*, 1992), which for many critics captures the spirit of "postmodernism" perfectly. The play, which is about incidents of state violence in Argentina, actually forces its audience to engage with the staged theater in a very powerful way. The play is staged in a house, with the audience broken up into small groups, each with a "guide." The guide moves the groups through the house, opening doors and witnessing scenes within rooms. As the groups progress, the boundaries between "performance" and "reality" blur until the audience is forced to question its role in both, and come to grips with its own culpability for allowing state violence to continue.

Among this generation of good writers, one should also include Eduardo Pavlovsky, a psychiatrist by profession, whose characters' psychological makeup (often one of twisted and perverse cruelty) is usually explored in a sociopolitical context, such as the Caribbean dictatorships of François Duvalier (Papa Doc) and Rafael Trujillo, as an allegory relevant to any country.

Strong social protest and revisions of history and myth are central to the works of the Colombian Enrique Buenaventura, whose plays can be a vicious indictment of class oppression, and whose *Los papeles del infierno* (pr. 1968; the papers of Hell) documents the terrible period of modern Colombian history known as "La Violencia" through a series of short plays about ordinary human beings caught in the whirlwind of political violence and repression.

In Venezuela, José Ignacio Cabrujas and Román Chalbaud have been leading contemporary authors who also see the stage as a vehicle for questioning history and politics. Cabrujas's work is more clearly one of protest, not merely against the corruption inherent in institutions, but also against the mechanisms that corrupt pure individuals who attain power. Although Cabrujas writes in the style of Brecht, Chalbaud has played with the soap opera, with games and rituals, and with eroticism and thus resists any easy label as a "protest" writer.

Sebastián Salazar Bondy of Peru wrote a series of social dramas, moving on in the early 1960's, immediately before his death, to a unique dramatic style all his own, filled with irony and with elements of farce and popular comedy. Manuel Galich of Guatemala, an exiled member of the Arbenz government deposed in the 1953 coup, persisted in a straight theater of denunciation, tempered only by sardonic humor; Galich's works are among the few to deal so specifically with United States involvement in Latin America.

Cuban theater has always been among the most active and progressive in the Americas, with many distinguished writers and directors. Individual playwrights such as Virgilio Piñera, José Triana, Manuel Reguera Saumell, and Carlos Felipe are typical of the best, and they all treat social themes through fairly solid texts and (with the exception of Triana) largely conventional techniques.

These four authors span the period immediately before and after the triumph of the revolution in 1959. Their main concerns are social; their main focus, the individual's interaction with his or her environment (family, a slum, the effects of the revolution, institutional corruption under Fulgencio Batista), and one even finds, in Felipe's *Réquiem por Yarini* (pr. 1960), a powerful portrait of a famous pimp.

Triana's works reflect society in a critical light. His chief works were created on the eve of the 1959 revolution and present darkly satiric visions of "sacred" institutions such as the Church and the family, using mythical allusion and ritual devices that sometimes make his work very reminiscent of that of French playwright Jean Genet. In fact, his award-winning *La noche de los asesinos* (pr. 1966; *The Criminals*, 1967), in which three young people enact

their parents' murder, bears a strong resemblance to Genet's *Les Bonnes* (pr. 1947; *The Maids*, 1954).

Puerto Rican drama has found its finest expression in the works of a number of authors since the 1950's. Francisco Arriví tackled such difficult subjects as racism, the role of the intellectual (at a time when intellectuals were highly vulnerable because of their pro-independence views), and the complexes that beset the Puerto Rican psyche. Arriví's best-known work perhaps is his trilogy that includes *Vejigantes* (pr. 1957; mummers). René Marqués pursued political themes more aggressively, always obsessed with the nature of Puerto Rican identity as a culture and as a nation. His *La carreta* (pr. 1952; *The Oxcart*, 1969) has become a classic portrayal of the migration of Puerto Ricans, from the country to San Juan to New York and a life of continued economic hardship compounded by social problems such as drugs and prostitution.

MODERN GENRES AND THEMES

The great majority of theatergoers in Latin America continue to flock to lighter fare, to comedy, to musicals. The tradition of the *género chico* is uninterrupted: The comedy of social customs, the farce, and the musical comedy or review have always been the mainstay. In the traveling *carpa* (tents) of Mexico and the southwestern United States and in the *sainete criollo* (Argentine version of the Spanish *sainete*, with tangos and social types from Buenos Aires), in the prolific production of the Alhambra Theatre of Havana (where some of Cuba's best playwrights and musicians exercised their profession), and of other locales around the continent where vaudeville coexisted with good, solid comic drama, and in far more reputable playhouses, such as the San Martín municipal theater of Buenos Aires, literally thousands of scripted plays have entertained millions. Many of the best playwrights still work in that style, while a great many also combine elements of this popular tradition with European conventions à la Georges Feydeau or Noël Coward (adapted to Latin American culture). Even in revolutionary Cuba, the *comedia musical* has thrived through the pen of such good playwrights as Héctor Quintero and José Brene.

Among authors who have worked on psychological drama or fantasy, certain popular names stand out: Conrado Nalé Roxlo and Carlos Gorostiza of Argentina; Celestino Gorostiza, Xavier Villaurrutia, Salvador Novo, Carlos Solórzano, Elena Garro, Maruxa Vilalta, Luisa Josefina Hernández, and Rafael Solana of Mexico; Isaac Chocrón of Venezuela; and Elena Portocarrero and Julio Ortega of Peru. Many, influenced by Eugene O'Neill and Tennessee Williams, have sought to create characters of great psychological complexity, while others have created outright fantasies in which the characters play in dreamworlds.

COLLECTIVE CREATIONS AND POLITICAL PERFORMANCE

The 1960's brought with its revolutionary politics a corresponding movement in the theater. Much as the workers' theater of the 1930's and 1940's and the popular theater (the products of the Mexican revolution in the 1910's and Fray Mocho in Argentina in the 1950's) had gone out in search of their audience, many of the young actors, directors, and writers in the 1960's chose to place their craft at the service of the revolution.

Following the example of Fray Mocho and Augusto Boal in Brazil, and Enrique Buenaventura and Santiago García in Colombia, dozens of theater groups established themselves in strategic relationship to the communities that they wished to serve and to "conscientize" (educate toward liberation). The internal process of each group was revolutionized, with collective sharing of responsibilities and with collective creation becoming the most significant single change in playwriting in centuries.

Buenaventura, for example, gave up individual playwriting to become an equal member of the collective that he had founded in Cali. A number of groups (such as El Aleph of Chile, Libre Teatro Libre of Argentina, and Grupo Escambray of Cuba) produced quality plays through this method. In a few cases, groups of playwrights collaborated on a single play, the most famous example perhaps being *El avión negro* (pr. 1970), a satire about Juan Perón's return to Argentina, coauthored by Roberto Cossa, Carlos Somigliana, Ricardo Talesnik, and Germán

Rozenmacher, all distinguished Argentine playwrights. Collective creation caught on particularly in the community-based theater groups, whose interest was mostly in theater as an instrument of education and social change; Latino theater groups in the United States (particularly in the Chicano groups through their association TENAZ) have been active promoters of the process to this day. Its limitations have been amply demonstrated, however, in the quality of the texts produced, and it has become clear that a good, strong playwright is necessary to produce the end product of a collective process.

Another of the "Three B's" of Latin American Theater (along with Brecht and Buenaventura) is Augusto Boal. Boal has explored the relationship between politics and performance possibly more intimately than any other contemporary theorist. In 1971, Boal was arrested, tortured, and exiled: Even during his imprisonment he continued writing, and his play *Torquemada* (pb. 1972) is an autobiographical account of those events, in which he compares his torturers to those who participated in the Spanish Inquisition. Boal's book *Teatro del oprimado y otras poéticas políticas* (1974; *The Theatre of the Oppressed*, 1979) is now included as standard reading for most advanced theater theorists. Boal as a director engaged in a variety of experiments to create the revolutionary theater he envisioned: These experiments blurred fantasy and reality, creating unexpected theater in unusual places, such as restaurants, to demonstrate the freedom of the individual.

Community-based groups continued to flourish in the 1980's despite political and economic difficulties. The movement has flourished in Cuba and Nicaragua in particular, where it receives considerable official support, with hundreds of amateur and semiprofessional groups from which talented individuals are routinely singled out for professional training.

LATINO THEATER IN NORTH AMERICA

Latino theater in the United States grew impressively during the last decades of the twentieth century, a result primarily of two factors: the immigration of large numbers of Cubans and Puerto Ricans to the New York area and the growth of community movements among the Chicano population. Many Cuban and Puerto Rican artists, actors, and writers moved to New York in the mid-1960's and assumed an active role in the cultural life of the city, founding theater groups and workshops and boosting the activity of such pioneering groups as the Puerto Rican Travelling Theatre. It became possible to attend different Spanish-language theater performances every night of the week in New York, ranging from Spanish classics to Latin American repertory to original works by local authors.

The Chicano movement in California in the 1960's grew out of the civil rights and the farmworkers' movements. El Teatro Campesino sprang directly from agitprop work with César Chávez's organization and from experience with the San Francisco Mime Troupe. Teatro de la Esperanza, and, later, other community-based groups developed along similar lines. Teatro Nacional de Aztlan continues to exist, with more than one hundred member groups from all over the United States, with links to Mexican theater; in these links it has restored a relationship that had existed well into the twentieth century between the theaters of the United States and Mexico, through the Mexican companies that toured the American Southwest and California.

The Chicano and other community theaters tend to use original material or adaptations of repertory and classics, and some individual authors, such as Luis Miguel Valdez, have moved into the mainstream with works that deal with the Mexican American experience and culture. The work of Valdez with El Teatro Campesino, stunningly visual and powerful, reaches back to the performance rituals of pre-Columbian Aztec cultures, thus ideologically and politically separating itself from the European conquerors. In addition, his work clearly associates the Anglo-dominated U.S. government with the Spanish imperialists. The community theaters have established good working relationships with Chicano studies programs at various universities, through which Chicano theater has become legitimized as a subject of research and scholarship.

Among the most popular of modern Mexican American theater artists since the 1990's is Guillermo Gomez-Peña, a poet and playwright as well as actor, and regular commentator on National Public Radio (NPR). His work, along with that of Coco Fusco, emphasizes the multiple ethnicities of American culture and attempts to dissolve borders between identities. His performances use modern imagery of supersophisticated technology combined with ancient Aztec iconography, creating bizarre hybrid characters like El Mexterminator, Cyber-Vato, and El Naftazteca.

Theater festivals continue to bring groups, directors, writers, and critics together. Now these festivals are held not only in Manizales, Colombia, in Havana, in Mexico, or in Caracas, but also in New York, in Montreal, and in other North American cities. Latin American theater has overcome the balkanization that had plagued it for centuries, as it had plagued all former Spanish colonies: Since the 1960's, writers and directors, companies, and scholars of different countries have met and shared their work and their experience. The historical tie between the Latino culture of the United States and the cultures of Latin America is being restored, thanks in part to the theater.

BIBLIOGRAPHY

Albuquerque, Severino J. *Violent Acts: A Study of Contemporary Latin American Theatre.* Detroit, Mich.: Wayne State University Press, 1991. Provides an extremely useful, if disturbing, model for uniting twentieth century Latin American "Theatre of Revolt" across many countries and cultures by pointing out the recurring themes of riot, murder, assassination, and state-sponsored torture.

Allen, Richard F. *Teatro hispanoamericano: Una bibliografía anotada (Spanish American Theatre: An Annotated Bibliography).* Boston: G. K. Hall, 1987. Allen's guide is a good place to start when searching for materials on this subject. It is superior to some earlier versions because of the content and usefulness of its notations, which give the reader some idea of where a particular listing will lead.

Dauster, Frank N. *Historia del teatro hispanoamericano: Siglos XIX y XX.* Mexico City, Mexico: Ediciones de Andrea, 1966. An early work by one of the established writers of the field, this work is generally held to be a comprehensive history of the era, although now dated. An important text for pre-1960's drama but not to be considered alone, especially if researching pre-Columbian performance roots. In Spanish.

_____, ed. *Perspectives on Contemporary Spanish American Theatre*. Lewisburg, Pa.: Bucknell University Press, 1996. Dauster is one of the most respected writers in the field and here he has assembled some excellent essays to help provide several good models for analyzing recent Latino drama.

Gardner, Joseph L., ed. *Mysteries of the Ancient Americas*. Pleasantville, N.Y.: Reader's Digest Association, 1986. Assembled by the editors at *Reader's Digest*, this is a good first book for those who are just beginning to study pre-Columbian America. Full of lush photographs and artwork, this book has great information about the performance rituals of the Aztecs and other indigenous peoples, and explores how those traditions merged with medieval and modern ones under Spanish influence.

Gomez-Peña, Guillermo. *The New World Border*. San Francisco, Calif.: City Lights Books, 1996. Winner of the American Book Award, a collection of satirical dramatic texts as well as essays and poems by the border-busting artist. At turns funny and thought-provoking, Gomez-Peña is one of the most prominent inheritors and innovators of the Latino "Theatre of Revolt" tradition, linking modern hip-hop Anglo-American culture and ancient Aztec religion in a fascinating mix.

Huerta, Jorge A. *Chicano Drama: Performance, Society, and Myth*. Cambridge, England: Cambridge University Press, 2001. Using informative biographies of playwrights and analyses of their plays, discusses the way in which Chicano and Chicana dramatists negotiate cultural differences.

Weiss, Judith A., and Leslie Damasceno. *Latin American Popular Theatre: The First Five Centuries*. Albuquerque, N.M.: University of New Mexico Press, 1993. Focuses on such specific topics as the urban theater; popular forms, characters, and ideology; theater in the 1960's; and new trends in drama from the region.

Woodyard, George W., and Leon F. Lyday, eds. *Dramatists in Revolt*. Austin: University of Texas Press, 1976. Although this is an older book, it has taken its place as one of the fundamental texts for understanding anti-government theatrical traditions in Latin America.

Judith A. Weiss,
updated by Michael M. Chemers

WEST INDIAN DRAMA

Since Christopher Columbus's voyage, the people of the West Indies (or the Caribbean, as the region is now more commonly known) have been sharply divided between the privileged and the dispossessed, the elite and the common, the rich and the poor. (Until 1838, there was also the division between the free and the enslaved.) The development of drama in the West Indies, or the Caribbean, closely follows the region's historical and cultural development, from its colonial beginnings, through the periods of slavery and emancipation, to the growing national consciousness in the twentieth century that led to political independence for most of the English-speaking islands. From the first theater in the region, in Jamaica in 1682, until the 1930's, drama in the West Indies largely followed English fashion, serving to maintain the colonizers' identity with their mother country. The goal of creating an indigenous West Indian drama—that is, one that addresses the West Indian experience and is created by and for the native West Indian—has determined the direction of theatrical endeavor since the 1930's.

The gradual blending of European and African cultural traditions over nearly five hundred years has produced the modern West Indian Creole languages and cultures. Thus, the question of what is and is not distinctively West Indian in drama is part of the larger issue of cultural heritage. African elements in the folk traditions are strongly dramatic, especially in the carnival and Calypso of Trinidad, the mummers in many smaller islands, and the pantomime and Pocomania in Jamaica. Participants in the carnival masquerade called "The Pierrot," for example, wear elaborate costumes, usually with headpieces and long trains held by small boys. Each man carries a whip. They set out through the city, and whenever they encounter one another, they exchange long speeches. If one falters in his elaborate oratory, he feels his rival's lash. The mummers of Nevis and Saint Kitts perform in the streets during Christmas and Easter holidays. They recite, play, dance, and mime stories, many of them derived from medieval English mumming plays,

Arthurian legends, and Renaissance drama. The argument that theater is a European institution and therefore alien to the West Indies ignores the significant assimilation of English custom into the culture.

Nevertheless, it is true that for the first 250 years of its existence, the West Indian theater was the property of the elite. The colonial theater existed for the privileged, for the plantation owners, the governors, and the young Englishmen who came in search of wealth and exotic experience. Actors and plays were English, performed for audiences whose cultural identity was still centered on Great Britain, rather than on the New World. Eighteenth century New York actors would proudly add to their credits a brief respite in the Jamaican theater: a theater almost wholly British in character and content. The few plays from that period that included West Indian characters or settings used them for exotic appeal or to support the antislavery movement, as in Richard Cumberland's *The West Indian* (pr. 1771) and the romantic comedy *Inkle and Yarico* (pr. 1787) by George Colman the Younger. More typical of the dramatic treatment of slave life is Thomas Southerne's *Oroonoko: Or, The Royal Slave* (pr. 1695), a Restoration tragicomedy, based on Aphra Behn's novel about an African prince who is kidnapped by an English captain and sold into slavery in Surinam. The prince's wife becomes the object of the deputy-governor's passion and the subject of a comic underplot.

FIRST THEATERS AND FORMAL PLAYS

Barbados had its first dramatic society in 1729, Antigua in 1788, and Saint Lucia in 1832. By the 1820's, Port of Spain, the capital of Trinidad, supported three theaters and five performing companies. The repertoire was imported, except for a few short plays by Edward Lanza Joseph, who came to Trinidad from Scotland in 1820 and wrote plays and poetry until his death in 1840. He was dubbed "the Bard of Trinidad" because his plays, notably *Martial Law* (pr. 1832), were set locally and dealt with timely subjects.

Through the nineteenth and early twentieth centuries, plays by local playwrights were generally written in the manner of William Shakespeare, with West Indian characters providing comic relief. The Jesuit C. W. Barrand wrote two such five-act plays in blank verse: *St. Thomas of Canterbury* (pr. 1892) and *St. Elizabeth of Hungary* (pr. 1890). The epic *San Gloria* (pr. 1920), by Tom Redcam (the pen name of Thomas H. MacDermott), a play about Columbus, is in a similarly Elizabethan vein, but Redcam's sympathetic treatment of the Afro-West Indian presents a marked contrast to the usual treatment of blacks as lowlife characters speaking comic, pidgin English. The few black characters appearing in West Indian drama of this period were always played by white actors in blackface, but even when the situation would appear to demand black characters, they were usually omitted. The 80 percent black majority of Trinidad had no part, for example, in the first West Indian historical drama, Lewis Osborn Iniss's *Carmelita: The Belle of San Jose* (pr. 1897). Written for the centenary of England's takeover of the island from Spain, the play concerns a young English officer who falls in love with the young Spanish beauty Carmelita. Their union is a symbol of England's affectionate husbandry of its colony, yet the black population whose labor sustained the colony had no part in the historical drama.

The playwright George Bernard Shaw visited Jamaica in 1911 and in a press interview told Jamaicans that they ought to nourish their own culture by, among other projects, building a theater and keeping the American and English traveling companies out of it. He said that if the Jamaicans would write their own plays and do their own acting, the English would soon send their children to Jamaica for culture, instead of the other way around.

EARLY TWENTIETH CENTURY

As he so often lamented, Shaw went unheard. For the next three decades, wealthy Jamaicans continued to travel to the United States and England to attend plays and maintain cultural connections, and in January of each year, a touring English company would stage plays at very high prices in Kingston.

Nevertheless, given the growing national consciousness of West Indians in the 1930's, Shaw's advice proved prophetic. The first play about the black experience in the New World to feature a historical figure of heroic stature was *Touissant l'Ouverture* (pr. 1936), by the Trinidadian writer C. L. R. James. The play was produced in London with Paul Robeson in the title role. A number of West Indians who had been studying or working in England at that time returned to the Caribbean with an interest in changing the theater to include working-class people who had largely been excluded from productions (except for Marcus Garvey's outdoor theater in Jamaica in the early 1930's). Una Marson returned to Jamaica in 1937 to produce her play *Pocomania* (pr. 1938), which was the first play to use the African-derived religion named in the title as dramatic material.

THE 1940's AND 1950's

Later, once again in England, Marson founded the British Broadcasting Corporation (BBC) program *Caribbean Voices* (1942), which, along with a number of new magazines and drama groups, gave strong impetus to a new generation of West Indian playwrights, poets, and novelists. Magazines that published local writers were founded: *The Beacon* (1931) in Trinidad, *Bim* (1942) in Barbados, *Focus* (1943) in Jamaica, and *Kyk-over-al* (1945) in Guyana. An upsurge of interest in drama created a number of groups, including the Little Theatre Movement (1941) in Jamaica, the White Hall Players (1946) in Trinidad, the Georgetown Dramatic Group (1948) in Guyana, and the St. Lucia Arts Guild (1950) in St. Lucia. Committed to developing an indigenous drama, such groups needed more work from local playwrights. Edna Manley in the 1948 edition of *Focus* published Cicely Howland's *Storm Signal* and George Campbell's *Play Without Scenery*, but lamented in the issue's foreword that the Little Theatre Movement was still in great need of Jamaican plays.

Little more than a decade later, the Trinidadian playwright Errol Hill claimed that there were twenty-seven West Indian dramatists writing at home or abroad, and twenty years later, the Georgetown Public Library published a list of more than one hundred

Guyanese plays, many of which had been produced by the Theatre Guild of Guyana, founded in 1957. The University of the West Indies has published its Caribbean Plays Editions from its extramural departments in Jamaica and Trinidad since the 1950's, and has made available scores of plays.

The theater groups have done a great deal to encourage both writing and production of West Indian plays. While strongly identified with the annual pantomime, the Little Theatre Movement of Jamaica has produced work by many West Indian playwrights, notably Errol Hill, Errol John, Barry Reckord, Trevor Rhone, and Dennis Scott. The Theatre Guild of Guyana gave the first Caribbean production of John's *Moon on a Rainbow Shawl* (pr. 1957), which won the London *Observer*'s play competition of 1957 and has been produced in Europe, North and South America, and Australia. The Guild also premiered Evan Jones's *In a Backward Country* (pr. 1959) as well as work by many Guyanese playwrights, most notably Frank Pilgrim's *Miriamy* (pr. 1962) and Sheik Sadeek's *Porkknockers* (pr. 1974).

THE WALCOTT BROTHERS

The St. Lucia Arts Guild has the distinction of having produced the two most prolific and important playwrights in the Caribbean, the twin brothers Derek and Roderick Walcott. Both are legendary in the region, Derek Walcott having won the 1992 Nobel Prize in Literature. Though less well-known outside the Caribbean than his brother, Roderick Walcott is highly regarded for his dramatically powerful use of the Creole of St. Lucia, as well as his integration of folk traditions and music in dramatic situations. His best-known plays include *The Harrowing of Benjy* (pr. 1958), *A Flight of Sparrows* (pr. 1966), *Banjo Man* (pr. 1972; performed at Carifesta, Guyana), and *Chanson Marianne* (pr. 1974), which was commissioned for the Conference of Prime Ministers of the West Indies meeting in St. Lucia in 1974. The commitment of a playwright of Roderick Walcott's stature to remain in the West Indies gives reason for hope that the exodus of writers that has plagued the region since Claude McKay left Jamaica in 1912 is at least slackening.

Derek Walcott is the one West Indian playwright of truly international stature; he is also widely regarded as one of the foremost contemporary English-language poets. He has written dozens of plays, nearly two dozen of which are available in print. His accomplishments are legion. The production of his verse play *Henri Christophe: A Chronicle* (pr. 1950), about the Haitian monarch, is widely regarded as the foundation of an indigenous West Indian drama. Though the production was staged in London, the cast and crew were West Indian, and included many of the region's leading writers. The Barbadian novelist George Lamming wrote the prologue; Hill, who directed the London production, and John, the lead actor, are both prominent Trinidadian playwrights. When the newly independent Caribbean nations attempted to unite under a federal government, Walcott was commissioned to write a play for the inauguration of the first Federal Parliament. The result was an epic drama, *Drums and Colours* (pr. 1958), that spans four hundred years of history in episodic scenes framed with interludes of carnival dancers. Walcott founded the Trinidad Theatre Workshop in 1959, after studying theater in New York under a Rockefeller Foundation Fellowship. In 1966, the workshop became the first company to produce a complete theatrical season with West Indian players, and in 1967, it became the first West Indian company to tour internationally. In those successive seasons, the workshop premiered two of Walcott's most ambitious plays, *The Sea at Dauphin* (pr. 1950) and *Dream on Monkey Mountain* (pr. 1967). Caribbean drama history widely acknowledges the impact of the latter, which is regarded as exemplary of Walcott's dramatic work. In 1972, the Royal Shakespeare Company commissioned his musical *The Joker of Seville* (pr. 1974).

The 1980's saw a further flourishing of Walcott's dramatic output. He continued to premiere his plays in Trinidad, where his social comedy *Beef, No Chicken* (pr. 1981) opened at the Little Carib Theatre. The play offers a light treatment of government corruption and public lethargy in a small Caribbean community. Symbolic of the people's unwillingness to make even small, easy steps toward further economic development, Otto's Auto-Repair and Authentic Roti

Shop, which gives the play its title, is content to offer only beef rotis. Walcott's next play, *The Last Carnival* (pr. 1982), premiered in Trinidad in spite of a controversy over the inclusion of some American actors. The play argues that white Creoles are as much a part of the Caribbean's culture and history as are people of other races. It views decolonization as an outgrowth of British socialist thought. Like many of Walcott's plays, it has been translated and performed abroad. The Swedish version, *Sista karnevalen* (pr. 1992), was very successful and contains a few significant changes by the playwright.

On November 25, 1983, Walcott opened *A Branch of the Blue Nile* (pr. 1983) at Queen's Park Theatre in Barbados. The play addresses the issues facing professional theater in the Caribbean, with its limited resources and limited indigenous plays. Ostensibly about the staging of Shakespeare's *Anthony and Cleopatra* (pr. c. 1606-1607) by a Caribbean troupe modeled after the Trinidad Theatre Workshop, the cast sees plenty of infighting and philosophical arguments. In addition to an illicit love affair, the play features introspective musings about the merits and dangers of staging a European masterpiece with local talent.

Ironically, *A Branch of the Blue Nile* was the last drama that Derek Walcott produced in the Caribbean in the 1990's and into the twenty-first century. Instead, he used England for the premiere of *The Odyssey: A Stage Version* (pr. 1992). An adaptation of the Homeric epic set in a contemporary Caribbean world, the play opened to favorable reviews. By 2002, it was Walcott's only new dramatic play after winning the Nobel Prize in Literature, which was awarded primarily for his poetry. Walcott's script for Paul Simon's controversial musical *The Capeman* (pr. 1998) depicts the story of a Puerto Rican teenager, Salvador Agron, who murders a white teenage couple on a dare from his gang. With the group "Parents of Murdered Children" protesting its Broadway premiere on January 29, the show folded by March 28, 1998.

THEORETICAL DEBATE AND INTERNATIONAL INFLUENCE

Although a truly indigenous West Indian drama began only in the 1930's, the centuries-old folk tradi-

tions have readily lent themselves to the creation of unique West Indian theatrical styles. Critical debate in the theater continues, however, over which heritage, the African or the European, best expresses the West Indian experience. Critical judgments continue to be based on the use of European and African elements in the work, such as metropolitan versus Creole English in dramatic speech. Using the poetic richness of Creole is to limit appeal outside the region, but using metropolitan English in favor of a larger audience is to falsify local character.

C. L. R. James, foremost scholar of Caribbean literature, died in May of 1989 and left behind a legacy of critical understanding of not only Caribbean literature but also world literature. In many respects, with the awarding of the 1992 Nobel Prize in Literature to Derek Walcott, West Indian drama came of age, and Walcott's work has been popular for some time since.

West Indian drama also became more popular and accessible in 1985 with the publication of *Caribbean Plays for Playing*, edited by Edith Noel, in which new West Indian playwrights were introduced to a more general public, and whose introduction gave the student of West Indian drama some valuable insights into the origins of experimental theater. The book explains the experimental basis of the folk comedies of Ed "Bim" Lewis and Aston "Bam" Wynter in Jamaica, Freddie Kissoon in Trinidad, and Dennis Scott, Rawle Gibbons, "Sistren" (the all-female Jamaican group that performs documentary theater), and the actors' theater of Ken Corsbie and Mark Mathews in Guyana. Younger writers such as Kendel Hippolyte of St. Lucia and the commercially oriented works of Trevor Rhone are also mentioned. Other playwrights represented in this important anthology are Zeno Obi Constance and Aldwyn Bully. Less well known is Earl Lovelace, primarily a novelist but also a playwright of several plays, including *Jestina's Calypso* (pr. 1976).

CHALLENGES OF THE 1990'S

In Barbados, the competitive drama festivals organized by the island's National Cultural Foundation continue to foster the emergence of local talent. Anthony Hinkson and Winston Farrell are well-known

local playwrights. The career of Glenville Lovell signifies the drain of local talent that has plagued theater
in the West Indies. In 1992, Lovell produced his political play dealing with the 1983 intervention by the
United States in Grenada, *When the Eagle Screams*,
with a premiere in Trinidad. By the middle of the decade, he had moved to New York to find a larger audience for his dramatic output. Too often, the local
stage is considered too small and provincial by ambitious Caribbean professionals, who dream of international success in New York or London. Those who remain involved in local productions often hold outside
jobs, such as Barbados's Jeannette Layne-Clark, a
playwright of successful satires like *Pampalan '89*
(pr. 1989), who also works as a journalist.

To combat the loss of local professional talent,
two complementary approaches emerged on Barbados and elsewhere. The first is the Popular Theatre
Movement, which seeks to bring theater to local communities and develop short plays dealing with social
topics of local relevance. The second are the efforts
of professional organizations such as Barbados's production companies Stage One Theatre Productions
and W. W. B. Productions, which seek to produce local plays with local dramatic talent and to tour the
Caribbean and the world with its most successful productions.

Within the Organization of Eastern Caribbean
States (OECS), a group of loosely allied Caribbean
island nations, professional theater remains underdeveloped. Local playwrights and performers quickly
desire larger venues for their talents once they rise
above the level of amateurs. Therefore, Derek
Walcott has not produced his plays in his native St.
Lucia for several years. Leon Symester, who took the
politically inspired name of Chaka Wacca, left his native Antigua for the United States after writing and
producing a series of protest plays in the 1970's. The
dramatic theater that has remained is often characterized by modest production values, drawing on talent
who do not rely exclusively on theater for their livelihood. Characteristic of many other such outfits is
Rick James's Theatre Ensemble on Antigua, which
performs brief, locally written plays with modest casts
at tourist hotels and resorts on the island. The Popular

Theatre Movement seeks to fulfil a social and educational community function and occasionally draws
funding from state or international sources. Lack
of accessible and affordable performance space has
plagued theater companies in Dominica and St. Lucia, for example. Local plays are staged in abandoned
schools or hurricane-damaged cinemas on Dominica.
Because the government of St. Lucia charges fees out
of the range of most producers for the use of its
cultural center, playwright-producers such as Kendal
Hippolyte have opened small theaters such as his
Lighthouse Theatre, which seats slightly more than
one hundred spectators.

TRINIDAD CARNIVAL

By 2000, formal theater had not yet recovered its
previous vitality in Trinidad and Tobago. This was
largely because of the government's disastrous 1999
decision to terminate the lease for the Old Fire Station Building, used by the famous Trinidad Theatre
Workshop since 1989 as a dramatic venue, effectively
derailing the most professionally successful theatrical
outlet in Trinidad. The decades of work that Derek
Walcott and his collaborators had invested in restoring the building and creating a thriving arts center
around this location were lost.

However, the Trinidad Carnival continues to
thrive. A dramatic event that is unique in its elaborate
quality, Trinidad Carnival has been celebrated annually for more than 220 years and has inspired the best
local talent. Key dramatic figures of the Carnival are
the Calypsonian, a professional singer whose satirical
lyrics often reflect on topical issues, and the masked
Revellers, who accompany the Calypsonian with
mimed sketches and pantomime performances.

In the 1990's, the Carnival was aesthetically influenced by the costume designs of Peter Minshall,
whose work freed the masked Revellers, including
the carnival King and Queen and other stock figures,
to perform elaborate pantomime routines while still
dressed in splendid attire. Minshall's political and
ecological concerns gave the Carnivals of the 1990's
a special flair. His costumed bands took on issues
such as protection of the environment, global warm-
ing, and the specter of nuclear holocaust. In 1992,

Minshall and his troupe performed *The Arrival of Christopher Columbus* (pr. 1992) during the opening acts for the Summer Olympics in Barcelona, Spain, using a ship to symbolize Columbus's arrival to the New World.

The Calypso, sung at the Carnival, with its emphasis on satirical song and accompanying pantomime, also inspired Caribbean playwrights beyond the Carnival event itself. Rawle Gibbons wrote a cycle of three plays about the Calypso theater experience, *Sing de Chorus* (pr. 1991), *Ah Wanna Fall* (pr. 1992), and *Ten to One* (pr. 1993), further attesting to the cultural impact of this unique dramatic form.

2000 AND BEYOND

By 2002, Jamaica, the largest English-speaking island of the Caribbean, offered one of the brightest spots for theater, with a diverse and flourishing dramatic scene. Most popular is the Jamaica pantomime, a combination of music, song, dance, and text focusing on realistic or fantastic subjects. Its audience appeal throughout the island is immense, and its shows at Kingston's Ward Theatre enjoy long, sell-out runs of many months.

Unique to Jamaica are the plays of "Roots" (short for "Grassroots") Theatre. These are original, locally written and produced plays with a strong focus on sexual issues. They follow the tradition of Jamaica's Bim and Bam shows of an earlier age, which also centered on sexual (mis)behavior and the sexual escapades of their comic characters. Jamaican "Roots" theater, as produced, for example, by Ralph Holness, can be outright explicit and bawdy. It is a traveling theater form and features a small cast, relatively few props and scenery, and can be performed in almost any venue, ranging from a school hall to a cinema converted for the occasion. While productions for the countryside rely most heavily on sexuality for their audience appeal, the more urbane productions of Ginger Knight and Balfour Anderson strive to add dramatic sophistication to their sexual humor.

Formal theater, based on plays written by Jamaican, Caribbean, or international playwrights remains popular among urban theatergoers. In Kingston, the Little Theatre, Barn Theatre, and the massive 1,200-seat Ward Theatre are filled with spectators during their seasons. Trevor Rhone, who founded the Barn Theatre with fellow Jamaican producer and actress Yvonne Brewster in 1971, still writes original plays that attract Caribbean-wide attention. Revivals of European and American plays are equally successful.

In Jamaica, government support for the arts and funding of the Jamaica School of Drama at Mona has remained stable, ensuring opportunities for the growth of local talent. Yet even under these favorable circumstances, the migration of exceptional dramatic talent, especially to English stages, has remained an unsolved problem. The situation is much worse elsewhere. In Guyana (formerly British Guiana), the 1990's saw an unfortunate decline of the once-vibrant theatrical scene as economic and political problems caused the departure of most well-known indigenous talent. Playwrights Michael Abbensetts, Jan Carew, and Ian Valz had all left by 1995.

Wherever there has not been committed official support for local drama, emerging playwrights, actors, or dancers have left their Caribbean countries, where opportunities are difficult to come by. One of the largest challenges for local drama is to develop and maintain a substantial pool of local theater talent so that the creative impulses shaped by the Caribbean's unique multiracial and multicultural environment will not be lost to the stage. The Reichhold Center for the Arts at the University of the Virgin Islands has become an important philanthropic venue dedicated to the promotion of local talent. Under the directorship of the Montserrat playwright David Edgecombe since 1992, the Reichhold Center has put on an impressive production schedule of Caribbean plays. Founded in 1972, the Carifesta, an artistic festival dedicated to showcasing the best of Caribbean arts and culture, saw its seventh installment in August, 1999, in St. Kitts and Nevis. Organized to run every few years at a different location, Carifesta VII featured more than one thousand artists from the Caribbean and abroad and produced plays and theatrical workshops as well as other artistic activities in an artists' village built for the occasion.

The future development of Caribbean drama is dependent on the ability of local playwrights to stay in tune with their original communities. Playwrights should feel able to draw further inspiration from topics and concerns emanating from their countries, rather than feeling forced to seek artistic fulfilment elsewhere. Once this condition is met, Caribbean theater can experience a new renaissance.

BIBLIOGRAPHY

Corsbie, Ken. *Theatre in the Caribbean*. London: Hodder and Stoughton, 1984. A perceptive insider's view of the development of Caribbean drama by one of Guyana's most active playwrights. Covers its origins through the tumultuous 1960's and 1970's.

Hill, Errol. *The Jamaican Stage, 1655-1900*. Amherst: University of Massachusetts Press, 1992. Groundbreaking study by a famous Caribbean playwright and critic, providing a fascinating historical overview of the origins of Jamaican dramatic traditions and the many multiracial and multicultural conflicts that accompanied the development of a genuine local dramatic tradition.

_____. "Perspectives in Caribbean Theatre: Ritual, Festival, and Drama." *Caribbean Quarterly* 46 (September-December, 2000): 1-11. Text of a lecture that offers fresh insights to the topic by Hill, who speaks from rich personal experience. Emphasis is on African roots of Caribbean theatrical forms.

Innis, Christopher. "Dreams of Violence: Moving Beyond Colonialism in Canadian and Caribbean Drama." In *Theatre Matters*, edited by Richard Boon and Jane Plastow. Cambridge, England: Cambridge University Press, 1998. Comparative analysis of Derek Walcott's play *Dream on Monkey Mountain* by a Canadian professor dedicated to the study of Caribbean theater.

King, Barnaby. "The African-Caribbean Identity and the English Stage." *New Theatre Quarterly* 16 (May 2000): 131-136. Discusses African-Caribbean theater in the United Kingdom, with an emphasis on the problems of obtaining funding for productions that do not attempt to transform Caribbean theater into one aspect of British multiculturalism. Interesting view of the fate of Caribbean productions abroad and their impact on British society.

Okagbue, Osita. "The Strange and the Familiar: Intercultural Exchange Between African and Caribbean Theater." *Theatre Research International* 22 (Summer, 1997): 120-129. Engaging look at what Okagbue terms an African world view and its transmission in African and Caribbean plays. Uses two models, "theater as storytelling" and "theater as dream-ritual," to offer a detailed analysis of plays by Caribbeans Derek Walcott and Trevor Rhone, who in turn are juxtaposed with African playwrights Wole Soyinka and Efua Sutherland.

Olaniyan, Tejumola. *Scars of Conquest/Masks of Resistance* Oxford, England: Oxford University Press, 1995. Somewhat theoretical study that includes a useful chapter on Derek Walcott in light of the playwright's work with historical Caribbean subject matter. Also touches on the theoretical conflict of writing plays in English or Creole. Bibliography and index.

Omotoso, Kole. *The Theatrical Into Theatre: A Study of the Drama and Theatre of the English-Speaking Caribbean*. London: New Beacon Books, 1982. Still one of the best studies of Caribbean theater from its origins to 1980. Offers background on Caribbean theater during the days following independence, which saw much dedicated dramatic activity. Chapters focus on the role of family, nationalism, and language. Bibliography and index.

Stone, Judy S.J. *Studies in West Indian Literature: Theater*. London: Macmillan, 1994. Excellent, in-depth study by a playwright and critic from the Caribbean. Offers a fascinating, well-researched view of Caribbean theater in English, with emphasis on the theater of the 1920's. Her comprehensive bibliography attempts to list every major published and unpublished play of the region. Bibliography of critical sources as well as an index.

Robert Bensen, updated by R. C. Lutz
and Thomas J. Taylor

DRAMATIC GENRES

DRAMATIC GENRES

The classification of Western dramatic works into genres owes less to playwrights than to critics and theorists. Every age has tried to redefine preexisting genres in terms of its own preoccupations or has tried to invent new genres in order to categorize novel phenomena that do not fit the terminology available. Occasionally playwrights themselves concur in using these labels and even, as in the Renaissance and neoclassical periods, meekly follow the guidelines set down for them by academicians. For the most part, however, whenever drama has thrived, the dramatist's creation has preceded or preempted the critical definition. Consequently, the study of dramatic genres is not so much that of taxonomy as an inquiry into theatrical and literary fashion, as reflections of a society's values and concerns.

TRAGEDY AND COMEDY

The ubiquity of the laughing and frowning masks as a symbol of drama is a constant reminder that the two major genres, tragedy and comedy, took on definitive shape in Attica in the fifth century B.C.E. Speculating on the origins of Greek tragedy has been a favorite pastime of scholars for more than two hundred years, and there are more points of contention than there are extant Greek tragedies. Aristotle's speculation, which has been supported or endorsed by most classical scholars, is that tragedy originated in the wild Thracian rites of Dionysus or, more specifically, out of the later lyric dithyramb, a cantilena performed in the god's honor. Dionysus is a complex deity who combines the contradictions of life giving and death dealing, therapeutic bliss and wanton cruelty, dynamic possession of his worshipers and passive destruction by them. In accordance with his manifold nature, the choral plaint expressed both exuberant joy and profound grief, though with joy predominating.

Aristotle asserted that the word "tragedy" derived from *tragōn oidē*, a song of goats, usually taken to mean a hymn sung by a chorus, clad in goatskins to resemble satyrs, as they danced around the altar of Dionysus. Gerald F. Else, in *The Origin and Early Form of Greek Tragedy* (1965), has pointed out that this is a linguistically impossible compound; a more likely etymology is a formation from *tragoidos*, "goat singer or goat bard," from the prize that he received in competition.

Whatever the case, tradition has assigned specific developments to specific individuals. Arion of Lesbos (seventh century B.C.E.) is said to have been the first to spurn improvisation and write a dithyramb in advance, and also the first to compose a dithyramb not about Dionysus but about a heroic subject. This narrative poem, sung to music, was a rudimentary drama, not unlike an operatic oratorio. Thespis of Athens, which was a chief seat of the Dionysian cult, is credited with composing the first tragedy, in 534 B.C.E., a work consisting of a prologue, a series of choral songs, and a dramatic set speech, or *rhesis*, which had a strict tripartite structure, so that the thought enunciated at the start was restated at the end. Thespis eliminated the satyrs and gave the choral leader, in this case himself, the part of *hypokritēs*, or expositor, performing these recitations as monologues and advancing the action by brief dialogues with the chorus. By wearing a series of masks, he could assume different characters. In opposition to the lyric recitations of the chorus, these narrative passages were logical exhortations or straightforward descriptions that in turn elicited the choral response.

According to Else's suppositions, Thespis based his tragedy not on divine myths but on the Homeric legends, more native to Athens and very much in the tradition of the rhapsodist's recitations from Homer. With Thespis's innovations, the epic hero, the idea of impersonation, and iambic verse combined to give Greek tragedy its special character.

Thespis's innovations were so well approved that they became a leading feature in the Athenian festival of Dionysus, where further development was to be concentrated. Later improvements were made by Phrynichus, who introduced an actor who was distinct from the chorus leader, known as the *prota-*

gonistēs; added female roles both in the chorus and for the *rhesis*; and modified the preponderance of the choral contribution, which at that time dominated the play. Aeschylus further subordinated the chorus, reducing its role by adding a second actor, the *deuteragonistēs*; finally, a third actor was introduced by Sophocles, completing what became the standard cast size: Any poet who entered the public competition would be subsidized only for up to three actors and a chorus of twelve (later expanded to fifteen by Sophocles). It should be made clear, however, that, by changing masks and costumes, the actors could portray many more than three characters; nonspeaking figurants were also employed.

At the dramatic competitions held during the City Dionysia of Athens, each poet staged a tetralogy, consisting of three tragedies followed by a satyr play. The tragic trilogy is believed to have originated as an expanded form of the prologue-*rhesis*-*rhesis* sequence, designed to accommodate the second actor. In Aeschylus's time, the three tragedies were internally connected by plot, as in his *Oresteia* (458 B.C.E.; English translation, 1777), an association that Sophocles is said to have discarded. The satyr play may have been a concession to public protests that the new tragic form had ousted the fun-loving roistering of the Dionysia. It was reputed to have been an invention of Pratinas of Phlius (c. 500 B.C.E.), who adapted the dithyramb to a tragic format but retained the choric dances performed exclusively by satyrs, as was customary in his birthplace. The satyr play provided comic contrast to the tragedies that preceded it and, by featuring Silenus and his goatish entourage, emphasized the link with Dionysus. The plot of a satyr play was not necessarily comic; indeed—deriving, like tragic plots, from epic or legend—it might be somber in tone. The merriment came from the intervention of the drunken, lecherous, impudent satyrs capering about. Aeschylus was considered a master of the form, but the only extant satyr play is Euripides' *Kyklōps* (c. 421 B.C.E.; *Cyclops*, 1782).

Any discussion of Greek tragedy must be qualified by an admission of the paucity of extant texts. Some fourteen hundred tragedies may have been composed and performed in Athens alone, yet of these, only thirty-two by three authors, all of Athens, survive intact, along with a number of fragments and allusions. In general, however, tragedy is concerned less with gods than with people and especially with the hero's "pathos," or moment of emotional crisis. In tragedy, death is seen very much as the inevitable end of mortals; transfiguration or transcendence is seldom a possibility.

Before Aeschylus, the fit subjects for tragedy were the Homeric heroes and their progeny; Aeschylus enlarged the subject matter to include the struggles between gods and Titans, as in *Prometheus desmōtēs* (date unknown; *Prometheus Bound*, 1777), and relatively current history, as in *Phoinissai* (c. 410 B.C.E.; *The Phoenician Women*, 1781) and *Persai* (472 B.C.E..; *The Persians*, 1777). He also intensified the conflict, or agon, between individuals and between the protagonist and the chorus, in order to lead up to the protagonist's pathos. For the most part, tragic poets recycled the same heroic stories but were free to formulate new motivations and variants. Agathon, a contemporary of Euripides, is said to be the first to have invented a purely original plot, in *Antheus* (pr. c. 425 B.C.E.; the flower), which is no longer extant.

Structurally, Greek tragedy generally consists of the *prologos*, a scene that precedes the first entrance of the chorus; the *parodos*, the first important choral sequence; the *epeisodion*, a scene of dialogue or monologue that divides the choral songs; the *stasimon*, the choral song following each episode; and finally, the *exodos*, or withdrawal, following the last chorus. (On an open-air stage, chorus and actors would have to make their exits in full view of the audience.) There are, however, numerous variations on this pattern, and over time the chorus's role was reduced until Agathon turned it into a mere intermezzo, whose songs were unrelated to the plot. The prologue, which had been a relevant part of the action, was often used by Euripides as a set speech informing the audience of antecedent action (for which he was ridiculed by Aristophanes). In later days, when actors became virtuosos who toured the Greek world with their repertories, solos were introduced as star turns.

Reflecting the rhetorical nature of Attic civilization, almost all tragic action is unfolded in speech. Because the story begins close to its culmination, a large amount of exposition is required, and heralds, messengers, and similar ancillary figures report off-stage occurrences at length. The chorus functioned as a moral regulator by which the spectator might gauge his reaction to events, a signpost to significant elements that might otherwise be overlooked, and a significant part of the spectacle. Most important, its songs abstracted the situation by drawing historical parallels and thus allowed time for reflection on past actions and on those to come.

Comedy shares with tragedy and satyr drama a common origin in Dionysian revels; its name is related to the song of the *kōmos*, or mirth-making procession of Dionysus, that followed a ritual banquet. The Dorians of Megara claimed to have been the first to elaborate into full-fledged farce this impromptu horseplay, with its flaunting of totemic phalluses and its vigorous raillery. The genre gained a literary patina in Sicily from Epicharmus (c. 540-450 B.C.E.), who probably added a formal chorus to what had become a blend of philosophical debate, rhetoric, and monkeyshines; he also varied the mythological plots with stories taken from real life. These products were known as *motoriae*, because of their loose structure and violent action.

The chief seat of the worship of Dionysus in Attica was Icaria, where a more polished form of the Megarian comedy was introduced, possibly by Susarion, about 580 B.C.E. Comedy remained a minor genre, however, until the Athenians, around the time of the Persian Wars, fused its phallo-phoric choruses to a structure based on that of tragedy. The state granted to the genre a subvention and status in an annual festival, possibly because of complaints that satyr plays were not sufficient to represent riotous license at the Dionysian holidays.

This form of comedy, known as Old Comedy, flourished during the heyday of Athenian democracy and its immediate aftermath. Indeed, only in such a liberal society could Old Comedy have developed, with its sharp political satire and unbridled humor. The actors sported leather phalluses and wallowed in scatology and sexual innuendo, in both word and gesture. As in some of the village festivals that still survive in Greece, personal abuse and invective played a major role. Old Comedy bristled with in-jokes and scurrilous assaults, even on members of the audience, to such a degree that the Athenians prudently banned both foreigners and slaves from attendance. The raw material of real life was present in Old Comedy, heightened to a pitch of grotesquerie and lyric fantasy.

Originally, comedy had probably opened with a choral dance and ended with the *kōmos*. Its mature structure followed the pattern of tragedy, with a prologue, episodes, choruses, and an exodus, but it also featured a parabasis, a production number that usually occurred in about the middle of the play and in which the enlarged chorus (twenty-four as opposed to tragedy's fifteen members) made a direct appeal to the audience. The author might use the parabasis to request the prize, or the chorus might harangue the public on a topical issue or offer advice on current events. In theory, it consisted of seven separate parts, but they were seldom all present. (As a rule, Greek comedy was a much more flexible and adaptable genre than tragedy.)

Unlike tragedy, which drew its stories from myth and legend, Old Comedy seldom began *in medias res*. The opening of the comedy would set forth the basic premise of the plot: Usually, a malcontent character sets out to remedy an abuse by an extreme measure. This convention is evident in the works of Aristophanes, the only comic dramatist of the period whose plays (eleven of them) have survived in complete form: In *Lysistratē* (411 B.C.E.; *Lysistrata*, 1837), the title character resorts to a sex strike to bring about peace; in *Ornithes* (414 B.C.E.; *The Birds*, 1824), two dissatisfied Athenians leave their hometown to found a new community with the aid of the feathered kingdom; in *Nephelai* (423 B.C.E.; *The Clouds*, 1708), a father sends his dissolute son to be enrolled in Socrates' school, only to find that the boy grows even more dishonest under this Sophistic tutelage. Once the plot point is established, the play's structure is open enough to accommodate all sorts of tangents and digressions. Aristophanes, and most likely his competitors at the comic contests, sought first and foremost to amuse the audience; careful plot making and artistic refinements were not prime considerations. Whole episodes and stretches of dialogue were fabricated to raise laughs, built as a joke is built, with the necessary repetitions, key words, odd dialects, and retards to evoke the maximal mirth.

Less subject to religious decorum than tragedy, comedy also displayed more violence and action onstage and thus reduced messengers and expository speeches to a minimum (except when used to poke fun at tragic conventions). On the other hand, the reconciliatory banquet was seldom brought to view, perhaps because it was too closely connected to the religious rites from which comedy sprang. If, as some scholars contend, this was the case, it runs counter to the blasphemous mockery of the gods and their service that characterized Old Comedy. More plausibly, it might be argued that the final banquet was kept offstage as an event to which the audience might be invited, at least figuratively; in this way, comedy brought together a whole community that it had previously shown to be divided.

Both tragedy and comedy were spectacles, considerably embellished with stylized speech, music and dance, and a quantum of scenic effect; these elements were crucial to the planning and financing of the festivals. In his *De poetica* (c. 334-323 B.C.E.; *Poetics*, 1705), Aristotle, who had little taste for "opsis," the physical aspect of theater, belittled its significance, treating it as a side issue, and in this he has been closely followed by literary critics for centuries. For the original audience, however, much of the chorus displayed to best advantage in the parabasis; similarly, the thrill of some plays lay partly in the horrific masks and gestures of the characters. If Euripides was mocked for his overreliance on machinery and costuming, the criticism came from conservative connoisseurs and not the popular audience.

ARISTOTLE'S DEFINITIONS

The mention of Aristotle brings this discussion to the first formal definitions of tragedy and comedy, based on the types of drama that had evolved by 340 B.C.E. In his esoteric and fragmentary *Poetics*, Aris-

totle proposed a taxonomy of literary forms that he believed to be solidly grounded on the organic nature of the phenomena under discussion. As a natural scientist, he took a biological approach to literature and, by inductive reasoning, hoped to synthesize his analyses of representative specimens into a conclusive scheme of differentiation. Aristotle examined the available works and decided that the tragedy of Aeschylus, Sophocles, Euripides, and their colleagues represented a fully evolved form of poetry, which had been achieved only after passing through such stages as the epic and the ode. The nature of tragedy, therefore, lay in its entelechy; its constituent parts existed to perform tragedy's primary function, which was philosophical. Almost as if demonstrating how the physical attributes of a fish conduce to its behavioral survival, Aristotle anatomized tragedy to show how its features were part of a rational, well-functioning whole, productive of pleasure and reflection.

Aristotle's definition of tragedy, found in the *Poetics* (and given here in the familiar 1902 translation of Samuel Butcher), is the *locus classicus* of Western discussions of tragedy. For Aristotle, tragedy is

> an imitation of an action that is serious, complete, and of a certain magnitude; in language embellished with each kind of artistic ornament, the several kinds being found in separate parts of the play, in the form of action, not of narrative; through pity and fear effecting the proper purgation of these emotions.

Through the centuries, every item in this definition has been subjected to intense scrutiny and interpretation, but in essence, Aristotle's formulation has been accepted as the standard by which to distinguish tragedy from lesser genres of drama. The preeminence of tragedy is vital. Aristotle was the first to proclaim it the ultimate and superior dramatic form. In that, as in his sharp distinction between tragedy and comedy, most thinkers have followed him unquestioningly.

The instinct for imitation, or mimesis, was a basic principle of Greek art, the artist striving not "to express himself" but to perceive and bring forth whatever was essential in nature. The imitation, a harmonized and purified version of the original, would thus complete nature by distilling its ideal qualities. In this way, it would transmit the abiding and universal Ideas or Forms to the observer and aid in what Plato called "sound opinion," the basis for wisdom. Plato himself had scorned art, seeing it as a reflection of the truth, but Aristotle exalted poetry as superior to "history, in that it deals with the universal." Tragedy chose only such actions to imitate as would best illustrate the persisting and permanent truths of human nature.

The "serious, complete action of a certain magnitude" is in turn imitated in action, through the actor's performance and byplay, as well as by the playwright's creation. This is less simplistic than it sounds, because, for Aristotle, action was the product of character and thought, the outward manifestation of inner motivation. Thought can only be represented onstage as speech, and in a culture as verbal as the Greek, this meant subtle argumentation and suasion rather than the cogitative soliloquies of a Hamlet. Indeed, in Greek tragedy there is nothing that can properly be called a soliloquy. A character explains his motives, intentions, or feelings to the chorus or to another character, to gain acceptance of his point of view. This rhetorical expertise confirms the tragic hero's intellectual prowess.

It has been argued that Aristotle's definition of tragedy is too narrow, that it fails to conceive of a "tragic vision" of the world or a dramatic work as a paradigm for existence. In fact, his proposal of purgation (catharsis) as the proper effect of tragedy is a fruitful place to look for a broader meaning. It is also the most debatable item in his definition, but all the other facets of tragedy are relevant only insofar as they discharge pity and fear. Among the Greeks, catharsis had manifold connotations. In medical theory, it was the flushing out of excessive and disproportionate humors in the body; in religion, it was a cleansing of the soul by expelling harmful psychic elements; in music, as Aristotle noted in his *Politica* (335-323 B.C.E; *Politics*, 1598), it soothed and healed by purging overdone feelings such as religious zeal. In his *Technē rhetorikēs* (335-323 B.C.E.; *Rhetoric*, 1686), pity and fear are seen as dangerous and painful emotions: Fear is defined as an apprehension of

disaster, proximate and inescapable, and pity is this fear applied to others who have not merited the disaster. Fear alone is a passive and deleterious state, and pity alone is a helpless and disaffected feeling. If one experiences merely the former, the result is the same gooseflesh with which one responds to a thriller. If one experiences merely the latter, the result is a warm bath of superficial emotion, the kind prompted by a melodrama or a soap opera. The combination, however, triggers and then expels emotions of identification, as one apprehends the common lot of humanity. It is unclear from Aristotle's comments whether these processes take place during or after the performance, or how the double action operates. What is clear is that the pleasure in watching tragic suffering comes partly from the delight in observing a well-conducted imitation and the aesthetic harmony of the tragedy, and partly from the purgation, which leaves one's mind unclouded and open to contemplation. As Stephan Dedalus put it in James Joyce's *A Portrait of the Artist as a Young Man* (1916), in true catharsis, "the mind is arrested and raised above desire and loathing."

There are optimal circumstances in which these effects can be achieved. Certain stories, personages, and events, according to Aristotle, are more conducive to catharsis than others, and the skill of the dramatic poet is to be judged by his choice and handling of material to this end. "The plot is soul and first principle," which the poet arranges into a sequence productive of tragic effect. The best plots are those already known to the audience, such as the history of a great house, which require less time in the exposition of antecedent information. Novelty and surprise come from the editing and rationalization of the familiar myth. Impossible probabilities (such as a convincing portrayal of a supernatural being) are preferred to improbable possibilities (such as a true but extraordinary coincidence) in securing the universality of the action.

Central characters must be of sufficient stature that, when they undergo a change of fortune for the worse, their plight has resonance, but they must not be of such exalted status as to be remote from the audience. To exact fear, they should be like the members of the audience; yet, to exact pity, they must be undeserving of their great downfall in some degree. This downfall is the result not of a crime (for then it would be a retributive punishment) or merely of an accident or misadventure. Rather, it springs from the protagonist's hamartia, a term that has been rendered as "tragic flaw" but actually derives from the technical vocabulary of archery and means "a near miss of the mark." The tragic protagonist has somehow mistaken his aim, his identity, his choice of values; his moral responsibility becomes a complex issue. A character such as Sophocles' Oedipus in *Oidipous Tyrannos* (c. 429 B.C.E.; *Oedipus Tyrannus*, 1715) is indeed foredoomed to incest and patricide (and in Aeschylus's lost tragedy on the subject, the curse entailed by a blasphemy was well to the fore). In Sophocles, however, the crimes have been committed before the play begins, and the action of the drama reveals Oedipus coming to self-knowledge of his hamartia, in his case having taken the form of headstrong self-assurance and heedlessness. As George Saintsbury pointed out, Aristotle's doctrine of hamartia was a stroke of genius in defining tragedy: The great tragic dramatists share "the sense that there is infinite excuse, but no positive justification, for the acts which bring their heroes and heroines to misfortune."

For Oedipus, the moment when he recognizes his lifelong misapprehension is also the moment of his true downfall; for this reason, Aristotle considered *Oedipus Tyrannus* to be a nearly perfect tragedy. The necessary peripeteia, or reversal of fortune, the ironic boomerang of an intended purpose, coincides and coalesces with the anagnorisis, the protagonist's realization of how badly he has gone wrong. In Greek tragedy, this realization is usually limited, on the protagonists' part, to an awareness of their own mistakes; it is left to the chorus to draw general principles from their plight. William Shakespeare and Jean Racine, on the other hand, allow their tragic heroes insight into their place in the universal scheme of things, thus ennobling or improving them. Later ages allowed tragic heroes to transcend the mundane reversals that caused their fall. The audience is left with a sense of reconciliation and, if not of justice, at least of balance in life. A genuine tragedy, predicated on those terms,

would be neither depressing nor revolting but would inspire the audience with a heightened awareness of human beings' ability to overcome their fate. Greek tragedy seldom permits this consolation and recognizes no rewards beyond the mortal sphere: Sophocles' *Oidipous epi Kolōnōi* (401 B.C.E.; *Oedipus at Colonus*, 1729) is the rare exception. Once Greek tragedy moved beyond Aeschylus's pious obeisance to the powers-that-be, it remained steadfastly anthropocentric.

Of Aristotle's other recommendations, the twenty-four-hour rule was regularly debated in later ages. He had desired a tragedy to be only as long as memory could embrace, and to preserve unity of action, by which he meant a unity of motive binding the characters together (as the crisis in *Oedipus Tyrannus* ensnares each character). The best means to accomplish this unity is to limit the length of the plot's action to a hypothetical day. Else postulated that Aristotle meant that the length of performance should not go beyond a day, but since the usual presentation of three tragedies and a satyr play had of necessity to end by nightfall, this seems unlikely.

In sum, Aristotle saw tragedy as a way of bringing people to thoughtful contemplation, through their observation of action and passion. As the protagonist passes through pathos, that moment of extreme and unreasoning emotion, to reach a higher plane of understanding, the audience's feelings are heightened, discharged, leaving the mind clear to ponder the meaning of these events. Pleasure was a means, not an end, in this process.

Aristotle is more dismissive of comedy, and in this he followed Plato, who thought it suited only for slaves and aliens. In his *Philēbos* (365-361 B.C.E.; *Philebus*, 1779), Plato argued that "those who are weak and unable to revenge themselves, when they are laughed at, may be truly called ridiculous. . . . Ignorance in the powerful is hateful and horrible, because hurtful to others both in reality and fiction; but powerless ignorance may be reckoned and, in truth, is ridiculous." In other words, one may safely laugh at the innocuous and impotent. Aristotle was more willing to grant that innocent amusement creates a relaxation that is a legitimate accompaniment of the pursuit of virtue. Even if laughter is a politically dangerous emotion, it may be safely purged through comedy. Comedy, Aristotle explained,

> is an imitation of characters of a lower type—not, however, in the full sense of the word bad, the ludicrous being merely a subdivision of the ugly. It consists of some defect or ugliness which is not painful and not destructive. To take an obvious example, the comic mask is ugly and distorted, but does not imply pain.

The emphasis on lower types of characters directed comedy toward a more realistic depiction of society—especially since, as Aristotle noted, comic poets did not borrow from mythology but invented their plots, building them along lines of probability. By Aristotle's time, Aristophanic comedy had long been extinct (Aristotle does not allow the mockery of individuals that was commonplace in Aristophanes), and Aristotle could have known only Middle Comedy. Comic types, with a fixed vice that could be portrayed typically by a mask, had become the usual stage fare.

Attempts have been made to show that Aristotle did not intend to divide comedy and tragedy into mutually exclusive genres because they presented different facets of the same elements. The hamartia in tragedy provokes pity and fear because the punishment is so vastly disproportionate to the error, whereas in comedy the hamartia is grossly exaggerated, but the punishment is trifling. Tragedy reveals the contradiction between the hero's view of himself and the universe around him; comedy reveals the contradiction between the hero's view of himself and the society around him. Tragedy effects a reconciliation in the audience's mind; comedy effects a reconciliation onstage. In an essay of 1948, titled "The Argument of Comedy," Northrop Frye went so far as to suggest that tragedy is comedy that has not fulfilled its entelechy:

> The tragic catharsis passes beyond moral judgment, and while it is quite possible to construct a moral tragedy, what tragedy gains in morality it loses in cathartic power. The same is true of the comic catharsis, which raises sympathy and ridicule on a moral basis, but passes beyond both. . . . The audience gains a vision of that resurrection whether the conclusion is joyful or ironic, just as in tragedy it gains a vision of a heroic death whether the hero is morally innocent or guilty . . . tragedy is really implicit or uncompleted comedy; . . . comedy contains a potential tragedy within itself.

Any sharp distinction between tragedy and comedy had already begun to blur by the time of Euripides, who has been censured by writers from Aristotle to Friedrich Nietzsche for not preserving the tragic "spirit" of his precursors. Many of his plays have happy endings (*Alkēstis*, 438 B.C.E.; *Alcestis*, 1781) or lack a downward peripeteia for the protagonist (*Helenē*, 412 B.C.E.; *Helen*, 1782), or edulcorate an otherwise tragic ending with a "euthanasia," or blessed death (*Hippolytos*, 428 B.C.E.; *Hippolytus*, 1781), effected by a *deus ex machina*. In this respect, Euripides foreshadows the tragicomedies of a later day while maintaining the outward form of tragedy; certain of his characters come perilously close to the comic.

It is clear from Aristotle's definition that his view of comedy is a normative one; to deviate too radically from the established social norm is to render oneself comic. The character types he listed in his ethics as examples of the vicious or deviant are suitable for ridicule, and two of them, the *eiron* and the *alazon*, are patterns for Western comic types. The *eiron* is the mock-modest man of cunning, an expert at sophistic argumentation, subtle, covert, and, as the term implies, ironic in attitude. Socrates, with his homely exterior and ironic humility concealing a razor-sharp mind, was Aristotle's prime example; the type recurs in the clever slaves of the New Comedy tradition, their servility masking their ingenuity. The *alazon* is the *eiron*'s dialectical opposite: the bullying braggart who claims to be more than he can validate, the boastful coward or would-be lady's man whose pretensions are exposed by the play's end. Aristotle lists variations ranging from the boorish loudmouth to the urbane wit, and in a complex comic figure such as Shakespeare's Falstaff, the *eiron* and the *alazon* are merged.

FROM OLD COMEDY TO NEW COMEDY

Aristophanic comedy had approached the normative only in the sense that Aristophanes himself, a conservative with strongly pronounced tastes for peace and the old-fashioned way, contrasted these ideals with the abuses and newfangled practices he saw around him. He did not necessarily speak for his society or set it up as an admirable model; his comic heroes, in fact, tend to be down-to-earth, plainspoken characters, comic only in terms of the physical situations into which they are thrust. A number of modifications to Old Comedy brought it inevitably closer to Aristotle's paradigm. The spectacular parabasis was omitted, in part as a result of financial considerations, in part as a result of a law instigated in 396 B.C.E. by the dithyrambic poet Cinesias, who had been personally attacked in a comedy. Gradually, the law took a firmer hand in moderating comedy's satiric excesses: In 414 B.C.E., a statute of Syracosius forbade poets from referring to current events in comedy, and in 404 B.C.E., a similar law prohibited the insertion of a personal name into comedy. By the time of Aristophanes' last play, *Ploutos* (388 B.C.E.; *Plutus*, 1651), with its diminished chorus and absent parabasis, the transition to Middle Comedy was well under way.

No entire plays of Middle Comedy are extant, but its distinguishing features can be reconstructed from surviving fragments and traces of its influence on its successors. It has been called a comedy of manners, although the manners shown are not very specific, since types govern the action. Certain recurring figures still connected with the festal origins of comedy—revelers, courtesans, cooks—as well as soldiers and parasites, are standard, and they speak a colloquial prose that never reaches heights of poetry or depths of scurrility but maintains an easy mean. For the most part, supernatural machinery is absent, although one style of Middle Comedy, invented by the Thasian Hegemon, specialized in parodies of tragic myths. Athenians were laughing at his *Gigantomaknia* (pr. late fifth century B.C.E.; war of the giants) when news of the Sicilian debacle reached them.

Essentially, the differences between tragedy and comedy were effaced less by Euripides' innovations than by the sentimental accretions of so-called New Comedy. This style, practiced by Menander (whose *Dyskolos*, 317 B.C.E.; *The Bad-tempered Man*, 1921; also known as *The Grouch*), is the only complete sample in existence), introduced a few new characters, such as the clever slave and the captain of mercenaries. Its plots, however, became stereotypical and unvaried. The central novelty of Menander and his colleagues was to place the emphasis on a love interest revolving around a sympathetic young man and young girl and to festoon the action with moral and sentimental reflections in the Euripidean fashion.

In Aristophanes, there had been plenty of sex but no love; even in Middle Comedy, romantic involvement remained peripheral. In contrast, the pivot of the action in New Comedy was the young man's love, thwarted by the will or business dealings of an old crank; by the play's end, matters had been worked out, often through the machinations of a cunning slave, to bring the lovers together. As in tragedy, there was a late point of attack, close to the climax, and the hamartia, or mistaking of one's identity, in New Comedy became an external and mechanical use of disguises and concealed identities, until matters were cleared up by anagnorisis, or recognition of the truth. The *kōmos* feast at the finale became a wedding banquet, and the sententious commentary replaced the chorus, which had, by this time, atrophied into irrelevancy, as a group of nondancing singers whose contribution smacked of variety entertainment.

Other, minor genres were practiced during the heyday of New Comedy. The mime, the only Greek dramatic form in which women performed, was basically a comic sketch spiced with the music of the cymbal, flute, and tambourine. In Doric regions, the mime was absorbed by local comedy, which tended either toward mythological fantasies treated bawdily (the *phlyakes*) or toward a tepid sort of realism. Rhinthon of Tarentum, around 300 B.C.E., wrote *phlyakographies*, more sophisticated recensions of the *phlyakes* farces, full of repartee and slapstick, and the almost apocryphal Sotades produced pornographic travesties. Yet these were side issues. The form in which Menander cast comedy was to become the basic mode for that genre (and later for straight drama) for two millennia.

THE ROMANS

Greek tragedy and New Comedy were transmitted by the Romans, who were not themselves adept at drama but were content to borrow what their neighbors had developed. In this habit they were not unlike the Victorian English, who regarded their French allies as immoral and frivolous but who pillaged, reworked, and prettified French dramatic works for decades. One of the reasons the Romans did not develop an indigenous and viable drama of their own was the lack of religious sanction. Early Roman religious rites were accompanied by revels and masquerades, part dance, part song, part backchat, mostly improvised; like the phallic Fescennine verses, later sung only at weddings, these quasi-dramatic rites never evolved into true drama. The Saturae (or goatish medleys) acted out comic stories to the sound of a flute, but they were not incorporated into a dramatic spectacle until, typically, non-Roman influence took hold. Etruscan dancers and mimes came to Rome in 364 B.C.E. and introduced the *ludi scenici*, or stage games, originally as part of the annual propitiatory rites. Later, the Saturae, reminiscent in this of the satyr plays, were tacked on as *exodia*, or farcical interludes.

The mime enjoyed a revival of popularity during the Roman Empire, although even then, the principal feature of the form was gesticulation, not dialogue. The same holds true for the *fabulae Atellanae*, or Atellan fables, simpleminded comedies of country life, with a gallery of stock characters. These included Pappus, the tyrannical father or husband; Maccus, the hunchbacked glutton; Bucco, the greedy and mendacious loudmouth; and Dossennus, the village pedant. To these occasionally were added other stock figures: dim-witted or tricky servants; Manducus, a jaw-snapping bogeyman; and the witch Lamia. Here, too, speech was improvised, the plots slender but full of complications (*tricae*, from which "intrigue" derives), and the actors' byplay the main ingredient for success. No wonder that under the empire, such stock figures were readily absorbed into the popular pantomimes. The rustic characters, under other names and guises, would reappear in much folk comedy and take on fully fleshed forms in the Renaissance *commedia dell'arte* (see below).

Drama, then, was for the Romans neither a meaningful outgrowth from their religious beliefs nor an expression of communal solidarity, but purely and simply a rude recreation. According to tradition, Livius Andronicus, a Tarentine freedman of Greek ancestry, was the first to adapt tragedies and comedies from Greek originals, around 240 B.C.E.; unlike Aristotle, he was not very exact in drawing distinctions. An attempt was made to naturalize tragedy by means of the *fabula praetexta* (literally, the purple-hemmed-robe fable, a reference to the garb of superior court judges), which dramatized patriotic historical subjects and was meant to be performed as a eulogy at the funeral rites of the heroes whose victories it celebrated. It seems to have failed to catch on because the playwrights were permitted no latitude in dealing with the venerated Roman past and were not free to turn respected ancestors into human characters.

The Romans did, however, invent the five-act structure, conventionalizing the episodes of Greek tragedy, with a standard prologue and epilogue. The chorus was retained but seldom took much part in the action, and the responsibilities of the performers became specialized. Dialogue was recited, often by a single actor, with intervals in which a boy, accompanied by a flute player, would sing while the actor mimed what was sung. This division of labor alienated performer from character and audience from action; dynamic interchanges between characters were sacrificed to rhetorical monologues, and the pity and fear discharged by a well-conducted plot were replaced by maudlin tear-jerking and sensational thrills.

Nevertheless, the tragedies of Seneca have value beyond their intrinsic merit, for their influence on Renaissance and Elizabethan drama. It is still debated whether Seneca's tragedies, founded on Greek myths, were meant to be performed onstage or recited before a patrician audience. The latter opinion was long prevalent, but revivals of Seneca in the contemporary theater have proved that the tragedies have many stage-worthy and appealing features. What seems especially modern is Seneca's taste for the gruesome and the horrendous, in which he takes an almost sadistic delight; also noteworthy in this context is the speed in the development of the story, which may argue a lack of interest in characterization but which conduces to excitement and urgency. What is least modern about Seneca is his *sententiae*, the ponderous and artificial moralizing that clogs the movement of the drama and, rather than evolving organically from the characters, seems patently applied by the author.

Comedy became better acclimated to the Roman stage in two varieties: the *fabula palliata* (Greek-cloak fable), based on Greek originals and set in Greece, and the *fabula togata* (toga fable), which drew on the lives of the Roman proletariat. All that is known of the latter genre is based on titles and scholastic commentary, from which it can be inferred that the form was mildly satiric and topical, simple in cast and structure, and sexually unbridled.

Gnaeus Naevius, who is credited with inventing the *fabula praetexta*, also introduced the *contaminatio*, the conflation of two Greek plots into a single Latin one, thereby establishing the Italian comic formula of a rapid and complicated intrigue. Greek comedy was truly naturalized by the quasi-legendary plebeian Plautus, who translated the plays of Menander and his fellows into Latin, with their frustrated lovers, angry cooks, wily slaves, and meretricious courtesans adapted wholesale. The chorus was replaced by a prologue in which leading comic actors would ingratiate themselves with the audience and fill in the background. The setting was standardized: a street with two (occasionally three) house frontages, one entrance leading to the harbor and another to the forum. Plautus's genius lay in the complications he introduced into the plots, the elaborate weaving and unraveling of the intrigue. He also had a flair for comic dialogue, not as fanciful as Aristophanes' but still breezy and exuberant, with plentiful asides, and arrangements that have been characterized as the prototypes of the arias, duets, trios, and ensembles of comic opera. His Machiavellian slaves were clearly discriminated from one another, and he could heighten a conventional type such as the braggart soldier into a vital and recognizable human being (as in the play of that title, *Miles Gloriosus*, pr. 205 B.C.E.; *The Braggart Soldier*, 1825).

Moreover, even though Plautus's stories allegedly took place in Greece, it was obviously Roman morals and values that were being flouted, with masters befooled, slaves in charge, and mendacity, adultery, and the pleasure principle the order of the day. To license these affronts to Latin *industrias* and *honestas*, Plautus emphasized what can be called the "one mad day" aspect of comedy: Just as during the Saturnalia and similar religious festivals or holidays, the norm is perverted or challenged only to be ultimately restored and affirmed at the holiday's close, so, during the time of a comedy, antisocial activity is permitted, for the regular order will be reconfirmed at the finale. Henpecked husbands can feather lovenests; impertinent underlings can rule the roost; men can dress as women, and whores as virgins. By the final curtain, the irregularities have been resolved, the deviant characters either expelled from or reintegrated into society, and the unifying bond of community sealed anew. This pattern would remain a constant in traditional comedy from Thomas Dekker to Thornton Wilder.

Plautus's successor Terence was less rambunctious and more pallid, and his characters had not the vivacity or the variety of the earlier writer's; as with Menander, the love interest stands foremost. Terence even managed, in his *Andria* (pr. c. 166 B.C.E.; *The Girl from Andros*, 1912) to introduce a situation in which the young man is smitten, not with a slave girl, but with a young lady of his own class. Terence's dialogue was so polished and elegant that he was preserved as a model for Latinists during the Middle Ages, and his influence on Renaissance comedy was as profound as Seneca's on Renaissance tragedy: He became an arsenal of plots and personae to be rifled and refurbished at will.

Terence's refinements on Plautus bespoke the increasing sophistication of the *palliatae*, but in the process they lost their broad comedy and also their appeal to the masses and were performed for private audiences. The *togatae*, which flourished between 170 and 80 B.C.E., also enjoyed only a limited vogue. Roman audiences, coarsened by the sanguinary spectacles of the arena, found the theater tame, and the bellicose and austere national character never regarded drama as more than a frivolity. Horace's famous dicta on the drama in his *Ars poetica* (c. 17 B.C.E.; *The Art of Poetry*, 1567), his insistence on clarity, common sense, fastidiousness, and decorum, were meant to groom a crude form of entertainment into one that was fit for the salon, since a discriminating patron of the arts should disdain vulgar amusements. Drama that conformed to Horace's urbanity would suit the taste of an elite class, but drama is by nature a public art, and the Roman public required stronger fare.

Consequently, in the early empire, tragedy and comedy both gave way to ballets (*fabulae salticae*), which related the amorous exploits of the gods and heroes in a manner that was explicitly obscene, tricked out with spectacular effects like a Las Vegas nightclub show. Attempts were made to introduce crowd-pleasing features into tragedy: real executions and a slave tossed from a real tower. Comedy came to rely more heavily on slapstick and buffoonery. The pantomime, a lyric tragedy recited to a mimed solo with chorus and instruments, regained popularity; the mimes, who had a reputation for effeminacy, changed masks to represent different characters and excelled in the portrayal of voluptuous passion. Literary drama could not keep pace with the allure of sex, spectacle, and female performers, and the pantomime remained the preeminent Roman dramatic form until the sixth century, at the time that it was banned by Empress Theodora—who, in her salad days, had performed in sex shows at the circus.

From the foregoing survey of Greek and Roman dramatic forms, it should be apparent that, at their inception, tragedy and comedy were not distinct in nature. They arose from similar primitive impulses, and only gradually, and at the hands of individual creators, did their concerns and outward aspects grow far enough apart for them to be classified as mutually exclusive genres. Aristotle tried to demonstrate that these differences were intrinsic and organic, but the inability of the genres themselves to remain stable or meaningful outside post-Periclean society reveals their contingency. The classical genres of tragedy and comedy were not needed by a Christian world, and the Middle Ages had no interest in reviving them.

MIDDLE AGES

The early Christians associated the theater with paganism and persecution. The only shows to be seen during the late Roman Empire were debased and sensual, and the playhouses were ornamented with idols of the gods whose loves were played out onstage, so that no self-respecting Christian would go near them. Furthermore, as Saint Augustine more subtly realized, if the spectator were to be moved to tears by a tragedy, he would waste the compassion that should be expended on actual objects. From such a perspective, plays leach off the fine emotions that human beings should reserve for real-life situations.

Greek drama, as noted, was anthropocentric, its interest focused on humans in their world. Christian thinking was metaphysical and theocratic and saw the function of art as a means of turning one's mind to God. The early fathers of the Church were vigorously outspoken in their contempt of the body and the world as snares and delusions, the instruments of Original Sin, the hindrances that bar souls from Heaven. When Saint Bernard of Clairvaux, in his *Meditationes Piissimae*, described humans as "nothing else than fetid sperm, a sack of dung, the food of worms," he was lending graphic images to a not uncommon attitude. It is ironic that Tertullian, who considered his belief heretical in that the soul's activity is manifested and conditioned by the flesh, should be the Church father most explicit in his denunciation of the theater: He condemned it as a temple of Satan and maintained that, because all Christians at their baptism renounce Satan, to step inside a playhouse is automatically an act of apostasy.

In addition, the Middle Ages knew the literature of the ancients only piecemeal, and, despite attempts to adapt certain forms to Christian orthodoxy, the discrepancy between form and content was too great for success. The Byzantine *Khristōs paskhon* (c. ninth century; *Christ's Passion*) turned episodes from the Old and New Testaments into tragedy for educational purposes; in it, the Virgin Mary makes her first appearance onstage, lamenting her son's death with Agave's plaint from *Bakchai* (405 B.C.E.; *The Bacchae*, 1781) of Euripides. Within the isolation of her cloister, the nun Hroswitha of Gandersheim composed plays to glorify martyrdom and chastity in the style of Terence's comedies, faithful even to the bawdiness. These, however, were idiosyncratic cases, which had no effect on the world at large.

Classical tragedy could not be easily adapted, because its worldview ran counter to Christian tenets: In a universe in which Christ has saved everyone and where his mercy is available on application by the sinner, no tragic fate is possible for the protagonist. Only if protagonists persist in their obstinacy and reject redemption can they be doomed; in that case, they are criminals and infidels who deserve damnation. Hamartia is simply not recognized. With Christ himself as the central figure in tragedy, a happy ending cannot be avoided, despite the torments of the Passion. Besides, as a divinity, Christ (not unlike Dionysus in *The Bacchae*) is incapable of hamartia, because he knows full well the import of his actions.

Consequently, all that the Middle Ages retained of the classical concept of tragedy was the notion of a fall from prosperity; the malevolent figure of Fortune spinning her wheel became a commonplace emblem. As Geoffrey Chaucer defined the genre in his poem *Troilus and Criseyde* (1372-1386), "Tragedye is to seyn, a dite of a prosperite for a tyme that endith in wrecchydnesse." The fall from high degree to misery was itself thought tragic, regardless of whether the protagonist was morally responsible. Tragedy had also lost its dramatic connotation, and the Monk in *The Canterbury Tales* (1387-1400) regarded his potted verse biographies of fallen greatness to be exemplary tragedies.

Similarly, comedy came to mean any dramatic presentation, with the Spanish *comedia*, the French *comédie*, and the Italian *commedia* frequently signifying the same broad range that the English word "play" does. Medieval plays were mixed in form, combining the sublime with the ridiculous and the grotesque. Dante titled his great poem a *Commedia* (*Divina* was added only after his death) not because it is humorous but because its vision comprehends both the violent emotions of the damned and the incandescent spirituality of paradise and divine love, presented in an extravagant and fantastical mode yet couched in the realistic eloquence of the vulgar tongue.

Medieval drama, then, when it did begin to take shape, developed irregularly and with a teleological character. It was meant to instruct and focus the mind on God. The celebration of the Mass was itself a kind of performance, with the priest acting as both stage manager and star performer, and the communicants as both chorus and audience. As early as the sixth century, Pope Gregory the Great had fixed the antiphonal chant, which alternated the voices of soloists and choir, and this form was popularized by the Benedictines. Tutelon, a monk of Saint Gall, is credited with inventing Scriptural paraphrases called tropes (from *tropos*, a turn), some time in the tenth century. These tropes were inserted—"smuggled in," in Léon Gautier's phrase—before or after the sung portions of the breviary office to serve as Introits. The most renowned of these is the tenth century *Quem quaeritis*, sung on Easter Sunday. Half of the choir intoned to the three Marys come to the tomb, "*Quem quaertitis in sepulchro, o christicolae?*" (What seek you in the tomb, O Christians?), to which the other half replied, "*Iesum Nazarenum crucifixum, o caelicolae*" (Jesus of Nazareth who was crucified, O heavenly beings). The angelic half of the choir then announced, "*Non est hic, surrexit, sicut praedixerat/ Ite, nuntiate quia surrexit de sepulchro*" (He is not here. He has arisen as he foretold./ Go forth and proclaim that he has risen from the tomb).

The impetus for these tropes may have come from wandering clerics, the Goliards, who had introduced well-sung embellishments to the monasteries. When the *Regularis Concordia* (c. 970) of Aethelwold, bishop of Winchester, recommended such devices "to fortify unlearned people in their faith," there was a sudden flowering of "dramatic" chanting and gesture (such as drawing the veil before the altar), as if the clergy had been suppressing for centuries an instinct for drama. Visual celebrations of the chief dates of the Church calendar became the rule. The earliest Latin liturgical play extant is based on the tale of the Magi and Herod, but by the eleventh century, plays were being produced in France on biblical subjects that had no connection with Church festivals: the

Wise and Foolish Virgins, Adam and the Fall of Lucifer, Daniel, and Lazarus. Such plays, known as mystery plays, or mysteries, were written in the vernacular; their predecessors, the liturgical mysteries, had been written in Latin verse with some prose passages.

The earliest example of the vernacular mystery play is the Norman *Le Jeu d'Adam* (1146-1174). Indeed, it was in France that the terminology used to identify such plays originated. Technically, the term "mystery" (French *mystère*, a conflation of the Latin *ministerium*, meaning office or ceremony, with *mysterium*) covered plays depicting incidents from the life of Christ, and plays that dramatized the lives of saints were referred to as miracle plays, or miracles. This distinction, however, was not hard and fast even in France and did not exist at all in England, where the term "mystery" was not applied to these plays until the eighteenth century (by which time they were fodder for antiquarians). In any case, Christ's life was interpreted broadly to entail those episodes in the Old Testament that foretold his advent or symbolically prefigured his deeds. The Fall of Man, the Flood, and the sacrifice of Isaac were taken to be important prophecies of the redemption of the world, fulfilled by the Nativity, the Passion, and the Resurrection.

As these plays grew more elaborate, they were thrust out of the churches—sometimes for reasons of space, sometimes at the behest of an irate clergy—and into the churchyard or the public square. This shift, along with the adoption of the vernacular as the linguistic medium, enabled the plays to become less reverent and more profane, with heavy admixtures of comedy. As Benjamin Hunningher suggests in *The Origin of the Theater: An Essay* (1955), "When definite dramatic forms have been established, a church, no matter how opposed it might have been to theatre, may see some desirability in employing that theatre and even in participating directly in its further development." Thus, the Church sanctified the plays by associating them with the Corpus Christi festival in 1264 and with the solemn procession in which the symbol of the mystery of the Incarnation was borne (hence the term *processus* in ecclesiastic use to describe the plays). Occasionally, a council or a bishop

would disown these spectacles and prohibit them on the grounds that they had lost their religious character and were distracting the populace from true worship. (Robert Mannyng of Brunne, in his poem *Handlyng Synne*, 1288-1338, revived the legend of dancers in a churchyard who were cursed by the priest and condemned to dance for twelve months, in order to advertise the desecration of holy ground by such performances.) Plays performed by the clergy as didactic aids to religion were gradually supplanted by plays performed by laymen as expressions of secular concerns. In the process, Latin ceased to be a viable theatrical tongue (although it persisted in the *commedia erudita* and even enjoyed a revival in the Jesuit school dramas of the seventeenth century). Chanted speech was replaced by spoken dialogue, and the familiar figures of the Bible were ousted by original and more contemporary types.

In France, the drama was soon coopted by the laity; Jean Bodel, who wrote a relatively realistic *Le Jeu de Saint-Nicolas* (pr. c. 1200; *Play of Saint Nicholas of Jean Bodel*, 1932), was not a priest but a poet. (Saints' lives were particularly popular, since they could be given a local coloration and brought closer to the audience.) The Faust theme makes its first showing in Rutebeuf's *Théophilus* (pr. c. 1260; *Le Miracle de Théophile*, 1971), a miracle play of Our Lady that was still in the tradition of explicitly liturgical drama. As early as the thirteenth century, the vernal *Le Jeu de la feuillée* (pr. c. 1275; *The Greenwood Play*, 1971) of Adam de la Halle introduced pastoral elements; it was soon followed by his *Le Jeu de Robin et Marion* (pr. c. 1283; *The Play of Robin and Marion*, 1928), which announced a secular drama, more sophisticated in its structure than even so polished a Passion mystery as Arnoul Greban's of the same period. By the end of the fourteenth century, the *Estoire de Griselidis* (pr. 1395; the tale of patient Griselda) by Philippe de Mézières appeared, a serious secular drama whose style was that of miracle plays of the Virgin but with a new Petrarchan Humanism conspicuous. Half a century later, Joan of Arc appeared for the first time on any stage in the tedious and overlong *Mystère du siège d'Orléans* (pr. c. 1450; mystery of the siege of Orleans, possibly by

Jacques Milet), an embryonic chronicle play that attempted to dramatize recent history. This relatively rapid secularization was assisted by the mime tradition—the old comic interludes and farcical scenes that had been preserved and spread by wandering minstrels and mountebanks from earliest times.

In England, the miracle plays did not begin to flourish until they came under the sponsorship of the trade guilds, which vied with one another in sumptuous staging and promotion. Many of the plays were translated from the French, but English authors also created their own reworkings of the Bible, the Apocrypha, and the lives of the saints. A characteristic of the English miracle plays was their grouping into series called cycles, which were performed in the course of one day, unfolding the totality of Scriptural history from Creation to the Day of Judgment. Some scholars believe that this synoptic approach was influenced by the Anglo-Saxon epics. It was certainly facilitated by the *pagonds*, or pageant wagons, which could trundle an episode from one end of a market town to another. The earliest English dramatic work, from the latter half of the thirteenth century, *The Harrowing of Hell*, comes from the East Midlands and exhibits a peculiarly English penchant for the gloomy. Indeed, each cycle bears the stamp of the locality in which it arose: The Towneley, or Wakefield, Cycle is exuberant and packed with humor and jocular invention and is not overly reverent in its treatment of religious figures; the York Cycle is more somber and dignified; and the Coventry Cycle is more finely wrought in a literary sense, is more dramatically powerful, and shows a new sophistication in its use of abstract characters.

This growing abstraction came to fruition in the form known as the morality play. Morality plays, like mystery and miracle plays, reflect not only the liturgical origins of medieval drama but also its increasing secularization; the distinctive feature of the form is the use of allegorical characters representing virtues, vices, warring spiritual principles, and so on. The genre is said to have been invented by Norman *trouvères* sometime before the thirteenth century, in an attempt to wrest dramatic control away from the ecclesiastical authorities, but morality plays did not appear onstage until the next century. In France, moralities were the first secular plays to be presented by university students (in 1426 and 1431).

A morality is constructed to depict a conflict among the personified qualities of the human soul, with the protagonist as a metaphor for all humankind. The French quickly adapted this scheme to nonreligious matters, such as political and social debates, and, with the clear-cut division between good and evil, injected a foretaste of melodrama. There is even a prototypal problem play: Nicolas de la Chesnaye's morality of hygienic abstinence, published in 1507, in which Banquet conspires with Apoplexy, Epilepsy, and similar diseases to endanger human health.

Genre diversification occurred in French drama because of increasing specialization among the performance groups. In 1402, the Confrérie de la Passion announced a monopoly on the mystery and miracle plays to prevent further contamination by the new secular Humanism. A lay group, the Union de la Basoche, founded to divert minds from the disastrous wars, concentrated on moralities and short political satires and on spoof sermons in the style of the Feast of Fools. They were the first to enact *Maître Pathelin* (pr. 1485), one of the earliest situation comedies based on contemporary life. The term farce itself comes from the word for stuffing; just as a fowl is stuffed with forcemeat, so a mystery was larded with a comic interlude. The independence of the farce from the mystery enabled it to exploit such true-to-life situations as marital strife, legal chicanery, or business shenanigans; it served as a springboard for modern comedies of character and of manners.

Another early-fifteenth century group, Les Enfants sans Souci, confined themselves to *sotties* (the word means "foolishness"): short, comical allegories made to serve both Church and State. For example, Pierre Gringoire, in his *Jeu du Prince des Sots et de mère Sotte* (pr. 1511; the prince of fools and mother fool), supported Louis XII in his dispute with Pope Julius II. In nature, *sotties* were closer to satiric revues than to social comedies. The audiences for *sotties* and moralities were never as homogeneous or as large as those for miracles and mysteries, but an elite patronage allowed authors to experiment with subject matter and treatment in a manner that would have been inadmissible in a more public situation.

In England, where the comic element had been strong in the mysteries, the Vice character of the morality won enduring popularity. Originally a henchman of the Devil, the Vice, with his crude jokes, phallic sword of lath, and inept evildoing, became a popular favorite and assumed the truth-telling aspects of the court fool. This tolerated malefactor can be seen in so simple a creation as the sheep stealer Mak in the *Secunda Pastorum* (fifteenth century; commonly known as *The Second Shepherds' Play*), as well as in the richly complex figure of Shakespeare's Falstaff.

The earliest English moralities were devoid of religious dogma, merely presenting the allegorical strife over the soul of an Everyman. After the rupture with Rome that occurred during the reign of Henry VIII, however, the morality play began to be used for propaganda. Under Elizabeth I, theological controversy was waged in *New Custome* (pb. 1573) and Nathaniel Woode's *The Conflict of Conscience* (pb. 1581), and intellectual progress was treated in John Rastell's *The Nature of the Four Elements* (pr. c. 1517) and John Redford's *Wit and Science* (pr. c. 1530-1547), which contains a hilarious spelling lesson carried on by Ignorance and Idleness. By this means, the new learning was vulgarized and disseminated. John Bale's *King Johan* (pb. 1538) made an antipapist, patriotic appeal, and by combining the allegorical abstractions of the morality with characters from England's history, he invented an embryonic chronicle play. The moral element can still be glimpsed in the figure of Rumour in Shakespeare's *Henry IV, Part II* (pr. 1598).

Others, such as Sir David Lyndsay of the Mount in his *Satyre of the Thrie Estaitis* (pr. 1540), mingled contemporary types with allegorical figures to produce an early version of the comedy of humors. This movement was also carried forward by John Heywood, whose interludes were usually based on French farces, with a dosage of British anticlericism added. An interlude, as its etymology implies (*inter* plus *ludi*, "between the plays") was originally a light, humorous presentation interpolated between the epi-

sodes of a protracted mystery. The Victorian Shakespearean scholar John Payne Collier claimed that Heywood's interludes were the earliest form of modern drama, and he was right, insofar as Heywood's plays eschew any allegorical characters and draw their people and language from the life around them. The actions and personalities were as familiar to their original audiences as were their next-door neighbors.

Medieval drama was most technically adept and variegated in France and England. Religious spectacles of various kinds existed throughout Europe but seldom matured into more complex forms. The German Corpus Christi plays, or *Frohnleichnamspiele*, were written in the vernacular, with an emphasis on the Last Judgment and plentiful dollops of moralizing, but audiences were too naïve to warrant the step up to the morality play. The only secular plays in Germany were the *Fastnachtspiele*, or Shrove Tuesday shows, comic interludes played by professional strollers.

In Italy, the religious drama had been subsumed by the ostentatious processionals, or *Trionfi*, the artificiality and pomp of which militated against dramatic development. The secular equivalent, the *festaiuoli*, in which opulent ornamented dishes were brought into courtly banquets to the accompaniment of dance and music, gave rise to ballet and masque. (This latter form was introduced into England as a private entertainment or masquerade around 1512-1513 and, as noted below, had an illustrious future.) The English version of the *Trionfi* were "pageants," patriotic equestrian processions of mythological heroes and allegorical abstractions, with men and horses gorgeously caparisoned. The pageant lingers on in an etiolated form in the Lord Mayor's Show, the Macy's and Rose Bowl parades, the New Orleans Mardi Gras, and the hero's ticker-tape welcome.

Contrary to Aristotle's hypothesis that dramatic forms evolve through inner necessity, medieval drama responded to external stimuli, transmuting and adapting to ecclesiastical regulations and audience demands. Relatively untrammeled by prescriptive rules, it still needed a fresh impetus to develop beyond the limited genres of morality and farce. This impetus was provided by the rediscovery of classical literature; at the same time, however, the example of the Greeks and Romans inhibited the dramatic energies of certain cultures.

The Middle Ages had known Horace's *The Art of Poetry*. Aristotle's *Poetics*, however, although available in an unabridged Latin version, was seldom consulted. After the fall of Constantinople in 1453 and the influx of Greek pedagogues into a Europe thirsting for contact with intellectual authorities outside the Church, the *Poetics* became a guidebook for every budding scholar. Within a century, it had been fully translated into both Latin and Italian, published in its original Greek, and thoroughly annotated. In the medieval period, Aristotle, although a pagan, had been respected by the scholastics for his knowledge in the fields of natural history and logic; the Renaissance merely extended his authority to the arts and, with its tacit assumption that the classical past had been a golden age to be emulated but never superseded, measured contemporary literature on an impossible scale. What in Aristotle had been deductions and inferences drawn from observation became, in the Humanist tradition, rigid rules to be disregarded at peril of contempt. The critics themselves were luminaries of courts and aristocratic circles. Their edicts thus were endorsed from above and integrated into the intellectual codes of the ruling society. Drama founded on the Humanist reinterpretation of Aristotle was fare intended for a powerful but narrow group of *cognoscenti* and took on prestige as a guide to right thinking and proper conduct at a time when the Church's authority was waning.

ITALIAN RENAISSANCE

These Aristotelian prescriptions were most stunting to the growth of tragedy in Italy. Throughout the Middle Ages, tragedy for the Italians had meant Seneca. The *Ecerinis* (pr. c. 1314; *The Tragedy of Ecerinis*, 1972) of Albertino Mussato, though written in Latin, had tried to convey contemporary relevance by warning the Paduans that Cane Grande della Scala had designs on them, through the example of the tyrant Ezzelino. Antonio Minturno, in his work on poetry *On the Poet* (1559), was still sufficiently medieval in his thinking to define tragedy as a fall from

prominence to misery, teaching one to distrust all things mortal and to bear one's griefs bravely. He was also sufficiently fashionable to explore catharsis as an unpleasant compulsion that, through pity and fear, purges the characters of such negative qualities as the mortal sins and endows the spectators with a heightened respect for virtue. This emphasis on the didactic aim of drama was less Aristotelian than Horatian, and the note would be struck ever louder by every theorist of the period.

The immensely influential Julius Caesar Scaliger pronounced that tragedy has its roots in real life and is distinguished from comedy by its unhappy ending and by the exalted rank of its characters because only royalty and nobility have tragic potential. To suit the elevated station of the protagonists, the diction must be lofty. The dramatist's task is to teach correct behavior through pleasurable emotion and convincing imitation. Scaliger invented what came to be called the "French scene," defining a scene as "part of the act in which two or more characters speak," but he did not, despite the term by which they are known, invent the so-called *unités scaligériennes*.

These pernicious rules were, in fact, codified by Lodovico Castelvetro, who had a low opinion of the theater and its audience and was dubious about the possibility of tragedy offering moral examples. In his view, poetry could not accommodate science and philosophy but would have to offer a surrogate world, sufficiently recognizable to be accepted by the crude commoners who beheld it. Therefore, unity of time and place are essential, though double plots are allowed in order to enhance pleasure. Misreading Aristotle's twenty-four-hour rule to mean the time of performance, Castelvetro insisted that no presentation should last long enough to frustrate the audience's "bodily necessities, such as eating, drinking, disposing of the superfluous contents of belly and bladder, sleeping and so on." Castelvetro contended that this stolid, dim-witted audience had an inelastic imagination that could not be stretched too far; it could believe only the most plausible and the most visible. The most plausible subject for a tragedy, then, is an imaginary story supported by realistic data, whose action "may admit of happening, but must never have happened." Anything that cannot be portrayed with verisimilitude, such as violence, should be deleted, and the tragedy should end happily.

Despite Castelvetro's scorn for the theater, his awareness that its entertainment value was paramount struck an especially Italian note. Tragedies that followed the ancients too closely lacked appeal, such as Cino da Pistoia's *Filostrato e Panfila* (pr. 1499), which was written in Italian and based on a story from Giovanni Boccaccio but which employed the Senecan five acts and a chorus and was even introduced by the ghost of Seneca. Giambattista Giraldi Cinthio, in a discourse of 1543, reiterated that there was no satisfaction in writing a play that met all the academic criteria and failed to please the public. He, too, recommended the *finta favola*, the invented story, both for tragedy (his *Orbecche*, pr. 1541, is a gruesome array of murder and incest on the Senecan plan) and for *tragedia mista*, "mixed tragedy," in which the characters are all of the same social class but reveal a variety of personalities. In mixed tragedy, horrific events may occur but the ending is happy, a result that is achieved through reliance on recognition scenes. Such a play, Giraldi Cinthio asserted, would rouse the audience's horror and compassion (his extremist reading of fear and pity) and purge them of the obsessions that plagued the characters. His own *Gli antivalomeni* (pr. 1546) is a telling example: Tyrannies and threatened deaths are dispelled by the revelation of a cradle switch and by the marriage of two pairs of lovers, once the true identities of the exchanged infants are made known.

This formula has become a staple of Western drama, sometimes used seriously (as in Shakespeare's *The Winter's Tale*, pr. c. 1610-1611), sometimes casually to tie up loose ends (as in Molière's *Les Fourberies de Scapin* (pr. 1671; *The Cheats of Scapin*, 1701), sometimes nonsensically, trading on the audience's awareness that the device is silly and stale (as in Oscar Wilde's *The Importance of Being Earnest: A Trivial Comedy for Serious People* (pr. 1895) and W. S. Gilbert's *H.M.S. Pinafore*, pr. 1878). The clichéd nature of this kind of anagnorisis was soon criticized even by Giraldi Cinthio's contemporaries. Anton Francesco, known as Il Lasca, noted

that the discovery scenes were "so irksome to the audience that, when they hear in the argument how at the taking of this city or the sack of that, children have been lost or kidnapped, they know only too well what is coming, and would fain leave the room."

Giraldi Cinthio's own plays were lent interest by his originality in concocting his plots, and tragicomedy, as mixed tragedy came to be known, caught on. The genre was defined in 1599 by Battista Guarini as a means of freeing the audience from melancholy and disposing its soul to relaxation by portraying great characters indulging in common actions, a blend of public and private affairs, the whole expressed in dulcet, ornate language.

> Whoever creates tragicomedies takes from tragedy its great charm but not its great actions, its verisimilar plot but not its historically true one, its stirred emotions, but not its furious ones, its delight but not its sadness, its danger but not its death. From comedy he takes laughter that is not immoderate, modest amusement, the fabricated complication, happy reversal and, above all, the comic order. . . .

In short, one finds the best of all dramatic worlds.

A favorite style of tragicomedy was the pastoral, originally a dramatic imitation of the bucolic idylls of Horace, Vergil, and Longus, and a neoclassical response to rustic folk comedies that also featured peasants and shepherds. The earliest Italian example is Poliziano's *Orfeo* (pr. c. 1480; English translation, 1875), which begins on an idyllic note and ends on a tragic one, and is performed to music—clearly an ancestor of opera. The comic element came to the fore in Agostino Beccari's *Il sagrifizio* (pr. 1554; the sacrifice), but the masterpiece of the genre is Battista Guarini's *Il pastor fido* (pr. 1596; *The Faithful Shepherd*, 1602), a tragicomedy based on a story by Pausanias. Set in Arcady, the basic plot is extremely complicated and somber in tone, involving a number of unrequited love affairs, jealous intrigues, and a threat of death looming over the protagonists. This is intermingled with a modicum of satiric comedy and ends with an anagnorisis of true relationships, love triumphant, and an oracle fulfilled. The influence of *The Faithful Shepherd* cannot be overemphasized:

Guarini's play was translated, adapted, and imitated throughout Europe, confirming the age's taste for idealized swains, Platonic romances, and abstractly classical settings.

Following Aristotle's example, the Renaissance critics wasted little time in analyzing comedy. Castelvetro, Scaliger, Giraldi Cinthio, and the rest all stressed the low station of the characters and the private nature of the events. Scaliger noted of the plot that it begins in confusion and ends in resolution; Castelvetro made the remarkable comment that comic characters have recourse to law, whereas tragic characters must defend their honor in other ways that lie outside the courts. He also astutely recognized that the comic characters' joy, transmitted to the audience, consisted in concealing a disgrace, saving oneself from shame, and the like. These minor victories were to remain the stuff of farcical situations. An Oedipus loses his eyes; a Monsieur Prud'homme loses his trousers. Oedipus chooses his disgrace; Monsieur Prud'homme exults in evading his.

The Italian imitation of the *palliatae* of Plautus and Terence resulted in the *commedia erudita*, or school comedy, which enlisted the conventional parasites, pedants, and so on, and tacked on snippets of morality. The slavish way in which many authors stuck to their originals was commented on by the sarcastic Lasca:

> Authors of such comedies jumble up the new and the old, antique and modern together, making a hodge-podge and confusion, without rhyme or reason, head or tail. They lay their scenes in modern cities and depict the manners of today, but foist in obsolete customs and habits of remote antiquity. Then they excuse themselves by saying: Plautus did thus, and this was Menander's way and Terence's; never perceiving that in Florence, Pisa and Lucca people do not live as they used to do in Rome and Athens.

Eventually, however, dramatists managed to adapt the five-act structure and the conventions of Roman comedy to the mores of their own times. Among others, Ludovico Ariosto in *La cassaria* (pr. 1508; *The Coffer*, 1975), Niccolò Machiavelli in *La mandragola* (pr. 1519; *The Mandrake*, 1911), and Pietro Aretino in *Il marescalco* (pb. 1533; *The Marescalco*, 1986) produced literate comedies in racy language about scabrous modern characters without doing damage to the classical unities. The best features of the *commedia erudita* are its well-observed types and its craftsmanlike handling of intricate imbroglios; for post-Renaissance audiences, its least effective feature is a windy verbosity, the need to tell rather than to show. It efficiently superseded such earlier forms of Italian comedy as the *contrasti*, which features disputations between pairs of allegorical characters, and the *frottola*, in which humans replace the abstractions.

The *commedia erudita* did not, however, manage to supplant forms of comedy that were firmly rooted in Italian soil. The *farsa*, an earthly medieval comedy of plebeian life, persisted, although it came to be redefined as a subcategory of tragicomedy which "accepts all subjects—grave and gay, profane and sacred, urbane and rude, sad and pleasant," and has no truck with the unities. "The scene," explained Cecchi of Florence, "may be laid in a church, or a public square, or where you will, and if one day is not long enough, two or three may be employed."

Commedia dell'arte might be translated as "plays performed by professionals," to distinguish it from the erudite drama acted by nobles and university students. Although a number of individuals, including Francesco Cherea and Angelo Beolco, have, at one time or another, been credited with inventing it, it is more likely that it originated among the wandering jugglers and entertainers who, from Egyptian times, have preserved the popular traditions of the professional theater. Many of the character types from the Atellan farces and even the Greek *phylakes* were preserved and transmuted in it, taking on distinctive dialects and mannerisms of the Italian regions. Pappus became Pantalone, a merchant of Venice, greedy, lustful, and crabbed; the hunchback, hooknosed Maccus transformed into Pulcinello, brutal and rapacious; the pedant reappeared as Il Dottore, a grandiloquent, stuttering lawyer from Bologna; the clever slave and the dim-witted slave recur as Brighella and Arlecchino (Harlequin), the latter a peasant from Bergamo, victim of his appetites. Different troupes and regions renamed the characters at will and modified their endowments, but the basic types were conspicuous throughout Italy. Sometime in the late fifteenth century, the *capitano spavente*, a fire-eating but cowardly braggart, was added, possibly by Venturino of Pesara, partly in imitation of Plautus, and partly to mock the Spanish mercenaries who engineered the sack of Rome.

"The *Commedia dell'arte* does not exist as an independent body of drama," states K. M. Lea in her classic *Italian Popular Comedy* (1934). The scripts were not finished literary products but rather scenarios (*soggetti*), offering a three-act plot line with a prologue and a sequence of incidents; within these guidelines, the players were free to improvise their dialogue, exploiting local personalities and issues, or to draw on their stockpile of comic devices. Many set pieces, especially the love scenes, the *concetti* or aphorisms, and the elaborate physical business, known as *lazzi* (for example, two servants tied back to back trying to eat a plate of pasta lying on the ground), were known by heart and interpolated as the spirit moved. Leather masks immediately established the character and compelled the performer to use his body and voice to express what his face could not (ordinarily, the lovers were not masked). The popularity of this improvisatory genre prompted playwrights and writers in other theatrical forms to co-opt its strategies and stock characters: Lecchino, Pantalone, and their crew popped up in court entertainments; Massimo Troiano and the composer Orlando de Lasso, in 1568, regaled the duke of Bavaria with a medley of music, *lazzi*, and *commedia* characters; and the *Ballet comique de la Reine* (pr. 1581) transported a similar divertissement to the French court. The *commedia dell'arte*'s influence on the history of comedy, dance, opera, mime, and every theatrical form in which text is subservient to performance was immense.

FRENCH RENAISSANCE

The transition from medieval to Renaissance genres occurred later in France. The *mystères* had been banned in 1548, at which time the Pléiade, that galaxy of poets and taste-makers, was canvassing for the classics and urging imitation of Greek and Latin models. Significantly, members of the Pléiade acted

in Étienne Jodelle's *Cléopâtre captive* (pr. 1552; Cleopatra in bondage). *Cléopâtre captive* was known as the first "regular" French tragedy, and *Eugène* (pr. 1552), the first "regular" French comedy. In 1572, in a preface to *Saül le furieux* (Saul gone mad), Jean de la Taille asserted that tragedy, that "most elegant, excellent and splendid" type of poetry, essentially required unity of time and place. *Cléopâtre captive* is unregenerately Senecan, highly declamatory, with the obligatory ghost and chorus. The verse is in couplets of iambic pentameter, with occasional lapses into Alexandrines. The Alexandrine couplet was established by J. B. de La Péruse, in his *Médée* (pr. c. 1553?), as the standard verse form for French tragedy.

The most interesting experiments at this time were in adapting the biblical material of the *mystères* to the new classical format, but Scriptural stories and saints' lives were rapidly effaced by Jacques Amyot's 1559 French translation of Plutarch's *Bioi paralleloi* (c. 105-115; *Parallel Lives*, 1579), a treasure trove of incident and character. It is curious that Alexandre Hardy's dramatization of Amyot's translation of a Greek romance, titled *Les Chastes et loyales amours de Théagène et Chariclée* (pr. 1623; the chaste and faithful loves of Theagenus and Chariclea), was divided into eight *journées*, or days, a unit of the medieval dramatic structure. It soon became clear that the public preferred five-act structures entailing one day's action, despite the occasional complaint, such as Pierre de Laudun's in 1559, that packing all the action into one day destroys illusion, while thinning the action to fit a day denudes the play.

Many of the changes were required by the physical restrictions of the playing space. The medieval *mystère*, taking place in the open, could be fluid in its movement and take advantage of numerous stage settings, such as the "mansions," emblematic indications of locale arranged to be traversed lineally. The Hôtel de Bourgogne, which very probably housed the first French professional acting troupe, had limited space, and mansions were replaced by symbolic stage properties. These proliferated to such an extent that the patrons complained that props were incapable of representing all the necessary locales; in compliance, actors and playwrights began to narrow the scope of the action and generalize the location. This they would later justify by appeal to the unities, but in reality the innovations were practical responses to public demand.

In the sixteenth century, the French theater was relatively free of control from above and could draw its subject matter from any source it chose. The first tragedy written on a contemporary subject was Gabriel Bounyn's *La Soltane* (pb. 1561; the Sultan). Under the Medicis, Italian influence made Giovanni Boccaccio and his fellow romancers the dramatist's main creditors, but Nicolas Filleul's introduction of the pastoral in his *Achille* (pr. 1563) was a failure. The biblical tragedies, infused with the Calvinist temper of the Huguenots, became more spare and took to imitating Seneca. As for comedy, it shared the subject matter of the farce, even as it strove to resemble a five-act *palliata* by Terence. It is significant that Jodelle's *Eugène* pivots on the theme of cuckoldry, which came to dominate French comedy and, later, drama for centuries. A troupe of Italian comedians settled in Paris in 1576, and suddenly French prose comedy was revitalized by a vivacious set of characters and plot devices. Basically, however, the most popular form remained tragicomedy. French tragedy and comedy would not assume their characteristic shapes until the seventeenth century.

SPANISH AND GERMAN RENAISSANCE

Of the other important literatures of the European Renaissance, the Spanish and the German remained relatively untouched by the classical infection, and the English managed to survive it and render it benign. The first Spanish play of any stature was a tragicomedy, *Comedia de Calisto y Melibea* (1499, rev. ed. 1502 as *Tragicomedia de Calisto y Melibea*; commonly known as *La Celestina*; *Celestina*, 1631), attributed to Fernando de Rojas and written more as a novel in dialogue than as a stage play. This realistic, almost cynical story of a tragic love affair, with its vivid characterization of the old bawd Celestina and her associates, proved so irresistible that later dramatists scaled down the twenty-one act version of 1499 to suit the exigencies of their own theaters. Shakespeare seems to have drawn on it for *Romeo and*

Juliet. Influential though it was, *Celestina* was an anomaly. The first true Spanish dramas are credited to Juan del Encina, religious and pastoral eclogues that he called *representaciones* and were imitated in Portugal by Gil Vicente.

Encina was followed by Bartolomeo de Torres Naharro, who, in 1517, published eight plays, divided into *comedias a noticia*, which dealt with actual events, and *comedias a fantasia*, which used imaginary events; each of these irregular and loosely knit pieces, uninhibited by the unities, began with an *introyto*, or argument, and was divided into three *jornadas*, equivalent to the French *journée*. Torres Naharro's influence was limited by the Inquisition, which prohibited his plays. Less ambitious and perhaps more indigenous were the *pasos*, short comedies founded on popular sayings, and the *coloquios* of Lope de Rueda, pastoral farces in the form of dialogues among shepherds and a shepherdess, which were occasionally spiced with comic interludes featuring familiar types such as the Blackamoor and the Biscayan. These *entremeses*, or interludes, were developed by Miguel de Cervantes into pungent and well-observed one-act comedies of real life; the grounding in reality was also present in his tragedies, in which he introduced a personified abstraction, as in the morality, to speak a "divine" or heightened language.

The earliest Spanish tragedies were stilted imitations of classical originals, but the genius of Lope de Vega Carpio, Pedro Calderón de la Barca, and Luis Veléz de Guevara transformed Spanish drama into a brilliantly idiosyncratic school with its own genres. The standard Spanish term for a play, *comedia*, implies a romantic drama that combines elements of comedy and tragedy. The innumerable *comedias* of Lope de Vega, for example, can be divided into several subgenres.

The *comedia de ingenio*, or cape and sword dramas (*capa y espada*), derived their name from the everyday costume of the main characters, persons of noble birth. Although the plots were seldom original, the titles were ethnically Hispanic, deriving from proverbs, and the intrigue revolved around gallantry. Action was plentiful, both in the main plot and in the subplot, which concerned the *gracioso*, or rustic fop. The *comedia heroica*, or *de teatro*, dealt with royal or high-ranking figures; historical, mythological, or national themes; or current events. Its tone was more serious than that of the cape and sword play, concerning as it did the *pundonor*, the code of honor by which a gentleman lived, but it, too, had a comic underplot. Lope de Vega also wrote undesignated plays of the common people. All three types are notable for an alacrity of rhythm, sprightly dialogue, and a minimum of static or analytic passages.

Tragedy in the classic sense could not exist in Spain for theological reasons: God and the believer were on chivalric terms with each other. Fate could not be inexorable because divine magnanimity left the field open to free will, and miracles could always supervene at the eleventh hour. Therefore, when all secular plays were prohibited between 1598 and 1600, Lope de Vega turned his attention to the *comedia de santos*, or *de cuerpo*, miracle plays, and the *auto sacramental*, a development from the open-air Corpus Christi pageant. These solemn proceedings in honor of the Sacrament followed a set pattern: two or more characters speaking a complimentary prologue (the *loa*), a lyric farce or two (the *entremeses*) allied in nature to the *paso*; and the *auto* itself, an allegorical depiction of the sinful soul wavering and transgressing until Divine Grace intervenes, the ultimate *deus ex machina*.

So rich and vital was the Spanish drama of this period that, well into the nineteenth century, playwrights, librettists, and novelists of other nations looted it for plots and characters. The French and English tragicomedies of the seventeenth century would have been impoverished without it, and Guiseppe Verdi would have had to look elsewhere for the stories of some of his most popular operas. The genres fixed by Calderón, Lope de Vega, and Miguel de Cervantes maintained their hold in Spain with little change until the eighteenth century endorsed French fashion. Augustín Moreto did modulate the cape and sword drama into the *comedia de figuron*, or comedy of character, which streamlined the plots, put the *gracioso* center stage, and claimed to cleave to nature. Similarly, the *entremes* became divorced from

the religious drama and evolved into the *saynete* (as Toribio de Benavente called it around 1645), which literally means "a tasty morsel of crackling" and was a clownish little farce, usually containing a piquant moral. The flourishing of the Spanish drama can be attributed to the inability of the academic strictures to take root there; the theater always remained close to popular tastes and national sentiments.

ELIZABETHAN AND JACOBIAN ENGLAND

A similar situation obtained in England, where the introduction of Seneca and Terence prompted imitation but never preempted the indigenous modes of dramatic presentation. The shapeless intermingling of these elements can be seen in the interminable tragedy *Gorboduc* (pr. 1561), by Thomas Norton and Thomas Sackville intended for performance by lawyers for lawyers. The argument is drawn from pre-Christian Britain, pays no heed to unity of time and place, and contains allegorical dumb shows (the term itself had entered the English language only in 1561, the year before *Gorboduc* was first performed). These mimic depictions, featured between the numerous acts of *Gorboduc*, may have originated in the popular Italian *intermedii* or in the city pageants and court masques. At the same time, *Gorboduc* features a Senecan chorus and verbose messengers, for its ample violence is kept offstage. *Gorboduc* initiated act division and the use of blank-verse dialogue into English drama. Iambic pentameter established its dominion so rapidly in the English theater that when the complete translation of Seneca appeared in 1581, it failed to get a stage hearing because it was cast in fourteen-syllable lines.

Gorboduc, with its mélange of ancient and modern devices, was not thought a good model by Sir Philip Sidney. In his *Defence of Poesie* (1595), he censured native dramatic forms such as the miracles and moralities as antiquated vestiges of popery, "vaine playes or enterludes," unfit to carry out the drama's Horatian purpose "to teach and delight." Judging by Italian canons, Sidney found that *Gorboduc* was not strict enough in its observance of the rules, even though he refused to endorse the unities and allowed a messenger or chorus to span the breaks in time and place. Tragicomedy had crept into English in Richard Edwards's *Damon and Pithias* (pr. 1564), but Sidney condemned the genre as "mungrell," mixing kings and clowns with neither decency nor discretion; he maintained that even comedy must go beyond scornful laughter if it is to teach delightfully. Sidney's aristocratic strictures, however, had no bearing on the actual state of playwriting even when they were first published, and they remain an elegant if vain attempt to foster neoclassical drama in England.

Sidney extolled the poet over the historian, not only because the poet's teachings are pleasurable ("sportive" is a favorite word of Sidney) but also because tragedy exercises its own justice to punish vice and reward virtue. Ironically, even as he penned that sentiment, English playwrights were delving into their own national past for plots, to develop a native genre, the chronicle history. The clumsy but vigorous play *The Famous Victories of Henry V* (pr. c. 1588) would be improved on by Shakespeare, who also lent a hand to the *Tragedy of Sir Thomas More* (pr. c. 1590), which added a tragic component to the chronicle by demonstrating the hamartia of the central character. This hybrid of tragedy and history was exceptionally successful in Shakespeare: *Hamlet, Prince of Denmark* (pr. 1600-1601), *Macbeth* (pr. 1606), and *King Lear* (pr. c. 1605-1606) all begin with a kernel of "factual" data from Raphael Holinshed or Saxo Grammaticus but expand to treat subjects of universal import. Furthermore, the expertise of Shakespeare and his fellows in theatricalizing English history gave them a fluency and ease in handling classical history (*Julius Caesar*, pr. c. 1599-1600; Ben Jonson's *Sejanus His Fall*, pr. 1603) that is lacking in their foreign contemporaries. Their treatment of classical topics was not restrained by classical rules.

When, in *Hamlet, Prince of Denmark*, Polonius reads the roster of entertainments that the players are prepared to offer, one can infer the relaxed attitude toward genres that was prevalent in Elizabethan and Jacobean drama: "tragedy, comedy, pastoral, pastoral-comical, historical-pastoral, tragical-historical, tragical-comical, historical-pastoral, scene individable, or poem unlimited." By Continental standards, Elizabethan and Jacobean tragedy, in particular, was shockingly irregular, with its blatant cruelty, rapid shifts in time and space, and the jostling of the sublime and the ridiculous. Its protagonists were extremists, exemplified by Christopher Marlowe's overreachers, the grandeur of whose ambition outweighs the failure or moral obloquy of their enterprise. Fate, viewed as contingency, rules over the passions—hence the frequent reference to astrology and omens, the strong hand of the supernatural in human affairs. Ghosts, especially, teem in the genre known as revenge tragedy, perhaps introduced by Thomas Kyd's *The Spanish Tragedy* (pr. c. 1585-1589) and the anonymous *Locrine* (1595), and honed to a fine edge by Shakespeare, John Webster, Cyril Tourneur, and Thomas Middleton. Motivated by a crime committed in the past, the lone avenger follows the thread of his vendetta through to a gory end, leaving the stage strewn with corpses.

The red-blooded (in every sense) form of Elizabethan and Jacobean tragedy was the direct result of theatrical conditions: The audience was heterogeneous, ranging from the groundlings in the pit to the exquisites in the boxes (or even onstage), and the coexistence of convoluted, image-packed poetry and exuberant action in the same play was meant to provide something for everyone. (Plays produced in the banquet halls display subtler effects and quieter moods.) In the open-air playhouse, the actors were so close to the public that soliloquies and asides could be intimately addressed to it; the two permanent doors at the back of the stage, which permitted one set of characters to enter as another departed, made for maximum overlap and speed of scene changes. (It should be remembered that the formal act and scene breakdowns of these plays were often supplied by the publishers and therefore do not reflect the actual unbroken continuity of stage action.) The doors also made for much "Look where he comes" and "But see who comes here" in the dialogue. As in the French theater of the time, limited space put greater emphasis on properties, so that crowns and mirrors, handkerchiefs and rings took on symbolic qualities. Dialogue served the function of scene painting ("This is Illyria, lady"; "This castle hath a pleasant seat") and stage directions ("See how it stalks away"; the cues for Malvolio's yellow stockings and cross garters). Duels, battles, murders, elaborate pageants, and shows were included to beguile the eye of the audience and make it attentive to the more subdued moments. With the proliferation of theaters and the need for new plays, speedy composition, often in collaboration, kept to a minimum a nice observation of literary regulations.

When Polonius jibs at a lengthy heroic speech, Hamlet derides him: "He's for a jig or a tale of bawdy, or he sleeps." The jig, a lively interlude or afterpiece, usually in rhyme and occasionally improvised, is barely distinguishable from the droll, a one-man farce full of topical references and catchphrases. The clowns who were the favored performers of jigs and drolls—such as Richard Tarlton, who became the first nationally known "star" in England—did not abandon their flair for improvisation even when participating in written comedies and so kept that form from congealing. Elizabethan comedy was a farrago of folkloric characters, romantic Italian plots, and mythological additives from the pastoral. The attempts to naturalize this latter genre by Ben Jonson, John Fletcher, and Samuel Daniel were not successful, any more than were Jonson's stern edicts that classical models were the best guide to playwriting.

The irrelevance of classic genre divisions for the English drama becomes clear after a glance at the way Shakespeare's first editors, John Heminge and Henry Condell, subdivided his plays into "Comedies, Histories and Tragedies." The comedies include Plautine imitations such as *The Comedy of Errors* (pr. c. 1592-1594), an Italianate farce such as *The Taming of the Shrew* (pr. c. 1593-1594), and pastoral adventures such as *As You Like It* (pr. c. 1599-1600) in the same company with *Measure for Measure* (pr. 1604), referred to by modern critics as a "problem comedy," and *The Winter's Tale* and *The Tempest* (pr. 1611), baptized "romances" by Samuel Taylor Coleridge and heavily alloyed with masque elements. The history category is more straightforward, limited exclusively to chronicle plays of the English past. With tragedies, the sense of an *omnium gatherum* is again felt: Dramas from Roman history rub elbows with a story of private calamity such as *Romeo and Juliet*

(pr. c. 1595-1596). A romantic treatment of early Britain such as *Cymbeline* (pr. c. 1609-1610) is grouped with a bleak vision of early Britain such as *King Lear*. The domestic disaster of *Othello, the Moor of Venice* (pr. 1604) is neighbored by the universal span of *Antony and Cleopatra* (pr. c. 1606-1607). Admittedly, Shakespeare was more various and ingenious than his colleagues, but it is clear that form fit function in the drama of the period. A play took on the shape it needed without attention to labels.

Although they were given their modern titles only by later writers, the genres of romance and domestic tragedy assumed characteristic profiles at this time. The romance was so called because its story came from a tale or novella (any source was fair game) and often employed supernatural machinery and magic to attain its happy end; love was a leading motif. The domestic tragedy was a diminution of the chronicle play. Usually founded on a current news item of conjugal murder, it applies the structure and occasionally the tone and language of high tragedy to household events. Works such as *Arden of Feversham* (pb. 1592), Thomas Heywood's *A Woman Killed with Kindness* (pr. 1603), and *A Yorkshire Tragedy* (pb. 1608; once attributed to Shakespeare, who seems never to have dabbled in the genre) were consciously chosen as forerunners by such founders of latter-day bourgeois tragedies as George Lillo, Denis Diderot, and Gotthold Ephraim Lessing.

The masque, as noted above, was an Italian import, a blend of music and spoken dialogue, dancing and dumb show, with sumptuous decorative trappings and usually performed by amateurs. It was allegorical: a dolled-up morality without the moral, one might say. The earliest masques were mute, with the performers miming and dancing to the music, but by the mid-sixteenth century, words—both spoken and sung—had become a leading feature. Masques were generally private affairs, performed at weddings, banquets, and similar special occasions, by and for the nobility and the upper-middle class, indoors. The earliest masque may be Thomas Nabbes's *Microcosmus* (pr. 1637), whose kinship with the morality play is abundantly evident. By the early seventeenth century, the masque was the favorite entertainment at the court of King James I, who subsidized first-rate dramatists such as Jonson to lend their talents to it. The antimasque, a grotesque interlude that contrasted violently with the beauty and harmony of the masque, was created by Jonson in 1613. Despite his successes, the testy playwright gave up writing masques because, he complained with some justice, poetry was sacrificed to the splendor of scenic design; certainly Inigo Jones's settings and costumes are among the glories of decorative art. John Milton's *Comus* (pr. 1634) is the last masque to qualify as great literature before the form was submerged in the nascent opera.

Jonson was also the chief promulgator and exponent of a new style of comedy, the comedy of humors. Fundamentally related to the medieval psycho-physiological scheme that the human body was composed of four elements, or "humors" (blood, phlegm, black bile, and yellow bile), which, in disproportion, incline the personality to one excess or another, the comedy of humors exhibited characters who were not so much social types as pathological freaks. In Jonson's earliest specimens, *Every Man in His Humour* (pr. 1598) and *Every Man Out of His Humour* (pr. 1599), the characters are living demonstrations of their names, and although the former play is set in Italy, Jonson had no difficulty in transferring its action to London because the types bear few national characteristics. Having proved popular, this style evolved into a comedy of manners that reflected contemporary life as no other dramatic form had yet done. Jonson himself, however, was somewhat restricted by his allegiance to the classical authorities: He intended to scourge vice with satire in the manner of Horace and Juvenal while keeping to the unities. In a comedy such as *The Alchemist* (pr. 1610), he restricts the action to one day and one house, even as he brags of the play's topicality in his prologue:

> Our scene is London, 'cause we would make known,
> No country's mirth is better than our own;
> No clime breeds better for your whore,
> Bawd, squire, imposter, many persons more,
> Whose manners, now call'd humours, feed the stage.

Following the rules when all about him were ignoring them, Jonson was forced continually to engage in contentious prologues and inductions in which he justified his clinging to or falling from ancient precepts. His fellow comic writers, insouciant of endorsement from the ancients, were able to develop a citizen comedy that was realistic in ambience and novel in its plotting and characterization, because it was based on observation. Such plays as Thomas Middleton's *A Trick to Catch the Old One* (pr. c. 1605) and *A Chaste Maid in Cheapside* (pr. 1611) are virtual panoramas of London life.

The drama of the English Renaissance failed to have any influence on the Continent, except in Germany and points east. Hans Sachs's remodeling of the *Fastnachtsspiel* had merely smartened dialogue and brought the tone into closer touch with the rising burgher class. The *Englische Komödianten*, London players who toured Northern Europe beginning in 1585 with simplified versions of Christopher Marlowe, Shakespeare, and other staples of the Elizabethan repertory, had an immense impact on the inexperienced spectators. In garbled versions, the works of the Elizabethans permeated German Baroque drama for more than a century, and traces of English mummeries and *Hamlet, Prince of Denmark* can even be found in Russian folk-plays. The residual impression was one of bloodletting and buffoonery, and the preeminence of the clown, under such names as Pickelherring, Hans Supp, and Jean Potage, was a lasting legacy.

Opera

In the seventeenth century, the scepter of artistic sway passed to France. Italy made no new experiments in dramatic form except to add music to tragedy, which was eventually swamped by the increasing popularity of opera. *Opera in musica*, Italian for "a musical work," was soon abbreviated elsewhere, while at various times it was known in Italy as *dramma per musica* (drama in music), *favola* (fable), and *melodrama* (song drama). As a form of drama wholly set to music, it may have begun as an amateur attempt to re-create Greek tragedy: According to one story, the form originated when Galileo's father,

Vincenzo Galilei, a dilettante dabbling in monody in Florence in the early sixteenth century, sang the tale of Ugolino's starvation to the lute, much as Greek rhapsodists recited Homer. This fusion of drama and music was at first approved more by literary coteries than by professional musicians. Jacopo Peri's *Euridice* (pr. 1600) was the first public performance in this mode, although Orazio Vecchi's *L'Amfiparnaso* (pr. 1594) cobbled a sort of musical comedy out of polyphonic madrigals, using characters from the *commedia dell'arte*.

The step taken from these inchoate experiments to Claudio Monteverdi's operas was gigantic, though accomplished in a few years' time, and the richness of orchestration, emotional eloquence, and immediacy that were to characterize the genre are already present in Monteverdi's *L'Orfeo* (pr. 1607; *Orfeo*, 1949; with a libretto by Alessandro Striggio) and *Il combattimento di Tancredi e Clorinda* (pr. 1624; the battle of Tancred and Clorinda), employing a classical myth and a Renaissance romance, respectively. Recitative—that is, free musical declamation—was thought the only worthy medium of expression. Gradually, however, as opera became more popular, moving out of the court and into the theaters, tunes and melodies were introduced, and by Alessandro Scarlatti's time, in the early seventeenth century, tunes had blossomed into arias.

"From this time, until the death of Handel," wrote Donald Tovey, "the history of opera is simply the history of the aria; except in so far as in France, under Lully, it is also the history of ballet-making, the other main theatrical occasion for the art of tune-making." The *opera seria* (serious opera) of the period was a formal affair, set in classical antiquity or in an exotic clime and reliant on lavish spectacle and the exhibitionistic vocalism of castrati and female sopranos. Henry Purcell, in such works as *Dido and Aeneas* (pr. 1689) and *King Arthur* (pr. 1691), infused operatic music with emotional chromatics, and the Neapolitan composers of burlesque operas also escaped the rigidity of the French school. Not until Christoph Gluck, however, did opera change significantly, by means of the sonata, then developing into the symphony; as orchestral coloration deepened, so,

too, did the possibility for musical drama. With Wolfgang Amadeus Mozart, opera achieved full theatrical citizenship. In his operas, every note of music, rather than being wholly an excuse for vocal display or instrumental virtuosity, makes a dramatic point, assists the characterizations, and contributes to the total effect. The arias and ensembles drive the action rather than impede it, and the subtlety of orchestration adds a richer texture to the script. Mozart was fortunate in having the witty Lorenzo Da Ponte as his librettist on *Le nozze di Figaro* (pr. 1786; *The Marriage of Figaro*, 1894), *Il dissoluto punito* (pr. 1787; *Don Giovanni*, 1817), and *Così fan tutte* (pr. 1790; *The Retaliation*, 1894), but even the messy text of Emmaneul Schikaneder's *Singspiel die Zauberflöte* (pr. 1791; *The Magic Flute*, 1829) is transfigured and given sublimity by the music.

After Mozart, the tight web of music and drama began to unravel, and, with the possible exception of Gioacchino Rossini, most composers neglected mood and plot in favor of display; the *bel canto* school of Vincenzo Bellini and Gaetano Donizetti was more interested in vocal pyrotechnics than in dramatic cogency, and however much one thrills to the beauty of their mad scenes and ensembles, one cannot take seriously the characters or their predicaments. Like the Romantic dramatists, these composers were inspired by Shakespeare and Sir Walter Scott, whose works they pillaged for librettos; every so often, real passion breaks through, as in Rossini's *Otello* (pr. 1816), or genuine fantasy takes over, as in Carl Maria von Weber's *Der Freischütz* (pr. 1821; the enchanted marksman). The last major school of opera as a dramatic genre, before Richard Wagner and the later Giuseppe Verdi changed the rules of the game, was that of Giacomo Meyerbeer, whose grand operas were massive machines, overloaded with flamboyant set pieces, lavish scenery, all-star ensembles, and glamorous locales; the lushness of the music and the savoir faire of the showmanship cannot disguise its quintessential, albeit enjoyable, vulgarity.

FRENCH PREEMINENCE

To return to the seventeenth century, the French preeminence in the arts had a political cause. While

England was wracked by civil strife and Germany by the Thirty Years' War and while Italy and Spain underwent disunion and economic distress, France was being stabilized and consolidated. The adventurous individualism of the Renaissance was giving way to the sedate orderliness of national consciousness, and unbridled fancy yielded to rationality. From 1622 on, Cardinal Richelieu, who had been centralizing the power of the French monarchy, applied the same principles to the arts. The foundation of the Académie Française marked a move to legislate for literature a code that would prevent deleterious pluralism; similarly, the theater was to be elevated and the dramatic poet patronized and honored. The unities and other conventional devices that had previously been adopted out of expediency or mutual consent would become doctrinaire.

In 1631, in a preface to his pastoral tragicomedy *La Silvanire: Ou, La Mortevive* (pr. 1630, pb. 1631), itself founded on a prose romance, Jean Mairet endorsed the unities of action, time, and place. His endorsement was in some ways a reply to François Ogier, the last French defender of dramatic license for the next two centuries. Ogier, in support of Jean de Schelandre's *Tyr et Sidon* (pr. 1608), an earlier drama that defied the unities, insisted that plausibility is offended by the packing of many events into one day and that messengers and expository narratives are boring. Athens and Rome were not modern France, and even if they were, the ancients themselves violated the rules. Ogier, however, was fighting a losing battle. In the 1634-1635 season, three tragedies written according to the rules were presented and acclaimed by the public. Pierre Corneille's *Médée* (pr. 1635), Georges de Scudéry's *La Mort de César* (pb. 1636), and, most significantly, Mairet's own *Sophonisbe* (pr. 1634; *Sophonisba*, pb. 1956), which the Académie had qualified as absolutely "correct."

During the next decades, theorists such as Jean Chapelain, René Rapin, Charles de Saint-Denis, Sieur de Saint-Évremond, and Nicolas Boileau would write the prescriptions for drama, eventuating in the Abbé d'Aubignac's handbook for dramatists, *Pratique du théâtre* (1657). This is not the place to examine the arguments for and against the rules and the various interpretations given to Aristotle, except insofar as they affected written and performed drama. It must be borne in mind that much of the theory was composed to justify a preexisting theatrical situation, and two elements were critical in this regard.

First, the stage itself continued to be cramped, which restricted physical action; with the possibility of spectacle or strenuous movement eliminated, the focus had to be on psychological action. Consequently, French comedy specialized in comedy of character, and French tragedy in the intensive anatomy of motives and passions. Second, the audience, a mixture of aristocracy and bourgeoisie, had its taste dictated from above, by court circles and salons. This public prided itself on a nice discrimination and a fastidious judgment; it preferred to exercise its rational faculties rather than its imagination in the theater (and since many of the cognoscenti were sitting on the stage, any elaborate stage illusion would be difficult to sustain). Hence the recurrence of the term *vraisemblance* (verisimilitude) as a critical tenet expressing the need for plausibility in drama.

Essentially, all the calls for unity of time, place, and action, the integrity of the genre, and the decorum of presentation aided plausibility, making a jaded and demanding audience accept what it sees—or rather, hears, because the audience had been trained in games in salon conversation—"Discourse for five minutes on the difference between self-love and selfless love"—and was alert to the subtleties of a moral disquisition. Whether it be Phaedra parsing the nuances of her guilt or Tartuffe caustically equating his lust with divine adoration, the characters of French neoclassical drama always reveal themselves in well-structured speeches, or tirades (that is, something spun out in one long filament).

The case of Corneille is revealing of the manner in which French dramatists tailored their plays to the demands of the critics. His immensely popular *Le Cid* (pr. 1637; *The Cid*, 1637) was attacked, partly for its very popularity, and submitted to the Académie for an opinion. This verdict (drawn up by the neoclassical propagandist Chapelain and redrafted at Richelieu's behest) upheld Corneille's choice in tampering with history but condemned him for breaching credibility by overloading his twenty-four hours with too much action and by outraging decorum by allowing the character of Chimene to favor passion over duty. The rest of Corneille's long career was devoted to answering this criticism and avoiding a recurrence of these so-called faults. As Saintsbury said, there is something bizarre in the picture of "a genius curbing himself to the tendencies of the times and the dictates of the wits." Can one picture Shakespeare bowing to Jonson's strictures or Milton revising *Paradise Lost* (1667, 1674) to suit John Dryden?

Corneille did, in fact, generate two new types of tragedy: The *tragédie héroique*, in fashion between 1640 and 1650, drew on Roman history and exhibited the will overcoming obstacles set by circumstance or personal penchants, with serious consequences to the state, religion, or family. Its set of values centers on humanistic self-respect (*gloire*), which regards each blow of implacable fate as a challenging ordeal, not as a disaster. *Polyeucte* (pr. 1642; *Polyeuctes*, 1655) is perhaps the most interesting of these in linking Christian mysticism to Roman heroism. With *Don Sanche d'Aragon* (pr. 1650; *The Conflict*, 1798), Corneille created the *tragédie romanesque*, in which "love" may be substituted for "will"; familial or civic duties, differences in rank, and merely mistaken identities are overcome by a lofty and gallant passion. Indebted to both the Spanish cape-and-sword dramas and the rambling romances of Georges de Scudéry and Gautier de Costes de la Calprenède, the romantic tragedy enjoyed theatrical popularity but was overshadowed by the heroic form. Corneille himself considered love to be too trivial to carry a tragedy, and he posited "heroic comedy" as a potential genre.

On a number of scores, Corneille refuted or modified Aristotle in order to expand the possibilities of tragedy. While accepting tragedy's moral intent, imposed by the critics, he insisted on both a just distribution of punishments and rewards to please the audience and a purgation of passion through pity and fear. The Renaissance had interpreted catharsis as the moderation of injurious emotions; Corneille denied that this occurs. In accord with a growing taste for sentiment, he suggested that one pities the protagonists and fears to fall into their dilemmas, and thus

one purges the excesses that led the protagonists to their plights. He asserted that both saints and criminals could be proper heroes of a tragedy, a doctrine that he illuminated by the devout Polyeucte, and the vicious Cléopâtre in *Rodogune* (pr. 1644-1645); the touchstone for heroism was the character's *grandeur*, a magnitude of soul. This is an early glimpse at a more modern notion of tragic sublimity. He also introduced a new unity, the unity of peril, which the hero must either triumph over or fall beneath.

Many of Corneille's innovations were reactions to actual work in the theater; neoclassical doctrine had not congealed when he began playwriting, and he tried to modify critical dogma with hands-on experience — hence his subtle explanation of the locale of the action (*le lieu théâtral*) as a vague and nondescript space, like an antechamber, which would allow the actors to infringe on unity of place and move from city to city by taking a few steps. His *liaison des scènes*, the relating of each incident within a tight sequential pattern, corresponded to his audience's finicky insistence on plausibility and linear thinking. He recommended music to cover the noise of scene changes, cliff-hanging conclusions for the acts to hold the public's attention, stage directions to aid the actors in their portrayals, and an elimination of sung intermezzi.

Corneille's desire to excite commiseration by exhibiting the misfortunes of ordinary mortals was refined and heightened by Jean Racine in his *tragédies passionnées*, a genre that can be defined as any play he wrote after 1667. Physical and external action is reduced to a minimum and the audience is confronted with the spectacle of hearts rent asunder by irrepressible passion, driven to commit crimes despite any outside influences or nobler impulses. Adapting, even thriving on, the stiff etiquette of court ritual, willingly embracing unity of action, time, and place, Racinian tragedy distills its catastrophe into an urgent quintessence. The plays always begin in the middle of a crisis, with the preliminaries omitted or reduced to rapid exposition (as if *Hamlet* were to commence with its fifth act); the tense atmosphere warns that conflicting passions are about to collide in a crescendo of disaster. The cast is boiled down to a few interrelated individuals, held in uneasy balance like a colloidal suspension: Upsetting the balance results in tragedy. In his preface to *Bajazet* (pr. 1672; English translation, 1717), Racine insisted that "tragic characters ought to be regarded with another eye than that we use to observe the usual characters we have beheld close up. It might be said that the respect we have for a hero increases in proportion to his distance from us." Consequently, Racine's heroes are usually royalty, the only persons in the world of Louis XIV who could be supposed to enjoy independence of action and moral choice and who are sufficiently free of external pressures to make their own uninfluenced decisions. They are presented against an abstract and undefined background, within doors of nondescript palaces, the better to divorce them from a distracting context. The *vraisemblance* derives from portraying passion with as much shading and "truth to nature" as possible. Death becomes the only issue for the possessed characters.

Racine was less interested in Aristotle's catharsis, which in his definition meant a moderation of pity and fear, than in hamartia. Like Oedipus, Racine's characters are highly intelligent and self-analytical; their misjudgments arise when their intellects are clouded by passion. Thus, their situations are all the more ghastly, since they perceive their errors even as they make them. For the sake of verisimilitude, Racine eschewed soliloquies and replaced them with confidants of both sexes who act as listening posts and choral commentators. In his late plays drawn from the Bible, *Esther* (pr. 1689; English translation, 1715) and *Athalie* (pr. 1691; *Athaliah*, 1722), Racine introduced a chorus as lyric element, but those productions were in the nature of private experiments performed by amateurs. With Racine, French tragedy lost entirely the medieval vestiges apparent in Hardy and the Spanish influence manifest in Corneille, and became something rarefied, elitist, and basically unexportable.

Comedy, as usual, escaped from the critical straitjacket, not least because the theorists had little to say on the subject. (They stressed its intrigue, for example, so Corneille recommended that it be governed by a so-called unity of intrigue.) In any case, popular tra-

dition was too strong to be entirely overridden. Before 1624, the favorite theaters of Paris had been the trestle stages of the Pont-Neuf, where racy dialogues known as *tabarinades* (after the famous clown Tabarin) were performed. High society's preciosity and fascination with affairs of the heart meant that the love interest of Menander and Terence would be given full value in French literary comedy. A writer such as Molière was free to draw on contemporary romances, popular street farce, the Spanish comedy of intrigue, the Italian *commedia dell'arte* with its stock types, and the French comedy of character. Corneille had tried combining intrigue and character in *Le Menteur* (pr. 1643; *The Mistaken Beauty: Or, The Liar*, 1671), which met with a storm of abuse.

Molière's popularity was founded on his recensions of farces, but he brought the stereotypes up to date by commenting on the manners of his own time. *Les Précieuses ridicules* (pr. 1659; *The Affected Young Ladies*, 1732) won the laughter of the public, even as it earned the hatred of the coteries it satirized. Satire was a major element in Molière's comedies, which fluctuate between barbed attacks on fashionable follies and mirth-making slapstick. Molière was, first and foremost, a man of the theater, who had little time for rules when they conflicted with the immediacy of pleasing an audience. His famous statement, "'Tis no easy matter to make decent people laugh," is the rationale of his method, the exaltation of nature above decorum, and common sense above theory.

Comedy, which had previously been considered a minor genre, rose in stature with Molière, not least because his royal allowance suddenly gave comic poets social prestige. Molière, who was a poor actor in tragedy but a superb comedian, had a vested interest in inflating comedy's stock. He mocked tragedy for being too easy to concoct, whereas comedy, he boasted, is based on observation and requires a genuine artist who is able to bring reality into conflict with the ideal so that their incompatibility will evoke laughter. Perhaps the play that confirmed comedy's growing importance was *L'École des femmes* (pr. 1662; *The School for Wives*, 1714), whose leading character, Arnolphe, deepens from the cliché of a wealthy old crank in love with a young girl into a three-dimensional, sympathetic portrait of a vulnerable if incorrigible human being. Moreover, Arnolphe is not a generalized eccentric but rather a recognizable Parisian bourgeois. In his *Critique de l'École des femmes* (pr. 1663; *The Critique of The School for Wives*, 1714), Molière replied to criticism that Arnolphe's amorous frenzy was overdrawn by having his character Dorante remark, "as if respectable folk, even the gravest among 'em, didn't do things in like situations—in short, if we were to take a good look at ourselves when we are really enamoured—." In other words, comedy is no longer punishment meted out to a few extraordinary social deviants; it is, as Ramón Fernandez says in his biography of Molière, "an outlook upon all mankind, a technique for arresting ourselves and others at any stage of intimacy or deep involvement. It is a mode of expression as viable as tragedy for every human reality that is to be expressed." Comedy was thus rendered capable of treating every aspect of the human experience; one could talk of a comic vision.

Molière also perfected the *comédie-ballet*, a union of farcical high jinks and musical spectacle that was especially to the king's taste. *Le Bourgeois Gentilhomme* (pr. 1670; *The Would-Be Gentleman*, 1675), with its concluding Turkish extravaganza, and *Le Malade imaginaire* (pr. 1673; *The Imaginary Invalid*, 1732), with its pageant of doctors and clysters, relegated the music to interludes and finales. In the composite *tragédie ballet* introduced by Philippe Quinault and exemplified by Molière's *Psyche* (pr. 1671), music prevailed. The increasing concentration of theatrical power in the hands of the composer Jean-Baptiste Lully put new constraints on comedy, and Molière found himself the junior partner in these collaborations, which were a step on the road to *opéra comique*.

BRITISH RESTORATION DRAMA

In England, the Puritan Interregnum interrupted the rich theatrical tradition, forcing the actors out of London and back to the impromptu, miscellaneous fare that had preceded the founding of the playhouses. When Charles II was restored to the throne in 1660, he brought with him French manners, tastes,

and techniques. Suddenly, tragedy and comedy were more sharply differentiated than they had been before. The afterpiece, a short farce to follow a serious play, which had been adopted in France by 1650, became standard practice in England, where, in 1676, Thomas Otway presented *Titus and Berenice*, his adaptation of Racine's *Bérénice* (pr. 1670; English translation, 1676), followed in 1677 by his translation of Molière's *The Cheats of Scapin*. Fortunately, the example of Shakespeare still loomed large (even though he was drastically remodeled to suit Restoration fashion), and English playwrights found themselves trying to mediate between European critical positions and native dramatic instincts.

The first plays staged under the new licences were "dramatic operas," such as Sir William Davenant's earlier *The Siege of Rhodes, Part I* (pr. 1656), compounds of John Fletcher's romances and Corneille's tragedies, lightened by masque and pastoral, aglow with flames of tender love and vaunts of civic rectitude, and pompous with the blare of trumpets and the panoply of stage machines, all of it in tune with the grandiose political ambitions of the period. The heroic play, or heroic tragedy, typified by *The Black Prince* (pr. 1669), by Roger Boyle, Lord Orrery, was heavily indebted to Corneillean models. The themes came from French romances and tragedies, and the rhyme scheme of the heroic couplet was an adaptation of the Alexandrine to English numbers. Unfortunately, to the English ear it is too reminiscent of nursery rhymes and ballad meter to conduce to the highflown atmosphere its practitioners hoped to achieve.

Also in accord with French emphases, the heroic play centered on a love-and-honor conflict, with the hero eventually sighing for his cake and eating it too, for endings were happy and the love portrayed exceedingly idealized and platonic. It was meant to appeal to the sentiments rather than the emotions, particularly since, as in France, audiences were skeptical and distrustful of high seriousness. The resulting form was bombastic, grandiloquent, and artificial to a fault, and it produced no masterpieces.

The critical utterances of John Dryden, who worked changes on the heroic play, reveal a tension between his awareness of imported canons of taste and his fondness for the English tradition. He began his career by championing the heroic drama and ended by abandoning it. He tried to reconcile the employment of rhymed verse with verisimilitude, but he eventually reverted to blank verse (*All for Love: Or, The World Well Lost*, pr. 1677, pb. 1678) despite the misgiving that Shakespeare, Jonson, and Fletcher had exhausted it. Dryden shared his age's desire for harmony and decorum in art, pruning all the extravagances from Shakespeare in his adaptations and adding fresh extravagances of symmetry and operatic spectacle in their stead, along with a unified plot.

Dryden favored poetic justice (a term invented by Thomas Rymer in his 1674 translation of Rapin), since the audience's sympathies lay with a basically virtuous hero. Catharsis thus was interpreted as an amelioration of aggressive emotions by the cultivation of tender emotions of fear and pity. This sentimental strain dominated the next century. For Dryden and his contemporaries, sentimentalism meant the presentation of a tragic hero as a "wondrous kind" and ordinary mortal, whose feelings could readily be understood by the spectator. Regrettably, the average protagonist of heroic tragedy was the sort later parodied by George Villiers, the second duke of Buckingham, in *The Rehearsal* (pr. 1671), and Henry Fielding in *Tom Thumb: A Tragedy* (pr. 1730): an overblown and mouthing helmet topped with plumes surmounting a powdered periwig.

Comedy similarly narrowed its focus. Because opera and heroic drama had taken over romance, comic writers adapted the intricate Spanish and French intrigues to English situations. The result was less derivative and more brilliant than might be expected. In France, courtly conversation had been the paradigm for the verse tirade; in England, it became the model for prose dialogue. Wit was the *sine qua non* of a well-bred gentleman, and dramatic speeches in comedy were made to coruscate with finely aimed volleys of repartee and badinage. This emphasis on wit for its own sake conflicted with the demands of plausible characterization because even the boobies and clodpolls were given clever things to say. If one reads the lesser comedies of the Restoration and not

simply the much-anthologized masterpieces, the mind reels at the wearying sameness of tone and subject matter.

Urbanity is at a premium in Restoration comedy: The admirable characters are the rakes and men-about-town who conduct their affairs with finesse. The laughingstocks are the elderly, the provincial, the married, the business-minded, the foppish, or the obsessed, who are debarred from playing the game of seduction and fortune hunting. Sex, next to money, is the prime mover, a preoccupation with most of the characters, who are evaluated by their sexual viability. The prototype of the Restoration comedy of manners is taken to be Sir George Etherege's *The Man of Mode: Or, Sir Fopling Flutter* (pr. 1676), whose hero, Dorimant, a thoroughly amoral profligate, is permitted to wed the rich and beautiful heiress at the play's end.

Restoration comedy partakes of an odd realism not to be found in the heroic plays. The comedy's locales were the haunts of the beau monde: Saint James' Park, Pall Mall, a young man's dressing room or a lady's boudoir, taverns, law courts, and china closets. Its terms of reference and allusion were more bounded than the Manhattan-minded brand-name jokes in a Neil Simon play. The plays' style and content were meant for immediate reception by an exclusive and limited audience, with no thought of posterity or foreign royalties. Comedy's only aim, Dryden opined, was to beget malicious pleasure, which could be gauged by the public's laughter: "The faults and vices are but the sallies of youth, and the frailties of human nature, and not premeditated crime."

One who did not agree and said so vociferously was the Reverend Jeremy Collier, whose vastly popular, often reprinted, and widely read *A Short View of the Immorality and Profaneness of the English Stage* (1698) heralded a change of attitude of the theatergoing public. Collier's circumstantial diatribe against the comedies of his time is one of the earliest English examples of criticism altering literature in a significant way. Attacking the lewdness, profanity, irreligion, and irregularity of the stage, he put playwrights on the defensive. William Congreve offered a response that failed to make a dent in Collier's spiky armor. For Collier, "the business of plays is to recommend virtue and discountenance vice . . . to make folly and falsehood contemptible, and to bring everything that is ill under infamy and neglect."

The acceptance of Collier's premise (which even Congreve did not question) marks a major turning point. Throughout the eighteenth century, the Aristotelian genres and their previous modifications would be shunted aside by a number of new hybrid genres that catered to the tastes and understandings of a middle-class audience, more moralistic, less classically educated, and less sophisticated than the aristocratic circles whose tastes had dictated to the seventeenth century. "The drama's laws the drama's patrons give," Samuel Johnson was to write later in the century, and the new forms proved it.

Comedy was an early mouthpiece for middle-class morality. Mrs. Susannah Centlivre reclaimed her loose-living characters in the fourth act; George Farquhar reiterated that comedy must not leave vice unpunished or virtue unrewarded if it is to be "utile"; and Colley Cibber not only reformed his characters in *Love's Last Shift* (pr. 1696) but also put a moral sentiment, pathetically handled, right at the center of a comedy in his *The Careless Husband* (pr. 1704). In some small measure, this was a return to the Horatian principles enunciated by Renaissance critics, that audiences must be moved into the self-awareness that leads to moral improvement. The difficulty was to sustain the interest of a public no longer interested in seduction and satire. In tragedy, the new decorum spelled frigidity. Although Voltaire called Joseph Addison's *Cato* (pr. 1713) "the first reasonable English tragedy," and Addison himself despised tragicomedy as a "monstrous invention, a motley of mirth and sorrow," regular blank-verse tragedy dealing with Roman heroes grew increasingly literary and static, whereas tragicomedy held the stage in numerous guises.

George Lillo's *The London Merchant: Or, The History of George Barnwell* (pr. 1731) is honored as the first true bourgeois tragedy; it professed connections with Elizabethan domestic tragedy, which Lillo knew well, but was also akin to the evolving form of the novel, the "romance of everyday life." Lillo was a Low Church goldsmith, in no way different from

much of his audience, and could identify with their concerns. The first audience came to the play intending to mock it and left with their handkerchiefs to their eyes; it became a traditional Christmas and holiday pastime for masters to send their apprentices to see. This gratified Lillo's intention of enlarging "the province of the graver kind of poetry" by plays "founded on moral tales in private life" with the force "to engage all the faculties and powers of the soul in the cause of virtue, by stifling vice in its first principles."

The concern with emotion and sympathy was timely; the ethical nature of tragedy had been proclaimed by thinkers more profound than Lillo to be a valuable form of responsory exercise. As one's passions are affected mournfully, one's nature softens and one becomes more charitable and altruistic, more prone to commiseration, caring, and benevolence. Because pity, without fear, marked the sentimental catharsis, the traditional protagonist of high degree was less effectual than Lillo's mercantile clerk George Barnwell and his low-born posterity.

Lillo also created the tragedy of fate, in which the moral lesson is subservient to the ironic pathos. In his *Fatal Curiosity* (pr. 1736), an elderly couple murder a traveler for his money, not knowing that he is their son. The misguided parents are not vicious criminals but rather decent folk driven to extremities by poverty. Lillo is no social critic, and he attacks neither the economic wellsprings of destitution nor the crime itself; rather, he is intent on provoking a sentimental frisson through pity for both the perpetrators and their victim. Very popular in Germany, this plucking of heartstrings would eventuate in the tragedy of "innocent misfortune," the tearjerkers of August von Kotzebue, in which virtuous characters suffer needlessly to allow the audience an object for its sympathies. By that time, the form had degenerated into sentimentalism. Nevertheless, Lillo's influence extended even into the twentieth century: Albert Camus was so taken with the ethical dilemma of *Fatal Curiosity* that he refashioned it as *Le Malentendu* (pr. 1944; *The Misunderstanding*, 1948).

What Lillo did for English tragedy, Sir Richard Steele had earlier done for comedy in *The Conscious*

Lovers (pr. 1722), and despite attacks from conservatives such as John Dennis, the example took hold. Steele defined meliorative modes of tragedy and comedy: Tragedy was to represent domestic virtues, such as modesty and chastity, and high conceptions of virtue and merriment; comedy was to present a virtuous, honorable, gallant man whose happiness and success were proper subjects. Such a niminy-piminy prescription perfectly sums up sentimental comedy, designed to warm the cockles, not to split the sides. Steele seemed to forecast Lillo's counterjumper hero when he protested that a tragic hero is marked by greatness of sentiment, not his external position in life. The dividing line between bourgeois tragedy and sentimental comedy was barely perceptible and was dependent chiefly on the characters' fates: If, after five acts of misunderstanding, quarrels, and heartrending, they married, it was comedy; if they died, it was tragedy. By 1772, Oliver Goldsmith could complain that such comedies were bastard tragedies that had driven true comedy—the sort that raises laughter by "ridiculously exhibiting the follies of the lower part of mankind"—from the stage. "If [the characters in sentimental comedy] happen to have faults or foibles, the spectator is taught, not only to pardon, but to applaud them, in consideration of the goodness of their hearts."

MINOR GENRES

In contrast to these pastel genres, colorful minor forms sprang up. Opera, which had almost been naturalized in England by Purcell, was too much associated with courtly entertainments and allegorical pieces to attract a popular audience; the name came to mean Italian opera, which further alienated the general public. Sterile heroic tragedies of love and honor, squalled in Italian by geldings and fat women (so the opera's enemies portrayed it), had only snob appeal as an aristocratic diversion, despite the attractions of George Frederick Handel's music. Opera was ripe for parody, which it received at the hands of the poet John Gay. Part of the incentive to write a "Newgate pastoral" (as Jonathan Swift called it) may have come from Allan Ramsay's transposition of the lovers Florizel and Perdita to the Pentland Hills

in his *The Gentle Shepherd* (pb. 1725). Yet Gay's *The Beggar's Opera* (pr. 1728) was so novel that its success came as a total surprise: It wound up as the most enduringly popular play of the century. Gay's mode was basically mock-heroic: He displayed highwaymen, fences, and whores in the predicaments and uttering the sentiments of tragedy and opera. The key to the work's success was the music; Gay wrote new, sardonic lyrics to popular tunes and catches. "The audience," someone once remarked, "went in whistling the music." The ballad opera, as the form came to be known, enjoyed considerable success, presenting humble figures from British life—dustmen, sailors, farmers—in simple and tuneful tales of love versus duty, the ultimate *reductio* of the heroic tragedy. In the next century, the form would be swallowed by the more elaborate comic opera or supplanted by the vaudeville. If it had equivalents on the Continent, they were the *opéra comique* and the *Singspiel*.

English pantomime had its start between 1702 and 1716, when actors from the French fairs arrived and initiated "night scenes" in which *commedia dell'arte* characters conducted their shenanigans. By 1716, the character Harlequin (the Arlecchino of *commedia dell'arte*) received British citizenship at Lincoln's Inn Fields Theatre, and soon pantomime was the rage. At this period, a pantomime usually began with a mythological mime ballet featuring *commedia* masks; the first such piece explicitly to be called a "pantomime" was John Weaver's *The Loves of Mars and Venus* (pr. 1717). Soon the serious and the grotesque components were separated: The first part would be spoken or sung around a trite love story; the second part would feature comic mime, often performed with complicated machinery and transformations. To accommodate the latter, improvisation had to be kept to a minimum and the byplay of the clowns carefully rehearsed. For many years, pantomime drew better houses than any other genre in London and, by the Regency period, it had taken on a distinctly national character.

Burlesque also thrived in the care of John Gay, Henry Carey, and Henry Fielding; Fielding defined it in his preface to *The History of the Adventures of Jo-*

seph Andrews and His Friend Mr. Abraham Adams* (1742) as "what is monstrous and unnatural, and where our delight, if we examine it, arises from the surprising absurdity, as in appropriating the manners of the highest to the lowest, or *e converso*." This kind of travesty had its antecedents in the amateur productions staged at the end of Shakespeare's *Love's Labour's Lost* (pr. c. 1594-1595) and *A Midsummer Night's Dream* (pr. c. 1595-1596), and in Francis Beaumont's *The Knight of the Burning Pestle* (pr. 1607). The eighteenth century coupled facetiousness with criticism in parodies of artistic fads, social divagations, and political abuses. This type of shaft, aimed too often and too accurately at Prime Minister Robert Walpole, brought about the Licensing Act of 1737 and the formation of the Lord Chamberlain's office; these instruments of dramatic censorship effectively reduced the political (and, later, the religious and sexual) content of English drama to blandness.

Deprived of its sting, burlesque's exuberance was channeled into farce, and comedy proper coalesced with domestic tragedy. Comedy continued to preach homespun morality, and farce was free to kick up its heels and poke fun at innocuous social misfits and the vagaries of fashion. David Garrick and Samuel Foote managed to turn farce into a genuinely witty, even acerbic commentary on their times, but it remained a one-act form until W. S. Gilbert's *Engaged* (pr. 1877) expanded it to two.

GENRE SÉRIEUX

In France, the old traditions died hard. Voltaire tried to breathe new life into Racinian tragedy, especially when he returned from England in 1729: After Voltaire had seen Shakespeare performed, the French stage, which allowed no more than three speaking characters at any one time, struck him as inhibiting. Nevertheless, while he introduced crowd scenes, exotic settings, and even a ghost (in *Sémiramis*, pr. 1748) to French tragedy, he loyally maintained the unities, the Alexandrine, and the trumpeting of civic virtue that he had inherited. Drawing on Chinese, Egyptian, Syrian, and medieval history for his subject matter, he never succeeded in creating tragic characters or red-blooded diction.

Voltaire had nothing but contempt for what he called *comédie pleurnichon* (sniveling comedy), but he could not prevent the well-named *comédie larmoyante* (sentimental, or tearful, comedy) from usurping Racine's prerogatives. He himself dabbled in it with his Richardsonian *Nanine* (pr. 1749; English translation, 1927). The comedy of Molière had already been refined of its farcical elements by Marivaux, who portrayed sophisticated servants and carefully balanced wit and sentiment. The tipping of the balance into the sentimental was achieved by Nivelle de La Chaussée, who had begun by writing smutty clown shows for private theaters but whose comedies are sanctifications of marriage in the manner of Samuel Richardson's tear-stained novels. (Marivaux and Carlo Goldoni were also imitators of Richardson, whose stories of virtue in danger chimed with the call for "naïve and touching love" in comedies.) Voltaire's patron Frederick the Great sneered at La Chaussée for turning the stage into a "central depot for mawkishness," and La Chaussée apologized for the genre in a critique attached to *La Fausse Antipathie* (pr. 1733; mistaken antipathy), but soon he was insisting that improbable intrigues, caricatured portraits, and overdrawn portrayals of society be banished from the comic stage. Elié Fréron went even further and proposed "purely touching" plays without any admixture of comedy—or, in other words, bourgeois tragedy.

The answering echo came from Denis Diderot, the main propagandist for *tragédie bourgeoise* in France. Diderot divided drama into four genres: merry comedy, whose object is to ridicule vice; serious comedy, whose object is virtue and human responsibility; bourgeois tragedy, whose object is domestic misfortunes; and tragedy proper, whose object is public catastrophes and the mishaps of the great. It was the third category, the *genre sérieux*, that he promulgated as an agency of social reform and a propagator of the doctrine of philanthropy. Its author must "take the tone we have in serious matters" and advance the action "by perplexity and difficulties"; the subject must be important, a "simple, domestic" intrigue close to real life. Heroes must not confide in their valets, and, indeed, the servants' roles must be much reduced;

monologues are allowable, but not episodic characters. Character must be unfolded not by personality traits so much as by a man's condition with "its duties, its advantages, its difficulties," including a portrayal of profession, status, and family situation. Consequently, the best device for such a portrayal is the tableau, in which, as in a genre painting, the *dramatis personae* are viewed in natural relationship to one another. *Coups de théâtre* (twists in the plot) are also permissible, because such accidental and coincidental surprises occur in life, and the theater must be true to nature.

Diderot was more an aesthetician than a man of the theater, and his plays failed to have the impact of those of Lillo and Edward Moore. *Le Fils: Ou, Les Épreuves de la vertu* (pb. 1757; *Dorval: Or, The Test of Virtue*, 1767) was simply the old love-and-duty tussle from heroic tragedy redecorated with middle-class furnishings. His most original suggestions came in throwaway comments about performance, with a strong emphasis on the importance of the actor's contribution, beyond the script. In the final analysis, Diderot remains a traditionalist in his view that comedy must foster morality, but he notes that genres can no longer be classified by their subject matter:

> It is less the subject which makes a play comic, serious or tragic, than the tone, the passions, the character or the central theme. The effects of love, jealousy, gambling, licentiousness, ambition, hatred, envy, may incite laughter, thoughtfulness or fear.

No spectator should be allowed to mistake the intended effect, for the theater must teach proper conduct and social concern, and reform humankind through the exhibition of what Madame de Staël was to call "the affectation of nature." This far exceeded Lillo, who simply wanted his audience to feel instructive pity; Diderot meant to disturb and provoke his audience, forcing it into a new way of thinking.

Pierre-Augustin Caron de Beaumarchais embraced the cause of the *genre sérieux* by pointing out that tragedy had the wrong effect on eighteenth century persons. A Greek tragedy is so far removed from nature, so overwhelming, that the only possible response is terror, yet drama must engage the heart and

remind the spectator of the rewards of practicing virtue. Therefore, said Beaumarchais in his preface to *Eugénie* (pr. 1767; *The School of Rakes*, 1795), "the closer the suffering man is to my station in life, the more I take his misfortune to heart." Like Diderot, Beaumarchais insisted that a serious drama—and he uses the term *drame*, first introduced by Alain-René Lesage in 1707, to describe his own *Les Deux Amis* (pr. 1770; *The Two Friends*, 1800)—be of a more urgent interest and a more direct moral than tragedy, and be written only in prose. Also like Diderot, Beaumarchais's own efforts in the field were mediocre, but his comic masterpiece *La Folle Journée: Ou, Le Mariage de Figaro* (pr. 1784; *The Marriage of Figaro*, 1784) achieved an equivalent result by putting a common man, a servant with his own rather than his master's interests at heart, at stage center.

An even more vigorous propagandist for the *genre sérieux* was Louis-Sébastien Mercier, who condemned traditional tragic and comic forms because of their irrelevance to modern society. "The Drama," as Mercier names his salvational genre, will reach the greatest number and bind people through "compassion and pity" to lead them to virtue:

> Fall, fall, walls, that separate the genres! May the poet cast an unfettered sight into a vast countryside, and not feel his genius enclosed in those partitions which circumscribe and attenuate art.

The inflammatory rhetoric is striking, coming as it does ten years before the taking of the Bastille, and it heralds Victor Hugo's Romantic manifesto of fifty years later. The Drama alone, according to Mercier, can present average characters with mixed natures, the sort who make up the bulk of the audience, and can thus reveal the "manners, character, genius of our nation and our age, the details of our private life," to "form a republic wherein the torch of morality will enlighten the virtues we are still allowed to practice." As for catharsis, Mercier contended that it works best when it provokes indignation at vice and pity at adversity.

Mercier's fervor as a polemicist is less evident in his plays. *Jenneval* (pb. 1767), a reworking of *The*

London Merchant, shies away from the portrayal of murder and execution and transmutes its hero into a sensitive but impressionable lad who never actually sheds blood, who marries the heroine, and who is reclaimed by society. There is something Rousseauian about Jenneval as a naturally good man who can be brought back to the fold. *La Brouette du vinaigrier* (pr. 1771) was an ancestor of the proletarian drama in its portrait of a workingman's family in difficulties. Mercier had a considerable influence on young German playwrights in his time, but the French theater was more impervious to change. The suggested reforms were attacked in a pamphlet that circulated at court, *La Dramaturgie: Ou, La Manie des drames sombres* (1776), and even the character Arlequin was teased for being "sensitive" in Jean-Pierre Claris de Florian's *Le Bon Ménage* (pr. 1782; the good household). It is ironic that during the French Revolution and the Napoleonic era, the most popular plays were neoclassical tragedies, selling the integrity and self-sacrifice of Roman heroes as examples for the citizens who filled the seats.

LIGHT COMEDIES

The theaters of the fairs generated a number of dynamic minor forms, variations on the Italian comedy. When pantomime was infiltrated by popular airs, it began to develop into the vaudeville, cultivated by François Ponsard and Jean-François Marmontel. The etymology of the word is obscure, the most likely derivation being a corruption of *vaux-de-vire*; the genre would gain importance in the nineteenth century. *Opérettes*, lesser or chamber operas, were composed by Marmontel and Jean-Jacques Rousseau, whose *Devin du village* (pr. 1752; *The Cunning-man*, 1766) was parodied by Mozart in *Bastien und Bastienne* (pr. 1768) as a bastard pastoral. A more enduring form was the *opéra comique*, created by Michel-Jean Sedaine; a throwback to Adam de la Halle's *The Play of Robin and Marion*, as it emerged from the fairground booths, it adapted musical farce to modern life.

Charles-Simon Favart popularized these light comedies, built around gallant love affairs and rural sweethearts, home-grown versions of "noble savages."

In the nineteenth century, Daniel-François Auber, François-Adrien Boïeldieu, and Jacques Offenbach expanded the range of the genre, but the French long upheld the distinction that in opera proper, everything was sung, whereas in *opéra comique* there were spoken passages of dialogue. Comedy had nothing to do with the matter, and even *Carmen* (pr. 1875) first qualified as an *opéra comique*.

GERMAN BOURGEOIS DRAMA

The sentimental bourgeois drama sent down deep roots in Germany, where the opposing traditions of literature and entertainment had long distrusted each other. They hobnobbed without marrying in the *Haupt-und Staatsaktionen* (literally, "lofty deeds of state"), whose plots came from everywhere—the *Englische Komödianten*, the Jesuit school drama, recent political history—and which paraded Hanswurst, the salty Tyrolian Harlequin, cheek-by-jowl with melancholy princes and distressed damsels. All of this was couched in a fustian and improbable diction and enlivened by the periodic deployment of stage machinery. A measure of discipline was instilled by Professor Johann Christoph Gottsched, who set out to purify German taste by administering French remedies. Gottsched's "literary cookbook," as Kuno Francke called it, taught that any event providing a moral lesson was acceptable to literature; what genre it became depended on "the names which you give to the persons who are to appear in it." In comedy, the persons are citizens, while in tragedy, they are princes and heroes; that, and the fact that the former evokes laughter, the latter wonder, terror, and pity, are the only real distinctions between the genres. Gottsched himself wrote tragedies and his wife, Luise Kulmus, comedies for Carolina Neuber's acting troupe, to serve as examples. He also banished Hanswurst from the stage to prevent him from polluting the newly cleansed genres and to keep the actors from improvising. Tame, declamatory, and backward-looking, these works laid no foundation for a German repertory, although his *Agis, König von Sparta* (pr. 1750; *King Agis of Sparta*) was the first treatment of a social problem in German drama. Similarly, Magister J. Veltheim copied Molière's comedies for the court of Saxony and, like Gottsched, hoped to impose French habiliments on awkward Teutonic bodies.

These attempts to set up the French as arbiters of dramatic taste were thwarted by Gotthold Ephraim Lessing, who dedicated his career to combating everything for which Gottsched stood, with the laudably patriotic goal of creating a national theater independent of foreign domination. For Lessing, the unities and similar rules were literary tyranny, repressing the natural forms that tragic poetry would take, given the chance. Tragedy should represent human character and fate and prompt a purifying, violent discharge of emotion. Dramatic poetry was the highest form of literature, according to Lessing, because it translated arbitrary signs (figures of speech, meter, and so on) into natural signs through its mimetic directness. Lessing was by no means as hostile to French drama as he has been painted, and he let the *comédie larmoyante* have a place in the German repertory, although he noted that what the French called tragedy was nothing of the sort.

According to Lessing, the only true practitioners of tragedy had been the ancients and Shakespeare, who were known to the Germans chiefly through the mangled renderings of the *Englische Komödianten*. Lessing pursued the line the Romantics were to take, seeing Shakespeare as a child of nature, the best possible antidote for an overdose of French rigor. Lessing's own plays followed different paths: *Miss Sara Sampson* (pr., pb. 1755) imitated English domestic tragedy and was what Gottsched had named *Bürgerliches Trauerspiel: Minna von Barnhelm* (pr. 1767) owed much to Farquhar and could be termed a *weinerliches Lustspiel*, the German *comédie larmoyante*. Lessing embraced middle-class heroes in accordance with his own dictum that small actions and personal relationships reveal character much more efficiently than do the formal postures of the *Staatsaktionen*. The only true unity was unity of moral. As to mixing the genres, "if a genius for higher purposes amalgamates several of them in one and the same work, let us forget our primer and only examine whether he has attained these higher purposes."

STURM UND DRANG DRAMA

In fact, Lessing was shocked by the deluge of pseudo-Shakespearean plays that spewed forth in the wake of his encouragement. The Sturm und Drang (Storm and Stress) drama—so called from a play of that title, *Sturm und Drang* (pb. 1776), by Friedrich Klinger, so overheated in its passions as to remind Donald Clive Stewart of August Strindberg—allegedly followed Shakespeare in its numerous scene changes, national subject matter, and tempestuous emotions. The first success in the mode was Johann Wolfgang von Goethe's *Götz von Berlichingen mit der eisernen Hand* (pr. 1774; *Gortz of Berlichingen with the Iron Hand*, 1799), a drama of the German Reformation, which boasted fifty-four separate locales, some scenes being as brief as six lines. Goethe forgot that Shakespeare's stage allowed continuous action, whereas his own required scene-shifting that chopped up the play and disrupted the mood; he overlooked Shakespeare's architectonics, the poetic and theatrical devices that unify his plays.

Indeed, the assumption that Shakespeare licensed total freedom was widespread among German dramatists of the period and can be seen in Friedrich Schiller's *Die Räuber* (pb. 1781; *The Robbers*, 1792), of epic length and prolixity: The handling of crowds was exceptionally effective, but Schiller, too, missed Shakespeare's economy and balance. For a time, *Ritterstücke*, or plays of chivalry, founded on Romantic tales but tailored to a more classical form, were in vogue, but they and the traditional tragedy (or *Trauerspiel*, play of grief) never shared the popularity of the Sturm und Drang school. Its emotional extravagance was seconded on the bourgeois plane by the vast corpus of plays by Kotzebue, with their maudlin moralizing and extenuated virtue.

The central theme of a typical Sturm und Drang drama was the conflict between an unbridled genius and the corrupt and inhibiting society around him. As Goethe and Schiller grew personally more conservative, however, they turned back to a more classical ideal. Germany had rediscovered and reclaimed ancient Greece through the writings of Johann Joachim Winckelmann, who interpreted Greek art as the reflex of an inner vision that transcends nature to create ideal forms of pure beauty, which raise the mind to ecstasy. Goethe, under the influence of Roman architecture, and Schiller, under the influence of Immanuel Kant's philosophy, both espoused neoclassicism. Goethe's *Torquato Tasso* (pb. 1790, pr. 1807; English translation, 1827) forced a man of genius to choose between social responsibility and madness, and his *Iphigenie auf Tauris* (pb. 1787, pr. 1800; *Iphigenia in Tauris*, 1793) scaled down the drama almost to Racinian contours. Schiller turned to *Oedipus Tyrannus* as a model, hoping to find suitable tragic material in European history; for him, Sophocles' play was a tragic analysis of past events, the unfolding of the irremediable, and consequently more terrifying than a play in which the viewer's apprehension that something might befall is at work. His tribute to Sophocles was *Die Braut von Messina* (pr. 1803; *The Bride of Messina*, 1837), which revived the Greek chorus.

The German reversion to the ancients was allied with the growing Romantic interest in self-revelation, exemplified in the thought of Georg Wilhelm Friedrich Hegel, who reduced the hamartia of tragedy to an ethical choice. The hero chooses a partial good, which he wrongly believes to be an absolute good. The tension between the partial goods espoused by the characters produces the tragedy. A synthesis or reconciliation between the opposing forces occurs not onstage, but in the minds of the audience. Hegel praised *Antigone* as the paragon of tragedies because it best exemplifies this pattern, and he dismissed those plays that did not fit his scheme. This emphasis on ethical conflict became the keynote of later, related attempts to create a modern tragedy, such as those of Henrik Ibsen and Arthur Miller; as Hegel explained, "modern tragedy is contained in a more subjective sphere, modern tragic characters contain *within themselves* both sides of their ethical conflicts." Fate or external motivation are at a discount; instead of Creon and Antigone debating their stands, a Karl von Moor or a Faust experiences a dynamic tension within his own nature.

NINETEENTH CENTURY MELODRAMA

The most important new genre at the beginning of the nineteenth century was not sponsored by philosophers or scholars. This was melodrama, which, in its various avatars, would infiltrate and finally dominate all of its rivals. Scorned by critics, it thrived in the theater because it consolidated many of the trends effected by social change: the middle-class milieu, the desire for poetic justice, the sentimental ethos, the visually illustrative, and the tolerance of mixed forms. Like so many other popular genres, it originated in the French fairground booths as a gallimaufry of pantomime and music: the *mélo-drame*, or music drama (the word first appears in 1772). It gained respectability from *Pygmalion* (pr. 1771), a *scène lyrique* by Jean-Jacques Rousseau, who found something inherently ridiculous about opera. In his playlet, he alternated words and music, each speech preceded by a mood-setting musical phrase. James L. Smith, in *Melodrama* (1973), has pointed out that the operatic melodrama survives in the grave-digging scene of Ludwig van Beethoven's *Fidelio* (pr. 1805) and in Francis Poulenc's *La Voix humaine* (pr. 1959; the human voice).

By 1800, the term had been reapplied by Guilbert de Pixérécourt to a certain type of music drama performed by the theaters of the Boulevard du Temple. His *Cœlina: Ou, L'Enfant du mystère* (pr. 1800; *The Tale of Mystery*, 1802), is usually cited as the first dramatic melodrama, although everything about it is derivative: Its morality and didacticism come from the *drama bourgeois*, its sensational scenic effects from the opera and ballet-spectacle, its characters from the *comédie larmoyante*, its singing peasants from the *opéra comique*, its eloquent pantomime sequences from the *ballet d'action*, and its tableaux of action and movement from the François-Thomas de Boulevard pantomimes. Even its gothic elements can be glimpsed as early as 1764 in Baculard d'Arnaud's tragedy *Le Comte de Comminges* (pr. 1764). *The Tale of Mystery* was in three acts and in prose, which became standard. Its immense popularity throughout Europe can be attributed to Pixérécourt's skill in blending his dramatic cocktail, but also to his timing.

The French Revolution churned up a new audience, semiliterate and artistically unsophisticated, impatient of the classical tirade and hairsplitting psychological analysis of tragedy. They came to the theater for amusement and excitement, less to hear than to see. Melodrama, by reducing dialogue to the essential minimum and substituting telling gesture, mood music, and detailed mime, by eliminating complex moral issues and substituting a clear-cut identification of good and evil, and by decking out the previously chaste stage with all the allurements of the circus and opera created a play easily accessible to the masses. It drew on fashions and trends, such as the Rousseauian "noble savage," for its self-sacrificing Indians and monkeys, and on Gothicism for its horrors.

The stock characters of hapless hero and heroine, unrelenting villain and helpful comedian formed a nucleus that could be endlessly recostumed yet retain the comfort of familiarity. The audience knew from experience that the outcome would be happy, so the thrills and chills provided along the way were relatively harmless and unproductive of any genuine catharsis. As Smith has remarked, "In melodrama we win or lose; in tragedy we lose in the winning like Oedipus Rex or Macbeth, or win in the losing like Hamlet or Antony or Cleopatra." These tragic ambivalences had no appeal for melodrama's audiences, whose freedom to fear safely was abetted by an optimistic and humanitarian outlook, with poetic justice eternally operative.

Because melodrama became the common currency of the nineteenth century stage, the term "melodramatic" soon was given a pejorative connotation by those who resented the supplanting of tragedy and high comedy; even today, "melodramatic" suggests cheap theatrics, inadmissible plot manipulation, maudlin sentimentality, crass moralizing, spine-tingling horrifics—all that is coarse, crude, and arbitrary. Nevertheless, the principles and techniques of melodrama have permeated modern drama at every level, from Henrik Ibsen's *Gengangere* (pb. 1881; *Ghosts*, 1884) to the American musical comedy, and to belittle the genre's influence would be pointless. Its importance has been restated by the structuralist critics, who see in its conventional patterns a splendid array of theatrical semiotics.

Romanticism

The lessons taught by melodrama were not lost on Romantic playwrights, who adapted its most striking features and bent them to the service of a new style of tragedy. Much of the color, violence, and broad characterization of this Romantic tragedy was purely melodramatic, including a sumptuous change of scene for each act. Shakespeare was enlisted as a precursor, especially after the publication of Stendhal's *Racine et Shakespeare* (1823) and the Parisian appearance of Harriet Smithson and Charles Kean in *Hamlet* and *Romeo and Juliet* in 1827. A large amount of Romantic drama was, however, of native French manufacture. The Romantics also returned verse declamation to its place, varying impassioned arias with intentionally jarring colloquialisms. The opening line of Victor Hugo's *Hernani* (pr. 1830; English translation, 1830), with its enjambment—"*Serait-ce déjà lui? C'est bien à l'escalier/ Dérobé*" "Might he be here already? 'Tis at the hidden/ Staircase")—shocked and startled an audience unprepared to hear an Alexandrine violated in its own home, the Comédie-Française.

The opening night of *Hernani* is the date given for the initial success of Romanticism in French drama, but, in fact, it merely confirmed an already entrenched development. As early as 1809, when Nepomucène Lemercier's *Christophe Colomb* flopped resoundingly, an effort had been made to advance the cause of historical tragedy. The effort was aided by François Guizot's *Vie de Shakespeare* (pr. 1821), which showed that the Bard's multiplicity of characters and incidents, the duration and diversity that seem to separate them, are actually bonded by a unity of "impression" or interest. Far from deploring Shakespeare's diffuseness as an unfortunate token of his "barbaric" times, as Goethe had done, Guizot provided the Romantics with an ideal theatrical technique to replace the neoclassical theory of genres. The German Romantics had already rediscovered the notion of drama as an organic entity, not a mechanical construct, in which, to use Samuel Taylor Coleridge's description of Shakespeare, "all is growth, evolution, genesis—each line, each word almost, begets the following—and the will of the writer is an interfusion, a continuous agency, no series of separate acts." Characters are organs or limbs of the whole, even when they have lives of their own. Furthermore, August Wilhelm Schlegel asserted, if tragedy was a sculptural group, Romantic drama (like Diderot's tableaux) is a painting in which the diverse elements of life are not rigorously categorized: "While the poet seems to be offering us only an accidental reunion, he satisfies the unnoticed desires of the imagination, and plunges us into a contemplative disposition by the feeling of that marvellous harmony which results . . . and lends a soul, so to speak, to the different aspects of nature."

Hugo absorbed and reshaped these provocative ideas in his contagiously enthusiastic preface to *Cromwell* (pr. 1827; English translation, 1896), a manifesto that is not new in its concepts, but is strikingly forceful in its expression. Hugo believed that the drama should have philosophic scope to encompass vast human problems—historical, social, and moral—with the numerous characters personifying and illuminating various aspects of the central idea through their own diversity: "True poetry, complete poetry is in the harmony of contrasts," a mystical alliance of soul and body, of the sublime and the grotesque. Later, in his preface to the prose-play *Lucrèce Borgia* (pr. 1833; *Lucretia Borgia*, 1842), he promoted the eighteenth century view that "the theatre is a tribune, a pulpit" with a social mission, and the poet has a cure of souls.

These stimulating proposals for a Romantic drama, along with those of Alfred de Vigny and Benjamin Constant, were not programmatically followed by dramatists but were realized sporadically. *Henri III et sa cour* (pr. 1829; *Henri III and His Court*, 1931), by Alexandre Dumas, *père*, set the tone with its historical local color, action-packed scenes, and brisk dialogue, and the impassioned fervor of Vigny's *Othello* (pr. 1829) astounded playgoers accustomed to the anemic mouthings of neoclassical tragedy. Hugo's *Hernani* was consciously Shakespearean with a considerable alloy of melodrama, though more important as a *succès de scandale* than for any original qualities of its own. More fertile was Dumas's *Antony* (pr. 1831; English translation, 1904), a prototypical problem play, which transported the gloomy and alienated Romantic hero from the past to contemporary society and, through a tale of illegitimacy and thwarted love, cast a gauntlet at the establishment. The terminal date for true Roman-

tic drama is often given as 1843, the year that Hugo's *Les Burgraves* (pr. 1843; *The Burgraves*, 1896) met with failure. In truth, it never left the popular theaters of the boulevard du Crime, where its flamboyant heroism, protestations of honor, and tear-stained miracles were the stuff of plebeian rejoicing; at the turn of the century, it enjoyed a resurgence in the poetic dramas of Edmond Rostand and Catulle Mendès. A new lease on life came for Romantic drama in the swashbucklers of the cinema, for the Zorros and Robin Hoods of Douglas Fairbanks, Jr., and Errol Flynn were merely Hernani and Ruy Blas stripped of their poetry. Romantic drama has also been preserved, like a fly in amber, in the librettos of operas by Gaetano Donizetti, Vincenzo Bellini, and Giuseppe Verdi.

THE SCRIBEAN WELL-MADE PLAY

The classicists by no means perished before the onslaught of the Romantics; instead, their love of order and regularity was requited by the emergent form of the *pièce bien faite*, or well-made play, perfected and embodied by the more than four hundred plays of Eugène Scribe. Like the melodrama, the well-made play gets short shrift from critics who characterize it as an efficient machine and, like a machine, without heart, soul, or brain. This fails to explain away the abiding influence of the genre, whose precepts continue to inform not only most works for the commercial theater but also the structure of film and television drama. Its rules, declared Francisque Sarcey, "are the rules of the theatre because they are the rules of logic."

Scribe has been criticized because, unlike the Romantics and, later, the naturalists, he had no interest in "real life" or "nature" in the theater. The theater, in his view, is an art of fiction that contradicts truth and can dispense with reality. In life, nothing is ever completed or rounded off, or has a clear beginning, middle, and end; to imitate the incoherence and mystery of life in a play is to baffle and frustrate the audience. The drama's function is to take complex, obscure, inconsequential life and reshape it through simplicity, clarity, logic, and coherence—confessing, in the process, that the theater is a conventional art form. The first law of the theater is to arrest and hold the audience's attention; all other laws follow from that.

What are the structural features of the well-made play? Reduced to a formula by Stephen S. Stanton in his introduction to *Camille and Other Plays* (1957), they are:

> 1) a plot based on a secret known to the audience but withheld from certain characters (who have long been engaged in a battle of wits) until its revelation (or the direct consequence thereof) in the climactic scene serves to unmask a fraudulent character and restore to good fortune the suffering hero, with whom the audience has been made to sympathize; 2) a pattern of increasingly intense action and suspense, prepared by exposition (this pattern assisted by contrived entrances and exits, letters, and other devices); 3) a series of ups and downs in the hero's fortunes, caused by his conflict with an adversary; 4) the counterpunch of peripeteia and *scène à faire* [that is, the reversal of fortunes and the climactic confrontation to which everything has built up] marking, respectively, the lowest and highest point in the hero's adventures, and brought about by the disclosure of secrets to the opposing side; 5) a central misunderstanding or quiproquo [that is, misconstruing a word or situation] made obvious to the spectator but withheld from the participants; 6) a logical and credible denouement; and 7) the reproduction of the overall action pattern in the individual acts.

In other words, to make a play well is to streamline the intrigues of the situation comedy and the Romantic drama; plot, often extremely convoluted, was the be-all and end-all. Characters, themes, and ideas, mood setting and language—all had to be sacrificed to the carefully prepared action. Reductive as this formula sounds, it was based on the demands of the audience rather than on critical theories, and it gave supportive shape to otherwise minor genres, such as vaudeville and the *comédie d'intrigue*. In France, vaudeville became a highly polished morsel of social comedy, enlivened by simple songs; in Russia, it developed into a pungently realistic farce, rife with topical commentary.

PROBLEM PLAY

Scribe's own dramaturgy cannot by any stretch of the imagination be called drama of ideas, although it

is allied to his own *idée-maîtresse*, that great events are dependent on piddling causes, the "if Cleopatra's nose had been shorter" theory of history. Although, as a thinker, Scribe had little to offer, his successors welded the *pièce bien faite* to intellectual trends. Alexandre Dumas, *fils*, and Émile Augier remade high comedy along Scribean lines to create the *pièce à thèse*, better known in English as the problem play. Following Dumas's motto of "moral and social action through dramatic literature," the problem play featured a particular case study, drawn from life, in order to deduce a general conclusion about an important social or moral issue.

Typical themes, pregnant with significance for the Victorian and Second Empire world, were the double standard, women's position in society, marriage for money, divorce, and the status of prostitutes. A natural amalgamation of the sentimental comedy and the comedy of manners, it proceeded in proper Scribean fashion: The first act would wittily introduce the characters, the second and third would burgeon with colorful incidents, the fourth would bring the action to a climax by the final curtain, and the fifth and final act would furnish an optimistic denouement (or unraveling, another technical term of the genre), to quote Auguste Filon, "just before midnight, the time appointed by the police for the closing of the playhouse."

The problem with the problem play was that the strict architectonics of the well-made play did not permit open-ended conclusions or the admission of unresolvable complexities; a serious matter would be trivialized or neatly tied up by the play's end in a manner that did not reflect the complexities of real life. To relate the social issue to the otherwise independent intrigue, dramatists had recourse to the *raisonneur*, a mouthpiece who expounded the correct views, guided the other characters to the right road, and kept the audience alert to what everything meant. Usually a doctor or lawyer, the repository of other persons' secrets yet on the periphery of their lives, the *raisonneur* was described by the Russian journalist Vasili Sleptsov as a bottle brought onstage at regular intervals to pour out a bit of message and then recorked and stored away until needed again.

MIXES AND CHANGES

This disparity between form and content and its outcome are well illustrated by the career of Henrik Ibsen. When he began to write plays of contemporary life in the 1870's, he fell back on the Scribean model, which he knew intimately from his experience as a dramaturge at the Bergen theater. The influence of this model can clearly be traced in *Samfundets støtter* (pr. 1877; *The Pillars of Society*, 1880), *Et dukkehjem* (pr. 1879; *A Doll's House*, 1880; also known as *A Doll House*), and even *Gengangere* (pr. 1882; *Ghosts*, 1885), but Ibsen broke loose of its restrictions and retained only its most useful elements in such works as *Vildanden* (pr. 1885; *The Wild Duck*, 1891) and *Hedda Gabler* (pr. 1891; English translation, 1891). By the last phase of his writing, in *John Gabriel Borkman* (pr. 1897; English translation, 1897) and *Naar vi døde vaagner* (pr. 1900; *When We Dead Awaken*, 1900), he had abandoned it totally, along with the pretense of dealing with "social problems."

A similar evolution took place with George Bernard Shaw, who gained a hearing for his plays of ideas by imitating such popular Scribean offshoots as the costume melodrama, the problem play, and the drawing-room comedy. Once he was established as a playwright whose works were regularly performed, he was emboldened to invent whatever forms he needed, such as the "metabiological pentateuch" that *Back to Methuselah* (pr. 1922) purports to be.

When, in 1884, Francisque Sarcey listed the "most significant evolutions and revolutions in dramatic art," the three plays he cited (all French) were *Un Chapeau de paille d'Italie* (pr. 1851; *The Italian Straw Hat*, 1873) by Eugène Labiche, *La Dame aux camélias* (pr. 1852; *The Lady of the Camellias*, 1930) by Alexandre Dumas, *fils*, and *Orphée aux enfers* (pr. 1858; *Orpheus in the Underworld*, 1865), a libretto by Henri Meilhac and Ludovic Halévy with music by Jacques Offenbach. It is a strange but telling selection. *The Italian Straw Hat* is a typical piece of vaudeville, with Parisian and provincial types caught up in a comic whirlwind, yet it is fashioned with a Scribean rigor and precision that keep the action moving with diabolic *entrain*. There are astute touches of character and satire, but the convolutions

of the plot are paramount. It was the forerunner of the "bedroom farce" perfected by Georges Feydeau, Armand de Caillavet, and Robert de Flers at the century's end, a fast-paced and intricate intrigue, scored for slamming doors and revolving four-posters.

The Lady of the Camellias is a crossbreeding of the *drame bourgeois* and Romantic social protest: The truehearted but misunderstood outcast and the blighted love affair were relocated amid drawing-room conversation and well-meaning editorializing on the evils of prostitution. Offenbach's *Orpheus in the Underworld*, an *opéra bouffe*, is a sparkling travesty of classical themes, both tragic and operatic, with a *raisonneur*, Public Opinion, who relates the stage buffoonery to the audience's expectations. None of these plays conformed to any established genre, and none could even tenuously be considered traditional comedy or tragedy.

As a matter of fact, by the mid-nineteenth century, questions of genre were no longer an overriding concern with drama critics. Scribe's technique served as a handy manual, which virtually all drama critics— for example, William Archer—took as a given. Interpretation of Aristotle was left to classical scholars and seemed to have no relevance to stage practice, despite Scribe's redefinitions of peripeteia and anagnorisis. By the twentieth century, classification was made not along generic lines, but according to schools of art (naturalism, expressionism) or principles of stagecraft (theatricality, total theater). In the meantime, nineteenth century drama split and subdivided into innumerable minor and ephemeral genres, often mere labels with no ideological rationale.

MID-NINETEENTH CENTURY GENRES

This efflorescence of demotic genres was particularly rich in England, where the licensing laws had, until 1843, restricted the performance of "legitimate" tragedy and comedy to two patent theaters; all other playhouses were constrained to put on musical farragos, farces, and burlettas. This last, a diminutive of the Italian *burla*, or joke, was a three-act piece featuring at least six songs. By setting Shakespeare to music, managers could circumvent the law. Nights were long and varied in the nineteenth century theater. The evening would open with a curtain raiser, usually a farce or two-act comedy; proceed to the main piece, a melodrama, burletta, or comic opera; and conclude with an afterpiece, usually a burlesque or vaudeville, to send the audience home merry, if groggy. By the Regency period, English pantomime had been relegated to the Christmas season, and a characteristic format had evolved. The opening was in rhyme and told a story from fairy-tale or nursery lore of separated lovers, ridiculous wooers, and evil geniuses. At the critical moment, a good genius would appear and metamorphose the characters into the English versions of *commedia dell'arte* types: Columbine, Harlequin, Pantaloon, and, most indigenous of all, Clown. There would ensue a harlequinade, a relatively mute series of slapstick scenes and magical transformations, at the end of which the apotheosis, a gorgeous scene change, would occur and the characters would return to their original shapes; love would triumph and wickedness be mildly rebuked.

In France, the harlequinades mutated into specialized types: the *pantomime mélodrame*, a throwback to Pixérécourt; the *pantomime réaliste*, set in everyday life; the *pantomime villageoise*, or rustic panto, a seedy descendant of the pastoral; and the *pantomime féerie*, or fairy-tale pantomime. This last became increasingly spectacular and opulent in presentation, with protracted dance interludes, operatic singing, and expensive scenery and costumes. A more homely version of this had been known in Austria as the *Zauberposse*, or magic farce; an outgrowth of folk comedy, it combined supernatural effects with plots of bourgeois life. A good example is Ferdinand Raimond's *Der Alpenkönig und der Menschenfeind* (pr. 1828; the mountain king and the misanthrope), in which a surly paterfamilias of the Biedermeier period is reformed through the agencies of an Alpine goblin. All of these magical genres may relate back to Count Carlo Gozzi's fantastic *fiabe*, or fables, of the 1760's, which tried to revive interest in the *commedia dell'arte* by putting its characters into exotic and nightmarish stories.

In England, the *féerie* fused with the pantomime proper and the burlesque travesty to become the "ex-travaganza," defined by V. C. Clinton-Baddeley in *The Burlesque Tradition* (1952) as "burlesque weakened into farce . . . a whimsical entertainment conducted in rhymed couplets or blank-verse, garnished with puns, and normally concerned with classical heroes, gods and goddesses, kings and queens." The form was perfected by the ingenious James Robinson Planché in charming revisions of fairy tales, and eventually it superseded the Regency pantomime; by the late nineteenth century, the pantomime opening had become fussily elaborate and the harlequinade had been reduced to a few perfunctory scenes of tomfoolery. The English stage also knew the subspecies of aquatic, equestrian, and dog drama, so defined by their principal attractions. In each case a melodrama, the type took its name from its external claptrap: If the action transpired around and in a great tank of water, it was aquatic; if the leading actors performed on horseback, it was equestrian; and if the denouement was effected by a canine savior, it was dog. (Aquatic drama had nothing to do with nautical drama, a sentimental melodrama about the life of a seaman that was enacted on an ordinary planked stage.)

A similar point can be made about the cup-and-saucer dramas introduced to the English stage by Thomas William Robertson, James Albery, and Henry James Byron in the 1860's. In essence, they were sentimental comedies that purported to give a faithful portrait of everyday life. The reality was mostly confined to the staging: Practicable doors and windows, three-dimensional furniture with operative props such as a tea service; comparatively unstilted dialogue, at least in the comic scenes; and a variegated stage picture—all providing a patina of realism, while the characters and plots remained stagy. As the audience oohed and aahed at real toast prepared onstage, the same inadmissible coincidences and the last-minute *deus ex machina* put in their appearance.

NATURALISM

A more genuine lease on life was given to domestic tragedy in Germany, where Friedrich Hebbel, in revolt against Schiller, realized that drama must conform to the spirit of its own time. In the modern age, Hebbel reasoned, the central problems of humankind lie in social and political institutions; therefore, modern tragedy must question institutions, but not in the superficial way the problem play did. The family and caste remain important factors, but instead of being seen as a hearth of virtue, the middle class is condemned for its narrow-mindedness. Sharing the Romantic contempt for the social establishment, especially when in conflict with the individual, Hebbel went one step further by turning society into the modern equivalent of fate that destroys the hero utterly. The bourgeois protagonist of Hebbel's tragedy never achieves transcendence, never gains supernal illumination, never benefits from poetic justice; the culmination is a proof of the emptiness of existence and the vindication of the all-prevailing law. This bleak picture, which is presented in Hebbel's *Maria Magdalena* (pr. 1846; English translation, 1935), had been foreshadowed by Georg Büchner's fragmentary tragedy of an inarticulate prole, *Woyzeck* (written in 1836 but not published until 1879, and first produced in 1913; English translation, 1927).

Hebbel's unrelentingly Prussian outlook was popularized not by his own plays, which tended to feature mythological or historical milieus, but through Hermann Hettner's influential book *Das Moderne Drama* (1852):

> In the struggle of our inner character-development, in the secrets of family life, shaken down to its innermost foundations, in the volcanically undermined soil of our social conditions there lies at this moment the deepest deeps of the moral spirit. But where there are deep moral struggles there is also fate, great and gigantic, and where there is a great, that is, an inwardly necessary, fate, there also is pure tragedy.

This statement of the possibility of a distinctively modern tragedy was instrumental in directing Ibsen away from historical drama and toward plays of contemporary life, which, despite their cup-and-saucer trappings, revealed the destinies of the characters. "A Titan in a restaurant, the ancient Greeks never dreamt of such a thing!" the Russian poet Andrey Bely exclaimed about Ibsen's *When We Dead Awaken*.

Hebbel had noted that, "for the poet, nature must be a starting point and not a landing stage," and he would have been annoyed by the naturalist takeover of the bourgeois drama engineered by Émile Zola. Presupposing a materialistic and mechanistic moral world, the naturalists aligned themselves with scientists and claimed for their literary work objectivity of observation and experimentation, all in the service of social improvement. Because, in their system, human character was determined by environment and heredity, the social milieu must be reproduced in detail, and a class or stratum might be better matter for dramatic treatment than an individual. Few choices are open to the naturalistic hero, who offers the audience the spectacle of his inevitably following the beaten track of antecedent causes.

This philosophy blew to bits the tidy mechanism of the well-made play. The plays of Henry Becque, a forerunner of the naturalists, for example, kept plot to a minimum and simply displayed segments of life, the interplay of characters in a given situation; the *raisonneur* was jettisoned, forcing the audience to make its own moral judgments after seeing the evidence. In *Les Corbeaux* (pr. 1882; *The Vultures*, 1913), money and the lack of it become a surrogate for destiny, and the merely passive will is subjugated by desires and appetites. The direction pointed out by Becque was taken by the Théâtre Libre, founded by André Antoine to promote naturalism in drama.

The whole superstructure of French drama—the *intrigue parallèle* or subplot, the coincidences, the neat denouement, the speeches to the house, the mechanical virtuosity—were discarded, along with the specious solution of social problems. The spectator was to be presented with a slice of life, closely observed and served up without authorial interference or forced conclusions.

The Théâtre Libre gave new significance to the one-act play; previously, such short plays were comic or musical, meant to introduce or conclude an evening in the theater, not to steal focus from the main attraction. At Antoine's theater, an evening's bill might be made up of three or four one-act plays of serious import, elucidated by a lecturer. Thus, the *raisonneur* became an external adjunct to the drama. As Strindberg pointed out in his famous preface to *Fröken Julie* (pr. 1889; *Miss Julie*, 1912), his play runs about an hour and a half to say what it has to say; it refuses to conform to the old rule of an act lasting as long as the candles burn in the hall. Strindberg's view of naturalism was not cut-and-dried, and in an essay on modern drama, he drew a distinction between

> the misunderstood naturalism which holds that art merely consists of drawing a piece of nature in a natural way . . . [and] the great naturalism which seeks out the points where the great battles are fought, which loves to see what you do not see every day, which delights in the struggle between natural forces, whether these forces are called love and hate, rebellious or social instincts, which finds the beautiful or ugly unimportant if only it is great.

GRAND GUIGNOL DRAMA

Strindberg claimed that the Théâtre Libre was fostering this kind of epic naturalism, but he was guilty of wishful thinking. The theater was content to present *comédies rosses* and *comédies cruelles*, gloating snapshots of the seamy side of life. A *comédie rosse* was a brief episode, not unlike a thirty-minute television drama of the 1950's, that presented an incident of crime, squalor, or passion from the lives of the underprivileged. A sort of climax was reached in Auguste Liner's *Conte de Noël* (pr. 1890; Christmas story), in which an illegitimate newborn is thrown to the pigs to the sound of Christmas carols. The sardonic tone was pervasive as well in the *comédies cruelles*, popularized by Georges Courteline, which featured sick jokes or nasty anecdotes and whose despicable characters were butts for laughter.

These plays influenced two later developments. The Grand Guignol Theatre, founded by one of Antoine's disciples, alternated hilarious short comedies with grisly melodramas of fear and pain, thus sending the audience on an emotional roller coaster. "Grand Guignol" came to mean any play in which horror was the desired end, and the means, skillfully naturalistic reproductions of operations, eye-gougings, amputations, acid burnings, and the like. Its apogee came, perhaps, in the "splatter" movies of the 1970's and 1980's, wherein everything is directed toward obligatory moments of visceral panic. The influence of Grand Guignol was also felt in the opera, in the school of *verismo*, led by Giacomo Puccini, Pietro Mascagni, and Ruggiero Leoncavallo, who fluctuated between musical treatments of well-made historical dramas and the short, sharp shocks of the one-act *comédie rosse*. The ever-popular *Cavalleria rusticana* (pr. 1884; *Cavalleria Rusticana: Nine Scenes from the Life of the People*, 1893) and *I pagliacci* (pr. 1892; the strolling players) also spring to mind; Puccini's less familiar *Il tabarro* (pr. 1918; the cloak), a drama of adultery and murder that is set aboard a barge in the river Seine, is an even more authentic example. Here, too, the tendency was toward ludicrous sensationalism: In Franco Leoni's play *L'Oracolo* (pr. 1905; the oracle), a San Francisco Chinese is strangled with his own pigtail.

WAGNERIAN MUSIC DRAMA

If the objectivist drama intended by the naturalists thus dwindled into a neo-Jacobeanism of blood-and-guts, another nineteenth century approach was more successful. Richard Wagner hoped to unite opera and drama into a synthesis that he called at one time *Musikdrama*, and at another time *Gesamtkunstwerk* (composite work of art), the product of one creative mind, where music would ultimately subordinate poetry. Rather than reject Scribe, Wagner planned to employ his technical prowess while he restored the tragic denouement, moved the action away from modern life toward myth and legend, and played out the drama in the music itself. "A perfect art form," he declared, "must start from the point at which these laws" (that is, the laws of expansion and movement, of tone and light) "coincide"—in the world of dreams. As Eric Bentley has shown in *The Playwright as Thinker* (1946), Wagner's concept of music drama united three important ideas: the national idea, to identify Germanism by drawing on Teutonic folklore; the symphonic idea, with the music as endless and overwhelming, usurping the drama from the dialogue; and the theatrical idea, with the dialogue as a slow and continuous counterpoint to the raging symphonic background.

These ideals were not perfectly realized in Wagner's own music dramas because he was a greater musician than a poet, and his pretentious librettos, often turgid and repetitious, defeated his dramatic purpose. Modern conductors and directors have tried to scrape off the accretions of tradition to reveal a hidden symbolism concerning nineteenth century industrialism, but this reinterpretation is not entirely convincing. It was what might be called Wagner's "auteur theory" that left its imprint most deeply on modern drama: his involvement in every aspect of production from stage design and casting to choral drill and audience regulation (no applause during an act, no latecomers, no encores), his relegation of the orchestra to invisibility so that the music seems to come from a "mystic gulf."

All of this conduced to make the theater a separate world of superhuman proportions and atmosphere, with the playwright/composer as the unique mind pervading it. The cooperation of music, drama, and staging, with quasi-religious overtones, was a move to bring the drama back to its Greek origins, to sever its connection with the mundane, commercial, and purely literary. Denuded of metaphysical mumbo jumbo, its synthesis of rhythm, color, and design would come to underlie much Broadway and Hollywood practice, while the Symbolists and the expressionists also tried to create dramatic atmosphere from consistency of scenic elements.

The bridge between Wagner's *Gesamtkunstwerk* and the ancient Greeks was built by Friedrich Nietzsche in *Die Geburt der Tragödie aus dem Geiste der Musik* (1872; *The Birth of Tragedy out of the Spirit of Music*, 1909). The first to return to the Dionysian origins of tragedy, Nietzsche rejected the eighteenth century notion of Greek art as placid or harmonized—a child of Apollo. Apollo was merely the mediating force that allowed the savage Dionysiac impulses to be channeled from ritual to drama. True tragedy could only be "a manifestation and illustration of Dionysian states, as the visible symbolization of music, as a dream-world of Dionysian ecstasy." In Nietzsche's conception, tragedy results from the tension between the Apollonian energies of painting, sculpture, and epic, and the Dionysian energies of acting, dancing, music, and lyric poetry: Ecstasy and incantation grapple with poise and contemplation to produce a tragic dynamism. The modern world, with its materialistic reliance on science, cannot engender tragedy, except if it be rooted in myth.

Despite the book's shortcomings—its faulty scholarship, its assumption that Wagnerian opera was a revival of Greek tragedy (a belief Nietzsche later abandoned), and its assertion that Euripides killed off tragedy—it was highly important as a catalyst. Nietzsche was the first to state that the Greeks exploited irrational forces in their art, rather than repressing them, that the tragic hero's certain annihilation clinched his heroism, and that catharsis was not a purge of emotions but a confrontation with the terrible truths of existence and the validation of human worth. Much twentieth century tragedy, with its exploration of myth, the dark side of the mind, and the braving of unknown forces, springs directly from these Nietzschean theses.

SYMBOLIST DRAMA

Both Wagnerian atmosphere and the awareness of irrational annihilation are present in Symbolist drama, without the possibility of heroism or the Dionysian exhilaration. The Symbolists saw human beings as trapped between the involuntary poles of birth and death: They cannot understand the meaning, if any, of the universe or their place in it, and they spend their span clocking the moments. Their very mortality nullifies any possibility of accomplishment, will, or purpose in life. For Maurice Maeterlinck, drama took place in the mind or soul of a character and could not be expressed by outward action; the "tragedy of everyday life," as he defined it, means that a higher life cannot exist in our humble reality. For Symbolist Stéphane Mallarmé, drama is a sacred and mysterious rite, which can evoke the arcane spiritual meaning of existence through dreams.

The Symbolists, therefore, eschewed all the traditional apparatus of play making: no strong, detailed characterizations or acting roles, no true crisis or conflict, no message or catharsis. An archetypical Symbolist play such as Maurice Maeterlinck's *L'Intruse* (pr. 1891; *The Intruder*, 1948) is brief, uses nameless characters with generic identities (the Grandfather, the Daughter, and so on) and incantatory dialogue, keeps its protagonist, Death, unseen, and creates a semblance of action through hints, allusions, suggestions, the symbolic use of doors and windows opening onto a higher reality, sound effects (the wind, a scythe mowing grass, the crunch of gravel), and narrowly focused lighting. The most intuitive characters are those, such as the old and blind, farthest removed from common life. Symbolist drama also exploited absences and pauses as major components and established waiting as a fundamental metaphor for life. Without Maeterlinck, much of the work of Anton Chekhov, Samuel Beckett, Harold Pinter, and even the *nouvelle vague* (New Wave) filmmakers would be unthinkable.

Mallarmé went beyond Maeterlinck in his rejection of spectacle; he demanded a one-man performance and an initiate audience of about twenty-four—essentially a closet drama. He was echoed in Ireland by William Butler Yeats, who looked to the Japanese Nō drama as an example of what ritualized poetic drama, performed in a drawing room for a select coterie, might be, and in Russia by Fedor Sologub, who argued for a "theater of a single will," with the dramatist reading his own works as the actors, puppetlike, illustrated his words. Such a performance actually occurred at the Théâtre de l'Œuvre in Paris in 1894, when *La Gardienne* (the wardress), by Henri de Regnier, was recited in the orchestra pit, with actors miming scenes behind green gauze, in front of a dream landscape by Jean-Édouard Vuillard. The dream itself as a dramatic structure was first employed by Strindberg in *Ett drömspel* (pr. 1907; *A Dream Play*, 1912); he stressed the subjectivity of the individual dream, the detail and grotesquerie of its images, and its lack of intelligibility to the uninitiate. The coalescence of private vision and public statement was to be influential on German expressionism.

Symbolism was also partly responsible for the drama of mood, in which the evocation of an ambience is more important than action, and for the monodrama. Drama of mood is not so much a distinct genre as a description used in association with such figures as Chekhov and Christopher Fry, who adopted it for his plays *The Lady's Not for Burning*

(pr. 1948) and *Venus Observed* (pr. 1950). It was first coined by the Moscow Art Theatre around 1899 to label their efforts in creating a psychological atmosphere onstage to convey to the spectator, through subtle transitional nuances and lengthy pauses, the characters' inner feelings. It became especially popular in the English-speaking theater in the 1940's and 1950's, when method acting encouraged inwardness onstage, and it left fingerprints all over Eugene O'Neill, Tennessee Williams, Terence Rattigan, and Paddy Chayefsky.

MONODRAMA AND EXPRESSIONISM

The word monodrama first appears in the late eighteenth century to describe the one-man comic lecture popularized by Samuel Foote and George Alexander Stevens. It was resuscitated in 1910 by the Russian director Nikolai Evreinov, who reinterpreted it as a play in which the spectator is meant to "co-experience" exclusively what the active protagonist is undergoing. To achieve this, everything onstage must transmutate according to the emotions of the leading character: The color of the lighting, the size and shape of set pieces, even the three-dimensionality of the other characters alter in accordance with his reactions and mood changes. The monodramatic experiment was carried out only in certain one-act plays for the Crook Mirror Theatre in St. Petersburg, such as Evreinov's *V kulisakh dushi* (pr. 1912; *The Theatre of the Soul*, 1915), and B. F. Geier's cabaret sketches.

Significantly, Evreinov's proposal appeared the same year that the first expressionist drama, Oskar Kokoschka's *Mörder, Hoffnung der Frauen* (pr. 1908; *Murderer, Hope of Women*, 1963), was staged. Expressionist drama shares monodrama's basic premise that the world is to be seen from a unique, usually skewed or abnormal, viewpoint, but it also boasts a social purpose: to reveal humankind struggling to escape the technocratic, soulless modern world. Protest can be as strident as a political cartoon, as in Georg Kaiser's *Von Morgens bis Mitternachts* (pb. 1916; *From Morn to Midnight*, 1962), while O'Neill's *The Emperor Jones* (pr. 1920) is, to all intents and purposes, an apolitical monodrama.

TWENTIETH CENTURY INTERPRETATIONS

By World War I, dramatic genres had lost their specificity, and new terms were devised to cover the latest innovations in stagecraft and literary fashion. Playwrights felt free to give personal inflections to the once pristine generic terminology. Chekhov subtitled his *Chayka*, pr. 1896; *The Seagull*, 1909), in which a leading character commits suicide, a "comedy," and simply denominated *Dyadya Vanya* (pr. 1899; *Uncle Vanya*, 1914) "scenes from country life." When twentieth century playwrights and critics came to redefine the dramatic genres, they either dusted off existing formulas, or they devised terms that were supererogatory. In the former case, Arthur Miller's attempt to explicate "a tragedy of the common man" is merely a rehashing of Diderot and Mercier without the profundity of a Hebbel. In the latter case, Lionel Abel's suggestion of a new genre, "metatheater," to define certain poetic plays of metaphysical import, is arbitrary and debatable in its coverage.

The dissolution of the traditional genres reflected the situation in the arts in general, as time-honored assumptions crumbled before scientific, technological, and philosophical onslaughts. A deep chasm formed between the commercial theater, controlled by entrepreneurs, landlords, and speculators intent on enlarging their audiences in competition with the newer cinema and mass media, and the experimental theater, which cared more for communicating its ideas than for entertaining in any traditional sense. While the commercial theater continued to purvey traditional genres in diversified ways (the well-made play splintered into the drawing-room comedy, the murder mystery, and the situation comedy), the experimental drama refused to be pigeonholed, and new forms proliferated.

One new form that did emerge in the commercial theater was the musical comedy. Although it bore traces of ballad opera, *opéra comique*, and burlesque, it rapidly took on a distinctive profile of its own. In the United States, where the form would reach its fullest flowering, many claimants have been put forth as the first. Traditionally, *The Black Crook* (pr. 1866), a melodramatic Faust story, ornamented with leggy dancers in glittering dance numbers, is cited as the

original, but it bears closer resemblance to the Victorian burlesque, a mock-heroic treatment of a mythological or literary story, performed primarily by women in tights and broken up by song-and-dance interludes. The early musical comedy was a combination of variety acts and choral numbers loosely strung on an inconspicuous plot, and its setting could range from ancient Egypt (*The Wizard of the Nile*, by Victor Herbert, pr. 1895) to fairyland (*The Wizard of Oz*, by L. Frank Baum, pr. 1903) to modern New York (*Forty-five Minutes from Broadway*, by George M. Cohan, pr. 1906). The English tried to erect a wall between comic opera and musical comedy, based on how ambitious the music was and how tight the plotting. The score and structure of a Gilbert and Sullivan opera allow no digressions or interpolations, while musical comedies can be opened out to fit the specialties of a music-hall comedian or a novelty dance number.

MUSICALS AND REVUES

France remained loyal to *opéra bouffe*, the German world to operetta, and the Spanish-speaking theater to its folkloric *zarzuela*, but musical comedy triumphed in England. Until the 1940's, it retained its baggy structure, allowing it to be dominated by clowns such as Ed Wynn and Bert Lahr. With Richard Rodgers and Oscar Hammerstein's *Oklahoma!* (pr. 1943), a serious plot began to subjugate the other elements—including the increasingly vestigial comedy and the increasingly aggressive ballet sequences—to the story line. By the 1970's, this had evolved into what might be called "the problem musical" ("comedy" had dropped out of the nomenclature), which pretended to treat social issues and personal interactions in an adult manner (as in Stephen Sondheim's *Company*, pr. 1970, and *Follies*, pr. 1971). A reaction came in a revival of the revue form.

The revue originated in France as a New Year's recapitulation of the past year's events and celebrities, presented in a lightly satiric vein. It was imitated by Planché in England and John Brougham in the United States, without much success; its format required a certain amount of up-to-date information to be shared by the popular audience. By the time the word "revue" had entered the English language, around 1913, a more sophisticated and urbane public was ready to welcome a collection of musical and dramatic scenes, often lightly satiric and roughly centered on a theme. German revues tended to be political in complexion, American revues to be more spectacular, but essentially, the form satisfied the perennial taste for variety and brevity in entertainment, with a veneer of smartness and contemporaneity.

The revue lent itself well to political propaganda, and groups such as the Blue Blouses in the Soviet Union and the Living Newspaper in the United States made revues into organs of public information and left-wing polemic. Sergey Tretyakov's "factographic" approach to drama, an insistence that one begin with raw field data and select the elements that best convey the desired message, resulted in documentary drama, or docudrama. Erwin Piscator pioneered the multimedia presentation, combining film clips, allegorical tableaux, and other heterogeneous elements, with dialogue scenes. Agitprop (from agitation-propaganda) drama was usually crude, since the medium was not allowed to get in the way of the message, and it seldom survived the circumstances that called it into being. After World War II, documentary drama became a German specialty, best exemplified by Heinar Kipphardt's *In der Sache J. Robert Oppenheimer* (pr. 1964; *In the Matter of J. Robert Oppenheimer*, 1967) and Peter Weiss's *Die Ermittlung* (pr. 1964; *The Investigation*, 1966), bald presentations of trial testimony with a minimum of authorial editing or manipulation, but chosen with an eye to the general conclusions to be drawn. The revue pattern persisted, however, in the United States, as in Martin Duberman's *In White America* (pr. 1963) and Jonathan Katz's *Coming Out* (pr. 1972), efforts to promote civil rights for African Americans and homosexuals, respectively.

IMPACT OF CINEMA

The discoveries made by the cinema were gradually absorbed into the drama, and experimental techniques that at first baffled and irritated theater audiences became standard operating procedure. Flashbacks, the fading in and out of momentary scenes, blackouts, rapid shifts from the public to the intimate (once known as Shakespearean contrasts)—all were intercut and spliced as needed. The popularization of Freudianism rejuvenated the well-made play by allowing the subconscious a role in the denouement: Dramas seemingly as different as Maxwell Anderson's *Bad Seed* (pr. 1954), about a homicidal child, and Peter Shaffer's *Equus* (pr. 1973), about a disturbed adolescent, are both gradual exfoliations of the truth about a mental state. Anderson's melodrama uses the basic drawing-room format with a Freudian criminologist as *raisonneur* and a neatly ironic ending; Shaffer employed a less confident exponent of R. D. Laing as his spokesperson and had the benefit of a trendy theatricalist production. Both plays, however, are informed by the Scribean ambition to provide a causal "explanation" for a complex action.

The invention of photography is said to have freed painters from having to reproduce reality in an objective manner, allowing them to put their inner visions on canvas. The same holds true of the relationship of cinema to drama, although the serious drama had already moved in the direction of subjectivity by the time the first motion pictures were shown. Whereas naturalism and the commercial theater were coopted and consummated by the film, nonrealistic drama has never taken hold on the screen and continues to be called "experimental." As motion pictures replaced theater as the most popular entertainment medium in Western society, so drama should have been freed from its need to purvey standard fare in conventional ways to the lowest common denominator. Unfortunately, it has not yet become fully aware of its freedom.

DADAISM AND SURREALISM

Early evidence of the liberty to shock expectation and provide drama that was disconcerting and unpredictable was Alfred Jarry's anarchic puppet play *Ubu roi* (pr. 1896; English translation, 1951), which Yeats deplored as the advent of the "Savage God," an announcement that the world was rapidly falling into chaos. Jarry was taken as patron saint by the post-World War I Dadaists and Surrealists, whose plays are acts of provocation and disorientation rather than works of theatrical merit. In his 1919 manifesto, Dada's founder Tristan Tzara advertised spontaneity and disgust with accepted values. His influence was later felt in the upsurge of improvisation that swept Western theater in the 1960's and 1970's, the "happenings," and the rejection of consecutively meaningful dialogue.

Even more influential, because better organized, was Dada's successor and rival, Surrealism. The term *drame surréaliste* had been coined by the poet Guillaume Apollinaire in 1917 to describe his play *Les Mamelles de Tirésias* (pr. 1917; *The Breasts of Tiresias*, 1964), which offered a fresh alternative to mimesis: "it was time to relate to nature, but without imitating it in a photographic manner. When man wanted to imitate walking action he invented the wheel, which bears no resemblance to a leg. Thus, he did something unwittingly surrealistic." Apollinaire's play, an exuberant lampoon of the French government's call for fecundity, was close to Jarry in its facetiousness and childish savagery.

Surrealism received more intellectual validation from psychologist Sigmund Freud: André Breton, called the Pope of Surrealism, determined that the hidden reservoirs of imagination could be tapped through the subconscious. Although he retained the name "Surrealist" in homage to Apollinaire, his movement was less deliberately comic, more earnestly psychoanalytic than his predecessor's pranks. The goal of Surrealism was to disorder the mind by practicing automatic writing and studying dreams; in that way, the other aspect of the real, what was called "magical reality," is restored to its true place, and Cartesian logic is replaced by a more flexible approach to life. (Clearly, Surrealism was a reaction to the French school system as much as to anything else.) Human beings will recover their totality once they are released from loyalties to an imaginary god or rational imperatives, and will rediscover "an inner fairyland."

Originally intended as a weapon in a struggle for the revolutionary transformation of the consciousness, Surrealist drama has been more influential in its theoretical manifestos than in performance. Only in Poland, where life itself offered an irrational model,

was Surrealist drama able to draw on certain preexisting popular traditions, as in the plays of Stanisław Witkiewicz and Tadeusz Różewicz. Many of Surrealism's devices—the abrupt juxtaposition of unrelated objects or moods, the reproduction of the dream state, the revelation of the marvelous within the mundane—were rapidly absorbed into more accessible works and have become mainstays of contemporary theater.

Federico García Lorca's *Bodas de sangre* (pr. 1933; *Blood Wedding*, 1939) effects a surrealistic shift when it moves from the world of marriage contracts to the figure of Death in the forest; Jean Cocteau's *Orphée* (pr. 1926; *Orpheus*, 1933) updates the Greek myth with theatrical trickery and the effacement of stage convention. Tom Stoppard has been particularly successful in harnessing surrealistic effects, such as the acrobatic team in a logic professor's bedroom in *Jumpers* (pr. 1972), to intellectual comedy. Finally, much that is labeled Theater of the Absurd is Surrealist displacement put in aid of an existentialist outlook, as with the growing corpse in Eugène Ionesco's *Amédée: Ou, Comment s'en débarrasser* (pr. 1954; *Amédée: Or, How to Get Rid of It*, 1955).

ARTAUD'S THEATER OF CRUELTY

The most provocative offshoot of Surrealism was Antonin Artaud. Taken in his lifetime to be a talented madman, a freak on the fringes of the art world, he became, through the good offices of Jean-Paul Sartre and, later, Charles Marowitz, Peter Brook, and Jerzy Grotowski, a totemic figure. Artaud's plays, such as *Le Jet de sang* (pb. 1925; *Spurt of Blood*, 1968), are mere scenarios for spectacles; it was his pronunciamentos and manifestos that were ransacked for theatrical incentives during the 1960's and 1970's. Artaud, like most modern would-be reformers of the theater, looked around him and saw that playgoing was a hollow social function and that plays were stale restatements of conventional truisms, incapable of changing the world. In response, he predicated a Theater of Cruelty, a phrase much misinterpreted by those who see it only as a Grand Guignolesque recreation of atrocity onstage. To put Artaud's thesis bluntly, the theater was to become an arena of shock therapy; in the process, the actors would undergo such intense physical and psychic extremity that the audience would be unable to estrange itself; its preconceptions, hostilities, anxieties, and inner aggression would all be jarred loose, and it would leave the theater cleansed. This new catharsis could not be effected by texts, for Artaud discounted all but the incantatory value of words. Noises, startling sounds, violent gestures, ceremonial costumes, and unnerving lighting would all contribute, in an unfamiliar environment, to the curative result.

Although much contemporary theater practice embodies Artaud's desiderata, a corresponding drama has not been forthcoming. At most, he stimulated the notion of playwrights creating in collaboration with acting companies, to re-create their rehearsal discoveries as scenarios. Jean-Claude Van Itallie's work with the Open Theatre wrought improvisations and *études* into episodic scripts of a ritual cast. The Living Theatre's more intentionally Artaudian creations, *Frankenstein* (pr. 1965) and *Paradise Now* (pr. 1968), were joint efforts that barely existed on the page but required an abundance of live bodies and stage electricity to make an impact on an audience. The plays of Jean Genet and Fernando Arrabal are Artaudian in their exploitation of ritual and sadism, both mental and physical, but both are too rational, too political, and too fond of lapidary language to fulfill Artaud's prescriptions.

BRECHT'S EPIC THEATER

Bertolt Brecht began with Artaud's premise that the modern drama, what Artaud called "culinary theater," was a *digestif* for the bloated bourgeoisie, but his solution was diametrically the reverse of Artaud's. While Artaud repudiated the brain and its reasoning faculties and extolled the purely visceral response, Brecht distrusted emotion and desired the spectator to keep his mind clear and keen throughout a performance. Brecht was a Marxist, though hardly an orthodox one, who intended to reveal through the staged scenes problems in capitalist society that could not be cured in the theater. The audience had to depart pondering the situations, challenged to find the

remedy in life. Schiller had declared that the best tragedy was one drawn from history, for an audience would be more harrowed by prior awareness that the disaster had not been averted.

Brecht, on the contrary, insisted on the audience's awareness that any disaster might be averted, depending on the choices made; that history was not fixed, but fluid and therefore capable of being altered. In a scene of a wedding proposal, the audience was to be informed at the start that the young girl would turn it down; in this way, the audience would not be caught up in emotive suspense over the outcome and would be free to observe how and why the outcome was reached. Similarly, characters must be seen in flux, their various facets revealed in given circumstances and, particularly, within the socioeconomic context: not the deterministic environment of the naturalists that reduced human beings to a passive residuum, but a context that permitted choice and adaptation. The idea of the "characterless character" forming and melting in response to outside stimuli had earlier been voiced by Strindberg, but in a psychological and Darwinian sense.

Where Brecht differed most from the run-of-the-mill Marxist writers was in his emphasis on epic theater to promote the proper estrangement (or alienation) of the audience from the drama. Most socialist drama was ploddingly realistic if not melodramatic, anxious to get the message across at all costs. Epic theater was a synthesis of elements from the avant-garde—Frank Wedekind, Igor Stravinsky, Luigi Pirandello, Paul Claudel—and Asian theater, forged by Brecht into a systematic and flexible tool of dialectic. As to dramatic construction, the "knots must be noticeable"; each scene exists in and of itself, to present an object lesson, a testing ground for the characters. This eliminates the sense of inevitability that comes in the course of a well-made act with its exposition, climax, and denouement. The core of the scene, as well as of each actor's characterization, is the *Gestus*, a strikingly theatrical action or expression that takes on emblematic significance. For example, in *Herr Puntila und sein Knecht Matti* (pr. 1948; *Mr. Puntila and His Man Matti*, 1977), the *Gestus* for the scene "Climbing Mt. Hatelma" is a masterful construction of a mountain from tables and chairs that the drunken landowner and his valet scale to a falsely poetic height.

As a young man, Brecht was more doctrinaire about the spareness of his means. To keep the audience at arm's length, uninvolved with the protagonist and prepared to debate issues, he created the *Lehrstück*, or didactic play, a bare, flat enactment of a moral dilemma. Later, he followed his own inclination for popular amusements and insisted on the importance of pleasure as a factor contributing to the audience's receptivity. "To entertain the children of the scientific age in a palpable manner and cheerfully," he required his actors to have the agility and improvisatory skill of a Charlie Chaplin or a Karl Valentin. The playing out of a situation should have the same gripping interest as a boxing match or a trapeze act, but without sentimental empathy.

For that reason, Brecht's own plays were never intended to be unalterably finished, and most of them exist in several versions: The meaning of a play can be defined only in performance, he believed, and it is legitimate to modify the play to suit the public's understanding. When Giorgio Strehler, directing the first Italian production of *Der Dreigroschenoper* (pr. 1928; *The Threepenny Opera*, 1964) after World War II, asked Brecht if he could change the locale from Victorian England to Chicago in the 1920's, the author gladly gave him permission. In this respect, he was the opposite of Shaw, who regarded every one of his words as sacrosanct and seldom left his plays open-ended—which is why so many of them have aged so badly.

A great deal of Brecht's theatrical technique has been absorbed by the modern theater, even when his dialectic is left outside. The linkage of disconnected scenes, the interpolation of song (not as in opera to heighten the emotion, but rather to generalize the situation, retard progress, and cool off emotion), the naked lighting, conspicuous musicians, set changes in full view, direct address to the audience, distressed costumes and realistic props in a nonrealistic setting, even the signboards to title scenes, are the common tools of the modern dramatist. They have been popularized in historical dramas such as Robert Bolt's *A Man for All Seasons* (pr. 1960) and even in musical comedy. It may be suggested that in its influence, ethics, and adaptable form, Brecht's play is the modern equivalent of classical tragedies, however different their styles and philosophies are. In both cases, the format has often been adopted and altered to accommodate ways of thinking foreign to that which made the genre necessary in the first place.

THEATER OF THE ABSURD

One further genre must be touched on, the Theater of the Absurd, a term, if not invented, then given currency by the critic Martin Esslin, in a much-read book of that title. In it, Esslin discusses the work of Samuel Beckett, Eugène Ionesco, Jean Genet, Harold Pinter, and a few others, although Esslin warns against the dangers of generalizing. The term "absurd" has since come into wide use to describe a play with an unrealistic or alogical complexion. "Absurd" originated as an existentialist term to express the bitterly ludicrous meaninglessness of life, its anomie and lack of causal relation. When used that way, it can apply to aspects of Beckett and Ionesco, which are also absurd in the traditional sense of grotesquely comic. True absurdism is hard to find in drama, because it takes great skill to dramatize breakdowns in communication and vacuousness without becoming incoherent and boring. Beckett has many affinities to the Symbolists as well as to the absurdists, with his characters held in suspension and his eloquent pauses, while Ionesco is related to the Surrealists and their own ancestors, the *fin de siècle* farceurs whose whirligig comedies gave fantastic guises to middle-class banality. More idiosyncratic forms of ambiguity are currently practiced by the Austrian Peter Handke, whose plays test the nature of reality from a solipsist's point of view.

Another term used similarly to "absurdism" is J. L. Styan's dark comedy, propounded in his book *The Dark Comedy* (1962, revised 1968) as a fresh definition of tragicomedy. Styan recognized that the modern counterpoint of tragedy and farce was not wholly a twentieth century phenomenon but had its origins in Euripides, the mystery plays, Molière, and Shakespeare. Dark comedy, he wrote, is drama which impels the spectator forward by stimulus to mind or heart, then distracts him, muddles him, so that time and time again he must review his own activity in watching the play. In these submissive, humiliating spasms, the drama redoubles its energy, the play's images take on other facets, the mind other aspects, and the spectator "collects the force which again carries him onward." But now progression is more cautious, and he is on guard. He is charged with a tension as a result of which he is a more alert and therefore responsive participant. This tension is one of dramatic irony.

Dark comedy (as distinct from black comedy, which strives to derive humor from the morbid or taboo) is broad enough to encompass most of the innovative works of the contemporary repertory. It reflects the existentialist belief in a disjunctive world where there is no possibility for heroism or tragedy. It is also realistic in its assumption that modern audiences are heterogeneous and cannot be expected to share common assumptions. It proposes a catharsis that occurs from moment to moment but that is not necessarily effective outside the playhouse—perhaps a token of the drama's relative irrelevance to the modern world. At any rate, the definition of drama by its effect on the spectator returns us to the Aristotelian ethos.

In 1817, William Hazlitt had casually predicted that "the progress of manners and knowledge has an influence on the stage, and will in time perhaps destroy both tragedy and comedy." This seems to have come to pass. In the mouth of a newscaster, tragedy means a streetcar accident or an avalanche. Comedy (and the ugly neologism "comedic") has come to mean anything that gets a laugh. Generic terms are taken so lightly that they are used as titles themselves, rather than as explanatory subtitles: Sir Alan Ayckbourn's comedy of marriage called *Bedroom Farce* (pr. 1975), Erich Segal's best-selling romance *Love Story* (1970), and Anthony Shaffer's thriller *Whodunit* (pr. 1982) tacitly assume that these are defunct and formulaic tags, useful only for the exploitation of their conventions. Playwrights themselves, when pressed to subtitle their works, given them the neutral designations "play" or "drama" (or "comedy," still a popular label to reassure the press and public that nothing disagreeable or brain-straining is in the

offing). Semioticians study plays by breaking them down to their constituent signs, and deconstructionists repudiate any frame of reference extraneous to the author's linguistic games. Still, the drama is too public and synthetic a phenomenon for its context to be ignored, and the pluralism of modern culture is such that, by determining its generic alliances, a play may be clarified and its effect understood, just as those effects may be investigated to shed light on its genre.

BIBLIOGRAPHY

Andrews, Richard. *Scripts and Scenarios: The Performed Comic Text in Renaissance Italy.* Cambridge, England: Cambridge University Press, 1993. Traces the rise of the unique theatrical form, *comedia dell'arte*, in Italy, examining its influence on European drama, its antecedents, and its audience reception.

Cicora, Mary A. *Wagner's Ring and German Drama.* Westport, Conn.: Greenwood Press, 1999. Critical study of the place of Wagner's musical drama masterpiece against the backdrop of dramatic trends in late 1800's German drama.

Daniels, Barry V., ed. *Revolution in the Theatre: French Romantic Theories of Drama.* Westport, Conn.: Greenwood Press, 1983. Collection of perceptive essays probing the shape of drama in French Romantic theater. Index.

Di Maria, Salvatore. *Italian Tragedy in the Renaissance: Cultural Realities and Theatrical Innovations.* Lewisburg, Pa.: Bucknell University Press, 2002. Analyzes the revival of Greek and Roman tragedy on the Italian Renaissance stage, examining the way in which playwrights modified dramatic elements to make the productions relevant to their audiences.

Haymes, Edward R. *Theatrum Mundum: Essays on German Drama and German Literature.* Munich, Germany: Fink Verlag, 1980. Excellent collection of a rich variety of individual essays covering major playwrights from all eras of German drama after 1600.

Innes, Christopher, ed. *A Sourcebook on Naturalist Theatre.* London: Routledge, 2000. Excellent collection of sources for the works of Ibsen, Chekhov, and Shaw, the three playwrights who shaped naturalism. Includes an overview of history and criticism of naturalism. Bibliography and index.

Lyons, John D. *Kingdom of Disorder: The Theory of Tragedy in Classical France*. West Lafayette, Ind.: Purdue University Press, 1999. Scholarly work of French tragic drama from 1600 to 1699. Perceptive and with significant discussion of how individual plays correspond to theoretical demands. Bibliography and index.

Owens, Susan J., ed. *Companion to Restoration Drama*. Malden, Mass.: Blackwell Publishers, 2002. Provides a comprehensive overview to the contextual history of Restoration drama. Explores a multitude of topics with chapters such as "The Restoration Actress," "Libertinism and Sexuality," "Masculinity in Restoration Drama," "Heroic Drama and Tragicomedy," while also closely examining the noted playwrights of the period.

Shiach, David. *American Drama, 1900-1990*. New York: Cambridge University Press, 2000. Emphasizes key periods, topics, themes, and comparisons in literature, rather than on individual authors or plays, thus calling attention to important literary, historical, and social contexts of the twentieth century.

Sutton, Dana Ferrin. *Ancient Comedy: The War of the Generations*. New York: Twayne, 1993. Overview chapter explores the origins of ancient comedy in Dionysiac festivals and the development of the comedic form. Subsequent chapters combine lively descriptions of the era's rowdy plays with analyses of the historical context and the ubiquitous theme of intergenerational conflict.

Tydeman, William, Louise M. Haywood, Michael J. Anderson, et al., eds. *Medieval European Stage, 500-1500*. Cambridge, England: Cambridge University Press, 2001. The editors bring together a comprehensive selection of documents and analyses to elucidate the survival of classical tradition and development of the liturgical drama, the growth of popular religious drama in the vernacular, and the pastimes and customs of the people.

Laurence Senelick

MELODRAMA

In its strictest sense, melodrama refers to a genre that developed in France shortly before 1800 and became extremely popular, soon making its way to England in its original form. The form then broadened to include similarities to conventional drama, including a reliance on spectacle, on the resolution of the plot in a just manner, and on heroic characters and villains in conflict with each other.

The term "melodrama" comes from the French *mélodrame*, a term derived from *melos*, the Greek word for song. *Drame* referred to minor forms that conformed to neither the neoclassical definition of comedy nor tragedy. As the name implies, music was used structurally. Songs and dances were built into the original score of a melodrama, were carefully rehearsed, and kept the orchestra busy throughout the play. Characters were provided with entrance music that gave a clear indication of their personality, and the mood was supported by the orchestra at all important points. In early melodrama, music and acting style were inseparable, and long sequences of silent action to musical accompaniment were frequent. Melodramatic acting was thus influenced by the music the orchestra provided. The music dictated much of the timing the actor used and at times gave the play a sense of being choreographed rather than being acted in the usual sense. The initial identification of melodrama as a minor form was an important fact because it allowed the melodrama to develop outside the monopolies of licensed companies in France and, later, in England.

EARLY CHARACTER TYPES

Early melodramatic characters often were not completely developed, serving instead as vehicles for the quick development of suspense and spectacle on which the plays relied. For example, the heroine typically epitomized goodness, her physical beauty reflecting her purity of heart. She was honest, loyal, respectful of her parents, and above pettiness of any kind. Unless she was married she was chaste, and if married she was faithful to her husband.

Less consistent than the heroine, the hero was at times as pure and noble as she, but at other times he was easily duped or possessed weaknesses that the villain was able to exploit. He might be outwitted but he was unlikely to lose to the villain in a fair fight. Despite the fact that historically audiences expected to see the hero rescue the heroine, in serious melodrama it was sometimes the heroine's unflinching faithfulness that saved him from his own weakness. Later in the melodrama's history, charming roguish characters emerged as heroes. The highwayman, the frontier roughneck, and the city fireman all took their turns in this role.

The villain was at the center of melodramatic action. He disrupted harmony and laid plots that brought real danger to the heroine and hero. Audiences saw no need for him to justify his actions. Other reasons might be given, but greed, lust, or simple malice was usually sufficient. The villain of the early melodrama was eloquent, well dressed, and cultured. In the United States he was often of European aristocratic descent (or claimed to be).

The heroine's father was often included. Through him the villain was apt to try to gain control of the heroine. The father could be gullible or vain enough to be swayed by the villain's smooth talk, but it was equally likely that there was something in his past that the villain might threaten to expose.

A comic servant or companion frequently was used as a device. Typically this comic servant or companion instantly saw through the villain, put the situation in perspective, and made light of the high standards of conduct by which other characters feel inconveniently bound.

STRUCTURE

The melodrama generally has been presented in three acts, although there can be as few as two and as many as five. In the first act, a happy domestic situation is introduced. The virtue of the heroine or hero is quickly established, principal characters are introduced, and exposition is provided. There is frequently a love interest between hero and heroine. The villain arrives on the scene proposing that he marry the heroine, but the playwright finds a way to assure the audience that his love will be rejected. In spite of the villain's confidence, his plans are thwarted and he leaves vowing revenge.

In the second act, the villain's plans are laid and begin to carry out the plot. The heroine, hero, or both are brought near destruction. In the third act the situation is resolved in favor of the heroine or hero. Fortunes lost to the villain's manipulations are restored and the villain is no longer a threat, having been unmasked and turned over to the authorities or killed by a trap he had intended for someone else.

EARLY APPEAL

The initial appeal of the melodrama came neither through characterization nor through plot but rather from the satisfaction the audience gained in seeing good ultimately rewarded and the guilty finally punished. This formula is familiar to modern audiences in forums as disparate as Saturday morning Westerns and Walt Disney films. That the heroine was able to escape the machinations of the villain unscathed reinforced for audiences the notion that justice ultimately prevails.

The second source of appeal emerged with the advent of stage technology in the mid- to late nineteenth century. Melodramas relied on visual spectacle and supernatural phenomena, and new technological developments such as lighting, revolving stages, elevators, cutaway flats, and moving scenery were elaborate, expensive, and well advertised. At least one spectacular effect of some sort was a virtual requirement of any melodrama.

EVOLUTION OF THE GENRE

Classic melodrama emerged in France some time around 1790. Several plays may be argued to be the first melodrama, but the first master of the form is firmly established: French playwright Guilbert de Pixérécourt is credited with making melodrama popular in the late eighteenth and early nineteenth centuries and became a significant force in theatrical history. Pixérécourt's first produced melodrama was

Victor: Ou, L'Enfant de la forêt (Victor, or the child of the forest) in 1798. His first great success followed three years later with *Cœlina: Ou, L'Enfant du mystère* (pr. 1800; *The Tale of Mystery*, 1802). Other successes quickly followed. Pixérécourt is credited with the authorship of more than one hundred plays, most of them melodramas. He remained the most popular author of this form until his death in 1844. Most of his successes were adapted for presentation in England and the United States by others. After Pixérécourt, Victor Ducange, Louis Charles Caigniez, and Adolphe Dennery were the most noteworthy French playwrights of the genre.

Melodrama debuted in England in 1802 with *A Tale of Mystery*, a play adapted from *Cœlina* by Thomas Holcroft. As traditional comedy and tragedy waned in popularity, British theaters turned increasingly to other forms to support themselves financially. Melodramas were offered as afterpieces to ensure the success of more revered offerings, including the work of William Shakespeare, or were combined with other forms of popular entertainment to make up a full evening. Melodramas not only provided the greatest revenue of any type of drama during this period but also may be credited with saving the patent houses from bankruptcy while keeping several other companies prosperous.

A number of specialized melodramas joined the French imports. "Aquatic" melodrama took advantage of theatrical machinery to create impressive water effects, including cataracts, lakes, rapids, and oceans, into which characters were placed for thrilling climaxes. The first of these spectacles may have been *The Siege of Gibraltar* by Charles Dibdin, presented at Covent Garden in 1802. The climax of the play was the destruction of a fleet of scale models, which burned and sank.

Crime melodramas were the staple at the Royal Victoria and the Royal Coburg theaters in the early to mid-nineteenth century. The plays presented were bloody to the extreme, with mutilation and murder as staples. Some plays, such as George Dibdin-Pitt's Sweeney Todd tale *The String of Pearls: The Fiend of Fleet Street* (pr. 1847) were fictional, but others were dramatizations of sensational crimes. When actual crimes were used, authors felt no obligation to confine themselves to the facts when alteration made for a more satisfying story. Melodramas with social themes appeared in the 1830's, beginning with Douglas Jerrold's *The Rent Day* (pr. 1832) and G. F. Taylor's *The Factory Strike* (pr. 1838).

In the nineteenth century, Dion Boucicault was the first melodramatist to rival Pixérécourt's skill or popularity. He divided his time between the United States and England, achieving a series of solid hits on both sides of the Atlantic. He achieved a notable first success with his adaptation of *The Corsican Brothers* (pr. 1852). His next resounding hit was *The Poor of New York* (pr. 1857), a social drama based on a French original, which he adapted for London as *The Poor of Liverpool* and *The Streets of London* (pr. 1864). He went on to write *The Octoroon: Or, Life in Louisiana* (pr. 1859, 1861), which dealt with the issue of slavery, and *The Long Strike* (wr. 1866), in which an innocent man is saved from false conviction by a telegraph message sent and received in the nick of time. With *The Colleen Bawn* (pr. 1860), Boucicault began his work with Irish plays, going on to create *Arrah-na-Pogue: Or, The Wicklow Wedding* (pr. 1864) and *The Shaughraun* (pr. 1874). Boucicault was probably the most popular author of the 1850's and 1860's. Thereafter his popularity waned, but he continued to write until his death.

AMERICAN MELODRAMA

As melodrama moved to the United States, it followed the pattern established in England. The earliest melodramas were English imports, many of them in turn adapted from French originals. Yet, original dramas relying on uniquely American themes began to appear in the 1820's. The frontier roughneck stock character made his first appearance in an 1827 production number, "The Hunter of Kentucky," by Noah Ludlow. Always ready for a fight, inclined to brag and drink, but with homespun morality, the native hero had a long history that continued to evolve: Future incarnations had the hero making his way across the country as a hapless bumpkin, a lovable Irishman, or a big-city fireman.

Temperance melodramas appeared in 1844 with *The Drunkard: Or, The Fallen Saved* by William H. Smith but presented and later published anonymously. *Ten Nights in a Barroom* by William Pratt followed. Both owe their formula to *Fifteen Years of a Drunkard's Life* (1828), by Douglas Jerrold. Alcohol was presented as a genuine evil in these pieces, making them attractive propaganda for the growing temperance movement and assuring continual production until Prohibition in the 1920's. Despite several attempts to break a drinking habit encouraged by the villain, the hero slides into increasing addiction while his domestic situation deteriorates. He is eventually saved by the love of his family, who refuse to give up on him.

When the Native American was presented in American plays in the 1820's it tended to be as the "noble savage" envisioned by author James Fenimore Cooper. The melodrama acquired a new vision of the Native American in 1838 with the staging of *The Jibbenainosay*. Based on a novel by Robert Montgomery Bird, *Nick of the Woods: Or, The Jibbenainosay, A Tale of Kentucky* (1837), the play depicts an ordinarily quiet man who kills any Native American he can catch, usually just as one is about to commit some atrocity. While popularizing a new image of Native Americans, the Nick plays laid the foundation for many plots involving settlers and evil Indians.

Harriet Beecher Stowe's *Uncle Tom's Cabin* deserves special note among melodramas. It was adapted for the stage in several versions, but the most popular was by George L. Aiken in 1852. Its plot followed classic melodramatic themes and gained international popularity. It ran continually, gaining prominence until the 1880's when it declined, although it continued to be performed with some regularity until the Great Depression of the 1930's. With its sympathetic heroine and her child, an evil, unrepentant villain, and visual spectacle, it had all the elements on which melodrama's success had been built. It was not unusual to find simultaneous productions in large cities. Some estimates make *Uncle Tom's Cabin* the most frequently performed play of any type in American history.

LEGACY

With its naïve sense of justice, its superficial stock characters, and its contrived resolutions, melodrama lost its appeal as theatrical tastes moved toward realism in the early twentieth century. Classical melodrama is viable today only as a historical offering or perhaps in a spoofed form, betraying the sincerity with which it was originally presented.

Nonetheless, melodrama has exerted a lasting impact on theater. Because melodrama made heavy use of the orchestra to deliver music written especially for this medium, it can be argued that the subsequent and thoughtful matching of musical material to emotional moments in musicals, films, and television shows derives from melodrama and supports the careful creation of underscoring in these artistic media.

Melodrama's influence also continues to be felt in the use of spectacle. Each melodrama contained at least one scene in which some elaborate stage effect was used. Among these were fire, collapsing buildings, running water, and avalanches. Merely suggestive at the beginning of the nineteenth century, the spectacle scene was impressive in its elaborateness and believability by the end of the century. Melodrama can be credited with spurring the inventiveness of set designers and set builders and with confirming the value of carefully created visual effects achieved at considerable expense.

BIBLIOGRAPHY

Booth, Michael R. *English Melodrama*. London: Herbert Jenkins, 1965. Serves as an excellent resource on melodrama as it developed in England.

_____. *Victorian Spectacular Theatre, 1850-1910*. Boston: Routledge and Kegan Paul, 1981. Excellent treatment of the use of spectacle and machinery in English theater, which was essential to the melodrama's success.

Brooks, Peter. *The Melodramatic Imagination: Balzac, Henry James, Melodrama, and the Mode of Excess*. New Haven, Conn.: Yale University Press, 1976. Studies the relationship between melodrama in its strictest definition and other works. Includes some interesting observations about the structure of melodrama.

Disher, M. Willson. *Melodrama: Plots That Thrilled*. New York: Macmillan, 1954. Focuses on a number of popular melodramatic forms.

Grimsted, David. *Melodrama Unveiled: American Theatre and Culture, 1800-1850*. Chicago: University of Chicago Press, 1968. A standard book in the field, it offers valuable insight into the background and structure of the melodrama. Well annotated and with appendices.

McConachie, Bruce A. *Melodramatic Foundations: American Theatre and Society, 1820-1870*. Iowa City: University of Iowa Press, 1992. Treats this limited time frame thoroughly and includes a number of quotations from original sources. Well annotated.

Rahill, Frank. *The World of Melodrama*. Philadelphia: University of Pennsylvania Press, 1967. A comprehensive examination of melodrama in France, England, and the United States.

Glenn Patterson

VAUDEVILLE

From the 1880's to the 1930's, the most popular form of entertainment in the United States was the live variety show known as vaudeville. It has been estimated that vaudeville employed approximately twenty-five thousand performers during its span of popularity, and during its peak in the 1910's and 1920's, two thousand vaudeville theaters existed across the United States and Canada. In spite of its great popularity, however, by the 1950's vaudeville as mass entertainment had been replaced by television, film, and radio.

Although its origins and meaning are debated, the word "vaudeville" might have come from the French phrase "val de Vire," referring to regional folk songs sung in the Vire River valley. "Vaudeville" may also have derived from the French "voix de ville" or "voice of the city," a reference to folk music performed in urban areas of France.

EARLY HISTORY

Vaudeville evolved as a mixture of several types of early theater. Many of vaudeville's classic acts had their origins in ancient forms of entertainment enacted by street performers, jesters, and clowns. As far back as the sixteenth century, "music halls" in England presented stage shows (called "pantos," an abbreviated form of "pantomime") that presented a variety of different acts in one show. A single performance might include slapstick physical comedy, humorous songs, and humorous short plays or skits. Immigrants brought elements of the English panto to the United States in the late nineteenth century.

Vaudeville was also influenced by American burlesque, a type of show popular from the mid-nineteenth century through the 1920's. A burlesque show was usually a series of comedy skits, alternating with women singing or performing dances designed to show off their legs. Burlesque shows were closely related to "concert saloon" shows popular during the Civil War. Concert saloons (also called "honky-tonks" or beer halls) often hired piano players, dancers, or singers to entertain their all-male patrons.

With the Industrial Revolution came the growth of an American middle class. In the mid- to late nineteenth century large numbers of people moved from the country to the cities, and immigration from other countries to the United States reached a peak. City dwellers and laborers in new industries had money and leisure time, and concert saloon owners saw an opportunity to attract more patrons by offering more respectable entertainment. Concert saloons and beer halls began to call themselves "music halls," revising the shows they offered to make them suitable for a wider audience.

Singer and comedian Tony Pastor, "the father of vaudeville," had performed for years in beer halls, but in 1881 he opened his own theater in New York City called Tony Pastor's Fourteenth Street Theater. Pastor forbade the sale of alcohol in his theaters and focused on entertainment alone. The shows he produced were designed to attract a middle-class audience including families and featured simple entertainment by singing ensembles and comedians.

Two years after Pastor opened his first theater, Benjamin Franklin Keith opened a "museum" in Boston with a second-floor theater where singers and animal acts performed. Keith would become one of the most powerful men in vaudeville. In the ensuing years he would open many more theaters and would offer, in addition to variety acts, short plays, silent films, operettas, and lectures.

Like Pastor, Keith hoped to attract middle-class families to the theater. Advertisements for Keith's theaters emphasized that his shows were appropriate for women and children. Keith moved vaudeville even further from the concert saloons by enforcing a family atmosphere, even backstage, where performers were forbidden to use crude language or wear revealing clothing. In their acts, performers were told not to use even potentially offensive words such as "liar," "slob," or "spit." By the late 1920's Keith's theater managers were keeping a list of more than seventy words and phrases that performers were not allowed to speak on the stage.

Keith purchased theaters across the eastern United States, forming a "circuit" or chain of theaters that would all book the same traveling acts. In the 1920's Keith's circuit was the largest of approximately twenty-two circuits in the United States. Keith joined forces with the Orpheum circuit of theaters in the western United States, and the Keith-Orpheum circuit became the largest and most powerful chain of vaudeville theaters. Theater managers kept up a constant stream of communication about the relative success or failure of each act, and could use this information to decide whether or not to book an act or where to position an act on the bill. Performers who wanted to play the Keith-Orpheum circuit not only had to follow Keith's rules for keeping their acts clean; they also risked being blacklisted if they played in theaters outside the circuit.

Beyond controlling the content of the acts, Keith tried to bring the traditionally rowdy concert saloon audience under control in his theaters. Audiences used to the beer hall atmosphere were often loud and boisterous, shouting at the performers and providing running commentary on each act. Keith worried that middle-class women might feel uncomfortable in his theaters unless the audience behaved. Keith would himself sometimes take the stage to make a short speech, asking the audience to be more polite. Theater employees carried signs through the audience asking them not to stamp their feet, talk during the performances, or laugh too loudly.

THE BILL

Vaudeville theater managers would arrange the "bill" for each show, deciding the order in which performers would take the stage. A vaudeville show might include anywhere from two to twenty-two acts; a typical show would have eight to ten. The audience would be taking their seats during the opening act, so the first performance was usually a "dumb act," something that was visually interesting but not dependent on music or dialogue—perhaps a juggler, tightrope walker, magician, or a trained animal act.

The second act might be a singing duo or song-and-dance team. The third act, called by vaudeville performers the "three-spot," could be a short play, a comedy skit, or a group of dancers. The three-spot was typically followed by either a famous performer who was not quite famous enough to be the headliner, or something elaborate and eye-catching—perhaps a large dance troupe—to thrill the audience just before intermission. The best act on the bill would appear next to last, followed by the closing spot, called "the chaser" or "playing to the haircuts" because most of the audience would leave after seeing the headlining act.

THE PERFORMERS

Vaudeville performers ran the gamut from celebrities such as Helen Keller, Babe Ruth, Charles Lindbergh, W. C. Fields, and Sarah Bernhardt to the Banana Man, whose act consisted of pulling large objects out of his coat. A 1913 mail-order course for hopeful performers suggested countless talents that might be developed into a vaudeville act. These included escaping from handcuffs, posing like a statue, imitating birds or simply whistling, performing feats of strength, yodeling, and reading minds.

Although vaudeville was considered a lower form of entertainment, designed for an unsophisticated audience, famous personalities often worked vaudeville circuits to keep their names before the public or to bolster failing careers. Playing a vaudeville circuit would bring the performer into contact with a vast number of people. Vaudeville performers included magicians such as Harry Houdini (who became famous for his ability to escape from handcuffs and straitjackets) and comedians such as George Burns, Bert Lahr (who later played the Cowardly Lion in the motion picture *The Wizard of Oz*, 1939), and the famed African American Bert Williams.

Novelty acts were also popular. These might include snake charmers, singing ducks, or dogs that could juggle. Hadji Ali was a popular "regurgitator" who swallowed a pint of kerosene and then spit it out, setting a small model house on fire. Teenage conjoined twins the Hilton Sisters played clarinet duets; the Albee Sisters sang and danced wearing evening gowns and fake mustaches.

Most vaudevillians were, like their audience, from immigrant and working-class backgrounds. If they became successful in larger vaudeville circuits (such as the Keith-Orpheum circuit) they could make two or three times the money they would earn as laborers. They often wrote their own material and designed their own costumes, sets, and props. A vaudeville performer would typically develop one act and play it over and over; the most successful created unique stage personalities and signature pieces that an audience would recognize. The best acts had "insurance"—material that was guaranteed to go over well. Enthusiasm and high energy would usually help put over an act, and speed was important. Vaudeville's success is often attributed to the great variety and short duration of its acts. Vaudeville managers preferred wild, fast-paced comedy to serious material and would make sure no performance ran over its allotted time.

Ethnic and racial acts

Most vaudeville bills included male or female comedians portraying Chinese, Jewish, Asian, or Italian immigrants. Their comedy skits usually involved an immigrant not knowing how to behave properly in American society. Immigrants in the audience would also have struggled to feel at home in the United States, and they seemed to enjoy these exaggerated portrayals of ethnic groups. Racial and ethnic humor fell out of favor with vaudeville managers as new organizations such as the United Irish Societies of New York and the Associated Rabbis of America objected to acts that made ethnic characters appear foolish.

Vaudeville also incorporated many elements of "minstrel shows," variety shows popular through the late nineteenth century. In early minstrel shows white performers entertained each other with comic portrayals of stereotypical African American characters. The performers wore "blackface"—dark black facial makeup with exaggerated mouths painted on in white lipstick. Minstrel shows included jokes, songs, comic dialogues, and short plays. Vaudeville often featured acts based on minstrel shows, and some African American performers even used the traditional blackface makeup.

Many vaudeville managers would not put more than one African American act in a show, and most did not want to book African American acts that offered serious material rather than stereotypical comic characters. Some African American acts refused to present these characters or to perform in the expected makeup or costumes. The teenage Nicholas Brothers sang and danced dressed in tailcoats. Cabaret musician Bobby Short performed in vaudeville as a child but quit after being made to perform his song "Shoe-Shine Boy" while shining the shoes of a line of chorus girls.

The decline of vaudeville

The release of the first talking films in the late 1920's heralded the end of vaudeville. Movies became more popular during the Great Depression, offering fantasy and escapism during hard times, and at a low price. Theaters originally built for the vaudeville circuits increasingly showed movies instead. Stars of vaudeville left the circuits to perform in movies, on radio, and eventually in television, where variety programs mirrored the vaudeville format. The growing popularity of radio and television programs also kept vaudeville's audience at home. By 1932 there was only one theater left in the United States devoted exclusively to vaudeville. Many former vaudeville acts became stars in radio, television, and films, including the Marx Brothers, Fields, Fred Astaire, Ginger Rogers, Mae West, and Bob Hope.

Bibliography

Alter, Judy. *Vaudeville: The Birth of Show Business*. New York: Franklin Watts, 1998. This introduction to vaudeville discusses the rise and fall of vaudeville, the types of performances that were popular in vaudeville, the theaters, and performers. Also looks at the influence of vaudeville on modern entertainment.

Laurie, Joe, Jr. *Vaudeville: From the Honky-Tonks to the Palace*. New York: Henry Holt, 1953. A detailed history, with profiles of the circuit owners and detailed descriptions of many typical vaudeville acts, presented through a series of letters between two fictional veteran vaudevillians.

Palmer, Greg. *Vaudeville*. New York: Fox/Lorber, 1997. Documentary explores the history of vaudeville through vintage clips of more than eighty vaudeville acts and interviews with many former vaudevillians. Originally produced as an episode of the PBS *American Masters* series.

Slide, Anthony. *The Encyclopedia of Vaudeville.* Westport, Conn.: Greenwood Press, 1994. Detailed historical and biographical entries covering performers, managers, composers, troupes, routines, and animal acts, as well as histories of important cities and theaters in the vaudeville genre.

Recounts some sample vaudeville routines, and includes comments from former vaudevillians and contemporary performers.

Stein, Charles W., ed. *American Vaudeville as Seen by Its Contemporaries.* New York: Alfred A. Knopf, 1984. A collection of magazine articles, performers' reminiscences, and descriptions of vaudeville acts, many originally published during vaudeville's heyday.

Maureen Puffer-Rothenberg

MUSICAL DRAMA

The musical drama, musical play, or simply the musical is an evening-length theater piece integrating spoken dialogue and sung music in order to tell a story. The story, or book, while it may take up serious matters, always has a significant, if not dominant, comic element, and the characters in the story are recognizable and accessible to all members of the audience. The music, usually a set of songs, is composed in a popular idiom.

The foremost criterion for evaluating a musical's artistic success is the integration of book and music. In the best musicals, songs are like compressed scenes of dialogue, revealing character and moving the plot along. A song should never impede the action of the story. Also, in the very best musicals there is a unity of style or tone to the songs; they constitute a musical suite.

Secondary criteria for judging musicals are often derived from the relation of the story and musical idiom to the audience. A story can stray too far from an audience's experience or expectations, either in the general nature of the narrative events or in the relative degree of comedy in the plot. Music similarly challenges an audience when it approaches the technical or conceptual complexity of classical forms. Such musicals, even if they come from Broadway or London's West End, are frequently denied the label "musical," sometimes by their composers. Instead, they are called operettas or even operas.

As *Porgy and Bess* (pr. 1935), *Sweeney Todd, the Demon Barber of Fleet Street* (pr. 1979), and, by some accounts, even *My Fair Lady* (pr. 1956) and *Oklahoma!* (pr. 1943) belong to this group of musicals, the confusion of terminology ought to give pause. Definitions and criteria for the musical cannot be rigidly fixed. At the most superficial level, many a musical with a weak or poor book has become fantastically successful at the box office. From the artistic viewpoint, it would seem almost inevitable that a creative integration of story and music will challenge an audience's experiences and expectations; this is the quality of good art. During the 1984-1985 season,

Porgy and Bess and *Sweeney Todd, the Demon Barber of Fleet Street* were taken into the repertories of, respectively, the Metropolitan Opera and the New York City Opera. Perhaps the two works are operas—or perhaps labels such as "musical" and "operetta" and "opera" have outlived their usefulness: There is only musical theater. Indeed, perhaps no works ever written fulfill the criteria outlined as essential to musicals as successfully as do Wolfgang Amadeus Mozart's comic operas, which even include spoken dialogue. It is instructive to recall that *The Magic Flute* (pr. 1791), which is called an opera, was written for the *Singspiel*, the German language vaudeville, and that it satisfied a commercial craving for music, story, and spectacle as great as any possessed by contemporary audiences.

EVOLUTION OF THE MUSICAL

Musical theater in English goes back to the court masques of the Renaissance—private productions that, in the case of Ben Jonson's works, achieved a highly wrought integration of poetry, music, and spectacle. William Shakespeare first made a musical production number part of public theater when he inserted a full masque into the action of *The Tempest* (pr. 1611).

Strangely, the vicissitudes that beset English drama over the next century had the effect of encouraging musical theater. The Puritan Commonwealth's proscription extended to plays only; while few dared to indulge in this loophole with impunity, opera in English first dates from this period. The first English opera was *The Siege of Rhodes* (pr. 1656) with songs by several composers. The Restoration authorities also restrained legitimate drama, this time by awarding exclusive patents to the Covent Garden and the Drury Lane theaters; again musical theater went unrestricted. Even when musical entertainment was finally brought under governmental regulation early in the eighteenth century through the issuing of burletta licenses, the effect was to further musical theater, for the licensing rules established a minimum of five musical numbers per act as a requirement for a license; the real purpose of the burletta licenses was to provide further protection for the two legitimate theaters.

With all this opportunity, one might suppose that musical theater in England matured rapidly during the reign of the Georges, but this is not so. The artistic success of John Gay's *The Beggar's Opera* (pr. 1728), the earliest theater piece identifiable as a musical drama or musical play, was singular. No exceptional work of popular musical theater appeared again for 150 years, until the musical plays of W. S. Gilbert and Sir Arthur Sullivan, which are most frequently labeled "comic operas."

Gay's purposes in *The Beggar's Opera* were satiric, his victim the Italianate opera made fashionable by George Frederick Handel, but his approach to musical theater clearly foreshadowed that of the modern musical play. For opera's knights and princesses, Gay substituted highwaymen and whores. Instead of recitative, Gay used spoken dialogue. Finally, the music for *The Beggar's Opera* was not classical; in sixty-nine numbers, Gay's characters sang lyrics set to the popular tunes of the day, including a few of Handel's.

Gay's success spawned many imitations. Indeed, burlesquing the pretentions of high art, whether opera or literature, never lost its popularity, although, after Gay, few of these works were evening-length pieces. Also popular were shows such as *Tom and Jerry: Or, Life in London* (pr. 1823), Pierce Egan's theater work, which was part comic sketch, part travelogue, part musical. Shorter early musicals were performed on bills in variety or vaudeville theaters. Variety was the most popular of all the musical theater forms; in and out of favor over the decades were pantomime (only partly mute) and the "extravaganza," a form that featured dance (frequently with an element of titillation), elaborate stage machinery, and, often, burlesque or parody.

The Beggar's Opera came to the United States in 1751. The first American musical was performed in 1796. *The Archers: Or, The Mountaineers of Switzerland*, based on the story of William Tell, had a book by William Dunlop and songs by Benjamin Carr. All the early musical entertainment forms flourished in the United States, except perhaps pantomime, which

was never as popular as in England. Early in the nineteenth century, The United States added its own indigenous musical theater form, the minstrel show, whose three-part structure allowed for musical sketches as the final feature of the performance. The larger import of the arrival of musical theater in the United States is that the history of musical theater in English thereafter became mostly an American story. Indeed, the popular musical drama is most often said to be an American art form.

During the second half of the nineteenth century, the distinctions among the various types of musical theater (never rigid to begin with) began to blur. *The Black Crook* (pr. 1866), by Charles M. Barras, often cited as the United States' first important musical theater production, was famed for its scandalous ballets but also included in its full evening's worth of entertainment a plot, dialogue, and songs. The opening night performance took more than five hours. When disapproving church authorities attacked it, box office receipts increased. The pantomime *Humpty-Dumpty* (pr. 1868) kept all the production values, and it added much-needed comedy. Edward Harrigan and Tony Hart's short plays with original songs about a group of New York Irish called the Mulligan Guard, which appeared regularly from 1877 to 1885, are often credited with popularizing the musical play's interest in the common folk. Probably the most commercially successful musical of the nineteenth century was an elaborate 1874 burlesque based on Henry Wadsworth Longfellow's poem *Evangeline* (1847) by J. Cheever Goodwin and Edward E. Rice. *Evangeline* incorporated nearly all the elements of all the forms of musical theater and had a full original score. *Adonis* (pr. 1884), William Gill's evening-length burlesque of the Pygmalion myth, was another proof that integration of plot and musical elements was well under way.

It is England, however, that is usually given credit for producing the first musical comedies. Ironically, George Edwardes, an English impresario, had seen a number of American theatrical imports in London and had been struck both by their integration of story and music and by their popularity. He created for his own theaters, the Gaiety and the Prince of Wales, a series of musical comedy plays whose use of musical elements to tell a story was subtle enough to seem original. His three principal productions, *In Town* (pr. 1892), *The Gaiety Girl* (pr. 1893), and *The Shop Girl* (pr. 1895), all employed the same plot: A poor girl, an actress or a shop girl, succeeds in marrying into the upper crust. By modern standards, the plot was simply an excuse for the musical numbers. Still, it was a beginning.

One of Edwardes's goals was to make the musical theater more respectable, and so more profitable. His chorus girls, the wildly popular Gaiety Girls, the ancestors of the Florodora and Follies girls, were fully and fashionably clothed. The general quest for respectability in musical theater had already banished "waiter girls" from the music hall, creating thereby both wholesome vaudeville and modern burlesque. Perhaps no other single event contributed to the moral legitimizing of popular musical theater as did the advent of the collaborative works of Gilbert and Sullivan; especially influential was their first success, *H.M.S. Pinafore: Or, The Lass That Loved a Sailor* (pr. 1878). The artistic superiority of their work was also quickly recognized, but curiously enough their influence on popular musical theater, despite a few quick-penned imitations, was not significant. Musical comedy went its own evolutionary way.

In part, the explanation of this may lie in the perception of Gilbert and Sullivan's works as operas, albeit comic operas or operettas. Continental comic opera shared a similar fate. Jacques Offenbach was popular but did not directly influence the progress of musical drama in England and the United States. Johann Strauss, Jr., was never popular; *Die Fledermaus: The Bat* (pr. c. 1870) was not even produced in England or the United States until decades into the twentieth century. Largely because of its famous waltz, Franz Lehár's *The Merry Widow* (pr. 1905) became one of the greatest stage successes in the English-speaking theater, but again, there was no sudden burst of English-language operettas. Behind musical comedy or musical drama looms opera, the foremost integration of plot and music. One cannot fail to wonder whether the popular musical establishment simply grew skittish about pursuing a course

that led, in its perception, away from the expectations and desires of its audience.

EARLY TWENTIETH CENTURY FIGURES

There was a kind of American operetta, or rather there was one composer. The English-language version of *The Merry Widow* did not appear until 1907. Victor Herbert's *Babes in Toyland* had been produced in 1903, and *The Red Mill* had appeared in 1906. The production of *Naughty Marietta* dates from 1910, and without question Herbert stands as one of two dominant figures in popular musical theater in the period from 1900 to World War I. A native of Ireland and trained in Stuttgart and Vienna, Herbert began his American career as a cellist with the Metropolitan Opera; his wife, Therese Förster, sang in the first American *Aida* (pr. 1871) in the late 1880's. Not surprisingly, his musical plays follow European models; there are lush melodies and improbable stories, mostly about Europeans. There is another element in Herbert's shows, however, perhaps most forthrightly apparent in *The Red Mill*. *The Red Mill* is a musical farce about two American tourists who have run out of money and are stuck in Katwyk-ann-Zee, Holland. The operetta part of the show is complemented by American show biz. The Americans were played by Fred Stone and Dave Montgomery, who made L. Frank Baum's *The Wizard of Oz* (1903) famous as a musical, and who, along with Joseph M. Weber and Lew Fields, were the most popular vaudeville-type comics of the age. The United States flirted again with operetta in the 1920's. Rudolf Friml's *Rose-Marie* (pr. 1924) and *The Vagabond King* (pr. 1925) and Sigmund Romberg's *The Student Prince* (pr. 1924) and *The Desert Song* (pr. 1926), among the most successful shows of the decade, are perhaps the closest counterparts to the Continental models of Offenbach and Lehár in American musical history.

The other major figure of the twentieth century's first musical theater decade was George M. Cohan. Cohan's roots were in vaudeville; his parents were headliners, and he and his sister grew up as part of the act. When he began to write and star in musical plays, he never lost a rousing affection for the vaudeville style of performing, and he admitted openly that he played to the balconies. In plays such as *Little Johnny Jones* (pr. 1904) and *Forty-five Minutes from Broadway* (pr. 1906), he also introduced songs such as "Yankee Doodle Dandy" and "Give My Regards to Broadway" and, along with Herbert, helped establish the dominance of the composer in popular musical theater. Cohan's productions are also notable for their flag-waving patriotism. What had been only popular entertainment now became American entertainment, and henceforth one of the recurrent criteria for the musical was its Americanness as expressed in subject and theme, American topics for an American art form, even though Cohan's overt chauvinism grew too simplistic for the sophisticated entertainments of the decades to come. His last successful play was *I'd Rather Be Right* (pr. 1937) in which he was forced to collaborate with George S. Kaufman, Moss Hart, Richard Rodgers, and Lorenz Hart, all younger men whom he resented, and portray Franklin D. Roosevelt, whom he detested.

In the second decade of the twentieth century, a series of musicals were produced at the small Princess Theatre in New York. *Nobody Home* (pr. 1915), *Very Good Eddie* (pr. 1915), and *Oh, Lady! Lady!* (pr. 1918) brought to prominence their composer, Jerome Kern. Just as important for the development of the musical play, the shows' librettist, Guy Bolton, publicly expressed his belief in the importance of integrating all theatrical elements into the plot of the musical. In particular, he pointed out with pride how comedy in the Princess shows evolved from the dramatic situation; heretofore, comic material in musicals had the quality of comic acts from vaudeville. Kern and the Princess musicals were seminal to the development of the modern book musical.

VAUDEVILLE AND THE REVUE

The plotless musical evening, though, was far from dead. Vaudeville went on more or less triumphantly, and the revue appeared. Unlike vaudeville acts, revue numbers were prepared especially for that edition of the revue. The most famous revue was the *Ziegfeld Follies* (originally as *Follies of 1907*), which began in 1907. Florenz Ziegfeld's imitators followed the same formula: lavishly produced song and dance numbers, pretty girls draped in elaborate costumes, and comedy sketches featuring the leading comics of the time. The big revues died out in the late 1930's, but smaller-scaled revues such as *The Garrick Gaieties* (pr. 1925), music and lyrics by then-newcomers Richard Rodgers and Lorenz Hart, and the *New Faces* series (various years from 1934 to 1952) were still popular. They did not die out until the emergence of television in the 1950's, when the average viewer could see the same kind of entertainment for free. One of the most famous revues was Kaufman and Howard Dietz's *The Band Wagon* (pr. 1931), with a score by Arthur Schwartz, lyrics by Dietz, and dancing by Fred and Adele Astaire. Revues are important to the history of musical theater, because nearly every major composer and performer important to the development of the musical play worked in revues.

ERA OF THE COMPOSERS

After World War I, English-speaking audiences were briefly infatuated with shows such as *Irene* (pr. 1919), new versions of the Cinderella tale so successful in the Gaiety musicals, and with, as noted, American-made operettas. The 1920's, however, will be remembered as the time when the great popular composers—George Gershwin, Richard Rodgers, Cole Porter, Irving Berlin, Noël Coward—came to dominate the musical stage. The subjects of their musical shows were for the most part drawn from the upbeat society of the jazz age. (Lest anyone credit audiences with a complete switch to musical sophistication, the most successful 1920's-type musicals were Vincent Youman's *No, No, Nanette* of 1925 and 1927's *Good News*, the apotheosis of college football musicals, with a score by Ray Henderson.) George Gershwin's *Lady, Be Good!* (lyrics by Ira Gershwin) opened in 1924. Rodgers and Lorenz Hart's *Dearest Enemy* followed in 1925. (Rodgers and Hart shows such as *Dearest Enemy* and the 1927 show *A Connecticut Yankee*, despite being set in the past, have modern scores.) Berlin had already been on the theatrical scene for nearly as long as Kern with revues, especially the wartime show *Yip, Yip, Yaphank* (pr. 1918); revues remained his favored form throughout the 1920's, while his success with musical comedy began with Moss Hart's *Face the Music* (pr. 1932) and the films of Fred Astaire. Porter's first successes came at the end of the 1920's, with *Paris* (pr. 1928) and *Fifty Million Frenchmen* (pr. 1929). Coward's romantic *Bitter Sweet* opened in London in 1929, before crossing the Atlantic. Songs from these 1920's shows and their 1930's cousins help form the backbone of the body of popular standards. Gershwin's "I Got Rhythm" comes from *Girl Crazy* (pr. 1930); Porter's "Night and Day" was first sung in Dwight Taylor's *The Gay Divorce* (pr. 1932)—the list can go on and on. As book musicals, however, these shows are less successful. The plots are trivial excuses for the songs; the songs are virtually interchangeable with the songs from every other show by the same composer.

The 1930's and the Depression changed very little for the musical theater. There was a small vogue for musicals with political satire. (One of these, the mild *Of Thee I Sing*, pr. 1931, by Kaufman and Morrie Ryskind with music and lyrics by the Gershwins, became, in 1932, the first musical to win the Pulitzer Prize.) Serious dance entered the popular theater, most memorably with George Ballanchine's ballet to Rodgers's "Slaughter on Tenth Avenue," but even this landmark work comes from a featherweight musical, Rodgers and Hart's *On Your Toes* (pr. 1936). It was the 1940's that brought major change—with two exceptions that not only prefigured what was to come but equaled it.

Kern's *Show Boat* was produced in 1927 and is most often credited with being the first modern book musical. Oscar Hammerstein II wrote the libretto (based on Edna Ferber's novel about life on a Mississippi riverboat) and most of the lyrics. (The words to "Bill" are by P. G. Wodehouse, Kern's Princess Theatre collaborator.) The theatrical setting of the story lent itself to musicalization; some of the songs, such as "Bill," are introduced during performances or rehearsals in the story, and somehow it seems natural in the play for the characters to go on singing and dancing offstage. The showboat setting also adds variety and balance to the bitter-sweet romance of the leads, and in particular the black characters, the workman Joe, who sings "Ol' Man River," and the mulatto

Julie, who sings "Bill," give the musical weight and insight. The story sprawls, the plot hinges on coincidence, the white characters are unoriginal, and the ending is unrealistic. However, *Show Boat* continues to be a successful musical drama, because its score and lyrics are among the best ever written for the stage. Any list of the standard repertory of musical plays must begin with it.

Gershwin's *Porgy and Bess*, based on the novel by Dubose Heyward and subsequent play by Heyward and his wife Dorothy, with lyrics by Ira Gershwin and Heyward, is a tighter musical play. The story of the black crippled beggar, a fancy woman, and a drug dealer has an inherent focus, which is lacking in the romantic tale of *Show Boat*. For some, Heyward's attitude toward African Americans is paternalistic. Such a view, though, fails to consider how libretto and music complement each other in the work, transfiguring the characters into outsized, commanding theatrical figures. Unfortunately, even in the first production, with Anne Brown and Todd Duncan, and in the most famous of the revivals, the touring *Porgy and Bess* of 1952 with Leontyne Price as Bess, there were compromises and deletions from the score. Not until the 1974 revival by the Houston Opera (which also toured and played Broadway) was the complete score performed. Although the all-black nature of the story may have affected the work's popularity, another difficulty for the play has been producers' distrust of the score's operatic character. In truth, opera seems an appropriate label for *Porgy and Bess*. There is no spoken dialogue; there is recitative. The arching vocal lines for the women or the interwoven vocal lines of the trio at the end of the work reflect a musical complexity unique among musical plays in both technique and concept until the mature works of Stephen Sondheim.

AFRICAN AMERICAN FIGURES AND THEMES

Black performers in both *Porgy and Bess* and *Show Boat* emphasize the place of African Americans in the history of the musical. Harrigan used black actors in his Mulligan Guard sketches, and Bert Williams was one of Ziegfeld's headliners. Black revues were a part of the Broadway experience throughout the 1920's and 1930's. Yet even the kindest interpretation of the facts sees the presence of institutional racism. The all-black label, the label of separateness, draws attention away from serious works such as *Porgy and Bess* and Vernon Duke's *Cabin in the Sky* (pr. 1940), and despite the limited integration of a show such as *Show Boat*, black actresses never played Julie, the mulatto accused of miscegenation. A notable exception was the revue *As Thousands Cheer* (pr. 1933) with songs by Berlin and sketches by Moss Hart. Black actress and singer Ethel Waters spoofed Josephine Baker and Coward and sang "Supper Time," a song about racism. Also part of black musical history are black versions of white sources such as *The Hot Mikado* (1939), a swing version of Gilbert and Sullivan's *The Mikado: Or, The Town of Titipu* (pr. 1885); *Carmen Jones* (pr. 1943); and all-black casts in white shows such as the 1967 Pearl Bailey version of *Hello, Dolly!* (pr. 1964) or Harold Arlen and Truman Capote's lovely *House of Flowers* (pr. 1954). In his first effort following the death of Hammerstein, Rodgers collaborated with Sam Taylor on *No Strings* (pr. 1962), which concerns an interracial romance. Starring black actress and singer Diahann Carroll, it had a respectable run but was not a hit by Rodgers's standards and had mixed reviews. The first major musical created by African Americans was *The Wiz* (pr. 1975), with a soul and disco score by Charlie Smalls. As a new version of *The Wizard of Oz*, the show was a great hit, but a serious look at black life, Melvin Van Peebles's *Ain't Supposed to Die a Natural Death* (pr. 1971), failed. Ossie Davis's *Purlie* (pr. 1970; based on his 1961 play *Purlie Victorious*) and *Raisin* (pr. 1973; based on Lorraine Hansberry's 1959 play *A Raisin in the Sun*) treated racism less angrily and were successful. Thereafter the black musical revue returned again with shows such as *Bubbling Brown Sugar* (pr. 1976), *Eubie!* (pr. 1978; based on the life of Eubie Blake), and, most popular of all, *Ain't Misbehavin'* (pr. 1978). These shows renewed interest in black composers such as Eubie Blake and Fats Waller, and the same period saw the first production of Scott Joplin's ragtime opera *Treemonisha* (pr. 1975). Michael Bennett's production of *Dreamgirls* (pr. 1981) marked a return to the book musical. All of these shows increased black theater audiences and opportunities for black performers. Still, the sociological element remains a conspicuous part of the black musical theater experience.

THE MODERN BOOK MUSICAL

The 1940's established the book musical as the dominant form of popular musical drama. *Pal Joey* (pr. 1940), the penultimate Rodgers and Hart musical collaboration with a libretto by John O'Hara, based on his series of short stories that appeared in *The New Yorker*, set the stage with its cynical romance about the anti-heroic, but charming Joey and the older, hard-edged Vera, who dumps him at the end. The show's songs were character studies and depictions of the gritty nightclub world of the story. The most important show of the decade, however, was *Oklahoma!*, which opened in New York on March 31, 1943.

Oklahoma!, based on the play *Green Grow the Lilacs* (pr. 1931) by Lynn Riggs, was not the first book musical. The production's real innovations were the integration of Agnes de Mille's dances into the drama, particularly Laurie's dream ballet, and the striking tonal unity of the song score. Throughout his career, Richard Rodgers recycled songs cut from earlier musicals. In *Oklahoma!*, on the other hand, the songs are so specific to the characters and the situations that this was impossible. For instance, in "Surrey with a Fringe on Top," Hammerstein's lyrics are sung to a clip-clop rhythm and Rodgers's melody suggests a carriage ride down a country road. Nevertheless, the show, which was Rodgers's first collaboration with his new partner Hammerstein, did establish the book musical, with its integration of story and music, as *the* form of popular musical theater. The songs from *Oklahoma!* were truly memorable, and the composer remained the principal creative force in musicals, but after *Oklahoma!* a composer was expected to put his music at the service of the drama rather than the other way around.

The heyday of the book musical coincides almost exactly with the years of the Rodgers and Hammerstein partnership, a partnership that ended only with Hammerstein's death in 1960. Their first four hits—*Oklahoma!*, *Carousel* (pr. 1945), *South Pacific* (pr. 1949), *The King and I* (pr. 1951)—raised the partners to a position of eminence and influence in the popular musical theater unknown before or since. In most people's minds, a musical play was a Rodgers and Hammerstein musical play. In addition, the partnership changed Rodgers's music. Instead of the worldly tunes that had accompanied Hart's lyrics, Rodgers wrote melodies less specific to the musical times, more in the style of Kern, and this generalized approach also influenced and continues to influence many a Broadway score.

Carousel, based on *Liliom* (pr. 1909; English translation, 1921) by Ferenc Molnar, is probably the most innovative of the Rodgers and Hammerstein plays. Whole scenes are set to music. Instead of an overture, the show opens with a musical pantomime performed to a waltz. *Carousel*'s big musical moment is nothing less than a full-blown musical soliloquy. By comparison, *South Pacific*, based on *Tales of the South Pacific* (1947) by James Michener, is best remembered for its songs and its stars, Mary Martin and Ezio Pinza. It was a great show, but as an integrated musical drama, *South Pacific* represents a falling-off from the level of its two predecessors. Even then, Rodgers, Hammerstein, and book co-author Joshua Logan were testing the boundaries of the form by breaking one of the unwritten rules of musical drama that goes back at least as far as *The Magic Flute*. Secondary romances are usually played for comedy, as in *Oklahoma!* and *Carousel*. In this play, that romance is tragic and resembles David Belasco's *Madame Butterfly* (pr. 1900). *The King and I* marked a successful return to a more seamless approach to musical storytelling, although its originality lies more in the choice of subject, Margaret Landon's novel *Anna and the King of Siam* (1944), based on the diaries of Anna Leonowens, than in the play's musical dramaturgy. The partners' last two commercial successes, *Flower Drum Song* (pr. 1958) and *The Sound of Music* (pr. 1959), do not equal the earlier landmark works. Still, Rodgers and Hammerstein's influence on the musical play's development did not lessen, and all the important musicals for twenty years show this influence.

Other great popular composers also wrote scores for the new book musical play. Berlin's *Annie Get Your Gun*, with Ethel Merman as Annie Oakley, opened in 1946. (Another Merman vehicle, *Call Me Madam*, followed in 1950.) Porter's finest work, *Kiss Me, Kate* (with the book by Bella and Samuel Spewack), appeared in 1948. Some would argue that both shows are throwbacks to the musicals of the 1920's and 1930's, and, in truth, *Annie Get Your Gun* is a lot of old-fashioned American show biz mounted on a lightweight (but serviceable) plot. *Kiss Me, Kate*, however, though similarly lighthearted, is a highly crafted theater piece about a warring theater couple cast in a musical version of Shakespeare's *The Taming of the Shrew* (pr. c. 1593-1594). Porter's memorable score was his first to belong to the characters and storyline. Among musicals, *Kiss Me, Kate* must be reckoned the equivalent of Oscar Wilde's *The Importance of Being Earnest: A Trivial Comedy for Serious People* (pr. 1895).

One other composer must be mentioned with Berlin and Porter: Kurt Weill is a giant in the history of musical drama, but he stands a bit to the side of this story, since his masterwork (with Bertolt Brecht), *The Threepenny Opera* (pr. 1928), and other works such as *Rise and Fall of the City of Mahagonny* (pr. 1930), were originally written in German and are most often grouped with operas. Weill fled Nazi Germany in 1935 and began writing American musicals, but until the 1940's his greatest success was "September Song," written for *Knickerbocker Holiday* (pr. 1938), a play based on a book by Maxwell Anderson and a deserved Broadway failure. In 1941, Weill collaborated with Moss Hart (book) and Ira Gershwin (lyrics) to create *Lady in the Dark* (pr. 1941), a successful book musical whose intriguing musical numbers were the dreams of a female fashion magazine editor undergoing psychoanalysis. Weill conceived of each dream as a little one-act opera. Although originally unsuccessful, the Weill-Maxwell Anderson collaboration *Lost in the Stars* (pr. 1949), based on Alan Paton's novel *Cry, the Beloved Country* (1948), earns respect today, and *Street Scene* (pr. 1947), based on Elmer Rice's 1947 play, entered the opera repertory, the frequent fate of ambitious works in the popular musical theater. In 1954, Marc Blitzstein's famous English translation of *The Threepenny Opera* began a long successful run with Weill's widow, Lotte Lenya, in the cast. This production would significantly influence the darker musicals of the following decade.

THE 1950'S

The 1950's added many works to the musical repertory. Following the lead of *Oklahoma!* and *South Pacific*, many if not the majority of the best shows were evocations of some part of Americana. The plots stressed comedy at the expense of sentiment, but perhaps audiences found a special kind of nourishment in recognizing an America in part real, in part based on popular fiction, even if that fiction embraced crooks and disreputable show business types, and even if there were, as there often was, a small amount of satire mixed in with all the celebration and fun.

Perhaps the two best-loved shows from this group, Frank Loesser's *Guys and Dolls* (pr. 1950) and Meredith Willson's *The Music Man* (pr. 1957), nearly bracket the decade. Both shows center on disreputable characters. *Guys and Dolls* sets to music Damon Runyan's New York world of showgirls and lovable crooks; Willson's *Music Man* is a traveling con man who preys on gullible Midwestern towns. With "Seventy-six Trombones" and "Till There Was You," *The Music Man* probably had the more memorable score. (One more often thinks of the musical action of the nightclub performances or the floating crap game in *Guys and Dolls* than "Take Back Your Mink" or "Luck, Be a Lady.") *Guys and Dolls* was unusual in that the leading male character, Guy Masterson, is romantically involved with the secondary female character, Sarah. The leading female character, Miss Adelaide, has been engaged for fourteen years to the secondary male character, Nathan Detroit. Both shows, while they poke fun at their essentially American subjects, do so affectionately; these are lighthearted entertainments.

Loesser's other hits were *Where's Charley?* (pr. 1948), based on the farce *Charley's Aunt* by Brandon Thomas (1892); *The Most Happy Fella* (pr. 1956), based on *They Knew What They Wanted* (1924) by Sidney Howard; and *How to Succeed in Business With-*

out Really Trying (pr. 1961), a satire on the business world that, once again, was only "joshing." Although *How to Succeed in Business Without Really Trying* won the Pulitzer Prize, *The Most Happy Fella* is much more interesting because it is closer to opera with its use of recitative, arias, duets, trios, and choral pieces in additional to popular songs. Willson is also remembered for *The Unsinkable Molly Brown* (pr. 1960).

There is a simple enjoyment to these shows and their fellows. *The Pajama Game* (pr. 1954) is a comedy about a garment workers' strike, and *Damn Yankees* (pr. 1955) is a comic setting of the Faust legend in the baseball world. Both (with books by George Abbott and songs by Richard Adler and Jerry Ross) are loud and brassy compared with *Carousel* or *The King and I*, but perhaps this hardworking zeal to entertain, which infects every aspect of the shows, is exactly what makes these musicals so winning. In the same category are *Fiorello!* (pr. 1959), a musical biography of Mayor Fiorello La Guardia by Abbott with songs by Jerry Bock and Sheldon Harnick, and *Bye Bye Birdie* (pr. 1960), the Charles Strouse musical that looked at the Elvis Presley phenomenon. Composer Jule Styne contributed his *Gentlemen Prefer Blonds* (pr. 1949), which made Carol Channing a star, *Bells Are Ringing* (pr. 1956), which added luster to the star of Judy Holliday, and *Gypsy* (pr. 1959). Of all the Americana musicals, *Gypsy*, based on the memoirs of Gypsy Rose Lee, is the darkest. Its central character is Mama Rose, the grasping stage mother. Arthur Laurents's book was funny; Styne's score (with lyrics by Sondheim) was strong, and there was a star at the center, Merman, but in *Gypsy*, Merman did more than merely perform; she acted, showing fully the abrasive, destructive side of Mama Rose, most memorably in the show's finale, "Rose's Turn." *Gypsy* showed some of the darker side of human nature and was one foreshadowing of musicals to come.

NEW DIRECTIONS

The 1940's and 1950's also produced musical orphans and distant cousins, plays nearly or completely removed from the musical theater vogue for things American. Burton Lane's *Finian's Rainbow* (pr. 1947) was an odd mix of the American South with an Irish leprechaun. After its debut on television, Mary Martin's version of *Peter Pan* (music by Styne and Carolyn Leigh) moved to Broadway in 1954, costarring Cyril Ritchard as Captain Hook. Two small Off-Broadway shows, Rick Besoyan's operetta spoof *Little Mary Sunshine* (pr. 1959) and *The Fantasticks* (pr. 1960) by Tom Jones and Harvey Schmidt, asked audiences to turn to a nostalgic past with a quieter kind of sentiment than that in the big noisy Broadway musicals. In 1956, Leonard Bernstein, who had written the music for two Americana shows, *On the Town* (pr. 1944) and *Wonderful Town* (pr. 1953), wrote one of the most famous and most atypical of musical scores, *Candide* (pr. 1956). Setting the Voltaire satire to music, Bernstein mocked many of the standard set pieces of both light and serious musical drama such as the soprano's aria and the lovers' duet, and in the process made memorable additions to their numbers. It is said that the book (by Lillian Hellman) and the staging (by Tyrone Guthrie) caused the show's failure, but at least a suspicion remains that the work appeared at the wrong time. (A 1974 revival by Hal Prince, with a new book and an environmental staging, was a success.)

Appearing at exactly the right time, though, was *West Side Story* (pr. 1957); the street-gang setting for a tale of a modern Romeo and Juliet both shocked and attracted audiences. Bernstein's song score (with lyrics by Sondheim) included "Tonight" and "Maria," but as important was the musical writing for director-choreographer Jerome Robbins's ballets and dances. No musical has ever made such integral dramatic use of dance as *West Side Story*, with its choreographed wars on both the dance floor and the asphalt.

Alan Jay Lerner and Frederick Loewe had also written an Americana musical, *Paint Your Wagon* (pr. 1951), and an oddfellow, *Brigadoon* (pr. 1947), a pseudo-Scottish fantasy. Neither show (nor their 1960 production of *Camelot*) hints at the artistic and popular success of Lerner and Loewe's *My Fair Lady* (pr. 1956), which starred Rex Harrison and Julie Andrews as the phonetics professor and the flower girl. While few of even Rodgers and Hammerstein's song scores can boast as many hits (which include "I Could Have Danced All Night" and "On the Street Where You Live"), the backbone of *My Fair Lady* is its book, adapted from George Bernard Shaw's screenplay for Gabriel Pascal's 1938 film *Pygmalion*, in turn based on Shaw's play of that name (pr. 1913). Lerner switched one scene from Mrs. Higgins's home to the Ascot racetrack (giving Cecil Beaton the opportunity to create one of the most famous settings and costumes in modern theater history), but he resolutely retained much of Shaw's text from the final authorized version (1941). Lerner's faith in Shaw was well-placed; *My Fair Lady* probably has the strongest musical book ever written. Certainly, few other musical plays approach so ideal an integration of music and plot. It inspired other musical adaptations of English classics, including Charles Dickens's *Oliver Twist* (1837-1839) as *Oliver!* (pr. 1963).

INFLUENCE OF ROCK MUSIC

By the 1960's, conditions no longer favored the book musical in the form dominant for twenty years. Almost all the major composers of shows were silent, or nearly so, or had given up the musical. More important for the musical's future, the arrival of rock and roll—and, later, the Beatles—had irrevocably split popular music in two. In *Bye Bye Birdie*, Broadway had observed the rock phenomenon from a bemused, secure distance, but once the theater realized that the musical play was nearly on the brink of obsolescence, a few rock shows came forward, the most famous being the nearly plotless *Hair* (pr. 1967), the religious *Godspell* (pr. 1971), and *Grease* (pr. 1972). All were very popular and continue to be performed, but even Galt MacDermot's fine score for *Hair* is more rock-influenced than it is rock. The musical has not historically been successful in competing with rock on rock's own terms. Perhaps this fact, as it revealed itself, was at least partly responsible for the outsized importance that directors of musicals assumed during the 1960's. If musical theater could no longer deliver the musical goods, it could still produce an evening of theatrical magic and wonder.

CONCEPT MUSICALS

Still, in the 1960's and the 1970's, and even into the 1980's, old-fashioned book musicals continued to appear. (Because the importance of the book seems to have been sacrificed to outsized production concerns, most of these shows seem old-fashioned even when set beside *Oklahoma!* or *My Fair Lady*.) The total number of shows produced during these years may have been fewer than in previous decades, but the financial bonanzas for shows such as *Hello, Dolly!*, *Mame* (pr. 1966), *Annie* (pr. 1977), or *La Cage aux Folles* (pr. 1983) were enormous. It is staging that made these shows theatrical events of note. Naturally, theatrical technology had advanced, but much of the credit for what happened onstage must be given to plain ingenuity. Suddenly the stage could do more, faster, and in cleverer ways than ever before. Gower Champion's staging of *Hello, Dolly!* was a model of the new staging. *Hello, Dolly!* had Jerry Herman's title song and Carol Channing's starring presence already working for it, but what made the show exciting was the sleek, elegant look and move of the thing, its theatrical élan. By comparison, the staging of even the original *My Fair Lady* was stodgy.

The directors who rose to stardom during this period—Gower Champion, Bob Fosse, Hal Prince, Michael Bennett—had worked in the musical theater throughout the 1950's. As they developed, they gave an individual flavor to the musicals they mounted, and in short order there appeared the "concept musical." At least the beginnings of the concept musical can be seen in *Fiddler on the Roof* (pr. 1964), based on the short story "Tevye's Daughters" by Sholom Aleichem, Robbins's last Broadway assignment before returning to classical choreography. The show had a tuneful score by Bock and Harnick and a star, Zero Mostel. It was Robbins's staging, however, that attracted critical comment. Anatefka and its inhabitants appeared out of the shadows. Boris Aronson's settings, inspired by Marc Chagall, were simple; most often Tevye's little toy house sat alone on the dark stage. Another unique feature was that the romantic characters, Tevye's three daughters and their future husbands, were not introduced at the outset. When Tevye rejects his daughter's marriage to a Gentile, he reprises the song "Tradition" and joins a hallucinatory march across the stage of all the town's inhabitants.

The musical plays that most often bear the label "concept musical" place less stress on plot than *Fiddler on the Roof* does. Prince's 1966 production of *Cabaret* (score by John Kander and Fred Ebb) is more typical. Set in Christopher Isherwood's Berlin of the 1930's, and based on John Van Druten's stage adaptation *I Am a Camera* (pr. 1951), the show alternated between two failed love stories and the musical numbers at the cabaret itself; the production numbers commented on the action. Influenced by Weill's *The Threepenny Opera*, the show's real subjects were Berlin's decadence and the rise of the Nazis. As must be apparent, *Cabaret* shares some common assumptions with the more densely plotted *Fiddler on the Roof* and *Man of La Mancha*, 1965's ambitious, if sentimental, musical adaptation of Miguel de Cervantes's *El ingenioso hidalgo don Quixote de la Mancha* (1605, 1615; *The History of the Valorous and Wittie Knight-Errant, Don Quixote of the Mancha*, 1612-1620). All three are played more in darkness than in light; all three end unhappily. Although comedy is present, all three insist on their seriousness.

Occasionally the seriousness might be relaxed, as in Fosse's 1972 production of *Pippin* (although after his film *Cabaret*, Fosse returned to the theater with the gritty *Chicago*, pr. 1975, notable for its anti-star turn by the great Gwen Verdon), but the aim of all of these works was to provide a gripping kind of experience that could be had nowhere else but in the theater. Interestingly, the setting for the most popular of these shows was the theater. Bennett's production of *A Chorus Line* was an instant hit in 1975. A collaborative production of Joseph Papp's New York Shakespeare Festival Theatre, it moved to Broadway in 1975 and held the record for the longest run of any musical (6,137 performances) when it closed on April 29, 1990. The setting was an audition for a Broadway dance line, and this idea seemed to triumph over a score by Marvin Hamlisch, over a book by James Kirkwood and Nicholas Dante that indulged unabashedly in the old-fashioned sentimentality of backstage musicals dating back to *The Gaiety Girl* (pr. 1893; music by Sidney Jones, lyrics by Harry Greenback, and libretto by Owen Hall), and over choreography that, as the estimable Arlene Croce noted, was curiously mundane for a musical about dancing. Bennett, who was both the director and the choreographer, saw the dancer's life as one of endless repetition in class, audition, rehearsal, performance, and he etched this idea in the audience's mind nowhere more memorably than the show's finale, the gold-lamé-costumed, high-kicking chorus line that to some audiences celebrated the musical theater and to others criticized the musical show for its dehumanization of the people who did the singing and the dancing. (Bennett's next two shows, 1979's *Ballroom* and 1981's *Dreamgirls*, while almost musical opposites, shared a greater concern with a linear plot.)

The evolution of the concept musical and the emphasis on a newer, bolder theatricality also confirmed England as a small reliable source of musical plays besides those of Coward. Sandy Wilson's 1920's spoof *The Boy Friend* (pr. 1954) had delighted New York audiences during the book musical's heyday, and Anthony Newley and Leslie Bricusse's *Stop the World—I Want to Get Off* (pr. 1962) and *Oliver!* were successfully imported to Broadway. The innovators were Marguerite Monnot's gentle *Irma la Douce* (pr. 1960), and Joan Littlewood's strong and lively antiwar revue *Oh, What a Lovely War* (pr. 1964), but it is the Andrew Lloyd Webber musicals in their New York productions—the "rock opera" *Jesus Christ Superstar* (pr. 1971), *Evita* (pr. 1979), and *Cats* (pr. 1983)—that permanently enlivened the British musical show. The stagecraft of these shows has been applauded loudly, but the reception of Webber as a composer has been less universal. He is an innovator—his works contain no spoken dialogue—and his melodies have proven enormously popular, but the musical writing does not achieve the complexity and sophistication of the operatic form to which it avowedly aspires.

STEPHEN SONDHEIM

The one composer to achieve greatness during the decades that have been dominated by the concept musical and the director-as-star is Stephen Sondheim. Sondheim wrote the lyrics for *West Side Story* and *Gypsy*, and his first musical score was the farcical *A Funny Thing Happened on the Way to the Forum* (pr.

1962); but his breakthrough work was *Company*, the 1970 landmark concept musical. *Company* was less a play than a set of situations about a bachelor and his married friends. The married couples also doubled as the singing-dancing chorus and in solos or trios sang commentary on the ensuing action. There were songs within the scenes. In any case though, Sondheim resisted the easy melody (a frequently heard criticism of all of his important works) in favor of musical and emotional sophistication.

Other concept shows followed: *Follies* (pr. 1971), which found Sondheim brilliantly imitating the styles of decades of musical theater for a reunion of old follies girls; *Pacific Overtures* (pr. 1976), a historical pageant about the modernization of Japan; and *Sunday in the Park with George* (pr. 1984), a musical about Georges Seurat's painting *Sunday Afternoon on the Island of La Grande Jatte* (1884-1886) in which Sondheim chose classical music's minimalism as an equivalent for Seurat's pointillism. All of these shows were theatrically compelling, all but the last staged by Prince, *Cabaret*'s star director, but although Sondheim's musicals are very much of his moment, the dominating force of his music recalls the older decades when musical theater was the composer's forum.

Two other Sondheim plays (both Prince collaborations), though they share the customary shadowed affinities with concept musicals, have, like *Fiddler on the Roof* before them, a vital story to tell. *A Little Night Music* (pr. 1973) is a musical setting of Ingmar Bergman's *Smiles of a Summer's Night* (1955) and includes the song "Send in the Clowns." *Sweeney Todd, the Demon Barber of Fleet Street* was adapted from Christopher Bond's version of the Victorian bogey story about the homicidal barber. Faithful to two strong dramatic sources, the books for these musicals rival that of *My Fair Lady*. Musically, the interwoven vocal lines, the rhythmic counterpoint, and the soaring quality of the music (especially in *Sweeney Todd, the Demon Barber of Fleet Street* where the music is almost continuous) rival Gershwin's equally ambitious vision for *Porgy and Bess*.

Sondheim's preeminence in musical theater during the 1970's and 1980's was unprecedented, yet while providing a just measure of his talent, his position also pointed out something about the health of the popular musical theater. The hoped-for show was the big new show, whether the stirring *Sweeney Todd, the Demon Barber of Fleet Street* or the brassy *La Cage aux Folles*, but with spiraling costs, the number of musicals decreased. Sensing that audiences still loved singing and dancing, producers backed a variety of revues, and a few small musicals appeared, including Cy Coleman's *I Love My Wife* (pr. 1977) and William Finn's *March of the Falsettos* (pr. 1981). Unique was Fosse's dance revue, called simply *Dancin'* (pr. 1978).

One of the most lucrative ventures in the musical theater became the revival, from *No, No, Nanette* to *My Fair Lady* and *The King and I* to *Man of La Mancha*, frequently starring leads from the original casts. Some of these revivals were sparkling; many, though, were tired. Freed from copyright restrictions, *The Pirates of Penzance* came out in a Broadway version in 1981, and some of the more forward-thinking opera companies talked about taking into their repertories not only musicals such as *Porgy and Bess* and *Sweeney Todd, the Demon Barber of Fleet Street* but also the regular solid book musicals such as the legendary *Oklahoma!*

In the last decades of the twentieth century, almost single-handedly keeping the concept musical intact, Sondheim paired with several book writers in musicals such as *Into the Woods* (pr. 1987, with James Lapine), which is based on fairy tales, and *Assassins* (pr. 1991, with John Weidman), a remarkable musical defense of the impulses of presidential assassins from John Wilkes Booth to Lee Harvey Oswald. Tributes to Sondheim included a staged concert revue of *Follies*, with an all-star cast of Sondheim's favorite vocalists, and a 1992 Carnegie Hall retrospective, featuring his greatest songs from a twenty-five-year career. Sondheim, however, is famous for the complex rhymes and high-intensity deliveries of his songs; his difficult lyrics, which are almost always integral to the play's dramatic moment, and the harmonic sophistication of the musical score, preclude extracting Sondheim songs for popular consumption.

GROWING SPLIT IN DRAMA

The later 1980's and the first years of the 1990's, however, witnessed a widening split between entertainment extravaganzas and more serious musical drama. The huge success of British imports such as *Cats* (Lloyd Webber's musical based on T. S. Eliot's 1939 poetry collection *Old Possum's Book of Practical Cats*) and *Les Misérables*, first produced in French in 1980 and in English in 1985 (by Alain Boublil, and Claude-Michel Schönberg, from Victor Hugo's famous 1847 novel), meant that the economics of Broadway theater had turned toward investment-and-return criteria, rather than theatrical complexity of character and integrity of vision. The ambitious *Chess* (pr. 1986), by Benny Andersson, Tim Rice, and Bjorn Ulvaeus, also moved from London to the United States, with a revised score and new cast but still burdened with a massive electronic backdrop of sixty-four television sets and a revolving chessboard stage.

Typical of the gaudy extravaganzas is *Phantom of the Opera* (pr. 1986), Lloyd Webber's musical version of the classic story, complete with a falling chandelier on which the phantom rides over the audience. Less successful were his *Starlight Express* (pr. 1991) and *Aspects of Love* (pr. 1989). In Lloyd Webber musicals, one strong theme song typically emerges as the signature of the musical itself: "Phantom of the Opera," a song that makes use of the famous musical line from the motion picture, and the recurring "Don't Cry for Me, Argentina," from *Evita*, are examples.

Broadway continued to see its share of revivals and remakes filling the ever-diminishing musical stage: The 1980's, 1990's and the early years of the twenty-first century witnessed restagings of *Gypsy, Guys and Dolls, Camelot, Carousel, Show Boat, The King and I, Cabaret, Annie Get Your Gun,* and *Oklahoma!* They became so numerous that in 1994 the Tony Awards created a new category called "Revival (Musical)." Professional theaters (part of the League of Resident Theatres) in other cities cashed in on the popularity of such revivals as *Bye Bye Birdie, House of Flowers,* and *Damn Yankees.* Sondheim musicals such as *Follies* and *Company* continued to be revived in all parts of the United States, with varying degrees of professionalism.

Given the expense of producing on Broadway, many shows went on the road quickly, often with multiple casts, and made their profit not on Broadway but from major-city tours and film rights. The Toronto staging of *The Phantom of the Opera*, within a half-day's drive of a large portion of the American population, became a mainstay vacation and group-ticket sellout, while other casts and production companies move from city to city with the play as well. *Les Misérables* broke all box-office records for touring shows, and Lucy Simon's *The Secret Garden* (pr. 1991) had a longer run on the road than on Broadway.

CONTEMPORARY INNOVATIONS

The musical plays of the 1990's and the first few years of the twenty-first century exhibited several differences from previous decades. The first was that Broadway looked to movies for source material. These included *Grand Hotel: The Musical* (pr. 1990), *Meet Me in St. Louis* (pr. 1990), *The Goodbye Girl* (pr. 1993), *Beauty and the Beast* (pr. 1994), *Sunset Boulevard* (pr. 1995), *The Lion King* (pr. 1998), *The Producers* (pr. 2001), *The Full Monty* (pr. 2001), *Thoroughly Modern Millie* (pr. 2002), and *The Sweet Smell of Success* (pr. 2002). Producers, especially corporations like the Walt Disney Company and Clear Channel Entertainment, strove to minimize the possibility of commercial flops by adapting stories with an existing fan base. It certainly did not hurt the commercial success of *Kiss of the Spider Woman: The Musical* (pr. 1993), *Cyrano: The Musical* (pr. 1994), *Ragtime* (pr. 1998), *The Scarlet Pimpernel* (pr. 1998), and *Jane Eyre* (pr. 2001) that successful movies had already been made from either the original novels or plays.

Another trend was the revival of the revue but with a twist. Instead of original songs, they featured the work of deceased artists or teams of artists. These include *A Grand Night for Singing* (pr. 1994; the music of Rodgers and Hammerstein), *Smokey Joe's Café* (pr. 1995; the rock music of Jerry Leiber and Mike Stoller), *Swinging on a Star* (1996; the songs of lyricist Johnny Burke), and *Fosse* (1999; the choreogra-

phy of Bob Fosse). Related to this trend were musical biographies of artists that featured their own work such as *Jelly's Last Jam* (1992; based on the life of jazz composer Jelly Roll Morton) and *A Class Act* (2001; based on the life of Ed Kleban, lyricist for *A Chorus Line*). Another use of unoriginal music was *Mamma Mia* (pr. 2002) for which a story was written around the songs of the pop music group ABBA.

This is not to say that there were no original book musicals in the 1990's and the first decade of the next century; new musicals included *Five Guys Named Moe* (pr. 1992), *Blood Brothers* (pr. 1993), *Rent* (pr. 1996), and *Urinetown* (pr. 2001). However, there continues to be a concern that the desire to preserve the image of companies such as Disney may prevent these companies from producing original, cutting-edge musicals. Moreover, as of the early twenty-first century, there were only fifteen theaters on Broadway capable of hosting big budget musicals, producing a tandem concern that the giant corporations will squeeze out the independent producers.

BIBLIOGRAPHY

Bach, Stephen. *Dazzler: The Life and Times of Moss Hart.* New York: Alfred A. Knopf, 2001. Besides his famous collaborations with Kaufman, the director and writer also worked with such noted figures as Berlin, Porter, Rogers, Ira Gershwin, and other important musical drama figures from 1925 to his death in 1962.

Greene, Stanley, and Kay Greene. *Broadway Musicals: Show by Show.* 5th ed. Milwaukee, Wis.: H. Leonard, 1997. Surveys musicals that have run for five hundred or more performances, starting with plays from the late 1800's through the 1990's. Provides facts, synopsis, credits, and photos of three hundred plays.

Hutchinson, James M. *Dubose Heyward: A Charleston Gentleman and the World of "Porgy and Bess."* Jackson: University Press of Mississippi, 2000. Chapter 7 concerns *Porgy and Bess*, for which Heyward wrote the book and some of the lyrics.

Loesser, Susan. *A Most Remarkable Fella: Frank Loesser and the Guys and Dolls in His Life.* New

York: Donald I. Fine, 1993. In this portrait of her father, the author devotes one chapter each to *Where's Charley?*, *Guys and Dolls*, *The Most Happy Fella*, the unsuccessful *Greenwillow*, and *How to Succeed in Business Without Really Trying.*

Logan, Joshua. *Josh: My Up and Down, In and Out Life.* New York: Delacorte Press, 1976. The author directed musicals with songs by Rodgers and Moss Hart, Weill, Berlin, Rodgers and Hammerstein, and others and co-authored *South Pacific* with Hammerstein.

Long, Robert Emmet. *Broadway, the Golden Years: Jerome Robbins and the Great Choreographer-Directors, 1940's to the Present.* New York: Continuum, 2002. Provides a series of short biographical essays on choreographer-directors such as Robbins, de Mille, Fosse, and more, in the process tracing the development of the musical from the mid- to late twentieth century.

Nolan, Frederick. *Lorenz Hart: A Poet on Broadway.* New York: Oxford University Press, 1994. Comprehensive biography of the lyricist who teamed with Rodgers to produce some of the more memorable musicals from 1925 to 1940.

Rodgers, Richard. *Musical Stages: An Autobiography.* New York: Random House, 1975. Most of this book concerns the author's many collaborations with Lorenz Hart and Hammerstein. Chapter 24 reports on the production of the interracial musical romance *No Strings.*

Skinner, Cornelia Otis. *Life with Lindsay and Crouse.* Boston: Houghton Mifflin, 1976. Although Howard Lindsay and Russel Crouse are best known for *Life with Father*, they also wrote the books for *Call Me Madam* (Berlin), *Anything Goes* (Porter), and *The Sound of Music* (Rodgers and Hammerstein).

Dale Silviria, updated by Thomas J. Taylor
and Thomas R. Feller

ENGLISH-LANGUAGE OPERA

The history of opera written to an English libretto or book (either sung throughout or with spoken dialogue interspersed between the musical numbers) is one of long, deep valleys separated by but a few noteworthy crests. Following the invention of opera as a recognizable form by the Florentine *camerata* (a Humanistic discussion group that met in the late 1570's and early 1580's in the Florentine palace of Giovanni Bardi, Count of Vernio) just before the start of the seventeenth century, first France and then Germany joined Italy in developing a distinctly national form both in content and sound. This was not to be the case in Great Britain and, collaterally, the United States until the early twentieth century. Pure chance and ill fortune, combined with less definable causes such as public taste, account for the absence of an ongoing tradition. Equally curious, however, is the development of a sturdy form of English opera since the 1930's and its dominance in international theater, so that without benefit of indigenous prototypes, a powerful force in the lyric theater has been produced out of the thinnest of rarefied air.

THE SEVENTEENTH AND EIGHTEENTH CENTURIES

At the beginning of the seventeenth century, after the accession of James I to the English throne, the masque, a court pastime combining an allegorical story, dialogue, and vocal and dance music with scenic and costume spectacle, became dominant as royal entertainment. Although none of the great Elizabethan composers contributed music, masques incorporated lyrics, accompanied recitative, and involved scenic and costume design that later would appear in the first acknowledged English operas. The mighty forces behind the masque were the scenarios and words of British playwright Ben Jonson and the scenery and costumes of designer-architect Inigo Jones, whose knowledge of Italian practices introduced the British to the stage picture and craft of Italian scene painters and machinists.

In 1617, Nicholas Lanier composed for Jonson's masque, *Lovers Made Men* (pr. 1617), what was most likely the first English recitative, a type of vocal composition patterned on the natural rhythms of speech, in the Italian style of Claudio Monteverdi. Although the music is lost, it is doubtful that it would have exerted much influence on an English public that had come to prefer the traditional structure of the masque, with its fast-moving dialogue separating the songs known as "ayres."

Even before the execution of Charles I, the Commonwealth government suppressed theater, but the ruling Puritans did not as vigorously oppose secular music. This situation led to the curious attempt by practitioners of theater to circumvent the harsh laws by presenting stage spectacles under the guise of musical concerts. It was in this context that, at Rutland House in 1656, William Davenant's *The Siege of Rhodes* (pr. 1656-1659) was given a private performance. Davenant's work was subtitled *A Representation by the Art of Prospective in Scenes and the Story Sung in Recitative Musick in Five Acts*; the music (now lost) was contributed by a number of composers, including Matthew Locke and Henry Lawes. The changeable scenery in the Italian style was designed by John Webb, a student of then recently deceased Inigo Jones.

The first irony in the development of English opera came with the restoration of Charles II four years later, when the ban on spoken drama was lifted. The English, including Davenant, who was given one of the two monopolies to present plays in London, returned to their love of words and virtually abandoned their earlier attempts at opera. Incidental music for the theater and interpolated songs persisted, as did remnants of masques, now heavily influenced by the court of Louis XIV of France, where the new English king and much of his court had found refuge during the interregnum of the Puritan Parliament. Chief among these influences was Jean-Baptiste Lully, the Italian-born composer who had become the titan of French music.

Indeed, that a native English music survived to the end of the seventeenth century was somewhat miraculous, considering the English tendency to look to the Continent for what they thought was true genius. The slim promise of an English school of opera in the closing years of the seventeenth century rested with three composers: the previously mentioned Locke, with his setting of Thomas Shadwell's adaptation of Lully's *tragédie lyrique* titled *Psyche* (pr. 1675); John Blow, with his one complete work for the musical stage, *Venus and Adonis* (pr. c. 1684); and, most important, Henry Purcell. Purcell's one complete work for the stage, *Dido and Aeneas* (pr. c. 1689) with a superb libretto by Nahum Tate, is the earliest English opera to achieve a place in the international standard repertory. Despite his short lifetime, with *Dido and Aeneas* and his incidental music for spoken drama, Purcell seemed to light the way for future generations of theater composers.

Such, however, was not to be the course followed by theatrical history. Between the time of Purcell's death and the arrival of George Frederick Handel and his *Rinaldo* in 1711, operatic as well as theatrical tastes changed radically in London. In the theater, the forty-year reign of the rather prurient comedy of manners came under successful attack and was replaced by a more sentimental comedy meant to inspire a higher moral tone. Even the continued revivals of William Shakespeare's plays were marked by adaptations to the prevailing sentimental tone found in the new comedy. Purcell's prototype of what might have been a truly national form of opera virtually disappeared, overwhelmed by the change in popular taste that saw French and French-inspired English music fall out of favor, succumbing to the wave of Italian music and musicians that flooded England. With this wave came a type of singer known as a castrato, who had been sexually neutered before puberty so that his voice would not change. The unique sound that these male sopranos or altos produced made them the most celebrated singers in eighteenth century Europe.

Another sign of the triumph of the Italian style was the unchallenged preeminence of the German-born Handel, whose four-decade dominance of English opera was to obscure other English stage composers from history's notice. Despite Handel's conquest of London's opera stage, his works fall outside the scope of this essay, because all of his operas composed in England were in Italian, adhering to the international craze for that genre known as *opera seria*. Although Handel wrote forty such operas, his dramatic oratorios, sung in English but similar in structure and style to his *opera seria*, proved his greatest legacy to English musical theater. A performance in 1732 of his greatly revised *Esther* (pr. 1718) initiated a long series of these quasi-dramatic works based on biblical subjects, such as *Samson* (pr. 1743), *Saul* (pr. 1739), *Judas Maccabaeus* (pr. 1747), and *Solomon* (pr. 1749). Originally intended to be presented during Lent, even in Handel's time these oratorios found their way out of season into more than one theater. Such was their success that the audiences of England have still not lost their taste for Handel's semioperatic works and their successors, including Sir Arthur Sullivan's *The Prodigal Son* (pr. 1869), Sir Edward Elgar's *The Dream of Gerontius* (pr. 1900), Sir William Walton's *Belshazzar's Feast* (pr. 1931), and Michael Tippett's *A Child of Our Time* (pr. 1941).

The attempt to write Italianate full-length operas continued through the 1760's. Thomas Augustine Arne, the most accomplished composer of his day, based his own English text of *Artaxerxes* (pr. 1762) on that of *opera seria*'s most prolific librettist, Pietro Metastasio. This isolated attempt to transfer Italian opera into the English language coincided with the last gasps of *opera seria* on the Continent, where comic opera had already begun to supplant and cause modification to the older form.

In England, as if in response to playwright and librettist Joseph Addison's anguished pleas about not allowing Italian music to "entirely annihilate and destroy" English music, new forms of English musical stage works appeared. The most successful of these new forms was known as ballad opera, and its first major author, John Gay, made a direct assault on the Italian norm with his satiric *The Beggar's Opera* (pr. 1728). Gay supplied the play and lyrics, and Johann Christoph Pepusch arranged sixty-nine popular tunes, including a march from Handel's *Rinaldo*. Although the play and lyrics of ballad operas were almost always original, the music was usually borrowed, in a popular vein, and often uncredited. The success of *The Beggar's Opera* inspired hundreds of other attempts in the same style.

For the next sixty years, the ballad opera was a uniquely English form of theater that combined dialogue (generally superior to that of any Continental comic or serious opera), catchy tunes, and a talent for satire seldom found elsewhere. Besides satire of politics and politicians, the middle classes, and the legal profession, *The Beggar's Opera* poked fun at Italian opera and its performers, who at the time so dominated the London musical scene. One of its successors, *The Devil to Pay* (pr. 1743), by Charles Coffey, is historically important as the direct progenitor of German comic opera. It was also one of the first operas performed in the American colonies, in Charleston, South Carolina, in 1736.

These works, all designed for their popular appeal, gradually came to be known under the generic title of ballad operas. They relied as much on the spoken word as their music, and they often had strongly satirical elements. A well-known engraving of the English artist William Hogarth, *The Enraged Musician*, satirizes the noise of an eighteenth century London street even as it satirizes ballad opera. A musician, by implication from a posted broadside next to his window, engaged to play a performance of Gay's *The Beggar's Opera*, holds his ears while the real-life urchins of the city make their respective noises beneath his window.

Ballad opera was considered the people's opera primarily because of its simple form, its use of colloquial speech, and its homely subject matter. Even before Gay's sensational *The Beggar's Opera*, the elder Allan Ramsay achieved wide success with his *The Gentle Shepherd* (pr. 1725). These two works spurred a shift in taste that led to a general decline in the interest of more refined compositions. They led to the eventual failure of Handel's Royal Academy of Music.

It is also likely that the relative production simplicity of ballad opera in England made it congenial to the American colonies. *Flora*, also known under the title *Hob-in-the-Well* (pr. 1735), was the first opera to be performed in the United States and was given in Charleston, South Carolina. The spoken sections derived from the farce by Colley Cibber (pr. 1711) and from *The Country Wake* by Thomas Doggett, published in 1698. The music used was by various composers rather than by one single artist, and this was often the case in productions of ballad opera. Here, as with *The Beggar's Opera*, commercial interests capitalized on the appeal of the work. The Meissen porcelain factories in both Holland and England marketed a pattern they called *Hob in the Well* from 1730 through 1755.

In the United States, as in England, ballad opera was essentially an irreverent reaction, though to the New England music tradition that through much of the eighteenth century presented vocal music based on psalmlike and religious themes. New York would see its first ballad opera only in mid-century: *The Mock Doctor: Or, The Dumb Lady Cur'd* (pr. 1732) a farce with the music of various composers based on the adaptation of a Molière play by the English novelist Henry Fielding.

A relative to the ballad opera was the *pasticcio*, which took pieces of successful works and tied them together on a very slender string. Usually the *pasticcio* was found as an afterpiece during the standard eighteenth century evening of entertainment that included a spoken drama. In the last decades of the century, both the ballad opera and the *pasticcio* were replaced in public favor by an English comic opera with spoken dialogue and original music by one or more composers. Of these, Richard Brinsley Sheridan's *The Duenna: Or, The Double Elopement* (pr. 1775), with music by Thomas Linley the elder and Thomas Linley the younger, was very popular and has remained of interest primarily because of the reputation of its playwright. Despite the bold success of ballad opera, the eighteenth century produced little of an enduring nature in terms of English opera. If this is true in the Old World, the fate of the few comic operas composed in the newly independent country of the United States was even less impressive.

THE NINETEENTH CENTURY

Around the beginning of the nineteenth century, ballad opera developed into a more Italianate form that came to be called burletta. Generally speaking its satirical elements more closely resembled farce and were gentler, broader, and less identifiably English than in the ballad operas. *Frederick of Prussia: Or, The Monarch and the Mimic* (pr. 1837), a one-act burletta by Charles Selby, is a good example of the form. Produced at the Queen's Theatre, it was a play of lovers and mistaken identity involving Frederick the Great and freely incorporating incidental music and recitatives as the production warranted. The musical passages in burlettas need not advance or even have anything directly to do with plot; but could simply be diversions to lighten an already light drama.

The transition between the eighteenth and nineteenth centuries was tumultuous both politically and culturally. The shock waves of the French Revolution, followed as it was by Napoleon Bonaparte's initially republican-inspired conquests, found artistic expression in so-called rescue operas, of which Ludwig van Beethoven's *Fidelio* (pr. 1805) is a major example. In prose, poetry, and dramatic literature, revolution found its expression in the Romantics' assault on the bastilles of neoclassical drama and the worn out *opera seria*.

Although England was one of the dominant forces in the new movement with the novels of Sir Walter Scott, the poetry of William Wordsworth, and the scenic designs for antiquarian, medieval productions of the now faithfully restored plays of Shakespeare, it was left to the Italians and the French to set these works in operatic form. Although the Germans were developing opera rooted in their own mythology and medieval history, what little that passed for English opera retained the form of comic opera with musical selections separated by spoken dialogue and introduced the style of semiserious opera emphasizing sentimentality over history and tragedy. During the first seventy years of the nineteenth century, England produced only a handful of successful or important musical works for the stage, and these were products of non-English composers and found little audience outside England.

The first of these works was by the influential founder of the German Romantic school of opera, Carl Maria von Weber, whose *Der Freischütz* (pr.

1821) was to set a standard for subsequent developments by Richard Wagner. In 1826, shortly before his death in London, Weber opened *Oberon: Or, The Elf-King's Oath* (pr. 1826), an opera in English to a libretto by James Robinson Planché. Its overture remains a concert favorite, and its fairy music became the model for popular future incarnations such as those found in W. S. Gilbert and Sir Arthur Sullivan's *Iolanthe: Or, The Peer and the Peri* (pr. 1882). With the exception of Giuseppe Verdi, who was commissioned to write an opera for Jenny Lind in Italian for a London production in 1847, this was the last work by a non-British composer to be specially written for London. That England went from a perpetual importer of European music, especially French and Italian in origin, to semi-isolation in less than sixty years is difficult to explain except as a consequence of cultural chauvinism.

The two works that were to prove the most enduring in England for the rest of the century were products of Ireland. Dating back to the time of Handel and even before, Dublin had been London's only rival as a center for works in English for the lyric stage, and it was from there that Michael William Balfe's *The Bohemian Girl* (pr. 1843) and William Vincent Wallace's *Maritana* (pr. 1845) emerged. Coupled with *Lily of Killarney* (pr. 1862), by Sir Julius Benedict, a German émigré, these works made up the trio of successful romantic dialogue-operas that neither broke new ground nor established a distinctive national style or sound because their music was based primarily on the approach of Gioacchino Rossini and Antonio Gaetano Donizetti. Only two through-composed operas of note during the nineteenth century must be mentioned: John Barnett's *The Mountain Sylph* (pr. 1834) and Sullivan's *Ivanhoe* (pr. 1891), the latter a failure but a notable attempt at English grand opera with an English subject.

Despite his failure at grand opera, Sullivan, working with established author W. S. Gilbert as librettist, was to create the most enduring works of the English musical theater. These comic operas or operettas, inspired by the *opéras bouffes* of Jacques Offenbach in Paris, became a regular feature of the London theatrical scene in 1875 when impresario Richard D'Oyly

Carte brought them together to write a short after-piece to his production of Offenbach's *La Périchole* (pr. 1868). The resulting one-act comic opera, *Trial by Jury* (pr. 1875), ushered in a string of artistic and financial hits, including *H.M.S. Pinafore: Or, The Lass That Loved a Sailor* (pr. 1878), *The Pirates of Penzance: Or, The Slave of Duty* (pr. 1879), *Patience: Or, Bunthorne's Bride* (pr. 1881), *The Mikado: Or, The Town of Titipu* (pr. 1885), and *The Gondoliers: Or, The King of Barataria* (pr. 1889). As had been the English tradition in comic operas since the days of Gay, the emphasis in these works was on the inventive, sparkling, and truly satiric words, which made Sullivan's role mostly subservient. Although Gilbert and Sullivan's works have failed to become as popular in Europe, where operetta tradition used words simply as a skeleton on which the composer draped the muscle of the music, in the English-speaking world the mercurial words and the close-fitting music continue to hold the stage as easily and delightfully as they did when they were first presented. Gilbert and Sullivan's comic operas represent the major legacy of English musical theater of the nineteenth century.

The fortunes of English opera in England are mirrored in the first hundred years of the history of the United States, although in the latter more interest was focused on native themes, as in George Frederick Bristow's *Rip Van Winkle* (pr. 1855). While imported operas in foreign languages were regularly performed in New Orleans after 1805 and in New York after 1820, it was difficult for American composers to get their works produced: Many organizations, such as the New York Philharmonic Society, were under the control of foreign-born musicians. With native opera expensive to produce, especially by reluctant theaters, many American stage composers turned to writing dramatic cantatas that were similar in form to the English dramatic oratorio. These works, which collectively concentrated on natural or sea disasters (and almost every incident in American history), were produced into the twentieth century. Examples include *The Pilgrim Fathers* (pr. 1854), by George F. Root, and *The Wreck of the Hesperus* (pr. 1887), by Arthur Foote. At the end of the century, the Indianist movement inspired a number of stage works, includ-ing Charles Wakefield Cadman's *Shanewis: Or, The Robin Woman* (pr. 1918) and Victor Herbert's *Natoma* (pr. 1911)—one of his two excursions away from popular operettas and Broadway shows into through-composed opera (that is, opera for which new music is composed for each stanza).

THE TWENTIETH CENTURY

The popular tradition in opera continued in the long overlooked ragtime compositions of Scott Joplin in the early twentieth century. His first opera *A Guest of Honor* (c. 1903), was never performed and subsequently lost. Though he never saw a staged version of his opera *Treemonisha*, a work he composed around 1907, the work has achieved wide audience popularity since its full professional staging by the Huston Grand Opera in 1975. The Joplin operatic phenomenon was three quarters of a century before its time.

The first thirty years of the twentieth century saw opera in both the United States and England dominated by neo-Wagnerian principles in structure and sound, although modified by the *Verismo* school of Italian operatic naturalism. Perhaps the closest of Wagner's disciples was the English composer Rutland Boughton, who conceived of a festival home modeled on Wagner's Bayreuth for his own works, based primarily on Celtic and Old English legends. Boughton completed a massive tetralogy based on the Arthurian legends and gave a performance of the second piece, *The Round Table*, in 1916 at the Glastonbury Festival, his Bayreuth. The entire work has never been produced, and Boughton's reputation rests on a much simpler work, *The Immortal Hour* (pr. 1914). Other composers influenced by Wagner, perhaps less ambitious than Boughton but equally or more successful, included the only internationally acknowledged female opera composer, Dame Ethel Smyth, whose works include *The Wreckers* (pr. 1906), which is still able to hold the stage in revivals. Frederick Delius, who lived most of his life outside England, wrote six operas, of which *A Village Romeo and Juliet* (pr. 1907) is still performed.

In the United States, the late German Romantic school was represented by Walter Damrosch's *The Scarlet Letter* (pr. 1896) and *The Man Without a*

Country (pr. 1937), as well as Deems Taylor's *The King's Henchman* (pr. 1927) and *Peter Ibbetson* (pr. 1931), both of which premiered at the Metropolitan Opera House in New York. Howard Hanson's *Merry Mount* (pr. 1933), based on a novel by Nathaniel Hawthorne, made its debut at the Metropolitan and remains one of the grandest of grand operas using an American setting.

Two trends in opera written to an English libretto were dominant beginning around 1930; the first was the introduction of folk elements or reworked folk music into the story, setting, and texture of the work; the second employed naturalistic psychological studies of characters and music that embodies the emotions generated from within them. To be sure, there have been experiments in impressionism and other non-naturalistic forms, but most of these have been found in French, German, and Italian works. Exceptions include Virgil Thomson and Gertrude Stein's collaborations on *Four Saints in Three Acts* (pr. 1934) and *The Mother of Us All* (pr. 1947), with their focus on stimulation of the senses rather than content; Igor Stravinsky's *The Rake's Progress* (pr. 1951), based on drawings of William Hogarth with music consciously aping the style of Wolfgang Amadeus Mozart; and Marc Blitzstein's agitprop opera, *The Cradle Will Rock* (pr. 1937), modeled on the style of Bertolt Brecht and Kurt Weill.

In the mainstream of folk opera, England saw the work of two major composers, Gustav Holst in *At the Boar's Head* (pr. 1925) and Ralph Vaughan Williams in *Hugh the Drover* (pr. 1924) and *Sir John in Love* (pr. 1929), and in the United States a steady stream of folk or folk-related operas appeared during the 1950's and 1960's. Many American composers' contributions in this field were given active encouragement and first performances at the New York City Opera. Included in the long list of works that fall into this category are *The Tender Land* (pr. 1954) by Aaron Copland, *The Ballad of Baby Doe* (pr. 1956) and *Carrie Nation* (pr. 1966) by Douglas Moore, *Susannah* (pr. 1955) by Carlisle Floyd, and *Lizzie Borden* (pr. 1965) by Jack Beeson.

The second trend, into psychological naturalism, is highlighted in the United States by Kurt Weill's setting of Elmer Rice's play *Street Scene* (pr. 1947), the highly charged *The Medium* (pr. 1946) and *The Consul* (pr. 1950) by Gian Carlo Menotti, and the lyric *Vanessa* (pr. 1958) by Samuel Barber. In England after World War II, a titan of English opera emerged within a month after the fall of Germany. On June 7, 1945, the Sadler's Wells Opera reopened with the premiere of *Peter Grimes* by composer Benjamin Britten, and onto the international scene burst a universally acknowledged operatic genius. In his twelve operas, Britten mixes rich orchestral textures, extensive choral music, and an almost unerring sense of characterization. In addition to *Peter Grimes*, Britten's *Billy Budd* (pr. 1951)—based on the Herman Melville story—and *Death in Venice* (pr. 1973)—based on Thomas Mann's novella—have found their way into the standard repertory of the world's major opera houses and have elevated English opera to a status unknown since Purcell. Two other major English opera composers have works approaching the same international status: Michael Tippett, with works such as *The Midsummer Marriage* (pr. 1955) and *The Knot Garden* (pr. 1970), and Peter Maxwell Davies, with *Taverner* (pr. 1972) and *The Lighthouse* (pr. 1979).

As the dividing lines among opera, operetta, and musical comedy have blurred in the United States, and to a lesser extent in England, the commercial theater has become the proving ground for new works. Beginning with George and Ira Gershwin's jazz-inspired collaboration with DuBose and Dorothy Heyward, *Porgy and Bess* (pr. 1935), which took fifty years to reach the stage of the Metropolitan Opera House, a long list of works originally produced on Broadway have taken their places in both European and American opera houses. Among these are Menotti's *The Medium* and *The Consul*, Blitzstein's *Regina* (pr. 1949), Lillian Hellman and Leonard Bernstein's *Candide* (pr. 1956), Arthur Laurents and Bernstein's *West Side Story* (pr. 1957), Frank Loesser's *The Most Happy Fella* (pr. 1956), and Stephen Sondheim's *A Little Night Music* (pr. 1973) and *Sweeney Todd, the Demon Barber of Fleet Street* (pr. 1979). With the growing acceptance of a broader definition of opera, the efforts of English and American composers have assumed a central position in the operatic centers of the world.

The dividing line between opera and musical theater has become more obscured as the two disciplines merge: musical theater demanding stronger voices with more complex melodic lines and more sung dialogue, and opera moving toward popular themes and more accessible librettos. Musicals such as *Les Misérables* (first produced in French in 1980 and in English in 1985) and *The Phantom of the Opera* (pr. 1986) can be described as operas, since a large part of the dialogue is sung. Similarly, *Miss Saigon* (pr. 1987) and *Chess* (pr. 1986) can be seen as opera and are regularly reviewed in such periodicals as *Opera News*. Musical composer Ned Rorem said in *Opera News* (July, 1991) that "the sole difference between opera and musical comedy is that one uses conservatory-trained voices while the other uses show-biz voices." Stanley Silverman put it less somberly, noting that "opera is merely musical comedy an octave higher."

As examples of popular themes in English language opera, the 1980's saw Henry James's *The Aspern Papers* (1888), John Steinbeck's *Of Mice and Men* (1937), James M. Cain's *The Postman Always Rings Twice* (1934), and Luigi Pirandello's *Six Characters in Search of an Author* (pr. 1921) all transformed into operas. As opera experiments with its forms, the now traditional English language operas of Gian Carlo Menotti continue to find their way into the seasons of regional companies. For example, the double bill of *Help! Help! The Gobolinks!* (pr. 1969) and *Amahl and the Night Visitors* (pb. 1952, pr. 1953) was part of the Buffalo, New York, opera season in 1990.

The best names in English language opera occur again and again. Carlisle Floyd's completely rewritten *Passion of Jonathan Wade* was performed in 1992 in Houston, Miami, San Diego, and Seattle; the tale of a Reconstruction-era clash between North and South, it was billed as a world premiere, despite its original production in 1962. Floyd became famous for his *Susanna* (pr. 1956) and the less successful *Willie Stark* (pr. 1981). Moore's *Ballad of Baby Doe* is also performed occasionally. Leonard Bernstein revised *Candide* in 1988 and recorded the new version in 1989.

Closer to the avant-garde are the productions of Judith Weir's *A Night at the Chinese Opera* (pr. 1987) and *The Vanishing Bridegroom* (pr. 1990), both performed in Scotland. Philip Glass's *Hydrogen Jukebox* (pr. 1990) continued this composer's assault on the definition of music; Peter Sellars's direction of John Adams's *Nixon in China* (pb. 1981) and *The Death of Klinghoffer* (pr. 1991) is notable for the plays' unusual staging and subject matter. *Atlas*, by Meredith Monk, was staged at the Houston Grand Opera in 1991, after being workshopped from 1988 to 1990. William M. Hoffman and John Corigliano collaborated to bring *The Ghosts of Versailles*, after Pierre-Augustin Caron de Beaumarchais's *L'Autre Tartuffe: Ou, La Mère coupable* (pr. 1792; *Frailty and Hypocrisy*, 1804), to broadcast form in 1992.

Finally, no discussion of modern English language opera can be complete without the mention of Robert Wilson, a writer/designer/director whose avant-garde, multifaceted works combine operatic size and musical complexity with the visual possibilities of the stage and the meditative concentration of philosophical speculation. Wilson began his experimental career with theater pieces, "demonstrations," workshops, and other alternative theater activities. Often he tried "sound" pieces, whose function was to experience pure sound rather than the contextual tyranny of words. After his early "sound" works gained acceptance, Wilson tried an actual opera, *The Life and Times of Joseph Stalin* (pr. 1973), with music by Alan Lloyd, Igor Demjen, and others. It previewed in Copenhagen as a production of the Byrd Hoffman School of Byrds and premiered at the Brooklyn Academy of Music in December of 1973. Truncated versions of the opera were subsequently performed, along with Wilson's next opera, *A Letter for Queen Victoria* (pr. 1974). The following years continued Wilson's collaborations with his team of composers, choreographers, visual artists, and actors: *Einstein on the Beach* (pr. 1976), one of the most successful of this series of works, with music by Philip Glass, premiered in France. Among several "plays," Wilson designed and directed *Medea* (pr. 1981) and *the CIVIL warS* (pr. 1983), as well as some operas in other languages.

From these ambitious operatic constructions, usually performed at the Brooklyn Academy of Music, Wilson became more and more accepted in the world of English language opera. Wilson's imaginative and demanding productions have forced opera to expand its self-definition to include works as far removed from nineteenth century notions as his collaborators—Meredith Monk, David Byrne, Allen Ginsberg, Christopher Knowles, Laurie Anderson, Richard Foreman, and many others—are different from their classical counterparts in dance, theater, and dramaturgy.

Possibly as a reaction to the minimalism of Glass and John Cage, opera composers such as Corigliano, Dominick Argento, and John Harbison have modified academic styles with elements of lyricism and literary sources already familiar to modern audiences. Argento, for example, composed *The Aspern Papers* (pr. 1988) using a libretto he adapted from Henry James's novella. This followed upon Argento's song cycle *From the Diary of Virginia Woolf* (pr. 1975). Argento's two-act opera, *The Dream of Valentino* (pr. 1994), his work for chorus, *Walden Pond* (pr. 1996) based on Henry David Thoreau's *Walden: Or, Life in the Woods* (1854), and his *Miss Havisham's Fire* (pr. 1979, rev. 2001), based on Charles Dickens's novel *Great Expectations* (1860-1861), all combine widely read literature or elements of popular culture with sophisticated musical lines that suit the dramatic action. Harbison's opera *The Great Gatsby* (pr. 1999), commissioned by the Metropolitan Opera shares a popular novel as its inspiration. The opera incorporates familiar jazz rhythms of the 1920's with the composer's own music and a libretto that remains faithful to the plot of the Scott Fitzgerald novel.

BIBLIOGRAPHY

Altieri, Joanne. *The Theatre of Praise: The Panegyric Tradition in Seventeenth Century English Drama.* Newark: University of Delaware Press, 1986. A comprehensive study that discusses the relationship of art to propaganda in the context of the theater and its operatic derivative. There is a full chapter on opera's relationship to politics, history, and the theater.

Dircks, Phyllis. *Eighteenth Century Burletta.* ELS Monograph Series 78. Victoria, B.C.: English Literary Studies, 1999. Traces the relationship of ballad opera and the more Italianate form known as the burletta and considers the composers and primary works written in this form in the eighteenth century, emphasizing English composers of the period.

Fiske, Roger. *English Theatre Music in the Eighteenth Century.* New York: Oxford University Press, 1973. This is the standard reference work on eighteenth century theater music; it provides a history of the English musical theater following the Restoration era.

Gagey, Edmund McAdoo. *Ballad Opera.* Columbia University Studies in English and Comparative Literature. New York: Columbia University Press, 1937. Reprint. New York: B. Blom, 1965. The availability of this work makes it worthwhile to consult on the history of the ballad opera form. Gagey surveys composers and representative works popular in England and as imported to the United States.

Gilman, Lawrence. *Nature in Music and Other Studies in the Tone-Poetry of Today.* Freeport, N.Y.: Books for Libraries, 1966. Reprint. Temecula, Calif.: Best Books, 2001. This classic study compares the development of program music and opera and features sections on the place of opera in English.

Warrack, John, and Ewan West, eds. *The Concise Dictionary of Opera.* New York: Oxford University Press, 1996. This convenient reference work has the advantages of entries complete enough for the generalist and ready availability. The revised edition has completely new articles on English and ballad opera.

White, Eric Walter. *The Rise of English Opera.* New York: Philosophical Library, 1951. Reprint. New York: DaCapo Press, 1972. This history of opera in English focuses on the eighteenth century. It is particularly strong on ballad and folk opera, though it also traces the development of English opera through the years immediately following World War II.

John R. Lucas, updated by Thomas J. Taylor and Robert J. Forman

WESTERN EUROPEAN OPERA

Like cinema, opera is a collaborative art, requiring the skills of poets, composers, choreographers, set and costume designers, singers, musicians, and assorted stage technicians. However, unlike film, opera at first was neither a popular entertainment, nor was it intended to be. Because of its luxuriousness and expensive production requirements, initially the genre needed a rich patron, even a prince, to support it. Little wonder then that opera—often considered the most aristocratic of the arts—had its beginnings in the Renaissance courts of Italy in the 1580's. Tragedies and comedies, and related dramatic forms, had been featured at the royal courts of Florence and Mantua in northern Italy throughout the sixteenth century. Many of these plays were based on or influenced by Roman and especially Greek models. The revitalized interest in Greek culture, in fact, played a key role in the Renaissance spirit of inquiry and experimentation in the arts.

These plays were often accompanied by music, an attempt by the dramatists and their fellow musicians to emulate what they believed to be an integral part of the classical dramas of the ancient Greeks. Greek drama provided numerous uses of the chorus, for example, and the Renaissance playwrights and musicians sought to produce appropriate music for their own "modern" versions of these plays.

There were some important precursors to these early musical dramas, direct ancestors in the evolution of the full-fledged opera. Most important was the *intermedio*, a theatrical entertainment intended to keep the audience amused between the acts of the play. The *intermedio* was often more inventive, more spectacular, than the play it was intended to complement. This mixture of song, music, and dance was generally accompanied by elaborate stage effects, often intended to serve as political allegories honoring the prince or patron whose financial backing supported the whole production. At the wedding of one of the Medici, for example, the *intermedio* featured a naked Venus descending from a cloud in a bejeweled car, surrounded by the three Graces, also nude, among a bevy of white swans. During Venus's descent, music and the aroma of fresh flowers filled the air.

Though an important forerunner of opera, the *intermedio* relied more on theatrical effect than on artistic integration of its parts. The music was simply an adornment to a poetic text and a luxurious stage set, while the action and characterization were never fully dramatically realized.

Another significant forerunner was the pastoral, a short, dramatic lyric poem glorifying the bucolic settings of nature and country life. Not as elaborate as the *intermedio*, the pastoral typically featured shepherds, nymphs, and sylvan deities as characters. Choruses, songs, and dances complemented the lyric quality of the poetry but on the whole the plot presented little dramatic action. The pastoral was more of a mood piece, a pleasant, idealized evocation of the mythical "Golden Age," a candied artifice celebrating the storied notions of natural innocence and earthly bliss.

With the success of the pastoral and the *intermedio*, coupled with the frequent academic discussions among scholars and poets about music's emotional contribution to drama, the time was ripe for the birth of opera. *Dafne*, first performed in 1598, is generally considered the first, though the music has been almost entirely lost. Based on the Greek myth of Daphne, who is turned into a laurel tree as she escapes the amorous advances of the god Apollo, the musical drama was the first to integrate fully the demands of plot with the emotional quality of music. Composed by Jacopo Peri, with a text by the poet Ottavio Rinuccini, the opera was performed only three or four times over the next two years, but it set a precedent in making music a major component of the drama. In *Dafne*, the god Apollo, the traditional voice of poetry, becomes a principal character, a figure effectively combining poetry with music.

Peri and Rinuccini's second opera, *Euridice*, was even more influential. Once again the pair turned to Greek myth, this time the story of Orpheus and Eurydice. First performed at the wedding of Maria de' Medici and Henry IV of France in October, 1600, the opera established some techniques that were to become permanent characteristics of the genre. Besides being the first to deal with a myth that was to be the subject of numerous operas, *Euridice* showed a clear understanding of the use of recitative, a form of musical declamation, first discussed by Peri in his published preface to the opera. As a kind of middle ground between song and speech, recitative verse, used for both action and dialogue, was a key innovation in early opera's attempt to mesh the flexibility of music with the formalities of verse.

THE SEVENTEENTH CENTURY

Within a decade after the introduction of opera as a legitimate artistic medium, its first great composer emerged. Claudio Monteverdi was already a masterful composer of madrigals—songs usually in five parts with sophisticated contrasts in structure—which revealed his command of polyphonic technique; that is, two or more melodic lines played at once and complementing each other. Seven years after *Euridice*, Monteverdi produced another version of the story. With a libretto by Alessandro Striggio, *L'Orfeo* (pr. 1607; *Orfeo*, 1949), the first great opera, broke fresh ground in its use of new kinds of arias and duet writing, culminating in Orfeo's act 3 aria as he enters the gates of Hades. The instrumental accompaniment is intensely dramatic, imaginative, and emotionally powerful, effectively complementing the action.

By the second quarter of the seventeenth century, Venice—where Monteverdi had come permanently to live and work—had become the opera capital of the world. The city's theatrical traditions, always geared more to public festivities than to private entertainments, encouraged the growth and prosperity of the new medium. By 1650 the city could boast four opera houses; tourists from all over Europe were captivated by Venetian opera. Monteverdi wrote three new operas in Venice. His last, composed in the year of his death, is arguably his finest. *L'incoronazione di Poppea* (pr. 1642; *The Coronation of Poppea*, 1964) tells the story of the scandalous and dishonorable love affair between the Roman emperor Nero and his mistress, Poppea. Despite the basic problem in pre-

senting murderers and unprincipled lovers as central characters, Monteverdi succeeded in writing music of extraordinary sensuousness, particularly in the arias and duets. The music is among some of the finest in the operatic repertory.

The last half of the seventeenth century saw Italian opera being exported to other countries. Opera was slow getting started in France, largely because of the nationalist policy of the royal court. However, with the arrival in Paris in 1646 of Jean-Baptiste Lully, Italian opera was to be adapted to French tastes. An Italian by birth—he changed his name from Lulli to the Gallic form—Lully became the chief composer for the court of Louis XIV and quickly showed his skill at identifying and integrating French qualities into his operas. Though his operas were meant largely as political allegories to the reigning spirit of Louis XIV, their musical depth and richness—particularly the powerful choruses and the clear, graceful melodic lines—are hallmarks of French opera of the period. A dancer in his youth, Lully added ballet as an integral part of the action. Such operas as *Armide* (pr. 1686), his last, are models of the French operatic tradition. An opulent musical score is supported by spectacular stage effects, as in act 5 in which the title character summons demons to destroy her palace while she returns to Syria on a chariot drawn by dragons.

Although England had a strong musical tradition dating from the middle ages, opera came to the nation late in the seventeenth century. Like France, England had its own musical genres supported by and primarily performed in the royal court. Notable among these was the masque, a blend of music, dance, spectacle, and poetic text. Strongly influenced by the Italian *intermedio* as well as French forms, the masque was more theatrical than dramatic. With the coming of the English Civil War in the 1640's and its aftermath, theaters were closed and drama stilled. However, musical entertainments were excluded from the ban, and with the commencement of the Restoration era after 1660, a full theatrical life was reborn. A number of small, courtly operas were produced, notably John Blow's *Venus and Adonis* in the 1680's, but the greatest English opera of this period—and of the century—is *Dido and Aeneas* (pr. 1689) by Henry Purcell. Based on a story from Vergil's Aeneid (c. 29-19 B.C.E.; English translation, 1553), the opera treats the love affair between the queen of Carthage and the Trojan hero, Aeneas, who is destined by the gods to leave the queen and continue his journey to Italy where he is to be the progenitor of the Roman state. Particularly brilliant is Dido's lament in the last scene, as she sees Aeneas boarding his ship, abandoning her to unrequited love and tragic suicide.

OPERA SERIA

The closing years of the seventeenth century saw opera suffering from those very excesses that to a lesser degree had prompted its birth. Poets and theater managers were more concerned with spectacular stage effects, including supernatural occurrences, than on plots that maintained at least a pretense to credibility and human motive. Texts had become degraded by scenes of low, coarse comedy, complicated plots, and irrelevant subplots and characters. Whereas opera had begun as an esteemed entertainment for the aristocracy, by this period it had become, in some ways, a vulgar amusement for the masses.

By the beginning of the eighteenth century, reform was inevitable. Librettists such as Apostolo Zeno and more important, Pietro Metastasio began to disabuse opera from its excesses. They drew their plots largely from ancient history rather than mythology, emphasizing a logical, efficient, dignified action and usually calling for a cast of fewer than ten characters. The subject matter was serious, the action restrained, and the music characterized by a simpler melodic line with a clearer distinction between recitative and aria. This shift from the improbable to the rational, from the exuberant to the controlled, from the complicated to the simple was given the term *opera seria*, "serious" or "Neapolitan" opera, so called because the Italian city of Naples was the cultural hub from which these reforms emanated.

In time, *opera seria* became the dominant form of the eighteenth century, and Metastasio its most influential practitioner. His work was of such quality that his librettos were sometimes performed as straight dramas, and he himself was often compared favorably to the great literary figures of the past. His themes announced an artistic reflection of Order and Monarchy, of a world controlled by reason and a distrust of the passions. His heroes and heroines are noble princes, kings, and queens who ultimately subdue their base "human" drives and adhere to an ideal—patriotism, duty, or honor. Conflicts in Metastasian drama are thus not physical but psychological. Characters often philosophize but rarely bleed. The action of such dramas revolves about the protagonist's resolution of the conflict, a resolution sometimes closed by death but more often also by happiness and salvation. In the end, dignity triumphs and order is restored. Metastasio even constructed his librettos in an almost mathematical balance: aria followed by recitative followed by aria.

One of the most popular composers of this period was Johann Hasse. Called "the beloved Saxon" by the Italians, Hasse was Metastasio's most devout follower. He wrote more than eighty operas, most of them set to a libretto by Metastasio. His operas were highly regarded, especially his arias, which were rich in elegant, if facile, melodies.

Three other German composers were to produce the finest examples of *opera seria*. The operas of George Frederick Handel remained largely unknown in the operatic capitals of Europe. Working in London throughout most of his career, Handel was free to compose in his own style, unhampered by the demands of making a living by following the popular musical fashion. Between 1712 and 1741 he composed some thirty-six operas. Though his later works, such as *Orlando* (pr. 1733), show the influence of the Neapolitan school (Handel had visited Italy in the late 1720's), his early works in the genre are among his best. In *Giulio Cesare* (pr. 1724) he composed an act 2 aria, for example, in which Cleopatra sings of her love in strongly expressive tones, a penetrating psychology suffusing a context of deep emotion. Though the least influenced by Metastasian principles—he set only three of Metastasio's librettos—his personal style proved the rule by being an exception to it.

While Handel came late to the methods of Metastasio, Christoph Willibald Gluck, who met Metastasio in Vienna in the late 1730's, based his first three operas on Metastasio's librettos. However, it was not until Gluck collaborated with the Italian poet Raniero de Calzabigi that he produced the first of his great reform operas. *Orfeo ed Euridice* (*Orpheus and Eurydice*, 1770), produced in Vienna in 1762, was a landmark in the development of *opera seria*. The work is characterized by a mood of calm repose. The action is simplified, almost austere, each scene musically depicting a specific emotion of the character. Like the libretto, the music is spare, economical, free of the ornamental phrases and vocal caprices typical of the period. It is a work in which the music perfectly complements the text, so that one is artistically dependant on and nourished by the other. *Orpheus and Eurydice* was a departure from Metastasian principles in that it used mythological rather than historical subjects and made greater use of the chorus and ballet.

Gluck's masterpiece was produced near the end of his life. In *Iphigénie en Tauride* (*Iphigenia in Tauris*, 1916), produced in 1779, the composer successfully combined the elements of aria, chorus, and ballet into a highly expressive musical drama. His use of the orchestra in the depiction of tone and mood showed what could result when a first-rate text is enhanced by a first-rate score.

The summit of *opera seria* was attained by Wolfgang Amadeus Mozart. His opera *Idomeneo* (pr. 1781; English translation, 1961) is generally considered a masterpiece of the form. It represents a synthesis of the major musical traditions of France, Germany, and Italy. The sonority of the arias is distinctly in the Italian mode, while the orchestral tone, particularly the dramatic use of the woodwinds, suggests an advanced conception of symphonic composition then being worked out by the famous orchestra in the German city of Mannheim.

OPERA BUFFA

While Metastasian principles provided the form and content of *opera seria* in the first part of the eighteenth century, the free-wheeling, boisterous humor of the comic opera, or *opera buffa*, existed side by side with its serious counterpart. In fact, comic

scenes, called *intermezzi* in Italy, were often used to divert the audience between the acts of a serious opera. Stock character types portrayed in spontaneous, improvisational incidents had been a feature of the Italian *commedia dell'arte*, the traditional national comedy. Yet during this period, the broad comic routines were performed with suitable music, and over the course of the century, the scenes themselves evolved into full-sized operas, the texts and music becoming perfectly teamed.

The most brilliant *intermezzo* of the first half of the eighteenth century is *La serva padrona* (*The Maid Mistress*, 1955) of 1733 by Giovanni Battista Pergolesi. Characterized by an infectious gaiety and an economy of effect, including a small orchestra and only two singers, the piece illustrated the artistic possibilities of a simple, rapidly moving score melded seamlessly with its text. The plot, revolving around a servant's attempt to outwit her master, became an archetype of the genre. The comic possibilities in the conflict between upper and lower classes appealed to a broader audience, especially as the language of the text was more realistic, vernacular, and dialectic than the idealized abstractions typical of *opera seria*.

A key figure in the development of comic opera in Italy was Carlo Goldoni. His librettos contain an array of characters—usually seven drawn from a broad cross-section of society. He introduced an important theatrical innovation of the "finale," an ensemble in which several actions unfold at the end of an act, allowing for a complex pattern of music and gesture.

One of the great figures in the history of *opera buffa* is Giovanni Paisiello. Among his more than one hundred operas, *La molinara* (pr. 1789), one of his best, displays his gift for orchestration and ensemble writing in which the music justly complements the action of the text.

Domenico Cimarosa, composer of more than eighty operas, wrote one of the most famous comic operas of the period. His *Matrimonio segreto* (pr. 1792; *The Secret Marriage*, 1877) was marked by a tuneful spontaneity and a witty, lively charm.

Just as he had brought *opera seria* to its highest levels, Mozart also produced three works generally considered the masterpieces of *opera buffa*, as well as landmarks in the entire operatic literature. *Le nozze di Figaro* (pr. 1786; *The Marriage of Figaro*, 1819) was the first of three operas composed to texts by Lorenzo Da Ponte. Da Ponte's libretto was based on a famous play by Pierre-Augustin Caron de Beaumarchais, *La Folle Journée: Ou, Le Mariage de Figaro* (pr. 1784; *The Marriage of Figaro*, 1784). The story about a barber who outwits a duke was a familiar one; a version of the story had already been set to music by Paisiello a few years earlier. However, Da Ponte's piece was sharper, more incisive, and intrinsically more dramatic from a musical point of view than any of its predecessors.

The score that Mozart produced brought its characters to life as few operas had ever done. Character delineation was subtly achieved by harmonic combinations and strategic use of particular instruments of the orchestra. Ensembles carry much of the characterization as well, especially in the finales. *Il dissoluto punito, ossia, Il Don Giovanni* (pr. 1787; *Don Giovanni*, 1817) was written to take advantage of the success of *The Marriage of Figaro*, but the darker aspects of both the plot—especially when the unrepentant Don is carried off to hell—and the music—which was less festive and more somber than was expected in a comic opera—disappointed and puzzled the audience.

Mozart's last comic opera was *Cosi fan tutte* (pr. 1790; *They All Do That*, 1811). Da Ponte's libretto about lovers testing each other's fidelity was light and cheerful, and Mozart's music was richly melodious. The last finale has been called "an apotheosis" of the spirit of eighteenth century comic opera.

Die Zauberflöte (pr. 1791; *The Magic Flute*, 1819) was Mozart's last opera. The absurdities of a confused fairy-tale plot by the librettist Emmanuel Schikaneder are deepened when, by act 2, the action turns into a symbolic presentation of the principles of Freemasonry. However, it is the music that redeems and even glorifies the opera. Mozart's use of tone color and melodic charm make the work a masterpiece of German *Singspiel*, a kind of folk vaudeville in which spoken dialogue, not recitative, advances the story line while music deepens the characterization.

GRAND OPERA

During the first half of the nineteenth century, Paris was the leading center of the operatic world. This was partly the result of the revolutionary fervor that gripped Europe during the last years of the previous century, beginning with the American and French revolutions and culminating in the reign of Napoleon Bonaparte. Many of the leading musicians found Paris congenial to their creative ambitions. Among the most influential of the early nineteenth century was Luigi Cherubini who produced *Les Deux Journées* (pr. 1800; *The Escaper*, 1801; also known as *The Water Carrier*, 1871), a superb example of the so-called rescue opera, a subgenre of the *opera buffa*, just then coming into vogue. It featured a plot replete with chase sequences, exhilarating escapes, and last minute rescues. Napoleon's own favorite composer was Gasparo Spontini, whose masterpiece, *La Vestale* (pr. 1807; *The Vestale*, 1925) offered spectacular and massive choral numbers.

In sheer theatricality, the opera was a forerunner to the large-scale works that have come to be called grand opera. Characterized by librettos on historical subjects involving protagonists of heroic stature and combined with lavish staging, singing, and orchestration, grand opera enjoyed its greatest popularity in the 1830's and 1840's. The leading composer of this period was Giacomo Meyerbeer: *Robert le diable* (pr. 1831; *Robert the Devil*, 1849); *Les Huguenots* (pr. 1836; *The Huguenots*, 1858), his masterpiece; and *Le Prophète* (pr. 1849; English translation, 1849), all with librettos by Eugène Scribe, the foremost librettist of his day, represent all those aspects of grand opera—good and bad—that became staples of the genre: long scores, irrelevant spectacle, improbabilities of plot and character, and a certain over-ripeness of the music.

One of the greatest French operas of the century is the five-act *Le Troyens* (pr. 1890, complete; *The Trojans*, 1957; two parts, *The Capture of Troy* and *The Trojans at Carthage*) by Hector Berlioz. For musical color and originality it stands as its composer's masterpiece, but it has hardly ever been performed in totality because of its excessive length and high production costs.

Charles Gounod produced one of the most popular French operas ever written. Based on the medieval German legend of the scholar who sells his soul to the devil, *Faust* (wr. 1852-1859) is filled with rich musical numbers combining solemn dignity with deep, lyrical feeling. *Faust* was performed in Paris more than two thousand times before World War II.

Georges Bizet wrote his famous *Carmen* (English translation, 1895) in 1875, and it was produced in the same year. His most distinctive work, *Carmen* scandalized Parisians with its exotic realism and bold characterization. The music is tuneful, vital, and dramatically appropriate.

ITALIAN OPERA

While grand opera was developing in France, Italy was cultivating its own nationalist style that combined a distinct melodic quality with a more prominent use of the orchestra. No Italian composer more typifies this style than Gioacchino Rossini. He wrote both serious and comic operas, retiring early after composing his most ambitious work, *Guillaume Tell* (*William Tell*, 1839) in 1829. Though the opera is not frequently performed, its famous overture is an orchestral staple. However, his masterpiece is *Barbiere di Siviglia* (pr. 1816; *The Barber of Seville*, 1818). Generally considered the greatest *opera buffa* next to Mozart's work, the work combines sunny, infectious melody with a clear, bright orchestration.

With Rossini's retirement, Gaetano Donizetti became Italy's leading composer in the 1830's and early 1840's. *Lucia di Lammermoor* (pr. 1835; English translation, 1856), a serious opera with a libretto based on a novel by Sir Walter Scott, was filled with melodramatic effects and vocal histrionics, but its melodic line has kept it in the standard repertory. His comic operas, *L'elisir d'amore* (pr. 1832; *The Elixir of Love*, 1848) and *Don Pasquale* (pr. 1843; English translation, 1848), are notable examples of effective theatrical music.

Vincenzo Bellini's short career was characterized by operas such as *La Sonnambula* (pr. 1831; English translation, 1838), *Norma* (pr. 1831; English translation, 1841) and *I Puritani* (pr. 1835; English transla-

tion, 1836), compositions rich in purity of style, suave melodic line, and elegance.

The dominant Italian composer of the nineteenth century—and one of the greatest in all opera—is Giuseppe Verdi. From his first early success, *Nabucco* (pr. 1842; English translation, 1960) to the masterpiece of his old age, *Falstaff* (pr. 1893; English translation, 1893), Verdi perfectly combined the melodic expressiveness of the human voice with a gradually sure command of orchestration. All but *Falstaff* are serious operas, and several, like *Sicilian Vespers* (pr. 1855) and *Aida* (pr. 1871; English translation, 1891), are supreme examples of the exuberant pageantry characteristic of grand opera. Though the plots of many of his operas like *Rigoletto* (pr. 1851; English translation, 1888) and *Il Trovatore* (pr. 1853; English translation, 1855) are complex and often violent, his insistence on economy of scoring and musical characterization place his work among the most appropriately dramatic in all opera. The key to Verdi's music is its spontaneity and its aptness in portraying the complexity of human passion. Such musical portrayal is most evident in his tragic masterpiece, *Otello* (pr. 1887; English translation, 1888) in which the voice and the orchestra unite, the voice nevertheless leading the way in rendering human emotion.

Verdi's spiritual successor was Giacomo Puccini. He represents a musical bridge between the lush, vocal melody typical of Italian opera and the orchestral expressiveness characteristic of Richard Wagner's musical drama. His most well-known operas are *La Boheme* (pr. 1896; English translation, 1896), *Tosca* (pr. 1900; English translation, 1899), and *Madama Butterfly* (pr. 1904; *Madam Butterfly*, 1906), each marked by lilting melody and rich, harmonic orchestration.

The school of *Verismo* (Verism), colorful, bleak realism, flourished briefly in the last decade or so of the nineteenth century and is represented by two famous one-act operas. *Cavalleria Rusticana* (pr. 1890; *Rustic Chivalry*, 1891) by Pietro Mascagni and *Pagliacci* (pr. 1892; *The Clowns*, 1892) by Ruggiero Leoncavallo were sensational successes, filled with excessive passion and explosive emotion. They are often paired on the same performance bill.

WAGNER AND THE MUSIC DRAMA

A significant figure in the history of opera is Richard Wagner whose dedication to the composition of the total artwork (*Gesamtkunstwerk*) gave opera a new direction and a new challenge. Among his innovations was the use of the leitmotif, musical themes or "sign posts" attached directly or indirectly to certain characters or situations. Although he did not invent the technique—Cherubini had used it in the late eighteenth century, for instance—Wagner developed it from opera to opera, so that it often took on highly suggestive and elusive patterns; the music connected emotionally and intellectually with the action and characterization. His early operas, *Der Fliegende Hollander* (pr. 1843; *The Flying Dutchman*, 1876), *Tannhäuser* (pr. 1845; English translation, 1891), and *Lohengrin* (pr. 1850; English translation, 1880), are examples of German Romantic opera, a modified blend of grand opera, with spectacle and choral sections, but already revealing an integration that subordinated the traditional structure of aria and recitative into a more composed musical whole.

With the completion of his Nibelungenlied Cycle—four operas composed over twenty-five years—Wagner defined his legacy to opera. As with all of his major work, Wagner wrote his own librettos—further emphasizing the artistic "wholeness" of the composition. Based on the medieval epic poem, the *Nibelungenlied* and various other Norse myths, the four operas—*Das Rheingold* (*The Rhinegold*, 1889), *Die Walküre* (*The Valkyrie*, 1882), *Siegfried* (English translation, 1882), and *Götterdämmerung* (*The Twilight of the Gods*, 1901)—were completed and first performed as a cycle in 1876. The theme of the works is the relationship of humankind to the gods and the interplay of forces, both human and divine, that affect that relationship. Much of the action is both grand and deeply symbolic. At times the didactic and heavy-handed pronouncements of the poetry get in the way of the music. Wagner, after all, had written numerous essays on the philosophy of art and music, especially *Oper und Drama* (1851; *Opera and Drama*, 1913), that serve as a self-justification for his later work. However, the cycle—together with his last works, *Tristan und Isolde* (pr. 1865; *Tristan and Isolde*, 1886), *Die Meistersinger von Nurnberg* (pr. 1868; *The Master-Singers of Nuremberg*, 1885) and *Parsifal* (pr. 1882; English translation, 1879) remain the finest example of Wagner's musical innovations. Aria, recitative, and other traditional elements of the number opera are eliminated. In their place a system of through-composed *Versmelodi*, a synthesis of music and poetry that grows organically within the work, resulting not in an opera—a term Wagner rejected—but in a music drama, all elements thoroughly integrated into one work of art.

THE TWENTIETH CENTURY

Composers of the new century could not ignore the innovations of Wagner, only react to them. Claude Debussy produced a new kind of opera by using a few leitmotifs combined with a story that is purposely vague or "impressionistic." *Pelléas et Mélisande* (pr. 1902; *Pelléas and Mélisande*, 1907) is a symbolic, dreamlike composition that emphasizes mood rather than direct meaning. Unlike Wagnerian operas, the vocal parts are spare and closely akin to natural speech, and the opera looks back to Renaissance methods by its use of orchestral interludes and preludes that are played between scenes.

Richard Strauss was a direct spiritual descendent of Wagner. His romantic opera *Der Rosenkavalier* (pr. 1911; *The Rose-Bearer*, 1912) is filled with rich, tuneful orchestration, particularly waltzes. All the vocal parts have clear musical themes, so that even minor characters have a certain individuality.

One of the most influential composers of the first half of the twentieth century was Arnold Schoenberg. He wrote only three operas, and the last, *Von Heute auf Morgen* (pr. 1930) was never finished. However, the three introduced the use of dissonance as a controlling musical idea. This idea was the famous "twelve-tone" system that defied the conventional notion of key or tone. A stunning example of this system is the work of Schoenberg's pupil, Alban Berg. His *Wozzeck* (pr. 1925; English translation, 1952) is a gloomy, shocking work with abrupt changes of tone emotionally punctuated by orchestral interludes. This opera, whose central character was a villain, lonely, confused and alienated, became a major influence on opera composers in the first half of the century.

The work of Igor Stravinsky shows another direction for opera in the twentieth century. *The Rake's Progress* (pr. 1951), with a libretto by the poet W. H. Auden, is an outright celebration of Mozartian opera. Musical references to *Don Giovanni* abound, but the work's eclectic character—its ironies, its cynical ambiguity, its emotional constraint—makes its theme or intention unclear.

Showing the influence of *Wozzeck* is *Peter Grimes* (pr. 1945) by the English composer Benjamin Britten. Notable here are the orchestral interludes suggesting musical seascapes and enhancing the mood of tortured doubt endured by the title character.

The last quarter of the twentieth century was marked by works that question traditional operatic methods and experiment with avant-garde techniques, including the use of atonality. Luigi Nono composed *Prometeo* (pr. 1984), a "tragedy of hearing," as an opera for the ears only, with the audience sitting in total darkness. His earlier *Intolleranza 1960* (pr. 1961) is called a "scenic action" containing quotations from Marxist writings, supported by electronic sound effects and music in the twelve-tone scale.

BIBLIOGRAPHY

Brener, Milton. *Opera Offstage*. New York: Walker, 1996. Presents historical accounts of the problems in bringing some famous operas to the stage, including battles involving censorship, political intrigue, and financial constraints. Good section on Wolfgang Amadeus Mozart's *The Marriage of Figaro*.

Grout, Donald J. *A Short History of Opera*. 2d. ed. New York: Columbia University Press, 1965. Standard basic history of opera to which later studies are indebted. Some knowledge of musical notation is helpful but not necessary. Concise account of the Renaissance origins of the art form.

Levin, David, ed. *Opera Through Other Eyes*. Stanford, Calif.: Stanford University Press, 1993. Presents a literary approach to the opera, stressing the importance of the libretto in understanding the theory and practice of the art form.

Robinson, Paul. *Opera and Ideas*. New York: Harper and Row, 1985. Discusses some of the great operas as manifestations of historical, social, or ethical ideas. Suggests, for example, that Berlioz's *Les Troyens* is one of the great operas of the nineteenth century in its embodiment of its era's "historical consciousness."

Sutcliffe, Tom. *Believing in Opera*. Princeton, N.J.: Princeton University Press, 1996. Interprets opera as an all-encompassing art form, particularly as a performing art: dance, acting, lighting, and stagecraft. Discussions of choreographers and producers, including operatic "bratpack" producer Peter Sellars.

Edward Fiorelli

DEAF THEATER

Historically, deaf theater in the United States was little more than signed skits, jokes, and pantomimes until the establishment of the National Theater of the Deaf in 1967. A niche-based, or culture-based theater is defined traditionally by its literature, the play script, and its intended audience. Universal cultural themes might then extend to a broader audience. However, these traits played a much lesser role in the development of deaf theater, which is unique because it is usually defined by its physical method of performance. Plays performed in American Sign Language (ASL), regardless of their source, content, or intended audience are said to delineate deaf theater. Spoken language scripts are translated into ASL, a process reverse from that found in other niche-based drama. Deaf theater is usually performed simultaneously in two languages, manual ASL and spoken English. The development and proliferation of deaf theater reflects first the joining of spoken and manual languages and then the struggle to separate them. As the twenty-first century dawned, deaf theater began to embody the ASL literature of the deaf culture.

EARLY ORIGINS

Beginning in the nineteenth century and continuing through the 1960's, deaf Americans gathered together at deaf clubs to enjoy games, sports, and fellowship. Their activities often included a variety of spontaneously performed skits, deaf folklore, anecdotes, and unique sign language forms such as ABC stories that require the hand shape of each letter of the alphabet to be used in sequence. On rare occasions a rehearsed play was adapted from English. One of the earliest of these was the sign language production in 1894 of William Shakespeare's *The Merchant of Venice* (pr. c. 1596-1597) by the All Souls Working Club of the Deaf. However, deaf audiences typically preferred more visual and active vaudeville types of entertainment rather than those based on literary plays, which typically contained too much dialogue and not enough action.

Deaf audiences flocked to silent movies, especially to see deaf actor Emerson Romero. When his film career ended with the advent of "talkies" (films with sound), Romero founded a theatrical guild in New York, which presented short plays and skits, relying primarily on pantomime. One of his actors, Wolf Bragg, began adapting stories for sign language presentations and, under the sponsorship of the New York Hebrew Association of the Deaf, toured to deaf Jewish congregations until 1948.

Even at Gallaudet, the liberal arts college established in Washington, D.C. for deaf students, theatrical productions were limited to student clubs. However, in 1940, professor Frederick Hughes noticed that there were a large number of postlingually deaf students (students who lost their hearing after the age at which spoken language is acquired, typically around the age of three) who were skilled in both English and sign language. He taught the first dramatics classes and began to involve faculty members in presenting sign language adaptations of classic plays. He is credited with the concept of presenting plays in manual sign language with voice actors speaking the lines simultaneously. As most educators of the deaf at that time were hearing, this concept became very popular and quickly spread to residential schools for the deaf all over America.

THE MIRACLE WORKER

In 1959, the dramatic treatment of deafness received major exposure. William Gibson's *The Miracle Worker* was preparing to open on Broadway. Anne Bancroft was cast in the role of Anne Sullivan who teaches the concept of language to ten-year-old deaf and blind Helen Keller. To prepare for this role, Bancroft began to visit schools for the deaf and then went to Edna S. Levine, a psychologist who worked with deaf clients. Levine had two passions, Broadway theater and the deaf community. She became close friends with Bancroft, who embraced sign language with an enthusiasm that soon carried over to her director, Arthur Penn, and the set designer, David Hays.

Seeing their interest, Levine invited the cast and production team to attend a 1959 Gallaudet production of Shakespeare's *Othello, the Moor of Venice* (pr. 1604). Their response was so positive that they approached Mary Switzer—the first administrator of the Social and Rehabilitation Service in the Department of Health, Education, and Welfare—for a grant to stage a Broadway play in sign language. The grant was rejected, but the group's enthusiasm for sign language and deaf culture remained strong. After a second grant request was rejected, the theater professionals moved on to other projects.

THE NATIONAL THEATER OF THE DEAF

In 1964, David Hays helped to establish the Eugene O'Neill Theatre Center outside New London, Connecticut, on an estate on which Eugene O'Neill often spent his summers. Hays convinced the O'Neill Foundation to sponsor a professional training center for deaf actors, so he approached Mary Switzer a third time. One of the reasons previous grants had been denied was based on the theory that deaf children were better off being forced to try to speak because sign language was merely an inferior representation of English. However, in 1960, Gallaudet professor William C. Stokoe, Jr., wrote *Sign Language Structure* that provided the breakthrough recognition of ASL as a language in its own right. Stokoe's work was supported by deaf educators, and by 1966, it had been accepted by prominent politicians. Congress was also in the process of establishing the National Technical Institute for the Deaf (NTID) at the Rochester Institute of Technology and had accepted the notion of adult education programs for a broader spectrum of deaf clientele. The idea of a professional theater training program for deaf actors who used sign language was now credible. Hays received a grant of $16,500 from the Rehabilitation Services Administration of the Department of Health, Education and Welfare to establish the National Theater of the Deaf.

Hays quickly gathered a group of talented actors, including Phyllis Frelich and Gilbert Eastman from Gallaudet's drama department; and Bernard Bragg, who had studied with Marcel Marceau, had his own successful television show in San Francisco, *The Quiet Man* (1958-1961), and who knew the pool of skilled deaf actors. Hearing sign-language expert Lou Fant was hired to adapt plays into ASL. Hays's colleagues from the professional theater were brought in to teach master classes and to consult on the business of running a theater school and touring troupe of actors.

The first year, a company of nineteen performed five short plays including William Saroyan's *My Hart's in the Highlands* (pr. 1939) and a nonoperatic version of Giacomo Puccini's *Gianni Schicchi* (pr. 1918). The National Theater of the Deaf continued the established precedent of presenting spoken language plays simultaneously in ASL and English. Hays wanted to achieve a high profile quickly in order to attract donations and foundation grants, so the troupe began to tour almost immediately and even enjoyed a highly acclaimed run on Broadway in the Longacre Theater.

After a center had been created for deaf theater professionals, they began to mature as artists and to explore deaf themes in their own language. For the first time literary works were created first in ASL and then translated into English. In 1971, they produced their first deaf theme play, *My Third Eye*, which was filled with humorous anecdotes about what it means to be deaf. This was also the first National Theater of the Deaf production that was directed and designed by deaf practitioners, and the first National Theater of the Deaf play to be warmly received by the deaf audience, who until this time complained that theater merely presented plays in sign language for hearing audiences. *Parade*, a more political work, followed in 1975. In it Billie Dove leads a parade of deaf characters through a variety of deaf political issues on a quest to Washington, D.C., optimistically striving for "deaf rights."

DEAF PLAYS AND PLAYWRIGHTS

Most deaf playwrights have a direct connection to the National Theater of the Deaf. Eastman's *Sign Me Alice* (pr. 1973) tells the story of Alice Gallaudet, whose father founded education for the deaf in the United States. Bragg and Eugene Bergman teamed up in 1980 to create *Tales from a Clubroom*. Shanny Mow became the first deaf artistic director of a professional theater company in the United States in 1990. At first he adapted classics such as the *Iliad* (c. 800 B.C.E.; English translation, 1616) by Homer, and *Gilgamesh*, after the Sumerian legend. His first original play to be performed was *The Ghost of Chastity Past: Or, The Incident at Sashimi Junction* (pr. 1981), which combined his Asian, American, and deaf cultures. The result was a hilarious Western-genre play with Kabuki characters dealing with deaf issues.

The National Theater of the Deaf founded a conference for deaf playwrights in 1977 to train deaf writers in the art of play creation. After five years, the program was discontinued for lack of funds. The conference was revived twice during the 1990's by the Performing Arts Department of the National Technical Institute for the Deaf, which also gave winning scripts professional workshop productions. By 2000, over one hundred scripts were developed by deaf playwrights, many of which have been performed for deaf audiences around the world.

As of early 2002, only hearing playwrights had been successful in bringing commercial plays on deaf themes to production. The first of these was Mark Medoff, a playwright and college educator, whose *Children of a Lesser God* appeared on Broadway in 1980. The play was based on the life of actress Phyllis Frelich and was infused with political issues relevant to deaf individuals. The play ran for two years on Broadway, earning a 1980 Tony Award, and was turned into a successful motion picture version, earning deaf actress Marlee Matlin the Academy Award for best actress in 1986.

DEAF WEST THEATER

A new professional deaf theater was established in 1991 when National Theater of the Deaf alumni Edward Waterstreet and his wife, Linda Bove, moved to California and opened Deaf West Theater in North Hollywood. Waterstreet starred in the National Broadcasting Company Hallmark movie *Love Is Never Silent* (1985), and Bove became arguably the most recognized deaf actor in the United States, hav-

ing spent nearly two decades as a permanent resident on *Sesame Street*. Using grants provided by the U.S. Department of Education, Deaf West Theater produces three plays annually in its own theater. The Deaf West Theater Children's Theater provides twelve-week workshops in elementary schools and regular ASL storytelling workshops. The Deaf West Theater Performing Arts Center for Deaf and Hard of Hearing Artists sponsors a four-week summer school taught by working professionals.

THE FUTURE OF DEAF THEATER

Competition in the performing arts has always been formidable, even for talented individuals with no obstacle greater than chance. However, for deaf theater artists, doors that were once closed have opened wide. There are ever increasing opportunities because of university degrees and professional training programs for deaf artists. Many of the communication barriers that once existed have been eliminated by telecommunication devices for the deaf: the Internet, e-mail, palm pilots, and computer conferencing. Freelance deaf artists are earning a living in all aspects of the professional and academic theater.

The time may also be ripe for successful commercial productions by deaf artists, on deaf themes, for the deaf audience. The proliferation of inexpensive video and digital recording equipment has led to the establishment of a new literary genre. The literature of American Sign Language, including stories, poetry, and plays, created in sign language and stored as performance media rather than print media, is a viable outlet for deaf theater. Publication companies, such as DawnSignPress in San Diego, California, market home videos and DVDs (digital video disks) to the deaf market. Deaf theater has been established not only as a method of presentation but also as a literary art form of a unique culture. It will continue to grow in popularity and influence until it is no longer possible to say there has never been a commercial production on a deaf theme by deaf artists.

BIBLIOGRAPHY

Baldwin, Stephen C. *Pictures in the Air: The Story of the National Theater of the Deaf*. Washington,

D.C.: Gallaudet University Press, 1993. This is the most complete history of deaf theater in America. It also describes the National Theater of the Deaf's unique style of sign language and provides a listing of all of its productions, company listings, and a bibliography of plays by deaf playwrights.

Bragg, Bernard. *Lessons in Laughter: The Autobiography of a Deaf Actor.* As signed to Eugene Bergman. Washington, D.C.: Gallaudet University Press, 1989. An anecdotal memoir by an actor who was involved in all aspects of deaf theater.

Conley, Willy. "From Lip-reading Ants to Flying over the Cuckoo Nests." *American Theater* 18, no. 4 (April, 2001): 34-37, 60-61. Updates deaf theater history and describes the state of professional theater opportunities for deaf actors in the new millennium.

Stratton, Jean. "The 'eye-music' of deaf actors fills stage eloquently." *Smithsonian* 6, no. 12 (March, 1976): 67-72. Provides a brief history of the origins of the National Theater of the Deaf and an examination of its production of *Parade.*

Gerald S. Argetsinger

EXPERIMENTAL THEATER

"Experimental theater" is an often-used term that has a variety of possible definitions. In a broad sense, every great artist is essentially an experimenter; in this sense, the plays of dramatists such as T. S. Eliot, Eugene O'Neill, and Tennessee Williams were demonstrably experimental. Clearly, this is not the sense of the term as it has come to be used to describe a kind of theater that has developed in the United States and in Europe from the 1960's to the present and by the early twenty-first century, had made its way onto the stages of the world. In this specialized sense, "experimental theater" seems to suggest a willingness, within a theater environment, to militate aggressively against social and aesthetic conventions.

The proximate cause for protest—the one most ardently espoused—by theater artists in the United States in the 1960's was a political and social one, the escalation of the war in Vietnam. Other targets of protest were racism, sexism, oppression of the disadvantaged, and bureaucratic intransigence. A popular means of expressing this protest was shock tactics, in the streets and on campuses, often involving personal insult or property destruction. On the stage, shock was effectively achieved through the use of unconventional theatrical techniques. Directors and writers often abandoned or directly attacked traditional aesthetic standards, looking for untried means of expression in staging and in writing, enabling audiences to reassess their own experience in fresh, illuminating perspectives.

Although the motivating causes may have shifted since the 1960's, the essential principles of experimental theater remain relatively unchanged: Robert Wilson's production of *the CIVIL warS* in 1984 qualified as "experimental theater" at least as validly as did Megan Terry's *Viet Rock* in 1966. So did Tadashi Suzuki's November, 2001, production of his *Dionysus* (pr. 1991) at the Zellerbach Playhouse in Berkeley, California. With its reinterpretation of Euripides' material, which Suzuki turned into a conflict between a religious cult and political authority, and with its

acting style close to the ideals of performance art, his production dramatically emphasized the concerns raised by the September 11, 2001, attacks on the United States.

THE UNITED STATES

The history of American experimental theater is conventionally dated from 1958, the year that Joseph Cino opened his coffeehouse in New York City, Caffé Cino. Begun mainly as a haven for artists and offering exhibits, poetry readings, and a café menu for its growing clientele, Caffé Cino soon expanded its fare to include, first, play readings and then productions of complete plays, evolving into a regularly operating theater. Perhaps its most enduring contribution to the development of experimental theater in New York was its influence: Other companies began to emerge following the Caffé Cino example (notable among them Ellen Stewart's Café La Mama).

Thus was Off-Off-Broadway born, reflecting some of the features of what had been called Off-Broadway (equity waiver, small house, low budget) theater, but containing one relatively new element: the will to experiment, to break rules—both aesthetic and, often, social. Small companies proliferated during the 1960's and 1970's, many achieving little more than the thrill of the ephemeral moment of artistic freedom (sometimes all that was desired), but a few achieving fame (desired or not). To this liberated milieu were attracted a new wave of writers whose work has left an enduring stamp on the American experimental theater: Jack Gelber, Rochelle Owens, Ed Bullins, Leonard Melfi, Adrienne Kennedy, and the brilliantly prolific Sam Shepard. The work of others, such as Arthur Kopit, Lanford Wilson, and Amiri Baraka, has also continued to nourish the growth of this theater. Still others, though perhaps less widely known, have been integrally involved in the development of experimental theater, both in the United States and abroad; it is these latter writers whose work will be discussed.

THE LIVING THEATRE

In 1959, a watershed event occurred: the production of Jack Gelber's *The Connection* by the Living Theatre of Julian Beck and Judith Malina. The history of the Living Theatre actually begins in 1951, when Beck and Malina, recently married, began theater productions in their New York City apartment. The couple soon moved into the Cherry Lane Theatre but were forced out because of fire-law violations. In 1954, they relocated to a rented loft. Forced out again in 1956 because of safety violations, they eventually reopened in a building of their own at the corner of Fourteenth Street and Avenue of the Americas.

One of their most significant offerings was Gelber's *The Connection*, a production that set important precedents for the emerging experimental theater movement in at least two respects. First, it dealt in a free and forthright manner with the still somewhat taboo subject of drug addiction. Second, it challenged the barriers that separate actors-characters from audience in conventional theater environments. It is not that the methods that Gelber and Beck and Malina used to accomplish this effect were new—their antecedents could be found in Antonin Artaud, Luigi Pirandello, Bertolt Brecht, and others. The particular distinction of *The Connection* was, rather, its ability to bring some of these unconventional techniques together in an especially forceful and memorable fashion, at a time that was marked by growing restlessness both within the theater community and in American society at large.

As *The Connection*'s audience entered the theater, they encountered an uncurtained stage—something relatively unknown at the time—with actors sprawled about in assorted postures (one sleeping on a bed, one slumped over a table). As the audience would soon discover, these were junkies waiting for their "connection"—the fix to be brought by their pusher, Cowboy. Others, musicians in this jazz play, were dozing in their places, also waiting for Cowboy. After the audience was seated, two men came down the aisle and jumped onto the stage: Jim, a film producer, and Jaybird, a writer. Jim explained that they were doing a documentary on narcotic addiction and that they had assembled the junkies for this purpose, with the

bait of the fix. This was, then, a play-within-a-play, and the audiences were often completely taken in by the realism of the conversations of the addicts, who later would mingle with them, at intermission, looking for handouts. It was this altering of the traditional actor-audience relationship—the blurring of the distinctions between actor-character and viewer, and the effective expansion of the stage environment to include spectators as participants—that became the Living Theatre's trademark and would powerfully influence the development of experimental theater not only in the United States but also in Europe.

Beck and Malina took their repertoire—William Carlos Williams's *Many Loves* (pr. 1959), Brecht's *In the Jungle of Cities* (pr. 1960), and *The Connection*—on a successful tour of six cities in France, Germany, and Italy that would prepare the way for their later years of expatriate work in Europe. After one more New York success, Kenneth Brown's *The Brig* (pr. 1963), Beck and Malina's chronic financial difficulties became overwhelming. The theater was ordered closed, and the couple was arrested and imprisoned (Beck for sixty days, Malina for thirty) for unauthorized use of the theater and for failure to pay taxes.

The European odyssey followed: four years in twelve countries, the performances reflecting continually changing ideas and techniques (*Mysteries and Smaller Pieces*, pr. 1964, and *Frankenstein*, pr. 1965, both developed by the company collectively, and Brecht's *Antigone*, pr. 1967, which focused on the actor as actor, rather than as character). These new dimensions, and Beck and Malina's ever-present anarchist disposition, were evident in the eight-section *Paradise Now* (pr. 1968), a "rite of guerrilla theatre" ending in "permanent revolution," first produced in Avignon, then, that same year, back in the United States. More arrests followed, more financial problems, but also a successful tour of American cities and universities, another visit to Europe (in 1970), then thirteen months in Brazil (ending in arrest). Among later productions, in the United States and Europe, were *The Legacy of Cain* cycle (pr. 1975), *The Money Tower* (pr. 1975), and *Prometheus* (pr. 1978). The Living Theatre continued its zealous campaign of revolution in traditional theaters as well as in street performances, but was often on the move, with brief stays in American cities (Pittsburgh, 1974 to 1975) and longer ones in Europe. In 1984, from their base in Paris, Beck and Malina brought four plays— *The Yellow Methuselah* (pr. 1984), *The Archaeology of Sleep* (pr. 1984), Ernst Toller's *The One and the Many* (pr. 1984), and *Frankenstein*—to New York. The critics were disappointed, noting with regret that Beck and Malina's group—now made up mainly of European actors—had not adequately adjusted to the changing needs of changing times.

After the death of Beck in 1985, the Living Theatre continued operations under the direction of Malina and the new codirector Hanon Reznikov. It moved into a permanent location on Third Street in Manhattan. When authorities closed down this space in 1992, the company continued its travels between Europe and America. In 1999, the Italian town of Rocchetta Ligure built a theater for the company, where it held workshops and performed plays, in addition to its busy touring schedule. Ideologically committed to a hard leftist line, the productions after 1985 have fascinated European as well as American critics and audiences. *Utopia* (pr. 1995) projected its message of a new world through the means of dance theater and tried to animate the spoken word to the rhythm of songs. *Capital Changes* (pr. 2002) featured thirteen characters, played by a cast of Europeans and Americans, who live through four hundred years of human history, as the world evolves into the capitalist system.

ELLEN STEWART AND LA MAMA

Ellen Stewart founded Café La Mama in 1960, partially influenced by her interest in the Caffé Cino operation. Like Cino, a former dancer, Stewart had no experience in theater production. With her background in retail clothing and fashion design, she opened a boutique in New York. From the boutique, Stewart ("La Mama" to some of her friends) began working with writer Paul Foster to produce plays, and Café La Mama came into existence (licensed as a café to accommodate city codes). Like Beck and Malina, Stewart was plagued by city officials and was forced to change the location of her theater a number

of times. Like the Living Theatre, Café La Mama went to Europe (under Tom O'Horgan's direction) and returned highly acclaimed. Back in New York, Café La Mama's production of Rochelle Owens's *Futz* (pr. 1965) received Obie Awards. Stewart took *Futz* and Paul Foster's *Tom Paine* (pr. 1968) on a second trip to Europe and returned with more raves. Suddenly Owens, Foster, O'Horgan, and Stewart were established figures in New York theater.

Throughout this period of its growth, Stewart dedicated her time and energy exclusively to the enterprise, which was sometimes barely existing. She performed every task from making soup and washing floors to selecting the plays for production and introducing each performance. She was completely in charge. The company continued to grow and to change and to move. In 1969, operating from a complex of two theaters, it became La Mama ETC (Experimental Theatre Club). As one of the most consistently prolific of the experimental companies, La Mama continues to wield an extraordinary influence. Playwrights whose plays have been produced at La Mama include—besides Owens, O'Horgan, and Foster—Tom Eyen, Megan Terry, Maria Irene Fornes, Leonard Melfi, Israel Horovitz, Lanford Wilson, and Sam Shepard. La Mama groups sprang up in other cities in the United States and in more than a dozen cities all over the world.

At the beginning of the twenty-first century, La Mama had become a vital New York City dramatic institution. It developed into an influential arts complex that houses three theater stages, a seven-story rehearsal studio and archive building, and an art gallery. For its creative, experimental work, which has consistently nourished the development of new, cutting-edge theatrical talent, La Mama has received more than thirty Obie Awards, as well as numerous Drama Desk, Bessie, and Villager Awards. In its more than forty years of existence, many American as well as international playwrights, artists, and theater troupes have worked at La Mama. Because Stewart has been a meticulous keeper of records of every production launched at La Mama; the archives are a treasure trove for any student or historian of the Off-Off-Broadway movement. In 1986, using the proceeds won from her MacArthur Foundation award, she founded La Mama Umbria, an international artists' retreat housed in a centuries-old former convent in Spoleto, Italy.

JOSEPH CHAIKIN

Joseph Chaikin began appearing in roles at the Living Theatre in 1959. He acted in *The Connection* during the first European tour and performed the role of Galy Gay in Brecht's *Mann ist Mann* (pr. 1926; *A Man's a Man*, 1961) on their return. In 1963, he left Beck and Malina and founded his Open Theatre. The main focus of Chaikin's work has been on the actor, not the character—what Chaikin called "presence." The performance itself concentrated on the "inside"—the interior of the person and the situation, a kind of subtext distinguished from the "outside" illusion of conventional theater. Chaikin's actors are required to work on "inside-outside" techniques, moving, for example, back and forth from nonverbal to verbal contexts.

The main productions of the Open Theatre were generated through workshops featuring such techniques—collectively developed performances to which the writer contributed but did not dominate. Terry's *Viet Rock* was developed in Open Theatre workshops, though it was presented in 1966 at Café La Mama. Other major productions were Jean-Claude van Itallie's *The Serpent* (pr. 1967); *Terminal* (pr. 1969), with a text written by Susan Yankowitz; and *The Mutation Show* (pr. 1971), written by Chaikin and Roberta Sklar. The Open Theatre toured extensively both in the United States and in Europe before closing in 1973.

Chaikin's techniques—actor-focused performance, collective workshop creation, and "transformations" (actors shifting into and out of roles)—grew out of early influences, such as Konstantin Stanislavsky, Brecht, and Artaud, as well as contacts with Jerzy Grotowski, Peter Brook, the Living Theatre, and interaction with his own actors. The Open Theatre, in turn, profoundly influenced the development of experimental theater during its years of operation and its influence has continued in acting workshops throughout the United States and Europe. Chaikin

himself, after recovering from a serious illness, has continued acting and directing in some relatively conventional productions. He coauthored (with Shepard) two experimental pieces, produced as *Tongues and Savage/Love* (pr. 1979) and collaborated (with former Open Theatre members and others) on productions for the Winter Project, such as *Tourists and Refugees* (pr. 1980-1981) and *Trespassing* (pr. 1982), performed at La Mama ETC.

In 1984, open-heart surgery left Chaikin in a temporary state of aphasia, or unable to use or understand common words. Recovering, he wrote many plays about his experience, often in collaboration with other playwrights, such as *The War in Heaven* (pr. 1984, with Shepard) and *Struck Dumb* (pr. 1988, with Jean-Claude van Itallie). In the 1980's and 1990's, Chaiken was active as director on international stages and gave workshops and seminars on a global scale, including the Middle East and post-apartheid South Africa. His productions, even though they tend to have become less experimental, continue to thrive on Chaikin's performance theories developed with the Open Theatre.

His play *When the World Was Green* (pr. 1996, with Shepard) premiered at the 1996 Summer Olympics in Atlanta, Georgia, and successfully toured Russia and Singapore in 1998. A lyrical tale of regret and memory, the play features only two characters, an old chef who has poisoned a man he believed was his hated cousin, and a reporter interviewing the chef in prison. The play features the poetic, nonlinear, and elliptic style characteristic of Chaikin's earlier work, and the dramatic work required of the two sole performers is substantial. By 2002, Chaikin had received several Obie Awards and two Guggenheim Fellowships. His influence on experimental theater in America has been decisive.

THE PERFORMANCE GROUP

Richard Schechner formed the Performance Group in 1967 at what he called the Performing Garage on Wooster Street in Manhattan. Schechner, a university professor, had moved from Louisiana, where he had been involved with a theater group and had edited the *Tulane Drama Review*, which also moved to New

York, becoming *The Drama Review*. Like Chaikin, Schechner had been influenced by Grotowski's laboratory methods. Another main Schechner interest was environmental theater, a chief dictum of which was that "all the space is used for performance; all the space is used for audience." His *Dionysus in '69* (pr. 1968; based on Euripides' *Bakchai*, 405 B.C.E.; *The Bacchae*, 1781) epitomized Schechner's Performance Group doctrines. Developed in rigorous workshop sessions, *Dionysus in '69* was language-transcending ritual theater in which the audience was encouraged to participate—chanting, dancing, or disrobing when the actors did. The "environment" consisted of three- to five-level scaffolding around an irregular central space. Audiences climbed the scaffolding or sat on the floor. Actors moved in and out of character, sometimes speaking and acting on their own, as themselves. *Dionysus in '69* was followed by *Makbeth* (pr. 1969), *Commune* (pr. 1970), and a variety of other works, including some by outside writers, such as Shepard's *The Tooth of Crime* (pr. 1972), Ted Hughes's adaptation of *Seneca's Oedipus* (pb. 1968), and Jean Genet's *The Balcony* (pr. 1979).

After Schechner left the group in 1980, it continued, quite actively and prominently, as the Wooster Group, directed by Elizabeth LeCompte and including some of the former Performance Group actors, notably Spalding Gray. Under LeCompte, the Wooster Group came to be identified with experimental plays that straddle the boundaries of traditional theater and other media. The use of film, video, and electronic sound has been a trademark of LeCompte's productions of the early twenty-first century.

INFLUENTIAL REGIONAL COMPANIES

Many other companies were noteworthy in the development of American experimental theater. The San Francisco Mime Troupe, begun in 1959, has continued to generate excitement with its abrasively original work. Quick to point out that its title does not refer to pantomime but a "miming," or satirizing, of the powerful in society, the company has become internationally known for its free street theater and, in 1987, won the Regional Theatre Tony Award. In the 1990's and early 2000's, the San Francisco Mime Troupe has

continued to produce its experimental branch of political theater and live music. It has reaped community awards for its Youth Theater Project, which seeks to involve troubled inner-city children in production and performance of new plays arising out of the circumstances of their lives.

Committed to visuals and non-narrative theater, Peter Schumann formed the Bread and Puppet Theatre in 1961, sharing bread with his audiences and using large sculptured bodies in his productions, which were frequently conducted outdoors, in streets, or fields. The company dissolved in 1974 but continued to reunite for periodic specific projects (*A Monument for Ishi* in 1975, *Ave Maris Stella* in 1978) and an annual one, *The Demonstration Resurrection Circus* (pr. 1974), at Schumann's Vermont farm. In 1993, Schumann built a stage for winter festivals on his farm and moved into the direction of antiglobalization protests. His self-chosen enemies include the World Bank and the International Monetary Fund (IMF), and his play *Mr. Budhoo's Letter of Resignation from the IMF* (pr. 1995) is directed against these organizations.

A collective originally formed by Lee Breuer, Ruth Maleczech, and JoAnne Akalaitis in San Francisco in the 1960's toured Europe until 1969, when it settled in New York, calling itself Mabou Mines (after a Nova Scotia mining town) and pioneering a variety of mixed-genre works; Mabou Mines quickly became a major force in New York avant-garde theater. By 2002, it was led by a five-person artistic directorate and committed to the production of new, creative theater pieces and the staging of the classics from a fresh, sustained perspective. Mabou Mines is also dedicated to performance art and fusion theater. Its gender-reversed *King Lear* (pr. 1990) was as successful as Frederick Newmann's multimedia *Reel to Real* (pr. 1994) or Breuer's *Ecco Porco* (pr. 2000), where a pig travels through Dante's purgatory.

Other early influential companies were the Judson Poets Theatre (JPT), founded at the Judson Memorial Church in New York by the Reverend Al Carmines in 1961 and existing until 1981. In the late 1970's, the JPT shocked its audience with radical performance art such as when Nam June Paik drew blood from his arms with a razor as he was accompanied on the cello by Charlotte Moorman, who played bare breasted. Among other companies active in the 1960's and 1970's were the Firehouse Theatre, begun in Minneapolis in 1963 and moved to San Francisco in 1969; Theatre Genesis, formed by Ralph Cook in 1964; The American Place Theatre, also formed in 1964, by Wynn Handman; the Play-House of the Ridiculous, founded by John Vaccaro in 1966; and Charles Ludlam's spinoff, the Ridiculous Theatrical Company. In 1967, the OM-Theatre Workshop was developed by a group at a Boston church. Richard Foreman began his Ontological-Hysteric Theatre in 1968, and Robert Wilson established his Byrd Hoffman Foundation in 1969. The Squat Theatre, originally formed in Budapest in 1969, arrived at New York's Twenty-third Street in 1977. Among other groups outside New York were the Iowa Theatre Lab, the Omaha Magic Theatre, the Empty Space Theatre in Seattle, and the Changing Scene in Denver.

In addition to the San Francisco Mime Troupe, a number of other important groups have developed in California. Laura Farabaugh and Christopher Hardman founded the Snake Theatre in 1972, working with "found space"; it divided into two companies in 1980: Farabaugh's Night-fire and Hardman's Antenna Theatre. Driven by its mission to involve the audience and to combine a variety of artistic disciplines and new technologies in their productions, the Antenna has incorporated infrared-transmitted sound, holographic slides, and interactive video in plays at their theater in Sausalito, north of San Francisco.

A major California theater for decades has been El Teatro Campesino, begun by Luis Miguel Valdez in 1965, in connection with the United Farm Workers' movement of César Chávez. By 1971, El Teatro Campesino had established itself as an authentic theater giving voice to a somewhat militant Latino experience and moved into permanent quarters at rural San Juan Bautista in central California. It opened its workshop and playhouse in 1981 with an acclaimed production of Valdez's musical *Corridos: Tales of Passion and Revolution* (pr. 1981). Every Christmas, the company stages a classic Spanish play about the holiday season and every year, it produces a new play

in the cycle of *The Miracle, Mystery, and Historical Cycle of San Juan Bautista* (begun 1975).

The Padua Hills Playwrights' Workshop/Festival was formed by Murray Mednick in La Verne, California, in 1978. Like the Snake Theatre, it made liberal use of "found" environments. Padua Hills moved to the California Institute of the Arts in Valencia in 1984. Other important California theaters have been the Magic Theatre in San Francisco and the Odyssey Theatre, the East-West Players, the Los Angeles Actors' Theatre, and the collective Provisional Theatre in Los Angeles. Indicative of the trend to stage drama in the most unlikely of new and provocative locations, in 1994, at Stanford University in Palo Alto, a student drama group staged a controversial version of Peter Weiss's play *Marat Sade* (1964) in one of the men's restrooms on campus. Spectators were led into the lavatory, which had been remodeled to resemble an insane asylum of the late 1700's, and sat on the stairs leading to the cages on the floor where one actor and two actresses performed entirely in the nude.

AMERICAN THEATER IN THE 1990'S

The proliferation of small companies on both coasts and across the United States notwithstanding, the need for social protest and the new, sometimes shocking techniques with which to express that protest dwindled by the early 1990's. In their place occurred a consolidation of sorts that is symbolized in the move, for example, of Akalaitis from the Off-Off-Broadway Mabou Mines to the Off-Broadway Public Theatre. In 1992, when Joseph Papp, founder and guide of the Public Theatre for many years, died, Akalaitis took over the leadership of the theater, but under her direction the theater lacked the energy and creativity that characterized it at the height of the Papp years. In fact, the play *The Sisters Rosensweig* (pr. 1992), by a feminist protégée of the Public Theatre, Wendy Wasserstein, was performed in 1993 in the more comfortable, uptown Mitzi E. Newhouse Theater at Lincoln Center in a fairly traditional and highly successful production.

Off-Off-Broadway groups continued to produce plays, but a quick run-through of their offerings in the 1990's reveals more classical than new dramas in their repertoire, with companies such as the Play-House of the Ridiculous remaining static with productions similar to those of the early days. Theatre Row on Forty-second Street—more than a half dozen tiny theaters, including Playwrights Horizons—continued to accommodate inexpensive productions of risky plays by new playwrights.

The Roundabout Theater went one step further in its move from a downtown New York City location to the Criterion Theater in the heart of the Broadway district, its production of *Anna Christie* in 1992 giving new life to an old play that even its author, Eugene O'Neill, did not consider important. Actor Tony Randall, feeling the need for a national theater for the classics, in 1991 opened the National Theater, its declared purpose to produce the classics—American as well as European. On the West Coast, the Mark Taper Forum, the La Jolla Playhouse, and the South Coast Repertory Theater function similarly in their "Off-Broadway" capacities—as do the Goodman Theater of Chicago, the Actors' Theater of Louisville, and the Seattle Repertory.

Consolidation of the traditional and the innovative is the modus operandum of the experimenters in the 1990's, as writers take advantage of the new without sacrificing the traditional. These playwrights, such as Larry Kramer, Wasserstein, August Wilson, and Tony Kushner, are to be found mostly in Off-Broadway houses and regional theaters. Ironically, what are perhaps the most influential American plays of the 1990's, Kushner's 1991 production of *Angels in America: A Gay Fantasia on National Themes* (*Part One: Millennium Approaches*) and its 1992 follow-up, *Angels in America: A Gay Fantasia on National Themes* (*Part Two: Perestroika*), both of which dealt with the acquired immunodeficiency syndrome (AIDS) crisis and homosexuality, would not have become Broadway hits even a decade earlier. Their success shows how deeply experimental theater has influenced the mainstream. By the new millennium, even that most commercial of theatrical venues, the Broadway theater, had incorporated many of the methods, styles, themes, and subjects that had originated in the alternative, experimental scene of American theater.

PLAYWRIGHTS

Jean-Claude van Itallie, Belgian-born, arrived in the United States in 1940. His first play, *War*, which had opened in 1963, was given a production in March of 1965 at the Caffé Cino. In April, *America Hurrah!* (the *Motel* sequence) was performed at Café La Mama. *War* had introduced some of the techniques that would characterize van Itallie's work: symbolic action, expressionistic mixing of visuals and dialogue, an emphasis on highly stylized antirealism. *Motel*, which would later be combined with *Interview* (pr. 1966) and *TV* (pr. 1966) to complete the *America Hurrah!* trilogy, remained, in the view of many, the play with which van Itallie would be most readily identified. With its exaggerated doll figures (designed by Robert Wilson) and its absurd counterpointing of violent behavior within cliché situation, it soon became a symbol of the avant-garde view of the American mid-1960's.

In *Motel*, while the voice of the Motel-Keeper carries on a rambling monologue of trivial patter, the Man and Woman (also doll figures) come into the room. As the Man begins his violent antics, jumping on the mattress, the Woman throws her clothes out from the bathroom, then reenters the room naked, marking her body with lipstick and blotting it on the walls. The Man and Woman eventually destroy everything in the room, drowning out the Motel-Keeper's voice, which has been droning on, oblivious to the violence. The play ends with the Man and Woman tearing off the Motel-Keeper's head and walking out via the theater aisle.

Most of van Itallie's subsequent work was done with Chaikin's Open Theatre: *I'm Really There, Almost Like Being, The Dream, The Hunter and the Bird*, all in 1966, and *The Serpent* in 1967-1968. In *The Serpent*, van Itallie had worked collectively with Chaikin and his group. In their workshop sessions, the actors had been considering doing episodes from the Bible book of Genesis. Van Itallie combined these ideas with others (sequences depicting the assassinations of President John F. Kennedy and Martin Luther King, Jr.) and developed them into a working script, with spaces to permit improvisation. Using the Adam and Eve/Cain and Abel archetypes, the performance included the audience, with the actors portraying the serpent, offering audience members bites from their apples so that the audience might share the sense of lost innocence. Van Itallie has continued his experiments in *Take a Deep Breath* (pr. 1969), *Photographs: Mary and Howard* (pr. 1969), *Eat Cake* (pr. 1971), *Mystery Play* (pr. 1973), *Nightwalk* (an Open Theatre collaboration with Terry and Shepard, pr. 1973), *The Sea Gull* (a 1973 adaptation of Anton Chekhov's play), *A Fable* (pr. 1975), and *The King of the United States* (pr. 1973), among others. *America Hurrah!* and *The Serpent* have remained his most influential works.

In the 1980's, van Itallie focused on experimental adaptations of Chekhov's plays while continuing to write new drama of his own. His interest in Tibetan Buddhism, a religion to which he eventually converted, is reflected in his *The Tibetan Book of the Dead: Or, How Not to Do It Again* (pr. 1983). His play *Ancient Boys* (pr. 1989), which premiered at the La Mama Annex, failed to live up to the standards of van Itallie and his critics. Intended as a deep-cutting probe of the effects of AIDS, the decision to have the friends of Ruben, an artist who just died of the disease, come to relive his life in a series of flashbacks while gathered at his artist's studio reminded too many critics of conventional family drama.

Van Itallie fared better with *Struck Dumb* (pr. 1991), his collaborate work with Chaikin that deals with the latter playwright's temporary aphasia. The play has been hailed for its sophisticated analysis of the role of language use in maintaining human identity. Van Itallie's adaptation of Mikhail Bulgakov's novel *Master i Margarita* (1940) for the Theatre for the New City in New York in 1993 represented a return to van Itallie's occupation with biblical themes mixed with contemporary and personal allusions that he had launched in *The Serpent*. All van Itallie's papers chronicling his experimental work have been collected at Kent State University, from which he received an honorary doctoral degree.

In May, 1966, a year after its production of the *Motel* sequence of *America Hurrah!*, Café La Mama produced another landmark work, Megan Terry's *Viet Rock*. Although presented at Café La Mama, *Viet Rock* was developed, much like *The Serpent*, in work-

shop sessions at Chaikin's Open Theatre. In their characteristic manner, Chaikin's actors developed material improvisationally, which was then finished as script by Terry. Chaikin's and Terry's shared interest in "transformations" was evident throughout this work. Actors moved freely from one character to another, assuming rapidly changing moods and outlooks to fit the roles and sometimes even becoming inanimate objects. In this rock opera (contemporary with the 1968 *Hair*), the actors entered to the music of "The Viet Rock." They became, first, infants crying, then children playing war games, then mothers and their drafted, Vietnam-bound sons, the mothers becoming an airplane carrying their sons off to war. Terry and Chaikin ended the performance with a "celebration of presence," the actors moving into the audience in what was becoming a typical gesture of communal touching, dissolving the barrier separating actors from audience.

Other of Terry's plays have been equally inventive, if ultimately less influential. *Keep Tightly Closed in a Cool Dry Place* (pr. 1965), her earlier experiment with transformations, was followed by *Comings and Goings* (pr. 1966). *The Gloaming, Oh My Darling* (pr. 1966) was an experiment with absurdism and feminist statement; *Sanibel and Captiva* (pr. 1968) was another absurdist effort, and *Approaching Simone* (pr. 1970) another feminist one, a historical portrait of Simone Weil. *The Tommy Allen Show* (pr. 1969) was social satire and television parody; *Hothouse* (pr. 1974) was a relatively conventional melodrama; *American King's English for Queens* (pr. 1978) and *Brazil Fado* (a 1977 musical) returned to the transformational style. Both of the latter plays were performed at the Omaha Magic Theatre, which Terry had joined in 1971.

At the Omaha Magic Theatre, Terry has written more than sixty plays reflecting ongoing social, political, and sexual issues. *Walking Through Walls* (pr. 1987, with Jo Ann Schmidman) focused on ecology and envisioned a humanity at peace with its planet. *Sound Fields: Are We Hear* (pr. 1992, with Schmidman and Sora Kimberlain) experimented with captured sound that reflected the sonic fabric of human habitations; this play reflects how much Terry has moved away from her earlier work with revolutionary lyrics. *Star Path Moon Stop* (pr. 1995) further combined Terry's feminist and ecological concerns.

Maria Irene Fornes is a Cuban who moved to the United States in 1945. Two of her early works, *Promenade* and *The Successful Life of Three*, opened in the same year, 1965—*Promenade* at the Judson Poets Theatre and *The Successful Life of Three* at the Open Theatre. *Promenade*, with music by Judson's Carmines, is a subtle, complicated satire depicting the adventures of two escaped prisoners, 105 and 106, whose elemental innocence remains untarnished throughout their bizarre travels. The play's mood is broadly comic and whimsically absurd by turns, its style partly lyric expressionism, partly popular entertainment. *The Successful Life of Three*, an altogether different vehicle with its constant shifts of character and situation, allowed the Open Theatre actors the opportunity of making extensive use of their "transformations" techniques. *Fefu and Her Friends* (pr. 1977), a feminist (all-women) excursion, requires for performance a series of different rooms, with the audience separated into four groups moving from room to room in order to follow the action.

Another multilocation play, *No Time* (pr. 1984), was performed by the California Padua Hills group in Valencia, on a roof patio at the California Institute of the Arts and in rolling fields below. The action of this play blends lyric dialogue and violence in a Latin American setting of romantic love and political intrigue. Other Fornes plays include *Tango Palace* (pr. 1964), *Aurora* (pr. 1974, anticipating the simultaneous scenes of *Fefu*), *A Vietnamese Wedding* (pr. 1967), and *Molly's Dream* (pr. 1968). By 2002, Fornes had won ten Obie Awards for her Off-Broadway plays. Her *Terra Incognita* (pr. 1992) and *Enter the Night* (pr. 1993) were hailed for Fornes's never-ending experimentation with form and her refusal to shift her style to accommodate current theatrical fashions. At the core of her work is a quest for wisdom and a desire for graciously gained insights.

THE FORMALISTS

Representing another side of experimental theater were the formalists—writers such as Robert Wilson,

Alan Finneran, and structuralist Michael Kirby. These were often artists of the minimalist and postmodernist schools who strove to free their subjects from all traditional, received content and styles, reducing them to their elementary forms. Of those working in theater, many came from other artistic disciplines (Wilson was originally a painter, Finneran a painter-sculptor, Kirby a sculptor).

Wilson's Byrd Hoffman School of Byrds, many of whose members were physically disabled, provided a rich environment for this work. By giving his performers freedom of interpretation, he was able to explore new and unexpected perspectives. Although most of his work since founding the Byrd Hoffman School in 1969 has been done by professionals, he has retained these perspectives in productions such as *Deafman Glance* (pr. 1970), which, with its prologue, *The Life and Times of Joseph Stalin* (pr. 1973), has a playing time of twelve hours. Wilson's *Ka Mountain*, performed at the Shiraz Festival in Iran in 1972, requires seven days and nights. *A Letter for Queen Victoria* followed in 1974, and *Einstein on the Beach*, perhaps Wilson's best-known work, followed in 1976.

Philip Glass composed the music for *Einstein on the Beach*, and Andrew de Groat and Wilson's longtime associate Lucinda Childs choreographed it. This work exemplifies many of Wilson's formalist techniques—the stressed slow motion by means of which Wilson hopes to engage the audience's "interior screen," the random language patterns, the repetition of movements and sounds. It consists of nine major sections connected by short "knee plays" (connecting sequences). The work touches the life and ideas of Albert Einstein indirectly, mainly through images suggesting the relationship between time and space. Other Wilson compositions include his two-person (Wilson and Childs) *I Was Sitting on My Patio This Guy Appeared I Thought I Was Hallucinating* in 1977 and *the CIVIL warS*, planned for the Los Angeles Olympic Arts Festival but aborted for lack of funding, although it has since been finished, and segments have been produced in various parts of the world, including a 1985 performance in Boston.

In the 1980's, Wilson produced most of his work in Europe. His *The Black Rider: The Casting of the*

Magic Bullets (pr. 1990) premiered in Hamburg, Germany, and the Brooklyn Academy of Music, and indicated Wilson's strong interest in musical collaboration, this time with songwriter Tom Waits. In the 1990's, Wilson experimented with operas and plays adapted from classical sources, and a grant from the Pew Charitable Trusts created an American home for Wilson at Houston's Alley Theater. Returning from musicals to dramatic work, Wilson's *Hamlet: A Monologue* (pr. 1995) was lauded for its postmodern deconstruction of William Shakespeare's brooding protagonist.

Boston artist Alan Finneran founded Soon 3 in San Francisco in 1972, as a group to present his "performance landscapes," theatrical renderings of his mobile sculptures. His productions have included *Desire Circus* (pr. 1975), *Black Water Echo* (pr. 1977), *A Wall in Venice/3 Women/Wet Shadows* (pr. 1978), *Tropical Proxy* (pr. 1979), *The Man in the Nile at Night* (pr. 1980), and *Renaissance Radar* (pr. 1980). In each of these, mobile sculptures have dominated the sets, with people moving through silent "tasks" against a background of music and taped dialogue.

Michael Kirby's structuralism has grown out of his 1975 manifesto. His works focus on structure—objects, scene fragments, unrelated language passages—to enable the audience to respond as nondirectively as possible. In his plays, *Revolutionary Dance* (pr. 1976), *Eight People* (pr. 1975), *Photoanalysis* (pr. 1976), and *Double Gothic* (pr. 1978), he has attempted to accomplish the objective of structural prominence by means of repetition of language, objects, and images. The work of Kirby and other formalists suggests, but is not limited to, the surreal, with echoes of Adolphe Appia, Vsevolod Meyerhold, and the Futurists.

THE TWENTY-FIRST CENTURY

The beneficiaries of experimental fervor (new feminist, gay, and African American dramatists), who in the 1960's would have had a hearing only Off-Off-Broadway, continued to have their works produced in the early twenty-first century in more comfortable Off-Broadway and even Broadway theaters. Since the 1980's, their subject matter has become increasingly accepted by regular theatergoers: for example, Was-

serstein's *The Sisters Rosensweig* with its three middle-aged Jewish sisters; Kramer's *The Destiny of Me* (pr. 1993), which, like his *The Normal Heart* (pr. 1985), sought to turn AIDS into a political issue and was a radical message by one of the founders of the activist gay group ACT UP; August Wilson's *Ma Rainey's Black Bottom* (pr. 1984), *Fences* (pr. 1985), winner of the 1987 Pulitzer Prize in Drama, and *The Piano Lesson* (pr. 1987), which won the Pulitzer Prize in 1990, and his *Seven Guitars* (pr. 1995) and *King Hedley II* (pr. 2001), all of which deal with the African American experience of the twentieth century; and Kushner's *Angels in America* productions (pr. 1991 and 1992), which represent a more magical response to AIDS than Kramer's angry plays, are all representative of plays that earlier would have been confined to the category of experimental theater.

Complementing this mainstream acceptance of the former avant-garde is the early twenty-first century emergence of new themes and concepts among the forerunners of contemporary experimental theater. Radical performance art by artists such as Karen Finley continues to seek to shock audiences and create a distance between the spectators and their comfortable assumptions about the everyday world, and their own bodies in particular. Feminist and gay theater seeks to advance beyond past issues while constantly vigilant for conservative backlash and attempts at censorship.

The use of multimedia technology, especially film, television, and the Internet, continues to influence the work of technically minded experimental theater such as Sausalito's company Antenna. Perhaps one of the most dynamic fields for experimental theater in the United States is the idea of fusion theater, which continues to critically combine elements of non-Western traditions regarding acting, dramatic and storytelling conventions, music, and performance styles with its Western counterparts. Amazing work is done here, for example, on the stages of La Mama or at the Zellerbach Playhouse in Berkeley, among many other avant-garde stages all over the United States. Fusion theater promises to provide artistic stimuli for a global experimental theater for the decades to come.

ENGLAND

In the fall of 1955, Peter Brook was astonishing traditional Shakespeare audiences with his bold version of *Titus Andronicus*, starring Sir Laurence Olivier and Vivien Leigh, at the Shakespeare Memorial Theatre in Stratford. In the same season, Samuel Beckett's *En attendant Godot* (pr. 1953; *Waiting for Godot*, 1954) was being given its London premiere. A few months later, in 1956, George Devine formed the English Stage Company at the Royal Court Theatre. A revolution was under way in English theater, and John Osborne, Harold Pinter, John Arden, Arnold Wesker, Edward Bond, and Tom Stoppard (to name a few of the major writers) began their domination of the stage. Also by 1956, Joan Littlewood's Theatre Workshop, which she had established in the Theatre Royal in London's East End in 1953, had garnered wide recognition as an alternative to mainstream theater, both attracting a working-class audience and developing an art-audience engagement radically different from the existing relationships of London's commercial stage.

New theaters were being erected and new companies continued to emerge in this fresh environment, which would become known as England's Fringe theater. The Belgrade Theatre, built in Coventry in 1958, was the first of many postwar theater buildings that would be constructed over the next ten years. The Chichester Festival Theatre was formed in 1962, and in 1963, Jim Haynes, an American, established the Traverse Theatre Workshop Company in Edinburgh. Haynes managed the Traverse as chairman (of the Theatre Club) and artistic director for the next three years, developing it into what would become an indispensable base for the eventual expansion of Fringe theater in England.

In the autumn of 1963, another American, Charles Marowitz, joined Peter Brook in developing the Theatre of Cruelty group, with the object of applying some of Antonin Artaud's theories and techniques in a series of experimental exercises. The group, comprising twelve actors and sponsored by the Royal Shakespeare Company, spent twelve weeks in rehearsal at the London Academy of Music and Dramatic Arts (LAMDA) Theatre Club, then presented

(in 1964) a five-week program consisting of the premiere of Artaud's three-minute *Spurt of Blood* (pb. 1925), some short "nonsense sketches" by Paul Ableman, a mimed dramatization of an Alain Robbe-Grillet short story, two collages written by Brook, three scenes from Jean Genet's *Les Paravents* (pr. 1961, Berlin) titled *The Screens*, the premiere of John Arden's short play *Ars Longa, Vita Brevis*, and Marowitz's collage *Hamlet* (1966).

In 1965, Jeff Nuttal began The People Show and Roland Muldoon and Claire Burnely formed their agitprop group CAST (Cartoon Archetypal Slogan Theatre). Both companies were to have considerable impact on the later development of London's alternative theater environment.

One of the most popular forms of alternative theater, lunchtime theater, began in 1966 with the founding of Quipu by David Halliwell and David Calderisi at the Arts Theatre Club. This midday phenomenon would foster two essential ingredients of the Fringe movement: low-budget production and an unfettered working environment for the artist.

The year 1967 was a crucial one in the development of London's Fringe; the visit of two important American companies to London galvanized the existing experimental English groups into a major theatrical phenomenon. Chaikin's Open Theatre performed van Itallie's *America Hurrah!* in the Royal Court Theatre in Sloane Square in the summer of 1967, and soon afterward, Stewart's Café La Mama arrived at the Mercury Theatre with Owens's *Futz*. Café La Mama's Tom O'Horgan also directed a brief run of *Tom Paine* at the Vaudeville Theatre in London's West End.

World events in 1967 and 1968 provided an atmosphere in which the flames of the American-inspired counterculture theater could be fanned. The student rioting in France, the turbulence of the Democratic Party's national convention in Chicago, the Soviet invasion of Czechoslovakia, and the continuing conflict in Vietnam all invited protest. The American theater companies had set exciting examples of how this protest might be articulated, and the British Fringe groups responded accordingly.

The flourishing of the Fringe theater movement was later given added impetus by the success of the unprecedented "Come Together" Festival of autumn, 1969. Like American experimental theater, the Fringe developed both through the willingness of producers and companies to present nontraditional performances or provide space for them, and through the innovative work of individual playwrights.

ENGLAND IN THE 1960'S AND 1970'S

Besides those already mentioned (Theatre Workshop, Belgrade Theatre, Chichester Festival Theatre, Traverse Theatre Workshop, People Show, CAST, Quipu, Royal Court, and Mercury Theatre), the main Fringe theaters by 1968 included the Arts Laboratory in Drury Lane, formed by Traverse founder Jim Haynes; Ed Berman's Inter-Action (which would spin off other influential sections such as the lunchtime Ambiance Basement, The Other Company, and the children-oriented Dogg's Troupe); and William Gaskill's Theatre Upstairs at the Royal Court Theatre. David Hare and Tony Bicat (later joined by Howard Brenton, Snoo Wilson, and Trevor Griffiths) began Portable Theatre; Nancy Meckler, also American, founded Freehold; and the Pip Simmons Theatre Group was formed—all in Haynes's Drury Lane. John Fox started The Welfare State in Leeds; performing in a variety of outdoor settings, Fox's Welfare State quickly became one of the strongest influences on theater outside the London area.

These were the major theater groups working in the key year of 1968. Other important theaters providing spaces for these companies from 1968 on were the Roundhouse, the Institute of Contemporary Art (ICA), The Half Moon, The Oval House, The Bush, and The King's Head. Other companies would continue to emerge, such as the Young Vic, 7:84 (7 percent of the population possessed 84 percent of the nation's wealth), and IOU, which had separated from its parent, Welfare State, in 1976.

The most prolific of the London groups were the Portable, Freehold, and Pip Simmons. Portable, as its name implies, designed its productions to allow flexibility, both in format and in playing space. For example, in 1971, Portable was able to put on three productions concurrently at the Edinburgh Festival. Portable also experimented, as had the Traverse ear-

lier, with collaborative productions in which one or more writers, along with other members of the company, would develop a performance script in a workshop environment, combining ideas of everyone involved, actors as well as writers; Brenton's *Hitler Dances* (pr. 1972) had been created in this way by the Traverse Workshop. From an actual incident that he had observed, Brenton suggested the idea of children playing around a bomb site to the Traverse actors. On a tour to Amsterdam's Mickery Theatre, the Traverse group then developed Brenton's concept into workable play elements that Brenton later finished as a script. The final product thus combined Brenton's ideas, such as a projected image of the children resurrecting the body of a German soldier from the bomb crater, with the actors' individual memories of their own wartime experiences in London, and other ideas mutually derived from film and news sources.

In contrast to the Traverse's writer-actors collaboration, the Portable Theatre's workshop plays were the efforts of writers only. The first and most celebrated of these was *Lay By* (pr. 1971). In 1971, during an informal get-together of writers at Gaskill's Royal Court Theatre, David Hare proposed the idea of writing a collaborative play. Trevor Griffiths found a newspaper item concerning a sensational event that had occurred on a motorway lay-by—an act of fellatio involving two women and a truck driver. In all, seven writers participated in the writing of the script, including Brenton and Stephen Poliakoff. Although unified in style, this first joint effort was thematically disjointed, superficial, and luridly sensational, providing no evident justification, aesthetically or otherwise, for its pornographic excesses. Other Portable collaborations, none more noteworthy than *Lay By*, were *England's Ireland* and *Point 101*, both produced in 1972. These early collective efforts, flaws notwithstanding, established a powerful precedent that influenced later group collaborations both in England and the United States.

Meckler's Freedhold, by contrast, used a script by one author only but worked it out communally in a laboratory environment. With her New York La Mama background, Meckler concentrated on expressionistic image statement, partly through the use of mime techniques. Freedhold's *Antigone* (pr. 1969), adapted from Sophocles by Peter Hulton, was galvanized in the intense discipline of Meckler's workshop into a powerful modern combination of feminist statement and antiwar protest. Other productions developed similarly in the Freedhold workshop were Roy Kift's *Mary Mary* and Meckler's own *Genesis*.

The Pip Simmons Theatre Group has been one of the consistently most popular of the Fringe companies. Having started in 1968 with the absurdist material of Jean Tardieu, Simmons soon began developing his own plays and his own style of theater. His *Superman* (pr. 1969), a group creation, was representative of the Simmons style, mixing cartoonlike, fast-paced action, characters reminiscent of cardboard caricatures, flashing strobe-light "framing," vaudeville situations, and rock music. *Superman* echoed American protest, satirizing American society and depicting aspects of the Civil Rights movement, with Superman coming to the rescue of the distressed. *Superman* was followed by *Do It!* (pr. 1971), adapted from Jerry Rubin's book of the same title; *George Jackson Black and White Minstrel Show* (pr. 1972), a powerful racial satire using a minstrel format; and *An Die Musik* (pr. 1975), exploiting—as did *George Jackson Black and White Minstrel Show*—audience voyeurism, but shifting the theme from racial bigotry to the Holocaust.

As in the United States, the focus for protest plays in Great Britain dissipated in the late 1980's, lunchtime theater having almost disappeared, other fringe theaters such as the King's Head (a pub) reviving plays by Noël Coward and the Victorian author of the "well-made" play Harley Granville-Barker, and the new little Almeida Theater in North London reviving in 1993 Harold Pinter's *No Man's Land*, with Pinter himself in one of the two leading roles. The tiny Pit Theater at London's Royal Shakespeare Theater and the Cottesloe at the Royal National have become homes for risky new plays, interestingly, by writers such as American Richard Nelson and Hare, respectively, and Brenton has become a mainstay on the big stages of the prestigious Royal National Theatre.

Playwrights

Howard Brenton's first play, *Ladder of Fools*, was performed while he was a student at Cambridge in 1965. This was a sprawling piece, which Brenton himself has described as "jokeless, joyless." From that point on, however, his work would be marked by tight, spare construction and fast-paced dialogue liberally sprinkled with humor. His next play was a farce titled *Winter Daddikins* (pr. 1965), written after his graduation from Cambridge; *Wesley* (pr. 1970) and *Gargantua* (pr. 1969) were among the plays that followed. In 1969, Brenton wrote his first full-length play, *Revenge* (pr. 1969), exploring what would become, for him, a central situation: the criminal versus the police in a morally blurred environment. *Christie in Love* (pr. 1969), written for the Portable Theatre, epitomizes this theme and demonstrates as well Brenton's technique of mixing the surreal (in his depiction of the social-moral milieu) and the naturalistic (the character of Christie).

Of the many plays he wrote during the next several years (*The Education of Skinny Spew*, pr. 1969; *Scott of the Antarctic*, pr. 1971; *A Sky-Blue Life*, pr. 1966, an adaptation of Shakespeare's *Measure for Measure* [pr. 1604]; and the aforementioned *Hitler Dances*), *Magnificence*, commissioned by Gaskill and performed in 1973 at the Royal Court Theatre, perhaps best reflects the deepening and maturing of Brenton's attitudes. The central character, Jed, personifies what for Brenton are the essential contradictions of modern life—the "magnificence" of extreme, violent social reaction as well as its utter stupidity and futility—and the uncontrollable frustrations that result from them. The urban terrorism of *Magnificence* reappeared in *The Saliva Milkshake* (pr. 1975) and *Weapons of Happiness* (pr. 1976), while its political satire was reprised in *The Churchill Play* (pr. 1974), commissioned by the Nottingham Playhouse. With *Weapons of Happiness*, presented in the new Lyttleton auditorium of the National Theatre, the seemingly inevitable blending of Brenton into mainstream theater was completed. His bold, caustic polemics continued in *The Romans in Britain* (pr. 1980), where it led to a private prosecution under the 1956 Sexual Offenses Act for its graphic, onstage depiction of the homosexual rape by a Roman soldier of a naked Druid priest. Eventually, his prosecution was withdrawn, but Brenton's work became no longer Fringe in a formal sense. His 1983 production, *The Genius*, is, by his earlier standards, quite conventional in both form and content.

Yet Brenton did not lose his political radicalism. Together with Tariq Ali, he wrote *Iranian Nights* (pr. 1989), which offers a critical look at the Iranian revolution. His *H.I.D. Hess Is Dead* (pr. 1989) dramatizes the suicide of Rudolf Hess, the last Nazi leader imprisoned in Spandau, Germany, following his conviction at the 1945-1946 Nuremberg trials. The fall of European communism in the late 1980's deeply shocked left-wing Brenton and he tried to come to terms with the practical failure of this ideology in *Moscow Gold* (pr. 1990, with Ali). Foregoing his trademark aggressive shock tactics, which Brenton reserves for his dramatic attacks on Western society, *Moscow Gold* is structured as a surreal farce with former Soviet leaders Vladimir Lenin and Mikhail Gorbachev floating in the air like weird angels and Gorbachev's body representing the former Soviet Union, with breakaway republics causing bodily anguish in his neck, back, and buttocks. In *Ugly Rumours* (pr. 1998, with Ali), Brenton returns to his aggressive condemnation of British society and his propagation of increasingly anachronistic socialist ideals.

David Hare wrote his first play, *How Brophy Made Good* (pr. 1969), to meet a crisis when a play promised by Snoo Wilson for the Portable Theatre failed to materialize. Two following efforts were both successes: *Slag* in 1970 and *The Great Exhibition* in 1972. Although not produced in the Fringe, but rather in the fashionable Hampstead Theatre Club, both plays reflected Hare's underground proclivities as director of the Portable Theatre. *Slag* offered a close look at three women, mistresses of a girls' school, each a unique study. *The Great Exhibition*, written while Hare was resident dramatist at the Royal Court Theatre, satirizes the tendencies, both in the mainstream and in the Fringe, of intellectuals and artists to court working-class audiences. In 1974, Hare helped found another Fringe group, the Joint Stock Theatre Group, for which he wrote *Fanshen* (pr. 1975, adapta-

tion of William Hinton's novel), a play set in revolutionary China. Hare's blind adulation of China's Communist Party—which from 1966 to 1976 had banned all Chinese theater with the exception of eight revolutionary operas commissioned by Jiang Qing, Mao Zedong's radical wife—makes Hare's fawning *Fanshen* something of an embarrassment for an audience aware of real Maoism, which China rejected in its radical form by late 1976.

Hare's work in the 1970's and 1980's, including the highly successful *Plenty* in 1978 and *A Map of the World* in 1983, has generally been in the mainstream of contemporary British theater as far as production styles are concerned, but far to the left of the politics of most British audiences. Dissatisfied with a less radical Labor Party, which sought to distance itself from its "Looney Left" in the early 1990's, Hare's *Absence of War* (pr. 1993) blamed Labor's loss of ideology for its electoral defeat in 1992. Increasingly, critics and audiences have become somewhat tired of Hare's relentless anti-British polemics, and *The Judas Kiss* (pr. 1998) and *Via Dolorosa* (pr. 1999), which also starred Hare reading his own monologues, have been less well received.

Brenton and Hare often collaborated, for example on *Brassneck*, a tour de force written for the Nottingham Playhouse in 1973. It enjoyed an extensive run in Nottingham and was highly acclaimed by critics, who saw the best talents of both artists combining to produce this family saga with its biting satire on capitalism. *Brassneck* was later made available to a much wider audience through a television performance.

A third member of the Portable group, Snoo Wilson, is generally regarded as the most characteristically Fringe in his personal philosophy as well as in the unrelenting originality of his work. Whereas both Brenton and Hare have, in different ways, moved into commercial theater, Wilson has steadfastly sought alternatives.

Wilson's first professional work was an adaptation of Shakespeare's *Pericles, Prince of Tyre* (pr. c. 1607-1608), titled *Pericles, The Mean Knight* (1970), in which he stripped the original play down to a one-hour program and darkened the tragicomic ending;

this was followed by *Device of Angels* (pr. 1970), written for the Portable Theatre. The techniques that have set Wilson's stamp indelibly on alternative theater—visual intrusions, incongruous juxtaposing of episodes, slapstick comedy, eloquent patches of carefully reasoned dialogue—first appeared in *Pignight* (pr. 1971). This breakthrough play deals with its subject—a family pig-raising farm gradually taken over by criminals—on many levels, centering on the problem of haves living off of have-nots and incorporating jolting images of animal slaughtering. *Blow Job* (pr. 1971), a more conventionally conceived play, also portrays the criminal element, this time raiding safes by blowing them up.

Wilson, a prolific writer whom Brenton has described as "a real voyager . . . a writer of nerve and daring," followed these plays with, among others, *The Beast* (pr. 1974), *Vampire* (pr. 1973), *The Pleasure Principle* (pr. 1973), *The Soul of the White Ant* (pr. 1975), *The Glad Hand* (pr. 1978), *A Greenish Man* (pr. 1975, 1978), and *Flaming Bodies* (pr. 1979). Each manifested the distinctive Wilsonian combination of intelligent social comment and outrageous or astonishing visuals—*Flaming Bodies*, for example, calling for a car to crash through a window. *Spaceache* (pr. 1984) and *Inside Babel* (pr. 1985) are considered genuine Fringe productions, experimental in style and content.

Heathcote Williams wrote only one important play, but that one, *AC/DC* (pr. 1970), has come to be widely regarded as one of the best and most influential plays produced by Fringe theater. It accomplished, in ways that perhaps eclipsed even Snoo Wilson's bold techniques, a kind of Artaudian nonrepresentational statement, an organic blending of subject matter and stage device. *AC/DC* presents two schizophrenics, Maurice and Perowne, and three hyped-up characters, one of whom—Sadie—becomes dominant by the end of the play. All the characters are ruled by electronically transmitted influences: rock music, television images, news reporting. In their electrically wired world, they become automatons, bereft of personality. Sadie finally exorcises the schizophrenics by tearing down their media icons and cutting Perowne's brain out of his skull.

Also an accomplished poet, Williams's long poem *Whale Nation* (pr. 1988) was made into a successful play, featuring facts that Williams had collected about the lives of whales. His interest in preserving endangered species was followed by two more volumes of poetry, including *Sacred Elephant* (1989).

The other major Fringe playwrights, Trevor Griffiths, David Edgar, John McGrath, Howard Barker, Stephen Poliakoff, Barrie Keeffe, John Grillo, Steven Berkoff, Charles Marowitz, and Peter Brook, although important in varying degrees to the growth of the movement, seem to have been less centrally influential than were Howard Brenton, David Hare, and Snoo Wilson. Griffiths, Edgar, McGrath, and Barker were more specifically political in their objectives—McGrath, for example, in his 7:84 Company; Griffiths with plays such as *Occupations* (pr. 1970), written for 7:84, and the award-winning *Comedians* (pr. 1975); and Edgar, with his highly acclaimed *Destiny* (pr. 1976). The plays of Poliakoff and Keeffe have tended to deal with the young and disadvantaged. Much of Brook's later work, though experimental, was performed outside the Fringe, in commercial theaters or in specialized productions abroad (on the Continent, in the Middle East, in Africa). Marowitz and Berkoff worked almost exclusively through their own companies—Marowitz in the Open Space (which closed in 1983, after which Marowitz returned to the United States and joined the Los Angeles Actors' Theatre in 1983) and Berkoff in the London Theatre Group.

BRITISH FRINGE IN THE TWENTY-FIRST CENTURY

Like New York's Off-Off-Broadway, by the early twenty-first century, London's Fringe had lost some of the vitality of its heyday in the 1960's and 1970's. The experiments, however, continued. Experimental theater remains at the vanguard of performance art in both countries. The "Theatre of Cruelty" experiment that Brook and Marowitz conducted in 1964, for example, had a direct influence on Brook's 1965 triumph, *The Persecution and Assassination of Jean-Paul Marat as Performed by the Inmates of the Asylum of Charenton Under the Direction of the Marquis de Sade (Marat/Sade)*, which in turn has had a continuing pronounced influence on the general development of theater in Europe and in the United States. For his part, in 1985, Marowitz returned to his Shakespeare collage experiments with a reworking of *A Midsummer Night's Dream*. It is true that, because of the vanguard position of experimental theater, many of its artists and productions have, after brief moments of triumph, either moved into other, less militant roles or simply faded from view.

By 1992, the last year of Prime Minister Margaret Thatcher's tenure, England had replaced the political subjects of earlier experiments with the subjects of writers as stylistically different as feminist Caryl Churchill—whose *Serious Money* (pr. 1987) added to her innovative *Cloud Nine* (pr. 1979) and *Top Girls* (pr. 1982)—and traditionalist Alan Ayckbourn (*A Small Family Business*, pr. 1987 and *Man of the Moment*, pr. 1990). Expanding her feminist subjects and her Brechtian techniques, Churchill in *Mad Forest* (pr. 1990) took on post-communist Eastern Europe in a gripping Brechtian-style play about life in Romania. Representative of newer playwrights from the working class is Willy Russell, with *Educating Rita* (pr. 1980).

The Marowitz-Brook directorial experiments, however they have loosened the strictures of conventional techniques, have themselves become history. The lines between experimental and traditional are increasingly blurred by easy transfers of plays among the Fringe, provincial, subsidized, and even commercial theaters.

Under Prime Minister Tony Blair, who came to power with his "New Labor" in 1997, experimental theater continued to receive relatively generous public funding in the United Kingdom. Yet the overall absence of major political conflicts and the general intellectual disillusionment with the ideology of communism in the light of its global failures have somewhat bereft the Fringe of issues and an intellectual counterstance to mainstream values. Antiglobalization, the environment, AIDS, feminism, and residual class issues remain the topic of Fringe plays of the early twenty-first century. There is also the emergence of a distinct performance art, which has invigorated the British avant-garde. Yet as mainstream the-

aters continue to incorporate many of the stylistic and thematic concerns of the Fringe, it becomes harder to identify a genuine, distinctive Fringe style. Experimentation continues on all levels of English stage productions, and plays in all forms remain a staple of British cultural activities.

BIBLIOGRAPHY

Blumenthal, Eileen. *Joseph Chaikin: Exploring the Boundaries of Theatre*. Cambridge, England: Cambridge University Press, 1984. Perceptive study of this influential American experimental dramatist, whose life is inevitably tied to the history of Off-Off Broadway theater. Bibliography and index.

Brater, Enoch, and Ruby Cohn, eds. *Around the Absurd: Essays on Modern and Postmodern Drama*. Ann Arbor.: University of Michigan Press, 1990. Essays include critical analyses of works by playwrights Maria Irene Fornes and Tom Stoppard, and a perceptive overview of experimental theater from 1959 to 1989.

Craig, Sandy, ed. *Dreams and Deconstructions: Alternative Theatre in Britain*. Ambergate, England: Amber Lane Press, 1980. Perceptive essays discussing the years of the artistic height of the British Fringe theater. Essays analyze key plays and the works of major playwrights. Bibliography and index.

Davies, Andrew. *Other Theatres: The Development of Alternative and Experimental Theatre in Britain*. Totowa, N.J.: Barnes and Noble, 1987. A thorough history of the movement in England with useful discussions of major ideas and theories, cultural background, and individual plays and playwrights. Bibliography and index.

Fuchs, Elinor. *The Death of Character: Perspectives on Theater After Modernism*. Bloomington: Indiana University Press, 1996. Explores experimental theater in the United States after World War II by a New York City theater critic. Rich on theoretical reflections. Contains excerpts of critical reviews and articles for nine experimental productions from 1979 to 1993. Bibliographic notes and index.

Innes, Christopher. *Avant Garde Theatre, 1892-1992*. London: Routledge, 1993. Excellent, comprehensive look at European and North American experimental theater. This is a thorough revision of his earlier book, *Holy Theatre* (1981), with many new chapters on influential experimental playwrights. Richly illustrated, with pictures from many famous productions. Notes, bibliography, index.

Kershaw, Baz. *The Politics of Performance: Radical Theatre as Cultural Intervention*. London: Routledge, 1992. Passionate discussion of radical theater as a correlative to the ills of contemporary Western society. Focus is on emergence, work, and development of the British Fringe theaters, their politics, and spectatorship. Bibliographical references and index.

Kirby, Michael. *A Formalist Theater*. Philadelphia: University of Pennsylvania Press, 1987. Describes general formalist theories regarding acting and performance, and discusses the social context for a formalist play. Concludes with an in-depth analysis of three American formalist plays, two of which were written by the author. Brief chapter on formalist film. Index.

Robinson, Marc. *The Other American Drama*. Baltimore, Md.: Johns Hopkins University Press, 1997. Detailed study of role and function of experimental drama in the United States. Focus is on the innovations that avant-garde theater has brought to the American stage. Bibliography and index.

Roose-Evans, James. *Experimental Theatre from Stanislavsky to Peter Brook*. 3d ed. New York: Universe Books, 1984. A classic by a British theater director dedicated to experimental plays, who is also known for successful West End, London, productions. Focuses on the early European background that laid the foundations for Britain's Fringe theater. Bibliography and index.

Szilassy, Zoltán. *American Theater of the 1960's*. Carbondale: Southern Illinois University Press, 1986. Still one of the best books on this exciting period in American drama, which saw the emergence of major experimental groups, playwrights, and performances, all of which are discussed in an accessible style.

Joseph H. Stodder,
updated by R. C. Lutz

FEMINIST THEATER

As long as theater has existed as a human endeavor, women have been involved in the creation of performances. In Western society, the earliest known plays were various types of fertility celebrations held in honor of the Greek god Dionysus; many of these rites were almost certainly first performed by women known as maenads. Eventually, when theater became a state-sponsored institution, women were no longer allowed to participate in public performance. Though this exclusion of women is unfortunately all too typical of theater history, during the twentieth century a new style of issue-oriented, female-centered theater began to emerge, led by pioneering feminist playwrights such as Alice Childress, Tina Howe, Caryl Churchill, and Marsha Norman, among others. Feminist theater can be defined as theater that works to highlight women's social and political struggles, while in the process exposing patriarchal structures in society and the politics of prevailing gender roles. Although feminist theater has waxed and waned throughout its history, feminist writers and performers have made a lasting mark on the world of contemporary theater.

The earliest known female playwright did not emerge in the twentieth century but much earlier, in the tenth century—Hroswitha of Gandersheim, a nun who wrote six comedies in Latin during her lifetime. Other early playwrights included Isabella Andreini, a famous star of the Italian *commedia dell'arte* (an improvisational style of theater popular during the Renaissance), and Aphra Behn, one of the most popular playwrights in England during the seventeenth century. However, though women were writing plays and participating in various ways in the theater, true feminist theater did not emerge as a genre until the twentieth century.

EARLY TWENTIETH CENTURY

Understandably, the topic that brought feminist theater to the foreground was one of the single most significant political issues of the twentieth century for women: gaining the vote. Suffragists used several means to work for their right to vote, including the creation of political drama. One such play was a three-act vehicle titled *Votes for Women*. This play, by the American expatriate actress Elizabeth Robins, was presented at London's Court Theatre in 1907. The play was a didactic work, with the express purpose of swaying the political opinions of the viewers. The issues Robins dealt with in the work included not only suffrage for women but also abortion, social justice for women workers, and relationships between women. Though now seen as somewhat simplistic, this complex and uncompromising play set the stage for a new type of drama by women. Other important plays in this vein are *How the Vote Was Won* (pr. 1909) by Cicely Hamilton, *Chains* (pr. 1910), by Elizabeth Baker, and *In the Workhouse* (pr. 1911) by Margaret Nevinson.

Once a woman's vote was deemed a constitutional right, however, the political fervor that marked the suffrage movements in both the United States and Great Britain was somewhat lessened. The effects of World War I and World War II also served to take the focus away from the issue of feminism. Although many female playwrights wrote during the period between 1900 and 1950, feminist drama did not fully emerge again until the 1950's.

THE 1950's

During the 1950's, the undercurrents of social revolution were being felt at all levels of American society, and once again women were deeply involved in the changes taking place. One of the pioneers of feminist theater in this era was Alice Childress, the first African American woman playwright to have a professional production of her work staged Off-Broadway; she also won a 1956 Obie Award (the first ever won by a woman playwright) for her pioneering work *Trouble in Mind* (pr. 1955). The main character in the play is an African American actress named Wilmetta Mayer, who represents the political and social aspirations of both women and African Americans in the stilted, stereotype-ridden world of the

United States in the 1950's. In later plays, such as *Wine in the Wilderness* (pr. 1976) and *Wedding Band: A Love/Hate Story in Black and White* (pr. 1966), Childress continued to treat the theme of African American women dealing with unjust social and economic conditions. Childress's work was extremely influential to her contemporaries, including Lorraine Hansberry.

Hansberry wrote a small handful of plays (two of which were incomplete when she died and were finished by her husband) before her untimely death from cancer in 1965. The best known of these is *A Raisin in the Sun* (pr. 1959), which won the New York Drama Critics Circle Award for best American play of the 1958-1959 season. The play was immensely popular: It enjoyed a two-year run on Broadway, was made into a popular film, and became a classic of the feminist genre. Like Childress, Hansberry deals simultaneously with the issues women face, particularly in society, and the more general issues of racial inequity, economic injustice, and a lack of political power for oppressed minorities. The mutual concern with justice for women and justice for all those on the margins of society's power structure continued to be a theme in women's writing, especially during the 1960's and 1970's, the most important period in the history of feminist theater.

THE 1960'S AND 1970'S

During the 1960's, the social protests that were in nascent form only a decade before exploded onto the scene, prompted by many converging developments—protests against the Vietnam War and for civil rights for African Americans, the increasing presence of women in the workplace, an emerging counterculture, and various other trends. Out of this mix emerged the most important single pioneer of feminist theater in the United States, Megan Terry.

Terry was an original founder of the Open Theatre of New York, one of the most noteworthy organizations in modern stagecraft. From 1963 to 1966, the Open Theatre conducted a series of workshops for actors and audiences, exploring the ideas of what constituted performance and how plays might be used in the service of social ideas. Terry's one-act play *Calm Down Mother* (pr. 1965) is considered by many to be the foundational play of modern feminist theater. In this experimental work, three actresses called simply "Woman One," "Woman Two," and "Woman Three" undergo a series of transformations, centering around mother-daughter and mother-sister relationships. The actresses portray famous characters such as Margaret Fuller, as well as stereotypical poor women and even subway turnstile doors. The concept of transformation—of women becoming "other," dynamically changing identities and moving fluidly through time and space—became a common theme in feminist drama. Later playwrights from Churchill to Norman have used this device to great effect. Terry's other important plays include *Ex-Miss Copper Queen on a Set of Pills* (pr. 1963), *Keep Tightly Closed in a Cool Dry Place* (pr. 1965), *Comings and Goings* (pr. 1966), *Viet Rock: A Folk War Movie* (pr. 1966), and *Hothouse* (pr. 1974).

The clearest heir of Terry's social protest writing style, Caryl Churchill, also emerged as a professional playwright during the 1960's but wrote her best-known works during the 1970's and 1980's. Churchill wrote many radio plays and other works for the British Broadcasting Corporation (BBC) in her native England as early as 1958, but first reached real renown as a playwright with the production of her play *Owners* in 1972 at London's Royal Court Theatre. She is best known for her masterwork, *Top Girls*, which was first produced in 1982. In this complex drama, various female characters from history and literature (including Isabella Bird, Lady Nijo, Dull Gret, Pope Joan, Patient Griselda) gather for a dinner party with Marlene, a modern career woman celebrating a promotion at work. The characters interact with each other, completely heedless of time and reality, as the fictional and artistic characters are treated exactly the same as Marlene herself. The characters discuss women's roles in their various societies over time, and Marlene deals with her own guilt over giving her daughter away to someone else to raise in order to move more quickly up the career ladder. Churchill pulls no punches in holding women accountable for all their choices, good and bad, marking a change from the "cheerleading" women's dramas of earlier periods. As the 1980's arrived, feminist theater was hitting its stride as a mature art form with a distinct voice.

THE 1980'S

By the 1980's, feminist theater was well established as a distinctive genre of drama, with its own venues, performers, and notable playwrights. Some of the most significant works of feminist drama emerged during this era. Leading the way was Marsha Norman, an American playwright who first garnered attention with her 1977 work *Getting Out*, about a young woman being released from prison, where she has spent eight years on charges of robbery, kidnapping, and murder. The play follows the central character through her first day of freedom and examines the obstacles that face her in her struggle to be a successful, independent woman. The subject matter is tough and uncompromising, once again including the familiar theme of mother-daughter conflict and the damage wrought by the failure of mother love. Norman also uses some of the transformational techniques pioneered by Terry. The main character, Arlene, has an alter ego, Arlie, a separate character who represents the hard exterior Arlene has traditionally presented to the world. Arlene and Arlie interact with each other, as Arlene tries to fight off the lure of easy money through crime and violence.

Although *Getting Out* was well received, Norman is best known for her most important play, entitled *'night, Mother*, which premiered in Cambridge, Massachusetts, at the American Repertory Theatre in 1982 and in New York City in 1983. The play won the Susan Smith Blackburn Prize and the Pulitzer Prize in Drama in 1983. Highly controversial, *'night, Mother* tells the story of Jessie Cates, a woman with epilepsy who is divorced, has a delinquent son, and lives with her mother, Thelma. The action takes place in real time on one Saturday night when Jessie suddenly announces to her mother that she is going to commit suicide. Jessie and Thelma argue about the suicide for the next two hours, with Jessie explaining why she feels she is justified in taking her life and Thelma trying to talk her out of it. Finally, Jessie completes the suicide at the play's end. The play was hailed as a masterwork by many critics and was a popular audience favorite, but many feminist critics were offended by the final suicide and complained that the play demeaned women's lives. The fact that Norman felt free to write such a brutally honest and highly negative play demonstrates the level of maturity that feminist theater had achieved in the seventy years since the earliest suffragist dramas, which were universally positive about women and their choices. With increasing economic, cultural, political, and social power, women were freer by this time to depict female lives in a more balanced fashion, rather than putting on a positive visage in the face of oppression.

Another popular and noteworthy writer of the 1980's was Beth Henley, whose comedy *Crimes of the Heart* (pr. 1979) opened on Broadway in 1981. The play went on to win the 1981 Pulitzer Prize in Drama, as well as the 1980-1981 New York Drama Critics Circle Award. A feature film was made of the play, and it continues to be popular in regional theater revivals. Though obviously a great deal more lighthearted than Norman's work, *Crimes of the Heart* deals with the three Magrath sisters. The youngest sister has shot her husband and is about to go on trial for attempted murder, the oldest sister is mourning the death of her pet horse, and the middle sibling is back home from Hollywood where she tried to start a singing career. As the sisters interact, they discuss their dead mother, who hanged the family cat and herself in the basement. Conflicts about family roles, men, and the nature of sisterhood arise, and all are treated in high comic fashion. Again, critics were divided about whether this play showcased positive or negative images of women, a debate that marked its maturity.

A final example of the high point reached by feminist theater in the 1980's is *My Sister in This House*, by Wendy Kesselman. The play premiered in New York in 1981 and was awarded the 1980 Susan Smith Blackburn Prize and the 1980 Playbill Award. The play is based on the same 1933 murder case that inspired Jean Genet's famous play *Les Bonnes* (pr. 1947; *The Maids*, 1954). The play re-imagines the events from the standpoint of the young women who serve as maids in a middle-class household. Controversial issues of class tyranny, lesbianism, and women's roles in violence are examined in this play, which ends with a violent confrontation and a grisly description of the murder scene from actual court records. Kesselman's play was viewed as enormously vital because it not only retold a familiar story from a different perspective but also dealt with other contentious issues in a matter-of-fact manner that was new at the time, especially for American feminist theater.

Though feminist theater reached new heights in the 1980's, the political and social conditions that led to its rise were constantly shifting and changing. As feminism itself matured and women gained more power in all arenas of public life, many writers argued that issue-oriented drama was no longer needed. Additionally, the changing economics of theater production made it more and more difficult to produce dramatic plays that did not have universal appeal to assure wide audiences. As the 1990's approached, an economic downturn exacerbated the problem, and feminist theater began to slip into a period of decline.

THE 1990'S

As the 1990's dawned, the general feeling among many theatrical professionals was that feminist theater was passé, a relic of a bygone era that seemed unnecessary given women's accomplishments in all areas of public life. However, a few playwrights continued to write plays about women's issues, and many of these plays won major awards and found popular success. One writer who flourished during the 1990's, Wendy Wasserstein, actually made her debut in the 1970's. Wasserstein first came to public attention with her 1977 play *Uncommon Women and Others*, an all-woman ensemble piece about students at Mount Holyoke College in the 1960's. The play was considered lightweight but found great popularity as a staple of college drama productions. In 1989 Wasserstein gained more critical acclaim with *The Heidi Chronicles*, another ensemble piece about a strong Jewish character facing the various trials of life. Most consider her masterwork her 1992 play, *The Sisters Rosensweig*, yet another ensemble piece

about the lives of Jewish women from New York. The play concerns three sisters from Brooklyn who meet in London to celebrate the fifty-fourth birthday of the oldest sister, Sara. The play won the Outer Critics Circle Award for Best Play of the 1992-1993 season. Although still concerned primarily with women's lives, the play is typical of the more mainstream, less didactic fare that became popular during the 1990's.

Another play that garnered attention during the 1990's was a 1998 play by Eve Ensler, *The Vagina Monologues*. The play became somewhat controversial when its extremely frank and explicit discussion of female sexuality and sexual anatomy caused some cultural critics to complain that it was senselessly exploitative. The play consists of a series of monologues, spoken by various characters, about vaginas and the various sexual situations in which women and girls find themselves. Rape, incest, masturbation, and other sensitive subjects are treated at length. During the play's run in New York, several famous television actresses, as well as former Mayor Rudy Giuliani's wife, Donna Hanover, were cast in the play, which was seen as a stunt by many serious drama critics. Many other critics found the play pointless and unnecessary. Nevertheless, the play continued to hold out the banner of feminist theater at a time when it was otherwise in serious decline.

THE TWENTY-FIRST CENTURY

As drama continues to develop during the modern era, the future of feminist theater is unclear. From its earliest beginnings in the suffrage era, women's drama has addressed the social injustices faced by women who were not allowed full participation in political, economic, or cultural life. As women overcame many of these obstacles during the twentieth century, the need for a distinct class of feminist theater has become less pressing. Some see the genre as hopelessly degraded, while others feel that a resurgence of women-centered drama is possible. In any case, the history of feminist theater demonstrates that women have created an exciting and powerful art form that reflects the vitality of women's changing lives and their constantly evolving roles in the modern world.

BIBLIOGRAPHY

Aston, Elaine. *An Introduction to Feminism and Theatre*. New York: Routledge, 1994. Provides a good overview of the many theories surrounding feminism and the theater and makes complicated theoretical material understandable to the general reader.

Canning, Charlotte. *Feminist Theaters in the U.S.A.: Staging Women's Experience*. London: Routledge, 1996. Canning interviewed thirty female playwrights in order to uncover insight into the struggles and successes of feminist theater during the 1970's and 1980's.

Flores, Yolanda. *The Drama of Gender: Feminist Theater by Women of the Americas*. New York: Peter Lang, 2000. Examines a number of feminist plays written by Hispanic women across Central and South America, discussing topics such as the intersections of race and gender, compulsory heterosexuality, and dramatic forms.

Keyssar, Helene. *Feminist Theatre: An Introduction to Plays of Contemporary British and American Women*. New York: Grove Press, 1985. This entry in the Grove Press Modern Dramatists series collects the most important scholarly ideas current at the time of its publication, the heyday of feminist theater criticism. Keyssar provides close readings of major works by Terry, Churchill, Wasserstein, Henley, Norman, and other key writers of feminist plays.

Moore, Honor, ed. *The New Women's Theatre: Ten Plays by Contemporary American Women*. New York: Vintage Books, 1977. This early text provides an introduction that has been tremendously influential on later scholars of feminist theater. The ten plays included are excellent examples from early feminist playwrights, including Childress and Howe.

Stowell, Sheila. *A Stage of Their Own: Feminist Playwrights of the Suffrage Era*. Ann Arbor: University of Michigan Press, 1992. Stowell provides a good overview of issue theater from the suffrage era and closely examines the influence of suffrage playwrights on later women dramatists.

Vicki A. Sanders

GAY AND LESBIAN THEATER

After Mart Crowley's *The Boys in the Band* was produced in 1968 and gained a following, gay drama came out of the closet in which it had endured for decades. This was the first openly gay play to be staged in New York the year after the state of New York relaxed its ban on presenting homosexuality onstage. The second event that paved the way for gay drama through the remainder of the twentieth century, the Stonewall Inn riots, followed close on the heels of the production of *The Boys in the Band*.

THE STONEWALL INN RIOTS

The gay liberation movement in the United States sprang to life in 1969. On June 27 of that year, a tactical force of the New York City Police Department raided the Stonewall Inn, a gay gathering place in New York City's Greenwich Village. Such raids, which had been a form of perpetual police harassment of gays, were frequent in New York and other large cities. They usually resulted in the arrests of a few people, causing them embarrassment and inconvenience, even though the charges against them frequently were dismissed. Records of these arrests, however, generally remained in police files and could be a source of concern for years to come among those who had been arrested.

June 27 was different from most Friday nights at the Stonewall Inn. The gay community was in mourning over the death of one of its icons, Judy Garland, five days earlier. Civil disobedience was in the air and had hung heavily over the country for some time as racial tensions, discontent over the involvement of the United States in the Vietnam War, and concern over the unequal treatment of minorities led to widespread protests. The boiling point was being approached in many areas in which social discontent was seething not far below the surface. On that Friday night, large numbers of homosexual men whom the police tried to herd into their vans resisted strenuously; rioting ensued.

BEFORE STONEWALL

In the first twenty-five years of the 1900's, Britain and the United States were shaking loose from the moral strictures that had pervaded and inhibited public life during the long reign of Great Britain's Queen Victoria, who was monarch from 1837 until her death in 1901. In the United States, an increasing bohemianism was sweeping avant-garde artistic circles. In New York, this bohemianism was centered in Greenwich Village and in Harlem, where the Harlem Renaissance was taking shape.

A tolerance for sexual freedom began to replace the Victorian restraints that had contributed to the downfall of Oscar Wilde toward the end of Victoria's reign. The Bloomsbury Group, which flourished in London, was peppered with male homosexuals and lesbians, among them some of the most gifted writers, artists, and intellectuals of that period.

The plays of Noël Coward, particularly *The Vortex* (pr. 1924) and *Design for Living* (pr. 1933)—while they did not deal explicitly with homosexuality—skated close to the edge in implying the subject in ways that homosexuals in Coward's audiences could scarcely miss. Among straight people, his naughtiness passed as "high camp" rather than out-and-out homosexuality. Throughout Coward's career, his plays were peppered with homosexual lyrics, such as "Mad About the Boy" in *Words and Music* (pr. 1932) and "Matelot" in the revue *Sigh No More* (pr. 1945). British playwrights such as Coward always had to contend with the British censors. Anything sexual had to be presented with sufficient subtlety to get it past the censors and make production on London's West End possible.

Oscar Wilde managed to evade the censors in *The Importance of Being Earnest: A Trivial Comedy for Serious People* (pr. 1895) when he invented the hypochondriacal Bunbury, whom Algernon had constantly to visit in the country. The word "bun" refers in British slang to a woman's sexual organ, but "bum," which is very close to it, refers to the buttocks. The censors apparently overlooked the sexual implications of Algernon's "Bunburying," which has since been interpreted in both heterosexual and homosexual contexts.

As early as 1894, in Alfred Jarry's play, *Haldernablou* (pr. 1894), the protagonist, Duke Haldern, tells his page that love can exist only outside sex. At the page's instigation, however, their relationship becomes sexual, leading the Duke to suffer such severe pangs of conscience that he eventually strangles the page. Henry B. Fuller's *At Saint Judas's* (pr. 1896) also addresses a homosexual topic. As the bridegroom and his best man await the bride in the church's sacristy immediately before she is to marry, it is revealed that the best man has calculatedly set up impediments to the marriage because he is in love with the groom. His duplicity, his being the Judas in the play's title, forces him eventually to commit suicide after he admits having been driven mad by the thought of his friend's marriage to a woman. Any plays in this period that present homosexuality even tangentially were not permitted to have happy outcomes.

LESBIAN PLAYS OF THE 1920'S AND 1930'S

Early twentieth century society was somewhat more accepting of lesbianism than it was of male homosexuality. Closeness between two women was not considered unusual. Nevertheless, the subject was clearly controversial and probably resulted in Lillian Hellman's not receiving the 1935 Pulitzer Prize in Drama for *The Children's Hour* (pr. 1934), which is generally conceded to be her best play. Because only one Pulitzer Prize in Drama can be awarded in a given year, the Pulitzer drama jury, which had several excellent plays to choose from in 1935, sidestepped the issue and awarded the 1935 prize to Zoë Atkins for *The Old Maid* (pr. 1934).

The Children's Hour focuses on two teachers, Karen and Martha, who have been close since college. They teach together in a school, where Mary, an emotionally disturbed student, accuses the two of having an "indecent" relationship. Karen, having a deep and genuine concern for Mary, recognizes her emotional problems. In the end, it is proved that the girl's accusations are false, but the veil of suspicion that has descended upon the two teachers has utterly destroyed them. The thorny ethical questions with which the play deals are compelling, but the taint of lesbianism made the play a controversial offering in its time and resulted in its being banned in Britain, although it was performed on Broadway in the United States.

Predating *The Children's Hour* by fifteen years is Edna St. Vincent Millay's *The Lamp and the Bell* (pr. 1921), written to be performed at the fiftieth anniversary of Vassar College's Alumnae Association, which was presumably its only production. In this play, Princess Beatrice and Bianca are two women clearly in love with each other, although each discusses her expectations of heterosexual matrimony. Beatrice becomes attached to King Mario, who is visiting, but he is puzzled by her because she acts so masculine. Meanwhile, Bianca, who has been sent away, returns, falls in love with Mario, and marries him. Beatrice, who steps aside, never marries but, on the death of her father, becomes queen. During a free-for-all with a band of brigands, Beatrice unintentionally kills Mario. She and Bianca, however, are not reunited until Bianca is on her deathbed. Beatrice comes to comfort her and Bianca dies in her arms during a final loving embrace.

Djuna Barnes's *The Dove* (pr. 1926) was performed at the Studio Theatre at Smith College and also at New York City's Bayes Theater, although it never made it to Broadway. Its three characters, Vera, Amelia, and the Dove, are clearly lesbians. The Dove falls in love with Amelia, forcing Vera to leave. Lesbian overtones pervade some of Barnes's other plays, such as *Two Ladies Take Tea* (pr. 1925) and *To the Dogs* (wr. 1929), in which a young man, rejected by a woman to whom he wants to make love, goes so far as to call her a queer woman, a description she accepts and acknowledges as apt.

The lesbian drama of this period, presenting the love of women for other women, does not, however, deal openly with the sexual aspects of their relationships. The focus of such plays is often on issues related only incidentally to lesbianism. A play like *The Children's Hour*, as Eric Bentley pointed out, is almost two plays: one in which the innocent are punished, the other in which lesbianism is punished, but the first concern in this play essentially overwhelms the second. Obviously, Karen is in love with Martha, but the two are innocent of the manufactured charges lodged against them by the mendacious and emotionally disturbed Mary.

LATENT HOMOSEXUALITY

Much of the prominent drama between the 1920's and the 1960's made veiled allusions to homosexuality but dealt with latency rather than with the overtly homosexual characters that were to occur in later plays. In *The Unknown* (pr. 1920), W. Somerset Maugham speaks lovingly of a friend lost in the war, but this sort of love more nearly reflects veneration than homosexuality. J. R. Ackerley in *The Prisoners of War* (pr. 1925), set in an internment camp in Switzerland, presents Conrad, whose complicated emotions are almost certainly linked to homosexuality. However, this is not the story of a love affair between two men. It is an account of the emotions that Conrad feels for the handsome young Grayle, who, presumably having no sexual interest in Conrad, shuns him.

Eugene O'Neill's plays were notably devoid of gay characters, although in *Strange Interlude* (pr. 1928), the presentation of Charles Marsden, a confirmed bachelor, suggests he might be gay. Likewise, in *Ah, Wilderness!* (pr. 1933), young Richard is extremely sensitive and is given to voluminous reading in works not only by Henrik Ibsen and George Bernard Shaw but also by Oscar Wilde and Algernon Charles Swinburne, suggesting at least his exposure to and interest in gay elements in what he chooses to read.

Much more directly homosexual were Coward's *Post Mortem* (pb. 1931), which, significantly, was not produced, and Keith Winter's *The Rats of Norway* (pr. 1933), which is set in an isolated boys' school in Northumbria, where Chetwood, one of the masters, is obviously gay and notably effeminate. The play, however, does not center on him so much as it focuses on Stevan, a new teacher in the school, who treats Chetwood badly, presumably because of his obviousness, and falls in love with a female colleague.

Among the most sensitive pre-Stonewall plays that deal with homosexuality is Robert Anderson's *Tea and Sympathy* (pr. 1953). This play deals with la-tency rather than with any fully developed manifestations of homosexuality. A sensitive youth, Tom, the play's protagonist, is a student at a boys' boarding school. He has twice played female roles in the school's dramatic productions. Now gossip is swirling around him because he was seen bathing nude with one of the school's junior masters, who is thought to be gay. His housemaster, Bill, calls him to account for this, but Bill's wife, Laura, in an attempt to help Tom prove to himself that he is "normal," has sex with him. She also quite presciently speculates that her husband's homophobia probably stems from fears about his own sexual identity.

In *Tea and Sympathy*, as in many of the plays of this period, homosexuality is presented as an abnormality but as something that must be understood, tolerated, and dealt with compassionately. Even the homosexual playwrights of the 1940's, 1950's, and 1960's—notably Tennessee Williams, William Inge, and Edward Albee—failed to write anything that depicted homosexual existence as being in any way satisfying.

In Williams's case, the protagonist, Tom, in *The Glass Menagerie* (pr. 1944), is not clearly homosexual even though he is an autobiographical character (Williams was gay). In *A Streetcar Named Desire* (pr. 1947), Williams reveals that Blanche Du Bois was once married to a young man who, obviously homosexual, ended up committing suicide after Blanche discovered him in a compromising situation with a man. In *Suddenly Last Summer* (pr. 1958), Sebastian, dead when the play opens, has been murdered in an unnamed developing country by young boys whom he was obviously using for sex. Brick, in *Cat on a Hot Tin Roof* (pr. 1955), is married to a voluptuous woman but produces no offspring, presumably because he is gay and, therefore, not sexually interested in his wife. The dialogue skirts the issue at times but the implications of Brick's homosexuality are clear.

William Inge's major dramas of the 1950's have no homosexual characters, although the author's own predilections are clear in his populating three of his four earliest plays with sexy young hunks who disturb the equilibrium of the frustrated women in the plays. Only in later plays like *A Loss of Roses* (pr. 1959) or *Natural Affection* (pr. 1963) does Inge treat homosexuality, but even then only incidentally, as when Donnie in *Natural Affection* makes it clear that he has been sexually abused in the reformatory to which he has been confined. Two one-act plays by Inge, written as exercises when he was undergoing psychoanalysis, treat homosexuality directly. In *The Tiny Closet* (pr. 1959) and *The Boy in the Basement* (pb. 1962), the protagonists are clearly gay but closeted and repressed.

In his plays, Edward Albee makes fewer direct allusions to homosexuality—save for a passing reference in *The Zoo Story* (pr. 1959)—than Inge or Williams, although one critic quite aptly dubbed *Who's Afraid of Virginia Woolf?* (pr. 1962) Albee's great gay closet play. Martha and Honey are caricatures of women, the latter having been appropriately compared by one critic to a screaming drag queen. Despite his not alluding directly to gay topics, the critics took Albee to task more than they did Inge or Williams for the veiled homosexuality in his plays. John Clum points out that at that time, the closet seemed to be an unspoken agreement between playwrights and their audiences and between playwrights and critics.

Arthur Miller, a heterosexual playwright, evades direct presentation of homosexuality in his plays, although Biff in *Death of a Salesman* (pr. 1949), because he does not have girlfriends and tends to be quite passive, has been seen by some critics as a latent homosexual. In *A View from the Bridge* (pr. 1955), Eddie Carbone kisses his wife's cousin, Rodolpho, full on the mouth, which was shocking to audiences, but the essence of the play and even of that action is not overtly homosexual.

Although some openly homosexual plays were produced in both Broadway or Off-Broadway venues before Stonewall—notably productions such as Lanford Wilson's *The Madness of Lady Bright* (pr. 1964) and Paddy Chayefsky's *The Latent Heterosexual* (pr. 1968), neither of which enjoyed much popular acceptance—the games that many of the most significant playwrights were forced to play during this closeted period did not survive long after

Crowley's *The Boys in the Band* attracted enthusiastic audiences and after the Stonewall Inn riots helped to bring about in drama a new candor regarding homosexuality.

The Boys in the Band centered on a homosexual character named Michael, who lived in a lower-Manhattan apartment, and his homosexual friends and former lovers. This group of men ranged from the cultured and effeminate to the athletic and virile and from the promiscuous to the monogamous. Crowley's portrayal of Michael's struggle with his homosexual identity brought criticism from those who charged that he perpetuated stereotypes about gay men being unhappy. However, as the first play about a group of homosexual men, Crowley's work opened the doors for many later homosexual playwrights.

POST-STONEWALL DRAMA

If *Who's Afraid of Virginia Woolf?* demolished middle-class conceptions of family values, post-Stonewall drama put the finishing touches on demolishing it completely. Lanford Wilson's *Fifth of July* (pr. 1978), like other gay plays of the era, brings homosexuality up front in making its protagonist clearly homosexual, a Vietnam veteran who, having lost both legs in the war, has returned home to small-town Missouri to teach school. The gay couple central to the play bring affirmation to a family relationship that is not based on procreation. Although theirs is a family, it greatly challenges the concept of the traditional family. The same can be said of Albee's George and Martha in *Who's Afraid of Virginia Woolf?*, but this play makes the point with no overt introduction of homosexuality.

The Boys in the Band paved the way for much more honest presentations of homosexuality in such plays as John Hopkins's *Find Your Way Home* (pr. 1970), Simon Gray's *Butley* (pr. 1971), David Rabe's *Streamers* (pr. 1976), Marvin Hamlisch and Edward Kleban's *A Chorus Line* (pr. 1975), and Harvey Fierstein's *La Cage aux Folles* (pr. 1983) and *Torch Song Trilogy* (pb. 1978-1979). The blatant opening sex scene of *Torch Song Trilogy* is living testimony to how far gay theater has come after the Stonewall Inn riots.

Dan Pruitt and Patrick Hutchison's *The Harvey Milk Show* (pr. 1991), a musical about the openly gay San Francisco city supervisor who was murdered by a homophobic off-duty policeman, Dan White, is essentially an allegorical attack on homophobia and on the sort of hatred engendered by people such as singer Anita Bryant in her Save the Children campaign. In this play, Harvey Milk emerges as a Christ figure, working miracles on earth, being murdered for what he represents, and returning spiritually as a positive presence in society.

THE DRAMA OF AIDS

No single element affected contemporary gay drama as much as the onset of the AIDS (acquired immunodeficiency syndrome) epidemic in the early 1980's. This widespread illness that claimed the lives of so many gay men became the stuff of which compelling drama had to be made. Perhaps no American playwright approached the topic more effectively than Tony Kushner in his pair of plays, *Angels in America: A Gay Fantasia on National Themes* (*Part One: Millennium Approaches*), first produced in 1991, and *Angels in America: A Gay Fantasia on National Themes* (*Part Two: Perestroika*), produced in 1992. These plays reached wide audiences throughout the Western world and served to enlighten straight society about many salient aspects of gay existence, as, somewhat earlier, had Ron Cowen's moving AIDS drama, *An Early Frost* (pr. 1985), which was aired on network television throughout the United States.

Paul Rudnick's *Jeffrey* (pr. 1993) deals with the difficult efforts of the protagonist, a food server in his thirties, to eschew the casual sex that has been so much a part of his life when the AIDS epidemic forces him to acknowledge that casual sex is no longer sensible. He essentially gives up sex until he meets Steve, to whom he is strongly attracted. Steve is HIV-positive, representing the very thing that Jeffrey most fears. Rudnick's conclusion is that AIDS does not cause Jeffrey the greatest difficulty but rather his reluctance to adjust to the compromised world that the AIDS scare has created.

The drama of AIDS essentially set out to show

that AIDS is not exclusively a gay disease, a form of heavenly retribution against those who are different. This kind of drama deals with the fear and the heartbreak of an epidemic that robs people of their sexual freedom and, in many cases, of those who mean the most to them.

As gay drama has advanced, it has made the statement to broad audiences in modern society that the problem is not homosexuality but rather homophobia, a pernicious form of prejudice. It would be naïve to suggest that homophobia no longer exists, but it is probably safe to say that, partly through the efforts of drama, it has become more socially acceptable in the Western world.

BIBLIOGRAPHY

Clum, John M. *Something for the Boys: Musical Theater and Gay Culture.* New York: St. Martin's Press, 1999. This consideration of musical theater and gay culture is unique in its field. The selective discography that follows the main text is particularly useful to scholars and researchers.

_____. *Still Acting Gay: Male Homosexuality in Modern Drama.* New York: St. Martin's Press, 2000. A remarkably comprehensive study of gay theater, extraordinarily well written at a level that non-experts in the field can easily comprehend.

_____, ed. *Staging Gay Lives: An Anthology of Contemporary Gay Theater.* New York: Westview Press, 1995. This collection of ten gay plays is carefully selected. It is enhanced by Tony Kushner's foreword as well as by the editor's preface. A good introduction to gay drama.

Furtado, Ken, and Nancy Hellner, eds. *Gay and Lesbian American Plays: An Annotated Bibliography.* Metuchen, N.J.: Scarecrow Press, 1993. The fullest list in existence of gay and lesbian drama up to the early 1990's. Useful for plays that fall within its time frame.

Shewey, Don, ed. *Out Front: Contemporary Gay and Lesbian Plays.* New York: Grove Press, 1988. This collection is helpful not only for the eleven gay plays it reproduces but for its valuable introduction, "Pride in the Name of Love: Notes on

Contemporary Gay Theater." Extensive bibliography.

Sinfield, Alan. *Out on Stage: Lesbian and Gay Theatre in the Twentieth Century.* New Haven, Conn.: Yale University Press, 1999. Among the most inclusive studies of gay theater. Sinfield writes well and his material is meticulously organized and presented in this important book in gay studies. Extensive index of plays.

R. Baird Shuman

POLITICAL THEATER

Theater has been political since its inception during the ancient Greek period because of its social nature and the power of the spoken word. From Aeschylus to Britain's Caryl Churchill, playwrights have long recognized theater's ability to provoke serious contemplation of social issues and invoke understanding of and sympathy for political causes. As a dynamic tool for public instruction, propaganda, and entertainment, theater examines, and sometimes even solves, the problems inherent in human society.

The word "politics" is usually connected to issues dealing with government or public social policy, but in a broader sense politics concerns how people handle, control, and manage power in groups. It refers to how society organizes power through informal as well as formal channels. There are many different varieties of political theater, but the two most common include plays used to make a statement in order to change public sentiment concerning a social issue and those used directly to instigate social change as an agent of propaganda. The term "political theater" may take a variety of definitions, but typically the term refers to any live production of a play that carries either an overt or covert sociopolitical message whose purpose is a means to change social attitudes or policies.

A STATEMENT THROUGH HISTORY

Plays that make political statements often do so to encourage the audience's serious consideration of a social issue. They may be used to change perceptions, challenge stereotypes, or simply provoke thought. Sometimes these plays depict historical or political events from the recent or distant past to allow the playwright to draw parallels and comment on contemporary issues. Plays that re-create historical events allow the author to highlight the significance of the event to then further his or her own political agenda. In her book *Polity and Theater in Historical Perspective* (1977), Karen Hermassi asserts that politics is the vocation of the theater and that the aim of most playwrights is to influence the audience's thinking with concern to social issues. She cites as an example the ancient Greek playwright Aeschylus, stating that he intended to reshape society's perception and memory of the myths he dramatized, not merely retell the story. When playwrights dramatize historical events in plays, they usually concern themselves with communicating what they see as true about the event, not necessarily what is factual.

One of the most powerful examples of this kind of political statement play comes from the McCarthy era in the United States. During the 1950's, Senator Joseph McCarthy took full advantage of America's fear of communism during the Cold War to make a name for himself as the avenging angel of democracy. He hoped to root out communism in the United States by heading the House Committee on Un-American Activities (HUAC), which held a series of trials accusing a variety of government workers, Hollywood artists, and others of being communists. Those identified and tried could escape persecution if they admitted their "guilt" and exposed communists. If they refused, however, they were cited for contempt of Congress and blacklisted in Hollywood. One such artist, Arthur Miller, himself a victim of the hearings, responded to the events by writing a play, *The Crucible* (pr. 1953), full of symbolic parallels to the HUAC hearings. Although Miller successfully appealed his contempt citation four years later, the careers and lives of many of the film industry's brightest talents were destroyed.

Miller sets *The Crucible* during the Salem witch-hunts of the late seventeenth century. He uses a historic example of witch-hunts for his dramatic condemnation of the injustice he witnessed and experienced in his own time. The play chronicles the terror-rousing activities of a young girl, Abigail, embittered by unrequited love. In her fury, she takes advantage of the irrational fear of witchcraft in her community by leading a group of young girls into performances of hysteria in order to appear bewitched by certain individuals in the community. The panic she induces eventually leads to the execution of many innocent people who refuse to admit guilt (because they are innocent) or to name others. Like the McCarthy hearings, the Salem trials resulted punishment only if the accused refused to admit his or her guilt and name others. Public record shows that no confessed "witch" was hanged in Salem, and even though most of those executed were exonerated in 1711 for the benefit of their families, four of the names were not cleared until 1957.

Miller's play speaks so powerfully and universally about the theme of witch-hunts that it has been used as public instruction for such historic eras as the period of Japanese American internment camps in the United States during World War II, apartheid in Africa, and even the backlash experienced by the North American Muslim community after the September 11, 2001, terrorist attacks on the World Trade Center and the Pentagon.

MARGINALIZED GROUPS

Another genre of political statement drama presents a variety of settings and characters and makes no attempt to re-create a historical event but nonetheless provokes serious consideration among the audience regarding a social issue. This kind of political statement play is probably the most common form of political theater; many playwrights throughout theater history have used the stage as a platform for espousing their political philosophy. Plays of this kind endeavor to raise public awareness or influence public opinion. In the last third of the twentieth century, the Western theater community experienced an explosion of "nonhistorical" political statement plays with the emergence of playwrights such as Tony Kushner, whose two Pulitzer Prize winning plays, *Angels in America: A Gay Fantasia on National Themes* (*Part One: Millennium Approaches*), first produced in 1991, and *Angels in America: A Gay Fantasia on National Themes* (*Part Two: Perestroika*), produced in 1992, challenged audiences to reexamine their opinions concerning the homosexual community and the phenomenon of AIDS (acquired immunodeficiency syndrome).

Moreover, within the realm of nonhistorical plays, marginalized groups found a forum to voice their opinions and experiences. African American playwrights such as Amiri Baraka and August Wilson explored the African American experience in plays such as Baraka's *Slave Ship: A Historical Pageant* (pr. 1967) and Wilson's *Fences* (pr. 1985). British playwright Caryl Churchill, a foremost pioneer of feminist drama, wrote plays that examined the roles and expectations of women and blacks in society. In her experimental work *Cloud Nine* (pr. 1979), she mixes race and gender in characters, having males play many women's roles (and vice versa), and blacks portray white characters. This particular brand of mixed casting forced audiences to reevaluate long-held sexual stereotypes and racial biases. Churchill has said that in *Cloud Nine* she was able to explore what fascinates her most: the internal emotions of people operating within external political limitations.

Other groups, such as Latino, Jewish, and Asian Americans, also recognize the ability of theater to sway audience sentiments. In the twentieth century, for the first time in Western theater, plays portrayed ethnic and minority groups as something other than sideline characters. The authenticity of the experience portrayed in these plays echoes beyond the confines of their cultural community and speaks to a greater human experience. In this way, diversity in plays has helped to shape public opinion and attitude, which in turn may lead to political actions on behalf of the previously disenfranchised.

One of the most well-known minority theaters is El Teatro Campesino, founded by Luis Miguel Valdez in 1965. Emphasizing activism through theater, El Teatro Campesino produced the newest, experimental, often confrontational works by Latino playwrights, thus starting an official phase in Latino theater that continued to awaken political consciousness in American-born Latino descendants. One of Valdez's plays produced by El Teatro Campesino, *Los Vendidos* (pr. 1967), gives examples of the ideological apparatus of American-born Latino artists. His cast, consisting of Mexican and Mexican American stereotypes (farmworker, urban Johnny, *revolucionario*) confronts the most uncomfortable myths about the people of Mexican heritage in both Anglo-American and Latino cultures.

David Henry Hwang's play *M. Butterfly* (pr. 1988) addresses uniquely Asian American social issues. Hwang uses the true story of a diplomat named Gallimard—who falls in love with an exotic performer portraying the title character, Song Liling, in Giacomo Puccini's opera, *Madama Butterfly* (pr. 1904)—as inspiration for his play. What separates it from historical drama is that Hwang does not attempt to re-create anything other than the personal relationship between the two characters. *M. Butterfly* is a provocative study of Western fantasy about Asia juxtaposed against its reality. Hwang uses Gallimard to represent the West and Song as the embodiment of the East to contrast not only the two cultures but also gender issues. Song says,

> The West has sort of an international rape mentality towards the East. . . . The West thinks of itself as masculine. . . . so the East is feminine. . . . The West believes the East, deep down, wants to be dominated—because a woman can't think for herself.

Gallimard is surprised near the end of the play to discover that his "Butterfly" is really a man, which in turn shatters his fantasy about submissive Asian women and challenges everything he holds to be true. Furthermore, the audience, along with Gallimard, must question its own delusions about sexual and racial stereotypes.

A STATEMENT THROUGH PRODUCTION

The third division of political statement theater can be found when a live production is used to make a statement—possibly one not even intended or inherent in the written play itself. In this form of political theater, the director and production artists are making the statement, not the playwright. It became popular during the twentieth century to set older plays in a contemporary setting, thereby making a political statement. The first important such production, and probably the beginning of the trend, was Orson Welles's 1937 production of a modern-dress *Julius Caesar.* William Shakespeare's *Julius Caesar* (pr. c. 1599-1600) itself combines history and tragedy, set against the backdrop of ancient Rome as it experiences political upheaval and civil unrest. The dichot-

omy between the liberal and conservative in the play makes *Julius Caesar* a popular work to use for political statement through production. In Welles's production, Caesar represented Benito Mussolini, Italy's fascist dictator, so that his murder in the play symbolically presented the hoped-for end of fascist rule in Europe. Most scholars contend, however, that Shakespeare's works are too complex to be so easily compartmentalized.

Nonetheless, during his work with the Depression-era Federal Theatre Project, Welles and his producer John Houseman regularly made headlines for their avant-garde approaches to theater. In 1936, Welles's production of Shakespeare's *Macbeth* made a political statement just by having an all-black cast, something quite uncommon in white theaters and in Shakespearean productions of the 1930's. Probably the most famous political statement made by Welles and Houseman, though, came with their spontaneous and unexpected production of the controversial musical *The Cradle Will Rock* in 1937.

Marc Blitzstein's left-wing opera remains one of the most politically charged musicals in theater history, but its premiere production gave it public attention never dreamed of by Welles and Houseman. *The Cradle Will Rock* is set in "Steeltown, USA," a small town run by the evil capitalistic dictator Mr. Mister. The musical presents a series of vignettes that depict the "selling out" of the local professionals—the newspaper editor, the minister, the artists, and the college president—who all sell their souls to Mr. Mister and become members of his Liberty Committee. The proletarian hero of the piece, Larry Foreman, leads a successful rebellion of factory workers to form unions and take power away from the corrupt capitalistic system, putting it back into the hands of the workers.

Welles and Houseman had mounted the production as part of the Federal Theatre Project Unit 891 at the Maxine Elliot Theater in New York City. After rehearsals at the venue, however, the government locked the building and canceled the production. A crowd of more than six hundred audience members clustered around the door the following evening, June 16, 1937, while Welles and Houseman frantically looked for another theater. Finally, they found an old piano, put it in the back of a truck, and drove up Broadway to the Venice Theater with cast and audience members alike following behind. Their union prohibited the actors from performing on stage, but Welles circumvented this ban by having them perform the opera in the aisles of the theater. Blitzstein sat alone on stage at the piano under one work light and began to play the opening number, and then the actors joined in. The phenomenal opening night garnered coverage on the front page of *The New York Times* the following morning—and a place in history. Although before the show began Welles made an impassioned speech that their protest was artistic, not political, critics and historians alike see this as one of the most political theatrical events in American history.

THEATER FOR SOCIOPOLITICAL CHANGE

A revolutionary new kind of theater, known generally as people's or workers' theater, evolved in Germany during the last half of the nineteenth century and into the 1920's. The League for Proletarian Culture, formed in 1920 by a group of intellectuals, artists, and workers in Berlin, established the first Proletarian Theater as a part of the Workers' Theater Movement (WTM). Many others would soon follow, but Erwin Piscator's Proletarian Theater was the most successful of these, laying the foundation for several important developments to come in the WTM.

The essential tenets of Piscator's Proletarian Theater called for simplicity of design and subordination of artistic goals to revolutionary objectives. It was important that the theater be mobile, which meant minimizing the technical aspects of production. The plays were called "agitprop," an abbreviation for the term agitation-propaganda, and the idea was to stir up the workers to make them emotionally fit for revolution. The plays moved out of established theater buildings and into halls and meeting places throughout Berlin. This new play structure contained a montage of dramatic or even comic scenes, often punctuated by music, in a style similar to German cabaret or newsreels. Piscator envisioned a workers' theater, journalistic in nature and highly stylized with person-

ification of social issues, rapid scene changes, and propagandistic dialogue.

The WTM spread quickly to Britain and inspired many proletarian theaters in the newly formed Soviet Union. The largest and most widespread of these was a group called the Blue Blouses, which offered two main theatrical forms: the Living Newspaper and agitprop plays. The Living Newspaper was improvised drama done on street corners and in warehouses, acting out current news of the day. The Russian population was largely illiterate, and the Living Newspaper performances raised public awareness of political and social events and concerns. The agitprop plays were usually performed in blue shirts (hence the title "Blue Blouses") and dungarees wherever people congregated. The Blue Blouses journal, *Sinyaya Bluza*, defined the movement as a theater born of revolution, both mobile and high-spirited.

The WTM became popular in the late 1920's in the United States when the stock market crash of 1929 brought a major economic depression and an unprecedented loss of jobs. By the time President Franklin D. Roosevelt took office in 1933, income had been cut in half and twelve million people were unemployed. The Depression had a profound impact on union membership, and many employees attempted to run their businesses without any workers' organizations, which led to several abuses of the workers. The oppressed, overworked, and underpaid workers of American industry soon realized that the only ones getting rich from the sweat of their labor were the business owners and company managers. The thought of unifying as a workforce became a very attractive idea, so many plays during this period focused on the establishment of unions to ensure worker safety, income, and fair treatment.

Probably the most notable American play from this period is Clifford Odets's one-act called *Waiting for Lefty*. The Group Theatre first produced it in 1935, and most theater historians consider it the best agitprop play ever written. *Waiting for Lefty* depicts a labor meeting of unionized cab drivers trying to decide if they should strike. Short scenes depicting cruelty to workers and explaining how each union member came to consider a radical path of disobedience interrupt the meeting periodically. Lefty, the play's hero, is killed, and the play ends with the strident scream from all the characters, "Strike! Strike! Strike!" At its first performance, the audience leapt to their feet and joined in, giving the actors a rousing standing ovation and forty curtain calls. Although not a particularly well-written drama, *Waiting for Lefty* spoke to and for a repressed workforce looking for validation for its political cause.

Agitprop and Living Newspaper plays produced by both the WTM and the Federal Theatre Project during the 1930's helped gel the spirit of solidarity among workers and deserve some credit for bringing immense changes to the industrial union scene in subsequent years. When the Congress of Industrial Organizations was formed in 1938, it began making significant improvements in working conditions and ran effective campaigns for union membership.

THEATRE OF THE OPPRESSED

No essay on political theater could be complete without a discussion of Augusto Boal, a Brazilian theater director with a revolutionary concept of using theater directly to explore and influence governmental policies. Boal has traveled extensively through Africa, Australia, Europe, and North and South America demonstrating his theater techniques through workshops and lectures. As founder of the Theatre of the Oppressed movement, he writes, teaches, directs, and theorizes about applying the art of theater to solving social problems.

Theatre of the Oppressed began in the 1960's when Boal would hold discussions following his plays to ask the audience members how they would have solved the problem differently. This custom progressed to a point where he asked the audience to stop the play at any time and propose a different direction for the plot. On one of these occasions, Boal could not understand the suggestion of one audience member so she went up to the stage to take the actor's place in order to explain. This was the birth of what Boal calls the "spect-actor," or spectator-actor. He contends that the audience members should not just be observers but participants. His Theater of the Oppressed theories coalesced in 1971 with the

publication of his book, *The Theatre of the Oppressed.*

As Boal's theories developed over the years, Theatre of the Oppressed evolved into three basic types: Image Theater, Invisible Theater, and Forum Theater. Image Theater occurs when acting teachers use games or exercises. Boal's, on the other hand, is specifically geared toward finding essential truths about people, societies, and cultures. Boal believes that pure imagination exercises can help free the actor of what he calls the "cop in the head," the internal censor that might prevent more liberated thinking.

Invisible Theater is a technique designed to involve the unsuspecting public in a piece of theater. A group of actors rehearses a scene and then takes it to the streets or any area where a large group may be spontaneously gathered. Some act out the scene while others pose as spectators who become involved in the action by commenting on it. For example, one actor may stand on the corner on a sunny day with an umbrella and overcoat, pretending that it is raining. A "spect-actor" comments to someone on the street that he must be crazy. Others make more comments and soon the public is unwittingly pulled into a discussion, free to express opinions or intervene in the action. Invisible Theater resembles agitprop performances, with the exception that Boal's actors never take a political stance. He prefers to allow the audience to come to its own conclusions through cooperative, creative work.

Forum Theater is a theatrical game that depicts the protagonist being oppressed by others. The audience is asked to solve the oppression—how can the person free himself from his oppressors? If one thinks she has the answer, she may come up and play the protagonist. The audience and performers work together as one body to solve the problem of oppression.

Boal's extensive travels to conduct workshops that teach his techniques have opened up a new avenue of interactive theater across the globe. He does not see Theatre of the Oppressed as the only way to do theater, but many share his enthusiasm in using theater in this purely political manner. In his introduction to Boal's second book, *Games for Actors and Non-Actors* (1992), translator Adrian Jackson describes

Theatre of the Oppressed as being about raising questions instead of answering them and challenging rather than accepting.

Since he began his work with the Theatre of the Oppressed, Augusto Boal has written many texts, including *The Rainbow of Desire: The Boal Method of Theatre and Therapy* (1995) and *Legislative Theater* (1998), and has become the subject of numerous scholarly essays and books. From 1993 to 1996, he served as Vereador (Member of Parliament) for his native Rio de Janeiro and used his revolutionary theater techniques to shape legislative decisions and policies.

BIBLIOGRAPHY

Berghaus, Gunter, ed. *Fascism and Theatre: Comparative Studies on the Aesthetics and Politics of Performance in Europe, 1925-1945*. Providence, R.I.: Berghahn Books, 1996. A collection of essays about the intimate connection between theater and politics in Italy, France, and Germany.

Colleran, Jeanne, and Jenny S. Spencer, eds. *Staging Resistance: Essays on Political Theater*. Ann Arbor: University of Michigan Press, 2001. A wide variety of essays on political theater and the work of Irish, English, French, Australian, and Asian directors and playwrights.

Goldstein, Malcolm. *The Political Stage: American Drama and Theater of the Great Depression*. New York: Oxford University Press, 1974. Good coverage of the American WTM, the Federal Theatre Project, the Group Theatre, the Theater Guild, and Broadway theater during the 1930's.

Himelstein, Morgan Y. *Drama Was a Weapon: The Left-Wing Theater in New York, 1929-1941*. New Brunswick, N.J.: Rutgers University Press, 1963. Comprehensive overview of the development of political theater during the Great Depression containing a very useful bibliography of plays, articles, and books on the subject.

Itzin, Catherine. *Stages in the Revolution: Political Theater in Britain Since 1968*. London: Methuen, 1982. Chapters cover important political playwrights, theater groups, and theater organizations in Britain, including Caryl Churchill, John Arden, and the Agitprop Street Players.

Scharine, Richard G. *From Class to Caste in American Drama: Political and Social Themes Since the 1930's*. New York: Greenwood Press, 1991. A study of American political theater from the 1930's through the postmodern period. Good coverage of World War II, the Cold War, and the Vietnam era, as well as civil rights issues for blacks, Latinos, women, and homosexuals.

Stourac, Richard, and Kathleen McCreery. *Theater as a Weapon: Workers' Theater in the Soviet Union, Germany, and Britain, 1917-1934*. London: Routledge and Kegan Paul, 1986. A thorough overview of the WTM throughout Germany, Britain, the Soviet Union, and America.

Jill Stapleton-Bergeron

CINEMA AND DRAMA

Live drama is an ancient art form with thousands of years of recorded history and ongoing cultural vitality. Cinema is a much newer art form, with a history dating back only to approximately 1895 but having a mass appeal that has pushed live theater into a secondary position in all but a handful of urban locations.

SIMILARITIES AND DIFFERENCES

As art forms, drama and cinema have important likenesses and intriguing differences. First, both are primarily story-based art forms. Second, both drama and cinema depend primarily on performers and performance to communicate the story to the audience. A stage play or a screenplay can be read like a novel, but only speaking, gesturing human actors can give the story its full, intended realization. Third, both drama and cinema share certain common supporting features. These include sets, props, costumes, and all the other elements that make up *mise en scène*; music and other sound effects; and a play script in which the primary thrust of the story is articulated through human speech or "dialogue." Even in the silent era, films relied heavily on human speech that was understood through contextual intuition; a combination of gesture, facial expression, and lip reading; and inserts of printed, projected text.

Despite—or, perhaps, because of—these many likenesses, much has been written about the differences between the two media. For instance, in cinema circles, the terms "talky" and "stagey" are negative adjectives that imply the film has not liberated itself from its stage-bound origins. In the world of motion pictures, "cinematic" is the primary form of praise, implying that the film makes use of the advantages (camera angles, editing, special effects) offered by the medium.

In part, these kinds of distinctions derive from the historical rivalry of the two forms. However, they also point to certain crucial conditions of production. Indeed, they can all be said to originate in one specific condition: dramatic scripts or "plays" are pro- duced on a stage, by actors performing directly and personally in the company of the audience. In cinema, however, the actors perform for the director and the camera. Their performance is recorded on an intermediary medium, traditionally celluloid film and increasingly digital formats, to be cut and manipulated for an audience who will be present for a performance of two-dimensional simulacra of the live actors. From this single difference—which can be located specifically in the intermediary function of camera and film—come nearly all of the much discussed differences between the two media.

For instance, the visual field of cinema is potentially much greater than that of stage production. This is a direct function of the wonderful mobility of modern camera equipment and advances in cinematic special effects. The stage is capable of splendid effects of spectacle, but no stage could convincingly deal with the events of films such as *2001: A Space Odyssey* (1968) or *Raiders of the Lost Ark* (1981).

Performers work in very different circumstances. The stage actor prepares his or her role to be performed sequentially, in real time, from beginning to end in a single developing sequence. The screen actor works piecemeal, creating the role in fragments that the director and editor stitch together in post-production to create the illusion of a sequential, emotionally evolving performance.

On the live stage, the performer is always conscious of playing directly and personally to the audience. Mistakes cannot be edited out in post-production, and charisma must be generated from within and projected throughout the house without the aid of lingering, larger-than-life closeups or other amplifications of effect that the camera is uniquely qualified to create.

Still, despite the differences between the two media, there are core abilities and practices that keep stage and screen united. Most screenwriters start out writing plays because, above all, they must master the art of creating character, plot, and theme through the spoken word. Most actors learn and perfect their craft on the stage before live audiences. Even though many actors leave the stage when the world of film calls, few can say they have made it without stage experience, and a surprising number return to the stage on a regular basis to refresh their art and to renew their acquaintance with their audience.

THE BEGINNINGS

Historically, the art of narrative cinema is intertwined with its great historical precursor, the live theater. The nature of this relationship has long been a contentious issue in film criticism and theory. Secure in the cinema's current dominance as the premiere source of performed story art, film theorists tend to stress the cinema's uniqueness and its independence from stage-bound limitations. However, filmmakers were not always so eager to stress such differences, and in the early days of movies often tried explicitly—and successfully—to appropriate the success of the live theater.

Although human speech is the core of stage drama, cinema, an almost silent medium for its first three decades, began from the start to incorporate elements of stage practice and personnel into the filmed product. During these years, vaudeville sketches and theatrical excerpts were routinely filmed and exhibited in cinema theaters and nickelodeons. A parallel development led to full-length stage plays appearing on screen in condensed versions. William Shakespeare was a favorite for such treatment, in part because the stories were well known and the written texts accessible. Additionally, as the silent film moved into its mature phase (1910-1927), the desire to put full-length plays on screen helped producers like Adolf Zuckor and Daniel Frohman and their Famous Players Film Company to break the industry's own self-imposed one- or two-reel (fifteen- to thirty-minute) limit on theatrical films. Thus the full-length stage play helped give rise to the full-length feature film.

Among the famous stage plays that found their way to the silent screen were Sir James Barrie's *Peter Pan: Or, The Boy Who Wouldn't Grow Up* (pr. 1904; film 1924), Owen Wister and Kirk La Shelle's stage adaptation of Wister's popular novel *The Virginian*

(1902; film 1914), Oscar Wilde's *Lady Windermere's Fan* (pr. 1892; film 1925), and Eugene O'Neill's *Anna Christie* (pr. 1921; film 1923), later pronounced by O'Neill as one of his two favorite screen adaptations of his own work.

THE EARLY SOUND ERA

Throughout the silent-film era, inventors were working to produce systems that would allow sound (particularly dialogue) to be recorded for synchronized reproduction with the film. This development came to fruition with the nearly simultaneous development of Vitaphone, Phonofilm, and Movietone. Vitaphone was the first to make it to the screen, in the Warner Bros. adaptation of Samson Raphaelson's stage hit *The Jazz Singer* (pr. 1925; film 1927).

Though sound now seems like an obvious asset to the film industry, it met with initial resistance from the major studios, who were reluctant to pay for the new equipment, and from some filmmakers, who feared sound would turn cinema into mere filmed theater. The believers were smaller commercial studios such as Warner Bros. and Fox which correctly predicted that synchronized sound would give them a competitive edge against the established major studios such as Paramount.

The immediate popularity of the new sound film also created an even more favorable market for scripts that had already proven themselves on the stage. John C. Tibbetts and James M. Welsh estimate that at least 28 percent of feature films released between 1928 and 1930 were based on stage plays.

The standard-bearer was Eugene O'Neill. *Anna Christie* was remade for sound to serve as Greta Garbo's talking debut in the role of Anna. The film stayed faithful to the stage play, with a minimal effort to "open up" with exterior scenes, and is now largely regarded as a classic example of a stage play that never quite became cinema, despite a powerful script and excellent cast. Other O'Neill plays that came to the screen during the 1930's and 1940's included *The Long Voyage Home* (pr. 1917; film 1940), *Strange Interlude* (pr. 1928; film 1932), and *The Emperor Jones* (pr. 1920; film *Emperor Jones*, 1933). The latter two were among O'Neill's most daring antirealistic theatrical experiments, and both of the subsequent films show the strain of the attempt to domesticate them for the screen.

In general, it proved easier to translate the more conventionally realistic playwrights to the screen than O'Neill, whose inventiveness derived from a deep rethinking of the expressive possibilities of the live theater. The pull of the movies of this era was toward realism, whether in comedy or drama. One playwright who made the transition successfully and frequently to the screen was Lillian Hellman with *The Little Foxes* (pr. 1939; film 1941), *Watch on the Rhine* (pr. 1941; film 1943), and *The Children's Hour* (pr. 1934), the latter filmed as *These Three* in 1936. Other 1930's and 1940's playwrights whose stage work made it to the screen were Ben Hecht and Charles MacArthur, Robert Sherwood, Maxwell Anderson, Claire Boothe, and Philip Barry.

THE 1950'S AND 1960'S

Despite the impressive list of plays that achieved both artistic and commercial success during the 1930's and 1940's, it would appear that the greatest era of this crossover activity came during the 1950's and early 1960's. Not only did a new generation of important writers of drama and comedy emerge on Broadway, but also that unique and distinctive New York invention, the Broadway musical, came fully into its own, both on the stage and in expensive, lavishly staged, star-studded, full-color Hollywood versions.

The main creative engine of the Broadway-to-Hollywood movement of nonmusical stage plays was undoubtedly Tennessee Williams. Among his stage works that came to the screen during this period were *The Glass Menagerie* (pr. 1944; film 1950), *A Streetcar Named Desire* (pr. 1947; film 1951), *The Rose Tattoo* (pr. 1951; film 1955), *Cat on a Hot Tin Roof* (pr. 1955; film 1958), *Suddenly Last Summer* (pr. 1958; film 1959), *Sweet Bird of Youth* (pr. 1959; film 1962), and *The Night of the Iguana* (pr. 1961; film 1964). With these seven theater-to-film plays, Williams stretched the American filmgoer's imagination in the dark areas of desire, passion, loneliness, and forbidden sex. The censors were able to soften the de-

tails of Williams's themes, but there was no way to hide them completely.

The plays of William Inge also made impressive transitions from stage to screen. These included *Come Back, Little Sheba* (pr. 1950; film 1952), *Picnic* (pr. 1953; film 1955), *Bus Stop* (pr. 1955; film 1956), and *The Dark at the Top of the Stairs* (pr. 1957; film 1960). Other strong plays that made good movies include George Axelrod's *The Seven Year Itch* (pr. 1952; film 1955), Donald Bevan's *Stalag 17* (pr. 1951; film 1953), Robert Anderson's *Tea and Sympathy* (pr. 1953; film 1956), William Gibson's *The Miracle Worker* (pr. 1959; film 1962), and Edward Albee's *Who's Afraid of Virginia Woolf?* (pr. 1962; film 1966). Two plays by African American authors that brought black concerns to a mainstream audience were Lorraine Hansberry's classic *A Raisin in the Sun* (pr. 1959; film 1961) and LeRoi Jones's (Amiri Baraka's) *Dutchman* (pr. 1964; film 1966), the latter bringing a distinctly Off-Broadway sensibility to the issues of race, class, and sex in the big city.

The 1950's and 1960's were also notable for the adaptation of Broadway musicals to the Hollywood screen. Musical films had been part of cinema since the development of commercially and technologically feasible synchronization processes, and the New York stage had always been home to a variety of musical stage shows, ranging from nonnarrative musical reviews to lightweight, formulaic musical comedies to the more narratively unified and musically refined operettas of Sigmund Romberg, Victor Herbert, and others. Many of these were turned into popular films, but in 1943, with the production of Richard Rodgers and Oscar Hammerstein II's *Oklahoma!*, the Broadway musical achieved a new level of musical and theatrical dynamism.

Eager for product that would fill its new widescreen technologies with color, music, and spectacle (and do something that the rising television medium could not match), Hollywood lavished talent, time, and money on a series of new musicals of unparalleled vitality and variety. The greatest names in American musical theater—Rodgers, Hammerstein, Cole Porter, Moss Hart, Jerome Kern, Leonard Bernstein, and more—were brought to screen audiences in the United States and around the world. Among the greatest productions during this era were *Annie Get Your Gun* (pr. 1946; film 1950), *Show Boat* (pr. 1927; film 1951), *Kiss Me, Kate* (1948; film 1953), *Oklahoma!* (film 1955), *The King and I* (pr. 1951; film 1956), *The Music Man* (pr. 1957; film 1962), *My Fair Lady* (pr. 1956; film 1964), *West Side Story* (pr. 1957; film 1961), *The Sound of Music* (pr. 1959; film 1965), and *Hello, Dolly!* (pr. 1964; film 1969).

AFTER THE 1960's

After 1969, mounting such spectacular shows and moving them to Hollywood seemed to grow more difficult. Bob Fosse became a force with *Sweet Charity* (1966; film 1969) and *Cabaret* (pr. 1966; film 1972), but the most creative single individual working on Broadway, Stephen Sondheim, seemed all but ignored by Hollywood (his *A Little Night Music* of 1973 was filmed for release in 1977 by a European production group). "New age" stage hits such as *Hair* (pr. 1968; film 1979), *Godspell* (pr. 1971; film 1973), and *Jesus Christ Superstar* (1971; film 1973) had bumpy roads to the screen. With a pair of notable exceptions—*Grease* (1972; film 1978) and *A Chorus Line* (1975; film 1985)—the great age of Broadway musical adaptation ended with the 1960's.

More in the traditional mode has been the work of Neil Simon, one of the very few stage playwrights whose work—like that of O'Neill, Hellman, Williams, and Inge before him—almost always brings a guaranteed audience with it. From *Barefoot in the Park* (pr. 1963; film 1967) to *Lost in Yonkers* (pr. 1991; film 1993), Simon has written stage comedies that Hollywood loves to screen, top stars love to act in, and audiences line up to see.

The younger generation of playwrights has produced some challenging plays that have been made into interesting, often critically and commercially successful films, but most have not sustained a cinema connection by playwriting alone. Those who have forged careers in stage and screen have done so in the manner of David Mamet and Aaron Sorkin, by becoming screenwriters, producers, and directors of their own work and that of others. In the case of

Sorkin, television has beckoned, and Sorkin has responded with the popular and critically successful television program *The West Wing* (1999).

SHAKESPEARE ON SCREEN

With the evident slippage of relationship between the stage playwright and the silver screen, it is noteworthy that one playwright who remains current is one of the classics, William Shakespeare, whose plays came to the screen in no fewer than one dozen theatrical screen releases since 1990 alone. Shakespearean screen production has a long and distinguished place in the history of the relationship between drama and cinema.

The filming of Shakespearean texts (not contemporary language adaptations) reframes the argument over whether the image should be more important than the word in filmmaking. The image remains primary, but such is the power and prestige of Shakespeare's poetic speech that it goes a long way to evening the balance in critical debates. In addition, because Shakespeare's imagination ranged freely beyond the limits of the physical stage, it rarely seems strange or forced to open up the texts to multiple locations or settings. Finally, although Shakespeareans and moviegoers may debate over whether to be "authentic" or modern in costume and setting, actual Elizabethan stage practice seemed to be tolerant of both approaches, and this invites experiment and innovation on both stage and film.

A short list of notable Shakespeare films would have to include the major works of such Shakespearean *auteurs* as Lawrence Olivier, *Hamlet* (pr. c. 1600-1601; film 1955), *Henry V* (pr. c. 1598-1599; film 1944); Orson Welles, *Othello* (pr. 1604; film 1952), *Chimes at Midnight* (1967; adaptation of several Shakepeare plays); Franco Zefferreli, *The Taming of the Shrew* (pr. c. 1593-1594; film 1966), *Romeo and Juliet* (pr. c. 1595-1596; film 1968); and Kenneth Brannagh, *Henry V* (film 1989), *Hamlet* (film 1996), *Much Ado About Nothing* (pr. pr. c. 1598-1599; film 1993). However, there are many other films of varying degrees of fidelity to or freedom from the Shakespearean text that capture on film the spirit of Shakespeare's multifaceted genius. Remaking Shakespeare keeps the cinema in a fruitful and honest relationship with its theatrical roots.

LEGACY OF THE STAGE

The complexities of the relationship between cinema and drama resist comfortable generalizations. As much as cinéastes may assert the independence of the cinema from the stage, there can be no doubt that historically the early filmmakers were dependent on the theater both for performing talent in all genres and for story material that brought with it strong conflicts, human dimensions, engaging stories, and storytelling techniques, and rich resources of character and character development. Scholarship in silent film shows this was as true before the coming of sound as it certainly was afterward. Experience has shown that the simple filming of a great play rarely makes a great movie. Experience makes it equally evident that a great movie is impossible without the inner, dramatic resources developed first for the live stage.

A review of the film industry's own major honors, the Academy Awards, is an interesting indicator of the high regard with which Hollywood still rewards a good stage play. Consider these winners of the Best Picture Award: *You Can't Take It with You* (1938), *Casablanca* (1943), *Hamlet* (1948), *West Side Story* (1961), *My Fair Lady* (1964), *A Man for All Seasons* (1966), *Oliver!* (1968), *Amadeus* (1984), and *Driving Miss Daisy* (1989). These outstanding theatrical films are just a small sampling of numerous other filmed plays in which directors, actors (lead and supporting), and other talented theater and film professionals were honored by their peers. Ultimately, the lesson is that while the cinema may have outgrown its theatrical precursor in entertainment industry power and prestige, it still recognizes the need to make use of the theater, to be renewed by it, and to honor it.

BIBLIOGRAPHY

Brady, Ben. *Principles of Adaptation for Film and Television.* Austin: University of Texas Press, 1998. A veteran television producer and screenwriter, Brady provides a vivid how-to book concerning all aspects of the adaptation process, from evaluating the potential of a written narrative, to character and dialogue development, to understanding "camera language."

Buhler, Stephen M. *Shakespeare in the Cinema.* Albany: State University of New York Press, 2001. Examines the history of Shakespearean film adaptations, with chapter titles that include "Shakespeare and the Screen Idol," "Ocular Proof: Three Versions of *Othello*," "The Revenge of the Actor-Manager," and "Documentary Shakespeare."

McAuliffe, Jody, ed. *Plays, Movies, and Critics.* Durham, N.C.: Duke University Press, 1994. A collection of essays exploring the interconnections between drama and cinema, including interviews with noted figures such as Martin Scorsese and Stanley Kaufman.

Manville, Roger. *Theater and Film.* Rutherford, N.J.: Fairleigh Dickinson University Press, 1979. After some concise theoretical chapters, this readable, informative book makes its main points through careful analyses of a small group of individual films.

Phillips, Gene D. *The Films of Tennessee Williams.* Philadelphia, Pa.: Art Alliance Press, 1980. Explores the adaptations of Williams's plays into film and looks at the portrayal of the American South in cinema.

Rothwell, Kenneth S. *A History of Shakespeare on Screen: A Century of Film and Television.* New York: Cambridge University Press, 1999. A wide-ranging, well-written, genuinely comprehensive historical overview of the top films from the 1890's to the 1990's.

Tibbets, John C., and James M. Welsh. *The Encyclopedia of Stage Plays into Film.* New York: Facts on File, 2001. A handsome, well-illustrated reference work with excellent overview essays and individual play entries. An indispensable source.

Roger J. Stilling

RADIO DRAMA

The first radio station in the United States, Pittsburgh's KDKA, began broadcasting in 1920. The idea of competing networks scheduling program slates to win listeners from one another was almost a decade away. By 1922, only thirty stations operated in the United States, but radio was already becoming the new-appliance phenomenon that later television, the videocassette recorder, and the personal computer would become: By 1923, 556 stations broadcast an assortment of programs. The production of receiver sets shows the same explosion of growth: From only a few receivers being produced in 1921, the Radio Corporation of America (RCA, incorporated on October 17, 1919) and others such as Atwater Kent and Westinghouse Electric Corporation manufactured one hundred thousand sets in 1922 and five hundred thousand in 1923. For the first time in 1923, both Sears, Roebuck, and Company and Montgomery Ward offered radios in their catalogs.

Tom Lewis's book on the genesis of radio further points out that the end of the 1920's saw another surge in the popularity of the medium, sparked by the public's desire to follow the heroics of Charles A. Lindbergh. When William S. Paley combined two small networks into the Columbia Broadcasting System (CBS) and named himself president, he established conditions that would affect not only the development of American radio drama but also the basic nature of the medium.

Paley sought to compete with the National Broadcasting Company (NBC) and its president David Sarnoff by widening the types of programs broadcast. NBC had until then been featuring programs that often played to the highest tastes of listeners. Paley eschewed classical concerts and educational fare and instead found a receptive audience that enjoyed jazz, vaudeville comics, and soap opera. It was NBC that eventually broadcast the most popular radio series ever, *Amos 'n' Andy* (beginning in 1926 as *Sam 'n' Henry* on Chicago's WGN, the show first aired on NBC under its familiar title on August 19, 1929), and the national sensation of that comedy spurred further sales of radios.

Worthington Miner wrote about the early days of the medium and how the expenses of creating a national industry were absorbed by the broadcasters, the manufacturers, and the sponsors. The listeners, however, had to pay too:

> [T]he price to the public was the stamp of a salesman's mind on the dramatic content and intent of every program put on the air. . . . [A] vigorous theater thrives on controversy, and in precisely those areas of prejudice and conviction—sex, politics, and religion—that are taboo for the salesman.

Miner added that "the wonder is that anything of quality or substance ever reached the public air."

His comments identify both the main propellant and the main obstacle for first-rate radio drama in the United States: commercialization. The revenues generated by the sale of airtime made possible innovative, intelligent plays such as those produced by Orson Welles, Norman Corwin, and Arch Oboler in the 1930's and 1940's; the need, however, for large audiences to satisfy the sponsors virtually guaranteed that most radio shows followed the safe rather than the experimental. Howard Fink tabulated the extreme imbalance toward the popular in American radio drama and concluded that during the twenty-year span from the rise of radio to the rise of television at most only twelve radio series (out of some six thousand listed by the *Variety Radio Directory*) attempted serious plays written expressly for the radio or adapted from other media. That comes to less than half of 1 percent.

The natural comparison to radio in Great Britain tells a different story. The work of John Reith as the first general manager of the British Broadcasting Corporation (BBC) saved British radio and later television from the American type of commercialization by having the BBC set up as a public utility partly paid for by the small fees of listeners. The history of serious radio drama in England has never been a summary of isolated plays and programs of merit but rather the story of the development of an art form that continued even after the rise of television.

It may be unfair to blame Paley for the paradox of American radio—how commercialization alternatively abetted and retarded literary drama. The facts support different readings. Paley may have lowered the quality of the airwaves by broadcasting to a wider audience, or he may have begun to recognize that the growth of the industry was great enough to make room for smaller audiences of different tastes. Paley, along with Irving Reis, for example, became the driving force behind *The Columbia Workshop* (1936), one of the best dramatic anthologies in American radio.

A half-hour "sustaining series" (that is, free from commercial sponsorship), *The Columbia Workshop* debuted with a suspense drama written by Reis, *Meridian 7-1212*, a work that Fink described as going "behind the mechanical illusions of realistic sound to show a real understanding of the *space* of the medium, especially the necessity of creating verbal and intellectual complications to replace the visual complexities of the theatre." The following year, *The Columbia Workshop* offered the first American verse play written for radio, Archibald MacLeish's *The Fall of the City: A Verse Play for Radio* (pr. 1937). MacLeish had written a polemic against fascism, and Reis cast young Welles as the narrator who describes the subjugation of thousands of people to a conqueror who turns out to be a fearful-sounding but empty suit of armor. The narrator's description of the lifting of the visor and the hollowness inside placed a vivid image in the minds of radio listeners.

The broadcast became the single most famous radio show until that time. Blending sound techniques and poetry to exploit the theater-of-the-mind capabilities of radio, Reis broadcast the show from an armory to approximate the acoustics of a town square. He recorded the sounds of two hundred extras and timed the playbacks during the performance so that, following the live cheers of the extras, the echoing crowd noise sounded overwhelming. Welles had to perform his lines in the quiet of an isolation booth, a change made out of necessity but one that created a type of verbal concerto through the balance of contrasting sounds of the crowd and the narrator.

ORSON WELLES

Just as *Amos 'n' Andy* fueled the growth of popular radio, the MacLeish broadcast made serious radio drama exciting and more popular. Soon writers of note such as W. H. Auden and Stephen Vincent Benét were crafting scripts directly for the radio; later, other literary figures such as Sherwood Anderson, Maxwell Anderson, Edna St. Vincent Millay, William Saroyan, and Dorothy Parker would work in the medium. Welles's next radio assignment continued the innovations. His seven-part version of Victor Hugo's *Les Misérables* (1862; English translation, 1862) for the Mutual Network was called by Welles a "projection" rather than an adaptation or dramatization. To prepare what may have been the first broadcast miniseries, Welles chose important selections from the novel to be read by himself as narrator or by actors performing the characters. He used sound effects and music to accompany Hugo's prose and also played the part of Jean Valjean. The result, according to Welles's biographer Frank Brady, was that "Welles developed the character of Jean Valjean more fully than it had been in the novel."

With his growing experiences in radio, Welles, unlike many radio actors, by now knew the difference between reading lines in front of a microphone and sounding on the air like a real person. In such a context in which sound is the only medium for communication, to refer to the actor's voice as an instrument risks understatement. Brady wrote that Welles would position himself before a microphone as if it were a kind of sonic mirror, and "he would seemingly be able to gesture with sound and move himself in space, creating illusions of intimacy or distance by employing only certain voice changes."

In 1938, CBS offered Welles total artistic control of a new sustaining series to begin on July 11. The network hoped that the program would receive enough favorable attention to bring in advertisers as continuing sponsors for the hour-long show. *First Person Singular*, the name that was eventually chosen, would also provide another vehicle for Welles's Mercury players, a repertory company performing in theater works that Welles and John Houseman were directing and producing. The limited budget and the weekly demands of radio (and also perhaps the satisfactions of total artistic control) kept Welles from commissioning original scripts, so he settled on the popular classics to adapt himself with the help of Houseman, Howard Koch, Richard Brooks, Abraham Polonsky, and Herman J. Mankiewicz. Their first offering was *Dracula* (1897), restructured from the letters-and-diary approach in which Bram Stoker had written it into a style more suited to radio. His other shows in his first season included adaptations of *Treasure Island* (1883; on July 18), *A Tale of Two Cities* (1859; July 25), *The Thirty-nine Steps* (1915; August 5), three short stories (August 8), *Hamlet, Prince of Denmark* (pr. c. 1600-1601; August 15), and Welles's favorite novel, G. K. Chesterton's *The Man Who Was Thursday: A Nightmare* (1908; September 5). CBS renewed the series for the fall and renamed it *Mercury Theatre on the Air*.

The most famous Mercury performance came later in 1938 on Halloween Eve, when CBS broadcast an adaptation by Koch of H. G. Wells's novel *The War of the Worlds* (1898). Welles decided to tell the story of the Martian invasion in the format of a special-report newcast. His inspiration may have partly been the popular show *The March of Time* (1931), which dramatized actual news events in a radio studio with sound effects and a live orchestra. Such a format smudged the line between the real and the fictional and testified to the power of drama on radio. In an age before the ubiquitous camcorder gave television newscasts their immediacy, radio simply manufactured its reality, re-creating baseball games and news events as needed. *The March of Time* was the most popular news program on the air. In interviews years later, Welles said he also intended in the broadcast to lampoon the seriousness of radio and the way listeners passively accepted everything they heard over the airwaves.

For the man-from-Mars broadcast, Welles wanted to develop the novel's science-fiction premise realistically. The actor playing a field reporter, for example, listened to the recordings of on-the-air accounts of the burning of the dirigible *Hindenburg* and tried to mimic the eyewitness panic. According to Houseman, the opening of the show was intentionally boring in its protracted use of simulated dance music from a Brooklyn hotel to contrast the later urgency of the supposed news bulletins. The show would switch its listeners from the network newsroom to remote feeds from the invasion sites. Welles played Professor Pierson, an astronomer at an observatory. Although the beginning of the broadcast explained that the program was a dramatization of *The War of the Worlds* and repeated that disclaimer later, the show nevertheless created widespread panic when many listeners thought that the world was actually being invaded. Welles and the Mercury players were front-page news the next morning. Ironically, for all Welles's ambitious literary efforts in the medium, this was the broadcast that eventually won the program a sponsor. On December 9, 1938, the *Mercury Theatre on the Air* became the *Campbell Playhouse*.

Although nothing matched the invasion broadcast for sensationalism, some of Welles's other shows perhaps illustrate better his mastery of radio as a storytelling medium. On the whole, he tended to think of the scripts for broadcast as stories rather than as plays. As Richard Wilson, of the Mercury actors, describes it: "Radio is the medium for the story. The best storyteller was Orson. . . . He likened radio listeners to the audience that gathered around a storyteller in the town square, held spellbound with imaginative and fanciful tales." The show for October 29, 1939, was a radio version of Booth Tarkington's novel *The Magnificent Ambersons* (1918).

In 1942, Welles would also choose Tarkington's novel as the subject for his second film, but he knew that he could not play the part of George Amberson Minafer on screen, since the tall Welles was too heavy and mature looking to portray convincingly a spoiled adolescent. On radio, however, Welles played George and succeeded at bringing out both the proud and the whiny sides of pampered youth. The overlapping dialogue and sound montage that Welles's early films *Citizen Kane* (1941) and *The Magnificent Ambersons* (1942) employ so effectively have their roots in the techniques of radio drama. (Certainly Welles's radio talents invigorated his own films and even motion pictures in general; the use of sound montage in radio, however, is sometimes mistakenly credited to Welles when the work of True Boardman on the CBS anthology *Sunday Afternoon Theatre*, 1937—also known as *Silver Theatre*—probably deserves that distinction.)

Welles adapted Joseph Conrad's *Heart of Darkness* (1902) twice for radio. The second Conrad broadcast, from March 13, 1945, appeared on the series *This Is My Best* (1944), for which Welles had become director as well as host. Welles, playing the narrator Marlow, used the grunts of the natives lugging ivory to suggest the ominous climate of Africa. After journeying up the river to find Kurtz, his predecessor, Marlow hears Kurtz's last anguished whisper "the horror, the horror" and senses the degree to which Kurtz has viewed, and become involved in, the dark side of human behavior. When Marlow, however, returns to meet with Kurtz's fiancée and is asked to relate the dying man's last words, he lies and says that Kurtz spoke his fiancée's name. The audience hears the ghostly echo of Kurtz, however, repeating "the horror, the horror" and understands in that single aural image that the evils experienced by Kurtz have found their way into the subconscious of Marlow.

Shows such as *The Mercury Theatre on the Air* owed part of their mystique to the live nature of the broadcasts. In the days before magnetic tape, scratchy acetate discs were the only way engineers could reproduce sound, and so programs were aired live. Colorful stories exist about Welles, who was widely employed as an actor in live radio, using a blaring ambulance as his crosstown transportation between one show and another. Sometimes still in his theater makeup, he would race from the ambulance into a private elevator to be whisked up to a broadcast studio and handed a script minutes before airtime. Photographs show him as director of his own program, standing on a raised platform before a podium and a microphone with an engineering booth in front of him, actors and the sound-effects staff to his left, and Bernard Herrmann and his orchestra behind him. Everyone wore headphones, and Welles worked the creative ensemble like a conductor of sorts, reading lines and cuing others in order to obtain the right sound mix. John Houseman deserves credit for disciplining Welles's productive but often uncontrolled

genius. In a rare surviving disc of a rehearsal session, Welles can be heard intoning perfectly the lines from a Shakespearean soliloquy and then bursting into a profane string of epithets because at the end of the speech he elided the *t* in "restless." Such a slip might not be noticed onstage or on film, where both the eye and the ear are occupied, but radio augmented the aural dimension to a degree that the speech had to be consonant perfect. Such dramatic heights were never far from the mercantile because Welles frequently read the commercials, too. One critic of the time lamented: "It's a shock to hear a plug for prune juice by someone who sounds like the Archbishop of Canterbury."

Just as fascinating as the way live shows were prepared are the accounts of resourcefulness of those in charge of sound effects. Before the invention of tape libraries of effects, sound engineers had to re-create live on the air the sounds needed for a particular show. For their broadcast of *A Tale of Two Cities*, Welles and Houseman, for example, experimented for hours in order to find the right vegetable to hack for the severing crunch of the guillotine (they finally selected a cabbage). The jobs of sound-effect engineers required them to cultivate a lore all their own. Trial and error taught them that a knife plunged into a potato or grapefruit close to the microphone made the sound of a stabbed torso. Shaking wheat stalks produced a whistle like wind blowing through brush. Squeezing a box of corn starch made scrunches like footsteps in snow. Hitting a sponge simulated the thud of a punch to the stomach.

CORWIN, OBOLER, AND POPULAR RADIO DRAMA

Along with Welles, Norman Corwin and Arch Oboler also stand out for their important work in creating serious radio drama. Corwin's first series was *Words Without Music* (1938), which combined Corwin's own scripts with adaptations of classics such as the poetry of Walt Whitman and Carl Sandburg. In setting free verse for the radio, Corwin let each poem suggest the best approach, but he is particularly remembered for using choral speech effectively. Corwin's next series, *Pursuit of Happiness* (1939), introduced what Corwin called a "radio opera," a blend of music, documentary, and drama. If Welles's gifts to radio were primarily those of the consummate actor-director, Corwin's legacies were those of the writer. His sensitivity to language aided in his broadcasts of poetry and in imparting a lyrical dimension to his own scripts. Like Welles, Corwin was associated with *The Columbia Workshop*. His radio script coauthored with Lucille Fletcher, *My Client Curley* (1940), about a luckless theatrical agent who happens on a boy with a dancing caterpillar, became one of the classics of radio and was later made into a film. Another series, *Columbia Presents Corwin* (1944), continued his originality and is regarded as perhaps his best work. Some of Corwin's memorable plots for this series include a story about a boy's visit to heaven in search of his lost dog and a dramatization of the return of Abraham Lincoln's body by train to Springfield, Illinois.

Oboler first gained attention in popular radio by working with performers such as Rudy Vallee, Eddie Cantor, Milton Berle, and Edgar Bergen. The incongruity of a ventriloquist performing on radio did not deter millions from enjoying Bergen (nor for that matter a radio dance show featuring Fred Astaire), and Oboler learned the techniques of radio drama in this apprenticeship. Oboler's first work as a writer-director came on the NBC suspense program *Lights Out* (1936), which made his name well known. His sustaining series *Arch Oboler's Plays* (1939) offered anthology programming and competed with both Welles and *The Columbia Workshop*. Oboler relied often on the psychological element of radio and explored the consciousness of the central character to carry forward the story. For example, Oboler's episode from *Lights Out* called "Oxychloride X" focuses on a college student hazed by fraternity men. The highlight of the show occurs when the student decides to get even and travels across campus at night to break into the science laboratory and concoct an all-powerful solvent. His wild mutterings organize the scene, reveal his insecurities, and establish an eerie tone. Like Corwin, Oboler worked during the war on propaganda plays for radio, which, more centered on messages, were less innovative in technique.

ATMOSPHERIC TECHNIQUES

The mainstream of American radio, though utilizing the dramatic form, featured almost exclusively popular rather than serious programs. Freed from seriousness of purpose and depth of thought, these shows nevertheless reveal at times aspects of technique that showcase the medium well. The sound effects and voice characterizations of Mel Blanc, for example, greatly enhanced the comedy of Jack Benny. When Benny started up his Maxwell, Blanc's exaggerated sputters all but gave the car a personality; when Benny opened his vault, Blanc's creaks and groans made the comedian's stinginess something that could be heard. Benny moved his show to television in the 1950's, and audiences actually saw a set designer's version of the famous vault. This reality, however, probably did not measure up to the medieval picture in the minds of listeners. Fibber McGee's closet of junk, the clip-clop of horse-drawn hansom cabs in Sherlock Holmes's Victorian London, and the Wild West of the Lone Ranger illustrate the power of radio serial drama to unlock the imagination.

One of the longest-running detective programs, *The Shadow* (1931), also used the medium well. The Shadow of the pulp magazines published during the run of the radio show was a sinister figure in black who used blazing revolvers to fight crime. The character on radio, however, was never seen. Having the power "to cloud men's minds," the hero seemed to appear and penetrate the psychological defenses of the criminals with his uncanny powers. In the episode titled "The White Legion," The Shadow (performed by Welles) intimidates a secret society by exposing its members' identities. The final scene takes place in open court, where suddenly the mysterious voice of The Shadow disrupts the proceedings and names the judge himself as the ringleader of the criminals. The series' atmosphere catered to the imaginative powers of its audience.

JOHN DICKINSON CARR AND VAL GIELGUD

Another gifted writer from the flowering of radio is John Dickson Carr. Carr is mainly remembered as a detective novelist whose books employ locked-room puzzles. Because he was also a master of atmosphere and mood, his talent thrived in radio. Carr wrote mystery plays on both sides of the Atlantic, and his experiences point out some of the differences between American and British radio drama. Carr submitted his first radio play, a three-part work featuring his Chestertonian hero Dr. Gideon Fell, to Val Gielgud, the head of drama programming for the BBC. In England, Carr learned, writing took precedence over time limits and genre. Gielgud did not feel obligated to adhere to the formula conventions of mysteries or even to preset lengths of programs. In addition, he wanted the writer present at rehearsals to explain his intentions and, if necessary, to make any revisions. Contrary to the American custom, Gielgud fostered a radio drama that minimized musical bridges, clichéd "knife-chords," and sound effects. In "The Black Minute," Carr's second script for the BBC, for example, a transition is accomplished by simply fading from a frightened woman's cries to the relaxed voice of the taxi driver who had brought her moments ago to a sinister house. The contrast between the sound of her anguish and the cabdriver's calm makes the heroine's plight more fretful for the audience. Carr's script also shows how sound effects, used sparingly, can assume greater force. The key scene in "The Black Minute" is a séance in which the characters join hands in a locked, darkened room. As the tense characters await the words of the medium, the only sound is the background scratch of a gramophone. As with the earlier transition, less becomes more. The methodical grinding of the gramophone makes the lengthening silence more unbearable.

With the United States' entry into World War II, Carr returned to the United States and wrote plays for the CBS series *Suspense* (1942). There, he encountered a work situation nearly the opposite of that in England. The American show was timed to the last second, and Carr's scripts were tailored to fit the predesigned pattern. With its own orchestra, *Suspense* also made generous use of background music and strident knife-chords as sonic punctuation. Carr wrote "The Dead Sleep Lightly" for *Suspense* in the thirty-minute format of most American shows, but when he returned to England in 1943, he expanded the script of forty minutes, added his detective Dr.

Fell as a foil, and boldly changed the ending to let the culprit, exposed by Fell, avoid arrest.

It is a mistake to imply that the worlds of American and British radio drama were irreconcilable. Though clear differences existed, Gielgud could also see the comparative merits of the other style. Carr served as a go-between when he offered Gielgud more of his scripts from *Suspense* to develop into a series on the BBC (*Appointment with Fear*, debuting on September 11, 1943, was the result). Gielgud's reaction to "all the trimmings of atmospheric bass-voiced narrator, knife-chords and other specially composed musical effects, and a regular length of half an hour timed to the split second" was that "the temptation to compete 'on the home ground' [was] irresistible." Carr's program proved to be a success.

THE BBC

The development of British radio plays can be traced to the broadcast of *Twelfth Night* on May 28, 1923. The first original work for British radio was Richard Hughes's *Danger* (1924), a fifteen-minute play about three characters trapped in the pitch black of a coal mine. Reginald Denny's *The White Chanteau* (1925) became the first original, full-length play on the BBC. In the 1930's, as technology improved, more attention to original programming brought forth the experimental play by Tyrone Guthrie *The Flowers Are Not for You to Pick* (1930). Guthrie's play takes place in the mind of the protagonist—a young missionary who drowns on his way to his first assignment in China—and breaks up the traditional linear plot by moving the audience via flashbacks through a number of formative moments in the hero's life. Guthrie understood that time could be manipulated more effectively by the radio dramatist than space, something that holds true even though stereo broadcasts in later years have made space a more important dimension. The emphasis on the psychological can also be seen in Louis MacNeice's verse play *Christopher Columbus* (1944), in which different actors voice different parts ("Doubt," "Faith") of the hero's mind. MacNeice's fantasy *The Dark Tower* (1947) emphasizes sound effects and music more than his previous plays and is sometimes mentioned as

MacNeice's best work. *Under Milk Wood: A Play for Voices* (pr. 1953) is Dylan Thomas's highly regarded radio play about small-town life in Wales. The broadcast elements of language, sound, and silence may in part explain the interest of Harold Pinter and Samuel Beckett in radio. Explorations of the ambiguities of communication and the richness of silence lend themselves ideally to the medium. Pinter's radio plays *A Slight Ache* (pr. 1959) and *A Night Out* (pr. 1960) preceded his first stage success, and Beckett's radio plays *All That Fall* (pr. 1957), *Embers* (pr. 1959), and *Words and Music* (pr. 1962) have taken a place in importance next to his stage works. The tradition continued. Robert Bolt's play about Sir Thomas More, *A Man for All Seasons* (pr. 1960), appeared first on BBC radio in 1954. John Arden, Tom Stoppard, and John Mortimer also made contributions to British radio drama.

SOUND DRAMA ON LONG-PLAYING RECORDS

If the term "radio drama" may be slightly altered to "sound drama," then the development of the genre can be charted through the rise of the long-playing record and audio cassettes. One of the first stage works preserved on sound recordings was Arthur Miller's 1949 play *Death of a Salesman*. Miller had written radio plays after graduating from the University of Michigan, and his expressionistic play about Willy Loman centers on Willy's mind and its slipping hold on reality, material well suited for sound drama. Columbia recorded the play with Thomas Mitchell as Willy; later, Caedmon Records issued a version with Lee J. Cobb as the salesperson. Eventually, technology permitted a nostalgic renaissance for radio drama when many old-time radio shows (such as Basil Rathbone's and Nigel Bruce's work as Sherlock Holmes and Dr. Watson, respectively) were issued as record albums and audio cassettes.

Both Caedmon Records and London Records have produced unabridged disc and cassette recordings of the complete plays of William Shakespeare. This should come as no surprise. Before CBS radio had begun *The Columbia Workshop*, it had experimented in the summer of 1937 with a series of adaptations and selected scenes from Shakespeare. Welles

worked on the *Hamlet* broadcast. While CBS prepared its series, NBC quickly signed John Barrymore for its own Shakespeare series to start in late June. Though the casting on CBS emphasized film stars rather than stage performers (Rosalind Russell as Beatrice, Edward G. Robinson as Petruchio, Humphrey Bogart as Hotspur), Shakespeare proved ideal for radio. With stage directions and action incorporated into much of the poetry, Shakespeare's dramaturgy minimized props and relied on the aural. The rhymed couplets signaled the close of a scene for radio listeners just as they did for their original spectators in Elizabethan England. In 1964, the Broadway cast of *Hamlet*, directed by John Gielgud and starring Richard Burton, recorded the play on a four-disc set for Columbia Records. BBC radio has often released some of its best Shakespeare productions on audio cassettes as well.

Caedmon Records, as it was producing its complete Shakespeare on long-playing records during the 1960's and early 1970's, also assembled an impressive series of performances of classic plays on disc. Most of these productions, as well as the majority of its Shakespeare recordings, were directed by Howard Sackler, author of the play *The Great White Hope* (pr. 1967), and an accomplished interpreter of stage works for sound media. These unabridged recordings helped to keep alive the tradition of sound drama after the popularity of radio waned. The Caedmon multidisc sets also found their way into the catalogs of countless public and academic libraries where they became a valuable educational resource for the flood of "baby boomers" entering high school and college. The advisory board for this project included, among others, distinguished figures in education (John Gassner, a Yale professor and an anthologist of numerous drama collections), in drama (Tyrone Guthrie and Eva Le Gallienne), and in the recording industry (Barbara Holdridge and Marianne Mantell, pioneering producers in spoken-word audio). The ongoing series was also marketed as a prestige subscription service called the Theatre Recording Society.

This Caedmon catalog of recorded drama contains some impressive performances that have gained historical stature. The National Theatre of Great Britain's 1964 production of Henrik Ibsen's *Bygmester Solness* (pr. 1893; *The Master Builder*, 1893) with Michael Redgrave, Maggie Smith, and Derek Jacobi, for example, was offered to Theatre Society subscribers in 1965. Laurence Olivier's production of Chekhov's *Dyadya Vanya* (pr. 1899; *Uncle Vanya*, 1914), first staged at the Chichester Festival Theatre and later performed for British pay television, also became a part of the series, as did the 1972 Lincoln Center production of Arthur Miller's *The Crucible* (pr. 1953) with Robert Foxworth and Pamela Payton-Wright.

The drama recordings that originated in the Caedmon studios were also memorable, featuring, for example, a classic and sensitive production of Tennessee Williams's *The Glass Menagerie* (pr. 1944) directed by Howard Sackler with Montgomery Clift, Jessica Tandy, Julie Harris, and David Wayne, as well as recordings of *The Front Page* (pr. 1928) with Robert Ryan and Bert Convy, the durable stage comedy by Ben Hecht and Charles MacArthur, and Eugene O'Neill's *The Emperor Jones* (pr. 1920) with James Earl Jones. This last recording included a fifty-minute rehearsal discussion of the play among director Theodore Mann and the actors. With the rise of the audio-book industry in the 1980's and 1990's, selections from the Caedmon archive, most of which had fallen out of print, found new audiences when the plays were reissued on audio cassettes and compact discs by Harper Audio, the subsequent copyright holders of the Caedmon collection.

THE LA THEATRE WORKS AND NEW MEDIA

In the late twentieth century the efforts of designing new productions of classic and contemporary plays for audio had been largely taken over by a group called the LA Theatre Works (LATW). Having originated in 1987 and broadcasting over several radio services (such as the group's associate producer, station KCRW-FM in Santa Monica, California, as well as National Public Radio, or NPR, and the BBC), this award-winning organization eventually assembled an audio theater collection of more than three hundred titles, reportedly the largest in the country. Their growing list of performers (Alan Alda,

Annette Bening, Richard Dreyfuss, Julie Harris, Amy Irving, Nathan Lane, and Jason Robards, among others) formed an American roster as noteworthy as the predominately British casts who had appeared on the Caedmon recordings. Typically the LATW presents its unabridged plays in radio-theater format before subscription patrons, and the live responses of these audiences enhance the listening experience. Most importantly, however, the recordings of the LATW illustrate further refinements in the art of recorded drama.

The LATW recording of David Henry Hwang's *M. Butterfly* (pr. 1988), for example, uses a richly textured sound design more elaborate than the left- and right-channel separation of early stereo recordings. To present the recollected flashbacks of John Lithgow's character, who addresses the audience from a prison cell, the recording alters the timbre and sonic depth of these remembered scenes as they are dramatized. Sometimes Lithgow's character narrates the beginning of a flashback (speaking close to the microphone for an immediacy that suggests the present-day) and then appears as a younger man in the flashback scene (speaking at a greater distance but also with greater separation of channels and a slight filter on the sound). The ever-shifting time structure of Hwang's play is thus clearly and effectively translated to the sound medium.

Two unabridged, dramatic readings of novels by the LATW (of Sinclair Lewis's *Babbitt*, 1922, and Frank Norris's *McTeague*, 1899) signaled further innovation by blending the characteristics of drama and fiction. Director Gordon Hunt assigned the third-person narration of Lewis's novel to a large number of voices rather than to only one narrator. In these passages a new voice takes over the narration with each alteration in thought, emotion, or psychology. This technique eventually becomes the sound equivalent of a cut or edit in a film so that important shifts in the tone or content of the storytelling are heightened. The listener's attention is also more easily engaged over the course of a fourteen-hour recording with such smooth gear-shifting of the audio narration. The strategy works in a near-intuitive way, suggesting that the subtleties in Lewis's novel were there for the careful reader to discern and that the changing narrators are simply italicizing a richness inherent in the text. The catalog of the LATW includes works by numerous classic (Shakespeare, George Bernard Shaw, Oscar Wilde, Ibsen) and contemporary (Neil Simon, Wendy Wasserstein, Sir Alan Ayckbourn, Athol Fugard) playwrights. In late 2001 and early 2002, the LATW took radio drama into a new arena by becoming one of the program providers for the XM digital satellite radio network.

As technology changes, so too does the delivery of recorded drama. The Internet as well has become a storehouse for many productions of drama on audio with the ever-improving capabilities of streaming media. The experience of radio drama can be a liberating one for performers and audiences. Actor Richard Dreyfuss's comment about the recordings of the LATW really applies to all creatively effective radio drama: "Film and theater are limited only by the eye. Audio theater is limited only by the imagination."

BIBLIOGRAPHY

Callow, Simon. *Orson Welles: The Road to Xanadu.* New York: Viking Penguin, 1996. Callow writes insightfully about Welles and his work in radio and includes a list of Welles's radio broadcasts.

Carr, John Dickson. *The Door to Doom and Other Detections.* Edited by Douglas G. Greene. New York: Harper and Row, 1980. Six radio plays by Carr, a bibliography of Carr's radio scripts, and a listing of other radio scripts based on Carr's novels.

Crook, Tim. *Radio Drama.* New York: Routledge, 1999. Traces the evolution of radio drama, from early broadcasts in 1914 to modern-day "media guerrilla" productions. Examines the techniques necessary for effective radio presentations.

Drakakis, John. *British Radio Drama.* Cambridge, England: Cambridge University Press, 1981. Offers a historical and critical examination of the development of British radio, focusing on the contributions of MacNiece, Beckett, Dylan Thomas, Dorothy L. Sayers, and many more.

Greene, Douglas G. "John Dickson Carr and the Radio Mystery." In *The Dead Sleep Lightly.* New York: Doubleday, 1983. Greene's expert essay surveys Carr's work in radio and introduces nine radio plays by Carr.

_____. *John Dickson Carr: The Man Who Explained Miracles.* New York: Otto Penzler, 1996. Provides a biography of Carr and includes a checklist of Carr's radio work with some annotations.

Lewis, Tom. *Empire of the Air: The Men Who Made Radio.* New York: HarperCollins, 1991. The story of the rise of radio focuses on the lives of Lee de Forest, Edward Howard Armstrong, and David Sarnoff.

Nevins, Francis M., Jr., and Ray Stanich. *The Sound of Detection: Ellery Queen's Adventures in Radio.* Madison, Ind.: Brownstone Books, 1983. The history of a single continuing radio series by authoritative writers on radio and mystery fiction.

Theatre of the Imagination: Radio Stories by Orson Welles and the Mercury Theatre. Six audio cassettes. Produced by Frank Beacham and Richard Wilson. Santa Monica, Calif.: Voyager, 1988. Audio recordings of Orson Welles's work in radio, the package also includes an audio documentary featuring members of the Mercury Theatre discussing the quality and style of their broadcasts.

Welles, Orson, and Peter Bogdanovich. *This Is Orson Welles.* New York: HarperCollins, 1992. Transcripts with annotations of Bogdanovich's many conversations with Welles about his career. This is perhaps the best source for Welles's own thoughts on his work in radio.

Glenn Hopp

TELEVISION DRAMA

In the early days of television broadcasting, there was little reason to suspect that the medium viewed by many as a passing novelty would in time become the single most pervasive and influential aspect of popular culture. Certainly, the grainy, problem-prone early broadcasts seemed to pose no real threat to radio, television's predecessor in American living rooms, and unlike radio and films, the technology of television did not catch on quickly with the public. Indeed, the necessary technical knowledge had existed since the 1920's, but it was not until the late 1940's that the medium began to become a real presence in American life.

In its earliest incarnation, television was a local phenomenon, with broadcasts limited to the East Coast of the United States, within easy range of New York City. Slow developments throughout the 1930's were largely put on hold during World War II. However, in the postwar years, the medium began to grow with a force and speed that surprised many skeptics. Both the National Broadcasting Company (NBC) and the Columbia Broadcasting System (CBS) had received commercial broadcasting licenses in 1941, and by 1946 commercial television had become a reality. Joined by the short-lived DuMont network and later by the American Broadcasting Company (ABC), the networks began searching for programs to fill their expanding schedules. By 1948, the four networks offered almost complete prime-time broadcasts—the hours between seven and eleven o'clock in the evening—seven nights a week.

THE RISE OF TELEVISION DRAMA

In the late 1940's, television was a technology in search of content. Yet radio, its closest relative, could provide only limited inspiration because of the key difference between the two mediums. Despite early predictions, television was not simply "radio with pictures." Actual radio with pictures would have offered the sight of actors speaking lines into a microphone while technicians supplied sound effects and music to one side. What television required of its content was that it provide the visual imagery that radio left to the listener's imagination. What had taken place in the mind of the radio listener would now take place on the screen of the television viewer.

With New York City as their headquarters, it was not surprising that the networks turned to the legitimate theater for programming ideas. The alliance between live theater and television was established early, when NBC in its experimental stages offered New York viewers a production of Rachel Crothers's play *Susan and God* (pr. 1937), with actress Gertrude Lawrence. DuMont, lobbying hard to prove its worthiness for a broadcasting license, offered the first regularly scheduled live dramatic series, *Television Workshop*, to a limited audience during the early 1940's. NBC followed suit with *NBC Television Theatre* in 1945 and later with *Kraft Television Theatre* in 1947, a show that would prove to be among the most important in shaping the face of television.

Sponsored by Kraft Foods, *Kraft Television Theatre* would remain on the air for eleven years and would help set the standard by which television drama would be judged. With generous budgets and talented people working both on and off camera, the series brought high-quality productions into American homes each Wednesday night, offering viewers classical and contemporary dramas and providing them with their first glimpses of such actors as Paul Newman, Joanne Woodward, James Dean, and Grace Kelly. Rod Serling, whose acclaimed teleplay *Patterns* aired in 1955, established his reputation as a writer on the show. The series was also one of the earliest to experiment with color in the mid-1950's.

The show's influence was also felt in another crucial area of television's development: the growing interest of commercial sponsors in the medium as a format for advertising their products. As the popularity of *Kraft Television Theatre* grew, sales of Kraft cheese skyrocketed, demonstrating conclusively that television had potential as a sales arena undreamed of by radio or print advertising. The impact of visual imagery offered a marketing tool that would be seized by every corporation that had a product to be sold and the advertising dollars needed to purchase airtime. Gradually, the influence of sponsors would become a shaping force in television's content and format. What had begun as an effort by Kraft Foods to associate its products with quality productions in viewers' minds would evolve into a relationship that would determine the future of commercial television in the decades to come.

In the early years, however, the ability to link company products to fine drama had a galvanizing effect on corporate America, and by 1948, Chevrolet, Philco Corporation, and Westinghouse Electric Corporation had all become sponsors of dramatic series. They were joined in the 1950's by Goodyear Tire and Rubber Company, Aluminum Company of America (Alcoa), Kaiser Aluminum, and U.S. Steel. All these companies believed—in tandem with the networks—that high-quality programming was the surest way to attract viewers.

TELEVISION'S GOLDEN AGE

By 1948, all four networks were offering their viewers live drama, and the period often referred to as television's golden age had begun. With hours of airtime to fill and budgets underwritten by powerful sponsors, live television drama became a testing ground for talented young actors and writers and a showcase for the kind of work that had previously been available only to paying audiences in theaters. Viewers could see Maurice Evans performing the plays of William Shakespeare, a live 1954 production of Reginald Rose's *Twelve Angry Men*, or a young Sidney Poitier—one of the first African American actors to appear on television in a leading role—in Robert Alan Arthur's *A Man Is Ten Feet Tall*.

During this era, in an attempt to distinguish themselves from their competitors and establish their own niche in a rapidly burgeoning field, several shows specialized in particular forms of television drama. *Robert Montgomery Presents* offered adaptations of popular films and managed to lure such Hollywood stars as James Cagney and Claudette Colbert to the small screen. *Philco TV Playhouse* began in association with Actors' Equity and presented adaptations of

Broadway plays before joining with Book-of-the-Month Club and featuring dramatizations of current novels. *The U.S. Steel Hour* also drew on the legitimate theater, offering a production of Henrik Ibsen's 1890 play *Hedda Gabler* starring Tallulah Bankhead, while *Goodyear TV Playhouse* offered a wide range of original teleplays, including several by the young Paddy Chayefsky. Chayefsky's *Marty*, telecast in 1953 and regarded as one of the finest dramas in television history, would reverse the trend of borrowing from other media when its feature-film adaptation received an Oscar as Best Picture in 1955.

Perhaps the two most highly acclaimed live dramatic series during the 1950's were *Playhouse 90* and *Studio One*. Each in its own way represented not only that which was best in television drama but also that which was unique. For five years, *Playhouse 90* produced weekly, ninety-minute live dramas, sparing no expense on either production values or talent and setting a standard of excellence that is still singled out as an example of the best that television's golden age had to offer. Incredibly, the series' second telecast was the landmark *Requiem for a Heavyweight*, written by Rod Serling and starring Jack Palance. With its combination of fine performances, careful staging, and well-crafted writing, the production proved to be a declaration of the course that the series would follow in the years to come.

The best teleplay writers were those who, like Serling and Chayefsky, realized that television was a medium particularly well suited to the staging of complex, intimate dramas. Unable to compete with feature films in scope, television could reach directly into its viewers' homes and present them with stories of ordinary individuals, so-called kitchen-sink dramas. If Hollywood represented glamour, then good teleplay writing was characterized by its ability to turn television's lack of glamour into an effective asset.

Studio One, on the other hand, concentrated less on its material and more on the manner in which it was staged. Although the series grew out of an unsuccessful radio program, under producer Worthington C. Miner the television version set out to explore the possibilities of the new visual medium and became one of the most highly praised dramatic series of the 1950's. Miner was one of the earliest television pioneers to grasp the fact that television's power lay in its images rather than its dialogue. Radio's complete reliance on words and sounds to tell a story led many early dramatic television series to offer productions in which the staging was an accompaniment to the story. Under Miner's guidance, however, *Studio One* explored ways in which to tell a story through visual means. Although good writing also characterized the show, its main emphasis was on its imagery. It is not surprising, therefore, that the series helped to launch the careers of a number of notable feature-film directors, including George Roy Hill, Franklin Schaffner, and Sidney Lumet.

Despite their individual differences, live dramatic series had several factors in common that were unique to the medium of television. Unlike motion pictures, teleplays were performed live, offering audiences an immediacy that films were unable to match, and "live" on television involved risks and complications that neither the radio nor the stage faced. The lack of pictures allowed radio performers to work from scripts, unseen by their audience, and mistakes that occurred could often be covered. Stage productions have long rehearsal periods, out-of-town tryouts, and the luxury of rewrites if a play contains material that does not work well when tested in front of a live audience. Additionally, mistakes made on a stage are seen by a limited audience; television actors faced the daunting prospect that their gaffes would take place in front of an audience that was literally nationwide.

The newness of the technology also brought its share of complications. The history of live television drama is filled with anecdotes of "dead" bodies that crawled offscreen or, conversely, actors who unwittingly stepped out of the picture, uncertain of the limits of the camera's range. As television technology developed and performers became more familiar with the medium, the potential for on-the-air mishaps lessened, but the rawness, the sense that anything might happen, is remembered with great fondness by participants and viewers alike.

Ironically, one of the boons of live television drama would eventually also prove to be a factor in its decline. With a burgeoning market of prime-time hours to fill, dramatic series gave many young and untested writers a forum for their talents. Young actors also benefited when many better-known performers expressed little interest in appearing in the new medium. Yet these same factors gradually led the networks to the realization that live drama was both costly and a strain on available resources. The growing success of shows such as *Dragnet* and *Gunsmoke*, which began in 1952 and 1955 respectively, heralded the development of what would become the core of television drama: the weekly filmed or taped dramatic series.

ANTHOLOGIES AND EPISODIC DRAMA

Although live television drama was at the heart of the medium's golden age, it was in the realm of the prerecorded dramatic series—and its comedic counterpart, the situation comedy—that television would find its most lasting voice. Episodic series, performed live, had also been a staple of radio programming, although the technological advantages of television and the longer running times of the shows allowed television drama series to develop in ways that had not been possible on the radio. That development took two distinct paths: the weekly anthology series and the weekly episodic drama.

Of the two, the anthology series is by far the road less traveled. Its earliest example was *Four Star Playhouse*, which each week offered a filmed, thirty-minute drama featuring one of its four stars, Charles Boyer, David Niven, Dick Powell, and Ida Lupino. In 1955, Alfred Hitchcock lent his considerable presence to the anthology format with *Alfred Hitchcock Presents*, which he hosted for ten years. Thirty-minute, and later hourlong, tales of suspense with surprise twists at the conclusion characterized the show, which also played with the medium of television itself in Hitchcock's droll introductions and conclusions of each episode. Often mocking his commercial sponsors, Hitchcock would also negate any possible censorship problems over an episode's content by adding a humorous coda that seemed to belie a story's message of evil triumphing over good.

The most ambitious and successful anthology series was Serling's *The Twilight Zone*, which used the genres of suspense and fantasy to tackle such subjects as intolerance, racial prejudice, and human beings' capacity for violence and greed. Introduced each week by Serling, the series combined the best elements of live television drama—solid writing, talented casts, serious subject matter—with the added advantages of filming. Often dismissed at the time of its initial run as simply a science-fiction or horror series, the show later grew in critical stature. In the early 1970's Serling would return to the anthology format with the horror series *Night Gallery*, the pilot of which contained a segment directed by a young Steven Spielberg.

EMERGING GENRES AND THEMES

The lack of widespread success for anthology-style shows, however, demonstrated what would become a truism of programming philosophy; viewing audiences prefer series with recurring casts of familiar characters. This piece of television wisdom is the motivating factor behind both episodic dramas and situation comedies, and it has shaped the style of programming that has dominated the airwaves since the early 1960's. The episodic dramatic series has taken many forms and covers a wide range of genres, from Westerns and crime shows to medical dramas and soap operas, and has managed at its best to surpass in quality the majority of Hollywood feature films released in any given year.

Of all the genres that have played an important part in television drama, none owes a greater debt to its radio forebears than the soap opera. Beginning in the 1950's, series such as *General Hospital*, *As the World Turns*, and *Days of Our Lives* became the backbone of daytime television, engaging loyal viewers with their ongoing emotional melodramas. Later popular additions to the genre included *One Life to Live*, *The Bold and the Beautiful*, *Another World*, and *All My Children*. If prime-time series concentrated on new stories each week, soap operas examined the loves and losses of their recurring casts of characters, and just as live television drama had helped launch the careers of many notable actors of the 1950's and

1960's, so daytime soaps provided a springboard for the careers of such performers as Meg Ryan, Morgan Freeman, and Demi Moore. Perhaps no form of television drama has shown the endurance of the soap opera, and although changing social mores and relaxed censorship restrictions have served to spice up their content, the shows themselves remain constant in their approach. Working under enormous time constraints, soap operas retain a degree of the rawness and immediacy of early live drama, although the quality of work involved is generally far lower.

In 1964, the first prime-time version of a soap opera made its appearance. Based on the best-selling novel by Grace Metalious, *Peyton Place* (1956) premiered on ABC in September of 1964 and was an immediate success. Telecast two to three nights per week during most of its five-year run, the show brought daytime television's blend of scandal, intrigue, and melodrama to a nighttime audience that watched in droves. The show launched the careers of Mia Farrow and Ryan O'Neal, among others, and paved the way for the later prime-time soap operas that would dominate television in the 1980's. Their arrival was heralded by *Dallas* in 1978, a series that would go on to achieve international popularity and make its central character, Larry Hagman's unscrupulous J. R. Ewing, one of the most famous characters in television history. Adding opulent wealth to the familiar soap-opera formula, *Dallas* inspired several imitators and garnered one of the highest television ratings ever with its much-hyped "Who Shot J. R.?" second-season opener. The show also inspired several imitators, including the popular *Dynasty* and the 1990's *Melrose Place*, and would give rise more than a decade later to a subgenre of teenage soaps that included *Beverly Hills 90210* and *Dawson's Creek*.

In the late 1950's and early 1960's, Westerns, long a favorite of Saturday matinee film audiences, became among the most popular shows on the air. If theater had been the chief inspiration for live television productions and radio the source for soap operas, Westerns, with their outdoor locations and action-based stories—not to mention livestock—had their roots directly in Hollywood. With the long-running *Gunsmoke* leading the way, such series as

Rawhide, starring Clint Eastwood; *Have Gun Will Travel*; *Wagon Train*; *Maverick*, with James Garner; *The Virginian*; and *Wanted-Dead or Alive*, starring Steve McQueen, were soon changing the format of television drama. They would be followed in the mid-1960's by *The Big Valley*, featuring Barbara Stanwyck as a Western matriarch, and *The High Chaparral*. The most successful Western was unquestionably *Bonanza*, which ran for a total of fourteen years starting in 1959 and established characters so well known and loved that the show was able to shift from an action emphasis to one of personal drama. *Bonanza* would prove to be the last of a dying breed, however, and—with the exception of the popular 1990's series, *Dr. Quinn, Medicine Woman*—fitful efforts to revive the Western in subsequent years met with little success.

Ironically, although *The Twilight Zone* proved to be among the last of the successful anthology series, it was the first entry in what would later become an extremely popular television genre: the science fiction/horror series. The 1960's saw the appearance of *The Outer Limits*, Serling's *Night Gallery*, and, in 1966, the original *Star Trek*. The brainchild of writer-producer Gene Roddenberry, *Star Trek* inspired such cultish loyalty among its viewers that it later spawned not only numerous television sequels and a popular series of big-budget motion pictures but also an ongoing series of conventions devoted to the show as well. The genre continued into the 1970's with shows featuring government agents equipped with powerful robotic body parts in *The Six Million Dollar Man* and *The Bionic Woman*. The 1990's marked the debut of *The X Files*, which combined science fiction and horror with government conspiracy theories, and *Buffy, the Vampire Slayer*, in which a teenage girl and her friends battle the forces of the "undead" while dealing with the issues of growing up.

The crime drama—and its cousin, the courtroom drama—borrowed heavily from both radio and motion pictures. Unlike Westerns, neither genre's popularity has diminished, and a look at any given period of television programming over the decades finds them among the highest-rated weekly shows. *The Untouchables*, beginning in 1959, was a fast-paced,

often violent thriller that drew on period settings and cinematic depictions of dramatic Feds-and-mobsters confrontations, while *Dragnet*, with its much-parodied deadpan style, had its roots in radio, a connection apparent in the show's static visual style and a reliance on dialogue over action to tell its stories. *Perry Mason*, begun in 1957, centered its action in the courtroom in mysteries that were enhanced by visual imagery but would have been easily rendered through dialogue alone. The 1970's *Kojak* and *Columbo* enjoyed immense popularity partly because of memorable performances by Telly Savalas and Peter Falk, respectively, in the title roles. Ensemble cast dramas, such as *Hill Street Blues*, *Homicide: Life on the Streets*, and *NYPD Blue*, a mainstay of 1980's and 1990's television, offered gritty portraits of urban crime while exploring the lives of their large cast of characters, and *L.A. Law* and *The Practice* offered the same approach to the legal system.

Although not as early a prime-time staple as the crime drama, medical shows have also had an enduring role in dramatic programming, and as episodic drama developed, a dominant storytelling device began to emerge that seemed particularly well-suited to the genre. On shows such as *Dr. Kildare*, *Ben Casey* (both running 1961-1966), and *Marcus Welby, M.D.* (1969-1976), the recurring star or central cast of characters remained constant while each new patient provided the springboard into that week's story or issue. The result was a format in which central characters showed little emotional change or growth, functioning instead as the anchor on which each week's story was hung. Although individual episodes might feature stories in which the series' star fell in love or suffered a loss, these events did not translate into internal changes that made themselves felt in later episodes.

Although later medical dramas would make use of new narrative devices, the format of the earlier shows proved adaptable to other types of series as well. "Road" shows such as *Route 66*, *Run for Your Life*, and *The Fugitive*—all prominent in the 1960's—also used the device, moving their central characters from place to place each week and setting up problems for a new set of individuals whom the hero would assist before once again moving on. The better shows adopting this device used it as a means of exploring a wide range of ideas and issues. The critically praised 1960's series *The Defenders*, starring E. G. Marshall, used its legal setting to examine not only personal dramas but also social problems; a direction also taken by the short-lived *East Side/West Side* (1963-1964), which starred George C. Scott as a social worker. The acclaimed 1990's program *Law and Order* took an in-depth look each week at criminal investigations and legal issues rather than the lives of its characters, often drawing on true stories for its plot lines. Although individual films and stage plays were forced by constraints of length to focus on one or two issues, a continuing television series could encompass a remarkable range of ideas in a single season. Television was also at an advantage in this area over radio, which had reached its zenith at a more restrictive period in broadcasting history.

FOCUS ON CHARACTER DEVELOPMENT

It was not until the 1970's, however, that television drama other than soap operas began to use the format of the episodic series to explore in depth the lives of the shows' permanent characters. The family drama *The Waltons*, with its Depression-era stories drawn from the childhood of writer Earl Hamner, Jr., managed after near cancellation in 1972 to find its viewers and engage them for eight years with its heartwarming tales of the series' large, close-knit country family. *The Waltons* soon opened the door to several similar family dramas, including *Little House on the Prairie*, *Eight Is Enough*, and the aptly named *Family*.

In 1978, television took a dramatic leap forward with the debut of *Hill Street Blues*. Produced by Steven Bochco, the series drew on the best elements from television drama in the past and combined them with not only innovative visual techniques and an original plotting structure. Set in an urban precinct, the show interwove the personal and professional lives of its large ensemble cast of characters with stories and issues often drawn from recent headlines. Each week's episode involved both limited subplots that were concluded by the hour's end and segments of ongoing plot lines that were often strung out over several weeks. Within this format, the lives of the characters underwent gradual yet substantial development, aided by exceptionally fine performances from a talented cast. The show frequently raised unresolvable social and political issues and explored the ways in which these conflicts affected individual lives. By the time it left the air in 1987, *Hill Street Blues* had become one of the most honored and acclaimed series in television history and a powerful influence on television drama as a whole.

In its ensemble cast, interlocking plot lines, and concentration on serious drama, *Hill Street Blues* had hit upon a formula that took full advantage of the specifics of television as a medium. Its documentary-like realism and densely staged scenes place it beyond the reach of radio, and its episodic structure allows for character development and continuing story lines that are not possible in film or theater. *St. Elsewhere* adapted the show's structure to a hospital setting in the 1980's and eventually went on to find its own strikingly original voice in episodes that featured fantasy sequences and a strong self-reflexive sense that obliquely called the viewer's attention to the subject of television itself. *L.A. Law* would prove to be the most successful of the shows to follow the format, consistently drawing high ratings with its wealthy law-firm setting and frequently outrageous plot lines.

The versatility of the structure was also demonstrated in late 1980's shows such as *thirtysomething* and the cult favorite *Twin Peaks*, with the former series using the format to explore the lives of six friends over a period of several years and the latter offering director David Lynch's dark, sometimes fantastic view of the hidden life of a small town. The highly popular *ER*, debuting in 1994, added breakneck pacing to the mix in its depiction of life-and-death drama in a Chicago hospital emergency room, while Bochco's 1990's series, *NYPD Blue*, pushed the limits of television censorship with its language, partial nudity, and adult themes. In the decades since its debut, *Hill Street Blues*—and the dramatic structure it introduced—has proven to be one of the lasting contributors to the shape of television drama.

MADE-FOR-TELEVISION MOVIES

Surprisingly, with Hollywood to draw on as an example, the concept of movies made for television did not keep pace with other forms of television drama. NBC began experimenting with the idea in 1964, but it was not until 1966, with *Fame Is the Name of the Game*, that the format really began to gain popularity. Aired as part of the network's popular *Saturday Night at the Movies*, which featured broadcasts of Hollywood films, the film earned impressive ratings, as did Serling's *Doomsday Flight* later that year.

The success of these two projects sparked what would become an important part of network broadcasting fare. Although many made-for-television movies are mundane and unexceptional—or, conversely, a format for titillating or headline-grabbing subjects—they have also done much to bring a variety of social and personal issues to the small screen. In the 1970's, several notable television movies were aired: *Brian's Song* drew praise for its touching story of football player Brian Piccolo's death from cancer; *My Sweet Charlie* dealt with the controversial subject of an interracial love affair; *The Autobiography of Miss Jane Pittman* traced the history of African Americans from the Civil War to the Civil Rights movement; and *That Certain Summer* presented the story of a young man dealing with his father's homosexuality.

The made-for-television movie proved to be a boon for television actors who longed to play serious roles outside their familiar series personas. In the mid-1970's *Sybil*, which was telecast over two nights, Sally Field offered a harrowing portrait of a young woman suffering from multiple personalities, while in 1984 both *The Burning Bed*, featuring Farrah Fawcett as a victim of domestic violence, and *Something About Amelia* with *Cheers* star Ted Danson in a drama about incest, engaged viewers with unnerving social issues. Abortion, acquired immunodeficiency syndrome (AIDS), Alzheimer's disease, school desegregation, homelessness, and the nuclear holocaust have also found their way to the small screen via television film, making their presence felt among less notable efforts.

THE MINISERIES

Once the idea of the television film was established, the groundwork was laid for a dramatic format eminently well suited to the medium: the miniseries. What the miniseries could offer was the opportunity to tell a complex story in greater depth than the traditional two-hour length of a feature or television film would permit. This structure lent itself especially well to adaptations of novels, which did not need to be drastically edited when presented in the miniseries form. NBC's *The Blue Knight* in 1973 defied conventional programming wisdom by scheduling its four installments on consecutive nights, paving the way for the popular *QB VII* and *Rich Man, Poor Man*, which at twelve episodes, was one of the longest miniseries.

In January of 1977, ABC broadcast the landmark miniseries *Roots*. Adapted from the best-selling book by Alex Haley, it would become one of the highest-rated series in television history, as audiences watched in unprecedented numbers the saga of a black family from the slave-trading days to the aftermath of the Civil War. Produced by David Lloyd Wolper, the series boasted an exceptional cast, a powerfully written script, and a subject of both sweeping historical scope and intimate emotional detail. The popularity of *Roots* stunned skeptics who doubted that television audiences would commit to better than a week's worth of viewing. *Shogun*, *Holocaust*, and *The Winds of War*, all of which followed *Roots* in the next decade, would also enjoy remarkable viewer response before the format began to fade in popularity. *War and Remembrance*, the latter series' sequel, failed to match the success of its predecessor, and the longer miniseries gave way gradually to two-night series. Given the proper subject, however, the format remained capable of resurrecting its earlier success, as in the case of *Lonesome Dove*. Not only a miniseries but a Western as well in a medium that had pronounced the genre officially dead, *Lonesome Dove* garnered not only critical acclaim but also a rapt viewing audience in the 1980's.

CABLE TELEVISION

After decades of relative stability, television as a whole underwent perhaps the most dramatic change since its inception with the emergence of cable networks in the early 1980's. Not surprisingly, the astonishing growth of cable television had a significant effect on the face of television drama. Originally seen primarily as forums for broadcasting theatrical feature films, cable channels such as Home Box Office (HBO) and Showtime expanded since the early 1990's to include significant amounts of original programming. HBO won acclaim for its films *The Positively True Adventures of the Alleged Texas Cheerleader-Murdering Mom, Barbarians at the Gates, And the Band Played On,* and *Miss Evers' Boys,* and the miniseries *From the Earth to the Moon* and *The Corner,* while Showtime garnered praise for its films *Bastard out of Carolina* and an adaptation of *Twelve Angry Men* and the miniseries *Hiroshima.*

Mining the realms of both the made-for-television movie and the weekly series, cable networks in the 1990's and early twenty-first century have taken advantage of their exemption from the censorship restrictions that apply to commercial networks to explore areas of drama that were previously untouchable on the small screen. HBO explored the topic of abortion in the film *If These Walls Could Talk,* while its sequel focused on the subject of lesbianism. Original cable series have also achieved critical acclaim, most notably HBO's *The Sopranos* with its complex, often violent look at the life of a Mafia don and his family.

BRITISH TELEVISION

No discussion of the miniseries—or indeed of television drama—would be complete without the inclusion of British television. The format of the miniseries did not originate with American television; it was borrowed after the success of such British dramas as *The First Churchills, The Six Wives of Henry VIII,* and *The Forsyte Saga* on American public television. *The Prisoner,* shown on CBS in 1968, also captivated viewers with its enigmatic tale of a former secret agent held against his will in a nameless village, as did the witty, sophisticated spy series *The Avengers* from the same period. Although British programming also featured episodic series that returned from year to year, programming philosophy

evolved in a markedly different fashion from that of its American counterpart. While American networks strive to establish popular series that will continue to draw viewers from year to year, British television has never balked at the idea of a successful series that is constructed to last for only one season.

The result has been a vast array of dramatic series that have found a home on public television. Through the umbrella series *Masterpiece Theatre* and *Mystery* on the Public Broadcasting Service (PBS) and later the Arts and Entertainment (A&E) cable network, much of the best of British television—with an emphasis on historical drama, literary adaptations, and elaborate period pieces—has made its way to American screens. In the 1970's, *Elizabeth R* introduced Glenda Jackson to American viewers and provided a compelling history of the monarch's reign. *Upstairs, Downstairs,* which ran for five seasons, traced the first three decades of the twentieth century through the lives of an upper-class family and their servants. The widely seen *I, Claudius, Masterpiece Theatre*'s most requested series, offered a vivid, witty, often gruesome look at the early Roman emperors, while 1984's *The Jewel in the Crown* took a scathing look at the last days of the British rule in colonial India. One of the most successful exports from England in the 1980's was the immensely popular *Brideshead Revisited,* an elegant adaptation of Evelyn Waugh's novel starring Jeremy Irons.

Adaptations of books by Agatha Christie, Dorothy L. Sayers, and P. D. James and the Sherlock Holmes stories of Arthur Conan Doyle have fed the American appetite for traditional English murder mysteries, and hard-edged crime dramas in the 1990's such as *Prime Suspect* and *Cracker* offered dark, well-written plot lines and complex characters. The relationship between British and American television programming has not been a one-way street, however, and many of the United States' most popular dramas have enjoyed great success in England as well.

REALITY OR UNSCRIPTED TELEVISION

An odd stepchild of television drama is the so-called reality show, a strange hybrid of soap opera, miniseries, game show, and documentary that has been the source of much critical controversy. While theoretically not a fictional storytelling format, the structure of shows at the turn of the twenty-first century such as *Survivor* and *Big Brother* is in fact as preplanned and controlled as any episodic television series and therefore merits a mention in the history of dramatic programming. Each episode's events unfold around a series of activities dictated by the shows' creators; only the dialogue and individual interactions are left to chance. Indeed, it can be argued that even these are in some measure predetermined through the selection of contestants whose personalities are likely to clash or bond in specific ways. Editing choices also manipulate the viewer's perceptions of each contestant/character while shaping the dramatic arc of each week's installment. The emergence of the reality show may be seen as part of an oft-criticized trend in television toward the blurring of the line between reality and fiction, or news and entertainment, and there is unquestionably a connection between news shows that use performers to reenact actual events and unscripted shows that use real people to provide dramatic entertainment.

BIBLIOGRAPHY

Hawes, William. *Live Television Drama, 1946-1951*. Jefferson, N.C.: McFarland, 2001. Covers the early years of live drama. Particularly valuable are the notes and appendices listing all episodes of many dramatic series.

Kisseloff, Jeff. *The Box: An Oral History of Television, 1920-1961*. New York: Viking, 1995. An interesting, informative oral history with actors, directors, writers, and producers; contains extensive coverage of the medium in the 1920's and 1930's.

McNeil, Alex. *Total Television*. New York: Penguin Books, 1996. A comprehensive show-by-show guide providing running dates, networks, and synopses.

Marschall, Rick. *History of Television*. New York: Gallery Books, 1986. Offers a decade-by-decade examination of television history.

Shulman, Arthur, and Roger Youman. *How Sweet It Was*. New York: Shorecrest, 1966. Explores the early decades of television through an examination of various television genres.

Slide, Anthony. *The Television Industry: A Historical Dictionary*. New York: Greenwood Press, 1991. Outlines the history of a comprehensive listing of television networks and production companies.

Smith, Anthony, ed. *Television: An International History*. London: Oxford University Press, 1995. A useful book for anyone interested in the development of television in countries outside of the United States.

Wilk, Max. *The Golden Age of Television*. New York: Delacorte Press, 1976. Offers a look at television's early years through a focus on a variety of individual shows.

Janet Lorenz

DRAMA TECHNIQUES

ACTING STYLES

Illuminating a play's text for the audience remains the primary task for actors, which they accomplish according to the nature of the literature they are called on to perform. A fiery melodrama with stock characters, for example, requires broad gestures and declamatory speech, whereas a realistic play with complex characterization necessitates a more lifelike approach. At the same time, actors, as the principal instruments of drama, reflect, as all artists do, the values, tastes, and fashions of the society in which they perform. Because a theater audience registers its approval or disapproval at the moment of artistic "creation" (in the sense that all stage plays are fully created only when performed), the actor remains one of the few artists who immediately responds to the demands of the public. Theater represents the most immediate of art forms, reflecting societal moods and anticipating change; thus, as society evolves, it creates new trends in dramatic literature, with acting styles reflecting those changes. A twenty-first century American audience viewing a nineteenth century melodrama would find the broad gestures and declamatory speech laughable; conversely, the nineteenth century audience would be bored and confused by the stark realism of twenty-first century American stage.

Actors are their own instruments. Whereas sculptors have clay with which to mold their art, actors use their voices, bodies, and individual characteristics as their clay. Actors' methodology—how they create a role—lies at the center of a debate that has raged for centuries. One theory holds that actors should create the role through mechanical means; that is, they should not experience the emotion of the character but should simulate it through logical and deliberate choice of gesture and vocal inflection. In contrast, the creative or psychological approach insists that actors should create from the inside, emphasizing motivation and emotion. The first theory, or external approach, presupposes the importance of characterization over the personality of the actor, whereas the second, or internal approach, emphasizes the importance of the actor's emotions projected through the character. In the early 1900's, the great Russian actor-teacher Konstantin Stanislavsky fused the two theories into one system.

RENAISSANCE ACTING

In the mid-twentieth century, scholars looking back at the Elizabethan stage focused on what acting styles may have looked like in plays such as Christopher Marlowe's *Doctor Faustus* (pr. c. 1585-1588) or William Shakepseare's *Hamlet, Prince of Denmark* (pr. c. 1600-1601) or *King Lear* (pr. c. 1605-1606), debating on the differences between a more formal style of acting—with an emphasis on the technical aspects of delivery—and a more natural style, emphasizing the internal, psychological life of the character. The two great actors from the English Renaissance—Richard Burbage, the leading actor of Shakespeare's company, the Lord Chamberlain's Men, and Edward Alleyn, leading actor of Marlowe's company, the Lord Admiral's Men—typified some of the differences in acting styles that characterized the period. Each was praised as the finest talent of his day; however, Burbage, as Hamlet, instructs the visiting players on proper playing, clearly distinguishing between poor acting—the tragedians who "strut and bellow" and "saw the air too much" with bad gestures, and the clowns who improvise and upstage fellow actors—and correct acting, suiting "the action to the word, the word to the action" so as to observe and not go beyond the "modesty of nature." (It must be added that relatively little is known about acting styles on the Elizabethan stage.) While the arguments about Elizabethan acting styles focused the debate between what constituted "formal" or "natural" acting, Alfred Harbage's seminal article in 1939, "Elizabethan Acting," argued for a more formal style, while Marvin Rosenberg's response to Harbage, "Elizabethan Actors: Men or Marionettes?" (1954) argued for the opposite. Shakespeare's company probably employed a more lifelike approach than that of its rivals. The Globe Playhouse, like other playhouses of its day, precluded the use of much scenery, thereby focusing the audience's attention on the actor. However, Burbage, using the lines written for him by Shakespeare, made an advertisement for a superior style of playing in the midst of *Hamlet*, and clearly the Chamberlain's Men believed they presented a more "realistic" style of play than that of other London acting companies.

The characters in Shakespeare's plays (especially in the later ones) are complex compared with those of his contemporaries. Burbage, who played Othello, Hamlet, and King Lear, must have employed a subtle style in order to capture the many nuances of those multifaceted heroes. Nowhere is the disparity in characterization more evident than in Marlowe's treatment of Barabas in *The Jew of Malta* (pr. c. 1589), a role played by Alleyn, and Shakespeare's treatment of Shylock, probably played by Burbage, in *The Merchant of Venice* (pr. c. 1596-1597). Compared with the complex Shylock, Barabas represents a one-dimensional arch villain roaring his way through a melodramatic revenge tragedy. Broad characters require the actor to use broad strokes, and Alleyn, like Burbage, must have adapted his delivery to suit the material. Perhaps Shakespeare had Alleyn in mind when Hamlet, in his advice to the players, speaks of actors who "tear a passion to tatters, to very rags, to split the ears of the groundlings . . . ."

RESTORATION ACTING

Acting styles on the Restoration stage borrowed heavily from the French Baroque theater. English audiences traveling to France to see plays during the Commonwealth expected similar fare when the English theaters reopened. One notable difference in the reign of Charles II was the appearance of women on the stage, heretofore portrayed by young men and boys. Interestingly, audiences had some trouble adapting to the change because real women seemed physically larger than the young men and boys to whom audiences were accustomed. Still, the actor's delivery, particularly in tragedy, was highly formalized and declamatory.

Reflecting the classical tastes of high society, aristocratic norms of decorum, temperance, politeness, and simplicity governed the actor; actor-playwright Colley Cibber, in *An Apology for the Life of Colley Cibber* (1740), said that the theater should be "a school of manners and virtue." Discussing the actor's methods, the leading actor of the period, Thomas Betterton, said that the actor carefully catalogs "the passions and habits of the mind [that] discover themselves in our looks, action and gestures." That the Restoration actors' approach to their roles was external and technical seems evident in Betterton's assertion that acting should "never transport the speaker out of himself." The actors played primarily on the wide apron, or forestage, in front of the proscenium arch, rarely doing something so informal as sitting. Scenery, almost never used as a function of action, served as a backdrop within the proscenium. In 1712, theater manager Christopher Rich, to increase audience capacity, removed the apron at the Theatre Royal, Drury Lane. This moved the actors farther from the audience and forced them to use the scenery.

Nevertheless, the grandiloquent style of acting flourished. In the early 1700's, James Quin specialized in vocal effects and formalized acting that exhibited the form rather than the content of tragedy. Versatility became nonexistent because actors were hired to play specific roles that then became their property, unlike the earlier Elizabethan stage, where actors demonstrated versatility by doubling roles. Gradually, however, some actors, such as Charles Macklin, referring to the "hoity-toity tone of the tragedy of that day," adopted a more natural delivery. Macklin taught his students first to speak the lines as they would in real life and then to add force to them for the stage.

The great actor-manager David Garrick thoroughly revolutionized acting. Criticizing the artificiality of oratorical delivery, Garrick emphasized the use of the correct gesture suited to the spoken line, as well as a more natural delivery (echoing Hamlet's advice to the visiting players, and underscoring that every age defines what it considers to be "natural"). A masterful technician, he observed people in real life, then meticulously cataloged gestures and movements for the stage. Garrick's natural delivery caused Quin to remark, "If this young fellow is right then we have all been wrong." A highly versatile actor, Garrick excelled at both tragedy and comedy, and although his style was considered fresh and natural, he was "not above the stops and starts and drawn-out death scenes that drew applause." Sarah Siddons, a protégé of Garrick, fulfilled the ideal of tragic acting espoused by François Talma; he described her style as "the union of grandeur without pomp and nature without triviality."

NINETEENTH CENTURY ACTING

Excessive emotional display, considered undesirable by actors throughout the Restoration and eighteenth century, became the norm with the rise of English melodrama and the nineteenth century tragedians. Melodrama, which flourished in both England and the United States, afforded the actor an opportunity, in Hamlet's condemnation, to "tear a passion to tatters." As a way to circumvent the consortium of London playhouses that held licenses for dramatic fare, melodrama, in its original sense, meant theater set to music. A continual musical accompaniment set a tone for emotional scenes on stage, and because the characters were stock villain, hero, heroine, comic man, and comic woman, characterization became simpler. So important did action become to the melodrama that authors wrote elaborate stage directions for the actors, including descriptions of facial expressions such as "revenge burning in his eye" or "his countenance disordered." Strict conventions governed each stock character, and each type was marked by its idiosyncrasies. The comic characters dressed ludicrously and indulged in such low comedy as face slapping, falling down, and bumping into one another. The villain generally sported a black top hat, frock coat, and cape and boots; his delivery was marked by facial contortions and furtive asides. William Brady, writing of New York's Bowery Theatre around 1870, recalled a special technique for the villain's death: "elbows stiff, spine rigid, then fall over backward square on the back of your head." Audience participation was not discouraged. The villain was regularly hissed and booed and the hero cheered on in his efforts, and it was not uncommon for audience members to comment aloud on an actor's per-

formance or a piece of stage business. In turn, audience involvement required the actors to become more aggressive in their style. Movement and gesture were performed as broadly as possible, and speech was marked by peculiar pronunciation and special rhythm. Each syllable was voiced with elaborate distinction and sometimes elongated for effect.

The flourishing of melodrama spawned a number of star actors in both England and the United States. These giants of the stage, most of whom got their start in melodrama, assayed the great Shakespearean tragic roles, developed their repertoires to include the parts in which they particularly excelled, and honed their talents to such a degree that their dramatic feats became legendary. The first of these great actors in England was Edmund Kean, whose powers were so great that he reportedly caused an actress playing a scene with him to faint; the Romantic poet George Gordon, Lord Byron, allegedly was so carried away by Kean's performance of Hamlet that he was seized with convulsions. Samuel Taylor Coleridge's comment that watching Kean act was like "reading Shakespeare by flashes of lightning," doubtless meant as a compliment, may provide some insight into the histrionics of Kean's acting style.

The first great American actor of the period was Edwin Forrest. The feud that developed between Forrest and the English actor William Charles Macready initiated a lively rivalry between English and American actors that continued into the twentieth century. Because Forrest was not as well trained as his English counterpart, his style was considered blunt, natural, and impulsive, while Forrest and other critics accused Macready of being artificial, cold, and mechanical. The feud culminated in 1849 when Macready, attempting to perform *Macbeth* (pr. 1606) at the Astor Place Theatre in New York City, was booed off the stage. A riot ensued, and 134 persons were killed. An interesting facet of the Forrest-Macready feud is how acting styles reflect the *Zeitgeist*. The United States was a young country living out a spirit of revolution and pioneering, and it was natural that Forrest's simplicity appealed to Americans, just as Macready's sophistication played successfully to a more complex English culture that had been developing for centuries. Consider, for example, the play President Abraham Lincoln saw at Ford's Theater when he was assassinated: *Our American Cousin* (pr. 1858) had the brash, uncouth American outsmart his English cousins, using such homespun language as "sockdologizing"—a word that assassin John Wilkes Booth, himself an actor, knew would draw laughter and conceal his gunshot. Booth's leap to the stage after shooting Lincoln emulated his own performance in *Macbeth* months before the assassination.

Versatility was of little importance to the nineteenth century tragedians. They adapted the character to suit their personalities, and unlike the leading actors on the twentieth century English stage, who would later play virtually every role of importance in the Shakespearean canon, these earlier stars played only a few parts and were best known for one or two portrayals. Kean was most famous for his King Lear, Macready for his Macbeth and his Hamlet, and Charles Kemble was regarded as the outstanding Mercutio of his day. Later in the century, Sir Henry Irving was acclaimed for his Hamlet, and in the United States, Edwin Booth, brother to John Wilkes, was most famous as Othello. Another American, Joseph Jefferson, achieved star status with his portrayal of Rip Van Winkle. Audiences did not go to the theater to see *King Lear* or *Othello*—they went to see Kean as Lear or Booth as Othello. English actress Ellen Terry noted that although Henry Irving "expressed himself in a multiplicity of parts, . . . he was always the same Irving."

This practice of infusing the part with the actor's personality was criticized by the French actor Benoit-Constant Coquelin. Writing for *Harper's Monthly* in 1887, he asserted that the English practice resulted in "revolting hideousness" and "naked realities. People do not go to the theatre for that sort of thing." This prompted a reply from Irving, who wrote that Coquelin "had lost sight of the fact that in tragedy . . . it is rather the *soul* of the artist than his form which is moulded by the theme." Dion Boucicault joined the debate, saying that although Shakespeare's great heroes suffer from different causes, they suffer alike, in the same historionic key: "Booth, Forrest, Macready, Kean, (Tommaso) Salvini always presented the same man in a different costume." Coquelin fired a parting salvo, saying that the French actors are great "generalizers," whereas the English concern themselves with the individual.

The French actress Sarah Bernhardt, when asked to list the requirements of great acting, replied "voice, voice, and more voice." Her English and American contemporaries probably concurred, as ample evidence suggests that vocal technique was the principal instrument of tragic acting of the late nineteenth century. Drama critic and author William Winter, commenting on the English actor James William Wallack, said that "his sonorous tones flowed over the action in a veritable silver torrent of musical sound." Shortly before his death in 1893, Edwin Booth recorded, on one of the earliest phonographs, some lines from Othello's senate speech. Booth employed a distinct vibrato—a slightly tremulous effect—in reading the lines. Booth's contemporaries doubtless used this vocal device, and the custom of "singing the lines" continued well into the twentieth century.

A number of factors caused the decline of melodramatic acting. With the increasing complexity of society, the trauma of World War I, and the twentieth century fascination with psychology, artists began focusing on the realistic and naturalistic aspects of life. The stately grandeur of the nineteenth century theater gave way as playwrights and actors began creating complex characters in real-life situations.

Another factor that contributed to the decline of melodramatic acting—perhaps the most significant—was the advent of the cinema. As the art of cinema developed, audiences expected actors to adopt cinematic techniques for the stage, and by the time sound motion pictures were made, the broad style of melodrama was considered cheap and hammy. Ironically, the earliest films were heavily influenced by melodrama, and some of the more famous melodramas were made into motion pictures, including *Uncle Tom's Cabin* (1903), *The Count of Monte Cristo* (1913), and *Under the Gaslight* (1914). The broad gestures that actors employed in the silent cinema provide an insight into the acting styles of the nineteenth century stage. In those silent films, audiences had to "read" the emotions of the actors before reading their dialogue, which lagged behind the action on the screen.

IMPACT OF STANISLAVSKY

In the early 1900's, disillusioned by the staleness of his own acting and in part inspired by the work of the Italian tragedian Salvini, Konstantin Stanislavsky set about to formulate a system of acting that would allow actors to develop their character properly and sustain the portrayal through many performances. The precepts that Stanislavsky set forth in *An Actor Prepares* (1936) and *Building a Character* (1949) did more to revolutionize acting styles on the English-speaking stage than any factor before that time. Stanislavsky divided his "System," as it came to be known, into roughly two parts: the actors' work on themselves and their work on their roles.

In *An Actor Prepares*, Stanislavsky asserts that actors must establish the inner life of the character through the use of realistic action combined with their own creative imagination, their concentration, and their physical relaxation. Stanislavsky points out that because emotion is a result of action, it cannot be acted; a correct lifelike action will produce a correct lifelike emotion. Actors stimulate the creative imagination through the use of the "magic if," postulating an imaginary situation, as in "What would I do if my father died?" It follows that actors can believe in imaginary or theatrical truth as sincerely as they can believe in real truth, just as a little girl believes in the existence of her doll. The System maintains that actors placing themselves in an imaginary situation similar to a real-life situation will experience a real emotion on stage. This concept of emotional memory later played a key role in the American adaptation of the System. To help the actor develop concentration, Stanislavsky introduces the concept of "public solitude": Even in a crowd, Stanislavsky notes, individuals have their own capsule of space, which moves with them. Tension, Stanislavsky emphasizes, becomes a barrier to natural action, and actors must relax their muscles.

Stanislavsky's chief teaching tool was improvisation, wherein the actors, working without a text, were given a set of lifelike circumstances and, using their creative imaginations, reacted accordingly. Improvisation became especially popular in the United States, so much so that by the 1960's some American groups used improvisation even in performance. However, improvisation must be aided by one's emotional memory or by external stimuli. One exercise had actors choose together the furniture for their stage home from the property room, much as if shopping; in this way, the scene when rehearsed or improvised held a stronger sense of the personal and familiar.

Building a Character addresses the external methods by which the actor creates a characterization. In this work, Stanislavsky stresses the importance of such technical factors as tempo and rhythm, voice and diction, fluidity of movement, and observation of nature. Stanislavsky asserts that the actor must cultivate a sense of aesthetics and likens the composition of a role to that of a musical opus.

By combining the internal or creative approach with the external or technical approach, Stanislavsky evidently thought he had defined the actor's creative process. He objected to its being called "his System," saying there is only one system—creative organic nature. Stanislavsky's teachings and their derivatives, especially as practiced by the Group Theatre and the Actors Studio, were the most important influence on acting styles in twentieth century America.

Although articles describing the System had appeared in American journals as early as 1906, it was not until Richard Boleslavsky (a protégé of Stanislavsky) came to the United States from Russia that the System became known to American actors. Boleslavsky was the first proponent of the System in the United States, teaching at the Neighborhood Playhouse in New York City in 1923. He also published an article, "Stanislavsky: The Man and His Methods," in the April, 1923, issue of *Theatre* magazine. That same year, American Lee Strasberg journeyed to Moscow to study the System and to attend performances at Stanislavsky's Moscow Art Theatre. Strasberg, an immigrant from Austro-Hungary, had grown up speaking only Yiddish and had spent his early years as an actor in the Yiddish theater. He became fascinated with the acting process and would spend his life teaching and writing on the subject.

THE GROUP THEATRE

In 1931, Strasberg, Harold Clurman, and Cheryl Crawford, united by a common interest in the System, founded the Group Theatre. Until that time, actors in American theater—following the nineteenth century practice—were cast by type. The Group Theatre founders believed that typecasting stifled the actor's artistic growth, and they set out to form an ensemble of actors who could express their creative imaginations in the tradition of Stanislavsky. The Group Theatre located a farm in Brookfield Center, Connecticut, and retreated there to live and work together. Some of the notable actors in the original Group Theatre were Franchot Tone, Elia Kazan, Sanford Meisner, Morris Carnovsky, and Stella Adler. Using improvisation as their principal rehearsal technique, the actors began preparations for the first production. Strasberg's insistence that emotion or affective memory was the most important element of an actor's creative life led to divisiveness among the Group Theatre's members and caused a controversy that lasted for many years. Nevertheless, the initial production of Pad Green's *The House of Connelly* (pr. 1931) was successful, with drama critic Stark Young pointing out that "there was not an instance of stage cheating for effect, or of hollowness."

Not all the actors, however, were happy with this approach. Stella Adler, an actress with a decided flair, felt out of place with what she called the "untheatrical" personalities of some of the others. Strasberg termed her style of acting "Jewish emotionalism," and a disenchanted Adler traveled to Russia to meet with Stanislavsky himself. In Moscow, she worked with Stanislavsky for five weeks, during which time she took careful notes. On her return to the Group, Adler accused Strasberg of misinterpreting Stanislavsky's writings. Some of the other actors agreed with her, and Strasberg and Crawford, angered by the revolt, promptly resigned.

The Group Theatre's influence on American acting style was enormous in that the Group Theatre introduced to the stage a new realism that evidently appealed to audiences. Elia Kazan's performance in Clifford Odets's *Waiting for Lefty* (pr. 1935) was so believable that many in the audience thought Kazan was a real cabdriver. The acting style of the Group Theatre was not without its detractors, however, and drama critic Brooks Atkinson accused Kazan of "getting to be a self-conscious actor with purple patches," who is "studiously spontaneous." Angered by Atkinson's review, Kazan quit acting and turned to directing. Other critics accused the Group Theatre of clannishness and of cultivating a mystical reverence for Stanislavsky. Actress Laurette Taylor, famous for the portrayal of the stifling mother Amanda in Tennessee Williams's *The Glass Menagerie* (pr. 1944), among her many roles, asked, "Why must they make acting a malady?" Hampered by continuing criticism and financial difficulties, the Group Theatre was forced to close its doors in 1941.

THE ACTORS STUDIO

Believing that the actor was undervalued in the American theater and united in a desire to pursue realism on the stage, Elia Kazan and Robert Lewis founded the Actors Studio in 1947. At their headquarters on West Forty-eighth Street in New York City, twenty-six actors gathered to study their craft. Marlon Brando, Montgomery Clift, Julie Harris, Kim Hunter, Karl Malden, E. G. Marshall, and Maureen Stapleton were among the original ensemble. Invited to join the Studio in 1951, Lee Strasberg eventually assumed control. Strasberg and Kazan continued the work they had begun at the Group Theatre, stressing improvisation and emotional memory. Actors were required to perform simple exercises such as threading a needle or peeling an orange—the goal of the tasks was not to achieve a mimetic effect but to capture the sense or emotion of the moment, paying attention to the seemingly unnoticed details of the experience. The emphasis on emotion and the private moment signaled a departure from Stanislavsky, with Strasberg referring to his technique as the "Method," or an "adaptation of the Stanislavsky system." The Method actor aimed for absolute verisimilitude on stage, especially in terms of the actor's own feelings. Thus, the audience became a kind of voyeur, and this unique actor-audience relationship bred in some Method actors a contempt for the audience.

In 1947, Brando, considered by many as the prototype of the Method actor, stunned the theater world with his remarkable performance as Stanley Kowalski in Tennessee Williams's *A Streetcar Named Desire*. Probably more than any other actor, Brando deeply affected the realistic acting style in both theater and cinema. Film actors were naturally intrigued by the Actors Studio and its Method, and in the 1970's actors such as Robert De Niro, Robert Duvall, and Jack Nicholson joined the Studio. Boleslavsky and Michael Chekhov (another of Stanislavsky's protégés) had been teaching the System in Hollywood for years, and in 1966, responding to a demand from the film community, Strasberg founded the Actors Studio West.

The Method created an enormous debate in American theater. Critic Robert Brustein described the Method as a "subjective, autobiographical approach to acting . . . through a mistaken reading of Stanislavski." Other critics complained that the Actors Studio's "torn T-shirt school" ignored the technical aspects of an actor's training, resulting in actors with poor diction and sloppy stage movement. The emphasis on emotional reality evidently caused some actors to hang on to an emotion at all costs, thus isolating them and preventing interaction with other players on the stage. Indeed, many non-Method actors believed that practicing the Method was neurotic, and indeed, Method actor James Dean called acting "the most logical way for people's neuroses to manifest themselves." By the 1970's, the Actors Studio catered more to film actors than to stage actors, and by the 1980's, the Method was so out of vogue in American theater that the stage actor generally used the term "Method actor" as an insult. In New York City, acting schools that tried to find a middle ground sprang up everywhere, with the Herbert Berghof School in the West Village, including such teacher/actors and writers as Austin Pendleton, Uta Hagen, and Horton Foote, as but one example. Hagen's book, *Respect for Acting* (1973), represents a solid integration of study, technique, and exercises for finding an emotional life for the actor.

ENGLISH VS. AMERICAN APPROACH

English actors, too, were influenced by the movement toward realism, though much less so than the Americans. The English had their acting schools, most notably the Royal Academy of Dramatic Art and the London Academy of Music and Dramatic Art, but the emphasis remained more focused on the technical aspects of acting. Courses in fencing, stage movement, and voice and diction were a regular part of the English student actor's curriculum. While the American theater had become indigenous, its actors performing in the heavily realistic style of their native drama, the English were more eclectic in their tastes. The proliferation of the repertory system and the founding of the National Theatre of Great Britain (1963-1964) allowed the English actors to continue their classical tradition. Twentieth century English actors gained respect for their important contributions to society: Actors such as Laurence Olivier, John Gielgud, Ralph Richardson, and Michael Redgrave, who worked their ways up through the repertory system to emerge as major stars, much like their nineteenth century predecessors, were awarded knighthoods, and Olivier was the first actor to be made Lord of the Realm.

Mid-twentieth century English and American actors regarded one another's styles with a mixture of admiration and scorn. While the Americans admired, and even envied, the English actors' ability to perform the classics, many believed that the English actors were cold and artificial. Conversely, the English admired the emotional exuberance of the American actors, but it was not in the English character to attempt such style. Here, perhaps, we might note an anecdote about two fine actors, one from the English tradition and the other the American—Olivier and Dustin Hoffman—who starred in the 1976 film *The Marathon Man*. Apparently Olivier, on learning that Hoffman had stayed awake all night and even screamed himself hoarse in preparation for a scene in which he shows the signs of torture, asked Hoffman if it were true; having been assured that it was, Olivier is said to have remarked, "My dear boy, why didn't you simply act?" The American theater in the first half of the twentieth century, however, with the possible exceptions of John Barrymore and Paul Robeson, produced no stars in the English classical tradition.

NEW APPROACHES TO SHAKESPEARE

The dramas of Shakespeare played a key role in changing acting styles. The twentieth century witnessed a renaissance in performances of Shakespeare's plays in both England and the United States, Shakespeare being the most frequently performed playwright. Shakespeare festivals had been held regularly since 1879 at Stratford-upon-Avon, Shakespeare's birthplace, and in 1961 the Royal Shakespeare Company was formed. Interest in performing Shakespeare quickly spread to Canada and the United States, the Bard's plays becoming so popular in the latter that by the 1980's virtually every state in the United States had at least one Shakespeare festival, many with facsimiles of the first Globe playhouse.

INNOVATIONS OF THE 1960'S AND 1970'S

By the 1960's, American actors, growing disillusioned with the Method, were searching for new techniques. The politicization of American society at that time led to the formation of agitprop theater companies such as the San Francisco Mime Troupe (formed in 1959 by R. G. Davis), whose chief aim was to make a political statement. The acting style of these groups was rough, broad, and forceful, borrowing from the Italian *commedia dell'arte*. The performances were often improvised, with the actors working only from a scenario. This kind of "street theater" was not in the mainstream of American theater; further, the orientation of such groups was political, not artistic.

By the 1960's, the American actor's training had fallen primarily into the hands of the universities. Most universities had a drama department, and some institutions, such as the Yale School of Drama and the University of Washington, were associated with professional companies. A renewed interest appeared in performing the classics, especially Shakespeare, and those universities with professional training programs provided the student actor with a broad base of classical training, including, like the English schools, courses in voice and diction and stage movement.

In 1962, as artistic director of the Royal Shakespeare Company, Peter Brook captured the attention of the theater world with his innovative staging of *King Lear* with Paul Scofield and Peter Weiss's production of *The Persecution and Assassination of Jean-Paul Marat as Performed by the Inmates of the Asylum of Charenton Under the Direction of the Marquis de Sade* (pr. 1964), commonly known as *Marat/ Sade*. The acting was rough, blunt, and simple, and Brook's work with the actors at the Royal Shakespeare Company resulted in a new physicality in acting style.

In the early 1970's, Brook's controversial production of Shakespeare's *A Midsummer Night's Dream* toured the United States. Brook staged the play metaphorically as a circus, requiring the actors to perform feats of tumbling, juggling, and trapeze-swinging. The idea of "physicalizing" the dramatic moment caught on, and the resultant acting style saw more physicality, simplicity, and clarity of expression. Brook's insistence that the only essentials for theater were an empty space, an actor, and someone to watch (that is, the audience) elevated the actor's role in theater to preeminence. The thrust stage became the most popular form of theater architecture because it brought the actor closer to the audience and minimized the use of scenery. The actor's task was to find the simplest form of expression. Conversely, the stage became more like its Elizabethan predecessor, where actors on the expansive stage were never more than a few feet away from spectators in the pit or those in the balconies before and above them.

Brook's ideas, as outlined in his book *The Empty Space* (1968), had the most significant influence on acting style since Stanislavsky. Brook asserts that only when the actor's work is "immediate" can it be fresh, compelling, and exciting. He argues that "Deadly Theatre," or bad theater, is made deadly in part by preconceived notions about how a particular play should be staged or how a particular role should be played, and "nowhere does the Deadly Theatre install itself so securely . . . as in the works of William Shakespeare." Brook points out that it is virtually impossible for actors to speak Hamlet's "To be or not to be"—probably the most famous line on the English-speaking stage—and make it sound fresh. Only by re-phrasing the line in their own words can actors begin to make the phrase live. Thus, improvisation is an important tool in that it forces the actor to create from moment to moment—a technique the actor must possess even in performance. Brook objects to the phrase "building a character," adding that only the mediocre actor builds a character the way a mason builds a wall, brick by brick, working up to a finished product. Truly creative actors, Brook asserts, must be willing to forsake all that they have learned, to "discard the hardened shells of [their] work," so that in performance they appear "in front of an audience, naked and unprepared." Only then will the actor's performance be immediate. Brook arrives at a formula: Theater = R r a. That is, theater is (R) repetition, (r) representation, and (a) assistance. Repetition means the mechanics of the actor's performance, the repeating night after night the same gestures and lines; representation is the actor's performance; and assistance is the communication that the actor receives from the audience.

Stanislavsky no doubt would have agreed with much of Brook's thesis. Both attempted to provide the actor with techniques that would allow the actor's performance to remain fresh and exciting. Both also shared a concern that the actor continue to explore new styles and techniques. Long after Stanislavsky's death, the Moscow Art Theatre continued to stage his productions exactly as he directed them. Stanislavsky would have disapproved of these carefully preserved museum pieces, since he cautioned actors that his System was itself subject to ceaseless revision, changing every day. Brook agreed, arguing that in theater "the slate is wiped clean all the time." He stressed the importance of Stanislavsky's "magic if," pointing out that while in life "if" implies fiction and evasion, in the theater it is truth. When the actor and audience "are persuaded to believe in this truth, then the theatre and life are one."

ROLE OF CINEMA

The most notable distinctions in modern acting styles have to do with the emergence of cinema as an art form. Acting schools across the country, and especially on both coasts, reflect the differences in acting formats: classes center on stage work, film acting, and even commercial and soap opera acting. Film schools, such as New York University among many others, offer classes in cinema, which include acting specifically geared toward film and television. Film remains a director's medium. Many successful film actors rely on the nuances of direction—in close-ups, editing, and camera work—to help them create a role. Film actors often, however, seek "legitimacy" by appearing on the stage. The Public Theatre's productions of Shakespeare in the Park in New York City's Central Park affords this opportunity to many actors. The founder, Joseph Papp, sought to make Shakespeare understandable and approachable to the everyday public, which meant using stars from the ubiquitous cinema to draw people to the free performances. As a result, audiences and critics alike were often confronted with well-known and highly praised film actors who had difficulty in delivering Shakespeare's poetic dialogue or moving comfortably on the stage. Audiences were forced to recognize the differences between the stage and film.

Actors in contemporary cinema rely on many technical aspects of film to popularize their abilities: action stars, handsome and beautiful actors, and even special effects, which emphasize the cult of personality rather than the inherent abilities in their craft. However, that is not to say that many popular stars of the cinema are not capable and talented actors in other venues. Rather, it serves as a reminder that the medium for the actor's art depends on the anticipated reception of society and its continuing reflection of what each era deems "natural" or "realistic."

BIBLIOGRAPHY

Benedetti, Jean, and Alice L. Crowley. *Stanislavski and the Actor: The Method of Physical Action.* New York: Routledge, 1998. Benedetti is a well-known Stanislavsky scholar and here provides the first English version of Stanislavsky's later notes and practical exercises. Benedetti adds his own analysis of Stanislavsky's acting approach and rehearsal methods.

Brestoff, Richard. *Great Acting Teachers and Their*

Methods. Lyme, N.H.: Smith and Kraus, 1995. A good introduction to some of theater's renowned teachers and an exploration of how their techniques are used today in universities and acting groups. Each chapter presents a sample "class" to provide the reader with insight into the ways in which methods have historically been taught.

Chekhov, Michael. *Lessons for the Professional Actor.* Edited by Deirdre Hurst Du Prey. New York: Performing Arts Journal Publications, 1985. Chekhov was an actor with the famed Moscow Art Theatre, who trained in the Stanislavsky system of acting and established a studio in New York to work with young Broadway actors. Chekhov's variation to the Stanislavsky system lay in his emphasis on physical movement, which both blocked "articulation" and could free an actor's emotions for his stage representations.

Hagen, Uta. *Respect for Acting.* New York: Macmillan, 1973. Offers acting students a solid starting point for balancing the necessities of technique, a study of the period and the literature to be acted, and exercises that develop an interior life, as well as underscoring the proper technical skills necessary for the actor.

Harbage, Alfred. "Elizabethan Acting." *PMLA* 54, no. 2 (1939): 685-708. Harbage's article began an interest in Elizabethan acting styles that grew in intensity for the next four decades. His contrasts between "formal" and "natural" established the terms in the debate.

Hill, John. *The Actor: Or, A Treatise on the Art of Playing.* 1755. Reprint. New York: Benjamin Blom, 1972. This reissue of Hill's 1755 work offers enjoyable insight as to what an Englishman in the eighteenth century saw as the "science of acting" and the rules whereby one could perfect the art.

Hirsch, Foster. *A Method to Their Madness: A History of the Actors Studio.* New York: Da Capo Press, 2001. Traces the evolution of Stanislavsky's methods from Moscow to the Group Theatre and finally to New York's Actors Studio. Examines Lee Strasberg's controversial techniques and the Studio's famous alumni and goes behind the scenes to observe its modern-day sessions, interview its members, and trace its internal politics.

Rosenberg, Marvin. "Elizabethan Actors: Men or Marionettes?" *PMLA* 69 (1954): 915-27. Rosenberg's essay presented a contrast to Harbage's "Elizabethan Acting," using some remarkable examples from the Shakespearean era to argue for a more natural approach to the acting on the Elizabethan stage.

Stanislavsky, Constantin. *An Actor Prepares.* Translated by Elizabeth Reynolds Hapgood. New York: Theatre Arts Books, 1936. Stanislavsky's first and most important work on the art of acting, dealing mostly with the actor's interior life.

_____. *Building a Character.* Translated by Elizabeth Reynolds Hapgood. New York: Theatre Arts Books, 1949. Argues that body, voice, and movement should be united in preparing the actor for his role.

William Frankfather,
updated by Wayne Narey

MONOLOGUE AND SOLILOQUY

Though the idea of monologue is simple—any solo speech delivered by an actor—the purpose and effect of monologue and soliloquy in the world of theater are anything but simple. Sometimes monologues provide essential narration and exposition, filling in the audience on past or offstage events; sometimes they serve to mediate between audience and action, much like the chorus of classical Greek drama; and sometimes they signal the passage of time or a change of location. A monologue may occur at any point in a play, as a prologue or epilogue, or as a part of the main action. Often monologues occur at moments of heightened emotion, but just as often they provide opportunity for dispassionate analysis. Traditionally words dominate in a monologue, regardless of whether other actions are occurring on stage. Indeed, during the Victorian era, Robert Browning and other poets took the stylized language of monologue out of the theater entirely, giving it a new life in "dramatic monologues," in which the poets spoke in the voices of fictional or historical figures.

Generally speaking, a theatrical monologue or soliloquy is a set piece, which allows for virtuoso performance and highlights the skill of both writer and actor. Handled poorly by either party, a monologue can break the spell of the theater, but when done well, a monologue can be among the most moving and enlightening moments in a production. It is perhaps for this reason that actors commonly are expected to prepare monologue recitations for auditions, and many books of great monologues have been compiled for this purpose. Depending on the context, monologues may be delivered to another character on stage, or they may be spoken directly to the audience, providing a sort of intimacy between speaker and auditors. They may also be delivered to an implied other who is absent from the stage (perhaps God, a spirit, or a character's other self). Still other times, monologues or soliloquies are performed in a more introspective mode, giving the illusion that the audience is simply allowed to overhear the character's words or thoughts.

Usually monologues are spoken by regular characters in the play, but occasionally they come from an "outside" presence, brought on specifically for the purpose—for instance, the Stage Manager in Thornton Wilder's *Our Town* (pr. 1938).

Though both refer to extended speeches delivered by a single character or actor, the terms "monologue" and "soliloquy" should not be taken as interchangeable. A soliloquy is a particular subset or type of monologue, in which the speaking character is alone (or believes himself or herself to be alone). As such, a soliloquy serves as a window into the character's mind and heart and is sometimes called an "interior monologue." Unlike other sorts of theatrical speeches, in which a character might have reason to deceive fellow characters, one can typically assume that whatever a character says in a soliloquy is the absolute truth. Soliloquies are most often used to express the character's most deeply held beliefs and concerns or to debate a future course of action.

Even more than other types of dramatic language, the soliloquy is an inherently theatrical convention. Although people do sometimes talk to themselves in real life, they rarely if ever do so with the conviction, fervor, or soul searching that typify a stage soliloquy. Encountering a person on the street behaving as does a character delivering a soliloquy—speaking, probably with heightened emotion, to no visible auditors—would likely bring into question that person's mental soundness. In theater, however, we enjoy this intimate peek into the character's mind and heart. Movies (and some modern stage productions) often use a recorded voice over to solve the problem of an otherwise sane character talking to himself or herself.

EARLY HISTORY

Monologues and soliloquies have played important roles throughout the history of Western theater, changing in style and substance as the theater itself evolved. The monologue was first introduced in classical Greek theater—always highly stylized in its conventions—in which it had several functions. Because violent action traditionally took place off stage, the Greek playwrights often employed a messenger to report significant offstage events (often including battles, murders, and the intercession of gods) to the principal characters. Additionally, playwrights such as Euripides and Aristophanes wrote tragic or comic monologues as rhetorical set pieces, to be delivered as prologues or in the lofty debates that often occur at the heart of Greek drama.

Medieval European drama, generally religious in nature and often highly allegorical, continued with some of these traditions, particularly in the prologues and epilogues common in morality plays. Playwrights of this period also used monologues to deliver the word of God and prayers to God.

In the Renaissance, many functions of the Greek chorus had been taken over by single characters, sometimes actually designated as "chorus," who were responsible for delivering monologues to inform the audience about the backgrounds and philosophical implications of plays. At this time, soliloquy also rose to a place of central importance in English drama. Indeed, many soliloquies of Elizabethan drama rank among the true gems of literary achievement. Christopher Marlowe's Dr. Faustus (*Doctor Faustus*, pr. c. 1588) is first seen alone in his study, arrogantly rejecting, one by one, each of the higher arts and sciences in favor of power and black magic. In the penultimate scene of the same play, Faustus is again alone in the same spot and this time delivers another moving soliloquy as he realizes, too late, the consequences of his earlier action. William Shakespeare, of course, is considered the master of the Renaissance soliloquy, particularly in his tragedies. Soliloquies such as Lady Macbeth's guilty speech while sleepwalking (*Macbeth*, pr. 1606) and King Lear's mad ravings in the storm (*King Lear*, pr. c. 1605) have made a profound mark on dramatic history. Hamlet's soliloquies are without equal in terms of their influence, with the "to be or not to be" speech, particularly, ranking as the most famous soliloquies in English literature (*Hamlet, Prince of Denmark*, pr. c. 1600-1601).

Modern and Contemporary Theater

Art, including theater, of the nineteenth and early twentieth centuries put an increasing emphasis on psychological explorations of individuals. It was, therefore, natural that monologue and soliloquy would be used in new ways to express psychological turmoil and growth in dramatic characters. In his early career especially, Henrik Ibsen rejected monologue as he sought a more naturalistic mode of discourse. On the other hand, August Strindberg and other playwrights who favored a more expressionistic mode were more likely to call upon the poetic power of monologue and soliloquy. For a number of American playwrights, including Eugene O'Neill and Arthur Miller, monologue acted to modulate the tension between naturalistic and nonnaturalistic performance strategies and provided a vehicle for characters to express their isolation and alienation from society and even those closest to them.

As the twentieth century progressed and more varieties of experimental theater emerged, playwrights found yet more ways to adapt the age-old techniques of monologue and soliloquy to their purposes. Bertolt Brecht, always seeking ways to disrupt the illusionary possibilities of theater, stressed the unreal nature of solo speech, directing his actors to step out of character and deliver critical lines directly to the audience, thus breaking the illusion and encouraging alienation. As antinaturalistic Brechtian techniques found their way into mainstream theater, similar approaches were adopted by a number of late twentieth century playwrights. During the intermission of Suzan-Lori Parks's *Venus* (pr. 1986), for example, a nineteenth century anatomist stands alone on stage and delivers a lecture on race and physiology. Caryl Churchill's *Vinegar Tom* (pr. 1976), a play set in the seventeenth century, carries the idea one step further as scenes are interrupted by characters in modern dress who directly address the audience in song.

Another hugely influential twentieth century playwright, Samuel Beckett, used monologue increasingly as his career progressed, anticipating and demonstrating as he did so the direction that the ancient technique was taking in the theatrical world as a whole. His first stage success, *En attendant Godot* (pr. 1953; *Waiting for Godot*, 1954), contains several well-known monologues, notably the confused rantings of the (perhaps) semi-imbecilic slave Lucky. His later works showcased the monologue talents of his actors. Winnie in *Happy Days* (pr. 1961), for instance, speaks all but a few lines of this two-act play, sometimes addressing her distracted husband, and other times merely filling her increasingly bleak life by talking to herself. The entire play *Krapp's Last Tape* (pr. 1958) is a monologue of sorts, as the title character "converses" with past versions of himself captured on audiotape. Beckett's later, more fragmentary works continue this attempt to capture the isolation of modern humans. One of these is actually called *A Piece of Monologue* (pr. 1979), with the single character called only Speaker. Better known is Beckett's teleplay *Not I* (pr. 1972), in which a character known as Mouth, masked by the theater curtain so that only her mouth is visible to the audience, addresses her frantic, self-defensive monologue to a silent, hooded Auditor.

FROM MONOLOGUE TO PERFORMANCE ART

Even though it became possible in the late twentieth century for monologue to be the entire basis of a theatrical work, plays for solo voices have never been more than a small minority of the total theatrical offerings. Still, these cutting-edge dramas offer particularly rich ground for examining that which makes a play a play. One-voice works such as Harold Pinter's *Monologue* (pr. 1973) and David Drake's *The Night That Larry Kramer Kissed Me* (pr. 1972), to give just two examples, have generally been referred to as plays, for they follow the basic structure and conventions of much theater, even though they lack the dialogue that is traditionally the primary communicative vehicle of a play. However, it is questionable whether the same can be said of Peter Handke's plotless stream of invective, *Publikumsbeschimpfung und andere Sprechstücke* (pr. 1966; *Offending the Audience*, 1969) or Ntozake Shange's "choreopoem," *for colored girls who have considered suicide/ when the rainbow is enuf* (pr. 1975). Should these be considered untraditional theater pieces, plays, or something else?

Performance art is the name most often given to work encompassing primarily monologue that seems to slip out of the loosely defined category of "play," though performance art also encompasses very different types of entertainment, which may be based on music, spectacle, or simple shock value. Indeed, even standup comedy is a variety of performance art and may be considered a type of monologue as well. The term "performance artist" has been applied productively to a wide range of late twentieth and twenty-first century artists who do indeed create some form of theatrical monologue, frequently on subjects of political or social importance.

For these monologuists, as they are sometimes called, an entire performance may be spoken from a single perspective, often though not always that of the performer, as with Spalding Gray's politically charged hit *Swimming to Cambodia* (pr. 1985), in which the author/performer recounts, with artistic flourishes, his time spent in Southeast Asia working on a movie project. In other cases, monologues may be polyvocal, as when Anna Deveare Smith recreates a range of voices in *Twilight: Los Angeles, 1992* (pr. 1993), a solo performance piece about racially motivated street riots in that city. It is with monologue performances such as these that the form comes full circle to return to its roots in storytelling, a performative art even more ancient than theater itself.

BIBLIOGRAPHY

Frieden, Ken. *Genius and Monologue*. Ithaca, N.Y.: Cornell University Press, 1985. Likely the most comprehensive study of the monologue—narrative, poetic, and theatrical—from its roots in classical antiquity to the modern era. Frieden's language, however, is intended for fellow scholars, so the book is not particularly inviting for a general reader.

Geis, Deborah R. *Post-Modern Theatrick(s): Monologue in Contemporary American Drama*. Ann Arbor: University of Michigan Press, 1993. Though she focuses her discussion on post World War II America, Geis grounds her study in a wider look at the roles of monologue, particularly in its narrative function.

Maher, Mary Zenet. *Modern Hamlets and Their Soliloquies*. Iowa City: University of Iowa Press, 1992. Unlike most academic studies of soliloquy, which tend to focus on the authors, this book gives voice to the actors' side of the story. Actors who played Hamlet in well-received twentieth century stage and screen performances discuss how they prepared and performed the melancholy Dane's most memorable moments.

Skiffington, Lloyd A. *A History of English Soliloquy: Aeschylus to Shakespeare*. Lanham, Md.: University Press of America, 1985. Skiffington traces the soliloquy's development in form and purpose through Western, and particularly English, drama, seeing Shakespeare's work as the crowning achievement of the technique.

Janet E. Gardner

STAGING AND PRODUCTION

Although plays are certainly a form of literature, they are actually intended for performance, not reading. A few plays are written exclusively to be read, and these are referred to as closet drama. It is important to the understanding of any play script to have a basic knowledge of the kind of performance the playwright had in mind when composing his or her drama. Performance practices vary from culture to culture and from one time period to another. These practices include such issues as acting styles, costumes, scenery, theatrical architecture, the relation of audience to performance, and, above all, the type of dramatic illusion the playwright sought to achieve, for the illusion sought will influence choices in all the other production elements. Although dramatic illusion varies considerably from playwright to playwright, even in the same culture and time period, the simplest method of analyzing the dramatic illusion is to place it on a continuum from realistic—or replication of the audience's sense of ordinary modes and manners—to presentational—or the deliberate distortion or stylization of what a given audience might consider to be ordinary modes and manners. Of course, one must always bear in mind that what seems realistic to one culture may seem highly stylized or distorted to another culture.

Theatrical production may be the most ancient of the human arts. As early as 20,000 years ago, cave paintings in Africa, Spain, and France depict people in what appear to be animal costumes. More than fifty Egyptian "pyramid texts" survive from the period around 4,000-2,000 B.C.E. The most famous of these, the Abydos passion play, depicts the life, death, and rebirth of the god Osiris. These pyramid texts are not complete plays, and there is not much information in Egyptian records to indicate how these plays were produced. However, there is no doubt that they were associated with religious ritual. Indeed, it is safe to say that almost all religious ritual is performative in some manner. Because Egypt had great influence on Greek culture in general, it is probable that Greek theatrical production contained surviving elements of Egyptian theater. Certainly both Greek and Egyptian theater were forms of religious ritual.

ANCIENT GREEK AND ROMAN THEATER

The religious festivals of the ancient Greeks provide the first complete dramatic texts and the first records about production and staging practices. The festivals of the city of Athens, especially the Lenaea, the rural Dionysia, and the City Dionysia, all featured performances of some type. These festivals were dedicated to Dionysus, the god of wine and fertility, who was said to die each year in the winter (as do the vines), only to be reborn again each spring. When the Athenian ruler, Pisistratus legalized the City Dionysia in 534 B.C.E., that festival became the virtual center of Greek drama. Aeschylus, Sophocles, Euripides, and Aristophanes wrote and directed plays for this festival. Because the festival was a state-sponsored religious ritual, all male citizens of Athens were expected to attend. Later, women were also allowed. The festival lasted five days. The first day consisted of prayers and other devout activities including parading the image of Dionysus through the streets and placing it on the altar in the theater.

The word "theater" is taken from the Greek *theatron* and means "a seeing place." In Athens the "seeing place" was a hillside near the Acropolis. Here the citizens gathered for the central three days of the Dionysia. During this time four or more plays were presented each day, along with other ceremonies. At least three tragedies and one or more comedies and satyr plays (sex farces) made up each day's performance. On the fifth day of the Great Dionysia a large prayer meeting was held to thank Dionysus for his blessings. The area of presentation of the plays was the orchestra or dancing circle, a huge circle in the center of which stood the *thymele* or altar to the god. Because the day was long, the spectators, uninhibited by any formal seating arrangements, moved about at will, eating, drinking, talking, and reacting strongly to the performances. At one performance, they became so angry with subject matter presented by the playwright Aeschylus that they rushed at him and would have injured him had he not taken refuge on the altar of Dionysus. Later, spectators were more confined by the erecting of wooden seats, but the stone seats with which we associate classical Greek theaters were not installed until after the high period of Greek drama.

This massive festival was produced each year by a head official known as the *archon* and supported in part by state funds and in part by wealthy citizens, known as *choregoi*, appointed each year by the Athenian ruler. It was the responsibility of these citizen sponsors to house, feed, train, and costume one or more of the choruses used in the various plays. The chorus was composed of a sizable group of young male dancers. The expense of supporting a group of male teenagers throughout the long rehearsal period must have been considerable.

The chorus was very important, for not only did it represent characters in the play, such as a group of birds in Aristophanes *Ornithes* (414 B.C.E.; *The Birds*, 1824), but it also served as the voice of the playwright and as the voice of the citizens of Athens. The chorus communicated not only through singing and speaking but also in elaborate dance patterns filled with special symbolic gestures known as *cheironomia*. In many ways, the chorus in Greek plays was very much like the chorus in a contemporary musical comedy.

Indeed, Greek theatrical production techniques were not unlike those used in contemporary opera and musical comedy. A good portion of the play was sung or chanted. The leading actors spoke or sung their lines to the accompaniment of a lyre, hence the term "lyrics." The chorus always chanted or performed in song and dance routines. Characters were usually drawn as slightly "larger than life." Part of this characterization technique can be accounted for by the size of the "seeing place" and the thousands of spectators in attendance. Actors wore elaborate costumes that included special boots known as *kothornos* and a large mask that covered the entire head. The mask was sometimes made to resemble an actual person as in an account of the production of Aristoph-

anes' *Nephelai* (423 B.C.E.; *The Clouds*, 1708) where an actor wore a mask that looked strikingly like the philosopher Socrates. A particular feature of comedies and satyr plays was the wearing of a large padded phallus in part for humor and in part to remind the audience that Dionysus was the god of fertility and procreation.

Playwrights were also expected to serve as the director of the plays. An author would submit his plays to a jury for selection in the annual Dionysia. If selected, he would be assigned a chorus and given a production team. The playwright-director would also be assigned three professional actors who would perform all the major roles. Changes in character would probably be facilitated by changing masks. Scenic elements were probably kept to a minimum. Although the remains of ancient Greek theaters sometimes feature a raised stage or *logion*, this was probably added much later or even installed by Greco-Roman architects. All the action took place in the dancing circle without much scenic statement, with the costumes and movement of the chorus providing visual intrigue. There is mention of the use of *skene graphia*, often translated as "scenic design." However the words actually mean "scenic writing. Perhaps there were banners or other symbolic devices placed about the dancing circle or carried by the chorus, in much the same way that these elements are used in Chinese and Indian theater.

There apparently was a small housing unit adjacent to the dancing circle known as the *skene*, from which we get our words scene and scenery. The word originally meant "a tent," and the structure was probably used to change costumes and masks, but it could represent a palace or a house of some type. Later the *skene* was made into a formal stone structure Two final production devices need mentioning. The first is the *ekkyklema*, a kind of cart used to show in tableau what took place out of the dancing circle. For instance, after Clytemnestra has killed her husband and his lover in the bath, the bodies are "rolled about" the stage for the spectators to see. Some kind of hoisting device was also used to raise gods or special mortals above the orchestra. The device was called the *machane* or machine, and when it was used for an entrance of a god, it became the *deus ex machina* or "god from the machine."

Considering its total staging and production practices, the ancient Greek theater may be called highly stylized or presentational. In its use of stylized costumes and sparse and symbolic scenic elements as well as its heavy dependence for theatrical excitement on the singing and dancing of the actors and chorus, the theater of the Greeks is not unlike modern musical theater or even, because of its ecstatic and mystical nature, akin to some rock concerts, for it is in the venues of rock concerts with their frank recognition of a surrounding and participating audience that one understands the appeal of ancient Greek theater. It is with a sense of all the Greek theater's movement and energy that one should read the tragedies of Aeschylus, Sophocles, and Euripides to realize the immediate power of the terrifying events portrayed.

Roman theater was influenced strongly by the Greeks, but the two cultures are quite different and hence theatrical practices differed as well. First, the theater was never accorded as important a place in Roman society as it was in Athens. Not surprisingly, most of the writing of the Roman tragedian Seneca is closet drama, plays intended to be read only. Moreover, Rome was always ruled by a monarchy, consequently the theater was less democratic in architecture and production. Unlike the Athenian theater with its orchestra and surrounding seeing place, reflecting democracy, the Roman theater was frontal, emphasizing autocracy and discouraging spectator participation. The Roman word for theater is not a "seeing place" but a listening space, an "auditorium."

The audience, the listeners, were there to hear and learn a lesson. It was, indeed, not uncommon for Roman actors to step out of character and address the audience directly with a sermon or observation. The chorus, which represented the people, was eliminated from most productions, while the logion or stage platform was used extensively and the *skene* was enlarged. The *skene* had three doors, which represented the doors to a palace or the doors to houses on a Roman street. As with the Greeks, Roman actors were still masked, and in tragedy, their boots had extremely high soles and heels, so that it is unlikely that they moved with any frequency or fluidity, but in a theater for listening, actor movement is less important. Roman comic actors, on the other hand, although masked, seemed to have worn the clothing of the day and to have moved about easily. Little wonder that comedy was more popular than tragedy. The most popular form of entertainment in Rome, however, was the war games of the gladiators, presented in great arenas, and the naval battles, staged in circular stadia flooded with water in the center.

INDIA, CHINA, AND SOUTHEAST ASIA

Theater disappeared in Greece and Rome with the spread of Christianity, while simultaneously there evolved in India a new form of theatrical art known as Sanskrit drama. Drawing material from the great Indian epics, *Mahābhārata* (c. 400 B.C.E.-400 C.E.; *The Mahabharata of Krishna-Dwaipayana Vyasa*, 1887-1896; also known as *The Mahabharata*) and *Rāmāyana* (c. 500 B.C.E.; English translation, 1870-1889), Sanskrit theater emerged in the first century of the current era.

Considerable evidence exists of production practices from a work called *Nāṭya-śāstra* (between 200 C.E. and 300 C.E.; *The Nāṭya shāstra*, 1950). This work indicates that Indian producers used three shapes of playhouses—square, rectangular, and triangular—with three sizes—small, medium and large—for each type of theater. In all there were nine theater shapes. The theater building in its totality symbolized the entire universe. It was divided into an acting area and an area for spectators. The spectator area was shaped like a cave and contained four pillars: red, white, blue, and yellow. These signified the four castes of society but also the four geographical regions of the world. The playing space was divided into an area for the musicians and another for the dancer-actors. There was no scenery, but the wall behind the performance area was highly decorated with symbolic carvings and paintings, reminding one of the *skene graphia* in the Greek theater. The actor was the central artist, but acting was not based on normal behavior. Instead, it was based on a number of symbolic movements signifying inner feelings and thoughts assigned to parts of the body. There were, for instance, thirteen movements of the head, thirty-six of the eyes, as well as many movements of the nose, cheek, and eyebrows. These movements were to be combined with speaking, singing, and dance to communicate a complex assortment of moods and thoughts to the spectators. Costume and makeup were strictly codified so that the clothing and makeup immediately identified the character's station in society. Properties were also symbolic. The presence of a horse, for example, was signified by a bit. Music was always present and was provided by a full orchestra, which included a vocalist who "sang out" expository information about characters and locale. This highly stylized, presentational theater would presage the even more presentational forms to develop in China and Japan. Ancient Indian plays continue to be popular throughout the world, especially *Mṛcchakaṭikā* (c. 300-600 C.E.; *Mrchhakatika*, 1898, also known as *The Little Clay Cart*).

Although theater existed in China as early as in Egypt, the evidence is slender until about 1500 B.C.E., when the Shang Dynasty ascended to power. From that point on, all the performing arts—dance, music, and religious ritual—flourished. After 1000 B.C.E. frequent references are made to dwarfs, buffoons, court jesters, mimes, and singers, and when the Han Dynasty came to power in 206 B.C.E., theater was so popular that nights at court came to be called the time of the "one hundred plays." Encouragement of theater continued and in 714 the emperor Ming Huang established a royal training school for actors known as "Students of the Pear Garden."

Little is known of the production details of ancient Chinese theater, but information indicates that performances were not unlike the contemporary form known as Beijing Opera. The playing area was bare and might indicate any given locale. Doors on either side of the staging area were used for entrances and exits. A fourteenth century wall painting from northwestern China shows an elaborately decorated curtain at the rear of the playing space. Actors and actresses are shown in highly decorated long robes with long, hanging sleeves, and carrying various hand properties including fans, umbrellas, and knives. A small orchestra is also present. From these begin-

nings, by the late eighteenth century emerged the Beijing Opera as it is known today. The plays are sung and danced more than spoken, with all speech governed by traditional rhythms. Extremely acrobatic movements are employed. An orchestra, usually in casual street clothing, sits about the rear of the stage. Scenic technicians or stagehands are also present in plain clothing. This is in contrast to the extraordinarily extravagant costumes of the performers, whose clothing includes intricate headdresses, jackets with high banners extending above the shoulders, and extremely stylized face painting. Fanciful beards are also common. Communication is dominated by a highly formalized system, which includes special hand, arm, and leg movements; twenty different types of pointing; and an extensive repertoire of sleeve and beard motions. Clearly, the Beijing Opera makes no attempt at realistic theater.

The theater of Southeast Asia is related to that of India, with dance-drama highly developed throughout the region. The most distinctive performance form is that practiced in Malaysia and Indonesia—the shadow puppet theater. These puppets are made of flat leather pieces cut and decorated so that intricate shadow patterns are cast on a screen when the figures are placed in front of a light. The figurines, which are mounted on a stick, range in height from 6 inches (15 centimeters) to more than 3 feet (91 centimeters). A single artist manipulates all the figures and also performs the speaking and singing related to the narrative. Performances are at night, and the audience sits on both sides of the screen, those on one side seeing the shadows and those on the other seeing the puppets themselves.

Clearly, the theaters of India, China, and southeast Asia fall more on the presentational rather than the representational side of the performance continuum, and it is this quality that has made them interesting to the nonrealistic theater artist of the twentieth and twenty-first centuries.

MEDIEVAL EUROPE

While theater was developing in India, the Christian church was resisting its formation in Europe. Of course, the Christian Mass was indeed a form of theater, retelling the story of the Last Supper, and it was certainly as highly stylized as any Sanskrit drama. It is not surprising, then, that theatrical variations would creep into the basic story of the Mass. Any variation in the Christian service was known as a trope, to which historians point to mark the rebirth of Western theater and its drama. The oldest extant Easter trope dates from 925, but undoubtedly the practice was initiated earlier. In the Easter trope, priests impersonating the three Marys approach a side altar that represents the tomb of Christ. A fourth priest, costumed as an angel, appears and asks "Whom seek ye?" The three Marys say they are looking for Christ, and the angel tells them he has risen.

Out of this tiny moment of dialogue develops most of modern Western drama and theater. It was not long before dramatic troping became extremely popular in churches, so much so that ultimately the hierarchy feared for corruption of the mass or serious sacrilege and excluded tropes from the church building. The new theater went no further than the church steps or at most the village square in front of the church. Here the religious performances were picked up by the town merchants as a means of entertainment and as a device to encourage business. Previously, clergy had been the theatrical performers and producers; now religious plays of all sorts were presented by amateurs throughout Europe. Indeed, huge festivals of plays were performed on certain feast days, especially the Feast of Corpus Christi.

The merchant class assumed responsibility for production, and certain guilds were assigned particular plays or locales. For instance, the blacksmiths would present the plays about hell because they had experience working with and controlling fire, while the bakers guild presented the Last Supper. The silk merchants would be assigned heaven, for they could provide the most edifying and glorious atmosphere. By 1400, play festivals were being presented throughout Europe.

Plays were short and always on a religious theme. Those plays dealing with Bible stories were called mystery plays; those dealing with the lives of saints were called miracle plays. The play festivals of any given town might last several days, during which cycles of mysteries or miracles were enacted. Plays were presented in a general area, either a public square or street corner. The actual locale or stage for an individual play was called a *sede* or mansion. In some areas in Europe, the *sedes* were arranged across the church steps, in others they were dispersed about the main square as in a contemporary church or school fair. In England it was not uncommon for the *sedes* to be placed on wheels, and these so-called pageant wagons would be rolled from street corner to street corner, where the mystery or miracle play was enacted over and over throughout the day.

Scenes might begin on one *sede*, then spread out to the public square or street corner, and then to one or more other *sedes* before the play was completed. For instance, stage directions for one play about the slaughter of the innocents indicate that "here Herod rageth in the street." Costumes for miracle and mystery plays were realistic in that they were the clothing of the time, but nonrealistic in that no effort was made to present the actual clothing worn by a saint or a Roman soldier. Thus Mary and Joseph might appear costumed as a medieval merchant and his wife. Devils and angels were highly stylized in costume and properties.

The scenery was very elaborate with each guild trying to outdo the other for religious as well as civic recognition. Special effects, such as hell fire or lightning, were attempted frequently. Newly invented machines, particularly the mechanical winch, provided for heavenly presences to be raised or lowered. A particular feature of the medieval theater was the concept of simultaneous locales. Floor plans such as those for the sixteenth century Lucerne Passion Play indicate that all *sedes* or mansions were distributed about the public arena so that the audience could at once see them all and move from locale to locale to attend the plays being enacted. Always present were the *sede* for heaven and that for hell, with the latter represented by Hell's Mouth, or a huge dragon's mouth out of which devils sprang. God was always watching events and sending angels out to intercede, and Satan also watched and sent devils out to seduce and interfere. Indeed, devils and angels would move about in the audience as well, bringing both joy and fear, delight and laughter. Obviously this was a theater in which the line between performer and spectator was not at all enforced.

In the English practice of pageant wagon production, the lower portion of the wagon was curtained-off and devils issued from this area. Sometimes a second wagon was used to represent heaven; sometimes a raised platform on the wagon itself connoted heaven. The Christian notion that God is present in all the universe, as is Satan, and that the two are present in all human history made the idea of simultaneous settings entirely real and acceptable in medieval theater.

Medieval acting was no doubt at first rather amateurish, but eventually there developed a tradition of acting that was satisfactory for the festival nature of the theater. By the late fifteenth century, a semi-professional theater was developing. Playwrights were emerging. The highly specific religious nature of certain productions was yielding to the new playwrights. First, as might be expected with all the devils running about playing tricks on the audience, an element of farce was added to plays such as the famous *Secunda Pastorum* (fifteenth century; commonly known as *The Second Shepherds' Play*) of the English Wakefield Cycle, which continues to be read and performed frequently.

This short play begins in the public arena, probably in and among the audience, where a group of shepherds lead in their sheep and then fall asleep. Mak, the mischievous shepherd, steals one of the sheep and runs to the *sede* that represents his hut, where he awakens his wife. The shepherds also awaken to discover the lost sheep and follow Mak to his hut. While they are knocking on the door, Mak tells his wife to hide the sheep in her bed. When the shepherds ask after the sheep Mak tells them that his wife has just had a baby. After some discussion of the strange look and hairy nature of the baby, the shepherds pull back the covers, take their sheep, and begin to punish Mak. From the Heaven *sede* an angel comes to announce the birth of Christ. The shepherds then walk through the public space and the spectators to the *sede* that represents the stable in Bethlehem, where the play ends with everyone worshiping the new little Jesus.

Along with farcical works, plays dealing with ethical situations, as opposed to Bible stories, began to evolve. A form known as the morality play, typified by such works as the fifteenth century *The Castle of Perseverance*, became popular as a device for teaching civic as well as religious values. Farces and moralities were not limited to Christian feast days and might be presented throughout the year. They were good advertisement for market days in the towns, they were excellent fare for the newly emerging grandeur of royal courts, and they demanded the development of part-time and full-time professional actors and scenic technicians. Talented people responded to the demand, and acting companies appeared throughout Europe.

JAPAN

As theater was reborn in Christian Europe, a parallel development was taking place in Japan with the form known as the Nō theater. Doubtless there were performing arts before the Nō theater, but records are few until the Nō emerged in Japan in the fourteenth century. Prior to that, there had existed a comic entertainment known as *sarugaku*. It was the *sarugaku* performer Kan'ami Kiotsugu who impressed the Ashikaga shogun so much that the shogun became his patron. When Kan'ami and his son Zeami Motokiyo set about to create a dramatic form that included the ideals of Zen Buddhism, Nō theater was born.

The written script of a Nō play is very short, and the focus of the art is entirely on the actor. Costumes are much less gaudy than in Chinese theater and are made of silk decorated with elaborate embroidery. On their faces, the major actors (all men) wear one of five types of wooden masks representing a man, a woman, an aged person, a deity, or a monster/demon. Each mask may have many minor variations, but the basic types are always clearly delineated. In addition to the actors, there is a group of musicians and a chanting chorus. All these performers are dressed in identical and simple robes. Also on stage in a basic costume is a stage attendant who aids the actor in changing or adjusting costumes or masks. The stage attendant is never considered part of the action. Fans are an important accessory and much information can be presented to the audience through conventionalized fan movements. Essentially the actor's motions follow the music and the story being chanted by the chorus.

Nō makes no effort at realistic representation; indeed its main thrust is to avoid any illusion of realism. Since the early seventeenth century, the Nō stage has been standardized, further contributing to the presentational character of the theater. It consists of a raised thrust platform that is surrounded by the audience on three sides. On the right side of the stage platform is a bridge on which all the characters of the play enter. Both the stage and the bridge are roofed over. The stage roof is supported by four pillars that have symbolic significance. On the back wall of the stage is a painting of a pine tree and a stand of bamboo. Off stage left is a small door used for the entrance of the chorus and musicians and for the exit of dead characters.

Paralleling the Nō theater are two other highly stylized Japanese entertainment forms: Bunraku and Kabuki. Bunraku is a puppet theater that traces its origins to 1100 but did not become firmly established until the turn of the seventeenth century, when narrations chanted to musical accompaniment were added to puppet performances. Puppets became ever more elaborate, evolving from a single head on a stick to full-body dolls each with three puppeteers, one to manipulate the head and right arm, another to manipulate the left arm, and a third to operate the feet. By 1736, the puppets were enlarged to their present size of 3 or 4 feet (0.9 or 1.2 meters). All the puppeteers were visible to the audience, although their black clothing signified that they were unseen. Unseen or not, the puppeteers were expected to involve themselves in the emotions and situation of the play their dolls were enacting.

Although Nō and Bunraku theater were forms intended mainly for the ruling class, the most popular type of early Japanese theater, and one still popular, was the Kabuki. Thought to be first performed in 1603 by Okuni, a female temple dancer, Kabuki grew into a mixture of Bunraku and Nō theater, and by 1616 there were several Kabuki theaters in Tokyo.

The Kabuki stage resembles that of Nō theater, except that in Kabuki the entrance bridge extends from the rear of the playhouse to the stage platform, much like the runway in modern burlesque theaters. The entrance of a performer along this runway, the *hanamichi*, was an exciting event taking a considerable period of time, for the actor was expected to move slowly while striking and holding a series of conventional poses called *mie*.

More like Beijing Opera than Nō theater, Kabuki actors wear gaudy and extravagant robes, so voluminous and heavy that stage attendants are often used to aid the actor in carrying and adjusting his costume. The roles in Kabuki are divided into several conventional types: brave men, mild men, villains, children, and women (who are all played by men as in Elizabethan theater). The masks of Nō theater are replaced by extensive face painting with symbolic meaning: A white face is used for most characters, while blue or brown is used for demons and villains. All facial characteristics are exaggerated, but women especially exaggerate their eyebrows and add rouge to the corners of their eyes.

While Kabuki may be said to be more realistic in illusion than other Japanese theater forms, it is still more presentational than Western theater. For example, a horse is actually a wooden form covered with a cloth and carried by two men whose legs clearly show. As in Nō, fans and scarves are used symbolically, with an extensive system of meanings and emotion attached to the varied positions of each.

Stage scenery is extensive, more decorative than realistic. Every locale is indicated by a change of scenery, and many scenic elements have conventional meanings: White mats indicate snow, blue mats water. Stage attendants move about in clear view adding or striking scenery as necessary. Musical accompaniment is always present. In the middle of the eighteenth century, mechanical trapdoors were added to the stage and soon thereafter two revolving stages were added.

Kabuki spectators are arranged on three sides of the stage platform, and performances last up to eight hours with the presentation of four separate pieces, including a lengthy dance program. The spectators are expected to eat, drink, and come and go as necessary.

ENGLISH ELIZABETHAN THEATER

As the Middle Ages gave way to the European Renaissance and commerce promoted the growth of towns into large cities, certain actors of miracle and mystery plays found that they could make a living performing almost daily in growing urban centers like London. Accordingly they organized into acting companies and sought royal patrons and financiers to aid them in production costs and legal procedures. One such company under the patronage of the earl of Leicester was organized by a successful carpenter named James Burbage who, in 1576, built the first theater in London, known simply as The Theatre. The Leicester's Men evolved into the Lord Chamberlain's Men, the company of which William Shakespeare was a member. It was this company that built the famous Globe Theatre in 1599. Actually, ten public theaters were built in London before 1642, in addition to private indoor theaters such the Blackfriars. At the end of the twentieth century, the Globe Theatre was restored based on the best evidence and scholarly opinion available and is used consistently to produce Shakespearean works.

The acting companies of Elizabethan England were small, capitalistic organizations of theatrical artists whose members owned whole or part shares in the income earned, although some artists were on salary or were apprentices who received a small stipend. A lead actor usually headed the company, such as James's son Richard Burbage in the Lord Chamberlain's Men, who performed all Shakespeare's major characters. Edward Alleyn, the partner of the financier, Phillip Henslowe, headed the rival company, the Lord Admiral's Men, who played at the Fortune Theatre. Christopher Marlowe, the great tragic dramatist who was to have such a strong influence on Shakespeare, was the major playwright for Henslowe's company.

Acting companies might number up to twenty-five members, including apprentices. Playwrights wrote with particular actors in mind, such as Burbage for the character of Hamlet and Will Kemp or later Robert Armin for the clown roles. Boy apprentices played the roles of women, hence the frequent disguising of women as men as in Shakespeare's *As You Like It* (pr. c. 1599-1600). Shakespeare was a full member of his company and his income as both an actor and a playwright made him a quite wealthy man.

In the summer months, the companies performed in their public theaters, which were open air, large, circular or polygonal structures accommodating two to three thousand spectators. The theater building surrounded an open courtyard in which stood the bulk of the spectators, known as "the groundlings," who paid the lowest price for admission. Built into three sides of the theater were mezzanine and balcony seats for the middle and upper classes, who were willing to pay higher prices to be able to sit and be protected by a roof from the sun's heat. The stage platform was a very large area, about 25 feet (7.6 meters) deep and 40 feet (12.2 meters) across, which jutted out into the courtyard. The groundlings surrounded the thrust stage on three sides, as did the seated spectators. Above the stage platform was a row of boxes occupied by special customers. For an additional fee, a few spectators could rent a stool and sit on the playing platform along with the actors. Young aristocrats and young men-about-town usually rented the stools to show off their importance. In all, the audience "swarmed about" the actors on all sides. It was a noisy, participatory group known for talking, eating, and rowdy behavior. Those who were seated on stage were expected to stand and intrude themselves into the action of the play.

Although the evidence is clear about the use of a surround stage, scholars disagree about other structural scenic elements. In the area at the top of the theater building above the stage was a small hut that housed the musicians who provided accompaniment to the action of the play; atop the hut was a pole on which a flag was flown on days when performances took place. Some portion of the playing area was covered with a roof, known as "the heavens," and in some theaters, the ceiling of this roof may have been painted with clouds and stars. "The heavens" was supported by two pillars that are clearly seen in surviving drawings of Elizabethan theaters. The wall immediately behind the playing platform was provided with some sort of device for actors to enter and exit. It may only have been two doors or two curtains, since plays mention one or another door and Polonius is hiding "behind the arras" or curtain when he is killed in *Hamlet, Prince of Denmark* (pr. c. 1600-1601). For many years, scholars—influenced perhaps by the modern proscenium arch with its front curtain—were convinced that the wall behind the stage featured a curtain that could be drawn to reveal an inner stage. Since the middle of the twentieth century, however, this practice has been questioned and even denied. There is no "inner stage" in London's restored Globe Theatre. Another hotly debated staging possibility is an opening in "the heavens" through which properties or even actors representing characters such as ghosts could be raised or lowered. Whether or not these devices were present, there is no doubt that the stage platform was pierced in one or more places to provide for trapdoors that were equipped with mechanical winches so that ghosts and devils could appear or disappear through the floor. Finally, much argument has arisen over whether there was a permanent balcony above the stage used for acting purposes such as the "balcony scene" in *Romeo and Juliet* (pr. c. 1595-1596). Balcony scenes may have been staged with actors appearing among the spectators seated above and at the rear of the stage platform, or a raised scenic unit representing a balcony may have been carried on the stage for special scenes.

Elaborate properties such as tables, thrones, and four-poster beds were also in frequent use, and these would have been brought to the stage platform through trapdoors or doors and curtains in the rear wall. Surviving stage directions call for beds to be "thrust upon the stage." Apparently no effort was made to hide the technicians used to transport such properties. In addition to large scenic elements, a number of common hand properties were in constant use: letters, swords, fans, knives and daggers, and small musical instruments. Except for some possible changes in large properties, no scenic divisions were indicated. Following the medieval practice, the stage platform was considered the *platea*, and scene locales

within this neutral space were usually indicated in the dialogue, by a musical interlude, or by a significant entrance or exit of one or more characters.

Because the stage was not opulently decorated for each play or scene and actors did not use elaborate makeup or masks as in Asian or ancient Western theater, costuming became the prime visual appeal of the theater. It was the tradition for actors to obtain costumes from the company's aristocratic patrons, such as Lord Chamberlain and his household, who would pass along used clothing to the performers. This made for richly clothed actors. No doubt the company also had to purchase some of its costuming. There was no attempt at historical accuracy. Macbeth did not appear in kilts but in the clothing of a mid-sixteenth century nobleman, as did the Roman general Julius Caesar.

Dancing and dueling were common aspects of most performances. Hence *Romeo and Juliet* contains a ballroom scene and *Hamlet* ends in a deadly duel. Actors were expected to sing and dance, as well as have powerful speaking voices to project above the noise of the spectators. The acting style probably was more oratorical and declamatory than it is in the modern era, but that would have been because the theaters were so large and the spectators so noisy. Also, the plays were written in verse, which is more formalized than ordinary conversation. Performers would have been trained in dueling with both sword and dagger as was the Elizabethan practice, and clowns would have had to possess mime and acrobatic skills. Although the many soliloquies of Elizabethan dramatic literature were usually thoughts spoken aloud, performers often would address the spectators directly in prologues or in the many asides, both visual and auditory, common to Elizabethan theater.

Performances in public theaters were in broad daylight, but there also were indoor venues that did require general lighting by torch or candle and that lighting could be used for some special effects. The indoor theaters were all considered private, whether they were the banqueting hall of a castle or such buildings as the Blackfriars Theatre, remodeled by Burbage in 1597 from an old building used to train choirboys in singing and acting. A much smaller space than the outdoor theaters, the Blackfriars was used only during the winter months and admission was much higher. There was no pit for the groundlings, and the spectators were seated on benches before the stage or in balconies rising on either side of the theater. Ben Jonson, Shakespeare's brilliant contemporary, had most of his plays staged at the Blackfriars. Indoor performances were also given at court for the queen and in the banqueting halls of nobility.

In addition to the plays of the public theater by writers such as Shakespeare, as the seventeenth century dawned, court theaters also made use of a special dramatic form known as the court masque or masquerade. Although both Henry VIII and Elizabeth supported the production of masques, the form was brought to a peak by James I who spent enormous sums of money to produce at least one masque a year. Most of the roles, especially those requiring special skills such as clowning or singing, were performed by professionals, but the dancing, which constituted the major burden of masque, was performed by courtiers and minor members of the nobility. Many of the court masques were written in large part by Jonson and designed, directed, and produced by the court architect, Inigo Jones.

Jones had recently returned from Italy where he had studied Italian architecture and scene design, and he introduced these matters into the court masque. Among his many innovations was indoor lighting, including the use of a "torchbearer" (the carrier of a candelabrum) to accompany each dancer. Jones also introduced fanciful and spectacular costume designs not seen before in Elizabethan theater. Devils, for instance, would be covered from head to toe in long flaming-red feathers and accompanied by torch bearers. The court masque, with its introduction of new Italian techniques and trends, marked the end of Elizabethan theater, with its practices steeped in the staging traditions of the Medieval theater. Indeed, Jonson, who finally realized that his traditions did not suit the new theatrical ideals of Jones, gave up collaborating with the fabled producer in 1631. That was just the beginning of the death of the Elizabethan theatrical tradition: When the Puritans came to power

a decade later, they closed all English theaters in 1642.

ITALIAN RENAISSANCE THEATER

The massive explosion of brilliant poetic drama that marked the English Renaissance theater was matched by an equal explosion in innovations in architecture, scenery, costume, and music that characterized the Italian Renaissance theater. The most important of these innovations was the invention of the proscenium arch theater building, which was to become the most pervasive form of theatrical architecture in Western civilization and would ultimately influence all world theater. The word "invention" is applied here because, even though the Italians thought they were reintroducing the theater building of the Greeks and the Romans, they were actually offering an entirely new performance space.

The story of this new invention begins with the formation of the Olympic Academy in Vicenza in 1555 to study Greek tragedy. The academy enlisted the services of the eminent architect Andrea Palladio to construct for them an ancient Greek theater. A student of Vitruvius, the Roman architect who wrote his *Iquattro libri dell'architettura* (1570; *The Four Books of Architecture*, 1721) in the first century, Palladio set out to build a Greek theater as he understood it from Vitruvius. However, Palladio could not escape the major visual innovation of his time—perspective painting. He designed a theater with a projecting playing platform surrounded on three sides by seating for an audience. In front of the playing platform was a pit, the remnants of the large dancing circle or orchestra of the Greeks.

Using the three traditional doorways of the classic Roman theater, Palladio designed three arches—a large central arch and two smaller side arches—in the back wall or *skene* of the playhouse. These would become the prototype for the now common architectural feature of a triple entrance known as the Palladian arch. Behind each of the open arches, Palladio displayed city street scenes that he deliberately built in perspective. Palladio's brilliant invention, the prototype of the proscenium theater, was called the Teatro Olimpico. The architect died before it could be completed and it was finished by his student Scamozzi, who then went on to build another such theater at Sabbionetta. Both theaters survive today.

The first true proscenium arch theater was the Teatro Farnese built at Parma in 1618 by Giovanni Aleotti. The Teatro Farnese completes the evolution begun by Palladio with a single arch placed in front of the playing area so that the whole performance is framed and the scenery used is capable of being designed in sharp perspective. The performers had to be kept in front of the proscenium arch because if they entered the area of painted scenery, they would destroy the forced perspective. All the techniques described by the designer Sebastiano Serlio in his *Tutte l'opera d'architettura: Libro 1-5* (1545; *The Five Books of Architecture*, 1611) were able to be realized within a working theater. Serlio had designed perspective pictures of what Vitruvius had described as the types of scenic backgrounds: tragic or lofty buildings or castles, comic or city street scenes, and satyric or pastoral scenes.

As described in Nicola Sabbattini's *Scene e macchine teatrali* (1638), the proscenium arch also provided effective hiding places for devices used for the rapid changing of scenery. These devices included the rotating triangular structures on whose three faces a different scene or part of a scene could be painted in perspective so that hidden stagehands could quickly flip it in unison to form an entirely new scene before the audience's very eyes. A second technique was the use of a "chariot and pole" mechanism in which flat pieces of scenery mounted on tracks like a trolley car were pulled in and out of sight by a winch. New experiments were also made in the use and control of lighting, including increasing the luminosity of candles with reflectors and the placing of glass containers filled with colored water in front of candles to change the mood of a scene or to indicate dawn or sunset. Metal cups were also lowered in unison over a bank of candles to create a dimming effect.

Many and seemingly magical changes of scenery and lights were now practiced regularly in Italy, though the great expense involved limited these scenic spectacles mainly to small theaters supported by the wealthy or the nobility, as was the case in the English court masque. The new theater offered such a rich potential for visual exploitation that some of Italy's greatest artists, including Leonardo da Vinci, designed scenery. Another major feature of the new proscenium theater was the extensive use of music to enhance scenic changes. Frequent changes of elaborate costumes also further enhanced the rich new visual experience in theater. Opera, which literally means "working scenery," was an inevitable development.

At first Italian drama turned away from the religious plays of the Middle Ages (*sacri representioni*) to translations of Roman comedy and tragedy, especially the works of Plautus and Seneca. The tragedies in particular were long and wordy. To hold the attention of the wealthy patrons who supported them, theatrical producers relieved the tediousness of the talking by interspersing entertainments of singing and dancing, called *intermezzi*, between the acts of the tragedy. When the proscenium arch was perfected, the *intermezzi* became ever more elaborated and ultimately were the main focus of the theatrical performance. The discovery by Italian literary scholars of Aristotle's book on drama, *De poetica* (c. 334-323 B.C.E.; *Poetics*, 1705), gave the invention of opera its final push. Mistranslating the Aristotelian term *melopoeia*, the scholars argued that the most crucial part of tragedy was song and music. Using the lavish visual styles developed by the scenic artists in the *intermezzi*, composers began to set whole theatrical works to music, the first of which was *Dafne* in 1598 (text by Ottavio Rinucci and Giulio Caccini; music by Jacobo Peri). The court quickly embraced the musically and visually gorgeous new form and opera came to dominate the Italian theater for the next century.

The exciting new directions in scenery were too expensive for the popular theater, characterized by the form of street theater known as *commedia dell'arte* (literally "the professional theater"). The *commedia* troupes were made up of a small company of professional actors and actresses who traveled from neighborhood to neighborhood and from city to city performing both serious and comic works. Each company member perfected a stock character type, which can be divided into four groups. The most realistic of the character groups were the young lovers whose attempts to be joined were usually frustrated by the old parents, Pantalone and his wife, or by other older characters such as the Capitano, a blustering military type more often than not a coward beneath all of his posturing; or the Dottore, who represented all the world's pedants who are more educated than they are bright. The young lovers were usually aided in their pursuit of romance by the *zanni* or servants, the most well known of whom are Francesca, the maid, and Arlecchino (Harlequin), the fellow who is "stupid like a fox." Using these stock characters, the *commedia* companies built plays around scenarios, or plot outlines, the dialogue to which they would improvise as the situation demanded, using one set of lines, perhaps in Florence and another in Rome. The plays were further fleshed out by *lazzi*, or performance routines, that might range from a comedian's deadpan or tag line to acrobatic tricks or song and dance routines. One of the most common *lazzi* was beating Arlecchino with a flat wooden sword built out of two pieces of board that make a loud noise when struck together, hence the term "slapstick comedy."

Costuming of each stock character was a stylized version of the usual clothing of the period. Arlecchino's clothing was simply an assemblage of rags and patches that might be worn by any tramp. These gradually became formalized into the diamond-shaped patterns now associated with the French harlequin. The Capitano wore an exaggerated version of a military uniform. The lovers were dressed in the latest fashions of the day, and Pantalone wore an outdated fashion featuring baggy pants or loose fitting tights and a large cod piece that echoed the phallus worn by Roman and Greek comic and satyric figures. The most famous of the *commedia* companies was the Gelosi, which in its most vigorous period was headed by a woman, Isabella Andrieni. The popularity of the *commedia dell'arte* spread across Italy and into France and even crossed the English Channel, where it influenced dramatists such as Jonson and Shakespeare.

SPANISH AND FRENCH THEATER TO 1800

As in England, Spain emerged from the Middle Ages into a renaissance known as the Golden Age of Spanish drama. More so than England, Spain was heavily influenced by other cultures, having been occupied by the Moors for more than five hundred years and having been the European discoverer of the New World in 1492. The Spanish royalty gave major support to the production of religious plays, known as *auto sacramentales*, at the feast of Corpus Christi. Cities supplied wagons or *carros* for the production of these sacred plays. These wagons, from two to four in number, were then placed next to a fixed platform to make a raised playing area for each play. The *carros* were decorated in various ways to provide the scenic atmosphere for the play.

When a play was finished, the wagons would be dragged away and others pulled up next to the fixed platform to make the new scene for the next play. The *carros* included two or three levels that could be used to indicate places such as Heaven or Hell. In addition to the sacred subject matter, the actors often performed short farces and other entertainments. It was the comic elements that eventually led to the banning of all *auto sacramentales* in the mid-eighteenth century.

Under the influence of the Italian Renaissance, Spain developed an interest in ancient Western culture, and this interest led naturally to drama. To perform secular theater, a group of professional actors had emerged from the *auto sacramentales*. By 1540 notices concerning professional actors were common and one of these professionals, first noted in 1542, is Lope de Rueda who became Spain's first important writer of secular plays. The stage for which Rueda wrote was so simple that according to Miguel de Cervantes, it consisted of a few boards set on benches with a blanket for a rear curtain. His costumes were four white sheepskins trimmed with gilded leather. Although there were no theater structures in 1540, there were permanent theater houses in most major cities by 1570 and major theatrical companies in Madrid and Seville. Some twenty years later, Lope de Vega Carpio, known as the Spanish Shakespeare, began to write secular poetic dramas, known as *come-*

dias, regularly for the theater. By the time of his death in 1635, he had written as many as eight hundred theater pieces.

The plays of Spain's dramatic renaissance were produced in theaters known as *corrales*, because they were adapted from open courtyards. At one end of the open court or patio a raised platform was erected for a stage. At the opposite end of the patio was a balcony, the *cazuela*, reserved especially for female spectators. Below the *cazuela* was an area occupied by standing spectators. Just below the stage was a small orchestra in which benches could be placed for special seating. To the left and right of the patio were sloped balconies with seating for the higher class customers. The larger theaters held about two thousand people. Spectators, as in Elizabethan theaters, were active and noisy, and the presence of the women segregated in the *cazuela* made for increased rowdiness.

As in England, acting companies were composed of shareholders and were headed by a leading actor-manager. Chief among these was Arias de Panefiel, considered the finest of his time, and Cosme Perez, the great comedian. As in England, female roles were played by boy apprentices until the late sixteenth century when women were admitted on to the stage. Among the actresses, Juespa Vaca was the most celebrated. Because of the verse dramas, actors were expected to develop strong speaking voices and excellent diction. They also were required to sing and dance, and dancing was a frequent element of the performance, especially for the women. Most productions also ended with the joyous, wild and licentious dance known as the *zarabanda*.

Visually, staging was much like that in England, except that in the more elaborate *corrales*, the facade behind the stage might contain two stories of playing areas and curtains that could be opened to reveal scenic elements. *Sedes* might also be placed on the stage to indicate specific locales. Costuming practices also resembled those in England with contemporary dress being worn no matter what historical period was being presented. Because of the tight religious control that was a heritage of the Inquisition, female costumes were always a source of difficulty with various

bans being placed on the type and cut of clothing allowed to actresses. Although plays from the public theater were presented in the royal court, court masques had been popular since the thirteenth century and became much more elaborate in costumes and scenery during the mid-seventeenth century reign of Phillip IV.

In 1621 Cosme Lotti, an Italian theatrical producer, was imported from Florence to introduce proscenium staging into court entertainment. Productions were presented in the banquet hall and often in the palace gardens. In 1635, for the production of a masque by Pedro de la Barca Calderón, Lotti built a floating stage on a lake. This production was filled with special effects such as a shipwreck and a chariot drawn across the water by mechanical dolphins. Lighting effects were created using three thousand lanterns. The king and his party watched the presentation from gondolas. In 1640, Lotti built a permanent theater, the Colesio, in the king's palace, Buen Retiro. It was the first enclosed theater in Spain and the first to have a proscenium arch. From this point on, the use of Italianate perspective scenery and lavish costuming became more and more common in Spain.

As elsewhere in Europe, French theater evolved from medieval religious performances, and as in Italy, the study of Roman culture led eventually to the translation and imitation of classical drama. At first classical plays were performed at court and at Jesuit schools throughout France. The French court, however, under the influence of the Italian Catherine de' Medici, queen mother of three French kings in the sixteenth century, embraced the new Italian techniques including perspective scenery, elaborate stage machinery, and lavish costumes. These productions ultimately developed into the famous *comédieballet*, not unlike our modern musical comedy, so popular with King Louis XIV. The Italian influence also included the encouragement of frequent visits to Paris by *commedia dell'arte* troupes.

All French theater, however, was greatly inhibited between 1540 and 1590 by the bloody civil war between the Catholics and the Protestants. When theatrical performances resumed, there emerged in Paris a major actor-manager, Valeran LeComte, who headed a company known as the King's Actors. With Valeran leading the way in Paris, more than four hundred professional acting companies appeared throughout France. As in England and Spain, actors were gathered in sharing companies that also included a few salaried actors and paid actresses and apprentices.

In the first thirty years of the seventeenth century, the major theater in Paris was the Hôtel de Bourgogne. It featured a long narrow house with a pit for a standing audience. Balconies on each side of the theater stood above the pit and extended into boxes above the stage where the wealthy and upper class were seated. The stage was raised six feet above the pit and was flanked on either side by a door for entrances. Later, benches were placed on either side of the stage for special seating. A facade with a decorative middle arch was at the rear of the stage. It is possible *sedes* or large properties were placed about the stage to indicate various locales. Companies who could not rent the Hôtel de Bourgogne often used tennis courts for performances. Roofed and enclosed, the long narrow tennis court with its side balconies for spectators was not unlike the architecture of the Bourgogne. A curtain was hung in front of one back wall and a raised stage placed in front of it. Spectators sat courtside or stood in the tennis court itself.

One of these tennis courts was made permanently into a theater and named Thêâtre du Marais. This structure burned in 1644 and was rebuilt into a more Italianate theater with a stage that sloped upward toward the back (raked) to better accommodate the new perspective scenery imported from Italy. A second level was added to the stage, and from this level it might have been possible to fly (that is, to raise and lower) scenic elements. Competition from the scenic grandeur of the Marais forced the Hôtel de Bourgogne to remodel in 1647, adding a second stage level and a raked stage. Meanwhile, the royal prime minister, Cardinal Richelieu, was building a completely equipped Italian proscenium theater, the Thêâtre du Palais Royal, in his castle. It now remained for both the public and court theaters of France completely to incorporate the new Italian ideal of a scenic theater.

In the mid-seventeenth century, the famous Italian scene designer, Giacomo Torelli, was imported from Italy by the French queen to design a production of the opera *La finta pazza* (pr. 1641), the 1645 performance of which was to be produced by a *commedia dell'arte* troupe. Torelli completely remodeled the king's banqueting room, the Salle du Petit-Bourbon, into an Italian theater. The king was so taken with the opera and the redesign of the Petit-Bourbon into a theater that he commissioned many productions to follow. Ballets were particularly popular, with Louis XIV himself dancing the leads. The joining of opera and ballet in the Petit-Bourbon established a tradition continued to the modern era. In 1659, the Italian ideal triumphed in French theater when the Petit-Bourbon was torn down and a new Italian theatrical designer, Gaspare Vigarani, replaced it with the world's most elaborate special effects theater, the Salle des Machines. In a 1662 opera production Vigarani placed Louis and the entire royal family on a 60-foot-by-45-foot (18.3-meter-by-13.7-meter) elevator and "flew" them past the clouds hung above the stage and into heaven. Vigarani died three years later and his son, Carlo, followed the king to his new palace in Versailles where ever more elaborate ballets and operas were staged.

Although quite different, the popular and court theater were finally joined through the talents of Molière, France's greatest writer and the leading actor-manager of his time. Born Jean-Baptiste Poquelin, Molière was the son of a prosperous merchant with the appointment of furniture maker to the king. Molière, however, left his father's profession to form a small acting company, which had gained quite a reputation by 1660 when it was allowed to use the Thêâtre du Palais Royal recently remodeled by Torelli. Molière, as the leading actor and writer for the company, so impressed Louis XIV that he gave them the title of the King's Troupe. Other major actors in the company were Molière's wife Armade Béjart; Michel Baron, the great tragedian; and LaGrange, who also kept the company records, and indeed his *Registre* is an excellent source of information about the finances, performances, and organization of the company.

The stars of the rival company at the Hôtel de Bourgogne were the tragic actor Montfleury and Mlle Champmeslé, considered the great tragic actress of the age. Tiberio Fiorello, who headed the *commedia delle'arte* troupe in Paris that often appeared at court, was Molière's chief comic rival. When Molière died, all French acting companies in Paris were joined by order of the king into a single troupe to be called the Comédie-Française, or the French National Theatre, which continues today. The *comedia dell'arte* and the *opéra comique* remained as separate companies until, for a reason still unknown, the Italians were expelled from France. The *opéra comique* remained.

Unlike that of the *opéra comique*, scenery in public theaters was simple and formalized. The typical scene for tragedies was a generalized background that might serve as a street, a vestibule, a square, or a palace. The scene for comedies was "the room with four doors," which differed little from the palace scene except it depicted general domestic architecture, usually an interior. Lighting was provided by chandeliers holding candles that hung over the stage and throughout the auditorium. In some theaters footlights, candles backed with reflectors, were used across the front of the playing area. Actors did not perform within the scenery, but on the forestage in front of the proscenium arch.

Acting techniques varied from comedy to tragedy. In the latter, actors apparently stood in a fixed formation, stepping forward in turn to deliver the long and elevated speeches typical of the genre. Comic acting may have been more casual in approach and probably borrowed many of the techniques of the popular *commedia dell'arte*. In both comedy and tragedy actors had to be particularly agile vocally because rhymed couplets and other atypical speech patterns were common. In the comedy ballets, the progenitor of the modern musical, singing and dancing were required. While some attempt was made to suggest historical clothing—in particular a "Roman habit" with a helmet with plums and a Roman skirt, and a Turban for Arab characters—costumes were usually the clothing of the times, except for the traditional stylized costumes worn by the *commedia dell'arte*. Men wore swords and carried walking sticks or long staffs. Fol-lowing the tradition set by Louis XIV, male pants ended at the knee and the well-turned male leg was further emphasized by high heeled shoes. Women frequently carried fans. Elaborate hats, as well as full shoulder length wigs usually completed male attire.

RESTORATION THEATER

Throughout the rule of the Puritan Commonwealth, which began in 1642, theatrical production was suppressed in England, and major theaters were torn down. When Charles II was returned from his exile in France and the monarchy restored in 1660, the king brought with him a taste for theater in the French style. He granted theatrical licenses to two producers, Sir William Davenant and Thomas Killigrew, both of whom built small indoor proscenium theaters that catered to the wealthy and exclusive society of London.

Because both Killigrew and Davenport had connections with Inigo Jones, the production practices resembled those of the court masque, especially in the use of the "wing and backdrop" procedure. In this scenic style, actors performed mainly on the forestage, and behind the proscenium arch was a movable set hidden by a curtain that rose at the start of the play to reveal a flat painted scene across the stage. This scene was actually two "trolley flats," set in grooves and joined at mid-stage. When a scene change was required, the flats either parted and slid to the sides or another pair of painted flats slid in front of them, creating a new scene.

On either side of the stage from the back wall to the proscenium arch were also wings or a series of painted flats that continued the general perspective view. These wings were either rotated or slid back and replaced by other wings when the scene changed. The whole change, as was done on the continent as well, was accomplished in full view of the audience. The actors themselves were always in front of, never inside, of the scenery, and they would enter or exit through two doors, known as proscenium doors, that were built into the proscenium arch. The scenery was grand and formalized: Whole battle scenes might be painted in still life on the backdrop for heroic tragedies and operas, but scenery was relatively simple for comedy, showing an interior or perhaps a rustic locale. The stage and the auditorium were lighted by chandeliers holding candles and by footlights.

The entire theater house was a small structure. The outside dimensions of the first Drury Lane Theatre, opened in 1674, were 112 feet (34.1 meters) by 58 feet (17.7 meters). This theater held only about seven hundred people and was intended for an elite audience. The highest ranks, including the king himself, sat in boxes that overlooked the forestage. Beneath these boxes was a row of benches that was often sold to the young dandies. In front of the forestage and occupying the length of the theater was the pit, in which the audience was seated on benches. On either side of the theater were galleries in which audience was seated. There might be two or three galleries. Unlike continental theaters, all English audiences were seated, for all came from the upper classes.

Despite their social status, the audience was not necessarily well behaved. In addition to eating, drinking, and conversation, there was considerable flirting between the men and women of the audience. Often there were also assignations, for numbers of prostitutes plied their trade in the theater, and sometimes the more daring ladies also wore vizards (masks). Adding to the general hubbub were the orange wenches who worked the theater aisles flirting with the audience and selling oranges that might be eaten or thrown at the actors if the play displeased the spectators. Nell Gwyn, the actress and infamous mistress of King Charles, began her theatrical career as an orange girl in Drury Lane Theatre.

People went to the theater to see and be seen, and each visit was a grand party. Adding to the party atmosphere was the presentation of dancing and singing between every act no matter whether the play were tragic or comic. There was also considerable interaction during performance between actors and audience, with smirks and barbs being tossed across the footlights in both directions. Gwyn made her first overtures to King Charles as she performed, and he leaned across to communicate to her from his royal box. Indeed one of the exciting features of Restoration theater in England is that women were seen on stage for the first time.

Although the new English audience would tolerate heroic tragedies in the French tradition, they much preferred to celebrate throwing off the Puritan yoke with comedy, especially the licentious plays that came to be known as Restoration comedy, which featured beautiful actresses playing lively and sophisticated young ladies who were possessed of a sparkling wit and given to naughty singing and dancing. These actresses were matched on stage by equally witty and attractive men. Both sexes were costumed and made up in the most outlandish fashions of the day. Men wore the outfits made popular in France. Actresses favored extremely low-cut dresses with long, full skirts and wore high peaked wigs on their heads. Men carried handkerchiefs that were flitted about to emphasize their speeches or to wipe the snuff from their noses and beards. Women carried fans that they used judiciously to conceal what was revealed by the low-cut gowns.

A favorite costume of the audience was that of the so-called breeches role. Following the tradition begun in the Elizabethan theater for other reasons, the plots of many Restoration comedies called for a woman to be disguised as a man and dress in breeches. The knee-length breeches displayed women's legs, a part of the female anatomy never revealed in public. There was usually a scene near the end where the ruse was uncovered by someone tearing open the vest of the disguised woman and revealing her bosom. As might be surmised from the participatory activity of the audience, the Restoration theater was not conducive to a strongly unified play or a distinct separation between artist and spectator.

Acting techniques were conventionalized. Thomas Betterton, the great actor-manager, is attributed with a manual for actors that includes such instruction as requiring tragic actors to point to their heads to indicate reason and to their hearts to indicate passion. He insisted that love be presented in a gay, soft, charming voice and that disappointment be in a sad, dull, and languishing tone. This advice might still be valid today. It is important not to judge any gesture or vocal quality as false or artificial because what seems natural to one time and age may seem false and artificial to another. Betterton was considered the greatest actor of his day, playing roles from Hamlet to Falstaff, as well as roles in contemporary plays. His fame was matched by his wife, Mary Saunderson, who appeared in roles from operatic heroines to Lady Macbeth and from Ophelia to light comedy. The title of Queen of Tragedy was reserved for Elizabeth Barry, Betterton's leading lady at the Drury Lane Theatre.

In Restoration England, the tradition of the stock company inherited from the days of Elizabeth was further developed and was fixed in the form that would hold true for Western theater until the early twentieth century. In the stock company tradition, a fixed group of actors, which changes only when a shareholder leaves the company and stock roles—the young lover, the grouchy father, the scheming villain, the grand dame, the clown—are virtually owned by one of the company members. A stock of plays is acquired and placed in the repertory, and the company must be ready, with little rehearsal, to perform any of the repertory plays. To make up for the brief rehearsal times, a standard set of movements or blocking was used by each company and such practices as "keeping an arm's length in all directions away from the leading lady or man" were strictly maintained. Because under-rehearsed productions put a burden on the performer's memory, a prompter was usually present backstage or in a box in the front of the pit or in a trap cut in the forestage.

EIGHTEENTH CENTURY BRITISH AND CONTINENTAL THEATER

The Restoration's sharp swing away from Puritan sexual manners and mores prompted a counter swing in the early eighteenth century known as sentimentalism. This new sentimentalism was greatly encouraged by the rise in the wealth and influence of the middle class, who wanted to see their own values reflected in theater. Sentimental comedy, dealing mainly with the middle class and stressing the triumph of love and virtue over adversity, began with Colley Cibber's *Love's Last Shift: Or, The Fool in Fashion* (pr. 1696) and was firmly established with Richard Steele's *The Conscious Lovers* (pr. 1722).

To accommodate the new middle class flocking to see an accurate portrayal of themselves, the London

theaters were gradually enlarged and by 1790 Drury Lane was rebuilt to hold thirty-six hundred spectators. Italian scenic practices were now common throughout Europe, and stages at theaters such as Drury Lane and the Haymarket were equipped with all sorts of moveable scenery and even devices for flying scenery. Improvements in lighting, which included use of lamps with powerful reflectors above the proscenium arch and in the wings, as well as a better design for footlights, made it possible throughout Europe to reduce the forestage and place the actors within the scenic environment behind the proscenium arch. Lighting reforms by David Garrick at the Drury Lane were said to be brighter than even those at the Comédie-Française.

To meet the demands of sentimental comedy and the new middle-class audience, a new generation of actors rejected the grand cadences of speech associated with heroic tragedy for what was considered a more natural style. This trend in acting reflected practices being taken up throughout Europe. In 1657 a very popular work by Michel Le Faucheur titled *Traité de l'action de l'orateur* (1657; *An Essay upon the Action of an Orator, as His Pronunciation and Gesture Useful Both for Divines and Lawyers, and Necessary for All Young Gentlemen, that Study How to Speak Well in Publick*, 1680) was issued by the French Academy. This publication was complemented by René Descartes's *Les Passions de l'âme* (1649; *The Passions of the Soul*, 1950), in which the philosopher argues that each of the six chief passions expresses itself by external signs. A debate followed arguing for the perfect outward sign for each emotion, which did point out that the actor who really feels the emotion will find the proper facial expression.

The English counterpart of these French theorists was John Bulwer who published in two volumes of studies of movement and emotions: *The Chirologia* (1644) and *The Chironomia* (1644). Although Bulwer and his fellow theorists felt that there was only one appropriate gesture for each emotional situation, their work furthered the study of the use of speech and movement by the actor to express and communicate the natural emotional range of normal humans.

In his *The Life of Mr. Thomas Betterton* (1710), Charles Gildon cites a conversation with Betterton in which the great actor insists that nature must be studied as the first guide for an actor, who would then adapt nature to the most beautiful and effective uses of gesture and speech. Newly emerging star actors such as Charles Macklin embraced the concept of bringing nature to the stage and even introduced what he considered more natural costuming, such as playing Macbeth in kilts instead of the traditional red uniform of a British army officer. Thus began an interest in historical accuracy that would be extended by practices in Continental theater as well. To meet the new taste for sentimentalism, Macklin broke with tradition and played Shylock as a sympathetic character. However, Macklin's reforms were to be realized completely in the triumph of David Garrick who, on his debut in the 1740's, brought to the stage an entirely new, vivid, energetic, and "real" style of acting. Within a decade, Garrick had taken control as actor-manager of Drury Lane, the company, which included Macklin, the tragic actress Hannah Pritchard, and great comic actress Peg Woffington.

In France, the rise of the bourgeoisie also provoked changes in the theater. *Comédies larmoyantes*, or crying comedies, the French version of sentimental comedy, became the norm, and a new group of performers emerged to present the new drama. Most of these new talents were at the Comédie-Française, and not surprisingly, because crying comedy stressed love and marriage, many were women. These included Adrienne Lecouvreur (called the "mistress of tears") Mlle Champmeslé, Mlle Dumesnil, and the greatest of her day, the woman known simply as Clairon. As the century drew to a close a new star arose, Madame Vestris. The male counterparts to these actresses were Michel Baron, Henri-Louis Cain ("Lekain"), the comic actor Preville, and the leader of the *commedia dell'arte*, Luigi Riccoboni.

With the publication of the philosopher Denis Diderot's book, *Paradoxe sur le comédien* (1773; *The Paradox of Acting*, 1883), it became more and more the custom throughout the eighteenth century for acting to be considered a fine art and for plays to be strictly rehearsed under the direction of a single actor-manager. Nowhere was this practice more adhered to than in Germany, where the dramatist and intellectual leader, Johann Christoph Gottsched, joined in 1727 with the actors Johann and Carolina Nueber to establish a company in Leipzig and later in Hamburg that would change the direction of German theater and ultimately give birth to such institutions as the Hamburg National Theatre and to the great dramatists of the Sturm und Drang movement, including Johann Wolfgang von Goethe and Friedrich Schiller. Opened in 1767, the Hamburg National Theatre hired Gotthold Ephraim Lessing as its literary advisor, and he produced his famous work on theatrical theory, *Hamburgische Dramaturgie* (1767-1769; *Hamburg Dramaturgy*, 1889).

The theater at Hamburg was also to give work to Germany's most important actor, F. L. Schröder, who is remembered for creating the "Hamburg school" of acting and production that placed great emphasis on creating emotional depth in character. Another German school of acting and production was created at the Weimar Court Theater by the two writer-directors Goethe and Schiller. Dedicated to recapturing the true spirit of ancient classicism, the two all but originated the modern Romantic movement in which an idealization of history is presented in a vivid but carefully controlled and graceful image. This image would include attempts to achieve historical accuracy, as least as well as the scholarship of the day could provide historical information. With Goethe as producer-director, many revivals of Shakespeare as well as new works by Schiller, such as *Wilhelm Tell* (pr. 1804; *William Tell*, 1841), made Weimar famous throughout Germany. To train his actors, Goethe wrote a set of one hundred rules, including fixed strictures for gesture and for standing on and moving about the proscenium stage. These rules include a prohibition against spitting on stage and an instruction that one should not reach between one's legs to pull up a chair on which to sit.

To accommodate the new middle-class audience, which made up in higher attendance numbers the income provided by the elite of the previous century, eighteenth century theaters grew larger and larger. Although this audience was much quieter than in the past, it could be provoked into riotous behavior, especially when conditions were overcrowded, because in order to gain as much income as possible from a popular production, managers would frequently squeeze in attendees until no space of any type remained. When this practice failed to secure sufficient income, prices would be raised. "Old price" riots would follow, as would other types of riots when an announced production was changed or even when an expected actor did not appear that day. Admission was high in relation to costs of the day, and an audience expected to be entertained for up to five hours on a single admission. In addition to a play, they expected to see a short opening farce, to enjoy dances and pantomimes between acts (sometimes the pantomime was a full evening production), and an afterpiece that included song and dance.

Another innovation used to control and direct audience attention and reaction was the paid claque. Introduced in France to support new plays, the claque, or group of audience members paid to laugh "in the right places" and to applaud at appropriate times, was soon a feature of Western theater. Spending so much time in a packed theater and being forced into a response by the claque could cause irritable tempers. The alternative was to build larger and larger theaters such as the Teatro Argentina, which opened in Rome in 1732 and contained an enormous pit as well as five stories of galleries that accommodated thousands of people. The Argentina was principally an opera house, but auditoria of all types began to grow ever larger throughout the century.

To enliven the huge stages of these grand structures, Western eighteenth century theater produced not only a century of great actors but also a large cadre of superb scenic artists. Chief among these were the Bibliena family of Italy whose designs transformed theaters throughout Europe, especially in Paris and Vienna. Bringing the curvilinear style of European baroque to a new height, the Biblienas also introduced the strongly perspective *scena d'angolo*, or single-point perspective, to the large stage. In this technique, a single vanishing point is established upstage center, and all scenery is built or painted to vanish in perspective toward that point, forcing an illu-sion of great depth on the visual image offered to the spectator.

The French scene designer Philip James de Loutherbourg worked in both France and England, placing an even greater emphasis on historical accuracy, as well as bringing to the production design a strong sense of unity and belonging. Lighting reforms were also instituted by Loutherbourg and others and included poles placed behind the walls of the proscenium arch and hung with rising tiers of lamps, as well as better designed footlights and the use of colored silk gauze in front of lamps to enhance moods on stage.

THEATER OF THE NINETEENTH CENTURY

Weimar Romanticism, with its emphasis on the historical and the magical, engulfed all of nineteenth century theater. The sense of the Romantic was greatly enhanced by the invention of gaslight that replaced candles as general illumination in 1823 in London's Covent Garden Theatre. Around 1817 limelight, used to create the spotlight effect, was also introduced. Gas footlights, with increased luminosity, could be sunk below the stage level and no longer glared in the spectators' eyes. Gaslight allowed the auditorium to be dimmed and thus meant that the stage image appeared all the more intense and magical. Special effects, such as a moonlit garden, could be achieved by placing blue silk filters in front of the backstage and overhead gas lamps and dimming them appropriately.

This technical invention allowed the new generation of actor-managers, such as Henry Irving, to make Shakespearean revivals all the more lush and romantic. An even more spectacular lighting invention, electric lights, were used in Paris Opera around 1847. The scenic image would be forever changed, and lighting would become the principal element of nineteenth century visual theater.

Acting did not suffer from the Romantic revolution. Indeed the emphasis on the power of personal and greatly felt emotion produced a new crop of stage personalities whose names continue to reverberate two centuries later. In Germany, one man rose to shine above the thousands of professional performers. Ludwig Devrient played some five hundred different characters, including many of Shakespeare's great figures such as King Lear. France, where Victor Hugo won the theater for Romanticism in 1830 with his play *Hernani* (pr. 1830; English translation, 1830), produced several actors of great fame including Francois Joseph Talma, Frédérick Lemaître, Mlle Mars, and the incomparable Rachel, who became famous in England as well. In England the Kemble family of actors, managers, and producers gave the public the fine "classical" actress Sarah Kemble Siddons, but her steely and reserved style was ultimately swept aside by the new Romantic sensation, Edmund Kean, who astonished and delighted the audience with his powerful presentations of villains such as Richard III and Shylock.

Kean was eclipsed in fame and stature only by the American actor Edwin Booth, whose revivals of Shakespeare, especially in the role of Hamlet, were sensational successes on both sides of the Atlantic. In the United States, Booth had been preceded by Edwin Forrest who excelled in the so-called American or "physical" school of acting. Another American theatrical invention, the minstrel show, grew out of African American slaves entertaining their masters in a vaudevillian presentation. The form was taken over by white performers with blackened faces, the most famous of which was Thomas D. Rice, who created a character and a dance named Jim Crow. One African American actor did, however, rise from humble beginnings to become famous: Ira Aldridge. Unable to practice his art in the United States, in 1825 he migrated to England where he became renowned as the "African Roscius." Aldridge toured throughout Europe in such roles as Othello, and he was decorated by the rulers of both Prussia and Russia. A third American actor should be noted, the fine comic Joseph Jefferson, who was famous for his portrayal of Rip Van Winkle. Finally, the British born Lydia Thompson brought her show, the "British Blondes," to New York in 1868. Although an actress and comic of considerable ability, Thompson and her "blonds" went on to create an entertainment that is now modern burlesque.

As the century progressed, more and more plays about the daily lives of ordinary people became the standard fare. These so-called melodramas built their conflict around the danger to virtuous and hardworking people posed by unscrupulous villains. Actors were asked to play ordinary people, but in theaters holding thousands of spectators. Therefore, gestures, speeches, and emotions were obviously and necessarily exaggerated to "get up to the top balcony." Although some acting techniques might seem odd to a modern audience, at the time certain techniques were part and parcel of melodramatic performance. For example, in a time when highly starched and stiff collars, together with tight vests, were commonly worn, it was unlikely that an actor, or any man on the street, would hang his head in despair and rub his forehead, rather it was more probable that an actor would throw his head back and rub his fist across his forehead. Likewise, in very large, modern theaters, actors wear hidden microphones so that they do not seem to be projecting so loudly; in the huge playhouses of the nineteenth century, performers needed to shout and disclaim to be heard.

The gains in technology that allowed for the expansion of lighting design also prompted ever more intricate stage machinery. Special effects such as fires or horse races on stage (accomplished by having the animals run on a revolving floor track) became more common. Scene changes could create realistic detail and were accomplished with revolving stages or multiple trapdoors, or even by using counterweights to "fly" scenic pieces into the scene house above the stage while other pieces were lowered. All of this could be done before the eyes of the audience, but a special kind of magic was produced by blacking out all the lights, lowering the curtain, and then raising the curtain on a newly changed and lighted visual field. With so much technology available, the replication of historical accuracy or the sense that "you are there" became an obsessive goal of theatrical producers. By the end of the nineteenth century, most plays and even some operas were done in a realistic manner so that gardens would have real, not painted, shrubbery. In 1832, the French actress Madame Vestris set a precedent by staging an interior with three continuous walls, the first box set, which established a precedent that was taken up throughout Western theater.

Realism was established as the major theatrical goal in the latter part of the nineteenth century by the German director, George II, duke of Saxe-Meiningen. Controlling every aspect of the production from the casting of the actors to the overseeing of the settings and costumes, Saxe-Meiningen created a sense of unity of production in his theater that became the ideal of all Europe. He was especially famous for his staging of large crowd scenes in which he as a director-choreographer clearly excelled. In 1887, an aspiring young French director, André Antoine, opened his Théâtre Libre in Paris. He had seen the Meiningen Players and wanted to incorporate the theatrical techniques into the plays of the new naturalistic writers: Henrik Ibsen, Émile Zola, and August Strindberg. Antoine created a setting that was a complete room with four walls and filled with real furniture and other ordinary objects: wine glasses, pen and paper, and books. He then removed one of the walls, and it was through this virtual fourth wall that the audience observed the actors. All contact between the audience and the actors was cut off, and Antoine even insisted that his actors turn their backs to the audience when it was natural to do so because of the configuration of the room. This was an entirely new custom in the theater. The ideal of modern fourth wall realism established by Antoine was to present all the world from an objective or external viewpoint in which the actors replicated the speech, gestures, dress, movements, and manners of everyday life.

Antoine's Théâtre Libre was a small, experimental space, but his techniques were soon imitated. In 1891, J. T. Grein founded the Independent Theatre in London to do the plays of George Bernard Shaw, and in 1889, Otto Brahm created Berlin's Freie Bühne (Free Theater). The next year Konstantin Stanislavsky, an actor and director, joined with Vladimir Nemirovich-Danchenko to form the Moscow Art Theatre, the most famous of all nineteenth century realist enterprises. A year earlier, Stanislavsky had also seen the Meiningen Players, and he set out to create a theater of realistic ensemble and unity. To achieve his goal, Stanislavsky turned to the work of the Russian playwright Anton Chekhov. This is not to say that Chekhov was completely delighted with Stanislav-

sky's approach. He continually complained about the director's insisting on too much realism in such sound effects as the croaking of frogs or the ticking of clocks.

Along with directorial concepts, Stanislavsky wrote several influential books on the art of acting. Most theater enthusiasts are familiar at least in part with Stanislavsky's theory of the "magic if," which argues that in order to portray a character honestly and realistically, actors must constantly ask if these are the facts of character and situation, what behavior might follow? In essence, actors are searching constantly for motivation or the hidden cause of characters' external actions. This is the "subtext" on which the external text is built. In rehearsal with an ensemble, the subtext for the entire assemblage of characters is sought out as a joint effort. The subtext is discovered more easily and made more vivid, argues Stanislavsky, if the actor searches out circumstances and attitudes in his or her own inner life that resemble those of the character. These "emotion recalls" can be found by improvising with other actors in rehearsal. The so-called Stanislavsky "method" was introduced into European and American acting schools, often without reference or knowledge of Stanislavsky's extensive work on pure vocal and physical techniques unrelated to character study as laid out in his book *An Actor Prepares* (1936).

With the Théâtre Libre, the Independent Theatre, and the Moscow Art Theatre leading the way, fourth wall realism flourished as the century turned and may be arguably called the dominant contemporary style, especially in more popular forms such as cinema and television drama. However, realism had hardly taken root in the theater when counter-realistic trends presented a challenge. In 1896 French director Aurélien-François Lugné-Poë produced Alfred Jarry's deliberately antirealistic work, *Ubu roi.* Concurrently prominent theater artists and theorists were calling for a return to the elemental and ritualistic adventure that lies at the basis of theater.

Adolphe Appia, the Swiss director, took up Richard Wagner's notion of total theater in which music, setting, costume, and performer all cohere to create a total art work. Appia argued that Wagner's use of realistic and representational settings did not cohere with the composer's idealistic music. To prove his point, in the 1890's, Appia published two books of stage designs he had created for Wagnerian operas. These designs made use of what Appia called "painting with light," and he showed examples of scenery composed only of various platforms and steps that could be changed constantly by the play of electrical lighting to reflect the rhythms of the Wagnerian music. Wagner never used the designs but theater artists throughout Europe and the United States were inspired by Appia to forego flat-painted, perspective scenery in favor of plastic, three-dimensional sculptured forms.

TWENTIETH CENTURY THEATER FORMS

Although realism is a widespread theatrical production style, it is matched in contemporary theater and other dramatic media by various nonrealistic approaches. In 1905 the English director Edward Gordon Craig published *The Art of the Theatre*, the first of his many essays calling for the establishment of the director as the major artist in a theater free of the restraints of realism. In such a theater, the director-artist would use the actor as an *Übermarionette*, or super puppet, to create visual, vocal, and kinetic rituals in a formalized setting. Vsevolod Meyerhold, a student of Stanislavsky's, was unhappy with the realism of his teacher and seized on the theories of Craig to create a new Moscow theater devoted to stylized movement in a formal scenic setting composed of swings and slides and other gymnastic equipment on which his actors performed. His new approach, "biomechanics," harkened back to the theaters of India, China, and Southeast Asia. Biomechanics became the ideal style for the plays of the Russian Symbolist, Nikolai Evreinov. Parallel developments in Germany, prompted by the plays of Georg Kaiser and Ernst Toller, helped to create the theater of expressionism, the aim of which was not to present external life but to express the inner feelings of the characters.

Expressionism flourished after World War I, particularly under the German directors Leopold Jessner and Max Reinhardt. Jessner created his plays on a set constructed of a series of steps or platforms (*Jessner treppen*) that broke through the plane of the proscenium arch and seemed literally to fling the actors into the laps of the spectators. Reinhardt produced lavish spectacles that featured stylized actions and frequent interruptions of the story by the performers in order to deliver speeches or songs directly to the audience. In a controversial production of Georg Büchner's *Dantons Tod* (pb. 1835; *Danton's Death*, 1927), he placed more than one hundred actors throughout the audience and during the play he had his "plants" leap up and shout support or opposition to the issues being presented. With this approach, he deliberately destroyed the line between spectator and performance.

Intrusions into and mingling with the spectators became standard theater practice in modern theaters with various types of agitprop "living newspaper" productions involving audience and actors occupying the same open space. One form of audience-actor intermingling was the epic theater of the German antirealistic advocates Erwin Piscator and Bertolt Brecht. Both men collaborated on a theatrical production process that was designed to force the audience to reflect constantly on solutions to issues of war and social injustice. Brecht introduced photographic slides and film clips into his plays to emphasize the jarring contrast between live actors and those in various media. He also insisted that his stage remain essentially empty of decoration and that the lighting instruments be always in plain view of the audience. Actors walked the aisles and even appeared on runways above the audience. All of this was to produce what Brecht called the "alienation effect," or the use of frankly theatrical devices to reduce the audience's sympathy or empathy for the characters in the play so that they may think, instead, of the message carried therein.

To achieve the "A-effect," Brecht trained his actors to distance themselves from their roles and to consider the role much like a hat that they took off or put on at whim. In rehearsal, he insisted that they speak of the characters in the third person and in the past tense. In this sense, Brecht represented the opposite pole from the Stanislavsky method, and advocates of the two approaches to acting maintain a lively debate even today. Brecht's productions swirled with activity and excitement and made his Berlin theater a place sought by theater lovers throughout the world. When the Nazi Party came to power, Brecht came to the United States, where—together with his composer Kurt Weill and his leading actress Lotta Lenya—he presented a highly successful production of his musical, *Der Dreigroschenoper* (pr. 1928; libretto; based on John Gay's play *The Beggar's Opera*; *The Threepenny Opera*, 1949).

It should not be surprising that Brecht produced musicals in his epic theater approach, for the opera as a theatrical form has always been antirealistic, and the American and British musical, which evolved from vaudeville in the late nineteenth century, never tends to be realistic. Indeed, the acting demands of the musical theater, with the need to break out in song and dance on cue, are closer in technique to Brecht's ideals than to those of Stanislavsky. Another important presentational theatrical approach was proposed by Antonin Artaud, a poet, writer, actor, and director who in his book, *Le Théâtre et son double* (1938; *The Theatre and Its Double*), argued that Western realist theater was devoted to a very narrow range—the social problems of groups or the known psychological problems of individuals.

The real problems, argued Artaud, are buried deep in the subconscious where they ferment and cause hatred and violence. Audiences must be made to face such problems, and to do so he advocated a Theater of Cruelty, or brutal honesty, where the audience was forced, through the invention of new theatrical rituals, to face the depths of their subconscious existence. Accordingly, the box set of the fourth wall theater was abolished, and open arenas with thrust stages or no particular stages at all were employed to present performances that were characterized by vibrating lights and vocal shrieks as well as cries and wails of emotional agony or joy. In short, the audience's senses should be assaulted, for Artaud was convinced that people conceptualize through their senses.

POSTMODERNISM

Contemporary theater includes both realism and antirealism, sometimes in the same production, as in Tennessee Williams's very realistic *A Streetcar Named Desire* (pr. 1947), in which, as Blanche is raped, the walls of the Kowalski apartment begin to fade and disappear to reveal a wildly contorted street scene outside. This same effect is often practiced in the most faithfully realistic of films, together with such other artificial techniques as close-ups, superimposed images, swish-pans, and jump cuts. Indeed, film with its manipulation of the actor by the director, the cinematographer, and the editor is the full realization of Craig's concept of the "super puppet." The combining of photographic slides and film clips with live performance, introduced by epic theater, is the feature of such directors as Robert Wilson in theater pieces such as *the CIVIL warS* (partial pr. 1983 and 1984), which also includes the use of laser beam lighting. The interweaving of film and live actors is the feature of the famous Prague theater known as the Laterna Magika, which began its experiments in 1958 under the guidance of the scene designer Josef Svoboda and the director Alfred Radok. Indeed, movement between a variety of dramatic mediums is common today.

Playwrights such as Arthur Miller see their stage works performed on film and television, or a film such as *The Full Monty* (1997) might be made into a stage musical. Actors, directors, and other theatrical artists move freely from live theater to the media. This mixing of several available forms and styles, often in fanciful ways, is now labeled postmodernism, a special form of which is performance art. Typified by artists such as Laurie Anderson, a performance art piece might include an artist working alone and presenting a statement through multimedia, music, singing, storytelling, and stand-up comedy. The postmodern audience no longer expects theater to be done in any particular architectural structure or in any particular style. One successful show might be presented in fourth wall realism; the next in a theater, such as the Guthrie Theater in Minneapolis, dominated by a massive thrust stage; a third in an arena space with the audience encircling the stage as in the Arena Theatre in Washington; and the fourth in a bare "black box" space employing live actors mixed with film or computer-generated images.

The postmodern theater of the twenty-first century does not hesitate to look beyond its culture or its time for new production forms, as is clearly demonstrated by the enormously successful contemporary adaptation of Malaysian puppet theater by Julie Taymor in her live epic theater staging of the animated film, *The Lion King* (pr. 1998), in a remodeled nineteenth century proscenium playhouse.

BIBLIOGRAPHY

Ashby, Clifford. *Classical Greek Theatre: New Views on an Old Subject.* Iowa City: University of Iowa Press, 2001. Reviews the issues connected with Greek theater and questions some of the traditional beliefs about staging and production.

Bamber, Gascoigne. *World Theatre.* Boston: Little, Brown, 1968. Still the best single collection of theatrical practices from the earliest times to the mid-twentieth century.

Banham, Martin, ed. *The Cambridge Guide to Theatre.* 2d ed. Cambridge, England: Cambridge University Press, 1995. An extensive reference source on world theater and drama from primitive rituals to contemporary theater.

Brockett, Oscar G., and Franklin J. Hildy. *History of the Theatre.* 9th ed. Boston: Alleyn and Bacon, 2002. The most frequently cited text on the history of theater and drama practices. Covers the entire spectrum of the art in a historical narrative.

Cole, Toby, and Helen Kirch Chinoy. *Actors on Acting.* New York: Crown, 1970. Collects in one source the writings and statements made by actors from the ancient Greek theater to those of the twentieth century.

Duerr, Edwin. *The Length and Depth of Acting.* Boston: Little, Brown, 1963. An extensive history of world actors and their practices from ancient Greece to the mid-twentieth century.

Hartol, Phyllis. *The Theatre: A Concise History.* New York: Thames and Hudson, 1998. An excellent short narrative of the history of theatrical art.

Wickham, Glynne. *A History of the Theatre.* Cambridge, England: Cambridge University Press, 1992. An especially good source on the staging practices of the Medieval, Elizabethan, and Renaissance theaters.

Wilmeth, Don B., and Tice L. Miller, eds. *The Cambridge Guide to American Theatre.* New York: Cambridge University Press, 1996. A comprehensive reference source on all matters related to American theater up to the end of the twentieth century.

Zarhy-Levo, Yael. *The Theatrical Critic as Cultural Agent.* New York: Peter Lang, 2001. Gives insight into the development of the contemporary absurdist theater and into the important function of critics and reviewers in establishing a theatrical tradition.

Elliott A. Denniston;
updated by August W. Staub

ADAPTING NOVELS TO THE STAGE

Plays are an older art form than novels, dating back to the ancient Greeks, but the theater often looks to the younger medium for new material. The most obvious challenge to adapting a novel to the stage arises from the fact that authors intend their novels to be read, whereas playwrights, with the exception of George Bernard Shaw, intend their plays to be seen and heard. A play is a visual and auditory experience, while reading a novel is a literary and imaginative one.

A great advantage of adapting a best-selling novel to the stage is that there is a ready-made audience for it. On the other hand, this fact can be a disadvantage as well, in that the members of that audience may have strong views of what the characters should look like and how they should sound, and (inevitably) what portions of plot and subplots should be retained or eliminated in the process of adapting a narrative originally designated for a different medium. When Andrew Lloyd Webber (music and book), Richard Stilgoe (book and lyrics), and Charles Hart (lyrics) adapted *The Phantom of the Opera* in 1988, both the advantages and disadvantages were even greater, because so many people had seen one or more of the movies previously adapted from Gaston Leroux's novel *Fantôme de l'opéra* (1910; *The Phantom of the Opera*, 1911).

Adapting a novel is no guarantee of success. Henry James attempted to adapt his 1876-1877 novel *The American* to the London stage in 1891. Unfortunately, it flopped, and he never tried again. Some of the most successful artists in theater failed miserably when they adapted novels. In 1928, Richard Rodgers (music) and Lorenz Hart (lyrics) adapted a now unknown novel by Charles Petit called *The Son of the Grand Eunuch*. The reviews of *Chee-Chee*, as it was renamed, were mostly negative, and it was only performed thirty-one times on Broadway before closing. This was the shortest run of any Rodgers or Hart musical, and *Chee-Chee* has never been revived. Evidently, even Rodgers and Hart could not make a play about castration palatable to a theater audience, even

if the subject provided Hart with the opportunity to write witty puns and double entendres into the script. Moss Hart's adaptation of Edgar Mittelholzer's *Shadows Move Among Them* (1951) as *The Climate of Eden* closed after twenty performances on Broadway in 1952, the shortest of that director-playwright's career.

An advantage of adapting a novel is that it may be easier to persuade financiers to back plays and musicals containing controversial material. One example is Edna Ferber's *Show Boat* (1926), adapted into the 1927 musical by Jerome Kern (music) and Oscar Hammerstein II (lyrics and book). In an era of lightweight comedies and melodrama, this musical changed Broadway by utilizing fully developed characters, songs integrated with the story, and a plot that dealt with the subjects of bad marriages, miscegenation, and the exploitation of black workers.

There is no formula for successfully adapting a novel to the stage, and every supposed rule has exceptions. In general, an adapter must simplify the story and reduce the number of characters. However, the theatrical medium also enables a playwright to take advantage of the auditory and visual nature of theater and explore aspects of a story impossible to examine in a novel.

EARLY ADAPTATIONS

Before the twentieth century, adaptations of famous novels in theater were more common because the concept of intellectual property was in its infancy, and adapters did not feel obligated to pay royalties to or get permission from the original authors. For instance, shortly after its publication, several playwrights adapted *The Vampyre* (1819), by John Polidori, to the stage in Great Britain and France because of an erroneous rumor that the famous Romantic George Gordon, Lord Byron, was the true author. James Fenimore Cooper's novels were popular as well. Ten of his first fourteen novels were adapted to the stage all over Europe. However, the single novel most often adapted in the United States was *Uncle*

Tom's Cabin: Or, Life Among the Lowly (1852), by Harriet Beecher Stowe. There are twelve known versions and at least four hundred touring companies that played nothing else. The most famous adaptation was by George Aiken, produced in 1852. It had six acts that were performed over two nights and required extensive scene construction and painting. Polidori, Stowe, and Cooper never received royalties.

PARING THE STORY

The average novel is longer and has more scenes than are practical to perform onstage. With a few exceptions, such as Eugene O'Neill's *The Iceman Cometh* (pr. 1946) and *Strange Interlude* (pr. 1928), modern audiences will not sit still for more than three hours. When Shaw's *Back to Methuselah* premiered in New York in 1922, it took three nights to stage and was a flop. Bram Stoker assembled a group of actors, including the famous actress Ellen Terry as Mina Murray, for a onetime reading of *Dracula* shortly after its publication in 1897. His production consisted of five acts and forty-seven scenes, lasting four hours. However, his purpose was to establish his legal ownership of the dramatic rights to the story, and he never repeated his attempt. In 1979, The Royal Shakespeare Company mounted an eight-and-one-half-hour production of Charles Dickens's *Nicholas Nickelby* that achieved some success as a theater "event" but in general, the limitation of audience attention span seems unlikely to change, arguably because a twenty-first century audience reared on cable television's fast-paced Music Television (MTV) channel may not be willing to sit still for even three hours.

One adaptation method is to strip the novel's plot down to the bare essentials. One of the longest novels ever adapted to the stage is *Les Misérables* (1862) by Victor Hugo: It is more than one thousand pages in the unabridged version. However, because the intricate plot threads sooner or later converge on the central character, Jean Valjean, the original French adapters Alain Boublil and Jean-Marc Natel chose to concentrate on him in their original 1980 adaptation. The lives of Fantine, the Bishop of Digne, Marius, and others before their meeting of Valjean are simply omitted in the musical. So, too, are the chapters de-

voted to the Battle of Waterloo, because Valjean was still in prison at the time, and King Louis-Philippe, because he never has any contact with Valjean.

Another approach is to cut or extract sections of the novel. When Hamilton Deane wrote the first successful adaptation of *Dracula* (pr. 1924) in 1923, he deleted the beginning and ending sections in Transylvania and transferred all the Whitby scenes to London. A 1928 musical adaptation of Alexandre Dumas's *Les Trois Mousquetaires* (1844; *The Three Musketeers*, 1846) produced by Florenz Ziegfeld with lyrics by P. G. Wodehouse used only the first half of that novel.

When Rodgers (music), Hammerstein (lyrics and book), and Joshua Logan (book and director) adapted *South Pacific* in 1949 from James Michener's *Tales of the South Pacific* (1947), they originally were going to use only the chapter "Fo' Dolla'." However, when they decided it would appear too derivative of Giacomo Puccini's *Madama Butterfly* (1904), they made it the secondary romance to the chapter "Our Heroine" and included bits and pieces from the rest of the book.

Herman Wouk extracted one portion of his novel *The Caine Mutiny* (1951) as *The Caine Mutiny Court-Martial* (pr. 1953). It consists of two acts: Act 1 presents the prosecution and act 2 presents the defense with a scene in a hotel banquet room to end the play. Using the courtroom testimony of the actors, Wouk was able to convey the information that readers of *The Caine Mutiny* would have learned before the court-martial section.

Alan Jay Lerner (lyrics and book) combined the two approaches when he adapted T. H. White's *The Once and Future King* (1958) as *Camelot* in 1960, with music by Frederick Loewe. First, he began with Arthur as an adult, which eliminated the first part of the book, "The Sword in the Stone." Then he stripped the rest of story down to the love triangle between Arthur, Guinevere, and Lancelot.

Sometimes it is necessary to tighten a book's plot. In Michener's *Tales of the South Pacific*, which is really a series of interconnected short stories, Joe Cable and Émile de Becque never meet. In *South Pacific*, they are partners on a dangerous mission behind enemy lines, which is taken from another chapter in

Michener's book, about a coast watcher. Nor does Nellie Forbush meet Bloody Mary, her daughter Liat, or Luther Billis in the book, but she comforts Liat over Cable's death and sings "Honey Bun" to Billis in the musical.

CHARACTERS

Most novels have more characters than are practical to show on the stage. Unnecessary characters can be eliminated. Lloyd Webber and Stilgoe eliminated the character of the Persian from *The Phantom of the Opera* because they felt he muddled the story. In his rewrite of the Deane version of *Dracula* for its 1927 New York staging, John L. Balderston completely eliminated Quincy Morris and Arthur Holmwood, two of Lucy Westenra's suitors. Boublil and Natel omitted the sister of the Bishop of Digne, Colette's biological father, Marius's entire family, and many other characters from their adaptation of *Les Misérables*, because they have no interaction with the central character, Jean Valjean.

Sometimes characters can be combined. In *Dracula*, Balderston combined the characters of Lucy Westenra and Mina Murray into a single character, Lucy Steward, for the New York version of the play. When Hammerstein and Logan sent Cable and de Becque on a dangerous mission behind enemy lines in *South Pacific*, they performed the function of the Remittance Man in Michener's novel.

It is common to change minor characters. In *Dracula*, Deane changed the part of Quincy Morris to a woman. Then in his rewrite, Balderston changed John Steward, another of Lucy's suitors, into her father. In *South Pacific*, Logan and Hammerstein promoted Ensign Harbison to commander and made him nicer, but also less important to the story and not at all cowardly. They also made Luther Billis less competent but funnier than he is in the book.

On rare occasions, the adapter can change a major character. One reason to change major characters is to make them less passive. In the 1927 nonmusical version of *Porgy*, based on Dubose Heyward's 1925 novel, Heyward and his wife Dorothy made the title character more action-oriented and less introspective and changed the ending. In the book, Porgy stares off into the distance when he learns that Sportin' Life has taken Bess away. In the play and subsequent opera, Porgy follows them to New York.

Unless the playwright has a purpose, as Samuel Beckett did in *En attendant Godot* (pr. 1953; *Waiting for Godot*, 1954), audiences generally expect a title character to be the central focus. It is difficult to imagine two novels more different than Thomas Heggen's *Mister Roberts* (1946) and *Dracula*, but they are similar in that the title characters stay mostly in the background. When Joshua Logan and Heggen adapted *Mister Roberts*, they rectified that weakness by bringing him to center stage and giving him more dialogue. He was too good in the book to make an appropriate stage character. Logan and Heggen gave him the flaw of reverse snobbery by having him believe that combat officers are superior to those in logistical support like him.

The most spectacularly successful change of a major character was *Dracula*. Except for the early scenes in Transylvania, which Deane cut, Dracula himself seldom appears in the novel. Deane brought him into the center of the action and changed his appearance. In the book, Dracula had hair on the palms of his hands, his breath smelled, and he dressed completely in black. Deane, on the other hand, made Dracula into a cultured member of the nobility and had him wear formal evening clothes and an opera cloak. It was the Deane conception of Dracula that captured the popular imagination rather than Stoker's, especially when combined with the thick Hungarian accent of Bela Lugosi, who played the character on the New York stage in 1927 and in the 1931 movie. In the 1977 revival starring Frank Langella, the romantic aspects of the Dracula character were emphasized. He wants to love women and be loved in return. In Stoker's novel, he regards women as objects and property.

DIALOGUE AND MUSIC

Many novels have little or no dialogue, while, with the exception of a few stage directions, a play is driven by and consists entirely of dialogue. When the Heywards adapted *Porgy*, for instance, they had to add dialogue because most of the novel consists of narrative.

It may be more important for dialogue to be faithful to the spirit of the original rather than to the letter, especially if the novelist's purpose was satire. The dialogue for Herbert Field's *A Connecticut Yankee* (pr. 1927), based on Mark Twain's *A Connecticut Yankee in King Arthur's Court* (1889), combined archaic English with 1920's slang, especially in the song "Thou Swell." King Arthur's lines are based on the utterances of President Calvin Coolidge, and Merlin's speech sounds like a mixture of thirteenth century Sir Thomas Mallory and twentieth century New York journalist Damon Runyon.

Because a play is heard, one way the stage can add value to the original novel is to include music. Even if electronic books become commonplace one day, it is unlikely they will include original music of the quality of a Rodgers or Lloyd Webber production. Furthermore, since musicals generally have a larger budget than nonmusicals, it may also be feasible to include more characters and scenes.

In *South Pacific*, songs reveal the character of the singer and take place logically within the action rather than interrupting it. Nellie Forbush's songs, such as "I'm in Love with a Wonderful Guy," are conversational, straightforward, and bright. Émile de Becque's songs, such as "Some Enchanted Evening," are complicated, passionate, and yet thoughtful. Marine First Lieutenant Joe Cable is a Princeton graduate, his fiancé attends Byrn Mawr College, and there is a job waiting for him after the war at the family's law firm of Cable, Cable, and Cable. However, he falls madly in love with Liat, a seventeen-year-old Tonkinese (Chinese-Vietnamese) girl who would be unacceptable to his family and social circle back home. He expresses his internal conflict in the songs "Younger than Springtime" and "You've Got to Be Carefully Taught." A recurring story line in the book was the absence of female companionship, especially for the enlisted men. This is reflected in the song "There Is Nothin' Like a Dame."

CHOREOGRAPHY AND SPECTACLE

In addition to the importance of dialogue and music, the visual experience is important in a play. If there are scenes that lend themselves to dance, the visual can enrich the experience. When Rodgers and Hammerstein adapted Margaret Landon's novel *Anna and the King of Siam* (1944), based on the diaries of Anna Leonowens, as *The King and I* in 1951, they engaged Jerome Robbins. He staged "Getting to Know You," "Shall We Dance?" and "March of the Siamese Children." The latter had no words, yet the music and body language reveal the relationships between the king and his children. His biggest challenge was the ballet sequence "The Small House of Uncle Thomas." Rodgers suggested he approach it from a comic perspective, and the result was the combination of Asian movements with the melodrama of the Stowe novel *Uncle Tom's Cabin* (1852), on which the ballet sequence is based.

The so-called megamusical enjoyed a boom in the 1970's, 1980's, and 1990's. Sometimes the producers used novels as sources. They were characterized by spectacle, mobile scenery, and computer-generated special effects for light and sound. Special effects are nothing new. When William Young adapted Lew Wallace's 1880 novel *Ben-Hur* in 1899, the production featured a treadmill to simulate the chariot race. In *Les Misérables*, the stage revolved, and the sets included a barricade to simulate the 1832 uprising. *The Phantom of the Opera* required extensive modification of the Majestic Theater in New York. The stage had to have ninety-six trapdoors to move scenery. A chandelier descends from the ceiling and crashes onstage. More than one hundred candles rise from their own little trapdoors in the Phantom's lair.

BIBLIOGRAPHY

Bach, Stephen. *Dazzler: The Life and Times of Moss Hart*. New York: Alfred A. Knopf, 2001. Covers the life of one of the theater's most successful playwright-directors of the mid-twentieth century. Chapter 23 examines Hart's adaptation of *Shadows Move Among Them*; chapter 24, his aborted attempt to adapt Edna Ferber's *Saratoga Trunk*; and chapter 27, the adaptation of *Camelot*, which he directed.

Douglas, Kirk. *The Ragman's Son*. New York: Simon and Schuster, 1988. Chapter 30 describes the author's unsuccessful attempt to bring Ken Kesey's

1962 novel *One Flew over the Cuckoo's Nest* to Broadway in 1963 with himself playing McMurphy, and the early chapters concern Douglas's early career as a New York stage actor.

Hutchinson, James M. *Dubose Heyward: A Charleston Gentleman and the World of "Porgy and Bess."* Jackson: University Press of Mississippi, 2000. Heyward and his wife Dorothy adapted two of his novels to the stage. Chapter 4 describes their first nonmusical adaptation of *Porgy* to the stage, chapter 7 concerns the much more famous George Gershwin opera *Porgy and Bess*, for which Heyward wrote the book and much of the lyrics, and the last chapter includes the less successful adaptation of his second novel, *Mamba's Daughters*.

Logan, Joshua. *Josh: My Up and Down, In and Out Life*. New York: Delacorte Press, 1976. The passages describing the adaptations of *Mister Roberts* and *South Pacific* are very detailed.

Nolan, Frederick. *Lorenz Hart: A Poet on Broadway*. New York: Oxford University Press, 1994. Describes the staging of *A Connecticut Yankee*, the ill-fated *Chee-Chee*, and *Pal Joey*, Hart's masterpiece.

Rodgers, Richard. *Musical Stages: An Autobiography*. New York: Random House, 1975. This book includes several accounts not only of adapting novels to musicals such as *A Connecticut Yankee* and *South Pacific*, but also of adapting novels to nonmusical plays that Rodgers produced.

Skinner, Cornelia Otis. *Life with Lindsay and Crouse*. Boston: Houghton Mifflin, 1976. Although Clarence Day's *Life with Father* (1935) is not a novel, but rather a series of personal reminiscences, the process by which Howard Lindsay and Russel Crouse adapted the book is the same as adapting a novel.

Thomas R. Feller

RESOURCES

BIBLIOGRAPHY

This bibliography lists works of a general nature under four broad subject headings: Criticism, Historical, World Regions, and Technique. For information on more specialized subjects, see the bibliographies at the ends of the articles on individual dramatists and overviews.

CRITICISM

Adler, Stella. *Stella Adler on Ibsen, Strindberg, and Chekhov.* Edited by Barry Paris. New York: Alfred Knopf, 1999. A collection of lectures from the famed acting teacher that examine the preeminent plays of modern theater, their playwrights, and the environments in which they were conceived.

Altshuler, Thelma C., and Richard Paul Janero. *Responses to Drama: An Introduction to Plays and Movies.* Boston: Houghton Mifflin, 1967. Student guide to such topics as "Popcorn and Caviar," "Page, Stage, and Film," and morality in drama.

Balmforth, Ramsden. *The Ethical and Religious Value of the Drama.* New York: Gordon Press, 1925. Opinionated, mostly outdated, but specialized essays on religious and moral themes in the drama.

Banks, Morwenna, and Amanda Swift. *The Joke's on Us: Women in Comedy from the Music Hall to the Present Day.* London: Pandora, 1987. This feminist-oriented survey provides an in-depth study of such topics as women in music halls and cabarets, male and female humor, and women in comedy. Illustrations, often provocative.

Barish, Jonas A. *The Antitheatrical Prejudice.* Berkeley: University of California Press, 1981. From Plato to Yvor Winters, the author examines critics and moralists who oppose certain freedoms of the theater.

Barnet, Sylvan, and William Burto, et al. *Types of Drama: Plays and Contexts.* 8th ed. New York: Longman, 2001. Provides a number of well-known plays from throughout the ages, each accompanied by an introduction, biographical notes of the dramatist, and stage histories. Book also includes an introductory chapter that provides critical tools for the reading and understanding of drama.

Bennett, Susan. *Theater Audiences: A Theory of Production and Reception.* 2d ed. New York: Routledge, 1997. Analyzes the audience as a cultural phenomenon and examines the practices of intercultural theaters and their audiences.

Benson, Carl Frederick, and Taylor Littleton. *The Idea of Tragedy.* Glenview, Ill.: Scott, Foresman, 1966. Benson divides his text into two parts—"Idea," treating critical theory by significant critics, and "Tragedy," covering six representative works—with useful comments by different authors.

Bentley, Eric. *The Playwright as Thinker: A Study of Drama in Modern Times.* New York: Reynal and Hitchcock, 1946. Reprint. San Diego: Harcourt Brace Jovanovich, 1987. Seminal book that includes essays titled "Bernard Shaw," "Varieties of Comic Experience," and "Broadway—and the Alternative."

_____. *The Theatre of Commitment, and Other Essays on Drama in Our Society.* New York: Atheneum, 1967. This book contains such essays as "The American Drama from 1944 to 1954" and "What Is Theatre?"

_____. *Thinking About the Playwright: Comments from Four Decades.* Evanston, Ill.: Northwestern University Press, 1990. A collection of Bentley essays, ranging in topics from the nature of theater, the pros and cons of political theater, theater as a form of group therapy, and much more.

_____. *The Theory of the Modern Stage: An Introduction to Modern Theatre and Drama.* Harmondsworth, Middlesex, England: Penguin Books, 1968. Collection of essays by notable drama commentators; chapters include "Ten Makers of Modern Theatre" and "Toward a Historical Over-View."

_____, ed. *Theory of Modern Stage.* New York: Applause Theater Books, 1997. A series of essays present the ideas of several prominent theater scholars about the art of the stage and the future possibilities of drama. The second part of the book contains excerpts from the writings of such seminal commentators as George Lukacs, Romain Rolland, and Alexis de Tocqueville.

Black, Michael. *Poetic Drama as Mirror of the Will.* London: Vision Press, 1977. Sound scholarly work that is particularly good on William Shakespeare.

Blau, Herbert. *Take Up the Bodies: Theatre at the Vanishing Point.* Champaign: University of Illinois Press, 1982. Primarily "a meditation," according to the author, this complex but original study includes chapters titled "Conspiracy Theory," "The Power Structure," "Missing Persons," and "The Future of an Illusion."

Boulton, Marjorie. *The Anatomy of Drama.* London: Routledge and Kegan Paul, 1960. Popularization of literary criticism, especially useful in its treatment of conventions.

Brockett, Oscar G., ed. *Studies in Theatre and Drama.* The Hague: Mouton, 1972. Scholarly essays written in honor of Hubert C. Heffner; most of the studies are specialized.

Brooks, Cleanth, and Robert B. Heilman. *Understanding Drama.* New York: Holt, Rinehart and Winston, 1945. This clearly written text on the theater was very influential during the late 1940's. It includes such general topics as dialogue and action, and special problems of the drama and how to solve them. Also contains representative scenes from plays.

Brown, John Russell, ed. *Drama and the Theatre, with Radio, Film, and Television: An Outline for the Student.* London: Routledge and Kegan Paul, 1971. Collection of essays, including J. F. Arnott's "Theatre History," Kenneth Muir's "Plays," John Fernald's "Acting," and George Brandt's "Radio, Film, and Television." Augmented by a few illustrations.

Brustein, Robert. *Cultural Calisthenics: Writings on Race, Politics, and Theatre.* Chicago: Ivan R. Dee, 1998. The theater critic for *The New Republic* takes on a number of timely issues related to theater, including segregated casting, political correctness, and the National Endowment· for the Arts.

_____. *Who Needs Theatre: Dramatic Opinions.* New York: Atlantic Monthly Press, 1987. Genial, sometimes controversial opinions on Shakespeare, modernism, apartheid, and other topics.

Burt, Richard. *Shakespeare After Mass-Media.* New York: Palgrave, 2002. Examines the contemporary cultural significance of William Shakespeare, exploring the way his plays have been presented and reinterpreted in modern-day radio, television, popular music, and electronic media.

Calderwood, James L., and Harold E. Toliver, eds. *Perspectives on Drama.* New York: Oxford University Press, 1968. Collection of critical essays ranging from Eric Bentley to Thornton Wilder; strong on aesthetics and dramatic theory.

Cameron, Kenneth M., and Theodore J. C. Hoffman. *The Theatrical Response.* New York: Macmillan, 1969. Brisk, readable account; especially effective are chapters titled "The Critical Analysis of Drama" and "Some Theater Futures."

Carlson, Marvin. *Theories of the Theatre: A Historical and Critical Survey from the Greeks to the Present.* Expanded ed. Ithaca, N.Y.: Cornell University Press, 1994. Massive scholarly work of great range, examines the aesthetic and philosophical movements that have shaped Western theater.

Clurman, Harold. *The Naked Image: Observations on the Modern Theater.* New York: Macmillan, 1966. Collection of reviews and essays by the noted critic.

Cohn, Ruby. *Currents in Contemporary Drama.* Bloomington: Indiana University Press, 1969. Scholarly treatment of English drama, as well as Continental and classical plays.

Cooper, Charles W. *Preface to Drama.* New York: Ronald Press, 1955. Some of the examples from this textbook for undergraduates are outdated, but Cooper's discussion is generally sound.

Davis, Walter A. *Get the Guests: Psychoanalysis, Modern American Drama, and the Audience.* Madison: University of Wisconsin Press, 1994. Provides a detailed reading of five classic twentieth century plays–by Arthur Miller, Edward Albee, Tennessee Williams, and two by Eugene O'Neill— and examines their psychological impact on audiences.

Dawson, S. W. *Drama and the Dramatic.* London: Methuen, 1970. Brief study of dramatic conventions, influenced in part by the method of F. R. Leavis; chapters on "Drama, Theatre, and Reality," "Action and Tension," "Character and Idea." Useful to actors as well as to students of the theater.

De los Reyes, Marie Philomene. *The Biblical Theme in Modern Drama.* Quezon City: University of the Philippines Press, 1978. Specialized study on aspects of the religious treatment in selected plays. Effective chapters on the language of biblical themes and on dramaturgy.

Dickinson, Hugh. *Myth on the Modern Stage.* Urbana: University of Illinois Press, 1969. Chapters on Robinson Jeffers, Eugene O'Neill, T. S. Eliot, and Tennessee Williams.

Ditsky, John. *The Onstage Christ: Studies in the Persistence of a Theme.* Totowa, N.J.: Barnes and Noble Books, 1980. Insightful essays on George Bernard Shaw, John Millington Synge, T. S. Eliot, John Osborne, Tennessee Williams, Harold Pinter, and others.

Dollimore, Jonathan. *Radical Tragedy: Religion, Ideology, and Power in the Drama of Shakespeare and his Contemporaries.* 2d ed. Durham, N.C.: Duke University Press, 1994. Originally published in 1984; still stands as a pioneer work in the criticism and reinterpretation of Renaissance drama.

Dyer, Richard. *Now You See It: Studies on Lesbian and Gay Film.* London: Routledge, 1990. Includes chapters titled "Shades of Genet," "Underground and After," and "Lesbian/Woman: Lesbian Cultural Feminist Film." Photographs and illustrations.

Ellis-Fermor, Una. *The Frontiers of Drama.* 2d ed. London: Methuen, 1964. This brief but valuable study by the noted critic treats such topics as "The Limitations of Drama," "Shakespeare's Political Plays," and "The Universe of *Troilus and Cressida.*"

Esslin, Martin. *The Theatre of the Absurd.* 3d ed. Harmondsworth, Middlesex, England: Penguin Books, 1980. Famous critical study that includes essays on Harold Pinter, Edward Albee, Arthur Kopit; brilliant treatment of Samuel Beckett.

Fergusson, Francis. *The Human Image in Dramatic Literature.* Garden City, N.Y.: Doubleday, 1957. Brief but stimulating series of essays by the noted critic. Includes essays on Bertolt Brecht, Thornton Wilder, and T. S. Eliot, on the American theater between the wars, and on Shakespeare.

Filewood, Alan D. *Collective Encounters: Documentary Theatre in English Canada.* Toronto: University of Toronto Press, 1987. Studies such matters as the evolution of Canada's documentary theater, collective creation, and documentary theater and politics. Bibliography.

Fortier, Mark. *Theory/Theater: An Introduction.* New York: Routledge, 1997. Explores theater from a number of contemporary theoretical perspectives, including postmodernism, feminism, postcolonialism, and materialism.

Freedman, Morris, ed. *Essays in the Modern Drama.* Lexington, Mass.: D. C. Heath, 1964. Collection of essays by notable commentators on a number of playwrights and a variety of themes.

Gassner, John. *Dramatic Soundings: Evaluations and Retractions Culled from Thirty Years of Dramatic Criticism.* New York: Crown, 1966. This memorial volume ranges widely, with particularly good sections on perspectives on American theater and on productions of the 1960's.

_____, ed. *Ideas in the Drama: Selected Papers from the English Institute.* New York: Columbia University Press, 1964. Excellent collection of essays by such authorities as Vivian Mercier, Edwin A. Engel, Victor Brombert, and others. "From Myth to Ideas—and Back" and "Ideas in the Plays of Eugene O'Neill" are some of the essays.

Gassner, John, and Ralph G. Allen. *Theater and Drama in the Making.* Boston: Houghton Mifflin, 1964. Excellent chapters on the medieval theater, the Renaissance theater, and the American theater; essays on theory, criticism, and stagecraft by playwrights and distinguished commentators.

Goldman, Michael. *On Drama: Boundaries of Genre, Borders of Self.* Ann Arbor: University of Michigan Press, 2000. Argues that drama should be viewed as a fluid experience and that genre should not be understood as establishing exclusive parameters but rather as a social practice that can provide a lens for better understanding drama.

Goodlad, J. S. R. *A Sociology of Popular Drama.* Totowa, N.J.: Rowman and Littlefield, 1971. Insightful and clearly written study of drama as ritual, with excellent chapters such as "Roles: Society as Unscripted Drama," "Drama as Mass Communication," and "The Drama of Reassurance."

Granville-Barker, Harley. *The Use of the Drama.* Princeton, N.J.: Princeton University Press, 1945. Brief but stimulating essays by the distinguished playwright and critic on such topics as "The Sort of Play to Study," "The Casting of a Play: Among Actors, Among Students," and "The Cooperative Task."

Grawe, Paul H. *Comedy in Space, Time, and the Imagination.* Chicago: Nelson-Hall, 1983. Genre study with such general chapters as "Theoretical," "Lucrative," "Popular," and "Sombre."

Grene, David. *Reality and the Heroic Pattern: Last Plays of Ibsen, Shakespeare, and Sophocles.* Chicago: University of Chicago Press, 1967. Brief but insightful essays; especially convincing in the studies of Shakespeare's *The Winter's Tale* and *The Tempest.*

Grossvogel, David I. *Four Playwrights and a Postscript: Brecht, Ionesco, Beckett, Genet.* Ithaca, N.Y.: Cornell University Press, 1962. The essay on Samuel Beckett is scholarly and precise; other essays are on Bertolt Brecht, Eugène Ionesco, and Jean Genet.

Guthke, Karl S. *Modern Tragicomedy.* New York: Random House, 1966. Excellent criticism, including material on "The Philosophy of the Tragicomedian."

Hobson, Harold. *Verdict at Midnight: Sixty Years of Dramatic Criticism.* New York: Longmans, Green, 1952. Particularly interesting essays, primarily from a historical rather than critical standpoint, on such playwrights as Henrik Ibsen and George Bernard Shaw.

Hogan, Robert Goode, and Sven Eric Molin. *Drama: The Major Genres: An Introductory Critical Anthology.* New York: Dodd, Mead, 1962. This collection of essays includes particularly useful sections on comedy and tragicomedy.

Hoy, Cyrus. *The Hyacinth Room: An Investigation into the Nature of Comedy, Tragedy, and Tragicomedy.* New York: Alfred A. Knopf, 1964. Directed to specialists in the history and criticism of the theater, this volume is written in a lively style that will appeal also to serious general students.

Huber, Werner, and Martin Middeke, eds. *Biofictions: The Rewriting of Romantic Lives in Contemporary Fiction and Drama.* Columbia, S.C.: Camden House, 1999. Explores how the lives of British Romantics and the myths surrounding them have been reincarnated in modern-day fiction and drama.

Innes, Christopher D. *Holy Theatre: Ritual and the Avant Garde.* New York: Cambridge University Press, 1981. Mostly treats European theater but includes sections on Samuel Beckett and Shakespearean adaptations.

Jonas, Susan, Michael Lipu, and Geoffrey S. Proehl, eds. *Dramaturgy in American Theater: A Source Book.* Fort Worth, Tex.: Harcourt Brace College, 1997. Brings together original essays from experts and noted figures in the field of dramaturgy. Reviews the history of the field, its European antecedents, and modern-day applications.

Jones, Thora Burnley, and Bernard de Bear Nicol. *Neo-Classical Dramatic Criticism, 1560-1770.* Cambridge, England: Cambridge University Press, 1976. Scholarly treatment of Restoration and early eighteenth century drama criticism.

Kernodle, George Riley. *Invitation to the Theatre.* 3d ed. San Diego: Harcourt Brace Jovanovich, 1985. This popular student introduction to theater contains such chapters as "The Performance Place," "Dramatic Action," "Black Liberation," and "Ethnic Theatre and the Realistic Impulse."

Kerr, Walter. *Tragedy and Comedy.* New York: Simon and Schuster, 1967. Clearly written chapters such as "The Tragic Source of Comedy," "The Tragic Ending," and "Comic Despair and Comic Solace."

Keyssar, Helene. *Feminist Theatre: An Introduction to Plays of Contemporary British and American Women.* New York: Grove Press, 1985. This entry in the Grove Press Modern Dramatists series collects the most important scholarly ideas current at the time of its publication, the heyday of feminist theater criticism. Keyssar provides close readings of major works by Megan Terry, Caryl Churchill, Wendy Wasserstein, Beth Henley, Marsha Norman, and other key writers of feminist plays.

Klein, Maxine. *Theatre for the Ninety-eighth Percent.* Boston: South End Press, 1978. Social-action study (often dogmatic but also insightful) of the popular theater, used to advance social and political concerns.

Kott, Jan. *Shakespeare Our Contemporary.* Translated by Boleslaw Taborski. Garden City, N.Y.: Doubleday, 1964. Of interest not only for the light that it casts on Shakespeare but also for its influence on both the production and ways of reading dramatic works.

_____. *The Theater of Essence, and Other Essays.* Evanston, Ill.: Northwestern University Press, 1984. Contains excellent discussions in chapters titled "Shakespeare's Riddle," "Ionesco: Or, A Pregnant Death," "Nō: Or, About Signs," and "The Icon of the Absurd." Introduction by Martin Esslin.

Kuritz, Paul. *The Making of Theatre History.* Englewood Cliffs, N.J.: Prentice-Hall, 1988. Succinct discussion of a wide range of topics, including theater and Buddhism, Confucianism, Zhan Buddhism, and mythology. Illustrations.

Leech, Clifford. *The Dramatist's Experience, with Other Essays in Literary Theory.* New York: Barnes and Noble Books, 1970. Scholarly, lucid treatment of such topics as "The Shaping of Time," "On Seeing a Play," and "The Dramatist's Experience."

Littlewood, Samuel Robinson. *Dramatic Criticism.* London: Sir I. Pitman and Sons, 1939. Once-influential study, with essays such as "To Meet the Puritans," "Criticism as a Profession," and "The Future of Criticism."

McCollom, William G. *Tragedy.* New York: Macmillan, 1957. Study of the general nature of tragedy as well as of tragic drama.

Matthews, Brander. *Playwrights on Playmaking, and Other Studies of the Stage.* 1923. Reprint. Freeport, N.Y.: Books for Libraries Press, 1967. Classic study by the distinguished scholar. Insightful chapters such as those titled "Tragedies with Happy Endings," "Mark Twain and the Theater," and "Memories of Actors."

_____. *Rip Van Winkle Goes to the Play, and Other Essays on Plays and Players.* New York: Charles Scribner's Sons, 1926. Reprint. Port Washington, N.Y.: Kennikat Press, 1967. Once-influential and still stimulating essays such as "The Question of the Soliloquy," "Second-Hand Situations," and "Memories of Actresses."

Michel, Laurence Anthony, and Richard B. Sewall, eds. *Tragedy: Modern Essays in Criticism.* 1963. Reprint. Westport, Conn.: Greenwood Press, 1978. Essays by notable commentators.

Moreno, J. L. *The Theatre of Spontaneity.* 1947. 3d ed. Ambler, Pa.: Beacon House, 1983. Translated by the author from the German, Moreno's specialized study includes such chapters as "Machine-Drama and the Spontaneity Principle" and "Psychocatharsis."

Morley, Sheridan. *Shooting Stars: Plays and Players, 1975-1983.* New York: Quartet Books, 1983. Provides twenty years of drama criticism and reviews.

Nathan, George Jean. *The Critic and the Drama.* New York: Alfred A. Knopf, 1922. Historically interesting views on the post-World War I American theater; essays, among others, on drama as art, the place of the theater, and dramatic criticism in America.

_____. *Materia Critica.* New York: Alfred A. Knopf, 1924. Collection of stimulating essays by the once-influential American drama critic. Contains opinionated chapters on "Certain Familiar Types of Entertainment" and "Certain Actors and Actresses."

Nelson, Robert J. *Play Within a Play: The Dramatist's Conception of His Art.* New Haven, Conn.:

Yale University Press, 1958. Study ranging from Shakespeare to Jean Anouilh, with such chapters as "The Drama: Ritual or Play?"

O'Connor, William Van. *Climates of Tragedy*. Baton Rouge: Louisiana State University Press, 1943. Reprint. New York: Russell and Russell, 1965. Treats the general psychology and aesthetic of tragedy, as well as its dramatic uses.

Pavis, Patrice. *Languages of the Stage: Essays in the Semiology of Theatre*. New York: Performing Arts Journal Publications, 1982. Treatment of such topics as "Gesture and Body Language" and "Examples of Semiotic Analysis."

Peacock, Ronald. *The Art of Drama*. New York: Macmillan, 1957. Reprint. Westport, Conn.: Greenwood Press, 1974. Excellent treatise on aesthetics of drama, with sound chapters titled "Images and Representation," "Imagery and the Interpretation of Experience in Art," and "Art and Experience."

Proehl, Geoffrey S. *Coming Home Again: American Family Drama and the Figure of the Prodigal*. Madison, N.J.: Fairleigh Dickinson University Press, 1997. Explores the representation of the family in American drama, especially the characterization of the prodigal husband or son. Traces the development of this character type from medieval times through the modern era.

Reinelt, Janelle G., and Joseph R. Roach, eds. *Critical Theory and Performance*. Ann Arbor: University of Michigan Press, 1994. Serving as an introduction to the contributions of critical theory to the study of drama, theater, and performance, the essays examine topics such as "Performance Theory, Hmong Shamans, and Cultural Politics," "Performing All Our Lives: AIDS, Performance, Community," and "Focus on the Body: Pain, Praxis, and Pleasure in Feminist Performance," among many others.

Reiss, Timothy J. *Tragedy and Truth: Studies in the Development of a Renaissance and Neoclassical Discourse*. New Haven, Conn.: Yale University Press, 1980. Scholarly work that treats, among other topics, plays by Shakespeare.

Roberts, Patrick. *The Psychology of Tragic Drama*.

Boston: Routledge and Kegan Paul, 1975. Studies of Harold Pinter and Shakespeare, among other writers.

Rosefeldt, Paul. *The Absent Father in Modern Drama*. New York: Peter Lang, 1996. Analyzes works by such noted playwrights as Henrik Ibsen, Anton Chekhov, Arthur Miller, Sam Shepard, Caryl Churchill, and many others to explore the role of the absent father or hidden father figure and the way in which it impacts the social, psychological, and metaphysical structure of modern dramas.

Schechner, Richard. *Public Domain: Essays on the Theatre*. Indianapolis: Bobbs-Merrill, 1969. Contains such provocative essays titled "Pornography and the New Expression," "Happenings," and "The Politics of Ecstasy."

Schleuter, June, ed. *Modern American Drama: The Female Canon*. Madison, N.J.: Fairleigh Dickinson University Press, 1996. Twenty essays examine the contribution of female playwrights to modern drama, looking at such themes as the drama of rebellion and rejection, African American and lesbian playwrights, and the important female predecessors to twentieth century playwrights.

Sedgewick, Garnett Gladwin. *Of Irony: Especially in Drama*. 1935. Reprint. Toronto: University of Toronto Press, 1967. Great series of lectures on irony.

Seltzer, Daniel, ed. *The Modern Theatre: Readings and Documents*. Boston: Little, Brown, 1967. Handbook that comprehensively treats aspects of theory, the actor, and the creative audience. Good selection of critics and playwrights.

Smiley, Sam. *Theatre: The Human Art*. New York: Harper and Row, 1987. Clear and copiously illustrated discussions in such chapters as "Classical and Medieval Drama," "The Rise of National Theatres," "The Modern Theatre," and "Contemporary Innovations."

Smith, Susan V. H. *Masks in Modern Drama*. Berkeley: University of California Press, 1984. Specialized scholarly study of ritual, myth, spectacle, satiric masks, and other topics.

States, Bert O. *Great Reckonings in Little Rooms: On*

the Phenomenology of the Theatre. Berkeley: University of California Press, 1985. Dedicated to Kenneth Burke, this profound study of the "theater phenomenon" treats rhetorical strategies originally articulated by Burke.

Styan, J. L. *The Dark Comedy: The Development of Modern Comic Tragedy.* 1962. 2d ed. London: Cambridge University Press, 1968. Interesting discussion of dark comedy as a fresh manifestation of tragicomedy. Traces the origins of this twentieth century genre to Euripides, the mystery plays, Molière, and Shakespeare.

_____. *The Elements of Drama.* Cambridge, England: Cambridge University Press, 1960. Among other subjects, the critic examines, with theatrical examples, "Dramatic Dialogue Is More Than Conversation," "The Behavior of the Words on the Stage," and "Tempo and Meaning."

Tennyson, G. B. *An Introduction to Drama.* New York: Holt, Rinehart and Winston, 1967. Helpful general essays titled "The Language of Plays," "Character," and "The Reader and the Play," among others.

Thomas, Geoffrey Arden. *The Theatre Alive.* London: C. Johnson, 1948. Outdated but sometimes insightful treatment of such topics as "War," "Fools, Fairies, and Fantasies," and "Thrillers and Killers."

Thompson, Alan Reynolds. *The Anatomy of Drama.* Berkeley: University of California Press, 1942. 2d ed. Freeport, N.Y.: Books for Libraries Press, 1968. Thompson treats such topics as drama as a narrative medium, reality and illusion, and sources of dramatic effect.

_____. *The Dry Mock: A Study of Irony in Drama.* Berkeley: University of California Press, 1948. This volume on irony contains such chapters as "Emotional Discord: The Nature of Irony," "Self-Mockery: Romantic Irony," and "Painful Laughter: Comic Irony."

Tornqvist, Egil. *Transposing Drama: Studies in Representation.* New York: St. Martin's Press, 1990. Questions what kinds of fundamental changes occur when a play text is translated in language or adapted to another medium.

Whitman, Robert. *The Play-Reader's Handbook.* Indianapolis: Bobbs-Merrill, 1966. Clearly defined instruction on "Concepts of Reality in the Great Periods of Drama."

Wickham, Glynne. *Drama in a World of Science, and Three Other Lectures.* Toronto: University of Toronto Press, 1962. Especially useful discussion of the postwar revolution in British drama and university theater; the title lecture ranges widely on intellectual background.

Williams, Raymond. *Modern Tragedy.* Stanford, Calif.: Stanford University Press, 1966. Treats the theme in fiction as well as drama; good material on Eugene O'Neill, Tennessee Williams, T. S. Eliot, and Samuel Beckett.

Wolter, Jurgen C., ed. *Dawning of American Dramatic Criticism, 1746-1915.* Traces the United States' historical search for a national drama, and theater and surveys the development of dramatic criticism in the United States through the use of contemporary writing that reflected the attitudes and values of the period.

Worthen, William B. *Modern Drama and the Rhetoric of Theater.* Berkeley: University of California Press, 1992. By examining noted British and American plays from the 1880's to the 1980's, Worthen explores the interplay between dramatic text and stage production and the way in which it impacts the audience's experience in modern theater.

HISTORICAL

Ackerman, Alan L. *The Portable Theater: American Literature and the Nineteenth Century Stage.* Baltimore, Md.: Johns Hopkins University Press, 2002. Investigates the central importance and representation of the stage in the works of Walt Whitman, Herman Melville, Louisa May Alcott, and Henry James and discusses the subtle genre shift from melodrama to quiet realism during the nineteenth century.

Adams, Joseph Quincy. *Shakespearean Playhouses: A History of English Theatres from the Beginnings to the Restoration.* Boston: Houghton Mifflin, 1917. Reprint. Gloucester, Mass.: P. Smith, 1960.

Classic scholarly work that is still basically reliable.

Agnew, Jean-Christophe. *Worlds Apart: The Market and the Theatre in Anglo-American Thoughts, 1550-1750.* Cambridge, England: Cambridge University Press, 1986. Specialized study of commercial aspects involved in theater production.

Albright, Victor E. *The Shakespearean Stage.* New York: Columbia University Press, 1909. Reprint. New York: AMS Press, 1965. Once-influential account of the theater. Although dated, it is still generally sound.

Bentley, Eric. *What Is Theater?* New York: Atheneum, 1968. Compilation of dramatic reviews, from 1944 to 1967, together with "The Dramatic Event"—important documents in the history of the modern theater.

Bentley, Gerald Eades. *The Jacobean and Caroline Stage.* Oxford, England: Clarendon Press, 1941-1968. 7 vols. Multivolume work that is still generally reliable.

_____, ed. *The Seventeenth-Century Stage.* Chicago: University of Chicago Press, 1968. Collection of essays such as "Shakespeare's Celibate Stage" by Michael Jamieson, "Elizabethan Actors: Men or Marionettes?" by Marvin Rosenberg, and "The Numbers of Actors in Shakespeare's Early Plays" by William A. Ringler, Jr.

Besset, Jean-Marie, et al. *Gay Plays: An International Anthology.* New York: Ubu Repertory Theater Publications, 1989. The preface, by Catherine Temerson and Francoise Kourilsky, sets the critical background for such works as Besset's *The Function*, Copi's *A Tower Near Paris*, and Hervé Dupuis' *The Return of the Young Hyppolytus*.

Booth, Michael R. *Victorian Spectacular Theatre, 1850-1910.* Boston: Routledge and Kegan Paul, 1981. Treats such topics as spectacle, melodrama, and pantomime.

Bordman, Gerald Martin. *American Musical Theater: A Chronicle.* 3d ed. London: Oxford University Press, 2000. Surveys the range of musical theater and its development, from the early eighteenth century through the 1999-2000 Broadway season. Includes analysis of non-Broadway productions,

trends and themes, and provides several useful indices.

Boughner, Daniel C. *The Braggart in Renaissance Comedy: A Study in Comparative Drama from Aristophanes to Shakespeare.* Minneapolis: University of Minnesota Press, 1954. Specialized scholarly criticism that illuminates certain conventions.

Bradbrook, M. C. *The Rise of the Common Player: A Study of Actor and Society in Shakespeare's England.* London: Chatto and Windus, 1962. Great work of scholarly reconstruction.

Bradby, David, Louis James, and Bernard Sharratt, eds. *Performance and Politics in Popular Drama: Aspects of Popular Entertainment in Theatre, Film, and Television, 1800-1976.* New York: Cambridge University Press, 1980. Especially useful to historians of the drama; valuable essay on spectacle, performance, and audience in nineteenth century theater, as well as essays on many specialized topics, such as water drama, by notable scholars.

Brandt, George W., ed. *Modern Theories of Drama: A Selection of Writings on Drama and Theatre, 1840-1990.* London: Oxford University Press, 1997. Chronicles the development of dramatic theory over the course of 150 years, examining theories that have grown outdated and some that have been resurrected from history.

Brockett, Oscar Gross, and Robert R. Findlay. *Century of Innovation: A History of American and European Theatre and Drama Since the Late Nineteenth Century.* 2d ed. Boston: Allyn and Bacon, 1991. Examines the rise of a number of genres, including realism, expressionism, and Surrealism; drama between the two World Wars, and mid- to late twentieth century dramatic developments.

Burroughs, Catherine. *Women in British Romantic Theatre: Drama, Performance, and Society, 1790-1840.* Cambridge, England: Cambridge University Press, 2000. Eleven essays explore the vast contributions of female playwrights, actors, translators, critics, and managers who worked in British theater during the Romantic era and question why they faded in importance.

Butsch, Richard. *The Making of American Audiences: From Stage to Television, 1750-1990*. New York: Cambridge University Press, 2000. Analyzes the evolution of audiences' theatrical tastes as the dramatic art form simultaneously evolved from melodrama, minstrelsy, and vaudeville, to movies, radio, and television.

Campbell, Lily Bess. *Scenes and Machines on the English Stage During the Renaissance: A Classical Revival*. Cambridge, England: Cambridge University Press, 1923. Classic study that treats English and Italian stage decoration at different times, from the sixteenth century to post-Restoration.

Cerasano, Susan P., and Marion Wynne-Davies. *Reading in Renaissance Women's Drama: Criticism, History, and Performance, 1594-1998*. London: Routledge, 1998. Focuses on contemporary critical reaction to women's drama, examining the way in which the critical history of the Renaissance woman dramatist has developed, the social context from which Renaissance women dramatists arose, and the contributions of individual female dramatists.

Chambers, E. K. *The Elizabethan Stage*. Oxford, England: Clarendon Press, 1923. Famous scholarly work that is still generally reliable.

_____. *The Medieval Stage*. 2 vols. London: Oxford University Press, 1903. Classic, comprehensive history of the drama and staging of the Middle Ages.

Clark, Barrett Harper, and George Freedley, eds. *A History of Modern Drama*. New York: D. Appleton-Century, 1947. Treats the drama of England, Ireland, and the United States, as well as Continental drama.

Conolly, L. W. *The Censorship of English Drama, 1737-1824*. San Marino, Calif.: Huntington Library, 1976. Specialized scholarly work that helps the reader understand problems in the playwright's licensing of plays.

Cook, Ann Jennalie. *The Privileged Playgoers of Shakespeare's London, 1576-1642*. Princeton, N.J.: Princeton University Press, 1981. Specialized study on aspects of the elite class who attended the theater.

Cunningham, Peter, ed. *Extracts from the Accounts of the Revels, in the Reigns of Queen Elizabeth and King James I*. London: The Shakespeare Society, 1842. Reprint. New York: Kraus Reprint, 1966. In spite of its date of publication, this classic text is still useful for its reproductions of the original "Office Books of the Masters and Yeomen."

Dent, Thomas C., Richard Schechner, and Gilbert Moses, eds. *The Free Southern Theater by the Free Southern Theater: A Documentary of the South's Radical Black Theater, with Journals, Letters, Poetry, Essays, and a Play Written by Those Who Built It*. Indianapolis: Bobbs-Merrill, 1969. As the title reflects, this volume examines black theater in the South.

Dobbs, Brian. *Drury Lane: Three Centuries of the Theatre Royal, 1663-1971*. London: Cassell, 1972. Surveys the theater from "Royal Favours" of the seventeenth century to "Shows and Stars 1939-71."

Donohue, Joseph. *Theatre in the Age of Kean*. Oxford, England: Basil Blackwell, 1975. Treats topics from "The Demise of Sheridan's Theatre" to "The Age of Kean and Its Prospects."

Dutton, Richard. *Mastering the Revels: The Regulation and Censorship of English Renaissance Drama*. Iowa City: University of Iowa Press, 1991. Scholarly study that grew out of Dutton's research on Ben Jonson.

Elsom, John. *Erotic Theatre*. New York: Taplinger, 1974. Contains an introduction by John Trevelyan. Covers a wide range of topics, from eroticism to theatrical performances.

_____. *Post-War British Theatre*. Boston: Routledge and Kegan Paul, 1976. "Language and Money," "The Search for Self," and "Breaking Out: The Angry Plays" are some of the chapters in this study.

Evans, Chad. *Frontier Theatre*. Victoria, British Columbia: Sono Nis Press, 1983. Scholarly study of such topics as "Early Amateur Theatricals," "Troupes of the Gold Era," and "The Northwest Reflection." Evans also discusses opera and the circus.

Evans, G. Blakemore, ed. *Elizabethan-Jacobean*

Drama: The Theatre in Its Time. New York: New Amsterdam, 1988. Contains discussions of London theaters, repertories, and the underworld. The sober text is enlivened by thirty black-and-white illustrations, some of them reproduced for the first time.

Flaumenhaft, Mera J. *The Civic Spectacle: Essays on Drama and Community*. Lanham, Md.: Rowman and Littlefield, 1994. In examining the plays of Aeschylus, Euripides, Machiavelli, and Shakespeare, Flaumenhaft argues that by revising well-known myths or histories, each of these playwrights reshaped the moral and political community to which he belonged.

Fuchs, Elinor, ed. *Plays of the Holocaust*. New York: Theatre Communications Group, 1987. This international anthology includes an annotated bibliography of Holocaust plays.

Gale, Maggie B., and Vivien Gardner, eds. *Women, Theatre, and Performance: New Histories, New Historiographies*. Manchester, England: Manchester University Press, 2001. A multinational panel of contributors examine topics surrounding theater, gender, geography, theatrical space, women's playwrighting, and much more.

Galloway, David, ed. *The Elizabethan Theatre, II*. Toronto: Macmillan of Canada, 1970. One of a series of volumes, edited by Galloway and other distinguished scholars, treating specialized papers.

Genest, John. *Some Account of the English Stage, from the Restoration in 1660 to 1830*. 1832. Reprint. New York: B. Franklin, 1965. Classic multivolume that should be read with some understanding of later scholarship.

Gildersleeve, Virginia. *Government Regulation of the Elizabethan Drama*. New York: Columbia University Press, 1908. Reprint. Westport, Conn.: Greenwood Press, 1975. Classic essay that treats censorship and related matters up to the "Puritan Victory."

Gilman, Robert. *The Making of Modern Drama*. New Haven, Conn.: Yale University Press, 1999. Presents a critical exploration of the development of modern drama by examining the works of playwrights such as Ibsen, Luigi Pirandello, and Bertolt Brecht, and Strinberg, among others.

Glasstone, Victor. *Victorian and Edwardian Theatres: An Architectural and Social Survey*. Cambridge, Mass.: Harvard University Press, 1975. Beautifully illustrated work that offers insight concerning the staging and audience reception of plays.

Greenwald, Michael L., Roger Schultz, Roberto D. Pomo. *The Longman Anthology of Drama and Theater: A Global Perspective*. New York: Longman, 2001. Comprehensive critical and historical material of twenty-three historically important plays taken from countries around the world. Additional topics range from folk rituals and ceremonies, the role of the storyteller, and staging conventions. Maps, lush illustrations, biographies, and more.

Gurr, Andrew. *The Shakespearean Stage, 1574-1642*. Cambridge, England: Cambridge University Press, 1970. Specialized work that brings later scholarship to supplement older sources.

Harbage, Alfred. *Shakespeare and the Rival Traditions*. New York: Macmillan, 1952. Reprint. Bloomington: Indiana University Press, 1970. Influential study that treats, among other topics, "The War of the Theatres."

Hartigan, Karelisa V. *Greek Tragedy on the American Stage: Ancient Drama in the Commercial Theater, 1882-1994*. Westport, Conn.: Greenwood, 1995. Explores the critical reception of Greek tragedy throughout several periods in the modern era, examining in particular the debates that have arisen from the staging of "classics" and the way political milieu influences the plays chosen for performance.

Henslowe, Philip. *Henslowe's Diary*. Edited by R. A. Foakes and R. T. Rickert. Cambridge, England: Cambridge University Press, 1961. Chief sourcebook for the theatrical history of the English stage between 1590 and 1604.

Herrick, Marvin T. *Tragicomedy: Its Origin and Development in Italy, France, and England*. 1955. Reprint. Urbana: University of Illinois Press, 1962. Scholarly treatise that covers English tragicomedy from before Francis Beaumont and John Fletcher through Sir William Davenant, along with other topics.

Hillebrand, Harold Newcomb. *The Child Actors: A Chapter in Elizabethan Stage History.* New York: Russell and Russell, 1964. Major scholarly work on the subject, examining various theaters and companies.

Hotson, Leslie. *The Commonwealth and Restoration Stage.* New York: Russell and Russell, 1962. Influential work that treats such topics as "The Playhouses," "The Duke's Company, 1660-1682," and "The King's Company, 1682-1694."

Hudson, Lynton Alfred. *The English Stage, 1850-1950.* London: Harrap, 1951. Brief but useful text, with selected illustrations.

Hughes, Leo. *The Drama's Patrons: A Study of the Eighteenth-Century London Audience.* Austin: University of Texas Press, 1971. Comprises chapters such as "A Varied Response," "Changing Tastes," and "Morality and Sensibility."

Hume, Robert D., ed. *The London Theatre World, 1660-1800.* Carbondale: Southern Illinois University Press, 1980. Collection of scholarly essays by notables.

Hunt, Hugh. *The Abbey: Ireland's National Theatre, 1904-1978.* New York: Columbia University Press, 1979. Survey of subjects such as "The Troubled Years, 1914-1923," "The Years of Exile, 1951-1966," and "The Abbey in the Seventies."

Innes, Christopher D. *Avant Garde Theatre, 1892-1992.* London: Routledge, 1993. Uses critical and intercultural theory, anthropology, and psychotherapy to explore the role of primitivism and ritual in the development of avant garde theater.

Joseph, Stephen. *The Story of the Playhouse in England.* London: Barrie and Rockliff, 1963. Not about plays and playwrights but a "history of the playhouse, the place where actors perform to their audiences." Illustrations.

Kelly, Linda. *The Kemble Era.* New York: Random House, 1980. Treats John Philip Kemble, Sarah Siddons, and the London stage.

Kemble, Fanny. *Journal of a Young Actress.* New York: Columbia University Press, 1990. "Proud, high-spirited, and, withal, not entirely unself-critical," Kemble embarked, with her father, the celebrated actor Charles Kemble, on an American acting tour. Her journal is a delight. Contains a foreword by Elizabeth Fox-Genovese.

King, Thomas James. *Shakespearean Staging, 1599-1942.* Cambridge, Mass.: Harvard University Press, 1971. Authoritative work that supplements and corrects older works on the same general subject.

Kitchin, Laurence. *Drama in the Sixties: Form and Interpretation.* London: Faber, 1966. Includes material on "Compressionism," "Epic," and "Malice Domestic."

Knapp, Bettina L. *Theatre and Alchemy.* Detroit: Wayne State University Press, 1980. Very specialized. A scholarly but fascinating work. Especially intriguing is the chapter titled "Spiritus Mundi/Anima Mundi."

Lancashire, Ian. *Dramatic Texts and Records of Britain: A Chronological Topography to 1558.* Cambridge, England: Cambridge University Press, 1984. This detailed, in-depth study contains a "finding list" that is a topographical guide to British dramatic records. Includes illustrations and many reproductions of rare documents.

Landa, M. J. *The Jew in Drama.* London: P. S. King and Son, 1926. Rev. ed. Port Washington, N.Y.: Kennikat Press, 1968. Scholarly treatment of such topics as "Hebrew Origins of Drama," "The Original of Fagin," and "The Yiddish Theatre."

Lawrence, William John. *The Elizabethan Playhouse and Other Studies.* Philadelphia: J. B. Lippincott, 1912. Once-influential work that is still useful for specialists, although the general reader must be cautious.

_____. *Pre-Restoration Stage Studies.* Cambridge, Mass.: Harvard University Press, 1927. Classic study that is, despite its older material, still generally sound.

Lowe, Robert W. *A Bibliographical Account of English Theatrical Literature: From the Earliest Times to the Present Day.* London: John C. Nimmo, 1888. Reprint. Detroit: Gale Research, 1966. This standard annotated bibliography (with brief commentary) contains some entries that are unique from a historical point of view.

Lumley, Frederick. *New Trends in Twentieth Century Drama: A Survey Since Ibsen and Shaw.* 1956.

Rev. ed. New York: Oxford University Press, 1972. Broad approach to the modern theater, with material on English, Irish, and American dramatists, as well as European writers.

McAfee, Helen. *Pepys on the Restoration Stage.* New Haven, Conn.: Yale University Press, 1916. Reprint. New York: B. Blom, 1964. Classic account of references in Samuel Pepys's diary to the Restoration theater.

McCollum, John I., ed. *The Restoration Stage.* Boston: Houghton Mifflin, 1961. Selections of historically significant critical texts by John Dryden and others.

McConachie, Bruce A., and Thomas Postlewait, eds. *Interpreting the Theatrical Past: Essays in the Historiography of Performance.* Iowa City: University of Iowa Press, 1994. Thirteen essays give historic information on specific people, events, social conditions, documents, and works of theater, in the process uncovering new methodological approaches and theoretical orientations.

MacKaye, Percy. *The Playhouse and the Play, and Other Addresses Concerning the Theatre and Democracy in America.* New York: Macmillan, 1909. Reprint. New York: Johnson Reprint, 1970. The addresses by the author are historically significant for the American theater prior to 1909.

Macqueen-Pope, Walter Jones. *The Curtain Rises: A Story of the Theatre.* Edinburgh, Scotland: Thomas Nelson, 1961. Good historical survey, with illustrations, of the stagecraft of the English theater. Chapters include "Burbage—The Father of the Theatre," "Giants of the Elizabethan Theatre," and "Victorian and Edwardian Pantomime."

Milhous, Judith. *Thomas Betterton and the Management of Lincoln's Inn Fields, 1695-1708.* Carbondale: Southern Illinois University Press, 1979. Excellent specialized material on "The Lincoln's Inn Fields Experiment" and other topics.

Montrose, Louis Adrian. *The Purpose of Playing: Shakespeare and the Cultural Politics of the Elizabethan Theatre.* Chicago: University of Chicago Press, 1996. Examines the social and cultural context in which Elizabethan theater was created, focusing specifically on the ways in which plays of the era reflected sociocultural events and attitudes, while at the same time, questioned the absolutist assertions of the Elizabethan state.

Mullaney, Steven. *The Place of the Stage: License, Play, and Power in Renaissance England.* Chicago: University of Chicago Press, 1988. This brief, cogent study contains such chapters as "Toward a Rhetoric of Space in Elizabethan London," "The Place of the Stage," and "Lying Like Truth: Riddle, Representation, and Treason."

Murphy, Brenda. *Congressional Theatre: Dramatizing McCathyism on Stage, Film, and Television.* Cambridge, England: Cambridge University Press, 1999. Explores the intersection of art and politics, first examining the political, historical, and social contexts of the McCarthy era and then discussing the way in which performers and playwrights responded to the contentious atmosphere.

Murray, John Tucker. *English Dramatic Companies, 1558-1642.* Boston: Houghton Mifflin, 1810. Reprint. New York: Russell and Russell, 1963. Multivolume work that treats "Greater Men's Companies," "Lesser Men's Companies," and "Children's Companies."

Murrie, Eleanore Boswell. *The Garrick Stage: Theatres and Audiences in the Eighteenth Century.* Edited by Sybil Rosenfeld. Athens: University of Georgia Press, 1980. Covered are such topics as the playhouses and old and new costumes.

_____. *Masks, Mimes, and Miracles: Studies in the Popular Theatre.* London: Harrap, 1931. Reprint. New York: Cooper Square, 1963. Classic, still useful work, with such chapters as "The Fate of the Mime in the Dark Ages" and "The *Commedia Dell'Arte*"—scholarly material that indirectly touches later English drama.

_____. *The Restoration Court Stage, 1660-1702, with a Particular Account of the Production of Calisto.* Cambridge, Mass.: Harvard University Press, 1932. Reprint. New York: Barnes and Noble Books, 1966. Based on previously unpublished material from the Accounts of His Majesty's Office of Works and other sources.

Novy, Marianne, ed. *Cross-Cultural Performances: Differences in Women's Re-Visions of Shakepeare.*

Urbana: University of Illinois Press, 1994. Emphasizes the intersections of theater, race, and colonialism in examining how female playwrights, novelists, and actors re-imagine Shakespearean drama.

Orgel, Stephen. *Impersonations: The Performance of Gender in Shakespeare's England*. New York: Cambridge University Press, 1996. In analyzing why England was the only country during the Renaissance not to use women on the stage, Orgel seeks to uncover gender conventions and the intersections of sexuality and power.

Ramírez, Elizabeth C. *Chicanas/Latinas in American Theatre: A History of Performance*. Bloomington: Indiana University Press, 2000. Traces the development and traditions of Latina theater, from its pre-Columbian and Mexican roots, to its role in social protest, to emerging Chicana playwrights and themes.

Ran-Moseley, Faye. *Tragicomic Passion: Clowns, Fools, and Madmen in Drama, Film, and Literature*. New York: Peter Lang, 1994. Explores the roles of tragicomic characters from the ancient Greeks through the twentieth century and argues that the tragicomic characters became more prevalent in the twentieth century than ever before, reflecting the universal and tragicomic encounter of self and society.

Rosenfeld, Sybil M. *Strolling Players and Drama in the Provinces, 1660-1765*. Cambridge, England: Cambridge University Press, 1939. Reprint. New York: Octagon Books, 1970. Classic scholarly study that treats different groups of players and various theaters.

Rowell, George. *Theatre in the Age of Irving*. Totowa, N.J.: Rowman and Littlefield, 1981. Studies "Setting the Scene," "Traditional Airs," and "Accolade."

_____. *The Victorian Theatre, 1792-1914: A Survey*. 2d ed. New York: Cambridge University Press, 1978. Covers "The New Drama," "The Return to Respectability," "The Era of Society Drama," and other subjects.

Schechner, Richard. *Between Theatre and Anthropology*. Philadelphia: University of Pennsylvania Press, 1985. Psychological-anthropological study that includes such essays as "Peter Brook's Company in Africa," "Balinese Dancer Demonstrating Her Walking Technique," and "Shakers Dancing in the Nineteenth Century." Foreword by Victor Turner.

_____. *The Living Book of the Living Theatre*. Greenwich, Conn.: New York Graphic Society, 1971. As much a photographic essay as a discussion on the social and improvisational theater during the late 1960's. Offers historical insight into the political and social concerns of the time, especially of the "street theater" of confrontation.

Seilhamer, George O. *History of the American Theatre*. New York: B. Blom, 1968. Massively documented and persuasive study, but difficult for the general reader.

Seller, Maxine Schwartz, ed. *Ethnic Theater in the United States*. Westport, Conn.: Greenwood Press, 1983. Comprehensive study examining ethnic theater from Armenian American to Yiddish.

Shapiro, Michael. *Children of the Revels: The Boy Companies of Shakespeare's Time and Their Plays*. New York: Columbia University Press, 1977. Scholarly account of "The Companies," "The Occasion," "The Style," and "The Plays." Fully annotated.

Smith, Irwin. *Shakespeare's Blackfriars Playhouse: Its History and Its Design*. New York: New York University Press, 1964. Specialized scholarly work that treats the Blackfriars from the origins in 1275 to 1642.

Southern, Richard. *The Medieval Theatre in the Round*. 2d ed. London: Faber, 1975. Scholarly, comprehensive study that provides an astonishing reconstruction of the age.

_____. *The Staging of Plays Before Shakespeare*. New York: Theater Arts Books, 1973. Monumental scholarly work that treats the earliest surviving interludes (1466-1508) and shows how their staging techniques affected those of later playwrights such as Shakespeare.

Steele, Richard. *The Theatre*. Edited by John Loftis. Oxford, England: Clarendon Press, 1962. Scholarly edition treating the distinguished eighteenth century essayist's views on the theater.

Stephens, John Russell. *The Censorship of English Drama, 1824-1901*. New York: Cambridge University Press, 1980. Specialized scholarly study.

Sturgess, Keith. *Jacobean Private Theatre*. London: Routledge and Kegan Paul, 1987. Scholarly account, with black-and-white illustrations. Devotes chapters to the audience, the Blackfriars, and the court theater.

Summers, Montague. *The Restoration Theatre*. 1934. Reprint. New York: Humanities Press, 1964. Once-influential work that must be read with some scholarly caution. Treats, among other topics, costume, realism on the stage, and the epilogue.

Taubman, Hyman Howard. *The Making of the American Theatre*. New York: McCann, 1965. Ambitious work that includes chapters on "Realism of a Sort," "Disarray in the Sixties," and "New Forces and New Hope."

Thompson, Elbert N. S. *The Controversy Between the Puritans and the Stage*. New York: H. Holt, 1903. Reprint. New York: Russell and Russell, 1966. In two parts: "The Puritan Attack" and "The Dramatists' Reply."

Thorndike, Ashley H. *Shakespeare's Theater*. New York: Macmillan, 1916. Influential study that is still generally sound.

Trewin, J. C. *The Edwardian Theatre*. Totowa, N.J.: Rowman and Littlefield, 1976. Brief but useful study on such topics as "The Drawing-Room," "The Study," and "Closing the Door."

_____. *The English Theatre*. London: P. Elek, 1948. Brief guide to plays and playwrights of the first quarter of the twentieth century. The chapter titled "College Wit-Crackers" includes discussions of Noël Coward, Frederick Lonsdale, A. A. Milne, and others.

Troubridge, St. Vincent. *The Benefit System in the British Theatre*. London: Society for Theatre Research, 1967. Scholarly account of payments and "benefits" to British actors, from the 1680's to the 1880's, with such chapters as "Patronage and Sale of Tickets," "Making Up the Bill," "The Bespeak," and "Stars and Benefits in the Provinces."

Watson, Charles S. *The History of Southern Drama*. Lexington: University Press of Kentucky, 1997. Provides a comprehensive discussion of the development of drama in the American South from its eighteenth century roots onward, examining historical contexts, themes and characteristics, and playwrights.

Wellwarth, George E. *The Theater of Protest and Paradox: Developments in the Avant-Garde Drama*. 1964. Rev. ed. New York: New York University Press, 1971. This fine critical survey treats twentieth century dramatists under "The Experimentalists" and "The Traditionalists"; "New American Drama" discusses Edward Albee and others.

Welsford, Enid. *The Court Masque*. Cambridge, England: Cambridge University Press, 1927. Reprint. New York: Russell and Russell, 1962. Massive work of scholarship that is still reliable.

Wickham, Glynne. *Early English Stages, 1300 to 1660*. New York: Columbia University Press, 1959-1981. 3 vols. Multivolume work of great utility to the student of English dramatic history.

Wilson, John Harold. *A Preface to Restoration Drama*. Boston: Houghton Mifflin, 1965. Concise study on such topics as "The Restoration Theater," "The Poets," "Villain Tragedy," and "Pathetic Tragedy."

Woods, Leigh. *Garrick Claims the Stage: Acting and Social Emblem in Eighteenth-Century England*. Westport, Conn.: Greenwood Press, 1984. More than an account of the remarkable David Garrick's historical contributions to the theater, Woods's book treats such topics as refinement in acting and illusionism on the stage.

Yamazaki, Masakazu. *Mask and Sword: Two Plays for the Contemporary Japanese Theater*. Translated by J. Thomas Rimer. New York: Columbia University Press, 1980. The plays are *Zeami* and *Sanetomo*. Includes an interview with Yamazaki, who discusses modern Japanese drama.

WORLD REGIONS

Albuquerque, Severino J. *Violent Acts: A Study of Contemporary Latin American Theatre*. Detroit, Mich.: Wayne State University Press, 1991. Examines twentieth-century Latin American "Theatre of Revolt" across many countries and cultures, noting the recurring themes of riot, murder, assassination, and state-sponsored torture.

Brandon, James R., and Martin Banham, eds. *The Cambridge Guide to Asian Theatre*. Cambridge, England: Cambridge University Press, 2000. Individual Asian countries and their respective theatrical developments and history are covered, with comprehensive listings of the most important aspects of each country's dramatic genres and styles.

Brockett, Oscar Gross, and Franklin J. Hardy. *History of the Theatre*. 9th ed. Boston: Allyn and Bacon, 2002. Examines the origins and social variations of the theater in several world regions, mixing historic accounts with interpretation.

Conteh-Morgan, John. *Theater and Drama in Francophone Africa: A Critical Introduction*. Cambridge, England: Cambridge University Press, 1994. In-depth analytical study of French-language drama and its evolution. Significant bibliographical references and index listing playwrights, theaters, theater companies, groups, and festivals.

Fey, Faye Chunfang. *Chinese Theories of Theater and Performance from Confucius to the Present*. Ann Arbor: University of Michigan Press, 1999. Analyzes the four major periods in Chinese theatrical history, starting with antiquity and ending with the twentieth century, much of which is presented in English for the first time.

Fischer-Lichte, Erika. *The History of European Drama and Theatre*. Translated by Jo Riley. London: Routledge, 2002. Comprehensive presentation of the evolution of European drama, from the Greeks to the twentieth century.

Gassner, John, and Edward Quinn, eds. *Readers Encyclopedia of World Drama*. Reprint. Dover, 2002. A comprehensive overview of drama that traces its early roots in ritual and follows its development through the modern era. The topics of national drama, playwrights, plays, and genres are covered exhaustively.

Greenwald, Michael L., Roger Schultz, and Roberto D. Pomo. *The Longman Anthology of Drama and Theater: A Global Perspective*. New York: Long-

man, 2001. Comprehensive critical and historical material of twenty-three historically important plays taken from countries around the world. Additional topics range from folk rituals and ceremonies, the role of the storyteller, and staging conventions. Maps, lush illustrations, biographies, and more.

Kavanagh, Robert Mshengu. *Theatre and Culture Struggle in South Africa*. London: Zed Books, 1985. Includes many excerpts from plays. Among the chapters are "Culture and Social Relations in South Africa Before 1976," "The Struggle for Social Hegemony," and "The Development of Theatre in South Africa up to 1976."

Kerr, David. *African Popular Theatre*. Riverside, Calif.: Ariadne, 1995. Traces the roots and development of African theater as enjoyed by the majority of Sub-Saharan African nations. Includes discussion of formal theater, folk rituals, and folk theater. Bibliography.

Leach, Robert, and Victor Borovsky. *A History of Russian Theatre*. Cambridge, England: Cambridge University Press, 1999. Comprehensive analysis of Russian drama and theater, covering the important playwrights, their plays, and all matters concerning the theater.

Lopez, Manuel D. *Chinese Drama*. Metuchen, N.J.: Scarecrow Press, 1991. An annotated bibliography of commentary, criticism, and plays in English translation consisting of two parts: the background and development of Chinese drama from pre-Han Dynasty to Post-Cultural Revolution China, and individual plays, anthologies, and collections.

Mackerras, Colin, ed. *Chinese Theater from Its Origins to the Present Day*. Honolulu: University of Hawaii Press, 1995. Examines the documented performances associated with shamanism as early as the third millennium B.C.E.

Mander, Raymond, and Joe Mitchenson. *A Picture History of the British Theatre*. London: Hulton Press, 1957. Remarkable, often rare illustrations, with brief commentary on such topics as the Elizabethan and Jacobean stage, the Restoration period, and the twentieth century.

Marker, Frederick J., and Lise-Lone Marker. *A History of Scandinavian Theatre*. Cambridge, England: Cambridge University Press, 1996. Comprehensive overview of Danish, Norwegian, and Swedish drama from the Middle Ages to the 1990's.

Olaniyan, Tejumola. *Scars of Conquests/Masks of Resistence: The Invention of Cultural Identities in African, African American, and Caribbean Drama*. London: Oxford University Press, 1995. Explores the way in which historical black performance has been a form of cultural struggle and an integral part of the black diaspora.

Ortolani, Benito. *The Japanese Theater, From Shamanistic Ritual to Contemporary Pluralism*. Princeton, N.J,: Princeton University Press, 1995. Focuses on a historical range of performing traditions in comprehensive overviews and offers a history of Western scholarship on the topic and a thorough bibliography of sources in Western languages.

Parker, Mary, ed. *Modern Spanish Dramatists*. Westport, Conn.: Greenwood Press, 2002. Comprehensive portraits of thirty-three playwrights, with full bibliography of their work, and a useful introduction to Spanish theater in the modern period.

Reiter, Seymour. *World Theater: The Structure and Meaning of Drama*. New York: Horizon Press, 1973. Critical resource of students of the Chinese and Japanese theater, as well as of the modern Continental drama; particularly good chapters on modern drama and play premises and audience response.

Richmond, Farley P., ed. *Indian Theatre: Traditions of Performance*. Honolulu: University of Hawaii Press, 1990. A varied collection that focuses on the performance of Sanskrit and folk theater.

Roose-Evans, James. *London Theatre: From the Globe to the National*. Oxford, England: Phaidon Press, 1977. Lively work that surveys the scene from 1567 to the twentieth century.

Rubin, Don, ed. *Canadian Theatre History: Selected Readings*. Toronto, Ont.: Copp Clark, 1996. A highly useful collection of original source materials covering developments from the early 1800's to the 1990's.

_____. *The World Encyclopedia of Contemporary Theatre*. Volume 3. London and New York: Routledge, 1997. Contains brief profile of all the nations of Africa followed by descriptive summaries of key moments in the historical development of their theater. Identifies important African theaters, playwrights, actors, and performances.

Scott, A. C. *The Kabuki Theatre of Japan*. London: George Allen & Unwin, 1955. Outlines the origins of Japanese drama, the importance of kabuki, and its similarities to the origins of Chinese drama.

Segel, Harold B. *20th Century Russian Drama from Gorky to the Present*. Rev. ed. Baltimore, Md.: John Hopkins University Press, 1993. Valuable survey of Russian drama from Maxim Gorky's prerevolutionary plays into the 1990's. Analyzes both the plays and the relevant background material impacting them, especially political and ideological factors.

Shepherd, Simon, and Peter Womack. *English Drama: A Cultural History*. Cambridge, Mass.: Blackwell, 1996. Traces the development of English drama, from the medieval era through the twentieth century, arguing that the development and eras were contradictory and uneven.

Shih, Chung-Wen. *The Golden Age of Chinese Drama: Yuan Tas-chu (Yuan Zaju)*. Princeton, N.J.: Princeton University Press, 1976. A rigorous discussion of various aspects of the plays in the Yuan Dynasty, including their historical background and social milieu, convention and structure, characterization and themes, and language and music.

Sommerstein, Alan H. *Greek Drama and Dramatists*. London: Routledge, 2002. Provides an overview of Greek drama, specifically examining the social and theatrical contexts and different characteristics of ancient Greek dramatic genres. Looks closely at noted authors from the period, such as Sophocles and Euripides, as well as sixty other authors.

Weiss, Judith A., and Leslie Damasceno. *Latin American Popular Theatre: The First Five Centuries*. Albuquerque, N.Mex.: University of New Mexico Press, 1993. Focuses on such specific topics as the urban theater; popular forms, characters, and ideology; theater in the 1960's; and new trends in drama from the region.

Winkler, John J., and Froma I. Zeitlin, eds. *Nothing to do with Dionysos? Athenian Drama in its Social Context*. Reprint. Princeton, N.J.: Princeton University Press, 1992. Essays elucidate the sociopolitical context of ancient Greek drama. Argues that theatrical productions, which initially served as civic events in honor of Dionysos, grew in complexity and turned to focus on the concerns of the body politic.

Yates, Frances A. *Theatre of the World*. Chicago: University of Chicago Press, 1969. Discussion of such masters of stage illustration as John Dee, Robert Fludd, and Inigo Jones, relating them historically with their contributions to the theater.

TECHNIQUE

Archer, William. *Play-Making: A Manual of Craftsmanship*. Boston: Small, Maynard, 1912. Reprint. New York: Dover, 1960. Historically interesting essays by the distinguished English drama critic who translated and popularized the work of Henrik Ibsen.

Allen, David. *Stanislavski for Beginners*. New York: Writers and Readers, 1999. Documents details of Konstantin Stanislavsky's life as well as his "system" of acting techniques, one that proved vitally important to twentieth century American dramatists and actors.

Baker, George P. *Dramatic Technique*. New York: Houghton Mifflin, 1919. Reprint. Westport, Conn.: Greenwood Press, 1970. Once-influential treatise by the distinguished teacher of a generation of American dramatists.

Ball, David. *Backwards and Forwards: A Technical Manual for Reading Plays*. Carbondale: Southern Illinois University Press, 1990. Provides direction for reading and interpreting plays, using several of Shakespeare's works to illustrate points.

Barranger, Milly S. *Theatre: A Way of Seeing*. 5th ed. Belmont, Calif.: Wadsworth, 2001. Through the use of numerous photographs, it illustrates and discusses theatrical genres, components, rituals, and practitioners.

Barton, Robert. *Acting: Onstage and Off*. 3d ed. Belmont, Calif.: Wadsworth, 2002. Includes many practical exercises and theoretical approaches to acting.

Beckerman, Bernard. *Dynamics of Drama: Theory and Methods of Analysis*. New York: Drama Book Specialists, 1979. Useful for both the actor and the student of theater; good chapters on foundations, variations, and response.

Benedetti, Robert L. *The Actor at Work*. 8th ed. Boston: Allyn and Bacon, 2000. Provides a thorough examination of the factors involved in the acting process and exercises to elucidate the physical, vocal, analytical, and ethical aspects of acting.

Berry, Cicely. *The Actor and the Text*. New York: Applause Theater Books, 1992. More than three hundred pages that examine such topics as sound and meaning, heightened versus naturalistic text, energy through the text, argument and emotion, scene structures, and using poetry.

Bloom, Michael. *Thinking Like a Director: A Practical Handbook*. New York: Faber and Faber, 2001. Highly engaging and useful look at directing, covering steps such as thinking like an artist, interpreting the action, developing the approach, the design process, casting, rehearsals, and the final stages.

Boal, Augusto. *The Rainbow of Desire: The Boal Method of Theatre and Therapy*. Translated by Adrian Jackson. London: Routledge, 1995. A seminal work in modern drama that fostered new ways to approach theater and performance. Boal asserts performers must create the future of theater rather than wait passively for it and provides a multitude of exercises to accomplish this goal.

Bogart, Anne. *A Director Prepares: Seven Essays on Art in the Theatre*. London: Routledge, 2001. Discusses the challenges of creating theater from a director's viewpoint, examining the use of memory, violence, eroticism, embarrassment, and stereotype, among others.

Bowman, Walter Parker. *Theatre Language*. New York: Theatre Arts Books, 1961. Dictionary of technical terms, some of them historical but most of them current, used by actors and stage directors.

Brook, Peter. *The Open Door: Thoughts on Acting and Theater.* New York: Random House, 1995. Three essays written by a preeminent stage director of the contemporary stage. Brooks discusses the selection of plays he directs, how he elicits performances from his actors, and his hopes for the dramatic medium in the years to come.

Brown, Dennis. *Actors Talk: Profiles and Stories from the Acting Trade.* New York: Limelight Editions, 1999. Eleven interviews with actors such as Lillian Gish, Gregory Peck, Danny Kaye, and José Ferrer, followed by brief conversations with twenty-two other actors.

Brown, Ivor John Carnegie. *What Is a Play?* London: Macdonald, 1964. Cogent essays such as "Play and Player," "The Play Screened," and "Playing with the Play."

Brown, John Russell. *Effective Theatre: A Study with Documentation.* London: Heinemann Educational, 1969. Includes useful material on actors, stage design, and production.

_____. *What is Theatre? An Introduction and Exploration.* Woburn, Mass.: Butterworth-Heinemann, 1996. An introductory textbook, assists students in reading a play text and gaining an optimal understanding of its performance. Second half presents the perspectives and advice of theater practitioners from several generations. Photographs and illustrations throughout.

Burgess, Charles O. *Drama: Literature on Stage.* Philadelphia: J. B. Lippincott, 1969. Directed to students of the drama, this clearly written book has useful chapters (with examples). Among them are "Symbolism and Other Devices," "Theme: Meaning in Drama," and "Judging Plays."

Burns, Elizabeth. *Theatricality: A Study of Convention in the Theatre and in Social Life.* New York: Harper and Row, 1972. Treats such topics as acting, spectators and critics, and "Roles, Symbolic Types, and Characters."

Busfield, Roger M. *The Playwright's Art: Stage, Radio, Television, Motion Pictures.* New York: Harper, 1958. Reprint. Westport, Conn.: Greenwood Press, 1971. Includes such topics as the play and fiction, playwrights and their audience, and finding dramatic material.

Campbell, Paul Newell. *Form and the Art of Theatre.* Bowling Green, Ohio: Bowling Green State University Popular Press, 1984. Treats such topics as the theater audience, the performers and the performance, and the genres of theater.

Carlson, Marvin A. *Performance: A Critical Introduction.* London: Routledge, 1996. Takes a cultural, anthropological, and ethnographic approach to the survey of the modern concept of performance, examining in the process issues of identity formation, historical contexts, linguistic approaches, and much more.

Cole, Toby. *Actors on Acting: The Theories, Techniques, and Practices of the World's Great Actors, Told in Their Own Words.* 4th ed. New York: Random House, 1995. One of the foremost texts on acting, this book is organized by essays, grouped by country and acting tradition, that explore the theories and viewpoints of more than 130 actors from ancient Greece to the twentieth century. Excellent bibliography.

Corrigan, Robert W., and James L. Rosenberg, eds. *The Context and Craft of Drama: Critical Essays on the Nature of Drama and Theatre.* San Francisco: Chandler, 1964. Excellent selection of theoretical and critical essays on dramaturgy, including sections on the actor, director, designer, and critic.

Culp, Ralph Borden. *The Theatre and Its Drama: Principles and Practices.* Dubuque, Iowa: Wm. C. Brown, 1971. Good material on children's theater and creative dramatics, playwrights and playwriting, playhouses and players.

Delgado, Maria M. *In Contact with the Gods? Directors Talk Theatre.* New York: St. Martin's Press, 1996. Eighteen noted stage directors from around the world were interviewed by an audience in 1994 and the resulting question-and-answer format brings to light a number of contemporary topics and their impact of theatrical considerations, including multiculturalism, theater companies and institutions, new technologies, the art of acting, and politics and aesthetics.

Delgado, Ramon. *Acting with Both Sides of Your Brain: Perspectives on the Creative Process.* New York: Holt, Rinehart and Winston, 1986. Using modern insights from brain hemisphere research, the author provides such chapters as "Touching Both Sides of Your Brain," "The Level of Words," "The Level of Unconscious Role-Playing," and "The Level of Aesthetic Distance."

Downer, Alan S., ed. *The Art of the Play: An Anthology of Nine Plays.* New York: Henry Holt, 1955. Clear, concise introduction to nine plays, with essays on the player and action.

England, Alan William. *Scripted Drama: A Practical Guide to Teaching Techniques.* New York: Cambridge University Press, 1981. Brief but pointed chapters on acting the text, planning a production, and improvisation.

George, Kathleen. *Rhythm in Drama.* Pittsburgh: University of Pittsburgh Press, 1980. Contains such chapters as "The Panoramic Stage," "The Symbolic Gesture," and "Repetition of Verbal Strategy."

Glover, J. Garrett. *The Cubist Theatre.* Ann Arbor, Mich.: UMI Research Press, 1983. Treats such topics as "Geometricization," "An Anti-Climactic Landscape," "Condensed Signs," and "Cubist Lighting."

Goldman, Michael. *The Actor's Freedom: Toward a Theory of Drama.* New York: Viking Press, 1975. Brief but stimulating essays on actors and audience and hero and play.

Goodridge, Janet. *Rhythm and Timing of Movement in Performance: Drama, Dance, Ceremony.* Philadelphia, Pa.: J. Kingsley, 1998. Examines how humans communicate through movement and performance. Generous illustrations.

Grebanier, Bernard. *Playwriting.* New York: Thomas Y. Crowell, 1961. Essays on such topics as "The Theater vs. Life," "Sources for Ideas for Plays," and "Plot and Character."

Greenwood, Ormerod. *The Playwright: A Study of Form, Method, and Tradition in the Theatre.* London: Pitman, 1950. Sections on the playwright's choices and kinds of theater.

Hagen, Uta. *A Challenge for the Actor.* New York: Charles Scribner's Sons, 1991. Provides sound techniques explained in simple language. Includes a list of acting exercises.

Hamilton, Clayton M. *The Theory of the Theatre and Other Principles of Dramatic Criticism.* New York: Henry Holt, 1939. Although the examples are outdated, this book provides a sound treatment of the theory of the theater and the problems of the playwright.

Harrison, Martin. *The Language of Theatre.* London: Routledge, 1998. Explores more than two thousand theater terms in depth, providing etymology, terms in use, and cross-references.

Hartnoll, Phyllis, and Peter Found, eds. *Concise Oxford Companion to the Theatre.* 2d ed. England: Oxford University Press, 1992. An essential reference guide, provides entries on a vast range of topics, including playwrights, actors, theaters, styles, and periods.

Hayman, Ronald. *The Set-up: An Anatomy of the English Theatre Today.* London: Eyre Methuen, 1973. Among the chapters are "The Actor's Motives," "The West End," "Repertory," and "The Fringe."

Hermassi, Karen. *Polity and Theatre in Historical Perspective.* Berkeley: University of California Press, 1977. Very specialized but cogent study, with excellent essays titled "Power Without Love," "Workable Pictures of the World," and "The Political Vocation of Theatre."

Holtan, Orley I. *Introduction to Theatre: A Mirror to Nature.* Englewood Cliffs, N.J.: Prentice-Hall, 1976. Valuable source for such subjects as the language of theater, the actor, theater space, and confrontation and communion.

Hull, S. Loraine. *Strasberg's Method as Taught by Lorrie Hull.* Woodbridge, Conn.: Ox Bow, 1985. Lucid account with many practical examples of relaxation techniques and sensory exercises. Among the chapters are "What Is Good Acting?" and "The Trained Actor."

Ingham, Rosemary. *From Page to Stage: How Theatre Designers Make Connections Between Scripts and Images.* Portsmouth, N.H.: Heinemann, 1998. Discusses the relationships between text analysis, imagination, and creation and examines how a designer's interpretation will affect the audience's perception and reaction to a staged performance.

Kernan, Robert. *Building Better Plots*. Cincinnati, Ohio: Writer's Digest Books, 1999. Kernan, an Emmy-award winning writer, provides an entertaining yet thorough how-to approach to plot writing, examining such topics as narrative and structure, rising action, using plot archetypes, character development, and subplots.

Kernodle, George R. *Invitation to the Theatre*. 3d ed. San Diego: Harcourt Brace Jovanovich, 1985. Useful textbook in clear language that treats kinds of plays, the play in production, and the mass media.

Kohansky, Mendel. *The Disreputable Profession: The Actor in Society*. Westport, Conn.: Greenwood Press, 1984. Contains clear and sometimes amusing discussions of the acting profession. Chapters include "The Bawdy Restoration Theatre" and "Salaries and Sex Symbols."

_____. *Fundamental Acting: A Practical Guide*. New York: Applause Theatre Book Publishers, 1997. Aimed at the beginning acting student, provides basic techniques in acting two of the stage's most enduring forms: comedy and Shakespearean verse.

Le Vay, John. *Margaret Anglin: A Stage Life*. Toronto: Simon and Pierre, 1989. More than a biography of this distinguished actor, the work makes clear the conventions of acting during the early decades of the twentieth century.

Mabley, Edward. *Dramatic Construction: An Outline of Basic Principles*. Philadelphia: Chilton, 1972. Analyses of the texts of classic and modern plays; material on realism and its predecessors and "The Revolt Against Realism."

McGrath, John. *A Good Night Out, Popular Theatre: Audience, Class, and Form*. London: Eyre Methuen, 1981. Includes "Toward a Working-Class Theatre," "Theatre as Political Forum," and "The Challenge of Cinema and Television."

Marx, Milton. *The Enjoyment of Drama*. New York: F. S. Crofts, 1940. 2d ed. New York: Appleton-Century-Crofts, 1961. Handbook on the theater, with clear exposition of such topics as the purpose and aim of drama and how to judge a play.

Mitchell, John D. *Actors Talk: About Styles of Acting*. Midland, Miss.: Northwood Institute Press, 1988. Contains interviews with such noted actors as Tony Randall, Jessica Tandy, and Stephen Daley, who discuss their craft. Also provides brief biographies of many actors, including European and Asian ones.

Rice, Elmer. *The Living Theatre*. New York: Harper and Row, 1959. Wide-ranging essays by the distinguished American playwright, including chapters titled "What Does the Public Want?" and "The Noncommercial Theatre."

Selden, Samuel. *The Stage in Action*. New York: Appleton-Century-Crofts, 1941. Reprint. London: Peter Owen, 1962. Treats such matters as "Magic in Rhythm and Tone" and "The Player Singing."

Simonson, Lee. *The Stage Is Set*. New York: Theatre Art Books, 1963. Comprehensive handbook that contains such general chapters as "Scenery in the Theatre of Ideas" and "Players in the Pulpit."

Smiley, Sam. *Playwriting: The Structure of Action*. Englewood Cliffs, N.J.: Prentice-Hall, 1971. Material on spectacle, problems of production, diction, and the writer's vision.

Spencer, Stuart. *The Playwright's Guidebook*. New York: Faber and Faber, 2002. A concise and insightful handbook, provides guidance for students in structure, conflict, character, and problem-solving.

Spolin, Viola. *Improvisation for the Theatre*. Edited by Paul Sills. 3d ed. Northwestern University Press, 1999. A well-known and used handbook by theater teachers and directors, presents the "game" approach of Spolin and offers more than two hundred creative group work techniques and games. Glossary of theater and coaching terms included.

Styan, John L. *Drama: A Guide to the Study of Plays*. New York: Peter Lang, 2000. Introduces the elements of drama, provides tools for understanding classical and modern plays, and emphasizes the role of the spectator and the theater for which the play was written. Helpful glossary, charts, and diagrams.

Taylor, Malcolm. *The Actor and the Camera*. London: A & C Black Limited, 1994. An easy-to-read and informative book on the specifics of acting techniques for the camera, including soap operas and commercials, as well as film, and even discussing the audition process and how to join the appropriate unions.

Thomas, James Michael. *Script Analysis for Actors, Directors, and Designers*. 2d ed. Boston: Focal Press, 1999. Using a formalist approach, assists students in the skills of script analysis. The parts of a play are presented progressively in order to foster an understanding of artistic unity. Appendix offers introductions to additional critical theories.

Van Druten, John. *Playwright at Work*. 1953. Reprint. Westport, Conn.: Greenwood Press, 1971. Informal but useful essays by the distinguished dramatist.

Van Laan, Thomas F. *The Idiom of Drama*. Ithaca, N.Y.: Cornell University Press, 1970. Scholarly treatment of "The Medium," "The Immediate Action," and "The Action of Depth."

Waxberg, Charles S. *The Actor's Script: Script Analysis for Performers*. Portsmouth, N.H.: Heinemann, 1997. Using a variety of plays to illustrate his points, Waxberg offers tools for script analysis and creation, including such topics as breaking scenes into playable beats and actions, character analysis techniques, and playwriting styles.

Wilson, Garff B. *A History of American Acting*. Bloomington: Indiana University Press, 1966. Treats such topics as "The School of Emotionalism," "The Comic Stage," and "Comedians in Transition."

Wolford, Lisa. *Grotowski's Objective Drama Research*. Jackson: University Press of Mississippi, 1996. Combines theoretical analysis and practical description of Jerzy Grotowski's dynamic and radical approach to theater, Objective Drama.

Worsley, T. C. *The Fugitive Art: Dramatic Commentaries, 1947-1951*. London: J. Lehmann, 1952. Brilliant essays, addressed to the technically advanced student, on the production of various plays, mostly those on the London stage for the designated years.

Wright, Edward A., and Lenthiel H. Downs. *A Primer for Playgoers*. 1958. 2d ed. Englewood Cliffs, N.J.: Prentice-Hall, 1969. Nontechnical, clear discussion of such topics as the script, the audience, and the production.

Leslie B. Mittleman,
updated by Sarah Hilbert

DRAMATIC TERMS AND MOVEMENTS

Absurdism. See *Theater of the Absurd.*

Academic drama. See *School plays.*

Act: One of the major divisions of a play or opera. The practice of dividing a play into acts probably began in Rome but is derived from Greek drama, which separated the episodes of a play by choral interludes. In classical theory (notably in France in the seventeenth century), a play is divided into five acts; since the eighteenth and nineteenth centuries, however, the typical number of acts has varied from four to one, while some plays have entirely eliminated structure by acts and use only scene division. (See also *Scene.*)

Action. See *Plot.*

African American drama: Drama written by or focusing on African Americans that emerged formally in the twentieth century but has precedents in the mid-nineteenth century. Playwrights in this vein include August Wilson, James Baldwin, Ed Bullins, Lorraine Hansberry, Adrienne Kennedy, and Suzan-Lori Parks.

Afterpiece: Short farce meant to follow a serious play, a practice adopted in France by 1650, which became a standard part of English drama during the Restoration.

Agitprop: Word combining "agitation" and "propaganda" to describe drama performed as social protest rather than for its dramatic or literary merit. A German labor group called the Prolet-Bühne first used this term in New York City in 1930. Agitprop drama was performed throughout the 1930's by the American labor movement and continues to be performed in Europe and in the United States.

Agon: Greek, meaning "contest." A segment of Greek drama in which two participants become involved in verbal conflict. The two participants may be a character and the chorus; two characters, each backed by part of the chorus; or two parts of the chorus.

Alazon: Impostor or braggart of Greek comedy. The type survives in Roman comedy, as with the *Miles gloriosus* (*The Braggart Warrior*, 1767) of Plautus. (See also *Miles gloriosus.*)

Alexandrine: In French, a verse of twelve syllables generally containing four accents (in English, the iambic hexameter is sometimes referred to as an "Alexandrine"). Established as the standard form for French tragedy in the mid-sixteenth century, the Neoclassical dramatists of the seventeenth century (Pierre Corneille and Jean Racine, for example) used the Alexandrine to create the serious, elevated tone that was theoretically considered proper for the tragic mode.

Alienation: German dramatist Bertolt Brecht developed the theory of alienation in his epic theater. Brecht sought to create an audience that was intellectually alert rather than emotionally involved in a play by using alienating techniques such as minimizing the illusion of reality onstage and interrupting the action with songs and visual aids. Brecht hoped an intellectually alert audience would relate the dramatic action to problems in the real world and seek solutions to those problems. (See also *Epic theater.*)

Allegory: By representing abstract ideas or concepts through the symbolic use of character, plot, and situation, allegories are intended to instruct the audience in moral or political values. Allegory is an important component of classical drama and medieval morality plays.

Anabasis: Greek, meaning "a going up." The rising of an action to its climax. (See also *Rising action.*)

Anagnorisis: Recognition or discovery. Aristotle uses this term in the *De poetica* (c. 334-323 B.C.E.; *Poetics*, 1705) to refer to the moment of recognition in which a character moves from a state of ignorance to one of knowledge. In Sophocles' *Oidipous Tyrannos* (c. 429 B.C.E.; *Oedipus Tyrannus*, 1715; also know as *Oedipus Rex*), which Aristotle considered the ideal example of tragedy, an anagnorisis occurs when Oedipus discovers that he himself is the slayer of his father, as predicted by the seer. This recognition is accompanied by a "peripeteia" (or reversal) in which the whole action of the play is reversed.

Antagonist: Major character in opposition to the protagonist or hero.

Antimasque: Grotesque interlude within a masque which contrasts violently to the beauty and harmony of the preceding episodes. Ben Jonson created the antimasque, which typically includes grotesque dances of clowns and monsters. (See also *Masque*.)

Antistrophe: In classical Greek drama, the antistrophe is a stanza-like unit of song and dance responding to the strophe and mirroring its structure. (See also *Strophe*.)

Apollonian and Dionysian: Friedrich Nietzsche proposed in *Die Geburt der Tragödie aus dem Geiste der Musik* (1872; *The Birth of Tragedy out of the Spirit of Music*, 1909) that Greek tragedy was composed of two opposing elements, which it held in tension and finally unified. One element, the Dionysian, represented the savage, frenzied, passionate nature of humanity. The Apollonian stood for reason, moderation, and order. Nietzsche believed that the choral songs provided the Dionysian element and the dialogue the Apollonian element. Characters were often torn between these opposing forces within their personalities, which personified larger philosophical and moral issues.

Apron stage: The apron is that part of the stage that extends beyond the proscenium arch. A stage that consists entirely or primarily of an apron and on which the action is not "framed" by a proscenium may be called an "apron stage."

Asian American drama: Form of drama that emerged from the identity politics and student radicalism of the 1960's and 1970's. "Asian American" was coined in the 1960's as a replacement for "Oriental," a term that many considered a demeaning colonialist description that exoticized all individuals to whom it was attached. Thematic orientation focuses on varied topics such as the struggle against racism, ethnic profiling, economic discrimination, shared cultural heritage and ethnic identity, and invisibility. Playwrights include Frank Chin, Philip Kan Gotanda, Jessica Hagedorn, Velina Hasu Houston, David Henry Hwang, Genny Lim, and Elizabeth Wong.

Aside: Short passage generally spoken by one character in an undertone, or directed to the audience, so as not to be heard by the other characters on stage.

Auto sacramental: Renaissance development of the medieval open-air Corpus Christi pageant in Spain. A dramatic, allegorical depiction of a sinful soul wavering and transgressing until the intervention of Divine Grace restores order.

Avant-garde: Term describing plays intended to expand the conventions of the theater through the experimental treatment of form and/or content.

Ballad opera: Type of burlesque opera popular in eighteenth century England and modeled upon (as well as parodying) contemporary Italian operatic conventions. The story is conveyed in both spoken dialogue and songs (the latter mirroring the arias of the more serious form) set to old folk songs or ballads. The most successful work in this genre was John Gay's *The Beggar's Opera* (pr. 1728).

Beijing Opera: Complex theatrical style of drama known in Chinese as *Jingju* (Wade-Giles, *ching-hsi*), commonly called Beijing Opera. It was begun by Anhui actors sometime in the 1830's, when two modes of music, *erhuang diao* and *xipidiao*, were brought together. By the 1870's it had become the predominant form of Chinese drama and remains the major force in modern-day Chinese theater. The form is characterized by lavish costumes, percussive music, acrobatic dance, and colloquial lyrics.

Black comedy: General term of modern origin that refers to a form of "sick humor" that is intended to produce laughter out of the morbid and the taboo. The term is sometimes inappropriately confused with "dark comedy."

Blank verse: Unrhymed iambic pentameter, blank verse that first appeared in drama in Thomas Norton and Thomas Sackville's *Gorboduc*, performed in 1561, and that later became the standard form of Elizabethan drama.

Boulevard drama: Body of plays produced in the mid- and late nineteenth century in Paris by writers such as Ludovic Halévy and Eugène Labiche. The term properly refers to comedies of some sophistication, designed as commercial products.

Bourgeois drama: Term generally used to describe the modern realistic drama which deals with the situations and social problems of the middle class.

Bunraku: Japanese puppet theater. It emerged in the twelfth century but did not become firmly established until the turn of the seventeenth century, when narrations chanted to musical accompaniment were added to puppet performances.

Burlesque: Work which, by imitating attitudes, styles, institutions, and people, aims to amuse. Burlesque is distinguished from a closely related form, satire, in that its aim is ridicule simply for the sake of amusement rather than for political or social change. An example of burlesque drama is Gilbert and Sullivan's comic opera *Patience: Or Bunthorne's Bride* (pr. 1881), which is a parody of the aesthetic movement in late nineteenth century England.

Burletta: Short comic play with music that was popular in eighteenth and nineteenth century English theater.

Buskin: Half boot covering the foot and calf, worn by actors in Greek tragedy, also known as a cothurnus. The purpose of the buskin was to designate the stature of the characters; while comic actors wore low, flat foot coverings, tragic figures wore platform buskins. "To put on buskins" became a term for performing or writing tragedy. (See also *Sock.*)

Capa y espada: Spanish for "cape and sword," a term referring to the Spanish theater of the sixteenth and seventeenth centuries dealing with love and intrigue among the aristocracy. The greatest practitioners were Lope de Vega and Pedro Calderón de la Barca. The term *comedia de ingenio* is also used.

Cape and sword play. See *Capa y espada.*

Caroline: Of or referring to the reign of King Charles I of England, lasting from 1625 to 1649. Political strife and the violent opposition to the theater by the Puritans informed Caroline drama with a rather decadent morality and generally a quality inferior to the plays of the preceding Jacobean and Elizabethan periods, although Caroline drama did produce the noted tragedian John Ford and his counterpart in Caroline comedy, James Shirley. Caroline drama was effectively halted in 1642, when the Puritans closed all public theaters for the next eighteen years.

Catastrophe: The conclusion of a play or narrative, especially tragedy, the catastrophe is more often called the "denouement," meaning the unknotting or resolution of the situation. (See also *Freytag's pyramid.*)

Catharsis: Term from Aristotle's *Poetics* referring to the purgation of the emotions of pity and fear in the spectator aroused by the actions of the tragic hero. The meaning and the operation of this concept have been a source of great, and unresolved, critical debate.

Cavalier drama: Type of play performed at court in the 1630's during the reign of Charles I of England until the ascendancy of Oliver Cromwell in 1642 and the closing of the theaters. The plays featured elaborate plots, political conflicts, lustful villains, beautiful and virtuous ladies, and their brave, honorable lovers. Dialogue was typically florid and artificial. The most notable dramatists in this genre were Thomas Killigrew and John Suckling.

Centre 42: Early 1960's British movement designed to bring theater to people outside London and to factory districts and areas where little or no theater was performed.

Character: Personage appearing in any literary or dramatic work.

Chorus: Originally a group of singers and dancers in religious festivals, the chorus evolved into the dramatic element that reflected the opinions of the masses or commented on the action in Greek drama. In its most developed form, the chorus consisted of fifteen members: seven reciting the strophe, seven reciting the antistrophe, and the leader interacting with the actors. The development of the role of the chorus is generally seen as one of diminishing importance: In Aeschylus, the chorus often takes part in the action; in Sophocles, it serves as a commentator; and in Euripides, its function is sometimes purely lyric. The Romans adapted the Greek chorus to their own stage, and the Elizabethans occasionally imitated the Roman chorus (reducing it to a single actor), but it never became an integral part of the structure. The chorus has been used during all periods, including the modern (for example, in T. S. Eliot's 1935 *Murder in the Cathedral*), but has survived most prominently in the opera and other forms of musical theater. (See also *Parodos.*)

Chronicle play: Dramatization of historical material (or material believed to be historical), the chronicle play became popular at the end of the sixteenth century. Drawing heavily on the chronicle histories of

Raphael Holinshed and Edward Hall, dramatists originally strung together loose scenes from history, but the form later developed greater unity in works such as Christopher Marlowe's *Edward II* (pr. c. 1592) and the *Henry IV* (pr. late sixteenth century) plays of William Shakespeare. Also termed "history plays," the chronicle plays developed into subtle studies of character and became more important as examinations of human strengths and frailties than as accounts of historical facts.

Classical drama: Classical drama originally referred to the literature and theater of ancient Greece and Rome, but later the term also included theater composed in imitation of the Greco-Roman tradition, which was often called "neoclassical." In more common usage, the term refers to art which possesses at least some of the following characteristics: balance, proportion, control, unity, and simplicity.

Climax: Moment in a drama at which the action reaches its highest intensity and is resolved. The major climax of a play may be preceded by several climaxes of lesser and varying intensity.

Closet drama: Play meant to be read rather than performed. Two examples of closet drama are Alfred de Musset's *Fantasio* (pb. 1834, pr. 1866; English translation, 1853) or George Gordon, Lord Byron's *Manfred* (pb. 1817, pr. 1834). Also, a play which, although meant for performance, has survived only as literature.

Comedia: Principal form of nonreligious drama during the Spanish Golden Age (*Siglio de Oro*) of the sixteenth century that mixed tragic and comic elements in a complex, suspenseful plot, used a variety of verse forms, and favored realistic language and action. The *comedias* of the early sixteenth century were written in five acts, but by the 1580's the number of acts had been reduced to three by playwrights such as Lope de Vega.

Comedia erudita: "Learned comedy." In the Renaissance, scholarly imitations of classical comedies (particularly Roman) were created by such writers as Pietro Aretino, Ludovico Ariosto, and Niccolò Machiavelli (the latter's *La mandragola*, pr. 1520; *The Mandrake*, 1911; is frequently cited as an example of the genre).

Comédie ballet: Theatrical form mixing elements of comedy, farce, and musical-balletic spectacle popular in seventeenth century France. Molière's *Le Bourgeois Gentilhomme* (pr. 1670; *The Would-Be Gentleman*, 1675) and *Le Malade imaginaire* (pr. 1673; *The Imaginary Invalid*, 1732; also known as *The Hypochondriac*) are the two best examples of the form.

Comédie larmoyante: French term meaning "tearful, or weeping, comedy." This sentimental comedy was popular in eighteenth century France. A development from the earlier style of comedy, *comédie larmoyante* aimed to produce not critical laughter (as in the earlier style exemplified by Molière) but pleasurable tears. The chief practitioners were Philippe Destouches and Pierre-Claude Nivelle de La Chaussée. (See also *Sentimental comedy*.)

Comedy: Generally, a lighter form of drama (as contrasted with tragedy) that aims chiefly to amuse and ends happily. Wit and humor are used to entertain. The comic effect typically arises from the recognition of some incongruity of speech, action, or character development. The comic range extends from coarse, physical humor (called low comedy) to a more subtle, intellectual humor (called high comedy). When comedy tends toward the judgmental or critical, it is referred to as satiric; when it is mixed with sympathy or pathos, it moves in the direction of tragedy. There are many specific comic forms and manifestations. (See also *Burlesque, Burletta, Comedia erudita, Comédie larmoyante, Comedy of humours, Comedy of manners, Commedia dell' arte, Dark comedy, Farce, High comedy, Interlude, Low comedy, New Comedy, Old Comedy, Romantic comedy, Satire, Sentimental comedy, Slapstick,* and *Tragicomedy*.)

Comedy, drawing room. See *Drawing room comedy*.

Comedy, laughing. See *Laughing comedy*.

Comedy, sentimental. See *Sentimental comedy*.

Comedy of humors: Type of drama developed in the late sixteenth and early seventeenth centuries by Ben Jonson and George Chapman that dealt with characters whose behavior is controlled by some single characteristic, or "humor." In medieval and Renaissance medicine, the humors were the four bodily fluids (blood, phlegm, yellow bile, and black bile), any excess of which created a distortion or imbalance of personality (by extension, the term came to mean "mood" or "disposition"). Jonson used this theory of character in several of his works, such as *Every Man in His Humour* (pr. 1598) and *Every Man out of His Humour* (pr. 1599).

Comedy of manners: Sometimes known as "genteel comedy" (in reference to its lack of coarseness), a form of comedy that arose during the eighteenth century, dealing with the intrigues (particularly the amorous intrigues) of sophisticated, witty members of the upper classes. The effect and appeal of these plays are primarily intellectual, depending upon quick-witted dialogue and cleverness and facility of language. The Restoration period was particularly fond of this form, as can be seen in the plays of such dramatists as William Congreve, Sir George Etherege, and William Wycherley.

Comic relief: Humorous incident or scene in an otherwise serious or tragic drama intended to release the audience's tensions through laughter without detracting from the serious material.

Commedia dell'arte: Dramatic comedy performed by troupes of professional actors, which became popular in the mid-sixteenth century in Italy. These troupes were rather small, consisting of perhaps a dozen actors who performed stock roles in mask and improvised upon skeletal scenarios (often derived from the traditional material of ancient Roman comedy). The tradition of the *commedia*, or masked comedy, was influential into the seventeenth century and still, in fact, exerts some influence. Some of the more famous stock roles are Pulchinella, Harlequin, Arlecchino, Pantalone, Il Dottore, and Il Capitano.

Commedia palliata: Roman comedy produced in Greek costume and refined by Plautus during the second century B.C.E.

Corpus Christi plays: These religious plays depicting biblical events were performed on Corpus Christi Day in England during the fourteenth, fifteenth, and sixteenth centuries. The plays originated in the liturgy of the Church, but they came to be staged outdoors on large wagons that moved through towns (such as York and Chester) in a procession, so that each play was performed before several different audiences. (See also *Liturgical drama, Miracle play, Trope.*)

Cothurnus. See *Buskin.*

Counterplot: Secondary action coincident with the major action of a play. The counterplot is generally a reflection on or variation of the main action and as such is strongly integrated into the whole of the play. A counterplot may also be referred to as a subplot, but this more general term may refer to a secondary action which is largely unrelated to the main action. (See also *Subplot.*)

Coup de théâtre: An unusual, striking, unexpected turn of events in the action of a play.

Cup-and-saucer drama: Type of play that furthers the illusion of reality onstage through the realistic portrayal of domestic situations among the upper classes and through the use of realistic sets and authentic properties. The English playwright Thomas William Robertson (1829-1871) was the chief practitioner of this type of drama.

Curtain raiser: An entertainment, sometimes a one-act play, performed at the beginning of a program. In the late nineteenth and early twentieth centuries, a curtain raiser often served to entertain an audience during the arrival of latecomers, thus avoiding disturbances when the main presentation began.

Cycle play. See *Miracle play.*

Dada drama: Short-lived but important experiment in the capacity of the stage to present something other than familiar reality was Dada, an early twentieth century movement which began as a cabaret experiment in Switzerland. The guiding spirit of Dada was the Romanian poet Tristan Tzara, who asserted that the first order of business for the new artist was to raze all existing structures, including logic itself, in order for a new world to be built on cleared ground. Consequently, the Dadas looked at reason and logic and proceeded to do the direct opposite. Tzara's *Le Coeur à gaz* (wr. 1921, pb. 1946; *The Gas Heart,* 1964), Guillaume Apollinaire's *Les Mamelles de Tiresias* (pr. 1917; *The Breasts of Tiresias,* 1961), and Jean Cocteau's ballet scenario, *Les Mariés de la tour Eiffel* (1921; *The Wedding on the Eiffel Tower,* 1937), are examples of Dada drama.

Dark comedy: Term coined by J. L. Styan in *The Dark Comedy* (1962), referring to the modern concept of the play between tragedy and farce (which evolved from the work of a wide range of predecessors, such as Euripides, medieval mystery plays, Shakespeare, and Molière). The concept reflects the existential belief in a disjunctive world where there is no possibility for conventional notions of heroism and tragedy. Such a concept imposed upon drama tends to produce a catharsis from moment to moment (not a climactic one). The term is broad enough to encompass most of the innovative works of the contemporary repertoire.

Deaf theater: Form of theater that is unique because it is typically defined by its physical method of performance rather than by its literature, play script, or intended audience. Plays performed in American Sign Language (ASL), regardless of their source, content, or intended audience are said to delineate deaf theater. Spoken language scripts are translated into ASL, a process reverse from that found in other niche-based drama. Deaf theater is usually performed simultaneously in two languages, manual ASL and spoken English. The development and proliferation of deaf theater reflects first the joining of spoken and manual languages and then the struggle to separate them. Deaf theater began to embody the ASL literature of the deaf culture in the early twenty-first century.

Denouement: Originally French, this word literally means "unknotting" or "untying" and is another term for the catastrophe or resolution of a dramatic action, the solution or clarification of a plot.

Deus ex machina: Latin, meaning "god out of a machine." In the Greek theater, the use of a god lowered by means of a mechanism called the *mechane* (usually a crane with rope and pulleys) onto the stage to untangle the plot or save the hero. In *Poetics*, Aristotle condemned the use of the *deus ex machina*, arguing that ideally the resolution of a dramatic action should grow out of the action itself. The term has come to signify any artificial device for the simple or easy resolution of any dramatic difficulties.

Deuteragonist: Second actor in Greek drama, the addition of whom was an innovation of Aeschylus.

The term is often synonymous with antagonist. In subsequent usage, the term has indicated a major character of secondary importance or position, such as Claudius in William Shakespeare's *Hamlet, Prince of Denmark* (pr. c. 1600-1601)

Dialogue: Speech exchanged between characters or even, in a looser sense, the thoughts of a single character.

Dionysia: An annual drama festival and play contest that began in the sixth century B.C.E in honor of the god, Dionysus, and is said to mark the beginnings of Greek drama. The Dionysia was celebrated in March and was eventually followed by a second festival in Dionysus's honor, the Lenaea ("wine press"), held in the winter.

Dionysian. See *Apollonian and Dionysian.*

Dithyramb: Originally a choral hymn sung and danced during the ancient Greek rites of Dionysus, the tone of which was passionate and excited. In *Poetics*, Aristotle postulates that the tragic form developed from the dithyramb.

Documentary drama: Also popularly referred to as "docudrama," this term refers to the dramatization of actual events in a journalistic style that explores the ethics and responsibility of issues of public concern. Documentary drama developed in West Germany in the 1960's and is represented by works such as German dramatist Rolf Hochhuth's *Der Stellvertreter: Ein Christliches Trauerspiel* (pr. 1963; *The Representation*, 1963; also known as *The Deputy*, 1964) and American dramatist Eric Bentley's *Are You Now, or Have You Ever Been: The Investigation of Show-Business by the Un-American Activities Committee, 1947-1958* (pr. 1972).

Domestic tragedy: Serious and usually realistic play, with lower-class or middle-class characters and milieu, typically dealing with personal or domestic concerns. The term has been used to refer to works from the Elizabethan age to the present. Examples of domestic tragedy include George Lillo's *The London Merchant: Or, The History of George Barnwell* (pr. 1731), Thomas Heywood's *A Woman Killed with Kindness* (pr. 1603), several of the plays of Henrik Ibsen, and Arthur Miller's *Death of a Salesman* (pr. 1949).

Drama: Generally speaking, any work designed to be represented on a stage by actors (Aristotle defined drama as "the imitation of action"). More specifically, the term has come to signify a play of a serious nature and intent which may end either happily (comedy) or unhappily (tragedy).

Dramatic irony: Irony is a means of expressing a meaning or significance contrary to the stated or ostensible one. Dramatic irony often lies more in the action or structure of a play than in the words of a character. Oedipus' search for the murderer of Laius (whom he later discovers to be himself) is an example of extended dramatic irony. Dramatic irony may also occur when the spoken lines of a character are perceived by the audience to have a double meaning.

Dramatis personae: Characters in a play. Often, a printed listing defining the characters and specifying their relationships.

Dramaturgy: Composition of plays. The term is occasionally used to refer to the performance or acting of plays.

Drame: French term employed chiefly by Louis-Sébastien Mercier (1740-1814) to denote plays that mixed realistic and comic elements with a serious, often tragic, plot. Such plays featured middle-class characters and situations and a preponderance of sentimentality.

Drame héroique. See *Heroic drama.*

Drawing room comedy: Nineteenth century form, related to the comedy of manners form, that elevated the comedy's moral tone by banishing much of the witty sexual innuendo that had long characterized the genre. The setting is usually the drawing room, in which the social games being played are exposed for the audience's amusement as well as for its admiration, the latter being reserved for characters who can best play the game. Dion Boucicault's *London Assurance* (pr. 1841) illustrates the type.

Dumb show: Dramatic performance communicated entirely through gestures, not words. The play-within-a-play in *Hamlet, Prince of Denmark* is a famous example of the dumb show. The term "pantomime" is occasionally used to signify the same type of performance. (See also *Play-within-a-play.*)

Elizabethan: Of or referring to the reign of Queen Elizabeth I of England, lasting from 1558 to 1603, a period of important developments and achievements in the arts in England, particularly in poetry and drama. The era included such literary figures as Edmund Spenser, Christopher Marlowe, William Shakespeare, Ben Jonson, and John Donne. Sometimes referred to as the English Renaissance.

Entr'acte: Brief performance, often musical, intended to entertain an audience between the acts or scenes of a drama.

Environmental theater: Production style developed by the experimental theater groups of the 1960's, emphasizing a flexible approach to the total theater space and aimed at eliminating the traditional separation between audience and stage. Environmental theater is often performed in "found" spaces such as streets, warehouses, and fields.

Epic theater: Style of drama in which the action is presented in loosely related episodes, often interspersed with song, that are designed to distance the audience from the drama. Epic theater was developed by the German director Ervin Piscator in the late 1920's but came to be associated chiefly with the work of Bertolt Brecht. (See also *Alienation.*)

Epilogue: Closing section of a play, or a speech by an actor or chorus at the end of a play, which makes some reflection upon the preceding action or simply, as in Puck's speech at the end of *A Midsummer Night's Dream* (pr. c. 1595-1596), requests the approval and applause of the spectators. The term is sometimes used to refer to the actor who recites such a closing speech.

Episode: In Greek tragedy, the segment between two choral odes. In the larger sense, an episode is a portion of a plot or dramatic action having its own coherence and integrity.

Exodos: Final scene in a classical Greek drama.

Expressionism: Movement dominant in the decade that followed World War I, particularly referring to German painting. External reality, including the appearance of objects, is consciously distorted in order to represent reality as it is felt or "viewed emotionally." Among examples of expressionist drama (which often used distorted scenery, props, music, and unrealistic lighting effects) are Frank Wedekind's

Die Büchse der Pandora (pr. 1904; *Pandora's Box*, 1918), Eugene O'Neill's *The Hairy Ape* (pr. 1922), and the operas of Alban Berg (*Wozzeck*, pr. 1925; English translation, 1952; and *Lulu*, pr. 1937, English translation, 1977). A play may contain expressionistic devices without being specifically expressionistic (for example, Tennessee Williams's *The Glass Menagerie*, pr. 1944, or his *A Streetcar Named Desire*, pr. 1947).

Extravaganza: James Robinson Planché (1796-1880) developed this form in England. An elaborate musical presentation, the extravaganza was usually based on a fairy tale.

Falling action: Part of a play following the climax. (See also *Freytag's pyramid*.)

Farce: From the Latin *farcire*, meaning "to stuff." Originally an insertion into established Church liturgy in the Middle Ages, "farce" later became the term for specifically comic scenes inserted into early liturgical drama. The term has come to refer to any play that evokes laughter by such low-comedy devices as physical humor, rough wit, and ridiculous and improbable situations and characters. A play may contain farcical elements without being, properly speaking, a farce.

Feminist theater: Theater that works to highlight women's social and political struggles, while in the process exposing patriarchal structures in society and the politics of prevailing gender roles. Feminist playwrights include Alice Childress, Tina Howe, Caryl Churchill, Megan Terry, Wendy Wasserstein, and Marsha Norman.

Flashback: Scene in a play (or in film or literature) depicting events that occurred at an earlier time.

Foil: Any character who sets off or contrasts with another by means of different behavior, philosophy, or purpose.

Folk drama: Generally, plays on folk themes performed at popular or religious festivals by amateurs. Sometimes the term is used to indicate plays written by sophisticated, practiced dramatists on folk themes or in "folk settings" and performed by professional actors. John Millington Synge's *The Playboy of the Western World* (pr. 1907) may be considered, in some sense, a folk drama by this latter definition.

Fourth wall: Theatrical convention intended to heighten the illusion of reality onstage and employed extensively in the late nineteenth century. An invisible fourth wall is imagined to exist between the audience and a stage, enclosed on three sides by the stage set and framed on the fourth by the proscenium arch. The audience, in effect, looks in on the action "through" the fourth wall.

Freytag's pyramid: In 1863, the German critic Gustave Freytag described the theoretical structure of a typical five-act play in *Die Technik des Dramas*. He categorized the dramatic action into the following segments: introduction, rising action, climax, falling action, and catastrophe—all of which can be diagramed in a pyramidal form with the climax at the apex.

Fusion theater: Form of experimental theater which combines elements of non-Western traditions of acting, dramatic and storytelling conventions, music, and performance styles with its Western counterparts. New York's Café La Mama and Berkeley's Zellerbach Playhouse are popular playhouses that promote fusion theater. (See also *Experimental theater*.)

Gay and lesbian drama: Dramatic works written by or focusing on gay issues and lifestyles. Early twentieth century playwrights that subtly treated the subject of homosexuality included Noël Coward, Lillian Hellman, Edna St. Vincent Millay, and, in the 1950's, Robert Anderson. Mart Crowley's *The Boys in the Band*, produced in 1968, paved the way for gay drama in the decades that followed. Among the most honest presentations of homosexuality since 1968 have been John Hopkins's *Find Your Way Home* (pr. 1970), Marvin Hamlisch and Edward Kleban's *A Chorus Line* (pr. 1975), Harvey Fierstein's *La Cage aux Folles* (pr. 1983), and Tony Kushner's pair of plays, *Angels in America: A Gay Fantasia on National Themes*, Part One: Millenium Approaches (1991) and Part Two: Perestroika (1992). The AIDS crisis, homophobia, and political representation have become modern thematic orientations of gay and lesbian drama.

Grand Guignol: Type of theatrical presentation in which horror is the desired effect. This is typically achieved by skillfully naturalistic depictions of situations causing physical pain, such as amputations, eye gougings, and burnings. The effect is invariably grisly and is sometimes meant to produce an uncomfortable sort of laughter.

Hamartia: Greek word for "error," specifically an error in judgment. Aristotle, in *Poetics*, states that a true tragic hero should be a character "preeminently virtuous and just, whose misfortune, however, is brought upon him not by vice and depravity but by some error." This error of judgment may proceed either from ignorance or from moral fault and is sometimes referred to as a "tragic flaw."

Harangue: Speech, usually of some length, often addressed to a crowd to influence the attitudes and actions of the addressees. Antony's ironic speech to the citizens of Rome over Caesar's body in William Shakespeare's *Julius Caesar* (pr. c. 1599-1600) is a well-known example.

Harlequinade: Play or pantomime in the *commedia dell'arte* tradition featuring Harlequin, the stock buffoon who has a shaved head and parti-colored tights, and carries a wooden sword.

Hero/Heroine: Most important character in a drama. Popularly, the term has come to refer to a character who possesses extraordinary prowess or virtue, but as a technical dramatic term it simply indicates the central participant in a dramatic action. (See also *Protagonist*.)

Heroic drama: Type of play usually written in heroic couplets and of elevated diction and seriousness of action (although there might be a happy ending). Heroic drama was popular for a short period, predominantly during the Restoration in England, and its practitioners were John Dryden, Bronson Howard, and Thomas Otway, among others. In France, the *drame héroïque* was likewise popular during the seventeenth century (here the verse form was the Alexandrine). The *drame héroïque* reached a level of accomplishment and art far surpassing its English counterpart. The great French practitioners were Pierre Corneille and Jean Racine.

High comedy: Term broadly used to refer to comedy whose impulse is often satiric and whose appeal is primarily intellectual. Intellect, wit, style, and sophistication are the trademarks of this type of comedy. Plays such as William Congreve's *The Way of the World* (pr. 1700), Molière's *Le Misanthrope* (pr. 1666; *The Misanthrope*, 1709), and Oscar Wilde's *The Importance of Being Earnest: A Trivial Comedy for Serious People* (pr. 1895) are all examples of high comedy.

History play. See *Chronicle play.*

Hubris: Greek term for "insolence" or "pride," the characteristic or emotion in tragic heroes of ancient Greek drama that causes the reversal of their fortune, leading them to transgress moral codes or ignore warnings. An example of hubris in Sophocles' *Antigonē* (441 B.C.E.; *Antigone*, 1729) is Creon's overweening pride, which, despite Tiresias' admonitions, brings about the deaths of Antigone as well as those of Creon's wife and son.

Humors, comedy of. See *Comedy of humors.*

Hypokritēs: An expositor performing recitations in early Greek tragedy that advance the action by brief dialogues with the chorus.

Imitation: From the Greek mimesis, used by Aristotle in his *Poetics* to describe tragedy as "an imitation of an action" of a good man. Aristotle perceived artistic imitation not as an exact replica of life but as an artistic representation that transcends reality to convey universal truths, which produces pleasure in the observer. This term has remained central to Western literary and dramatic criticism, although it has been subject to various interpretations through the centuries.

Improvisational theater: Performance in which action and dialogue are created spontaneously by the actors, and which is often based upon a rough scenario rather than a written, rehearsed script. The *commedia dell'arte* of the Italian Renaissance featured improvisation, and many contemporary theater groups use improvisation both as a performance and as a training technique.

Interlude: Short play, often a farce, popular in fifteenth and sixteenth century England. The English interlude has Continental counterparts in such works as the anonymous French farce *Pierre Patelin* and the comedies of the German mastersinger Hans Sachs. Henry Medwall and John Heywood were practitioners of the interlude in England.

Intrigue: Incidents that make up the plot or action of a play. The term is most frequently applied to plots that are elaborate and in which the schemes of various characters are involved. A play such as William Congreve's *The Way of the World* is sometimes referred to as a "comedy of intrigue."

Irony. See *Dramatic irony.*

Jacobean: Of or pertaining to the reign of James I of England, who ruled from 1603 to 1625, the period following the death of Elizabeth I, which saw tremendous literary activity in poetry and drama. Many writers who achieved fame during the Elizabethan age were still composing (notably William Shakespeare, Ben Jonson, and John Donne). Other dramatists, such as John Webster and Cyril Tourneur, achieved success almost entirely during the reign of James I. The theater of this period is particularly noted for its interest in the violent and the fantastical.

Kabuki: Form of theater in Japan which was, traditionally, established by a former priestess of the early seventeenth century, Okuni. Okuni organized a troupe of actors that included both men and women. Kabuki enjoyed immediate popular success, and the number of companies (with both male and female performers) increased rapidly. As early as 1629, the presence of female performers caused a scandal and was banned. Female impersonators kept the tradition alive and remain very popular. Kabuki actors wear no masks (unlike the performers of the aristocratic Nō theater). The Kabuki drama is typically melodramatic and violent, with complex plotting.

Latino drama: Drama that emerged in the 1950's and 1960's, written by or focusing on the numerous groups that belong to Latino culture in the United States: Mexican Americans or Chicanos (American-born Mexicans), Puerto Ricans or Nuyoricans (New York Puerto Ricans), and Cuban Americans, whose modern theater has acquired several names, including Cuban American and Cuban exile theater. Identity issues, immigration, socioeconomic status, and a postmodern political consciousness of "the other" as both outsider and insider typically grounds the thematic orientation of Latino drama.

Laughing comedy: Term coined in 1772 by English playwright Oliver Goldsmith to describe a comedy, such as his *She Stoops to Conquer* (pr. 1773) or Richard Brinsley Sheridan's *The Rivals* (pr. 1775), that exposes human follies and vices for the amusement and edification of the audience, as opposed to the sentimental comedy, which dominated eighteenth century drama and which was intended to move audiences to pleasurable tears with sentimental stories about the middle class. The respective merits of these two types of comedy were hotly debated throughout the 1770's.

Lazzo: Improvised comic dialogue or action in the *commedia dell'arte*. Lazzi (plural) were among the prime resources of the *commedia* actors, consisting of verbal asides on current politics, literary topics, manifestations of terror, pratfalls, and similar actions.

Leitmotif: From the German, meaning "leading motif." Any repetition—of a word, phrase, situation, or idea—which occurs within a single work or group of related works and which serves to unify the work or works. The term has special meaning in musical drama (a signal melody or phrase of music), and the technique was used by the nineteenth century composer and theoretician Richard Wagner not only to unify his operas (most notably the four-opera cycle *Der Ring des Nibelungen*, pr. 1876; *The Nibelung's Ring*, 1877; also known as *The Ring of the Nibelung*, 1910) but also to add dramatic and psychological resonance and depth to the action.

Libretto: Italian for "little book." The text or script of an opera, operetta, or other form of musical theater.

Liturgical drama: Plays performed as part of the liturgy of the Church during the Middle Ages. The origin of these plays was in the tropes or interpolations into the Latin text of the liturgy, which was chanted by the clergy. These interpolations were expanded and eventually developed into independent performances in the vernacular. The performances eventually moved out of the church proper and were performed by members of the laity. While the plays ceased to be liturgical, they continued to deal with religious themes, particularly drawn from the Old and New Testaments. (See also *Corpus Christi plays, Miracle play, Trope.*)

Low comedy: Term broadly used to refer to the coarse elements in a play designed to arouse laughter. Such elements include physical comedy (slapstick, practical jokes) and off-color humor. Low comedy elements are to be found not only in such comic forms as farce but also in plays of high artistic repute, such as William Shakespeare's *A Midsummer Night's Dream* and *The Merry Wives of Windsor* (pr. 1597).

Manners, comedy of. See *Comedy of manners.*

Masque: Courtly entertainment popular during the first half of the seventeenth century in England. Derived from Italian court entertainments, it spanned from the latter part of the reign of Elizabeth I through that of James I and into that of Charles I. It was a particularly sumptuous form of spectacle including music (song and dance) and lavish costumes and scenery (the great Baroque architect Inigo Jones and the great Baroque composer Henry Purcell were frequently involved in the nonliterary aspects of these productions). Masques often dealt with mythological or pastoral subjects, and the dramatic action often took second place to pure spectacle. Ben Jonson was the greatest writer of masques during this period, and even the young John Milton composed a masque, *Comas* (pr. 1634), whose interest was, atypically, more literary than spectacle-oriented. (See also *Antimasque.*)

Melodrama: Originally a drama with occasional songs, or with music of any kind (*melos* is Greek for "song"). It was also one of the original Italian terms for opera. By the early nineteenth century, the term acquired a new meaning: a play in which characters are clearly either virtuous or evil and are pitted against one another in suspenseful, often sensational situations. Late eighteenth century French playwright Guilbert de Pixérécourt was a well known melodramatist, best remembered for his *Sélico: Ou, Les Nègres généreux* (pr. 1793). This type of play became so common that the term took on a pejorative meaning which it still retains today: any dramatic work characterized by stereotyped characters and sensational, sometimes improbable situations.

Method, the: An approach to acting developed by the Russian director Konstantin Stanislavsky. Commonly referred to as "the Method," this approach emphasizes a realistic acting style based on each actor's self-knowledge and on the entire cast's careful analysis of the script. An understanding of the motivation behind the character's speech and actions is essential to a believable performance, according to the rules of the Method, which was popularized in the United States by the noted acting instructor Lee Strasberg.

Miles gloriosus: Braggart soldier character type found in many plays from antiquity to the modern age, particularly in Elizabethan and Jacobean drama. The term derives from Plautus's play of the same title. Nicholas Udall's *Ralph Roister Doister* (pr. c. 1552) and William Shakespeare's *Sir John Falstaff* are quintessential examples of the type in sixteenth century English drama. (See also *Alazon.*)

Mime: Dramatic action portrayed by means of gesture and movement without speech. An actor who performs such actions is also called a "mime."

Mimesis. See *Imitation.*

Miracle play: In English drama, this term refers to medieval religious plays dramatizing the lives of the saints and divine miracles. The term "mystery play" (derived from the French term *mystère*) is used to designate plays derived from the Scriptures as opposed to those dealing with saints' lives. These plays were originally associated with the celebration of saints' feast days and with religious processions (particularly the Corpus Christi festival) and were performed in Latin as part of the liturgical services. Later, these plays were expanded, performed in the vernacular, and moved into the streets. Trade guilds were often responsible for the performance of a particular play, so that in time a series of performances by various guilds would create a cycle of plays. Some examples of subjects derived from Scripture include Christ's Passion, the Fall of Man, and the story of Noah. This form of dramatic entertainment reached its height in the fifteenth and sixteenth centuries. (See also *Corpus Christi plays*, *Liturgical drama*, *Trope.*)

Mise-en-scène: Staging of a drama, including scenery, costumes, movable furniture (properties), and, by extension, the positions (blocking) and gestures of the actors.

Modernism: An international movement in the arts that began in the early years of the twentieth century. Although the term is used to describe artists of widely varying persuasions, modernism in general was characterized by its international idiom, by its interest in cultures distant in space or time, by its emphasis on formal experimentation, and by its sense of dislocation and radical change. Seeking to revolutionize dramatic structure, playwrights often presented fantasies, hallucinations, nightmares, and other subjective experiences. In addition, they developed new lighting and staging techniques—particularly the turntable stage—that portrayed myriad moods rather than a single mood, and they excluded irrelevancy. Influenced by German expressionism, Symbolism, and Sigmund Freud, many of these playwrights were antinaturalistic. (See also *Symbolism, Expressionism, Naturalism.*)

Monodrama: Theatrical presentation featuring only one character. Jean Cocteau's *La Voix humaine* (pr. 1930; *The Human Voice*, 1951) is an example of this form.

Monologue: An extended speech by one character in a drama. If the character is alone onstage, unheard by other characters, the monologue is more specifically referred to as a soliloquy. (See also *Soliloquy.*)

Morality play: Dramatic form of the late Middle Ages and the Renaissance containing allegorical figures (most often virtues and vices) that are typically involved in the struggle over a person's soul. The anonymously written *Everyman* is one of the most famous medieval examples of this form.

Motoriae: Loosely structured play, refined by the Greek writer Epicharmus of Cos during the fifth century B.C.E., the violent action of which combines mythological plots with realistic stories.

Mummery: This term refers broadly to a theatrical presentation in which actors or dancers are masked or in disguise. The term is occasionally used to refer to acting in general.

Musical comedy: Theatrical form mingling song, dance, and spoken dialogue which was developed in the United States in the twentieth century and is derived from vaudeville and operetta. In its earliest stages, the music often had little to do with the libretto (the text or script), but a closer integration of these elements has occurred since the early 1940's. (See also *Musical theater, Opera.*)

Musical theater: Dramatic production in which music, lyrics, and sometimes dance are fundamental elements. Opera, operetta, and musical comedy are all forms of musical theater. Proponents of this genre include Claudio Monteverdi, George Frederick Handel, Wolfgang Amadeus Mozart, Gioacchino Rossini, Vincenzo Bellini, Giuseppe Verdi, Richard Wagner, Richard Strauss, and Giacomo Puccini. (See also *Musical comedy, Opera.*)

Mystery play. See *Miracle play.*

Native American drama: Dramatic works by Native Americans and/or about their experience in North America, which began in the 1960's and has continued. The search for identity in the United States and the hope of rectifying the cultural image of the Native American commonly held in American society are often thematic poles of such works. Works often integrate religious themes, rituals, and dances that began to perish at the end of the nineteenth century with the increasing removal of Indian peoples to reservations. Representative playwrights include Hanay Geiogamah, William S. Yellow Robe, Jr., Roxy Gordon, and Leanne Howe.

Naturalism: Naturalism was a type of realism, aimed at overturning theatrical convention, created in the late nineteenth century by a school of French and American writers including Émile Zola and Theodore Dreiser, who elevated the style nearly to a philosophical movement. As a genre, it professed to be unsentimental and, consequently, antibourgeois. Naturalistic drama sought to mirror life, even at its seamiest, in all its cruelty and degradation. Henry Becque and Gerhart Hauptmann were two naturalistic playwrights. (See also *Realism.*)

Neoclassicism: Aesthetic movement that influenced seventeenth century French and English drama and was characterized by an admiration for and an emulation of classical Greek and Roman culture. French neoclassical drama is best represented by the tragedies of Pierre Corneille and Jean Racine, who followed the strict rules of unity and verisimilitude advocated by the Académie Française. In England, neoclassical dramatists such as John Dryden wrote heroic tragedies, which were highly artificial dramas featuring exotic settings, improbable and spectacular action, and high-flown language, usually written in heroic couplets. (See also *Renaissance drama*.)

New Comedy: Greek comedy of the third and fourth centuries B.C.E. that coincided with the decline of Greek political power and with the decline of the satiric comic theater of Aristophanes. The New Comedy featured stereotyped plots and characters: courtesans, young lovers, foolish miserly old men, and scheming servants. After many amorous intrigues, the plays typically ended in a happy marriage. Menander was the chief proponent of the form, and the Romans Terence and Plautus were much influenced by it, finding in it an abundant source for material.

Nō: Form of theater developed in fourteenth century Japan from ritual dance associated with Shinto worship. The plays were designed for aristocratic audiences and were highly restrained and stylized. The plays are typically mysterious and gloomy in plot and atmosphere. Performers (who are always male) wear masks and employ a distinctly unrealistic form of acting. The text is sung or chanted to musical accompaniment in low- and high-pitched voices. The influence of this Eastern form can be seen in the West in certain twentieth century works such as William Butler Yeats's *At the Hawk's Well* (pr. 1916) and *The Only Jealousy of Emer* (pr. 1922).

Obligatory scene: Scene that a playwright has led an audience to expect (usually an emotional confrontation between characters) and without which the audience would be disappointed (also called a *scene a faire*).

Old Comedy: Greek comedy of the fifth century B.C.E. that originated in the fertility festivals in honor of Dionysus. Of the plays in this form, only those of Aristophanes survive. His work is notable for its biting personal and political satire as well as its lyric beauty. The chorus takes an important role in the action, notably delivering the parabasis, an extended speech usually expressing the views of the playwright. With the decline of Greek political power in the fourth century B.C.E., this form was replaced by New Comedy. The plays in this form relied heavily on stock characters and situations.

One-act play: Although there have been short, unified dramatic works that might properly be termed one-act dramas earlier on, this term has typically been employed for such works written since the late nineteenth century. The one-act play is usually quite limited in number of characters and scene changes, and the action often revolves around a single incident or event.

Opera: Form of dramatic entertainment consisting of a play set to music. Opera is the most important and most sophisticated form that combines music with theatrical representation. It is a complex combination of various art forms—music (both vocal and instrumental), drama, poetry, acting, stage design, dance, and so on. Like other art forms, it has its own conventions; these are sometimes derived more from a musical perspective than from a purely theatrical perspective or tradition. The origin of opera in the late sixteenth and early seventeenth centuries in Italy resulted from the attempts of certain Humanist literary figures and musicians to recreate classical Greek drama, with its combination of speech, music, and dance. From its inception through the present, opera has undergone a diverse history of its own (which sometimes mirrors the history of purely spoken drama). Practitioners of the form include Claudio Monteverdi, George Frederick Handel, Wolfgang Amadeus Mozart, Gioacchino Rossini, Vincenzo Bellini, Giuseppe Verdi, Richard Wagner, Richard Strauss, Giacomo Puccini, and Alban Berg. (See also *Musical comedy, Musical theater*.)

Pageant: Originally the platform or movable stage upon which medieval miracle and mystery plays were performed, the term has come to refer to any large-scale outdoor procession or performance.

Pantomime: Dramatic action communicated entirely by gesture and movement but not speech. Also, a type of theatrical entertainment developed in England in the eighteenth century. The story was usually acted out in both song and dance, and the scenery and stage effects could be quite lavish and spectacular. The form still survives in England in special Christmas entertainments designed for children.

Parabasis: Seven-part choral number occurring toward the middle of a Greek comedy that makes a direct appeal to the audience, requesting a prize or offering advice on current events.

Parodos: In classical Greek tragedy, the first scene in which the chorus appears and the first ode that the chorus sings are called *parodos*. The name derives from the entryway used by the chorus for entrances and exits. (See also *Chorus.*)

Passion play: Play that depicts the life, or incidents from the life, of a god. These plays had their origin in the pagan rites of ancient Egypt and the Near East. In Christian Europe, many medieval plays presented episodes from the life of Christ and are also referred to as Passion plays. The form still survives in various pageants in Europe and the Americas (particularly notable is the famous Oberammergau Passion play of Germany, performed every ten years).

Pastoral drama: Form of tragicomedy that was popular in the sixteenth and seventeenth centuries, originally a dramatic imitation of the bucolic idylls of Horace and Vergil. Pastoral drama represented a neoclassical vision of the rustic, Arcadian life and typically mingled such elements as unrequited love, intrigues of jealousy, and threats of death to the protagonists. These tragic elements are often happily resolved by the revelation of true relationships between characters or the triumph of love. The masterpiece of the genre (and one of the most influential theatrical works of the sixteenth century) is Battista Guarini's *Il pastor fido* (pr. 1596; *The Faithful Shepherd*, 1602). Another famous example is Torquato Tasso's sixteenth century play *Aminta* (pr. 1573).

Pathos: Quality in a dramatic character that evokes pity or sorrow from the audience.

Peripeteia: Sudden reversal of situation in a dramatic action. Aristotle gives as an example the arrival of the messenger in *Oedipus Tyrannus*, who believes he will relieve Oedipus's anxiety and accomplishes the reverse effect.

Pièce bien faite. See *Well-made play.*

Pièce de thèse. See *Problem play.*

Play-within-a-play: Play or dramatic fragment, performed as a scene or scenes within a larger drama, typically performed or viewed by the characters of the larger drama, such as the farcical "whodunit" in Tom Stoppard's *The Real Inspector Hound* (pr. 1968). In Elizabethan drama, the play-within-a-play was often performed as a dumb show, as in the play-

ers' scene in *Hamlet, Prince of Denmark*. (See also *Dumb show.*)

Plot: Sequence of the occurrence of events in a dramatic action. A plot may be unified around a single action, but it may also consist of a series of disconnected incidents—it is then referred to as "episodic."

Political theater: Broad term that typically refers to any production of a play that carries either an overt or covert sociopolitical message, provokes serious contemplation of social issues, or invokes an understanding of and sympathy for political causes. Often a dynamic tool for public instruction, propaganda, and entertainment, political theater instigates, examines, and sometimes even solves the problems inherent in human society. The two most common types of political theater include plays used to make a statement in order to change public sentiment concerning a social issue and those used directly to instigate social change as an agent of propaganda. Arthur Miller's *The Crucible* (pr. 1953), Amiri Baraka's *Slave Ship: A Historical Pageant* (pr. 1967), and Caryl Churchill's *Cloud Nine* (pr. 1979) are examples of political theater.

Postcolonial theater: Theatrical works primarily driven by, focused on, or concerned with the political, social, or cultural effects or aftermath of colonial dominance after a nation's independence. Postcolonial literature and theater often focuses on the "subaltern" (that is, those who are in a subordinate power position who fight, or have fought, the process and results of colonialism) finding their voice. Themes revolving around the intersections of nationalism, identity, and race, as well as protest and cultural revival, are often present in postcolonial dramatic works. Examples includes David Henry Hwang's *M. Butterfly* (pr. 1988), which studies the issues of Western colonialism, and Athol Fugard's *MASTER HAROLD . . . and the Boys* (pr. 1982) or *My Children! My Africa!* (pr. 1990), which examine the colonial legacy in South Africa.

Postmodernism: Term loosely applied to the various artistic movements that followed the era of so-called high modernism, represented by such giants as James Joyce and Pablo Picasso. The term typically refers to a work that calls attention to itself as an artifice rather than a mirror held up to external reality. In drama, the mixing of several available forms and styles, often in fanciful, experimental ways, is now labeled postmodernism, a special form of which is performance art. Typified by artists such as Laurie Anderson, a performance art piece might include an artist working alone and presenting a statement through multimedia, music, singing, storytelling, and stand-up comedy. Examples of postmodern plays include Dario Fo's *Morte accidentale di un anarchico* (pr. 1970; *Accidental Death of an Anarchist*, 1979), Caryl Churchill's *Top Girls* (pr. 1982), and Edward Albee's *Three Tall Women* (pr. 1991).

Presentationalism: An approach to playwriting and stage production that presents drama as an artificial, theatrical event rather than as a realistic representation of life. For example, classical Greek drama, with its masks, chorus, and circular stage, and Elizabethan drama, with its stark stage sets and blank verse, are presentational. (See also *Representationalism*.)

Problem play: Drama in which a social problem is illustrated and, usually, a solution is suggested. This form is also referred to as a thesis play (from the French *pièce de thèse*) and originated in the mid-nineteenth century in France. *Le Fils naturel* (pr. 1858; *The Natural Son*, 1879), by Alexandre Dumas, *fils*, is an early example. A number of Henrik Ibsen's plays can be categorized broadly as problem plays.

Prologue: Opening section of a play that often provides introductory information concerning the central action of the play. Also, a speech by an actor or chorus at the beginning of a play of an expository nature. The term is sometimes used to refer to the actor who recites such an introductory speech.

Properties: Usually abbreviated as "props." Properties are the movable objects (other than scenery or costumes) that appear on stage during a dramatic performance.

Proscenium: Part of a stage in front of the curtain. Also, the wall that separates the stage from the auditorium of a theater and provides the arch that frames the stage.

Protagonist: Originally, in the Greek drama, the first actor, who played the leading role. In a more general sense, the term has come to signify the most important character, usually a hero, in a drama or story. It is not unusual for there to be more than one protagonist in a play. (See also *Hero/Heroine*.)

Protasis: Section of a classical drama in which the characters are introduced and the dramatic situation is explained. The term "protatic character" has come to signify a character used only to assist in the exposition of a play and appearing nowhere else in the action.

Proverbe dramatique: Play—typically of one act—illustrating an aphorism that forms the play's title. This form began in France in the eighteenth century and was developed by Carmontelle, but its most famous practitioner was the nineteenth century poet and dramatist Alfred de Musset.

Psychological realism: Sigmund Freud's analysis of the complex psychological motivations behind human behavior led dramatists in the late nineteenth century to try to reproduce this psychological complexity in their characters rather than relying on character types. One of the earliest proponents of this psychological realism was August Strindberg (1849-1912), who argued that since human actions are caused by complex motivations in real life, they should be similarly portrayed on the stage.

Radio drama: Drama written for and performed over radio and popular in the United States between 1920 and 1940. Orson Welles was a well-known practitioner of radio drama.

Raisonneur: Character in a play, typically somewhat detached from the action, who acts as a spokesman for the author. This character observes the other characters involved more directly in the action and comments upon the action, expressing the author's views.

Realism: Broadly, any mode of art that attempts to present a replica of real life (as opposed to a fantastic or an ideal vision of life) and engage the audience in a reaction to the work as though it were real life. Particularly, realism was a reaction, beginning in the late nineteenth and early twentieth centuries, to fantastic, superhuman, melodramatic, idealistic, and otherwise Romantic forms of art and theater. Because realism sought to put forth the actual over the ideal, it necessarily replaced the exotic with the ordinary, the superhuman with the human, poetic and elevated language with familiar dialogue, the overblown and spectacular with the understated and domestic, and exaggerated or grandiose actions with those that are more plausible and often verbal or cerebral. Realist theater—characterized by a well-devised dramatic plot, with its emphasis on psychological truth and human pathos—tended to be sentimental and moralistic and to preach social reform. Realist playwrights rejected the idea of the well-made play with its mechanical artifices and slick plotting, as well as exaggerated theatricalism. Henrik Ibsen is considered the leader of this revolution in drama, and chief pioneers of dramatic realism in the twentieth century included Eugene O'Neill, Tennessee Williams, Arthur Miller, and Edward Albee. (See also *Romanticism, Russian realism, Well-made play.*)

Recognition. See *Anagnorisis.*

Renaissance drama: European drama produced from the early sixteenth to the late seventeenth centuries and often characterized by a concern for the classical ideals of composition and structure that are set forth in Aristotle's *Poetics* and are demonstrated in the works of classical dramatists such as Seneca, whose five-act plays were considered to epitomize the classical structure. Renaissance drama was also characterized by a humanitarian interest in secular subjects such as history, politics, and social issues, and this interest constituted a quite marked departure from the exclusively religious/allegorical concerns of medieval drama, evidenced in the miracle and morality plays. Renaissance drama first appeared in Italy during the early and mid-sixteenth century with playwrights such as Niccoló Machiavelli, Ludovico Ariosto, and Giangiorgio Trissino.

Repertory: Theater troupe or company that presents several different plays in alternation during the course of a season.

Representationalism: An approach to playwriting and staging that seeks to create the illusion of reality onstage through realistic characters and situations and/or through the use of realistic stage sets, properties, and acting styles. The Naturalistic drama advocated by the French novelist Émile Zola (1840-1902) and

practiced by French director André Antoine (1858-1943) at the turn of the twentieth century is an example of representationalism. The opposite approach to drama is presentationalism, which presents drama as a stylized, theatrical event. (See also *Presentationalism.*)

Restoration: Period in English history beginning with the restoration of Charles II to the throne, bringing an end to the Puritan interregnum, which had abolished the monarchy in 1649 and closed the theaters. The Restoration period has no precise end but is commonly held to have ended about 1700. As a result of the reopening of the London theaters, there was a surge of theatrical activity, and the period was known for the wealth of new drama produced by such dramatists as William Congreve, Sir George Etherege, William Wycherley, George Farquhar, and Oliver Goldsmith.

Revenge tragedy: Type of drama, particularly associated with the Elizabethan and Jacobean periods, in which revenge is the central motive. Thomas Kyd's *The Spanish Tragedy* (pr. c. 1585-1589) is said to have established the genre in English drama. Some other examples are Christopher Marlowe's *The Jew of Malta* (pr. c. 1589) and John Marston's *Antonio's Revenge* (pr. 1599). William Shakespeare's *Hamlet, Prince of Denmark* is, in an enlarged and very sophisticated sense, an example of this type of drama.

Reversal. See *Peripeteia.*

Revue: Theatrical production, typically consisting of sketches, song, and dance, which often comments satirically upon personalities and events of the day. Generally there is no plot involved, although some semblance of a unifying action or theme may unite the individual sketches and musical numbers.

Rising action: Part of a play preceding the climax. (See also *Anabasis, Freytag's pyramid.*)

Romantic comedy: Play in which love is the central motive of the dramatic action. The term often refers to plays of the Elizabethan period, such as William Shakespeare's *As You Like It* (pr. c. 1599) and *A Midsummer Night's Dream*, but it has also been applied to any modern work that contains similar features.

Romanticism: Broad term that at times fails to capture the complexity and multiplicity of European

Romanticism, which was manifested in different ways and different periods in European regions during the late eighteenth and nineteenth centuries. Generally, the genre exalted individualism over collectivism, revolution over conservatism, innovation over tradition, imagination over reason, and spontaneity over restraint. Romanticism regarded art as self-expression; it strove to heal the cleavage between object and subject and expressed a longing for the infinite in all things. It stressed the innate goodness of human beings and the evils of the institutions that would stultify human creativity. Other values associated with various schools of Romanticism include primitivism, an interest in folklore, a reverence for nature, and a fascination with the demoniac and the macabre.

Russian realism: Beginning in the mid-nineteenth century, a movement whose leaders included Ivan Turgenev, Aleksandr Ostrovsky, Leo Tolstoy, and later, Maxim Gorky. Anton Chekhov's plays *Chayka* (pr. 1896; *The Seagull*, 1909), *Dyadya Vanya* (pr. 1899; *Uncle Vanya*, 1914), *Tri sestry* (pr. 1901; *The Three Sisters*, 1920), and *Vishnyovy sad* (pr. 1904; *The Cherry Orchard*, 1908) are the best examples.

Satire: Dramatic satire employs the comedic devices of wit, irony, and exaggeration to expose and condemn human folly, vice, and stupidity. Although subject to political and societal repression throughout the centuries, dramatic satire appears in the classical Greek comedies of Aristophanes, in the personification of vices in the medieval morality plays, in the Renaissance plays of William Shakespeare and Ben Jonson, in the social satires of Oscar Wilde and George Bernard Shaw in the late nineteenth and early twentieth centuries, and in the twentieth century dramas of such dissimilar playwrights as Sean O'Casey and Harold Pinter.

Satyr play: In Greek drama, a performance composed of choric dances performed exclusively by actors dressed as satyrs. Not necessarily comic, the story was often derived from epics or legends and was associated with Dionysus.

Scenario: An outline of the dramatic action (plot) of a theatrical work, specifying the characters and the order of acts and scenes.

Scene: Division of action within an act (some plays are divided only into scenes instead of acts). Sometimes scene division indicates a change of setting or locale; sometimes it simply indicates the entrances and exits of characters; this latter case was, for example, the typical practice of the French neoclassical dramatists such as Pierre Corneille and Jean Racine. (See also *Act.*)

Scène à faire. See *Obligatory scene.*

School plays: Plays performed at secondary schools in sixteenth century England. These plays showed the influence of the classical comedy of Terence and Plautus and were composed both in Latin and in English. The earliest known example of the form in English, of about 1566, is Nicholas Udall's *Ralph Roister Doister.*

Sentimental comedy: With the rise of the middle class in the eighteenth century, a "new" audience patronized the theater, demanding drama which related to their social class and milieu and which upheld the traditionally accepted moral code that had brought them into increased position and power. The sentimental comedy was a type of play generally centered on the distresses of the middle class and intended to evoke the sympathies of the audience. Good and bad characters were often presented in a very schematic way without psychological complexity. Pleasurable tears, not laughter, were the mark of the successful sentimental drama. In England, the Restoration playwright George Farquhar anticipated some of the features of the sentimental comedy, but the true practitioners of the unadulterated form were playwrights such as Sir Richard Steele, Hugh Kelly, and Richard Cumberland. The corresponding development in French eighteenth century drama was the *comédie larmoyante* (tearful comedy), of which Philippe Destouches and Pierre-Claude Nivelle de La Chaussée are the chief proponents. (See also *Comédie larmoyante.*)

Set speech: Long, uninterrupted speech made by a single character to set forth a number of points. This device is prevalent in verse drama.

Setting: Time and place in which the action of a play happens. The term also applies to the physical elements of a theatrical production, such as scenery and properties.

Slapstick: Low comedy in which physical action (such as a kick in the rear, tripping, and knocking over people or objects) evokes laughter.

Social realism: Philosophical movement, begun in the early twentieth century, that raised political consciousness of the working classes and often criticized governments and regimes. By focusing on topics of social justice, the attitudes and problems of several social classes, and émigré identity, the form became popular with many "ethnic" dramatists by the 1960's and 1970's, including Latino, Native American, and Asian American playwrights.

Sock: Flat foot covering worn by actors in Greek comedy. In contrast, tragic actors wore high platform boots (buskins), which endowed them with increased stature, both physically and metaphorically. The sock was literally more down-to-earth. (See also *Buskin.*)

Soliloquy: Properly, an extended speech delivered by a character alone on stage, unheard by other characters. Soliloquy is a form of monologue, and it typically reveals the intimate thoughts and emotions of the speaker. (See also *Monologue.*)

Sottie: Form of medieval French farce that presented political, religious, or social satire.

Stasimon: Term for the odes sung by the chorus in classical Greek tragedy after the chorus had taken its place on the stage.

Stichomythia: In dramatic dialogue, a term referring to single lines, spoken alternately by two characters, which are characterized by repetitive patterns and antithesis. The Elizabethans, modeling after classical drama, used this type of dialogue with some frequency.

Stock character/situation: Frequently recurring dramatic type or dramatic incident or situation.

Strophe: In the choral odes of Greek drama, the strophe is a structural unit of lyric song and dance, similar to the stanza. The chorus sang and danced a strophe, followed by an antistrophe, which corresponded in form to the strophe. (See also *Antistrophe.*)

Sturm und Drang: Dramatic and literary movement in Germany during the late eighteenth century that took its name from Friedrich Maximilian Klinger's play of that title, published in 1777. Translated in English as "Storm and Stress," the movement was a reaction against classicism and a forerunner of Romanticism, characterized by extravagantly emotional language and sensational subject matter.

Subplot: Secondary action coincident with the main action of a play. A subplot may be a reflection (by means of contrast or similarity) upon the main action, but it may also be largely unrelated. (See also *Counterplot.*)

Surrealist drama: The term *drame surréaliste* (literally, "superrealistic drama") was originally coined in 1918 by Guillaume Apollinaire to describe his play *The Breasts of Tiresias* and was later modified and expanded by André Breton to describe a form of drama that focuses upon subconscious reality. The composition of such drama was often achieved by the practice of "automatic writing" and the study of dreams. The goal of Surrealist work is to restore the neglected subconscious to its rightful place alongside conscious perception.

Symbolism: Term commonly signifying a literary movement that originated in France in the latter part of the nineteenth century. Symbols have always been used in literature and drama, but as a conscious movement and practice, Symbolism achieved its most highly developed and defined form in the poetry of Stéphane Mallarmé and Arthur Rimbaud and in the plays of Maurice Maeterlinck. Drama was conceived as taking place in the mind and soul and was not felt to be truly expressed by outward action. The Symbolists, therefore, avoided the more traditional apparatus of dramatic construction: There are no strong, detailed characterizations; no true locus of crisis or conflict; no message or catharsis is intended. Action exists almost exclusively on a symbolic level and is conveyed through symbolic language, settings, lighting, sound effects, and so on. The influence of Symbolism was widespread and appears in the work of dramatists such as Leonid Andreyev, William Butler Yeats, Sean O'Casey, Anton Chekhov, and Eugene O'Neill.

Tableau. Silent, stationary grouping of performers in a theatrical performance. Also, an elaborate stage presentation featuring lavish settings and costumes as well as music and dance.

Theater of Cruelty: Term coined by French playwright and theorist Antonin Artaud to signify a vision in which theater becomes an arena for shock therapy. The characters undergo such intense physical and psychic extremities that the audience cannot ignore the cathartic effect in which its preconceptions, fears, and hostilities are brought to the surface and, ideally, purged. Startling noises, violent gestures, incantatory words or phrases, and unnerving lighting, music, and scenic effects all contribute to an atmosphere conducive to this curative goal.

Theater of the Absurd: General name given to a group of plays that share a basic belief that life is illogical, irrational, formless, and contradictory, and that human beings are without meaning or purpose. This philosophical perspective led to the abandonment of traditional theatrical forms and coherent dialogue. Practitioners have included writers as diverse as Eugene Ionesco, Samuel Beckett, Jean Genet, Harold Pinter, Edward Albee, and Arthur Kopit.

Theater of the Unspoken: (Théâtre de L'Inexprimé): A form of theater developed in France after World War I that emphasized the nonverbal elements of drama. It was created in response to the perception that earlier French theater was too verbose, containing too much dialogue. Practitioners include Jean-Jacques Bernard.

Théâtre Libre: French for "free theater." A private theater club founded by André Antoine in Paris in 1887 for the production of new Naturalistic plays. The innovations in settings, dramaturgy, direction, and acting had a great influence on the modern theater, helping liberate the stage from its early and mid-nineteenth century artificiality.

Thesis play. See *Problem play.*

Thespian: Another term for an actor; also, of or relating to the theater. The word derives from Thespis, by tradition the first actor of the Greek theater.

Three unities. See *Unities.*

Tirade: Technical term used in French drama (and particularly associated with the seventeenth century neoclassical theater) for a long set piece or uninterrupted speech delivered by a single character to other characters on stage. A tirade is not necessarily of an

angry or violent nature, as signified by the English cognate. The English term "harangue" is sometimes used as the technical equivalent.

Tragedy: In its broadest sense, a form of drama that is serious in action and intent. More specifically, Aristotle defined tragedy as an imitation of an action that is serious, complete in itself, and of a certain magnitude. He also specified that this action rouses pity and fear in the audience and purges these emotions. These rather broad criteria originally had specific meanings, which have undergone tremendous evolution from their inception through the present age—a single example is the notion of the tragic hero. Where in the ancient Greek theater the tragic heroes were typically personages of high rank and position (a king, queen, or nobleman), in the modern concept (particularly since the rise of the middle class in the eighteenth century) he or she would be a member of the middle or lower class. There has been much debate on the issue of whether "true tragedy" is even possible in the modern theater, and playwrights such as Eugene O'Neill and Arthur Miller have tried to incorporate the criteria of Aristotelian concepts in evoking tragic feeling or effects.

Tragedy, heroic. See *Heroic drama*

Tragedy, revenge. See *Revenge tragedy.*

Tragic flaw. See *Hamartia.*

Tragicomedy: Play in which the dramatic action, which ostensibly is leading to a tragic outcome, is reversed and concluded happily. This somewhat loose form mingled elements theoretically associated with tragedy (such as noble characters and an action ending in death) and those theoretically associated with comedy (such as lower-class or trivial characters and an action ending happily in celebration). The term is often associated with the early seventeenth century plays of Francis Beaumont and John Fletcher. Wolfgang Amadeus Mozart's opera *Don Giovanni* (pr. 1787) is a famous example of this form in musical theater.

Trope: Brief dialogue, often accompanied by music, used in early medieval religious services to dramatize certain portions of the liturgy. As tropes became more elaborate, they were separated from the religious service and evolved into liturgical drama, which later evolved into the medieval mystery and morality plays. (See also *Corpus Christi plays, Liturgical drama, Miracle play.*)

Unities: Set of rules for proper dramatic construction formulated by Italian and French Renaissance dramatic critics (particularly Ludovico Castelvetro), purported to be derived from the *Poetics* of Aristotle. The "three unities" were concerned with the standards governing the action, time, and setting of a drama: A play should have no scenes or subplots irrelevant to the central action, should not cover a period of more than twenty-four hours, and should not occur in more than one place or locale. In reality, Aristotle insists only upon unity of action in tragedy, and simply observes that most extant examples of Greek tragedy covered a period of less than a full day (there is absolutely no indication of the concept of unity of place). This formulation held particular sway over dramaturgy in France in the seventeenth century and persisted there virtually unchallenged until the introduction of the Romantic drama in the early nineteenth century.

Vaudeville: Variety show popular in the United States and Europe from the 1890's to the 1930's, vaudeville featured songs, comic playlets, animal acts, and sketches. These theatrical entertainments were a refined version of the nineteenth century form of burlesque.

Verse drama: Written in a poetic form and intended primarily as theater rather than as literature, verse drama was the prevailing form for Western drama throughout most of its history, comprising all the drama of classical Greece and continuing to dom-inate the stage through the Renaissance, when it was best exemplified by the blank verse of Elizabethan drama. In the seventeenth century, however, prose comedies became popular, and in the nineteenth and twentieth centuries verse drama became the exception rather than the rule.

Weeping comedy. See *Comédie larmoyante.*

Well-made play: From the French term *pièce bien faite,* a type of play constructed according to a "formula" which originated in nineteenth century France. The most prolific practitioner of the form was Eugene Scribe (1791-1861). Scribe took dramatic devices, which had been part of comedy and tragedy since the classical theater, and wove them into a formula that he repeated with little or no variation as the underlying frame for the plot construction of his enormous theatrical canon. The plot of a *pièce bien faite* often revolves around a secret known only to some of the characters, which is revealed at the climax and leads to catastrophe for the villain and vindication or triumph for the hero. Misunderstanding, suspense, and coincidence are some of the devices used in the unraveling of the plot. The well-made play provided a form for the developing social drama of such playwrights as Emile Augier and Alexandre Dumas, *fils,* and influenced later playwrights such as Henrik Ibsen and George Bernard Shaw.

Zanni: Stock buffoon character from the *commedia dell'arte* representing the madcap comic servant. Harlequin is the best known of this type.

Theodore Baroody,
revised by the editors

MAJOR AWARDS

PULITZER PRIZE IN DRAMA WINNERS

In 1903, Joseph Pulitzer, a prominent American journalist and owner of two major newspapers, made a gift of $2 million to New York's Columbia University. His will stipulated that $550,000 of that sum be reserved to fund prizes in journalism, letters, and music. In 1912, an Advisory Board of the School of Journalism (later renamed the Pulitzer Prize Board) was created to administer the prizes.

The drama award was added in 1917, although no prize was awarded that year. Stipulations asserted that a play could be considered only if it has been performed in New York during the twelve months between March 2 of a given year to March 1 of the following year, and only if it represented the educational value and power of the stage in raising the standard of good morals, good taste, and good manners. Plays original in their sources and that dealt with American life were given preference. No award was given in years when the Pulitzer Prize board deemed its standard of excellence was not met by the field of potential competitors.

1917 (No award)
1918 *Why Marry?* by Jesse Lynch Williams
1919 (No award)
1920 *Beyond the Horizon* by Eugene O'Neill
1921 *Miss Lulu Bett* by Zona Gale
1922 *Anna Christie* by Eugene O'Neill
1923 *Icebound* by Owen Davis
1924 *Hell-Bent fer Heaven* by Hatcher Hughes
1925 *They Knew What They Wanted* by Sidney Howard
1926 *Craig's Wife* by George Kelly
1927 *In Abraham's Bosom* by Paul Green
1928 *Strange Interlude* by Eugene O'Neill
1929 *Street Scene* by Elmer L. Rice
1930 *The Green Pastures* by Marc Connelly
1931 *Alison's House* by Susan Glaspell
1932 *Of Thee I Sing* by George S. Kaufman, Morrie Ryskind, and Ira Gershwin
1933 *Both Your Houses* by Maxwell Anderson
1934 *Men in White* by Sidney Kingsley
1935 *The Old Maid* by Zoe Akins
1936 *Idiot's Delight* by Robert E. Sherwood
1937 *You Can't Take It with You* by Moss Hart and George S. Kaufman
1938 *Our Town* by Thornton Wilder
1939 *Abe Lincoln in Illinois* by Robert E. Sherwood
1940 *The Time of Your Life* by William Saroyan
1941 *There Shall Be No Night* by Robert E. Sherwood
1942 (No award)
1943 *The Skin of Our Teeth* by Thornton Wilder
1944 (No award)
1945 *Harvey* by Mary Chase
1946 *State of the Union* by Russel Crouse and Howard Lindsay

1947   (No award)

1948   *A Streetcar Named Desire* by Tennessee Williams

1949   *Death of a Salesman* by Arthur Miller

1950   *South Pacific* by Richard Rodgers, Oscar Hammerstein II, and Joshua Logan

1951   (No award)

1952   *The Shrike* by Joseph Kramm

1953   *Picnic* by William Inge

1954   *The Teahouse of the August Moon* by John Patrick

1955   *Cat on a Hot Tin Roof* by Tennessee Williams

1956   *Diary of Anne Frank* by Albert Hackett and Frances Goodrich

1957   *Long Day's Journey into Night* by Eugene O'Neill

1958   *Look Homeward, Angel* by Ketti Frings

1959   *J. B.* by Archibald Macleish

1960   *Fiorello!* (book by Jerome Weidman and George Abbott, music by Jerry Bock, and lyrics by Sheldon Harnick)

1961   *All the Way Home* by Tad Mosel

1962   *How to Succeed in Business Without Really Trying* by Frank Loesser and Abe Burrows

1963   (No award)

1964   (No award)

1965   *The Subject Was Roses* by Frank D. Gilroy

1966   (No award)

1967   *A Delicate Balance* by Edward Albee

1968   (No award)

1969   *The Great White Hope* by Howard Sackler

1970   *No Place to Be Somebody* by Charles Gordone

1971   *The Effect of Gamma Rays on Man-in-the-Moon Marigolds* by Paul Zindel

1972   (No award)

1973   *That Championship Season* by Jason Miller

1974   (No award)

1975   *Seascape* by Edward Albee

1976   *A Chorus Line* (book by James Kirkwood and Nicholas Dante, music by Marvin Hamlisch, and lyrics by Edward Kleban)

1977   *The Shadow Box* by Michael Cristofer

1978   *The Gin Game* by Donald L. Coburn

1979   *Buried Child* by Sam Shepard

1980   *Talley's Folly* by Lanford Wilson

1981   *Crimes of the Heart* by Beth Henley

1982   *A Soldier's Play* by Charles Fuller

1983   *'Night, Mother* by Marsha Norman

1984   *Glengarry Glen Ross* by David Mamet

1985   *Sunday in the Park with George* (book by James Lapine, music and lyrics by Stephen Sondheim)

1986   (No award)

1987   *Fences* by August Wilson

1988   *Driving Miss Daisy* by Alfred Uhry

1989   *The Heidi Chronicles* by Wendy Wasserstein

1990   *The Piano Lesson* by August Wilson
1991   *Lost in Yonkers* by Neil Simon
1992   *The Kentucky Cycle* by Robert Schenkkan
1993   *Angels in America: A Gay Fantasia on National Themes* (*Part One: Millennium Approaches*) by Tony
           Kushner
1994   *Three Tall Women* by Edward Albee
1995   *The Young Man From Atlanta* by Horton Foote
1996   *Rent* by Jonathan Larson
1997   (No award)
1998   *How I Learned to Drive* by Paula Vogel
1999   *Wit* by Margaret Edson
2000   *Dinner with Friends* by Donald Margulies
2001   *Proof* by David Auburn
2002   *Topdog/Underdog* by Suzan-Lori Parks

OBIE AWARDS

The Village Voice Obie Awards were instituted during the 1955-1956 theatrical season, and were established to recognize the important and significant dramatic activities that flourished Off-Broadway in the dozens of small venues that were used for the presentation of plays that could not, for various reasons, be performed on Broadway. The Obies are unique in that they do not limit the number of honorees in any category and are not tightly bound by structured and immutable categories. From year to year, categories are added while others are dropped.

AWARD FOR PLAYWRITING

1974-1975   Sam Shepard for *Action*
                    Wallace Shawn for *Our Late Night*
                    Lanford Wilson for *The Mound Builders*
                    Ed Bullins for *The Taking of Miss Janie*

1975-1976   (No award)
1976-1977   David Rudkin for *Ashes*
                    Albert Innaurato for *Gemini* and *The Transfiguration of Benno Blimpie*
                    Willam Hauptman for *Domino Courts*
                    Maria Irene Fornes for *Fefu and Her Friends*
                    David Berry for *G. R. Point*

1977-1978   (No award)
1978-1979   Sam Shepard for *Buried Child*
                    Bernard Pomerance for *The Elephant Man*
                    Richard Nelson for *Vienna Notes*
                    Susan Miller for *Nasty Rumors and Final Remarks*
                    Rosalyn Drexler for *The Writer's Opera*

1979-1980　Jeff Weiss for *That's How the Rent Gets Paid (Part Three)* (script and direction)
　　　　　　Roland Muldoon for *Full Confessions of a Socialist* (script and direction)
　　　　　　Romulus Linney for *Tennessee*
　　　　　　Christopher Durang for *Sister Mary Ignatius Explains It All for You*
　　　　　　Lee Breuer for *A Prelude to Death in Venice*

1980-1981　Len Jenkin for *Limbo Tales* (script and direction)
　　　　　　Amlin Gray for *How I Got That Story: A Play in Two Acts*
　　　　　　Charles Fuller for *Zooman and the Sign*
　　　　　　Caryl Churchill for *Cloud Nine*
　　　　　　Robert Auletta for *Stops* and *Virgins*

1982-1983　Tina Howe, Distinguished Playwriting award
　　　　　　Harry Kondoleon, Most Promising Young Playwright
　　　　　　Caryl Churchill for *Top Girls*

1983-1984　Ted Tally for *Terra Nova*
　　　　　　Franz Xaver Kroetz for *Wer durchs Laub geht . . . (Through the Leaves)* and *Mensch Meier*
　　　　　　Len Jenkin for *Five of Us*
　　　　　　Václav Havel for *A Private View*
　　　　　　Maria Irene Fornes for *The Danube, Sarita,* and *Mud*
　　　　　　Samuel Beckett for *Ohio Imromptu, What Where, Catastrophe,* and *Pocket*

1984-1985　William M. Hoffman for *As Is*
　　　　　　Rosalyn Drexler for *Transients Welcome*
　　　　　　Christopher Durang for *The Marriage of Bette and Boo*

1985-1986　Lee Nagrin for *Bird/Bear*
　　　　　　Tadeusz Kantor for *Niech sczeną artykci (Let the Artists Die)*
　　　　　　John Jesurun for *Deep Sleep*
　　　　　　Martha Clarke for *Vienna: Lusthaus*
　　　　　　Eric Bogosian for *Drinking in America*

1986-1990　(No awards)
1990-1991　Mac Wellman for *Sincerity Forever*
　　　　　　John Guare for *Six Degrees of Separation*

1991-1992　Romulus Linney, Sustained Excellence in Playwriting
　　　　　　Neal Bell, Sustained Excellence in Playwriting

1992-1993　Paul Rudnick for *Jeffrey*
　　　　　　José Rivera for *Marisol*
　　　　　　Larry Kramer for *The Destiny of Me*
　　　　　　Harry Kondoleon for *The Houseguests*

1993-1994　Howard Korder for *The Lights*
　　　　　　Eric Bogosian for *Pounding Nails in the Floor with My Forehead*

1994-1995 Susan Miller for *My Left Breast*
           Terrence McNally for *Love! Valor! Compassion!* and *A Perfect Ganesh*
           Tony Kushner for *Slavs! (Thinking About the Longstanding Problems of Virtue and Happiness)*
           David Hancock for *The Convention of Cartography*

1995-1996 Doug Wright for *Quills*
           Suzan-Lori Parks for *Venus*
           Donald Margulies for *The Model Apartment*
           Ain Gordon for *Wally's Ghost*

1996-1997 Lanford Wilson for *Sympathetic Magic*
           Paula Vogel for *How I Learned to Drive*
           David Henry Hwang for *Golden Child*
           Eve Ensler for *The Vagina Monologues*

1997-1999 (No awards)
1999-2000 Harley Granville Barker for *Waste*

2000-2001 José Rivera for *References to Salvador Dali Make Me Hot*

2001-2002 Tony Kushner for *Homebody/Kabul*
           Melissa James Gibson for *[sic]*

AWARD FOR BEST PLAY

1957-1958 *The Brothers Karamazov* by Boris Tumarin and Jack Sydow

1963-1964 *Play* by Samuel Beckett

1993-1994 *Twilight: Los Angeles 1992* by Anna Deavere Smith

1994-1995 *Cryptogram* by David Mamet

1996-1997 *One Flea Spare* by Naomi Wallace

1997-1998 *Pearls for Pigs and Benita Canova* by Richard Foreman

2000-2001 *The Syringa Tree* by Pamela Glen

BEST NEW AMERICAN PLAY

1974-1975 *The First Breeze of Summer* by Leslie Lee

1975-1976 *American Buffalo* and *Sexual Perversity in Chicago* by David Mamet

1976-1977 *Curse of the Starving Class* by Sam Shepard

1977-1978 *Shaggy Dog Animation* by Lee Breuer

1978-1979 *Josephine, the Mouse Singer* by Michael McClure

1980-1981 *F.O.B.* by David Henry Hwang

1981-1982 *Mr. Dead and Mrs. Free* (theater piece, no playwright)
           Metamorphosis in Miniature (theater piece, no playwright)

1982-1983 *Edmond* by David Mamet

1983-1984 *Fool for Love* by Sam Shepard

1984-1985 *The Conduct of Life* by Maria Irene Fornes

1986-1987   *The Cure* and *Film Is Evil: Radio Is Good* by Richard Foreman

1987-1988   *Abingdon Square* by Maria Irene Fornes
            Serious Money by Caryl Churchill

1989-1990   *Bad Penny, Crowbar,* and *Terminal Hip* by Mac Wellman
            Imperceptible Metabolites in the Third Kingdom by Suzan-Lori Parks
            Prelude to a Kiss by Craig Lucas

1990-1991   *The Fever* by Wallace Shawn

1991-1992   *The Baltimore Waltz* by Paula Vogel
            Sally's Rape by Robbie McCauley
            Sight Unseen by Donald Margulies

1995-1996   *Sleep Deprivation Chamber* and *June and Jean in Concert* by Adrienne Kennedy (no later awards)

TONY AWARDS

The American Theatre Wing's Antoinette Perry Awards, popularly known as the Tony Awards, have been presented for distinguished achievement in the theater since 1947. Tony Award categories have changed and grown through the years. To be eligible for a Tony Award, a play must have opened during the current Broadway season in a Broadway theater with a minimum of 499 seats.

1947   Author   Arthur Miller for *All My Sons*

1948   Play   *Mister Roberts* by Thomas Heggen and Joshua Logan; based on the Thomas Heggen novel
       Author   Thomas Heggen and Joshua Logan for *Mister Roberts*

1949   Play   *Death of a Salesman* by Arthur Miller
       Author   Arthur Miller for *Death of a Salesman*
       Musical   *Kiss Me Kate.* Book by Bella and Samuel Spewack. Music and lyrics by Cole Porter

1950   Play   *The Cocktail Party* by T.S. Eliot. Produced by Gilbert Miller
       Musical   *South Pacific.* Book by Oscar Hammerstein II and Joshua Logan. Music by Richard
                 Rodgers, lyrics by Oscar Hammerstein II

1951   Play   *The Rose Tattoo* by Tennessee Williams. Produced by Cheryl Crawford
       Musical   *Guys and Dolls.* Book by Jo Swerling and Abe Burrows. Music and lyrics by Frank
                 Loesser

1952   Play   *The Fourposter* by Jan de Hartog
       Musical   *The King and I.* Book and lyrics by Oscar Hammerstein II. Music by Richard Rodgers

1953   Play   *The Crucible* by Arthur Miller. Produced by Kermit Bloomgarden
       Musical   *Wonderful Town.* Book by Joseph Fields and Jerome Chodorov. Music by Leonard
                 Bernstein, lyrics by Betty Comden and Adolph Green

1954   Play   *The Teahouse of the August Moon* by John Patrick. Produced by Maurice Evans and George
                 Schaefer
       Musical   *Kismet.* Book by Charles Lederer and Luther Davis. Music by Alexander Borodin, adapted
                 and with lyrics by Robert Wright and George Forrest

1955   Play   *The Desperate Hours* by Joseph Hayes. Produced by Howard Erskine and Joseph Hayes
        Musical *The Pajama Game.* Book by George Abbot and Richard Bissell. Music and lyrics by Richard Adler and Jerry Ross

1956   Play   *The Diary of Anne Frank* by Frances Goodrich and Albert Hackett. Produced by Kermit Bloomgarden
        Musical *Damn Yankees.* Book by George Abbot and Douglass Wallop. Music by Richard Adler and Jerry Ross

1957   Play   *Long Day's Journey into Night* by Eugene O'Neill. Produced by Leigh Connell, Theodore Mann, and José Quintero
        Musical *My Fair Lady.* Book and lyrics by Alan Jay Lerner. Music by Frederick Loewe

1958   Play   *Sunrise at Campobello* by Dore Schary. Produced by Lawrence Langner, Theresa Helburn, Armina Marshall, and Dore Schary
        Musical *The Music Man.* Book by Meredith Willson and Franklin Lacey. Music and lyrics by Meredith Willson

1959   Play   *J. B.* by Archibald MacLeish. Produced by Alfred de Liagre, Jr.
        Musical *Redhead.* Book by Herbert and Dorothy Fields, Sidney Sheldon, and David Shaw. Music by Albert Hague, lyrics by Dorothy Fields

1960   Play   *The Miracle Worker* by William Gibson. Produced by Fred Coe
        Musical (tie) *The Sound of Music.* Book by Howard Lindsay and Russel Crouse. Music by Richard Rodgers, lyrics by Oscar Hammerstein II
        Fiorello! Book by Jerome Weidman and George Abbot. Music by Jerry Bock, lyrics by Sheldon Harnick

1961   Play   *Beckett* by Jean Anouilh, translated by Lucienne Hill. Produced by David Merrick
        Musical *Bye, Bye, Birdie.* Book by Michael Stewart. Music by Charles Strouse, lyrics by Lee Adams

1962   Play   *A Man for All Seasons* by Robert Bolt. Produced by Robert Whitehead and Roger L. Steven
        Musical *How to Succeed in Business Without Really Trying.* Book by Abe Burrows, Jack Weinstock, and Willie Gilbert. Music and lyrics by Frank Loesser

1963   Play   *Who's Afraid of Virginia Woolf?* by Edward Albee. Produced by Theatre 1963, Richard Barr, and Clinton Wilder
        Musical *A Funny Thing Happened on the Way to the Forum.* Book by Burt Shevelove and Larry Gelbart. Music and lyrics by Stephen Sondheim

1964   Play   *Luther* by John Osborne. Produced by David Merrick
        Musical *Hello, Dolly!* Book by Michael Stewart. Music and lyrics by Jerry Herman

1965   Play   *The Subject Was Roses* by Frank Gilroy. Produced by Edgar Lansbury
        Musical *Fiddler on the Roof.* Book by Joseph Stein. Music by Jerry Bock, lyrics by Sheldon Harnick

1966   Play   *Marat/Sade* by Peter Weiss. English version by Geoffrey Skelton. Produced by the David Merrick Arts Foundation
        Musical *Man of La Mancha.* Book by Dale Wasserman. Music by Mitch Leigh, lyrics by Joe Darion

1967	Play	*The Homecoming* by Harold Pinter. Produced by Alexander H. Cohen
	Musical	*Cabaret*. Book by Joe Masteroff. Music by John Kander, lyrics by Fred Ebb
1968	Play	*Rosencrantz and Guildenstern Are Dead* by Tom Stoppard. Produced by the David Merrick Arts Foundation
	Musical	*Hallelujah, Baby!* Book by Arthur Laurents. Music by Jule Styne, lyrics by Betty Comden and Adolph Green
1969	Play	*The Great White Hope* by Howard Sackler. Produced by Herman Levin
	Musical	*1776*. Book by Peter Stone. Music and lyrics by Sherman Edwards
1970	Play	*Borstal Boy* by Frank McMahon. Produced by Michael McAloney and Burton C. Kaiser
	Musical	*Applause*. Book by Betty Comden and Adolph Green. Music by Charles Strouse, lyrics by Lee Adams
1971	Play	*Sleuth* by Anthony Shaffer. Produced by Helen Bonfils, Morton Gottlieb, and Michael White
	Musical	*Company*. Book by George Furth. Music and lyrics by Stephen Sondheim
1972	Play	*Sticks and Bones* by David Rabe. Produced by the New York Shakespeare Festival and Joseph Papp
	Musical	*Two Gentlemen of Verona*. Book adapted by John Guare and Mel Shapiro. Music by Galt MacDermot, lyrics by John Guare
1973	Play	*That Championship Season* by Jason Miller. Produced by the New York Shakespeare Festival and Joseph Papp
	Musical	*A Little Night Music*. Book by Hugh Wheeler. Music and lyrics by Stephen Sondheim
1974	Play	*The River Niger* by Joseph A. Walker. Produced by the Negro Ensemble Company
	Musical	*Raisin*. Book by Robert Nemiroff and Charlotte Zaltzberg. Music by Judd Woldin, lyrics by Robert Brittan
1975	Play	*Equus* by Peter Shaffer. Produced by Kermit Bloomgarden and Doris Cole Abrahams
	Musical	*The Wiz*. Book by William F. Brown. Music and lyrics by Charlie Smalls
1976	Play	*Travesties* by Tom Stoppard. Produced by David Merrick, Doris Cole Abrahams, and Burry Fredrik in association with S. Spencer Davids and Eddie Kulukundis
	Musical	*A Chorus Line*. Music by Marvin Hamlisch, lyrics by Edward Kleban
1977	Play	*The Shadow Box* by Michael Cristofer. Produced by Allan Francis, Ken Marsolais, Lester Osterman, and Leonard Soloway
	Musical	*Annie*. Book by Thomas Meehan. Music by Charles Strouse, lyrics by Martin Charnin
1978	Play	*Da* by Hugh Leonard. Produced by Lester Osterman, Marilyn Strauss, and Marc Howard
	Musical	*Ain't Misbehavin'*. Based on an idea by Richard Maltby, Jr. and Murray Horwitz. Music by Thomas "Fats" Waller, featuring songs by numerous artists
1979	Play	*The Elephant Man* by Bernard Pomerance. Produced by Richmond Crinkley, Elizabeth I. McCann, and Nelle Nugent
	Musical	*Sweeney Todd*. Book by Hugh Wheeler. Music and lyrics by Stephen Sondheim

1980	Play	*Children of a Lesser God* by Mark Medoff. Produced by Emanuel Azenberg, the Shubert Organization, Dasha Epstein, and Ron Dante
	Musical	*Evita*. Book by Tim Rice. Music by Andrew Lloyd Webber, lyrics by Tim Rice
1981	Play	*Amadeus* by Peter Shaffer. Produced by the Shubert Organization, Elizabeth I. McCann, Nelle Nugent, and Roger S. Berlind
	Musical	*42nd Street*. Book by Michael Stewart and Mark Bramble. Music by Harry Warren, lyrics by Al Dubin
1982	Play	*The Life and Adventures of Nicholas Nickleby* by David Edgar. Produced by James M. Nederlander, the Shubert Organization, Elizabeth I. McCann, and Nelle Nugent
	Musical	*Nine*. Book by Arthur Kopit. Music and lyrics by Maury Yeston
1983	Play	*Torch Song Trilogy* by Harvey Fierstein. Produced by Kenneth Waissman, Martin Markinson, Lawrence Lane, John Glines, BetMar, and Donald Tick
	Musical	*Cats*. Book by T. S. Eliot. Music by Andrew Lloyd Webber, lyrics by T. S. Eliot, additional lyrics by Trevor Nunn and Richard Stilgoe
1984	Play	*The Real Thing* by Tom Stoppard. Produced by Emanuel Azenberg, the Shubert Organization, Icarus Productions, Byron Goldman, Ivan Bloch, Roger Berlind, and Michael Codron
	Musical	*La Cage aux folles*. Book by Harvey Fierstein. Music and lyrics by Jerry Herman
1985	Play	*Biloxi Blues* by Neil Simon. Produced by Emanuel Azenberg, and the Center Theater Group/Ahmanson Theatre, Los Angeles
	Musical	*Big River*. Book by William Hauptman. Music and lyrics by Roger Miller
1986	Play	*I'm Not Rappaport* by Herb Gardner. Produced by James Walsh, Lewis Allen, and Martin Heinfling
	Musical	*The Mystery of Edwin Drood*. Book, music, and lyrics by Rupert Holmes
1987	Play	*Fences* by August Wilson. Produced by Carole Shorenstein Hays and the Yale Repertory Theatre
	Musical	*Les Misérables*. Book by Alain Boublil and Claude-Michel Schönberg. Music by Claude-Michel Schönberg, lyrics by herbert Kretzmer
1988	Play	*M. Butterfly* by David Henry Hwang. Produced by Stuart Ostrow and David Geffen
	Musical	*The Phantom of the Opera*. Book by Richard Stilgoe and Andrew Lloyd Webber. Music by Andrew Lloyd Webber, lyrics by Charles Hart and Richard Stilgoe
1989	Play	*The Heidi Chronicles* by Wendy Wasserstein. Produced by the Shubert Organization, Suntory International Corp., James Walsh, and Playwrights Horizons
	Musical	*Jerome Robbins Broadway*. Music orchestrated by Sid Ramin and William D. Brohn, music continuity by Scott Frankel. Featuring songs from numerous artists
1990	Play	*The Grapes of Wrath* by Frank Galati. Produced by the Shubert Organization, Steppenwolf Theater Co., Suntory International Corp, and Jujamcyn Theaters
	Musical	*City of Angels*. Book by Larry Gelbart. Music by Cy Coleman, lyrics by David Zippel
1991	Play	*Lost in Yonkers* by Neil Simon. Produced by Emanuel Azenberg
	Musical	*The Will Rogers Follies*. Book by Peter Stone. Music by Cy Coleman, lyrics by Betty Comden and Adolph Green

1992	Play	*Dancing at Lughnasa* by Brian Friel. Produced by Noel Pearson, Bill Kenwright, and Joseph Harris
	Musical	*Crazy for You.* Book by Ken Ludwig. Music by George Gershwin, lyrics by Ira Gershwin
1993	Play	*Angels in America: A Gay Fantasia on National Themes* (*Part One: Millennium Approaches*) by Tony Kushner. Produced by Jujamcyn Theaters, Mark Taper Forum/Gordon Davidson, Margo Lion, Susan Quint Gallin, Jon B. Platt, the Baruch-Frankel-Viertel Group, Frederick Zollo, and Herb Alpert
	Musical	*Kiss of the Spider Woman—The Musical.* Book by Terrence McNally. Music by John Kander, lyrics by Fred Ebb
1994	Play	*Angels in America, A Gay Fantasia on National Themes* (*Part Two: Perestroika*) by Tony Kushner. Produced by Jujamcyn Theaters, Mark Taper Forum/Gordon Davidson, Margo Lion, Susan Quint Gallin, Jon B. Platt, The Baruch-Frankel-Viertel Group, and Frederick Zollo, in association with the New York Shakespeare Festival, Mordecai/Cole Productions, and Herb Alpert
	Musical	*Passion.* Book by James Lapine. Music and lyrics by Stephen Sondheim
1995	Play	*Love! Valour! Compassion!* By Terrence McNally. Produced by Manhattan Theatre Club, Lynne Meadow, Barry Grove, and Jujamcyn Theatres
	Musical	*Sunset Boulevard.* Book by Don Black and Christopher Hampton. Music by Andrew Lloyd Webber, lyrics by Don Black and Christopher Hampton
1996	Play	*Master Class* by Terrence McNally. Produced by Robert Whitehead, Lewis Allen, Spring Sirkin
	Musical	*Rent.* Book, music, and lyrics by Jonathan Larson
1997	Play	*The Last Night of Ballyhoo* by Alfred Uhry. Produced by Jane Harmon, Nina Keneally, Liz Oliver
	Musical	*Titanic.* Book by Peter Stone. Music and lyrics by Maury Yeston
1998	Play	*Art* by Yasmina Reza. Produced by David Pugh, Sean Connery, Joan Cullman
	Musical	*The Lion King.* Book by Roger Allers and Irene Mecchi. Music by Elton John, lyrics by Tim Rice
1999	Play	*Side Man* by Warren Leight. Produced by Weissberger Theater Group, Jay Harris, Peter Manning, Roundabout Theatre Company, Todd Haimes, Ellen Richard, Ron Kastner, James Cushing, Joan Stein
	Musical	*Fosse.* Music orchestrated by Ralph Burns and Douglas Besterman, music arranged by Gordon Lowry Harrell and featuring songs by numerous artists
2000	Play	*Copenhagen* by Michael Frayn. Produced by Michael Codron, Lee Dean, the Royal National Theatre, James M. Nederlander, Roger Berlind, Scott Rudin, Elizabeth I. McCann, Ray Larson, Jon B. Platt, Byron Goldman, Scott Nederlander
	Musical	*Contact.* Book by John Weidman

2001	Play	*Proof* by David Auburn. Produced by Manhattan Theatre Club, Lynne Meadow, Barry Grove, Roger Berlind, Carole Shorenstein Hays, Jujamcyn Theaters, Ostar Enterprises, Daryl Roth, Stuart Thompson
	Musical	*The Producers, the New Mel Brooks Musical.* Book by Mel Brooks and Thomas Meehan. Music and lyrics by Mel Brooks
2002	Play	*The Goat: Or, Who is Sylvia?* by Edward Albee. Producers: Elizabeth Ireland McCann, Daryl Roth, Carole Shorenstein Hays, Terry Allen Kramer, Scott Rudin, Bob Boyett, Scott Nederlander, Sine/ZPI
	Musical	*Thoroughly Modern Millie.* Book by Richard Morris and Dick Scanlan. Music by Jeanine Tesori, lyrics by Dick Scanlan

TIME LINE

c. 30,000 B.C.E	Protodramas performed by Ice Age peoples.
c. 20,000-15,000 B.C.E	Cave drawings in France, Spain, and Africa show performers in animal costumes.
c. 4,000-2,000 B.C.E	"Pyramid texts" confirm existence of drama in ancient Egypt.
c. 2,000 B.C.E	Beginning of Egyptian Abydos passion play, dedicated to the god Osiris, as detailed on the Ikhernofret stele.
1500 B.C.E	Chinese emperors sponsor dramatic presentations at court.
534 B.C.E	Pisistratus, ruler of Athens, legalizes the Dionysia, an annual drama festival and play contest in honor of the god Dionysus. Thespis is named the first *archon* (producer) of the festival and is first to win a prize for a tragedy production.
499-408 B.C.E	Aeschylus, Sophocles, and Euripides write the great Greek tragedies.
487 B.C.E	Comedies are added to the Dionysian drama contests.
429 B.C.E	Sophocles writes his tragic masterpiece, *Oidipous Tyrannos* (*Oedipus Tyrannus*, 1715).
411 B.C.E	Aristophanes writes his comic masterpiece, *Lysistraté* (*Lysistrata*, 1837).
400-300 B.C.E	Greek tragedy declines.
c. 342-291 B.C.E	Life of Menander, important writer of Greek New Comedy genre, whose masterpiece is *Dyskolos* (317 B.C.E.; *The Bad-tempered Man*).
c. 334-323 B.C.E	Aristotle writes *De poetica* (*Poetics*, 1705), the first major work of literary and drama criticism.
c. 254-184 B.C.E	Plautus and Terence bring Roman comedy to its heights.
c. 17 B.C.E	Horace writes *Ars poetica* (*The Art of Poetry*, 1567), which will influence literary and dramatic theory during the Renaissance.
c. 4 B.C.E-65 C.E.	Life of Roman tragedian Seneca, whose work is influential in the Renaissance.
200 B.C.E-300 C.E.	*Nātya-śāstra* (*The Nātya śastra*, 1950), a study on dramaturgy, appears in India.
c. 300-600	Sanskrit drama, such as *Mŗcchakaţikā* (*Mrchhakatika*, 1898, also known as *The Little Clay Cart*, 1905), emerges in India.
527	Conversion of Byzantine empress Theodora to Christianity draws all dramatic performances to an end.
550-900	Drama is discouraged in Europe by the Christian Church.
714	Chinese rulers establish a drama school known as the Pear Garden.
c. 925	The first dramatic trope, or sacred play, presented inside a church as part of a Christian mass.
c. 935-972	Life of Hrosvitha of Gandersheim, a Christian nun and writer of six religious comedies in the style of Roman dramatist Terence.

c. 1000   Javanese shadow puppet plays are presented at the Javanese court.

c. 1100   Tropes move out of European churches to be presented in village squares.

1151   Hildegard of Bingen writes the first morality play, *Ordo Virtutum*.

c. 1200   Mature Chinese drama emerges.

c. 1200-1500   Medieval cycle plays, mysteries, and moralities are staged in village squares throughout Europe. Among these plays is *Secunda Pastorum* (commonly known as *The Second Shepherds' Play*), later known as part of the English Wakefield Cycle.

1363-1443   Japan's Zeami Motokiyo writes more than one hundred Nō plays, giving rise to this important dramatic form.

c. 1495   *Everyman*, the most famous English morality play, is first presented.

1500-1550   Rise of the Italian *commedia dell'arte*, or professional street theater.

1508   First Italian secular comedy, *La cassaria* (*The Coffer*, 1975), by Ludovico Ariosto.

1513   Bernardo Dovizi da Bibbiena's comedy *La calandria* is produced.

1519   Niccolò Machiavelli's produces his comic masterpiece, *La mandrogola* (*The Mandrake*, 1911).

1541   Giambattista Giraldi Cinthio's *Orbecche*, the first modern Italian tragedy, is produced.

1550-1571   Italian Renaissance drama critics Antonio Sebastiani Minturno, Julius Caesar Scaliger, and Lodovico Castelvetro contribute to the revival of classicism by publishing translations and adaptations of Aristotle and Horace.

1562-1635   Life of the "Spanish Shakespeare," Lope de Vega Carpio, author of eleven hundred plays.

1564-1616   William Shakespeare lives, writes thirty-nine verse plays.

1573   Torquato Tasso's *Aminta* (English translation, 1591) is the first dramatic pastoral, influencing plays such as Shakespeare's *As You Like It* (c. 1599-1600).

1580-1584   Teatro Olimpico, first permanent proscenium theater, built in Venice by Andrea Palladio and his student Vincenzo Scamozzi.

c. 1588   The University Wits emerge in England to give life to Elizabethan verse drama with works such as Christopher Marlowe's *Doctor Faustus*.

c. 1598   Jacobo Peri and Ottavio Rinuccini's *Dafne*, the first full-length Italian opera, is produced.

1599   Shakespeare's company, headed by actor Richard Burbage, opens the Globe Theatre.

c. 1600-1601   Shakespeare's *Hamlet, Prince of Denmark*, is produced.

1605   Ben Jonson's *Volpone: Or, The Fox* is produced.

c. 1610   Flaminio Scala becomes prolific publisher of *commedia dell'arte* scenarios.

1610-1642   Second generation of English verse playwrights, known informally as the Tudor dramatists, including Shakespeare.

1622-1673   Life of playwright Molière, one of France's greatest dramatists.

1636   Spanish playwright Pedro Calderón de la Barca publishes *La vida es sueño* (*Life Is a Dream*, 1830).

1640	Pierre Corneille, French tragedian, writes *Horace* (English translation, 1656) in accord with the three classic unities of time, place, and action, establishing the ideal of French classicism.
1642	Puritans seize control of English government; Oliver Cromwell closes all theaters.
c. 1650-1700	Japanese Kabuki drama emerges.
1653	Chikamatsu Monzaemon, Japan's greatest puppet theater playwright, is born.
1660	The English monarchy restored, and theaters are reopened.
1660-1696	English Restoration comedy dominates theaters, influenced by French theater, with witty, cynical works by John Dryden, William Wycherley, and Aphra Behn.
1664	Molière produces his masterpiece, *Tartuffe: Ou, L'Imposteur* (*Tartuffe*, 1732).
1665	First American play, *Ye Bare and Ye Cubb*, by William Darby, is performed in Virginia.
1677	French tragedian Jean Racine brings French classicism to its height with his play *Phèdre* (*Phaedra*, 1701).
1680	The Comédie-Française, the French national theater, is established.
1684	Bunraku, Japanese puppet theater, emerges.
1696	Colley Cibber's *Love's Last Shift: Or, The Fool in Fashion* signals the end of Restoration Comedy and the beginning of English middle-class sentimentalism.
1722	Sir Richard Steele's English sentimental masterpiece, *The Conscious Lovers*, is produced.
1728	John Gay's ballad opera, *The Beggar's Opera*, a progenitor of musical comedy and operetta and the basis for Bertolt Brecht's *Die Dreigroschenoper* (pr. 1928; *The Threepenny Opera*, 1949), is produced.
1730	Sentimentalism triumphs in France with Marivaux's *Le Jeu de l'amour et du hasard* (*The Game of Love and Chance*, 1907).
1755	Gotthold Ephraim Lessing, one of Germany's first significant playwrights, creates middle-class tragedy with *Miss Sara Sampson* (English translation, 1933).
1758	Denis Diderot's critical work, *Discours sur la poésie dramatique* (*Dramatic Essays of the Neoclassical Age*, 1950) rejects the three unities of classicism.
1762	Italian Carlo Goldoni recalls *commedia dell'arte* with *Il servitore di due padroni* (*A Servant of Two Masters*, 1952).
1767-1769	Gotthold Ephraim Lessing's work on drama criticism, *Hamburgische Dramaturgie* (*Hamburg Dramaturgy*, 1889), stresses for Germany the superiority of Shakespeare and rejects French classical theorists and dramatists.
1767-1845	Life of August Schlegel, considered the father of the German Romantic movement, who translated seventeen of Shakespeare's plays into German.
1767-1787	Germany's Sturm und Drang (storm and stress) movement characterized by emotional and sensational drama, foresees the German Romantic movement.
1772	Paris Opéra is established.

1773   Oliver Goldsmith rejuvenates Restoration comedy with *She Stoops to Conquer: Or, The Mistakes of a Night*.

1784   Pierre-Augustin Caron de Beaumarchais's *La Folle Journée: Ou, Le Mariage de Figaro* (*The Marriage of Figaro*, 1784) brings French new sentimentalism to a peak. It becomes the basis for the later Mozart opera of the same name.

1787   *The Contrast*, American Royall Tyler's comedy, introduces the character of the Yankee.

1789   Friedrich Schiller is appointed to the faculty of University of Jena.

1791   Establishment of the Weimar National Theatre, neighboring the University of Jena, with Johann Wolfgang von Goethe as its director. Schiller and Goethe unite to write and produce at Weimar and create Romanticized German classicism.

1797   *Castle Spectre*, written by Matthew Gregory Lewis (also known as Monk Lewis), begins the Romantic tradition of gothic melodramas.

1804   Schiller publishes *Wilhelm Tell* (*William Tell*, 1841).

1808   *Faust: Eine Tragödie* (*The Tragedy of Faust*, 1823) is published by Goethe.

1809   Zacharias Werner writes *Der 24 Fenruar* (*The Twenty-fourth of February*), the first Romantic "horror" play, about a curse falling on that date in February.

1821   English Romantic poet, George Gordon, Lord Byron, has *Marino Faliero, Doge of Venice* produced.

1823-1825   French literary critic Stendhal publishes *Racine et Shakespeare* (*Racine and Shakespeare*, 1962), in which he argues that Shakespeare's plays are more important than those of French tragedian Racine.

1827   Victor Hugo, French dramatist and critic, argues in the preface to his play *Cromwell* (English translation, 1896) that the classic unities of time, place, and action should be abandoned.

1828   Thomas D. Rice, originator of the Jim Crow character, creates first "Ethiopian operas," or black minstrel shows.

1830   The Comédie-Française brings Romanticism to France with its production of Victor Hugo's *Hernani* (English translation, 1830), which precipitates riots in the theater.

            American playwright George Washington Parke Custis gives expression to the concept of the "noble savage" with his play *Pocahontas*.

1832   William Dunlap publishes *A History of American Theatre*.

1833   Goethe publishes *Faust: Eine Tragödie, zweiter Teil* (*The Tragedy of Faust, Part Two*, 1838).

1834   Alfred de Musset publishes his masterpiece, the love story *On ne badine pas avec l'amour* (*No Trifling with Love*, 1890).

1835   Georg Büchner, leader of the Young Germany movement, publishes *Dantons Tod* (*Danton's Death*, 1927), a Romantic work about the French Revolution.

1836   Russian Nikolai Gogol's satire on the corruption of public officials, *Revizor* (*The Inspector General*, 1890), is presented in St. Petersburg.

1837	*Hamlet, Prince of Denmark* is first presented in Russia.
1845	Anna Cora Mowatt, America's first major female playwright, wins fame with her comedy *Fashion*.
1849	*Adrienne Lecouvreur* (English translation, 1855), by Eugène Scribe is published. It is the best known example of his well-made play concept, which stresses a pyramid structure with exposition and rising action, followed by a major climax, followed by falling action, and a denouement.
	Alexandre Dumas, *père*, dramatizes his novel *Les Trois Mousquetaires* (*The Three Musketeers*, 1846) as *La Jeunesse des mousquetaires*.
1852	The first dramatization of Harriet Beecher Stowe's novel *Uncle Tom's Cabin: Or, Life Among the Lowly* begins a tradition of touring "Tom Shows" across the United States.
	Alexandre Dumas, *fils*, produces a dramatization of his novel *La Dame aux camélias* (dramatized in English as *Camille*, 1856), about a prostitute with a heart of gold.
1859	Dion Boucicault's *The Octoroon: Or, Life in Louisiana* is produced, with its theme of an interracial love affair.
1863	German drama critic Gustave Freytag publishes *The Technique of the Drama: An Exposition of Dramatic Composition and Art*, which describes in detail the "well-made play."
1866	*The Black Crook*, considered by some to be the first American musical presented, opens in New York.
1879	Henrik Ibsen publishes first modern realistic drama, *Et dukkehjem* (*A Doll's House*, 1880).
1881	Émile Zola argues for realism in drama in his essay *Le Naturalisme au théâtre* (*Naturalism on the Stage*, 1893).
1888	August Strindberg publishes his realistic masterpiece *Fröken Julie* (*Miss Julie*, 1912).
1890	Ibsen's realistic masterpiece *Hedda Gabler* (English translation, 1891) is produced.
1891	German playwright Frank Wedekind's *Frühlings Erwachen* (*Spring Awakening*, 1909) is a subjective study of adolescent sexual awakening.
1892	Gerhart Hauptmann's drama of poverty, *Die Weber* (*The Weavers*, 1899), is published.
1892	Maurice Maeterlinck's *Pelléas et Mélisande* (*Pelléas and Mélisande*, 1894) introduces nonrealistic Symbolist drama.
1895	Oscar Wilde's *The Importance of Being Earnest: A Trivial Comedy for Serious People* is produced.
1896	Alfred Jarry publishes *Ubu roi* (English translation, 1951), a Surrealistic forerunner of absurdist theater.
1899	Konstantin Stanislavsky produces Anton Chekhov's *Chayka* (*The Seagull*, 1909) at the Moscow Art Theatre.
1900	Arthur Schnitzler publishes the frankly sexual *Reigen* (*Hands Around*, 1920; also as *La Ronde*, 1959).

1903   Bjørnstjerne Bjørnson wins the Nobel Prize in Literature.

1904   Sir James M. Barrie's *Peter Pan: Or, The Boy Who Wouldn't Grow Up* is produced.

            José Echegaray y Eizaguirre wins the Nobel Prize in Literature

1907   Dramatic expressionism is introduced with August Strindberg's *Spöksonaten* (*The Ghost Sonata*, 1916).

            John Millington Synge's masterpiece *The Playboy of the Western World* is produced in Ireland.

            Florenz Ziegfeld develops the modern American musical with his Ziegfeld Follies.

1908   Maeterlinck produces his Symbolist masterpiece, *L'Oiseau bleu* (*The Blue Bird*, 1909).

1912   Gerhart Hauptmann wins the Nobel Prize in Literature.

1913   Rabindranath Tagore wins the Nobel Prize in Literature.

1915-1917   Nikolai Evreinov's *Teatr dlya sebya* (*The Theatre in Life*, 1927) introduces expressionism to Russia.

1916   Georg Kaiser's German work, *Von morgens bis mitternachts* (*From Morn to Midnight*, 1920), is published.

1918   First year the Pulitzer Prize in Drama is awarded.

1920   Eugene O'Neill's first expressionistic drama, *The Emperor Jones*, is produced.

1921   Luigi Pirandello's expressionistic masterpiece, *Sei personaggi in cerca d'autore* (*Six Characters in Search of an Author*, 1922) is produced.

            Zona Gale becomes the first woman to win the Pulitzer Prize in Drama, with *Miss Lulu Bett*.

1922   Jacinto Benavente y Martínez wins the Nobel Prize in Literature.

1923   William Butler Yeats wins the Nobel Prize in Literature.

1925   George Bernard Shaw wins the Nobel Prize in Literature.

1928   Bertolt Brecht creates epic theater with the musical *Die Dreigroschenoper* (*The Threepenny Opera*, 1949), with music by Kurt Weill.

            Jerome Kern and Oscar Hammerstein II create the first modern American musical, *Show Boat*, based on the novel by Edna Ferber.

1929   Jean Giraudoux's myth-based work, *Amphitryon 38* (English translation, 1938), is produced.

1932   John Galsworthy wins the Nobel Prize in Literature.

1933   O'Neill writes *Ah, Wilderness!* a gentle, realistic play about coming of age in the United States.

            Spain's Federico García Lorca's poetic *Bodas de sangre* (*Blood Wedding*, 1939) is produced.

1934   Lillian Hellman deals with lesbianism in *The Children's Hour*.

            Cole Porter's *Anything Goes* is produced.

            Luigi Pirandello wins the Nobel Prize in Literature.

1935   George and Ira Gershwin produce *Porgy and Bess*, based on Du Bose Heyward's play.

1936	O'Neill wins the Noble Prize in Literature.
1938	French drama theorist Antonin Artaud writes *Le Théâtre et son double* (*The Theatre and Its Double*, 1958), calling for a "theatre of cruelty," which would directly assault the senses in nonrealistic ways.
	Thornton Wilder writes his gentle American classic play *Our Town*.
1941	Lillian Hellman's anti-Nazi play, *Watch on the Rhine*, is produced.
1943	Existentialist philosopher Jean-Paul Sartre publishes *Les Mouches* (*The Flies*, 1946), illustrating his philosophy.
	Rodgers and Hammerstein's *Oklahoma!* is produced.
1946	O'Neill writes *The Iceman Cometh*.
1947	Tennessee Williams's *A Streetcar Named Desire* is produced.
	The annual Tony Awards are established for best work in New York theater.
1948	T. S. Eliot wins the Nobel Prize in Literature.
1949	Arthur Miller blends realism and expressionism in *Death of a Salesman*.
1950	Eugène Ionesco's absurdist play *La Cantatrice chauve* (*The Bald Soprano*, 1956) is produced.
1951	Pär Lagerkvist wins the Nobel Prize in Literature.
1952	Agatha Christie's *The Mousetrap* opens, later becoming the longest running show in the history of London theater.
	Samuel Beckett's absurdist comedy *En attendant Godot* (*Waiting for Godot*, 1954) is produced.
	François Mauriac wins the Nobel Prize in Literature.
1955	Tennessee Williams creates steamy realism in *Cat on a Hot Tin Roof*.
1956	John Osborne's *Look Back in Anger* sees a return to realism for English theater.
	The Obie Awards are established for best Off-Broadway work.
1957	Albert Camus wins the Nobel Prize in Literature.
1959	Harold Pinter's *The Dumb Waiter* is produced.
1959	African American playwright Lorraine Hansberry writes her Broadway hit, *A Raisin in the Sun*.
1960	Arthur Kopit's absurdist work *Oh Dad, Poor Dad, Mamma's Hung You in the Closet and I'm Feelin' So Sad* is produced.
1960-2002	Harvey Schmidt and Tom Jones's *The Fantasticks* runs, eventually becoming the longest-running show in American history with 17,162 performances.
1961	Martin Esslin publishes his influential critical work *The Theatre of the Absurd*.
1962	Edward Albee's hit play *Who's Afraid of Virginia Woolf?* is produced.
1963	Václav Havel, who later becomes president of the Czech Republic, publishes *Zahradni slavnost* (*The Garden Party*, 1969).

1964   Amiri Baraka's play about the terrors of the black experience in the United States, *Dutchman*, is produced.

            Jerry Herman's *Hello, Dolly!* is produced.

            Jean-Paul Sartre wins the Nobel Prize in Literature.

1966   John Kander's *Cabaret* is produced.

            Megan Terry's anti-Vietnam War play, *Viet Rock: A Folk War Movie* is produced.

            Tom Stoppard's absurdist work *Rosencrantz and Guildenstern Are Dead* is produced.

1967   Miguel Ángel Asturias wins the Nobel Prize in Literature.

1968   Ed Bullins emerges as a major African American dramatist with *The Electronic Nigger*.

            Galt MacDermot, James Rado, and Gerome Ragni's hippie musical *Hair* debuts on Broadway.

            Towards a Poor Theatre, an English translation of Jerzy Grotowski's influential book *Możliwośćteatru* (1962) is published.

            Peter Handke produces his postmodernist work, *Kaspar*.

1969   Samuel Beckett wins the Nobel Prize in Literature.

1970   Italy's Dario Fo's postmodern *Morte accidentale di un anarchico* (*Accidental Death of an Anarchist*, 1979) is produced.

1972   Sir Alan Ayckbourn's *Absurd Person Singular* blends realism and absurdism.

1973   Patrick White wins the Nobel Prize in Literature.

1974   The Bread and Puppet Theatre's radical *Domestic Resurrection Circus* is produced.

1975   David Mamet's realistic *American Buffalo* is produced.

1975-1990   *A Chorus Line* runs on Broadway, becoming one of the longest-running Broadway shows with 6,137 performances.

1981   Beth Henley wins the Pulitzer Prize for *Crimes of the Heart*.

1982   Caryl Churchill's postmodern work *Top Girls* examines feminist issues by blending past and present realities.

1983   Sam Shepard's realistic *Fool for Love* is produced.

            Robert Wilson, director and playwright, presents the first of his famous postmodern pieces, *the CIVIL warS*.

1984   August Wilson, multiple award-winning dramatist, writes *Ma Rainey's Black Bottom*, the first of his series on African American history.

1986   Wole Soyinka wins the Nobel Prize in Literature.

1988   *M. Butterfly*, David Henry Hwang's study of the issues of Western colonialism, is produced.

            Wendy Wasserstein marks a new female presence in American drama with *The Heidi Chronicles*.

1991   First American production of *Hungarian Medea*, a play by the president of Hungary, Árpád Göncz.

        Tony Kushner writes his two-part expressionistic work, *Angels in America: A Gay Fantasia on National Themes* dealing with hypocrisy about homosexuality and AIDS.

        Derek Walcott wins the Nobel Prize in Literature

1994   Edward Albee's postmodern play *Three Tall Women* wins the Pulitzer Prize.

1996   Irish writer Martin McDonagh's *The Beauty Queen of Leenane* is produced.

1997   Julie Taymor's modern "shadow puppet" work, *The Lion King*, is presented at the renovated New Amsterdam Theatre.

        Dario Fo wins the Nobel Prize in Literature.

1998   British dramatist Michael Frayn's *Copenhagen* presents the postmodern world of quantum physics.

        French playwright Yasmina Reza wins the Tony Award for *Art*.

1999   Margaret Edson wins the Pulitzer Prize for her first play, *Wit*, in which a woman chats with the audience as she dies of cancer.

        Günter Grass wins the Nobel Prize in Literature.

2001   A new production of Mel Brooks's *The Producers* becomes the year's most successful show on Broadway, and wins a record-setting twelve Tony Awards.

2002   Suzan-Lori Parks becomes the first African American woman to win the Pulitzer Prize in Drama.

August W. Staub

CHRONOLOGICAL LIST OF DRAMATISTS

This chronology lists authors covered in these volumes in order of their dates of birth. This arrangement serves as a supplemental time line for those interested in the development of drama from ancient to modern times. For another chronological perspective, see the Time Line on page 4543.

BEFORE THE COMMON ERA

Aeschylus (525-524 B.C.E.)
Sophocles (c. 496 B.C.E.)
Euripides (c. 485 B.C.E.)
Aristophanes (c. 450 B.C.E.)
Menander (c. 342 B.C.E.)
Gnaeus Naevius (c. 270 B.C.E.)
Plautus (c. 254 B.C.E.)
Quintus Ennius (239 B.C.E.)
Terence (c. 190 B.C.E.)
Kālidāsa (c. 100 B.C.E. or c. 340 C.E.)
Seneca (4 B.C.E.)

FOURTEENTH CENTURY

Gao Ming (c. 1303)
Zeami Motokiyo (1363)

FIFTEENTH CENTURY

Gómez Manrique (c. 1412)
Wakefield Master (c. 1420)
Gil Vicente (c. 1465)
Juan del Encina (July 12, 1468?)
Niccolò Machiavelli (May 3, 1469)
Ludovico Ariosto (September 8, 1474)
Giangiorgio Trissino (July 8, 1478)
Bartolomé de Torres Naharro (c. 1485)
Henry Medwall (fl. 1486-1500)
Pietro Aretino (April 19 or 20, 1492)
Hans Sachs (November 5, 1494)
John Bale (November 21, 1495)
John Heywood (c. 1497)

SIXTEENTH CENTURY

Giambattista Giraldi Cinthio (November, 1504)
Nicholas Udall (December, 1505?)
Lope de Rueda (1510?)

António Ferreira (1528)

Thomas Norton (1532)
Giambattista Della Porta (1535)
Thomas Sackville (1536)
Battista Guarini (1538)
George Gascoigne (c. 1539)

Robert Garnier (1544?)
Torquato Tasso (March 11, 1544)
Miguel de Cervantes (September 29, 1547)

John Lyly (c. 1554)
George Peele (baptized, July 27, 1556)
Thomas Lodge (1558?)
Robert Greene (July, 1558)
Thomas Kyd (baptized, November 6, 1558)
George Chapman (c. 1559)

Lope de Vega Carpio (November 25, 1562)
Christopher Marlowe (February 6, 1564)
William Shakespeare (April 23, 1564)
Thomas Nashe (November, 1567)

Thomas Dekker (c. 1572)
Thomas Heywood (c. 1573)
Ben Jonson (June 11, 1573)
Cyril Tourneur (c. 1575)
John Marston (baptized, October 7, 1576)
John Webster (fl. c. 1577-1580)
John Fletcher (December, 1579)

Tirso de Molina (1580?)
Thomas Middleton (baptized, April 18, 1580)

Juan Ruiz de Alarcón (1581)
Philip Massinger (baptized, November 24, 1583)
Francis Beaumont (c. 1584)
John Ford (baptized, April 17, 1586)
Joost van den Vondel (November 17, 1587)
Richard Brome (c. 1590)

James Shirley (baptized, September 7, 1596)
Pedro Calderón de la Barca (January 17, 1600)

SEVENTEENTH CENTURY

Tristan L'Hermite (c. 1601)
Jean Mairet (baptized, May 10, 1604)
Sir William Davenant (February, 1606)
Pierre Corneille (June 6, 1606)
Jean de Rotrou (August 21, 1609)

Andreas Gryphius (October 2, 1616)
Agustín Moreto y Cabaña (1618)

Molière (baptized, January 15, 1622)
George Villiers (January 30, 1628)

John Dryden (August 19, 1631)
Sir George Etherege (c. 1635)
Philippe Quinault (June, 1635)
Jean Racine (December, 1639)
John Crowne (c. 1640)
Thomas Shadwell (1640?)
Aphra Behn (July, 1640)

William Wycherley (May 28, 1641?)
Sor Juana Inés de la Cruz (November, 1648)

Thomas Otway (March 3, 1652)
Nathaniel Lee (c. 1653)
Chikamatsu Monzaemon (1653)
Jean-François Regnard (February 8, 1655)

Sir John Vanbrugh (baptized, January 24, 1664)
Mrs. Susannah Centlivre (c. 1667)

Alain-René Lesage (December 13, 1668)
William Congreve (January 24, 1670)

Colley Cibber (November 6, 1671)
Sir Richard Steele (March, 1672)
Joseph Addison (May 1, 1672)
Nicholas Rowe (June 20, 1674)
Francesco Scipione Maffei (June 1, 1675)
George Farquhar (1678?)

Ludvig Holberg (December 3, 1684)
John Gay (June 30, 1685)
Marivaux (February 4, 1688)

Pierre-Claude Nivelle de La Chaussée (1692)
George Lillo (February 4, 1693)
Voltaire (November 21, 1694)
Pietro Metastasio (January 3, 1698)

EIGHTEENTH CENTURY

Carlo Goldoni (February 25, 1707)
Henry Fielding (April 22, 1707)

Denis Diderot (October 5, 1713)
Aleksandr Petrovich Sumarokov (November 25, 1717)
Samuel Foote (baptized, January 27, 1720)
Carlo Gozzi (December 13, 1720)

Friedrich Gottlieb Klopstock (July 2, 1724)
Oliver Goldsmith (November 10, 1728 or 1730)
Gotthold Ephraim Lessing (January 22, 1729)

Pierre-Augustin Caron de Beaumarchais (January 24, 1732)
Richard Cumberland (February 19, 1732)
Louis-Sébastien Mercier (June 6, 1740)

Denis Ivanovich Fonvizin (April 3, 1745)
Vittorio Alfieri (January 16, 1749)
Johann Wolfgang von Goethe (August 28, 1749)

Jakob Michael Reinhold Lenz (January 12, 1751)
Richard Brinsley Sheridan (October 30, 1751)

Elizabeth Inchbald (October 15, 1753)
Royall Tyler (July 18, 1757)
Friedrich Schiller (November 10, 1759)
Leandro Fernández de Moratín (March 10, 1760)

August von Kotzebue (May 3, 1761)
Joanna Baillie (September 11, 1762)
William Dunlap (February 19, 1766)

Guilbert de Pixérécourt (January 22, 1773)
Ludwig Tieck (May 31, 1773)
Matthew Gregory Lewis (July 9, 1775)
Heinrich von Kleist (October 18, 1777)
Adam Gottlob Oehlenschläger (November 14, 1779)

Giovanni Battista Niccolini (October 29, 1782)
James Sheridan Knowles (May 12, 1784)
James Nelson Barker (June 17, 1784)
Francisco Martínez de la Rosa, (March 10, 1787)
George Gordon, Lord Byron (January 22, 1788)
Ferdinand Raimund (June 1, 1790)

Franz Grillparzer (January 15, 1791)
Angel de Saavedra (March 10, 1791)
John Howard Payne (June 9, 1791)
Johan Ludvig Heiberg (December 14, 1791)
Eugène Scribe (December 24, 1791)
Percy Bysshe Shelley (August 4, 1792)
Aleksander Fredro (June 20, 1793)
Carl Jonas Love Almqvist (November 28, 1793)
Alexander Griboyedov (January 15, 1795)
James Robinson Planché (February 27, 1796)
Alexander Pushkin (June 6, 1799)

NINETEENTH CENTURY

Johann Nestroy (December 7, 1801)
Christian Dietrich Grabbe (December 11, 1801)
Victor Hugo (February 26, 1802)
Alexandre Dumas, *père* (July 24, 1802)
Edward Bulwer-Lytton (May 25, 1803)
Robert Montgomery Bird (February 5, 1806)
Nikolai Gogol (March 31, 1809)
Alfred, Lord Tennyson (August 6, 1809)

Juliusz Słowacki (September 4, 1809)
Alfred de Musset (December 11, 1810)

Zygmunt Krasiński (February 19, 1812)
Robert Browning (May 7, 1812)
Otto Ludwig (February 12, 1813)
Friedrich Hebbel (March 18, 1813)
Georg Büchner (October 17, 1813)
François Ponsard (June 1, 1814)
Mikhail Lermontov (October 15, 1814)
Eugène Labiche (May 5, 1815)
José Zorrilla y Moral (February 21, 1817)
Alexander Sukhovo-Kobylin (September 17, 1817)
Ivan Turgenev (November 9, 1818)
Émile Augier (September 17, 1820)
Dion Boucicault (December 27, 1820?)

Imre Madách (January 21, 1823)
Alexander Ostrovsky (April 12, 1823)
George H. Boker (October 6, 1823)
Alexandre Dumas, *fils* (July 27, 1824)
Henrik Ibsen (March 20, 1828)
Thomas William Robertson (January 9, 1829)
Manuel Tamayo y Baus (September 15, 1829)

Victorien Sardou (September 5, 1831)
José Echegaray y Eizaguirre (April 19, 1832)
Bjørnstjerne Bjørnson (December 8, 1832)
Aleksis Kivi (October 10, 1834)
W. S. Gilbert (November 18, 1836)
Algernon Charles Swinburne (April 5, 1837)
Henry Becque (April 18, 1837)
Ludwig Anzengruber (November 29, 1839)
Émile Zola (April 2, 1840)
Thomas Hardy (June 2, 1840)
Giovanni Verga (September 2, 1840)

Bronson Howard (October 7, 1842)
Henry James (April 15, 1843)
Benito Pérez Galdós (May 10, 1843)
Minna Canth (March 19, 1844)
Giuseppe Giacosa (October 21, 1847)
August Strindberg (January 22, 1849)

Henry Arthur Jones (September 20, 1851)
Ion Luca Caragiale (January 30, 1852)
Lady Augusta Gregory (March 15, 1852)
David Belasco (July 25, 1853)
François de Curel (June 10, 1854)
Oscar Wilde (October 16, 1854)
Arthur Wing Pinero (May 24, 1855)
George Bernard Shaw (July 26, 1856)
Henrik Pontoppidan (July 24, 1857)
Hermann Sudermann (September 30, 1857)
Gunnar Heiberg (November 18, 1857)
Eugène Brieux (January 19, 1858)
Edward Martyn (January 31, 1859)
Anton Chekhov (January 29, 1860)
Sir James Barrie (May 9, 1860)

Rabindranath Tagore (May 7, 1861)
Arthur Schnitzler (May 15, 1862)
Maurice Maeterlinck (August 29, 1862)
Roberto Bracco (November 10, 1862)
Gerhart Hauptmann (November 15, 1862)
Georges Feydeau (December 8, 1862)
Gabriele D'Annunzio (March 12, 1863)
Israel Zangwill (February 14, 1864)
Frank Wedekind (July 24, 1864)
Miguel de Unamuno y Jugo (September 29, 1864)
Herman Heijermans (December 3, 1864)
Clyde Fitch (May 2, 1865)
William Butler Yeats (June 13, 1865)
Paul Ernst (March 7, 1866)
Jacinto Benavente y Martínez (August 12, 1866)
Ramón María del Valle-Inclán (October 28, 1866)
Luigi Pirandello (June 28, 1867)
John Galsworthy (August 14, 1867)
Maxim Gorky (March 28, 1868)
Edmond Rostand (April 1, 1868)
Paul Claudel (August 6, 1868)
Stanisław Wyspiański (January 15, 1869)

Serafín Alvarez Quintero (March 26, 1871)
John Millington Synge (April 16, 1871)
Leonid Andreyev (August 9, 1871)
Félix-Henry Bataille (April 4, 1872)
Joaquín Alvarez Quintero (1873)
Alfred Jarry (September 8, 1873)

W. Somerset Maugham (January 25, 1874)
Owen Davis (January 29, 1874)
Hugo von Hofmannsthal (February 1, 1874)
Gordon Bottomley (February 20, 1874)
Karl Kraus (April 28, 1874)
María Martínez Sierra (December 28, 1874)
Antonio Machado (July 26, 1875)
Henry Bernstein (January 20, 1876)
Susan Glaspell (July 1, 1876)
Harley Granville-Barker (November 25, 1877)
Ferenc Molnár (January 12, 1878)
Carl Sternheim (April 1, 1878)
John Masefield (June 1, 1878)
Rudolf Besier (July 2, 1878)
Lord Dunsany (July 24, 1878)
Mikhail Artsybashev (November 5, 1878)
Georg Kaiser (November 25, 1878)
Nikolai Evreinov (February 26, 1879)
Sean O'Casey (March 30, 1880)
Luigi Chiarelli (July 7, 1880)
Guillaume Apollinaire (August 16, 1880)
Aleksandr Blok (November 28, 1880)

Frederick Lonsdale (February 5, 1881)
Gregorio Martínez Sierra (May 6, 1881)
Padraic Colum (December 8, 1881)
Henri-René Lenormand (May 3, 1882)
John Drinkwater (June 1, 1882)
Jean Giraudoux (October 29, 1882)
Hjalmar Bergman (September 19, 1883)
St. John Ervine (December 28, 1883)
Yevgeny Zamyatin (February 1, 1884)
Stanisław Ignacy Witkiewicz (February 24, 1885)
Edna Ferber (August 15, 1885)
DuBose Heyward (August 31, 1885)
Jules Romains (August 26, 1885)
Franz Theodor Csokor (September 6, 1885)
François Mauriac (October 11, 1885)
Lennox Robinson (October 4, 1886)
Arnold Zweig (November 10, 1887)
James Bridie (January 3, 1888)
Jean-Jacques Bernard (July 30, 1888)
T. S. Eliot (September 26, 1888)
Eugene O'Neill (October 16, 1888)
Maxwell Anderson (December 15, 1888)

Friedrich Wolf (December 23, 1888)
Jean Cocteau (July 5, 1889)
George S. Kaufman (November 16, 1889)
Karel Čapek (January 9, 1890)
Franz Werfel (September 10, 1890)
Marc Connelly (December 13, 1890)

Mikhail Bulgakov (May 15, 1891)
Pär Lagerkvist (May 23, 1891)
Sidney Howard (June 26, 1891)
Ferdinand Bruckner (August 26, 1891)
Ugo Betti (February 4, 1892)
Edna St. Vincent Millay (February 22, 1892)
Archibald MacLeish (May 7, 1892)
Elmer Rice (September 28, 1892)
S. N. Behrman (June 9, 1893?)
Merrill Denison (June 23, 1893)
Vladimir Mayakovsky (July 19, 1893)
Ernst Toller (December 1, 1893)
Paul Green (March 17, 1894)
J. B. Priestley (September 13, 1894)
Lorenz Hart (May 2, 1895)
Robert E. Sherwood (April 4, 1896)
Henry de Montherlant (April 21, 1896)
Austin Clarke (May 9, 1896)
R. C. Sherriff (June 6, 1896)
Philip Barry (June 18, 1896)
Yevgeny Shvarts (October 21, 1896)
Carl Zuckmayer (December 27, 1896)
Thornton Wilder (April 17, 1897)
Kaj Munk (January 13, 1898)
Bertolt Brecht (February 10, 1898)
Michel de Ghelderode (April 3, 1898)
Federico García Lorca (June 5, 1898)
Tawfiq al-Hakim (October 9, 1898)
Yury Olesha (March 3, 1899)
Lynn Riggs (August 31, 1899)
Miguel Angel Asturias (October 19, 1899)
Noël Coward (December 16, 1899)
Eduardo De Filippo (May 24, 1900)

TWENTETH CENTURY

John William van Druten (June 1, 1901)
Jack Kirkland (July 25, 1901?)

Kjeld Abell (August 25, 1901)
Marieluise Fleisser (November 23, 1901)
Ödön von Horváth (December 9, 1901)
Halldór Laxness (April 23, 1902)
Alejandro Casona (March 23, 1903)
Frank Sargeson (March 23, 1903)
Witold Gombrowicz (August 4, 1904)
Graham Greene (October 2, 1904)
Moss Hart (October 24, 1904)
John Patrick (May 17, 1905)
Lillian Hellman (June 20, 1905)
Jean-Paul Sartre (June 21, 1905)
Rodolfo Usigli (November 17, 1905)
Emlyn Williams (November 26, 1905)
Samuel Beckett (April 13, 1906)
Clifford Odets (July 18, 1906)
Dino Buzzati (October 16, 1906)
Sidney Kingsley (October 22, 1906)
W. H. Auden (February 21, 1907)
Mary Chase (February 25, 1907)
Alberto Moravia (November 28, 1907)
Christopher Fry (December 18, 1907)
Arthur Adamov (August 23, 1908)
William Saroyan (August 31, 1908)
Eugène Ionesco (November 26, 1909)
Jean Anouilh (June 23, 1910)
Jean Genet (December 19, 1910)

Tennessee Williams (March 26, 1911)
Max Frisch (May 15, 1911)
Fritz Hochwälder (May 28, 1911)
Terence Rattigan (June 10, 1911)
Paul Willems (April 4, 1912)
István Örkény (April 5, 1912)
Patrick White (May 28, 1912)
Donagh MacDonagh (November 22, 1912)
Irwin Shaw (February 27, 1913)
William Inge (May 3, 1913)
Aimé Césaire (June 25, 1913)
Robertson Davies (August 28, 1913)
Albert Camus (November 7, 1913)
Marguerite Duras (April 4, 1914)
George Tabori (May 24, 1914)
Dylan Thomas (October 27, 1914)
William Gibson (November 13, 1914)

Owen Dodson (November 28, 1914)
Tadeusz Kantor (April 6, 1915)
Arthur Miller (October 17, 1915)
Horton Foote (March 14, 1916)
Antonio Buero Vallejo (September 29, 1916)
Alice Childress (October 12, 1916)
Peter Weiss (November 8, 1916)
Carson McCullers (February 19, 1917)
Robert Anderson (April 28, 1917)
John Whiting (November 15, 1917)
Arthur Laurents (July 14, 1918)
Isidora Aguirre (March 22, 1919)
Robert Pinget (July 19, 1919)

Friedrich Dürrenmatt (January 5, 1921)
Ray Lawler (May 23, 1921)
Tadeusz Różewicz (October 9, 1921)
Heinar Kipphardt (March 8, 1922)
Tad Mosel (May 1, 1922)
Brendan Behan (February 9, 1923)
John Mortimer (April 21, 1923)
Elizabeth Jolley (June 4, 1923)
James Purdy (July 14, 1923)
Abe Kōbō (March 7, 1924)
James Baldwin (August 2, 1924)
Robert Bolt (August 15, 1924)
James Ene Henshaw (August 29, 1924)
Yukio Mishima (January 14, 1925)
Frank D. Gilroy (October 13, 1925)
Tankred Dorst (December 19, 1925)
Alfonso Sastre (February 20, 1926)
Dario Fo (March 24, 1926)
Peter Shaffer (May 15, 1926)
James Reaney (September 1, 1926)
Hugh Leonard (November 9, 1926)
Murray Schisgal (November 25, 1926)
Bernard Kops (November 28, 1926)
Martin Walser (March 24, 1927)
Neil Simon (July 4, 1927)
Peter Nichols (July 31, 1927)
Günter Grass (October 16, 1927)
Edward Albee (March 12, 1928)
Peter Hacks (March 21, 1928)
William Trevor (May 24, 1928)
Pavel Kohout (July 20, 1928)

Griselda Gambaro (July 28, 1928)
Brian Friel (January 9, 1929)
Heiner Müller (January 9, 1929)
Willis Hall (April 6, 1929)
Henry Livings (September 20, 1929)
John Osborne (December 12, 1929)
Howard Sackler (December 19, 1929)
Derek Walcott (January 23, 1930)
Stephen Sondheim (March 22, 1930)
Bernard Slade (May 2, 1930)
Maria Irene Fornes (May 14, 1930)
Lorraine Hansberry (May 19, 1930)
Sławomir Mrożek (June 26, 1930)
Romulus Linney (September 21, 1930)
Harold Pinter (October 10, 1930)
John Arden (October 26, 1930)
A. R. Gurney, Jr. (November 1, 1930)

Peter Barnes (January 10, 1931)
Thomas Bernhard (February 10, 1931)
Rolf Hochhuth (April 1, 1931)
Adrienne Kennedy (September 13, 1931)
Fay Weldon (September 22, 1931)
Lonne Elder III (December 26, 1931)
Vassily Aksyonov (1932)
Jack Gelber (April 12, 1932)
Arnold Wesker (May 24, 1932)
Ronald Ribman (May 28, 1932)
Athol Fugard (June 11, 1932)
Megan Terry (July 22, 1932)
George Ryga (July 27, 1932)
Fernando Arrabal (August 11, 1932)
Maruxa Vilalta (September 23, 1932)
Joe Orton (January 1, 1933)
David Storey (July 13, 1933)
Michael Frayn (September 8, 1933)
Wole Soyinka (July 13, 1934)
Edward Bond (July 18, 1934)
Sonia Sanchez (September 9, 1934)
Amiri Baraka (October 7, 1934)
Joseph A. Walker (February 23, 1935)
John Pepper Clark-Bekederemo (April 6, 1935)
John McGrath (June 1, 1935)
Larry Kramer (June 25, 1935)
Ed Bullins (July 2, 1935)

Earl Lovelace (July 13, 1935)
Mart Crowley (August 21, 1935)
Rochelle Owens (April 2, 1936)
Preston Jones (April 7, 1936)
Paul Zindel (May 15, 1936)
Václav Havel (October 5, 1936)
Simon Gray (October 21, 1936)
Luis Rafael Sánchez (November 17, 1936)
Alfred Uhry (December 3, 1936)
Lanford Wilson (April 13, 1937)
Arthur Kopit (May 10, 1937)
Richard Foreman (June 10, 1937)
JoAnne Akalaitis (June 29, 1937)
Tom Stoppard (July 3, 1937)
Robert Patrick (September 27, 1937)
Tina Howe (November 21, 1937)
Ngugi wa Thiong'o (January 5, 1938)
John Guare (February 5, 1938)
Ola Rotimi (April 13, 1938)
Caryl Churchill (September 3, 1938)
Charles Fuller (March 5, 1939)
Israel Horovitz (March 31, 1939)
Sir Alan Ayckbourn (April 12, 1939)
Volker Braun (May 7, 1939)
Terrence McNally (November 3, 1939)
Shelagh Delaney (November 25, 1939)
Bernard Pomerance (1940)
Frank Chin (February 25, 1940)
David Rabe (March 10, 1940)
Mark Medoff (March 18, 1940)
Luis Miguel Valdez (June 26, 1940)

Spalding Gray (June 5, 1941)
Robert Wilson (October 4, 1941)
David Williamson (February 24, 1942)
Michel Tremblay (June 25, 1942)
Steve Tesich (September 29, 1942)
Peter Handke (December 6, 1942)
Howard Brenton (December 13, 1942)
Charles Ludlam (April 12, 1943)
Sam Shepard (November 5, 1943)
Wallace Shawn (November 12, 1943)
Martha Clarke (June 3, 1944)

Alexander Buzo (July 23, 1944)
Botho Strauss (December 2, 1944)
Michael Cristofer (January 22, 1945)
August Wilson (April 27, 1945)
Timberlake Wertenbaker (1946?)
Franz Xaver Kroetz (February 25, 1946)
David Hare (June 5, 1947)
Marsha Norman (September 21, 1947)
David Mamet (November 30, 1947)
Albert Innaurato (June 2, 1948)
Ntozake Shange (October 18, 1948)
Jessica Hagedorn (1949)
Christopher Durang (January 2, 1949)
Lee Blessing (October 4, 1949)
John Patrick Shanley (October 13, 1950)
Wendy Wasserstein (October 18, 1950)

David Ives (1951)
Craig Lucas (April 30, 1951)
Eric Overmyer (September 25, 1951)
Paula Vogel (November 16, 1951)
Beth Henley (May 8, 1952)
Robert Schenkkan (March 19, 1953)
Eric Bogosian (April 24, 1953)
Harvey Fierstein (June 6, 1954)
Eduardo Machado (June 11, 1953)
Donald Margulies (September 2, 1954)
Tony Kushner (July 16, 1956)
Paul Rudnick (1957)
David Henry Hwang (August 11, 1957)
Caryl Phillips (March 13, 1958)
Steven Dietz (June 23, 1958)
Yasmina Reza (May 1, 1959)

Kenneth Lonergan (1961)
Jon Robin Baitz (November 4, 1961)
Rebecca Gilman (1964)
Patrick Marber (September 19, 1964)
Marina Carr (November 17, 1964)
Martin McDonagh (1970)

Sarah Kane (February 3, 1971)

CRITICAL SURVEY
OF
DRAMA

GEOGRAPHICAL INDEX OF DRAMATISTS

CATEGORIZED INDEX OF DRAMATISTS

Categories used in the index that follows.

ABSURDISM

Abe, Kōbō, 1

Abell, Kjeld, 5

Adamov, Arthur, 12

Albee, Edward, 49

Arrabal, Fernando, 146

Beckett, Samuel, 273

Bernhard, Thomas, 333

Camus, Albert, 557

Carr, Marina, 585

Cristofer, Michael, 749

Dorst, Tankred, 865

Durang, Christopher, 917

Dürrenmatt, Friedrich, 930

Frisch, Max, 1158

Gambaro, Griselda, 1199

Gelber, Jack, 1244

Genet, Jean, 1251

Grass, Günter, 1395

Guare, John, 1468

Hakim, Tawfiq al-, 1501

Henley, Beth, 1606

Horovitz, Israel, 1662

Howe, Tina, 1687

Ionesco, Eugène, 1738

Kopit, Arthur, 1883

Kroetz, Franz Xaver, 1927

Laxness, Halldór, 1985

McNally, Terrence, 2165

Mrożek, Sławomir, 2412

Örkény, István, 2538

Pinget, Robert, 2639

Pinter, Harold, 2644

Rabe, David, 2718

Tabori, George, 3260

Tesich, Steve, 3305

Tremblay, Michel, 3357

Walser, Martin, 3518

Wilson, Lanford, 3650

AESTHETIC MOVEMENT

Swinburne, Algernon Charles, 3245

Valle-Inclán, Ramón María del, 3428

Wilde, Oscar, 3592

AFRICAN AMERICAN CULTURE

Baldwin, James, 198

Baraka, Amiri, 214

Bullins, Ed, 511

Childress, Alice, 645

Dodson, Owen, 861

Elder, Lonne, III, 944

Fuller, Charles, 1186

Hansberry, Lorraine, 1523

Kennedy, Adrienne, 1824

Parks, Suzan-Lori, 2589

Sanchez, Sonia, 2901

Shange, Ntozake, 3026

Walker, Joseph A., 3514

Wilson, August, 3644

AGE OF GOETHE. *See* **GOETHE, AGE OF**

AGE OF JOHNSON. *See* **JOHNSON, AGE OF**

AGE OF SENSIBILITY. *See* **SENSIBILITY, AGE OF**

AGITPROP THEATER

Behan, Brendan, 285

Bond, Edward, 399

Brecht, Bertolt, 436

Brenton, Howard, 447

Fo, Dario, 1081

Hacks, Peter, 1490

Mayakovsky, Vladimir, 2294

Odets, Clifford, 2511

Sastre, Alfonso, 2932

Valdez, Luis Miguel, 3422

ALGONQUIN ROUND TABLE
Connelly, Marc, 726
Kaufman, George S., 1818

AMERICAN EARLY NATIONAL PERIOD
Barker, James Nelson, 225
Bird, Robert Montgomery, 355
Dunlap, William, 905
Tyler, Royall, 3393

AMERICAN LOCAL COLOR
Bird, Robert Montgomery, 355
Ferber, Edna, 1013
Glaspell, Susan, 1322
Green, Paul, 1417
Henley, Beth, 1606
Inge, William, 1723
Linney, Romulus, 2059
McCullers, Carson, 2112
Wilson, Lanford, 3650

ANGRY YOUNG MEN
Arden, John, 120
Delaney, Shelagh, 831
Kops, Bernard, 1893
Osborne, John, 2550
Pinter, Harold, 2644
Wesker, Arnold, 3571

ASIAN AMERICAN CULTURE
Chin, Frank, 649
Hagedorn, Jessica, 1495
Hwang, David Henry, 1700

ATHENIAN TRAGEDY
Aeschylus, 25
Euripides, 991
Sophocles, 3159

AUGUSTAN AGE, ENGLISH
Addison, Joseph, 18
Centlivre, Mrs. Susannah, 595
Congreve, William, 713
Fielding, Henry, 1033
Foote, Samuel, 1103
Gay, John, 1239
Rowe, Nicholas, 2840
Steele, Sir Richard, 3179
Vanbrugh, Sir John, 3436

AVANT-GARDE THEATER
Akalaitis, JoAnne, 39

Apollinaire, Guillaume, 115
Barry, Philip, 249
Cocteau, Jean, 696
Evreinov, Nikolai, 1002
García Lorca, Federico, 1215
Handke, Peter, 1516
Lenormand, Henri-René, 1994
Pinget, Robert, 2639
Shvarts, Yevgeny, 3117
Valle-Inclán, Ramón María del, 3428
Witkiewicz, Stanisław Ignacy, 3664

BAROQUE AGE
Cruz, Sor Juana Inés de la, 766
Gryphius, Andreas, 1460
Mairet, Jean, 2190

BLACK ARTS MOVEMENT
Baldwin, James, 198
Baraka, Amiri, 214
Bullins, Ed, 511
Elder, Lonne, III, 944
Fuller, Charles, 1186
Hansberry, Lorraine, 1523
Sanchez, Sonia, 2901
Wilson, August, 3644

BOULEVARD THEATER
Bataille, Félix-Henry, 257
Bernstein, Henry, 339
Brieux, Eugène, 463
Feydeau, Georges, 1025

CAPE AND SWORD PLAY
Calderón de la Barca, Pedro, 548
Tirso de Molina, 3326
Vega Carpio, Lope de, 3448

CAROLINE AGE
Brome, Richard, 470
Davenant, Sir William, 796
Ford, John, 1109
Heywood, Thomas, 1627
Jonson, Ben, 1785
Massinger, Philip, 2274
Shirley, James, 3107

CAVALIER DRAMA
Beaumont, Francis, 268
Davenant, Sir William, 796
Shirley, James, 3107

CLASSICISM
Ennius, Quintus, 967
Naevius, Gnaeus, 2446
Terence, 3294

CLASSICISM: RENAISSANCE
Della Porta, Giambattista, 836
Ferreira, António, 1020
Trissino, Giangiorgio, 3371

CLASSICISM: SEVENTEENTH AND EIGHTEENTH CENTURIES
Addison, Joseph, 18
Congreve, William, 713
Corneille, Pierre, 733
Dryden, John, 876
Jonson, Ben, 1785
Lee, Nathaniel, 1990
Marivaux, 2216
Metastasio, Pietro, 2328
Molière, 2366
Quinault, Philippe, 2713
Racine, Jean, 2727
Rotrou, Jean de, 2833
Shadwell, Thomas, 2979
Sumarokov, Aleksandr Petrovich, 3239
Tristan L'Hermite, 3377
Voltaire, 3486

CLASSICISM: NINETEENTH CENTURY
Grillparzer, Franz, 1452
Kleist, Heinrich von, 1858
Knowles, James Sheridan, 1870
Ponsard, François, 2682
Pushkin, Alexander, 2706
Rostand, Edmond, 2818
Schiller, Friedrich, 2944

CLASSICISM: TWENTIETH CENTURY
Anouilh, Jean, 97
Clark-Bekederemo, John Pepper, 667
Cocteau, Jean, 696
Davies, Robertson, 802
Eliot, T. S., 949
Hochwälder, Fritz, 1642
Mauriac, François, 2290
Rostand, Edmond, 2818
Tremblay, Michel, 3357

Machado, Eduardo, 2142
Mamet, David, 2196
Martin, Jane, 2245
Mishima, Yukio, 2359
Müller, Heiner, 2421
Nichols, Peter, 2478
Örkény, István, 2538
Orton, Joe, 2543
Overmyer, Eric, 2576
Owens, Rochelle, 2581
Parks, Suzan-Lori, 2589
Patrick, Robert, 2600
Pomerance, Bernard, 2678
Purdy, James, 2702
Reaney, James, 2752
Reza, Yasmina, 2770
Różewicz, Tadeusz, 2846
Rudnick, Paul, 2855
Ryga, George, 2873
Schisgal, Murray, 2953
Shange, Ntozake, 3026
Shanley, John Patrick, 3032
Shawn, Wallace, 3053
Shepard, Sam, 3070
Stoppard, Tom, 3191
Strauss, Botho, 3211
Terry, Megan, 3299
Tesich, Steve, 3305
Vilalta, Maruxa, 3472
Vogel, Paula, 3483
Walcott, Derek, 3506
Wasserstein, Wendy, 3527
Weiss, Peter, 3548
Weldon, Fay, 3554
Wertenbaker, Timberlake, 3565
White, Patrick, 3580
Whiting, John, 3585
Williams, Tennessee, 3621
Wilson, Lanford, 3650
Zindel, Paul, 3713

POSTSTRUCTURALISM
Brenton, Howard, 447
Wilson, Robert, 3658

PRE-RAPHAELITES
Bottomley, Gordon, 407
Swinburne, Algernon Charles, 3245

PROBLEM PLAY
Aksyonov, Vassily, 44
Anzengruber, Ludwig, 109

Augier, Émile, 170
Blessing, Lee, 370
Brieux, Eugène, 463
Dumas, Alexandre, *fils*, 885
Galsworthy, John, 1193
Gilman, Rebecca, 1293
Ibsen, Henrik, 1708
Jones, Henry Arthur, 1774
Martin, Jane, 2245
Pinero, Arthur Wing, 2629
Robertson, Thomas William, 2794
Sardou, Victorien, 2905
Storey, David, 3201
Tamayo y Baus, Manuel, 3271

PSYCHOLOGICAL REALISM
Anderson, Robert, 83
Benavente y Martínez, Jacinto, 315
Bergman, Hjalmar, 321
Bracco, Roberto, 421
Davis, Owen, 812
Gilroy, Frank D., 1297
Ibsen, Henrik, 1708
Inge, William, 1723
Laurents, Arthur, 1970
Miller, Arthur, 2346
Williams, Emlyn, 3614
Wilson, August, 3644
Zweig, Arnold, 3744

REALISM
Almqvist, Carl Jonas Love, 69
Artsybashev, Mikhail, 155
Augier, Émile, 170
Becque, Henry, 280
Bjørnson, Bjørnstjerne, 364
Blessing, Lee, 370
Bracco, Roberto, 421
Bulgakov, Mikhail, 504
Caragiale, Ion Luca, 580
Chekhov, Anton, 622
Cristofer, Michael, 749
Denison, Merrill, 842
Dumas, Alexandre, *fils*, 885
Fitch, Clyde, 1050
Fleisser, Marieluise, 1058
Fonvizin, Denis Ivanovich, 1089
Galsworthy, John, 1193
Gogol, Nikolai, 1337
Grabbe, Christian Dietrich, 1381
Greene, Graham, 1424
Hebbel, Friedrich, 1576

Heiberg, Gunnar, 1581
Heijermans, Herman, 1592
Henshaw, James Ene, 1611
Howard, Bronson, 1677
Howard, Sidney, 1683
Ibsen, Henrik, 1708
Jolley, Elizabeth, 1770
Kingsley, Sidney, 1830
Kroetz, Franz Xaver, 1927
Kushner, Tony, 1937
Laxness, Halldór, 1985
Lonergan, Kenneth, 2075
Ludwig, Otto, 2100
Marber, Patrick, 2209
Medoff, Mark, 2302
Mosel, Tad, 2408
Ostrovsky, Alexander, 2558
Pérez Galdós, Benito, 2618
Priestley, J. B., 2691
Rice, Elmer, 2781
Robertson, Thomas William, 2794
Robinson, Lennox, 2803
Schnitzler, Arthur, 2958
Scribe, Eugène, 2965
Turgenev, Ivan, 3384
Walker, Joseph A., 3514
Wolf, Friedrich, 3671

REALISM, MAGICAL. *See* **MAGICAL REALISM**

REALISM, PSYCHOLOGICAL. *See* **PSYCHOLOGICAL REALISM**

REFORMATION
Bale, John, 205
Sachs, Hans, 2887

RENAISSANCE
Aretino, Pietro, 127
Ariosto, Ludovico, 134
Beaumont, Francis, 268
Brome, Richard, 470
Cervantes, Miguel de, 601
Dekker, Thomas, 822
Della Porta, Giambattista, 836
Encina, Juan del, 960
Garnier, Robert, 1226
Gascoigne, George, 1231
Guarini, Battista, 1477
Heywood, John, 1622
Lyly, John, 2103

SURREALIST MOVEMENT
Apollinaire, Guillaume, 115
Arrabal, Fernando, 146
Buzzati, Dino, 532
Cocteau, Jean, 696
Saroyan, William, 2916
Vilalta, Maruxa, 3472
Witkiewicz, Stanisław Ignacy, 3664

SYMBOLIST MOVEMENT
Andreyev, Leonid, 91
Bataille, Félix-Henry, 257
Blok, Aleksandr, 375
Claudel, Paul, 687
Gorky, Maxim, 1366
Hofmannsthal, Hugo von, 1649
Jarry, Alfred, 1763
Maeterlinck, Maurice, 2181
Sukhovo-Kobylin, Alexander, 3234
Tagore, Rabindranath, 3263
Yeats, William Butler, 3694

THEATER OF CRUELTY
Abell, Kjeld, 5
Adamov, Arthur, 12
Bernhard, Thomas, 333
Gambaro, Griselda, 1199
Orton, Joe, 2543
Weiss, Peter, 3548

THEATER OF THE ABSURD. See ABSURDISM

THEATER OF THE GROTESQUE
Buzzati, Dino, 532
Chiarelli, Luigi, 633

THEATER OF THE UNSPOKEN
Bernard, Jean-Jacques, 328
Maeterlinck, Maurice, 2181

THEATRE WORKSHOP
Behan, Brendan, 285
Delaney, Shelagh, 831

TRAGEDY
Alfieri, Vittorio, 62
Buero Vallejo, Antonio, 495
Carr, Marina, 585
Chapman, George, 611

Corneille, Pierre, 733
Giraldi Cinthio, Giambattista, 1309
Klopstock, Friedrich Gottlieb, 1866
Maffei, Francesco Scipione, 2187
Mauriac, François, 2290
Naevius, Gnaeus, 2446
Seneca, 2972
Shakespeare, William, 2997
Trissino, Giangiorgio, 3371
Voltaire, 3486
Vondel, Joost van den, 3494
Webster, John, 3533

TRAGEDY, DOMESTIC. See DOMESTIC TRAGEDY

TRAGICOMEDY
Fletcher, John, 1071
Lenz, Jakob Michael Reinhold, 1998
Torres Naharro, Bartolomé de, 3343

TUDOR AGE
Bale, John, 205
Chapman, George, 611
Heywood, John, 1622
Kyd, Thomas, 1941
Marston, John, 2238
Norton, Thomas, 2494
Sackville, Thomas, 2494
Tourneur, Cyril, 3349
Udall, Nicholas, 3400

UNIVERSITY WITS
Greene, Robert, 1433
Lodge, Thomas, 2070
Lyly, John, 2103
Marlowe, Christopher, 2225
Nashe, Thomas, 2449
Peele, George, 2612

UNSPOKEN, THEATER OF. See THEATER OF THE UNSPOKEN

VAUDEVILLE
Feydeau, Georges, 1025
Heiberg, Gunnar, 1581
Heiberg, Johan Ludvig, 1585
Labiche, Eugène, 1950

VERISM
Giacosa, Giuseppe, 1269
Verga, Giovanni, 3457

VERSE PLAY
Anderson, Maxwell, 79
Augier, Émile, 170
Bale, John, 205
Bjørnson, Bjørnstjerne, 364
Bottomley, Gordon, 407
Calderón de la Barca, Pedro, 548
Clarke, Austin, 673
Cruz, Sor Juana Inés de la, 766
D'Annunzio, Gabriele, 790
Dodson, Owen, 861
Drinkwater, John, 871
Eliot, T. S., 949
Encina, Juan del, 960
Fry, Christopher, 1166
Garnier, Robert, 1226
Giacosa, Giuseppe, 1269
Giraldi Cinthio, Giambattista, 1309
Gozzi, Carlo, 1374
Griboyedov, Alexander, 1447
Hacks, Peter, 1490
Hardy, Thomas, 1531
Hugo, Victor, 1693
Kālidāsa, 1803
Lee, Nathaniel, 1990
Lodge, Thomas, 2070
MacDonagh, Donagh, 2119
MacLeish, Archibald, 2156
Masefield, John, 2267
Millay, Edna St. Vincent, 2342
Regnard, Jean-François, 2762
Rostand, Edmond, 2818
Shirley, James, 3107
Swinburne, Algernon Charles, 3245
Tagore, Rabindranath, 3263
Tennyson, Alfred, Lord, 3287
Thomas, Dylan, 3310
Yeats, William Butler, 3694

VICTORIAN AGE
Boucicault, Dion, 414
Browning, Robert, 475
Bulwer-Lytton, Edward, 520
Gilbert, W. S., 1283
James, Henry, 1756
Jones, Henry Arthur, 1774
Pinero, Arthur Wing, 2629

SUBJECT INDEX

Boldface entries are article topics.

Purcell, Henry, 4315, 4367, 4376
Purdy, James, 2702-2706; *Children Is All*, 2703; *Day After the Fair, A*, 2704; *In the Night of Time and Four Other Plays*, 2705; *Proud Flesh*, 2704
Purgatory (Yeats), 3698
Purple Dust (O'Casey), 2509
Purpurgrefven (Almqvist), 72
Pushkin, Alexander, 2706-2712, 4111; *Boris Gudunov*, 2708; *Covetous Knight, The*, 2709; *Feast in Time of the Plague, The*, 2711; *Mozart and Salieri*, 2710; *Stone Guest, The*, 2710; *Stseny iz rytsarskikh vryemen*, 2711; *Water Nymph, The*, 2711
Puss-in-Boots (Tieck), 3320
Pygmalion (Hakim, al-), 1507
Pyo lsandae, 4248
Pyo lsin-gut, 4249
Pyramid Texts, 3943

Qing shan lei (Ma), 4206
Quality Street (Barrie), 243
Quantrill in Lawrence (Pomerance), 2680
Quare Fellow, The (Behan), 288
Quartermaine's Terms (Gray), 1411
Que van quedando en el camino, Los. See *Ranquil*
Queen After Death (Montherlant), 2383
Queen Mary (Tennyson), 3290
Queen's Comedy, The (Bridie), 461
Queen's Husband, The (Sherwood), 3101
Queen's Men, 3839
Queen's Theatre, 3438, 3877
Quem quaeritis, 3823, 3990, 4302
Question of Mercy, A (Rabe), 2725
Quin, James, 3880
Quinault, Philippe, 2713-2717, 4319; *Alceste*, 2716; *Astrate*, 2715; *Comédie sans comédie, La*, 2714
Quinn, Arthur Hobson, 3753
Quintero, Joaquín Álvarez. *See* Álvarez Quintero, Joaquín
Quintero, Serafín Álvarez. *See* Álvarez Quintero, Serafín
Quinto, José María de, 2933
Quintuples. See *Quintuplets*

Quintuplets (Sánchez), 2900
Quipu, 4396

Rabbit Race, The (Walser), 3523
Rabe, David, 2718-2727, 3765; *Basic Training of Pavlo Hummel*, 2721; *Dog Problem, The*, 2726; *Hurlyburly*, 2725; *In the Boom Boom Room*, 2723; *Orphan, The*, 2722; *Question of Mercy, A*, 2725; *Sticks and Bones*, 2721; *Streamers*, 2724; *Those the River Keeps*, 2725
Rabourdin Heirs, The (Zola), 3726
Rachel (Grimke), 3776
Racine, Jean, 2727-2736, 3890, 4028, 4054, 4317; *Athaliah*, 2735; *Bajazet*, 2733; *Bérénice*, 2733; *Britannicus*, 2732; *Esther*, 2735; *Iphigenia in Aulis*, 2734; *Litigants, The*, 2732; *Mithridates*, 2733; *Phaedra*, 2734
Racing Demon (Hare), 1546
Radio drama, 4425-4433
Rafale, La. See *Whirlwind, The*
Raft, The (Clark-Bekederemo), 670
Raft of the Medusa, The (Kaiser), 1802
Raimann, Jakob. *See* Raimund, Ferdinand
Raimund, Ferdinand, 109, 2736-2744, 4081; *Barometer-Maker on the Magic Island, The*, 2741; *Diamond of the Spirit King, The*, 2741; *Maid from Fairyland, The*, 2742; *Mountain King and Misanthrope*, 2742; *Spendthrift, The*, 2743; *Unheilbringende Krone, Die*, 2743
Raisin in the Sun, A (Hansberry), 1527, 3777
Rake's Progress, The (Auden *and* Kallman), 168
Ralph Roister Doister (Udall), 3403, 3832, 3836
Rame, Franca, 4106
Ramido Marinesco (Almqvist), 72
Ramírez de Santillana, Juana Inés de Asbaje y. *See* Cruz, Sor Juana Inés de la
Ramos, José Antonio, 4274
Ranch, Hieronymus Justesen, 4120
Ranquil (Aguirre), 36

Rape upon Rape (Fielding), 1039
Raquel encadenada (Unamuno y Jugo), 3413
Raspberry Picker, The (Hochwälder), 1647
Rastell, John, 3833, 4305
Rats (Horovitz), 1666
Rat's Mass, A (Kennedy), 1827
Ratés, Les. See *Failures*
Rattigan, Terence, 2745-2752; *Adventure Story, The*, 2750; *Deep Blue Sea, The*, 2750; *French Without Tears*, 2748; *In Praise of Love*, 2751; *Playbill*, 2749
Räuber, Die. See *Robbers, The*
Raven, The (Gozzi), 1379
Ravenhill, Mark, 3927
Razgovor na bolshoy doroge. See *Conversation on the Highway, A*
Re cervo, Il. See *King Stag, The*
Reade, Hamish. *See* Gray, Simon
Reading Group, The (Weldon), 3556
Real Thing, The (Stoppard), 3198
Real World?, The (Tremblay), 3365
Realidad (Pérez Galdós), 4146
Realism, 1195, 4081; French, 4059
Realism, psychological. *See* Psychological realism
Reaney, James, 2752-2761, 4267; *Colours in the Dark*, 2759; *Donnellys, The*, 2760; *Killdeer, The*, 2757; *Listen to the Wind*, 2758
Rebellion (Drinkwater), 873
Recensenten og dyret (Heiberg), 1588
Recitative, 4375
Reckless (Lucas), 2093
Recruiting Officer, The (Farquhar), 1011
Red Magic (Ghelderode), 1267
Red Mill, The (Herbert), 4354
Red Noses (Barnes), 237
Red Oleanders (Tagore), 3269
Red Robe, The (Brieux), 467
Red Roses for Me (O'Casey), 2509
Red Sun at Morning (Cusack), 4259
Redcam, Tom, 4282
Reeves, John, 4267
Regional theater, American, 3763, 3797-3803
Regnard, Jean-François, 2762-2770, 3883, 4054;

Starke Stamm, Der (Fleisser), 1069
State of Revolution (Bolt), 397
State of Siege (Camus), 563
States of Shock (Shepard), 3077
Statius, Publius Papinius, 3982, 3986
Steele, Sir Richard, 3179-3184, 3857, 3881, 3932, 4321; *Conscious Lovers, The*, 3182; *Tender Husband, The*, 3181
Steffens, Henrik, 2521
Stellvertreter, Der. See *Deputy, The*
Stenvall, Aleksis. *See* Kivi, Aleksis
Step-in-the-Hollow (MacDonagh), 2123
Stephen Joseph Theatre-in-the-Round, 180
Stern Young Man, A (Olesha), 2527
Sternheim, Carl, 3184-3191; *Bloomers, The*, 3187; *Fossil, The*, 3189; *1913*, 3188; *Paul Schippel Esq.*, 3190; *Snob, The*, 3187; *Strongbox, The*, 3189
Stevenson, William, 3836
Stevie in the Bloodbath (Örkény), 2541
Stevie Wants to Play the Blues (Machado), 2148
Stewart, Douglas, 4260
Stewart, Ellen, 3810, 4388
Sticks and Bones (Rabe), 2721
Stodola, Ivan, 4048
Stone Guest, The (Pushkin), 2710
Stop It, Whoever You Are (Livings), 2068
Stoppard, Tom, 3191-3201, 3922, 3927; *Arcadia*, 3200; *Artist Descending a Staircase*, 3196; *Dirty Linen and New-Found-Land*, 3198; *Every Good Boy Deserves Favour*, 3198; *Hapgood*, 3199; *Indian Ink*, 3199; *Invention of Love, The*, 3200; *Jumpers*, 3195; *Night and Day*, 3198; *Real Thing, The*, 3198; *Rosencrantz and Guildenstern Are Dead*, 3194; *Travesties*, 3197
Storey, David, 3201-3211; *Caring*, 3210; *Changing Room, The*, 3208; *Contractor, The*, 3205; *Home*, 3207; *In Celebration*, 3204
Storm, The (Drinkwater), 873
Storm, The (Ostrovsky), 2563

Storm and Stress. *See* Sturm und Drang
Stormy Night, A (Caragiale), 583
Story of Him, The (Vilalta), 3475
Straight as a Line (Alfaro), 3790
Strange Fruit (Phillips), 2628
Strange One, A (Lermontov), 2018
Stranger, The (Kotzebue), 1905
Stranitzky, Josef Anton, 2457
Stranny chelovek. See *Strange One, A*
Strasberg, Lee, 3761, 4449
Strashimirov, Anton, 4050
Straumrof (Laxness), 1987
Strauss, Botho, 3211-3215, 4091; *Big and Little*, 3214; *Kalldewey, Farce*, 3214; *Narr und seine Frau heute abend in Pancomedia, Der*, 3214; *Park, The*, 3214; *Three Acts of Recognition*, 3213; *Time and the Room*, 3214
Straussler, Tomas. *See* Stoppard, Tom
Stravinsky, Igor, 4381
Streamers (Rabe), 2724
Street, Emmet. *See* Behan, Brendan
Street Scene (Rice), 2786
Street Sounds (Bullins), 516
Streetcar Named Desire, A (Williams), 3625
Strife (Glasworthy), 1197
Strindberg, August, 3215-3224, 4127, 4165, 4333; *Dream Play, A*, 3221; *Father, The*, 3219; *Ghost Sonata, The*, 3222; *Miss Julie*, 3220
String Game, The (Owens), 2584
Striptease (Mrożek), 2418
Strogiy yunosha. See *Stern Young Man, A*
Strompleikurinn (Laxness), 1988
Strong Are Lonely, The (Hochwälder), 1645
Strong Breed, The (Soyinka), 3173
Strongbox, The (Sternheim), 3189
Stronger, The (Giacosa), 1275
Stseny iz rytsarskikh vryemen (Pushkin), 2711
Students' Repertory Theater, 2096
Studio One, 4435
Stundesløse, Den. See *Fussy Man, The*
Sturm und Drang, 1328, 1998, 3894, 4075, 4326

Sturmgeselle Sokrates, Der (Sudermann), 3231
Subject Was Roses, The (Gilroy), 1303
Submission of Rose Moy, The (Li), 3784
Substance of Fire, The (Baitz), 193
subUrbia (Bogosian), 382
Subway Circus (Saroyan), 2917
Successful Life of Three, The (Fornes), 4394
Such Things Are (Inchbald), 1721
Sudermann, Hermann, 3224-3233, 4083; *Blumenboot, Das*, 3230; *Fires of St. John*, 3232; *Honor*, 3228; *Joy of Living, The*, 3230; *Magda*, 3230; *Man and His Picture, A*, 3229; *Sturmgeselle Sokrates, Der*, 3231
Śūdraka, 4223
Suds in Your Eye (Kirkland), 1848
Sueño de la razón, El. See *Sleep of Reason, The*
Sugimori Nobumori. *See* Chikamatsu Monzaemon
Sukhovo-Kobylin, Alexander, 3234-3239, 4111; *Case, The*, 3236; *Death of Tarelkin, The*, 3238; *Krechinsky's Wedding*, 3235
Sulayman al-hakim. See *Wisdom of Solomon, The*
Sullen Lovers, The (Shadwell), 2982
Sullivan, Sir Arthur, 1285, 3902, 4354, 4369
Sultan al-ha'ir, al-. See *Sultan's Dilemma, The*
Sultan's Dilemma, The (Hakim, al-), 1506
Sumarokov, Aleksandr Petrovich, 3239-3245, 4109; *Dimitri the Imposter*, 3244; *Gamlet*, 3243; *Khorev*, 3243
Summer Folk (Gorky), 1372
Summer of the Seventeenth Doll (Lawler), 1981, 4260
Summer's Last Will and Testament (Nashe), 2452, 3841
Sump'n Like Wings (Riggs), 2791
Sunday in the Park with George (Sondheim), 3157
Sun's Darling, The (Ford), 1111
Superstition (Barker), 231
Suppliants, The (Aeschylus), 3953

Throbbing, 3485; *How I Learned to Drive*, 3486
Voice in the Wilderness, A (Vilalta), 3476
Voice of the Turtle, The (Van Druten), 3447
Voinikov, Dobri, 4050
Vojnović, Ivo, 4052
Voleur, Le. See Thief, The
Volksstück, 112, 1671
Volpone (Jonson), 1789, 3851
Voltaire, 3486-3494, 3892, 4056, 4323; *Alzire*, 3492; *Mérope*, 3492; *Oedipus*, 3491; *Zaïre*, 3491
Volunteers (Friel), 1154
Von Goethe, Johann Wolfgang. *See* Goethe, Johann Wolfgang von
Von Hofmannsthal, Hugo. *See* Hofmannsthal, Hugo von
Von Horváth, Ödön. *See* Horváth, Ödön von
Von Kleist, Heinrich. *See* Kleist, Heinrich von
Von Kotzebue, August. *See* Kotzebue, August von
Von morgens bis mitternachts. See From Morn to Midnight
Von Schiller, Johann Christoph Friedrich. *See* Schiller, Friedrich
Vondel, Joost van den, 3494-3498, 4016; *Gijsbrecht van Aemstel*, 3496; *Jeptha*, 3497; *Lucifer*, 3497
Vor Sonnenaufgang. See Before Dawn
Vörösmarty, Mihály, 4047
Vošnjak, Jože, 4052
Votes for Women (Robins), 4403
Voyage de M. Perrichon, Le. See Journey of Mr. Perrichon, The
Voyage Round My Father, A (Mortimer), 2404
Voyage to Tomorrow (Hakim, al-), 1508
Voyageur sans bagage, Le. See Traveller Without Luggage
Voyna. See War (Artsybashev)
Voysey Inheritance, The (Granville-Barker), 1391
Voz en el desierto, Una. See Voice in the Wilderness, A
Vragi. See Enemies
Vrai Monde?, Le. See Real World?, The

Vrchlický, Jaroslav, 4049
Vsegda v prodazhe (Aksyonov), 46
Vujić, Joakim, 4051
Vultures, The (Becque), 283
Vybor guvernera. See Choice of a Tutor, The
Vyrozumění. See Memorandum, The

Waga tomo Hittorā. See My Friend Hitler
Wager, The (Giacosa), 1271
Wager, The (Medoff), 2305
Wagner, Heinrich Leopold, 3894, 4076
Wagner, Richard, 4081, 4334, 4380
Waiting for Dolphins (McGrath), 2136
Waiting for Godot (Beckett), 275, 3919, 4069, 4168
Waiting for Lefty (Odets), 2514, 4417
Wake of Jamey Foster, The (Henley), 1610
Wakefield Cycle, 3825
Wakefield Master, 3499-3506, 3827; *Buffeting, The*, 3505; *First Shepherds' Play, The*, 3503; *Herod the Great*, 3505; *Killing of Abel, The*, 3502; *Noah*, 3503; *Second Shepherds' Play, The*, 3504
Walcott, Derek, 3506-3514, 4283; *Dream on Monkey Mountain*, 3509; *Haitian Trilogy, The*, 3512; *Joker of Seville, The*, 3510; *O Babylon!*, 3510; *Odyssey, The*, 3512; *Pantomime*, 3511; *Remembrance*, 3511; *Three Plays*, 3512; *Ti-Jean and His Brothers*, 3509
Walcott, Roderick, 3507, 4283
Walk in the Woods, A (Blessing), 373
Walker, George F., 4268
Walker, Joseph A., 3514-3517; *District Line*, 3517; *Harangues, The*, 3516; *River Niger, The*, 3516; *Yin Yang*, 3516
Walker, London (Barroe), 243
Wallensteins Lager. See Camp of Wallenstein, The
Wallensteins Tod. See Death of Wallenstein, The
Walls Have Ears, The (Ruiz de Alarcón), 2869
Walser, Martin, 3518-3527; *Detour, The*, 3522; *Home Front*, 3524; *In

Goethes Hand, 3526; *Kaschmir in Parching*, 3526; *Kinderspiel, Ein*, 3524; *Ohrfeige, Die*, 3526; *Rabbit Race, The*, 3523; *Sauspiel, Das*, 3525; *Schwarze Schwan, Der*, 3523; *Überlebensgross Herr Krott*, 3523; *Wir werden schon noch handeln*, 3524
Waltz of the Toreadors, The (Anouilh), 106
Wandlung, Die. See Transfiguration
Wang Shicheng, 4211
Wang Shifu, 4206
War (Artsybashev), 157
War (van Itallie), 4392
War on Tatem, The (Medoff), 2305
War Plays, The (Bond), 405
Ward, Theodore, 3777
Wars of Caesar and Pompey, The (Chapman), 617
Wartah, al-. See Incrimination
Wasps, The (Aristophanes), 3970
Wasserstein, Wendy, 3527-3532, 3771, 4406; *Heidi Chronicles, The*, 3530; *Isn't It Romantic*, 3530; *Sisters Rosenweig, The*, 3531; *Uncommon Women and Others*, 3529
Waste (Granville-Barker), 1392
Watch on the Rhine (Hellman), 1604
Water Hen, The (Witkiewicz), 3669
Water Nymph, The (Pushkin), 2711
Waterhouse, Keith, 1510, 1512; *Billy Liar*, 1513; *Who's Who*, 1515
Waterloo Bridge (Sherwood), 3102
Watermill Center, 3660
Waters of Babylon, The (Arden), 124
Waverly Gallery, The (Lonergan), 2077
Way of the World, The (Congreve), 723
Wayang kulit, 4232
Wayside Motor Inn, The (Gurney), 1487
We (Fuller), 1190
We Can't Pay! We Won't Pay! (Fo), 1087
Wealth (Jones), 1778
Weapons of Happiness (Brenton), 452
Weather Breeder, The (Denison), 847
Weaver, John, 3888